ANNUAL 2007–2008

Published by Invincible Press, an imprint of HarperCollins*Publishers*, 77-85 Fulham Palace Rd, London W6 8JB

First published in 1887

2

A CIP catalogue record for this book is available from the British Library

The HarperCollins website address is: www.harpercollins.co.uk

Editorial compilation by Hayters-Teamwork, Image House, Station Rd, London, N17 9LR

Typesetting by Letterpart Limited, Reigate, Surrey

Printed and bound in Great Britain by Clays Ltd, St Ives plc

ISBN-13 978-0-00-725555-9

ISBN-10 0-00-725555-1

CONTENTS

MOORE THE MAN TO SET THE RIGHT EXAMPLE

BY STUART BARNES

Immaculate footballer. Imperial defender. Immortal hero of 1966. First Englishman to raise the World Cup aloft. Favourite son of London's East End. Finest legend of West Ham United. National treasure. Master of Wembley. Lord of the game. Captain extraordinary. Gentleman for all time.

This tribute to Bobby Moore, engraved on a statue of the World Cup winner outside Wembley, provides a perfect link between the old stadium where he captained England to glory all those years ago and the new arena where John Terry will lead the current national side in tricky European Championship qualifying matches in the weeks ahead. The statue faces Olympic Way and there could be no more fitting position for the man who skippered his country 90 times, won a total of 108 caps and drew respect and admiration all round the world. 'I'm delighted that Bobby's career has been recognised in such an appropriate way,' said his widow Stephanie at the unveiling ceremony. 'He belongs to football and to the fans. He used to tell me that playing at Wembley was like walking on air.'

So, as Moore gazes down at supporters on their way into the stadium, what would he make of the way the game has changed out of all recognition, not just since he was in his prime but also since he died of cancer in 1993 at the age of 51? Of England's failure to come close to matching those heady days of 66; of a game in which the biggest clubs are in foreign ownership; of a Premiership and its players awash with more money than ever before. Not to mention the managerial merry-go-round in which nearly half of the 92 league clubs now change the man in charge every season.

He would probably concur with some of the concerns expressed during the course of last season by three senior figures, whose forthright opinions should be noted by everyone connected with the game. In an article headlined 'Our Game Is Losing Its Soul,' Sir Bobby Robson admitted to feeling 'uneasy and a little depressed' about the shortage of British companies and business leaders willing to invest in the top clubs. Paul Jewell, at the time manager of Wigan Athletic, questioned whether football had lost touch with the working man. And Michel Platini, the new president of Europe's governing body UEFA, warned that the game ran the risk of being 'poisoned' by violence on and off the pitch.

Platini spoke out after Arsenal and Chelsea were each fined £100,000 for a mass brawl which scarred one of the season's showpiece matches, the Carling Cup Final. The former captain of France, like Moore one of the most respected players of his era, has written to all the associations under his control voicing those fears, and it is to be hoped that his promise to ensure they use their disciplinary powers to the full will be carried through. Jewell's concern will strike a chord with many fans, who fear they are being priced out of watching their favourite teams, believe the gap between the elite and the smaller clubs continues to grow and worry that some players on six-figure weekly salaries are no longer fully committed to the cause — at league and international level.

While Manchester United's success in denying Chelsea a third Premiership title dominated the headlines last season, there were some major achievements lower down the ladder. Reading proved a breath of fresh air in the top flight and who would argue with the League Managers' Association's choice of Steve Coppell as their Manager of the Year for a second successive season? Colchester United, everyone's favourite to go straight back down, showed that a club with gates of less than 6,000 can prosper in the Championship. Another side upsetting the odds were Scunthorpe United, who returned, as champions, to the game's second tier for the first time since 1963-64. Then there was Gretna completing a remarkable rise from the Scottish Third Division to the Premier League in three seasons in true fairy story fashion – a last-minute winner by 36-year-old James Grady against Ross County on the final day of the season.

All showed that the game's heart continues to beat strongly away from the big stage and there are sure to be more heroics in 2007-08. The immediate target, however, is for England to regain the confidence of the fans after some poor performances under Steve McClaren, prosper in Wembley's magnificent new surroundings and give every level of the game a lift by reaching the finals of Euro 2008 in some style.

Meanwhile, big-spending Manchester United will start favourites to retain the title, with Owen Hargreaves set to prove a particularly influential signing. This could be the season when Liverpool finally deliver a meaningful challenge and there will be plenty of attention, too, on events in North London, where Tottenham are keen to break into the top four at the expense of an Arsenal side having to come to terms without Thierry Henry. And what of Bobby Moore's old club West Ham? Alan Curbishley worked wonders keeping them in the Premiership, albeit with a huge helping hand from Carlos Tevez, but the controversy lingers. What would Bobby have made of it all?

ROBERT FREDERICK CHELSEA (BOBBY) MOORE

(This is the obituary which appeared in the *News of the World Football Annual* in 1993)

England's World Cup-Winning captain in 1966, died from cancer at his Putney home. His 108 caps stand as a British record for an outfield player, and he played 47 times at Wembley: 44 for England, in two Cup finals for West Ham and one for Fulham. In successive years, he lifted the F.A. Cup and Cup-Winners' Cup for West Ham, then the World Cup, a unique hat-trick. He began as a wing-half, and the switch by West Ham manager Ron Greenwood made him one of the finest centre-backs in the game's history. The secret of his tackling was perfect timing. He read the game beautifully, distributed masterfully from the back, never better than when he hit the pass from which Geoff Hurst completed his World Cup Final hat-trick. As a captain, he was calm, unflappable and authoritative. He gave English football qualities that are in short supply today – dignity and style. Despite his illness, he willed himself to be at Wembley to broadcast on London Capital Gold on England's World Cup match against San Marino. It was as if he wanted to bid farewell to his old stamping ground, to be involved with England and the World Cup just one more time. A week later, he left us. And suddenly became what England had never been seen to appreciate while he was alive, a legend. In a club tribute, West Ham "retired" the No. 6 shirt he made famous. In their first home match after his death, against Wolves. Ian Bishop, who would normally have worn it, pulled on a No. 12 shirt instead.

BOBBY MOORE – MILESTONES

- Born during the blitz at Barking, Essex, April 12, 1941.
- Signed professional for West Ham, June 1958. League debut, aged 17, away to Manchester United, September 8, 1958.
- Final appearance, for Fulham at Blackburn (Div. 2), May 14, 1977.
- Appearances – clubs: West Ham 642 (1958-74); Fulham 157 (1974-77);
- England 108 senior Internationals. (1962-73); equalled Billy Wright's record as captain 90 times. 18 youth caps, 8 for England Under-23s.
- Manager: Oxford City (1979-81); Southend (May 1984-April 1986). Honours:
- FA Cup-winning captain, West Ham 1964; Cup-winners' Cup, winning captain, West Ham 1965; England World Cup-winning captain 1966;
- Footballer of Year 1964. BBC TV Sports Personality of Year 1966. Awarded OBE 1967.
- More than 1,800 attended the memorial service in Westminster Abbey on June 28, including all Moore's World Cup-winning team-mates, but Sir Alf Ramsey was not able to join them.

SOCCER DIARY 2006-07

JULY 2006

21 Mick McCarthy, former Sunderland and Republic of Ireland manager, is named the new boss of Wolves.

22 Arsenal open their new Emirates Stadium with Dennis Bergkamp's testimonial match, which attracts a crowd of 54,000 and raises around £1m. for good causes.

23 Looking for regular first-team football, Damien Duff leaves champions Chelsea for Newcastle in a £5m. deal.

24 Niall Quinn assumes the dual role of chairman and manager at Sunderland after heading the consortium taking over the club.

25 Lazio and Fiorentina, originally relegated along with Juventus in Italian football's corruption scandal, are reinstated to Serie A on appeal.

26 Liverpool sign Jermaine Pennant from Birmingham for £6.7m. Joey Barton and 18-year-old Micah Richards, both linked with other clubs during the summer, sign four-year deals with Manchester City.

28 Ruud van Nistelrooy, unsettled at Manchester United since being left out of the Carling Cup Final against Wigan, joins Real Madrid for £10.2m. Geraint Williams, Colchester's caretaker-manager, is given the job on a permanent basis.

29 Celtic open their defence of the Scottish Premier League title with a 4-1 victory over Kilmarnock.

30 Former Newcastle and England striker Alan Shearer turns down the chance to join Steve McClaren's England coaching staff. William Gallas is fined by Chelsea for not turning up for a pre-season tour of the United States and loses his No 13 shirt to new signing Michael Ballack.

31 Worries that work on the new Wembley will be delayed further and that the new stadium will not be ready for the 2007 F.A. Cup Final are raised by builders Multiplex.

AUGUST 2006

1 Michael Carrick joins Manchester United from Tottenham for £18.6m., a record fee for the London club and six times the figure they paid West Ham for the player in August 2004. Steve McClaren begins work as the new England coach.

3 Wrexham, with new owners after a consortium led by former director Neville Dickens buys the club, come out of administration and get the go-ahead to start the new season.

4 Martin O'Neill ends 15 months out of football by becoming the new manager of Aston Villa. Wayne Rooney, sent off in England's World Cup quarter-final against Portugal, is dismissed in Manchester United's win over FC Porto in the Amsterdam Tournament.

5 The Football League's new boys experience mixed fortunes on the opening day of the season, Hereford winning 2-0 at Stockport and Accrington going down 2-0 at Chester.

6 Sir Bobby Robson is discharged from hospital after being taken ill while watching Ipswich's match against Crystal Palace.

7 Gary Breen announces his retirement from international football after winning 63 caps with the Republic of Ireland.

8 Newcastle's Stephen Carr, who retired from international football after the Republic of Ireland's failure to reach the World Cup Finals, changes his mind and is named in their squad for a friendly against Holland.

9 Steve McClaren names Chelsea's John Terry as the new England captain to succeed David Beckham.

10 Terry Venables, England coach from 1994-96, becomes Steve McClaren's assistant. After winning 94 caps, David Beckham is omitted from McClaren's squad for the friendly against Greece.

11 Nationwide Building Society become sole sponsor of the England team in a four-year deal worth around £25m.

13 Liverpool win the new season's first silverware, beating Chelsea 2-1 in the Community Shield.

14 Aston Villa are taken over by American billionaire Randy Lerner in a £62m. deal, which ends the 36-year era of chairman Doug Ellis.

15 On the eve of what should have been his England debut against Greece, West Ham's Dean Ashton sustains a broken ankle in training. Wayne Rooney and Paul Scholes, sent off in Manchester United's match against FC Porto in the Amsterdam Tournament, have appeals against three-match Premiership bans turned down by the F.A.
16 Steve McClaren makes a flying start as England coach with a 4-0 win over Greece, new captain John Terry scoring one of the goals. David Healy, on his 50th appearance for Northern Ireland, is on the mark in a 2-1 away win over Finland, but the Republic of Ireland suffer their heaviest home defeat for 20 years, 4-0 to Holland.
17 Liverpool sign the Holland World Cup striker Dirk Kuyt from Feyenoord for £10.2m.
19 Peter Ridsdale, Cardiff's former Leeds chairman, is ordered from the boardroom at Elland Road after celebrating his side's 1-0 Championship victory.
21 Chelsea pay £6m. for Hamburg's Holland World Cup defender Khalid Boulahrouz.
22 Liverpool confirm a place in the group stage of the Champions League in Kiev – the neutral venue ordered by UEFA for the second leg of their qualifier against Maccabi Haifa because of the situation in war-torn Israel. Nine Championship teams are beaten by League Two opposition in the first round of the Carling Cup, including Sunderland whose 2-0 defeat by Bury – their fifth in five matches – prompts chairman-manager Niall Quinn to accelerate his search for a new manager.
23 Arsenal reach the Champions League group stage at the expense of Dinamo Zagreb, but Hearts go out against AEK Athens. Owen Hargreaves is fined £17,000 by Bayern Munich after stating publicly that he wants to join Manchester United.
24 Manchester City's Ben Thatcher apologises to Pedro Mendes for an elbow which left the Portsmouth player unconscious on the running track at the City of Manchester Stadium. Obafemi Martins takes over Alan Shearer's No 9 shirt at Newcastle after a £10m. move from Inter Milan. Celtic sign the PSV Eindhoven striker Jan Vennegoor of Hesselink for £5m.
25 Bolton shatter their transfer record by paying the Turkish club Fenerbahce £8m. for the former Arsenal and Real Madrid striker Nicolas Anelka.
27 Roy Keane is appointed Sunderland's new manager by chairman Niall Quinn, the man he called a 'muppet' after being sent home from the Republic of Ireland's 2002 World Cup training camp.
28 The Football League put an end to the practice of having matches controlled by demoted Premiership referees.
29 Bradley Orr is sent off for butting Bristol City team-mate Louis Carey during their team's 3-1 win at Northampton.
30 Manchester City ban Ben Thatcher for six matches, two of them suspended, and fine him six weeks' wages, with two of those also suspended, for the challenge that put Portsmouth's Pedro Mendes in hospital. Doncaster's Dave Penney becomes the season's first managerial casualty.
31 West Ham pull off the most eye-catching – and intriguing – deal on transfer deadline-day by signing Argentine World Cup players Carlos Tevez and Javier Mascherano from Corinthians of Brazil, with neither club disclosing the fees involved. Wigan receive a club-record £4.5m. from Tottenham for Pascal Chimbonda. Arsenal's Ashley Cole joins Chelsea in exchange for William Gallas, while Sunderland's new manager Roy Keane signs six new players. Sir Clive Woodward, England's World Cup-winning rugby coach, ends his foray into football at Southampton after 13 months to set up a consultancy. Three Bristol City players are jailed over a nightclub brawl – Wales international David Partridge for two months and Steve Brooker and Bradley Orr for 28 days. A fourth player, Scott Brown, is ordered to undertake 100 hours of community service.

SEPTEMBER 2006

1 Chelsea are fined £40,000 for breaking F.A. doping control rules by conducting their own tests on players.
2 Peter Crouch takes his England tally to ten goals in 13 appearances with a brace in the 5-0 European Championship qualifying win over Andorra, Steve McClaren's first competitive game as coach. In his first one in charge, Steve Staunton is sent to the stands as the Republic of Ireland lose 1-0 to Germany. Scotland score their biggest win for 30 years, 6-0 against the Faroe Islands. But Wales lose 2-1 to a goal by the Czech Republic in the

last minute of normal time, while Northern Ireland's chances of collecting a £1m. bonus for reaching the finals already look slim after a 3-0 home defeat by Iceland. Tranmere goalkeeper Gavin Ward scores with a free-kick from just outside his own penalty area, against Leyton Orient.

3 A near-capacity crowd of 59,000 at Arsenal's Emirates Stadium see Brazil beat Argentina 3-0 in a friendly international.

4 Four days after moving from Chelsea to Arsenal, William Gallas is accused by the Premiership champions of having threatened to score an own goal or get himself sent off if selected for the season's opening game against Manchester City – an allegation he denies.

5 Wales are beaten 2-0 by Brazil in a friendly international played at Tottenham's White Hart Lane. Craig Levein, sacked by Leicester in January, is appointed manager of Raith.

6 Peter Crouch maintains his impressive scoring record for England with the only goal against Macedonia in a European Championship qualifier. David Healy's hat-trick enables Northern Ireland to bounce back after defeat by Iceland with a 3-2 win over Spain, while Scotland beat Lithuania 2-1.

7 Sean O'Driscoll ends a 22-year association with Bournemouth by taking over as manager of Doncaster.

8 Liverpool receive council approval to build a new 60,000-seater stadium in Stanley Park, a few hundred yards from Anfield. Mark McGhee is sacked as Brighton manager.

9 Roy Keane's managerial career gets off to a successful start as Sunderland win 2-1 at Derby.

11 Manchester City's Ben Thatcher is banned for eight matches by the F.A., with a further 15 games suspended, for elbowing Portsmouth's Pedro Mendes.

12 The Manchester United shirt worn by George Best when he scored six goals against Northampton in an F.A. Cup fifth round tie in 1970 is sold at Christie's for £24,000.

13 Arsenal set a Champions League record by fielding 11 players of different nationalities for part of the game against Hamburg.

14 Cesc Fabregas, Arsenal's 19-year-old midfielder, agrees a new eight-year contract with the club.

15 Lord Sebastian Coe, chairman of the London 2012 Olympic Committee, agrees to head FIFA's new anti-corruption watchdog.

18 Bryan Robson is dismissed as West Bromwich Albion manager after an indifferent start to the season.

19 Sam Allardyce is accused in a BBC *Panorama* programme of taking illegal payments in transfer deals. The Bolton manager denies the charge. Wigan, last season's beaten finalists, lose 2-0 to League One side Crewe in the second round of the Carling Cup.

20 Two Championship managers are sacked – Kevin Blackwell at Leeds and Gary Waddock at Queens Park Rangers. John Gregory, former Aston Villa and Derby manager, replaces Waddock. Three more Premiership teams are knocked out of the Carling Cup by lower-division opposition – Manchester City by Chesterfield, Fulham by Wycombe and Middlesbrough by Notts County.

21 Milan Mandaric, who took Portsmouth out of administration and into the Premiership before selling out to Alexandre Gaydamak, announces that he is stepping down as non-executive chairman.

22 Newcastle's Celestine Babayaro is banned for three games by the F.A. for striking Liverpool's Dirk Kuyt, an incident which went unseen by referee Mark Halsey and his officials. Steve Thompson, Notts County manager, is given a two-match touchline ban and fined £300 for abusive language at the game against MK Dons.

24 After four months in the job, Millwall manager Nigel Spackman pays the price for only one win in ten league matches.

25 Kevin Bond is sacked as Newcastle assistant manager following allegations made against him in the BBC *Panorama* programme.

26 Jonathan Barnett, Ashley Cole's agent, is banned from football matters for 18 months – half of them suspended – and fined £100,000 by the F.A. for his role in the 'tapping up' affair involving the player and Chelsea. Barclays extend their sponsorship of the Premier League until 2010 for £65.8m, nearly £9m. more than the current three-year deal. Arsene Wenger celebrates ten years as Arsenal manager with a 2-0 Champions League victory over FC Porto.

27 Colin Gordon, agent of England coach Steve McClaren, claims in a newspaper interview that the majority of agents are corrupt. Didier Drogba scores a hat-trick in Chelsea's 3-1 Champions League victory over Levski Sofia.
28 Blackburn, Newcastle, Tottenham and Rangers reach the group stage of the UEFA Cup, but West Ham and Hearts are knocked out. Watford unveil a £32m. plan to redevelop Vicarage Road.
29 Dean Wilkins, a former captain of the club, is appointed Brighton's new manager after a spell as caretaker.
30 England qualify for the women's World Cup Finals with a 1-1 draw against France.

OCTOBER 2006

1 Nigel Worthington is sacked as Norwich manager after the 4-1 home defeat by Burnley. Macclesfield, bottom of the Football League, dismiss their manager Brian Horton.
2 Premiership clubs give Lord Stevens and his team an extra two months to continue their investigations into transfer dealings.
4 Merseyside Police decide to take no action against Manchester City's Joey Barton for dropping his shorts at the end of the game at Everton. Darlington dismiss manager David Hodgson.
5 Brentford manager Leroy Rosenior receives a two-match touchline ban and is fined £500 by the F.A. for abusive language at the game against Luton.
6 Leighton Baines gives England Under 21s victory in the first leg of their European Championship play-off against Germany.
7 Gary Caldwell's goal earns Scotland a notable victory over France, while Northern Ireland gain a creditable goalless draw in Denmark. But there is gloom elsewhere in European Championship qualifying matches. England are held 0-0 by Macedonia, Wales are turned over 5-1 by Slovakia in Craig Bellamy's first game as captain and the Republic of Ireland have Richard Dunne sent off when suffering one of their most embarrassing defeats – 5-2 in Cyprus
8 Crystal Palace owner Simon Jordan buys the freehold of Selhurst Park from former chairman Ron Noades for £12m.
10 Two goals by Theo Walcott enable England Under 21s to complete a 3-0 aggregate win over Germany and secure a place in the European Championship Finals. Joey Barton is fined £2,000 by the F.A. but escapes a ban for dropping his shorts at the end of Manchester City's game at Everton.
11 Gary Neville's back pass bobbles past Paul Robinson as England drop more European Championship qualifying points in a 2-0 defeat in Croatia. Scotland have Steven Pressley sent off when losing by the same margin in the Ukraine. David Healy's matchwinner against Latvia continues Northern Ireland's revival, Wales beat Cyprus 3-1 and the Republic of Ireland also restore some pride with a 1-1 draw against the Czech Republic.
12 Kevin Bond, dismissed by Newcastle last month, is appointed manager of Bournemouth, the club his father John managed in the early 1970s. Hull manager Phil Parkinson is fined £1,000 by the F.A. for abusive language during the game against Derby.
13 Peter Grant, assistant to Alan Pardew at West Ham, is named the new Norwich manager. Hibernian's Tony Mowbray takes over at West Bromwich Albion.
14 Chelsea goalkeeper Petr Cech suffers a depressed fracture of the skull in a first-minute collision with Reading's Stephen Hunt.
16 Reading and the Ambulance Service reject claims by Chelsea manager Jose Mourinho that they took too long to respond to Petr Cech's injury.
17 Darlington allege a breach of the rules about payments to agents for the sacking of manager David Hodgson.
18 The F.A. decide to take no action against Stephen Hunt over the incident with Petr Cech. The Scottish Premier League sign an £8m., four-year sponsorship with Clydesdale Bank running from July 2007, when their agreement with Bank of Scotland runs out.
19 Agreement is reached in the long-running dispute between the F.A. and builders Multiplex over the new Wembley Stadium. Paul Sturrock, given a new three-year contract five weeks ago, is sacked by Sheffield Wednesday after a 4-0 defeat at Colchester.
20 Robert Earl, who founded the Planet Hollywood chain of restaurants, becomes the latest big-money investor in the Premiership, acquiring 23% of Everton.

21 Nationwide announce the end to their nine-year sponsorship of the Conference after this season.
22 Sam Hammam agrees to sell his majority shareholding in Cardiff to a consortium and is replaced as chairman by his deputy, the former Leeds chairman Peter Ridsdale.
23 Paul Ince, former Manchester United and England midfielder, takes his first step in management at Macclesfield, bottom of the Football League.
24 Pressure builds on Alan Pardew as West Ham are knocked out of the Carling Cup by Chesterfield – their eighth successive defeat. Chelsea goalkeeper Petr Cech is allowed home from hospital, ten days after suffering a depressed fracture of the skull against Reading.
25 Hearts are fined £10,000 by the Scottish F.A. after criticism of referees by majority shareholder Vladimir Romanov. The Football League extend a long-standing sponsorship agreement with Mitre to 2011.
26 Dennis Wise leaves Swindon to become the new Leeds manager. Alan Shearer hands out cheques totalling £1.64m., the proceeds of his testimonial season at Newcastle, to 14 charities and good causes. Jim Leishman steps down as Dunfermline manager to revert to his previous job of director of football.
27 The F.A. Council agree to back proposals to reform the game's governing body put forward in a structural review by Lord Burns. Chelsea agree to pay Leeds a reported £5m. compensation over the alleged 'tapping-up' of three youth players.
28 Sol Davis, the Luton defender, suffers a stroke on the team coach travelling to Ipswich Town.
29 Craig Brewster is sacked as manager of bottom-of-the-table Dundee United after nine months in the job.
30 Former Leicester manager Craig Levein takes over the Dundee United job. Dave Penney, formerly with Doncaster, becomes Darlington manager.
31 Rafael Benitez fields an unchanged Liverpool team for the first time in 100 games and a 3-0 win over Bordeaux puts them into the first knock-out round of the Champions League with two group fixtures remaining.

NOVEMBER 2006

1 John Collins, who left Hibernian to become Celtic's first £1m. player in 1990, returns to Easter Road as manager.
2 The F.A. decide to bring in tough new regulations on agents from the beginning of 2007.
3 Chelsea's Didier Drogba signs a new four-year contract.
5 Brian Laws, the Football League's second longest-serving manager to Crewe's Dario Gradi, leaves Scunthorpe after nearly ten years to take over at Sheffield Wednesday.
6 Sir Alex Ferguson completes 20 years as manager of Manchester United. Graham Rodger is sacked by struggling Grimsby after five months as manager.
7 Sir Alex sees his holders of the Carling Cup knocked out by Freddy Eastwood's goal for Southend in the fourth round. Three weeks after being sacked by Sheffield Wednesday, Paul Sturrock becomes Swindon's new manager.
8 Alan Buckley, in charge between 1988-94 and 1997-2000, begins a third spell as Grimsby manager.
9 The F.A. are fined £4,200 by UEFA for the behaviour of England fans before last month's game against Croatia in Zagreb. The Croatian Federation are fined £21,000 for poor organisation at the stadium.
10 Stephen Kenny, manager of Irish club Derry, becomes Dunfermline's new boss.
11 Fourth official Alan Sheffield is knocked unconscious and taken to hospital with a split forehead after being hit by a coin thrown from the crowd at the Newport-Swansea F.A. Cup first round tie.
13 Iain Dowie becomes the season's first managerial casualty in the Premiership, sacked by Charlton after 12 league matches with his side bottom of the table.
14 Dowie is replaced by his assistant, Les Reed. Chris Llewellyn scores his first goal for Wales in a 4-0 win over Liechtenstein.
15 Manchester City's Micah Richards, at 18 years and 144 days, becomes England's youngest-ever defender when starting the 1-1 friendly international draw in Holland. Robbie Keane scores a hat-trick as the Republic of Ireland score their first European

Championship qualifying win, 5-0 against San Marino in Lansdowne Road's final match before the stadium is redeveloped. Luton manager Mike Newell is reprimanded by the club for criticising assistant referee Amy Rayner and his own chairman Bill Tomlins.
17 Ferenc Puskas, the 'Galloping Major' who became a legend for Hungary and Real Madrid, dies aged 79.
18 Leroy Rosenior, manager of Brentford for little more than five months, is sacked after their 16th successive match with a victory.
20 West Ham are taken over by an Icelandic consortium, headed by UEFA executive committee member Eggert Magnusson, in a £108m. deal.
21 Celtic reach the Champions League knock-out stage for the first time with 1-0 win over Manchester United, earned by Shunsuke Nakamura's spectacular free-kick and Artur Boruc's penalty save from Louis Saha. Andy Ritchie is dismissed by second-from-bottom Barnsley, a month after the club blocked Sheffield Wednesday's request to approach him about becoming their manager.
22 Chelsea qualify from their Champions League Group, despite a 1-0 defeat by Werder Bremen. Gareth Southgate is given permission by the Premier League to remain as Middlesbrough manager until the end of the season while he pursues the required coaching qualifications. Caretaker Willie Donachie is given the Millwall manager's job on a permanent basis.
23 Blackburn, Newcastle and Tottenham all secure places in the first knock-out stage of the UEFA Cup.
24 Chief executive Peter Kenyon predicts that Chelsea will eventually become the biggest club in the world.
25 Motherwell's Scott McDonald scores the Scottish Premier League's 5,000th goal during the game against Falkirk.
26 Fabio Cannavaro, Italy's World Cup-winning captain, is named European Footballer of the Year, ahead of international team-mate Gianluigi Buffon and Arsenal's Thierry Henry.
27 Former Czech Republic international Lubos Kubik becomes Torquay's fourth manager of 2006, replacing Ian Atkins who turns down a new position as director of football and leaves the club.
28 A week after the takeover of West Ham by Eggert Magnusson's Iceandic consortium, FIFA set up a working group to look at the growing number of foreign buyers into the Premiership.
29 Liverpool's Craig Bellamy is cleared of assaulting two women in a Cardiff nightclub.
30 West Bromwich Albion midfielder Ronnie Wallwork, on loan at Barnsley, is stabbed several times in a Manchester bar.

DECEMBER 2006

1 Manchester United announce a three-month loan deal for 35-year-old Henrik Larsson while his Swedish club Helsingborgs take their winter break. Jonathan Barnett, Ashley Cole's agent, loses his appeal against an F.A. ban and fine for his role in the 'tapping up affair' involving the player and Chelsea, but has the ban reduced.
4 Phil Parkinson is sacked by struggling Hull, less than six months after leaving promoted Colchester to become their manager.
5 Boston, with debts of more than £1m., admit to an uncertain future after plans to move to a new ground are rejected by the local council.
6 Arsenal and Manchester United join Chelsea and Liverpool as Champions League group winners. Macclesfield, the only team without a league win, beat Rochdale 1-0.
7 Caretaker Nigel Adkins, who once took Welsh side Bangor into the European Cup, is confirmed as Scunthorpe manager.
9 Steve Claridge, 40, makes his 1,000th career appearance when he plays for Bournemouth, the club where he started his career
10 Arsenal's Theo Walcott is named the BBC's Young Sports Personality of the Year.
11 Alan Pardew is sacked as manager of struggling West Ham after the 4-0 defeat at Bolton.
13 Pardew is replaced by former Charlton manager Alan Curbishley, who returns to management after a seven-month break from the game.
14 Arsenal manager Arsene Wenger is fined £10,000 by the F.A. for pushing and swearing at Pardew on the Upton Park touchline after Marlon Harewood's late winner for West Ham.

15 Newcastle are awarded the Intertoto Cup for progressing further than any other club in the subsequent UEFA Cup.
16 Steve Parkin is sacked by Rochdale after a run of seven defeats in eight League Two matches.
18 Three weeks after being named European Footballer of the Year, Fabio Cannavaro is chosen as World Player of the Year, the first defender to win the trophy in its 16-year history.
19 Troubled Charlton lose 1-0 at home to Wycombe in a Carling Cup quarter-final. Wigan's Lee McCulloch is suspended for three matches by the F.A. after being caught on camera punching Sheffield United skipper Chris Morgan. Struggling Mansfield dismiss their manager Peter Shirtliff.
20 After an eight-month investigation into alleged illegal transfer payments, Lord Stevens criticises the way football is regulated and asks for more time to pursue 17 deals. Chelsea manager Jose Mourinho apologises for accusing Everton's Andy Johnson of diving. John Gorman resigns as manager of Northampton. Bury are thrown out of the F.A. Cup for fielding an ineligible player in their second round win over Chester.
21 Caretaker Scott Fitzgerald is given the manager's job at Brentford on a permanent basis.
22 The League Managers' Association warn that the growing number of foreign players, coaches and managers will inflict long-term damage on the England team.
23 Mark Crossley, Sheffield Wednesday's on-loan goalkeeper, heads a last-minute equaliser against Southampton. Doncaster end 84 years of football at Belle Vue before moving to a new stadium with a 1-0 victory over top-of-the-table Nottingham Forest.
24 Charlton sack Les Reed after 41 days in charge and replace him with the former West Ham manager Alan Pardew.
26 Tom Huddlestone signs a new four-and-a-half-year contract with Tottenham. A record Conference crowd of 11,065 see the leaders Oxford held 0-0 by Woking.
27 Billy Dearden is appointed manager of Mansfield for the second time, having been in charge between 1999-2002.
28 Bury's appeal against being thrown out of the FA Cup is turned down.
29 Charlton sign the captain of China, Zheng Zhi, on loan from the Shandong Zhi club.
31 Caretaker Simon Davey, head of the club's Academy, is given the Barnsley manager's job on a permanent basis. Stevenage midfielder George Boyd joins Peterborough for a record Conference fee of £260,000.

JANUARY 2007

1 Liverpool captain Steven Gerrard receives an MBE in the New Year's Honours List. Doncaster make a successful start in their £32m. Keepmoat Stadium, beating Huddersfield 3-0 watched by a near-capacity crowd of 14,470.
2 Stuart Gray, who had a brief spell in charge of Southampton in 2001, is appointed Northampton's new manager.
3 In the week he stripped Barry Ferguson of the Rangers captaincy, manager Paul Le Guen is sacked with his team trailing Celtic by 17 points in the SPL. Two players, Charlton's Osei Sankofa and Grimsby's Nick Fenton, both have one-match suspensions for red card offences doubled for what the F.A. calls 'frivolous' appeals.
Caretaker Keith Hill is confirmed as Rochdale manager until the end of the season.
4 Alan Pardew is cleared by the F.A. over his part in the touchline row with Arsene Wenger during the West Ham – Arsenal game in November. Sheffield United skipper Chris Morgan is banned by the F.A. for three games for appearing to punch Arsenal's Robin van Persie in an incident caught on camera. Caretaker Phil Brown, formerly in charge of Derby, is appointed Hull manager until the end of the season.
5 Luis Boa Morte is the first major signing in the January transfer window, joining West Ham from Fulham for £4.5m.
7 Rangers, also-rans in the title race and knocked out of the CIS Insurance Cup by St Johnstone, suffer a further blow when losing 3-2 to Dunfermline in round three of the Scottish Cup.
8 Walter Smith is refused permission by the Scottish FA to be released from his contract as national team manager to return to Rangers. Aaron Lennon signs a new contract keeping him at Tottenham until 2012.

9 John Terry is fined £10,000 by the F.A. for questioning the integrity of referee Graham Poll after Chelsea's defeat at Tottenham. Julio Baptista scores four times as Arsenal return to Anfield three days after a 3-1 F.A. Cup third round success and register a 6-3 victory over Liverpool in the quarter-finals of the Carling Cup.
10 The Scottish F.A. threaten legal action after the resignation of Walter Smith, who is unveiled as Rangers manager with former Ibrox striker Ally McCoist as his assistant.
11 David Beckham agrees a five-year deal to join Los Angeles Galaxy from Real Madrid. Wrexham, two points off a relegation place, sack manager Denis Smith. Barrow defender James Cotterill is jailed for four months for breaking the jaw of Sean Rigg in an F.A. Cup first round tie against Bristol Rovers.
12 Brian Carey, former captain and coach at the club, is appointed Wrexham manager until the end of the season.
15 Six successive league defeats cost Keith Alexander his job as Peterborough manager after seven months in charge.
16 The Football League announce a no-smoking policy at all grounds from the start of the 2007-08 season.
17 Coventry sack manager Micky Adams after a run of poor results, culminating in a 2-0 home defeat by Bristol City in an F.A. Cup third round replay.
18 The Belgravia Group announce they are no longer pursuing a takeover of Newcastle. Life-long supporter Matthew Benham takes over almost £3m. worth of Brentford's loans, saving the club £150,000 a year in interest charges.
19 Manchester United have a bid for England midfielder Owen Hargreaves turned down by Bayern Munich. Chelsea's Glen Johnson, on loan at Portsmouth, and Millwall's Ben May receive £80 fixed fines for stealing from a store in Dartford.
20 Wrexham midfielder Darren Ferguson, son of Sir Alex Ferguson, becomes Peterborough's new manager.
22 Ron Atkinson, 67, is appointed director of football at Kettering, where he began his managerial career in 1971.
23 Aston Villa sign Watford's Ashley Young for £9.6m., a record for both clubs. Chelsea reach the Carling Cup Final with a 5-1 aggregate win over Wycombe.
24 Charlton's Jimmy Floyd Hasselbaink is fined £5,000 by the F.A. for accusing, in his autobiography, one of his former clubs Chelsea of making illegal payments to players. Southend receive local council approval for a new 22,000-seater stadium.
25 Peter Taylor steps down as the England Under-21 coach to concentrate on his club duties at Crystal Palace.
26 Michel Platini, former captain and coach of France, becomes the most powerful man in European football after ending Lennart Johansson's 17-year tenure as president of UEFA. Chester and Shrewsbury are both fined £3,000 by the F.A. for a players' brawl.
28 Owen Hargreaves is named England's Player of the Year for 2006 in a poll of supporters.
29 Alex McLeish, who played 77 times for his country, is appointed Scotland's new manager.
30 Dubai International Capital withdraw their £450m. offer to buy Liverpool.
31 Matthew Upson's £7.5m. move from Birmingham to West Ham, a record for both clubs, is the biggest deal on transfer deadline day. Arsenal's youthful Carling Cup team reach the final with a 5-3 aggregate win over Tottenham.

FEBRUARY 2007

1 Manchester City manager Stuart Pearce is appointed part-time manager of the England Under-21 team
2 Argentine midfielder Javier Mascherano is given dispensation by FIFA to join Liverpool, despite playing for two clubs – Corinthians, of Brazil, and West Ham – in one 12-month period.
3 Holders Hearts lose 1-0 to bottom-of-the-table Dunfermline in round four of the Scottish Cup.
5 Torquay part company with manager Lubos Kubik after one win in his 12 league games.
6 American tycoons George Gillett and Tom Hicks finalise a £450m. takeover of Liverpool – a sum which includes the cost of a new stadium. London stages four internationals,

including Portugal's 2-0 victory over Brazil watched by a capacity 60,000 crowd at the Emirates Stadium. Other games are: Australia 1, Denmark 3 (Loftus Road); Ghana 4, Nigeria 1 (Griffin Park); Greece 0, South Korea 1 (Craven Cottage). In another friendly, Northern Ireland and Wales finish goalless.
7 England are beaten 1-0 by Spain in a friendly international – their fourth successive game without a victory. Stephen Ireland's first international goal, a last-minute winner against San Marino, spares the Republic of Ireland from embarrassment in a European Championship qualifier.
8 The F.A. fine Liverpool £14,000 and Everton £10,000 for a players' confrontation in a reserve match. Former England defender Terry Butcher parts company with Sydney F.C. after nine months in the job. Keith Curle, former Mansfield and Chester manager, takes over at Torquay until the end of the season.
9 Tottenham receive a bye into the last 16 of the UEFA Cup when Feyenoord's appeal against expulsion for crowd trouble at their group game against Nancy is rejected by the Court of Arbitration for Sport in Lausanne.
10 Darren Anderton scores the first hat-trick of a 17-year career in Bournemouth's 5-0 victory over Leyton Orient.
12 Bradford sack Colin Todd after a run of one win in ten matches, the 30th manager to go this season.
13 After more than three months of talks, former Portsmouth owner Milan Mandaric completes his takeover of Leicester. Luton manager Mike Newell is fined £6,500 by the F.A. for comments about assistant referee Amy Rayner and the role of women match officials generally. The F.A. fine Tottenham £8,000 and Middlesbrough £4,000 – with half the sums suspended for a year – over a players' confrontation at White Hart Lane.
14 Manchester United and Everton agree a £3m. fee for goalkeeper Tim Howard to stay at Goodison Park at the end of his season-long loan.
15 Kenny Jacket steps down as Swansea manager by mutual agreement after their push for promotion falters.
16 Fulham manager Chris Coleman is fined £2,500 by the F.A. for confronting referee Mike Dean and his assistants after the home game against Tottenham.
17 Craig Bellamy is fined a fortnight's wages by Liverpool after allegedly attacking team-mate John Arne Riise with a golf club during a training camp in Portugal. Other players are also reportedly fined.
18 Iain Dowie, formerly in charge at Oldham, Crystal Palace and Charlton, is appointed Coventry's new manager.
19 Chelsea post annual losses of £80.2m. – down from £140m. the previous year.
21 Craig Bellamy scores an equaliser and sets up the winner for John Arne Riise for Liverpool in the Champions League against Barcelona in the Nou Camp. Referee Mike Riley shows 11 yellow cards in the game between Roma and Lyon, equalling the record for the competition.
22 Newcastle overcome Zulte-Waregem in the first knock-out round of the UEFA Cup. Blackburn are knocked out by Bayer Leverkusen.
23 Swansea name their Spanish-born former midfield player Roberto Martinez as the club's new manager.
24 Huddersfield's Matt Glennon saves three penalties against Crewe – and still finishes on the losing side.
25 Chelsea's 2-1 win over Arsenal in the Carling Cup Final is soured when three players – John Obi Mikel, Kolo Toure and Emmanuel Adebayor – are sent off following a mass brawl.
26 Blackburn's David Bentley signs a new contract which will keep him at Ewood Park until the summer of 2011.
27 England's chances of hosting the 2018 World Cup take a knock when FIFA president Sepp Blatter favours North America for the tournament.
28 Alan Knill is sacked as Rotherham manager after a run of 14 matches without a victory.

MARCH 2007

2 An American consortium, with interests in financial services and property, invest £5m. in Millwall.

3 Stockport set a Football League record by scoring a ninth successive win with a ninth clean sheet – 3-0 against Swindon.
4 Kevin Nolan, the Bolton captain, signs a new four-year contract with the club.
5 The F.A. fine Chester £8,000, with £5,000 suspended for 12 months, for failing to control their players in the match against MK Dons.
6 Liverpool overcome holders Barcelona and Chelsea edge past FC Porto to reach the quarter-finals of the Champions League. Peter Jackson is sacked as Huddersfield manager after a 5-1 defeat by Nottingham Forest.
7 Arsenal's last chance of a trophy disappears when they are knocked out of the Champions League by PSV Eindhoven. Henrik Larsson signs off at Old Trafford with the goal against Lille that ensures Manchester United's passage to the quarter-finals.
9 Arsenal's Emmanuel Adebayor is fined £7,500 and given an extra one-game ban by the F.A. for failing to leave the pitch immediately after his dismissal in the Carling Cup Final.
10 The keys to the new £800m.Wembley are handed over to the F.A. by builders Multiplex, six-and-a-half-years after contracts were first signed and with the cost of the project having more than doubled.
11 Michael Essien agrees a new five-year contract with Chelsea. Chesterfield, a point above the relegation zone, sack manager Roy McFarland.
12 The Football League announce a three-year extension to their sponsorship deal with Coca-Cola.
14 Tottenham reach the quarter-finals of the UEFA Cup with victory over Braga, but Rangers go out against Osasuna. An F.A. Youth Cup record crowd of 38,187 watch the semi-final first leg between Arsenal and Manchester United at the Emirates Stadium.
15 Manager Mike Newell is sacked by relegation-threatened Luton after more criticism of the board. Newcastle lose a 4-2 lead from the first leg and are knocked out of the UEFA Cup by AZ Alkmaar.
16 Football League chairmen meet widespread opposition after agreeing to consider penalty shoot-outs for drawn matches.
18 Hibernian beat Kilmarnock 5-1 in the CIS Insurance Cup Final at Hampden Park. Head coach Valdas Ivanauskas leaves Hearts by mutual agreement, the fourth team chief to go in two years.
19 Newcastle midfielder Emre is cleared of an F.A. charge of racial abuse. Hampshire businessman Jeff Mostyn heads a £750,000 takeover of League One club Bournemouth.
20 The Football League reject a call from Liverpool manager Rafael Benitez for Premiership clubs to be allowed to field their reserve teams in the Championship.
21 UEFA fine Lille £42,000 for security breaches and Manchester United £6,300 for misbehaviour by fans after trouble at their Champions League game.
22 Two Premiership managers are disciplined by the F.A. Wigan's Paul Jewell is fined £2,000 and given a suspended two-match touchline ban for his behaviour towards referee Phil Dowd at Arsenal. Portsmouth's Harry Redknapp receives a £750 fine for abusive language at the home game against Manchester City.
23 Former West Bromwich Albion midfield player Michael Appleton is awarded £1.5m. damages after suing a surgeon for unnecessary knee surgery which ruined his career.
24 England continue to struggle in their European Championship qualifying campaign with a goalless draw in Israel. David Healy becomes the first Northern Ireland player to score two international hat-tricks, following up his treble against Spain six months earlier with three in the 4-1 victory away to Liechtenstein. Substitute Craig Beattie's 89th minute goal gives Alex McLeish a successful start in charge of Scotland, 2-1 against Georgia, while Stephen Ireland follows up his matchwinner against San Marino with the only goal for the Republic of Ireland against Wales in the first soccer match at Dublin's Croke Park, the home of Gaelic sport. A crowd of 55,700 at the first international at the new Wembley see Giampaolo Pazzini score a hat-trick for Italy in a 3-3 draw with England in an Under-21 match.
26 An 18-point deduction for Ryman Premier League club AFC Wimbledon for fielding an ineligible player is reduced to three by an F.A. appeals panel after Prime Minister Tony Blair and nearly 100 MPs deem it 'excessive.'
27 Arsenal and Chelsea are both fined £100,000 for the mass brawl at the end of the Carling Cup Final. Soho Square announce that the F.A. Cup Final will return to Wembley this season after a safety certificate is granted for the new stadium. Former Leeds manager Kevin Blackwell takes charge of his home-town club Luton.

28 David Nugent scores on his England debut, but supporters continue to give coach Steve McClaren a hard time during the 3-0 European Championship qualifying win over Andorra. David Healy scores two more for Northern Ireland, who go top of their group by beating Sweden 2-1, taking the Leeds striker's tally to nine of his team's ten goals in the tournament so far. There are also victories for Wales (3-0 v San Marino) and the Republic of Ireland (1-0 v Slovakia), but Scotland go down 2-0 away to Italy.
29 The BBC and Sky lose TV rights for England's home matches and F.A. Cup ties when the F.A. accept an offer of £425m. from ITV and the Irish broadcaster Setanta for a new four-year contract – an increase of £125m.
30 Accrington are fined £12,000 by the Football League – half of it suspended – for fielding two ineligible players, but escape a points deduction.
31 Darlington's Tommy Wright is sent off after 43 seconds at Barnet for an elbowing offence.

APRIL 2007

1 In the Millennium Stadium's last final before England's showpiece club matches return to Wembley, a crowd of 59,024 see an extra-time goal by skipper Graeme Lee give Doncaster the Johnstone's Paint Trophy with a 3-2 victory over Bristol Rovers.
2 Newcastle unveil plans for a £300m. development at St James' Park, including raising the capacity from 52,000 to 60,000.
3 Steven Gerrard overtakes Ian Rush as Liverpool's leading European Cup scorer with his 15th goal in a 3-0 quarter-final victory against PSV Eindhoven. Tottenham escape punishment over the fan who aimed a punch at Frank Lampard after the F.A. Cup replay against Chelsea. Coventry's Kevin Kyle is given 120 hours of community service for a street brawl while celebrating Scotland's European Championship qualifying victory over France.
4 Fans clash with riot police during Manchester United's Champions League quarter-final with Roma in the Olympic Stadium. Phil Parkinson, Charlton's No 2, turns down the Huddersfield manager's job an hour before the club plan to announce his appointment.
5 More crowd trouble, this time at Tottenham's UEFA Cup quarter-final in Seville. The F.A. fine Leeds manager Dennis Wise £4,000 for pushing West Bromwich Albion's Diomansy Kamara off the pitch and Birmingham's Steve Bruce £1,500 for improper conduct towards doping control officials at Plymouth.
6 Former Manchester United striker Mark Robins is named Rotherham's new manager after a spell as caretaker.
7 Dagenham and Redbridge win promotion to the Football League as Conference champions with five games still remaining.
9 Among Dagenham's opponents in the new season will be Brentford, the first side to be relegated. Grimsby defender John McDermott makes his 750th appearance for the club he joined straight from school.
10 Manchester United record the biggest-ever win in a Champions League knock-out match, beating Roma 7-1 in the second leg of their quarter-final. Chelsea also go through by overcoming Valencia. Struggling Fulham sack Chris Coleman and appoint Northern Ireland manager Lawrie Sanchez until the end of the season. Relegated Brentford dismiss Scott Fitzgerald after less than four months as manager.
11 Liverpool join their Premiership rivals in the semi-finals by beating PSV Eindhoven. With their Championship status under threat, Leicester sack manager Rob Kelly.
12 Tottenham are unable to round off a successful week for English clubs, losing to Sevilla in the UEFA Cup quarter-finals. FIFA announce that the 2014 World Cup will be held in Brazil. Chester chairman Stephen Vaughan is fined £1,000 by the F.A. for violent conduct after the game at Shrewsbury.
13 Cristiano Ronaldo signs a new contract, reported to be worth £120,000 a week, keeping him at Manchester United until 2012. Reading's Leroy Lita is banned for three matches for violent conduct after the F.A. review an incident with Charlton's Talal El Karkouri which went unpunished.
14 Manchester United beat Watford 4-1 to reach the F.A. Cup Final for a record 18th time. Torquay are relegated to the Conference, ending 80 years' membership of the Football League.

15 An extra-time goal by Michael Ballack against Blackburn puts Chelsea into the F.A. Cup Final.
16 The F.A. come under fire from supporters' groups claiming that ticket prices for the F.A. Cup Final are too high.
17 Arsenal manager Arsene Wenger is fined £2,500 by the F.A. for berating match officials during the 2-2 draw with Portsmouth.
18 David Dein, one of the most influential men in British football, is ousted as Arsenal vice-chairman in a power struggle. UEFA award the 2012 European Championship Finals to Poland and the Ukraine.
19 The F.A. fine Sheffield United £10,000, Reading £5,000 and Reading coach Wally Downes £2,000 with a one-match touchline ban for a fracas at the Madejski Stadium.
20 Crewe announce that Dario Gradi, the game's longest-serving manager with 24 years in charge, will become the club's technical director at the end of the season, with academy manager Steve Holland promoted to first-team coach. Ron Atkinson resigns as director of football at Kettering less than three months after taking over.
21 Cristiano Ronaldo wins the PFA Player of the Year award and the Young Player accolade, the first to complete the double since Aston Villa's Andy Gray in 1977.
22 A stoppage-time winner by Shunsuke Nakamura against Kilmarnock confirms Celtic as Scottish Premier League champions for the second successive year. Portsmouth's David James overtakes David Seaman's Premiership record of 141 clean sheets.
23 More honours for Celtic. Shunsuke Nakamura is named Scottish PFA Player of the Year and manager Gordon Strachan is Manager of the Year for the second successive season. Former England captain Terry Butcher is appointed Brentford's new manager.
24 Portsmouth unveil plans for a new 36,000-seater waterfront stadium to replace run-down Fratton Park. Burnley manager Steve Cotterill is fined £2,000 by the F.A. for remarks to Derby's Mo Camara.
25 Alan Ball, England's youngest player in their 1966 World Cup-winning team, dies aged 61. UEFA fine Roma £31,000 and Manchester United £14,500 following crowd trouble at their Champions League game in the Olympic Stadium. The F.A. fine Stephen Bywater (Derby) £2,000 and Alex Bruce (Ipswich) £1,500 for an altercation after being sent off.
26 On-loan Jonathan Woodgate agrees a £7m. permanent move from Real Madrid to Middlesbrough. Former Chesterfield midfielder Lee Richardson is appointed manager after a spell as caretaker. The F.A. fine Luton £5,000, half of it suspended, and Queens Park Rangers £2,500 for a players' fracas.
27 West Ham are fined a record £5.5m. by an independent Premier League commission for breaches of regulations involving 'dishonesty and deceit' over Argentinian signings Carlos Tevez and Javier Mascherano. But the club escape having points deducted.
28 Scunthorpe, 66-1 outsiders, are crowned League One champions. Gretna complete a remarkable rise to the Scottish Premier League with a third successive title win, thanks to a last-minute winner by James Grady against Ross County.
29 Sam Allardyce resigns after seven years as Bolton manager. Mark Wright is sacked as Chester manager after poor results. Arsenal become the first British club to win the UEFA Women's Cup.
30 Bolton appoint Sam Allardyce's assistant, Sammy Lee, as his replacement as manager.

MAY 2007

1 Two saves by Jose Reina in a penalty shoot-out enable Liverpool to overcome Chelsea and reach the Champions League Final. Manchester City suspend Joey Barton until the end of the season after a training ground incident leaves team-mate Ousmane Dabo needing hospital treatment.
2 Manchester United go down 3-0 in the second leg of their Champions League semi-final with AC Milan and lose 5-3 on aggregate.
3 Arsenal manager Arsene Wenger is fined by the F.A. for the third time this season – £2,500 for remarks to an assistant referee after the stormy Carling Cup Final with Chelsea. UEFA fine Osasuna £31,000 and Rangers £8,200 for misbehaving fans at their UEFA Cup tie in Spain. Chelsea's Andriy Shevchenko accepts substantial libel damages over articles in the *Daily Mirror.*

4 Ken Bates puts Leeds into administration before they are officially relegated, ensuring that a ten-point penalty applies this season and not the new one. Cristiano Ronaldo adds the Football Writers' Association Footballer of the Year award to his PFA trophy. Scotland defender Andy Webster is ordered by FIFA to pay Hearts £650,000 for breaking his contract to join Wigan.
5 Boston also go into adminstration before they go down – this time back to the Conference.
6 Manchester United are crowned Premiership champions, while their former captain Roy Keane celebrates Sunderland's title win in the Championship in his first season as manager. Glenn Roeder bows to pressure and resigns as Newcastle manager.
7 Charlton are relegated from the Premiership. Arsenal's women's team complete an unprecedented quadruple success – Premier League, F.A. Cup, League Cup and UEFA Cup.
8 Adrian Boothroyd, manager of relegated Watford, signs a new three-year contract.
10 The F.A. ban two players for three matches for violent conduct not spotted by match officials – City's Michael Ball for stamping on United's Cristano Ronaldo in the Manchester derby and Fulham captain Michael Brown for butting Liverpool's Xabi Alonso.
11 Lawrie Sanchez resigns as Northern Ireland manager to take charge of Fulham after a month as caretaker. Bobby Williamson, formerly in charge of Plymouth, Hibernian and Kilmarnock, is appointed Chester's new manager. Sir Bobby Charlton unveils a statue of his World Cup-winning captain Bobby Moore at the new Wembley.
12 A record F.A. Trophy crowd of more than 53,000 see Stevenage come from two goals down to beat Kidderminster 3-2 in the new Wembley's first final. Dunfermline are relegated from the Scottish Premier League.
13 On a dramatic final day of the Premiership season, West Ham and Wigan survive while Sheffield United go down amid threats of legal action over the league's decision not to dock West Ham points for breaching regulations when signing Carlos Tevez. Fulham defender Matthew Briggs, aged 16 years and 65 days, becomes the Premiership's youngest-ever player. Another record crowd at Wembley, this time nearly 28,000 for the F.A. Vase Final, won by Truro City who beat AFC Totton 3-1.
14 The pressures of management are highlighted as Paul Jewell quits Wigan and Stuart Pearce is sacked by under-achieving Manchester City. Jewell's No 2, Chris Hutchings, replaces him – just as he did at Bradford seven years earlier. Shrewsbury play their final game at Gay Meadow before moving to a new stadium.
15 A fortnight after leaving Bolton, Sam Allardyce is named Newcastle's new manager. FIFA president Sepp Blatter promises to review the punishment handed out to West Ham over the Carlos Tevez affair. Aston Villa miss out on a UEFA Cup place in the competition's 'fair play' draw.
16 Neil Warnock calls time on seven years as Sheffield United manager, three days after relegation. Sevilla retain the UEFA Cup in a penalty shoot-out against Espanyol at Hampden Park.
17 A record transfer between Scottish clubs takes the Hibernian midfielder Scott Brown to Celtic for a fee of £4.4m.
19 A goal by Didier Drogba four minutes from the end of extra-time gives Chelsea victory over Manchester United in the F.A. Cup Final.
20 Morecambe win a place in the Football League for the first time by beating Exeter 2-1 in the Conference Play-off Final.
21 Liverpool businessman Steve Morgan agrees a takeover of Wolves, paying Sir Jack Hayward a nominal £10 for his shares and promising a £30m. investment in the club.
22 Bryan Robson, formerly in charge at Middlesbrough and West Bromwich Albion, is named Neil Warnock's successor as Sheffield United manager. Stuart McCall, Warnock's assistant at Bramall Lane, becomes manager of Bradford, where he had two spells as a player.
23 Liverpool lose 2-1 to AC Milan in the Champions League Final. Sir John Hall, former Newcastle chairman, and his family sell their 41.6% shareholding to businessman Mike Ashley, triggering a takeover bid for the club.
24 Liverpool fans blame UEFA for ticket chaos at the Champions League Final, which led to overcrowding and clashes with riot police.

25 Michael Owen returns to international football for the first time since the World Cup Finals in a 3-1 win by England B against Albania. Martin Allen leaves MK Dons to become Leicester manager. Yossi Benayoun signs a new five-year contract with West Ham.
26 Coach Steve McClaren restores David Beckham to the England squad for matches against Brazil and Estonia. A record crowd of 61,589 see Bristol Rovers beat Shrewsbury 3-1 in the League Two Play-off Final at Wembley. An 85th minute goal by Jean-Joel Perrier Doumbe, a defender on loan from Rennes, breaks Dunfermline resistance and gives Celtic the Scottish Cup. Shane Long scores his first goal for the Republic of Ireland, who draw 1-1 with Bolivia on their American tour in Boston.
27 Blackpool defeat Yeovil 2-0 in the League One Play-off Final. Steve Evans, manager of relegated Boston, resigns.
28 Derby beat West Bromwich Albion 1-0 in the Championship Play-off Final, a victory reputedly worth between £50m. and £60m. to the club. Tottenham's Robbie Keane signs a contract committing him to the club until 2012.
29 The F.A. receive the go-ahead from shareholders to implement plans for modernisation, including the appointment of an independent chairman, as recommended by the Burns Report.
30 Accountants Deloitte, in their annual review of football's finances, predict there will be the first £200,000-a-week player before 2010. Portsmouth pay a club-record fee of £7m. for Udinese's Ghana World Cup midfield player Sulley Muntari.
31 Manchester United announce that Owen Hargreaves will join them from Bayern Munich on July 1. The fee — £17m. Geoff Thompson, chairman of the F.A., is appointed Britain's FIFA vice-president after Scotland's John McBeth loses his chance of the position over criticism of African and Caribbean associations.

JUNE 2007

1 David Beckham, on his international return, sets up a goal for John Terry, but England are denied victory by a last minute Brazil equaliser at Wembley. Nigel Worthington, who won 66 caps with Northern Ireland, is appointed manager in succession to Lawrie Sanchez. Maurice Malpas parts company with Motherwell after a year as manager.
2 Ryan Giggs retires from international football after his 64th appearance for Wales in a goalless European Championship qualifier against the Czech Republic.
3 Steven Gerrard and Jamie Carragher pledge their futures to Liverpool by agreeing new four-year contracts.
4 Ken Bates regains control of Leeds at a creditors' meeting after putting the club in administration.
5 Newcastle sell Scott Parker to West Ham for £7m. and agree a £5.5m. fee for Manchester City's Joey Barton.
6 David Beckham continues his England renaissance, creating goals for Peter Crouch and Michael Owen in a 3-0 European Championship qualifying win over Estonia. Shaun Maloney scores his first for Scotland, who also win away, 2-0 against the Faroe Islands. Steven Gerrard accepts undisclosed libel damages over an article in *Sport* magazine.
7 Liverpool goalkeeper Jose Reina signs a new five-year contract.
8 The Football League close a loophole which enables clubs going into administration to avoid having the mandatory ten-point deduction apply to the following season. Xabi Alonso becomes the fourth Liverpool player in a week to sign a new long-term deal.
9 Blackburn's David Bentley withdraws from England's squad on the eve of the European Under-21 Championship in Holland, blaming fatigue.
10 Adam Pearson sells control of Hull to a business consortium, headed by former media chief Paul Duffen, for around £10m.
11 England have to be satisfied with a goalless draw against the Czech Republic after Leroy Lita misses a late penalty in their opening match of the European Under-21 Championship.
13 Businessman David Pinkney takes over Luton and unveils plans for a new 25,000-seater stadium.
14 Crystal Palace chairman Simon Jordan wins a High Court victory over Iain Dowie after claiming that he was deceived over the manager's departure from Selhurst Park. England lead Italy 2-0 but are held 2-2 in the European Under-21 Championship.

15 Five Premiership clubs – Bolton, Chelsea, Middlesbrough, Newcastle and Portsmouth – are named by Lord Stevens in his final report into alleged transfer irregularities. He also names 15 agents ands third parties involved in 17 deals. Ryan Giggs receives an OBE and Teddy Sheringham an MBE in the Queen's Birthday Honours. There is also an OBE for former F.A. chairman Geoff Thompson.
17 David Beckham bids farewell to Real Madrid with a Championship medal after a 3-1 win over Mallorca on the final day of the season. England qualify for the semi-finals of the European Under-21 Championship with a 2-0 win over Serbia & Montenegro, but the victory is soured by racist abuse against some of their players.
18 Mark McGhee, former Aberdeen and Celtic striker, returns to Scotland as Motherwell's new manager after spells in charge of five English clubs.
19 A three-man arbitration panel, headed by a retired High Court judge, ends a two-day hearing into the Carlos Tevez affair and announces its judgement will be made at the end of the month.
20 England's penalty jinx strikes again, this time in the semi-finals of the European Under-21 Championship with a 13-12 defeat on spot-kicks against Holland. Former Football League club Scarborough go out of business with debts of £2.5m.
21 Chelsea's John Obi Mikel is suspended indefinitely from playing for Nigeria by the country's F.A. after pulling out of an African Nations Cup qualifier against Uganda, citing a hamstring injury.
22 Queens Park Rangers are fined £20,000 and assistant manager Richard Hill is banned from football for three months by the F.A. for a brawl during a match against China's Olympic team at the club's training ground. Iain Dowie is ordered to pay costs estimated at more than £500,000 following his High Court defeat by Crystal Palace chairman Simon Jordan.
23 Thierry Henry calls time on eight years at Arsenal with a £16m. move to Barcelona.
25 Newcastle claim victory against FIFA and the F.A. over a claim for £10m. compensation for Michael Owen's knee injury sustained during the World Cup. Paul Ince, who led Macclesfield away from the threat of relegation last season, is appointed the new manager of MK Dons.
26 Former England coach Sven-Goran Eriksson agrees to a return to club management with Manchester City.
27 Hong Kong businessman Carson Yeung Ka-Sing pays £14.7m. for a 29.9% stake in Birmingham.
28 Liverpool extend the Premiership's longest-running sponsorship, launched with Carlsberg in 1992, until 2010 at around £8m. a year. Coach Fabio Capello is sacked, 11 days after leading Real Madrid to the Spanish League title. First-team coach Ian Brightwell is appointed Macclesfield's new manager. UEFA chose Manchester City to host the 2008 UEFA Cup Final. Everton's Tim Cahill and Mikel Arteta sign new five-year contracts.
29 After turning down a move to West Ham, Charlton's Darren Bent joins Tottenham for £16.5m. – a record for both clubs.
30 Former Tottenham defender Graham Roberts is awarded £32,000 compensation after being sacked as manager of Clyde over claims that he made racist comments.

JULY 2007

1 Billionaire businessman Mike Ashley seals a £133m. takeover of Newcastle.
2 Manchester United take their summer spending to nearly £50m. by signing FC Porto midfielder Anderson for £18m. and Sporting Lisbon winger Nani for £12m. Arsenal replace Thierry Henry by paying Dinamo Zagreb £8m. for Croatia striker Eduardo da Silva.
3 Sheffield United lose their legal fight against relegation – although an arbitration panel declare that West Ham should have been docked points over the Carlos Tevez affair.
4 Liverpool sign Atletico Madrid striker Fernando Torres for £22m. Former Fulham manager Chris Coleman takes charge of Real Sociedad.
5 Manchester United's bid to sign Carlos Tevez runs into opposition from West Ham and the Premier League.
6 Former Thai prime Minister Thaksin Shinawatra completes an £81m. takeover of Manchester City. The future of Leeds hangs in the balance after administrators put the debt-ridden club up for sale.
10 Chelsea sign Lyon's French international winger Florent Malouda for £13.5m.

ENGLISH TABLES 2006–07

BARCLAYS PREMIERSHIP

			HOME					AWAY						
		P	W	D	L	F	A	W	D	L	F	A	GD	Pts
1	Manchester Utd.	38	15	2	2	46	12	13	3	3	37	15	56	89
2	Chelsea	38	12	7	0	37	11	12	4	3	27	13	40	83
3	Liverpool	38	14	4	1	39	7	6	4	9	18	20	30	68
4	Arsenal	38	12	6	1	43	16	7	5	7	20	19	28	68
5	Tottenham	38	12	3	4	34	22	5	6	8	23	32	3	60
6	Everton	38	11	4	4	33	17	4	9	6	19	19	16	58
7	Bolton Wand.	38	9	5	5	26	20	7	3	9	21	32	–5	56
8	Reading	38	11	2	6	29	20	5	5	9	23	27	5	55
9	Portsmouth	38	11	5	3	28	15	3	7	9	17	27	3	54
10	Blackburn Rov.	38	9	3	7	31	25	6	4	9	21	29	–2	52
11	Aston Villa	38	7	8	4	20	14	4	9	6	23	27	2	50
12	Middlesbrough	38	10	3	6	31	24	2	7	10	13	25	–5	46
13	Newcastle Utd.	38	7	7	5	23	20	4	3	12	15	27	–9	43
14	Manchester City	38	5	6	8	10	16	6	3	10	19	28	–15	42
15	West Ham Utd.	38	8	2	9	24	26	4	3	12	11	33	–24	41
16	Fulham	38	7	7	5	18	18	1	8	10	20	42	–22	39
17	Wigan Athletic	38	5	4	10	18	30	5	4	10	19	29	–22	38
18	Sheffield Utd.	38	7	6	6	24	21	3	2	14	8	34	–23	38
19	Charlton Athletic	38	7	5	7	19	20	1	5	13	15	40	–26	34
20	Watford	38	3	9	7	19	25	2	4	13	10	34	–30	28

Manchester Utd. and Chelsea go into Champions League group stage; Liverpool and Arsenal into third qualifying round; Tottenham, Everton and Bolton Wand. into UEFA Cup.
Prize-money: 1 £9.73m, 2 £9.22m, 3 £8.75m, 4 £8.27m, 5 £7.78m, 6 £7.29m, 7 £6.81m, 8 £6.32m, 9 £5.83m, 10 £5.35m, 11 £4.86, 12 £4.37m, 13 £3.89m, 14 £3.40m, 15 £2.91m, 16 £2.43m, 17 £1.94, 18 £1.45m, 19 £973,126, 20 £486,500.
Biggest win: Reading 6, West Ham Utd. 0.
Highest attendance: 76,098 (Manchester Utd. v Blackburn Rov.).
Lowest attendance: 14,636 (Wigan Athletic v Reading).
Manager of Year: Sir Alex Ferguson (Manchester Utd.).
Golden Boot: 20 Didier Drogba (Chelsea).
Golden Glove: Jose Reina (Liverpool).
Football Writers' Player of Year: Cristiano Ronaldo (Manchester Utd.).
P.F.A. Player of Year: Cristiano Ronaldo.
P.F.A. Team of Year: Van der Sar (Manchester Utd.), Neville (Manchester Utd.), Ferdinand (Manchester Utd.), Vidic (Manchester Utd.), Evra (Manchester Utd.), Ronaldo (Manchester Utd.), Gerrard (Liverpool), Scholes (Manchester Utd.), Giggs (Manchester Utd.), Drogba (Chelsea), Berbatov (Tottenham).
Leading scorers (all club competitions): 33 Drogba (Chelsea); 24 McCarthy (Blackburn Rov.); 23 Berbatov (Tottenham), Ronaldo (Manchester Utd.), Rooney (Manchester Utd.); 22 Keane (Tottenham); 21 Lampard (Chelsea); 19 Viduka (Middlesbrough); 18 Crouch (Liverpool), Defoe (Tottenham); 17 Martins (Newcastle Utd.); 16 Yakubu (Middlesbrough); 15 Bent, D (Charlton Athletic); 14 Kuyt (Liverpool), Lita (Reading), Shevchenko (Chelsea); 13 Doyle (Reading), Van Persie (Arsenal); 12 Anelka (Bolton Wand.), Johnson (Everton), Kanu (Portsmouth), McBride (Fulham).
Others: 16 Hoskins (Watford) – 16 for Rotherham Utd.; 14 Folan (Wigan Athletic) – 12 for Chesterfield.

COCA-COLA CHAMPIONSHIP

			HOME					AWAY						
		P	W	D	L	F	A	W	D	L	F	A	GD	Pts
1	Sunderland	46	15	4	4	38	18	12	3	8	38	29	29	88
2	Birmingham City	46	15	5	3	37	18	11	3	9	30	24	25	86
3	Derby Co.†	46	13	6	4	33	19	12	3	8	29	27	16	84
4	W.B.A.	46	14	4	5	51	24	8	6	9	30	31	26	76
5	Wolves	46	12	5	6	33	28	10	5	8	26	28	3	76
6	Southampton	46	13	6	4	36	20	8	6	9	41	33	24	75
7	Preston N.E.	46	15	4	4	38	17	7	4	12	26	36	11	74
8	Stoke City	46	12	8	3	35	16	7	8	8	27	25	21	73
9	Sheffield Wed.	46	10	6	7	38	36	10	5	8	32	30	4	71
10	Colchester Utd.	46	15	4	4	46	19	5	5	13	24	37	14	69
11	Plymouth Argyle	46	10	8	5	36	26	7	8	8	27	36	1	67
12	Crystal Palace	46	12	3	8	33	22	6	8	9	26	29	8	65
13	Cardiff City	46	11	7	5	33	18	6	6	11	24	35	4	64
14	Ipswich Town	46	13	2	8	40	29	5	6	12	24	30	5	62
15	Burnley	46	10	6	7	35	23	5	6	12	17	26	3	57
16	Norwich City	46	10	5	8	29	25	6	4	13	27	46	–15	57
17	Coventry City	46	11	4	8	30	25	5	4	14	17	37	–15	56
18	Q.P.R.	46	9	6	8	31	29	5	5	13	23	39	–14	53
19	Leicester City	46	6	8	9	26	31	7	6	10	23	33	–15	53
20	Barnsley	46	9	4	10	27	29	6	1	16	26	56	–32	50
21	Hull City	46	8	3	12	33	32	5	7	11	18	35	–16	49
22	Southend Utd.	46	6	6	11	29	38	4	6	13	18	42	–33	42
23	Luton Town	46	7	5	11	33	40	3	5	15	20	41	–28	40
24	Leeds Utd.*	46	10	4	9	27	30	3	3	17	19	42	–26	36

(† Also promoted)
(* 10 points deducted for administration)

Biggest win: W.B.A. 7, Barnsley 0.
Highest attendance: 44,448 (Sunderland v Burnley).
Lowest attendance: 4,249 (Colchester Utd.v Barnsley).
Manager of Year: Roy Keane (Sunderland).
Player of Year: Jason Koumas (W.B.A.)
Top League scorer: 23 Jamie Cureton (Colchester Utd.).
P.F.A. Team of Year: Murray (Wolves), Alexander (Preston N.E.), Moore (Derby Co.), Davies (W.B.A.), Bale (Southampton), McSheffrey (Birmingham City), Whitehead (Sunderland), Edwards (Sunderland), Koumas (W.B.A.), Chopra (Cardiff City), Kamara (W.B.A.)
Leading scorers (all club competitions): 24 Cureton (Colchester Utd.); 23 Kamara (W.B.A.); 22 Chopra (Cardiff City), Phillips (W.B.A.); 21 Rasiak (Southampton); 19 Earnshaw (Norwich City), Howard (Derby Co.); 18 Iwelumo (Colchester Utd.); 17 Lee (Ipswich Town), McSheffrey (Birmingham City) – 1 for Coventry City; Nugent (Preston N.E.); 16 Eastwood (Southend Utd.), Jones (Southampton); 15 Vine (Birmingham City) – 14 for Luton Town; 14 Blackstock (Q.P.R.), Gray (Burnley), Hayles (Plymouth Argyle), Hume (Leicester City). **Others:** 20 Windass (Hull City) – 12 for Bradford City; 14 Kandol (Leeds Utd.) – 13 for Barnet.

COCA-COLA LEAGUE ONE

			HOME					AWAY						
		P	W	D	L	F	A	W	D	L	F	A	GD	Pts
1	Scunthorpe Utd.	46	15	6	2	40	17	11	7	5	33	18	38	91
2	Bristol City	46	15	5	3	35	20	10	5	8	28	19	24	85
3	Blackpool†	46	12	6	5	40	25	12	5	6	36	24	27	83
4	Nott'm. Forest	46	14	5	4	37	17	9	8	6	28	24	24	82
5	Yeovil Town	46	14	3	6	22	12	9	7	7	33	27	16	79
6	Oldham Athletic	46	13	4	6	36	18	8	8	7	33	29	22	75
7	Swansea City	46	12	6	5	36	20	8	6	9	33	33	16	72
8	Carlisle Utd.	46	12	5	6	35	24	7	6	10	19	31	–1	68
9	Tranmere Rov.	46	13	5	5	33	22	5	8	10	25	31	5	67
10	Millwall	46	11	8	4	33	19	8	1	14	26	43	–3	66
11	Doncaster Rov.	46	8	10	5	30	23	8	5	10	22	24	5	63
12	Port Vale	46	12	3	8	35	26	6	3	14	29	39	–1	60
13	Crewe Alexandra	46	11	4	8	39	38	6	5	12	27	34	–6	60
14	Northampton Town	46	8	5	10	27	28	7	9	7	21	23	–3	59
15	Huddersfield Town	46	9	8	6	37	33	5	9	9	23	36	–9	59
16	Gillingham	46	14	2	7	29	24	3	6	14	27	53	–21	59
17	Cheltenham Town	46	8	6	9	25	27	7	3	13	24	34	–12	54
18	Brighton & H.A.	46	5	7	11	23	34	9	4	10	26	24	–9	53
19	Bournemouth	46	10	5	8	28	27	3	8	12	22	37	–14	52
20	Leyton Orient	46	6	10	7	30	32	6	5	12	31	45	–16	51
21	Chesterfield	46	9	5	9	29	22	3	6	14	16	31	–8	47
22	Bradford City	46	5	9	9	27	31	6	5	12	20	34	–18	47
23	Rotherham Utd.*	46	8	4	11	37	39	5	5	13	21	36	–17	38
24	Brentford	46	5	8	10	24	41	3	5	15	16	38	–39	37

(† Also promoted)
(* 10 points deducted for administration)

Biggest win: Bournemouth 5, Leyton Orient 0; Carlisle Utd. 5, Gillingham 0; Oldham Athletic 5, Nott'm. Forest 0; Swansea City 5, Carlisle Utd. 0.
Highest attendance: 27,875 (Nott'm. Forest v Rotherham Utd.).
Lowest attendance: 3,036 (Cheltenham Town v Scunthorpe Utd.).
Manager of Year: Russell Slade (Yeovil Town).
Player of Year: Billy Sharp (Scunthorpe Utd.).
Top League scorer: 30 Billy Sharp.
P.F.A. Team of Year: Murphy (Scunthorpe Utd.), Otsemobor (Crewe Alexandra), Breckin (Nott'm. Forest), Skiverton (Yeovil Town), Lockwood (Leyton Orient), Hoolahan (Blackpool), Jarvis (Gillingham), Wellens (Oldham Athletic), Shuker (Tranmere Rov.), Varney (Crewe Alexandra), Sharp (Scunthorpe Utd.).
Leading scorers (all club competitions): 32 Sharp (Scunthorpe Utd.); 26 Constantine (Port Vale); 25 Varney (Crewe Alexandra); 23 Porter (Oldham Athletic); 21 Heffernan (Doncaster Rov.); 20 Morrell (Blackpool), Trundle (Swansea City); 19 Greenacre (Tranmere Rov.), Maynard (Crewe Alexandra),18 Holt, Grant (Nott'm. Forest); 17 Jevons (Bristol City); 16 Byfield (Millwall), Parker (Blackpool), Sodje (Port Vale); 15 Beckett (Huddersfield Town), Odejayi (Cheltenham Town), Showunmi (Bristol City); 14 Kuffour (Brentford), Vernon (Blackpool).

COCA-COLA LEAGUE TWO

			HOME					AWAY						
		P	W	D	L	F	A	W	D	L	F	A	GD	Pts
1	Walsall	46	16	4	3	39	13	9	10	4	27	21	32	89
2	Hartlepool Utd.	46	14	5	4	34	17	12	5	6	31	23	25	88
3	Swindon Town	46	15	4	4	34	17	10	6	7	24	21	20	85
4	MK Dons	46	14	4	5	41	26	11	5	7	35	32	18	84
5	Lincoln City	46	12	4	7	36	28	9	7	7	34	31	11	74
6	Bristol Rov.†	46	13	5	5	27	14	7	7	9	22	28	7	72
7	Shrewsbury Town	46	11	7	5	38	23	7	10	6	30	23	22	71
8	Stockport Co.	46	14	4	5	41	25	7	4	12	24	29	11	71
9	Rochdale	46	9	6	8	33	20	9	6	8	37	30	20	66
10	Peterborough Utd.	46	10	6	7	48	36	8	5	10	22	25	9	65
11	Darlington	46	10	6	7	28	30	7	8	8	24	26	–4	65
12	Wycombe Wand.	46	8	11	4	23	14	8	3	12	29	33	5	62
13	Notts Co.	46	8	6	9	29	25	8	8	7	26	28	2	62
14	Barnet	46	12	5	6	35	30	4	6	13	20	40	–15	59
15	Grimsby Town	46	11	4	8	33	32	6	4	13	24	41	–16	59
16	Hereford Utd.	46	9	7	7	23	17	5	6	12	22	36	–8	55
17	Mansfield Town	46	10	4	9	38	31	4	8	11	20	32	–5	54
18	Chester City	46	7	9	7	23	23	6	5	12	17	25	–8	53
19	Wrexham	46	8	8	7	23	21	5	4	14	20	44	–22	51
20	Accrington Stanley	46	10	6	7	42	33	3	5	15	28	48	–11	50
21	Bury	46	4	7	12	22	35	9	4	10	24	26	–15	50
22	Macclesfield Town	46	8	7	8	36	34	4	5	14	19	43	–22	48
23	Boston Utd.*	46	9	5	9	29	32	3	5	15	22	48	–29	36
24	Torquay Utd.	46	5	8	10	19	22	2	6	15	17	41	–27	35

(† Also promoted)
(* 10 points deducted for administration)

Biggest win: Boston Utd. 0, Grimsby Town 6; Lincoln City 7, Rochdale 1.
Highest attendance: 14,731 (Swindon Town v Walsall).
Lowest attendance: 1,234 (Accrington Stanley v Mansfield Town).
Manager of Year: Danny Wilson (Hartlepool Utd.).
Player of Year: Izale McLeod (MK Dons).
Top League scorer: 21 Richie Barker (Hartlepool Utd.) – 12 for Mansfield Town, Izale McLeod.
P.F.A. Team of Year: Ince (Walsall), Pead (Walsall), Nelson (Hartlepool Utd.), Westwood (Hartlepool Utd.), Humphreys (Hartlepool Utd.), Frecklingon (Lincoln City), Keates (Walsall), Monkhouse (Harlepool Utd.), Doherty (Wycombe Wand.), McLeod (MK Dons), Easter (Wycombe Wand.).
Leading scorers (all club competitions): 24 Barker (Hartlepool Utd.) – 15 for Mansfield Town, Easter (Wycombe Wand.), McLeod (MK Dons); 23 Walker (Bristol Rov.); 20 Bishop (Bury); 19 Murray (Rochdale) – 3 for Stockport Co.; 18 Dagnall (Rochdale), Forrester (Lincoln City); Platt (MK Dons); 17 Stallard (Lincoln City); 16 Elding (Stockport Co.) – 5 for Boston Utd., Lee (Notts Co.), Mullin (Accrington Stanley); 13 Hurst (Bury), Joachim (Darlington) – 3 for Boston Utd., Keates (Walsall), Mooney (Wycombe Wand. Wand), Roberts (Swindon Town), Symes (Shrewsbury Town).

BARCLAYS PREMIERSHIP RESULTS 2006-07

	Arsenal	Aston Villa	Blackburn Rov.	Bolton Wand.	Charlton Athletic	Chelsea	Everton	Fulham	Liverpool	Manchester City	Manchester Utd.	Middlesbrough	Newcastle Utd.	Portsmouth	Reading	Sheffield Utd.	Tottenham	Watford	West Ham Utd.	Wigan Athletic
Arsenal	–	1–1	6–2	2–1	4–0	1–1	1–1	3–1	3–0	3–1	2–1	1–1	1–1	2–2	2–1	3–0	3–0	3–0	0–1	2–1
Aston Villa	0–1	–	2–0	0–1	2–0	0–0	1–1	1–1	0–0	1–3	0–3	1–1	2–0	0–0	2–1	3–0	1–1	2–0	1–0	1–1
Blackburn Rov.	0–2	1–2	–	0–1	4–1	0–2	1–1	2–0	1–0	4–2	0–1	2–1	1–3	3–0	3–3	2–1	1–1	3–1	1–2	2–1
Bolton Wand.	3–1	2–2	1–2	–	1–1	0–1	1–1	2–1	2–0	0–0	0–4	0–0	2–1	3–2	1–3	1–0	2–0	1–0	4–0	0–1
Charlton Athletic	1–2	2–1	1–0	2–0	–	0–1	1–1	2–2	0–3	1–0	0–3	1–3	2–0	0–1	0–0	1–1	0–2	0–0	4–0	1–0
Chelsea	1–1	1–1	3–0	2–2	2–1	–	1–1	2–2	1–0	3–0	0–0	3–0	1–0	2–1	2–2	3–0	1–0	4–0	1–0	4–0
Everton	1–0	0–1	1–0	1–0	2–1	2–3	–	4–1	3–0	1–1	2–4	0–0	3–0	3–0	1–1	2–0	1–2	2–1	2–0	2–2
Fulham	2–1	1–1	1–1	1–1	2–1	0–2	1–0	–	1–0	1–3	1–2	2–1	2–1	1–1	0–1	1–0	1–1	0–0	0–0	0–1
Liverpool	4–1	3–1	1–1	3–0	2–2	2–0	0–0	4–0	–	1–0	0–1	2–0	2–0	0–0	2–0	4–0	3–0	2–0	2–1	2–0
Manchester City	1–0	0–2	0–3	0–2	0–0	0–1	2–1	3–1	0–0	–	0–1	1–0	0–0	0–0	0–2	0–0	1–2	0–0	2–0	0–1
Manchester Utd.	0–1	3–1	4–1	4–1	2–0	1–1	3–0	5–1	2–0	3–1	–	1–1	2–0	3–0	3–2	2–0	1–0	4–0	0–1	3–1
Middlesbrough	1–1	1–3	0–1	5–1	2–0	2–1	2–1	3–1	0–0	0–2	1–2	–	1–0	0–4	2–1	3–1	2–3	4–1	1–0	1–1
Newcastle Utd.	0–0	3–1	0–2	1–2	0–0	0–0	1–1	1–2	2–1	0–1	2–2	0–0	–	1–0	3–2	0–1	3–1	2–1	2–2	2–1
Portsmouth	0–0	2–2	3–0	0–1	0–1	0–2	2–0	1–1	2–1	2–1	2–1	0–0	2–1	–	3–1	3–1	1–1	2–1	2–0	1–0
Reading	0–4	2–0	1–2	1–0	2–0	0–1	0–2	1–0	1–2	1–0	1–1	3–2	1–0	0–0	–	3–1	3–1	0–2	6–0	3–2
Sheffield Utd.	1–0	2–2	0–0	2–2	2–1	0–2	1–1	2–0	1–1	0–1	1–2	2–1	1–2	1–1	1–2	–	2–1	1–0	3–0	1–2
Tottenham	2–2	2–1	1–1	4–1	5–1	2–1	0–2	0–0	0–1	2–1	0–4	2–1	2–3	2–1	1–0	2–0	–	3–1	1–0	3–1
Watford	1–2	0–0	2–1	0–1	2–2	0–1	0–3	3–3	0–3	1–1	1–2	2–0	1–1	4–2	0–0	0–1	0–0	–	1–1	1–1
West Ham Utd.	1–0	1–1	2–1	3–1	3–1	1–4	1–0	3–3	1–2	0–1	1–0	2–0	0–2	1–2	0–1	1–0	3–4	0–1	–	0–2
Wigan Athletic	0–1	0–0	0–3	1–3	3–2	2–3	0–2	0–0	0–4	4–0	1–3	0–1	1–0	1–0	1–0	0–1	3–3	1–1	0–3	–

Read across for home results, down for away.

COCA-COLA CHAMPIONSHIP RESULTS 2006–07

	Barnsley	Birmingham City	Burnley	Cardiff City	Colchester Utd.	Coventry City	Crystal Palace	Derby Co.	Hull City	Ipswich Town	Leeds Utd.	Leicester City	Luton Town	Norwich City	Plymouth Argyle	Preston N.E.	Q.P.R.	Sheffield Wed.	Southampton	Southend Utd.	Stoke City	Sunderland	W.B.A.	Wolves
Barnsley	–	1–0	1–0	1–2	0–3	0–1	2–0	1–2	3–0	1–0	3–2	0–1	1–2	1–3	2–2	0–1	2–0	0–3	2–2	2–0	2–2	0–2	1–1	1–0
Birmingham City	2–0	–	0–1	1–0	2–1	3–0	2–1	1–0	2–1	2–2	1–0	1–1	2–2	0–1	3–0	3–1	2–1	2–0	2–1	1–3	1–0	1–1	2–0	1–1
Burnley	4–2	1–2	–	2–0	1–2	1–2	1–1	0–0	2–0	1–0	2–1	0–1	0–0	3–0	4–0	3–2	2–0	1–1	2–3	0–0	0–1	2–2	3–2	0–1
Cardiff City	2–0	2–0	1–0	–	0–0	1–0	0–0	2–2	0–1	2–2	1–0	3–2	4–1	1–0	2–2	4–1	0–1	1–2	1–0	0–1	1–1	0–1	1–1	4–0
Colchester Utd.	1–2	1–1	0–0	3–1	–	0–0	0–2	4–3	5–1	1–0	2–1	1–1	4–1	3–0	0–1	1–0	2–1	4–0	2–0	3–0	3–0	3–1	1–2	2–1
Coventry City	4–1	0–1	1–0	2–2	2–1	–	2–4	1–2	2–0	1–2	1–0	0–0	1–0	3–0	0–1	0–4	0–1	3–1	2–1	1–1	0–0	2–1	0–1	2–1
Crystal Palace	2–0	0–1	2–2	1–2	1–3	1–0	–	2–0	1–1	2–0	1–0	2–0	2–1	3–1	0–1	3–0	3–0	1–2	0–2	3–1	0–1	1–0	0–2	2–2
Derby Co.	2–1	0–1	1–0	3–1	5–1	1–1	1–0	–	2–2	2–1	2–0	1–0	1–0	0–0	1–0	1–1	1–1	1–0	2–2	3–0	0–2	1–2	2–1	0–2
Hull City	2–3	2–0	2–0	4–1	1–1	0–1	1–1	1–2	–	2–5	1–2	1–2	0–0	1–2	1–2	2–0	2–1	2–1	2–4	4–0	0–2	0–1	0–1	2–0
Ipswich Town	5–1	1–0	1–1	3–1	3–2	2–1	1–2	2–1	0–0	–	1–0	0–2	5–0	3–1	3–0	2–3	2–1	0–2	2–1	0–2	0–1	3–1	1–5	0–1
Leeds Utd.	2–2	3–2	1–0	0–1	3–0	2–1	2–1	0–1	0–0	1–1	–	1–2	1–0	1–0	2–1	2–1	0–0	2–3	0–3	2–0	0–4	0–3	2–3	0–1
Leicester City	2–0	1–2	0–1	0–0	0–0	3–0	1–1	1–1	0–1	3–1	1–1	–	1–1	1–2	2–2	0–1	1–3	1–4	3–2	1–0	2–1	0–2	1–1	1–4
Luton Town	0–2	3–2	0–2	0–0	1–1	3–1	2–1	0–2	1–2	0–2	5–1	2–0	–	2–3	1–2	2–0	2–3	3–2	0–2	0–0	2–2	0–5	2–2	2–3
Norwich City	5–1	1–0	1–4	1–0	1–1	1–1	0–1	1–2	1–1	1–1	2–1	3–1	3–2	–	1–3	2–0	1–0	1–2	0–1	0–0	1–0	1–0	1–2	0–1
Plymouth Argyle	2–4	0–1	0–0	3–3	3–0	3–2	1–0	3–1	1–0	1–1	1–2	3–0	1–0	3–1	–	2–0	1–1	1–2	1–1	2–1	1–1	0–2	2–2	1–1
Preston N.E.	1–0	1–0	2–0	2–1	1–0	1–1	0–0	1–2	2–1	1–0	4–1	0–1	3–0	2–1	3–0	–	1–1	0–0	3–1	2–3	3–2	4–1	1–0	0–1
Q.P.R.	1–0	0–2	3–1	1–0	1–0	0–1	4–2	1–2	2–0	1–3	2–2	1–1	3–2	3–3	1–1	1–0	–	1–1	0–2	2–0	1–1	1–2	1–2	0–1
Sheffield Wed.	2–1	0–3	1–1	0–0	2–0	2–1	3–2	1–2	1–2	2–0	0–1	2–1	0–1	3–2	1–1	1–3	3–2	–	3–3	3–2	1–1	2–4	3–1	2–2
Southampton	5–2	4–3	0–0	2–2	1–2	2–0	1–1	0–1	0–0	1–0	1–0	2–0	2–1	2–1	1–0	1–1	1–2	2–1	–	4–1	1–0	1–2	0–0	2–0
Southend Utd.	1–3	0–4	1–0	0–3	0–3	2–3	0–1	0–1	2–3	1–3	1–1	2–2	1–3	3–3	1–1	0–0	5–0	0–0	2–1	–	1–0	3–1	3–1	0–1
Stoke City	0–1	0–0	0–1	3–0	3–1	1–0	2–1	2–0	1–1	0–0	3–1	4–2	0–0	5–0	1–1	1–1	1–0	1–2	2–1	1–1	–	2–1	1–0	1–1
Sunderland	2–0	0–1	3–2	1–2	3–1	2–0	0–0	2–1	2–0	1–0	2–0	1–1	2–1	1–0	2–3	0–1	2–1	1–0	1–1	4–0	2–2	–	2–0	2–1
W.B.A.	7–0	1–1	3–0	1–0	2–1	5–0	2–3	1–0	2–0	2–0	4–2	2–0	3–2	0–1	2–1	4–2	3–3	0–1	1–1	1–1	1–3	1–2	–	3–0
Wolves	2–0	2–3	2–1	1–2	1–0	1–0	1–1	0–1	3–1	1–0	1–0	1–2	1–0	2–2	2–2	1–3	2–0	2–2	0–6	3–1	2–0	1–1	1–0	–

Read across for home results, down for away.

COCA-COLA LEAGUE ONE RESULTS 2006–07

	Blackpool	Bournemouth	Bradford City	Brentford	Brighton & H.A.	Bristol City	Carlisle Utd.	Cheltenham Town	Chesterfield	Crewe Alexandra	Doncaster Rov.	Gillingham	Huddersfield Town	Leyton Orient	Millwall	Northampton Town	Nottm. Forest	Oldham Athletic	Port Vale	Rotherham Utd.	Scunthorpe Utd.	Swansea City	Tranmere Rov.	Yeovil Town
Blackpool	–	2–0	4–1	1–3	0–0	0–1	2–1	2–1	1–1	2–1	3–1	1–1	3–1	3–0	0–1	4–1	0–2	2–2	2–1	0–1	3–1	1–1	3–2	1–1
Bournemouth	1–3	–	1–1	1–0	1–0	0–1	0–1	2–1	0–3	1–0	2–0	1–1	1–2	5–0	1–0	0–0	2–0	3–2	0–4	1–3	1–1	2–2	2–0	0–2
Bradford City	1–3	0–0	–	1–1	2–3	2–1	1–1	2–2	1–0	0–1	0–1	4–2	0–1	0–2	2–2	1–2	2–2	1–1	2–0	1–1	0–1	2–2	2–0	0–2
Brentford	1–0	0–0	2–1	–	1–0	1–1	0–0	0–2	2–1	0–4	0–4	2–2	2–2	2–2	1–4	0–1	2–4	2–2	4–3	0–1	0–2	0–2	1–1	1–2
Brighton & H.A.	0–3	2–2	0–1	2–2	–	0–2	1–2	2–1	1–2	1–4	0–2	1–0	0–0	4–1	0–1	1–1	2–1	1–2	0–0	0–0	1–1	3–2	0–1	1–3
Bristol City	2–4	2–2	2–3	1–0	1–0	–	1–0	0–1	3–1	2–1	1–0	3–1	1–1	2–1	1–0	1–0	1–1	0–0	2–1	3–1	1–0	0–0	3–2	2–0
Carlisle Utd.	2–0	3–1	1–0	2–0	3–1	1–3	–	2–0	0–0	0–2	1–0	5–0	1–1	3–1	1–2	1–1	1–0	1–1	3–2	1–1	0–2	1–2	1–0	1–4
Cheltenham Town	1–2	1–0	1–2	2–0	1–1	2–2	0–1	–	0–0	1–1	0–2	1–1	2–1	2–1	3–2	0–2	0–2	1–2	0–1	2–0	1–1	2–1	1–0	1–2
Chesterfield	2–0	0–1	3–0	3–1	0–1	1–3	0–0	1–0	–	2–1	1–1	0–1	0–0	0–1	5–1	0–0	1–2	2–1	3–0	2–1	0–1	2–3	0–2	1–1
Crewe Alexandra	1–2	2–0	0–3	3–1	1–1	0–1	5–1	3–1	2–2	–	2–1	4–3	2–0	0–4	1–0	2–2	1–4	2–1	2–1	1–0	1–3	1–3	1–1	2–3
Doncaster Rov.	0–0	1–1	3–3	3–0	1–0	0–1	1–2	0–2	1–0	3–1	–	1–2	3–0	0–0	1–2	2–2	1–0	1–1	1–0	3–2	2–2	2–2	0–0	0–0
Gillingham	2–2	1–1	1–0	2–1	0–1	1–0	2–0	2–1	2–1	1–0	0–2	–	2–1	2–1	2–1	0–1	0–1	0–3	3–2	1–0	0–2	3–1	2–0	0–2
Huddersfield Town	0–2	2–2	2–0	0–2	0–3	2–1	2–1	2–0	1–1	1–2	0–0	3–1	–	3–1	4–2	1–1	1–1	0–3	2–2	3–0	1–1	3–2	2–2	2–3
Leyton Orient	0–1	3–2	1–2	1–1	1–4	1–1	1–1	2–0	0–0	1–1	1–1	3–3	1–0	–	2–0	0–2	1–3	2–2	2–1	2–3	2–2	0–1	3–1	0–0
Millwall	0–0	1–0	2–0	1–1	0–1	1–0	2–0	2–0	2–1	2–2	2–2	4–1	0–0	2–5	–	0–1	1–0	1–0	1–1	4–0	0–1	2–0	2–2	1–1
Northampton Town	1–1	3–1	0–0	0–1	0–2	1–3	3–2	2–0	1–0	1–2	0–2	1–1	1–1	0–1	3–0	–	0–1	2–3	0–2	3–0	2–1	1–0	1–3	1–1
Nottm. Forest	1–1	3–0	1–0	2–0	2–1	1–0	0–0	3–0	4–0	0–0	0–1	1–0	5–1	1–3	3–1	1–0	–	0–2	3–0	1–1	0–4	3–1	1–1	1–0
Oldham Athletic	0–1	1–2	2–0	3–0	1–1	0–3	0–0	0–2	1–0	1–0	4–0	4–1	1–1	3–3	1–2	3–0	5–0	–	0–1	2–1	1–0	1–0	1–0	1–0
Port Vale	2–1	2–1	0–1	1–0	2–1	0–2	0–2	1–1	3–2	3–0	1–2	2–0	1–2	3–0	2–0	1–0	1–1	3–0	–	1–3	0–0	0–2	2–3	4–2
Rotherham Utd.	1–0	0–2	4–1	2–0	0–1	1–1	0–1	2–4	0–1	5–1	0–0	3–2	2–3	2–2	2–3	1–2	1–1	2–3	1–5	–	2–1	1–2	2–1	3–2
Scunthorpe Utd.	1–3	3–2	2–0	1–1	1–2	1–0	3–0	1–0	1–0	2–2	2–0	3–1	2–0	3–1	3–0	1–0	1–1	1–1	3–0	1–0	–	2–2	1–1	1–0
Swansea City	3–6	4–2	1–0	2–0	2–1	0–0	5–0	1–2	2–0	2–1	2–0	2–0	1–2	0–0	2–0	2–1	0–0	0–1	3–0	1–1	0–2	–	0–0	1–1
Tranmere Rov.	2–0	1–0	1–1	3–1	2–1	1–0	0–2	2–2	2–0	1–0	1–0	2–3	2–2	3–0	3–1	1–1	0–0	1–0	1–2	2–1	0–2	0–2	–	2–1
Yeovil Town	0–1	0–0	0–0	1–0	2–0	2–1	2–1	0–1	1–0	2–0	1–0	2–0	3–1	2–1	0–1	0–0	0–1	1–0	1–0	1–0	0–2	1–0	0–2	–

Read across for home results, down for away.

COCA-COLA LEAGUE TWO RESULTS 2006–07

	Accrington Stanley	Barnet	Boston Utd.	Bristol Rov.	Bury	Chester City	Darlington	Grimsby Town	Hartlepool Utd.	Hereford Utd.	Lincoln City	Macclesfield Town	Mansfield Town	MK Dons	Notts Co.	Peterborough Utd.	Rochdale	Shrewsbury Town	Stockport Co.	Swindon Town	Torquay Utd.	Walsall	Wrexham	Wycombe Wand.
Accrington Stanley	–	2-1	2-1	1-1	1-1	0-1	0-2	4-1	1-2	2-0	2-2	3-2	3-2	3-4	1-2	3-2	1-1	3-3	0-1	1-1	1-0	1-2	5-0	2-1
Barnet	1-2	–	3-3	1-1	2-1	1-0	2-1	0-1	2-1	3-0	0-5	1-0	2-1	3-3	2-3	1-0	3-2	0-0	3-1	1-0	0-1	1-1	1-2	2-1
Boston Utd.	1-0	2-1	–	2-1	0-1	1-0	4-1	0-6	0-1	1-1	1-0	4-1	1-1	0-1	3-3	0-1	0-3	0-3	2-1	1-3	1-1	1-1	4-0	0-1
Bristol Rov.	4-0	2-0	1-0	–	2-0	0-0	1-2	1-0	0-2	2-1	0-0	0-0	1-0	1-1	2-0	3-2	0-0	1-0	2-1	1-0	1-0	1-2	0-1	1-2
Bury	2-2	2-2	2-1	0-2	–	1-3	1-1	3-0	0-1	2-2	2-2	1-1	1-1	0-2	0-1	0-3	0-1	1-2	2-0	0-1	0-1	1-2	1-0	0-4
Chester City	2-0	2-0	3-1	2-0	1-0	–	1-1	0-2	2-1	1-1	4-1	0-3	1-1	0-3	0-0	1-1	0-1	0-0	1-1	0-2	1-1	0-0	1-2	0-1
Darlington	2-1	2-0	2-0	1-1	1-0	1-0	–	2-2	0-3	1-0	1-1	4-0	0-2	1-0	0-1	3-1	0-5	1-2	0-5	1-2	1-1	0-0	1-1	3-2
Grimsby Town	2-0	5-0	3-2	4-3	2-0	0-2	0-1	–	1-4	2-1	0-0	1-1	1-1	1-3	0-2	0-2	0-4	2-1	0-1	1-0	2-0	2-1	2-1	2-2
Hartlepool Utd.	1-0	0-1	2-1	1-2	2-0	3-0	0-0	2-0	–	3-2	1-1	3-2	2-0	1-0	1-1	1-0	1-0	0-3	1-1	0-1	1-1	3-1	3-0	2-0
Hereford Utd.	1-0	2-0	3-0	0-0	1-0	2-0	1-1	0-1	3-1	–	1-2	1-0	1-3	0-0	3-2	0-0	0-0	0-1	0-2	0-0	1-1	0-1	2-0	1-2
Lincoln City	3-1	1-0	2-1	1-0	0-2	2-0	1-3	2-0	2-0	1-4	–	2-1	1-2	2-3	1-1	1-0	7-1	1-1	0-0	2-3	1-0	2-2	0-3	1-0
Macclesfield Town	3-3	2-3	2-3	0-1	2-3	1-1	1-1	2-1	0-0	3-0	2-1	–	2-3	1-2	1-1	2-1	1-0	2-2	2-0	2-1	3-3	0-2	2-0	0-2
Mansfield Town	2-2	2-1	1-2	0-1	0-2	2-1	1-0	1-2	0-1	4-1	2-4	1-2	–	2-1	2-2	0-2	1-2	1-1	1-1	2-0	5-0	2-1	3-0	3-2
MK Dons	3-1	3-1	3-2	2-0	2-1	1-2	1-0	1-2	0-0	1-3	2-2	3-0	1-1	–	3-2	0-2	2-1	2-0	2-0	0-1	3-2	1-1	2-1	3-1
Notts Co.	3-2	1-1	2-0	1-2	0-1	1-2	0-1	2-0	0-1	0-1	3-1	1-2	0-0	2-2	–	0-0	1-2	1-1	1-0	1-1	5-2	1-2	2-1	1-0
Peterborough Utd.	4-2	1-1	1-1	4-1	0-1	0-2	1-3	2-2	3-5	3-0	1-2	3-1	2-0	4-0	2-0	–	3-3	2-1	0-3	1-1	5-2	0-2	3-0	3-3
Rochdale	4-2	0-2	4-0	0-1	1-3	0-0	0-0	1-0	2-0	1-1	2-0	5-0	2-0	5-0	0-1	0-1	–	1-1	1-3	0-0	2-0	0-1	2-2	0-2
Shrewsbury Town	2-1	0-1	5-0	0-0	1-3	2-1	2-2	2-2	1-1	3-0	0-1	2-1	2-2	2-1	2-0	2-1	3-0	–	4-2	1-2	1-0	1-1	0-1	0-0
Stockport Co.	1-1	2-0	2-0	2-1	0-0	2-0	5-2	3-0	3-3	0-2	2-0	1-1	1-0	1-2	2-0	0-1	2-7	0-3	–	3-0	1-0	1-0	5-2	2-0
Swindon Town	2-0	2-1	1-1	2-1	2-1	1-0	1-1	3-0	0-1	1-2	0-1	2-0	2-0	2-1	1-1	0-1	1-0	2-1	2-0	–	2-1	1-1	2-1	2-1
Torquay Utd.	0-2	1-1	0-1	0-0	2-2	2-2	0-1	4-1	0-1	0-0	1-2	0-1	1-0	0-2	0-1	1-1	1-0	0-0	1-0	0-1	–	1-2	1-1	3-0
Walsall	3-2	4-1	1-1	2-2	0-1	1-0	1-0	2-0	2-0	1-0	1-2	2-0	4-0	0-0	2-1	5-0	1-1	1-0	2-0	0-2	1-0	–	1-0	2-0
Wrexham	1-3	1-1	3-1	2-0	1-1	0-0	1-0	3-0	1-1	1-0	2-1	0-0	0-0	1-2	0-1	0-0	1-2	1-3	0-1	2-1	1-0	1-1	–	0-2
Wycombe Wand.	1-1	1-1	0-0	0-1	3-0	1-0	1-0	1-1	0-1	0-0	1-3	3-0	1-0	0-2	0-0	2-0	1-1	1-1	2-0	1-1	2-0	0-0	1-1	–

Read across for home results, down for away.

HOW MANCHESTER UNITED REGAINED THE TITLE

AUGUST 2006

20 Manchester Utd. 5 (Saha 6, Pearce 14 og, Rooney 15, 63, Ronaldo 19), Fulham 1 (Ferdinand 40 og). Att: 75,115.
23 Charlton Athletic 0, Manchester Utd. 3 (Fletcher 49, Saha 80, Solskjaer 90). Att: 25,422.
26 Watford 1 (Francis 34), Manchester Utd. 2 (Silvestre 13, Giggs 52). Att: 19,453.

SEPTEMBER 2006

9 Manchester Utd. 1 (Giggs 9), Tottenham 0. Att: 75,453.
17 Manchester Utd. 0, Arsenal 1 (Adebayor 85). Att: 75,595.
23 Reading 1 (Doyle 48 pen), Manchester Utd. 1 (Ronaldo 73). Att: 24,098.

OCTOBER 2006

1 Manchester Utd. 2 (Solskjaer 41, 49), Newcastle Utd. 0. Att: 75,664.
14 Wigan Athletic 1 (Baines 5), Manchester Utd. 3 (Vidic 62, Saha 66, Solskjaer 90). Att: 20,631.
22 Manchester Utd. 2 (Scholes 38, Ferdinand 65), Liverpool 0. Att: 75,828.
28 Bolton Wand. 0, Manchester Utd. 4 (Rooney 10, 16, 89, Ronaldo 82). Att: 27,229.

NOVEMBER 2006

4 Manchester Utd. 3 (Saha 3 pen, Ronaldo 10, Vidic 66), Portsmouth 0. Att: 76,004.
11 Blackburn Rov. 0, Manchester Utd. 1 (Saha 64). Att: 26,162.
18 Sheffield Utd. 1 (Gillespie 13), Manchester Utd. 2 (Rooney 30, 75). Att: 32,584.
26 Manchester Utd. 1 (Saha 29), Chelsea 1 (Ricardo Carvalho 69). Att: 75,948.
29 Manchester Utd. 3 (Ronaldo 39, Evra 63, O'Shea 89), Everton 0. Att: 75,723.

DECEMBER 2006

2 Middlesbrough 1 (Morrison 66), Manchester Utd. 2 (Saha 19 pen, Fletcher 68). Att: 31,238.
9 Manchester Utd. 3 (Rooney 6, Saha 45, Ronaldo 84), Manchester City 1 (Trabelsi 72). Att: 75,858.
17 West Ham Utd. 1 (Reo-Coker 75), Manchester Utd. 0. Att: 34,966.
23 Aston Villa 0, Manchester Utd. 3 (Ronaldo 58, 85, Scholes 64). Att: 42,551.
26 Manchester Utd. 3 (Ronaldo 47, 51, Solskjaer 59), Wigan Athletic 1 (Baines 90 pen). Att: 76,018.
30 Manchester Utd. 3 (Solskjaer 33, Ronaldo 59, 77), Reading 2 (Sonko 38, Lita 90). Att: 75,910.

JANUARY 2007

1 Newcastle Utd. 2 (Milner 33, Edgar 74), Manchester Utd. 2 (Scholes 40, 45). Att: 52,302.
13 Manchester Utd. 3 (Park 11, Carrick 13, Ronaldo 35), Aston Villa 1 (Agbonlahor 52). Att: 76,078.
21 Arsenal 2 (Van Persie 83, Henry 90), Manchester Utd. 1 (Rooney 53). Att: 60,128.
31 Manchester Utd. 4 (Ronaldo 20 pen, Doyley 61 og, Larsson 70, Rooney 71), Watford 0. Att: 76,032.

FEBRUARY 2007

4 Tottenham 0, Manchester Utd. 4 (Ronaldo 45 pen, Vidic 48, Scholes 54, Giggs 77). Att: 36,146.

10 Manchester Utd. 2 (Park 24, Fletcher 82), Charlton Athletic 0. Att: 75,883.
24 Fulham 1 (McBride 17), Manchester Utd. 2 (Giggs 29, Ronaldo 88). Att: 24,459.

MARCH 2007

3 Liverpool 0, Manchester Utd. 1 (O'Shea 90). Att: 44,403.
17 Manchester Utd. 4 (Park 14, 25, Rooney 17, 74), Bolton Wand. 1 (Speed 87 pen). Att: 76,058
31 Manchester Utd. 4 (Scholes 61, Carrick 73, Park 83, Solskjaer 90), Blackburn Rov. 1 (Derbyshire 29). Att: 76,098.

APRIL 2007

7 Portsmouth 2 (Taylor 30, Ferdinand 89 og), Manchester Utd. 1 (O'Shea 90). Att: 20,223.
17 Manchester Utd. 2 (Carrick 4, Rooney 50), Sheffield Utd. 0. Att: 75,540.
21 Manchester Utd. 1 (Richardson 3), Middlesbrough 1 (Viduka 45). Att: 75,967.
28 Everton 2 (Stubbs 12, Fernandes 50), Manchester Utd. 4 (O'Shea 61, Neville 68 og, Rooney 79, Eagles 90). Att: 39,682.

MAY 2007

5 Manchester City 0, Manchester Utd. 1 (Ronaldo 34 pen). Att: 47,244.
9 Chelsea 0, Manchester Utd. 0. Att: 41,794.
13 Manchester Utd. 0, West Ham Utd. 1 (Tevez 45). Att: 75,927.

QUOTE-UNQUOTE

'Our objective is to keep Arsenal English, albeit with a lot of foreign players' – **Peter Hill-Wood**, club chairman, on a possible takeover by American billionaire Stanley Kroenke.

'I won't be a manager who sits in the directors' box – the walls are too high for me to see over' – **Sammy Lee** after succeeding Sam Allardyce at Bolton.

'It is very easy to say it is not a suitable stadium, coming from the man who invented the poll tax' – **William Gaillard**, UEFA communications' director, responding to criticism about the Olympic Stadium in Athens by former Tory leader and Liverpool supporter Michael Howard.

'If Rafa said he wanted to buy Snoogy Doogy, we would back him' – **George Gillett**, Liverpool co-owner, on his manager's demand for new signings.

'We have a spending plan but it will not be just spending like a drunken sailor' – **George Gillett** on reflection.

'Arsenal will always be in my blood and in my heart' – **Thierry Henry** after joining Barcelona.

'I had fifteen messages after the game. The best one was from my mum which said "Come outside and get some sweets" ' – **Nedum Onouha**, England Under-21 defender, after being subject to racial abuse from Serbian supporters at the European Championship Finals.

'Would you phone the president of Ghana?' – **Jose Mourinho**, Chelsea manager, asked by a Ghanaian journalist if he ever phoned owner Roman Abramovich to see how he was.

'It's sod's law, isn't it' – **Sam Allardyce**, Newcastle manager, after being handed an opening day Premiership match at former club Bolton.

HIGHLIGHTS OF THE PREMIERSHIP SEASON 2006-07

AUGUST 2006

19 Reading take pride of place on the opening day of the season by retrieving a 2-0 deficit to beat Middlesbrough 3-2 with goals by Dave Kitson, Steve Sidwell and Leroy Lita. Sheffield United hold Liverpool 1-1, but the third promoted side, Watford, lose 2-1 at Everton after unluckily conceding a penalty when the ball hits full-back Chris Powell in the face. Martin O'Neill makes a satisfactory start as Aston Villa manager with a point at Arsenal's new Emirates Stadium, while Kanu is all smiles after a two-goal debut for Portsmouth in a 3-0 win over Blackburn – a penalty save by Brad Friedel denying the Nigerian striker a hat-trick. Blackburn have Lucas Neill and Andy Todd sent off. Also dismissed, on his debut, is Djimi Traore in Charlton's 3-1 reversal at West Ham.
20 John Terry's header sets up defending champions Chelsea for a 3-0 success against Manchester City, who have Bernado Corradi sent off in his first game for the club. Manchester United are also convincing winners, 5-1 against Fulham with Wayne Rooney scoring twice in front of the Premiership's first 70,000-plus crowd.
22 Dimitar Berbatov opens his account for Tottenham in a 2-0 victory over Sheffield United. Marlon King's 25-yard drive earns Watford their first point, against West Ham.
23 Andriy Shevchenko's first goal for Chelsea looks to be enough at the Riverside until Emanuel Pogatetz and Mark Viduka turn the game on its head for Middlesbrough in the final ten minutes. Ibrahima Sonko sees red as Reading lose 2-1 at Aston Villa, while Manchester City's Ben Thatcher is lucky not to do so for an elbow in the face of Pedro Mendes, which renders the Portsmouth player unconscious during the goalless draw. Ole Solskjaer, dogged by injury for three years, rounds off Manchester United's 3-0 win at Charlton with his first league goal since April 2003.
26 Two more elbowing incidents result in dismissals at the Valley – Charlton's Hermann Hreidarsson and Bolton's Kevin Davies in the home side's 2-0 success. Kevin Kilbane is also sent off in what proves his final match for Everton before a move to Wigan. But Everton claim their first league success over Tottenham at White Hart Lane for 21 years by a 2-0 margin. A first goal for Wigan by Emile Heskey on his 500th career appearance brings victory over Reading, while Daniel Agger's 30-yarder for Liverpool, his first for the club, comes in a 2-1 win over West Ham.
28 Another brace by Kanu keeps Portsmouth's momentum going in a 4-0 success at Middlesbrough.

SEPTEMBER 2006

9 Two goals by Andy Johnson, bringing his tally to four in four matches for his new club, enable Everton to overcome Liverpool 3-0 – their biggest Merseyside derby win for 40 years. Blackburn's Brad Friedel saves penalties from David Unsworth and Rob Hulse, while Sheffield United's Paddy Kenny is equal to a spot-kick from Lucas Neill to keep the scoresheet blank at Bramall Lane. Influential new-signing Jimmy Bullard sustains a serious knee injury, which keeps him out for the rest of the season, but Fulham score twice in the last ten minutes through Brian McBride and Carlos Bocanegra for a 2-1 win at Newcastle. Middlesbrough also do well after the sending-off of George Boateng with a 1-1 draw at Arsenal.
11 Ivar Ingimarsson is knocked out scoring the only goal for Reading against Manchester City, who have another of their new signings, Ousmane Dabo, sent off.
16 Portsmouth's early-season bandwagon rolls on, a Lomana LuaLua goal at Charlton coupled to a fifth successive clean sheet putting them on top of the table. Kevin Doyle finds the net after 18 seconds to point Reading to a 2-1 victory at Sheffield United. Wigan twice come from behind to earn a point at Everton, with Paul Scharner on the mark each time.

17 After a stuttering start to the season, Arsenal come good at Old Trafford with Emmanuel Adebayor's 85th minute winner. Chelsea have Michael Ballack sent off against Liverpool, but prevail thanks to Didier Drogba's stunning volley. Obefami Martins scores his first goal for Newcastle in the 2-0 win at West Ham, for whom Argentinian signings Carlos Tevez and Javier Mascherano make their first league starts.
20 Xabi Alonso, who scored from inside his own half against Luton in the F.A. Cup last season, does it again in the 2-0 win over Newcastle, Dirk Kuyt having earlier netted his first goal for the club.
23 Three players score in the Premiership for the first time for their new clubs. William Gallas helps Arsenal to their first win at the Emirates Stadium, 3-0 against Sheffield United. Mark Gonzalez launches Liverpool's 3-0 victory over Tottenham and Shabani Nonda nets the only goal of the game for Blackburn at Middlesbrough. Kevin Doyle, a boyhood Manchester United fan, earns Reading a point from the penalty spot against Sir Alex Ferguson's team.
24 Newcastle's Titus Bramble and Everton's Tony Hibbert are sent off in separate incidents during a 1-1 draw.
25 Portsmouth's bid to equal Chelsea's six-match start to a season without conceding a goal comes to grief when Kevin Nolan fires the winner for Bolton at Fratton Park.
30 Robin van Persie's stunning volley, an early contender for goal of the season, points Arsenal to a 2-1 success at Charlton. Another spectacular effort, Phil Jagielka's 30-yarder in stoppage-time, brings Sheffield their first victory in the top flight – 2-1 against Middlesbrough. Gary Speed marks his 750th club appearance with Bolton's first in the 2-0 win over Liverpool.

OCTOBER 2006

1 Manchester United go back to the top, on goal difference from Chelsea, when two goals by Ole Solskjaer see off Newcastle.
2 Watford look to be heading for their first Premiership win when leading Fulham 2-0, but end up needing an 89th minute Ashley Young goal, his second of the game, for a 3-3 scoreline.
14 England captain John Terry dons the goalkeeper's jersey after Chelsea's Petr Cech and Carlo Cudicini are both taken to hospital with injuries sustained against Reading. The champions also have John Obi Mikel sent off, but hold out for a 1-0 victory against a side who have Andre Bikey dismissed. Gareth Barry's equaliser against Tottenham spares some of the embarrassment of Aston Villa team-mate Juan Pablo Angel, who misses a penalty then heads into his own net in the space of two second half minutes. Calum Davenport sees red for conceding the spot-kick, but the dismissal is later rescinded. Andy Cole opens his account for Portsmouth in a 2-0 victory over West Ham, while Nemanja Vidic heads his first in English football as Manchester United come from behind to prevail 3-1 at Wigan.
21 Michael Ballack scores his Premiership goal and Andriy Shevchenko his first at Stamford Bridge as Chelsea beat Portsmouth 2-1. Antonio Valencia opens his account by rounding off Wigan's 4-0 win over Manchester City, while Moritz Volz's equaliser at Aston Villa is his first in the league for Fulham. Sheffield United have Claude Davis sent off in the 2-0 defeat at Everton.
22 Paul Scholes, on his 500th appearance, and Rio Ferdinand give Manchester United victory over Liverpool, who trail the leaders by 11 points as a result and may have seen their title chances ended, even at this early stage of the season. Arsenal win 4-0 at Reading and Tottenham defeat troubled West Ham with Mido's first goal since he returned to the club.
28 In the week of his 21st birthday, Wayne Rooney registers the first Premiership hat-trick of the season as Manchester United sweep Bolton aside 4-0 at the Reebok. Sheffield United pay for Danny Webber's failure from the penalty spot as Chelsea win 2-0. Watford are still without a victory, but a point against Tottenham could have been three had Ashley Young's strike not been wrongly disallowed for offside.
29 After eight successive league and cup defeats, West Ham beat Blackburn 2-1 with goals by 40-year-old Teddy Sheringham and Hayden Mullins. Manchester United stay ahead of Chelsea at the top on goal difference.

NOVEMBER 2006

4 Watford are hit by the news that Marlon King is out for the season with a knee injury, but break their Premiership duck by beating Middlesbrough 2-0 thanks to Ashley Young's strike and Jonathan Woodgate's own goal. Two other struggling sides score welcome wins, Danny Webber's goal for Sheffield United accounting for Newcastle at St James' Park and Darren Bent giving Charlton a 1-0 success against Manchester City.
5 A day of high drama in the capital. At Upton Park, Arsene Wenger confronts Alan Pardew on the touchline as the West Ham manager celebrates Marlon Harewood's 89th minute winner against Arsenal. At White Hart Lane, John Terry is sent off as Chelsea lose to Tottenham, 2-1, for the first time in the league since 1990.
11 In-form Didier Drogba nets a hat-trick and lays on Chelsea's fourth for Andriy Shevchenko against Watford. Chris Sutton's first for Aston Villa sets up victory at Everton. Colin Kazim-Richards comes off the bench to score his first for Sheffield United, who retrieve a 2-0 deficit to earn a point against Bolton. Henri Camara celebrates the birth of his son with a goal as Wigan make it four wins on the trot – 3-2 against Charlton in what proves to be Iain Dowie's last match as manager.
12 Liverpool's title hopes are written off completely after a 3-0 defeat at Arsenal, for whom central defenders Kolo Toure and William Gallas are both on the mark. Reading end a run of four successive defeats with a 3-1 win over Tottenham, Nicky Shorey opening the scoring with his first in the Premiership.
18 Les Reed admits the severity of Charlton's position after his first match in charge – a 2-0 defeat at Reading. A rare goal by Geremi, a superb free-kick, is enough to give Chelsea victory over West Ham, while a more familiar name on the scoresheet, Wayne Rooney, scores both for Manchester United, who come from behind to win at Sheffield United. Bernardo Corradi opens his account with two goals for Manchester City to set up a 3-1 victory over Fulham, while the injured-dogged Kieron Dyer's first in the Premiership since March 2005 earns Newcastle a point at Arsenal.
19 Blackburn's Tugay, after a stunning strike, and Tottenham's Hossam Ghaly are sent off in separate incidents in a 1-1 draw.
25 Malcolm Christie, another player unlucky with injuries, gets his first goal since February 2005 as Middlesbrough secure a point at Aston Villa. Steven Gerrard's first of the season in the league breaks the deadlock for Liverpool against Manchester City, while Andy Reid's first for Charlton, against Everton, provides Les Reed with his first point. But pride of place goes to Bolton's record-signing Nicolas Anelka. After firing blanks in the first ten Premiership matches for his new club, the Frenchman scores twice against his old one, Arsenal, in a 3-1 success.
26 The meeting of the top two ends all square, Louis Saha putting Manchester United ahead at Old Trafford and Ricardo Carvalho equalising.
28 Danny Webber's late goal against his former club gives Sheffield United victory at Watford, who have Chris Powell dismissed.
29 Darius Vassell maintains the knack of scoring against his old team and Sylvain Distin runs almost the length of the pitch to net his first goal for 18 months as Manchester City prevail 3-1 at Villa Park. Arsenal have Philippe Senderos sent off in a 2-1 defeat at Fulham, leaving Manchester United (38) and Chelsea (35) streets ahead of the rest. Patrice Evra nets for United for the first time in a 3-0 win over Everton.

DECEMBER 2006

2 Three days after being cleared of assault charges in court, Craig Bellamy is on the mark twice as Liverpool win 4-0 at Wigan, all the goals coming in the first half for a side who had not scored away from home in the league since the opening day of the season. Two disputed penalties by Gilberto Silva ease Arsenal to a 3-0 success against Tottenham, while Portsmouth's Matthew Taylor and Aston Villa's Gareth Barry also convert spot-kicks in a 2-2 scoreline. Portsmouth have Pedro Mendes sent off.

5 A stoppage-time winner against Blackburn by Talal El Karkouri, his first goal for nearly two years, breathes life into Charlton's troubled season. Didier Zokora and George Boateng are sent off after clashing in Tottenham's 2-1 win over Middlesbrough. Boateng's red card is later rescinded.
6 Two days after his 19th birthday, David Cotterill scores his first goal for Wigan in the 2-0 victory at West Ham. James Harper nets his first two of the campaign at Newcastle, but Reading go down 3-2 to Emre's late strike, his first of the campaign.
9 Gary Speed becomes the first player to appear in 500 Premiership games and has a hand in three of Bolton's four goals against West Ham, a result which marks the end of Alan Pardew's three years as manager. Kevin Davies doubles his tally for the season in that match. So too does Obafemi Martins in Newcastle's 3-1 success at Blackburn, who have Stephane Henchoz sent off. Wayne Rooney nets his 50th in the Premiership as United overcome City 3-1 in the Manchester derby. City's Bernardo Corradi is dismissed for the second time this season. Matthew Taylor volleys in from 45 yards to set up Portsmouth's 2-0 win over Everton and it's also a red-letter day for Jamie Carragher, whose goal in Liverpool's 4-0 victory over Fulham is his first since January 1999. Steed Malbranque claims his first for Tottenham in the 5-1 thrashing of Charlton.
10 Arsenal take the lead through Matthieu Flamini at Stamford Bridge, but Michael Essien earns Chelsea a point.
16 Arsene Wenger is ordered from the dug-out for comments to match officials before Arsenal pull back a 2-0 deficit to earn a point at home against Portsmouth, for whom Noe Pamarot scores his first goal. Newcastle continue to improve on the back of goals by Obafemi Martins, whose brace in the 2-1 success against Watford bring his tally to five in four games.
17 Alan Curbishley makes a dream start as West Ham manager, Nigel Reo-Coker's goal proving enough to see off Manchester United. Chelsea twice come from behind to win 3-2 at Everton with a late Didier Drogba strike, while Tom Huddlestone's first league goal for Tottenham comes in a 2-1 victory at Manchester City.
23 Another 3-2 scoreline for Chelsea and another late decider, this time from Arjen Robben at Wigan after his side surrender a 2-0 lead to two Emile Heskey goals. Also on the mark for the champions, for the first time in the Premiership, is Salomon Kalou. Cristiano Ronaldo nets two of Manchester United's three second half goals at Villa Park and there are three other two-goal performances – Robin van Persie, in Arsenal's 6-2 win over Blackburn, Shabani Nonda for Rovers in that match and Nicolas Anelka as Bolton prevail 2-0 at Manchester City. Joey Barton, of City, is sent off, along with Paul Konchesky in West Ham's goalless draw at Fulham. Two players celebrate first goals for their clubs, Sol Campbell for Portsmouth, who come from behind to beat Sheffield United 3-1, and Julio Arca in Middlesbrough's 2-0 victory over Charlton – Les Reed's last game of a brief spell in charge of the London club.
26 Mixed fortunes for the top two. Cristiano Ronaldo comes off the bench to fire another double in Manchester United's 3-1 win over Wigan, but Chelsea are held 2-2 at home by Reading after an 85th minute own goal by Michael Essien. Two years to the day since his last Premiership goal, Linvoy Primus heads two for Portsmouth for a 2-1 victory at West Ham. Stephen Ireland's first for Manchester City brings three points at Sheffield United.
27 Alan Pardew's first match in charge of Charlton is spoiled by Franck Queudrue's disputed stoppage-time free-kick which earns Fulham a 2-2 result at the Valley.
30 Moritz Volz registers the Premiership's 15,000th goal, earning £15,000 for charity from sponsors Barclays, as Fulham hold Chelsea 2-2 at Stamford Bridge. So Manchester United, with Cristiano Ronaldo scoring twice for the third successive match, go into the New Year six points clear at the top after beating Reading 3-2. Central defender Phil Jagielka replaces injured goalkeeper Paddy Kenny for the final half an hour and preserves Sheffield United's 1-0 advantage over Arsenal, established by Christian Nade's first Premiership goal. Substitute DaMarcus Beasley opens his account to give Manchester City victory at West Ham, while Phil Neville's strike for Everton in a 3-0 scoreline against Newcastle is his first in the league for four years. A stoppage-time winner by Bryan Hughes against Aston Villa gives Alan Pardew his first success as Charlton manager.

JANUARY 2007

1 Reading record the season's biggest victory, scoring four times in the first 36 minutes and going on to overwhelm West Ham 6-0, with Brynjar Gunnarsson and Stephen Hunt netting in the Premiership for the first time. David Edgar, a 19-year-old defender making only his second appearance, deprives Manchester United of victory with a 25-yard equaliser for a Newcastle side missing 12 players through injury. Matt Derbyshire, 20, also celebrates his first goal as Blackburn overcome faltering Wigan 3-0 at the JJB Stadium.

13 Michael Carrick registers his first goal for the club and Ji-Sung Park his first of the season as Manchester United beat Aston Villa for the third time in three weeks in the league and F.A. Cup, this time 3-1. Two other players are off the mark. Philippe Christanval's stoppage-time effort secures a 3-3 draw for Fulham at West Ham, who have Bobby Zamora sent off, while Stephen Quinn earns a point for Sheffield United against Portsmouth. Arsenal's Gilberto Silva is dismissed after 13 minutes at Blackburn, but Thierry Henry sets up a goal for Kolo Toure, then scores himself for a 2-0 victory against the odds.

20 Petr Cech, back for Chelsea three months after suffering a fractured skull, is beaten twice in the first 18 minutes by Dirk Kuyt and Jermaine Pennant as Liverpool win 2-0. Aston Villa score twice late on – Gavin Mahon's own goal and Gabriel Agbonlahor – for their first win in 12 games, 2-0 against Watford. Stewart Downing sets up three goals, then gets one himself, as Middlesbrough sweep aside Bolton 5-1, El-Hadji Diouf's dismissal compounding a bad day for Sam Allardyce's team. Fulham's Heidar Helguson sees red, but Vincenzo Montella opens his account from the penalty spot in a 1-1 draw against Tottenham. Trouble on and off the pitch at Reading. Sheffield United's Keith Gillespie is sent off for flattening Stephen Hunt seconds after coming off the bench. Then, Mark Halsey sends United manager Neil Warnock and Steve Coppell's assistant Wally Downes to the stands after a confrontation. Reading win 3-1, Ulises De La Cruz scoring for the first time for the club and Shane Long claiming his first in the Premiership. Midway through his fourth season in England, Amdy Faye breaks his duck to give Charlton a surprise success at Portsmouth.

21 Manchester United look set to go nine points clear of Chelsea at the top when leading through Wayne Rooney at the Emirates Stadium. But Robin van Persie equalises for Arsenal after 83 minutes and Thierry Henry heads a stoppage-time winner.

FEBRUARY 2007

3 Wigan bring to an end their worst-ever league run of eight successive defeats with a Lee McCulloch winner against Portsmouth. John Carew fires his first for Aston Villa, who also win 1-0, against West Ham. Stephen Warnock is sent off on his home debut for Blackburn, who nevertheless beat Sheffield United 2-1 with two Morten Gamst Pedersen goals. Also dismissed is Philippe Senderos in Arsenal's 1-1 draw at Middlesbrough. Everton frustrate Liverpool in a goalless derby at Anfield.

4 Cristiano Ronaldo's controversial penalty sets Manchester United on the way to a 4-0 romp at Tottenham and wins a £400 bet with Sir Alex Ferguson for reaching 15 goals for the season.

10 Darius Henderson finally breaks his Premiership duck in a tale of two penalties at Upton Park. Henderson scores from the spot, Marlon Harewood misses, so Watford overcome West Ham in a bottom-of-the-table game. Steve Sidwell doubles his tally for the season with both goals in Reading's 2-0 win over Aston Villa. Portsmouth's Pedro Mendes, victim of a tackle from behind by Joey Barton, is carried off in the 2-1 success against Manchester City – just as he had been earlier in the season when flattened by Ben Thatcher.

11 Skipper Kevin Nolan marks his 200th Premiership appearance with a goal in Bolton's 2-1 win over Fulham. Wigan, poised to go eight points clear of the third relegation spot, are left fuming over refereeing decisions after losing a 1-0 lead to two late goals at Arsenal.

24 Manchester United move nine points clear of Chelsea at the top, from an extra game played, after Cristiano Ronaldo's 88th minute winner at Fulham. Alan Curbishley has a

miserable return to the Valley as West Ham Utd. leak three first half goals to Charlton Athletic and lose their relegation battle 4-0. It also looks curtains for Watford after a 3-0 home defeat by Everton in which Manuel Fernandes scores his first goal for the club.
25 Robbie Keane nets twice in Tottenham's 4-1 victory over Bolton and is then sent off for handling on the line. Blackburn reverse a 3-0 defeat at Portsmouth on the opening day of the season and, just like Kanu in that match, Shabani Nonda has a penalty saved with a hat-trick beckoning.

MARCH 2007

4 Outplayed for most of the game and down to ten men when Paul Scholes is sent off, Manchester United pull off an improbable victory at Anfield, thanks to John O'Shea's last-minute strike. Chelsea respond with a 2-0 win at Portsmouth to stay in touch. Caleb Folan's first goal for Wigan earns victory at Manchester City, while Charlton retrieve a 2-0 half-time deficit for a point at Watford.
5 In one of the games of the season, Mark Noble and Carlos Tevez score their first Premiership goals for West Ham, who lead Tottenham 2-0 and then 3-2. But they surrender both leads and are beaten in stoppage time by Paul Stalteri's effort.
17 A 90-yard punt by Paul Robinson sails over the head of his rival for the England goalkeeper's spot, Ben Foster, for Tottenham's second goal in a 3-1 win over Watford. Cristiano Ronaldo runs almost as far to set up Wayne Rooney for another spectacular goal in Manchester United's 4-1 victory over Bolton. Rob Hulse suffers a broken leg as Sheffield United go down 3-0 at Chelsea, but two of United's relegation rivals prosper away from home. Emile Mpenza scores his first for Manchester City, who end a run of five successive defeats by beating Middlesbrough 2-0, while fortune favours West Ham at Blackburn. Carlos Tevez converts a disputed penalty, Bobby Zamora's winner clearly does not cross the line and Rovers have David Bentley unluckily sent off.
18 Charlton keep alive their hopes of beating the drop with a 2-0 win over Newcastle, the captain of China Zheng Zhi netting his first goal for the club.
31 Peter Crouch hits a hat-trick as Liverpool beat Arsenal 4-1 and gain a measure of revenge for three league and cup defeats earlier in the season. Manchester United come from behind to master Blackburn 4-1, but Chelsea need a stoppage-time winner by substitute Salomon Kalou at Watford to keep the deficit down to six points. Darren Bent's 86th penalty against Wigan maintains Charlton's revival, while a hobbling Ian Pearce and Croatian Niko Kranjcar score for the first time for Fulham and Portsmouth respectively in a 1-1 draw.

APRIL 2007

7 The gap at the top narrows to three points as Rio Ferdinand concedes an own goal in Manchester United's 2-1 defeat at Portsmouth and Ricardo Carvalho nets the only goal for Chelsea against Tottenham. Three players score for the first time for their clubs. Bolton's Iranian midfielder Teymourian Andranik is on the mark twice in a 3-1 success at Wigan, for whom Emile Heskey's opener is his 100th league goal. Spaniard Alvaro Arbeloa helps Liverpool win 2-1 at Reading, while the Czech Republic's Patrik Berger strikes for Aston Villa in a 2-1 scoreline at Blackburn. West Ham inflict Arsenal's first defeat at the Emirates, 1-0, to give themselves a lifeline.
9 Fulham's 3-1 home defeat by Manchester City has major repercussions – sucking Chris Coleman's team into relegation trouble and proving to be the manager's last game before he is sacked. Watford enjoy rare success in a disappointing season, captain Gavin Mahon scoring his first Premiership goal in the 4-2 win over Portsmouth.
14 Arsenal edge out Bolton 2-1 in a match between teams contesting a Champions League qualifying place, thanks to a first Premiership goal of the season for Cesc Fabregas. Bolton's Ivan Campo is sent off. Craig Gardner scores a career first for Aston Villa, who win 3-1 at Middlesbrough. Sheffield United overcome West Ham 3-0 in a vital relegation game, while Fulham slide further into trouble when beaten by the only goal at Reading in Lawrie Sanchez's first match as caretaker manager.

15 Charlton's revival is halted by James McFadden's stoppage-time goal which gives Everton a 2-1 verdict. Wigan lead Tottenham three times, but have to settle for a point.
21 Watford's fate is sealed when they share the points with Manchester City, but Bobby Zamora keeps West Ham's chances of beating the drop alive with the only goal against Everton. At the Valley, Sheffield United draw more encouragement than Charlton from a 1-1 scoreline. Tension also begins to take a toll at top, with. Manchester United held 1-1 by Middlesbrough. Jermaine Jenas rescues a point for Tottenham with a stoppage-time strike against Arsenal, while the day's biggest turnaround is at Bolton, where Reading come from behind to score three times in the final ten minutes, Kevin Doyle netting twice.
22 Frustration for Chelsea, who miss the chance to cut Manchester United's lead to a single point when held to a goalless draw at Newcastle. In another 0-0 scoreline at Villa Park, David James overtakes David Seaman's Premiership record of 141 clean sheets.
28 A dramatic, defining day in the title race ends with Manchester United moving five points clear with three games left. They retrieve a 2-0 deficit to win 4-2 at Everton, Chris Eagles rounding off the comeback with a goal on his debut, while Chelsea are held 2-2 at home by Bolton in a game that marks the end of Sam Allardyce's seven years as the Wanderers manager. At the bottom, West Ham move level on points with Wigan by winning 3-0 at the JJB Stadium, while Ben Thatcher is sent off as Charlton lose 4-1 at Blackburn.
30 A year and a day after he last pulled on a Newcastle shirt, Michael Owen returns at Reading and plays the whole game. His side lose 1-0.

MAY 2007

5 Cristiano Ronaldo's penalty in the Manchester derby takes United to the brink of the title. Everton overcome Portsmouth 3-0 in a match between UEFA Cup aspirants, while Blackburn, another team holding European ambitions, prevail 2-0 at Newcastle in what proves to be Glenn Roeder's final game in charge of the home team before his resignation. Fulham have Papa Bouba Diop sent off but end a run of ten games without a victory against a second-string Liverpool, thanks to Clint Dempsey's first goal for the club. Carlos Tevez scores twice and sets up one for Mark Noble as revitalised West Ham win 3-1 against Bolton, who have Sammy Lee in charge for the first time. That success increases the pressure on Wigan, beaten by the only goal at home to Middlesbrough, and Sheffield United, who go down 3-0 at Aston Villa.
6 Manchester United become champions after Chelsea are held 1-1 at Arsenal, despite a brave effort to overcome the dismissal of Khalid Boulahrouz.
7 Charlton go down after a 2-0 home defeat by Tottenham extends their lean run at the most important stage of the season to six matches.
10 Jason Roberts is sent off as Blackburn's chance of finishing high enough for a UEFA Cup spot is ended in a 1-1 draw at Tottenham.
11 West Ham complete a great escape with their seventh win in nine games, thanks to a Carlos Tevez goal against Manchester United at Old Trafford. But the feat is accompanied by controversy as rival clubs threaten legal action over the Premier League's decision not to take points away from West Ham as punishment for breaches of regulations when signing Tevez. Wigan, despite having Lee McCulloch sent off, also stay up with a 2-1 victory over Sheffield United, who are relegated with an inferior goal difference. A penalty at Bramall Lane by David Unsworth, who missed a vital one earlier in the season when he was with United, proves decisive. Tottenham, 2-1 winners over Manchester City, Everton, who hold Chelsea 1-1 at Stamford Bridge, and Bolton, who draw 2-2 with Aston Villa, confirm UEFA Cup places. But Portsmouth miss out after Graham Poll, refereeing his last game in the top flight, disallows a goal by Nico Kranjcar against Arsenal. So do Reading, despite coming from behind three times to draw 3-3 at Blackburn.

LEAGUE AND CONFERENCE PLAY-OFFS 2007

Derby County, Blackpool and Bristol Rovers took the honours as record crowds, plenty of goals and a return to Wembley for the finals made for some eventful and entertaining matches. Stephen Pearson, signed from Celtic for £650,000 in the January transfer window, took Derby back to the Premiership after an absence of five seasons with a goal estimated to be worth between £50m. and £60m. to the club. His first in their colours, which saw off the challenge of West Bromwich Albion, came in the 61st minute, three minutes after the introduction of 18-year-old Giles Barnes. The gifted youngster, left out of the starting line-up because of a lack of match fitness after injury, took a pass from leading scorer Steve Howard and delivered a telling low cross which Pearson touched past Dean Kiely as he slid in. It was third time lucky for manager Billy Davies, who had led Preston North End into the play-offs, without success, in the two previous years, before taking over at Pride Park.

Blackpool rounded off a remarkable end-of-season run by claiming a place in the game's second tier for the first time for 30 years, beating Yeovil Town 2-0 in the League One Final. It was the tenth successive victory for a team evoking memories of Blackpool's most famous Wembley appearance, the F.A. Cup Final dominated by Stanley Matthews in 1953. This time, their man-of-the-match was Keigan Parker, who added to a Robbie Williams strike close to half-time with a delightful shot into the far corner after 52 minutes. Yeovil enjoyed their big moment in the semi-finals against Nottingham Forest, wiping out a 3-1 aggregate deficit in the last eight minutes at the City Ground and going on to prevail in extra-time.

Richard Walker took his tally to 23 for the season with two goals in Bristol Rovers' 3-1 victory over Shrewsbury Town in the League Two Final, watched by a crowd of more than 61,000. Rovers, who went through by beating Lincoln 7-4 on aggregate, fell behind to Stewart Drummond's third minute header, but Walker turned things around by half-time. Shrewsbury had Marc Tierney sent off before Sammy Igoe ran half the length of the pitch to confirm victory in stoppage-time.

Morecambe, underdogs in the Conference play-offs, upset the odds by dismissing York, then coming from behind to beat Exeter City 2-1 in the final to claim a place in the Football League for the first time. Manager Sammy McIlroy, who led Macclesfield Town into the league in 1997, saw his side fall behind to an early goal by Lee Phillips and fail from the penalty spot when Wayne Curtis had his spot-kick saved by Paul Jones. But Garry Thompson equalised shortly before half-time and Danny Carlton's drive for the winner nine minutes from time was worthy of the new Wembley. Exeter had Matt Gill sent off in stoppage time.

SEMI-FINALS, FIRST LEG

COCA-COLA CHAMPIONSHIP

Southampton 1 (Surman 7), **Derby Co.** 2 (Howard, 36, 58 pen). Att: 30,602. **Wolves** 2 (Craddock 44, Olofinjana 52), **W.B.A.** 3 (Phillips 25, 54, Kamara 73). Att: 27,750.

LEAGUE ONE

Oldham Athletic 1 (Liddell 75 pen), **Blackpool** 2 (Barker 52, Hoolahan 87). Att: 12,154. **Yeovil Town** 0, **Nott'm. Forest** 2 (Commons 23 pen, Perch 90 pen). Att: 8,935.

LEAGUE TWO

Bristol Rov. 2 (Disley 10, Walker 54), **Lincoln City** 1 (Hughes 31). Att: 10,654. **Shrewsbury Town** 0, **MK Dons** 0. Att: 7,126.

NATIONWIDE CONFERENCE

Exeter City 0, **Oxford Utd.** 1 (Taylor 40 og). Att: 8.659. **York City** 0, **Morecambe** 0. Att: 6,660.

SEMI-FINALS, SECOND LEG

COCA-COLA CHAMPIONSHIP

Derby Co. 2 (Moore 3, Best 66 og), **Southampton** 3 (Viafara 4, 54, Rasiak 89). Att: 31,569 (aet, agg 4-4, **Derby Co.** won 4-3 on pens). **W.B.A.** 1 (Phillips 65), **Wolves** 0. Att: 27,415 (**W.B.A.** won 4-2 on agg).

LEAGUE ONE

Blackpool 3 (Southern 28, Morrell 75, Parker 90), **Oldham Athletic** 1 (Wolfenden 83). Att: 9,453 (Blackpool won 5-2 on agg). **Nott'm. Forest** 2 (Dobie 47, Gary Holt 93), **Yeovil Town** 5 (Davies 22, 109, Wright 82 og, Stewart 87, Morris 92). Att: 27,819 (aet, **Yeovil Town** won 5-4 on agg).

LEAGUE TWO

Lincoln City 3 (Hughes 25, 90, Stallard 43), **Bristol Rov.** 5 (Campbell 3, Lambert 11, Walker 36, Igoe 82, Rigg 90). Att: 7,694 (**Bristol Rov.** won 7-4 on agg). **MK Dons** 1 (Andrews 74), **Shrewsbury Town** 2 (Cooke 58, 76). Att: 8,212 (**Shrewsbury Town** won 2-1 on agg).

NATIONWIDE CONFERENCE

Oxford Utd. 1 (Odubade 27), **Exeter City** 2 (Phillips 39, Stansfield 70). Att: 10,691 (aet, agg 2-2, **Exeter City** won 4-3 on pens). **Morecambe** 2 (Curtis 40, 48), **York City** 1 (Bowey 20 pen). Att: 5,567 (**Morecambe** won 2-1 on agg).

FINALS – WEMBLEY

COCA-COLA CHAMPIONSHIP – MAY 28, 2007

Derby Co. 1 (Pearson 61), **W.B.A.** 0. Att: 74,993.
Derby Co. (4-4-2): Bywater, Mears, Moore, Leacock, McEveley, Fagan (Edworthy 82), Oakley, S. Johnson (Jones 87), Pearson, Howard, Peschisolido (Barnes 58). **Subs not used:** Camp, Macken. **Booked:** Peschisolido, Mears, Jones, Oakley, Bywater. **Manager:** Billy Davies.
W.B.A. (4-4-2): Kiely, McShane (Ellington 71), Perry, Sodje (Clement 80), Robinson, Gera (Carter 71), Koren, Greening, Koumas, Phillips, Kamara. **Subs not used:** Daniels, Chaplow. **Booked:** Sodje, McShane, Perry. **Manager:** Tony Mowbray.
Referee: G. Poll (Herts). **Half-time:** 0-0.

LEAGUE ONE – MAY 27, 2007

Yeovil Town 0, **Blackpool** 2 (Williams 43, Parker 52). Att: 59,313.
Yeovil Town (4-4-1-1): Mildenhall, Lindegaard (Lynch 77), T. Forbes, Guyett, Jones, Gray, Barry, Cohen (Kalala 40), Davies, Stewart, Morris (Knights 72). **Subs not used:** Rose, Skiverton. **Booked:** Barry, Morris. **Manager:** Russell Slade.
Blackpool (4-4-2): Rachubka, Barker, Jackson, Evatt, Williams, A. Forbes (Fox 78), Southern, Jorgensen, Hoolahan (Vernon 86), Morrell, Parker (Gillett 90). **Subs not used:** Coid, Burgess. **Booked:** Barker. **Manager:** Simon Grayson.
Referee: A. D'Urso (Essex). **Half-time:** 0-1.

LEAGUE TWO – MAY 26, 2007

Bristol Rov. 3 (Walker 21, 35, Igoe 90), **Shrewsbury Town** 1 (Drummond 3). Att: 61,589 (rec).
Bristol Rov. (4-4-2): Phillips, R. Green, Anthony, Elliott, Carruthers, Igoe, Campbell, Disley, Haldane (Rigg 65), Walker, Lambert. **Subs not used:** M. Green, Lines, Sandell, Lescott. **Booked:** Campbell, Walker. **Manager:** Paul Trollope.
Shrewsbury Town (4-4-2): MacKenzie, Herd (Burton 85), Langmead, Hope, Tierney, Asamoah, Drummond, Hall, Ashton, Cooke (Humphrey 73), Symes (Fortune-West 80). **Subs not used:** Esson, Leslie. **Booked:** Cooke, Tierney. **Sent-off:** Tierney. **Manager:** Gary Peters.
Referee: M. Jones (Cheshire). **Half-time:** 2-1.

NATIONWIDE CONFERENCE – MAY 20, 2007

Exeter City 1 (Phillips 8), **Morecambe** 2 (Thompson 42, Carlton 82). Att: 40,043
Exeter City (4-4-2): P. Jones, Tully, Todd, Edwards, B. Jones, Carlisle (Logan 53), Taylor, Gill, Elam (Mackie 56), Challinor, Phillips (Stansfield 36). **Subs not used:** Richardson, Buckle. **Booked:** Todd. **Sent-off:** Gill. **Manager:** Paul Tisdale.
Morecambe (4-4-1-1): Davies, Yates, Blackburn, Bentley, Adams, Curtis, Stanley, Sorvel, Thompson (Brannan 86), Twiss (Hunter 71), Carlton (McNiven 87). **Subs not used:** Howard, Neal. **Manager:** Sammy McIlroy.
Referee: M. Oliver (Northumberland). **Half-time:** 1-1.

PLAY-OFF FINALS – HOME & AWAY

1987 Divs. 1/2: **Charlton Athletic** beat Leeds Utd. 2-1 in replay (Birmingham City) after 1-1 agg (1-0h, 0-1a). Charlton Athletic remained in Div. 1. Losing semi-finalists: Ipswich Town and Oldham Athletic. **Divs. 2/3**: **Swindon Town** beat Gillingham 2-0 in replay (Crystal Palace) after 2-2 agg (0-1a, 2-1h). Swindon Town promoted to Div. 2. Losing semi-finalists: Sunderland and Wigan Athletic; Sunderland relegated to Div. 3. **Divs. 3/4**: **Aldershot** beat Wolves 3-0 on agg (2-0h, 1-0a) and promoted to Div. 3. Losing semi-finalists: Bolton Wand. and Colchester Utd.; Bolton Wand. relegated to Div.4.

1988 Divs. 1/2: **Middlesbrough** beat Chelsea 2-1 on agg (2-0h, 0-1a) and promoted to Div. 1; Chelsea relegated to Div. 2. Losing semi-finalists: Blackburn Rov. and Bradford City. **Divs. 2/3**: **Walsall** beat Bristol City 4-0 in replay (h) after 3-3 agg (3-1a, 0-2h) and promoted to Div. 2. Losing semi-finalists: Sheffield Utd. and Notts Co; Sheffield Utd. relegated to Div. 3. **Divs. 3/4**: **Swansea City** beat Torquay Utd. 5-4 on agg (2-1h, 3-3a) and promoted to Div. 3. Losing semi-finalists: Rotherham Utd. and Scunthorpe Utd.; Rotherham Utd. relegated to Div.4.

1989 Div. 2: **Crystal Palace** beat Blackburn Rov. 4-3 on agg (1-3a, 3-0h). Losing semi-finalists: Watford and Swindon Town. **Div. 3**: **Port Vale** beat Bristol Rov. 2-1 on agg (1-1a, 1-0h). Losing semi-finalists: Fulham and Preston N.E. **Div.4**: **Leyton Orient** beat Wrexham 2-1 on agg (0-0a, 2-1h). Losing semi-finalists: Scarborough and Scunthorpe Utd.

PLAY-OFF FINALS AT WEMBLEY

1990 Div. 2: **Swindon Town** 1, Sunderland 0 (att: 72,873). Swindon Town promoted, then demoted for financial irregularities; Sunderland promoted. Losing semi-finalists: Blackburn Rov. and Newcastle Utd. **Div. 3**: **Notts Co.** 2, Tranmere Rov. 0 (att: 29,252). Losing semi-finalists: Bolton Wand. and Bury. **Div. 4**: **Cambridge Utd.** 1, Chesterfield 0 (att: 26,404). Losing semi-finalists: Maidstone and Stockport Co.

1991 Div. 2: **Notts Co.** 3, Brighton & H.A. 1 (att: 59,940). Losing semi-finalists: Middlesbrough and Millwall. **Div. 3**: **Tranmere Rov.** 1, Bolton Wand. 0 (att: 30,217).

Losing semi-finalists: Brentford and Bury. **Div. 4**: **Torquay Utd.** 2, Blackpool 2 – Torquay Utd. won 5-4 on pens (att: 21,615). Losing semi-finalists: Burnley and Scunthorpe Utd.

1992 Div. 2: **Blackburn Rov.** 1, Leicester City 0 (att: 68,147). Losing semi-finalists: Derby Co. and Cambridge Utd. **Div. 3**: **Peterborough Utd.** 2, Stockport Co. 1 (att: 35,087). Losing semi-finalists: Huddersfield Town and Stoke City. **Div. 4**: **Blackpool** 1, Scunthorpe Utd. 1, aet, Blackpool won 4-3 on pens (att: 22,741). Losing semi-finalists: Barnet and Crewe Alexandra.

1993 Div. 1: **Swindon Town** 4, Leicester City 3 (att: 73,802). Losing semi-finalists: Portsmouth and Tranmere Rov. **Div. 2**: **W.B.A.** 3, Port Vale 0 (att: 53,471). Losing semi-finalists: Stockport Co. and Swansea City. **Div. 3**: **York City** 1, Crewe Alexandra 1, aet, York City won 5-3 on pens (att: 22,416). Losing semi-finalists: Bury and Walsall.

1994 Div. 1: **Leicester City** 2, Derby Co. 1 (att: 73,671). Losing semi-finalists: Millwall and Tranmere Rov. **Div. 2**: **Burnley** 2, Stockport Co. 1 (att: 44,806). Losing semi-finalists: Plymouth Argyle and York City. **Div. 3**: **Wycombe Wand.** 4, Preston N.E. 2 (att: 40,109). Losing semi-finalists: Carlisle Utd. and Torquay Utd.

1995 Div. 1: **Bolton Wand.** 4, Reading 3 (att: 64,107). Losing semi-finalists: Tranmere Rov. and Wolves. **Div. 2**: **Huddersfield Town** 2, Bristol Rov. 1 (att: 59,175). Losing semi-finalists: Brentford and Crewe Alexandra. **Div. 3**: **Chesterfield** 2, Bury 0 (att: 22,814). Losing semi-finalists: Mansfield Town and Preston N.E.

1996 Div. 1: **Leicester City** 2, Crystal Palace 1, aet (att: 73,573). Losing semi-finalists: Charlton Athletic and Stoke City. **Div. 2**: **Bradford City** 2, Notts Co. 0 (att: 39,972). Losing semi-finalists: Blackpool and Crewe Alexandra. **Div. 3**: **Plymouth Argyle** 1, Darlington 0 (att: 43,431). Losing semi-finalists: Colchester Utd. and Hereford.

1997 Div. 1: **Crystal Palace** 1, Sheffield Utd. 0, (att: 64,383). Losing semi-finalists: Ipswich Town and Wolves. **Div. 2**: **Crewe Alexandra** 1, Brentford 0 (att: 34,149). Losing semi-finalists: Bristol City and Luton Town. **Div. 3**: **Northampton Town** 1, Swansea City 0 (att: 46,804). Losing semi-finalists: Cardiff City and Chester City.

1998 Div. 1: Charlton Athletic 4, Sunderland 4, aet, Charlton Athletic won 7-6 on pens (att: 77, 739). Losing semi-finalists: Ipswich Town and Sheffield Utd. **Div. 2: Grimsby Town** 1, Northampton Town 0 (att: 62,988). Losing semi-finalists: Bristol Rov. and Fulham. **Div. 3: Colchester Utd.** 1, Torquay Utd. 0 (att: 19,486). Losing semi-finalists: Barnet and Scarborough.

1999 Div. 1: Watford 2, Bolton Wand. 0, (att: 70,343). Losing semi-finalists: Ipswich Town and Birmingham City. **Div. 2: Manchester City** 2, Gillingham 2, aet, Manchester City won 3-1 on pens (att: 76,935). Losing semi-finalists: Preston N.E. and Wigan Athletic. **Div. 3: Scunthorpe Utd.** 1, Leyton Orient 0, (att: 36,985). Losing semi-finalists: Rotherham Utd. and Swansea City.

2000 Div. 1: Ipswich Town 4, Barnsley 2 (att: 73,427). Losing semi-finalists: Birmingham City and Bolton Wand. **Div. 2: Gillingham** 3, Wigan Athletic 2, aet (att: 53,764). Losing semi-finalists: Millwall and Stoke City. **Div. 3: Peterborough Utd.** 1, Darlington 0 (att: 33,383). Losing semi-finalists: Barnet and Hartlepool Utd.

PLAY-OFF FINALS AT MILLENNIUM STADIUM

2001 Div. 1: Bolton Wand. 3, Preston N.E. 0 (att: 54,328). Losing semi-finalists: Birmingham City and W.B.A. **Div. 2: Walsall** 3, Reading 2, aet (att: 50,496). Losing semi-finalists: Stoke City and Wigan Athletic. **Div. 3: Blackpool** 4, Leyton Orient 2 (att: 23,600). Losing semi-finalists: Hartlepool Utd. and Hull City.

2002 Div. 1: Birmingham City 1, Norwich City 1, aet, Birmingham City won 4-2 on pens. (att: 71,597). Losing semi-finalists: Millwall and Wolves. **Div. 2: Stoke City** 2, Brentford

0 (att: 42,523). Losing semi-finalists: Cardiff City and Huddersfield Town. **Div. 3: Cheltenham Town** 3, Rushden & Diamonds 1 (att: 24,368). Losing semi-finalists: Hartlepool Utd. and Rochdale.

2003 Div. 1: Wolves 3, Sheffield Utd. 0 (att: 69,473). Losing semi-finalists: Nott'm. Forest and Reading. **Div. 2: Cardiff City** 1, Q.P.R. 0, aet (att: 66,096). Losing semi-finalists: Bristol City and Oldham Athletic. **Div. 3: Bournemouth** 5, Lincoln City 2 (att: 32,148). Losing semi-finalists: Bury and Scunthorpe Utd.

2004: Div. 1: Crystal Palace 1, West Ham Utd. 0 (att: 72,523). Losing semi-finalists: Ipswich Town and Sunderland. **Div. 2: Brighton & H.A.** 1, Bristol City 0 (att: 65,167). Losing semi-finalists: Hartlepool Utd. and Swindon Town. **Div. 3: Huddersfield Town** 0, Mansfield Town 0, aet, **Huddersfield Town** won 4-1 on pens (att: 37,298). Losing semi-finalists: Lincoln City and Northampton Town.

2005: Championship: West Ham Utd. 1 Preston N.E. 0 (att: 70,275). Losing semi-finalists: Derby Co. and Ipswich Town. **League 1: Sheffield Wed.** 4, Hartlepool Utd. 2, aet (att: 59,808). Losing semi-finalists: Brentford and Tranmere Rov. **League 2: Southend Utd.** 2, Lincoln City 0, aet (att: 19532). Losing semi-finalists: Macclesfield Town and Northampton Town.

2006: Championship: Watford 3, Leeds Utd. 0 (att: 64,736). Losing semi-finalists: Crystal Palace and Preston N.E. **League 1: Barnsley** 2, Swansea City 2, aet, **Barnsley** won 4-3 on pens. Losing semi-finalists: Huddersfield Town and Brentford. **League 2: Cheltenham Town** 1, Grimsby Town 0 (att: 29,196). Losing semi-finalists: Wycombe Wand. and Lincoln City.

HISTORY OF THE PLAY-OFFS

Play-off matches were introduced by the Football League to decide final promotion and relegation issues at the end of season 1986-87.

A similar series styled "Test Matches" had operated between Divisions One and Two for six seasons from 1893-98, and was abolished when both divisions were increased from 16 to 18 clubs.

Eighty-eight years later, the play-offs were back in vogue. In the first three seasons (1987-88-89), the Finals were played home-and-away, and since they were made one-off matches in 1990, they have featured regularly in Wembley's spring calendar, until the old stadium closed its doors and the action switched to the Millennium Stadium in Cardiff in 2001.

Through the years, these have been the ups and downs of the play-offs:

1987 Initially, the 12 clubs involved comprised the one that finished directly above those relegated in Divisions One, Two and Three and the three who followed the sides automatically promoted in each section. Two of the home-and-away Finals went to neutral-ground replays, in which **Charlton Athletic** clung to First Division status by denying Leeds Utd. promotion while **Swindon Town** beat Gillingham to complete their climb from Fourth Division to Second in successive seasons, via the play-offs, Sunderland fell into the Third and Bolton Wand. into Division Four, both for the first time. **Aldershot** went up after finishing only sixth in Division Four; in their Final, they beat Wolves, who had finished nine points higher and missed automatic promotion by one point.

1988 Chelsea were relegated from the First Division after losing on aggregate to **Middlesbrough**, who had finished third in Division Two. So Middlesbrough, managed by Bruce Rioch, completed the rise from Third Division to First in successive seasons, only two years after their very existence had been threatened by the bailiffs. Also promoted via the play-offs: **Walsall** from Division Three and **Swansea City** from the Fourth. Relegated, besides Chelsea: Sheffield Utd. (to Division Three) and Rotherham Utd. (to Division Four).

1989 After two seasons of promotion-relegation play-offs, the system was changed to involve the four clubs who had just missed automatic promotion. That format has remained. Steve Coppell's **Crystal Palace**, third in Division Two, returned to the top flight after eight years, beating Blackburn Rov. 4-3 on aggregate after extra time. Similarly, **Port Vale** confirmed third place in Division Three with promotion via the play-offs. For **Leyton Orient**, promotion seemed out of the question in Division Four when they stood 15th. on March 1. But eight wins and a draw in the last nine home games swept them to sixth in the final table, and two more home victories in the play-offs completed their season in triumph.

1990 The play-off Finals now moved to Wembley over three days of the Spring Holiday week-end. On successive afternoons, **Cambridge Utd.** won promotion from Division Four and **Notts Co.** from the Third. Then, on Bank Holiday Monday, the biggest crowd for years at a Football League fixture (72,873) saw Ossie Ardiles' **Swindon Town** beat Sunderland 1-0 to reach the First Division for the first time. A few weeks later, however, Wembley losers **Sunderland** were promoted instead, by default; Swindon were found guilty of "financial irregularities" and stayed in Division Two.

1991 Again, the season's biggest League crowd (59,940) gathered at Wembley for the First Division Final in which **Notts Co.** (having missed promotion by one point) still fulfilled their ambition, beating Brighton & H.A. 3-1. In successive years, County had climbed from Third Division to First via the play-offs – the first club to achieve double promotion by this route. Bolton Wand. were denied automatic promotion in Division Three on goal difference, and lost at Wembley to an extra-time goal by **Tranmere Rov.** The Fourth Division Final made history, with Blackpool beaten 5-4 on penalties by **Torquay Utd.** – first instance of promotion being decided by a shoot-out. In the table, Blackpool had finished seven points ahead of Torquay.

1992 Wembley that Spring Bank Holiday was the turning point in the history of **Blackburn Rov**. Bolstered by Kenny Dalglish's return to management and owner Jack Walker's millions, they beat Leicester City 1-0 by Mike Newell's 45th-minute penalty to achieve their objective – a place in the new Premier League. Newell, who also missed a second-half penalty, had recovered from a broken leg just in time for the play-offs. In the Fourth Division Final **Blackpool** (denied by penalties the previous year) this time won a shoot-out 4-3 against Scunthorpe Utd., who were unlucky in the play-offs for the fourth time in five years. **Peterborough Utd.** climbed out of the Third Division for the first time, beating Stockport Co. 2-1 at Wembley.

1993 The crowd of 73,802 at Wembley to see **Swindon Town** beat Leicester City 4-3 in the First Division Final was 11,000 bigger than that for the F.A. Cup Final replay between Arsenal and Sheffield Wed. Leicester rallied from three down to 3-3 before Paul Bodin's late penalty wiped away Swindon Town's bitter memories of three years earlier, when they were denied promotion after winning at Wembley. In the Third Division Final, **York City** beat Crewe Alexandra 5-3 in a shoot-out after a 1-1 draw, and in the Second Division decider, **W.B.A.** beat Port Vale 3-0. That was tough on Vale, who had finished third in the table with 89 points – the highest total never to earn promotion in any division. They had beaten Albion twice in the League, too.

1994 Wembley's record turn-out of 158,586 spectators at the three Finals started with a crowd of 40,109 to see Martin O'Neill's **Wycombe Wand.** beat Preston N.E. 4-2. They thus climbed from Conference to Second Division with successive promotions. **Burnley**'s 2-1 victory in the Second Division Final was marred by the sending-off of two Stockport Co. players, and in the First Division decider **Leicester City** came from behind to beat Derby Co. and end the worst Wembley record of any club. They had lost on all six previous appearances there – four times in the F.A. Cup Final and in the play-offs of 1992 and 1993.

1995 Two months after losing the Coca-Cola Cup Final to Liverpool, Bruce Rioch's **Bolton Wand.** were back at Wembley for the First Division play-off Final. From two goals down to Reading in front of a crowd of 64,107, they returned to the top company after 15 years, winning 4-3 with two extra-time goals. **Huddersfield Town** ended the first season at their new £15m. home with promotion to the First Division via a 2-1 victory against Bristol Rov. – manager Neil Warnock's third play-off success (after two with

Notts Co.). Of the three clubs who missed automatic promotion by one place, only **Chesterfield** achieved it in the play-offs, comfortably beating Bury 2-0.

1996 Under new manager Martin O'Neill (a Wembley play-off winner with Wycombe Wand. in 1994), **Leicester City** returned to the Premiership a year after leaving it. They had finished fifth in the table, but in the Final came from behind to beat third-placed Crystal Palace by Steve Claridge's shot in the last seconds of extra time. In the Second Division **Bradford City** came sixth, nine points behind Blackpool (3rd), but beat them (from two down in the semi-final first leg) and then clinched promotion by 2-0 v Notts Co. at Wembley. It was City's greatest day since they won the Cup in 1911. **Plymouth Argyle** beat Darlington in the Third Division Final to earn promotion a year after being relegated. It was manager Neil Warnock's fourth play-off triumph in seven seasons after two with Notts Co. (1990 and 1991) and a third with Huddersfield Town in 1995.

1997 High drama at Wembley as **Crystal Palace** left it late against Sheffield Utd. in the First Division play-off final. The match was scoreless until the last 10 seconds when David Hopkin lobbed Blades' keeper Simon Tracey from 25 yards to send the Eagles back to the Premiership after two seasons of Nationwide action. In the Second Division play-off final, **Crewe Alexandra** beat Brentford 1-0 courtesy of a Shaun Smith goal. **Northampton Town** celebrated their first Wembley appearance with a 1-0 victory over Swansea City thanks to John Frain's injury-time free-kick in the Third Division play-off final.

1998 In one of the finest games ever seen at Wembley, **Charlton Athletic** eventually triumphed 7-6 on penalties over Sunderland. For Charlton Athletic, Wearside-born Clive Mendonca scored a hat-trick and Richard Rufus his first career goal in a match that lurched between joy and despair for both sides as it ended 4-4. Sunderland defender Michael Gray's superb performance ill deserved to end with his weakly struck spot kick being saved by Sasa Ilic. In the Third Division, the penalty spot also had a role to play, as **Colchester Utd.**'s David Gregory scored the only goal to defeat Torquay Utd., while in the Second Division a Kevin Donovan goal gave **Grimsby Town** victory over Northampton Town.

1999: Elton John, watching via a personal satellite link in Seattle, saw his **Watford** side overcome Bolton Wand. 2-0 to reach the Premiership. Against technically superior opponents, Watford prevailed with application and teamwork. They also gave Bolton a lesson in finishing through match-winners by Nick Wright and Allan Smart. **Manchester City** staged a remarkable comeback to win the Second Division Final after trailing to goals by Carl Asaba and Robert Taylor for Gillingham. Kevin Horlock and Paul Dickov scored in stoppage time and City went on to win on penalties. A goal by Spaniard Alex Calvo-Garcia earned **Scunthorpe Utd.** a 1-0 success against Leyton Orient in the Third Division Final.

2000: After three successive play-off failures, **Ipswich Town** finally secured a place in the Premiership. They overcame the injury loss of leading scorer David Johnson to beat Barnsley 4-2 with goals by 36-year-old Tony Mowbray, Marcus Stewart and substitutes Richard Naylor and Martijn Reuser. With six minutes left of extra-time in the Second Division Final, **Gillingham** trailed Wigan Athletic 2-1. But headers by 38-year-old player-coach Steve Butler and fellow substitute Andy Thomson gave them a 3-2 victory. Andy Clarke, approaching his 33rd birthday, scored the only goal of the Third Division decider for **Peterborough Utd.** against Darlington.

2001: Bolton Wand., unsuccessful play-off contenders in the two previous seasons, made no mistake at the third attempt. They flourished in the new surroundings of the Millennium Stadium to beat Preston N.E. 3-0 with goals by Gareth Farrelly, Michael Ricketts – his 24th of the season – and Ricardo Gardner to reach the Premiership. **Walsall**, relegated 12 months earlier, scored twice in a three-minute spell of extra time to win 3-2 against Reading in the Second Division Final, while **Blackpool** capped a marked improvement in the second half of the season by overcoming Leyton Orient 4-2 in the Third Division Final.

2002: Holding their nerve to win a penalty shoot-out 4-2, **Birmingham City** wiped away the memory of three successive defeats in the semi-finals of the play-offs to return to the top division after an absence of 16 years. Substitute Darren Carter completed a fairy-tale first season as a professional by scoring the fourth spot-kick against Norwich City. **Stoke City** became the first successful team to come from the south dressing room in 12 finals since football was adopted by the home of Welsh rugby, beating Brentford 2-0 in the Second Division Final with Deon Burton's strike and a Ben Burgess own goal. Julian Alsop's 26th goal of the season helped **Cheltenham Town** defeat League newcomers Rushden & Diamonds 3-1 in the Third Division decider.

2003: Wolves benefactor Sir Jack Hayward finally saw his £60m. investment pay dividends when the club he first supported as a boy returned to the top flight after an absence of 19 years by beating Sheffield Utd. 3-0. It was also a moment to savour for manager Dave Jones, who was forced to leave his previous club Southampton because of child abuse allegations, which were later found to be groundless. **Cardiff City**, away from the game's second tier for 18 years, returned with an extra-time winner from substitute Andy Campbell against Q.P.R after a goalless 90 minutes in the Division Two Final. **Bournemouth**, relegated 12 months earlier, became the first team to score five in the end-of-season deciders, beating Lincoln City 5-2 in the Division Three Final.

2004: Three tight, tense Finals produced only two goals, the lowest number since the Play-offs were introduced. One of them, scored by Neil Shipperley, gave **Crystal Palace** victory over West Ham Utd., the much-travelled striker tapping in a rebound after Stephen Bywater parried Andy Johnson's shot. It completed a remarkable transformation for Crystal Palace, who were 19th in the table when Iain Dowie left Oldham Athletic to become their manager. **Brighton & H.A.** made an immediate return to Division One in a poor game against Bristol City which looked set for extra-time until Leon Knight netted his 27th goal of the campaign from the penalty spot after 84 minutes. **Huddersfield Town** also went back up at the first attempt, winning the Division Three Final in a penalty shoot-out after a goalless 120 minutes against Mansfield Town.

2005: Goals were few and far between for Bobby Zamora during **West Ham Utd.**'s Championship season – but what a difference in the Play-offs. The former Brighton & H.A. and Tottenham striker scored three times in the 4-2 aggregate win over Ipswich Town in the semi-finals and was on the mark again with the only goal against Preston N.E. at the Millennium Stadium. **Sheffield Wed.** were eight minute away from defeat against Hartlepool Utd. in the League One decider when Steven MacLean made it 2-2 from the penalty spot and they went on to win 4-2 in extra-time. **Southend Utd.**, edged out of an automatic promotion place, won the League Two Final 2-0 against Lincoln City, Freddy Eastwood scoring their first in extra-time and making the second for Duncan Jupp. **Carlisle Utd.** beat Stevenage 1-0 with a goal by Peter Murphy in the Conference Final to regain their League place 12 months after being relegated.

2006: From the moment Marlon King scored his 22nd goal of the season to set up a 3-0 win over Crystal Palace in the semi-final first leg, **Watford** had the conviction of a team going places. Sure enough, they went on to beat Leeds just as comfortably in the final. Jay DeMerit, who was playing non-league football 18 months earlier, headed his side in front. James Chambers fired in a shot that hit a post and went in off goalkeeper Neil Sullivan. Then Darius Henderson put away a penalty after King was brought down by Shaun Derry, the man whose tackle had ended Boothroyd's playing career at the age of 26. **Barnsley** beat Swansea City on penalties in the League One Final, Nick Colgan making the vital save from Alan Tate, while Steve Guinan's goal earned **Cheltenham Town** a 1-0 win over Grimsby Town in the League Two Final. **Hereford Utd.** returned to the Football League after a nine-year absence with Ryan Green's extra-time winner against Halifax in the Conference Final.

LEAGUE PLAY-OFF CROWDS YEAR BY YEAR

YEAR	MATCHES	AGG. ATT.
1987	20	310,000
1988	19	305,817
1989	18	234,393
1990	15	291,428
1991	15	266,442
1992	15	277,684
1993	15	319,907
1994	15	314,817
1995	15	295,317
1996	15	308,515
1997	15	309,085
1998	15	320,795
1999	15	372,969
2000	15	333,999
2001	15	317,745
2002	15	327,894
2003	15	374,461
2004	15	388,675
2005	15	353,330
2006	15	340,804
2007	15	405,278 (record)

QUOTE-UNQUOTE

'Believe me, no one wants England to be more successful than I do' – **Gary Lineker** on claims that criticism of the national team by him and fellow pundit Alan Hansen cost the BBC the rights for live internationals and the F.A. Cup.

'The link between the common man and the player has gone. It's almost become a them-and-us situation' – **Paul Jewell**, Wigan manager, after bitter criticism by fans of poor England performances in European Championship qualifying games.

'It made you feel quite humble to hear the bloody-minded response from our fans' – **Mick McCarthy**, Wolves manager, after Molinuex supporters kept the faith despite watching their team lose 6-0 to Southampton.

'Our game is under serious threat from violence – on the field, in the stands and outside the stadiums. It is poisoning football' – **Michel Platini**, new president of UEFA.

'You stop taking notes and just start clapping' – **Adrian Boothroyd**, Watford manager, watching his team's F.A. Cup semi-final opponents Manchester United overwhelm Roma 7-1 in the Champions League.

'We're living the dream and loving every minute of it' – **Nigel Adkins**, Scunthorpe manager, on the way to winning the League One title.

'I'm like a badger at the start of the pairing-up season' – Ian Holloway, **Plymouth** manager, after reaching the F.A. Cup quarter-finals.

'Sometimes you want to crack open the champagne and sometimes you want to kick the dog' – **Paul Ince** on the trials and tribulations of his first manager's job with Macclesfield.

ENGLISH HONOURS LIST

F.A. PREMIER LEAGUE

	First	Pts.	Second	Pts.	Third	Pts.
1992-3*a*	Manchester Utd.	84	Aston Villa	74	Norwich City	72
1993-4*a*	Manchester Utd.	92	Blackburn Rov.	84	Newcastle Utd.	77
1994-5*a*	Blackburn Rov.	89	Manchester Utd.	88	Nott'm. Forest	77
1995-6*b*	Manchester Utd.	82	Newcastle Utd.	78	Liverpool	71
1996-7*b*	Manchester Utd.	75	Newcastle Utd.	68	Arsenal	68
1997-8*b*	Arsenal	78	Manchester Utd.	77	Liverpool	65
1998-9*b*	Manchester Utd.	79	Arsenal	78	Chelsea	75
1999-00*b*	Manchester Utd.	91	Arsenal	73	Leeds Utd.	69
2000-01*b*	Manchester Utd.	80	Arsenal	70	Liverpool	69
2001-02*b*	Arsenal	87	Liverpool	80	Manchester Utd.	77
2002-03*b*	Manchester Utd.	83	Arsenal	78	Newcastle Utd.	69
2003-04*b*	Arsenal	90	Chelsea	79	Manchester Utd.	75
2004-05*b*	Chelsea	95	Arsenal	83	Manchester Utd.	77
2005-06*b*	Chelsea	91	Manchester Utd.	83	Liverpool	82
2006-07	Manchester Utd.	89	Chelsea	83	Liverpool	68

Maximum points: *a*, 126; *b*, 114.

FOOTBALL LEAGUE

FIRST DIVISION

	First	Pts.	Second	Pts.	Third	Pts.
1992-3	Newcastle Utd.	96	West Ham Utd.	88	††Portsmouth	88
1993-4	Crystal Palace	90	Nott'm. Forest	83	††Millwall	74
1994-5	Middlesbrough	82	††Reading	79	Bolton Wand.	77
1995-6	Sunderland	83	Derby Co.	79	††Crystal Palace	75
1996-7	Bolton Wand.	98	Barnsley	80	††Wolves	76
1997-8	Nott'm. Forest	94	Middlesbrough	91	††Sunderland	90
1998-9	Sunderland	105	Bradford City	87	††Ipswich Town	86
1999-00	Charlton Athletic	91	Manchester City	89	Ipswich Town	87
2000-01	Fulham	101	Blackburn Rov.	91	Bolton Wand.	87
2001-02	Manchester City	99	W.B.A.	89	††Wolves	86
2002-03	Portsmouth	98	Leicester City	92	††Sheffield Utd.	80
2003-04	Norwich City	94	W.B.A.	86	††Sunderland	79

CHAMPIONSHIP

	First	Pts.	Second	Pts.	Third	Pts.
2004-05	Sunderland	94	Wigan Athletic	87	††Ipswich Town	85
2005-06	Reading	106	Sheffield Utd.	90	Watford	81
2006-07	Sunderland	88	Birmingham City	86	Derby Co.	84

Maximum points: 138. ††Not promoted after play-offs.

SECOND DIVISION

	First	Pts.	Second	Pts.	Third	Pts.
1992-3	Stoke City	93	Bolton Wand.	90	††Port Vale	89
1993-4	Reading	89	Port Vale	88	††Plymouth Argyle	85
1994-5	Birmingham City	89	††Brentford	85	††Crewe Alexandra	83
1995-6	Swindon Town	92	Oxford Utd.	83	††Blackpool	82
1996-7	Bury	84	Stockport Co.	82	††Luton Town	78
1997-8	Watford	88	Bristol City	85	Grimsby Town	72
1998-9	Fulham	101	Walsall	87	Manchester City	82
1999-00	Preston N.E.	95	Burnley	88	Gillingham	85
2000-01	Milwall	93	Rotherham Utd.	91	††Reading	86
2001-02	Brighton & H.A.	90	Reading	84	††Brentford	83

2002-03	Wigan Athletic 100	Crewe Alexandra 86	††Bristol City 83
2003-04	Plymouth Argyle 90	Q.P.R. 83	††Bristol City 82

LEAGUE ONE

2004-05	Luton Town 98	Hull City 86	††Tranmere Rov. 79
2005-06	Southend Utd. 82	Colchester Utd. 79	††Brentford 76
2006-07	Scunthorpe Utd. 91	Bristol City 85	Blackpool 83

Maximum points: 138. †† Not promoted after play-offs.

THIRD DIVISION

1992-3*a*	Cardiff City 83	Wrexham 80	Barnet 79
1993-4*a*	Shrewsbury Town 79	Chester City 74	Crewe Alexandra 73
1994-5*a*	Carlisle Utd. 91	Walsall 83	Chesterfield 81
1995-6*b*	Preston N.E. 86	Gillingham 83	Bury 79
1996-7*b*	Wigan Athletic 87	Fulham 87	Carlisle Utd. 84
1997-8*b*	Notts Co. 99	Macclesfield Town .. 82	Lincoln City 75
1998-9*b*	Brentford 85	Cambridge Utd. 81	Cardiff City 80
1999-00*b*	Swansea City 85	Rotherham Utd. 84	Northampton Town . 82
2000-01*b*	Brighton & H.A. 92	Cardiff City 82	*Chesterfield 80
2001-02*b*	Plymouth Argyle ... 102	Luton Town 97	Mansfield Town 79
2002-03*b*	Rushden & Diamonds .. 87	Hartlepool Utd. 85	Wrexham 84
2003-04*b*	Doncaster Rov. 92	Hull City 88	Torquay Utd. 81

LEAGUE TWO

2004-05*b*	Yeovil Town 83	Scunthorpe Utd. 80	Swansea City 80
2005-06*b*	Carlisle Utd. 86	Northampton Town . 83	Leyton Orient 81
2006-07*b*	Walsall 89	Hartlepool Utd. 88	Swindon Town 85

Maximum points: *a*, 126; *b*, 138; * Deducted 9 points for financial irregularities.

FOOTBALL LEAGUE 1888-1992

	First	Pts.	Second	Pts.	Third	Pts.
1888-89*a*	Preston N.E.	40	Aston Villa	29	Wolves	28
1889-90*a*	Preston N.E.	33	Everton	31	Blackburn Rov.	27
1890-1*a*	Everton	29	Preston N.E.	27	Notts Co.	26
1891-2*b*	Sunderland	42	Preston N.E.	37	Bolton Wand.	36

OLD FIRST DIVISION

	First	Pts.	Second	Pts.	Third	Pts.
1892-3*c*	Sunderland	48	Preston N.E.	37	Everton	36
1893-4*c*	Aston Villa	44	Sunderland	38	Derby Co.	36
1894-5*c*	Sunderland	47	Everton	42	Aston Villa	39
1895-6*c*	Aston Villa	45	Derby Co.	41	Everton	39
1896-7*c*	Aston Villa	47	Sheffield Utd.	36	Derby Co.	36
1897-8*c*	Sheffield Utd.	42	Sunderland	39	Wolves	35
1898-9*d*	Aston Villa	45	Liverpool	43	Burnley	39
1899-1900*d*	Aston Villa	50	Sheffield Utd.	48	Sunderland	41
1900-1*d*	Liverpool	45	Sunderland	43	Notts Co.	40
1901-2*d*	Sunderland	44	Everton	41	Newcastle Utd.	37
1902-3*d*	The Wednesday	42	Aston Villa	41	Sunderland	41
1903-4*d*	The Wednesday	47	Manchester City	44	Everton	43
1904-5*d*	Newcastle Utd.	48	Everton	47	Manchester City	46
1905-6*e*	Liverpool	51	Preston N.E.	47	The Wednesday	44
1906-7*e*	Newcastle Utd.	51	Bristol City	48	Everton	45
1907-8*e*	Manchester Utd.	52	Aston Villa	43	Manchester City	43
1908-9*e*	Newcastle Utd.	53	Everton	46	Sunderland	44
1909-10*e*	Aston Villa	53	Liverpool	48	Blackburn Rov.	45

1910-11*e*	Manchester Utd.	52	Aston Villa	51	Sunderland	45
1911-12*e*	Blackburn Rov.	49	Everton	46	Newcastle Utd.	44
1912-13*e*	Sunderland	54	Aston Villa	50	Sheffield Wed.	49
1913-14*e*	Blackburn Rov.	51	Aston Villa	44	Middlesbrough	43
1914-15*e*	Everton	46	Oldham Athletic	45	Blackburn Rov.	43
1919-20*f*	W.B.A.	60	Burnley	51	Chelsea	49
1920-1*f*	Burnley	59	Manchester City	54	Bolton Wand.	52
1921-2*f*	Liverpool	57	Tottenham	51	Burnley	49
1922-3*f*	Liverpool	60	Sunderland	54	Huddersfield Town	53
1923-4*f*	*Huddersfield Town	57	Cardiff City	57	Sunderland	53
1924-5*f*	Huddersfield Town	58	W.B.A.	56	Bolton Wand.	55
1925-6*f*	Huddersfield Town	57	Arsenal	52	Sunderland	48
1926-7*f*	Newcastle Utd.	56	Huddersfield Town	51	Sunderland	49
1927-8*f*	Everton	53	Huddersfield Town	51	Leicester City	48
1928-9*f*	Sheffield Wed.	52	Leicester City	51	Aston Villa	50
1929-30*f*	Sheffield Wed.	60	Derby Co.	50	Manchester City	47
1930-1*f*	Arsenal	66	Aston Villa	59	Sheffield Wed.	52
1931-2*f*	Everton	56	Arsenal	54	Sheffield Wed.	50
1932-3*f*	Arsenal	58	Aston Villa	54	Sheffield Wed.	51
1933-4*f*	Arsenal	59	Huddersfield Town	56	Tottenham	49
1934-5*f*	Arsenal	58	Sunderland	54	Sheffield Wed.	49
1935-6*f*	Sunderland	56	Derby Co.	48	Huddersfield Town	48
1936-7*f*	Manchester City	57	Charlton Athletic	54	Arsenal	52
1937-8*f*	Arsenal	52	Wolves	51	Preston N.E.	49
1938-9*f*	Everton	59	Wolves	55	Charlton Athletic	50
1946-7*f*	Liverpool	57	Manchester Utd.	56	Wolves	56
1947-8*f*	Arsenal	59	Manchester Utd.	52	Burnley	52
1948-9*f*	Portsmouth	58	Manchester Utd.	53	Derby Co.	53
1949-50*f*	*Portsmouth	53	Wolves	53	Sunderland	52
1950-1*f*	Tottenham	60	Manchester Utd.	56	Blackpool	50
1951-2*f*	Manchester Utd.	57	Tottenham	53	Arsenal	53
1952-3*f*	*Arsenal	54	Preston N.E.	54	Wolves	51
1953-4*f*	Wolves	57	W.B.A.	53	Huddersfield Town	51
1954-5*f*	Chelsea	52	Wolves	48	Portsmouth	48
1955-6*f*	Manchester Utd.	60	Blackpool	49	Wolves	49
1956-7*f*	Manchester Utd.	64	Tottenham	56	Preston N.E.	56
1957-8*f*	Wolves	64	Preston N.E.	59	Tottenham	51
1958-9*f*	Wolves	61	Manchester Utd.	55	Arsenal	50
1959-60*f*	Burnley	55	Wolves	54	Tottenham	53
1960-1*f*	Tottenham	66	Sheffield Wed.	58	Wolves	57
1961-2*f*	Ipswich Town	56	Burnley	53	Tottenham	52
1962-3*f*	Everton	61	Tottenham	55	Burnley	54
1963-4*f*	Liverpool	57	Manchester Utd.	53	Everton	52
1964-5*f*	*Manchester Utd.	61	Leeds Utd.	61	Chelsea	56
1965-6*f*	Liverpool	61	Leeds Utd.	55	Burnley	55
1966-7*f*	Manchester Utd.	60	Nott'm. Forest	56	Tottenham	56
1967-8*f*	Manchester City	58	Manchester Utd.	56	Liverpool	55
1968-9*f*	Leeds Utd.	67	Liverpool	61	Everton	57
1969-70*f*	Everton	66	Leeds Utd.	57	Chelsea	55
1970-1*f*	Arsenal	65	Leeds Utd.	64	Tottenham	52
1971-2*f*	Derby Co.	58	Leeds Utd.	57	Liverpool	57
1972-3*f*	Liverpool	60	Arsenal	57	Leeds Utd.	53
1973-4*f*	Leeds Utd.	62	Liverpool	57	Derby Co.	48
1974-5*f*	Derby Co.	53	Liverpool	51	Ipswich Town	51
1975-6*f*	Liverpool	60	Q.P.R.	59	Manchester Utd.	56
1976-7*f*	Liverpool	57	Manchester City	56	Ipswich Town	52
1977-8*f*	Nott'm. Forest	64	Liverpool	57	Everton	55
1978-9*f*	Liverpool	68	Nott'm Forest	60	W.B.A.	59

1979-80*f*	Liverpool	60	Manchester Utd.	58	Ipswich Town	53
1980-1*f*	Aston Villa	60	Ipswich Town	56	Arsenal	53
1981-2*g*	Liverpool	87	Ipswich Town	83	Manchester Utd.	78
1982-3*g*	Liverpool	82	Watford	71	Manchester Utd.	70
1983-4*g*	Liverpool	80	Southampton	77	Nott'm. Forest	74
1984-5*g*	Everton	90	Liverpool	77	Tottenham	77
1985-6*g*	Liverpool	88	Everton	86	West Ham Utd.	84
1986-7*g*	Everton	86	Liverpool	77	Tottenham	71
1987-8*h*	Liverpool	90	Manchester Utd.	81	Nott'm. Forest	73
1988-9*j*	††Arsenal	76	Liverpool	76	Nott'm. Forest	64
1989-90*j*	Liverpool	79	Aston Villa	70	Tottenham	63
1990-1*j*	Arsenal	83	Liverpool	76	Crystal Palace	69
1991-2*g*	Leeds Utd.	82	Manchester Utd.	78	Sheffield Wed.	75

Maximum points: *a*, 44; *b*, 52; *c*, 60; *d*, 68; *e*, 76; *f*, 84; *g*, 126; *h*, 120; *j*, 114.
*Won on goal average. †Won on goal diff. ††Won on goals scored. No comp. 1915-19 – 1939-46

OLD SECOND DIVISION 1892-1992

	First	Pts.	Second	Pts.	Third	Pts.
1892-3*a*	Small Heath	36	Sheffield Utd.	35	Darwen	30
1893-4*b*	Liverpool	50	Small Heath	42	Notts Co.	39
1894-5*c*	Bury	48	Notts Co.	39	Newton Heath	38
1895-6*c*	*Liverpool	46	Manchester City	46	Grimsby Town	42
1896-7*c*	Notts Co.	42	Newton Heath	39	Grimsby Town	38
1897-8*c*	Burnley	48	Newcastle Utd.	45	Manchester City	39
1898-9*d*	Manchester City	52	Glossop	46	Leicester Fosse	45
1899-1900*d*	The Wednesday	54	Bolton Wand.	52	Small Heath	46
1900-1*d*	Grimsby Town	49	Small Heath	48	Burnley	44
1901-2*d*	W.B.A.	55	Middlesbrough	51	Preston N.E.	42
1902-3*d*	Manchester City	54	Small Heath	51	Woolwich Arsenal	48
1903-4*d*	Preston N.E.	50	Woolwich Arsenal	49	Manchester Utd.	48
1904-5*d*	Liverpool	58	Bolton Wand.	56	Manchester Utd.	53
1905-6*e*	Bristol City	66	Manchester Utd.	62	Chelsea	53
1906-7*e*	Nott'm. Forest	60	Chelsea	57	Leicester Fosse	48
1907-8*e*	Bradford City	54	Leicester Fosse	52	Oldham Athletic	50
1908-9*e*	Bolton Wand.	52	Tottenham	51	W.B.A.	51
1909-10*e*	Manchester City	54	Oldham Athletic	53	Hull City	53
1910-11*e*	W.B.A.	53	Bolton Wand.	51	Chelsea	49
1911-12*e*	*Derby Co.	54	Chelsea	54	Burnley	52
1912-13*e*	Preston N.E.	53	Burnley	50	Birmingham City	46
1913-14*e*	Notts Co.	53	Bradford P.A.	49	Woolwich Arsenal	49
1914-15*e*	Derby Co.	53	Preston N.E.	50	Barnsley	47
1919-20*f*	Tottenham	70	Huddersfield Town	64	Birmingham City	56
1920-1*f*	*Birmingham City	58	Cardiff City	58	Bristol City	51
1921-2*f*	Nott'm. Forest	56	Stoke City	52	Barnsley	52
1922-3*f*	Notts Co.	53	West Ham Utd.	51	Leicester City	51
1923-4*f*	Leeds Utd.	54	Bury	51	Derby Co.	51
1924-5*f*	Leicester City	59	Manchester Utd.	57	Derby Co.	55
1925-6*f*	Sheffield Wed.	60	Derby Co.	57	Chelsea	52
1926-7*f*	Middlesbrough	62	Portsmouth	54	Manchester City	54
1927-8*f*	Manchester City	59	Leeds Utd.	57	Chelsea	54
1928-9*f*	Middlesbrough	55	Grimsby Town	53	Bradford City	48
1929-30*f*	Blackpool	58	Chelsea	55	Oldham Athletic	53
1930-1*f*	Everton	61	W.B.A.	54	Tottenham	51
1931-2*f*	Wolves	56	Leeds Utd.	54	Stoke City	52
1932-3*f*	Stoke City	56	Tottenham	55	Fulham	50
1933-4*f*	Grimsby Town	59	Preston N.E.	52	Bolton Wand.	51
1934-5*f*	Brentford	61	Bolton Wand.	56	West Ham Utd.	56

1935-6*f*	Manchester Utd. 56	Charlton Athletic 55	Sheffield Utd. 52
1936-7*f*	Leicester City 56	Blackpool 55	Bury 52
1937-8*f*	Aston Villa 57	Manchester Utd. 53	Sheffield Utd. 53
1938-9*f*	Blackburn Rov. 55	Sheffield Utd. 54	Sheffield Wed. 53
1946-7*f*	Manchester City 62	Burnley 58	Birmingham City 55
1947-8*f*	Birmingham City 59	Newcastle Utd. 56	Southampton 52
1948-9*f*	Fulham 57	W.B.A. 56	Southampton 55
1949-50*f*	Tottenham 61	Sheffield Wed. 52	Sheffield Utd. 52
1950-1*f*	Preston N.E. 57	Manchester City 52	Cardiff City 50
1951-2*f*	Sheffield Wed. 53	Cardiff City 51	Birmingham City 51
1952-3*f*	Sheffield Utd. 60	Huddersfield Town .. 58	Luton Town 52
1953-4*f*	*Leicester City 56	Everton 56	Blackburn Rov. 55
1954-5*f*	*Birmingham City 54	Luton Town 54	Rotherham Utd. 54
1955-6*f*	Sheffield Wed. 55	Leeds Utd. 52	Liverpool 48
1956-7*f*	Leicester City 61	Nott'm. Forest 54	Liverpool 53
1957-8*f*	West Ham Utd. 57	Blackburn Rov. 56	Charlton Athletic 55
1958-9*f*	Sheffield Wed. 62	Fulham 60	Sheffield Utd. 53
1959-60*f*	Aston Villa 59	Cardiff City 58	Liverpool 50
1960-1*f*	Ipswich Town 59	Sheffield Utd. 58	Liverpool 52
1961-2*f*	Liverpool 62	Leyton Orient 54	Sunderland 53
1962-3*f*	Stoke City 53	Chelsea 52	Sunderland 52
1963-4*f*	Leeds Utd. 63	Sunderland 61	Preston N.E. 56
1964-5*f*	Newcastle Utd. 57	Northampton Town . 56	Bolton Wand. 50
1965-6*f*	Manchester City 59	Southampton 54	Coventry City 53
1966-7*f*	Coventry City 59	Wolves 58	Carlisle Utd. 52
1967-8*f*	Ipswich Town 59	Q.P.R. 58	Blackpool 58
1968-9*f*	Derby Co. 63	Crystal Palace 56	Charlton Athletic 50
1969-70*f*	Huddersfield Town .. 60	Blackpool 53	Leicester City 51
1970-1*f*	Leicester City 59	Sheffield Utd. 56	Cardiff City 53
1971-2*f*	Norwich City 57	Birmingham City 56	Millwall 55
1972-3*f*	Burnley 62	Q.P.R. 61	Aston Villa 50
1973-4*f*	Middlesbrough 65	Luton Town 50	Carlisle Utd. 49
1974-5*f*	Manchester Utd. 61	Aston Villa 58	Norwich City 53
1975-6*f*	Sunderland 56	Bristol City 53	W.B.A. 53
1976-7*f*	Wolves 57	Chelsea 55	Nott'm. Forest 52
1977-8*f*	Bolton Wand. 58	Southampton 57	Tottenham 56
1978-9*f*	Crystal Palace 57	Brighton & H.A. 56	Stoke City 56
1979-80*f*	Leicester City 55	Sunderland 54	Birmingham City 53
1980-1*f*	West Ham Utd. 66	Notts Co. 53	Swansea City 50
1981-2*g*	Luton Town 88	Watford 80	Norwich City 71
1982-3*g*	Q.P.R. 85	Wolves 75	Leicester City 70
1983-4*g*	†Chelsea 88	Sheffield Wed. 88	Newcastle Utd. 80
1984-5*g*	Oxford Utd. 84	Birmingham City 82	Manchester City 74
1985-6*g*	Norwich City 84	Charlton Athletic 77	Wimbledon 76
1986-7*g*	Derby Co. 84	Portsmouth 78	††Oldham Athletic .. 75
1987-8*h*	Millwall 82	Aston Villa 78	Middlesbrough 78
1988-9*j*	Chelsea 99	Manchester City 82	Crystal Palace 81
1989-90*j*	†Leeds Utd. 85	Sheffield Utd. 85	†† Newcastle Utd. .. 80
1990-1*j*	Oldham Athletic 88	West Ham Utd. 87	Sheffield Wed. 82
1991-2*j*	Ipswich Town 84	Middlesbrough 80	†† Derby Co. 78

Maximum points: *a*, 44; *b*, 56; *c*, 60; *d*, 68; *e*, 76; *f*, 84; *g*, 126; *h*, 132; *j*, 138. * Won on goal average. † Won on goal difference. †† Not promoted after play-offs.

THIRD DIVISION 1958-92

	First Pts.	Second Pts.	Third Pts.
1958-9	Plymouth Argyle 62	Hull City 61	Brentford 57
1959-60	Southampton 61	Norwich City 59	Shrewsbury Town 52
1960-1	Bury 68	Walsall 62	Q.P.R. 60

1961-2	Portsmouth	65	Grimsby Town	62	Bournemouth	59
1962-3	Northampton Town	62	Swindon Town	58	Port Vale	54
1963-4	*Coventry City	60	Crystal Palace	60	Watford	58
1964-5	Carlisle Utd.	60	Bristol City	59	Mansfield Town	59
1965-6	Hull City	69	Millwall	65	Q.P.R.	57
1966-7	Q.P.R.	67	Middlesbrough	55	Watford	54
1967-8	Oxford Utd.	57	Bury	56	Shrewsbury Town	55
1968-9	*Watford	64	Swindon Town	64	Luton Town	61
1969-70	Orient	62	Luton Town	60	Bristol Rov.	56
1970-1	Preston N.E.	61	Fulham	60	Halifax Town	56
1971-2	Aston Villa	70	Brighton & H.A.	65	Bournemouth	62
1972-3	Bolton Wand.	61	Notts Co.	57	Blackburn Rov.	55
1973-4	Oldham Athletic	62	Bristol Rov.	61	York City	61
1974-5	Blackburn Rov.	60	Plymouth Argyle	59	Charlton Athletic	55
1975-6	Hereford	63	Cardiff City	57	Millwall	56
1976-7	Mansfield Town	64	Brighton & H.A.	61	Crystal Palace	59
1977-8	Wrexham	61	Cambridge Utd.	58	Preston N.E.	56
1978-9	Shrewsbury Town	61	Watford	60	Swansea City	60
1979-80	Grimsby Town	62	Blackburn Rov.	59	Sheffield Wed.	58
1980-1	Rotherham Utd.	61	Barnsley	59	Charlton Athletic	59
†1981-2	**Burnley	80	Carlisle Utd.	80	Fulham	78
†1982-3	Portsmouth	91	Cardiff City	86	Huddersfield Town	82
†1983-4	Oxford Utd.	95	Wimbledon	87	Sheffield Utd.	83
†1984-5	Bradford City	94	Millwall	90	Hull City	87
†1985-6	Reading	94	Plymouth Argyle	87	Derby Co.	84
†1986-7	Bournemouth	97	Middlesbrough	94	Swindon Town	87
†1987-8	Sunderland	93	Brighton & H.A.	84	Walsall	82
†1988-9	Wolves	92	Sheffield Utd.	84	Port Vale	84
†1989-90	Bristol Rov.	93	Bristol City	91	Notts Co.	87
†1990-1	Cambridge Utd.	86	Southend Utd.	85	Grimsby Town	83
†1991-2	Brentford	82	Birmingham City	81	††Huddersfield T	78

* Won on goal average. ** Won on goal difference. † Maximum points 138 (previously 92). †† Not promoted after play-offs.

FOURTH DIVISION 1958-92

	First	Pts.	Second	Pts.	Third	Pts.	Fourth	Pts.
1958-9	Port Vale	64	Coventry City	60	York City	60	Shrewsbury Town	58
1959-60	Walsall	65	Notts Co.	60	Torquay Utd.	60	Watford	57
1960-1	Peterborough Utd.	66	Crystal Palace	64	Northampton Town	60	Bradford P.A.	60
1961-2	Millwall	56	Colchester Utd.	55	Wrexham	53	Carlisle Utd.	52
1962-3	Brentford	62	Oldham Athletic	59	Crewe Alexandra	59	Mansfield Town	57
1963-4	*Gillingham	60	Carlisle Utd.	60	Workington	59	Exeter City	58
1964-5	Brighton & H.A.	63	Millwall	62	York City	62	Oxford Utd.	61
1965-6	*Doncaster Rov.	59	Darlington	59	Torquay Utd.	58	Colchester Utd.	56
1966-7	Stockport Co.	64	Southport	59	Barrow	59	Tranmere Rov.	58
1967-8	Luton Town	66	Barnsley	61	Hartlepool Utd.	60	Crewe Alexandra	58
1968-9	Doncaster Rov.	59	Halifax Town	57	Rochdale	56	Bradford City	56
1969-70	Chesterfield	64	Wrexham	61	Swansea City	60	Port Vale	59
1970-1	Notts Co.	69	Bournemouth	60	Oldham Athletic	59	York City	56
1971-2	Grimsby Town	63	Southend Utd.	60	Brentford	59	Scunthorpe Utd.	57
1972-3	Southport	62	Hereford	58	Cambridge Utd.	57	Aldershot	56
1973-4	Peterborough Utd.	65	Gillingham	62	Colchester Utd.	60	Bury	59
1974-5	Mansfield Town	68	Shrewsbury Town	62	Rotherham Utd.	58	Chester City	57
1975-6	Lincoln City	74	Northampton Town	68	Reading	60	Tranmere Rov.	58
1976-7	Cambridge Utd.	65	Exeter City	62	Colchester Utd.	59	Bradford City	59
1977-8	Watford	71	Southend Utd.	60	Swansea City	56	Brentford	59
1978-9	Reading	65	Grimsby Town	61	Wimbledon	61	Barnsley	61
1979-80	Huddersfield Town	66	Walsall	64	Newport	61	Portsmouth	60

1980-1	Southend Utd. 67	Lincoln City 65	Doncaster Rov. 56	Wimbledon 55
†1981-2	Sheffield Utd. 96	Bradford City 91	Wigan Athletic 91	Bournemouth 88
†1982-3	Wimbledon 98	Hull City 90	Port Vale 88	Scunthorpe Utd. 83
†1983-4	York City 101	Doncaster Rov. 85	Reading 82	Bristol City 82
†1984-5	Chesterfield 91	Blackpool 86	Darlington 85	Bury 84
†1985-6	Swindon Town 102	Chester City 84	Mansfield Town 81	Port Vale 79
†1986-7	Northampton Town . 99	Preston N.E. 90	Southend Utd. 80	††Wolves 79
†1987-8	Wolves 90	Cardiff City 85	Bolton Wand. 78	††Scunthorpe Utd. . 77
†1988-9	Rotherham Utd. 82	Tranmere Rov. 80	Crewe Alexandra 78	††Scunthorpe Utd. . 77
†1989-90	Exeter City 89	Grimsby Town 79	Southend Utd. 75	††Stockport Co. 74
†1990-1	Darlington 83	Stockport Co. 82	Hartlepool Utd. 82	Peterborough Utd. .. 80
1991-2*a*	Burnley 83	Rotherham Utd. 77	Mansfield Town 77	Blackpool 76

* Won on goal average. Maximum points: †, 138; *a*, 126; previously 92. †† Not promoted after play-offs.

THIRD DIVISION – SOUTH 1920-58

	First	Pts.	Second	Pts.	Third	Pts.
1920-1*a*	Crystal Palace	59	Southampton	54	Q.P.R.	53
1921-2*a*	*Southampton	61	Plymouth Argyle	61	Portsmouth	53
1922-3*a*	Bristol City	59	Plymouth Argyle	53	Swansea City	53
1923-4*a*	Portsmouth	59	Plymouth Argyle	55	Millwall	54
1924-5*a*	Swansea City	57	Plymouth Argyle	56	Bristol City	53
1925-6*a*	Reading	57	Plymouth Argyle	56	Millwall	53
1926-7*a*	Bristol City	62	Plymouth Argyle	60	Millwall	56
1927-8*a*	Millwall	65	Northampton Town .	55	Plymouth Argyle	53
1928-9*a*	*Charlton Athletic	54	Crystal Palace	54	Northampton Town .	52
1929-30*a*	Plymouth Argyle	68	Brentford	61	Q.P.R.	51
1930-31*a*	Notts Co.	59	Crystal Palace	51	Brentford	50
1931-2*a*	Fulham	57	Reading	55	Southend Utd.	53
1932-3*a*	Brentford	62	Exeter City	58	Norwich City	57
1933-4*a*	Norwich City	61	Coventry City	54	Reading	54
1934-5*a*	Charlton Athletic	61	Reading	53	Coventry City	51
1935-6*a*	Coventry City	57	Luton Town	56	Reading	54
1936-7*a*	Luton Town	58	Notts Co.	56	Brighton & H.A.	53
1937-8*a*	Millwall	56	Bristol City	55	Q.P.R.	53
1938-9*a*	Newport	55	Crystal Palace	52	Brighton & H.A.	49
1946-7*a*	Cardiff City	66	Q.P.R.	57	Bristol City	51
1947-8*a*	Q.P.R.	61	Bournemouth	57	Walsall	51
1948-9*a*	Swansea City	62	Reading	55	Bournemouth	52
1949-50*a*	Notts Co.	58	Northampton Town .	51	Southend Utd.	51
1950-1*d*	Nott'm. Forest	70	Norwich City	64	Reading	57
1951-2*d*	Plymouth Argyle	66	Reading	61	Norwich City	61
1952-3*d*	Bristol Rov.	64	Millwall	62	Northampton Town .	62
1953-4*d*	Ipswich Town	64	Brighton & H.A.	61	Bristol City	56
1954-5*d*	Bristol City	70	Leyton Orient	61	Southampton	59
1955-6*d*	Leyton Orient	66	Brighton & H.A.	65	Ipswich Town	64
1956-7*d*	*Ipswich Town	59	Torquay Utd.	59	Colchester Utd.	58
1957-8*d*	Brighton & H.A.	60	Brentford	58	Plymouth Argyle	58

THIRD DIVISION – NORTH 1921-58

	First	Pts.	Second	Pts.	Third	Pts.
1921-2*b*	Stockport Co.	56	Darlington	50	Grimsby Town	50
1922-3*b*	Nelson	51	Bradford P.A.	47	Walsall	46
1923-4*a*	Wolves	63	Rochdale	62	Chesterfield	54
1924-5*a*	Darlington	58	Nelson	53	New Brighton	53
1925-6*a*	Grimsby Town	61	Bradford P.A.	60	Rochdale	59
1926-7*a*	Stoke City	63	Rochdale	58	Bradford P.A.	57
1927-8*a*	Bradford P.A.	63	Lincoln City	55	Stockport Co.	54

1928-9*a*	Bradford City 63	Stockport Co. 62	Wrexham 52
1929-30*a*	Port Vale 67	Stockport Co. 63	Darlington 50
1930-1*a*	Chesterfield 58	Lincoln City 57	Wrexham 54
1931-2*c*	*Lincoln City 57	Gateshead 57	Chester City 50
1932-3*a*	Hull City 59	Wrexham 57	Stockport Co. 54
1933-4*a*	Barnsley 62	Chesterfield 61	Stockport Co. 59
1934-5*a*	Doncaster Rov. 57	Halifax Town 55	Chester City 54
1935-6*a*	Chesterfield 60	Chester City 55	Tranmere Rov. 54
1936-7*a*	Stockport Co. 60	Lincoln City 57	Chester City 53
1937-8*a*	Tranmere Rov. 56	Doncaster Rov. 54	Hull City 53
1938-9*a*	Barnsley 67	Doncaster Rov. 56	Bradford City 52
1946-7*a*	Doncaster Rov. 72	Rotherham Utd. 64	Chester City 56
1947-8*a*	Lincoln City 60	Rotherham Utd. 59	Wrexham 50
1948-9*a*	Hull City 65	Rotherham Utd. 62	Doncaster Rov. 50
1949-50*a*	Doncaster Rov. 55	Gateshead 53	Rochdale 51
1950-1*d*	Rotherham Utd. 71	Mansfield Town 64	Carlisle Utd. 62
1951-2*d*	Lincoln City 69	Grimsby Town 66	Stockport Co. 59
1952-3*d*	Oldham Athletic 59	Port Vale 58	Wrexham 56
1953-4*d*	Port Vale 69	Barnsley 58	Scunthorpe Utd. 57
1954-5*d*	Barnsley 65	Accrington 61	Scunthorpe Utd. 58
1955-6*d*	Grimsby Town 68	Derby Co. 63	Accrington 59
1956-7*d*	Derby Co. 63	Hartlepool Utd. 59	Accrington 58
1957-8*d*	Scunthorpe Utd. 66	Accrington 59	Bradford City 57

Maximum points: *a*, 84; *b*, 76; *c*, 80; *d*, 92. * Won on goal average.

TITLE WINNERS

F.A. PREMIER LEAGUE
Manchester Utd. 9
Arsenal 3
Chelsea 2
Blackburn Rov. 1

FOOTBALL LEAGUE CHAMPIONSHIP
Sunderland 2
Reading 1

DIV.1 (NEW)
Sunderland 2
Bolton Wand. 1
Charlton Athletic 1
Crystal Palace 1
Fulham 1
Manchester City 1
Middlesbrough 1
Newcastle Utd. 1
Norwich City 1
Nott'm. Forest 1
Portsmouth 1

DIV.1 (ORIGINAL)
Liverpool 18
Arsenal 10
Everton 9
Aston Villa 7
Manchester Utd. 7
Sunderland 6
Newcastle Utd. 4
Sheffield Wed. 4
Huddersfield Town 3
Leeds Utd. 3
Wolves 3
Blackburn Rov. 2
Burnley 2
Derby Co. 2
Manchester City 2
Portsmouth 2
Preston N.E. 2
Tottenham 2
Chelsea 1
Ipswich Town 1
Nott'm. Forest 1
Sheffield Utd. 1
W.B.A. 1

LEAGUE ONE
Luton Town 1
Scunthorpe Utd. 1
Southend Utd. 1

DIV.2 (NEW)
Birmingham City 1
Brighton & H.A. 1
Bury 1
Fulham 1
Millwall 1
Plymouth Argyle 1
Preston N.E. 1
Reading 1
Stoke City 1
Swindon Town 1
Watford 1
Wigan Athletic 1

DIV.2 (ORIGINAL)
Leicester City 6
Manchester City 6
Sheffield Wed. 5
Birmingham City 4
Derby Co. 4
Liverpool 4
Ipswich Town 3
Leeds Utd. 3
Middlesbrough 3
Notts County 3
Preston N.E. 3
Aston Villa 2
Bolton Wand. 2
Burnley 2
Chelsea 2
Grimsby Town 2
Manchester Utd. 2
Norwich City 2
Nott'm Forest 2
Stoke City 2
Tottenham 2
W.B.A. 2
West Ham Utd. 2
Wolves 2

Blackburn Rov. 1	Fulham 1	Sunderland 1
Blackpool 1	Huddersfield Town 1	
Bradford City 1	Luton Town 1	**LEAGUE TWO**
Brentford 1	Millwall 1	Carlisle Utd. 1
Bristol City 1	Newcastle Utd. 1	Walsall 1
Bury 1	Oldham Athletic 1	Yeovil Town 1
Coventry City 1	Oxford Utd. 1	
Crystal Palace 1	Q.P.R. 1	
Everton 1	Sheffield Utd. 1	

APPLICATIONS FOR RE-ELECTION

(System discontinued 1987)

14	Hartlepool Utd.	4	Norwich City	2	Oldham Athletic
12	Halifax Town	3	Aldershot	2	Q.P.R.
11	Barrow	3	Bradford City	2	Rotherham Utd.
11	Southport	3	Crystal Palace	2	Scunthorpe Utd.
10	Crewe Alexandra	3	Doncaster Rov.	2	Southend Utd.
10	Newport	3	Hereford	2	Watford
10	Rochdale	3	Merthyr Tyd.	1	Blackpool
8	Darlington	3	Swindon Town	1	Brighton & H.A.
8	Exeter City	3	Torquay Utd.	1	Bristol Rov.
7	Chester City	3	Tranmere Rov.	1	Cambridge Utd.
7	Walsall	2	Aberdare	1	Cardiff City
7	Workington	2	Ashington	1	Carlisle Utd.
7	York City	2	Bournemouth	1	Charlton Athletic
6	Stockport Co.	2	Brentford	1	Mansfield Town
5	Accrington	2	Colchester Utd.	1	Port Vale
5	Gillingham	2	Durham C.	1	Preston N.E.
5	Lincoln City	2	Gateshead	1	Shrewsbury Town
5	New Brighton	2	Grimsby Town	1	Swansea City
4	Bradford P.A.	2	Millwall	1	Thames
4	Northampton Town	2	Nelson	1	Wrexham

RELEGATED CLUBS (TO 1992)

1892-3 In Test matches, Darwen and Sheffield Utd. won promotion in place of Accrington and Notts Co.
1893-4 Tests, Liverpool and Small Heath won promotion. Darwen and Newton Heath relegated.
1894-5 After Tests, Bury promoted, Liverpool relegated.
1895-6 After Tests, Liverpool promoted, Small Heath relegated.
1896-7 After Tests, Notts Co. promoted, Burnley relegated.
1897-8 Test system abolished after success of Burnley and Stoke City, League extended. Blackburn Rov. and Newcastle Utd. elected to First Division. Automatic promotion and relegation introduced.

FIRST DIVISION TO SECOND DIVISION

1898-9 Bolton Wand., Sheffield Wed.
1899-00 Burnley, Glossop
1900-1 Preston N.E., W.B.A.
1901-2 Small Heath, Manchester City
1902-3 Grimsby Town, Bolton Wand.
1903-4 Liverpool, W.B.A.
1904-5 League extended. Bury and Notts Co., two bottom clubs in First Division, re-elected.
1905-6 Nott'm. Forest, Wolves

1906-7	Derby Co., Stoke City
1907-8	Bolton Wand., Birmingham City
1908-9	Manchester City, Leicester Fosse
1909-10	Bolton Wand., Chelsea
1910-11	Bristol City, Nott'm. Forest
1911-12	Preston N.E., Bury
1912-13	Notts Co., Woolwich Arsenal
1913-14	Preston N.E., Derby Co.
1914-15	Tottenham, *Chelsea
1919-20	Notts Co., Sheffield Wed.
1920-1	Derby Co., Bradford P.A.
1921-2	Bradford City, Manchester Utd.
1922-3	Stoke City, Oldham Athletic
1923-4	Chelsea, Middlesbrough
1924-5	Preston N.E., Nott'm. Forest
1925-6	Manchester City, Notts Co.
1926-7	Leeds Utd., W.B.A.
1927-8	Tottenham, Middlesbrough
1928-9	Bury, Cardiff City
1929-30	Burnley, Everton
1930-1	Leeds Utd., Manchester Utd.
1931-2	Grimsby Town, West Ham Utd.
1932-3	Bolton Wand., Blackpool
1933-4	Newcastle Utd., Sheffield Utd.
1934-5	Leicester City, Tottenham
1935-6	Aston Villa, Blackburn Rov.
1936-7	Manchester Utd., Sheffield Wed.
1937-8	Manchester City, W.B.A.
1938-9	Birmingham City, Leicester City
1946-7	Brentford, Leeds Utd.
1947-8	Blackburn Rov., Grimsby Town
1948-9	Preston N.E., Sheffield Utd.
1949-50	Manchester City, Birmingham City
1950-1	Sheffield Wed., Everton
1951-2	Huddersfield Town, Fulham
1952-3	Stoke City, Derby Co.
1953-4	Middlesbrough, Liverpool
1954-5	Leicester City, Sheffield Wed.
1955-6	Huddersfield Town, Sheffield Utd.
1956-7	Charlton Athletic, Cardiff City
1957-8	Sheffield Wed., Sunderland
1958-9	Portsmouth, Aston Villa
1959-60	Luton Town, Leeds Utd.
1960-61	Preston N.E., Newcastle Utd.
1961-2	Chelsea, Cardiff City
1962-3	Manchester City, Leyton Orient
1963-4	Bolton Wand., Ipswich Town
1964-5	Wolves, Birmingham City
1965-6	Northampton Town, Blackburn Rov.
1966-7	Aston Villa, Blackpool
1967-8	Fulham, Sheffield Utd.
1968-9	Leicester City, Q.P.R.
1969-70	Sheffield Wed., Sunderland
1970-1	Burnley, Blackpool
1971-2	Nott'm. Forest, Huddersfield Town
1972-3	W.B.A., Crystal Palace
1973-4	Norwich City, Manchester Utd., Southampton
1974-5	Chelsea, Luton Town, Carlisle Utd.

1975-6 Sheffield Utd., Burnley, Wolves
1976-7 Tottenham, Stoke City, Sunderland
1977-8 Leicester City, West Ham Utd., Newcastle Utd.
1978-9 Q.P.R., Birmingham City, Chelsea
1979-80 Bristol City, Derby Co., Bolton Wand.
1980-1 Norwich City, Leicester City, Crystal Palace
1981-2 Leeds Utd., Wolves, Middlesbrough
1982-3 Manchester City, Swansea City, Brighton & H.A.
1983-4 Birmingham City, Notts Co., Wolves
1984-5 Norwich City, Sunderland, Stoke City
1985-6 Ipswich Town, Birmingham City, W.B.A.
1986-7 Leicester City, Manchester City, Aston Villa
1987-8 Chelsea**, Portsmouth, Watford, Oxford Utd.
1988-9 Middlesbrough, West Ham Utd., Newcastle Utd.
1989-90 Sheffield Wed., Charlton Athletic, Millwall
1990-1 Sunderland, Derby Co.
1991-2 Luton Town, Notts Co., West Ham Utd.

* Subsequently re-elected to First Division when League extended after the war.
** Relegated after play-offs.

SECOND DIVISION TO THIRD DIVISION

1920-1 Stockport Co.
1921-2 Bradford City, Bristol City
1922-3 Rotherham Utd., Wolves
1923-4 Nelson, Bristol City
1924-5 Crystal Palace, Coventry City
1925-6 Stoke City, Stockport Co.
1926-7 Darlington, Bradford City
1927-8 Fulham, South Shields
1928-9 Port Vale, Clapton Orient
1929-30 Hull City, Notts County
1930-1 Reading, Cardiff City
1931-2 Barnsley, Bristol City
1932-3 Chesterfield, Charlton Athletic
1933-4 Millwall, Lincoln City
1934-5 Oldham Athletic, Notts Co.
1935-6 Port Vale, Hull City
1936-7 Doncaster Rov., Bradford City
1937-8 Barnsley, Stockport Co.
1938-9 Norwich City, Tranmere Rov.
1946-7 Swansea City, Newport
1947-8 Doncaster Rov., Millwall
1948-9 Nott'm. Forest, Lincoln City
1949-50 Plymouth Argyle, Bradford P.A.
1950-1 Grimsby Town, Chesterfield
1951-2 Coventry City, Q.P.R.
1952-3 Southampton, Barnsley
1953-4 Brentford, Oldham Athletic
1954-5 Ipswich Town, Derby Co.
1955-6 Plymouth Argyle, Hull City
1956-7 Port Vale, Bury
1957-8 Doncaster Rov., Notts Co.
1958-9 Barnsley, Grimsby Town
1959-60 Bristol City, Hull City
1960-1 Lincoln City, Portsmouth
1961-2 Brighton & H.A., Bristol Rov.
1962-3 Walsall, Luton Town

1963-4	Grimsby Town, Scunthorpe Utd.
1964-5	Swindon Town, Swansea City
1965-6	Middlesbrough, Leyton Orient
1966-7	Northampton Town, Bury
1967-8	Plymouth Argyle, Rotherham Utd.
1968-9	Fulham, Bury
1969-70	Preston N.E., Aston Villa
1970-1	Blackburn Rov., Bolton Wand.
1971-2	Charlton Athletic, Watford
1972-3	Huddersfield Town, Brighton & H.A.
1973-4	Crystal Palace, Preston N.E., Swindon Town
1974-5	Millwall, Cardiff City, Sheffield Wed.
1975-6	Portsmouth, Oxford Utd., York City
1976-7	Carlisle Utd., Plymouth Argyle, Hereford Utd.
1977-8	Hull City, Mansfield Town, Blackpool
1978-9	Sheffield Utd., Millwall, Blackburn Rov.
1979-80	Fulham, Burnley, Charlton Athletic
1980-1	Preston N.E., Bristol City, Bristol Rov.
1981-2	Cardiff City, Wrexham, Orient
1982-3	Rotherham Utd., Burnley, Bolton Wand.
1983-4	Derby Co., Swansea City, Cambridge Utd.
1984-5	Notts Co., Cardiff City, Wolves
1985-6	Carlisle Utd., Middlesbrough, Fulham
1986-7	Sunderland**, Grimsby Town, Brighton & H.A.
1987-8	Sheffield Utd.**, Reading, Huddersfield Town
1988-9	Shrewsbury Town, Birmingham City, Walsall
1989-90	Bournemouth, Bradford City, Stoke City
1990-1	W.B.A., Hull City
1991-2	Plymouth Argyle, Brighton & H.A., Port Vale

** Relegated after play-offs.

THIRD DIVISION TO FOURTH DIVISION

1958-9	Rochdale, Notts Co., Doncaster Rov., Stockport Co.
1959-60	Accrington, Wrexham, Mansfield Town, York City
1960-1	Chesterfield, Colchester Utd., Bradford City, Tranmere Rov.
1961-2	Newport, Brentford, Lincoln City, Torquay Utd.
1962-3	Bradford P.A., Brighton & H.A., Carlisle Utd., Halifax Town
1963-4	Millwall, Crewe Alexandra, Wrexham, Notts Co.
1964-5	Luton Town, Port Vale, Colchester Utd., Barnsley
1965-6	Southend Utd., Exeter City, Brentford, York City
1966-7	Doncaster Rov., Workington, Darlington, Swansea City
1967-8	Scunthorpe Utd., Colchester Utd., Grimsby Town, Peterborough Utd. (demoted)
1968-9	Oldham Athletic, Crewe Alexandra, Hartlepool Utd., Northampton Town
1969-70	Bournemouth, Southport, Barrow, Stockport Co.
1970-1	Gillingham, Doncaster Rov., Bury, Reading
1971-2	Mansfield Town, Barnsley, Torquay Utd., Bradford City
1972-3	Scunthorpe Utd., Swansea City, Brentford, Rotherham Utd.
1973-4	Cambridge Utd., Shrewsbury Town, Rochdale, Southport
1974-5	Bournemouth, Watford, Tranmere Rov., Huddersfield Town
1975-6	Aldershot, Colchester Utd., Southend Utd., Halifax Town
1976-7	Reading, Northampton Town, Grimsby Town, York City
1977-8	Port Vale, Bradford City, Hereford, Portsmouth
1978-9	Peterborough Utd., Walsall, Tranmere Rov., Lincoln City
1979-80	Bury, Southend Utd., Mansfield Town, Wimbledon
1980-1	Sheffield Utd., Colchester Utd., Blackpool, Hull City
1981-2	Wimbledon, Swindon Town, Bristol City, Chester City
1982-3	Reading, Wrexham, Doncaster Rov., Chesterfield

1983-4 Scunthorpe Utd., Southend Utd., Port Vale, Exeter City
1984-5 Burnley, Orient, Preston N.E., Cambridge Utd.
1985-6 Lincoln City, Cardiff City, Wolves, Swansea City
1986-7 Bolton Wand.**, Carlisle Utd., Darlington, Newport
1987-8 Doncaster Rov., York City, Grimsby Town, Rotherham Utd.**
1988-9 Southend Utd., Chesterfield, Gillingham, Aldershot
1989-90 Cardiff City, Northampton Town, Blackpool, Walsall
1990-1 Crewe Alexandra, Rotherham Utd., Mansfield Town
1991-2 Bury, Shrewsbury Town, Torquay Utd., Darlington

** Relegated after plays-offs.

DEMOTED FROM FOURTH DIVISION TO CONFERENCE

1987 Lincoln City
1988 Newport
1989 Darlington
1990 Colchester Utd.
1991 No demotion
1992 No demotion

DEMOTED FROM THIRD DIVISION TO CONFERENCE

1993 Halifax Town
1994-6 No demotion
1997 Hereford
1998 Doncaster Rov.
1999 Scarborough
2000 Chester City
2001 Barnet
2002 Halifax Town
2003 Exeter City, Shrewsbury Town
2004 Carlisle Utd., York City

DEMOTED FROM LEAGUE TWO TO CONFERENCE

2005 Kidderminster Harr., Cambridge Utd.
2006 Oxford Utd., Rushden & Diamonds
2007 Boston Utd., Torquay Utd.

RELEGATED CLUBS (SINCE 1993)

1993

Premier League to Div. 1: Crystal Palace, Middlesbrough, Nott'm. Forest
Div. 1 to Div. 2: Brentford, Cambridge Utd., Bristol Rov.
Div. 2 to Div. 3: Preston N.E., Mansfield Town, Wigan Athletic, Chester City

1994

Premier League to Div. 1: Sheffield Utd., Oldham Athletic, Swindon Town
Div. 1 to Div. 2: Birmingham City, Oxford Utd., Peterborough Utd.
Div. 2 to Div. 3: Fulham, Exeter City, Hartlepool Utd., Barnet

1995

Premier League to Div. 1: Crystal Palace, Norwich City, Leicester City, Ipswich Town
Div. 1 to Div. 2: Swindon Town, Burnley, Bristol City, Notts Co.
Div. 2 to Div. 3: Cambridge Utd., Plymouth Argyle, Cardiff City, Chester City, Leyton Orient

1996

Premier League to Div. 1: Manchester City, Q.P.R., Bolton Wand.
Div. 1 to Div. 2: Millwall, Watford, Luton Town
Div. 2 to Div. 3: Carlisle Utd., Swansea City, Brighton & H.A., Hull City

1997

Premier League to Div. 1: Sunderland, Middlesbrough, Nott'm. Forest
Div. 1 to Div. 2: Grimsby Town, Oldham Athletic, Southend Utd.
Div. 2 to Div. 3: Peterborough Utd., Shrewsbury Town, Rotherham Utd., Notts Co.

1998

Premier League to Div. 1: Bolton Wand., Barnsley, Crystal Palace
Div. 1 to Div. 2: Manchester City, Stoke City, Reading
Div. 2 to Div. 3: Brentford, Plymouth Argyle, Carlisle Utd., Southend Utd.

1999

Premier League to Div. 1: Charlton Athletic, Blackburn Rov., Nott'm. Forest
Div. 1 to Div. 2: Bury, Oxford Utd., Bristol City
Div. 2 to Div. 3: York City, Northampton Town, Lincoln City, Macclesfield Town

2000

Premier League to Div. 1: Wimbledon, Sheffield Wed., Watford
Div. 1 to Div. 2: Walsall, Port Vale, Swindon Town
Div. 2 to Div. 3: Cardiff City, Blackpool, Scunthorpe Utd., Chesterfield

2001

Premier League to Div. 1: Manchester City, Coventry City, Bradford City
Div. 1 to Div. 2: Huddersfield Town, Q.P.R., Tranmere Rov.
Div. 2 to Div. 3: Bristol Rov., Luton Town, Swansea City, Oxford Utd.

2002

Premier League to Div. 1: Ipswich Town, Derby Co., Leicester City
Div. 1 to Div. 2: Crewe Alexandra, Barnsley, Stockport Co.
Div. 2 to Div. 3: Bournemouth, Bury, Wrexham, Cambridge Utd.

2003

Premier League to Div. 1: West Ham Utd., W.B.A., Sunderland
Div. 1 to Div. 2: Sheffield Wed., Brighton & H.A., Grimsby Town
Div. 2 to Div. 3: Cheltenham Town, Huddersfield Town, Mansfield Town, Northampton Town

2004

Premier League to Div. 1: Leicester City, Leeds Utd., Wolves
Div. 1 to Div. 2: Walsall, Bradford City, Wimbledon
Div. 2 to Div. 3: Grimsby Town, Rushden & Diamonds, Notts Co., Wycombe Wand.

2005

Premier League to Championship: Crystal Palace, Norwich City, Southampton
Championship to League 1: Gillingham, Nott'm. Forest, Rotherham Utd.
League 1 to League 2: Torquay Utd., Wrexham, Peterborough Utd., Stockport Co.

2006

Premier League to Championship: Birmingham City, W.B.A., Sunderland
Championship to League 1: Crewe Alexandra, Millwall, Brighton & H.A.
League 1 to League 2: Hartlepool Utd., MK Dons, Swindon Town, Walsall

2007

Premier League to Championship: Sheffield Utd., Charlton Athletic, Watford
Championship to League 1: Southend Utd., Luton Town, Leeds Utd.
League 1 to League 2: Chesterfield, Bradford City, Rotherham Utd., Brentford

QUOTE-UNQUOTE

'If there is a trophy for "Man of the Year" it should go to him' – **Petr Cech**, Chelsea goalkeeper, acclaims John Terry, who returned for the club's Carling Cup celebrations after being knocked out during the final.

'Arsene Wenger is a good manager, but he has never won the Champions League' – **Jose Mourinho**, Chelsea boss, in another dig at his rival.

'Plenty of managers who have won the Champions League will not be considered great managers' – **Arsene Wenger** responds.

'I can now consider myself a Red Devil' – **Javier Mascherano**, Argentine midfielder, gets his nicknames mixed up after signing for Liverpool.

'When I play Manchester City I need special insurance' – **Pedro Mendes**, Portsmouth midfielder, twice the victim last season of heavy challenges from Ben Thatcher and Joey Barton.

'Gary Neville told me I've achieved his dream' – **John O'Shea**, Manchester United midfielder, after his last-minute winner against Liverpool at Anfield.

'We threw everything we could at them – the kitchen sink, golf clubs, the contents of my garage' – **Ian Holloway**, Plymouth manager, after his side's F.A. Cup defeat by Watford.

'They were so early they brought the milk in' – **Roy Keane**, Sunderland manager, on three of his players who made sure they were on time for training after missing the team bus and being left behind for the game at Barnsley.

'We've gone down by one goal and the thickness of a post. I was that close to my biggest achievement as a manager' – **Neil Warnock** after Sheffield United's relegation.

'Losing our status because we played by the rules when another club haven't is a kick in the teeth' – **Kevin McCabe**, Sheffield United chairman, on the Premier League's decision not to take points off West Ham for breaching regulations over the signing of Carlos Tevez.

'We have set off on the road to justice and we will not come off that road until we get it' – **Dave Whelan**, Wigan chairman, leading legal moves against the league's decision.

'I find the suggestion that we wanted to keep West Ham in the Premiership at the expense of so-called smaller clubs one of the most offensive things I have heard' – **Richard Scudamore**, chief executive of the Premier League.

'We have been Public Enemy No 1. Everyone has jumped on the bandwagon. But it's over now' – **Alan Curbishley**, West Ham manager, after his side survive and Sheffield United go down.

ANNUAL AWARDS

FOOTBALL WRITERS' ASSOCIATION

Footballer of the Year: **1948** Stanley Matthews (Blackpool); **1949** Johnny Carey (Manchester Utd.); **1950** Joe Mercer (Arsenal); **1951** Harry Johnston (Blackpool); **1952** Billy Wright (Wolves); **1953** Nat Lofthouse (Bolton Wand.); **1954** Tom Finney (Preston N.E.); **1955** Don Revie (Manchester City); **1956** Bert Trautmann (Manchester City); **1957** Tom Finney (Preston N.E.); **1958** Danny Blanchflower (Tottenham); **1959** Syd Owen (Luton Town); **1960** Bill Slater (Wolves); **1961** Danny Blanchflower (Tottenham); **1962** Jimmy Adamson (Burnley); **1963** Stanley Matthews (Stoke City); **1964** Bobby Moore (West Ham Utd.); **1965** Bobby Collins (Leeds Utd.); **1966** Bobby Charlton (Manchester Utd.); **1967** Jack Charlton (Leeds Utd.); **1968** George Best (Manchester Utd.); **1969** Tony Book (Manchester City) & Dave Mackay (Derby Co.) – shared; **1970** Billy Bremner (Leeds Utd.); **1971** Frank McLintock (Arsenal); **1972** Gordon Banks (Stoke City); **1973** Pat Jennings (Tottenham); **1974** Ian Callaghan (Liverpool); **1975** Alan Mullery (Fulham); **1976** Kevin Keegan (Liverpool); **1977** Emlyn Hughes (Liverpool); **1978** Kenny Burns (Nott'm Forest); **1979** Kenny Dalglish (Liverpool); **1980** Terry McDermott (Liverpool); **1981** Frans Thijssen (Ipswich Town); **1982** Steve Perryman (Tottenham); **1983** Kenny Dalglish (Liverpool); **1984** Ian Rush (Liverpool); **1985** Neville Southall (Everton); **1986** Gary Lineker (Everton); **1987** Clive Allen (Tottenham); **1988** John Barnes (Liverpool); **1989** Steve Nicol (Liverpool); Special award to the Liverpool players for the compassion shown to bereaved families after the Hillsborough Disaster; **1990** John Barnes (Liverpool); **1991** Gordon Strachan (Leeds Utd.); **1992** Gary Lineker (Tottenham); **1993** Chris Waddle (Sheffield Wed.); **1994** Alan Shearer (Blackburn Rov.); **1995** Jurgen Klinsmann (Tottenham); **1996** Eric Cantona (Manchester Utd.); **1997** Gianfranco Zola (Chelsea); **1998** Dennis Bergkamp (Arsenal); **1999** David Ginola (Tottenham); **2000** Roy Keane (Manchester Utd.); **2001** Teddy Sheringham (Manchester Utd.); **2002** Robert Pires (Arsenal); **2003** Thierry Henry (Arsenal); **2004** Thierry Henry (Arsenal); **2005** Frank Lampard (Chelsea); **2006** Thierry Henry (Arsenal); **2007** Cristiano Ronaldo (Manchester Utd.).

PROFESSIONAL FOOTBALLERS' ASSOCIATION

Player of the Year: **1974** Norman Hunter (Leeds Utd.); **1975** Colin Todd (Derby Co.); **1976** Pat Jennings (Tottenham); **1977** Andy Gray (Aston Villa); **1978** Peter Shilton (Nott'm Forest); **1979** Liam Brady (Arsenal); **1980** Terry McDermott (Liverpool); **1981** John Wark (Ipswich Town); **1982** Kevin Keegan (Southampton); **1983** Kenny Dalglish (Liverpool); **1984** Ian Rush (Liverpool); **1985** Peter Reid (Everton); **1986** Gary Lineker (Everton); **1987** Clive Allen (Tottenham); **1988** John Barnes (Liverpool); **1989** Mark Hughes (Manchester Utd.); **1990** David Platt (Aston Villa); **1991** Mark Hughes (Manchester Utd.); **1992** Gary Pallister (Manchester Utd.); **1993** Paul McGrath (Aston Villa); **1994** Eric Cantona (Manchester Utd.); **1995** Alan Shearer (Blackburn Rov.); **1996** Les Ferdinand (Newcastle Utd.); **1997** Alan Shearer (Newcastle Utd.); **1998** Dennis Bergkamp (Arsenal); **1999** David Ginola (Tottenham); **2000** Roy Keane (Manchester Utd.); **2001** Teddy Sheringham (Manchester Utd.); **2002** Ruud van Nistelrooy (Manchester Utd.); **2003** Thierry Henry (Arsenal); **2004** Thierry Henry (Arsenal); **2005** John Terry (Chelsea); **2006** Steven Gerrard (Liverpool); **2007** Cristiano Ronaldo (Manchester Utd.).

Young Player of the Year: **1974** Kevin Beattie (Ipswich Town); **1975** Mervyn Day (West Ham Utd.); **1976** Peter Barnes (Manchester City); **1977** Andy Gray (Aston Villa); **1978** Tony Woodcock (Nott'm Forest); **1979** Cyrille Regis (W.B.A.); **1980** Glenn Hoddle (Tottenham); **1981** Gary Shaw (Aston Villa); **1982** Steve Moran (Southampton); **1983** Ian Rush (Liverpool); **1984** Paul Walsh (Luton Town); **1985** Mark Hughes (Manchester Utd.); **1986** Tony Cottee (West Ham Utd.); **1987** Tony Adams (Arsenal); **1988** Paul Gascoigne (Newcastle Utd.); **1989** Paul Merson (Arsenal); **1990** Matthew Le Tissier (Southampton);

1991 Lee Sharpe (Manchester Utd.); **1992** Ryan Giggs (Manchester Utd.); **1993** Ryan Giggs (Manchester Utd.); **1994** Andy Cole (Newcastle Utd.); **1995** Robbie Fowler (Liverpool); **1996** Robbie Fowler (Liverpool); **1997** David Beckham (Manchester Utd.); **1998** Michael Owen (Liverpool); **1999** Nicolas Anelka (Arsenal); **2000** Harry Kewell (Leeds Utd.); **2001** Steven Gerrard (Liverpool); **2002** Craig Ballamy (Newcastle Utd.); **2003** Jermaine Jenas (Newcastle Utd.); **2004** Scott Parker (Chelsea); **2005** Wayne Rooney (Manchester Utd.); **2006** Wayne Rooney (Manchester Utd.); **2007** Cristiano Ronaldo (Manchester Utd.).

Merit Awards: 1974 Bobby Charlton & Cliff Lloyd; **1975** Denis Law; **1976** George Eastham; **1977** Jack Taylor; **1978** Bill Shankly; **1979** Tom Finney; **1980** Sir Matt Busby; **1981** John Trollope; **1982** Joe Mercer; **1983** Bob Paisley; **1984** Bill Nicholson; **1985** Ron Greenwood; **1986** England 1966 World Cup-winning team; **1987** Sir Stanley Matthews; **1988** Billy Bonds; **1989** Nat Lofthouse; **1990** Peter Shilton; **1991** Tommy Hutchison; **1992** Brian Clough; **1993** Manchester Utd., 1968 European Champions; Eusebio; **1994** Billy Bingham; **1995** Gordon Strachan; **1996** Pele; **1997** Peter Beardsley; **1998** Steve Ogrizovic; **1999** Tony Ford; **2000** Gary Mabbutt; **2001** Jimmy Hill; **2002** Niall Quinn; **2003** Sir Bobby Robson; **2004** Dario Gradi; **2005** Shaka Hislop; **2006** George Best; **2007** Sir Alex Ferguson.

MANAGER OF THE YEAR (1)

(Chosen by a panel from the governing bodies, media and fans.)

1966 Jock Stein (Celtic); **1967** Jock Stein (Celtic); **1968** Matt Busby (Manchester Utd.); **1969** Don Revie (Leeds Utd.); **1970** Don Revie (Leeds Utd.); **1971** Bertie Mee (Arsenal); **1972** Don Revie (Leeds Utd.); **1973** Bill Shankly (Liverpool); **1974** Jack Charlton (Middlesbrough); **1975** Ron Saunders (Aston Villa); **1976** Bob Paisley (Liverpool); **1977** Bob Paisley (Liverpool); **1978** Brian Clough (Nott'm Forest); **1979** Bob Paisley (Liverpool); **1980** Bob Paisley (Liverpool); **1981** Ron Saunders (Aston Villa); **1982** Bob Paisley (Liverpool); **1983** Bob Paisley (Liverpool); **1984** Joe Fagan (Liverpool); **1985** Howard Kendall (Everton); **1986** Kenny Dalglish (Liverpool); **1987** Howard Kendall (Everton); **1988** Kenny Dalglish (Liverpool); **1989** George Graham (Arsenal); **1990** Kenny Dalglish (Liverpool); **1991** George Graham (Arsenal); **1992** Howard Wilkinson (Leeds Utd.); **1993** Alex Ferguson (Manchester Utd.); **1994** Alex Ferguson (Manchester Utd.); **1995** Kenny Dalglish (Blackburn Rov.); **1996** Alex Ferguson (Manchester Utd.); **1997** Alex Ferguson (Manchester Utd.); **1998** Arsene Wenger (Arsenal); **1999** Alex Ferguson (Manchester Utd.); **2000** Sir Alex Ferguson (Manchester Utd.); **2001** George Burley (Ipswich Town); **2002** Arsene Wenger (Arsenal); **2003** Sir Alex Ferguson (Manchester Utd.); **2004** Arsene Wenger (Arsenal); **2005** Jose Mourinho (Chelsea); **2006** Jose Mourinho (Chelsea); **2007** Sir Alex Ferguson (Manchester Utd.).

MANAGER OF THE YEAR (2)

(As chosen by the League Managers' Association and awarded to 'the manager who has made best use of the resources available to him'.)

1993 Dave Bassett (Sheffield Utd.); **1994** Joe Kinnear (Wimbledon); **1995** Frank Clark (Nott'm Forest); **1996** Peter Reid (Sunderland); **1997** Danny Wilson (Barnsley); **1998** David Jones (Southampton); **1999** Alex Ferguson (Manchester Utd.); **2000** Alan Curbishley (Charlton Athletic); **2001** George Burley (Ipswich Town); **2002** Arsene Wenger (Arsenal); **2003** David Moyes (Everton); **2004** Arsene Wenger (Arsenal); **2005** David Moyes (Everton); **2006** Steve Coppell (Reading); **2007** Steve Coppell (Reading).

SCOTTISH FOOTBALL WRITERS' ASSOCIATION

Player of the Year: 1965 Billy McNeill (Celtic); **1966** John Greig (Rangers); **1967** Ronnie Simpson (Celtic); **1968** Gordon Wallace (Raith); **1969** Bobby Murdoch (Celtic); **1970** Pat

Stanton (Hibernian); **1971** Martin Buchan (Aberdeen); **1972** David Smith (Rangers); **1973** George Connelly (Celtic); **1974** World Cup Squad; **1975** Sandy Jardine (Rangers); **1976** John Greig (Rangers); **1977** Danny McGrain (Celtic); **1978** Derek Johnstone (Rangers); **1979** Andy Ritchie (Morton); **1980** Gordon Strachan (Aberdeen); **1981** Alan Rough (Partick Thistle); **1982** Paul Sturrock (Dundee Utd.); **1983** Charlie Nicholas (Celtic); **1984** Willie Miller (Aberdeen); **1985** Hamish McAlpine (Dundee Utd.); **1986** Sandy Jardine (Hearts); **1987** Brian McClair (Celtic); **1988** Paul McStay (Celtic); **1989** Richard Gough (Rangers); **1990** Alex McLeish (Aberdeen); **1991** Maurice Malpas (Dundee Utd.); **1992** Ally McCoist (Rangers); **1993** Andy Goram (Rangers); **1994** Mark Hateley (Rangers); **1995** Brian Laudrup (Rangers); **1996** Paul Gascoigne (Rangers); **1997** Brian Laudrup (Rangers); **1998** Craig Burley (Celtic); **1999** Henrik Larsson (Celtic); **2000** Barry Ferguson (Rangers); **2001** Henrik Larsson (Celtic); **2002** Paul Lambert (Celtic); **2003** Barry Ferguson (Rangers); **2004** Jackie McNamara (Celtic); **2005** John Hartson (Celtic); **2006** Craig Gordon (Hearts); **2007** Shunsuke Nakamura (Celtic).

SCOTTISH PROFESSIONAL FOOTBALLERS' ASSOCIATION

Player of the Year: 1978 Derek Johnstone (Rangers); **1979** Paul Hegarty (Dundee Utd.); **1980** Davie Provan (Celtic); **1981** Mark McGhee (Aberdeen); **1982** Sandy Clarke (Airdrieonians); **1983** Charlie Nicholas (Celtic); **1984** Willie Miller (Aberdeen); **1985** Jim Duffy (Morton); **1986** Richard Gough (Dundee Utd.); **1987** Brian McClair (Celtic); **1988** Paul McStay (Celtic); **1989** Theo Snelders (Aberdeen); **1990** Jim Bett (Aberdeen); **1991** Paul Elliott (Celtic); **1992** Ally McCoist (Rangers); **1993** Andy Goram (Rangers); **1994** Mark Hateley (Rangers); **1995** Brian Laudrup (Rangers); **1996** Paul Gascoigne (Rangers); **1997** Paolo Di Canio (Celtic) **1998** Jackie McNamara (Celtic); **1999** Henrik Larsson (Celtic); **2000** Mark Viduka (Celtic); **2001** Henrik Larsson (Celtic); **2002** Lorenzo Amoruso (Rangers); **2003** Barry Ferguson (Rangers); **2004** Chris Sutton (Celtic); **2005** John Hartson (Celtic) and Fernando Ricksen (Rangers); **2006** Shaun Maloney (Celtic); **2007** Shunsuke Nakamura (Celtic).

Young Player of Year: 1978 Graeme Payne (Dundee Utd.); **1979** Ray Stewart (Dundee Utd.); **1980** John McDonald (Rangers); **1981** Charlie Nicholas (Celtic); **1982** Frank McAvennie (St. Mirren); **1983** Paul McStay (Celtic); **1984** John Robertson (Hearts); **1985** Craig Levein (Hearts); **1986** Craig Levein (Hearts); **1987** Robert Fleck (Rangers); **1988** John Collins (Hibernian); **1989** Billy McKinlay (Dundee Utd.); **1990** Scott Crabbe (Hearts); **1991** Eoin Jess (Aberdeen); **1992** Phil O'Donnell (Motherwell); **1993** Eoin Jess (Aberdeen); **1994** Phil O'Donnell (Motherwell); **1995** Charlie Miller (Rangers); **1996** Jackie McNamara (Celtic); **1997** Robbie Winters (Dundee Utd.); **1998** Gary Naysmith (Hearts); **1999** Barry Ferguson (Rangers) ; **2000** Kenny Miller (Hibernian); **2001** Stilian Petrov (Celtic); **2002** Kevin McNaughton (Aberdeen); **2003** James McFadden (Motherwell); **2004** Stephen Pearson (Celtic); **2005** Derek Riordan (Hibernian); **2006** Shaun Maloney (Celtic); **2007** Steven Naismith (Kilmarnock).

SCOTTISH MANAGER OF THE YEAR

1987 Jim McLean (Dundee Utd.); **1988** Billy McNeill (Celtic); **1989** Graeme Souness (Rangers); **1990** Andy Roxburgh (Scotland); **1991** Alex Totten (St. Johnstone); **1992** Walter Smith (Rangers); **1993** Walter Smith (Rangers); **1994** Walter Smith (Rangers); **1995** Jimmy Nicholl (Raith); **1996** Walter Smith (Rangers); **1997** Walter Smith (Rangers); **1998** Wim Jansen (Celtic); **1999** Dick Advocaat (Rangers); **2000** Dick Advocaat (Rangers); **2001** Martin O'Neill (Celtic); **2002** John Lambie (Partick Thistle); **2003** Alex McLeish (Rangers); **2004** Martin O'Neill (Celtic); **2005** Alex McLeish (Rangers); **2006** Gordon Strachan (Celtic); **2007** Gordon Strachan (Celtic).

EUROPEAN FOOTBALLER OF THE YEAR

(Poll conducted by *France Football*) 1956 Stanley Matthews (Blackpool); **1957** Alfredo di Stefano (Real Madrid); **1958** Raymond Kopa (Real Madrid); **1959** Alfredo di Stefano

(Real Madrid); **1960** Luis Suarez (Barcelona); **1961** Omar Sivori (Juventus); **1962** Josef Masopust (Dukla Prague); **1963** Lev Yashin (Moscow Dynamo); **1964** Denis Law (Manchester Utd.); **1965** Eusebio (Benfica); **1966** Bobby Charlton (Manchester Utd.); **1967** Florian Albert (Ferencvaros); **1968** George Best (Manchester Utd.); **1969** Gianni Rivera (AC Milan); **1970** Gerd Muller (Bayern Munich); **1971** Johan Cruyff (Ajax); **1972** Franz Beckenbauer (Bayern Munich); **1973** Johan Cruyff (Barcelona); **1974** Johan Cruyff (Barcelona); **1975** Oleg Blokhin (Dynamo Kiev); **1976** Franz Beckenbauer (Bayern Munich); **1977** Allan Simonsen (Borussia Moenchengladbach); **1978** Kevin Keegan (SV Hamburg); **1979** Kevin Keegan (SV Hamburg); **1980** Karl-Heinz Rummenigge (Bayern Munich); **1981** Karl-Heinz Rummenigge (Bayern Munich); **1982** Paolo Rossi (Juventus); **1983** Michel Platini (Juventus); **1984** Michel Platini (Juventus); **1985** Michel Platini (Juventus); **1986** Igor Belanov (Dynamo Kiev); **1987** Ruud Gullit (AC Milan); **1988** Marco van Basten (AC Milan); **1989** Marco van Basten (AC Milan); **1990** Lothar Matthaus (Inter Milan); **1991** Jean-Pierre Papin (Marseille); **1992** Marco van Basten (AC Milan); **1993** Roberto Baggio (Juventus); **1994** Hristo Stoichkov (Barcelona); **1995** George Weah (AC Milan); **1996** Matthias Sammer (Borussia Dortmund); **1997** Ronaldo (Inter Milan); **1998** Zinedine Zidane (Juventus); **1999** Rivaldo (Barcelona); **2000** Luis Figo (Real Madrid); **2001** Michael Owen (Liverpool); **2002** Ronaldo (Real Madrid); **2003** Pavel Nedved (Juventus); **2004** Andriy Shevchenko (AC Milan); **2005** Ronaldinho (Barcelona); **2006** Fabio Cannavaro (Real Madrid).

FIFA WORLD FOOTBALLER OF YEAR

(Voted by national coaches): 1991 Lothar Matthaus (Inter Milan and Germany); **1992** Marco van Basten (AC Milan and Holland); **1993** Roberto Baggio (Juventus and Italy); **1994** Romario (Barcelona and Brazil); **1995** George Weah (AC Milan and Liberia); **1996** Ronaldo (Barcelona and Brazil); **1997** Ronaldo (Inter Milan and Brazil); **1998** Zinedine Zidane (Juventus and France); **1999** Rivaldo (Barcelona and Brazil); **2000** Zinedine Zidane (Juventus and France); **2001** Luis Figo (Real Madrid and Portugal); **2002** Ronaldo (Real Madrid and Brazil); **2003** Zinedine Zidane (Real Madrid and France); **2004** Ronaldinho (Barcelona and Brazil); **2005** Ronaldinho (Barcelona and Brazil); **2006** Fabio Cannavaro (Real Madrid and Italy).

OLD AND NEW FOR GUPPY AND KENNA

Steve Guppy and Jeff Kenna will provide sporting quiz nights with a Wembley teaser after becoming the first two players to feature in a competitive match at both the old and the new stadiums. They were on opposing sides when Stevenage Borough beat Kidderminster Harriers 3-2 in last season's F.A. Trophy Final. Ironically, Guppy's first appearance under the twin towers was also against Kidderminster, in the 1991 Trophy Final when he was with Wycombe Wanderers. The former England winger, who was also on the winning team that day, went on to play there a further five times, the last one in 2000 when Leicester City beat Tranmere Rovers in the Worthington Cup Final. Full-back Kenna, a former Republic of Ireland international, lost with Southampton in the 1992 Zenith Data Systems Cup Final against Nottingham Forest and with Blackburn Rovers in the 1995 Charity Shield against Everton when he was injured early on and had to go off.

RECORD HAT-TRICK FOR MANAGER STIMSON

Mark Stimson completed a record managerial hat-trick when his Stevenage Borough side beat Kidderminster Harriers 3-2 at Wembley to win last season's F.A. Trophy. The 39-year-old former Tottenham, Newcastle United and Portsmouth full-back had led Grays Athletic to victory in the final in the two previous years.

ENGLISH LEAGUE ROLL-CALL

REVIEW, APPEARANCES, SCORERS 2006-07

(Figures in brackets = appearances as substitute)

BARCLAYS PREMIERSHIP

ARSENAL

Arsene Wenger has always been fiercely protective of his team, but he was forced to concede that this time they were not equipped to deliver any silverware. The admission wasn't particularly surprising. Wenger had to reshape his squad after the summer departure of several senior players, while the move to a spacious new stadium from the tighter confines of Highbury presented its own problems. Too many points were dropped at the Emirates in the first half of the season, leaving the gap opened up by Manchester United and Chelsea too substantial to close. Then, injuries to Thierry Henry and Robin van Persie ruled out the two leading scorers for most of the second half when, in quick succession, Arsenal were removed from the F.A. Cup by Blackburn and the Champions League by PSV Eindhoven. The young side Wenger fielded in the Carling Cup went all the way, but lost 2-1 to Chelsea after taking the lead through Theo Walcott.

Adebayor, E .... 21(8)
Aliadiere, J .... 4(7)
Almunia, M 1
Baptista, J .... 11(13)
Clichy, G .... 26(1)
Denilson .... 4(6)
Diaby, V .... 9(3)
Djourou, J .... 18(3)
Eboue, E .... 23(1)
Fabregas, F .... 34(4)
Flamini, M .... 9(11)
Gallas, W 21
Gilberto Silva 34
Henry, T .... 16(1)
Hleb, A .... 27(6)
Hoyte, J .... 18(4)
Lehmann, J 36
Ljungberg, F .... 16(2)
Poom, M 1
Rosicky, T .... 22(4)
Senderos, P .... 9(5)
Song, A .... 1(1)
Toure, K 35
Van Persie, R .... 17(5)
Walcott, T .... 5(11)

League goals (63): Van Persie 11, Gilberto Silva 10, Henry 10, Adebayor 8, Baptista 3, Flamini 3, Gallas 3, Rosicky 3, Toure 3, Fabregas 2, Hleb 2, Diaby 1, Hoyte 1, Opponents 3.

F.A. Cup goals (7): Adebayor 2, Rosicky 2, Henry 1, Ljungberg 1, Toure 1. **Carling Cup goals (15):** Baptista 6, Aliadiere 4, Adebayor 2, Song 1, Walcott 1, Opponents 1. **Champions League goals (13):** Fabregas 2, Van Persie 2, Baptista 1, Eboue 1, Flamini 1, Gilberto Silva 1, Henry 1, Hleb 1, Ljungberg, 1, Rosicky 1, Opponents 1.

Average home league attendance: 60,045. **Player of Year:** Cesc Fabregas.

ASTON VILLA

With a new owner in Randy Lerner and new manager in Martin O'Neill, there was a fresh sense of optimism surrounding Villa Park. When their team climbed to third in the table with victory at Everton three months into the season, supporters were full of anticipation. O'Neill counselled caution, urging them to ignore any prospect of Champions League football, and he proved spot on, his team hitting a bad patch and going 11 matches without another victory. They went on to flirt with the fringes of the relegation zone before regrouping for a strong finish which brought 15 points from the last 21 and 11th position in the table, five higher than a year earlier. O'Neill aims for further progress in the new campaign in which winter signings John Carew and Ashley Young, along with the fast-emerging Gabriel Agbonlahor, are expected to play leading roles.

Agathe, D .... –(5)
Agbonlahor, G .... 37(1)
Angel, J-P .... 18(5)
Bardsley, P 13
Baros, M .... 10(7)
Barry, G 35
Berger, P .... 5(8)
Bouma, W .... 23(2)
Cahill, G .... 19(1)
Carew, J 11
Davis, S .... 17(11)
Djemba-Djemba, E .... –(1)
Gardner, C .... 11(2)
Hendrie, L .... –(1)
Hughes, A .... 15(4)

Kiraly, G 5	Moore, L .... 7(6)	Sorensen, T 29
Laursen, M .... 12(2)	Osbourne, I .... 6(5)	Sutton, C .... 6(2)
Maloney, S .... 5(3)	Petrov, S 30	Taylor, S .... 4(2)
McCann, G .... 28(2)	Ridgewell, L .... 19(2)	Whittingham, P .... 2(1)
Mellberg, O 38	Samuel, J .... 2(2)	Young, A .... 11(2)

League goals (43): Agbonlahor 9, Barry 8, Angel 4, Moore 4, Carew 3, Berger 2, Gardner 2, Petrov 2, Young 2, Baros 1, Maloney 1, McCann 1, Mellberg 1, Ridgewell 1, Sutton 1, Opponents 1.
F.A. Cup goals (1): Baros 1. **Carling Cup goals (5):** Angel 3, Agbonlahor 1, Barry 1.
Average home league attendance: 36,214. **Player of Year:** Gareth Barry.

BLACKBURN ROVERS

Benni McCarthy, a £2m. signing from FC Porto, ranked highly in a list of the season's best acquisitions with 23 goals in all competitions. His tally of 18 in the Premiership was not quite enough to ensure a second successive season of European football, despite a haul of 11 points from the final five matches. Three successive defeats before that had left Blackburn with too much ground to make up. But at least they kept the campaign alive almost to the end and with sharper finishing could have wrested the initiative away from Chelsea in a tight F.A. Cup semi-final. McCarthy also scored three times in the UEFA Cup, where his team headed their group before going out to Bayer Leverkusen 3-2 on aggregate after a frustrating goalless draw in the second leg at Ewood Park. Mark Hughes did not have the best of luck with injuries, losing Steven Reid after three games and Robbie Savage and Andre Ooijer from January onwards.

Bentley, D 36	Jeffers, F .... 3(7)	Pedersen, M 36
Berner, B 1	Khizanishvili, Z ...... 17(1)	Peter, S .... 1(8)
Brown, J .... –(1)	Kuqi, S .... –(1)	Reid, S 3
Derbyshire, M .... 8(14)	McCarthy, B 36	Roberts, J .... 9(9)
Dunn, D .... 7(4)	McEveley, J .... 3(1)	Samba, C .... 13(1)
Emerton, B .... 32(2)	Mokoena, A .... 18(9)	Savage, R 21
Friedel, B 38	Neill, L 20	Todd, A .... 6(3)
Gallagher, P .... 2(14)	Nelsen, R 12	Tugay, K .... 26(4)
Gray, M .... 10(1)	Nonda, S .... 17(9)	Warnock, S 13
Henchoz, S .... 10(2)	Ooijer, A 20	

League goals (52): McCarthy 18, Nonda 7, Pedersen 6, Derbyshire 5, Bentley 4, Roberts 4, Samba 2, Gallagher 1, Tugay 1, Warnock 1, Opponents 3.
F.A. Cup goals (12): Derbyshire 4, McCarthy 3, Pedersen 2, Gallagher 1, Mokoena 1, Roberts 1. **Carling Cup goals:** None. **UEFA Cup goals (12):** Bentley 3, McCarthy 3, Savage 2, Jeffers 1, Neill 1, Nonda 1, Tugay 1.
Average home league attendance: 21,275. **Player of Year:** David Bentley.

BOLTON WANDERERS

Sammy Lee faces the daunting task of following in the footsteps of Sam Allardyce after the manager who established Bolton as a force in the top flight decided that seven years in charge was long enough. Whether Allardyce would have stayed if his team had sustained a challenge for a Champions League place will remain a moot point. A faltering Arsenal were in their sights with a month of the season remaining. But Bolton lost a crucial game 2-1 at the Emirates after taking the lead through Nicolas Anelka and failed to win any of their last six fixtures. The consolation was a second UEFA Cup spot in three seasons, although it was a close thing, with Reading finishing one point behind and Portsmouth two. Victories over Arsenal, Liverpool and Tottenham were highlights at the Reebok, while a 4-0 defeat there by Manchester United proved a sharp reminder that Bolton still have some way to go before they can think about moving up to the next level.

Anelka, N 35	Cesar Martin .... –(1)	Faye, A .... 29(3)
Ben Haim, T .... 30(2)	Davies, K 30	Fortune, Q .... 5(1)
Campo, I .... 31(3)	Diouf, E-H .... 32(1)	Gardner, R .... 13(5)

Giannakopoulos, S . 11(12)	Nolan, K 31	Tal, I .... 4(12)
Hunt, N .... 32(1)	Pedersen, H .... 10(8)	Teymourian, A .... 6(11)
Jaaskelainen, J 38	Sinclair, J .... –(2)	Thompson, D .... 3(5)
Meite, A 35	Smith, J .... –(1)	Vaz Te, R .... 2(23)
Michalik, L .... 3(1)	Speed, G 38	

League goals (47): Anelka 11, Davies 8, Speed 8, Diouf 5, Campo 4, Nolan 3, Faye 2, Teymourian 2, Michalik 1, Pedersen 1, Opponents 2.
F.A. Cup goals (6): Teymourian 2, Davies 1, Meite 1, Nolan 1, Tal 1. **Carling Cup goals (3):** Anelka 1, Campo 1, Nolan 1.
Average home league attendance: 23,606. **Player of Year:** Jussi Jaaskelainen.

CHARLTON ATHLETIC

A club renowned for stability on and off the pitch were relegated after a season of turmoil in both areas. Alan Curbishley had spent 15 years as manager before stepping down at the end of the previous campaign. Iain Dowie, Curbishley's successor, lasted until mid November when he was sacked with the team rock bottom. Les Reed's tenure lasted only until Christmas Eve, by which time things were not much better. In came Alan Pardew, a fortnight after he himself had been fired by West Ham, and out went leading scorer Darren Bent with a knee injury. Pardew banked on Bent's return sparking a revival and victories over West Ham, Newcastle and Wigan changed the whole complexion in the relegation zone. But Charlton were unable to maintain the momentum, failing to win again and going down after a 2-0 home defeat by Tottenham in the penultimate fixture.

Ambrose, D .... 21(5)	Holland, M .... 27(6)	Sam, L .... 3(4)
Bent, D 32	Hreidarsson, H .... 30(1)	Sankofa, O 9
Bent, M .... 17(13)	Hughes, B .... 15(9)	Song, A 12
Bougherra, M .... 2(3)	Kishishev, R .... 6(8)	Sorondo, G .... –(1)
Carson, S 36	Lisbie, K .... 1(7)	Thatcher, B .... 10(1)
Diawara, S .... 18(5)	Myhre, T 1	Thomas, J .... 16(4)
El Karkouri, T 36	Pouso, O 1	Traore, D 11
Faye, A .... 25(3)	Randolph, D 1	Young, L 29
Fortune, J .... 6(2)	Reid, A .... 15(1)	Zheng Zhi .... 8(4)
Hasselbaink, J ...... 11(14)	Rommedahl, D .... 19(9)	

League goals (34): Bent, D 13, Ambrose 3, El Karkouri 3, Thomas 3, Hasselbaink 2, Reid 2, Bent, M 1, Faye 1, Holland 1, Hughes 1, Young 1, Zheng Zhi 1, Opponents 2.
F.A. Cup goals: None. **Carling Cup goals (5):** Bent, D 2, Hasselbaink 2, Bent, M 1.
Average home league attendance: 26,195. **Player of Year:** Scott Carson.

CHELSEA

Jose Mourinho completed a full set of domestic trophies thanks to Didier Drogba's extra-time winner against Manchester United in the F.A. Cup Final. His team also overcame Arsenal to lift the Carling Cup, but the double was overshadowed, to some extent, by his uneasy relationship with club owner Roman Abramovich, which clearly spilled over into the dressing room and heightened speculation about the manager's future. Mourinho bemoaned injuries to Petr Cech and John Terry – along with Abramovich's refusal to sanction paying for cover in the January transfer window – and their absence clearly hampered efforts to keep pace in the Premiership with United, who denied them a third successive title. Chelsea also fell short in the Champions League, losing in the semi-finals to Liverpool for the second time in three years. Drogba, however, could do little wrong, his precise finish at Wembley taking his tally for the season to 33, which included a hat-trick against Levski Sofia.

Ballack, M .... 23(3)	Cole, J .... 3(10)	Geremi, N .... 15(4)
Boulahrouz, K .... 10(3)	Cudicini, C .... 7(1)	Hilario, H 11
Bridge, W .... 17(5)	Diarra, L .... 7(3)	Hutchinson, S .... –(1)
Cech, P 20	Drogba, D .... 32(4)	Kalou, S .... 19(14)
Cole, A .... 21(2)	Essien, M 33	Lampard, F .... 36(1)

Makelele, C .... 26(3)
Mikel, J .... 10(12)
Morais, N .... –(2)
Paulo Ferreira .... 18(6)
Ricardo Carvalho 31
Robben, A .... 16(5)
Sahar, B .... –(3)
Shevchenko, A .... 22(8)
Sinclair, S .... 1(1)
Terry, J .... 27(1)
Wright-Phillips, S . 13(14)

League goals (64): Drogba 20, Lampard 11, Kalou 7, Ballack 5, Shevchenko 4, Ricardo Carvalho 3, Essien 2, Robben 2, Wright-Phillips 2, Geremi 1, Makelele 1, Terry 1, Opponents 5.
F.A. Cup goals (21): Lampard 6, Drogba 3, Shevchenko 3, Wright-Phillips 3, Mikel 2, Ballack 1, Essien 1, Kalou 1, Ricardo Carvalho 1. **Carling Cup goals (14):** Drogba 4, Lampard 3, Shevchenko 3, Bridge 1, Cole, J 1, Essien 1, Kalou 1.
Champions League goals (17): Drogba 6, Shevchenko 3, Ballack 2, Essien 2, Cole, J 1, Lampard 1, Robben 1, Wright-Phillips 1. **Community Shield goals (1):** Shevchenko 1.
Average home league attendance: 41,541. **Player of Year:** Michael Essien.

EVERTON

Everton's biggest victory in the Merseyside derby for 40 years, Andy Johnson scoring twice in a 3-0 scoreline, helped lay the foundations for a solid season's work, which earned a sixth-place finish and a UEFA Cup spot. A goalless draw at Anfield confirmed local bragging rights, along with the satisfaction of answering Rafael Benitez's dismissal of Everton as 'a small club.' They clinched a place in Europe by beating rivals Portsmouth 3-0 at Goodison, a week after the disappointment of surrendering a two-goal lead and losing 4-2 to Manchester United on the defining day of the race for the championship. Johnson's contribution in his first season, the raw young talent of James Vaughan and Victor Anichebe and the prospect of a return from an injury-dogged campaign by Tim Cahill all offer David Moyes the prospect of more good things to come.

Anichebe, V .... 5(14)
Arteta, M 35
Beattie, J .... 15(18)
Cahill, T .... 17(1)
Carsley, L 38
Da Silva, A .... –(1)
Davies, S .... 13(2)
Fernandes, M .... 8(1)
Hibbert, T .... 12(1)
Howard, T 36
Hughes, M .... –(1)
Johnson, A 32
Kilbane, K 2
Lescott, J .... 36(2)
McFadden, J .... 6(13)
Naysmith, G .... 10(5)
Neville, P 35
Nuno Valente .... 10(4)
Osman, L .... 31(3)
Stubbs, A 23
Turner, I 1
Van der Meyde, A ..... 5(3)
Vaughan, J .... 7(7)
Weir, D .... 2(3)
Wright, R 1
Yobo, J 38

League goals (52): Johnson 11, Arteta 9, Cahill 5, Vaughan 4, Anichebe 3, Osman 3, Beattie 2, Fernandes 2, Lescott 2, McFadden 2, Stubbs 2, Yobo 2, Carsley 1, Naysmith 1, Neville 1, Opponents 2.
F.A. Cup goals (1): Johnson 1. **Carling Cup goals (6):** Cahill 2, Anichebe 1, McFadden 1, Opponents 2.
Average home league attendance: 36,738. **Player of Year:** Mikel Arteta.

FULHAM

Fulham were somewhat fortunate to emerge unscathed from an end-of-season slump after Rafael Benitez, with the Champions League Final against AC Milan uppermost in his mind, fielded what was virtually a Liverpool reserve team in the penultimate match at Craven Cottage. Substitute Clint Dempsey's first Premiership goal clinched their first victory in 11 matches and ensured survival by a single point. Northern Ireland manager Lawrie Sanchez, who took over on a caretaker basis when Chris Coleman was sacked, then sacrificed his international ambitions by accepting the job on a permanent basis. It was ironic that Coleman's dogged pursuit of Dempsey had finally brought the American midfielder to the club in the January transfer window. Sanchez, noting Fulham's failure to record back-to-back victories after the opening month of the campaign, promised major changes in personnel to try to avoid a similar struggle.

Boa Morte, L .... 12(3)
Bocanegra, C .... 26(4)
Briggs, M .... –(1)
Brown, M 34
Bullard, J 4
Christanval, P .... 19(1)

Davies, S 14	Lastuvka, J .... 7(1)	Radzinski, T .... 25(10)
Dempsey, C .... 1(9)	McBride, B .... 34(4)	Rosenior, L 38
Diop, P B .... 20(3)	Montella, V .... 3(7)	Routledge, W .... 13(10)
Helguson, H .... 16(14)	Niemi, A 31	Runstrom, B .... –(1)
Jensen, C .... 10(2)	Pearce, I 22	Smertin, A .... 6(1)
John, C .... 9(14)	Queudrue, F .... 28(1)	Volz, M .... 24(5)
Knight, Z .... 22(1)		

League goals (38): McBride 9, Bocanegra 5, Helguson 3, Bullard 2, Davies 2, Jensen 2, Knight 2, Montella 2, Radzinski 2, Volz 2, Christanval 1, Dempsey 1, John 1, Pearce 1, Queudrue 1, Opponents 2.
F.A. Cup goals (9): McBride 3, Montella 3, Radzinski 1, Routledge 1, Volz 1. **Carling Cup goals (1):** Helguson 1.
Average home league attendance: 22,273. **Player of Year:** Brian McBride.

LIVERPOOL

A long-overdue championship challenge was as good as over by the end of October, another indifferent start to the season leaving Liverpool 11 points adrift of Manchester United and Chelsea with little prospect of making up the leeway. Interest in the F.A. Cup and Carling Cup disappeared with two crushing home defeats by Arsenal in the space of four days in January. So that left a second Champions League success in three years as the sole target. Victories over holders Barcelona, PSV Eindhoven and Chelsea augured well. So, too, did the way they took the final to AC Milan. But the Italians in general, and two-goal Filippo Inzaghi in particular, were too wily in the end. Rafael Benitez had insisted that, whatever the outcome, he needed to spend the millions made available by the club's new owners George Gillett and Tom Hicks on some major signings in order to give his side added quality and impetus. Defeat in Athens merely reinforced that belief.

Agger, D .... 23(4)	Gerrard, S .... 35(1)	Padelli, D 1
Arbeloa, A .... 8(1)	Gonzalez, M .... 14(11)	Paletta, G .... 2(1)
Aurelio, F .... 10(7)	Guthrie, D .... –(3)	Pennant, J .... 20(14)
Bellamy, C .... 23(4)	Hyypia, S 23	Reina, J 35
Carragher, J .... 34(1)	Insua, E 2	Riise, J A .... 29(4)
Crouch, P .... 19(13)	Kewell, H .... –(2)	Sissoko, M .... 15(1)
Dudek, J 2	Kronkamp, J 1	Warnock, S 1
El Zhar, N .... –(3)	Kuyt, D .... 27(7)	Xabi Alonso .... 29(3)
Finnan, S .... 32(1)	Luis Garcia .... 11(6)	Zenden, B .... 9(7)
Fowler, R .... 6(10)	Mascherano, J 7	

League goals (57): Kuyt 12, Crouch 9, Bellamy 7, Gerrard 7, Xabi Alonso 4, Fowler 3, Luis Garcia 3, Agger 2, Gonzalez 2, Hyypia 2, Arbeloa 1, Carragher 1, Kewell 1, Pennant 1, Riise 1, Opponents 1.
F.A. Cup goals (1): Kuyt 1. **Carling Cup goals (8):** Fowler 2, Agger 1, Crouch 1, Gerrard 1, Hyypia 1, Paletta 1, Riise 1. **Champions League goals (22):** Crouch 7, Gerrard 3, Luis Garcia 3, Bellamy 2, Fowler 2, Riise 2, Agger 1, Gonzalez 1, Kuyt 1. **Community Shield goals (2):** Crouch 1, Riise 1.
Average home league attendance: 43,561.

MANCHESTER CITY

A poor season for City ended, predictably, with the dismissal of manager Stuart Pearce. His team were particularly impotent at home, where ten goals in 19 matches proved two fewer than the previous Premiership low by relegated Sunderland in 2005-06. Defeat in the final game at Eastlands, in which Manchester United effectively clinched the title, just rubbed it in. Pearce's three main strikers, Darius Vassell, Georgios Samaras and new-signing Bernado Corradi rarely delivered. Emile Mpenza came in to liven things up in the second half of the campaign, but City's problems seemed too deep-rooted for any major improvement. Joey Barton's suspension by the club following a nasty training ground incident with Ousmane Dabo proved the final straw. City enjoyed a measure of success in the F.A. Cup, overcoming Sheffield Wednesday, Southampton and Preston before losing at Blackburn in the quarter-finals, but there was more embarrassment in the Carling Cup with defeat by Chesterfield. Former England coach Sven-Goran Eriksson replaced Pearce and was promised funds for rebuilding by new owner Thaksin Shinawatra.

Ball, M 12	Ireland, S .... 14(10)	Richards, M 28
Barton, J 33	Isaksson, A .... 12(2)	Samaras, G .... 16(20)
Beasley, D .... 11(7)	Johnson, M 10	Sinclair, T .... 14(4)
Corradi, B .... 19(6)	Jordan, S .... 12(1)	Sturridge, D .... –(2)
Dabo, O .... 10(3)	Miller, I .... 3(13)	Sun Jihai .... 10(3)
Dickov, P .... 9(7)	Mills, D .... –(1)	Thatcher, B 11
Distin, S 37	Mills, M 1	Trabelsi, H .... 16(4)
Dunne, R 38	Mpenza, E .... 9(1)	Vassell, D .... 28(4)
Hamann, D .... 12(4)	Onuoha, N .... 15(3)	Weaver, N 25
Hart, J 1	Reyna, C .... 12(3)	

League goals (29): Barton 6, Samaras 4, Beasley 3, Corradi 3, Mpenza 3, Vassell 3, Distin 2, Dunne 1, Ireland 1, Richards 1, Trabelsi 1, Opponents 1.
F.A. Cup goals (9): Ireland 2, Vassell 2, Ball 1, Barton 1, Beasley 1, Samaras 1, Opponents 1. **Carling Cup goals (1):** Samaras 1.
Average home league attendance: 39,997. **Player of Year:** Richard Dunne.

MANCHESTER UNITED

Sir Alex Ferguson completed 20 years in charge with a ninth title triumph. Indeed, at one stage, his team promised a repeat of the golden treble of 1999, particularly after routing Roma 7-1 on an unforgettable Champions League night at Old Trafford. But the growing demands of challenging for honours on three fronts proved beyond them. AC Milan were too good in the semi-finals, while tiredness was clearly evident in the extra-time defeat by Chelsea in the F.A. Cup Final. United, however, were not to be denied in the Premiership, halting Chelsea's bid for a third successive title, with an expansive brand of football not even Jose Mourinho could counter. Cristiano Ronaldo's failure to impose himself in the Wembley showpiece did nothing to detract from a magnificient season in which he matured into a player of genuine world class and claimed both major domestic Player of the Year awards. Ronaldo and Wayne Rooney both finished with 23 goals to their credit in all competitions.

Brown, W .... 17(5)	Ji-Sung Park .... 8(6)	Rooney, W .... 33(2)
Carrick, M .... 29(4)	Kuszczak, T 6	Saha, L .... 18(6)
Dong Fangzhou 1	Larsson, H .... 5(2)	Scholes, P .... 29(1)
Eagles, C .... 1(1)	Lee, K 1	Silvestre, M .... 6(8)
Evra, P .... 22(2)	Neville, G 24	Smith, A .... 6(3)
Ferdinand, R 33	O'Shea, J .... 16(16)	Solskjaer, O .... 9(10)
Fletcher, D .... 16(8)	Richardson, K .... 8(7)	Van der Sar, E 32
Giggs, R .... 25(5)	Ronaldo, C .... 31(3)	Vidic, N 25
Heinze, G .... 17(5)		

League goals (83): Ronaldo 17, Rooney 14, Saha 8, Solskjaer 7, Scholes 6, Park 5, Giggs 4, O'Shea 4, Carrick 3, Fletcher 3, Vidic 3, Eagles 1, Evra 1, Ferdinand 1, Larsson 1, Richardson 1, Silvestre 1, Opponents 3.
F.A. Cup goals (15): Rooney 5, Ronaldo 3, Solskjaer 2, Carrick 1, Heinze 1, Larsson 1, Richardson 1, Saha 1. **Carling Cup goals (2):** Lee 1, Solskjaer 1. **Champions League goals (23):** Rooney 4, Saha 4, Ronaldo 3, Carrick 2, Giggs 2, Evra 1, Larsson 1, O'Shea 1, Richardson 1, Scholes 1, Smith 1, Solskjaer 1, Vidic 1.
Average home league attendance: 75,826. **Player of Year:** Cristiano Ronaldo.

MIDDLESBROUGH

Gareth Southgate's first season as manager got off to a topsy-turvy start – and continued in much the same vein on the way to a 12th-place finish, an improvement of two on Steve McClaren's final campaign. Middlesbrough lost their opening match at Reading after surrendering a two-goal lead, overcame Chelsea, were hammered by Portsmouth, then claimed a point against Arsenal at the Emirates. The only time they looked like settling into a sustained run of success came around the turn of the year when three matches yielded 11 goals, including a 5-1 victory over Bolton. Jonathan Woodgate's decision to turn his loan spell into a permanent move from Real Madrid was a major boost, although there were question marks about the future of Mark Viduka and Yakubu. The pair scored consistently in the league and the F.A. Cup, where Middlesbrough came through three successive replays before falling in a fourth to Manchester United at the quarter-final stage.

Arca, J .... 18(3)
Bates, M .... –(1)
Boateng, G 35
Cattermole, L .... 22(9)
Christie, M .... 4(9)
Davies, A .... 21(2)
Dong Gook Lee .... 3(6)
Downing, S 34
Euell, J .... 9(8)
Graham, D .... –(1)
Huth, R .... 8(4)
Johnson, A .... 3(9)
Jones, B 2
Maccarone, M .... 1(6)
Mendieta, G .... 4(3)
Morrison, J .... 15(13)
Parnaby, S .... 9(9)
Pogatetz, E 35
Riggott, C .... 5(1)
Rochemback, F ...... 17(3)
Schwarzer, M 36
Taylor, A 34
Viduka, M .... 22(7)
Wheater, D .... 1(1)
Woodgate, J 30
Xavier, A 14
Yakubu, A .... 36(1)

League goals (44): Viduka 14, Yakubu 12, Arca 2, Downing 2, Morrison 2, Pogatetz 2, Rochemback 2, Boateng 1, Cattermole 1, Christie 1, Huth 1, Maccarone 1, Wheater 1, Xavier 1, Opponents 1

F.A. Cup goals (14): Viduka 5, Yakubu 4, Arca 1, Boateng 1, Cattermole 1, Christie 1, Hines, S 1. **Carling Cup goals:** None.

Average home league attendance: 27,729. **Player of Year:** Jonathan Woodgate.

NEWCASTLE UNITED

Will Sam Allardyce have any more joy in bringing the good times back to St James' Park than any of his distinguished predecessors? The question is one of the most intriguing of the new season, not least because of the way Roy Keane has promised to make his promoted Sunderland side a Premiership force in the north east. Allardyce, who took over after Glenn Roeder's resignation, is under no illusion about the size of the task. Newcastle had another indifferent season, inconsistent in the league, dumped out of the F.A. Cup 5-1 in front of their own fans by Birmingham and losing the chance to make a real impact in the UEFA Cup. They held a potentially decisive 4-1 lead in the first leg against AZ Alkmaar, yet finished up losing the tie on away goals with a place in the quarter-finals beckoning. To be fair, Newcastle again lost key players to injuries, the most severe ruling out Michael Owen until the final three matches.

Ameobi, S .... 9(3)
Babayaro, C 12
Bramble, T 17
Butt, N .... 27(4)
Carr, S 23
Carroll, A .... –(4)
Duff, D .... 20(2)
Dyer, K .... 20(2)
Edgar, D .... 2(1)
Emre, B .... 21(3)
Given, S 22
Harper, S .... 15(3)
Huntington, P .... 10(1)
Luque, A .... –(7)
Martins, O .... 32(1)
Milner, J .... 31(4)
Moore, C 17
N'Zogbia, C .... 10(12)
O'Brien, A .... 1(1)
Onyewu, O .... 7(4)
Owen, M 3
Parker, S .... 28(1)
Pattison, M .... 2(5)
Ramage, P .... 20(1)
Rossi, G .... 3(8)
Sibierski, A .... 14(12)
Solano, N .... 25(3)
Srnicek, P .... 1(1)
Taylor, S .... 26(1)

League goals (38): Martins 11, Dyer 5, Ameobi 3, Milner 3, Parker 3, Sibierski 3, Emre 2, Solano 2, Taylor 2, Butt 1, Duff 1, Edgar 1, Huntington 1.

F.A. Cup goals (3): Dyer 1, Milner 1, Taylor 1. **Carling Cup goals (5):** Solano 2, Parker 1, Rossi 1, Sibierski 1. **Intertoto Cup/UEFA Cup goals (20):** Martins 6, Sibierski 4, Ameobi 2, Luque 2, Bramble 1, Dyer 1, Emre 1, Taylor 1, Opponents 2.

Average home league attendance: 50,686.

PORTSMOUTH

Harry Redknapp reshaped his squad shrewdly after narrowly escaping relegation the previous season and was rewarded with the club's highest league placing, ninth, for half a century. David James, who overtook David Seaman's Premiership record of 141 clean sheets, and Sol Campbell, resurrecting a career that looked to be going nowhere, both had a major infuence. With the evergreen Kanu enjoying a prolific first half of the campaign, Portsmouth laid strong foundations for a UEFA Cup spot. But with Kanu's goals drying up and inconsistency creeping in, they were not the same force in the New Year. Even so, only a controversial decision by Graham Poll who, in his final Premiership game before retiring ruled out an effort from Nico Kranjcar against Arsenal, denied them the chance of a place in Europe for the first time. With Redknapp aiming to take them to a new level on the back of some major summer buys and a new stadium in the pipeline, there is every chance of the momentum continuing.

Campbell, S 32
Cole, A .... 5(13)
Davis, S .... 29(2)
Douala, R .... 1(6)
Fernandes, M .... 7(3)
Hughes, R .... 11(7)
James, D 38
Johnson, G .... 25(1)
Kanu, N .... 32(4)
Koroman, O .... –(1)
Kranjcar, N .... 11(13)
Lauren .... 9(1)
LuaLua, L .... 8(14)
Mendes, P .... 25(1)
Mvuemba, A .... 25(6)
Mwaruwari, B .... 25(6)
O'Brien, A .... 1(2)
O'Neil, G 35
Pamarot, N .... 21(2)
Primus, L 36
Stefanovic, D 20
Taylor, M .... 30(5)
Thompson, ... 5(7)
Todorov, S .... 1(3)
Traore, D 10

League goals (45): Kanu 10, Taylor 8, Mwaruwari 6, Cole 3, Kranjcar 2, LuaLua 2, Mendes 2, Pamarot 2, Primus 2, Todorov 2, Campbell 1, Mvuemba 1, O'Neil 1, Opponents 3.
F.A. Cup goals (3): Kanu 2, Cole 1. **Carling Cup goals (2):** Fernandes 1, Taylor 1
Average home league attendance: 19,862. **Player of Year:** David James.

READING

From first to last, promoted Reading won acclaim all round, not just for meeting head-on the challenges of the Premiership but overcoming most of them them in some style. They retrieved a two-goal deficit to beat Middlesbrough on the opening day of the season and came from behind three times to earn a point at Blackburn on the final day. That result confirmed eighth place in the table, one away from a UEFA Cup spot that Steve Coppell publicly insisted would have come too soon for his side, yet privately felt they would certainly have merited. A 6-0 victory over West Ham was the season's biggest in the division, while a 3-1 success against Tottenham, delivered with another display of brisk, attacking football, was another to savour by Coppell, who was named Manager of the Year for the second successive year by the League Managers' Association.

Bikey, A .... 7(8)
Convey, B .... 8(1)
De la Cruz, U 9
Doyle, K .... 28(4)
Duberry, M 8
Federici, A .... –(2)
Gunnarsson, B ..... 10(13)
Hahnemann, M 38
Halford, G .... 2(1)
Harper, J .... 36(2)
Hunt, S .... 28(7)
Ingimarsson, I 38
Kitson, D .... 9(4)
Lita, L .... 22(11)
Little, G .... 18(6)
Long, S .... 9(12)
Murty, G 23
Oster, J .... 6(19)
Seol K-H .... 22(5)
Shorey, N 37
Sidwell, S 35
Sodje, S .... 2(1)
Sonko, I 23

League goals (52): Doyle 13, Lita 7, Hunt 4, Seol 4, Sidwell 4, Gunnarsson 3, Harper 3, Ingimarsson 2, Kitson 2, Long 2, De la Cruz 1, Oster 1, Shorey 1, Sonko 1, Opponents 4.
F.A. Cup goals (9): Lita 4, Kitson 2, Gunnarsson 1, Long 1, Sodje 1. **Carling Cup goals (6):** Lita 3, Bikey 1, Long 1, Mate, P 1,
Average home league attendance: 23,829. **Player of Year:** Ivar Ingimarsson.

SHEFFIELD UNITED

So near, yet so far. Sheffield United went straight back down to the Championship with an inferior goal difference of one after losing a make-or-break match at Bramall Lane on a tense final day of the season. Defeat by Wigan, who stayed up as a result, also brought an end to Neil Warnock's seven years in charge, the manager choosing to step down and being replaced by Bryan Robson. The bitter irony was that Wigan's winner was a penalty by David Unsworth, who had missed from the spot in a goalless draw with Blackburn when wearing United colours earlier in the season. Even harder for United to take was West Ham's great escape and the way it was engineered by Carlos Tevez, the player whose controversial signing the club felt should have led to West Ham being docked points. The loss of leading scorer Rob Hulse for the final two months was a blow, although Warnock and his team were forced to shoulder some blame, having at one stage been ten points clear of trouble.

Akinbiyi, A .... 2(1)
Armstrong, C .... 24(3)
Bennett, I 2
Bromby, L .... 12(5)
Davis, C .... 18(3)
Fathi, A .... 2(1)
Geary, D 26
Gerrard, P 2
Gillespie, K .... 27(4)
Hulse, R .... 28(1)
Ifill, P 3
Jagielka, P 38
Kabba, S .... –(7)
Kazim-Richards, C .... 15(12)
Kenny, P 34
Kilgallon, M 6
Kozluk, R .... 17(2)
Law, N .... 2(2)
Leigertwood, M ...... 16(3)
Lucketti, C 8
Montgomery, N .... 22(4)
Morgan, C .... 21(3)
Nade, C .... 7(18)
Quinn, A .... 11(8)
Quinn, S 15
Shelton, L .... 2(2)
Sommeil, D .... 4(1)
Stead, J .... 12(2)
Tonge, M .... 23(4)
Unsworth, D 5
Webber, D .... 13(9)
Wright, A 1

League goals (32): Hulse 8, Stead 5, Jagielka 4, Nade 3, Webber 3, Gillespie 2, Quinn, S 2, Tonge 2, Kazim-Richards 1, Morgan 1, Opponents 1.
F.A. Cup goals: None. **Carling Cup goals (3):** Akinbiyi 1, Montgomery 1, Nade 1.
Average home league attendance: 30,684. **Player of Year:** Phil Jagielka.

TOTTENHAM HOTSPUR

Tottenham finished fifth for the second successive season in a manner which suggested that if anyone can mount a sustained challenge to the big four it will be Martin Jol's team. They might have done so this time but for a dreadful start which delivered just two goals and four points from the opening six matches. After that, Dimitar Berbatov began to live up to his £10.9m. price tag, scoring 23 goals in all competitions and bringing a new skilful, stylish cutting edge to White Hart Lane. Seven of those came in the UEFA Cup, where Tottenham topped their group with maximum points and restricted the holders, Sevilla, to a 2-1 advantage in the first leg of the quarter-finals. But two goals conceded in the first eight minutes of the return, left them with too much to do. They also missed out on the chance of F.A. Cup success when surrendering a two-goal lead to Chelsea at Stamford Bridge and losing the replay.

Assou-Ekotto, B 16
Berbatov, D .... 30(3)
Chimbonda, P 33
Davenport, C .... 8(2)
Davids, E .... 6(3)
Dawson, M 37
Defoe, J .... 20(14)
Gardner, A .... 6(2)
Ghaly, H .... 17(4)
Huddlestone, T ...... 15(6)
Ifil, P 1
Jenas, J .... 24(1)
Keane, R .... 18(9)
King, L 21
Lee Young-Pyo .... 20(1)
Lennon, A .... 22(4)
Malbranque, S .... 18(7)
Mido, A .... 7(5)
Murphy, D .... 5(7)
Robinson, P 38
Rocha, R 9
Stalteri, P .... 1(5)
Taarabt, A .... –(2)
Tainio, T .... 20(1)
Ziegler, R .... –(1)
Zokora, D .... 26(5)

League goals (57): Berbatov 12, Keane 11, Defoe 10, Jenas 6, Lennon 3, Malbranque 2, Tainio 2, Chimbonda 1, Davenport 1, Dawson 1, Ghaly 1, Huddlestone 1, Mido 1, Murphy 1, Robinson 1, Stalteri 1, Opponents 2.
F.A. Cup goals (15): Keane 5, Berbatov 3, Defoe 1, Ghaly 1, Jenas 1, Lennon 1, Malbranque 1, Mido 1, Opponents 1. **Carling Cup goals (12):** Defoe 4, Mido 3,

Huddlestone 2, Berbatov 1, Keane 1, Opponents 1. **UEFA Cup goals (20):** Berbatov 7, Keane 5, Defoe 3, Malbranque 2, Ghaly 1, Jenas 1, Lennon 1.
Average home league attendance: 35,739. **Player of Year:** Dimitar Berbatov.

WATFORD

Adrian Boothroyd brought a refreshing openness and honesty to the Premiership and made no attempt to disguise the fact that his team simply weren't good enough to survive in the top flight. Not many opponents really turned them over, but nine drawn games at Vicarage Road underlined the extra bit of quality required. It might have been different had Marlon King been allowed to test himself at this level after scoring 21 goals in their promotion campaign. But King sustained a knee injury eight games into the season and by the time he returned, Watford were all but down. In his absence, they had no-one able to score with any frequency. Hameur Bouazza was their leading marksman with five and that told its own story. The consolation was a run to the semi-finals of the F.A. Cup, where a 4-1 defeat by Manchester United perhaps did not reflect the way they fought hard to upset the odds.

Ashikodi, M .... –(2)
Avinel, C 1
Bangura, A .... 12(4)
Bouazza, H .... 27(5)
Carlisle, C 4
Cavalli, Y .... 2(1)
Chamberlain, A .... –(1)
Chambers, J .... 8(4)
DeMerit, J .... 29(3)
Doyley, L .... 17(4)
Foster, B 29
Francis, D .... 28(4)
Henderson, D .... 24(10)
Hoskins, W .... 4(5)
Jarrett, A .... –(1)
Kabba, S .... 6(5)
King, M .... 12(1)
Lee, R .... 9(1)
Mackay, M .... 13(1)
Mahon, G .... 33(1)
Mariappa, A .... 17(2)
McNamee, A .... 4(3)
Powell, C .... 9(6)
Priskin, T .... 7(9)
Rinaldi, D .... 6(1)
Robinson, T .... –(1)
Shittu, D .... 27(3)
Smith, T 32
Spring, M .... 2(4)
Stewart, J .... 30(1)
Williams, G .... 2(1)
Williamson, L .... 4(1)
Young, A 20

League goals (29): Bouazza 5, Francis 4, King 4, Henderson 3, Young 3, DeMerit 2, Priskin 2, Mahon 1, Rinaldi 1, Shittu 1, Smith 1, Opponents 2.
F.A. Cup goals (8): Bouazza 2, Mackay 2, Ashikodi 1, Francis 1, McNamee 1, Smith 1.
Carling Cup goals (4): Francis 1, Priskin 1, Shittu 1, Young 1.
Average home league attendance: 18,750. **Player of Year:** Ben Foster.

WEST HAM UNITED

Alan Curbishley began what proved to be an eventful return to management with a 1-0 victory over Manchester United. Five months later he supervised an identical success over the champions at Old Trafford that completed West Ham's remarkable – and highly controversial – escape from relegation. A goal by Argentine World Cup star Carlos Tevez on that final day of the season delivered a seventh victory in nine matches for a team seemingly dead and buried when ten points away from safety in mid-March. It was accompanied by anger from rival clubs over the Premier League's decision not to have taken points off West Ham for breaching regulations when signing Tevez, who did more than anyone to keep his side up. Amid all the threats of legal action, Curbishley won widespread acclaim for transforming the club's fortunes after taking over from Alan Pardew, dismissed by the new Icelandic owners in the wake of a 4-0 defeat at Bolton.

Benayoun, Y .... 25(4)
Blanco, K .... 1(7)
Boa Morte, L .... 8(6)
Bowyer, L .... 18(2)
Carroll, R 12
Cole, C .... 5(12)
Collins, J 16
Dailly, C .... 10(4)
Davenport, C .... 5(1)
Etherington, M .... 24(3)
Ferdinand, A 31
Gabbidon, D 18
Green, R 26
Harewood, M .... 19(13)
Konchesky, P 22
Mascherano, J .... 3(2)
McCartney, G .... 16(6)
Mears, T .... 3(2)
Mullins, H .... 21(9)
Neill, L 11
Newton, S .... –(3)
Noble, M 10
Pantsil, J .... 3(2)
Quashie,N 7
Reo-Coker, N 35
Sheringham, T .... 4(13)
Spector, J .... 17(8)
Tevez, C .... 19(7)
Upson, M 2
Zamora, B .... 27(5)

League goals (35): Zamora 11, Tevez 7, Benayoun 3, Harewood 3, Cole 2, Mullins 2, Noble 2, Sheringham 2, Blanco 1, Boa Morte 1, Reo-Coker 1.
F.A. Cup goals (3): Cole 1, Mullins 1, Noble 1. **Carling Cup goals (1):** Harewood 1. **UEFA Cup goals:** None.
Average home league attendance: 34,722. **Player of Year:** Carlos Tevez.

WIGAN ATHLETIC

Paul Jewell and his team held their nerve on an afternoon of high drama and were rewarded with a 2-1 win at Bramall Lane that kept them up and sent Sheffield United down. David Unsworth's penalty – he had missed a crucial one when playing for United earlier in the season – proved decisive. Despite the dismissal of Lee McCulloch, Wigan held on to the lead at the end of a rollercoaster season which still had a sting in the tail – a drained Jewell stepping down the following day to be replaced immediately by his No 2, Chris Hutchings. Successive single goal wins over Newcastle and Manchester City had given Wigan an eight-point cushion. But a failure to win any of the next eight fixtures, even against Tottenham after leading three times, dragged them into trouble. That game highlighted Wigan's Achilles heel – the inability to hold on to potential match-winning positions.

Aghahowa, J .... 3(3)
Baines, L 35
Boyce, E 34
Camara, H .... 18(5)
Chimbonda, P .... –(1)
Connolly, D .... –(2)
Cotterill, D .... 5(11)
De Zeeuw, A 21
Filan, J 10
Folan, C .... 8(5)
Haestad, K .... 1(1)
Hall, F .... 22(2)
Heskey, E .... 33(1)
Jackson, M .... 17(3)
Johansson, A .... 4(8)
Kavanagh, G .... –(2)
Kilbane, K .... 26(5)
Kirkland, C 26
Landzaat, D .... 29(4)
McCulloch, L .... 25(4)
Pollitt, M .... 2(1)
Scharner, P .... 22(3)
Skoko, J .... 24(4)
Taylor, R .... 12(4)
Teale, G .... 7(5)
Todorov, S .... 2(3)
Unsworth, D .... 6(4)
Valencia, L .... 17(5)
Webster, A .... 3(1)
Wright, D .... 6(6)

League goals (37): Heskey 8, Camara 6, McCulloch 4, Baines 3, Scharner 3, Folan 2, Landzaat 2, Cotterill 1, Jackson 1, Kilbane 1, Taylor 1, Unsworth 1, Valencia 1, Opponents 3.
F.A. Cup goals (1): McCulloch 1. **Carling Cup goals:** None.
Average home league attendance: 18,158. **Player of Year:** Arjan De Zeeuw.

COCA-COLA CHAMPIONSHIP

BARNSLEY

Just when an immediate return to League One looked to be on the cards, Barnsley demonstrated how quickly football's fortunes can change. Two days after a 5-1 defeat at Ipswich sent them into the bottom three with a month of the season remaining, Danny Nardiello scored the only goal against promotion-chasing Birmingham at Oakwell. The former Manchester United striker then netted four times in wins over fellow strugglers Southend and Crystal Palace to lift his side to safety. It was a successful introduction to management for Simon Davey, promoted from head of the club's Academy after Andy Ritchie was sacked in late November and confirmed as manager after a spell as caretaker. While a 7-0 thrashing by West Bromwich Albion in their final match proved embarrassing, it did not detract from the satisfaction Davey derived from keeping them up.

Atkinson, R 6
Austin, N .... 21(3)
Colgan, N .... 43(1)
Coulson, M .... –(2)
Devaney, M .... 37(4)
Eckersley, A 6
Ferenczi, I .... 14(2)
Hassell, B .... 37(2)
Hayes, P .... 25(5)
Healy, C .... –(8)
Heckingbottom, P ... 28(3)
Heslop, S .... –(1)
Howard, B 42
Jones, R .... 1(3)
Kay, A .... 31(1)
Knight, L .... 6(3)
Lucas, D .... 2(1)
Mannone, V .... 1(1)
Mattis, D 3
McCann, G .... 17(5)
McIndoe, M 18

Nardiello, D .... 19(11)	Reid, P .... 36(1)	Wallwork, R 2
Nyatanga, L 10	Richards, M .... 22(9)	Williams, R .... 8(7)
Potter, L 1	Togwell, S 44	Wright, T .... 4(13)
Rajczi, P 8 (7)	Tonge, D .... 2(4)	Wroe, N .... –(3)
Reid, K .... 12(14)		

League goals (53): Nardiello 9, Howard 8, Ferenczi 6, Richards 6, Devaney 5, Hayes 5, McIndoe 4, Hassell 2, Reid, K 2, Kay 1, McCann 1, Nyatanga 1, Rajczi 1, Togwell 1, Wright 1.
F.A. Cup goals (1): Coulson 1. **Carling Cup goals (3):** Devaney 1, McIndoe 1, Williams 1.
Average home league attendance: 12,733. **Player of Year:** Brian Howard.

BIRMINGHAM CITY

The knives were out for Steve Bruce on more than one occasion when indifferent form suggested his side were not ready for an immediate return to the Premiership. Bruce – and more significantly his directors – kept faith and were rewarded with the runners-up place behind Sunderland. Typically, Birmingham made hard work of it, defeats by Burnley and Barnsley over Easter suggesting they would have to be satisfied with a place in the play-offs. The manager then played a crucial card by bringing in Andy Cole on loan from Portsmouth. Four straight wins reflected the impact the 35-year-old striker had on the team and a 2-0 win over Sheffield Wednesday, achieved despite the dismissal of Fabrice Muamba, clinched promotion in front of a full house at St Andrews. A fifth on the final day of the season at Preston would have brought the title, but a single-goal defeat meant they finished two points behind.

Bendtner, N .... 38(4)	Jaidi, R 38	Nafti, M .... 18(14)
Campbell, D .... 15(17)	Jerome, C .... 20(18)	Painter, M 1
Clemence, S .... 31(3)	Johnson, D .... 24(2)	Sadler, M 36
Cole, A 5	Kelly, S .... 35(1)	Taylor, Maik 27
Danns, N .... 11(18)	Kilkenny, N .... –(8)	Taylor, Martin .... 29(2)
Doyle, C 19	Larsson, S .... 27(16)	Tebily, O .... 5(1)
Dunn, D .... 9(2)	McSheffrey, G 40	Upson, M .... 8(1)
Forssell, M .... 3(5)	Muamba, F .... 30(4)	Vine, R .... 10(7)
Gray, J .... 2(5)	N'Gotty, B 25	

League goals (67): McSheffrey 13, Bendtner 11, Campbell 9, Jerome 7, Jaidi 6, Clemence 4, Larsson 4, Danns 3, Upson 2, Cole 1, Dunn 1, Forssell 1, Johnson 1, N'Gotty 1, Vine 1, Opponents 2.
F.A. Cup goals (9): Larsson 3, Campbell 2, McSheffrey 1, N'Gotty 1, Taylor, Martin 1, Opponents 1. **Carling Cup goals (9):** Bendtner 2, Jerome 2, Larsson 2, McSheffrey 2, Campbell 1.
Average home league attendance: 22,273. **Player of Year:** Stephen Clemence.

BURNLEY

A bright start and a flourishing finish offset a mid-season slump which could have proved costly. Steve Cotterill joked about 'freezing teletext' after his side briefly topped the table and for much of the first half of the season they more than held their own. But as winter set in, Burnley began to seize up and it was four long months before the thaw set in. Eighteen matches without a victory – plus an F.A. Cup defeat by Reading – left them only three points away from the bottom three. The big chill ended with a 4-0 win over Plymouth, followed by a single goal success against Birmingham. Another promotion-chasing team, West Bromwich Albion, were also seen off and by the time Burnley made it five victories out of six, they were well clear of trouble.

Akinbiyi, A .... 15(5)	Djemba-Djemba, E . 13(2)	Gudjonsson, J .... 9(2)
Branch, G .... –(5)	Duff, M .... 42(2)	Harley, J .... 44(1)
Caldwell, S .... 16(1)	Elliott, W .... 40(2)	Hyde, M .... 19(4)
Coughlan, G .... 1(1)	Foster, S .... 7(10)	Jensen, B .... 30(1)
Coyne, D 12	Gray, A .... 34(1)	Jones, S .... 37(4)

Lafferty, K .... 15(20)	McVeigh, P .... 6(2)	Pollitt, M 4
Mahon, A .... 10(15)	Noel-Williams, G .... 19(4)	Sinclair, F .... 16(3)
McCann, C .... 24(14)	O'Connor, G .... –(8)	Spicer, J .... –(11)
McGreal, J .... 21(1)	O'Connor, J .... 39(4)	Thomas, W 33

League goals (52): Gray 14, Jones 5, McCann 5, Noel-Williams 5, Elliott 4, Lafferty 4, O'Connor, J 3, McVeigh 3, Akinbiyi 2, Duff 2, Mahon 2, Harley 1, Spicer 1, Opponents 1.
F.A. Cup goals (2): Akinbiyi 1, O'Connor, G 1. **Carling Cup goals:** None.
Average home league attendance: 11,956. **Player of Year:** Wade Elliott.

CARDIFF CITY

When Michael Chopra was scoring goals, Cardiff looked the part; when they dried up, his team were not the same force. That was the story of a side who, approaching the half-way point of the campaign, bore the hallmark of genuine promotion contenders. They were top of the table and Chopra was the Championship's most prolific marksman. When the former Newcastle striker hit his first barren patch, Cardiff started to slide. When he found his touch again in the New Year – nine goals in six games including a hat-trick against Leicester – promotion prospects were resurrected. If there was a moment then which defined the season it came as Chopra went off with a hamstring injury at Derby. His team, right in contention until then, lost 3-1, did not win any of their last eight fixtures and finished 11 points adrift of the top six.

Alexander, N 39	Forde, D 7	McPhail, S 43
Blake, D .... 3(7)	Gilbert, K .... 21(3)	Parry, P .... 41(1)
Byrne, J .... 2(8)	Glombard, L .... 1(5)	Purse, D 31
Campbell, K .... 4(15)	Green, M .... –(6)	Ramsey, A .... –(1)
Chambers, J 7	Gunter, C .... 9(6)	Redan, I .... –(2)
Chopra, M 42	Johnson, R .... 26(6)	Scimeca, R 35
Cooper, K .... –(4)	Kamara, M .... 3(12)	Thompson, S .... 39(4)
Feeney, W .... 4(2)	Ledley, J 46	Walton, S .... 5(1)
Ferretti, A .... –(1)	Loovens, G 30	Whittingham, P ...... 18(1)
Flood, W .... 5(20)	McNaughton, K ...... 39(3)	Wright, A .... 6(1)

League goals (57): Chopra 22, Parry 6, Thompson 6, Scimeca 5, Purse 4, Whittingham 4, Ledley 3, Johnson 2, Byrne 1, Flood 1, Kamara 1, Loovens 1, Opponents 1.
F.A. Cup goals: None. **Carling Cup goals:** None.
Average home league attendance: 15,223. **Player of Year:** Roger Johnson.

COLCHESTER UNITED

Colchester had upset the odds by winning promotion to the game's second tier for the first time and did so again by not only surviving but flourishing. They accomplished it with a new manager, Geraint Williams taking over after Phil Parkinson left for what proved to be an ill-fated spell at Hull, and after a dreadful start which left them second from bottom after four straight defeats. Jamie Cureton's hat-trick turned the tide, bringing a 4-3 win over Derby, and after that there was no looking back. Cureton claimed a second hat-trick, against Southend, on his way to 23 league goals for the season. Chris Iwelumo weighed in with 18 and such was the all-round confidence and conviction of their team, particularly at home, that they were a single point away from a play-off place with two matches remaining after overcoming champions-to-be Sunderland 3-1. Defeat in both meant a tenth place finish, still a commendable achievement.

Baldwin, P .... 35(3)	Ephraim, H .... 5(16)	Jackson, J .... 24(8)
Barker, C 38	Garcia, R .... 33(3)	Jones, R .... –(6)
Brown, W 46	Gerken, D 27	McLeod, K .... 13(11)
Cureton, J 44	Guy, J .... 1(31)	Mills, M .... 8(1)
Davison, A 19	Halford, G 28	Richards, G .... 3(2)
Duguid, K .... 42(1)	Iwelumo, C .... 41(5)	Watson, K .... 38(2)
Elokobi, G .... 8(2)	Izzet, K 45	White, J .... 8(8)

League goals (70): Cureton 23, Iwelumo 18, Garcia 7, Duguid 5, Guy 3, Halford 3, McLeod 3, Jackson 2, Baldwin 1, Brown 1, Ephraim 1, Izzet 1, Richards 1, Watson 1.
F.A. Cup goals (1): Cureton 1. **Carling Cup goals:** None.
Average home league attendance: 5,466. **Player of Year:** Jamie Cureton.

COVENTRY CITY

Ten summer signings by Micky Adams raised hopes that Coventry would improve on their eighth place from the previous season and mount a serious challenge for, at least, a play-off place. It was not to be. Inconsistency dogged his every move, with the team unable to put together any meaningful form. Adams was sacked after an F.A. Cup third round home defeat by Bristol City and replaced by Iain Dowie, whose appointment had an immediate impact with his first six games in charge yielding 14 points. Then Coventry slipped back into their bad old ways, failed to win another match until the final one against Burnley and slipped to 17th. Dowie faced a busy summer looking for new blood and a fresh approach.

Adebola, D .... 28(12)
Andrews, W .... –(3)
Birchall, C .... 17(11)
Bischoff, M .... 2(1)
Cameron, C .... 16(8)
Clarke, C 12
Currie, D .... 6(2)
Davis, L .... 1(2)
Doyle, M 40
Duffy, R 13
El Idrissi, F .... –(1)
Fadiga, K .... 1(5)
Giddings, S .... –(1)
Hall, M .... 38(2)
Hawkins, C 13
Heath, M 7
Hildreth, L .... –(1)
Hughes, S .... 36(1)
Hutchison, D .... 3(11)
John, S .... 19(4)
Kyle, K .... 18(13)
Marshall, A 41
McKenzie, L .... 23(8)
McNamee, D 16
McSheffrey, G 3
Mifsud, M .... 12(7)
Osbourne, I .... 16(3)
Page, R .... 28(1)
Steele, L 5
Tabb, J .... 22(9)
Thornton, K .... 5(6)
Turner, B 1
Virgo, A .... 10(5)
Ward, E 39
Whing, A .... 15(1)

League goals (47): Adebola 8, McKenzie 7, John 5, Mifsud 4, Doyle 3, Kyle 3, Tabb 3, Ward 3, Birchall 2, Cameron 2, Andrews 1, Hughes 1, McSheffrey 1, Thornton 1, Virgo 1, Opponents 2.
F.A. Cup goals (3): Cameron 1, John 1, McKenzie 1. **Carling Cup goals (1):** Adebola 1.
Average home league attendance: 20,342. **Player of Year:** Andy Marshall.

CRYSTAL PALACE

Peter Taylor insisted that had Palace displayed a 'meaner' side to their game they could have mounted a significant challenge for promotion. It was small comfort to supporters for a disappointing campaign spent largely in mid-table after victories in the opening three matches had Selhurst Park full of anticipation. Shefki Kuqi, a £2.5m. buy from Blackburn, failed to maintain that momentum, his partnership with Clinton Morrison generally not living up to expectations. Palace fared better around the turn of the year and Taylor held out hope of a late charge similar to the one that took them up three seasons earlier. His team did finish on a high note with wins over Derby and Colchester, but by then it was too late to make a difference, too many home defeats having proved a major stumbling block.

Borrowdale, G .... 24(1)
Butterfield, D .... 25(3)
Cort, L 37
Fletcher, C .... 33(4)
Flinders, S .... 7(1)
Freedman, D .... 11(23)
Grabban, L .... –(8)
Granville, D 15
Green, S .... 5(9)
Hudson, M .... 38(1)
Hughes, M .... 12(4)
Ifill, P .... 6(7)
Kennedy, M .... 34(4)
Kiraly, G 29
Kuqi, S .... 24(11)
Lawrence, M .... 31(3)
Macken, J 1
Martin, D .... –(5)
McAnuff, J .... 31(3)
Morrison, C .... 31(10)
Reich, M .... 4(2)
Scowcroft, J .... 26(9)
Soares, T .... 32(5)
Spence, L .... 1(1)
Speroni, J 5
Turner, I 5
Ward, D 20
Watson, B .... 19(6)

League goals (59): Morrison 12, Cort 8, Kuqi 7, McAnuff 5, Scowcroft 5, Hudson 4, Fletcher 3, Freedman 3, Soares 3, Watson 3, Green 2, Ifill 2, Grabban 1, Kennedy 1. **F.A. Cup goals (2):** Kuqi 1, McAnuff 1. **Carling Cup goals (1):** Hughes 1.
Average home league attendance: 17,541. **Player of Year:** Leon Cort.

DERBY COUNTY

Derby started the season with modest expectations. They finished it in a blaze of glory with Stephen Pearson's first goal for the club bringing victory over West Bromwich Albion at Wembley and a return to the Premiership after an absence of five seasons. Billy Davies worked wonders in his first season in charge at Pride Park after twice missing out in the play-offs with Preston. The manager kept faith with Steve Howard when many maintained that the former Luton striker was not up to the task and was rewarded with 16 league goals, plus two in the semi-final win over Southampton. Davies spent shrewdly in the January transfer window – including £650,000 on Pearson from Celtic – after telling the board that without investment in new players his side would not maintain the momentum. And he made a key substitution in the final, bringing on gifted 18-year-old Giles Barnes, who promptly laid on the winner for Pearson.

Barnes, G .... 31(8)	Howard, S 43	Mears, T .... 8(5)
Bisgaard, M .... 17(15)	Idiakez, I .... 4(1)	Moore, D .... 28(7)
Boertien, P .... 10(1)	Jackson, R .... 3(2)	Nyatanga, L .... 5(2)
Bolder, A .... 9(4)	Johnson, M .... 22(7)	Oakley, M .... 36(1)
Bywater, S 37	Johnson, S .... 21(6)	Pearson, S .... 6(3)
Camara, M 19	Jones, D .... 27(1)	Peschisolido, P ...... 3(11)
Camp, L 3	Leacock, D .... 36(2)	Smith, R .... 5(10)
Currie, D .... 4(3)	Lupoli, A .... 18(17)	Smith, T .... 4(1)
Edworthy, M 38	Macken, J .... 4(4)	Stead, J .... 15(2)
Fagan, C .... 12(5)	Malcolm, R .... 6(3)	Teale, G .... 11(5)
Grant, L .... 6(1)	McEveley, J 15	

Play-offs –appearances: Bywater 3, Fagan 3, Howard 3, Johnson, S 3, Leacock 3, McEveley 3, Mears 3, Moore 3, Oakley 3, Pearson 3, Macken 2, Peschisolido 1, Barnes –(2), Jones –(2), Currie –(1), Edworthy –(1), Nyatanga –(1), Teale –(1),
League goals (62): Howard 16, Barnes 8, Lupoli 7, Jones 6, Oakley 6, Peschisolido 3, Stead 3, Bisgaard 2, Moore 2, Currie 1, Fagan 1, Johnson, M 1, Johnson, S 1, Mears 1, Nyatanga 1, Smith, T 1, Teale 1, Opponents 1. **Play-offs – goals (5):** Howard 2, Moore 1, Pearson 1, Opponents 1.
F.A. Cup goals (4): Lupoli 3, Peschisolido 1. **Carling Cup goals (4):** Howard 1, Johnson, M 1, Moore 1, Lupoli 1.
Average home league attendance: 25,944. **Player of Year:** Steve Howard.

HULL CITY

Dean Windass returned to his home-town club on loan from Bradford City to play a leading role in seeing off the threat of relegation. Approaching his 38th birthday, Windass scored seven goals in seven games, including a hat-trick against fellow-strugglers Southend to steer Hull towards safety. An eighth at Cardiff finally provided some much-needed breathing space. They had been up against it from the start, registering a single point from the opening six matches. Phil Parkinson, who had led Colchester to an improbable promotion to the Championship the previous season, paid the price in early December, not long after a 5-1 defeat by his former club. Former Derby manager Phil Brown replaced him, initially as caretaker, then to the end of the season, and finally on a permanent basis as the reward for supervising this escape route.

Andrews, K .... –(3)	Coles, D .... 16(5)	Duffy, D .... 4(5)
Ashbee, I 35	Collins, S 6	Duke, M .... –(1)
Barmby, N .... 7(13)	Dawson, A 38	Elliott, S .... 20(12)
Bridges, M .... 8(7)	Delaney, D .... 36(1)	Fagan, C 27
Burgess, B .... –(3)	Doyle, N 1	Featherstone, N .... –(2)

Forster, N .... 26(9)	Mills, D 9	Thelwell, A 2
France, R .... 13(11)	Myhill, B 46	Turner, M .... 42(1)
Jarrett, J 3	Parkin, J .... 22(7)	Vaz Te, R .... 1(5)
Livermore, D .... 24(1)	Parlour, R .... 14(1)	Welsh, J .... 9(9)
Marney, D .... 26(11)	Peltier, L .... 5(2)	Windass, D .... 15(3)
McPhee, S .... 9(3)	Ricketts, S 40	Yeates, M .... 2(3)

League goals (51): Windass 8, Fagan 6, Parkin 6, Elliott 5, Forster 5, Barmby 4, Livermore 4, Turner 3, Bridges 2, Dawson 2, Marney 2, Ashbee 1, Delaney 1, Ricketts 1, Welsh 1.
F.A. Cup goals (4): Dawson 2, Forster 1, Parkin 1. **Carling Cup goals (3):** Barmby 1, Burgess 1, Duffy 1.
Average home league attendance: 18,583. **Player of Year:** Andy Dawson.

IPSWICH TOWN

Jim Magilton rode a rollercoaster in his first taste of management. It could hardly have started any worse – one point from the opening four games. Just as quickly, his side turned things round with 13 points accumulated in the next five – and that was how it went for much of the season. This inconsistency meant Ipswich never seriously threatened a play-off place, or came close to slipping into trouble. Alan Lee's 16 league goals included a hat-trick in the 5-0 win over Luton. His team also scored five against Hull and Barnsley, while conceding five to West Bromwich Albion. They reached the fifth round of the F.A. Cup and were unlucky not to go further, outplaying Watford despite the dismissal of George O'Callaghan but losing to an 88th minute goal.

Bates, M 2	Lee, A .... 38(3)	Price, L 34
Bowditch, D .... 3(6)	Legwinski, S .... 31(1)	Richards, M .... 20(8)
Bruce, A .... 40(1)	Macken, J .... 13(1)	Roberts, G .... 30(3)
Clarke, B .... 10(17)	Miller, I .... –(1)	Sito, L .... 6(2)
Currie, D .... 6(7)	Moore, S .... –(1)	Supple, S .... 11(1)
De Vos, J 39	Naylor, R .... 21(4)	Walters, J .... 11(5)
Forster, N 4	Noble, M .... 12(1)	Walton, S .... 13(6)
Garvan, O .... 24(3)	O'Callaghan, G .... 3(8)	Williams, G .... 25(4)
Harding, D .... 40(2)	Parkin, S .... –(2)	Wilnis, F .... 19(2)
Haynes, D .... 4(27)	Peters, J .... 20(3)	Wright, D 19
Jeffers, F .... 7(2)	Pollitt, M 1	

League goals (64): Lee 16, Haynes 7, Legwinski 5, Jeffers 4, Walters 4, Clarke 3, Macken 3, Roberts 3, Walton 3, De Vos 2, Peters 2, Richards 2, Williams 2, Bowditch 1, Currie 1, Forster 1, Garvan 1, Noble 1, O'Callaghan 1, Wright 1, Opponents 1.
F.A. Cup goals (2): Lee 1, Richards 1. **Carling Cup goals (2):** Clarke 1, De Vos 1.
Average home league attendance: 22,444. **Player of Year:** Sylvain Legwinski.

LEEDS UNITED

A club that six years earlier had finished fourth in the Premiership and contested a Champions League semi-final against Valencia slipped into the game's third tier amid dark days at Elland Road. Their final match at Elland Road against Ipswich came close to being abandoned when hundreds of fans invaded the pitch. Then, before relegation was confirmed, owner Ken Bates put Leeds into administration, ensuring that a mandatory ten-point deduction applied this season and not next. It was not the scenario Dennis Wise expected when he left Swindon to take over as manager in October following the dismissal of Kevin Blackwell. Wise brought in former Chelsea team-mate Gus Poyet as his assistant and chopped and changed the team in search of a winning formula. It looked as if they had finally found it when Leeds won three out of four matches to move to within a point of safety with three weeks of the campaign remaining. But a late goal conceded at Southampton and that 1-1 draw with Ipswich cast them adrift.

Ankergren, C 14	Armando Sa, M .... 6(5)	Bakke, E .... 2(1)

Bayly, R 1
Beckford, J .... 1(4)
Blake, R .... 27(9)
Butler, P 16
Carole, S .... 7(10)
Crainey, S .... 18(1)
Cresswell, R .... 18(4)
Delph, F .... –(1)
Derry, S 23
Douglas, J .... 34(1)
Ehiogu, U 6
Einarsson, G .... –(3)
Elliott, R .... 5(2)
Elliott, T .... –(3)
Flo, T A 1
Foxe, H .... 12(6)
Gray, M 6
Gregan, S 1
Healy, D .... 31(10)
Heath, M 26
Horsfield, G .... 11(3)
Howson, J .... 6(3)
Johnson, A .... 4(1)
Johnson, J .... 3(2)
Kandol, T .... 11(7)
Kelly, G 16
Kilgallon, M .... 18(1)
Kishishev, R 10
Lewis, E .... 40(1)
Michalik, L 7
Moore, I .... 14(19)
Nicholls, K .... 12(1)
Richardson, F .... 19(3)
Rui Marques, M ..... 14(3)
Stack, G 12
Stone, S .... 5(5)
Sullivan, N 7
Thompson, A .... 9(2)
Warner, T 13
Westlake, I .... 19(8)
Wright, A 1

League goals (46): Healy 10, Blake 8, Cresswell 4, Heath 3, Lewis 3, Horsfield 2, Moore 2, Thompson 2, Butler 1, Derry 1, Douglas 1, Ehiogu 1, Flo 1, Foxe 1, Howson 1, Kandol 1, Michalik 1, Stone 1, Opponents 2.
F.A. Cup goals (1): Opponents 1. **Carling Cup goals (5):** Moore 3, Bakke 1, Blake 1.
Average home league attendance: 21,613. **Player of Year:** Eddie Lewis.

LEICESTER CITY

When former Portsmouth owner Milan Mandaric took over the club in mid-February, Leicester looked to be comfortably cushioned against any threat of relegation. Instead, form dipped, the slide assumed serious proportions and manager Rob Kelly paid the price. Mandaric turned to Nigel Worthington, whose first match as caretaker was against his former side Norwich. Defeat in that one and in the next against Birmingham meant Leicester had taken just four points from ten fixtures. Then they found salvation in successive 1-0 victories against Preston and Barnsley, which rescued what had become a critical situation and enabled a 4-1 home defeat by Wolves on the last day of the season to be absorbed without further worry. Worthington departed without being entrusted with the job on a permanent basis and in came the MK Dons manager Martin Allen, charged with building a brighter future.

Cadamarteri, D .... –(9)
Fryatt, M .... 21(11)
Glombard, L .... –(1)
Hammond, E .... 17(14)
Henderson, P 28
Horsfield, G .... 9(4)
Hughes, S .... 34(7)
Hume, I .... 39(6)
Jarrett, J 13
Johansson, N-E 36
Johnson, A .... 21(1)
Kenton, D .... 20(3)
Kisnorbo, P 40
Logan, C 18
Low, J .... 12(4)
Mattock, J .... 3(1)
Maybury, A .... 25(2)
McAuley, G .... 27(3)
McCarthy, P .... 20(2)
Newton, S 9
O'Grady, C .... 6(4)
Porter, L .... 26(8)
Stearman, R .... 23(12)
Sylla, M .... 3(3)
Tiatto, D .... 24(1)
Welsh, A .... 4(3)
Wesolowski, J .... 11(8)
Williams, G .... 12(2)
Yeates, M .... 5(4)

League goals (49): Hume 13, Hammond 5, Kisnorbo 5, Fryatt 3, Hughes 3, McAuley 3, Porter 3, Horsfield 2, Kenton 2, Johansson 1, Johnson 1, McCarthy 1, Newton 1, Stearman 1, Tiatto 1, Williams 1, Yeates 1, Opponents 2.
F.A. Cup goals (5): Cadamarteri 1, Fryatt 1, Kisnorbo 1, McAuley 1, Wesolowski 1.
Carling Cup goals (7): Stearman 2, Hammond 1, Hume 1, Kisnorbo 1, McCarthy 1, O'Grady 1.
Average home league attendance: 23,205. **Player of Year:** Iain Hume.

LUTON TOWN

Relegation seemed a distant prospect when Mike Newell's side climbed to fifth after a bright start to the season, highlighted by a 5-1 victory over Leeds. But it all went wrong, on and off the field. That success was followed by a 5-0 setback at Ipswich – and six more defeats in succession. The sale of more key players – leading scorer Rowan Vine and midfielder Carlos Edwards – in the January transfer window did nothing to improve Newell's frosty relationship with his chairman Bill Tomlins. It eventually led to his dismissal after further criticism of the board, leaving new manager Kevin Blackwell with little chance of saving his home-town club from going down. Luton paid the price for a repeated failure to hold on to the lead. They won only twice in 2007 and the drop was confirmed by a 1-0 defeat at Derby, one of many matches they lost by a single goal margin.

Andrew, C .... 5(2)
Barnett, L 39
Bell, D .... 28(6)
Beresford, M 26
Boyd, A .... 5(14)
Brill, D .... 9(2)
Brkovic, A .... 14(6)
Carlisle, C .... 4(1)
Coyne, C .... 11(7)
Davis, S .... 20(4)
Edwards, C 26
Emanuel, L .... 39(1)
Feeney, W .... 15(14)
Foley, K .... 38(1)
Heikkinen, M 37
Holmes, P .... 3(2)
Idrizaj, B .... 3(4)
Keane, K .... 17(2)
Kiely, D 11
Langley, R .... 18(11)
Morgan, D .... 21(15)
O'Leary, S .... 5(2)
Parkin, S .... 7(1)
Perrett, R .... 8(2)
Robinson, S .... 37(1)
Runstrom, B .... 7(1)
Spring, M 14
Talbot, D .... 13(2)
Vine, R 26

League goals (53): Vine 12, Edwards 6, Morgan 4, Barnett 3, Bell 3, Brkovic 3, Talbot 3, Emanuel 2, Feeney 2, Runstrom 2, Andrew 1, Boyd 1, Coyne 1, Heikkinen 1, Idrizaj 1, Keane 1, Langley 1, O'Leary 1, Parkin 1, Perrett 1, Spring 1, Opponents 2.
F.A. Cup goals (3): Feeney 1, Vine 1, Opponents 1. **Carling Cup goals (4):** Boyd 1, Feeney 1, Morgan 1, Vine 1.
Average home league attendance: 8,580. **Player of Year:** Leon Barnett.

NORWICH CITY

A change of manager two months into the season did little to improve Norwich's prospects of a return to the Premiership. Amid growing unrest among supporters, Nigel Worthington's six years in charge at Carrow Road came to an end after a run of one point from five games. Peter Grant, assistant to Alan Pardew at West Ham, came in to find Robert Earnshaw in prolific form, the Wales striker scoring 17 goals before a groin operation ruled him out for more than three months. Norwich, however, leaked too many to have a realistic chance of challenging for a play-off place, conceding three or more goals on 12 occasions. By the time Earnshaw returned to fitness, they were playing out a disappointing campaign. The Wales striker still managed to increase his league tally to 19, beaten only by Jamie Cureton (Colchester), Michael Chopra (Cardiff) and Diomansy Kamara (West Bromwich Albion), all of whom played many more matches.

Ashdown, J 2
Boyle, P 3
Brown, C .... 3(1)
Camp, L 3
Chadwick, L .... 1(3)
Colin, J .... 30(3)
Croft, L .... 33(3)
Doherty, G 34
Drury, A 39
Dublin, D .... 22(11)
Eagle, R .... 3(7)
Earnshaw, R .... 28(2)
Etuhu, D .... 42(1)
Fleming, C .... 4(6)
Fotheringham, M ...... 9(5)
Gallacher, P .... 26(1)
Henderson, I .... –(2)
Huckerby, D 40
Hughes, A .... 28(8)
Jarvis, R .... 1(4)
Lappin, S 14
Marshall, D 2
Martin, C .... 13(5)
McKenzie, L .... –(4)
McVeigh, P .... 6(15)
Renton, K .... 1(2)
Robinson, C .... 26(1)
Safri, Y .... 30(5)
Shackell, J .... 42(1)
Smart, B .... –(1)
Spillane, M .... 4(1)
Thorne, P .... 4(11)
Warner, T 13

League goals (56): Earnshaw 19, Huckerby 8, Etuhu 6, Dublin 5, Martin 4, Croft 3, Shackell 3, Robinson 2, Chadwick 1, Lappin 1, Safri 1, Opponents 3.
F.A. Cup goals (8): Huckerby 5, Dublin 2, Martin 1. **Carling Cup goals (6):** Jarvis, Ryan 2, Etuhu 1, Fleming 1, McKenzie 1, Thorne 1.
Average home league attendance: 24,544. **Player of Year:** Darren Huckerby.

PLYMOUTH ARGYLE

Ian Holloway returned to management after an acrimonious departure from Queens Park Rangers to take Plymouth into the top half of the table and into the quarter-finals of the F.A. Cup. Their progress to the last eight may not have been particularly spectacular – wins over Peterborough, Barnet and Derby – but they were certainly up for it against Watford and were somewhat unfortunate to go down by the only goal after enjoying more of the play. As with many teams, they suffered a reaction after that defeat, (winning only four of the next five games) and losing touch with a play-off place Holloway felt could have been achieved. At least the season finished on a high note, with the following five producing maximum points, lifting Plymouth to 11th.

Aljofree, H .... 22(3)
Barness, A 1
Buzsaky, A .... 27(9)
Capaldi, T .... 30(1)
Chadwick, N .... 9(7)
Connolly, P 38
Dickson, R .... –(2)
Djordjic, B .... 8(9)
Doumbe, M 29
Ebanks-Blake, S ... 30(11)
Fallon, R .... 5(10)
Gallen, K .... 6(7)
Gosling, D .... 8(4)
Halmosi, P .... 14(2)
Hayles, B .... 37(2)
Hodges, L .... 11(4)
Larrieu, R 6
McCormick, L 40
Nalis, L .... 39(3)
Norris, D 41
Reid, R .... 1(5)
Samba, C .... 1(12)
Sawyer, G .... 19(3)
Seip, M .... 36(1)
Sinclair, S .... 8(7)
Summerfield, L .... 11(12)
Timar, K .... 8(1)
Wotton, P .... 21(1)

League goals (63): Hayles 13, Ebanks-Blake 10, Norris 6, Halmosi 4, Nalis 4, Wotton 4, Buzsaky 3, Djordjic 3, Chadwick 2, Gosling 2, Seip 2, Sinclair 2, Fallon 1, Gallen 1, Samba 1, Summerfield 1, Timar 1, Opponents 3.
F.A. Cup goals (7): Aljofree 2, Sinclair 2, Gallen 1, Hayles 1, Norris 1. **Carling Cup goals:** None.
Average home league attendance: 13,009. **Player of Year:** Lilian Nalis.

PRESTON NORTH END

For the third successive year Preston's bid for a Premiership place came to grief. Twice under Billy Davies they lost in the play-offs. This time, with Paul Simpson in charge, they looked a decent bet for an automatic promotion place for much of the season. But after winning his first England cap, leading scorer David Nugent suffered a loss of form, which seemed to spread throughout the team. There was a crushing home defeat by struggling Southend, who scored twice in the final three minutes, and although Preston responded commendably by winning 4-0 at Coventry next time out, it was their only success in a damaging run of seven matches. Victory over promoted Birmingham in the final match was not enough to restore a place in the top six, Southampton finishing ahead of them by a single point.

Agyemang, P .... 10(21)
Alexander, G 42
Anyinsah, J .... –(3)
Chilvers, L 45
Davidson, C .... 12(3)
Dichio, D .... 16(14)
Henderson, W 4
Hill, M .... 37(1)
Jarrett, J .... 4(1)
Lonergan, A 13
McCormack, A .... –(3)
McKenna, P .... 32(1)
Mellor, N .... 2(3)
Miller, T .... 4(3)
Nash, C 29
Neal, L .... 3(21)
Nowland, A .... –(1)
Nugent, D .... 43(1)
Ormerod, B .... 16(13)
Pergl, P 6
Pugh, D 45
Ricketts, M .... 7(7)
Sedgwick, C .... 41(2)
Soley, S 6
Songo'o, F .... 4(2)
St Ledger, S .... 40(1)
Stock, B .... 1(1)
Whaley, S .... 31(9)
Wilson, K .... 13(8)

League goals (64): Nugent 15, Ormerod 8, Agyemang 7, Alexander 6, Whaley 6, Dichio 5, Pugh 4, Chilvers 2, McKenna 2, Mellor 1, Neal 1, Pergl 1, Ricketts 1, Sedgwick 1, St Ledger 1, Wilson 1, Opponents 2.
F.A. Cup goals (4): Nugent 2, Ormerod 1, Wilson 1. **Carling Cup goals (1):** Whaley 1.
Average home league attendance: 14,429. **Player of Year:** Matt Hill.

QUEENS PARK RANGERS

John Gregory knew the size of the task facing him when returning to the club he once served as a player following the dismissal of Gary Waddock. Six weeks into what had already turned into a difficult season, chairman Gianni Paladini told him nothing less than survival would suffice. Rangers responded to the new manager with a run of improved form, before sinking back into trouble, a 5-0 defeat at Southend underlining their problems. But the return from injury of Gareth Ainsworth and some important goals from Dexter Blackstock helped turn the tide. Rangers battled for a point at Derby, then won four of the next five matches. By the time Cardiff were seen off at Loftus Road, Rangers had pulled clear and Gregory could look forward to building towards a more productive campaign.

Ainsworth, G .... 18(4)
Baidoo, S .... 2(7)
Bailey, S .... 7(3)
Bignot, M .... 32(1)
Bircham, M .... 12(5)
Blackstock, D .... 37(2)
Bolder, A 16
Camp, L 11
Cole, J 3
Cook, L 37
Cullip, D 13
Czerkas, A .... 2(1)
Donnelly, S .... –(3)
Furlong, P .... 9(13)
Gallen, K .... 9(9)
Idiakez, I .... 4(1)
Jones, P 12
Jones, R .... 17(14)
Kanyuka, P .... 7(4)
Lomas, S .... 26(8)
Mancienne, M .... 26(2)
Milanese, M 14
Moore, S 3
Nygaard, M .... 17(6)
Oliseh, E 2
Rehman, Z .... 23(2)
Ricketts, R .... –(2)
Rose, M .... 10(1)
Rowlands, M .... 27(2)
Royce, S 20
Shimmin, D 1
Smith, J .... 22(7)
Stewart, D 45
Timoska, S .... 11(3)
Ward, N .... 11(8)

League goals (54): Blackstock 13, Rowlands 10, Smith 6, Jones, R 5, Cook 3, Gallen 3, Nygaard 3, Furlong 2, Lomas 2, Ainsworth 1, Baidoo 1, Idiakez 1, Stewart 1, Ward 1, Opponents 2.
F.A. Cup goals (2): Baidoo 1, Blackstock 1. **Carling Cup goals (5):** Cook 1, Gallen 1, Nygaard 1, Jones, R 1, Stewart 1.
Average home league attendance: 12,936. **Player of Year:** Lee Cook.

SHEFFIELD WEDNESDAY

After nearly ten years at Scunthorpe, Brian Laws seized the chance to manage at a bigger club when Paul Sturrock was dismissed in the wake of a 4-0 defeat at Colchester, which left Wednesday facing the prospect of a relegation struggle, having won only two of their opening 12 matches. Laws, who played under Brian Clough at Nottingham Forest, got off on the right foot with a victory at Ipswich, took his new team up to mid-table, then supervised an 11-match unbeaten run yielding 27 points. It raised the prospect of a place in the play-offs and had Kenny Lunt's shot gone in, instead of crashing off the Birmingham crossbar, they might have gone into the final game with the dream still alive. Instead, Wednesday went down 2-0 to a side who clinched promotion, leaving Laws to look forward to building on what he felt were the right foundations for the new season.

Adams, S .... 2(1)
Adamson, C .... 3(1)
Andrews, W .... 7(2)
Beevers, M 2
Boden, L .... –(1)
Bougherra, M 28
Brunt, C .... 42(2)
Bullen, L .... 33(5)
Burton, D .... 35(7)
Clarke, L .... 3(7)
Corr, B .... –(1)
Coughlan, G .... 14(4)
Crossley, M 17
Folly, Y .... 20(9)
Gilbert, P .... 5(1)
Graham, D .... –(4)
Hills, J .... 15(1)
Johnson, J .... 5(2)
Jones, B 15
Lekaj, R .... –(2)
Lunt, K .... 30(7)
MacLean, S .... 20(21)
McAllister, S .... –(6)
McArdle, R .... –(1)
O'Brien, B .... 13(9)
Sam, L 4
Simek, F 41
Small, W .... 13(7)
Spurr, T .... 31(5)
Talbot, D .... 2(6)
Tudgay, M .... 37(3)
Turner, I 11
Watson, S 11
Whelan, G .... 35(3)
Wood, R 12

League goals (70): Burton 13, MacLean 12, Tudgay 11, Brunt 10, Whelan 7, Bougherra 2, Johnson 2, Small 2, Andrews 1, Clarke 1, Coughlan 1, Crossley 1, McAllister 1, O'Brien 1, Simek 1, Opponents 4.
F.A. Cup goals (2): Bullen 1, MacLean 1. **Carling Cup goals (1):** Whelan 1.
Average home league attendance: 23,638. **Player of Year:** Glenn Whelan.

SOUTHAMPTON

George Burley had his share of setbacks in the play-offs when manager of Ipswich and suffered more disappointment when Southampton lost out on penalties to another of his former clubs, Derby, in a dramatic second semi-final at Pride Park. Trailing 2-1 from the first leg, they levelled the tie with an 89th minute goal by Grzegorz Rasiak, but lost out when Inigo Idiakez failed from the spot. Burley had no complaints about the efforts of his players at the end of a season in which they lacked the consistency required for an automatic promotion spot but generally proved good value for money. They scored more goals, 41, than anyone away from home, including six with a less than full strength side against Wolves at Molineux in which on-loan Marek Saganowski netted a hat-trick.

Baird, C 44
Bale, G 38
Belmady, D .... 9(5)
Best, L .... 6(3)
Bialkowski, B 8
Cranie, M .... –(1)
Davis, K 38
Dyer, N .... 10(8)
Fuller, R 1
Guthrie, D .... 8(2)
Idiakez, I .... 12(2)
Jones, K .... 25(9)
Lallana, A 1
Licka, M .... 7(8)
Lundekvam, C 33
Makin, C .... 19(3)
McGoldrick, D .... 1(8)
Ostlund, A .... 17(3)
Pele, P .... 34(3)
Powell, D 8
Prutton, D .... 1(2)
Rasiak, G .... 32(7)
Saganowski, M .... 11(2)
Skacel, R .... 32(5)
Surman, A .... 26(11)
Viafara, J .... 29(7)
Wright, J .... 41(1)
Wright-Phillips, B . 15(24)

Play-offs-appearances: Baird 2, Guthrie 2, Pele 2, Saganowski 2, Surman 2, Viafafa 2, Best 1(1), Belmadi 1(1), Skacel 1(1), Bale 1, Bialkowski 1, Cranie 1, Davis 1, Ostlund 1, Jones 1, Makin 1, Rasiak – (2), Idiakez –(1),
League goals (77): Rasiak 18, Jones 14, Saganowski 10, Wright-Phillips 8, Bale 5, Best 4, Surman 4, Baird 3, Skacel 3, Viafara 2, Idiakez 1, Licka 1, Pele 1, Prutton 1, Wright 1, Opponents 1. **Play-offs – goals (4):** Viafara 2, Rasiak 1, Surman 1.
F.A. Cup goals (3): Rasiak 2, Jones 1. **Carling Cup goals (9):** Wright-Phillips 3, Belmadi 1, Dyer 1, Jones 1, McGoldrick 1, Skacel 1, Opponents 1.
Average home league attendance: 23,556. **Player of Year:** Chris Baird.

SOUTHEND UNITED

Three successive home defeats at a time when the battle against relegation was at its peak sent Southend straight back down to League One. They looked capable of surviving after late goals from Alan McCormack and Kevin Maher delivered a shock success at Preston. But form suddenly deserted them at Roots Hall where, earlier in the season, the likes of Sunderland, Southampton, Stoke and West Bromwich Albion had all been overcome. Colchester Utd. and Barnsley went away with maximum points, the latter in a vital match between two teams in trouble. When the drop was confirmed by Luton's victory, manager Steve Tilson admitted that his team had come up short when it mattered most. That was certainly not the case when they took on Manchester United in the Carling Cup, Freddie Eastwood's goal accounting for the holders and setting up a quarter-final tie at Tottenham, who needed extra-time before finding a winner.

Ademeno, C .... –(1)
Barrett, A .... 26(2)
Bradbury, L .... 28(3)
Campbell-Ryce, J ... 38(5)
Clarke, P .... 34(3)
Cole, M .... 1(3)
Collis, S .... –(1)
Eastwood, F .... 41(1)
Flahavan, D 46
Foran, R .... 9(6)
Francis, S .... 32(8)
Gower, M 43
Guttridge, L .... 15(2)
Hammell, S .... 38(1)
Harrold, M .... 13(23)
Hooper, G .... 3(16)
Hunt, L .... 30(5)
Lawson, J .... –(2)
Maher, K 41
McCormack, A .... 20(2)
Moussa, F .... 2(2)
Paynter, B .... 5(4)
Prior, S .... 15(2)
Ricketts, M .... –(2)

Riera, A .... 1(1)	Sodje, E .... 23(1)	Wilson, C 2
Sam, L .... –(2)		

League goals (47): Eastwood 11, Gower 8, Maher 5, Bradbury 4, Barrett 3, Harrold 3, McCormack 3, Campbell-Ryce 2, Clarke 2, Hunt 2, Foran 1, Francis 1, Hammell 1, Sodje 1.
F.A. Cup goals (4): Bradbury 1, Eastwood 1, Gower 1, Maher 1. **Carling Cup goals (10):** Eastwood 4, Hooper 2, Gower 1, Hammell 1, Hunt 1, Paynter 1.
Average home league attendance: 10,024. **Player of Year:** Kevin Maher.

STOKE CITY

Tony Pulis and his team introduced a measure of success to a club more noted for managerial upheaval and boardroom manoeuvring than achievements on the pitch in recent years. They put together a profitable late run which offered the chance of securing a place in the play-offs on the last day of the season. Stoke were level on points with sixth-place Southampton, but experienced a frustrating afternoon at Loftus Road, where a 1-1 scoreline against Queens Park Rangers was overshadowed by victory for their rivals over Southend. Even so, eighth place was the highest since 1996. It came after a miserable start which yielded only one win in the opening ten matches before a 4-0 win at Leeds and a 5-0 success against Norwich pointed them in the right direction.

Bangoura, S .... 1(3)	Griffin, A .... 32(1)	Pericard, V .... 17(12)
Berger, P .... 1(6)	Harper, K .... –(3)	Pulis, A .... –(1)
Brammer, D .... 11(11)	Hendrie, L .... 26(2)	Rooney, A .... –(10)
Buxton, L 1	Higginbotham, D 44	Russell, D .... 40(3)
Chadwick, L .... 13(2)	Hill, C .... 15(3)	Sidibe, M .... 42(1)
Delap, R 2	Hoefkens, C .... 42(3)	Sigurdsson, H .... –(2)
Diao, S 27	Lawrence, L 27	Simonsen, S 46
Dickinson, C .... 5(8)	Martin, L .... 4(9)	Sweeney, P .... 10(3)
Duberry, M 29	Matteo, D 9	Whitley, J .... –(3)
Eustace, J .... 7(8)	Parkin, J .... 5(1)	Wilkinson, A .... 2(2)
Fortune, J 14	Paterson, M .... –(9)	Zakuani, G 9
Fuller, R .... 25(5)		

League goals (62): Fuller 10, Sidibe 9, Higginbotham 7, Russell 7, Lawrence 5, Chadwick 3, Hendrie 3, Parkin 3, Griffin 2, Hill 2, Hoefkens 2, Pericard 2, Fortune 1, Martin 1, Matteo 1, Paterson 1, Sweeney 1, Opponents 2.
F.A. Cup goals (2): Fuller 1, Opponents 1. **Carling Cup goals (1):** Pericard 1.
Average home league attendance: 15,749. **Player of Year:** Danny Higginbotham.

SUNDERLAND

Regaining a Premiership place was the last thing on the minds of supporters as Sunderland lost their first four games under chairman/manager Niall Quinn. When defeat by Bury in the Carling Cup followed, they feared another grim season. But what a transformation after Quinn persuaded his old Republic of Ireland team-mate Roy Keane to take on his first managerial position. The former Manchester United stalwart steered his side into mid-table by the end of the year, strengthened his squad in the transfer widow, then proved unstoppable. Their only league defeat of 2007, at Colchester, offered some encouragement to rivals Derby and Birmingham. Instead, a crowd of more than 44,000 saw Sunderland regain the initiative by beating Burnley. Then, a handsome 5-0 success at Luton, along with Birmingham's 1-0 defeat at Preston on the final day, left them champions by a two-point margin. Keane, unchallenged as the division's Manager of the Year, immediately began to target the players he felt were needed to prevent another return to the Championship.

Alnwick, B 11	Clarke, C .... 2(2)	Connolly, D .... 30(6)
Brown, C .... 10(6)	Collins, D .... 36(2)	Cunningham, K 11
Caldwell, S 11	Collins, N .... 6(1)	Delap, R 6

Edwards, C 15	Kyle, K .... –(2)	Simpson, D .... 13(1)
Elliott, R 7	Lawrence, L .... 10(2)	Stead, J .... 1(4)
Elliott, S .... 15(9)	Leadbitter, G .... 24(20)	Stokes, A .... 7(7)
Evans, J 18	Miller, L .... 24(6)	Varga, S 20
Fulop, M 5	Miller, T .... 3(1)	Wallace, R .... 20(12)
Hartley, P .... –(1)	Murphy, D .... 27(11)	Ward, D 30
Hysen, T .... 15(11)	Nosworthy, N .... 27(2)	Whitehead, D .... 43(2)
John, S .... 10(5)	Nyatanga, L .... 9(2)	Wright, S .... 2(1)
Kavanagh, G .... 10(4)	Riera, A .... –(1)	Yorke, D .... 28(4)

League goals (76): Connolly 13, Murphy 10, Leadbitter 7, Wallace 6, Edwards 5, Elliott, S 5, Yorke 5, Hysen 4, John 4, Whitehead 4, Brown 3, Miller, L 2, Stokes 2, Evans 1, Kavanagh 1, Collins, N 1, Stead 1, Varga 1, Opponents 1.
F.A. Cup goals: None. **Carling Cup goals:** None.
Average home league attendance: 31,887. **Player of Year:** Nyron Nosworthy.

WEST BROMWICH ALBION

A season that promised so much ended with so little for Albion, the highest scorers in the Championship but a team riddled with inconsistency in the latter stages of the season when the pressures began to mount. They had been virtually untouchable at the Hawthorns until a 2-1 reversal against Sunderland was followed by three more defeats there. Tony Mowbray, who had left Hibernian to take over as manager when Bryan Robson was sacked early on, stabilised the ship and a 7-0 rout of Barnsley, in which Kevin Phillips netted his second hat-trick of the season, sent them into the play-offs on a high. Phillips scored three times in the semi-final against Wolves, taking his total for the season to 22, but neither he nor striker partner Diomansy Kamara, who totalled 23, made an impact in the final against Derby, a 1-0 defeat raising fears that some key players would decide to leave during the summer.

Albrechtsen, M .... 26(5)	Hodgkiss, J .... –(5)	Nicholson, S .... –(2)
Carter, D .... 19(14)	Hoult, R 14	Perry, C 23
Chaplow, R .... 16(12)	Inamoto, J .... –(3)	Phillips, K .... 31(5)
Clement, N .... 14(6)	Kamara, D .... 33(1)	Quashie, N .... 17(3)
Davies, C 32	Kiely, D 17	Robinson, P 42
Ellington, N .... 19(15)	Koren, R .... 15(3)	Sodje, S 7
Gera, Z .... 28(12)	Koumas, J .... 34(5)	Wallwork, R .... 9(1)
Greening, J .... 40(2)	MacDonald, S .... –(9)	Watson, S .... 10(2)
Hartson, J .... 14(7)	McShane, P .... 31(1)	Zuberbuhler, P 15

Play-offs – appearances: Greening 3, Kamara 3, Kiely 3, Koren 3, Koumas 3, McShane 3, Perry 3, Phillips 3, Robinson 3, Sodje 3, Gera 2(1), Chaplow 1, Ellington –(3), Carter –(2), Clement –(1), MacDonald –(1),
League goals (81): Kamara 20, Phillips 16, Ellington 10, Koumas 9, Gera 5, Hartson 5, Carter 3, Greening 2, McShane 2, Robinson 2, Albrechtsen 1, Chaplow 1, Clement 1, Koren 1, Sodje 1, Wallwork 1, Opponents 1. **Play-offs – goals (4):** Phillips 3, Kamara 1.
F.A. Cup goals (9): Phillips 3, Kamara 2, Carter 1, Gera 1, Hartson 1, McShane 1.
Carling Cup goals (6): Nicholson 2, Carter 1, Ellington 1, Greening 1, Wallwork 1.
Average home league attendance: 20,471. **Player of Year:** Diomansy Kamara.

WOLVERHAMPTON WANDERERS

Mick McCarthy was disappointed but not downhearted when his side lost to West Bromwich Albion in both legs of their play-off semi-final. The Wolves manager saw enough promise from his emerging young team to predict a bright future. Players like Michael Kightly, Andy Keogh and Stephen Ward added a new dimension and McCarthy believes they can mature into influential players. Kightly, in particular, made a major impact after moving from Conference club Grays, scoring eight goals in little more than half a season. Wolves had lost two of their three league and F.A. Cup matches to Albion during the regular campaign and again found it hard coping with the Diomansy

Kamara/Kevin Phillips spearhead of their Black Country rivals. A 3-2 defeat at Molineux was followed by a 1-0 reversal in the second leg.

Bothroyd, J .... 19(14)
Breen, G 40
Budtz, J .... 2(2)
Clapham, J .... 21(5)
Clarke, L .... 11(11)
Clyde, M 3
Collins, N .... 20(2)
Cort, C .... 7(3)
Craddock, J .... 28(6)
Davies, C .... 6(17)
Davies, M .... –(7)
Edwards, R .... 24(9)
Fleming, C 1
Gleeson, S .... –(3)
Gobern, L .... 6(6)
Henry, K 34
Ikeme, C .... –(1)
Johnson, J .... 14(6)
Jones, D 8
Keogh, A 17
Kightly, M 24
Little, M .... 19(7)
McIndoe, M .... 25(2)
McNamara, J 19
Mulgrew, C .... 5(1)
Murray, M 44
Naylor, L 3
O'Connor, K 3
Olofinjana, S .... 41(3)
Potter, D .... 35(3)
Ricketts, R .... 15(4)
Ward, S .... 11(7)
Wheater, D 1

Play-offs – appearances: Bothroyd 2, Breen 2, Collins 2, Craddock 2, Hennessey 2, Keogh 2, Kightly 2, McIndoe 2, McNamara 2, Olofinjana 2, Potter 2, Ward –(2), Gleeson –(1), Little –(1), Mulgrew –(1).
League goals (59): Bothroyd 9, Kightly 8, Olofinjana 8, Clarke 5, Keogh 5, Craddock 4, Henry 3, Johnson 3, McIndoe 3, Ward 3, Gobern 2, Collins 2, Breen 1, Opponents 3.
Play-offs – goals (2): Craddock 1, Olofinjana 1.
F.A. Cup goals (4): Davies, C 2, Olofinjana 1, Potter 1. **Carling Cup goals:** None.
Average home league attendance: 20,967. **Player of Year:** Matt Murray.

COCA-COLA LEAGUE ONE

BLACKPOOL

A season that looked like developing into a battle against relegation ended with Blackpool celebrating in front of a near-60,000 crowd at the new Wembley after claiming a place in the game's second tier for the first time for 30 years. A 2-0 victory over Yeovil in the Play-off Final, achieved with goals from Robbie Williams just before half-time and Keigan Parker just after, climaxed a remarkable transformation in fortunes for Simon Grayson's team. It was a club-record tenth successive win – a run that embraced a 6-3 defeat of Swansea in which Andy Morrell scored four times, almost brought the second automatic promotion spot and left Oldham beaten 5-2 on aggregate in the semi-finals. It was a far cry from the opening 11 matches, which produced a single win and left Blackpool scrambling in the bottom four.

Barker, S 45
Bean, M .... 2(4)
Blinkhorn, M .... –(2)
Brandon, C .... 4(1)
Burgess, B .... 13(14)
Coid, D .... 15(3)
Dickinson, C 7
Edge, L 1
Evans, R 32
Evatt, I .... 42(2)
Farrelly, G .... –(1)
Fernandez, V .... –(1)
Forbes, A .... 26(8)
Fox, D .... 33(4)
Gillett, S .... 20(11)
Gorkss, K .... 8(2)
Graham, D .... 1(3)
Hart, J 5
Hoolahan, W .... 37(5)
Jackson, M .... 42(1)
Jorgensen, C .... 21(10)
Joseph, M .... 3(5)
Morrell, A .... 34(6)
Parker, K .... 24(21)
Prendergast, R .... 3(2)
Rachubka, P 8
Southern, K .... 37(2)
Tierney, P .... 8(2)
Vernon, S .... 21(17)
Wilkinson, A .... 5(2)
Williams, R 9

Play-offs – appearances: Barker 3, Evatt 3, Forbes 3, Hoolahan 3, Jackson 3, Jorgensen 3, Morrell 3, Parker 3, Rachubka 3, Southern 3, Williams 3, Fox –(2), Gillett –(2), Burgess –(1), Vernon –(1).
League goals (76): Morrell 16, Parker 13, Vernon 11, Hoolahan 8, Southern 5, Fox 4, Williams 4, Barker 3, Brandon 2, Burgess 2, Jorgensen 2, Forbes 1, Gillett 1, Graham 1, Jackson 1, Opponents 2. **Play-offs – goals (7):** Parker 2, Barker 1, Hoolahan 1, Morrell 1, Southern 1, Williams 1.
F.A. Cup goals (10): Morrell 3, Barker 1, Burgess 1, Evatt 1, Hoolahan 1, Jackson 1, Parker 1, Vernon 1. **Carling Cup goals (2):** Vernon 2. **Johnstone's Paint Trophy goals (4):** Burgess 2, Barker 1, Gillett 1.

Average home league attendance: 6,876. **Player of Year:** Shaun Barker.

BOURNEMOUTH

Darren Anderton's first hat-trick in a career spanning more than 500 matches helped preserve Bournemouth's League One status. It came in a 5-0 win over Leyton Orient and lifted his team out of the bottom four. The former Tottenham and England winger made another important contribution with the only goal against Millwall, the first of three successive wins in March which took Kevin Bond's team clear of trouble. By then, they had sufficient points in the bag to compensate for a failure to win any of the final six games. Bond followed in the footsteps of his father, John Bond, who managed the club in the 1970s, when Sean O'Driscoll joined Doncaster after six years in charge, a month into the season.

Ainsworth, L .... 2(5)
Anderton, D 28
Bertrand, R 5
Best, L .... 12(3)
Broadhurst, K .... 25(2)
Browning, M .... 17(4)
Claridge, S 1
Connolly, M .... 3(2)
Cooke, S .... 6(4)
Cooper, S .... 29(4)
Cork, J 7
Cummings, W .... 26(5)
Fletcher, S .... 32(9)
Foley, S .... 15(3)
Gillett, S 7
Gowling, J .... 25(8)
Hart, C 8
Hayter, J .... 41(1)
Hollands, D .... 14(19)
Howe, E .... 14(1)
Lawson, J .... 2(2)
Maher, S .... 5(2)
McGoldrick, D 12
McQuoid, J .... –(2)
Moss, N 27
Pitman, B .... 8(20)
Purches, S .... 38(5)
Songo'o, F .... 3(1)
Standing, M .... –(1)
Stewart, G 19
Summerfield, L .... 5(3)
Vidarsson, B .... 4(2)
Vokes, S .... 8(5)
Walker, J .... 5(1)
Wilson, M 19
Young, N 34

League goals (50): Hayter 10, Anderton 6, McGoldrick 6, Pitman 5, Vokes 4, Best 3, Wilson 3, Browning 2, Connolly 1, Cooke 1, Fletcher 1, Foley 1, Gillett 1, Gowling 1, Hollands 1, Howe 1, Purches 1, Summerfield 1, Vidarsson 1.
F.A. Cup goals (5): Fletcher 2, Hayter 2, Hollands 1. **Carling Cup goals (1):** Fletcher 1.
Johnstone's Paint Trophy goals: None.
Average home league attendance: 6,028. **Player of Year:** Darren Anderton.

BRADFORD CITY

Stuart McCall was an influential figure in Bradford's rise to the Premiership, a forceful and fully-committed midfielder who led by example. Now, he has been asked to devote that energy and enthusiasm into restoring the fortunes of a club who have slipped from the top-flight to League Two in seven seasons. He became their eighth manager in that time, two more having tried unsuccessfully to halt the slide last season – Colin Todd and defensive stalwart David Wetherall. Todd's side were fourth after a dozen matches. By the time he was sacked in mid-February, they were in freefall. Wetherall, given the job until the end of the season, was unable to halt the slide and a single point from the last three games left them four points adrift, a home defeat by relegation rivals Leyton Orient proving particularly damaging.

Ainge, S .... 5(4)
Ashikodi, M 8
Barrau, X .... 1(2)
Bentham, C .... 12(6)
Black, T 4
Bower, M 46
Bridge-Wilkinson, M 39
Brown, J .... 1(5)
Clarke, M .... 5(3)
Colbeck, J .... 14(18)
Daley, O .... 13(1)
Doyle, N .... 25(3)
Dyer, B .... 2(3)
Edghill, R .... 20(4)
Graham, D .... 17(5)
Healy, C 2
Hibbert, D .... 4(4)
Holmes, L 16
Johnson, E .... 17(15)
Johnson, J .... 26(1)
Logan, C .... 3(1)
Muirhead, B .... 1(3)
Osborne, L .... –(1)
Parker, B .... 35(4)
Paynter, B 15
Penford, T .... 1(2)
Ricketts, D 46
Rogers, A .... 4(4)
Schumacher, S 44
Swift, J .... 1(1)
Weir-Daley, S .... 2(3)
Wetherall, D 41
Windass, D 25
Youga, K 11

League goals (47): Windass 11, Schumacher 6, Bridge-Wilkinson 4, Johnson, J 4, Paynter 4, Bower 3, Graham 3, Johnson, E 3, Ashikodi 2, Barrau 2, Daley 2, Dyer 1, Weir-Daley 1, Wetherall 1.
F.A. Cup goals (4): Bridge-Wilkinson 1, Schumacher 1, Windass 1, Opponents 1. **Carling Cup goals (1):** Johnson, E 1. **Johnstone's Paint Trophy goals (1):** Brown 1
Average home league attendance: 5,599. **Player of Year:** Nathan Doyle.

BRENTFORD

Terry Butcher's appointment offered a rare moment of optimism for Brentford fans, who saw their team finish bottom 12 months after reaching the play-offs for the second successive season. The former England captain promised a new attitude and a new-look squad after becoming the club's third manager in less than a year. He succeeded Scott Fitzgerald, who followed Leroy Rosenior out of Griffin Park when results showed no sign of improving. Ironically, the season had started encouragingly enough under Rosenior, with Brentford unbeaten and up to fourth in the table after seven matches. The decline was startling – the next 17 games failing to deliver a victory. Two solid away successes, at Blackpool and Huddersfield, provided some hope, but form dipped again and Brentford became the first side to be relegated, with five games remaining.

Abbey, N 16
Brooker, P .... 24(10)
Carder-Andrews, K .... 2(3)
Charles, D .... 9(8)
Cox, S .... 11(2)
Dark, L .... 2(1)
Frampton, A 32
Griffiths, A .... 32(5)
Heywood, M .... 25(3)
Ide, C .... 24(2)
Keith, J .... 17(1)
Kuffour, J .... 38(1)
Leary, M 17
Masters, C 11
Montague, R .... –(4)
Moore, C .... 8(8)
Mousinho, J .... 29(5)
Nelson, S 19
O'Connor, K .... 38(1)
Onibuje, F .... –(2)
Osborne, K .... 17(4)
Owusu, L .... 4(3)
Partridge, D 3
Peters, R .... –(13)
Pinault, T .... 24(3)
Rhodes, A .... 8(7)
Richards, G 10
Shipperley, N 11
Skulason, O 10
Taylor, S .... 3(3
Tillen, S .... 28(6
Tomlin, G .... 6(6
Wijnhard, C .... 7(2
Willock, C .... 18(10
Wilson, C 3

League goals (40): Kuffour 12, Ide 7, O'Connor 6,Willock 3, Keith 2, Moore 2, Charles 1, Frampton 1, Griffiths 1, Heywood 1, Pinault 1, Richards 1, Skulason 1, Tillen 1.
F.A. Cup goals: None. **Carling Cup goals (2):** Kuffour 1, O'Connor 1. **Johnstone's Paint Trophy goals (1):** Kuffour 1.
Average home league attendance: 5,599. **Player of Year:** Jo Kuffour.

BRIGHTON AND HOVE ALBION

Mark McGhee had admitted after relegation the previous season that Brighton would continue to find it hard going without a proper stadium to call their own – and amid continuing uncertainty about the proposed move to Falmer, this proved another tough season for the club, not least for the manager himself. He was dismissed after three early defeats, making way for youth coach Dean Wilkins, whose initial appointment until the end of the campaign was followed by a three-year deal. Brighton were up to 11th going into the final part of the season, but then slipped seven places after winning only one of their final 12 games. Earlier, Academy product Jake Robinson had scored two hat-tricks in the space of a fortnight, against Huddersfield (3-0) and in an 8-0 F.A. Cup win over Northwich.

Bertin, A .... 15(1)
Bowditch, D .... 1(2)
Butters, G 31
Carpenter, R .... 13(2)
Cox, D .... 40(2)
El-Abd, A .... 39(3)
Elder, N .... 1(12)
Elphick, T .... 2(1)
Flinders, S 12
Fraser, T .... 18(9)
Frutos, A .... 5(5)
Gatting, J .... 10(13)
Hammond, D 37
Hart, G .... 18(7)
Henderson, W 20
Hinshelwood, A ...... 10(1)
John, A .... 1(3)
Kazim-Richards, C .... –(1)
Kuipers, M 1
Loft, D .... 5(6
Lynch, J .... 34(5
Mayo, K .... 28(2
Molango, M .... –(1
O'Cearuill, J .... 6(2
Rehman, Z ....
Reid, P 1
Rents, S .... 19(6

Revell, A .... 34(4)
Robinson, J .... 28(10)
Santos, G .... 7(4)
Savage, B .... 14(1)
Stokes, T .... 5(1)
Ward, N .... 6(2)
Whing, A 12
Williams, S 3

League goals (49): Hammond 8, Revell 7, Cox 6, Robinson 6, Savage 6, Gatting 4, Hart 2, Bowditch 1, El-Abd 1, Elder 1, Fraser 1, Loft 1, Reid 1, Ward 1, Williams 1, Opponents 2.

F.A. Cup goals (11): Robinson 4, Cox 2, Revell 2, Gatting 1, Hammond 1, Rents 1. **Carling Cup goals (3):** Cox 1, El-Abd 1, Reid 1. **Johnstone's Paint Trophy goals (7):** Hammond 2, Revell 2, Robinson 2, Cox 1.

Average home league attendance: 6,047. **Player of Year:** Dean Hammond.

BRISTOL CITY

Two first half goals by former West Ham and Arsenal youngster David Noble and a third by Alex Russell clinched promotion for Gary Johnson's side in front of a near-20,000 crowd. The 3-1 win over Rotherham enabled City to hold on to the runners-up position behind Scunthorpe in the face of a sustained late challenge from Blackpool, which had threatened them with having to settle for the play-offs. It was another success for Johnson, who had taken Yeovil from the Conference to League One in the space of three years before accepting the challenge of bringing the good times back to Ashton Gate. After losing three of the of the first four games, City moved into their stride and over the course of the season proved a shade more consistent than their main rivals, Nottingham Forest.

Andrews, W .... 3(4)
Basso, A 45
Betsy, K .... 16(1)
Brooker, S .... 19(4)
Brown, S .... 12(3)
Carey, L .... 36(2)
Corr, B .... 1(2)
Cotterill, D .... 3(2)
Fontaine, L .... 23(7)
Jevons, P .... 31(10)
Johnson, L .... 41(1)
Keogh, R .... 20(11)
McAllister, J .... 29(2)
McCombe, J .... 38(3)
Murray, S .... 21(7)
Myrie-Williams, J .. 15(10)
Noble, D .... 18(8)
Orr, B .... 29(6)
Ruddy, J 1
Russell, A .... 20(8)
Showunmi, E .... 28(5)
Skuse, C .... 31(11)
Smith, A .... 3(7)
Weale, C .... –(1)
Wilson, B .... 17(2)
Woodman, C .... 5(6)
Wright, N .... 1(3)

League goals (63): Jevons 11, Showunmi 10, Murray 7, Johnson 5, Brown 4, McCombe 4, Orr 4, Noble 3, Andrews 2, Brooker 2, Carey 2, Keogh 2, Myrie-Williams 2, Russell 2, Betsy 1, Cotterill 1, McAllister 1.

F.A. Cup goals (14): Jevons 4, Showunmi 3, McCombe 2, Murray 2, Brooker 1, Keogh 1, Noble 1. **Carling Cup goals (1):** Cotterill 1. **Johnstone's Paint Trophy goals (7):** Jevons 2, Showunmi 2, Andrews 1, Corr 1, Keogh 1.

Average home league attendance: 12,818. **Player of Year:** Jamie McCombe.

CARLISLE UNITED

A third successive promotion was probably too much to ask of a club whose rise had been so well chartered by Paul Simpson, particularly with the manager moving on to take charge at Preston. But under the former Newcastle and Everton player Neil McDonald they certainly gave it a go, despite heavy defeats at the hands of Crewe (5-1), Swansea (5-0) and Yeovil (4-1). Each time, his side responded well and a run of five successive victories, sparked by a 5-0 success of their own against Gillingham, left them single point off a play-off place. The fixture list, however, had left them with a tough run-in and successive defeats by promotion rivals Bristol City and Swansea ended their chances.

Aranalde, Z 43
Arnison, P .... 6(5)
Beckford, J 4
Billy, C .... 16(4)
Bridges, M 5
Gall, K .... 44(1)
Garner, J .... 17(1)
Graham, D 11
Grand, S .... 1(3)
Gray, K .... 27(4)
Hackney, S .... 14(4)
Harper, K 7
Hawley, K .... 30(2)
Hindmarch, S .... –(7)
Holmes, D .... 8(28)
Joyce, L .... 7(9)
Krause, J 3
Liversey, D .... 29(2)

Lumsdon, C .... 36(3)
McDermott, N .... 6(9)
Murphy, P 40
Murray, G .... –(1)
Murray, P 14
Raven, D 36
Smith, Jeff 17
Smith, Johann .... 9(5)
Thirlwell, P .... 29(1)
Vipond, S .... 1(3)
Westwood, K 46

League goals (54): Hawley 12, Gall 8, Graham 7, Garner 5, Gray 3, Holmes 3, McDermott 3, Hackney 2, Lumsdon 2, Murphy 2, Aranalde 1, Beckford 1, Smith, Jeff 1, Smith, Johann 1, Joyce 1, Liversey 1, Murray, P 1.
F.A. Cup goals (1): Gray 1. **Carling Cup goals (1):** Holmes 1. **Johnstone's Paint Trophy goals (1):** Holmes 1.
Average home league attendance: 7.906. **Player of Year:** Zigor Aranalde.

CHELTENHAM TOWN

The achievement may have seemed a modest one, but John Ward took plenty of pride in the way his promoted team ensured their League One status in a season of fluctuating fortunes. Cheltenham started brightly, climbing to sixth in the first few weeks. By mid-season they had slid to second from bottom and were still in deep trouble after losing 3-0 at Nottingham Forest with little more than a month of the season left. But a strong finish brought crucial wins over relegation rivals Leyton Orient and Brentford, followed by a big victory at Oldham. Another away success, 4-2 at Rotherham, completed the recovery.

Armstrong, C 42
Bell, M .... 5(2)
Bird, D .... 26(5)
Brown, Scott (Gk) ... 10(1)
Brown, Scott (Mid) 4
Caines, G .... 26(13)
Connolly, A .... 6(2)
Connor, P .... 9(6)
Duff, S 34
Elvins, R .... –(5)
Finnigan, J 40
Gallinagh, A .... –(1)
Gill, J .... 38(1)
Gillespie, S .... 13(10)
Guinan, S .... 17(2)
Higgs, S 36
Lowe, K .... 14(2)
McCann, G 15
Melligan, J .... 38(5)
O'Leary, K 5
Odejayi, K .... 38(7)
Reid, C .... –(6)
Rosa, D .... 3(1)
Smith, A 2
Spencer, D .... 23(4)
Townsend, M .... 27(3)
Victory, J .... 7(3)
Vincent, A .... –(5)
Wilson, B .... 22(3)
Wylde, M .... 4(3)
Yao, S .... 2(13)

League goals (49): Odejayi 13, Finnigan 7, Melligan 7, Gillespie 5, McCann 5, Spencer 3, Bird 2, Wilson 2, Connor 1, Lowe 1, O'Leary 1, Townsend 1, Victory 1.
F.A. Cup goals: None. **Carling Cup goals (3):** Guinan 1, Odejayi 1, Wilson 1. **Johnstone's Paint Trophy goals (5):** McCann 2, Finnigan 1, Melligan 1, Odejayi 1.
Average home league attendance: 4,358. **Player of Year:** Shane Higgs.

CHESTERFIELD

Chesterfield were full of cheer during an eventful Carling Cup run but increasingly low on spirit in the league and finished fourth from bottom. Goals were hard to come by after the sale of leading scorer Caleb Folan to Wigan in the January transfer window, particularly during the last month of the season when a 3-0 win over fellow strugglers Bradford was not enough to offset four other matches in which they failed to score. Although former midfielder Lee Richardson had not been able to halt the slide after replacing Roy McFarland as manager on a caretaker basis, he was given the job on a permanent basis. Folan played a key role in cup wins over Wolves, Manchester City and West Ham. Another battling performance came in round four at the Valley, where Charlton were grateful to go through on penalties.

Allison, W .... 13(23)
Allott, M 39
Bailey, A .... 25(5)
Boertien, P 4
Critchell, K .... 6(4)
Daniels, C 2
Davies, G .... 6(8)
Downes, A 45
Folan, C .... 19(4)
Grimaldi, S 8
Hall, P .... 40(6)
Hazell, R 39
Holmes, P 10
Hughes, M 2
Hurst, K 25
Jackson, J .... 1(13)
Jordan, M 6
Kovacs, J .... 5(2)
Larkin, C .... 27(12)
Lowry, J .... 6(2)
Meredith, J 1

Nicholson, S .... –(2)	Picken, P .... 38(1)	Shaw, P .... 23(7)
Niven, D 45	Rizzo, N .... 2(2)	Smith, A .... 5(8)
O'Hare, A .... 16(1)	Roche, B 40	Ward, J .... 8(1)

League goals (45): Folan 8, Allison 5, Hall 5, Larkin 4, Shaw 4, Downes 3, Hurst 3, Niven 3, Ward 3, O'Hare 2, Hazell 1, Holmes 1, Hughes 1, Picken 1, Opponents 1.
F.A. Cup goals: None. **Carling Cup goals (7):** Folan 3, Larkin 2, Allison 1, Niven 1.
Johnstone's Paint Trophy goals (7): Downes 2, Folan 1, Hall 1, Niven 1, Shaw 1, Smith 1.
Average home league attendance: 4,234. **Player of Year:** Aaron Downes.

CREWE ALEXANDRA

Dario Gradi's 24th and final year as manager concluded with another talented young player he brought through the ranks moving on to bigger things. Luke Varney joined Charlton for a fee rising to £2.5m. after scoring 25 times in all competitions, a tally that would have been even more impressive had he not been forced to miss part of the season through injury. Nicky Maynard contributed 19, while a dozen by Ryan Lowe included a hat-trick in the 5-1 win over Carlisle. But Crewe also leaked plenty of goals. Their for-and-against columns totalled 138, preventing Gradi from securing more than a mid-table finish before becoming the club's technical director and handing over more responsibility for team affairs to newly-promoted first team coach Steve Holland.

Baudet, J 42	Lowe, R .... 31(6)	Rix, B .... 24(7)
Bignot, P .... 9(2)	Matthews, L .... –(10)	Roberts, G .... 41(2)
Carrington, M .... –(3)	Maynard, N .... 27(4)	Rodgers, L .... 5(7)
Coo, C .... –(1)	McNamee, A 5	Suhaj, P .... –(2)
Cox, N .... 29(2)	Miller, S .... 2(5)	Taylor, A 4
Flynn, C .... –(1)	Moss, D .... 18(4)	Tomlinson, S 7
Grant, T .... 3(1)	O'Connor, M .... 25(4)	Varney, L .... 31(3)
Higdon, M .... 13(12)	O'Donnell, D .... 21(4)	Vaughan, D .... 26(3)
Jack, R .... 19(11)	Osbourne, I 2	Williams, B 39
Jones, B 41	Otsemobor, J 27	Woodards, D .... 9(2)
Kempson, D .... 6(1)	Pope, T .... –(4)	

League goals (66): Varney 17, Maynard 16, Lowe 8, Vaughan 4, Higdon 3, Miller 3, Rodgers 3, Roberts 3, Moss 2, Rix 2, Baudet 1, Cox 1, Jack 1, Jones 1, O'Donnell 1.
F.A. Cup goals: None. **Carling Cup goals (6):** Maynard 2, Jack 1, Lowe 1, O'Connor 1, Varney 1. **Johnstone's Paint Trophy goals (13):** Varney 7, Lowe 3, Jack 1, Maynard 1, Moss 1.
Average home league attendance: 5,461. **Player of Year:** Luke Varney.

DONCASTER ROVERS

Dave Penney's dismissal, the move from Belle Vue and victory in the Johnstone's Paint Trophy spelled an eventful season for the club, on and off the field. Penney became the first managerial casualty with just six league and Carling Cup matches gone. His last one in charge was, ironically, against Bournemouth, who provided his replacement when Sean O'Driscoll decided to switch to the Keepmoat Stadium. A near-capacity crowd of more than 14,000 saw the first game there – a 3-0 win over Huddersfield. Rovers were unable to follow it up by pressing home a promotion challenge, but went all the way to the Millennium Stadium, where a 59,000 crowd saw skipper Graeme Lee's extra-time goal give them a 3-2 victory over Bristol Rovers in the final of the knock-out competition for teams in the lower two divisions.

Blayney, A 8	Forte, J .... 31(10)	Hird, S .... –(5)
Budtz, J .... 6(1)	Gilbert, P 4	Horlock, K 2
Cadamarteri, D 6	Green, L .... –(2)	Lee, G .... 36(3)
Coppinger, J .... 34(5)	Green, P .... 36(5)	Lockwood, A .... 42(2)
Di Piedi, M .... 1(2)	Griffith, A 2	McCammon, M .... 14(8)
Dyer, B .... 9(6)	Guy, L .... 19(17)	McDaid, S .... 16(4)
Filan, J 3	Heffernan, P .... 23(6)	Nelthorpe,C .... 2(4)

O'Connor, J .... 39(1)
Price, J .... 19(12)
Roberts, G .... 28(2)
Roberts, S .... 15(6)
Smith, B 13
Stock, B .... 35(1)
Streete, T .... 2(4)
Sullivan, N 16
Thornton, S .... 15(15)
Wilson, M .... 17(5)
Worley, H 10
Wright, A 3

League goals (52): Heffernan 11, Price 6, Forte 5, Coppinger 4, Guy 4, Lee 4, Stock 3, Green, P 2, Lockwood 2, McCammon 2, Cadamarteri 1, Dyer 1, Horlock 1, Nelthorpe 1, O'Connor 1, Roberts, G 1, Streete 1, Wilson 1, Opponents 1.
F.A. Cup goals (4): Guy 1, Heffernan 1, McCammon 1, Stock 1. **Carling Cup goals (8):** Forte 3, McCammon 2, Coppinger 1, Lee 1, Stock 1. **Johnstone's Paint Trophy goals (18):** Heffernan 9, Price 4, Forte 1, Guy 1, Lee 1, Stock 1, Thornton 1.
Average home league attendance: 7,725. **Player of Year:** Paul Heffernan.

GILLINGHAM

Gillingham have made a habit in recent seasons of struggling away from home and this one was no exception. They leaked 53 goals on their travels, conceding four or more in five league games and once in the F.A. Cup against Bristol City. Manager Ronnie Jepson sympathised with travelling supporters, particularly those who made the seven-hour coach trip to Carlisle and saw a 5-0 defeat. That left their team two places away from the bottom four and there was further concern after defeat at Rotherham. But a 1-0 success against promotion-chasing Bristol City, followed by wins against Chesterfield and Port Vale, took them clear of trouble.

Bastians, F 5
Bentley, M 41
Brill, D 8
Chorley, B .... 24(3)
Clohessy, S .... 3(3)
Collin, F .... –(3)
Cox, I 33
Crofts, A 43
Cumbers, L .... –(1)
Easton, C .... 26(6)
Flinders, S 9
Flynn, M .... 44(1)
Howell, L .... –(1)
Jack, K 9
Jackman, D .... 30(1)
Jarvis, M .... 34(1)
Johnson, L .... 23(1)
Jupp, D .... 26(1)
Larrieu, R 14
McDonald, D .... 16(10)
Mulligan, G .... 37(1)
Ndumbu-Nsungu, G .... 14(18)
Pouton, A .... 3(5)
Pugh, A .... –(3)
Randolph, D 3
Royce, S 3
Sancho, B .... 19(7)
Savage, B .... 8(6)
Southall, N 15
Spiller, D .... 11(14)
Stone, C .... 2(1)
Tonge, D 3

League goals (56): Flynn 10, Crofts 8, Mulligan 7, Jarvis 6, McDonald 6, Bentley 4, Cox 3, Ndumbu-Nsungu 3, Bastians 1, Chorley 1, Easton 1, Jackman 1, Johnson 1, Pouton 1, Savage 1, Opponents 2.
F.A. Cup goals (7): Bentley 2, Flynn 2, Ndumbu-Nsungu 2, Mulligan 1. **Carling Cup goals (1):** Crofts 1. **Johnstone's Paint Trophy goals (1):** Mulligan 1.
Average home league attendance: 6,281. **Player of Year:** Andrew Crofts.

HUDDERSFIELD TOWN

Peter Jackson had not been far away from achieving promotion in the two previous seasons, so much was expected this time, not least when his board indicated that a place in the play-offs was the minimum requirement. But things never really came together for the manager and his team, whose inconsistency left them marooned in mid-table for much of the time. When a 5-1 defeat by Nottingham Forest ended any realistic chance of a top-six finish, Jackson's second spell in charge was brought to an end and Andy Ritchie came in, having himself been fired – by Barnsley – four months earlier. Defeat in the first round of all three cup competitions compounded a disappointing campaign.

Abbott, P .... 8(10)
Adams, D 23
Ahmed, A .... 4(5)
Akins, L .... –(2)
Beckett, L .... 32(9)
Berrett, J .... –(2)
Booth, A .... 29(5)
Brandon, C .... 17(6)
Clarke, N 16
Clarke, T .... 6(3)
Collins, M .... 39(4)
Glennon, M 46
Hand, J .... –(1)
Hardy, A .... 5(4)
Hayes, P 4

Holdsworth, A 35	Mirfin, D 38	Taylor, A .... 7(1)
Hudson, M .... 30(2)	Racchi, D .... –(3)	Taylor-Fletcher, G 39
McAliskey, J .... 3(5)	Schofield, D .... 25(10)	Worthington, J .... 27(1)
McCombe, J .... 5(2)	Sinclair, F 13	Young, M .... 16(13)
McIntosh, M .... 24(2)	Skarz, J .... 15(2)	

League goals (60): Beckett 15, Taylor-Fletcher 11, Booth 7, Abbott 5, Schofield 5, Collins 4, Hudson 3, Holdsworth 2, Worthington 2, Young 2, Brandon 1, Hayes 1, McAliskey 1, Mirfin 1.
F.A. Cup goals: None. **Carling Cup goals:** None. **Johnstone's Paint Trophy goals (1):** Booth 1.
Average home league attendance: 10,572. **Player of Year.** David Mirfin.

LEYTON ORIENT

Martin Ling guided promoted Orient to safety at the end of a tough season and was rewarded with a new two-year contract. They were bottom at the beginning of December after leaking three or more goals in virtually every other game, and still in a relegation place two months later when conceding nine in two defeats by Bournemouth and Brighton. The tide turned when Ryan Jarvis, on loan from Norwich, scored five times in back-to-back wins over Millwall (5-2) and Tranmere (3-1) to lift them clear. There was still plenty of work to do, but a 2-0 victory away to Bradford, another struggling team, proved decisive. Full-back Matt Lockwood's 11 goals included a hat-trick against Gillingham and six penalties.

Alexander, G .... 42(2)	Hooper, G .... 2(2)	Palmer, A 6
Barnard, D .... 9(10)	Ibehre, J .... 12(18)	Partridge, D 1
Chambers, A .... 36(2)	Jarvis, R 14	Saah, B .... 30(2)
Connor, P .... 5(13)	Keith, J .... 8(3)	Shields, S .... –(1)
Corden, W .... 36(6)	Lockwood, M 41	Simpson, M 15
Demetriou, J .... 2(13)	Mackie, J .... 33(2)	Steele, L .... 9(2)
Duncan, D .... –(3)	McMahon, D .... 3(5)	Tann, A .... 13(8)
Easton, C .... 29(1)	Miller, J .... 28(3)	Thelwell, A .... 20(2)
Echanomi, E .... –(3)	Morris, G 3	Till, P 4
Fortune, C 9	Mulryne, P .... 1(1)	Tudor, S .... 28(5)
Garner, G 43	Page, J .... –(1)	Walker, J .... 9(5)
Guttridge, L .... 15(2)		

League goals (61): Alexander 12, Lockwood 11, Jarvis 6, Chambers 4, Ibehre 4, Steele 4, Corden 3, Connor 2, Demetriou 2, Hooper 2, Miller 2, Tudor 2, Walker 2, Easton 1, Guttridge 1, Simpson 1, Tann 1, Thelwell 1.
F.A. Cup goals (4): Corden 2, Miller 1, Walker 1. **Carling Cup goals:** None. **Johnstone's Paint Trophy goals (1):** Duncan 1.
Average home league attendance: 4,848. **Player of Year:** Matt Lockwood.

MILLWALL

Willie Donachie resurrected the fortunes of a side staring at a second successive relegation after a lacklustre first half of the season. Donachie, appointed manager initially on a caretaker basis after the sacking of Nigel Spackman, took a while to get things right. When he did, Darren Byfield's goals sparked a run of five straight wins which enabled Millwall to move clear of trouble and eventually to a position in the top half of the table. Byfield scored a hat-trick in the 4-1 win over his former team Gillingham, two against Rotherham (4-0) and one against Brenford (4-1). This improvement also proved significant for team-mate Neil Harris, who replaced Teddy Sheringham as the club's all-time leading marksman with one against Rotherham that took his tally to 94.

Ardley, N .... 15(5)	Brighton, T .... 13(3)	Dunne, A .... 29(3)
Bakayogo, Z .... 3(2)	Byfield, D .... 28(3)	Elliott, M .... 40(2)
Brammer, D 17	Craig, T 30	Fuseini, A .... 5(2)
Braniff, K .... 5(2)	Day, C .... 4(1)	Grant, G .... 1(3)

Hackett, C 21(12)
Harris, N 21
Haynes, D 5
Hubertz, P 14(20)
Lee, C 4(1)
Mawene, S 4
May, B 7(6)
McInnes, D 7(6)
Morais, F 8(4)
Morris, J 1(3)
Phillips, M 8(4)
Pidgeley, L 42
Robinson, P 37(1)
Ross, M 14(1)
Senda, D 34(2)
Shaw, R 41
Smith, R 5(1)
Trotter, L 1(1)
Whitbread, Z 13(1)
Williams, M 19(10)
Zebroski, C 10(15)

League goals (59): Byfield 16, Hubertz 9, Dunne 6, Harris 5, Hackett 3, Robinson 3, Williams 3, Zebroski 3, Haynes 2, May 2, Brammer 1, Braniff 1, Brighton 1, Craig 1, McInnes 1, Morais 1, Opponents 1.
F.A. Cup goals (3): Dunne 1, May 1, Opponents 1. **Carling Cup goals (2):** Braniff 1, Hubertz 1. **Johnstone's Paint Trophy goals (3):** Hackett 1, May 1, Robinson 1.
Average home league attendance: 9,233. **Player of Year:** Richard Shaw.

NORTHAMPTON TOWN

Promoted Northampton consolidated satisfactorily amid a change of manager midway through the season. John Gorman stepped down, citing 'personal' reasons, five days before Christmas and was replaced by Stuart Gray, who once had a short spell in charge of Southampton. Gray gave the team a sharper attacking edge, which led to their strike rate almost doubling in the second part of campaign. It left them comfortably placed just below mid-table, helped by a particularly notable victory over Easter when champions-elect Scunthorpe had a 19-match unbeaten run ended by a stoppage-time goal from Bradley Johnson at Sixfields.

Aiston, S 14(7)
Bojic, P 19(7)
Bunn, M 42
Burnell, J 24
Chambers, L 29
Cole, M 6(2)
Cox, S 6(2)
Crowe, J 43
Deuchar, K 14(3)
Doig, C 39
Dolman, L 1
Dyche, S 20(1)
Gilligan, R 14(9)
Harper, L 4
Holt, A 33(2)
Hughes, M 17
Hunt, D 20(9)
Jess, E 22(4)
Johnson, Bradley 21(6)
Johnson, Brett 2(2)
Kirk, A 29(15)
Laird, M 2(4)
May, D 2(1)
McGleish, S 24(1)
Pearce, A 15
Quinn, J 5(13)
Robertson, J 9(8)
Taylor, I 26(7)
Watt, J 2(8)
Wright, N 2(2)

League goals (48): McGleish 12, Kirk 7, Johnson, Bradley 5, Cox 3, Crowe 3, Deuchar 3, Robertson 3, Holt 2, Hughes 2, Burnell 1, Chambers 1, Cole 1, Jess 1, Pearce 1, Quinn 1, Taylor 1, Opponents 1.
F.A. Cup goals (3): Burnell 1, McGleish 1, Opponents 1. **Carling Cup goals (2):** Kirk 1, Watt 1. **Johnstone's Paint Trophy goals:** None.
Average home league attendance: 5,573. **Player of Year:** Mark Bunn.

NOTTINGHAM FOREST

When Forest led the division by six points approaching the midway point of the season, all the indications were of a long-overdue change in fortunes for this once successful club. In the event, it was a case of flattering to deceive. Weaknesses exposed by Scunthorpe's 4-0 win at the City Ground were evident again in a 5-0 defeat by another promotion-minded team, Oldham. A growing inconsistency left Colin Calderwood's team playing catch-up and ultimately having to rely on the play-offs. Again, hopes were high after penalties by Kris Commons and James Perch set up a 2-0 win at Yeovil in the semi-final first leg. Again they were dashed, this time as Forest surrendered a 3-1 aggregate lead in the last ten minutes of the return and lost 5-4 in extra-time.

Agogo, J 20(9)
Bastians, F –(2)
Bennett, J 24(6)
Breckin, I 46
Chambers, L 10(4)
Clingan, S 25(3)
Commons, K 28(4)
Cullip, D 19(1)
Curtis, J 38(3)
Dobie, S 2(17)
Harris, N 11(8)
Henry, J –(1)
Holt, Gary 30(9)
Holt, Grant 34(12)
Hughes, R –(2)

Lester, J .... 24(11)	Perch, J .... 43(3)	Thompson, J .... 6(8)
McGugan, L .... 11(2)	Prutton, D .... 11(1)	Tyson, N .... 12(12)
Moloney, B .... –(1)	Smith, P 45	Weir-Daley, S .... –(1)
Morgan, W .... 31(7)	Southall, N .... 26(1)	Wright, A 9
Pedersen, R 1		

Play-offs – appearances: Breckin 2, Chambers 2, Commons 2, Curtis 2, Dobie 2, Holt, Gary 2, Lester 2, McGugan 2, Perch 2, Smith 2, Wright 2, Morgan –(2), Bennett –(1), Holt, Grant –(1), Prutton –(1), Weir-Daley –(1)
League goals (65): Holt, Grant 14, Commons 9, Agogo 7, Tyson 7, Lester 6, Perch 5, Southall 5, Breckin 3, Bennett 2, McGugan 2, Prutton 2, Holt, Gary 1, Harris 1, Opponents 1. **Play-offs-goals (4):** Commons 1, Dobie 1, Holt, Gary 1, Perch 1.
F.A. Cup goals (10): Agogo 3, Commons 3, Tyson 2, Holt, Grant 1, Southall 1. **Carling Cup goals:** None. **Johnstone's Paint Trophy goals (6):** Holt, Grant 3, Lester 1, Morgan 1, Southall 1.
Average home league attendance: 20,617. **Player of Year:** Grant Holt.

OLDHAM ATHLETIC

John Sheridan's first season in charge was on course to deliver something special when his blend of youthful exuberance and seasoned campaigners gradually built up a head of steam after overcoming a poor start. With Chris Porter in prolific form, Oldham went into the New Year on a high having scored 14 goals in four games, including a 5-0 victory over Nottingham Forest. They went top after beating another promotion-minded team, Swansea, but it proved a brief stay as form disappeared and four successive defeats followed. After that, Oldham did enough to hold on to a top six place, but were second best to Blackpool in the play-offs losing both semi-final legs. Porter became the club's first player to score 20 league goals for 29 years, finishing with 23 in all competitions.

Aljofree, H 5	Howarth, C .... 2(1)	Smith, T .... –(1)
Blayney, A .... 2(1)	Knight, D 2	Stam, S .... 19(3)
Charlton, S 34	Liddell, A .... 44(2)	Swailes, C 4
Clarke, L 5	Lomax, K .... 3(6)	Taylor, C .... 40(4)
Cywka, T .... –(4)	McDonald, G .... 39(4)	Tierney, M .... 1(4)
Eardley, N 36	Molango, M .... 3(2)	Trotman, N .... –(1)
Edwards, P .... 10(16)	Pearson, M .... –(1)	Turner, B 1
Glombard, L .... 3(5)	Pogliacomi, L 40	Warne, P .... 42(4)
Grabban, L .... 1(8)	Porter, C .... 34(1)	Wellens, R 42
Gregan, S 27	Rocastle, C .... 17(18)	Wolfenden, M .... –(6)
Haining, W 44	Roque, M .... 1(3)	Wood, N .... 3(2)
Hall, C .... 2(17)	Smalley, D .... –(2)	

Play-offs – appearances: Gregan 2, Haining 2, Liddell 2, Porter 2, Taylor 2, Warne 2, Wellens 2, Blayney 1(1), Edwards 1(1), McDonald 1(1), Charlton 1, Eardley 1, Lomax 1, Pogliacomi 1, Rocastle 1, Glombard –(2), Wolfenden –(1),
League goals (69): Porter 21, Liddell 10, Warne 9, McDonald 7, Taylor 4, Wellens 4, Clarke 3, Eardley 2, Haining 2, Rocastle 2, Charlton 1, Glombard 1, Hall 1, Molango 1, Stam 1. **Play-offs – goals(2):** Liddell 1, Wolfenden 1.
F.A. Cup goals (8): Hall 3, Warne 2, Gregan 1, Porter 1, Trotman 1. **Carling Cup goals (1):** Rocastle 1. **Johnstone's Paint Trophy goals:** None.
Average home league attendance: 6,334. **Player of Year:** Paul Warne.

PORT VALE

Prolific scoring by Leon Constantine and a four-goal match haul by Akpo Sodje were the highlights of Vale's season. Only Scunthorpe's Billy Sharp, the League One Player of the Year, bettered Constantine's tally of 26 in all competitions. Sodje had his big moment against Rotherham, netting three times in 19 first half minutes and adding another after the break in a 5-1 victory at Millmoor. That gave his side an outside chance of closing the gap on the top six, but home defeats by Tranmere and Carlisle meant they had to be satisfied with a mid-table finish, one better than the previous season.

Abbey, G .... 18(6)	Humphreys, R .... 5(2)	Smith, J .... 24(3)
Anyon, J .... 21(1)	Husbands, M .... 3(20)	Smith, C .... –(1)
Cardle, J .... 1(6)	Kamara, M .... 14(4)	Sodje, A .... 38(5)
Constantine, L .... 41(1)	Lowndes, N .... 1(11)	Sonner, D 33
Fortune, C .... 11(2)	McGregor, M .... 26(6)	Talbot, J .... 18(4)
Gardner, R .... 12(4)	Miles, C .... 23(6)	Walker, R .... 12(4)
Goodlad, M 25	Moore, S .... 8(4)	Walsh, M .... 16(2)
Harsley, P .... 29(3)	Pilkington, G 46	Weston, R 15
Hulbert, R .... 16(4)	Rodgers, L .... 6(2)	Whitaker, D .... 44(1)

League goals (64): Constantine 22, Sodje 14, Pilkington 6, Whitaker 6, Smith, J 3, Rodgers 3, Gardner 2, Abbey 1, Harsley 1, Hulbert 1, Husbands 1, Kamara 1, Moore 1, Sonner 1, Opponents 1.
F.A. Cup goals (2): Sodje 1, Whitaker 1. **Carling Cup goals (6):** Constantine 2, Smith, J 1, Sodje 1, Walker 1, Whitaker 1. **Johnstone's Paint Trophy goals (2):** Constantine 2.
Average home league attendance: 4,724. **Player of Year:** Akpo Sodje.

ROTHERHAM UNITED

Will Hoskins scored freely as Rotherham attacked a ten-point deduction for going into administration with plenty of gusto. Alan Knill's team gathered 31 points from 20 matches to climb out of the bottom four, but were unable to maintain that momentum, and slipped back over the Christmas and New Year programme. Their chances of making up ground for a second time were then undermined when Hoskins and midfielder Lee Williamson joined Watford during the January transfer window. Club finances received a boost, but results continued to suffer, costing Knill his job after this lean run extended to 14 games without a win. Caretaker Mark Robins enjoyed a measure of success, enough for a permanent appointment as manager but not enough to stave off the drop.

Bopp, E .... 24(5)	Hurst, P .... 11(1)	Robertson, G .... 16(2)
Brogan, S .... 19(4)	Jarvis, R 10	Sharps, I 38
Cochrane, J .... 29(2)	Keane, M .... 16(6)	Streete, T 4
Cutler, N 41	Kerr, N .... 1(2)	Taylor, R .... 1(9)
Diagouraga, T .... 4(3)	King, L .... 4(2)	Williamson, L .... 17(2)
Duncum, S .... –(2)	Mills, P .... 27(4)	Wilson, C .... 5(1)
Facey, D .... 37(3)	Montgomery, G .... 5(1)	Wiseman, S .... 9(9)
Fleming, C 17	Murdock, C 4	Woods, M .... 31(5)
Henderson, I 18	Newsham, M .... 3(13)	Worrell, D .... 38(3)
Hibbert, D .... 12(9)	O'Grady, C .... 11(2)	Yates, J .... 2(1)
Hoskins, W .... 22(2)	Partridge, R .... 30(3)	

League goals (58): Hoskins 15, Facey 10, Bopp 5, Williamson 5, O'Grady 4, Woods 4, Newsham 3, Partridge 3, Hibbert 2, Sharps 2, Cochrane 1, Henderson 1, Mills 1, Wiseman 1, Opponents 1.
F.A. Cup goals: None. **Carling Cup goals (5):** Hoskins 1, Keane 1, Partridge 1, Sharps 1, Williamson 1. **Johnstone's Paint Trophy goals (1):** Facey 1.
Average home league attendance: 4,762. **Player of Year:** Martin Woods.

SCUNTHORPE UNITED

Scunthorpe upset all the odds in a memorable, title-winning season and will be playing Championship football for the first time since 1963-64. Three years after escaping relegation to the Conference, the 66-1 outsiders scattered all their bigger rivals – and a host of club records – with a squad short on star names but brimming with confidence and conviction. They lost long-serving manager Brian Laws to Sheffield Wednesday in early November and key player Andy Keogh to Wolves without breaking stride. Club physio Nigel Adkins succeeded Laws to supervise a run of seven successive victories which saw off the chasing pack, while on-loan Jermaine Beckford proved an ideal replacement for Keogh alongside the prolific Billy Sharp. No-one in the four divisions matched the 30 league goals accumulated by Sharp, League One's Player of the Year. Scunthorpe also boasted the meanest defence and the division's best goalkeeper in Joe Murphy.

Baraclough, I	25(8)	Hinds, R	37(7)	Murphy, J	45
Beckford, J	17(1)	Hurst, K	11(2)	Ridley, L	15(3)
Butler, A	4(7)	Keogh, A	25(3)	Sharp, B	45
Byrne, C	18(6)	Lillis, J	1	Sparrow, M	27(2)
Crosby, A	36(3)	MacKenzie, N	10(14)	Talbot, D	2(1)
Ferretti, A	–(4)	McBreen, D	1(6)	Taylor, C	42(3)
Foster, S	44	Morris, I	18(10)	Torpey, S	5(9)
Foy, R	1(4)	Mulligan, D	20(4)	Williams, M	32(3)
Goodwin, J	25(6)				

League goals (73): Sharp 30, Beckford 8, Keogh 7, Crosby 5, Sparrow 4, Morris 3, Taylor 3, Hinds 2, MacKenzie 2, Baraclough 1, Goodwin 1, Mulligan 1, Talbot 1, Torpey 1, Opponents 4.

F.A. Cup goals (2): Baraclough 1, Sharp 1. **Carling Cup goals (5):** Baraclough 1, Mulligan 1, Paul, S 1, Sharp 1, Torpey 1. **Johnstone's Paint Trophy goals (2):** Foy 1, Goodwin 1. **Average home league attendance:** 5,668. **Player of Year:** Steve Foster.

SWANSEA CITY

Swansea's hopes of bringing Championship football to the Liberty Stadium again ended in disappointment. Twelve months earlier, Barnsley had denied them on penalties in the Play-off Final. This time, they missed out completely after a bizarre 6-3 home defeat by Blackpool on the final day of the regular season, Oldham confirming sixth place by beating Chesterfield. Manager Kenny Jackett had been confident of going one better this time. But he grew increasingly disillusioned with his team's inconsistency, along with criticism from supporters and the media, and walked away from the job in mid-February after a home defeat by Oldham. His replacement was former Swansea midfielder Roberto Martinez.

Abbott, P	9(9)	Gueret, W	42	Oakes, A	4(1)
Akinfenwa, A	12(13)	Iriekpen, E	31(1)	Painter, M	22(1)
Allen, J	–(1)	Jones, C	–(7)	Pratley, D	25(3)
Amankwaah, K	23(6)	Knight, L	10(1)	Robinson, A	33(6)
Austin, K	26(4)	Lawrence, D	37(2)	Tate, A	36(2)
Britton, L	39(2)	MacDonald, S	3(5)	Trundle, L	31(3)
Butler, T	17(13)	McLeod, K	2(2)	Tudur-Jones, O	3
Craney, I	24(3)	Meslien, S	–(1)	Watt, S	–(1)
Duffy, D	5(3)	Monk, G	2	Way, D	4(5)
Duffy, R	8(3)	O'Leary, K	19(4)	Williams, T	17(12)
Fallon, R	22(2)				

League goals (69): Trundle 19, Fallon 8, Knight 7, Robinson 7, Akinfenwa 5, Duffy, D 5, Lawrence 5, Iriekpen 4, Britton 2, Abbott 1, Butler 1, O'Leary 1, Pratley 1, Tate 1, Opponents 2.

F.A. Cup goals (9): Britton 3, Butler 2, Akinfenwa 1, Iriekpen 1, Robinson 1, Trundle 1. **Carling Cup goals (2):** Pratley 1, Opponents 1. **Johnstone's Paint Trophy goals (1):** Tudur-Jones 1.

Average home league attendance: 12,720. **Player of Year:** Leon Britton.

TRANMERE ROVERS

New manager Ronnie Moore entertained high hopes of marking his return to the club where he made nearly 300 appearances as a player with a promotion challenge. Instead, he had to be satisfied with an improvement of nine places on the previous season's finish of 18th after his team failed to sustain the form that took them into the top four approaching the midway point of the campaign. Only once after that were Tranmere able to register back-to-back victories and slipped back in the pack. The season, however, ended on a high for 18-year-old prospect Craig Curran, who scored all three goals in the 3-1 win over Brentford, having previously netted on his home debut.

Achterberg, J .... 3(1)	Hinchcliffe, B .... 1(1)	Shuker, C .... 45(1)
Curran, C .... 2(2)	Jennings, S .... –(2)	Stockdale, R .... 35(1)
Davies, S .... 16(12)	McAteer, J .... 10(8)	Taylor, G .... 36(1)
Ellison, K .... 26(8)	McCready, C 42	Thompson, J 12
Goodison, I 40	McLaren, P 42	Tremarco, C .... 14(9)
Greenacre, C .... 39(5)	Mullin, J .... 39(1)	Ward, G .... 36(2)
Harrison, D .... 7(5)	Sherriff, S .... 40(3)	Zola, C .... 15(14)
Hart, J 6		

League goals (58): Greenacre 17, Taylor 7, Shuker 6, Mullin 5, Zola 5, Curran 4, Ellison 4, Sherriff 3, Davies 1, Harrison 1, McCready 1, McLaren 1, Ward 1, Opponents 1.
F.A. Cup goals (5): Greenacre 2, Taylor 2, Sherriff 1. **Carling Cup goals (1):** Sherriff 1. **Johnstone's Paint Trophy goals (2):** Jennings 1, Shuker 1.
Average home league attendance: 6,930. **Player of Year:** Ian Goodison.

YEOVIL TOWN

A 2-0 defeat by Blackpool in the Play-off Final did nothing to disguise a solid season's work by Yeovil. Russell Slade kept them in contention for a top six place all season and was rewarded with League One's Manager of the Year title from the League Managers' Association for making the most of the resources at his disposal. His team reached Wembley with victory against-the-odds over Nottingham Forest in the semi-finals. Forest looked to have the tie all sewn up after winning 2-0 at Huish Park and leading 3-1 on aggregate ten minutes from the end of the second leg. Instead, an own goal followed by Marcus Stewart's strike took it into extra-time and a 5-4 success was clinched by Arron Davies with his second of the game and Lee Morris.

Alcock, C .... –(1)	Harrold, M .... 2(3)	Morris, L .... 23(10)
Barry, A .... 13(11)	James, K .... 2(4)	Poole, D .... 1(3)
Best, L .... 14(1)	Jones, N 42	Rooney, A .... 1(2)
Brittain, M .... 12(3)	Kalala, J .... 35(3)	Rose, M .... 7(2)
Clarke, T 1	Knights, D .... –(4)	Skiverton, T 39
Cohen, C 44	Law, N .... 5(1)	Stewart, M 31
Cooper, K 4	Lindegaard, A .... 12(2)	Sweeney, P .... 5(3)
Cranie, M .... 11(1)	Lynch, M 17	Terry, P 20
Davies, A .... 34(5)	Maher, S .... –(1)	Tonkin, A .... 1(4)
Forbes, T 46	McCallum, G .... –(1)	Webb, D .... –(4)
Gray, W .... 24(22)	Mildenhall, S 46	Welsh, I .... 4(14)
Guyett, S .... 10(6)		

Play-offs – appearances: Barry 3, Cohen 3, Davies 3, Forbes 3, Gray 3, Guyett 3, Jones 3, Lindegaard 3, Mildenhall 3, Morris 3, Stewart 3, Kalala –(2), Knights –(1), Lynch –(1)
League goals (55): Gray 11, Best 10, Stewart 8, Cohen 6, Davies 6, Morris 5, Skiverton 2, Terry 2, Jones 1, Kalala 1, Welsh 1, Opponents 2. **Play-offs – goals (5):** Davies 2, Morris 1, Stewart 1, Opponents 1.
F.A. Cup goals (1): Cohen 1. **Carling Cup goals (2):** Gray 1, Harrold 1. **Johnstone's Paint Trophy goals (1):** Barry 1.
Average home league attendance: 5,764. **Player of Year:** Steve Mildenhall.

COCA-COLA LEAGUE TWO

ACCRINGTON STANLEY

Manager John Coleman dreamt that the threat of an immediate return to the Conference would be lifted by a 4-2 win over Macclesfield in the penultimate match of the season – and he wasn't far off the mark. Two goals by Andy Proctor helped secure a 3-2 success, which left Paul Ince's side sweating on relegation instead. It was the most important of 10 home victories in which a total of 42 goals was beaten only by Peterborough in the division. But although Accrington usually gave good value for money, it was hard going at the turnstiles for a club back in the Football League 44 years after resigning for financial reasons. An average crowd of just over 2,200 was much less than they had hoped for.

Almeida, M	5	Elliot, R	7	Mullin, P	46
Antwi, G	9	Fleetwood, S	3	N'da, J	–(3)
Bains, R	2(1)	Grant, R	1	Proctor, A	38(5)
Boco, R	28(4)	Grant, T	6	Richardson, L	34(4)
Brown, D	8(9)	Harris, J	26(6)	Roberts, G	14
Byron, J	–(1)	Jacobson, J	6	Rogers, A	6
Cavanagh, P	26	Kazimierczak, P	7(1)	Todd, A	44(2)
Craney, I	18	Mangan, A	6(28)	Ventre, D	4(2)
Doherty, S	14(6)	Mannix, D	1	Welch, M	25(6)
Dugdale, A	2	Martin, D	10	Whalley, S	13(7)
Dunbavin, I	22(1)	McGivern, L	3(4)	Williams, R	43
Edwards, P	29(4)	McGrail, C	–(2)		

League goals (70): Mullin 14, Todd 10, Roberts 8, Brown 5, Craney 5, Cavanagh 4, Mangan 4, Boco 3, Proctor 3, Welch 3,Williams 3, Harris 2, Whalley 2, Doherty 1, Edwards 1, Jacobson 1, McGivern 1.
F.A. Cup goals: None. **Carling Cup goals (1):** Mullin 1. **Johnstone's Paint Trophy goals (4):** Craney 1, Mullin 1, Todd 1, Williams 1.
Average home league attendance: 2,260. **Player of Year:** Andy Todd.

BARNET

A climb of four places to 14th represented some progress for Barnet after a dodgy start to the season which bought three straight defeats. They were up and running after seeing off Hereford 3-0 and did enough at Underhill to stay clear of trouble. Tresor Kandol scored a hat-trick against Rochdale before joining Leeds and there were wins over promotion-minded Hartlepool, Swindon and Stockport in the second half of the campaign. Kandol had also made an impact with both goals in a Carling Cup upset at Cardiff, while Barnet also overcame Colchester in the F.A. Cup on the way to the fourth round when their run was ended by Plymouth.

Allen, O	7(7)	Grazioli, G	7(10)	Lewis, S	2(2)
Bailey, N	43(1)	Gross, A	27	Nicolau, N	17(5)
Birchall, A	22(1)	Harrison, L	28	Norville, J	1(2)
Burch, R	6	Hatch, L	18(13)	Puncheon, J	34(3)
Charles, A	13(4)	Hendon, I	25(1)	Sinclair, D	42
Cogan, B	33(6)	Hessenthaler, A	19(5)	Vieira, M	8(13)
Devera, J	23(3)	Ioannou, N	1(1)	Warhurst, P	11(8)
Flitney, R	12(3)	Kandol, T	14(2)	Yakubu, I	28(1)
Graham, R	22(12)	King, S	43		

League goals (55): Birchall 6, Kandol 6, Sinclair 6, Bailey 5, Puncheon 5, Allen 4, Hendon 4, Cogan 3, Hatch 3, Vieira 3, Graham 2, Grazioli 2, King 2, Gross 1, Hessenthaler 1, Nicolau 1, Yakubu 1.
F.A. Cup goals (9): Kandol 2, Sinclair 2, Birchall 1, Hendon 1, Puncheon 1, Vieira 1, Yakubu 1. **Carling Cup goals (3):** Kandol 2, Vieira 1. **Johnstone's Paint Trophy goals (3):** Kandol 3.
Average home league attendance: 2,279. **Player of Year:** Simon King.

BOSTON UNITED

Five seasons of league football ended for Boston amid serious financial problems. Players went weeks without being paid, they travelled to some away games in their own cars and for one match there were only three substitutes. Not surprisingly, they were always struggling. A 4-1 win over relegation rivals Macclesfield over Easter offered some hope, but the drop was confirmed by a 3-1 defeat at Wrexham on the last day of the season. When it became clear in that match that there would be no escape, officials put the club into administration in an attempt to ensure that accompanying ten-point deduction applied immediately and not from the start of the 2007-08 Conference season. In fact, they suffered a double demotion to the Conference South, and lost manager Steve Evans as well.

Albrighton, M 12	Galbraith, D .... 21(9)	Nunn, B .... –(1)
Benjamin, T .... 2(1)	Greaves, M .... 38(1)	Richards, J 3
Broughton, D 25	Green, F .... 35(4)	Ryan, R .... 9(4)
Canoville, L .... 15(1)	Holland, C .... 12(2)	Rowntree, A .... –(3)
Clarke, J .... 30(6)	Jarrett, A 5	Rowson, D 6
Cooksey, E .... 11(5)	Kennedy, J 13	Rusk, S .... 2(1)
Cotton, D .... –(2)	Joachim, J 3	Ryan, T 23
Cryan, C 15	Joynes, N .... 9(1)	Stevens, J .... 11(1)
Davidson, B .... 3(6)	Marriott, A 46	Tait, P .... 9(5)
Elding, A .... 18(1)	Maylett, B .... 4(17)	Talbot, S .... 16(2)
Ellender, P .... 40(2)	Miller, I 12	Thomas, B 11
Farrell, D .... 23(17)	N'Guessan, D .... 13(10)	Vaughan, S .... 6(1)
Forbes, N .... –(1)	Nicholson, S .... 5(1)	

League goals (51): Broughton 8, Elding 5, N'Guessan 5, Green 4, Ryan 4, Greaves 3, Joachim 3, Clarke 2, Galbraith 2, Jarrett 2, Stevens 2, Tait 2, Thomas 2, Ellender 1, Farrell 1, Kennedy 1, Joynes 1, Talbot 1, Opponents 2.
F.A. Cup goals: None. **Carling Cup goals:** None. **Johnstone's Paint Trophy goals:** None.
Average home league attendance: 2,151. **Player of Year:** Mark Greaves.

BRISTOL ROVERS

A season to remember for Rovers ended with victory at Wembley in front of a record crowd of more than 61,000 for the League Two Play-off Final. Two goals by Richard Walker, taking his tally for the season to 23, delivered a 3-1 victory over Shrewsbury, their promotion following hard on the heels of Bristol City's move up from League One. Walker also scored in each of the semi-final legs against Lincoln – after Rickie Lambert had secured a place in the play-offs with an 86th minute winner at Hartlepool on the final day of the regular season. Lambert's strike also proved significant in the return leg of the Johnstone's Paint Trophy semi-final against their neighbours. His team went on to retrieve a two-goal deficit, inflicted in the first five minutes at the final at the Millennium Stadium, before going down 3-2 to Doncaster in extra-time.

Agogo, J 3	Haldane, L .... 32(13)	Nicholson, S .... 12(10)
Anthony, B .... 20(3)	Hinton, C .... 28(2)	Oji, S 5
Campbell, S .... 35(6)	Hunt, J .... 12(2)	Phillips, S 44
Carruthers, C .... 33(5)	Igoe, S .... 35(5)	Rigg, S .... 1(17)
Disley, C .... 42(3)	Jacobson, J .... 9(2)	Sandell, A .... 20(16)
Easter, J .... 1(2)	Lambert, R .... 28(8)	Shearer, S 2
Elliott, S 39	Lescott, A .... 30(4)	Walker, J .... 3(1)
Green, R .... 29(4)	Lines, C .... 4(3)	Walker, R .... 39(7)

Play-offs – appearances: Anthony 3, Campbell 3, Carruthers 3, Disley 3, Elliott 3, Green 3, Haldane 3, Lambert 3, Phillips 3, Walker, R 3, Jacobson 2, Igoe 1(2), Rigg –(3), Lines –(1).
League goals (49): Walker, R 12, Lambert 8, Haldane 6, Nicholson 6, Elliott 5, Disley 4, Sandell 3, Campbell 1, Hunt 1, Igoe 1, Rigg 1, Walker, J 1. **Play-offs – goals (10):** Walker, R 4, Igoe 2, Campbell 1, Disley 1, Lambert 1, Rigg 1.
F.A. Cup goals (6): Walker, R 4, Anthony 1, Disley 1. **Carling Cup goals (1):** Walker, R 1.
Johnstone's Paint Trophy goals (8): Igoe 2, Walker, R 2, Anthony 1, Easter 1, Lambert 1, Nicholson 1.
Average home league attendance: 5,480. **Player of Year:** Steve Phillips.

BURY

Four successive defeats at the start of the season suggested another difficult campaign for Bury and it proved the case in more ways than one. They eventually finished four points clear of trouble after struggling throughout on their own ground, where only four of the 23 matches produced victories. Fortunately there were twice as many on their travels, including a crucial 1-0 success, achieved by a goal from Tom Youngs, against champions-to-be Walsall when the pressure was at its peak. Previously the club had been expelled from the F.A. Cup for fielding an ineligible player, on-loan Hartlepool midfielder Stephen Turnbull, in the 3-1 win over Chester in a second round replay. Their appeal against the decision was turned down. So too was manager Chris Casper's offer to the board to resign.

Adams, N .... 11(8)
Baker, R .... 34(5)
Barry-Murphy, B .... 8(6)
Bedeau, A .... 2(1)
Bishop, A 43
Blinkhorn, M .... 1(9)
Brass, C .... 20(2)
Buchanan, D .... 36(5)
Challinor, D 43
Edge, L 1
Fettis, A 9
Fitzgerald, J .... 20(3)
Flitcroft, D .... 3(1)
Goodfellow, M .... 2(2)
Grundy, A .... –(1)
Hurst, G .... 32(3)
Jones, L 2
Kempson, D 12
Kennedy, J 12
Kennedy, T .... 35(2)
Mattis, D 22
Mocquet, W 9
Parrish, A .... 6(3)
Pittman, J .... 5(4)
Pugh, M .... 27(8)
Rouse, D .... –(2)
Schmeichel, K 14
Scott, P .... 45(1)
Speight, J .... –(12)
Stephens, D .... 2(1)
Taylor, D .... 1(3)
Turnbull, S .... 4(1)
Warrington, A 20
Woodthorpe, C .... 12(4)
Worrall, D .... –(1)
Wroe, N .... 4(1)
Youngs, T .... 9(10)

League goals (46): Bishop 14, Hurst 12, Baker 5, Youngs 4, Fitzgerald 3, Pugh 3, Scott 2, Adams 1, Mattis 1, Pittman 1.

F.A. Cup goals (11): Bishop 5, Mattis 3, Baker 1, Hurst 1, Pugh 1. **Carling Cup goals (2):** Bishop 1, Fitzgerald 1. **Johnstone's Paint Trophy goals:** None.

Average home league attendance: 2,588. **Player of Year:** Paul Scott.

CHESTER CITY

Bobby Williamson, formerly in charge at Plymouth, Kilmarnock and Hibernian was named Chester's seventh manager in eight years after Mark Wright parted company with the club for the second time. Wright, whose first departure was in August 2004, left following the penultimate game of the season, a 1-1 draw against his former side Peterborough, which extended Chester's indifferent form in the second half of the season. Youth team manager Simon Davies took charge for the final fixture at Lincoln, where a 2-0 defeat meant they had won only one of the last 14 and slipped from a healthy top-half position to 18th.

Allen, G .... 2(1)
Artell, D .... 42(1)
Bennett, D .... 27(5)
Blundell, G .... 21(6)
Bolland, P .... 23(3)
Broughton, D .... 9(5)
Brownlie, R .... 3(1)
Cronin, G .... 1(3)
Danby, J 46
Hand, J 43
Hessey, S .... 22(4)
Holroyd, C .... 7(15)
Kearney, A .... 4(2)
Kelly, S .... –(2)
Linwood, P .... 33(4)
Marples, S .... 24(6)
Martinez, R 31
Maylett, B .... 3(2)
McSporran, J .... –(1)
Meechan, A .... 2(6)
Ravenhill, R .... 1(2)
Rutherford, P .... 6(3)
Sandwith, K .... 27(5)
Semple, R .... –(3)
Steele, L .... 11(9)
Vaughan, J .... 5(1)
Vaughan, S 20
Walters, J .... 24(2)
Westwood, A 21
Wilson, L .... 34(7)
Yeo, S .... 14(1)

League goals (40): Walters 9, Blundell 6, Yeo 4, Martinez 3, Westwood 3, Broughton 2, Hand 2, Sandwith 2, Artell 1, Bennett 1, Bolland 1, Linwood 1, Maylett 1, Steele 1, Wilson 1, Opponents 2.

F.A. Cup goals (7): Steele 2, Wilson 2, Blundell 1, Hand 1, Walters 1. **Carling Cup goals:** None. **Johnstone's Paint Trophy goals (7):** Blundell 2, Wilson 2, Bolland 1, Hand 1, Linwood 1.

Average home league attendance: 2,473. **Player of Year:**

DARLINGTON

Dave Penney described it as a 'transitional' time for a team he took over at the end of October, two months after becoming the first managerial casualty of the season (at Doncaster). Barry Conlon's hat-trick against Macclesfield had given Darlington a flying start under David Hodgson. But one of the favourites for promotion were soon showing inconsistent form, which contributed to Hodgson's dismissal days after the club launched an inquiry into his conduct. Penney enjoyed a productive start, with six successive victories in the league and cup competitions before the honeymoon ended and eight successive defeats followed. A 5-0 home defeat by Stockport on the final day of the season pushed them down to 11th.

Albrighton, M 3
Armstrong, A 16(13)
Blundell, G 14(1)
Burgess, K –(1)
Clarke, M 2
Close, B 26(1)
Collins, P 28(3)
Conlon, B 12(7)
Cummins, M 38(1)
Duke, D 4(9)
Giallanza, G 12(2)
Griffith, A 2(2)
Hardman, L –(1)
Holloway, D 14(7)
Horwood, E 20
Hutchinson, J 13
James, C 22(1)
Joachim, J 26(10)
Johnson, S 8(16)
Jones, L 9
Keltie, C 25(2)
Logan, C –(9)
Martis, S 2
McLeod, M 2
Miller, I 7
Ngoma, K 15(3)
Phillips, M 7(1)
Prendergast, R 5(3)
Ravenhill, R 13(2)
Reay, S 1(2)
Rowson, D 20(4)
Russell, S 31
Ryan, T 4(1)
Smith, M 30(4)
Stockdale, D 6
Vaisanen, V 5
Wainwright, N 30(11)
Wheater, D 15
Wiseman, S 10
Wright, J –(1)
Wright, T 9(4)

League goals (52): Joachim 7, Conlon 6, Smith 6, Wainwright 5, Cummins 4, Wright, T 4, Blundell 3, Giallanza 3, Johnson 2, Rowson 2, Wheater 2, Armstrong 1, Holloway 1, Keltie 1, Miller 1, Ngoma 1, Ravenhill 1, Ryan 1, Opponents 1.
F.A. Cup goals (5): Smith 3, Collins 1, Ngoma 1. **Carling Cup goals (4):** Joachim 3, Johnson 1. **Johnstone's Paint Trophy goals (2):** Giallanza 1, Smith 1.
Average home league attendance: 3,813. **Player of Year:** Neil Wainwright.

GRIMSBY TOWN

Alan Buckley returned for a third spell as manager to lead Grimsby away from trouble and into a position of some comfort just below mid-table. Buckley had been in charge at Blundell Park between 1988-94 and again from 1997-2000. This time, following the departure of Graham Rodger in early November, he had an immediate impact on results, but then a run of seven successive defeats left his team second from bottom. The tide turned a week after a 4-1 defeat at Torquay. They swept aside Lincolnshire rivals Boston 6-0 away from home, with Peter Bore scoring three times, overcame Bristol Rovers 4-3 and also won five of the next six matches. Later, there was a second hat-trick, from Danny North as Barnet were beaten 5-0.

Barnes, P 46
Beagrie, P 6(3)
Bennett, R 3(2)
Bloomer, M 5(4)
Bolland, P 37(2)
Bore, P 21(11)
Boshell, D 23(6)
Butler, A 4
Croft, G 26(2)
Fenton, N 37(1)
Futcher, B 3(1)
Grand, S 4(3)
Harkins, G 11(6)
Hegarty, N 9(6)
Hunt, J 15
James, K 2
Jones, G 29(10)
Lawson, J –(1)
McDermott, J 20(3)
McIntosh, M 4
Newey, T 42(1)
North, D 12(8)
Paterson, M 15
Pulis, A 9
Rankin, I 15(5)
Ravenhill, R 15(2)
Reddy, M 4(6)
Rizzo, N 1
Taylor, A 2(9)
Thorpe, T 5(1)
Till, P 17(5)
Toner, C 31(2)
Whittle, J 33(4)

League goals (57): Bore 8, Jones 8, Toner 8, North 6, Paterson 6, Bolland 5, Fenton 4, Boshell 2, Hunt 2, Rankin 2, Ravenhill 2, Taylor 2, Newey 1, Whittle 1.
F.A. Cup goals: None. **Carling Cup goals:** None. **Johnstone's Paint Trophy goals:** None.
Average home league attendance: 4,379. **Player of Year:** Danny North.

HARTLEPOOL UNITED

Danny Wilson's side came from nowhere to regain a place in League One at the first attempt and almost went up as champions. Victory over Bristol Rovers would have clinched the title, but a home defeat by Bristol Rovers in the last game meant they had to be satisfied with the runners-up spot behind Walsall. Hartlepool, at one stage 18 points behind their rivals, established a club-record run of 23 matches without losing, their ability to come up with late goals often proving crucial. It included eight successive wins without a goal conceded, equalling the Football League record before Stockport went one better two months later. This success brought Danny Wilson the division's Manager of the Year award from the League Managers' Association, while Richie Barker, the player he signed from Mansfield in the January transfer window, was its joint top scorer with 24 in all competitions.

Barker, R 18
Barron, M .... 26(3)
Boland, W .... 25(2)
Brackstone, J .... 6(2)
Brown, J .... 29(7)
Bullock, L .... 8(17)
Clark, B 40
Daly, J .... 14(5)
Duffy, D 10
Foley, D .... 4(21)
Gibb, A .... 12(13)
Hignett, C .... –(2)
Humphreys, R .... 37(1)
Konstantopoulos, D 46
Liddle, G 42
Mackay, M .... –(1)
Maidens, M .... –(4)
Monkhouse, A 26
Nelson, M 42
Porter, J .... 14(8)
Proctor, M .... 1(1)
Robson, M .... 18(2)
Strachan, G .... 2(2)
Sweeney, A .... 31(4)
Tinkler, M .... 4(2)
Williams, D .... 19(7)
Williams, E .... 32(8)

League goals (65): Barker 9, Daly 9, Monkhouse 7, Brown 6, Williams, E 6, Duffy 5, Porter 5, Sweeney 4, Clark 3, Humphreys 3, Liddle 3, Robson 2, Bullock 1, Nelson 1, Opponents 1.
F.A. Cup goals (2): Brown 1, Opponents 1. **Carling Cup goals (1):** Porter 1. **Johnstone's Paint Trophy goals (4):** Bullock 1, Foley 1, Humphreys 1, Liddle 1.
Average home league attendance: 5,087. **Player of Year:** Michael Nelson.

HEREFORD UNITED

A chronic shortage of goals at the tail end of the season undermined the club's return to the Football League after a nine-year absence. Hereford failed to score in ten of the last 13 games and won only once – a 3-0 success against Boston. Until then, they had been going along nicely, a 4-1 victory at Lincoln achieved with their best performance of the season and capped by Steve Guinan's hat-trick, keeping alive an outside chance of making the play-offs. The loss of form meant they had to be satisfied with 16th in the table. It was a disappointing finish, yet a position they would probably have taken gladly had it been on offer at the beginning of the campaign.

Beckwith, D 32
Brown, W 39
Connell, A .... 33(11)
Eustace, J 8
Ferrell, A .... 15(6)
Fitzpatrick, J .... –(1)
Fleetwood, S .... 21(6)
Giles, M .... 11(2)
Guinan, S 16
Gulliver, P .... 24(2)
Harrison, P .... –(1)
Jeannin, A .... 11(1)
Jennings, S 11
MacKenzie, N 7
McClenahan, T .... 24(2)
Mkandawire, T 39
Osborn, S .... –(1)
Palmer, M .... 1(2)
Purdie, R .... 43(1)
Rose, R .... 29(4)
Sheldon, G .... 3(5)
Sills, T .... 22(14)
Smith, B 18
Thomas, D 15
Travis, S .... 34(2)
Tynan, S 7
Wallis, J .... –(2)
Webb, L .... 13(8)
Williams, A .... 30(11)

League goals (45): Connell 9, Williams 8, Guinan 7, Purdie 6, Fleetwood 3, Mkandawire 2, Sills 2, Thomas 2, Jeannin 1, McClenahan 1, Rose 1, Sheldon 1, Smith 1, Opponents 1.
F.A. Cup goals (6): Purdie 2, Webb 2, Connell 1, Ferrell 1. **Carling Cup goals (4):** Fleetwood 3, Purdie 1. **Johnstone's Paint Trophy goals (1):** Williams 1.
Average home league attendance: 3,327. **Player of Year:** Rob Purdie.

LINCOLN CITY

With Jamie Forrester in prolific form, Lincoln gave every indication of overcoming their promotion jinx. Forrester scored all four goals at Mansfield (4-2) recorded hat-tricks against Barnet (5-0) and Rochdale (7-1) and received solid support from strike partner Mark Stallard. But neither could maintain that momentum in the second part of the season when a run of seven games without a win meant they had to be satisfied with a fifth successive place in the play-offs. The first leg of the semi-final against Bristol Rovers was tight – a 2-1 defeat. The second, at Sincil Bank, proved a nightmare, with two goals conceded in the opening 11 minutes and more poor defending resulting in a 5-3 reversal.

Amoo, R .... 35(8)
Bacon, D 1
Beevers, L .... 42(2)
Birley, M .... 3(1)
Brown, N .... 26(2)
Cryan, C .... –(4)
Eaden, N .... 32(1)
Forrester, J .... 39(2)
Frecklington, L .... 38(4)
Green, P .... 11(4)
Gritton, M .... 5(12)
Holmes, P 5
Hughes, J .... 37(4)
Kell, R .... –(1)
Kerr, S 44
Marriott, A 46
Mayo, P .... 28(6)
Mendes, J .... 4(5)
Mettam, L .... 1(3)
Morgan, P .... 27(6)
Moses, A .... 26(6)
N'Guessan, D .... 4(5)
Nicholson, S .... 7(1)
Ryan, O .... –(7)
Semple, R .... –(4)
Stallard, M 41
Warlow, O .... –(5)
Weir-Daley, S .... 4(7)

Play-offs – appearances: Beevers 2, Eaden 2, Forrester 2, Frecklington 2, Green 2, Hughes 2, Kerr 2, Marriott 2, Morgan 2, Stallard 2, Brown 1 (1), Amoo 1, Gritton –(2), Mayo –(1), Mendes –(1).
League goals (70): Forrester 18, Stallard 15, Frecklington 8, Hughes 6, Beevers 5, Weir-Daley 5, Kerr 3, Amoo 2, Gritton 2, Brown 1, Green 1, Mayo 1, Mettam 1, Morgan 1, Moses 1. **Play-offs – goals (4):** Hughes 3, Stallard 1.
F.A. Cup goals (1): Frecklington 1. **Carling Cup goals (3):** Beevers 1, Frecklington 1, Stallard 1. **Johnstone's Paint Trophy goals:** None.
Average home league attendance: 5,175. **Player of Year:** Lee Beevers.

MACCLESFIELD TOWN

Finishing third from bottom in your first season may not represent much of an achievement for a new manager. For Paul Ince, however, it was one to savour. When the former Manchester United and England stalwart took over after Brian Horton was dismissed, Macclesfield had collected only five points from their first 15 matches. By the time Ince had the first win under his belt – 1-0 against Rochdale despite having Alan Navarro sent off – nearly half the season had gone and the survival odds were stacked against them. Yet such was the new sense of confidence and conviction he instilled into his players that they built on that victory and went on a run which netted 19 points from seven games. There was still plenty to do and further dips in form to come. But Macclesfield did just enough to offset a lean run-in and finish two points clear. Ince left in the summer to take over at MK Dons and was replaced by coach Ian Brightwell.

Begovic, A .... 2(1)
Benjamin, R .... –(2)
Blackman, N .... –(1)
Brain, J 9
Brightwell, I 4
Bullock, M .... 38(5)
D'Laryea, N 1
Doyle, R .... –(2)
Hadfield, J .... 30(7)
Heath, C .... 16(9)
Holgate, A .... 2(4)
Ince, P .... –(1)
Jennings, J .... 5(4)
Lee, T 34
McIntyre, K .... 43(1)
McNeil, M .... 29(6)
McNulty, J 15
Miles, J .... 23(7)
Morley, D 35
Murphy, J .... 25(4)
Murray, A .... 8(3)
Navarro, A .... 28(4)
Rankin, I .... 1(3)
Regan, C .... 36(2)
Reid, I .... 2(6)
Robinson, M 5
Rouse, D 1
Scott, R .... 22(4)
Swailes, D 38
Teague, A .... 10(3)
Tipton, M .... 15(18)
Tolley, J .... 22(1)
Weir-Daley, S .... 5(2)
Wiles, S .... 2(5)

League goals (55): McIntyre 9, Murphy 7, Miles 5, Tipton 5, Bullock 4, Heath 4, McNeil 4, Morley 3, Swailes 3, Navarro 2, Scott 2, Weir-Daley 2, Hadfield 1, Holgate 1, Regan 1, Teague 1, Tolley 1.
F.A. Cup goals (4): Murphy 2, McIntyre 1, McNulty 1. **Carling Cup goals:** None. **Johnstone's Paint Trophy goals:** None.
Average home league attendance: 2,427. **Player of Year:** Kevin McIntyre.

MANSFIELD TOWN

Another modest season in lower mid-table for Mansfield, who sacked manager Peter Shirtliff in December after some poor results and brought in Billy Dearden for his second spell at the club. Dearden, in charge between 1999-2002, enjoyed marginally more success, Martin Gritton netting a hat-trick in the 5-0 win against his old club Torquay and his team enjoying victories over Walsall, Wycombe and Lincoln. But injuries contributed to a lean spell of two points from eight matches which pushed them down the table, until Barry Conlon stabilised things by scoring once and setting up another for Simon Brown in victory over Barnet.

Arnold, N	6(16)	Conlon, B	16(1)	McGhee, J	–(2)
Baptiste, A	46	D'Laryea, J	37	McIntosh, A	1
Barker, R	24	Dawson, S	32(2)	Muggleton, C	16(1)
Beardsley, C	3(7)	Gritton, M	14(5)	Mullins, J	39(4)
Birchall, A	1(4)	Hamshaw, M	38(2)	Reet, D	8(12)
Boulding, M	25(14)	Hjelde, J	25(3)	Sheehan, A	9(1)
Boulding, R	–(9)	Hodge, B	9	Sleath, D	3(4)
Brown, S	30(4)	Jelleyman, G	39(1)	Trimmer, L	–(1)
Buxton, J	27(3)	Kitchen, A	3	White, J	30
Charlton, A	3(1)	Lloyd, C	6(13)	Wood, C	1
Coke, G	15(6)				

League goals (58): Barker 12, Conlon 6, Gritton 6, Reet 6, Brown 5, Boulding, M 5, Hamshaw 4, Arnold 3, Baptiste 3, Mullins 2, Buxton 1, Coke 1, D'Laryea 1, Dawson 1, Hjelde 1, Opponents 1.
F.A. Cup goals (2): Barker 2. **Carling Cup goals (3):** Barker 1, Boulding, M 1, Reet 1. **Johnstone's Paint Trophy goals (3):** Beardsley 1, Opponents 1.
Average home league attendance: 3,176. **Player of Year:** Richie Barker.

MILTON KEYNES DONS

The new season will kick off in a new ground with a new manager in Paul Ince. But there is no change in status for a team who missed out narrowly on automatic promotion, then failed to live up to expectations in the play-offs. Dons went into the semi-final against Shrewsbury with plenty of momentum after four successive victories had closed the gap on third place Swindon to a single point. A goalless draw in the first leg at Gay Meadow made them favourites to go through in the final game at the National Hockey Stadium before the move to a 30,000-capacity stadium. Instead, they lost it 2-1, another near miss for Martin Allen who had reached the play-offs in the two previous seasons with Brentford. A week after this latest setback, Allen left to take charge of Leicester. At least there was success for 24-goal Izale McLeod, named League One's Player of the Year.

Andrews, K	34	Edds, G	26(9)	Morgan, C	3
Baines, A	19	Harper, L	22	O'Hanlon, S	33(3)
Baldock, S	–(1)	Hastings, J	–(7)	Page, S	–(1)
Bankole, A	5(1)	Hayes, J	–(11)	Platt, C	37(5)
Blizzard, D	8	Jarrett, A	2(3)	Rizzo, N	–(3)
Butler, P	17	Knight, L	7(9)	Smith, G	9(14)
Chorley, B	12(1)	Lewington, D	45	Smith, J	16(1)
Crooks, L	3(9)	McGovern, J-P	40(4)	Stirling, J	5(11)
Diallo, D	40	McLeod, I	33(1)	Taylor, S	6(22)
Dyer, L	39(2)	Mitchell, P	13(7)	Tillen, J	–(1)

Watts, A .... 1(1)
Wilbraham, A .... 31(1)

Play-offs – appearances: Andrews 2, Bankole 2, Blizzard 2, Edds 2, Diallo 2, Hayes 2, Lewington 2, McLeod 2, O'Hanlon 2, Stirling 2, McGovern 1, Platt 1, Dyer –(2), Knight –(2), Taylor –(1).
League goals (76): McLeod 21, Platt 18, Wilbraham 7, Andrews 6, Dyer 5, O'Hanlon 4, McGovern 3, Edds 2, Taylor 2, Chorley 1, Smith, G 1, Knight 1, Lewington 1, Stirling 1, Opponents 3. **Play-offs goals (1):** Andrews 1.
F.A. Cup goals (2): McLeod (2) **Carling Cup goals (3):** Wilbraham 2, McLeod 1. **Johnstone's Paint Trophy goals (1):** Page 1.
Average home league attendance: 6,033. **Player of Year:** Clive Platt.

NOTTS COUNTY

Indifferent home form denied County the chance to make an impact on the promotion race. More games were lost than won at Meadow Lane, where performances against teams in the lower reaches of the table proved particularly disappointing. Even so, there was an improvement of eight places on the previous season's finish of 21st to accompany an eventful run to the fourth round of the Carling Cup in which they excelled against higher grade opposition. Crystal Palace and Middlesbrough were both beaten on their own ground. County then knocked out Southampton, before a home tie against Wycombe that seemed to offer a real chance of a place in the quarter-finals went against them.

Byron, M .... 2(1)
Curtis, T .... –(2)
Deeney, S 7
Dudfield, L .... 29(12)
Edwards, M .... 44(1)
Gleeson, D .... 16(1)
Hunt, S .... 24(8)
Lee, J .... 37(1)
Martin, D .... 12(17)
McCann, A 43
McMahon, D .... 3(4)
Mendes, J .... 22(15)
N'Toya, T .... 4(17)
Needham, L .... –(1)
Parkinson, A .... 40(5)
Pilkington, K 39
Pipe, D 39
Ross, I .... 26(10)
Sheridan, J .... –(3)
Silk, G .... 24(6)
Smith, J .... 25(2)
Somner, M .... 35(3)
Walker, J .... 2(6)
Weston, M .... 1(3)
White, A .... 32(3)

League goals (55): Lee 15, Dudfield 7, Mendes 5, Parkinson 5, White 5, Martin 4, Smith 4, Edwards 3, Hunt 1, N'Toya 1, Ross 1, Somner 1, Opponents 3.
F.A. Cup goals (1): Dudfield 1. **Carling Cup goals (5):** Dudfield 1, Edwards 1, Lee 1, Martin 1, N'Toya 1. **Johnstone's Paint Trophy goals:** None.
Average home league attendance: 4,973. **Player of Year:** Mike Edwards.

PETERBOROUGH UNITED

Six successive defeats cost Keith Alexander his job in mid-January and opened the way for Wrexham midfielder Darren Ferguson to launch his managerial career. There was no dream start for Sir Alex Ferguson's son, with three more setbacks in quick succession ending any interest Peterborough had in a play-off place. But Ferguson gradually began to exert his influence on the team. His first win came, ironically, against his old club and this 3-0 result was followed by several more free-scoring performances which led to a place in the top half of the table. With a busy summer in the transfer market behind him, Ferguson will be looking for something better in 2007-08.

Arber, M .... 31(3)
Benjamin, T .... 15(12)
Blackett, S .... 12(1)
Blanchett, D .... –(3)
Boyd, G .... 19(1)
Branston, G .... 23(1)
Butcher, R .... 35(8)
Carden, P .... 1(1)
Crow, D .... 22(13)
Davis, L 7
Day, J .... 17(7)
Futcher, B .... 22(3)
Gain, P .... 26(8)
Ghaichem, J .... 1(1)
Holden, D .... 20(1)
Huke, S .... 9(9)
Hyde, M 18
Jalal, S 1
Low, J .... 17(2)
Mackail-Smith, C .... 13(2)
McLean, A 16
Morgan, C .... 22(1)
Newton, A 43
Opapa, L .... 6(5)
Plummer, C 7
Rachubka, P 4
Richards, J .... 4(9)
Smith, A .... 5(4)
Stirling, J .... 14(8)
Strachan, G .... 13(3)

Turner, B .... 7(1)	White, A 7	Yeo, S .... 8(5)
Tyler, M 41		

League goals (70): Mackail-Smith 8, Benjamin 7, McLean 7, Boyd 6, Crow 6, Gain 6, Butcher 4, Futcher 3, Strachan 3, White 3, Yeo 2, Arber 1, Blanchett 1, Day 1, Holden 1, Huke 1, Low 1, Morgan 1, Newton 1, Opara 1, Richards 1, Smith 1, Opponents 4. **F.A. Cup goals (7):** Crow 3, McLean 3, Butcher 1. **Carling Cup goals (3):** Benjamin 2, Branston 1. **Johnstone's Paint Trophy goals (1):** Crow 1.
Average home league attendance: 4,662. **Player of Year:** Aaron McLean.

ROCHDALE

Keith Hill was rewarded with a three-year contract after steering Rochdale away from relegation trouble to the fringe of a play-off place. They were third from bottom after seven defeats in eight matches when the former centre-half replaced Steve Parkin as manager in mid-December. The transformation was considerable for a team whose slide had embraced a 7-1 defeat at Lincoln. Under Hill, appointed initially as caretaker, they lost only three times and scored 48 goals in the second half of the season. A 7-2 win at Stockport was accompanied by 5-0 scorelines against MK Dons and Macclesfield and four-goal performances against Boston, Grimsby and Accrington. Chris Dagnall netting a hat-trick against Macclesfield.

Barker, K .... 11(1)	Gilks, M 46	Poole, G .... 1(5)
Bates, T .... –(2)	Goodall, A 46	Prendergast, R .... 4(1)
Boardman, J .... 3(1)	Jackson, M .... 8(4)	Ramsden, S .... 32(2)
Brown, G .... 14(7)	Jones, G .... 26(1)	Reet, D .... –(6)
Christie, I .... 4(1)	Lambert, R 3	Reid, R .... –(2)
Clarke, D .... 5(7)	Le Fondre, A 7	Rundle, A .... 20(9)
Cooksey, E .... 10(9)	McArdle, R 25	Sako, M .... 14(3)
Crooks, L .... 26(5)	Mocquet, W .... 6(1)	Sharp, J 12
Dagnall, C .... 32(5)	Moyo-Modise, C ...... 1(18)	Stanton, N 35
Dodds, L .... 6(6)	Muirhead, B 12	Thompson, J .... 5(8)
Doolan, J 40	Murray, G .... 29(2)	Turnbull, S .... 2(2)
Etuhu, K .... 3(1)	Perkins, D .... 14(4)	Warburton, C 4

League goals (70): Dagnall 17, Murray 16, Le Fonde 4, Rundle 4, Doolan 3, Goodall 3, Jones 3, Muirhead 3, Ramsden 3, Sako 3, Etuhu 2, Dodds 2, Clarke 1, Mocquet 1, Moyo-Modise 1, Prendergast 1, Sharp 1, Opponents 2.
F.A. Cup goals (1): Doolan 1. **Carling Cup goals (2):** Doolan 1, Rundle 1. **Johnstone's Paint Trophy goals (2):** Barker 1, Dagnall 1.
Average home league attendance: 2,897. **Player of Year:** Glenn Murray.

SHREWSBURY TOWN

Shrewsbury Town drew a blank on their final appearance at Gay Meadow before moving to a new stadium, sharing a goalless draw with MK Dons. It left their rivals favourites to reach the League Two Play-off Final, but two goals by substitute Andy Cooke won the day in the second leg. Shrewsbury were also underdogs against Bristol Rovers at Wembley and this time they found the task too great, despite leading after three minutes through Ross Drummond's header. The consolation was playing in front of a record crowd of more than 61,000 at the end of a good season in which an unbeaten run of 14 matches was instrumental in claiming sixth place on goal difference. Cooke scored two hat-tricks, home and away against Stockport.

Asamoah, D .... 34(5)	Drummond, S .... 43(1)	Hope, R 33
Ashton, N .... 42(1)	Edwards, D .... 39(6)	Humphrey, C .... –(12)
Burton, S .... 26(2)	Esson, R 6	Jones, L .... 4(3)
Canoville, L .... 6(1)	Fortune-West, L ...... 10(9)	Jones, M .... 3(10)
Cooke, A .... 21(13)	Hall, D .... 21(6)	Keith, J 1
Cowan, G .... 3(1)	Herd, B .... 29(2)	Langmead, K 45
Davies, B 43	Hogg, S .... –(1)	Leslie, S .... 1(4)

Shearer, S 20
Sorvel, N .... 15(3)
Symes, M .... 20(13)
Thomas, D .... 3(3)
Tierney, M 18
Williams, D .... –(2)

Play-offs – appearances: Ashton 3, Drummond 3, Hope 3, Langmead 3, Tierney 3, Fortune-West 2(1), Asamoah 2, Davies 2, Hall 2, Jones, L 2, Shearer 2, Symes 2(1), Cooke 1(2), Humphrey 1(1), Herd 1, MacKenzie 1, Burton –(2).
League goals (68): Davies 12, Asamoah 10, Cooke 10, Symes 9, Fortune-West 7, Edwards 5, Drummond 4, Langmead 3, Ashton 2, Burton 1, Herd 1, Jones, M 1, Sorvel 1, Opponents 2. **Play-offs – goals (3):** Cooke 2, Drummond 1.
F.A. Cup goals: None. **Carling Cup goals:** None. **Johnstone's Paint Trophy goals (7):** Symes 4, Asamoah 1, Edwards 1, Opponents 1.
Average home league attendance: 4,729. **Player of Year:** Kelvin Langmead.

STOCKPORT COUNTY

A Football League record run was not enough for Stockport, who lost out on a play-off place on goal difference. Despite winning 5-0 at Darlington on the last day of the season, they were pipped at the post by Shrewsbury, who secured a point in their final match to make sure of sixth spot. Stockport looked a safe bet to make it when recording nine straight wins, without conceding a single goal, after bringing in on loan Wolves keeper Wayne Hennessey, who until then had not played a league game. But they won only one of the next ten, a 7-2 defeat at Rochdale underlining how quickly fortunes changed. Early in the campaign, Adam Le Fondre had scored four times in a 5-2 win over Wrexham.

Allen, D .... 1(6)
Blizzard, D 7
Bowler, M .... 5(3)
Bramble, T .... 19(12)
Briggs, K .... 16(4)
Clare, R .... 29(1)
Crowther, R 1
Dickinson, L .... 11(22)
Dinning, T .... 27(5)
Elding, A 20
Ellis, D .... –(2)
Gleeson, S 14
Griffin, A .... 29(13)
Hennessey, W 15
Kane, T 4
Le Fondre, A .... 14(7)
Lewis, J 5
Malcolm, M .... 10(8)
Murray, G 11
Nolan, E .... 2(2)
Owen, G 39
Pilkington, A .... 18(6)
Poole, D .... 30(1)
Proudlock, A .... 14(9)
Raynes, M .... 7(2)
Robinson, M .... 11(2)
Rose, M .... 22(3)
Rowe, T .... 1(3)
Ruddy, J 11
Spencer, J 15
Tansey, G .... 2(1)
Taylor, J .... 44(1)
Treacy, K .... 2(2)
Tunnicliffe, J .... 4(1)
Williams, A 46

League goals (65): Elding 11, Dickinson 7, Le Fondre 7, Bramble 6, Pilkington 5, Poole 4, Griffin 3, Murray 3, Proudlock 3, Rose 3, Briggs 2, Dinning 2, Gleeson 2, Malcolm 2, Robinson 2, Taylor 1, Williams 1, Opponents 1.
F.A. Cup goals (5): Proudlock 3, Bramble 1, Poole 1. **Carling Cup goals:** None. **Johnstone's Paint Trophy goals (1):** Malcolm 1.
Average home league attendance: 5,514. **Player of Year:** Gareth Owen.

SWINDON TOWN

Swindon took the loss of Dennis Wise in their stride and made an immediate return to League One. Under Wise, they won their opening six matches and lost only two of the first 15 before the manager left to take over at Leeds. Under his successor, Paul Sturrock, the team stayed in the thick of a promotion race which stretched to the final day of the season. There were some late wobbles, defeat by Bristol Rovers giving MK Dons the chance to deny them third place. But despite conceding a last-minute equaliser to leaders Walsall, Swindon secured the required point in front of a crowd of nearly 15,000 on the last day of the season. It was the third time in four years that Sturrock had been involved with a promotion-winning team.

Brezovan, P 14
Brown, A .... 13(17)
Brownlie, R .... 6(8)
Caton, A .... 3(2)
Comyn-Platt, C 2
Corr, B 8
Evans, P .... 11(4)
Grimes, A .... –(4)
Holgate, A .... –(1)
Ifil, J 40
Ince, P .... 2(1)
James, K .... –(2)

Jutkiewicz, L .... 13(20)
Lonergan, A 1
Monkhouse, A .... 9(1)
Nicholas, A .... 30(5)
Noubissie, P .... 1(2)
Onibuje, F .... 6(8)
Peacock, L .... 40(2)
Pook, M .... 32(6)
Rhodes, A .... –(4)
Roberts, C .... 39(3)
Shakes, R .... 26(6)
Smith, J 41
Smith, P 31
Sturrock, B .... 7(12)
Timlin,M .... 18(6)
Vincent, J 34
Wells, B .... –(1)
Weston, C .... 21(6)
Westwood, A .... 8(1)
Williams, A 27
Zaaboub, S .... 23(4)

League goals (58): Peacock 10, Roberts 10, Jutkiewicz 5, Corr 3, Evans 3, Smith, J 3, Sturrock 3, Brown 2, Brownlie 2, Monkhouse 2, Nicholas 2, Onibuje 2, Pook 2, Shakes 2, Ifil 1, Timlin 1, Weston 1, Zaaboub 1, Opponents 3.

F.A. Cup goals (5): Roberts 3, Ifil 1, Opponents 1. **Carling Cup goals (2):** Evans 1, Nicholas 1. **Johnstone's Paint Trophy goals:** None.

Average home league attendance: 7,419. **Player of Year:** Phil Smith.

TORQUAY UNITED

Eighty years of Football League membership came to an end for Torquay after a season of constant managerial changes and boardroom turmoil. Ian Atkins, who saved the club from going down 12 months earlier, was replaced after a 5-2 defeat by Peterborough in late November by one-time Czech Republic defender Lubos Kubik. He departed after one win in 12 and former Mansfield and Chester manager Keith Curle took on the survival effort. Curle fared little better, a lack of scoring power continuing to undermine the team's chances, and relegation was confirmed with three games still to play. The upheaval continued. Leroy Rosenior's 'return' as manager reportedly lasted ten minutes after another takeover of the club, leading to former midfielder John Buckle coming in.

Abbey, N 24
Andrews, L 46
Angus, S .... 33(3)
Baxter, D .... –(1)
Cooke, S .... 9(4)
Critchell, K .... 6(1)
Dickson, R .... 7(2)
Easter, J .... 8(2)
Evans, M 14
Fortune-West, L .... 2(3)
Garner, D 8
Gordon, D 8
Graham, D 7
Halliday, M 3
Hapgood, L .... –(1)
Hill, K .... 24(12)
Hockley, M .... 25(12)
Horsell, M .... 5(1)
Jarvis, R .... 2(2)
John, A .... 6(1)
Kerry, L .... 6(1)
Leary, M .... –(2)
Mansell, L .... 43(2)
McKoy, N .... 1(3)
McPhee, C .... 11(26)
Motteram, C .... 1(6)
Miller, K 7
Murray, A 21
Oliver, D .... –(1)
Phillips, M .... 10(4)
Rayner, S 10
Reed, S .... 10(5)
Reid, R .... 4(3)
Robertson, C 9
Robertson, J .... 5(4)
Robinson, M 18
Smith, P .... 5(3)
Taylor, C .... 11(2)
Thorpe, L .... 39(2)
Villis, M .... 3(3)
Ward, J .... 21(4)
Williams, M 2
Woods, S 32

League goals (36): Ward 9, Thorpe 8, Mansell 4, Reid 2, Robertson, J 2, Angus 1, Cooke 1, Dickson 1, Evans 1, Garner 1, Hill 1, Kerry 1, Phillips 1, Robertson, C 1, Taylor 1, Williams 1.

F.A. Cup goals (5): Robertson, J 2, Ward 2, McPhee 1. **Carling Cup goals:** None. **Johnstone's Paint Trophy goals:** None.

Average home league attendance: 2,633. **Player of Year:** Lee Mansell.

WALSALL

Walsall crowned an immediate return to League One when Dean Keates volleyed a championship-clinching equaliser with seconds remaining of the final game at Swindon. It was the reward for a season's great consistency and the way their nerve held during the run-in. Hartlepool had overtaken them at the top with an impressive charge, but lost momentum at a crucial time and finished a point behind after being unable to regain it. Leading scorer Keates and defender Chris Westwood played key roles in the success of a side who forced the pace from the start and were beaten only once in their first 20 matches. Both, however, declined the chance to step up, signing instead during the summer for another League Two promotion push, this time with Peterborough.

Bedeau, A .... 8(10)
Benjamin, T 8
Bossu, B 1
Bradley, M .... –(1)
Butler, M 44
Cederqvist, P .... 3(8)
Constable, J .... 2(4)
Cooper, K 8
Dann, S .... 24(6)
Deeney, T .... –(1)
Demontagnac, I ...... 2(17)
Dobson, M 39
Fangueiro, C .... 2(3)
Fox, D 44
Gerrard, A .... 31(4)
Harper, K 10
Ince, C 45
Keates, D .... 36(3)
Kinsella, M .... 8(3)
Pead, C .... 26(15)
Picken, A .... 1(1)
Roper, I 27
Sam, H .... 28(14)
Smith, E .... 1(2)
Taylor, K .... 27(8)
Westwood, C .... 38(2)
Wrack, D .... 7(11)
Wright, M .... 31(6)
Wright, T .... 5(1)

League goals (66): Keates 13, Butler 11, Sam 7, Dann 4, Harper 4, Roper 4, Dobson 3, Fox 3, Wright, M 3, Benjamin 2, Westwood 2, Wright, T 2, Bedeau 1, Demontagnac 1, Fangueiro 1, Gerrard 1, Kinsella 1, Taylor 1, Wrack 1, Opponents 1.
F.A. Cup goals: None. **Carling Cup goals (2):** Butler 1, Dann 1. **Johnstone's Paint Trophy goals (1):** Wrack 1.
Average home league attendance: 5,642. **Player of Year:** Dean Keates.

WREXHAM

Brian Carey, a stalwart of more than 350 appearances for Wrexham as a player, marked his managerial debut by steering the club away from relegation trouble. He took over after Denis Smith, League Two's longest-serving manager was sacked, amid growing worries about their position, after six years in charge. It proved a tough baptism for former skipper Carey, who won only one of his first 12 matches and saw his side slide to second from bottom. But they came good with four victories in the last five games games, two of them against fellow-strugglers Torquay and Boston. Carey, appointed initially as caretaker, was rewarded with a two-year contract.

Barron, S 3
Carvill, M .... 1(5)
Craddock, T 1
Crowell, M .... 10(5)
Done, M .... 27(7)
Evans, G .... 9(3)
Evans, S .... 34(1)
Ferguson, D .... 19(1)
Fleming, A .... 1(1)
Garrett, R 10
Ingham, M 31
Johnson, J .... 10(12)
Jones, Mark .... 29(1)
Jones, Michael 1
Lawrence, D 3
Llewellyn, C 39
Mackin, L .... 1(7)
McAliskey, J 3
McEvilly, L .... 18(10)
Mitchell, P 5
Molango, M 3
Morgan, C 1
Newby, J .... 2(9)
Pejic, S 33
Proctor, M 9
Reed, J .... –(4)
Roberts, N .... 17(2)
Roche, L .... 26(2)
Ruddy, J 5
Samba, C .... 1(2)
Smith, K .... 5(3)
Spender, S .... 23(2)
Ugarte, J .... –(2)
Valentine, R .... 32(2)
Walker, R 3
Whitley, J 11
Williams, A 9
Williams, D 40
Williams, Marc .... 11(5)
Williams, Mike ..... 20(10)

League goals (43): Llewellyn 9, McEvilly 7, Jones, Mark 5, Roberts 3, Williams, D 3, Evans 2, Proctor 2, Spender 2, Valentine 2, Craddock 1, Done 1, Johnson 1, Smith 1, Whitley 1, Williams, Marc 1, Opponents 2.
F.A. Cup goals (4): Jones, Mark 1, McEvilly 1, Smith 1, Williams, D 1. **Carling Cup goals (5):** Llewellyn 2, Done 1, Jones, Mark 1, Roberts 1. **Johnstone's Paint Trophy goals (1):** Crowell 1.
Average home league attendance: 5,030. **Player of Year:** Danny Williams.

WYCOMBE WANDERERS

For the third successive season Wycombe came up short after setting a fast early pace. This time they were top with 22 points from the opening nine matches before indifferent home form caught up with them. Eleven games at the Causeway were drawn, too many for a team wanting to stay in contention. High point of the campaign came with victories over Fulham and Charlton in the Carling Cup and a 1-1 result against Chelsea in the first leg of the semi-finals before the Premiership side exerted their authority by winning the return match 4-0. Jermaine Easter's six goals in the competition featured in a total of 24, ranking him as the division's leading marksmen alongside Hartlepool's Richie Barker and Izale McLeod of MK Dons. It included a hat-trick in the 3-0 win over Bury.

Ainsworth, L .... 3(4)	Doherty, T .... 23(3)	O'Halloran, S .... 9(2)
Antwi, W 25	Easter, J .... 30(8)	Oakes, S .... 29(6)
Anya, I .... 1(12)	Fernandez, V 1	Onibuje, F .... 1(4)
Barnes-Homer, M ...... –(1)	Golbourne, S .... 31(3)	Palmer, C .... 22(10)
Batista, R 29	Grant, A .... 39(1)	Pettigrew, A 1
Betsy, K 29	Gregory, S .... –(3)	Stockley, S .... 33(1)
Bloomfield, M .... 39(2)	Martin, R .... 32(10)	Stonebridge, I .... 1(8)
Christon, L .... 5(1)	McGleish, S .... 11(3)	Torres, S .... 8(12)
Crooks, L 11	McParland, A .... 1(3)	Williamson, M 33
Dixon, J .... 1(9)	Mooney, T .... 41(1)	Young, J .... 17(2)

League goals (52): Easter 17, Mooney 12, Betsy 5, McGleish 5, Bloomfield 4, Doherty 2, Martin 2, Antwi 1, Dixon 1, Golbourne 1, Stockley 1, Williamson 1.
F.A. Cup goals (3): Antwi 1, Easter 1, Oakes 1. **Carling Cup goals (10):** Easter 6, Oakes 2, Mooney 1, Williamson 1. **Johnstone's Paint Trophy goals (1):** Stonebridge 1.
Average home league attendance: 4,983. **Player of Year:** Jermaine Easter.

QUOTE-UNQUOTE

'It's like anything else. If you want a nice meal, you have to pay the money. If you want a cheap meal, you go to the chippy' – **Roy Keane**, Sunderland manager, on the £2m. fee for Arsenal's Anthony Stokes.

'I'd rather have a big crowd than the TV money. I know what it's like to be roared on' – **Niall Quinn**, Sunderland chairman, turning down televised coverage of the game against Championship leaders Derby.

'If it was a boxing match it would be Muhammad Ali against Jimmy Krankie' – **Adrian Boothroyd**, Watford manager, on the match against Manchester United.

'If I see an empty seat in the stands, I'll sit there. Maybe I'll get lynched, but I'd rather get lynched among the people' – **George Gillett**, new Liverpool owner.

'I'd like to see agents removed from the game. A guy can go in and ask for your wage and expect to be given thousands and even millions' – **Gary Neville**, Manchester United captain, on why he believes football should cut out the middle man.

'He has a glittering career ahead of him, even though he looks only 12-years-old' – **Martin O'Neill**, Aston Villa manager, on £9.6m. new signing Ashley Young.

'Dear oh dear, that's on the M61' – **Mark Lawrenson**, BBC pundit, after Arsenal's Gilberto Silva fires a penalty high over the crossbar in the F.A. Cup replay at Bolton.

'What was incredible was going into the Chelsea dressing room to have a chat and swop shirts. It's bigger than my house' – **Dickson Etuhu**, Norwich midfielder, after his side's F.A. Cup tie at Stamford Bridge.

'We're building a strong squad in a hurry. Half my players are struggling to find hotels, houses, schools for the kids – or even the names of their team-mates' – **Billy Davies**, Derby manager.

'The only way we will be getting into Europe is on Easyjet in the summer' – **Steve Coppell**, Reading manager, plays down his side's chances of European football.

LEAGUE CLUB MANAGERS

Figure in brackets = number of managerial changes at club since the War.

BARCLAYS PREMIERSHIP

Arsenal (11)	Arsene Wenger	October 1996
Aston Villa (19)	Martin O'Neill	August 2006
Birmingham City (21)	Steve Bruce	December 2001
Blackburn Rov. (22)	Mark Hughes	September 2004
Bolton Wand. (18)	Sammy Lee	April 2007
Chelsea (19)	Jose Mourinho	June 2004
Derby Co. (19)	Billy Davies	June 2006
Everton (16)	David Moyes	March 2002
Fulham (24)	Lawrie Sanchez	May 2007
Liverpool (10)	Rafael Benitez	June 2004
Manchester City (26)	Sven-Goran Eriksson	June 2007
Manchester Utd. (8)	Sir Alex Ferguson	November 1986
Middlesbrough (17)	Gareth Southgate	June 2006
Newcastle Utd. (20)	Sam Allardyce	May 2007
Portsmouth (24)	Harry Redknapp†	December 2005
Reading (16)	Steve Coppell	October 2003
Sunderland (21)	Roy Keane	August 2006
Tottenham (18)	Martin Jol	November 2004
West Ham Utd. (10)	Alan Curbishley	December 2006
Wigan Athletic (16)	Chris Hutchings	May 2007

† Second spell at club. Number of changes since elected to Football League: Wigan Athletic 1978.

COCA-COLA LEAGUE – CHAMPIONSHIP

Barnsley (19)	Simon Davey	December 2006
Blackpool (23)	Simon Grayson	January 2006
Bristol City (20)	Gary Johnson	September 2005
Burnley (20)	Steve Cotterill	June 2004
Cardiff City (26)	Dave Jones	May 2005
Charlton Athletic (15)	Alan Pardew	December 2006
Colchester Utd. (21)	Geraint Williams	July 2006
Coventry City (27)	Iain Dowie	February 2007
Crystal Palace (32)	Peter Taylor	June 2006
Hull City (23)	Phil Brown	January 2007
Ipswich Town (10)	Jim Magilton	June 2006
Leicester City (21)	Martin Allen	May 2007
Norwich City (22)	Peter Grant	October 2006
Plymouth Argyle (28)	Ian Holloway	June 2006
Preston N.E. (23)	Paul Simpson	June 2006
Q.P.R. (23)	John Gregory	September 2006
Scunthorpe Utd. (22)	Nigel Adkins	December 2006
Sheffield Utd. (30)	Bryan Robson	May 2007
Sheffield Wed. (24)	Brian Laws	November 2006
Southampton (18)	George Burley	December 2005
Stoke City (22)	Tony Pulis†	June 2006
Watford (24)	Adrian Boothroyd	March 2005
W.B.A. (26)	Tony Mowbray	October 2006
Wolves (20)	Mick McCarthy	July 2006

† Second spell at club.

COCA-COLA LEAGUE ONE

Bournemouth (19)	Kevin Bond	October 2006
Brighton & H.A (27)	Dean Wilkins	October 2006
Bristol Rov. (22)	Paul Trollope	November 2005
Carlisle Utd. (1)	Neil McDonald	June 2006
Cheltenham Town (3)	John Ward	November 2003
Crewe Alexandra (18)	Steve Holland	May 2007
Doncaster Rov. (1)	Sean O'Driscoll	September 2006
Gillingham (19)	Ronnie Jepson	November 2005
Hartlepool Utd. (29)	Danny Wilson	June 2006
Huddersfield Town (22)	Andy Ritchie	April 2007
Leeds Utd. (20)	Dennis Wise	October 2006
Leyton Orient (20)	Martin Ling	October 2003
Luton Town (20)	Kevin Blackwell	March 2007
Millwall (27)	Willie Donachie	November 2006
Northampton Town (27)	Stuart Gray	January 2007
Nott'm. Forest (15)	Colin Calderwood	May 2006
Oldham Athletic (22)	John Sheridan	June 2006
Port Vale (18)	Martin Foyle	February 2004
Southend Utd. (26)	Steve Tilson	March 2004
Swansea City (28)	Roberto Martinez	February 2007
Swindon Town (23)	Paul Sturrock	November 2006
Tranmere Rov. (17)	Ronnie Moore	June 2006
Walsall (30)	Richard Money	May 2006
Yeovil Town (2)	Russell Slade	June 2006

Number of changes since elected to Football League: Cheltenham Town 1999; Yeovil Town 2003. Since returning: Doncaster Rov. 2003, Carlisle Utd. 2005.

COCA-COLA LEAGUE TWO

Accrington Stanley (-)	John Coleman	July 1999
Barnet (-)	Paul Fairclough	May 2004
Bradford City (30)	Stuart McCall	May 2007
Brentford (28)	Terry Butcher	April 2007
Bury (21)	Chris Casper	October 2005
Chester City (4)	Bobby Williamson	May 2007
Chesterfield (17)	Lee Richardson	April 2007
Dagenham & Redbridge (-)	John Still	April 2004
Darlington (31)	Dave Penney	October 2003
Grimsby Town (29)	Alan Buckley†	November 2006
Hereford Utd. (-)	Graham Turner	August 1995
Lincoln City (24)	John Schofield	June 2006
Macclesfield Town (7)	Ian Brightwell	June 2007
Mansfield Town (25)	Billy Dearden†	December 2006
Milton Keynes Dons (13)	Paul Ince	June 2007
Morecambe (-)	Sammy McIlroy	May 2006
Notts Co. (29)	Steve Thompson	June 2006
Peterborough Utd. (23)	Darren Ferguson	January 2007
Rochdale (29)	Keith Hill	January 2007
Rotherham Utd. (21)	Mark Robins	April 2007
Shrewsbury Town (1)	Gary Peters	November 2004
Stockport Co. (32)	Jim Gannon	January 2006
Wrexham (18)	Brian Carey	January 2007
Wycombe Wand. (7)	Paul Lambert	July 2006

† Third spell at club. Number of changes since elected to Football League: Peterborough Utd. 1960; Wycombe Wand. 1993; Macclesfield Town 1997; Dagenham & Redbridge 2007, Morecambe 2007. Since returning: Chester City 2004, Shrewsbury Town 2004; Barnet 2005; Accrington Stanley 2006, Hereford Utd. 2006.

MANAGERIAL INS AND OUTS: 2006-07

BARCLAYS PREMIERSHIP

Bolton Wand.: Out – Sam Allardyce (April 07); In – Sammy Lee.
Charlton Athletic: Out – Iain Dowie (November 06); In – Les Reed; Out – Les Reed (December 06); In – Alan Pardew.
Fulham: Out – Chris Coleman (April 07); In – Lawrie Sanchez.
Manchester City: Out – Stuart Pearce (May 07).
Newcastle Utd.: Out – Glenn Roeder (May 07); In – Sam Allardyce.
Sheffield Utd.: Out – Neil Warnock (May 07); In – Bryan Robson.
West Ham Utd.: Out – Alan Pardew (December 06); In – Alan Curbishley.
Wigan Athletic: Out – Paul Jewell (May 07); In – Chris Hutchings.

COCA-COLA CHAMPIONSHIP

Barnsley: Out – Andy Ritchie (November 06); In – Simon Davey.
Coventry City: Out – Micky Adams (January 07); In – Iain Dowie.
Hull City: Out – Phil Parkinson (December 06); In – Phil Brown.
Leeds Utd.: Out – Kevin Blackwell (September 06); In – Dennis Wise.
Leicester City: Out – Rob Kelly (April 07); In – Martin Allen.
Luton Town: Out – Mike Newell (March 07); In – Kevin Blackwell.
Norwich City: Out – Nigel Worthington (October 07); In – Peter Grant.
Q.P.R: Out – Gary Waddock (September 06); In – John Gregory.
Sheffield Wed.: Out – Paul Sturrock (October 06); In – Brian Laws.
Sunderland: Out – Niall Quinn (August 06); In – Roy Keane.
W.B.A: Out – Bryan Robson (September 06); In – Tony Mowbray.

COCA-COLA LEAGUE ONE

Bournemouth: Out – Sean O'Driscoll (September 06); In – Kevin Bond.
Bradford City: Out – Colin Todd (February 07); In: David Wetherall; Out – David Wetherall (May 07); In – Stuart McCall.
Brentford: Out – Leroy Rosenior (November 06); In – Scott Fitzgerald; Out – Scott Fitzgerald (April 07); In – Terry Butcher.
Brighton & H.A.: Out – Mark McGhee (September 06); In – Dean Wilkins.
Chesterfield: Out – Roy McFarland (March 07); In – Lee Richardson.
Crewe Alexandra: Out – Dario Gradi (May 07); In – Steve Holland.
Doncaster Rov.: Out – Dave Penney (August 06); In – Sean O'Driscoll.
Huddersfield Town: Out – Peter Jackson (March 07); In – Andy Ritchie.
Millwall: Out – Nigel Spackman (September 06); In – Willie Donachie.
Northampton Town: Out – John Gorman (December 06); In – Stuart Gray.
Rotherham Utd.: Out – Alan Knill (March 07); In – Mark Robins.
Scunthorpe Utd.: Out – Brian Laws (November 06); In – Nigel Adkins.
Swansea City: Out – Kenny Jackett (February 07); In – Roberto Martinez .

COCA-COLA LEAGUE TWO

Boston Utd.: Out Steve Evans (May 07).
Chester City: Out Mark Wright (April 07); In – Bobby Williamson.
Darlington: Out – David Hodgson (October 06); In – Dave Penney.
Grimsby Town: Out – Graham Rodger (November 06); In – Alan Buckley.
Macclesfield Town: Out – Brian Horton (October 06); In – Paul Ince.
Mansfield Town: Out – Peter Shirtliff (December 07); In – Billy Dearden.

MK Dons: Out – Martin Allen (May 07).
Peterborough Utd.: Out – Keith Alexander (January 07); In – Darren Ferguson.
Rochdale: Out – Steve Parkin (December 06); In – Keith Hill.
Swindon Town: Out – Dennis Wise (October 06); In – Paul Sturrock.
Torquay Utd.: Out – Ian Atkins (November 06); In – Lubos Kubik; Out – Lubos Kubik (February 07); In – Keith Curle; Out – Keith Curle (May 07); In – Paul Buckle.
Wrexham: Out – Denis Smith (January 07); In – Brian Carey.

QUOTE-UNQUOTE

'There was one point when he cut back inside Billy Wright and took him so far out of the game that he had to pay three and six to get back into the ground' – **Sir Alex Ferguson** on the late Ferenc Puskas, who inspired Hungary to become the first Continental side to beat England at Wembley.

'I'm on first-name terms with about half the crowd' – **John McDermott**, Grimsby defender, on his 736th appearance for the club.

'It's your throat that's going to be cut if you don't produce results' – **Eggert Magnusson**, West Ham's new chairman, warns manager Alan Pardew . . . a week before sacking him.

'We have every confidence in the team we have put together. We won't be making another change this season' – **Peter Varney**, Charlton chief executive.

'I hold my hands up. We have gone back on something we said and it's not nice to do that. We are not normally that type of club, but that's the position we were in' – **Peter Varney** a week later after the sacking of Les Reed.

'We played like a bunch of drunks' – **Yossi Benayoun**, West Ham winger, after the 6-0 defeat by Reading.

'He is the one player all the other Premership managers would love to have in their team' – Steve Coppell, **Reading** manager, on Manchester United's Cristiano Ronaldo.

'This is the best night in all the seven years I've been manager here. It reminded me of when I was a kid, walking to the ground and smelling the excitement' – **Neil Warnock,** Sheffield United manager, after the 1-0 victory over Arsenal.

'There are times in this league when you feel like you're a water pistol up against multi-million pound cannons' – **Adrian Boothroyd**, Watford manager on struggling to cope with the Premiership.

'He must be made of gold' – **Chris Coleman**, Fulham manager, on the £10m. valuation Hearts put on goalkeeper Craig Gordon.

'Beckham is going to be half a film actor living in Hollywood. Despite being free, no club in the world wanted him' – **Ramon Calderon**, Real Madrid president, on the former England captain's move to LA Galaxy.

'Beckham is an elite footballer and has always shown exemplary behaviour. Sorry a thousand times' – **Ramon Calderon** has a change of heart.

'I'm a Geordie and I'll get a tough time off my family in the next few days' – **Steve Bruce**, Birmingham manager, after his team's 5-1 F.A. Cup win over Newcastle at St James' Park.

'Our bad results have only one explanation – the poor atmosphere around the club. Not everyone is pulling in the same direction and that is immensely dangerous' – **Didier Drogba**, Chelsea striker, on unrest at Stamford Bridge.

NATIONAL REFEREES 2007-08

SELECT GROUP

Bennett, Steve (Kent)
Clattenburg, Mark (Tyne and Wear)
Dean, Mike (Wirral)
Dowd, Phil (Staffs)
D'Urso, Andy (Essex)
Foy, Chris (Merseyside)
Halsey, Mark (Lancs)
Knight, Barry (Kent)
Rennie, Uriah (Yorks)
Riley, Mike (Yorks)
Styles, Rob (Hants)
Walton, Peter (Northants)
Webb, Howard (Yorks)
Wiley, Alan (Staffs)

NATIONAL GROUP

Armstrong, Paul (Berks)
Atkinson, Martin (Yorks)
*Attwell, Stuart (Warwicks)
Bates, Tony (Staffs)
Beeby, Richard (Northants)
Booth, Russell (Notts)
Boyeson, Carl (Yorks)
Bratt, Steve (West Midlands)
*Cook, Steven (Surrey)
Crossley, Phil (Kent)
Deadman, Darren (Cambs)
Dorr, Steve (Worcs)
Drysdale, Darren (Lincs)
*East, Roger (Wilts)
*Evans, Karl (Gtr Manchester)
*Foster, David (Tyne & Wear)
Friend, Kevin (Leics)
Graham, Fred (Essex)
*Haines, Andy (West Midlands)
Hall, Andy (West Midlands)
Haywood, Mark (Yorks)
Hegley, Grant (Herts)
Hill, Keith (Herts)
*Horwood, Graham (Beds)
Ilderton, Eddie (Tyne & Wear)
Jones, Michael (Cheshire)
Joslin, Phil (Notts)
Kettle, Trevor (Rutland)
Laws, Graham (Tyne & Wear)
Lee, Ray (Essex)
*Lewis, Gary (Cambs)
Lewis, Rob (Shrops)
Marriner, Andre (West Midlands)
Mason, Lee (Lancs)
Mathieson, Scott (Cheshire)
McDermid, Danny (London)
Melin, Paul (Surrey)
Miller, Nigel (Co Durham)
Miller, Pat (Beds)
Moss, Jon (Yorks)
Oliver, Clive (Northumberland)
Oliver, Michael (Northumberland)
Penn, Andy (West Midlands)
Penton, Clive (Sussex)
Pike, Mike (Cumbria)
Probert, Lee (Wilts)
Russell, Mike (Herts)
Salisbury, Graham (Lancs)
Shoebridge, Rob (Derbys)
Singh, Jarnail (Middx)
Stroud, Keith (Hants)
Swarbrick, Neil (Lancs)
Tanner, Steve (Somerset))
Taylor, Anthony (Gtr Manchester)
Taylor, Paul (Herts)
Thorpe, Mike (Suffolk)
*Ward, Gavin (Surey)
Webster, Colin (Tyne & Wear)
Whitestone, Dean (Northants)
Williamson, Iain (Berks)
Woolmer, Andy (Northants)
Wright, Kevin (Cambs)

(*New appointments)

F.A. CUP 2006-07

FIRST ROUND

Barrow 2, Bristol Rov. 3
Bishop's Stortford 3, King's Lynn 5
Bournemouth 4, Boston Utd. 0
Bradford City 4, Crewe Alexandra 0
Brentford 0, Doncaster Rov. 1
Brighton & H.A. 8, Northwich 0
Burton 1, Tamworth 2
Cheltenham Town 0, Scunthorpe Utd. 0
Chelmsford 1, Aldershot 1
Chesterfield 0, Basingstoke 1
Clevedon 1, Chester City 4
Exeter 1, Stockport Co. 2
Farsley 0, MK Dons 0
Gainsborough 1, Barnet 3
Gillingham 4, Bromley 1
Havant 1, Millwall 2
Huddersfield Town 0, Blackpool 1
Kettering 3, Oldham Athletic 4
Lewes 1, Darlington 4
Leyton Orient 2, Notts Co. 1
Macclesfield Town 0, Walsall 0
Mansfield Town 1, Accrington Stanley 0
Morecambe 2, Kidderminster Harr. 1
Newport 1, Swansea City 3
Northampton Town 0, Grimsby Town 0
Nott'm. Forest 5, Yeading 0
Peterborough Utd. 3, Rotherham Utd. 0
Port Vale 2, Lincoln City 1
Rochdale 1, Hartlepool Utd. 1
Rushden 3, Yeovil Town 1
Salisbury 3, Fleetwood 0
Shrewsbury Town 0, Hereford Utd. 0
Stafford 1, Maidenhead 1
Swindon Town 3, Carlisle Utd. 1
Torquay Utd. 2, Leatherhead 1,
Tranmere Rov. 4, Woking 2
Weymouth 2, Bury 2
Wrexham 1, Stevenage 0
Wycombe Wand. 2, Oxford 1
York City 0, Bristol City 1

FIRST ROUND REPLAYS

Aldershot 2, Chelmsford 0
Bury 4, Weymouth 3
Grimsby Town 0, Northampton Town 2
Hereford Utd. 2, Shrewsbury Town 0
Maidenhead 0, Stafford 2
MK Dons 2, Farsley 0
Scunthorpe Utd. 2, Cheltenham Town 0
Walsall 0, Macclesfield Town 1
Harlepool Utd 0, Rochdale 0
(aet, Hartlepool Utd. won 4-2 on pens)

SECOND ROUND

Aldershot 1, Basingstoke 1
Barnet 4, Northampton Town 1
Bradford City 0, Millwall 0
Brighton & H.A. 3, Stafford 0
Bristol City 4, Gillingham 3
Bristol Rov. 1, Bournemouth 1
Bury 2, Chester City 2
Darlington 1, Swansea City 3
Hereford Utd. 4, Port Vale 0
King's Lynn 0, Oldham Athletic 2
Macclesfield Town 2, Hartlepool Utd. 1
Mansfield Town 1, Doncaster Rov. 1
MK Dons 0, Blackpool 2
Rushden 1, Tamworth 2
Salisbury 1, Nott'm. Forest 1
Scunthorpe Utd. 0, Wrexham 2
Stockport Co. 2, Wycombe Wand. 1
Swindon Town 1, Morecambe 0
Torquay Utd. 1, Leyton Orient 1
Tranmere Rov. 1, Peterborough Utd. 2

SECOND ROUND REPLAYS

Basingstoke 1, Aldershot 3
Bournemouth 0, Bristol Rov. 1
Chester City 1, Bury 3
(Bury expelled for ineligible player – Chester City reinstated)
Doncaster Rov. 2, Mansfield Town 0
Leyton Orient 1, Torquay Utd. 2
Millwall 1, Bradford City 0 (aet)
Nott'm. Forest 2, Salisbury 0

DROGBA GOAL GIVES MOURINHO FULL SET OF TROPHIES

THIRD ROUND	FOURTH ROUND	FIFTH ROUND	SIXTH ROUND	SEMI-FINALS	FINAL
***Chelsea** 6	***Chelsea** 3				
Macclesfield Town 1		***Chelsea** 4			
*Nottm. Forest 2	Nottm. Forest 0				
Charlton Athletic 0			***Chelsea** 3:2		
*Blackpool 4	*Blackpool 1:2				
Aldershot 2		Norwich City 0			
*Tamworth 1	Norwich City 1:+3				
Norwich City 4				**Chelsea** +2	
*Leicester City 2:3	*Fulham 3				
Fulham 2:4		*Fulham 0			
*Stoke City 2	Stoke City 0				
Millwall 0			Tottenham 3:1		
*Cardiff City 0:0	*Tottenham 3				
Tottenham 0:4		Tottenham 4			
*Southend Utd. 1:2	Southend Utd. 1				
Barnsley 1:0					**Chelsea** +1
*Liverpool 1	*Arsenal 1:3				
Arsenal 3		*Arsenal 0:0			
*Doncaster Rov. 0	Bolton Wand. 1:1				
Bolton Wand. 4			*Blackburn Rov. 2		
*Q.P.R. 2:0	*Luton Town 0				
Luton Town 2:1		Blackburn Rov. 0:1			
*Everton 1	Blackburn Rov. 4				
Blackburn Rov. 4				Blackburn Rov. 1	
*Crystal Palace 2	*Crystal Palace 0				
Swindon Town 1		*Preston N.E. 1			
*Preston N.E. 1	Preston N.E. 2				
Sunderland 0			Manchester City 0		
*Sheffield Wed. 1:1	*Manchester City 3				
Manchester City 1:2		Manchester City 3			
*Torquay Utd. 0	Southampton 1				
Southampton 2					

*Barnet 2
Colchester Utd. 1
*Peterborough Utd. . 1:1
Plymouth Argyle 1:2
*Derby Co. 3
Wrexham 1
*Bristol Rov. 1
Hereford Utd. 0
*West Ham Utd. 3
Brighton & H.A. 0
*Watford 4
Stockport Co. 1
*Chester City 0:0
Ipswich Town 0:1
*Sheffield Utd. 0
Swansea City 3
*Bristol City 3:2
Coventry City 3:0
*Hull City 1:3
Middlesbrough 1:4
*Wolves 2:2
Oldham Athletic 2:0
*W.B.A. 3
Leeds Utd. 1
*Birmingham City .. 2:5
Newcastle Utd. 2:1
*Reading 3
Burnley 2
*Portsmouth 2
Wigan Athletic 1
Aston Villa 1
***Manchester Utd.** 2

*Barnet 0
Plymouth Argyle 2
*Derby Co. 1
Bristol Rov. 0
*West Ham Utd. 0
Watford 1
*Ipswich Town 1
Swansea City 0
*Bristol City 2:2
Middlesbrough ... 2:+A2
*Wolves 0
W.B.A. 3
*Birmingham City 2
Reading 3
Portsmouth 1
***Manchester Utd.** 2

*Plymouth Argyle 2
Derby Co. 0
*Watford 1
Ipswich Town 0
*Middlesbrough . 2:+B1
W.B.A. 2:1
Reading 1:2
***Manchester Utd.** 1:3

*Plymouth Argyle 0
Watford 1
*Middlesbrough 2:0
Manchester Utd. 2:1

Watford 1
Manchester Utd. 4

Manchester Utd. 0

*Drawn at home. +After extra-time. A – Middlesbrough won 5-4 on pens. B – Middlesbrough won 5-4 on pens. Semi-finals: Chelsea v Blackburn Rov. at Old Trafford. Manchester Utd. v Watford at Villa Park.

ROUND BY ROUND HIGHLIGHTS

FIRST ROUND

Basingstoke, bottom of the Conference South, deliver the biggest surprise when Matt Warner's goal knocks out a Chesterfield side fresh from Carling Cup successes against Wolves, Manchester City and West Ham. Yeovil, who in their non-league days were the F.A. Cup's most successful giant-killers, are beaten 3-1 by Rushden & Diamonds, for whom Michael Rankine scores twice. Two players register hat-tricks, Jake Robinson in Brighton's 8-0 romp against Northwich and Kris Commons as Nottingham Forest overcome Yeading 5-0. Chris Hall's stoppage-time goal gives Oldham a 4-3 win in one of the best matches of the day, at Kettering. But the programme is soured when fourth official Alan Sheffield is taken to hospital after being struck on the head by a coin during Swansea's 3-1 victory at Newport.

SECOND ROUND

Seven clubs from League Two overcome League One opposition. Barnet and Hereford score four against Northampton and Port Vale respectively, while Wrexham win 2-0 at high-flying Scunthorpe. Little Salisbury also earn praise, taking Nottingham Forest to a replay before bowing out 2-0 at the City Ground. Macclesfield's reward for beating Hartlepool is a visit to Chelsea. Phil Jevons's prize is the match ball for his hat-trick for Bristol City in the 4-3 victory over Gillingham.

THIRD ROUND

Tom Butler takes pride of place, scoring twice and winning a penalty as Swansea beat Sheffield United 3-0 at Bramall Lane. Nottingham Forest also knock out Premiership opposition, goals by Junior Agogo and Grant Holt accounting for Charlton. Macclesfield's big day is going well until goalkeeper Tommy Lee is sent off for bringing down Andriy Shevchenko, opening the way for Frank Lampard to complete a hat-trick from the penalty spot in Chelsea's 6-1 victory. Loanee Arturo Lupoli also scores three, in Derby's 3-1 win over Wrexham. Arturo's parent club, Arsenal, take the honours in the heavyweight tie of the round as Tomas Rosicky nets twice in a 3-1 success over holders Liverpool at Anfield. Two replays prove eventful. Birmingham are 5-1 winners at Newcastle, who have Steven Taylor sent off. Wayne Routledge delivers a stoppage-time winner after Fulham retrieve a 3-1 deficit against Leicester with two goals from Vincenzo Montella, his first for the club.

FOURTH ROUND

Arsenal overcome missed penalties by Gilberto Silva and Julio Baptista to prevail 3-1 in an eventful replay at Bolton after extra-time. Emmanuel Adebayor scores twice and other two-goal marksmen are Leroy Lita, in Reading's 3-2 success at Birmingham, Matt Derbyshire as Blackburn ease through 4-0 at Luton and Wayne Rooney for Manchester United who overcome Portsmouth 2-1. The Black Country derby proves a one-sided affair, with West Bromwich Albion mastering Wolves 3-0 at Molineux.

FIFTH ROUND

Manchester United score three times in the first six minutes of a replay against Reading, but are clinging on to a 3-2 lead at the end. In another replay, Benni McCarthy's 87th minute strike for Blackburn ends Arsenal's interest in the competition. Chelsea, against Norwich, and Tottenham, at Fulham, record 4-0 victories. Michael Ball scores his first goal for Manchester City in their 3-1 success at Preston. Unluckiest team are ten-man Ipswich, who continue to dominate at Watford after George O'Callaghan's dismissal but go out to Damien Francis's 88th minute goal.

SIXTH ROUND

Chelsea retrieve a 3-1 half-time deficit against Tottenham and win the replay 2-1 at White Hart Lane. Blackburn's Aaron Mokoena also experiences highs and lows, scoring his first goal for the club but then receiving a second yellow card in the 2-0 victory over Manchester City. Hameur Bouazza gives Watford a hard-earned victory at Plymouth, while Cristiano Ronaldo's penalty for Manchester United sees off Middlesbrough in a replay.

SEMI-FINALS

Manchester United overcome a spirited challenge from Watford at Villa Park in the first of two sharply-contrasting ties. Wayne Rooney gives them an early lead and although Hameur Bouazza levels, Cristiano Ronaldo quickly restores United's lead. Then second half goals from Rooney and Kieran Richardson confirm their superiority. Chelsea look as if they are set for a comfortable passage when leading Blackburn at Old Trafford through Frank Lampard's strike. But Jason Roberts equalises and Morten Gamst Pedersen has a golden opportunity to win it with a header. But he is off target and Rovers are punished by Michael Ballack's extra-time winner.

FINAL

A gleaming new stadium, but a tired old final. Perhaps we should not have been surprised that instead of match in keeping with Wembley's splendid new surroundings, the Premiership's top two teams delivered a sterile, unsatisfactory encounter. Chelsea were playing their 64th game of the season. They had gone all the way in the Carling Cup, reached the semi-finals of the Champions League and chased their rivals most of the way to the title. Manchester United, in their 60th match, had poured so much into regaining the title and trying to give Sir Alex Ferguson the second European Cup he craved.

A spongy, stamina-sapping pitch and a period of extra-time placed even greater demands on both sets of players. No wonder there were some tired legs by the time Steve Bennett brought proceedings to a close. Having to negotiate 107 steps to the Royal Box for the presentations was the last thing the players needed, although John Terry and his team at least were able to forget their weariness after Didier Drogba's 33rd goal of the season provided a rare moment of quality to settle the issue in their favour.

Drogba was beaten to the PFA and football writers' Player of the Year awards by the consistent brilliance of Cristiano Ronaldo. This time, however, the Ivory Coast striker had the final say at a time when the prospect of a third successive penalty shoot-out to decide the trophy was uppermost in everyone's mind. Wayne Bridge, preferred to a not fully-fit Ashley Cole at left-back, played an angled cross into the middle, where John Obi Mikel knocked it into the path of Drogba. A one-two with Frank Lampard gave Drogba the extra half-yard he exploited to the full by touching a volley past the advancing Edwin van der Sar.

So, seven years after Chelsea brought down the F.A. Cup curtain at the old Wembley by beating Aston Villa, they began a new era by grinding out victory against a side who were rarely allowed to play the expansive football that delivered the title. Paul Scholes worked hard searching for openings and Wayne Rooney threatened sporadically. But Ronaldo was shackled from start to finish and for long spells the teams cancelled each other out. United's best chance embraced the game's one major talking point, Ryan Giggs sliding in on Rooney's cross and his momentum carrying Petr Cech, along with the ball, over the line. Ferguson insisted Giggs had been nudged by Michael Essien. For many neutrals, the claim owed more to a sense of frustration that his side had not been good enough on the day than anything else.

CHELSEA 1, MANCHESTER UNITED 0 (aet)

Wembley (89,826), Saturday, May 19, 2007

Chelsea (4-1-4-1): Cech, Paulo Ferreira, Essien, Terry, Bridge, Makelele, Wright-Phillips (Kalou 93), Mikel, Lampard, J. Cole (Robben 46, A. Cole 107), Drogba. **Subs not used:** Cudicini, Diarra. **Scorer:** Drogba (116). **Booked:** Makelele, Kalou, Paulo Ferreira, A. Cole. **Manager:** Jose Mourinho.

Manchester Utd. (4-4-1-1): Van der Sar, Brown, Ferdinand, Vidic, Heinze, Fletcher (Smith 92), Carrick (O'Shea 112), Scholes, Ronaldo, Giggs (Solskjaer 112), Rooney. **Subs not used:** Kuszczak, Evra. **Booked:** Scholes, Smith, Vidic. **Manager:** Sir Alex Ferguson.

Referee: S. Bennett (Kent). **Half-time:** 0-0.

HOW THEY REACHED THE FINAL

CHELSEA

Round 3: 6-1 home to Macclesfield Town (Lampard 3, 1 pen, Wright-Phillips, Mikel, Ricardo Carvalho)
Round 4: 3-0 home to Nott'm. Forest (Shevchenko, Drogba, Mikel)
Round 5: 4-0 home to Norwich City (Wright-Phillips, Drogba, Essien, Shevchenko)
Round 6: 3-3 home to Tottenham (Lampard 2, Kalou); 2-1 away to Tottenham (Shevchenko, Wright-Phillips)
Semi-final: 2-1 v Blackburn Rov. (aet, Lampard, Ballack).

MANCHESTER UNITED

Round 3: 2-1 home to Aston Villa (Larsson,, Solskjaer)
Round 4: 2-1 home to Portsmouth (Rooney 2)
Round 5: 1-1 home to Reading (Carrick), 3-2 away to Reading (Heinze, Saha, Solskjaer)
Round 6: 2-2 away to Middlesbrough (Rooney, Ronaldo pen), 1-0 home to Middlesbrough (Ronaldo pen)
Semi-final: 4-1 v Watford (Rooney 2, Ronaldo, Richardson)

LEADING SCORERS (FROM FIRST ROUND)

6 Lampard (Chelsea); 5 Bishop (Bury), Huckerby (Norwich City), Keane (Tottenham), Rooney (Manchester Utd.), Viduka (Middlesbrough); 4 Derbyshire (Blackburn Rov.), Jevons (Bristol City), Lita (Reading), Robinson (Brighton & H.A.), Walker (Bristol Rov.), Yakubu (Middlesbrough).

FINAL FACTS AND FIGURES

* Chelsea had not beaten Manchester United in the F.A. Cup since 1950 when goals by Robert Campbell and Roy Bentley brought a 2-0 win in a sixth round tie at Stamford Bridge, watched by a crowd of 70,362.

* Didier Drogba's match-winner was the first time he had scored against United.

* Jose Mourinho completed a full set of trophies at the end of his third season in English football, having won two Premiership titles, the Carling Cup twice and the Community Shield once.

* Chelsea became the third team to complete an F.A. Cup/League Cup double after Arsenal (1993) and Liverpool (2001).

* United were making a record 18th appearance in the final, one more than Arsenal.

* Ryan Giggs joined eight players who had appeared in five F.A. Cup Finals at Wembley – Joe Hulme, Johnny Giles, Pat Rice, Frank Stapleton, Ray Clemence, Mark Hughes, John Barnes and Roy Keane.

* Giggs also equalled Keane's record of seven finals at Wembley and the Millennium Stadium, having appeared in two in Cardiff.

* The last time the top two teams in the top division contested the final was in 1986 when champions Liverpool defeated runners-up Everton 3-1.

* Prince William, president of the F.A. officially opened the new Wembley and welcomed the F.A. Cup back to its 'rightful home.'

* The F.A. defended the cost of tickets, ranging from £35 to £95, and prices inside the stadium, which included £10 for a programme and £5 for a burger.

QUOTE-UNQUOTE

'Officials are being pilloried right, left and centre for decisions they do or do not give. We need a cultural change. The game will die without referees and we need to show them more respect' – **David Elleray**, former top Premiership official.

'I promise you that if one day I have a ball that is two metres inside my goal and the referee doesn't allow it, I won't speak about referees for two years' – **Jose Mourinho**, Chelsea manager.

'Enjoy the second half of the Uriah Rennie Show' – Deepdale's public address announcement at the Preston – Crystal Palace game after referee Rennie dismisses two Preston penalty claims.

'We bought 23 single tickets at Hanger Lane station' – **Micky Adams**, Coventry manager, after his squad had to use the London Underground to complete their journey to play Q.P.R. when their coach was stuck in traffic.

'Every player dives, not just me. It's just because it is me that people talk about it' – **El-Hadji Diouf**, Bolton striker.

'Chelsea as a football club and a brand are more dynamic, more relevant' – **Peter Kenyon**, chief executive, predicting they will eventually become the biggest club in the world.

'We are going to quake and tremble about that' – **Sir Alex Ferguson**, Manchester United manager, in response to Peter Kenyon's thoughts.

'Football's a difficult business and aren't they all prima donnas?' – **The Queen** talking to Premier League chairman Sir David Richards.

'I think my wife was having serious doubts about whether I was a footballer or not. At least I can show her a bit of proof' – **Malcolm Christie**, Middlesbrough striker, on scoring on his comeback after a long lay-off through injury.

'The wife told me it looked as if I knew what I was doing a bit more' – **Gareth Southgate**, Middlesbrough manager, after switching to wearing a suit on the touchline.

'I'll wake up tomorrow and find someone has scored an extra goal against us somewhere' – **Gordon Strachan** after Celtic reach the Champions League knock-out stage for the first time.

F.A. CUP FINAL TEAMS 1900-2006

1900 BURY – Thompson; Darrock, Davidson, Pray, Leeming, Ross, Richards, Wood, McLuckie, Sagar, Plant. **SOUTHAMPTON** – Robinson; Meehan, Durber, Meston, Chadwick, Petrie, Turner, Yates, Farrell, Wood, Milward. **Scorers:** Bury – McLuckie 2, Wood, Plant.

1901 TOTTENHAM – Clawley; Erentz, Tait, Norris, Hughes, Jones, Smith, Cameron, Brown, Copeland, Kirwan. **SHEFFIELD UTD.** – Foulke; Thickett, Boyle, Johnson, Morren, Needham, Bennett, Field, Hedley, Priest, Lipsham. **Scorers:** (first match) Tottenham – Brown 2, Sheff. Utd. – Bennett, Priest. **Scorers:** (second match) Tottenham – Cameron, Smith, Brown, Sheff. Utd. – Priest.

1902 SHEFFIELD UTD. – Foulke; Thickett, Boyle, Needham, Wilkinson, Johnson, Barnes, Common, Hedley, Priest, Lipsham. (Bennett injured in first match and Barnes took his place in the replay). **SOUTHAMPTON** – Robinson; C. B. Fry, Molyneux, Bowman, Lee, A. Turner, Wood, Brown, Chadwick, J. Turner, Metson. **Scorers:** (first match) Sheff. Utd. – Common, Southampton – Wood. **Scorers:** (second match) Sheff. Utd. – Hedley, Barnes, Southampton – Brown.

1903 BURY – Monteith; Lindsey, McEwan, Johnson, Thorpe, Ross, Richards, Wood, Sagar, Leeming, Plant. **DERBY CO.** – Fryer; Methven, Morris, Warren, Goodall (A.), May, Warrington, York, Boag, Richards, Davis. **Scorers:** Bury – Ross, Sagar, Leeming 2, Wood, Plant.

1904 MANCHESTER CITY – Hillman; McMahon, Burgess, Frost, Hynde, S. B. Ashworth, Meredith, Livingstone, Gillespie, Turnbull (A.), Booth. **BOLTON WAND.** – D. Davies; Brown, Struthers, Clifford, Greenhalgh, Freebairn, Stokes, Marsh, Yenson, White, Taylor. **Scorer:** Manchester City – Meredith.

1905 ASTON VILLA – George; Spencer, Miles, Pearson, Leake, Windmill, Brawn, Garratty, Hampton, Bache, Hall. **NEWCASTLE UTD.** – Lawrence; McCombie, Carr, Gardner, Aitken, McWilliam, Rutherford, Howie, Appleyard, Veitch, Gosnell. **Scorer:** Aston Villa – Hampton 2.

1906 EVERTON – Scott; Balmer (W.), Crelly, Makepeace, Taylor, Abbott, Sharp, Bolton, Young, Settle, H. P. Hardman. **NEWCASTLE UTD.** – Lawrence; McCombie, Carr, Gardner, Aitken, McWilliam, Rutherford, Howie, Veitch, Orr, Gosnell. **Scorer:** Everton – Young.

1907 SHEFFIELD WED. – Lyall; Layton, Burton, Brittleton, Crawshaw, Bartlett, Chapman, Bradshaw, Wilson, Stewart, Simpson. **EVERTON** – Scott; Balmer (W.), Balmer (R.), Makepeace, Taylor, Abbott, Sharp, Bolton, Young, Settle, H. P. Hardman. **Scorers:** Sheff. Wed. – Stewart, Simpson, Everton – Sharp.

1908 WOLVES – Lunn; Jones, Collins, Rev. K. R. G. Hunt, Wooldridge, Bishop, Harrison, Shelton, Hedley, Radford, Pedley. **NEWCASTLE UTD.** – Lawrence; McCracken, Pudan, Gardner, Veitch, McWilliam, Rutherford, Howie, Appleyard, Speedle, Wilson. **Scorers:** Wolves – Hunt, Hedley, Harrison, Newcastle Utd. – Howie.

1909 MANCHESTER UTD. – Moger; Stacey, Hayes, Duckworth, Roberts, Bell, Meredith, Halse, Turnbull (J.), Turnbull (A.), Wall. **BRISTOL CITY** – Clay; Annan, Cottle, Hanlin, Wedlock, Spear, Staniforth, Hardy, Gilligan, Burton, Hilton. **Scorer:** Manchester Utd. – Turnbull (A.).

1910 NEWCASTLE UTD. – Lawrence; McCracken, Carr, Veitch, Low, McWilliam, Rutherford, Howie, Shepherd, Higgins, Wilson. (Whitson was injured in first match and Carr took his place in the replay). **BARNSLEY** – Mearns; Downs, Ness, Glendinning, Boyle, Utley, Bartrop, Gadsby, Lillycrop, Tufnell, Forman. **Scorers:** (first match) Newcastle Utd. – Rutherford, Barnsley – Tufnell. **Scorer:** (second match) Newcastle Utd. – Shepherd 2 (1 pen.).

1911 BRADFORD CITY – Mellors; Campbell, Taylor, Robinson, Torrance, McDonald, Logan, Spiers, O'Rourke, Devine, Thompson. (Gildea played centre half in the first match). **NEWCASTLE UTD.** – Lawrence; McCracken, Whitson, Veitch, Low, Willis, Rutherford, Jobey, Stewart, Higgins, Wilson. **Scorer:** Bradford City – Spiers.

1912 BARNSLEY – Cooper; Downs, Taylor, Glendinning, Bratley, Utley, Bartrop, Tufnell, Lillycrop, Travers, Moore. **W.B.A.** – Pearson; Cook, Pennington, Baddeley, Buck, McNeal, Jephcott, Wright, Pailor, Bower, Shearman. **Scorer:** Barnsley – Tufnell.

1913 ASTON VILLA – Hardy; Lyons, Weston, Barber, Harrop, Leach, Wallace, Halse, Hampton, Stephenson (C.), Bache. **SUNDERLAND** – Butler; Gladwin, Ness, Cuggy, Thompson, Low, Mordue, Buchan, Richardson, Holley, Martin. **Scorer:** Aston Villa – Barber.

1914 BURNLEY – Sewell; Bamford, Taylor, Halley, Boyle, Watson, Nesbit, Lindley, Freeman, Hodgson, Mosscrop. **LIVERPOOL** – Campbell; Longworth, Pursell, Fairfoul, Ferguson, McKinlay, Sheldon, Metcalfe, Miller, Lacey, Nicholl. **Scorer:** Burnley – Freeman.

1915 SHEFFIELD UTD. – Gough; Cook, English, Sturgess, Brelsford, Utley, Simmons, Fazackerley, Kitchen, Masterman, Evans. **CHELSEA** – Molyneux; Bettridge, Harrow, Taylor, Logan, Walker, Ford, Halse, Thompson, Croal, McNeil. **Scorers:** Sheff. Utd. – Simmons, Fazackerley, Kitchen.

1920 ASTON VILLA – Hardy; Smart, Weston, Ducat, Barson, Moss, Wallace, Kirton, Walker, Stephenson (C.), Dorrell. **HUDDERSFIELD TOWN** – Mutch; Wood, Bullock, Slade, Wilson, Watson, Richardson, Mann, Taylor, Swan, Islip. **Scorer:** Aston VIlla – Kirton.

1921 TOTTENHAM – Hunter; Clay, McDonald, Smith, Walters, Grimsdell; Banks, Seed, Cantrell, Bliss, Dimmock. **WOLVES** – George; Woodward, Marshall, Gregory, Hodnett, Riley, Lea, Burrill, Edmonds, Potts, Brooks. **Scorer:** Tottenham – Dimmock.

1922 HUDDERSFIELD TOWN – Mutch; Wood, Wadsworth, Slade, Wilson, Watson, Richardson, Mann, Islip, Stephenson, Smith (W.H.). **PRESTON N.E.** – J. F. Mitchell; Hamilton, Doolan, Duxbury, McCall, Williamson, Rawlings, Jefferis, Roberts, Woodhouse, Quinn. **Scorer:** Huddersfield Town – Smith (pen.).

1923 BOLTON WAND. – Pym; Haworth, Finney, Nuttall, Seddon, Jennings, Butler, Jack, Smith (J. R.), Smith (J.), Vizard. **WEST HAM UTD.** – Hufton; Henderson, Young, Bishop, Kay, Tresadern, Richards, Brown, Watson (V.), Moore, Ruffell. **Scorers:** Bolton Wand. – Jack, Smith (J. R.).

1924 NEWCASTLE UTD. – Bradley; Hampson, Hudspeth, Mooney, Spencer, Gibson, Low, Cowan, Harris, McDonald, Seymour. **ASTON VILLA** – Jackson; Smart, Mort, Moss, Dr. V. E. Milne, Blackburn, York, Kirton, Capewell, Walker, Dorrell. **Scorers:** Newcastle Utd. – Harris, Seymour.

1925 SHEFFIELD UTD. – Sutcliffe; Cook, Milton, Pantling, King, Green, Mercer, Boyle, Johnson, Gillespie, Tunstall. **CARDIFF CITY** – Farquharson; Nelson, Blair, Wake, Keenor, Hardy, Davies (W.), Gill, Nicholson, Beadles, Evans (J.). **Scorer:** Sheff. Utd. – Tunstall.

1926 BOLTON WAND. – Pym; Haworth, Greenhalgh, Nuttall, Seddon, Jennings, Butler, Jack, Smith (J. R.), Smith (J.), Vizard. **MANCHESTER CITY** – Goodchild; Cookson, McCloy, Pringle, Cowan, McMullan, Austin, Browell, Roberts, Johnson, Hicks. **Scorer:** Bolton Wand. – Jack.

1927 CARDIFF CITY – Farquharson; Nelson, Watson, Keenor, Sloan, Hardy, Curtis, Irving, Ferguson, Davies (L.), McLachlan. **ARSENAL** – Lewis; Parker, Kennedy, Baker, Butler, John, Hulme, Buchan, Brain, Blyth, Hoar. **Scorer:** Cardiff City – Ferguson.

1928 BLACKBURN ROV. – Crawford; Hutton, Jones, Healless, Rankin, Campbell, Thornewell, Puddefoot, Roscamp, McLean, Rigby. **HUDDERSFIELD TOWN** – Mercer; Goodall, Barkas, Redfern, Wilson, Steele, Jackson (A.), Kelly, Brown, Stephenson, Smith (W.H.). **Scorers:** Blackburn Rov. – Roscamp 2, McLean, Huddersfield Town – Jackson.

1929 BOLTON WAND. – Pym; Haworth, Finney, Kean, Seddon, Nuttall, Butler, McClelland, Blackmore, Gibson, Cook (W.). **PORTSMOUTH** – Gilfillan; Mackie, Bell, Nichol, McIlwaine, Thackeray, Forward, Smith (J.), Weddle, Watson, Cook (F.). **Scorers:** Bolton Wand. – Butler, Blackmore.

1930 ARSENAL – Preedy; Parker, Hapgood, Baker, Seddon, John, Hulme, Jack, Lambert, James, Bastin. **HUDDERSFIELD TOWN** – Turner; Goodall, Spence, Naylor, Wilson, Campbell, Jackson (A.), Kelly, Davies, Raw, Smith (W. H.). **Scorers:** Arsenal – James, Lambert.

1931 W.B.A. – Pearson; Shaw, Trentham, Magee, Richardson (W.), Edwards, Glidden, Carter, Richardson (W. G.), Sandford, Wood. **BIRMINGHAM CITY** – Hibbs; Liddell, Barkas, Cringan, Morrall, Leslie, Briggs, Crosbie, Bradford, Gregg, Curtis. **Scorers:** W.B.A. – Richardson (W. G.) 2, Birmingham City – Bradford.

1932 NEWCASTLE UTD. – McInroy; Nelson, Fairhurst, McKenzie, Davidson, Weaver, Boyd, Richardson, Allen, McMenemy, Lang. **ARSENAL** – Moss; Parker, Hapgood, Jones

(C.), Roberts, Male, Hulme, Jack, Lambert, Bastin, John. **Scorers:** Newcastle Utd. – Allen 2, Arsenal – John.

1933 **EVERTON** – Sagar; Cook, Cresswell, Britton, White, Thomson, Geldard, Dunn, Dean, Johnson, Stein. **MANCHESTER CITY** – Langford; Cann, Dale, Busby, Cowan, Bray, Toseland, Marshall, Herd, McMullan, Brook. **Scorers:** Everton – Stein, Dean, Dunn.

1934 **MANCHESTER CITY** – Swift; Barnett, Dale, Busby, Cowan, Bray, Toseland, Marshall, Tilson, Herd, Brook. **PORTSMOUTH** – Gilfillan; Mackie, Smith (W.), Nichol, Allen, Thackeray, Worrall, Smith (J.), Weddle, Easson, Rutherford. **Scorers:** Manchester City – Tilson 2, Portsmouth – Rutherford.

1935 **SHEFFIELD WED.** – Brown; Nibloe, Catlin, Sharp, Millership, Burrows, Hooper, Surtees, Palethorpe, Starling, Rimmer. **W.B.A.** – Pearson; Shaw, Trentham, Murphy, Richardson (W.), Edwards, Glidden, Carter, Richardson (W. G.), Sandford, Boyes. **Scorers:** Sheff. Wed. – Rimmer 2, Palethorpe, Hooper, W.B.A. – Boyes, Sandford.

1936 **ARSENAL** – Wilson; Male, Hapgood, Crayston, Roberts, Copping, Hulme, Bowden, Drake, James, Bastin. **SHEFFIELD UTD.** – Smith; Hooper, Wilkinson, Jackson, Johnson, McPherson, Barton, Barclay, Dodds, Pickering, Williams. **Scorer:** Arsenal – Drake.

1937 **SUNDERLAND** – Mapson; Gorman, Hall, Thomson, Johnston, McNab, Duns, Carter, Gurney, Gallacher, Burbanks. **PRESTON N.E.** – Burns; Gallimore, Beattie (A.), Shankly, Tremelling, Milne, Dougal, Beresford, O'Donnell (F.), Fagan, O'Donnell (H). **Scorers:** Sunderland – Gurney, Carter, Burbanks, Preston N.E. – O'Donnell (F.).

1938 **PRESTON N.E.** – Holdcroft; Gallimore, Beattie (A.), Shankly, Smith, Batey, Watmough, Mutch, Maxwell, Beattie (R.), O'Donnell (H.). **HUDDERSFIELD TOWN** – Hesford; Craig, Mountford, Willingham, Young, Boot, Hulme, Isaac, McFadyen, Barclay, Beasley. **Scorer:** Preston N.E. – Mutch (pen.).

1939 **PORTSMOUTH** – Walker; Morgan, Rochford, Guthrie, Rowe, Wharton, Worrall, McAlinden, Anderson, Barlow, Parker. **WOLVES** – Scott; Morris, Taylor, Galley, Cullis, Gardiner, Burton, McIntosh, Westcott, Dorsett, Maguire. **Scorers:** Portsmouth – Barlow, Anderson, Parker 2, Wolves – Dorsett.

1946 **DERBY CO.** – Woodley; Nicholas, Howe, Bullions, Leuty, Musson, Harrison, Carter, Stamps, Doherty, Duncan. **CHARLTON ATHLETIC** – Bartram; Phipps, Shreeve, Turner (H.), Oakes, Johnson, Fell, Brown, A. A. Turner, Welsh, Duffy. **Scorers:** Derby Co. – Turner (H.) (o.g.), Doherty, Stamps 2, Charlton Athletic – Turner (H.).

1947 **CHARLTON ATHLETIC** – Bartram; Croker (P.), Shreeve, Johnson, Phipps, Whittaker, Hurst, Dawson, Robinson (W.), Welsh, Duffy. **BURNLEY** – Strong; Woodruff, Mather, Attwell, Brown, Bray, Chew, Morris, Harrison, Potts, F. P. Kippax. **Scorer:** Charlton Athletic – Duffy.

1948 **MANCHESTER UTD.** – Crompton; Carey, Aston, Anderson, Chilton, Cockburn, Delaney, Morris, Rowley, Pearson, Mitten. **BLACKPOOL** – Robinson; Shimwell, Crosland, Johnston, Hayward, Kelly, Matthews, Munro, Mortensen, Dick, Rickett. **Scorers:** Manchester Utd. – Rowley 2, Pearson, Anderson, Blackpool – Shimwell (pen.), Mortensen.

1949 **WOLVES** – Williams; Pritchard, Springthorpe, Crook (W.), Shorthouse, Wright, Hancocks, Smyth, Pye, Dunn, Mullen. **LEICESTER CITY** – Bradley; Jelly, Scott, Harrison (W.), Plummer, King, Griffiths, Lee, Harrison (J.), Chisholm, Adam. **Scorers:** Wolves – Pye 2, Smyth, Leicester City – Griffiths.

1950 **ARSENAL** – Swindin; Scott, Barnes, Forbes, Compton (L.), Mercer, Cox, Logie, Goring, Lewis, Compton (D.). **LIVERPOOL** – Sidlow; Lambert, Spicer, Taylor, Hughes, Jones, Payne, Baron, Stubbins, Fagan, Liddell. **Scorer:** Arsenal – Lewis 2.

1951 **NEWCASTLE UTD.** – Fairbrother; Cowell, Corbett, Harvey, Brennan, Crowe, Walker, Taylor, Milburn, Robledo (G.), Mitchell. **BLACKPOOL** – Farm; Shimwell, Garrett, Johnston, Hayward, Kelly, Matthews, Mudie, Mortensen, W. J. Slater, Perry. **Scorer:** Newcastle Utd. – Milburn 2.

1952 **NEWCASTLE UTD.** – Simpson; Cowell, McMichael, Harvey, Brennan, Robledo (E.), Walker, Foulkes, Milburn, Robledo (G.), Mitchell. **ARSENAL** – Swindin; Barnes, Smith (L.), Forbes, Daniel, Mercer, Cox, Logie, Holton, Lishman, Roper. **Scorer:** Newcastle Utd. – Robledo (G.).

1953 **BLACKPOOL** – Farm; Shimwell, Garrett, Fenton, Johnston, Robinson, Matthews, Taylor, Mortensen, Mudie, Perry. **BOLTON WAND.** – Hanson; Ball, Banks (R.), Wheeler,

Barrass, Bell, Holden, Moir, Lofthouse, Hassall, Langton. **Scorers:** Blackpool – Mortensen 3, Perry, Bolton Wand. – Lofthouse, Moir, Bell.

1954 W.B.A. – Sanders; Kennedy, Millard, Dudley, Dugdale, Barlow, Griffin, Ryan, Allen, Nicholls, Lee. **PRESTON N.E.** – Thompson; Cunningham, Walton, Docherty, Marston, Forbes, Finney, Foster, Wayman, Baxter, Morrison. **Scorers:** W.B.A. – Allen 2 (1 pen.), Griffin, Preston N.E. – Morrison, Wayman.

1955 NEWCASTLE UTD. – Simpson; Cowell, Batty, Scoular, Stokoe, Casey, White, Milburn, Keeble, Hannah, Mitchell. **MANCHESTER CITY** – Trautmann; Meadows, Little, Barnes, Ewing, Paul, Spurdle, Hayes, Revie, Johnstone, Fagan. **Scorers:** Newcastle Utd. – Milburn, Mitchell, Hannah, Manchester City – Johnstone.

1956 MANCHESTER CITY – Trautmann; Leivers, Little, Barnes, Ewing, Paul, Johnstone, Hayes, Revie, Dyson, Clarke. **BIRMINGHAM CITY** – Merrick; Hall, Green, Newman, Smith, Boyd, Astall, Kinsey, Brown, Murphy, Govan. **Scorers:** Manchester City – Hayes, Dyson, Johnstone, Birmingham City – Kinsey.

1957 ASTON VILLA – Sims; Lynn, Aldis, Crowther, Dugdale, Saward, Smith, Sewell, Myerscough, Dixon, McParland. **MANCHESTER UTD.** – Wood; Foulkes, Byrne, Colman, Blanchflower, Edwards, Berry, Whelan, Taylor (T.), Charlton, Pegg. **Scorers:** Aston Villa – McParland 2, Manchester Utd. – Taylor.

1958 BOLTON WANDERERS – Hopkinson; Hartle, Banks (T.), Hennin, Higgins, Edwards, Birch, Stevens, Lofthouse, Parry, Holden. **MANCHESTER UTD.** – Gregg; Foulkes, Greaves, Goodwin, Cope, Crowther, Dawson, Taylor (E.), Charlton, Viollet, Webster. **Scorer:** Bolton Wand. – Lofthouse 2.

1959 NOTT'M FOREST – Thomson; Whare, McDonald, Whitefoot, McKinlay, Burkitt, Dwight, Quigley, Wilson, Gray, Imlach. **LUTON TOWN** – Baynham; McNally, Hawkes, Groves, Owen, Pacey, Bingham, Brown, Morton, Cummins, Gregory. **Scorers:** Nott'm. Forest – Dwight, Wilson, Luton Town – Pacey.

1960 WOLVES – Finlayson; Showell, Harris, Clamp, Slater, Flowers, Deeley, Stobart, Murray, Broadbent, Horne. **BLACKBURN ROV.** – Leyland; Bray, Whelan, Clayton, Woods, McGrath, Bimpson, Dobing, Dougan, Douglas, MacLeod. **Scorers:** Wolves – McGrath (o.g.), Deeley 2.

1961 TOTTENHAM – Brown; Baker, Henry, Blanchflower, Norman, Mackay, Jones, White, Smith, Allen, Dyson. **LEICESTER CITY** – Banks; Chalmers, Norman, McLintock, King, Appleton, Riley, Walsh, McIlmoyle, Keyworth, Cheesebrough. **Scorers:** Tottenham – Smith, Dyson.

1962 TOTTENHAM – Brown; Baker, Henry, Blanchflower, Norman, Mackay, Medwin, White, Smith, Greaves, Jones. **BURNLEY** – Blacklaw; Angus, Elder, Adamson, Cummings, Miller, Connelly, McIlroy, Pointer, Robson, Harris. **Scorers:** Tottenham – Greaves, Smith, Blanchflower (pen.), Burnley – Robson.

1963 MANCHESTER UTD. – Gaskell; Dunne, Cantwell, Crerand, Foulkes, Setters, Giles, Quixall, Herd, Law, Charlton. **LEICESTER CITY** – Banks; Sjoberg, Norman, McLintock, King, Appleton, Riley, Cross, Keyworth, Gibson, Stringfellow. **Scorers:** Manchester Utd. – Law, Herd 2, Leicester City – Keyworth.

1964 WEST HAM UTD. – Standen; Bond, Burkett, Bovington, Brown, Moore, Brabrook, Boyce, Byrne, Hurst, Sissons. **PRESTON N.E.** – Kelly; Ross, Smith, Lawton, Singleton, Kendall, Wilson, Ashworth, Dawson, Spavin, Holden. **Scorers:** West Ham Utd. – Sissons, Hurst, Boyce, Preston N.E. – Holden, Dawson.

1965 LIVERPOOL – Lawrence; Lawler, Byrne, Strong, Yeats, Stevenson, Callaghan, Hunt, St. John, Smith, Thompson. **LEEDS UTD.** – Sprake; Reaney, Bell, Bremner, Charlton, Hunter, Giles, Storrie, Peacock, Collins, Johanneson. **Scorers:** Liverpool – Hunt, St. John, Leeds Utd. – Bremner.

1966 EVERTON – West; Wright, Wilson, Gabriel, Labone, Harris, Scott, Trebilcock, Young, Harvey, Temple. **SHEFFIELD WED.** – Springett; Smith, Megson, Eustace, Ellis, Young, Pugh, Fantham, McCalliog, Ford, Quinn. **Scorers:** Everton – Trebilcock 2, Temple, Sheff. Wed. – McCalliog, Ford.

1967 TOTTENHAM – Jennings; Kinnear, Knowles, Mullery, England, Mackay, Robertson, Greaves, Gilzean, Venables, Saul. **CHELSEA** – Bonetti; Harris (A.), McCreadie, Hollins, Hinton, Harris (R.), Cooke, Baldwin, Hateley, Tambling, Boyle. **Scorers:** Tottenham – Robertson, Saul, Chelsea – Tambling.

1968 W.B.A. – Osborne; Fraser, Williams, Brown, Talbut, Kaye (Clarke), Lovett, Collard, Astle, Hope, Clark. **EVERTON** – West; Wright, Wilson, Kendall, Labone, Harvey, Husband, Ball, Royle, Hurst, Morrissey. **Scorer:** W.B.A. – Astle.

1969 MANCHESTER CITY – Dowd; Book, Pardoe, Doyle, Booth, Oakes, Summerbee, Bell, Lee, Young, Coleman. **LEICESTER CITY** – Shilton; Rodrigues, Nish, Roberts, Woollett, Cross, Fern, Gibson, Lochhead, Clarke, Glover (Manley). **Scorer:** Manchester City – Young.

1970 CHELSEA – Bonetti; Webb, McCreadie, Hollins, Dempsey, Harris (R.) (Hinton), Baldwin, Houseman, Osgood, Hutchinson, Cooke. **LEEDS UTD.** – Sprake; Madeley, Cooper, Bremner, Charlton, Hunter, Lorimer, Clarke, Jones, Giles, Gray. **Scorers:** Chelsea – Houseman, Hutchinson, Leeds Utd. – Charlton, Jones. **Replay: CHELSEA** – Bonetti; Harris (R.), McCreadie, Hollins, Dempsey, Webb, Baldwin, Cooke, Osgood (Hinton), Hutchinson, Houseman. **LEEDS UTD.** – Harvey; Madeley, Cooper, Bremner, Charlton, Hunter, Lorimer, Clarke, Jones, Giles, Gray. **Scorers:** Chelsea – Osgood, Webb, Leeds Utd. – Jones.

1971 ARSENAL – Wilson; Rice, McNab, Storey (Kelly), McLintock, Simpson, Armstrong, Graham, Radford, Kennedy, George. **LIVERPOOL** – Clemence; Lawler, Lindsay, Smith, Lloyd, Hughes, Callaghan, Evans (Thompson), Heighway, Toshack, Hall. **Scorers:** Arsenal – Kelly, George, Liverpool – Heighway.

1972 LEEDS UTD. – Harvey; Reaney, Madeley, Bremner, Charlton, Hunter, Lorimer, Clarke, Jones, Giles, Gray. **ARSENAL** – Barnett; Rice, McNab, Storey, McLintock, Simpson, Armstrong, Ball, Radford (Kennedy), George, Graham. **Scorer:** Leeds Utd. – Clarke.

1973 SUNDERLAND – Montgomery; Malone, Guthrie, Horswill, Watson, Pitt, Kerr, Hughes, Halom, Porterfield, Tueart. **LEEDS UTD.** – Harvey; Reaney, Cherry, Bremner, Madeley, Hunter, Lorimer, Clarke, Jones, Giles, Gray (Yorath). **Scorer:** Sunderland – Porterfield.

1974 LIVERPOOL – Clemence; Smith, Lindsay, Thompson, Cormack, Hughes, Keegan, Hall, Heighway, Toshack, Callaghan. **NEWCASTLE UTD.** – McFaul; Clark, Kennedy, McDermott, Howard, Moncur, Smith (Gibb), Cassidy, Macdonald, Tudor, Hibbitt. **Scorers:** Liverpool – Keegan (2), Heighway.

1975 WEST HAM UTD. – Day; McDowell, Lampard, Bonds, Taylor (T.), Lock, Jennings, Paddon, Taylor (A.), Brooking, Holland. **FULHAM** – Mellor; Cutbush, Fraser, Mullery, Lacy, Moore, Mitchell, Conway, Busby, Slough, Barrett. **Scorer:** West Ham Utd. – Taylor (A.) 2.

1976 SOUTHAMPTON – Turner; Rodrigues, Peach, Holmes, Blyth, Steele, Gilchrist, Channon, Osgood, McCalliog, Stokes. **MANCHESTER UTD.** – Stepney; Forsyth, Houston, Daly, Greenhoff (B.), Buchan, Coppell, McIlroy, Pearson, Macari, Hill (McCreery). **Scorer:** Southampton – Stokes.

1977 MANCHESTER UTD. – Stepney; Nicholl, Albiston, McIlroy, Greenhoff (B.), Buchan, Coppell, Greenhoff (J.), Pearson, Macari, Hill (McCreery). **LIVERPOOL** – Clemence; Neal, Jones, Smith, Kennedy, Hughes, Keegan, Case, Heighway, McDermott, Johnson (Callaghan). **Scorers:** Manchester Utd. – Pearson, Greenhoff (J.), Liverpool – Case.

1978 IPSWICH TOWN – Cooper; Burley, Mills, Talbot, Hunter, Beattie, Osborne (Lambert), Wark, Mariner, Geddis, Woods. **ARSENAL** – Jennings; Rice, Nelson, Price, O'Leary, Young, Brady (Rix), Sunderland, Macdonald, Stapleton, Hudson. **Scorer:** Ipswich Town – Osborne.

1979 ARSENAL – Jennings; Rice, Nelson, Talbot, O'Leary, Young, Brady, Sunderland, Stapleton, Price (Walford), Rix. **MANCHESTER UTD.** – Bailey; Nicholl, Albiston, McIlroy, McQueen, Buchan, Coppell, Greenhoff (J.), Jordan, Macari, Thomas. **Scorers:** Arsenal – Talbot, Stapleton, Sunderland, Manchester Utd. – McQueen, McIlroy.

1980 WEST HAM UTD. – Parkes; Stewart, Lampard, Bonds, Martin, Devonshire, Allen, Pearson, Cross, Brooking, Pike. **ARSENAL** – Jennings; Rice, Devine (Nelson), Talbot, O'Leary, Young, Brady, Sunderland, Stapleton, Price, Rix. **Scorer:** West Ham Utd. – Brooking.

1981 TOTTENHAM – Aleksic; Hughton, Miller, Roberts, Perryman, Villa (Brooke), Ardiles, Archibald, Galvin, Hoddle, Crooks. **MANCHESTER CITY** – Corrigan; Ranson, McDonald, Reid, Power, Caton, Bennett, Gow, Mackenzie, Hutchison (Henry), Reeves. **Scorer:** Tottenham – Hutchison (o.g.), Manchester City – Hutchison. **Replay: TOTTENHAM** – Aleksic; Hughton, Miller, Roberts, Perryman, Villa, Ardiles, Archibald, Galvin, Hoddle,

Crooks. **MANCHESTER CITY** – Corrigan; Ranson, McDonald (Tueart), Reid, Power, Caton, Bennett, Gow, Mackenzie, Hutchison, Reeves. **Scorers:** Tottenham – Villa 2, Crooks, Manchester City – Mackenzie, Reeves (pen.).

1982 TOTTENHAM – Clemence; Hughton, Miller, Price, Hazard (Brooke), Perryman, Roberts, Archibald, Galvin, Hoddle, Crooks. **Q.P.R.** – Hucker; Fenwick, Gillard, Waddock, Hazell, Roeder, Currie, Flanagan, Allen (Micklewhite), Stainrod, Gregory. **Scorers:** Tottenham – Hoddle, Q.P.R. – Fenwick. **Replay: TOTTENHAM** – Clemence; Hughton, Miller, Price, Hazard (Brooke), Perryman, Roberts, Archibald, Galvin, Hoddle, Crooks. **Q.P.R.** – Hucker; Fenwick, Gillard, Waddock, Hazell, Neill, Currie, Flanagan, Micklewhite (Burke), Stainrod, Gregory. **Scorer:** Tottenham – Hoddle (pen.).

1983 MANCHESTER UTD. – Bailey; Duxbury, Albiston, Wilkins, Moran, McQueen, Robson, Muhren, Stapleton, Whiteside, Davies. **BRIGHTON & H.A.** – Moseley; Ramsey (Ryan), Pearce, Grealish, Gatting, Stevens, Case, Howlett, Robinson, Smith, Smillie. **Scorers:** Manchester Utd. – Stapleton, Wilkins, Brighton & H.A. – Smith, Stevens. **Replay: MANCHESTER UTD.** – Bailey; Duxbury, Albiston, Wilkins, Moran, McQueen, Robson, Muhren, Stapleton, Whiteside, Davies. **BRIGHTON & H.A.** – Moseley; Gatting, Pearce, Grealish, Foster, Stevens, Case, Howlett (Ryan), Robinson, Smith, Smillie. **Scorers:** Manchester Utd. – Robson 2, Whiteside, Muhren (pen.).

1984 EVERTON – Southall; Stevens, Bailey, Ratcliffe, Mountfield, Reid, Steven, Heath, Sharp, Gray, Richardson. **WATFORD** – Sherwood; Bardsley, Price (Atkinson), Taylor, Terry, Sinnott, Callaghan, Johnston, Reilly, Jackett, Barnes. **Scorers:** Everton – Sharp, Gray.

1985 MANCHESTER UTD. – Bailey; Gidman, Albiston (Duxbury), Whiteside, McGrath, Moran, Robson, Strachan, Hughes, Stapleton, Olsen. **EVERTON** – Southall; Stevens, Van den Hauwe, Ratcliffe, Mountfield, Reid, Steven, Sharp, Gray, Bracewell, Sheedy. **Scorer:** Manchester Utd. – Whiteside. **Sent-off:** Moran.

1986 LIVERPOOL – Grobbelaar; Lawrenson, Beglin, Nicol, Whelan, Hansen, Dalglish, Johnston, Rush, Molby, MacDonald. **EVERTON** – Mimms; Stevens (Heath), Van den Hauwe, Ratcliffe, Mountfield, Reid, Steven, Lineker, Sharp, Bracewell, Sheedy. **Scorers:** Liverpool – Rush 2, Johnston, Everton – Lineker.

1987 COVENTRY CITY – Ogrizovic; Phillips, Downs, McGrath, Kilcline (Rodger), Peake, Bennett, Gynn, Regis, Houchen, Pickering. **TOTTENHAM** – Clemence; Hughton (Claesen), Thomas (M.), Hodge, Gough, Mabbutt, Allen (C.), Allen (P.), Waddle, Hoddle, Ardiles (Stevens). **Scorers:** Coventry City – Bennett, Houchen, Mabbutt (o.g.), Tottenham – Allen (C.), Mabbutt.

1988 WIMBLEDON – Beasant; Goodyear, Phelan, Jones, Young, Thorn, Gibson (Scales), Cork (Cunningham), Fashanu, Sanchez, Wise. **LIVERPOOL** – Grobbelaar; Gillespie, Ablett, Nicol, Spackman (Molby), Hansen, Beardsley, Aldridge (Johnston), Houghton, Barnes, McMahon. **Scorer:** Wimbledon – Sanchez.

1989 LIVERPOOL – Grobbelaar; Ablett, Staunton (Venison), Nicol, Whelan, Hansen, Beardsley, Aldridge (Rush), Houghton, Barnes, McMahon. **EVERTON** – Southall; McDonald, Van den Hauwe, Ratcliffe, Watson, Bracewell (McCall), Nevin, Steven, Sharp, Cottee, Sheedy (Wilson). **Scorers:** Liverpool – Aldridge, Rush 2, Everton – McCall 2.

1990 MANCHESTER UTD. – Leighton; Ince, Martin (Blackmore), Bruce, Phelan, Pallister (Robins), Robson, Webb, McClair, Hughes, Wallace. **CRYSTAL PALACE** – Martyn; Pemberton, Shaw, Gray (Madden), O'Reilly, Thorn, Barber (Wright), Thomas, Bright, Salako, Pardew. **Scorers:** Manchester Utd. – Robson, Hughes 2, Crystal Palace – O'Reilly, Wright 2. **Replay: MANCHESTER UTD.** – Sealey; Ince, Martin, Bruce, Phelan, Pallister, Robson, Webb, McClair, Hughes, Wallace. **CRYSTAL PALACE** – Martyn; Pemberton, Shaw, Gray, O'Reilly, Thorn, Barber (Wright), Thomas, Bright, Salako (Madden), Pardew. **Scorer:** Manchester Utd. – Martin.

1991 TOTTENHAM – Thorstvedt; Edinburgh, Van den Hauwe, Sedgley, Howells, Mabbutt, Stewart, Gascoigne (Nayim), Samways (Walsh), Lineker, Allen. **NOTT'M FOREST** – Crossley; Charles, Pearce, Walker, Chettle, Keane, Crosby, Parker, Clough, Glover (Laws), Woan (Hodge). **Scorers:** Tottenham – Stewart, Walker (o.g.), Nott'm. Forest – Pearce.

1992 LIVERPOOL – Grobbelaar; Jones (R.), Burrows, Nicol, Molby, Wright, Saunders, Houghton, Rush (I.), McManaman, Thomas. **SUNDERLAND** – Norman; Owers, Ball,

Bennett, Rogan, Rush (D.) (Hardyman), Bracewell, Davenport, Armstrong (Hawke), Byrne, Atkinson. **Scorers:** Liverpool – Thomas, Rush (I.).

1993 ARSENAL – Seaman; Dixon, Winterburn, Linighan, Adams, Parlour (Smith), Davis, Merson, Jensen, Wright (O'Leary), Campbell. **SHEFFIELD WED.** – Woods; Nilsson, Worthington, Palmer, Hirst, Anderson (Hyde), Waddle (Bart-Williams), Warhurst, Bright, Sheridan, Harkes. **Scorers:** Arsenal – Wright, Sheff. Wed. – Hirst. **Replay: ARSENAL** – Seaman; Dixon, Winterburn, Linighan, Adams, Davis, Jensen, Merson, Smith, Wright (O'Leary), Campbell. **SHEFFIELD WED.** – Woods; Nilsson (Bart-Williams), Worthington, Palmer, Hirst, Wilson (Hyde), Waddle, Warhurst, Bright, Sheridan, Harkes. **Scorers:** Arsenal – Wright, Linighan, Sheff. Wed. – Waddle.

1994 MANCHESTER UTD. – Schmeichel; Parker, Bruce, Pallister, Irwin (Sharpe), Kanchelskis (McClair), Keane, Ince, Giggs, Cantona, Hughes. **CHELSEA** – Kharine; Clarke, Johnsen, Kjeldbjerg, Sinclair, Burley (Hoddle), Newton, Wise, Peacock, Stein (Cascarino), Spencer. **Scorers:** Manchester Utd. – Cantona 2 (2 pens.), Hughes, McClair.

1995 EVERTON – Southall; Jackson, Watson, Unsworth, Ablett, Horne, Parkinson, Hinchcliffe, Stuart, Limpar (Amokachi), Rideout (Ferguson). **MANCHESTER UTD.** – Schmeichel; Neville (G.), Bruce (Giggs), Pallister, Irwin, Butt, Keane, Ince, Sharpe (Scholes), McClair, Hughes. **Scorer:** Everton – Rideout.

1996 MANCHESTER UTD. – Schmeichel; Irwin, May, Pallister, Neville (P.), Beckham (Neville, G.), Keane, Butt, Giggs, Cantona, Cole (Scholes). **LIVERPOOL** – James; McAteer, Scales, Wright, Babb, Jones (Thomas), McManaman, Redknapp, Barnes, Collymore (Rush), Fowler. **Scorer:** Manchester Utd. – Cantona.

1997 CHELSEA – Grodas; Sinclair, Lebouef, Clarke, Minto, Petrescu, Di Matteo, Newton, Wise, Zola (Vialli), Hughes (M.). **MIDDLESBROUGH** – Roberts; Blackmore, Pearson, Festa, Fleming, Stamp, Emerson, Mustoe (Vickers), Hignett (Kinder), Juninho, Ravanelli, (Beck). **Scorers:** Chelsea – Di Matteo, Newton.

1998 ARSENAL – Seaman; Dixon, Adams, Keown, Winterburn, Parlour, Petit, Vieira, Overmars, Wreh (Platt), Anelka. **NEWCASTLE** – Given; Barton (Watson), Dabizas, Howey, Pearce (Andersson), Pistone, Batty, Lee, Speed, Shearer, Ketsbaia (Barnes). **Scorers:** Arsenal – Overmars, Anelka.

1999 MANCHESTER UTD. – Schmeichel; Neville (G.), Johnsen, May, Neville (P.); Beckham, Scholes (Stam), Keane (Sheringham), Giggs; Cole (Yorke), Solskjaer. **NEWCASTLE UTD.** – Harper; Griffin, Charvet, Dabizas, Domi; Lee, Hamann (Ferguson), Speed, Solano (Maric); Ketsbaia (Glass), Shearer. **Scorers:** Manchester Utd. – Sheringham, Scholes.

2000 CHELSEA – De Goey; Melchiot, Desailly, Leboeuf, Babayaro, Di Matteo, Wise, Deschamps, Poyet, Weah (Flo), Zola (Morris). **ASTON VILLA** – James; Ehiogu, Southgate, Barry, Delaney. Taylor (Stone), Boateng, Merson, Wright (Hendrie), Dublin, Carbone (Joachim). **Scorer:** Chelsea – Di Matteo.

2001 LIVERPOOL – Westerveld; Babbel, Henchoz, Hyypia, Carragher, Murphy (Berger), Hamann (McAllister), Gerrard, Smicer (Fowler), Heskey, Owen. **ARSENAL** – Seaman; Dixon (Bergkamp), Keown, Adams, Cole, Ljungberg (Kanu), Grimandi, Vieira, Pires, Henry, Wiltord (Parlour). **Scorers:** Liverpool – Owen 2, Arsenal – Ljungberg.

2002 ARSENAL – Seaman; Lauren, Campbell, Adams, Cole, Wiltord (Keown), Parlour, Vieira, Ljungberg, Bergkamp (Edu), Henry (Kanu). **CHELSEA** – Cudicini; Melchiot, Desailly, Gallas, Babayaro (Terry), Gronkjaer, Lampard, Petit, Le Saux, Hasselbaink (Zola), Gudjohnsen. **Scorers:** Arsenal – Parlour, Ljungberg.

2003 ARSENAL – Seaman; Lauren, Keown, Luzhny, Cole, Ljungberg, Parlour, Gilberto Silva, Pires, Bergkamp (Wiltord), Henry. **SOUTHAMPTON** – Niemi (Jones); Baird (Fernandes), Lundekvam, Svensson (M.), Bridge, Telfer, Oakley, Svensson (A.) (Tessem), Marsden, Beattie, Ormerod. **Scorer:** Arsenal – Pires.

2004 MANCHESTER UTD. – Howard (Carroll); G. Neville, Brown, Silvestre, O'Shea, Fletcher (Butt), Keane, Ronaldo (Solskjaer), Scholes, Giggs, Van Nistelrooy. **MILLWALL:** Marshall; Elliott, Lawrence, Ward, Ryan (Cogan), Wise (Weston), Ifill, Cahill, Livermore, Sweeney, Harris (McCammon). **Scorers:** Manchester Utd. – Van Nistelrooy (2), Ronaldo.

2005 ARSENAL – Lehmann; Lauren, Toure, Senderos, Cole, Fabregas (Van Persie), Gilberto Silva, Vieira, Pires (Edu), Reyes, Bergkamp (Ljungberg). **MANCHESTER UTD.** – Carroll; Brown, Ferdinand, Silvestre, O'Shea (Fortune), Fletcher (Giggs), Keane, Scholes, Rooney, Van Nistelrooy, Ronaldo.

2006 LIVERPOOL – Reina; Finnan, Carragher, Hyypia, Riise, Gerrard, Xabi Alonso (Kronkamp), Sissoko, Kewell (Morientes), Cisse, Crouch (Hamann). **WEST HAM UTD.** – Hislop; Scaloni, Ferdinand, Gabbidon, Konchesky, Benayoun, Fletcher (Dailly), Reo-Coker, Etherington (Sheringham), Ashton (Zamora), Harewood. **Scorers:** Liverpool – Gerrard 2, Cisse, West Ham Utd. – Ashton, Konchesky, Carragher (o.g.).

F.A. CUP FINALS – COMPLETE RESULTS

AT KENNINGTON OVAL

1872 The Wanderers beat Royal Engineers (1-0)

AT LILLIE BRIDGE, LONDON

1873 The Wanderers beat Oxford University (2-1)

AT KENNINGTON OVAL

1874 Oxford University beat Royal Engineers (2-0)
1875 Royal Engineers beat Old Etonians (2-0 after a 1-1 draw)
1876 The Wanderers beat Old Etonians (3-0 after a 0-0 draw)
1877†† The Wanderers beat Oxford University (2-1)
1878* The Wanderers beat Royal Engineers (3-1)
1879 Old Etonians beat Clapham Rov. (1-0)
1880 Clapham Rov. beat Oxford University (1-0)
1881 Old Carthusians beat Old Etonians (3-0)
1882 Old Etonians beat Blackburn Rov. (1-0)
1883†† Blackburn Olympic beat Old Etonians (2-1)
1884 Blackburn Rov. beat Queen's Park (Glasgow) (2-1)
1885 Blackburn Rov. beat Queen's Park (Glasgow) (2-0)
1886†*a* Blackburn Rov. beat W.B.A. (2-0 after a 0-0 draw)
1887 Aston Villa beat W.B.A. (2-0)
1888 W.B.A. beat Preston N.E. (2-1)
1889 Preston N.E. beat Wolves (3-0)
1890 Blackburn Rov. beat Sheffield Wed. (6-1)
1891 Blackburn Rov. beat Notts Co. (3-1)
1892 W.B.A. beat Aston Villa (3-0)

AT FALLOWFIELD, MANCHESTER

1893 Wolves beat Everton (1-0)

AT GOODISON PARK

1894 Notts Co. beat Bolton Wand. (4-1)

AT CRYSTAL PALACE

1895 Aston Villa beat W.B.A. (1-0)
1896 Sheffield Wed. beat Wolves (2-1)
1897 Aston Villa beat Everton (3-2)
1898 Nott'm. Forest beat Derby Co. (3-1)
1899 Sheffield Utd. beat Derby Co. (4-1)
1900 Bury beat Southampton (4-0)
1901††† Tottenham beat Sheffield Utd. (3-1 after a 2-2 draw)
1902 Sheffield Utd. beat Southampton (2-1 after a 1-1 draw)
1903 Bury beat Derby Co. (6-0)

1904	Manchester City beat Bolton Wand. (1-0)
1905	Aston Villa beat Newcastle Utd. (2-0)
1906	Everton beat Newcastle Utd. (1-0)
1907	Sheffield Wed. beat Everton (2-1)
1908	Wolves beat Newcastle Utd. (3-1)
1909	Manchester Utd. beat Bristol City (1-0)
1910**	Newcastle Utd. beat Barnsley (2-0 after a 1-1 draw)
1911*b*	Bradford City beat Newcastle Utd. (1-0 after a 0-0 draw)
1912*c*	Barnsley beat W.B.A. (1-0 after a 0-0 draw)
1913	Aston Villa beat Sunderland (1-0)
1914	Burnley beat Liverpool (1-0)

AT OLD TRAFFORD

1915	Sheffield Utd. beat Chelsea (3-0)

AT STAMFORD BRIDGE

1920††	Aston Villa beat Huddersfield Town (1-0)
1921	Tottenham beat Wolves (1-0)
1922	Huddersfield Town beat Preston N.E. (1-0)

AT WEMBLEY

1923	Bolton Wand. beat West Ham Utd. (2-0)
1924	Newcastle Utd. beat Aston Villa (2-0)
1925	Sheffield Utd. beat Cardiff City (1-0)
1926	Bolton Wand. beat Manchester City (1-0)
1927	Cardiff City beat Arsenal (1-0)
1928	Blackburn Rov. beat Huddersfield Town (3-1)
1929	Bolton Wand. beat Portsmouth (2-0)
1930	Arsenal beat Huddersfield Town (2-0)
1931	W.B.A. beat Birmingham City (2-1)
1932	Newcastle Utd. beat Arsenal (2-1)
1933	Everton beat Manchester City (3-0)
1934	Manchester City beat Portsmouth (2-1)
1935	Sheffield Wed. beat W.B.A. (4-2)
1936	Arsenal beat Sheffield Utd. (1-0)
1937	Sunderland beat Preston N.E. (3-1)
1938††	Preston N.E. beat Huddersfield Town (1-0)
1939	Portsmouth beat Wolves (4-1)
1946††	Derby Co. beat Charlton Athletic (4-1)
1947††	Charlton Athletic beat Burnley (1-0)
1948	Manchester Utd. beat Blackpool (4-2)
1949	Wolves beat Leicester City (3-1)
1950	Arsenal beat Liverpool (2-0)
1951	Newcastle Utd. beat Blackpool (2-0)
1952	Newcastle Utd. beat Arsenal (1-0)
1953	Blackpool beat Bolton Wand. (4-3)
1954	W.B.A. beat Preston N.E. (3-2)
1955	Newcastle Utd. beat Manchester City (3-1)
1956	Manchester City beat Birmingham City (3-1)
1957	Aston Villa beat Manchester Utd. (2-1)
1958	Bolton Wand. beat Manchester Utd. (2-0)
1959	Nott'm. Forest beat Luton Town (2-1)
1960	Wolves beat Blackburn Rov. (3-0)
1961	Tottenham beat Leicester City (2-0)
1962	Tottenham beat Burnley (3-1)
1963	Manchester Utd. beat Leicester City (3-1)
1964	West Ham Utd. beat Preston N.E. (3-2)
1965††	Liverpool beat Leeds Utd. (2-1)

1966	Everton beat Sheffield Wed. (3-2)
1967	Tottenham beat Chelsea (2-1)
1968††	W.B.A. beat Everton (1-0)
1969	Manchester City beat Leicester City (1-0)
1970††•	Chelsea beat Leeds Utd. (2-1 after a 2-2 draw)
1971††	Arsenal beat Liverpool (2-1)
1972	Leeds Utd. beat Arsenal (1-0)
1973	Sunderland beat Leeds Utd. (1-0)
1974	Liverpool beat Newcastle Utd. (3-0)
1975	West Ham Utd. beat Fulham (2-0)
1976	Southampton beat Manchester Utd. (1-0)
1977	Manchester Utd. beat Liverpool (2-1)
1978	Ipswich Town beat Arsenal (1-0)
1979	Arsenal beat Manchester Utd. (3-2)
1980	West Ham Utd. beat Arsenal (1-0)
1981	Tottenham beat Manchester City (3-2 after a 1-1 draw)
1982	Tottenham beat Q.P.R. (1-0 after a 1-1 draw)
1983	Manchester Utd. beat Brighton & H.A. (4-0 after a 2-2 draw)
1984	Everton beat Watford (2-0)
1985††	Manchester Utd. beat Everton (1-0)
1986	Liverpool beat Everton (3-1)
1987††	Coventry City beat Tottenham (3-2)
1988	Wimbledon beat Liverpool (1-0)
1989††	Liverpool beat Everton (3-2)
1990	Manchester Utd. beat Crystal Palace (1-0 after a 3-3 draw)
1991††	Tottenham beat Nott'm. Forest (2-1)
1992	Liverpool beat Sunderland (2-0)
1993††	Arsenal beat Sheffield Wed. (2-1 after a 1-1 draw)
1994	Manchester Utd. beat Chelsea (4-0)
1995	Everton beat Manchester Utd. (1-0)
1996	Manchester Utd. beat Liverpool (1-0)
1997	Chelsea beat Middlesbrough (2-0)
1998	Arsenal beat Newcastle Utd. (2-0)
1999	Manchester Utd. beat Newcastle Utd. (2-0)
2000	Chelsea beat Aston Villa (1-0)

AT MILLENNIUM STADIUM

2001	Liverpool beat Arsenal (2-1)
2002	Arsenal beat Chelsea (2-0)
2003	Arsenal beat Southampton (1-0)
2004	Manchester Utd. beat Millwall (3-0)
2005††	Arsenal beat Manchester Utd. (5-4 on pens after a 0-0 draw)
2006††	Liverpool beat West Ham Utd. (3-1 on pens after a 3-3 draw)

AT WEMBLEY

2007	Chelsea beat Manchester Utd. (1-0)

†† After extra time. * Won outright but restored to the Association. *a* Replayed at Baseball Ground. † A special trophy was awarded for the third consecutive win. ††† Replayed at Burnden Park. ** Replayed at Goodison Park. *b* Replayed at Old Trafford. new trophy provided. *c* Replayed at Bramall Lane. • Replayed at Old Trafford.
(All replays since 1981 played at Wembley.)

SUMMARY OF F.A. CUP WINS

Manchester Utd.	11	Liverpool	7	The Wanderers	5
Arsenal	10	Blackburn Rov.	6	W.B.A.	5
Tottenham	8	Newcastle Utd.	6	Bolton Wand.	4
Aston Villa	7	Everton	5	Chelsea	4

Manchester City 4
Sheffield Utd. 4
Wolves 4
Sheffield Wed. 3
West Ham Utd. 3
Bury 2
Nott'm. Forest 2
Old Etonians 2
Preston N.E. 2
Sunderland 2
Barnsley 1
Blackburn Olympic 1
Blackpool 1
Bradford City 1
Burnley 1
Cardiff City 1
Charlton Athletic 1
Clapham Rov. 1
Coventry City 1
Derby Co. 1
Huddersfield Town 1
Ipswich Town 1
Leeds Utd. 1
Notts Co. 1
Old Carthusians 1
Oxford University 1
Portsmouth 1
Royal Engineers 1
Southampton 1
Wimbledon 1

APPEARANCES IN FINALS

(Figures do not include replays)

Manchester Utd. 18
Arsenal 17
Liverpool 13
Newcastle Utd. 13
Everton 12
Aston Villa 10
W.B.A. 10
Tottenham 9
Blackburn Rov. 8
Chelsea 8
Manchester City 8
Wolves 8
Bolton Wand. 7
Preston N.E. 7
Old Etonians 6
Sheffield Utd. 6
Sheffield Wed. 6
Huddersfield Town 5
The Wanderers* 5
West Ham Utd. 5
Derby Co. 4
Leeds Utd. 4
Leicester City 4
Oxford University 4
Royal Engineers 4
Southampton 4
Sunderland 4
Blackpool 3
Burnley 3
Nott'm. Forest 3
Portsmouth 3
Barnsley 2
Birmingham City 2
Bury* 2
Cardiff City 2
Charlton Athletic 2
Clapham Rov. 2
Notts Co. 2
Queen's Park (Glas.) 2
Blackburn Olympic* 1
Bradford City* 1
Brighton & H.A. 1
Bristol City 1
Coventry City* 1
Crystal Palace 1
Fulham 1
Ipswich Town* 1
Luton Town 1
Middlesbrough 1
Millwall 1
Old Carthusians* 1
Q.P.R. 1
Watford 1
Wimbledon* 1
(* Denotes undefeated)

APPEARANCES IN SEMI-FINALS

(Figures do not include replays)

Arsenal 25, Manchester Utd. 25, Everton 23, Liverpool 22, Aston Villa 19, W.B.A. 19, Blackburn Rov. 18, Chelsea 17, Newcastle Utd. 17, Tottenham 17, Chelsea 16, Sheffield Wed. 16, Wolves 14, Bolton Wand. 13, Derby Co. 13, Sheffield Utd. 13, Nott'm. Forest 12, Sunderland 12, Southampton 11, Manchester City 10, Preston N.E. 10, Birmingham City 9, Burnley 8, Leeds Utd. 8, Huddersfield Town 7, Leicester City 7, West Ham Utd. 7, Fulham 6, Old Etonians 6, Oxford University 6, Notts Co. 5, Portsmouth 5, The Wanderers 5, Watford 5, Luton Town 4, Millwall 4, Queen's Park (Glasgow) 4, Royal Engineers 4, Blackpool 3, Cardiff City 3, Clapham Rov. 3, *Crystal Palace 3, Ipswich Town 3, Middlesbrough 3, Norwich City 3, Old Carthusians 3, Oldham Athletic 3, Stoke City 3, The Swifts 3, Barnsley 2, Blackburn Olympic 2, Bristol City 2, Bury 2, Charlton Athletic 2, Grimsby Town 2, Swansea City Town 2, Swindon Town 2, Wimbledon 2, Bradford City 1, Brighton & H.A. 1, Cambridge University 1, Chesterfield 1, Coventry City 1, Crewe Alexandra 1, Darwen 1, Derby Co. Junction 1, Hull City 1, Marlow 1, Old Harrovians 1, Orient 1, Plymouth Argyle 1, Port Vale 1, Q.P.R. 1, Rangers (Glasgow) 1, Reading 1, Shropshire Wand. 1, Wycombe Wand. 1, York City 1.

*(*A previous and different Crystal Palace club also reached the semi-final in season 1871-72)*

FOOTBALL'S CHANGING HOMES

Hard on the heels of completion of the new Wembley Stadium, two clubs are scheduled to kick off the 2007-08 season in new grounds. Seven others are planning moves, while several more have announced major development at their current homes. After four seasons at the National Hockey Stadium in Milton Keynes, **MK Dons** take up residency in a 30,000-capacity arena which has received a four-star UEFA rating. Masterminded by the club's chairman, music promoter and property developer Pete Winkelman, Stadium:MK is in the Denbigh area of the town and cost £42m. **Shrewsbury Town** are leaving cramped Gay Meadow on the banks of the River Severn after 97 years for a 10,000-capacity home. The New Meadow is on a greenfield site on the outskirts of the town.

Portsmouth are the latest Premiership club to unveil plans to move. Owner Alexandre Gaydamak wants to replace run-down Fratton Park with a £600m. development on reclaimed land in the docklands area. Work is scheduled to start in 2009 on a 36,000-capacity stadium, 1,500 apartments, restaurants and cafes. It will be designed by the architects responsible for Bayern Munich's Allianz Arena. New owners George Gillett and Tom Hicks have reaffirmed plans by **Liverpool** to build a 60,000-seater stadium in nearby Stanley Park, ending any prospect of ground-sharing with **Everton**. Their neighbours, meanwhile, are consulting with residents of the Kirkby area of the city, where a 55,000-capacity new home is earmarked, along with superstore and shopping complex.

Work has started on **Cardiff City**'s £38m., 30,000-capacity ground, close to Ninian Park on the site of the Leckwith athletics track. The track will be replaced as part of the project, which also involves retail development and is scheduled for completion in February 2009. **Southend United** have received planning approval for a new ground holding 22,000 and for a new training complex. **Colchester United** hope to have their new £14m. 10,000-seater Community Stadium at Cuckoo Farm in the north of the town ready for the 2008-09 season. A £10m. loan from the borough council will fund the project. The remainder comes from the Football Foundation and local government development agencies. **Nottingham Forest** are looking at building a 50,000-capacity stadium, with the latest in green technology, at Clifton on the outskirts of the city. The club will consult local people about the £125m. project which has a provisional 2014 completion date. Football's longest-running stadium saga may be nearing its end, with a Government decision imminent on **Brighton and Hove Albion**'s seven-year battle for a 23,000-seater home at Falmer. The club have been told that the South East England Development Agency are prepared to invest £5.3m. in the stadium.

A £300m. scheme to develop St James' Park has been unveiled by **Newcastle United**. It involves extending the Gallowgate end to raise capacity to 60,000, hotels, conference centre and apartments. Promoted **Derby County** plan a hotel, bars, restaurant and office space, costing £20m., at Pride Park. The 'Pride Plaza' project incorporates two squares named after Derby legends Brian Clough and Steve Bloomer. **Watford** have received planning permission for a £32m. development of Vicarage Road. This involves the construction of a new East Stand to raise capacity to 24,000 and low-cost housing. Reading, who enjoyed a successful first season in the Premiership, have also been given the go-ahead to raise capacity of the Madejski Stadium, to around 38,000, while **Fulham** are rebuilding the Hammersmith end of Craven Cottage, adding 1,100 seats, a restaurant overlooking the Thames and office space.

Bristol Rovers received planning permission to turn the Memorial Stadium they share with Bristol Rugby Club into an 18,500-seater arena. They are scheduled to share Cheltenham's Whaddon Road ground from January 2008 while work takes place. **Scunthorpe United** are seeking approval for a three-tier development at Glanford Park, incorporating leisure and conference facilities and raising the capacity to 11,000. **Leyton Orient** will have a four-sided stadium again for the new season after construction of the new North Stand at Brisbane Road.

RED CARDS MAR DROGBA'S WINNING DOUBLE FOR CHELSEA

THIRD ROUND	FOURTH ROUND	FIFTH ROUND	SEMI-FINALS	FINAL
***Arsenal** 2	**Arsenal** 1	**Arsenal** 6	**Arsenal** .... 2:+3	**Arsenal** 1
W.B.A. 0				
*Everton 4	*Everton 0			
Luton Town 0				
*Sheffield Utd. 2	*Birmingham City 0	*Liverpool 3		
Birmingham 4				
*Liverpool 4	Liverpool 1			
Reading 3				
*MK Dons 0	*Tottenham .... +3	*Tottenham .... +1	*Tottenham 2:1	
Tottenham 5				
*Port Vale .... +A0	Port Vale 1			
Norwich City 0				
*Leeds Utd. 1	*Southend Utd. 1	Southend Utd. 0		
Southend Utd. 3				
*Crewe Alexandra 1	Manchester Utd. 0			
Manchester Utd. .... +2				
*Chesterfield 2	*Chesterfield 3	*Charlton Athletic 0	*Wycombe Wand. 1:0	
West Ham Utd. 1				
*Charlton Athletic 1	Charlton Athletic ..... +C3			
Bolton Wand. 0				
*Notts Co. 2	*Notts Co. 0	Wycombe Wand. 1		
Southampton 0				
*Wycombe Wand. ..... +B2	Wycombe Wand. 1			
Doncaster Rov. 2				

*Watford .... 2 Hull City 1	*Watford 2			
		*Newcastle Utd. 0		
*Newcastle Utd. .... 3 Portsmouth 0	Newcastle Utd. .... +D2			
			Chelsea 1:4	
*Leicester City .... 2 Aston Villa .... +3	Aston Villa 0			**Chelsea** 2
		Chelsea 1		
*Blackburn Rov. .... 0 **Chelsea** 2	***Chelsea** 4			

*Drawn at home; in semi-finals, first leg. +After extra-time. A – Port Vale won 3-2 on pens. B – Wycombe Wand. won 3-2 on pens. C – Charlton Athletic won 4-3 on pens. D – Newcastle Utd. won 5-4 on pens.

FIRST ROUND: Accrington Stanley 1, Nott'm. Forest 0; Birmingham City 1, Shrewsbury Town 0; Blackpool 2, Barnsley 2 (aet, Barnsley won 4-2 on pens); Bournemouth 1, Southend Utd. 3; Brighton & H.A. 1, Boston Utd. 0; Bristol Rov. 1, Luton Town 1 (aet, Luton Town won 5-3 on pens); Burnley 0, Hartlepool Utd. 1; Bury 2, Sunderland 0; Cardiff City 0, Barnet 2; Carlisle Utd. 1, Bradford City 1 (aet, Carlisle Utd.won 4-3 on pens); Cheltenham Town 2, Bristol City 1; Chesterfield 0, Wolves 0 (aet, Chesterfield won 6-5 on pens); Crystal Palace 1, Notts Co. 2; Doncaster Rov. 3, Rochdale 2; Grimsby Town 0, Crewe Alexandra 3; Hereford Utd. 3, Coventry City 1; Huddersfield Town 0, Mansfield Town 2; Hull City 2, Tranmere Rov. 1 (aet); Leeds Utd. 1, Chester City 0; Leicester City 2, Macclesfield Town 0; Leyton Orient 0, W.B.A. 3; Millwall 2, Gillingham 1; MK Dons 1, Colchester Utd. 0 (aet); Peterborough Utd. 2, Ipswich Town 2 (aet, Peterborough Utd. won 4-2 on pens); Plymouth Argyle 0, Walsall 1; Port Vale 2, Preston N.E. 1; Q.P.R. 3, Northampton Town 2; Rotherham Utd. 3, Oldham Athletic 1; Scunthorpe Utd. 4, Lincoln City 3 (aet); Sheffield Wed. 1, Wrexham 4; Southampton 5, Yeovil Town 2; Stockport Co. 0, Derby Co. 1; Stoke City 1, Darlington 2; Swansea City 2, Wycombe Wand. 3 (aet); Swindon Town 2, Brentford 2 (aet, Brentford won 4-3 on pens); Torquay Utd. 0, Norwich City 2.

SECOND ROUND: Barnsley 1, MK Dons 2; Birmingham City 4, Wrexham 1 (aet); Brentford 0, Luton Town 3; Charlton Athletic 1, Carlisle Utd. 0; Chesterfield 2, Manchester City 1; Crewe Alexandra 2, Wigan Athletic 0; Doncaster Rov. 3, Derby Co. 3 (aet, Doncaster Rov. won 8-7 on pens); Fulham 1, Wycombe Wand. 2; Hereford Utd. 1, Leicester City 3; Hull City 0, Hartlepool Utd. 0 (aet, Hull City won 3-2 on pens); Leeds Utd. 3, Barnet 1; Mansfield Town 1, Portsmouth 2; Middlesbrough 0, Notts Co. 1; Millwall 0, Southampton 4; Peterborough Utd. 1, Everton 2; Port Vale 3, Q.P.R. 2; Reading 3, Darlington 3 (aet, Reading won 4-2 on pens); Rotherham Utd. 2, Norwich City 4; Scunthorpe Utd. 1, Aston Villa 2; Sheffield Utd. 1, Bury 0; Southend Utd. 3, Brighton & H.A. 2; Walsall 1, Bolton Wand. 3; Watford 0, Accrington Stanley 0 (aet, Watford won 6-5 on pens); W.B.A. 3, Cheltenham Town 1.

CARLING CUP FINAL

ARSENAL 1, CHELSEA 2

Millennium Stadium (70,073), Sunday, February 25, 2007

Arsenal (4-4-2): Almunia, Hoyte, Toure, Senderos, Traore (Eboue 67), Walcott, Fabregas, Denilson, Diaby (Hleb 68), Aliadiere (Adebayor 81), Baptista. **Scorer:** Walcott (12). **Booked:** Denilson, Eboue, Fabregas. **Sent-off:** Toure, Adebayor. **Manager:** Arsene Wenger.

Chelsea (4-1-3-2): Cech, Diarra, Ricardo Carvalho, Terry (Mikel 63), Bridge, Makelele (Robben 46), Essien Ballack, Lampard, Drogba, Shevchenko (Kalou 90). **Scorer:** Drogba (20, 84). **Sent-off:** Mikel. **Manager:** Jose Mourinho.

Referee: H. Webb (South Yorks). **Half-time:** 1-1.

Didier Drogba's 27th and 28th goals of a prolific season proved too much for Arsene Wenger's accomplished young side on an afternoon of compelling entertainment. Yet the last final to be played at the Millennium Stadium before English football's showpiece matches returned to Wembley will be remembered most for all the wrong reasons. With Chelsea clinging on to their slender advantage, a mass brawl broke out following John Obi Mikel's challenge on Kolo Toure. When the Arsenal defender retaliated, players from all parts of the pitch dived in, prompting Wenger and Jose Mourinho to run on to try to separate them.

When referee Howard Webb restored order, he dismissed the two protagonists, along with Arsenal striker Emmanuel Adebayor. The repercussions from the F.A.'s discplinary commission for all parties were severe — a £100,000 fine for each club and bans for the players. Chelsea had previously lost their captain John Terry, who was knocked unconscious when accidentally kicked in the face by Abou Diaby. This time, the outcome was a positive one, with Terry returning from hospital to claim the trophy during his team's celebrations.

Wenger's decision to start with the bulk of the side that had successfully negotiated some testing ties en route to the final looked to be a wise one when 17-year-old Theo Walcott, without a goal all season, exchanged passes with Diaby before curling his shot wide of Petr Cech after 12 minutes. Chelsea were level eight minutes later as Drogba ran on to Michael Ballack's pass, beating first the offside trap and then Manuel Almunia. Frank Lampard struck the crossbar, but Arsenal continued to play with great confidence until the 84th minute when substitute Arjen Robben crossed and Drogba's mastery of Philippe Senderos in games between these sides was further underlined when he outmuscled the Swiss defender to head the winner.

HOW THEY REACHED THE FINAL

ARSENAL

Round 3: 2-0 away to W.B.A. (Aliadiere 2, 1 pen)
Round 4: 1-0 away to Everton (Adebayor)
Round 5: 6-3 away to Liverpool (Baptista 4, Aliadiere, Song)
Semi-finals: v Tottenham – first leg, 2-2 away (Baptista 2); second leg, 3-1 home, aet (Adebayor, Aliadiere, Chimbonda og)

CHELSEA

Round 3: 2-0 away to Blackburn Rov. (Kalou, Joe Cole)
Round 4: 4-0 home to Aston Villa (Drogba, Essien, Lampard, Shevchenko)
Round 5: 1-0 away to Newcastle Utd. (Drogba)
Semi-finals: v Wycombe Wand. – first leg, 1-1 away (Bridge); second leg, 4-0 home (Lampard 2, Shevchenko 2)

LEADING SCORERS

6 Baptista (Arsenal), Easter (Wycombe Wand.); **4** Aliadiere (Arsenal), Defoe (Tottenham), Drogba (Chelsea), Eastwood (Southend Utd.).

LEAGUE CUP – COMPLETE RESULTS

LEAGUE CUP FINALS

1961*	Aston Villa beat Rotherham Utd. 3-2 on agg. (0-2a, 3-0h)
1962	Norwich City beat Rochdale 4-0 on agg. (3-0a, 1-0h)
1963	Birmingham City beat Aston Villa 3-1 on agg. (3-1h, 0-0a)
1964	Leicester City beat Stoke City 4-3 on agg. (1-1a, 3-2h)
1965	Chelsea beat Leicester City 3-2 on agg. (3-2h, 0-0a)
1966	W.B.A. beat West Ham Utd. 5-3 on agg. (1-2a, 4-1h)

AT WEMBLEY

1967	Q.P.R. beat W.B.A. (3-2)
1968	Leeds Utd. beat Arsenal (1-0)
1969*	Swindon Town beat Arsenal (3-1)
1970*	Manchester City beat W.B.A. (2-1)
1971	Tottenham beat Aston Villa (2-0)
1972	Stoke City beat Chelsea (2-1)
1973	Tottenham beat Norwich City (1-0)
1974	Wolves beat Manchester City (2-1)
1975	Aston Villa beat Norwich City (1-0)
1976	Manchester City beat Newcastle Utd. (2-1)
1977†*	Aston Villa beat Everton (3-2 after 0-0 and 1-1 draws)
1978††	Nott'm. Forest beat Liverpool (1-0 after 0-0 draw)
1979	Nott'm. Forest beat Southampton (3-2)
1980	Wolves beat Nott'm. Forest (1-0)
1981†††	Liverpool beat West Ham Utd. (2-1 after 1-1 draw)

MILK CUP

1982*	Liverpool beat Tottenham (3-1)
1983*	Liverpool beat Manchester Utd. (2-1)
1984**	Liverpool beat Everton (1-0 after *0-0 draw)
1985	Norwich City beat Sunderland (1-0)
1986	Oxford Utd. beat Q.P.R. (3-0)

LITTLEWOODS CUP

1987	Arsenal beat Liverpool (2-1)
1988	Luton Town beat Arsenal (3-2)
1989	Nott'm. Forest beat Luton Town (3-1)
1990	Nott'm. Forest beat Oldham Athletic (1-0)

RUMBELOWS CUP

1991	Sheffield Wed. beat Manchester Utd. (1-0)
1992	Manchester Utd. beat Nott'm. Forest (1-0)

COCA-COLA CUP

1993	Arsenal beat Sheffield Wed. (2-1)
1994	Aston Villa beat Manchester Utd. (3-1)
1995	Liverpool beat Bolton Wand. (2-1)
1996	Aston Villa beat Leeds Utd. (3-0)
1997	Leicester City beat Middlesbrough (*1-0 after *1-1 draw) ★
1998	Chelsea beat Middlesbrough (2-0)

WORTHINGTON CUP (AT MILLENNIUM STADIUM FROM 2001)

1999	Tottenham beat Leicester City (1-0)
2000	Leicester City beat Tranmere Rov. (2-1)
2001	Liverpool beat Birmingham City (5-4 on pens after *1-1 draw)
2002	Blackburn Rov. beat Tottenham (2-1)
2003	Liverpool beat Manchester Utd. (2-0)

CARLING CUP

2004	Middlesbrough beat Bolton Wand. (2-1)
2005*	Chelsea beat Liverpool (3-2)
2006	Manchester Utd. beat Wigan Athletic (4-0)
2007	Chelsea beat Arsenal (2-1)

* After extra time. † First replay at Hillsborough, second replay at Old Trafford. †† Replayed at Old Trafford. ††† Replayed at Aston Villa Park. ** Replayed at Maine Road. ★ Replayed at Hillsborough

SUMMARY OF LEAGUE CUP WINNERS

Liverpool	7	Manchester Utd.	2	Middlesbrough	1
Aston Villa	5	Norwich City	2	Oxford Utd.	1
Chelsea	4	Wolves	2	Q.P.R.	1
Nott'm Forest	4	Blackburn Rov.	1	Sheffield Wed.	1
Leicester City	3	Birmingham City	1	Stoke City	1
Tottenham	3	Leeds Utd.	1	Swindon Town	1
Arsenal	2	Luton Town	1	W.B.A.	1
Manchester City	2				

LEAGUE CUP FINAL APPEARANCES

10 Liverpool; **7** Aston Villa; **6** Arsenal, Manchester Utd., Nott'm. Forest; **5** Chelsea, Leicester City, Tottenham; **4** Norwich City; **3** Manchester City, Middlesbrough, W.B.A.; **2** Birmingham City, Bolton Wand., Everton, Leeds Utd., Luton Town, Q.P.R., Sheffield Wed., Stoke City, West Ham Utd., Wolves; **1** Blackburn Rov., Newcastle Utd., Oldham Athletic, Oxford Utd., Rochdale, Rotherham Utd., Southampton, Sunderland, Swindon Town, Tranmere Rov., Wigan Athletic. **(Figures do not include replays).**

LEAGUE CUP SEMI-FINAL APPEARANCES

13 Liverpool; **12** Arsenal, Aston Villa; **11** Tottenham; **10** Manchester Utd.; **9** Chelsea; **7** West Ham Utd.; **6** Nott'm Forest; **5** Blackburn Rov., Leeds Utd., Leicester City, Manchester City, Middlesbrough, Norwich City; **4** Birmingham City, Bolton Wand., Sheffield Wed., W.B.A.; **3** Burnley, Crystal Palace, Everton, Ipswich Town, Q.P.R., Sunderland, Swindon Town, Wolves; **2** Bristol City, Coventry City, Luton Town, Oxford Utd., Plymouth Argyle, Southampton, Stoke City, Tranmere Rov., Watford, Wimbledon; **1** Blackpool, Bury, Cardiff City, Carlisle Utd., Chester City, Derby Co., Huddersfield Town, Newcastle Utd., Oldham Athletic, Peterborough, Rochdale, Rotherham Utd., Sheffield Utd., Shrewsbury Town, Stockport Co., Walsall, Wigan Athletic, Wycombe Wand. **(Figures do not include replays).**

OTHER COMPETITIONS 2006-07

JOHNSTONE'S PAINT TROPHY

FIRST ROUND

Northern: Accrington Stanley 1, Carlisle Utd. 1 (Accrington Stanley won 3-1 on pens); Bradford City 1, Scunthorpe Utd. 2; Bury 0, Tranmere Rov. 2; Hartlepool Utd. 3, Rotherham Utd. 1; Huddersfield Town 1, Doncaster Rov. 2; Lincoln City 0, Grimsby Town 0 (Grimsby Town won 5-3 on pens); Macclesfield Town 0, Stockport Co. 1; Wrexham 1, Rochdale 1 (Rochdale won 5-3 pens).
Southern: Brighton & H.A. 2, Boston Utd. 0; Bristol Rov. 1, Torquay Utd. 0; Gillingham 1, Nott'm. Forest 2; Hereford Utd. 1, Shrewsbury Town 2; Northampton Town 0, Brentford 0 (Brentford won 4-2 on pens); Notts Co. 0, Barnet 1; Walsall 1, Swansea City 1 (Swansea City won 4-3 on pens); Wycombe Wand. 1, Swindon Town 0.

SECOND ROUND

Northern: Accrington Stanley 4, Blackpool 4 (Accrington Stanley won 4-2 on pens); Chester City 3, Stockport Co. 0; Hartlepool Utd. 1, Doncaster Rov. 3; Mansfield Town 3, Grimsby Town 0; Oldham Athletic 0, Chesterfield 1; Rochdale 1, Crewe Alexandra 1 (Crewe Alexandra won 2-0 on pens); Scunthorpe Utd. 0, Port Vale 0 (Port Vale won 5-3 on pens); Tranmere Rov. 0, Darlington 1.
Southern: Brighton & H.A. 4, MK Dons 1; Cheltenham Town 3, Barnet 2; Leyton Orient 1, Bristol City 3; Millwall 2, Bournemouth 0; Nott'm. Forest 2, Brentford 1; Peterborough Utd. 1, Swansea City 0; Shrewsbury Town 2, Yeovil Town 1; Wycombe Wand. 0, Bristol Rov. 2.

THIRD ROUND

Northern: Chesterfield 4, Chester City 4 (Chesterfield won 3-1 on pens); Darlington 1, Mansfield Town 0; Doncaster Rov. 2, Accrington Stanley 1; Port Vale 2, Crewe Alexandra 3.
Southern: Bristol Rov. 1, Peterborough Utd. 0; Cheltenham Town 2, Shrewsbury Town 3; Millwall 1, Brighton & H.A. 1 (Brighton & H.A. won 3-2 on pens); Nott'm. Forest 2, Bristol City 2 (Bristol City won 4-2 on pens).

SEMI-FINALS

Northern: Chesterfield 2, Crewe Alexandra 4; Doncaster Rov. 2, Darlington 0.
Southern: Bristol City 2, Brighton & H.A. 0; Shrewsbury Town 0, Bristol Rov. 1.

AREA FINALS

Northern first leg: Crewe Alexandra 3 (Moss 51, Lowe 63, Varney 86), Doncaster Rov. 3 (Heffernan 29, 74, Stock 40). Att: 4,631. **Second leg:** Doncaster Rov. 3 (Heffernan 63, 83, Price 89), Crewe Alexandra 2 (Varney 32, Lowe 36). Att: 12,561 (Doncaster Rov. won 6-5 on agg).
Southern first leg: Bristol City 0, Bristol Rov. 0. Att: 18,730. **Second leg:** Bristol Rov. 1 (Lambert 65), Bristol City 0. Att: 11,530 (Bristol Rov. won 1-0 on agg).

FINAL

BRISTOL ROVERS 2, DONCASTER ROVERS 3 (aet)

Millennium Stadium (59,024), Sunday, April 1, 2007

Bristol Rov. (4-4-2): Phillips, Lescott, Hinton, Elliott, Carruthers, Igoe (Sandell 100), Campbell, Disley, Haldane (Lines 105), Lambert, Walker (Nicholson 100). **Subs not used:** Green, Anthony. **Scorers:** Walker (49 pen), Igoe (62). **Manager:** Paul Trollope.

Doncaster Rov. (4-4-2): Sullivan, O'Connor, Lockwood, Lee, McDaid, Stock (Wilson 102), Coppinger, Green, Price (Thornton 60), Forte (Guy 87), Heffernan. **Subs not used:** Roberts, Dyer. **Scorers:** Forte (1), Heffernan (5), Lee (110). **Booked:** Coppinger, Stock. **Manager:** Sean O'Driscoll.

Referee: G. Laws (Tyne and Wear). **Half-time:** 0-2.

FINALS – RESULTS

Associated Members' Cup
1984 (Hull City) Bournemouth 2, Hull City 1
Freight Rover Trophy
1985 (Wembley) Wigan Athletic 3, Brentford 1
1986 (Wembley) Bristol City 3, Bolton Wand. 0
1987 (Wembley) Mansfield Town 1, Bristol City 1 (aet; Mansfield Town won 5-4 on pens.)
Sherpa Van Trophy
1988 (Wembley) Wolves 2, Burnley 0
1989 (Wembley) Bolton Wand. 4, Torquay Utd. 1
Leyland Daf Cup
1990 (Wembley) Tranmere Rov. 2, Bristol Rov. 1
1991 (Wembley) Birmingham City 3, Tranmere Rov. 2
Autoglass Trophy
1992 (Wembley) Stoke City 1, Stockport Co. 0
1993 (Wembley) Port Vale 2, Stockport Co. 1
1994 (Wembley) Huddersfield Town 1, Swansea City 1 (aet; Swansea City won 3-1 on pens.)
Auto Windscreens Shield
1995 (Wembley) Birmingham City 1, Carlisle Utd. 0 (Birmingham City won in sudden-death overtime)
1996 (Wembley) Rotherham Utd. 2, Shrewsbury Town 1
1997 (Wembley) Carlisle Utd. 0, Colchester Utd. 0 (aet; Carlisle Utd. won 4-3 on pens.)
1998 (Wembley) Grimsby Town 2, Bournemouth 1 (Grimsby Town won with golden goal in extra time)
1999 (Wembley) Wigan Athletic 1, Millwall 0
2000 (Wembley) Stoke City 2, Bristol City 1
LDV Vans Trophy
2001 (Millennium Stadium) Port Vale 2, Brentford 1
2002 (Millennium Stadium) Blackpool 4, Cambridge Utd. 1
2003 (Millennium Stadium) Bristol City 2, Carlisle Utd. 0
2004 (Millennium Stadium) Blackpool 2, Southend Utd. 0
2005 (Millennium Stadium) Wrexham 2, Southend Utd. 0
Football League Trophy
2006 (Millennium Stadium) Swansea City 2, Carlisle Utd. 1
Johnstone's Paint Trophy
2007 (Millennium Stadium) Doncaster Rov. 3, Bristol Rov. 2 (aet)

OTHER LEAGUE CLUBS' CUP COMPETITIONS

FINALS – AT WEMBLEY

Full Members' Cup (Discontinued after 1992)
1985-86 Chelsea 5, Manchester City 4
1986-87 Blackburn Rov. 1, Charlton Athletic 0

Simod Cup
1987-88 Reading 4, Luton Town 1
1988-89 Nott'm. Forest 4, Everton 3
Zenith Data Systems Cup
1989-90 Chelsea 1, Middlesbrough 0
1990-91 Crystal Palace 4, Everton 1
1991-92 Nott'm. Forest 3, Southampton 2

ANGLO-ITALIAN CUP (Discontinued after 1996: * Home club)

1970 *Napoli 0, Swindon Town 3
1971 *Bologna 1, Blackpool 2 (aet)
1972 *AS Roma 3, Blackpool 1
1973 *Fiorentina 1, Newcastle Utd. 2
1993 Derby Co. 1, Cremonese 3 (at Wembley)
1994 Notts Co. 0, Brescia 1 (at Wembley)
1995 Ascoli 1, Notts Co. 2 (at Wembley)
1996 Port Vale 2, Genoa 5 (at Wembley)

F.A. VASE FINALS

At Wembley (until 2001)
1975 Hoddesdon Town 2, Epsom & Ewell 1
1976 Billericay Town 1, Stamford 0*
1977 Billericay Town 2, Sheffield 1 (replay Nottingham, after a 1-1 draw at Wembley)
1978 Blue Star 2, Barton Rov. 1
1979 Billericay Town 4, Almondsbury Greenway 1
1980 Stamford 2, Guisborough Town 0
1981 Whickham 3, Willenhall Town 2*
1982 Forest Green Rov. 3, Rainworth Miners' Welfare 0
1983 V.S. Rugby 1, Halesowen Town 0
1984 Stansted 3, Stamford 2
1985 Halesowen Town 3, Fleetwood Town 1
1986 Halesowen Town 3, Southall 0
1987 St. Helens Town 3, Warrington Town 2
1988 Colne Dynamoes 1, Emley 0*
1989 Tamworth 3, Sudbury Town 0 (replay Peterborough Utd., after a 1-1 draw at Wembley)
1990 Yeading 1, Bridlington 0 (replay Leeds Utd., after 0-0 draw at Wembley)
1991 Guiseley 3, Gresley Rov. 1 (replay Bramall Lane, Sheffield, after a 4-4 draw at Wembley)
1992 Wimborne Town 5, Guiseley 3
1993 Bridlington Town 1, Tiverton Town 0
1994 Diss Town 2, Taunton Town 1*
1995 Arlesey Town 2, Oxford City 1
1996 Brigg Town 3, Clitheroe 0
1997 Whitby Town 3, North Ferriby Utd. 0
1998 Tiverton Town 1, Tow Law Town 0
1999 Tiverton Town 1, Bedlington Terriers 0
2000 Deal Town 1, Chippenham Town 0

2001 Taunton Town 2, Berkhamsted 1 (Villa Park)
2002 Whitley Bay 1, Tiptree Utd. 0* (Villa Park)
2003 Brigg Town 2, AFC Sudbury 1 (Upton Park)
2004 Winchester City 2, AFC Sudbury 0 (St Andrews)
2005 Didcot Town 3, AFC Sudbury 2 (White Hart Lane
2006 Nantwich Town 3, Hillingdon Borough 1 (St Andrews)
2007 Truro City 3, AFC Totton 1 (Wembley)

* After extra time

F.A.TROPHY

SECOND ROUND

Eastbourne 0, Northwich 1; Exeter 0, Kidderminster 1; Farnborough 0, Braintree 2; Gravesend 0, *Wimbledon 1; Morecambe 5, Mangotsfield 0; Newport 0, Histon 0; Oxford 2, Halifax 2; Redditch 3, Dagenham 2; Salisbury 2, Southport 1; Stalybridge 1, Kettering 1; Stevenage 3, Leigh 1; Tamworth 1, Welling 1; Worcester 2, Burton 1; Weston SM 0, Grays 4; Witton 0, Rushden 1; Yeading 2, Bishop's Stortford 0. **Replays:** Halifax 2, Oxford 1; Histon 3, Newport 1; Kettering 3, Stalybridge 1; Welling 2, Tamworth 1. * Wimbledon fielded ineligible player – Gravesend through.

THIRD ROUND

Gravesend 2, Rushden 1; Grays 2, Yeading 1; Halifax 3, Redditch 1; Histon 1, Northwich 2; Kettering 0, Salisbury 2; Kidderminster 0, Braintree 0; Morecambe 1, Stevenage 1; Welling 2, Worcester 1. **Replays:** Braintree 1, Kidderminster 3; Stevenage 3, Morecambe 0 (aet).

FOURTH ROUND

Kidderminster 3, Halifax 1; Northwich 3 Gravesend 0; Stevenage 3, Salisbury 0; Welling 1, Grays 4.

SEMI-FINALS

First leg: Grays 0, Stevenage 1; Kidderminster 2, Northwich 0. **Second leg:** Northwich 3, Kidderminster 2 (Kidderminster won 4-3 on agg); Stevenage 2, Grays 1 (aet, Stevenage won 3-1 on agg).

FINAL

KIDDERMINSTER HARRIERS 2, STEVENAGE BOROUGH 3

Wembley (53,262 – comp rec), Saturday, May 12, 2007

Kidderminster Harriers (4-4-2): Bevan, Kenna, Creighton, Whitehead, Smikle (Reynolds 90), Russell, Hurren, Penn, Blackwood, Christie (White 76), Constable. **Subs not used:** Taylor, McGrath, Sedgemore. **Scorers:** Constable (31, 37). **Booked:** Penn, Hurren. **Manager:** Mark Yates.

Stevenage Borough: (4-4-2): Julian, Fuller, Gaia, Henry, Nutter, Guppy (Dobson 63), Miller, Beard, Cole, Oliver, Morison. **Subs not used:** Potter, Slabber, Nurse, McMahon. **Scorers:** Cole (51), Dobson (74), Morison (88). **Booked:** Oliver, Fuller. **Manager:** Mark Stimson.

Referee: C. Foy (Merseyside). **Half-time:** 2-0.

F.A. TROPHY FINALS

At Wembley

1970 Macclesfield Town 2, Telford Utd. 0
1971 Telford Utd. 3, Hillingdon Borough 2
1972 Stafford Rangers 3, Barnet 0
1973 Scarborough 2, Wigan Athletic 1*
1974 Morecambe 2, Dartford 1
1975 Matlock Town 4, Scarborough 0
1976 Scarborough 3, Stafford Rangers 2*
1977 Scarborough 2, Dagenham 1
1978 Altrincham 3, Leatherhead 1
1979 Stafford Rangers 2, Kettering Town 0
1980 Dagenham 2, Mossley 1
1981 Bishop's Stortford 1, Sutton Utd. 0
1982 Enfield 1, Altrincham 0*
1983 Telford Utd. 2, Northwich Victoria 1
1984 Northwich Victoria 2, Bangor City 1 (replay Stoke City, after a 1-1 draw at Wembley)
1985 Wealdstone 2, Boston Utd. 1
1986 Altrincham 1, Runcorn 0
1987 Kidderminster Harriers 2, Burton Albion 1 (replay W.B.A., after a 0-0 draw at Wembley)
1988 Enfield 3, Telford Utd. 2 (replay W.B.A., after a 0-0 draw at Wembley)
1989 Telford Utd. 1, Macclesfield Town 0*
1990 Barrow 3, Leek Town 0
1991 Wycombe Wand. 2, Kidderminster Harriers 1
1992 Colchester Utd. 3, Witton Albion 1
1993 Wycombe Wand. 4, Runcorn 1
1994 Woking 2, Runcorn 1
1995 Woking 2, Kidderminster 1
1996 Macclesfield Town 3, Northwich Victoria 1
1997 Woking 1, Dagenham & Redbridge 0*
1998 Cheltenham Town 1, Southport 0
1999 Kingstonian 1, Forest Green Rov. 0
2000 Kingstonian 3, Kettering Town 2

At Villa Park

2001 Canvey Island 1, Forest Green Rov. 0
2002 Yeovil Town 2, Stevenage Borough 0
2003 Burscough 2, Tamworth 1
2004 Hednesford Town 3, Canvey Island 2
2005 Grays Athletic 1, Hucknall Town 1* (Grays Athletic won 6-5 on pens)

At Upton Park

2006 Grays Athletic 2, Woking 0

At Wembley

2007 Stevenage Borough 3, Kidderminster Harriers 2

(* After extra-time)

F.A. YOUTH CUP WINNERS

Year	Winners	Runners-up	Aggregate
1953	Manchester Utd.	Wolves	9-3
1954	Manchester Utd.	Wolves	5-4
1955	Manchester Utd.	W.B.A.	7-1

1956	Manchester Utd.	Chesterfield	4-3
1957	Manchester Utd.	West Ham Utd.	8-2
1958	Wolves	Chelsea	7-6
1959	Blackburn Rov.	West Ham Utd.	2-1
1960	Chelsea	Preston N.E.	5-2
1961	Chelsea	Everton	5-3
1962	Newcastle Utd.	Wolves	2-1
1963	West Ham Utd.	Liverpool	6-5
1964	Manchester Utd.	Swindon Town	5-2
1965	Everton	Arsenal	3-2
1966	Arsenal	Sunderland	5-3
1967	Sunderland	Birmingham City	2-0
1968	Burnley	Coventry City	3-2
1969	Sunderland	W.B.A.	6-3
1970	Tottenham	Coventry City	4-3
1971	Arsenal	Cardiff City	2-0
1972	Aston Villa	Liverpool	5-2
1973	Ipswich Town	Bristol City	4-1
1974	Tottenham	Huddersfield Town	2-1
1975	Ipswich Town	West Ham Utd.	5-1
1976	W.B.A.	Wolves	5-0
1977	Crystal Palace	Everton	1-0
1978	Crystal Palace	Aston Villa	*1-0
1979	Millwall	Manchester City	2-0
1980	Aston Villa	Manchester City	3-2
1981	West Ham Utd.	Tottenham	2-1
1982	Watford	Manchester Utd.	7-6
1983	Norwich City	Everton	6-5
1984	Everton	Stoke City	4-2
1985	Newcastle Utd.	Watford	4-1
1986	Manchester City	Manchester Utd.	3-1
1987	Coventry City	Charlton Athletic	2-1
1988	Arsenal	Doncaster Rov.	6-1
1989	Watford	Manchester City	2-1
1990	Tottenham	Middlesbrough	3-2
1991	Millwall	Sheffield Wed.	3-0
1992	Manchester Utd.	Crystal Palace	6-3
1993	Leeds Utd.	Manchester Utd.	4-1
1994	Arsenal	Millwall	5-3
1995	Manchester Utd.	Tottenham	†2-2
1996	Liverpool	West Ham Utd.	4-1
1997	Leeds Utd.	Crystal Palace	3-1
1998	Everton	Blackburn Rov.	5-3
1999	West Ham Utd.	Coventry City	9-0
2000	Arsenal	Coventry City	5-1
2001	Arsenal	Blackburn Rov.	6-3
2002	Aston Villa	Everton	4-2
2003	Manchester Utd.	Middlesbrough	3-1
2004	Middlesbrough	Aston Villa	4-0
2005	Ipswich Town	Southampton	3-2
2006	Liverpool	Manchester City	3-2
2007	Liverpool	Manchester Utd.	††2-2

(* One match only; † Manchester Utd. won 4-3 on pens, †† Liverpool won 4-3 on pens.)

WELSH CUP FINAL

Camarthen 3, Afan Lido 2 (at Llanelli).

WOMEN'S F.A. CUP FINAL

Arsenal 4, Charlton Athletic 1 (at City Ground).

WOMEN'S PREMIER LEAGUE CUP FINAL

Arsenal 1, Leeds Utd. 0 (at Glanford Park).

F.A. SUNDAY CUP FINAL

Coundon Conservative Club (Durham) 5, Lebeq Tavern Courage (Bristol) 0 (at Anfield).

F. A. COMMUNITY SHIELD

LIVERPOOL 2, CHELSEA 1

Millennium Stadium (56,275), Sunday, August 13, 2006

Liverpool (4-2-3-1): Reina, Finnan, Carragher, Agger, Riise, Sissoko, Zenden (Xabi Alonso 60), Pennant (Gerrard 60), Luis Garcia (Bellamy 66), Gonzalez (Aurelio 57), Crouch (Sinama Pongolle 88). **Subs not used:** Dudek, Hyypia. **Scorers:** Riise (9), Crouch (80). **Booked:** Xabi Alonso.

Chelsea (4-1-3-2): Cudicini, Geremi (Bridge 54), Terry, Ricardo Carvalho, Paulo Ferreira (Mikel 81), Essien, Ballack (Kalou 25), Lampard, Robben (Diarra 63), Drogba (Wright-Phillips 72), Shevchenko. **Subs not used:** Hilario, Mancienne. **Scorer:** Shevche-kno (43). **Booked:** Ballack, Lampard, Diarra.

Referee: M. Atkinson (West Yorkshire). **Half-time:** 1-1.

CHARITY SHIELD RESULTS (POST WAR)

Year	Winners	Runners-up	Score
1948	Arsenal	Manchester Utd.	4-3
1949	Portsmouth	Wolves	*1-1
1950	England World Cup XI	F.A. Canadian Tour Team	4-2
1951	Tottenham	Newcastle Utd.	2-1
1952	Manchester Utd.	Newcastle Utd.	4-2
1953	Arsenal	Blackpool	3-1
1954	Wolves	W.B.A.	*4-4
1955	Chelsea	Newcastle Utd.	3-0
1956	Manchester Utd.	Manchester City	1-0
1957	Manchester Utd.	Aston Villa	4-0
1958	Bolton Wand.	Wolves	4-1
1959	Wolves	Nott'm. Forest	3-1
1960	Burnley	Wolves	*2-2
1961	Tottenham	F.A. XI	3-2
1962	Tottenham	Ipswich Town	5-1
1963	Everton	Manchester Utd.	4-0
1964	Liverpool	West Ham Utd.	*2-2
1965	Manchester Utd.	Liverpool	*2-2
1966	Liverpool	Everton	1-0
1967	Manchester Utd.	Tottenham	*3-3
1968	Manchester City	W.B.A.	6-1
1969	Leeds Utd.	Manchester City	2-1
1970	Everton	Chelsea	2-1
1971	Leicester City	Liverpool	1-0

1972	Manchester City	Aston Villa	1-0
1973	Burnley	Manchester City	1-0
1974	Liverpool	Leeds Utd.	1-1
	(Liverpool won 6-5 on penalties)		
1975	Derby Co.	West Ham Utd.	2-0
1976	Liverpool	Southampton	1-0
1977	Liverpool	Manchester Utd.	*0-0
1978	Nott'm. Forest	Ipswich Town	5-0
1979	Liverpool	Arsenal	3-1
1980	Liverpool	West Ham Utd.	1-0
1981	Aston Villa	Tottenham	*2-2
1982	Liverpool	Tottenham	1-0
1983	Manchester Utd.	Liverpool	2-0
1984	Everton	Liverpool	1-0
1985	Everton	Manchester Utd.	2-0
1986	Everton	Liverpool	*1-1
1987	Everton	Coventry City	1-0
1988	Liverpool	Wimbledon	2-1
1989	Liverpool	Arsenal	1-0
1990	Liverpool	Manchester Utd.	*1-1
1991	Arsenal	Tottenham	*0-0
1992	Leeds Utd.	Liverpool	4-3
1993	Manchester Utd.	Arsenal	1-1
	(Manchester Utd. won 5-4 on penalties)		
1994	Manchester Utd.	Blackburn Rov.	2-0
1995	Everton	Blackburn Rov.	1-0
1996	Manchester Utd.	Newcastle Utd.	4-0
1997	Manchester Utd.	Chelsea	1-1
	(Manchester Utd. won 4-2 on penalties)		
1998	Arsenal	Manchester Utd.	3-0
1999	Arsenal	Manchester Utd.	2-1
2000	Chelsea	Manchester Utd.	2-0
2001	Liverpool	Manchester Utd.	2-1

COMMUNITY SHIELD RESULTS

Year	Winners	Runners-up	Score
2002	Arsenal	Liverpool	1-0
2003	Manchester Utd.	Arsenal	1-1
	(Manchester Utd. won 4-3 on penalties)		
2004	Arsenal	Manchester Utd.	3-1
2005	Chelsea	Arsenal	2-1
2006	Liverpool	Chelsea	2-1

(Fixture played at Wembley since 1974. Millennium Stadium since 2001.
*Trophy shared)

FAMILY DOUBLE FOR THE OLIVERS

Michael Oliver, a 22-year-old student from Northumberland, became the Football League's youngest referee when he took charge of last season's Hereford United-Grimsby Town match. At the same time his father Clive officiated at the game between Chesterfield and Leyton Orient. It was the first time a father and son had refereed league fixtures on the same day.

SCOTTISH FINAL TABLES 2006-07

BANK OF SCOTLAND PREMIER LEAGUE

			HOME					AWAY						
		P	W	D	L	F	A	W	D	L	F	A	GD	Pts
1	Celtic	38	16	1	2	36	13	10	5	4	29	21	31	84
2	Rangers	38	11	6	2	35	10	10	3	6	26	22	29	72
3	Aberdeen	38	11	3	5	33	21	8	5	6	22	17	17	65
4	Hearts	38	9	4	6	26	19	8	6	5	21	16	12	61
5	Kilmarnock	38	7	5	6	24	22	9	2	9	23	32	–7	55
6	Hibernian	38	9	6	4	32	20	4	4	11	24	26	10	49
7	Falkirk	38	10	2	8	24	19	5	3	10	25	28	2	50
8	Inverness CT	38	8	6	5	25	20	3	7	9	17	28	–6	46
9	Dundee Utd.	38	5	8	6	17	24	5	4	10	23	35	–19	42
10	Motherwell	38	5	3	11	25	34	5	5	9	16	27	–20	38
11	St Mirren	38	3	6	10	13	23	5	6	8	18	28	–20	36
12	Dunfermline	38	6	4	9	17	28	2	4	13	9	27	–29	32

(After 33 matches, League split into top six and bottom six teams, each playing five further games and staying in their respective section, regardless of points won)

Leading scorers (all club competitions): 26 Boyd (Rangers); 19 Naismith (Kilmarnock); 16 McDonald (Motherwell), Stokes (Falkirk), Vennegoor of Hesselink (Celtic); 15 Killen (Hibernian); 14 Adam (Rangers), Benjelloun (Hibernian), Foran (Motherwell), Nish (Kilmarnock); 13 Mackie (Aberdeen), Sutton (St Mirren); 12 Dargo (Inverness CT), Fletcher (Hibernian), Robson (Dundee Utd.); 11 Nakamura (Celtic), Velicka (Hearts).

FIRST DIVISION

			HOME					AWAY						
		P	W	D	L	F	A	W	D	L	F	A	GD	Pts
1	Gretna	36	10	4	4	35	18	9	5	4	35	22	30	66
2	St Johnstone	36	13	3	2	39	17	6	5	7	26	25	23	65
3	Dundee	36	11	2	5	27	19	5	3	10	21	23	6	53
4	Hamilton Acad.	36	9	7	2	30	17	5	4	9	16	30	–1	53
5	Clyde	36	8	4	6	24	14	3	10	5	22	21	11	47
6	Livingston	36	3	7	8	20	24	8	5	5	21	22	–5	45
7	Partick Thistle	36	6	6	6	25	33	6	3	9	22	30	–16	45
8	Queen of South	36	6	6	6	19	24	4	5	9	15	30	–20	41
9	Airdrie Utd.†	36	6	3	9	19	25	5	4	9	20	25	–11	40
10	Ross Co.	36	6	6	6	22	25	3	4	11	18	32	–17	37

† Also relegated

Play-offs (on agg) – Semi-finals: Airdrie Utd. 6, Brechin City 1; Stirling Alb. 3, Raith Rov. 1. **Final:** Stirling Alb. 5, Airdrie Utd. 4.

Leading scorers (all club competitions): 26 McMenamin (Gretna), Scotland (St Johnstone); 16 Offiong (Hamilton Acad.), Roberts (Partick Thistle); 15 Hardie (St Johnstone), Lyle (Dundee); 14 Milne (St Johnstone); 13 O'Neill (Queen of the South), 12 Twigg (Airdrie Utd.); 11 Dobbie (Queen of the South); 10 Arbuckle (Clyde), Craig (Livingston).

SECOND DIVISION

			HOME					AWAY						
		P	W	D	L	F	A	W	D	L	F	A	GD	Pts
1	Morton	36	13	4	1	41	13	11	1	6	35	19	44	77
2	Stirling Alb.†	36	12	2	4	37	17	9	4	5	30	22	28	69
3	Raith Rov.	36	7	5	6	22	18	11	3	4	28	15	17	62
4	Brechin City	36	9	2	7	30	24	9	4	5	31	21	16	60
5	Ayr Utd.	36	7	3	8	21	23	7	5	6	25	24	–1	50
6	Cowdenbeath	36	7	4	7	36	35	6	2	10	23	21	3	45
7	Alloa Athletic	36	5	6	7	24	27	6	3	9	23	43	–23	42
8	Peterhead	36	6	5	7	34	27	5	3	10	26	35	–2	41
9	Stranraer††	36	8	2	8	29	38	2	7	9	16	36	–29	39
10	Forfar Athletic	36	4	3	11	21	31	0	4	14	16	59	–53	19

† Also promoted. †† Also relegated.

Play-offs (on agg) – Semi-finals: East Fife 4, Stranraer 2; Queen's Park 4, Arbroath 1. **Final:** Queen's Park 7, East Fife 2.

Leading scorers (all club competitions): 23 Buchanan (Cowdenbeath), Russell (Brechin City); 18 Weatherson (Morton); 16 Cramb (Stirling Alb.), Moore (Stranraer); 15 Clark (Cowdenbeath); 14 Templeman (Morton); 13 Gribben (Forfat Athletic), 12 Aitken (Stirling Alb.), Bavidge (Peterhead), 11 Hamilton (Stranraer), Linn (Peterhead), Paateleianen (Cowdenbeath).

THIRD DIVISION

			HOME					AWAY						
		P	W	D	L	F	A	W	D	L	F	A	GD	Pts
1	Berwick Rangers	36	12	3	3	29	14	12	0	6	22	15	22	75
2	Arbroath	36	9	4	5	27	20	13	0	5	34	13	28	70
3	Queen's Park†	36	12	3	3	33	13	9	2	7	24	15	29	68
4	East Fife	36	10	4	4	26	15	10	3	5	33	22	22	67
5	Dumbarton	36	12	2	4	30	15	6	3	9	22	22	15	59
6	Albion Rov.	36	8	2	8	30	29	6	4	8	26	32	–5	48
7	Stenhousemuir	36	9	1	8	36	31	4	4	10	17	32	–10	44
8	Montrose	36	6	2	10	20	27	5	2	11	22	35	–20	37
9	Elgin City	36	7	0	11	24	30	2	2	14	15	39	–30	29
10	East Stirling	36	3	1	14	11	37	3	2	13	16	41	–51	21

† Also promoted.

Leading scorers (all club competitions): 23 Chaplain (Albion Rov.); 21 Johnston (Elgin City); 18 Weatherston (Queen's Park); 17 O'Reilly (East Fife); 13 Martain (Arbroath); 12 Ferry (Queen's Park), Wood (Berwick Rangers); 11 Dobbie (Dumbarton), Jablonski (East Fife), Rogers (Montrose), Sellars (Arbroath), Trouten (Queen's Park).

SCOTTISH LEAGUE RESULTS 2006-07

BANK OF SCOTLAND PREMIER LEAGUE

	Aberdeen	Celtic	Dundee Utd.	Dunfermline	Falkirk	Hearts	Hibernian	Inverness CT	Kilmarnock	Motherwell	St Mirren	Rangers
Aberdeen	–	0–1	3–1	1–0	2–1	1–3	2–1	1–1	3–1	2–1	2–0	1–2
	–	1–2	2–4	3–0	–	1–0	2–2	1–1	3–0	–	–	2–0
Celtic	1–0	–	2–2	1–0	1–0	2–1	2–1	3–0	4–1	2–1	2–0	2–0
	2–1	–	–	2–1	–	1–3	1–0	–	2–0	1–0	5–1	0–1
Dundee Utd.	3–1	1–4	–	0–0	1–2	0–1	0–3	3–1	1–0	1–1	1–0	2–1
	–	1–1	–	0–0	1–5	–	0–0	1–1	–	1–1	0–2	–
	–	–	–	–	–	–	–	–	–	0–0	–	–
Dunfermline	0–3	1–2	2–1	–	0–3	1–2	0–4	0–0	3–2	0–2	2–1	1–1
	–	–	1–0	–	0–3	0–1	1–0	–	1–1	4–1	0–0	0–1
Falkirk	0–2	0–1	5–1	1–0	–	1–1	2–1	3–1	1–2	0–1	1–1	1–0
	1–2	1–0	2–0	1–0	–	–	–	1–0	0–2	1–2	2–0	–
	–	–	–	–	–	–	–	–	–	–	0–2	–
Hearts	0–1	2–1	4–0	1–1	0–0	–	3–2	4–1	0–2	4–1	0–1	0–1
	1–1	1–2	0–4	–	1–0	–	2–0	1–0	1–0	–	1–1	–
Hibernian	1–1	2–2	2–1	2–0	0–1	2–2	–	2–0	2–2	3–1	5–1	2–1
	0–0	2–1	–	–	2–0	0–1	–	–	0–1	2–0	–	0–2
	–	–	–	–	–	–	–	–	–	–	–	3–3
Inverness CT	1–1	1–1	0–0	1–0	3–2	0–0	0–0	–	3–4	0–1	1–2	2–1
	–	1–2	1–0	1–3	1–1	–	3–0	–	–	2–0	2–1	–
	–	–	–	2–1	–	–	–	–	–	–	–	–
Kilmarnock	1–0	1–2	0–0	5–1	2–1	0–0	2–1	1–1	–	1–2	1–1	2–2
	1–2	1–2	1–0	–	–	1–0	0–2	3–2	–	–	–	1–3
Motherwell	0–2	1–1	2–3	2–1	4–2	0–1	1–6	1–4	5–0	–	0–0	1–2
	0–2	–	–	2–0	3–3	0–2	–	1–0	0–1	–	2–3	0–1
St Mirren	1–1	1–3	1–3	0–0	1–0	2–2	1–0	1–1	0–1	2–0	–	2–3
	0–2	–	0–1	0–1	–	–	1–1	0–1	0–2	0–0	–	0–1
Rangers	1–0	1–1	2–2	2–0	4–0	2–0	3–0	0–1	3–0	1–1	1–1	–
	3–0	2–0	5–0	–	2–1	0–0	–	1–1	–	–	–	–
	–	–	–	–	–	2–1	–	–	0–1	–	–	–

Read across for home results, down for away

BELL'S FIRST DIVISION

	Airdrie Utd.	Clyde	Dundee	Gretna	Hamilton Acad.	Livingston	Partick Thistle	Queen of South	Ross Co.	St Johnstone
Airdrie Utd.	–	2–1	0–1	4–2	1–2	0–1	1–2	2–2	0–2	2–1
	–	1–0	0–3	0–0	1–0	3–1	1–1	0–2	0–1	1–2
Clyde	0–0	–	2–1	1–2	2–1	1–1	0–0	4–0	3–0	1–0
	0–1	–	1–1	2–0	3–0	0–1	2–0	0–1	2–4	0–1
Dundee	1–0	3–0	–	1–3	1–1	0–1	0–1	2–1	3–1	1–1
	2–1	1–4	–	0–1	1–0	2–0	3–1	1–0	3–2	2–1
Gretna	0–2	3–3	0–4	–	6–0	1–1	4–0	5–0	2–1	2–0
	0–0	0–0	1–0	–	1–0	4–1	2–0	0–3	4–1	0–2
Hamilton Acad.	2–1	3–1	1–0	3–1	–	1–1	1–2	1–1	0–0	2–2
	3–0	1–1	1–0	0–0	–	3–0	2–1	2–2	1–0	3–4
Livingston	3–0	1–1	2–3	1–2	0–1	–	2–2	2–0	0–0	1–1
	1–3	0–0	1–3	1–1	1–2	–	0–1	0–1	1–1	3–2
Partick Thistle	4-2	1–1	3–1	0–6	3–1	2–3	–	1–1	3–2	1–5
	0–1	0–4	2–1	2–2	0–2	0–0	–	0–0	1–1	2–0
Queen of South	1–1	0–2	2–0	0–3	1–1	2–0	0–2	–	2–0	0–1
	0–3	0–0	2–2	0–4	1–1	1–1	4–3	–	2–0	1–0
Ross Co.	2–1	1–1	1–0	0–1	0–1	0–3	2–5	1–0	–	2–2
	1–1	2–2	0–0	2–3	4–1	0–2	2–1	1–0	–	1–1
St Johnstone	1–0	0–0	2–1	3–3	0–0	1–2	2–0	5–0	3–1	–
	4–3	2–1	2–0	2–1	4–2	1–2	2–0	3–0	2–1	–

Read across for home results, down for away

BELL'S SECOND DIVISION

	Alloa Athletic	Ayr Utd.	Brechin City	Cowdenbeath	Forfar Athletic	Morton	Peterhead	Raith Rov.	Stirling Alb.	Stranraer
Alloa Athletic	–	0–1	2–2	2–1	2–0	3–2	1–1	1–2	1–2	1–1
	–	1–1	2–3	0–0	2–0	0–3	2–4	2–3	1–1	1–0
Ayr Utd.	0–1	–	1–2	0–4	5–0	0–1	1–2	1–0	0–0	0–2
	4–3	–	1–1	0–2	3–1	1–0	0–0	0–2	3–2	1–0
Brechin City	2–0	0–2	–	4–2	4–2	2–3	1–0	1–0	0–1	3–0
	2–3	2–0	–	1–0	2–2	0–1	3–1	1–2	1–4	1–1
Cowdenbeath	6–1	1–1	1–3	–	3–2	1–2	4–2	1–2	2–2	4–2
	5–2	3–1	0–3	–	2–1	1–1	0–3	1–5	1–2	0–0
Forfar Athletic	0–2	0–1	1–2	1–1	–	1–3	2–3	1–1	0–2	2–1
	0–2	1–1	3–2	2–0	–	0–4	1–2	1–2	0–2	5–0
Morton	4–0	0–0	1–0	1–0	1–1	–	4–2	2–0	1–1	3–0
	2–1	4–2	0–2	3–0	9–1	–	2–1	1–0	2–1	1–1
Peterhead	1–2	3–1	1–1	1–0	8–0	0–4	–	0–1	2–3	5–2
	0–0	2–2	1–4	0–2	2–2	1–2	–	0–0	2–1	5–0
Raith Rov.	0–0	1–0	1–1	1–3	0–0	1–3	5–2	–	1–3	1–1
	3–0	0–1	1–0	1–2	2–1	2–0	2–0	–	0–1	0–0
Stirling Alb.	5–0	1–3	2–1	1–0	3–0	2–1	2–0	1–1	–	3–3
	4–0	4–2	0–1	1–0	4–0	2–1	2–1	0–1	–	0–2
Stranraer	2–2	1–3	3–1	1–0	3–2	0–3	2–1	1–4	2–1	–
	3–4	0–3	0–2	1–6	4–1	1–0	1–1	0–2	3–1	–

Read across for home results, down for away

BELL'S THIRD DIVISION

	Albion Rov.	Arbroath	Berwick Rangers	Dumbarton	East Fife	East Stirling	Elgin City	Montrose	Queens Park	Stenhousemuir
Albion Rov.	–	1–3	0–1	2–1	0–1	4–0	3–1	3–1	1–1	2–5
	–	0–3	0–1	0–1	0–3	2–1	6–2	2–2	2–1	2–1
Arbroath	2–3	–	0–1	0–0	1–1	1–2	2–1	3–1	1–2	2–0
	0–0	–	1–0	2–2	1–3	3–2	2–1	1–0	1–0	4–1
Berwick Rangers	1–1	3–2	–	3–0	2–1	2–2	3–1	1–2	1–0	0–1
	3–0	1–0	–	2–1	2–0	2–0	0–0	1–0	0–2	2–1
Dumbarton	3–1	0–2	2–0	–	2–1	2–0	3–1	2–0	0–0	4–0
	3–1	1–0	1–2	–	0–2	2–1	1–0	2–1	1–2	1–1
East Fife	2–2	2–1	2–0	1–0	–	5–0	1–1	2–0	1–0	0–0
	1–3	1–2	0–2	1–0	–	0–2	3–1	2–0	1–0	1–1
East Stirling	0–1	0–2	0–3	0–2	0–4	–	2–1	0–3	2–1	5–0
	0–0	1–5	0–1	1–5	0–2	–	0–2	0–2	0–2	0–1
Elgin City	0–3	0–4	1–2	0–2	1–2	5–0	–	3–2	1–2	2–0
	3–0	0–1	2–1	0–1	2–3	2–1	–	0–2	0–3	2–1
Montrose	2–1	0–1	0–1	1–1	1–0	1–0	2–0	–	0–3	0–1
	2–3	0–1	1–2	0–5	3–3	4–0	0–1	–	0–2	3–2
Queen's Park	2–1	0–3	1–0	1–0	3–0	1–3	3–0	1–1	–	1–1
	5–0	1–0	0–2	2–0	1–1	2–1	3–0	5–0	–	1–0
Stenhousemuir	3–2	1–2	2–3	1–0	0–1	2–0	2–0	5–0	2–1	–
	0–4	1–2	2–0	5–1	3–5	1–1	3–2	2–5	1–2	–

Read across for home results, down for away

HOW CELTIC RETAINED THE TITLE

JULY 2006

29 Celtic 4 (Zurawski 25, 90, Jarosik 38, Nakamura 75), Kilmarnock 1 (Naismith 87) Att: 54,620.

AUGUST 2006

6 Hearts 2 (Bednar 49, 87), Celtic 1 (Petrov 65). Att: 16,822.
12 Celtic 2 (McManus 28, Petrov 65), St Mirren 0. Att: 56,579.
20 Inverness CT 1 (Munro 80), Celtic 1 (Pearson 26). Att: 7,332.
26 Celtic 2 (Zurawski 62, Vennegoor of Hesselink 66), Hibernian 1 (Brown 8). Att: 58,078.

SEPTEMBER 2006

9 Aberdeen 0, Celtic 1 (Vennegoor of Hesselink 79). Att: 15,304.
16 Celtic 1 (McManus 31), Dunfermline Athletic 0. Att: 55,894.
23 Celtic 2 (Gravesen 35, Miller 74), Rangers 0. Att: 59,341.

OCTOBER 2006

1 Falkirk 0, Celtic 1 (McGeady 84). Att: 7,139.
14 Dundee Utd. 1 (Hunt 5), Celtic 4 (Nakamura 44, 48, 58, Vennegoor of Hesselink 52). Att: 10,504.
21 Celtic 2 (Craigan 16 og, Zurawski 66), Motherwell 1 (McDonald 77). Att: 57,742.
29 Kilmarnock 1 (Nish 49), Celtic 2 (Nakamura 55, Miller 75). Att: 10,083.

NOVEMBER 2006

4 Celtic 2 (Jarosik 86, Gordon 90 og), Hearts 1 (Velicka 72). Att: 58,971.
12 St Mirren 1 (Sutton 56), Celtic 3 (Gravesen 2, 21, 69). Att: 8,445.
18 Celtic 3 (Dods 43 og, Vennegoor of Hesselink 72, Jarosik 85), Inverness CT 0. Att: 56,637.
26 Hibernian 2 (Sproule 12, Thomson 63), Celtic 2 (Sno 70, McGeady 74). Att: 16,747.

DECEMBER 2006

2 Celtic 1 (Zurawski 72), Aberdeen 0. Att: 58,911.
10 Dunfermline Athletic 1 (Simmons 90), Celtic 2 (McGeady 49, Zurawski 68). Att: 7,080.
17 Rangers 1 (Hemdani 88), Celtic 1 (Gravesen 38). Att: 50,418.
23 Celtic 1 (Gravesen 24), Falkirk 0. Att: 55,000.
26 Celtic 2 (O'Dea 78, Nakamura 80), Dundee Utd. 2 (Robertson 17, Samuel 58). Att: 57,343.
30 Motherwell 1 (Smith 90), Celtic 1 (Riordan 37). Att: 9,769.

JANUARY 2007

2 Celtic 2 (O'Dea 39, McGeady 90), Kilmarnock 0. Att: 57,236.
14 Hearts 1 (Mikoliunas 28), Celtic 2 (Vennegoor of Hesselink 59, Jarosik 81). Att: 17,129.

20 Celtic 5 (Vennegoor of Hesselink 16, 61 pen, 75, McGeady 69, Miller 82), St Mirren 1 (McGinn 47). Att: 58,382.
28 Inverness CT 1 (Bayne 57), Celtic 2 (Riordan 37, Vennegoor of Hesselink 90). Att: 7,484.

FEBRUARY 2007

10 Celtic 1 (Beattie 54), Hibernian 0. Att: 59,659.
17 Aberdeen 1 (Mackie 90), Celtic 2 (Beattie 9, Nakamura 20). Att: 16,711.

MARCH 2007

3 Celtic 2 (Miller 4, Vennegoor of Hesselink 76), Dunfermline Athletic 1 (Hammill 87). Att: 59,131.
11 Celtic 0, Rangers 1 (Ehiogu 50). Att: 59,425.
18 Falkirk 1 (Thomson 16), Celtic 0. Att: 6,438.
31 Dundee Utd. 1 (Daly 90), Celtic 1 (Nakamura 48). Att: 11,363.

APRIL 2007

7 Celtic 1 (Riordan 52), Motherwell 0. Att: 58,654.
22 Kilmarnock 1 (Nish 50), Celtic 2 (Vennegoor of Hesselink 24, Nakamura 90). Att: 13,623.
29 Celtic 1 (Pressley 63), Hearts 3 (Ivaskevicius 57, Driver 61, Pospisil 71 pen). Att: 59,510.

MAY 2007

5 Rangers 2 (Boyd 34, Adam 55), Celtic 0. Att: 50,384.
12 Celtic 2 (Vennegoor of Hesselink 33, 49), Aberdeen 1 (Mackie 41). Att: 59,510.
20 Hibernian 2 (Brown 60, Spoule 90), Celtic 1 (Riordan 56). Att: 13,885.

QUOTE-UNQUOTE

'I looked at the table for a minute or two, then duly ignored what I saw. Champions League football remains an impossible dream this season' – **Martin O'Neill**, Aston Villa manager, after victory at Everton elevated his side to third.

'I want them to show bit of nastiness, to be like the Leeds United of before because they were horrible on the pitch' – **Dennis Wise** on the task of resurrecting the fortunes of the Elland Road club.

'I don't know where the years have gone' – **Sir Alex Ferguson** on 20 years as Manchester United manager.

'It's a great reminder to everyone at the club that football can smack you in the face' – **Sir Alex Ferguson** on the shock defeat by Southend in the Carling Cup.

'We didn't see Sir Alex, but we could hear him. The old hairdryer must have been out' – **Steven Hammell**, Southend defender.

'She shouldn't be here. I know that sounds sexist, but I am sexist' – **Mike Newell**, Luton manager, objecting to assistant referee Amy Rayner running the line in his team's match against Q.P.R and about women officials generally.

'I probably need to hold my tongue sometimes' – **Mike Newell** apologises for his outburst which later brings him a £6,500 fine from the F.A.

SCOTTISH HONOURS LIST

PREMIER DIVISION

	First	Pts.	Second	Pts.	Third	Pts.
1975-6	Rangers	54	Celtic	48	Hibernian	43
1976-7	Celtic	55	Rangers	46	Aberdeen	43
1977-8	Rangers	55	Aberdeen	53	Dundee Utd.	40
1978-9	Celtic	48	Rangers	45	Dundee Utd.	44
1979-80	Aberdeen	48	Celtic	47	St Mirren	42
1980-81	Celtic	56	Aberdeen	49	Rangers	44
1981-2	Celtic	55	Aberdeen	53	Rangers	43
1982-3	Dundee Utd.	56	Celtic	55	Aberdeen	55
1983-4	Aberdeen	57	Celtic	50	Dundee Utd.	47
1984-5	Aberdeen	59	Celtic	52	Dundee Utd.	47
1985-6	*Celtic	50	Hearts	50	Dundee Utd.	47
1986-7	Rangers	69	Celtic	63	Dundee Utd.	60
1987-8	Celtic	72	Hearts	62	Rangers	60
1988-9	Rangers	56	Aberdeen	50	Celtic	46
1989-90	Rangers	51	Aberdeen	44	Hearts	44
1990-1	Rangers	55	Aberdeen	53	Celtic	41
1991-2	Rangers	72	Hearts	63	Celtic	62
1992-3	Rangers	73	Aberdeen	64	Celtic	60
1993-4	Rangers	58	Aberdeen	55	Motherwell	54
1994-5	Rangers	69	Motherwell	54	Hibernian	53
1995-6	Rangers	87	Celtic	83	Aberdeen	55
1996-7	Rangers	80	Celtic	75	Dundee Utd.	60
1997-8	Celtic	74	Rangers	72	Hearts	67

PREMIER LEAGUE

	First	Pts.	Second	Pts.	Third	Pts.
1998-99	Rangers	77	Celtic	71	St Johnstone	57
1999-2000	Rangers	90	Celtic	69	Hearts	54
2000-01	Celtic	97	Rangers	82	Hibernian	66
2001-02	Celtic	103	Rangers	85	Livingston	58
2002-03	*Rangers	97	Celtic	97	Hearts	63
2003-04	Celtic	98	Rangers	81	Hearts	68
2004-05	Rangers	93	Celtic	92	Hibernian	61
2005-06	Celtic	91	Hearts	74	Rangers	73
2006-07	Celtic	84	Rangers	72	Aberdeen	65

Maximum points: 72 except 1986-8, 1991-4 (88), 1994-2000 (108), 2001-07 (114).
* Won on goal difference.

FIRST DIVISION (Scottish Championship until 1975-76)

	First	Pts.	Second	Pts.	Third	Pts.
1890-1*a*	††Dumbarton	29	Rangers	29	Celtic	24
1891-2*b*	Dumbarton	37	Celtic	35	Hearts	30
1892-3*a*	Celtic	29	Rangers	28	St Mirren	23
1893-4*a*	Celtic	29	Hearts	26	St Bernard's	22
1894-5*a*	Hearts	31	Celtic	26	Rangers	21
1895-6*a*	Celtic	30	Rangers	26	Hibernian	24
1896-7*a*	Hearts	28	Hibernian	26	Rangers	25
1897-8*a*	Celtic	33	Rangers	29	Hibernian	22
1898-9*a*	Rangers	36	Hearts	26	Celtic	24
1899-1900*a*	Rangers	32	Celtic	25	Hibernian	24

Season	First	Pts	Second	Pts	Third	Pts
1900-1*c*	Rangers	35	Celtic	29	Hibernian	25
1901-2*a*	Rangers	28	Celtic	26	Hearts	22
1902-3*b*	Hibernian	37	Dundee	31	Rangers	29
1903-4*d*	Third Lanark	43	Hearts	39	Rangers	38
1904-5*a*	†Celtic	41	Rangers	41	Third Lanark	35
1905-6*a*	Celtic	46	Hearts	39	Rangers	38
1906-7*f*	Celtic	55	Dundee	48	Rangers	45
1907-8*f*	Celtic	55	Falkirk	51	Rangers	50
1908-9*f*	Celtic	51	Dundee	50	Clyde	48
1909-10*f*	Celtic	54	Falkirk	52	Rangers	49
1910-11*f*	Rangers	52	Aberdeen	48	Falkirk	44
1911-12*f*	Rangers	51	Celtic	45	Clyde	42
1912-13*f*	Rangers	53	Celtic	49	Hearts	41
1913-14*g*	Celtic	65	Rangers	59	Hearts	54
1914-15*g*	Celtic	65	Hearts	61	Rangers	50
1915-16*g*	Celtic	67	Rangers	56	Morton	51
1916-17*g*	Celtic	64	Morton	54	Rangers	53
1917-18*f*	Rangers	56	Celtic	55	Kilmarnock	43
1918-19*f*	Celtic	58	Rangers	57	Morton	47
1919-20*h*	Rangers	71	Celtic	68	Motherwell	57
1920-1*h*	Rangers	76	Celtic	66	Hearts	56
1921-2*h*	Celtic	67	Rangers	66	Raith	56
1922-3*g*	Rangers	55	Airdrieonians	50	Celtic	40
1923-4*g*	Rangers	59	Airdrieonians	50	Celtic	41
1924-5*g*	Rangers	60	Airdrieonians	57	Hibernian	52
1925-6*g*	Celtic	58	Airdrieonians	50	Hearts	50
1926-7*g*	Rangers	56	Motherwell	51	Celtic	49
1927-8*g*	Rangers	60	Celtic	55	Motherwell	55
1928-9*g*	Rangers	67	Celtic	51	Motherwell	50
1929-30*g*	Rangers	60	Motherwell	55	Aberdeen	53
1930-1*g*	Rangers	60	Celtic	58	Motherwell	56
1931-2*g*	Motherwell	66	Rangers	61	Celtic	48
1932-3*g*	Rangers	62	Motherwell	59	Hearts	50
1933-4*g*	Rangers	66	Motherwell	62	Celtic	47
1934-5*g*	Rangers	55	Celtic	52	Hearts	50
1935-6*g*	Celtic	68	Rangers	61	Aberdeen	61
1936-7*g*	Rangers	61	Aberdeen	54	Celtic	52
1937-8*g*	Celtic	61	Hearts	58	Rangers	49
1938-9*f*	Rangers	59	Celtic	48	Aberdeen	46
1946-7*f*	Rangers	46	Hibernian	44	Aberdeen	39
1947-8*g*	Hibernian	48	Rangers	46	Partick	46
1948-9*i*	Rangers	46	Dundee	45	Hibernian	39
1949-50*i*	Rangers	50	Hibernian	49	Hearts	43
1950-1*i*	Hibernian	48	Rangers	38	Dundee	38
1951-2*i*	Hibernian	45	Rangers	41	East Fife	37
1952-3*i*	*Rangers	43	Hibernian	43	East Fife	39
1953-4*i*	Celtic	43	Hearts	38	Partick	35
1954-5*f*	Aberdeen	49	Celtic	46	Rangers	41
1955-6*f*	Rangers	52	Aberdeen	46	Hearts	45
1956-7*f*	Rangers	55	Hearts	53	Kilmarnock	42
1957-8*f*	Hearts	62	Rangers	49	Celtic	46
1958-9*f*	Rangers	50	Hearts	48	Motherwell	44
1959-60*f*	Hearts	54	Kilmarnock	50	Rangers	42
1960-1*f*	Rangers	51	Kilmarnock	50	Third Lanark	42
1961-2*f*	Dundee	54	Rangers	51	Celtic	46
1962-3*f*	Rangers	57	Kilmarnock	48	Partick	46
1963-4*f*	Rangers	55	Kilmarnock	49	Celtic	47
1964-5*f*	*Kilmarnock	50	Hearts	50	Dunfermline	49

1965-6*f*	Celtic	57	Rangers	55	Kilmarnock	45
1966-7*f*	Celtic	58	Rangers	55	Clyde	46
1967-8*f*	Celtic	63	Rangers	61	Hibernian	45
1968-9*f*	Celtic	54	Rangers	49	Dunfermline	45
1969-70*f*	Celtic	57	Rangers	45	Hibernian	44
1970-1*f*	Celtic	56	Aberdeen	54	St Johnstone	44
1971-2*f*	Celtic	60	Aberdeen	50	Rangers	44
1972-3*f*	Celtic	57	Rangers	56	Hibernian	45
1973-4*f*	Celtic	53	Hibernian	49	Rangers	48
1974-5*f*	Rangers	56	Hibernian	49	Celtic	45

* Won on goal average. †Won on deciding match. ††Title shared.
Competition suspended 1940-46 (Second World War).

SCOTTISH CHAMPIONSHIP WINS

Rangers	*51	Hibernian	4	Kilmarnock	1
Celtic	41	Dumbarton	*2	Motherwell	1
Aberdeen	4	Dundee	1	Third Lanark	1
Hearts	4	Dundee Utd.	1	(* Incl. 1 shared)	

FIRST DIVISION

(Since formation of Premier Division)

	First	Pts.	Second	Pts.	Third	Pts.
1975-6*d*	Partick	41	Kilmarnock	35	Montrose	30
1976-7*j*	St Mirren	62	Clydebank	58	Dundee	51
1977-8*j*	*Morton	58	Hearts	58	Dundee	57
1978-9*j*	Dundee	55	Kilmarnock	54	Clydebank	54
1979-80*j*	Hearts	53	Airdrieonians	51	Ayr Utd.	44
1980-1*j*	Hibernian	57	Dundee	52	St Johnstone	51
1981-2*j*	Motherwell	61	Kilmarnock	51	Hearts	50
1982-3*j*	St Johnstone	55	Hearts	54	Clydebank	50
1983-4*j*	Morton	54	Dumbarton	51	Partick	46
1984-5*j*	Motherwell	50	Clydebank	48	Falkirk	45
1985-6*j*	Hamilton	56	Falkirk	45	Kilmarnock	44
1986-7*k*	Morton	57	Dunfermline	56	Dumbarton	53
1987-8*k*	Hamilton	56	Meadowbank	52	Clydebank	49
1988-9*j*	Dunfermline	54	Falkirk	52	Clydebank	48
1989-90*j*	St Johnstone	58	Airdrieonians	54	Clydebank	44
1990-1*j*	Falkirk	54	Airdrieonians	53	Dundee	52
1991-2*k*	Dundee	58	Partick	57	Hamilton	57
1992-3k	Raith	65	Kilmarnock	54	Dunfermline	52
1993-4*k*	Falkirk	66	Dunfermline	65	Airdrieonians	54
1994-5*l*	Raith	69	Dunfermline	68	Dundee	68
1995-6*l*	Dunfermline	71	Dundee Utd.	67	Greenock Morton	67
1996-7*l*	St Johnstone	80	Airdrieonians	60	Dundee	58
1997-8*l*	Dundee	70	Falkirk	65	Raith	60
1998-9*l*	Hibernian	89	Falkirk	66	Ayr Utd.	62
1999-2000*l*	St Mirren	76	Dunfermline	71	Falkirk	68
2000-01*l*	Livingston	76	Ayr Utd.	69	Falkirk	56
2001-02*l*	Partick Thistle	66	Airdie	56	Ayr Utd.	52
2002-03*l*	Falkirk	81	Clyde	72	St Johnstone	67
2003-04*l*	Inverness CT	70	Clyde	69	St Johnstone	57
2004-05*l*	Falkirk	75	St Mirren	60	Clyde	60
2005-06*l*	St Mirren	76	St Johnstone	66	Hamilton Acad.	59
2006-07*l*	Gretna	66	St Johnstone	65	Dundee	53

Maximum points: a, 36; *b*, 44; *c*, 40; *d*, 52; *e*, 60; *f*, 68; *g*, 76; *h*, 84; *i*, 60; *j*, 78; *k*, 88; *l*, 108. * Won on goal difference.

SECOND DIVISION

	First	Pts.	Second	Pts.	Third	Pts.
1921-2*a*	Alloa	60	Cowdenbeath	47	Armadale	45
1922-3*a*	Queen's Park	57	Clydebank	52	St Johnstone	50
1923-4*a*	St Johnstone	56	Cowdenbeath	55	Bathgate	44
1924-5*a*	Dundee Utd.	50	Clydebank	48	Clyde	47
1925-6*a*	Dunfermline	59	Clyde	53	Ayr Utd.	52
1926-7*a*	Bo'ness	56	Raith	49	Clydebank	45
1927-8*a*	Ayr Utd.	54	Third Lanark	45	King's Park	44
1928-9*b*	Dundee Utd.	51	Morton	50	Arbroath	47
1929-30*a*	*Leith Athletic	57	East Fife	57	Albion	54
1930-1*a*	Third Lanark	61	Dundee Utd.	50	Dunfermline	47
1931-2*a*	*East Stirling	55	St Johnstone	55	Stenhousemuir	46
1932-3*c*	Hibernian	55	Queen of South	49	Dunfermline	47
1933-4*c*	Albion	45	Dunfermline	44	Arbroath	44
1934-5*c*	Third Lanark	52	Arbroath	50	St Bernard's	47
1935-6*c*	Falkirk	59	St Mirren	52	Morton	48
1936-7*c*	Ayr Utd.	54	Morton	51	St Bernard's	48
1937-8*c*	Raith	59	Albion	48	Airdrieonians	47
1938-9*c*	Cowdenbeath	60	Alloa	48	East Fife	48
1946-7*d*	Dundee Utd.	45	Airdrieonians	42	East Fife	31
1947-8*e*	East Fife	53	Albion	42	Hamilton	40
1948-9*e*	*Raith	42	Stirling	42	Airdrieonians	41
1949-50*e*	Morton	47	Airdrieonians	44	St Johnstone	36
1950-1*e*	*Queen of South	45	Stirling	45	Ayr Utd.	36
1951-2*e*	Clyde	44	Falkirk	43	Ayr Utd.	39
1952-3*e*	Stirling	44	Hamilton	43	Queen's Park	37
1953-4*e*	Motherwell	45	Kilmarnock	42	Third Lanark	36
1954-5*e*	Airdrieonians	46	Dunfermline	42	Hamilton	39
1955-6*b*	Queen's Park	54	Ayr Utd.	51	St Johnstone	49
1956-7*b*	Clyde	64	Third Lanark	51	Cowdenbeath	45
1957-8*b*	Stirling	55	Dunfermline	53	Arbroath	47
1958-9*b*	Ayr Utd.	60	Arbroath	51	Stenhousemuir	46
1959-60*b*	St Johnstone	53	Dundee Utd.	50	Queen of South	49
1960-1*b*	Stirling	55	Falkirk	54	Stenhousemuir	50
1961-2*b*	Clyde	54	Queen of South	53	Morton	44
1962-3*b*	St Johnstone	55	East Stirling	49	Morton	48
1963-4*b*	Morton	67	Clyde	53	Arbroath	46
1964-5*b*	Stirling	59	Hamilton	50	Queen of South	45
1965-6*b*	Ayr Utd.	53	Airdrieonians	50	Queen of South	47
1966-7*b*	Morton	69	Raith	58	Arbroath	57
1967-8*b*	St Mirren	62	Arbroath	53	East Fife	49
1968-9*b*	Motherwell	64	Ayr Utd.	53	East Fife	48
1969-70*b*	Falkirk	56	Cowdenbeath	55	Queen of South	50
1970-1*b*	Partick	56	East Fife	51	Arbroath	46
1971-2*b*	*Dumbarton	52	Arbroath	52	Stirling	50
1972-3*b*	Clyde	56	Dunfermline	52	Raith	47
1973-4*b*	Airdrieonians	60	Kilmarnock	58	Hamilton	55
1974-5*b*	Falkirk	54	Queen of South	53	Montrose	53

SECOND DIVISION (MODERN)

	First	Pts.	Second	Pts.	Third	Pts.
1975-6*d*	*Clydebank	40	Raith	40	Alloa	35

1976-7*f*	Stirling	55	Alloa	51	Dunfermline	50
1977-8*f*	*Clyde	53	Raith	53	Dunfermline	48
1978-9*f*	Berwick Rangers	54	Dunfermline	52	Falkirk	50
1979-80*f*	Falkirk	50	East Stirling	49	Forfar	46
1980-1*f*	Queen's Park	50	Queen of South	46	Cowdenbeath	45
1981-2*f*	Clyde	59	Alloa	50	Arbroath	50
1982-3*f*	Brechin	55	Meadowbank	54	Arbroath	49
1983-4*f*	Forfar	63	East Fife	47	Berwick Rangers	43
1984-5*f*	Montrose	53	Alloa	50	Dunfermline	49
1985-6*f*	Dunfermline	57	Queen of South	55	Meadowbank	49
1986-7*f*	Meadowbank	55	Raith	52	Stirling	52
1987-8*f*	Ayr Utd.	61	St Johnstone	59	Queen's Park	51
1988-9*f*	Albion	50	Alloa	45	Brechin	43
1989-90*f*	Brechin	49	Kilmarnock	48	Stirling	47
1990-1*f*	Stirling	54	Montrose	46	Cowdenbeath	45
1991-2*f*	Dumbarton	52	Cowdenbeath	51	Alloa	50
1992-3*f*	Clyde	54	Brechin	53	Stranraer	53
1993-4*f*	Stranraer	56	Berwick Rangers	48	Stenhousemuir	47
1994-5*g*	Greenock Morton	64	Dumbarton	60	Stirling	58
1995-6*g*	Stirling	81	East Fife	67	Berwick Rangers	60
1996-7*g*	Ayr Utd.	77	Hamilton	74	Livingston	64
1997-8*g*	Stranraer	61	Clydebank	60	Livingston	59
1998-9*g*	Livingston	77	Inverness Cal.	72	Clyde	53
1999-2000*g*	Clyde	65	Alloa	64	Ross County	62
2000-01*g*	Partick Thistle	75	Arbroath	58	Berwick Rangers	54
2001-02*g*	Queen of South	67	Alloa Athletic	59	Forfar Athletic	53
2002-03*g*	Raith Rov.	59	Brechin City	55	Airdrie Utd.	54
2003-04*g*	Airdrie Utd.	70	Hamilton	62	Dumbarton	60
2004-05*g*	Brechin City	72	Stranraer	63	Morton	62
2005-06*g*	Gretna	88	Morton	70	Peterhead	57
2006-07g	Morton	77	Stirling	69	Raith	62

Maximum points: *a*, 76; *b*, 72; *c*, 68; *d*, 52; *e*, 60; *f*, 78; *g*, 108. * Won on goal average.

THIRD DIVISION (MODERN)

	First	Pts.	Second	Pts.	Third	Pts.
1994-5	Forfar	80	Montrose	67	Ross County	60
1995-6	Livingston	72	Brechin	63	Caledonian Th.	57
1996-7	Inverness Cal.T.	76	Forfar	67	Ross County	77
1997-8	Alloa	76	Arbroath	68	Ross County	67
1998-9	Ross County	77	Stenhousemuir	64	Brechin	59
1999-2000	Queen's Park	69	Berwick Rangers	66	Forfar	61
2000-01	*Hamilton	76	Cowdenbeath	76	Brechin	72
2001-02	Brechin City	73	Dumbarton	61	Albion Rov.	59
2002-03	Morton	72	East Fife	71	Albion Rov.	70
2003-04	Stranraer	79	Stirling	77	Gretna	68
2004-05	Gretna	98	Peterhead	78	Cowdenbeath	51
2005-06	*Cowdenbeath	76	Berwick Rangers	76	Stenhousemuir	73
2006-07	Berwick Rangers	75	Arbroath	70	Queen's Park	68

Maximum points: 108. * Won on goal difference.

RELEGATED FROM PREMIER DIVISION

1975-6	Dundee, St Johnstone	1977-8	Ayr, Clydebank
1976-7	Kilmarnock, Hearts	1978-9	Hearts, Motherwell

1979-80	Dundee, Hibernian	1993-4	St J'stone, Raith, Dundee
1980-1	Kilmarnock, Hearts	1994-5	Dundee Utd.
1981-2	Partick, Airdrieonians	1995-6	Falkirk, Partick Thistle
1982-3	Morton, Kilmarnock	1996-7	Raith
1983-4	St Johnstone, Motherwell	1997-8	Hibernian
1984-5	Dumbarton, Morton	1998-9	Dunfermline
1985-6	No relegation	1999-2000	No relegation
1986-7	Clydebank, Hamilton	2000-01	St Mirren
1987-8	Falkirk, Dunfermline, Morton	2001-02	St Johnstone
1988-9	Hamilton	2002-03	No relegation
1989-90	Dundee	2003-04	Partick Thistle
1990-1	No relegation	2004-05	Dundee
1991-2	St Mirren, Dunfermline	2005-06	Livingston
1992-3	Falkirk, Airdrieonians	2006-07	Dunfermline

RELEGATED FROM FIRST DIVISION

1975-6	Dunfermline, Clyde	1992-3	Meadowbank, Cowdenbeath
1976-7	Raith, Falkirk	1993-4	Dumbarton, Stirling Alb.,
1977-8	Alloa, East Fife		Clyde, Morton, Brechin
1978-9	Montrose, Queen of South	1994-5	Ayr, Stranraer
1979-80	Arbroath, Clyde	1995-6	Hamilton, Dumbarton
1980-1	Stirling, Berwick Rangers	1996-7	Clydebank, East Fife
1981-2	East Stirling, Queen of South	1997-8	Partick, Stirling Alb.
1982-3	Dunfermline, Queen's Park	1998-9	Hamilton, Stranraer
1983-4	Raith, Alloa	1999-2000	Clydebank
1984-5	Meadowbank, St Johnstone	2000-01	Morton, Alloa
1985-6	Ayr, Alloa	2001-02	Raith Rov.
1986-7	Brechin, Montrose	2002-03	Alloa Athletic, Arbroath
1987-8	East Fife, Dumbarton	2003-04	Ayr, Brechin
1988-9	Kilmarnock, Queen of South	2004-05	Partick Thistle, Raith Rov.
1989-90	Albion, Alloa	2005-06	Brechin, Stranraer
1990-1	Clyde, Brechin	2006-07	Airdrie Utd., Ross Co.
1991-2	Montrose, Forfar		

RELEGATED FROM SECOND DIVISION

1993-4	Alloa, Forfar, E. Stirling,	1999-2000	Hamilton
	Montrose, Queen's Park,	2000-01	Queen's Park, Stirling Alb.
	Arbroath, Albion,	2001-02	Morton
	Cowdenbeath	2002-03	Stranraer, Cowdenbeath
1994-5	Meadowbank, Brechin	2003-04	East Fife, Stenhousemuir
1995-6	Forfar, Montrose	2004-05	Arbroath, Berwick Rangers
1996-7	Dumbarton, Berwick Rangers	2005-06	Dumbarton
1997-8	Stenhousemuir, Brechin	2006-07	Stranraer, Forfar
1998-9	East Fife, Forfar		

HIGHS AND LOWS FOR HENNESSEY

Wayne Hennessey experienced the highs and lows of goalkeeping after being loaned by Wolves to Stockport last season. In his first nine matches, Hennessey helped create a Football League record with nine clean sheets in nine successive wins. But the 20-year-old then conceded 15 in his next four, including a 7-2 home defeat inflicted by Rochdale.

BANK OF SCOTLAND PREMIER LEAGUE ROLL CALL

APPEARANCES AND SCORERS 2006-07

(Figures in brackets = appearances as substitute)

ABERDEEN

Ground: Pittodrie Stadium, Pittodrie Street, Aberdeen, AB24 5QH. **Capacity:** 21,421. **Telephone:** 01224 650400. **Colours:** Red and white. **Nickname:** Dons.

Anderson, R 35
Brewster, C .... 6(6)
Byrne, R .... 4(1)
Clark, C 37
Considine, A .... 23(10)
Crawford, S 4
Daal, D .... 1(6)
Dempsey, G .... 20(6)
Diamond, A .... 13(8)
Foster, R .... 35(2)
Hart, M 34
Langfield, J 38
Lovell, S .... 15(12)
Mackie, D .... 31(5)
Maguire, C .... 3(16)
Miller, L .... 25(6)
Nicholson, B 31
Severin, S .... 34(1)
Smith, D .... 3(3)
Smith, J .... 19(2)
Stewart, J .... 1(3)
Touzani, K .... 6(5)

League goals (55): Mackie 13, Lovell 9, Nicholson 6, Miller 4, Severin 4, Crawford 3, Foster 3, Anderson 2, Considine 2, Daal 2, Dempsey 2, Clark 1, Smith, J 1, Maguire 1, Opponents 2.
Tennents Cup goals (3): Nicholson 2, Brewster 1. **CIS Insurance Cup goals:** None.
Average home league attendance: 12,475.

CELTIC

Ground: Celtic Park, Glasgow, G40 3RE. **Capacity:** 60,355. **Telephone:** 0871 226 1888. **Colours:** Green and white. **Nickname:** Bhoys.

Balde, B 6
Beattie, C .... 9(7)
Bjarnason, T 1
Boruc, A 36
Brown, M 1
Caldwell, G .... 20(1)
Camara, M 1
Gravesen, T .... 18(4)
Hartley, P 10
Jarosik, J .... 18(7)
Kennedy, J 3
Lennon, N .... 30(1)
Maloney, S .... 7(2)
Marshall, D .... 1(1)
McGeady, A .... 22(12)
McManus, S 31
Miller, K .... 20(11)
Nakamura, S 37
Naylor, L 32
O'Dea, D .... 9(5)
Pearson, S .... 3(10)
Perrier Doumbe, J .... 3(1)
Petrov, S 3
Pressley, S 14
Riordan, D .... 6(10)
Sheridan, C .... –(1)
Sno, E .... 7(11)
Telfer, P .... 20(1)
Vennegoor of Hesselink, J 17(4)
Wallace, R 2
Wilson, M 12
Zurawski, M .... 19(7)

League goals (65): Vennegoor of Hesselink 13, Nakamura 9, Gravesen 6, Zurawski 6, McGeady 5, Jarosik 4, Miller 4, Riordan 4, Beattie 2, McManus 2, O'Dea 2, Petrov 2, Pearson 1, Pressley 1, Sno 1, Opponents 3.
Tennents Cup goals (13): Vennegoor of Hesselink 4, Riordan 3, Zurawski 2, Miller 1, O'Dea 1, Perrier Doumbe 1, Pressley 1. **CIS Insurance Cup goals (3):** Zurawski 2, Beattie 1. **Champions League goals (8):** Miller 3, Nakamura 2, Jarosik 1, Pearson 1, Vennegoor of Hesselink 1.
Average home league attendance: 57,928.

DUNDEE UNITED

Ground: Tannadice Park, Tannadice Street, Dundee, DD3 7JW. **Capacity:** 14,223. **Telephone:** 01382 833166. **Colours:** Tangerine and white. **Nickname:** Terrors.

Archibald, A .... 14(2)
Brewster, C .... 1(2)
Burnett, G 1

Cameron, G .... 20(5)
Conway, C .... 22(8)
Daly, J .... 10(1)
Dillon, S 15
Duff, S .... 22(6)
Easton, W .... 1(6)
Gomis, M .... 9(3)
Goodwillie, D .... 3(14)
Hunt, N .... 25(3)
Kalvenes, C 29
Kenneth, G 11
Kerr, M .... 35(1)
Mair, L .... 17(1)
McCracken, D .... 32(1)
McLean, E 1
Miller, L .... 1(2)
Proctor, D .... 9(3)
Robb, S .... 8(7)
Robertson, D .... 21(5)
Robson, B 29
Russell, J .... –(1)
Russell, W .... –(1)
Samuel, C .... 27(10)
Smith, G .... 4(2)
Stillie, D 37
Watson, K .... –(1)
Wilkie, L 14

League goals (40): Robson 11, Hunt 10, Samuel 5, Robertson 3, Cameron 2, Daly 2, Duff 1, Kalvenes 1, Kenneth 1, Mair 1, McCracken 1, Robb 1, Oppponents 1.
Tennents Cup goals (3): Kenneth 1, Robertson 1, Robson 1. **CIS Insurance Cup goals (1):** Robertson 1.
Average home league attendance: 7,147.

DUNFERMLINE ATHLETIC

Ground: East End Park, Halbeath Road, Dunfermline, KY12 7RB. **Capacity:** 11,780. **Telephone:** 01388 724295. **Colours:** Black and white. **Nickname:** Pars.

Bamba, S .... 21(2)
Burchill, M .... 12(8)
Campbell, I .... –(1)
Crawford, S .... 22(3)
Daquin, F .... 8(12)
De Vries, D 27
Glass, S 11
Hamilton, J .... 17(8)
Hammill, A .... 9(4)
Harris, J .... –(1)
Labonte, A .... 11(2)
Mason, G .... 35(1)
McCunnie, J .... 8(6)
McGuire, P .... 22(2)
McIntyre, J .... 7(3)
McKenzie, R .... 11(1)
McManus, T .... 6(2)
Morrison, O .... 12(12
Morrison, S 12
Muirhead, S .... 20(6)
O'Brien, J 13
Ross, G .... 16(10)
Ryan, B .... 2(3)
Shields, G 29
Simmons, S .... 22(1)
Smith, C .... –(1)
Tod, A .... 5(5)
Whelan, N 1
Williamson, I .... –(4)
Wilson, C .... –(3)
Wilson, S 31
Woods, C .... 9(3)
Young, D .... 19(2)

League goals (26): Crawford 5, Glass 3, Hamilton 2, Mason 2, McIntyre 2, McManus 2, Simmons 2, Young 2, Hammill 1, Morrison, O 1, McGuire 1, O'Brien 1, Shields 1, Wilson, S 1.
Tennents Cup goals (7): Simmons 3, Hamilton 1, McGuire 1, McIntyre 1, Wilson 1. **CIS Insurance Cup goals:** None.
Average home league attendance: 6,106.

FALKIRK

Ground: Falkirk Stadium, Westfield, Falkirk, FK2 9DX. **Capacity:** 7,975. **Telephone:** 01324 624121. **Colours:** Navy blue and white. **Nickname:** Bairns.

Allison, B .... 1(2)
Barr, D 36
Craig, L .... 17(10)
Cregg, P 32
Dodd, D .... 14(3)
Finnigan, C .... 10(1)
Gow, A .... 34(2)
Higgins, S .... 14(1)
Holden, D .... 8(1)
Lambers, J 9
Latapy, R .... 36(1)
Lescinel, J-F .... –(1)
Lima, V .... 17(5)
McManus, T .... –(5)
McStay, R .... –(4)
Milne, K 34
Moutinho, P .... 14(7)
O'Donnell, S .... 20(5)
Robertson, D .... –(2)
Ross, J 36
Schmeichel, K 15
Scobbie, T .... 16(5)
Stewart, J .... 4(14)
Stokes, A 16
Thomson, S .... 17(5)
Twaddle, M .... 10(6)
Uras, C .... 8(1)

League goals (49): Stokes 14, Gow 7, Latapy 6, Cregg 3, Finnigan 3, Craig 2, Moutinho 2, O'Donnell 2, Thomson 2, Twaddle 2, Barr 1, Holden 1, Milne 1, Scobbie 1, Opponents 2.
Tennents Cup goals (2): Craig 1, Gow 1. **CIS Insurance Cup goals (7):** Stokes 2, Moutinho 2, Craig 1, Stewart, M 1, Twaddle 1.
Average home league attendance: 5,387.

HEARTS

Ground: Tynecastle Stadium, Gorgie Road, Edinburgh, EH11 2NL. Capacity: 17,402. **Telephone:** 0870 787 1874. **Colours:** Maroon and white. **Nickname:** Jam Tarts.

Aguiar, B	20(4)	Glen, G	–(1)	McCann, N	14(7)
Banks, S	4	Goncalves, J	9(2)	Mikoliunas, S	29(2)
Barasa, N	7(3)	Gordon, C	34	Mole, J	7(3)
Bednar, R	14(4)	Hartley, P	18(3)	Neilson, R	12(2)
Berra, C	34(1)	Ivaskevicius, K	9	Pilibaitis, L	4(1)
Beslija, M	2(3)	Jankauskas, E	8(5)	Pinilla, M	2(1)
Brellier, J	16(6)	Jonsson, E	–(3)	Pospisil, M	12(12)
Cesnauskis, D	5(4)	Kancelsku, T	3(2)	Pressley, S	13
Costa, T	1	Karipidis, C	10(2)	Tall, I	17(6)
Driver, A	17(3)	Kingston, L	10	Velicka, A	23(4)
Elliot,C	5(5)	Klimek, A	1(1)	Wallace, L	13(4)
Fyssas, J	18(3)	Makela, J	1(8)	Zaliukas, M	26(1)

League goals (47): Velicka 8, Pospisil 6, Bednar 4, Mikoliunas 4, Driver 3, Hartley 3, Mole 3, Aguiar 2, Pinilla 2, Zaliukas 2, Berra 1, Fyssas 1, Ivaskevicius 1, Jankauskas 1, Kingston 1, Makela 1, Tall 1, Opponents 3.
Tennents Cup goals (4): Velicka 3, Bednar 1. **CIS Insurance Cup goals: (4):** Makela 3, Aguiar 1. **Champions League Goals (4):** Bednar 1, Mikoliunas 1, Tall 1, Opponents 1.
Average home league attendance: 16,937.

HIBERNIAN

Ground: Easter Road Stadium, Albion Place, Edinburgh EH7 5QG. **Capacity:** 17,400. **Telephone:** 0131 661 2159. **Colours:** Green and white. **Nickname:** Hibees.

Benjelloun, A	16(17)	Jones, R	34	Murphy, D	33
Beuzelin, G	18(7)	Killen, C	17(1)	Shields, J	2(1)
Brown, Scott	30	Konde, O	2(1)	Shiels, D	13(11)
Brown, Simon	4	Konte, A	–(1)	Sowunmi, T	2(3)
Campbell, R	2(1)	Lynch, S	2(1)	Sproule, I	16(16)
Chisholm, R	5(1)	Malkowski, Z	19	Stevenson, L	13(3)
Dalglish, P	–(2)	Martis, S	27	Stewart, M	23(6)
Fletcher, S	24(7)	McCaffrey, D	1	Thomson, K	22(1)
Glass, S	2(8)	McCann, K	7(1)	Whittaker, S	34(1)
Gray, D	2(1)	McCluskey, J	1(4)	Zemmama, M	17(6)
Hogg, C	15	McNeil, A	15		

League goals (56): Killen 13, Shiels 7, Sproule 7, Benjelloun 6, Fletcher 6, Brown, Scott 5, Jones 4, Zemmama 2, Beuzelin 1, Gray 1, McCann 1, Stewart 1, Thomson 1, Whittaker 1.
Tennents Cup goals (11): Benjelloun 3, Fletcher 1, Jones 1, Killen 1, Murphy 1, Sowunmi 1, Sproule 1, Stewart 1, Opponents 1. **CIS Insurance Cup goals (19):** Benjelloun 5, Fletcher 4, Jones 3, Brown, Scott 2, Shiels 2, McCluskey 1, Murphy 1, Opponents 1. **Intertoto Cup goals (10):** Konte 2, Sproule 2, Brown, Scott 1, Dalglish 1, Fletcher 1, Jones 1, Killen 1, Murphy 1.
Average home league attendance: 14,587.

INVERNESS CALEDONIAN THISTLE

Ground: Tulloch Caledonian Stadium, Stadium Road, Inverness, IV1 1FF. **Capacity:** 7,400. **Telephone:** 01463 222880. **Colours:** Royal blue. **Nickname:** Caley Thistle.

Bayne, G	29(9)	Fraser, M	15(1)	McBain, R	30(2)
Black, I	22(4)	Golabek, S	1	McCaffrey, S	9(4)
Brown, M	23	Hart, R	8(8)	McSwegan, G	2(7)
Dargo, C	25(2)	Hastings, R	37	Morgan, A	1(5)
Dods, D	35	Keogh, L	1(7)	Munro, G	36
Duncan, R	22(6)	McAllister, R	5(14)	Paatelainen, M	6(5)

Rankin, J .... 32(2)	Tokely, R 34	Wyness, D .... 14(6)
Sutherland, Z .... 1(4)	Wilson, B .... 30(4)	

League goals (42): Dargo 10, Bayne 6, Rankin 6, Dods 4, Wilson 4, McAllister 2, Munro 2, Paatelainen 2, Tokely 2, Hastings 1, McBain 1, McCaffrey 1, Wyness 1.
Tennents Cup goals (8): Dargo 2, Bayne 1, Duncan 1, McBain 1, Morgan 1, Wilson 1, Wyness 1. **CIS Insurance Cup goals (3):** Bayne 1, McAllister 1, Wyness 1.
Average home league attendance: 4,879.

KILMARNOCK

Ground: Rugby Park, Kilmarnock, KA1 2DP. **Capacity:** 18,128. **Telephone:** 01563 545300. **Colours:** White and blue. **Nickname:** Killie.

Barrowman, A .... –(3)	Hamill, J .... 2(2)	Murray, S .... –(9)
Combe, A 11	Hay, G .... 28(1)	Naismith, S .... 35(2)
Di Giacomo, P .... 8(14)	Invincible, D .... 24(1)	Nish, C .... 24(9)
Dodds, R .... 3(6)	Johnston, A .... 25(3)	O'Leary, R .... 5(2)
Fernandez, D .... 7(1)	Koudou, A .... 2(3)	Quinn, R 6
Ford, S .... 12(4)	Leven, P .... 20(7)	Smith, G 27
Fowler, J 38	Lilley, D 7	Sylla, M .... 10(1)
Gibson, W .... 1(6)	Locke, G .... 4(8)	Wales, G .... 21(7)
Greer, G 33	Murray, G 30	Wright, F 35

League goals (47): Naismith 15, Nish 13, Di Giacomo 6, Wales 4, Invincible 2, Greer 1, Hay 1, Leven 1, Wright 1, Opponents 3.
Tennents Cup goals (1): Nish 1. **CIS Insurance Cup goals (11):** Naismith 4, Wright 3, Greer 1, Invincible 1, Murray, G 1, Wales 1.
Average home league attendance: 6,807.

MOTHERWELL

Ground: Fir Park, Firpark Street, Motherwell ML1 2QN. **Capacity:** 13,677. **Telephone:** 01698 333333. **Colours:** Claret and amber. **Nickname:** Well.

Clarkson, D .... 19(10)	Kerr, B 35	Molloy, T .... –(6)
Coakley, A .... –(2)	Kinniburgh, W .... 4(2)	Murphy, D .... 12(1)
Connolly, K .... 1(1)	Lasley, K 14	Murphy, J .... 1(1)
Corrigan, M .... 19(3)	Maguire, S 3	O'Donnell, P 3
Craigan, S 34	McBride, K .... 10(7)	Paterson, J 34
Donnelly, R 2	McCormack, R .... 6(6)	Quinn, P .... 24(2)
Elliot, C .... 10(5)	McDonald, S .... 30(2)	Reynolds, M 35
Fitzpatrick, M ...... 13(11)	McGarry, S .... 19(7)	Smith, D .... 12(5)
Foran, R .... 22(1)	McLean, B .... 1(3)	Smith, G .... 23(1)
Hamilton, J .... 2(1)	Meldrum, C .... 15(1)	Vadocz, K 11
Keegan, P .... 4(4)		

League goals (41): McDonald 15, Foran 7, Clarkson 2, Elliot 2, Kerr 2, McCormack 2, Reynolds 2, Smith, D L, 2, Fitzpatrick 1, Maguire 1, Murphy, D 1, O'Donnell 1, Paterson 1, Smith, D 1, Opponents 1.
Tennents Cup goals (4): Foran 1, Kerr 1, McCormack 1, McDonald 1. **CIS Insurance Cup goals (8):** Foran 6, Clarkson 1, McGarry 1.
Average home league attendance: 5,877.

RANGERS

Ground: Ibrox Park, Edmison Drive, Glasgow, G51 2XD. **Capacity:** 51,082. **Telephone:** 0870 600 1972. **Colours:** Royal blue and white. **Nickname:** Gers.

Adam, C 32	Burke, C .... 10(12)	Hemdani, B 36
Bardsley, P 5	Clement, J 19	Hutton, A .... 32(1)
Boyd, K .... 25(7)	Ehiogu, U 9	Lennon, S .... –(3)
Buffel, T .... 9(8)	Ferguson, B .... 31(1)	Letizi, L 7

Martin, L .... 4(3)	Prso, D .... 23(5)	Sionko, L .... 14(4)
McGregor, A 31	Rae, G .... 3(7)	Smith, S 17
Murray, I .... 12(1)	Rodriguez, J .... 12(1)	Svensson, K .... 20(1)
N'Diaye, M .... –(1)	Sebo, F .... 4(20)	Thomson, K .... 8(1)
Novo, N .... 22(6)	Shinnie, A .... –(2)	Weir, D 14
Papac, S .... 19(2)		

League goals (61): Boyd 20, Adam 11, Novo 5, Ferguson 4, Prso 4, Buffel 3, Sionko 3, Burke 2, Sebo 2, Bardsley 1, Ehiogu 1, Hemdani 1, Hutton 1, Rae 1, Smith 1, Opponents 1.
Tennents Cup goals (2): Boyd 2. **CIS Insurance Cup goals (2):** Boyd 1, Opponents 1. **UEFA Cup goals (16):** Novo 4, Adam 3, Boyd 3, Ferguson 3, Buffel 1, Hemdani 1, Hutton 1.
Average home league attendance: 49,955.

ST MIRREN

Ground: St Mirren Park, Love Street, Paisley, PA3 2EA. **Capacity:** 10,866. **Telephone:** 0141 889 2558. **Colours:** Black and white. **Nickname:** Buddies.

Brady, G .... 26(3)	Lawson, P 4	Millen, A 23
Brittain, R .... 26(5)	Mackay, B .... –(4)	Molloy, C .... 6(5)
Broadfoot, K 37	Malone, E .... 4(2)	Murray, H 31
Bullock, T 17	Maxwell, I 16	O'Donnell, S 5
Burke, A .... 4(9)	McCay, R .... –(1)	Potter, J .... 25(1)
Corcoran, M .... 10(17)	McGinn, S .... 1(3)	Reid, A .... 20(2)
Gemmill, S .... –(5)	McGowne, K 19	Smith, C 21
Kean, S .... 21(10)	McKenna, D .... 1(9)	Sutton, J .... 29(4)
Lappin, S 24	Mehmet, B .... 11(14)	Van Zanten, D 37

League goals (31): Sutton 11, Kean 5, Broadfoot 3, Brady 2, Mehmet 2, Brittain 1, Corcoran 1, Lappin 1, McGinn 1, Murray 1, O'Donnell 1, Van Zanten 1, Opponents 1.
Tennents Cup goals (2): Brittain 1, Sutton 1. **CIS Insurance Cup goals (3):** Mehmet 2, Sutton 1.
Average home league attendance: 5,609.

DOUBLE PENALTY SAVE ON DEBUT

Slovakian goalkeeper Peter Brezovan marked his debut for Swindon Town by saving penalties from Joel Porter and Richie Humphreys in a 1-0 win at Hartlepool on the opening day of last season.

LANDMARK GOAL COMES IN STYLE

Huddersfield Town's Gary Taylor-Fletcher scored the 500,000th goal in English league football last season – and he did it in style with a 25-yard drive in the 3-0 home win over Rotherham United. The first was credited to Aston Villa's Gershom Cox, an own goal against Wolves in September 1888.

MIGHTY TAXI BILL FOR QUINN

Sunderland chairman Niall Quinn paid £8,000 for taxis to take home fans left stranded by the cancellation of their flight after the team's 1-0 victory at Cardiff last season.

HIBERNIAN HIT FIVE IN CIS INSURANCE CUP FINAL

SECOND ROUND	THIRD ROUND	FOURTH ROUND	SEMI-FINALS	FINAL
***Hibernian** 4	***Hibernian** 6	***Hibernian** 1	**Hibernian** +3	**Hibernian** 5
Peterhead 0	Gretna 0	Hearts 0	St Johnstone 1	
• Bye	*Alloa Athletic 0	*Rangers 0	Falkirk 0	
*Alloa Athletic 2	Hearts 4	St Johnstone 2		
Ross Co. 1	*Dunfermline Ath. 0	*Celtic 1		
• Bye	Rangers 2	Falkirk +C1		
*Ayr Utd. 0	*St Johnstone 3			
Dunfermline Ath. +A0	Dundee Utd. 0			
• Bye	*Celtic 2			
*St Johnstone 4	St Mirren 0			
Elgin City 0	*Inverness C T 0			
*Dundee Utd. +1	Falkirk 1			
Airdrie Utd. 1				
• Bye				
*St Mirren 3				
Stenhousemuir 1				
*Inverness C T 3				
Dumbarton 1				
*Cowdenbeath 0				
Falkirk 5				

*Queen's Park .... +B0	*Queen's Park 0		**Kilmarnock** 1
Aberdeen 0		Motherwell 2	
*Motherwell 3	Motherwell 3		
Partick Thistle 2			
*Brechin City 0		**Kilmarnock** 3	
Livingston 3	*Livingston 1		
*Queen of the South 1		***Kilmarnock** 3	
Kilmarnock 2	**Kilmarnock** .... +2		

FIRST ROUND: Albion Rov. 1, Stenhousemuir 2; Arbroath 0, Elgin City 1; Ayr Utd. 2, Berwick Rangers 0; Brechin City 2, Morton 1; Cowdenbeath 4, East Stirling 1; Dumbarton 3, Stirling Alb. 0; Dundee 1, Partick Thistle 3; Forfar Athletic 1, Alloa Athletic 2 (aet); Montrose 1, Peterhead 2; Queen of the South 4, Clyde 2; Queen's Park 2, Hamilton Acad 1 (aet); Raith Rov. 1, Airdrie Utd. 2; Ross Co. 4, Stranraer 2; St Johnstone 3, East Fife 1.
*Drawn at home. + After extra-time. A – Dunfermline Ath. won 7-6 on pens. B – Queen's Park won 5-3 on pens. C – Falkirk won 5-4 on pens. Semi-finals: Hibernian v St Johnstone at Tynecastle. Kilmarnock v Falkirk at Rugby Park.

CIS INSURANCE CUP FINAL

HIBERNIAN 5, KILMARNOCK 1

Hampden Park (52,000), Sunday, March 18, 2007

Hibernian (4-4-2): McNeil, Whittaker (Martis 90), Hogg (McCann 90), Jones, Murphy, Sproule (Zemmama 79), Scott Brown, Beuzelin, Stevenson, Benjelloun, Fletcher. **Subs not used:** Simon Brown, Stewart. **Scorers:** Jones (28), Benjelloun (59, 85), Fletcher (66, 87). **Manager:** John Collins.

Kilmarnock (4-4-2): Combe, Wright, Greer, Ford, Hay, Di Giacomo (Locke 76), Johnston, Fowler, Leven (Wales 57), Nish, Naismith. **Subs not used:** Smith, Murray, O'Leary. **Scorer:** Greer (77). **Booked:** Hay, Di Giacomo. **Manager:** Jim Jefferies.

Referee: D. McDonald. **Half-time:** 0-1.

SCOTTISH LEAGUE CUP FINALS

1946 Aberdeen beat Rangers (3-2)
1947 Rangers beat Aberdeen (4-0)
1948 East Fife beat Falkirk (4-1 after 0-0 draw)
1949 Rangers beat Raith Rov. (2-0)
1950 East Fife beat Dunfermline Athletic (3-0)
1951 Motherwell beat Hibernian (3-0)
1952 Dundee beat Rangers (3-2)
1953 Dundee beat Kilmarnock (2-0)
1954 East Fife beat Partick Thistle (3-2)
1955 Hearts beat Motherwell (4-2)
1956 Aberdeen beat St Mirren (2-1)
1957 Celtic beat Partick Thistle (3-0 after 0-0 draw)
1958 Celtic beat Rangers (7-1)
1959 Hearts beat Partick Thistle (5-1)
1960 Hearts beat Third Lanark (2-1)
1961 Rangers beat Kilmarnock (2-0)
1962 Rangers beat Hearts (3-1 after 1-1 draw)
1963 Hearts beat Kilmarnock (1-0)
1964 Rangers beat Morton (5-0)
1965 Rangers beat Celtic (2-1)
1966 Celtic beat Rangers (2-1)
1967 Celtic beat Rangers (1-0)
1968 Celtic beat Dundee (5-3)
1969 Celtic beat Hibernian (6-2)
1970 Celtic beat St Johnstone (1-0)
1971 Rangers beat Celtic (1-0)
1972 Partick Thistle beat Celtic (4-1)
1973 Hibernian beat Celtic (2-1)
1974 Dundee beat Celtic (1-0)
1975 Celtic beat Hibernian (6-3)
1976 Rangers beat Celtic (1-0)
1977† Aberdeen beat Celtic (2-1)
1978† Rangers beat Celtic (2-1)
1979 Rangers beat Aberdeen (2-1)
1980 Dundee Utd. beat Aberdeen (3-0 after 0-0 draw)
1981 Dundee Utd. beat Dundee (3-0)
1982 Rangers beat Dundee Utd. (2-1)
1983 Celtic beat Rangers (2-1)
1984† Rangers beat Celtic (3-2)
1985 Rangers beat Dundee Utd. (1-0)
1986 Aberdeen beat Hibernian (3-0)
1987 Rangers beat Celtic (2-1)
1988† Rangers beat Aberdeen (5-3 on pens. after 3-3 draw)
1989 Rangers beat Aberdeen (3-2)
1990† Aberdeen beat Rangers (2-1)
1991† Rangers beat Celtic (2-1)
1992 Hibernian beat Dunfermline Athletic (2-0)
1993† Rangers beat Aberdeen (2-1)
1994 Rangers beat Hibernian (2-1)
1995 Raith Rov. beat Celtic (6-5 on pens. after 2-2 draw)
1996 Aberdeen beat Dundee (2-0)
1997 Rangers beat Hearts (4-3)
1998 Celtic beat Dundee Utd. (3-0)
1999 Rangers beat St Johnstone (2-1)

2000	Celtic beat Aberdeen (2-0)
2001	Celtic beat Kilmarnock (3-0)
2002	Rangers beat Ayr Utd. (4-0)
2003	Rangers beat Celtic (2-1)
2004	Livingston beat Hibernian (2-0)
2005	Rangers beat Motherwell (5-1)
2006	Celtic beat Dunfermline Athletic (3-0)
2007	Hibernian beat Kilmarnock (5-1)

(† After extra time; Skol Cup 1985-93, Coca-Cola Cup 1995-97, CIS Insurance Cup 1999)

SUMMARY OF SCOTTISH LEAGUE CUP WINNERS

Rangers	24	Dundee	3	Livingston	1
Celtic	13	East Fife	3	Motherwell	1
Aberdeen	6	Hibernian	3	Partick Thistle	1
Hearts	4	Dundee Utd.	2	Raith Rov.	1

SCOTTISH LEAGUE CHALLENGE CUP 2006-07

First round: Ayr Utd. 2, Livingston 1; Brechin City 1, Arbroath 2; Cowdenbeath 4, Stirling Alb. 0; Dumbarton 1, Morton 2 (aet); East Stirling 0, Queen's Park 5; Forfar Athletic 2, Dundee 1; Hamilton Acad. 3, Berwick Rangers 1; Partick Thistle 1, Albion Rov. 2; Queen of the South 1, Stranraer 0; St Johnstone 3, Raith Rov. 1 (aet); Airdrie Utd. 0, Gretna 3; East Fife 0, Ross Co. 3; Elgin City 2, Stenhousemuir 0; Montrose 2, Peterhead 0.

Second round: Albion Rov. 5, Elgin City 2; Forfar Athletic 1, Abroath 3; Morton 3, Cowdenbeath 2; Ross Co. 2, Alloa Athletic 1; St Johnstone 3, Queen's Park 0; Gretna 3, Hamilton Acad. 1; Montrose 0, Clyde 3; Queen of the South 2, Ayr Utd. 2 (aet, Ayr Utd. won 5-4 on pens).

Third round: Albion Rov. 3, Arbroath 3 (aet, Albion Rov. won 5-3 on pens); Clyde 1, Ayr Utd. 0; Morton 3, St Johnstone 2; Ross Co. 3, Gretna 2 (aet).

Semi-finals: Clyde 3, Morton 1; Ross Co. 4, Albion Rov. 1.

FINAL

ROSS COUNTY 1, CLYDE 1

(aet, Ross County won 5-4 on pens)
McDiarmid Park (4,062), Sunday, November 12, 2006

Ross Couty: Samson, Irvine, McKinlay, Dowie, Keddie, Gardyn, Adams, Cowie (capt) (Robertson 102), Scott (Anderson 117), Caimi (Crooks 115), Gunn. **Subs not used:** McCulloch, Malin. **Scorer:** Dowie (80). **Booked:** Caimi, Scott, Dowie. **Manager:** Scott Leitch.

Clyde: Hutton, McKeown, McGregor, Higgins, Bryson, McCann, McHale (capt), O'Donnell, Malone, Hunter (McKenna 78), Ferguson (Bradley 78). **Subs not used:** Harris, Miller, Cherrie. **Scorer:** Hunter (43). **Booked:** O'Donnell, Malone, McCann, Higgins, McGregor. **Sent-off:** Malone. **Manager:** Joe Miller.

Referee: C. Thomson. **Half-time:** 0-1.

DOGGED DUNFERMLINE BEATEN BY LATE WINNER

THIRD ROUND		FOURTH ROUND		FIFTH ROUND		SEMI-FINALS		FINAL	
***Celtic**	4	**Celtic**	4	**Celtic**	2	**Celtic**	2	**Celtic**	1
Dumbarton	0								
*Hamilton Acad.	2	*Livingston	1						
Livingston	4								
*Stirling Alb.	1	*Inverness CT	1	*Inverness CT	1				
Inverness CT	6								
*Dundee Utd.	3	Dundee Utd.	0						
St Mirren	2								
*Airdrie Utd	0	*Motherwell	2	*Motherwell	1	St Johnstone	1		
Motherwell	1								
*Morton	3	Morton	0						
Kilmarnock	1								
*Berwick Rangers	0	*Falkirk	0	St Johnstone	2				
Falkirk	2								
*St Johnstone	0+2	St Johnstone	3						
Ayr Utd.	0:1								
*Dundee	1:3	*Queen of the South	2	*Queen of the South	1	Hibernian	0+0		
Queen of the South	1:+A3								
*Cowdenbeath	1:1	Cowdenbeath	0						
Brechin City	1:0								
*Aberdeen	2:1	*Hibernian	3	Hibernian	2				
Hibernian	2:4								
*Clyde	0	Gretna	1						
Gretna	3								

Fifth round	Quarter-finals	Semi-finals	Final (replay)	Final
*Deveronvale 5	*Deveronvale 0			Dunfermline Ath. 0
Elgin City 4		Patrick Thistle 0		
*Ross Co. 0	Partick Thistle 1			
Partick Thistle 1			Dunfermline Ath. 0:1	
*Stranraer 0	Hearts 0			
Hearts 4		*Dunfermline Ath. 2		
Rangers 2	*Dunfermline Ath. 1			
*Dunfermline Ath. 3				

FIRST ROUND: Arbroath 2, Albion Rov. 1; Brechin City 1, Queen's Park 1. Deveronvale 3, Montrose 2; East Fife 1, Berwick Rangers 3; Edinburgh Univ. 2, Keith 1; East Stirling 0, Stirling Alb. 2; Preston Athletic. 2, Stenhousemuir 0; Stranraer 4, Alloa Athletic 2. **REPLAY:** Queen's Park 1, Brechin City 2.

SECOND ROUND: Annan Athletic 0, Morton 3; Berwick Rangers 2, Arbroath 0; Brechin City 2, Preston Athletic 1; Cowdenbeath 5, Edinburgh Univ. 1; Deveronvale 2, Fraserburgh 1; Edinburgh City 0, Stirling Alb. 1; Elgin City 1, Buckie Thistle 0; Peterhead 0, Ayr Utd. 2; Raith Rov. 0, Dumbarton 1; Stranraer 3, Forfar Athletic 1.

*Drawn at home. +After extra-time. A – Queen of the South won 4-2 on pens. Semi-finals at Hampden Park.

TENNENTS SCOTTISH CUP FINAL

CELTIC 1, DUNFERMLINE ATHLETIC 0

Hampden Park (49,600), Saturday, May 26, 2007

Celtic (4-4-2): Boruc, Perrier Doumbe, Pressley, McManus, Naylor, Nakamura, Hartley, Lennon (Caldwell 66), McGeady, Miller (Beattie 55), Vennegoor of Hesselink. **Subs not used:** McGovern, Riordan, Bjarnason. **Scorer:** Perrier Doumbe (85). **Booked:** McGeady, Perrier Doumbe. **Manager:** Gordon Strachan.

Dunfermline Athletic (4-4-2): De Vries, Shields, Bamba, Wilson, Morrison (Crawford 72), Hammill, Young, McCunnie, Muirhead, McIntyre (Hamilton 81), Burchill (Williamson 89). **Subs not used:** McKenzie, McGuire. **Booked:** Burchill. **Manager:** Stephen Kenny.

Referee: K. Clark. **Half-time:** 0-0.

SCOTTISH F.A. CUP FINALS

1874	Queen's Park beat Clydesdale (2-0)
1875	Queen's Park beat Renton (3-0)
1876	Queen's Park beat Third Lanark (2-0 after 1-1 draw)
1877	Vale of Leven beat Rangers (3-2 after 0-0, 1-1 draws)
1878	Vale of Leven beat Third Lanark (1-0)
1879	Vale of Leven awarded Cup (Rangers withdrew after 1-1 draw)
1880	Queen's Park beat Thornlibank (3-0)
1881	Queen's Park beat Dumbarton (3-1)
1882	Queen's Park beat Dumbarton (4-1 after 2-2 draw)
1883	Dumbarton beat Vale of Leven (2-1 after 2-2 draw)
1884	Queen's Park awarded Cup (Vale of Leven withdrew from Final)
1885	Renton beat Vale of Leven (3-1 after 0-0 draw)
1886	Queen's Park beat Renton (3-1)
1887	Hibernian beat Dumbarton (2-1)
1888	Renton beat Cambuslang (6-1)
1889	Third Lanark beat Celtic (2-1)
1890	Queen's Park beat Vale of Leven (2-1 after 1-1 draw)
1891	Hearts beat Dumbarton (1-0)
1892	Celtic beat Queen's Park (5-1)
1893	Queen's Park beat Celtic (2-1)
1894	Rangers beat Celtic (3-1)
1895	St. Bernard's beat Renton (2-1)
1896	Hearts beat Hibernian (3-1)
1897	Rangers beat Dumbarton (5-1)
1898	Rangers beat Kilmarnock (2-0)
1899	Celtic beat Rangers (2-0)
1900	Celtic beat Queen's Park (4-3)
1901	Hearts beat Celtic (4-3)
1902	Hibernian beat Celtic (1-0)
1903	Rangers beat Hearts (2-0 after 0-0, 1-1 draws)
1904	Celtic beat Rangers (3-2)
1905	Third Lanark beat Rangers (3-1 after 0-0 draw)
1906	Hearts beat Third Lanark (1-0)
1907	Celtic beat Hearts (3-0)
1908	Celtic beat St Mirren (5-1)
1909	Cup withheld because of riot after two drawn games in Final between Celtic and Rangers (2-2, 1-1)
1910	Dundee beat Clyde (2-1 after 2-2, 0-0 draws)
1911	Celtic beat Hamilton Acad. (2-0 after 0-0 draw)
1912	Celtic beat Clyde (2-0)
1913	Falkirk beat Raith Rov. (2-0)
1914	Celtic beat Hibernian (4-1 after 0-0 draw)
1915-19	No competition (World War 1)
1920	Kilmarnock beat Albion Rov. (3-2)
1921	Partick Thistle beat Rangers (1-0)
1922	Morton beat Rangers (1-0)
1923	Celtic beat Hibernian (1-0)
1924	Airdrieonians beat Hibernian (2-0)
1925	Celtic beat Dundee (2-1)
1926	St. Mirren beat Celtic (2-0)
1927	Celtic beat East Fife (3-1)
1928	Rangers beat Celtic (4-0)
1929	Kilmarnock beat Rangers (2-0)
1930	Rangers beat Partick Thistle (2-1 after 0-0 draw)
1931	Celtic beat Motherwell (4-2 after 2-2 draw)
1932	Rangers beat Kilmarnock (3-0 after 1-1 draw)

1933	Celtic beat Motherwell (1-0)
1934	Rangers beat St. Mirren (5-0)
1935	Rangers beat Hamilton Acad. (2-1)
1936	Rangers beat Third Lanark (1-0)
1937	Celtic beat Aberdeen (2-1)
1938	East Fife beat Kilmarnock (4-2 after 1-1 draw)
1939	Clyde beat Motherwell (4-0)
1940-6	No competition (World War 2)
1947	Aberdeen beat Hibernian (2-1)
1948†	Rangers beat Morton (1-0 after 1-1 draw)
1949	Rangers beat Clyde (4-1)
1950	Rangers beat East Fife (3-0)
1951	Celtic beat Motherwell (1-0)
1952	Motherwell beat Dundee (4-0)
1953	Rangers beat Aberdeen (1-0 after 1-1 draw)
1954	Celtic beat Aberdeen (2-1)
1955	Clyde beat Celtic (1-0 after 1-1 draw)
1956	Hearts beat Celtic (3-1)
1957†	Falkirk beat Kilmarnock (2-1 after 1-1 draw)
1958	Clyde beat Hibernian (1-0)
1959	St. Mirren beat Aberdeen (3-1)
1960	Rangers beat Kilmarnock (2-0)
1961	Dunfermline Athletic beat Celtic (2-0 after 0-0 draw)
1962	Rangers beat St. Mirren (2-0)
1963	Rangers beat Celtic (3-0 after 1-1 draw)
1964	Rangers beat Dundee (3-1)
1965	Celtic beat Dunfermline Athletic (3-2)
1966	Rangers beat Celtic (1-0 after 0-0 draw)
1967	Celtic beat Aberdeen (2-0)
1968	Dunfermline Athletic beat Hearts (3-1)
1969	Celtic beat Rangers (4-0)
1970	Aberdeen beat Celtic (3-1)
1971	Celtic beat Rangers (2-1 after 1-1 draw)
1972	Celtic beat Hibernian (6-1)
1973	Rangers beat Celtic (3-2)
1974	Celtic beat Dundee Utd. (3-0)
1975	Celtic beat Airdrieonians (3-1)
1976	Rangers beat Hearts (3-1)
1977	Celtic beat Rangers (1-0)
1978	Rangers beat Aberdeen (2-1)
1979†	Rangers beat Hibernian (3-2 after two 0-0 draws)
1980†	Celtic beat Rangers (1-0)
1981	Rangers beat Dundee Utd. (4-1 after 0-0 draw)
1982†	Aberdeen beat Rangers (4-1)
1983†	Aberdeen beat Rangers (1-0)
1984†	Aberdeen beat Celtic (2-1)
1985	Celtic beat Dundee Utd. (2-1)
1986	Aberdeen beat Hearts (3-0)
1987†	St. Mirren beat Dundee Utd. (1-0)
1988	Celtic beat Dundee Utd. (2-1)
1989	Celtic beat Rangers (1-0)
1990†	Aberdeen beat Celtic (9-8 on pens. after 0-0 draw)
1991†	Motherwell beat Dundee Utd. (4-3)
1992	Rangers beat Airdrieonians (2-1)
1993	Rangers beat Aberdeen (2-1)
1994	Dundee Utd. beat Rangers (1-0)
1995	Celtic beat Airdrieonians (1-0)
1996	Rangers beat Hearts (5-1)

1997	Kilmarnock beat Falkirk (1-0)
1998	Hearts beat Rangers (2-1)
1999	Rangers beat Celtic (1-0)
2000	Rangers beat Aberdeen (4-0)
2001	Celtic beat Hibernian (3-0)
2002	Rangers beat Celtic (3-2)
2003	Rangers beat Dundee (1-0)
2004	Celtic beat Dunfermline Athletic (3-1)
2005	Celtic beat Dundee Utd. (1-0)
2006†	Hearts beat Gretna (4-2 on pens after 1-1 draw)
2007	Celtic beat Dunfermline Athletic (1-0)

(† After extra time; Cup sponsored by Tennents since season 1989-90)

SUMMARY OF SCOTTISH CUP WINNERS

Celtic 34, Rangers 31, Queen's Park 10, Aberdeen 7, Hearts 7, Clyde 3, Kilmarnock 3, St. Mirren 3, Vale of Leven 3, Dunfermline Ath. 2, Falkirk 2, Hibernian 2, Motherwell 2, Renton 2, Third Lanark 2, Airdrieonians 1, Dumbarton 1, Dundee 1, Dundee Utd. 1, East Fife 1, Morton 1, Partick Thistle 1, St. Bernard's 1.

QUOTE-UNQUOTE

'I am regarding this season as a pause in a career that has plenty of years left' – **Michael Owen**, Newcastle striker, in positive mood while recovering from a serious knee injury.

'For me, the jury's still out. I think he's got a hell of a lot to do' – **Roy Keane**, Sunderland manager, on former Manchester United team-mate Wayne Rooney.

'The goal of a lifetime' – **Arsene Wenger**, Arsenal manager, on Robin van Persie's spectacular volley on the run against Charlton.

'Are agents corrupt? Not all – but the majority. We pretend we are holier than thou, but the English game is considered the dirty man of Europe' – **Colin Gordon**, agent of England coach Steve McClaren.

'I'm not joining in with that debate' – **Steve McClaren** when asked about Gordon's allegation.

'I've javelined the crutches about 80 yards' – **Michael Owen**, Newcastle striker, takes a step towards recovery from a serious knee injury.

'Make no mistake, the players, staff and myself are, like you, all hurting today. There are no excuses and I accept full responsibility' – **Steve McClaren**, England coach, in an e-mail to members of the England Supporters' Club after the 2-0 defeat by Croatia.

'He was nibbling his arm' – **Martin Jol**, Tottenham manager, after Jermain Defoe is accused of biting West Ham's Javier Mascherano.

'There is no evidence that sacking a manager gives you success. There is good evidence that sticking with your manager works' – **Sir Alex Ferguson**, in charge at Manchester United for 20 years, urges more job security in the game.

'We know about injuries in our job' – **Arsene Wenger**, Arsenal manager, after The Queen is unable to officially open the club's Emirates Stadium because of a back problem.

CONFERENCE FINAL TABLES 2006-2007

NATIONWIDE CONFERENCE

			HOME					AWAY						
		P	W	D	L	F	A	W	D	L	F	A	GD	Pts
1	Dag. & Red.	46	16	4	3	50	20	12	7	4	43	28	45	95
2	Oxford	46	11	9	3	33	16	11	6	6	33	17	33	81
3	Morecambe†	46	11	7	5	29	20	12	5	6	35	26	18	81
4	York	46	10	6	7	29	22	13	5	5	36	23	20	80
5	Exeter	46	14	7	2	39	19	8	5	10	28	29	19	78
6	Burton	46	13	3	7	28	21	9	6	8	24	26	5	75
7	Gravesend	46	12	6	5	33	25	9	5	9	30	31	7	74
8	Stevenage	46	12	4	7	46	30	8	6	9	30	36	10	70
9	Aldershot	46	11	7	5	40	31	7	4	12	24	31	2	65
10	Kidderminster	46	7	5	11	19	26	10	7	6	24	24	–7	63
11	Weymouth	46	12	6	5	35	26	6	3	14	21	47	–17	63
12	Rushden	46	10	5	8	34	24	7	6	10	24	30	4	62
13	Northwich	46	9	2	12	26	33	9	2	12	25	36	–18	58
14	Forest Green	46	10	5	8	34	33	3	13	7	25	31	–5	57
15	Woking	46	8	8	7	34	26	7	4	12	22	35	–5	57
16	Halifax	46	12	8	3	40	22	3	2	18	15	40	–7	55
17	Cambridge	46	8	4	11	34	33	7	6	10	23	33	–9	55
18	Crawley*	46	10	6	7	27	20	7	6	10	25	32	0	53
19	Grays	46	8	9	6	29	21	5	4	14	27	34	1	52
20	Stafford	46	7	4	12	25	33	7	6	10	24	38	–22	52
21	Altrincham	46	9	4	10	28	32	4	8	11	25	35	–14	51
22	Tamworth	46	8	6	9	24	27	5	3	15	19	34	–18	48
23	Southport	46	7	4	12	29	30	4	10	9	28	37	–10	47
24	St Albans	46	5	5	13	28	49	5	5	13	29	40	–32	40

† Also promoted, * Deducted 10 pts

Manager of Year: John Still (Dag. & Red.). **Goalscorer of Year:** Paul Benson (Dag. & Red.). **Player of Year:** Paul Benson. **Fair Play award:** Forest Green. **Leading scorers:** 28 Benson (Dag. & Red.); 27 MacDonald (Gravesend); 24 Donaldson (York), Morison (Stevenage); 19 Jackson (Rushden); 18 Duffy (Oxford); 17 Grant (Aldershot), Simpson (Cambridge); 16 Clare (Burton); 15 McAllister (Grays); 13 Grayson (Stafford); 12 Atieno (Tamworth), Brayson (Northwich), Madjo (Stafford), McNiven (Morecambe), Sole (Woking), Thompson (Morecambe).

CONFERENCE CHAMPIONS

1979-80	Altrincham	1993-94	Kidderminster Harriers
1980-81	Altrincham	1994-95	Macclesfield Town
1981-82	Runcorn	1995-96	Stevenage Borough
1982-83	Enfield	1996-97*	Macclesfield Town
1983-84	Maidstone Utd.	1997-98*	Halifax Town
1984-85	Wealdstone	1998-99*	Cheltenham Town
1985-86	Enfield	1999-2000*	Kidderminster Harriers
1986-87*	Scarborough	2000-01*	Rushden & Diamonds
1987-88*	Lincoln City	2001-02*	Boston Utd.
1988-89*	Maidstone Utd.	2002-03*	Yeovil Town
1989-90*	Darlington	2003-04*	Chester City
1990-91*	Barnet	2004-05*	Barnet
1991-92*	Colchester Utd.	2005-06*	Accrington
1992-93*	Wycombe Wand.	2006–07*	Dagenham & Redbridge

(* Promoted to Football League)

Conference – Record Attendance: 11,065, Oxford v Woking, December 26, 2006.

NATIONWIDE CONFERENCE RESULTS 2006-07

	Aldershot	Altrincham	Burton	Cambridge	Crawley	Dag. & Red.	Exeter	Forest Green	Gravesend	Grays	Halifax	Kidderminster	Morecambe	Northwich	Oxford	Rushden	Southport	St Albans	Stafford	Stevenage	Tamworth	Weymouth	Woking	York
Aldershot		0–0	3–2	0–1	0–2	1–1	3–2	2–1	3–2	1–0	1–0	4–2	0–1	1–3	1–1	2–2	2–2	2–0	4–2	4–0	3–3	1–0	2–2	0–2
Altrincham	0–0		2–3	5–0	1–1	0–5	1–2	2–2	0–2	1–0	1–0	0–1	0–2	3–0	0–3	2–1	2–1	2–0	0–1	2–1	2–0	0–0	2–3	0–4
Burton	1–3	2–1		2–1	2–1	0–2	1–0	1–0	0–1	3–0	1–0	1–1	2–1	2–0	1–2	1–2	0–1	1–0	0–0	2–1	1–0	1–1	2–1	1–2
Cambridge	2–0	2–2	1–2		1–2	4–2	1–3	1–1	3–0	2–0	1–2	1–1	1–3	0–1	0–3	0–1	2–2	0–2	0–1	1–0	1–0	7–0	3–0	0–5
Crawley	1–2	1–1	1–0	1–1		0–0	0–3	3–1	1–1	0–1	2–0	0–0	4–0	0–2	0–1	1–0	2–1	2–1	1–2	3–0	1–0	0–3	0–0	3–0
Dag. & Red.	2–1	4–1	3–0	2–0	2–1		4–1	1–1	2–1	0–0	1–0	1–3	2–1	5–0	0–1	1–2	0–0	4–2	1–1	2–0	4–0	4–1	3–2	2–1
Exeter	0–0	2–1	3–0	2–0	1–1	3–2		1–0	1–3	2–1	4–1	1–1	1–0	1–1	2–1	0–0	2–1	4–2	1–2	1–1	1–0	4–0	1–0	1–1
Forest Green	3–0	2–2	1–0	1–1	1–0	0–1	2–1		0–1	0–0	2–0	2–1	1–3	2–1	1–5	0–2	1–2	2–2	2–1	4–4	2–0	3–2	2–3	0–1
Gravesend	1–1	3–1	0–0	2–0	1–0	0–0	2–2	1–1		2–0	2–0	1–3	2–1	3–0	1–0	1–0	0–4	3–2	1–4	1–1	4–1	1–3	1–0	0–1
Grays	1–2	1–1	0–1	1–1	0–0	0–1	2–2	1–1	0–2		1–0	3–0	0–1	1–0	2–2	3–1	4–0	2–1	1–1	0–2	1–0	2–2	3–0	0–0
Halifax	2–0	1–1	1–2	1–0	2–1	3–1	2–1	2–2	1–1	0–2		2–0	1–1	0–2	1–1	0–0	1–1	4–1	3–1	2–1	3–1	4–1	3–0	1–1
Kidderminster	0–0	3–2	0–0	1–0	0–1	1–4	0–2	2–2	1–2	2–1	1–0		0–1	0–1	0–0	0–0	2–0	1–3	2–0	1–2	0–2	0–1	0–1	2–1
Morecambe	2–1	0–1	0–1	2–2	1–0	1–1	2–2	1–1	1–0	1–0	4–0	0–1		2–1	0–3	1–0	0–0	2–0	1–0	3–3	0–0	2–0	2–0	1–3
Northwich	1–3	1–1	0–3	0–4	2–1	2–0	1–0	2–0	1–2	0–3	3–2	0–1	0–2		1–0	4–1	3–1	0–3	4–0	0–0	0–1	0–1	0–2	1–2
Oxford	2–0	1–1	0–0	1–1	1–1	2–2	1–0	0–2	1–0	1–1	2–0	0–1	0–0	5–1		0–1	2–2	2–1	2–0	2–0	2–1	4–1	0–0	2–0
Rushden	0–1	3–0	1–2	3–1	1–1	2–3	3–0	2–0	0–0	1–3	0–1	0–1	2–2	1–0	1–0		2–3	1–0	2–1	2–2	1–1	4–1	2–0	0–1
Southport	1–0	2–1	3–1	1–2	3–1	1–4	0–1	1–2	2–2	3–1	1–1	0–1	1–2	1–2	0–1	1–2		1–1	5–1	1–2	1–0	0–1	0–0	0–1
St Albans	3–5	1–5	0–1	0–0	2–2	1–2	1–2	0–0	2–3	0–6	3–2	1–1	0–2	1–3	0–2	3–2	2–2		0–3	2–3	1–0	1–0	0–1	4–2
Stafford	0–3	1–0	1–1	1–2	0–1	1–2	0–1	0–1	3–1	4–2	2–3	1–2	1–3	2–0	0–1	1–1	1–0	2–2		1–3	0–4	2–0	1–0	0–0
Stevenage	3–2	0–1	2–1	4–1	2–3	1–2	0–0	3–3	3–0	1–0	2–1	1–2	3–3	0–2	2–2	1–0	3–1	1–2	6–0		3–0	1–0	3–2	1–2
Tamworth	2–0	1–0	0–1	0–1	0–1	0–2	1–0	1–1	2–1	4–2	1–0	0–0	0–1	0–1	1–3	1–4	1–1	1–1	0–0	2–1		1–3	3–1	2–2
Weymouth	1–0	1–2	1–1	2–1	3–2	1–1	2–1	1–0	2–1	3–2	1–0	1–1	2–1	1–1	1–1	1–1	2–0	2–1	1–2	0–1	3–1		2–3	1–2
Woking	2–0	2–0	0–0	0–1	1–2	2–2	0–2	3–3	2–2	1–0	2–2	3–0	1–1	3–2	1–0	3–0	1–1	1–2	1–1	0–1	0–2	4–0		1–2
York	1–0	1–0	3–2	1–2	5–0	2–3	0–0	0–0	0–2	2–2	2–0	1–0	2–3	2–1	1–0	3–1	2–2	0–0	0–0	0–1	0–2	1–0	0–1	

Read across for home results, down for away

NATIONWIDE NORTH

		P	W	D	L	F	A	GD	Pts
1	Droylsden	42	23	9	10	85	55	30	78
2	Kettering	42	20	13	9	75	58	17	73
3	Workington	42	20	10	12	61	46	15	70
4	Hinckley	42	19	12	11	68	54	14	69
5	Farsley†	42	19	11	12	58	51	7	68
6	Harrogate	42	18	13	11	58	41	17	67
7	Blyth	42	19	9	14	57	49	8	66
8	Hyde	42	18	11	13	79	62	17	65
9	Worcester	42	16	14	12	67	54	13	62
10	Nuneaton	42	15	15	12	54	45	9	60
11	Moor Green	42	16	11	15	53	51	2	59
12	Gainsborough	42	15	11	16	51	57	–6	56
13	Hucknall	42	15	9	18	69	69	0	54
14	Alfreton	42	14	12	16	44	50	–6	54
15	Vauxhall	42	12	15	15	62	64	–2	51
16	Barrow	42	12	14	16	47	48	–1	50
17	Leigh	42	13	10	19	47	61	–14	49
18	Stalybridge	42	13	10	19	64	81	–17	49
19	Redditch	42	11	15	16	61	68	–7	48
20	Scarborough*	42	13	16	13	50	45	5	45
21	Worksop	42	12	9	21	44	62	–18	45
22	Lancaster*	42	2	5	35	27	110	–83	1

† Also promoted * Deducted 10 pts

NATIONWIDE SOUTH

		P	W	D	L	F	A	GD	Pts
1	Histon	42	30	4	8	85	44	41	94
2	Salisbury†	42	21	12	9	65	37	28	75
3	Braintree	42	21	11	10	51	38	13	74
4	Havant	42	20	13	9	75	46	29	73
5	Bishop's Stortford	42	21	10	11	72	61	11	73
6	Newport	42	21	7	14	83	57	26	70
7	Eastbourne	42	18	15	9	58	42	16	69
8	Welling	42	21	6	15	65	51	14	69
9	Lewes	42	15	17	10	67	52	15	62
10	Fisher	42	15	11	16	77	77	0	56
11	Farnborough*	42	19	8	15	59	52	7	55
12	Bognor Regis	42	13	13	16	56	62	–6	52
13	Cambridge	42	15	7	20	44	52	–8	52
14	Sutton	42	14	9	19	58	63	–5	51
15	Eastleigh	42	11	15	16	42	52	–5	48
16	Yeading	42	12	9	21	56	78	–22	45
17	Dorchester	42	11	12	19	49	77	–28	45
18	Thurrock	42	11	11	20	58	79	–21	44
19	Basingstoke	42	9	16	17	46	58	–12	43
20	Hayes	42	11	10	21	47	73	–26	43
21	Weston S-Mare	42	8	11	23	49	77	–28	35
22	Bedford	42	8	7	27	43	82	–39	31

† Also promoted * Deducted 10 pts – also relegated for financial reasons.

OTHER LEAGUES 2006-07

WELSH PREMIER LEAGUE

		P	W	D	L	F	A	GD	Pts
1	New Saints	32	24	4	4	81	20	61	76
2	Rhyl	32	20	9	3	67	35	32	69
3	Llanelli	32	18	9	5	72	33	39	63
4	Welshpool	32	17	9	6	54	33	21	60
5	Connah's Quay	32	16	8	8	49	40	9	56
6	Carmarthen	32	14	8	10	57	50	7	50
7	Port Talbot	32	15	5	12	42	39	3	50
8	Aberystwyth	32	13	9	10	47	37	10	48
9	Bangor	32	14	6	12	55	47	8	48
10	Haverfordwest	32	10	9	13	49	46	3	39
11	Porthmadog	32	8	11	13	40	52	–12	35
12	Airbus	32	7	8	17	40	67	–27	29
13	Cefn Druids	32	7	7	18	41	66	–25	28
14	Caersws	32	6	9	17	34	59	–25	27
15	Caernarfon	32	6	8	18	41	73	–32	26
16	Newtown	32	6	6	20	30	63	–33	24
17	Cwmbran	32	4	8	20	36	75	–39	20

RYMAN PREMIER DIVISION

		P	W	D	L	F	A	GD	Pts
1	Hampton	42	24	10	8	77	53	24	82
2	Bromley	42	23	11	8	83	43	40	80
3	Chelmsford	42	23	8	11	96	51	45	77
4	Billericay	42	22	11	9	71	42	29	77
5	Wembledon†*	42	21	15	6	76	37	39	75
6	Margate	42	20	11	11	79	48	31	71
7	Boreham Wood	42	19	12	11	71	49	22	69
8	Horsham	42	18	14	10	70	57	13	68
9	Ramsgate	42	20	5	17	63	63	0	65
10	Heybridge	42	17	13	12	57	40	17	64
11	Tonbridge	42	20	4	18	74	72	2	64
12	Staines	42	15	12	15	64	64	0	57
13	Carshalton	42	14	12	16	54	59	–5	54
14	Hendon	42	16	6	20	53	64	–11	54
15	Leyton	42	13	10	19	55	77	–22	49
16	East Thurrock	42	14	6	22	56	70	–14	48
17	Ashford Town	42	11	13	18	59	71	–12	46
18	Folkestone	42	12	10	20	45	66	–21	64
19	Harrow	42	13	6	23	61	71	–10	45
20	Worthing	42	8	11	23	57	82	–25	35
21	Walton & H	42	9	6	27	38	83	–45	33
22	Slough	42	4	6	32	26	123	–97	18

†Also promoted *Deducted 3 pts

UNIBOND PREMIER DIVISION

		P	W	D	L	F	A	GD	Pts
1	Burscough*	42	23	12	7	80	37	43	80
2	Witton Albion	42	24	8	10	90	48	42	80
3	Telford†	42	21	15	6	72	40	32	78
4	Marine	42	22	8	12	70	53	17	74
5	Matlock	42	21	9	12	70	43	27	72
6	Guiseley	42	19	12	11	71	49	22	69
7	Hednesford	42	18	14	10	49	41	8	68
8	Fleetwood	42	19	10	13	71	60	11	67
9	Gateshead	42	17	14	11	75	57	18	65
10	Ossett	42	18	10	14	61	52	9	64
11	Whitby	42	18	6	18	63	78	–15	60
12	Ilkeston	42	16	11	15	66	62	4	59
13	North Ferriby	42	15	9	18	54	61	–7	54
14	Prescot	42	13	14	15	52	56	–4	53
15	Lincoln	42	12	15	15	40	58	–18	51
16	Frickley	42	13	10	19	50	69	–19	49
17	Leek	42	13	9	20	49	61	–12	48
18	Ashton	42	13	9	20	52	72	–20	48
19	Kendal	42	12	11	19	59	79	–20	47
20	Mossley	42	10	5	27	48	79	–31	35
21	Radcliffe	42	7	11	24	39	71	–32	32
22	Grantham	42	3	8	31	39	94	–55	17

†Also promoted *Deducted 1 pt

BRITISH GAS SOUTHERN PREMIER DIVISION

		P	W	D	L	F	A	GD	Pts
1	Bath City	42	27	10	5	84	29	55	91
2	Team Bath	42	23	9	10	66	42	24	78
3	King's Lynn	42	22	10	10	69	40	29	76
4	Maidenhead†	42	20	10	12	58	36	22	70
5	Hemel Hempstead	42	19	12	11	79	60	19	69
6	Halesowen	42	18	13	11	66	53	13	67
7	Chippenham	42	19	9	14	61	56	5	66
8	Stamford	42	16	11	15	65	62	3	59
9	Mangotsfield	42	13	19	10	44	45	–1	58
10	Gloucester	42	15	13	14	67	70	–3	58
11	Hitchin	42	16	9	17	55	68	–13	57
12	Merthyr Tydfil	42	14	14	14	47	46	1	56
13	Banbury	42	15	10	17	60	64	–4	55
14	Yate	42	14	12	16	59	71	–12	54
15	Tiverton	42	14	8	20	56	67	–11	50
16	Cheshunt	42	14	7	21	56	71	–15	49
17	Rugby	42	15	4	23	58	79	–21	49
18	Clevedon	42	12	12	18	60	61	–1	48
19	Wealdstone	42	13	9	20	69	82	–13	48
20	Corby	42	10	9	23	52	69	–17	39
21	Cirencester	42	9	12	21	46	76	–30	39
22	Northwood	42	8	10	24	44	74	–30	34

†Also promoted

SCOT-ADS HIGHLAND LEAGUE

		P	W	D	L	F	A	GD	Pts
1	Keith	28	20	4	4	67	26	641	64
2	Inverurie	28	20	4	4	62	33	29	64
3	Buckie	28	16	8	4	54	28	26	56
4	Deveronvale	28	17	4	7	77	35	42	55
5	Huntly	28	17	4	7	67	39	28	55
6	Cove	28	13	6	9	52	36	16	45
7	Nairn	28	13	4	11	57	42	15	43
8	Fraserburgh	28	11	8	9	48	42	6	41
9	Clachnacuddin	28	9	6	13	43	42	1	33
10	Rothes	28	10	2	16	42	57	–15	32
11	Wick	28	10	2	16	44	61	17	32
12	Forres	28	7	7	14	454	60	–6	28
13	Brora	28	8	2	18	38	84	–46	26
14	Lossiemouth	28	3	5	20	25	64	–39	14
15	Fort William	28	3	0	25	26	107	–81	9

BARCLAYS PREMIERSHIP RESERVE LEAGUE

NORTH

		P	W	D	L	F	A	GD	Pts
1	Bolton Wand.	18	10	3	5	21	16	5	33
2	Manchester Utd.	18	9	4	5	24	17	7	31
3	Middlesbrough	18	9	3	6	31	25	6	30
4	Manchester City	18	9	2	7	27	24	3	29
5	Liverpool	18	8	2	8	24	19	5	26
6	Blackburn Rov.	18	7	5	6	16	15	1	26
7	Sheffield Utd.	18	8	2	8	23	23	0	26
8	Newcastle Utd.	18	6	5	7	29	29	0	23
9	Everton	18	3	7	8	18	25	7	16
10	Wigan Athletic	18	2	5	11	8	28	20	11

SOUTH

		P	W	D	L	F	A	GD	Pts
1	Reading	18	12	2	4	45	15	30	38
2	Watford	18	11	2	5	26	20	6	35
3	Chelsea	18	10	3	5	26	11	15	33
4	Aston Villa	18	9	3	6	38	26	12	30
5	Tottenham	18	8	6	4	22	18	4	30
6	Charlton Athletic	18	7	4	7	28	24	4	25
7	West Ham Utd.	18	5	3	10	18	28	–10	18
8	Fulham	18	4	5	9	16	30	–14	17
9	Arsenal	18	4	4	10	15	29	–14	16
10	Portsmouth	18	2	4	12	12	45	–33	10

PONTIN'S HOLIDAY'S LEAGUE

DIVISION ONE CENTRAL

		P	W	D	L	F	A	GD	Pts
1	Birmingham City	22	13	5	4	38	21	17	44
2	Nottm. Forest	22	13	4	5	44	23	21	43
3	Walsall	22	12	4	6	41	23	18	40
4	Sheffield Wed.	22	12	4	6	36	25	11	40
5	W.B.A.	22	11	3	8	36	30	6	36
6	Leeds Utd.	22	7	7	8	33	35	–2	28
7	Barnsley	22	7	5	10	44	47	–3	26
8	Stoke City	22	6	7	9	25	37	–12	25
9	Huddersfield Town	22	6	6	10	25	32	–7	24
10	Port Vale	22	6	5	11	25	35	–10	23
11	Shresbury Town	22	5	5	12	29	44	–15	20
12	Bradford City	22	4	5	13	19	43	–24	17

DIVISION ONE WEST

		P	W	D	L	F	A	GD	Pts
1	Oldham Athletic	20	10	7	3	39	18	21	37
2	Preston N.E.	20	11	2	7	48	32	16	35
3	Bury	20	10	5	5	43	32	11	35
4	Accrington Stanley	20	9	3	8	38	36	2	30
5	Tranmere Rov.	20	9	2	9	30	31	–1	29
6	Blackpool	20	9	1	10	32	34	–2	28
7	Manchester City	20	7	5	8	26	32	–6	26
8	Rochdale	20	8	1	11	32	39	–7	25
9	Wrexham	20	7	4	9	21	33	–12	25
10	Carlisle Utd.	20	6	4	10	28	38	–10	22
11	Chester City	20	6	2	12	21	33	–12	20

DIVISION ONE EAST

		P	W	D	L	F	A	GD	Pts
1	Rotherham Utd.	18	12	3	3	46	23	23	39
2	Grimsby Town	18	12	2	4	35	22	13	38
3	Hartlepool Utd.	18	10	6	2	40	17	23	36
4	Hull City	18	11	1	6	35	22	13	34
5	York City	18	6	7	5	32	21	11	25
6	Sheffield Utd.	18	6	4	8	28	33	–5	22
7	Scunthorpe Utd.	18	6	2	10	24	32	–8	20
8	Doncaster Rov.	18	4	3	11	19	46	–27	15
9	Darlington	18	3	3	12	14	33	–19	12
10	Lincoln City	18	3	3	12	14	38	–24	12

PONTINS HOLIDAY'S COMBINATION

CENTRAL DIVISION

		P	W	D	L	F	A	GD	Pts
1	Brighton & H.A.	14	12	1	1	44	10	34	37
2	Southampton	14	12	0	2	36	13	23	36
3	Crystal Palace	14	7	1	6	29	25	4	22
4	Q.P.R.	14	6	2	6	22	31	–9	20
5	Millwall	14	4	3	7	15	16	–1	15
6	Bournemouth	14	4	2	8	21	36	–15	14
7	Wycombe	14	4	1	9	15	26	–11	13
8	Aldershot	14	1	2	11	14	39	–25	5

EAST DIVISION

		P	W	D	L	F	A	GD	Pts
1	Ipswich	18	13	2	3	45	18	27	41
2	Colchester Utd.	18	8	8	2	21	10	11	32
3	Luton Town	18	9	3	6	32	24	8	30
4	Southend Utd.	18	9	2	7	32	28	4	29
5	Leyton Orient	18	6	8	4	29	21	8	26
6	Northampton Town	18	7	4	7	22	23	–1	25
7	Norwich City	18	6	6	6	30	26	4	24
8	M.K. Dons	18	7	2	9	26	35	–9	23
9	Stevenage	18	2	5	11	18	37	–19	11
10	Oxford Utd.	18	1	4	13	13	46	–33	7

WALES AND WEST DIVISION

		P	W	D	L	F	A	GD	Pts
1	Cheltenham Town	18	11	5	2	42	22	20	38
2	Bristol City	18	8	6	4	42	23	19	30
3	Cardiff City	18	7	7	4	26	25	1	28
4	Bristol Rov.	18	8	4	6	18	19	–1	28
5	Plymouth Argyle	18	7	5	6	31	28	3	26
6	Exeter City	18	7	3	8	26	14	12	24
7	Swindon Town	18	6	4	8	26	25	1	22
8	Yeovil Town	18	6	3	9	31	38	–7	21
9	Swansea City	18	4	4	10	15	29	–14	16
9	Weymouth	18	4	3	11	11	745	–34	15

F.A. WOMEN'S PREMIER LEAGUE

		P	W	D	L	F	A	GD	Pts
1	Arsenal	22	22	0	0	119	10	109	66
2	Everton	22	17	4	1	56	15	41	52
3	Charlton Athletic	22	16	4	2	63	32	31	50
4	Bristol Academy	22	13	8	1	53	41	12	40
5	Leeds Utd.	22	12	9	1	50	44	6	37
6	Blackburn Rov.	22	10	10	2	37	36	1	32
7	Birmingham City	22	8	10	4	34	29	5	28
8	Chelsea	22	8	10	4	33	34	–1	28
9	Doncaster Rov.	22	7	13	2	29	54	–25	23
10	Cardiff City	22	3	16	3	26	64	–38	12
11	Sunderland	22	3	17	2	15	72	–57	11
12	Fulham	22	1	19	2	12	96	–84	5

IRISH FOOTBALL 2006-07

EIRCOM LEAGUE

PREMIER DIVISION

		P	W	D	L	F	A	Pts
1	Shelbourne	30	18	8	4	60	27	62
2	Derry City	30	18	8	4	46	20	62
3	Drogheda Utd.	30	16	10	4	37	23	58
4	Cork City	30	15	11	4	37	15	56
5	Sligo Rov.	30	11	7	12	33	42	40
6	U.C.D.	30	9	11	10	26	26	38
7	St Patrick's Ath.	30	9	10	11	32	29	37
8	Longford Town	30	8	10	12	23	27	34
9	Bohemians *	30	9	5	16	29	34	29
10	Bray Wand.	30	3	8	19	22	64	17
11	Waterford Utd.	30	2	6	22	20	58	12

(* Deducted 3 points)

Leading scorer: 15 Jason Byrne (Shelbourne). **Player of Year:** Joseph Ndo (Shelbourne). **Young Player of Year:** Kevin Deery (Derry City). **Goalkeeper of Year:** David Forde (Derry City). **Personality of Year:** Pat Fenlon (Shelbourne).

FIRST DIVISION

		P	W	D	L	F	A	Pts
1	Shamrock Rov.† *	36	21	12	3	53	13	72
2	Dundalk	36	22	5	9	57	33	71
3	Galway Utd.†	36	19	12	5	57	25	69
4	Cobh Ramblers	36	16	10	10	50	33	58
5	Limerick	36	14	5	17	38	48	47
6	Finn Harps	36	12	10	14	49	45	46
7	Kildare Co.	36	11	10	15	38	55	43
8	Athlone Town	36	11	9	16	29	47	42
9	Monaghan Utd.	36	6	9	21	32	64	27
10	Kilkenny City	36	3	8	25	25	65	17

(† Shamrock Rov. and Galway Utd. both promoted. * Deducted 3 points)

Leading scorer: 18 Philip Hughes (Dundalk). **Player of Year:** Philip Hughes.

FAI CARLSBERG CUP FINAL

Derry City 4 (Farren, Brennan, Hutton, S. Brennan og), **St. Patrick's Ath.** 3 (Mulcahy, Molloy, O'Connor), aet – Lansdowne Road, December 3, 2006.

Derry City: Forde, McCallion, K. Brennan, Hutton, Delaney, McCourt, Higgins (McHugh), Molloy, Deery (McGlynn), Beckett (Hargan), Farren.

St. Patrick's Ath: Ryan, S. Quigley, Frost, S. Brennan, Mulcahy, C. Foley, Murphy (O'Connor), M. Foley (Armstrong), Keegan (M. Quigley), Molloy, Rutherford.

Referee: D. Hancock (Dublin).

EIRCOM LEAGUE CUP FINAL

Derry City 0, **Shelbourne** 0, aet, **Derry City** won 3-0 on pens – The Brandywell, September 17, 2006.

SETANTA SPORTS CUP FINAL

Linfield 1 (McAreavey), **Drogheda Utd.** (Grant), aet, **Drogheda Utd.** won 4-3 on pens – Windsor Park, May 12, 2007.

CARNEGIE IRISH LEAGUE

PREMIER DIVISION

		P	W	D	L	F	A	Pts
1	Linfield	30	21	8	1	73	19	71
2	Glentoran	30	20	3	7	76	33	63
3	Cliftonville	30	18	7	5	47	26	61
4	Portadown	30	17	7	6	49	26	58
5	Lisburn Distillery	30	14	6	10	50	39	48
6	Crusaders	30	14	5	11	50	42	47
7	Coleraine	30	13	6	11	55	50	45
8	Dungannon Swifts	30	13	5	12	41	41	44
9	Ballymena Utd.	30	12	7	11	46	40	43
10	Limavady Utd.	30	10	5	15	39	54	35
11	Armagh City	30	11	2	17	42	66	35
12	Newry City	30	8	7	15	39	54	31
13	Donegal Celtic	30	6	9	15	33	51	27
14	Larne	30	7	5	18	33	60	26
15	Glenavon	30	5	10	15	40	58	25
16	Loughall	30	1	8	21	23	77	11

Leading scorer: 27 Gary Hamilton (Glentoran). **Player of Year:** William 'Winkie' Murphy (Linfield). **Young Player of Year:** Mark McAllister (Dungannon Swifts). **Manager of Year:** David Jeffrey (Linfield).

FIRST DIVISION

		P	W	D	L	F	A	Pts
1	Institute	22	17	3	2	50	14	54
2	Bangor	22	14	5	3	49	23	47
3	Banbridge Town	22	13	4	5	45	31	43
4	Carrick Rangers	22	12	6	4	38	27	42
5	Ards	22	11	5	6	42	25	38
6	Dundela	22	8	5	9	33	35	29
7	H&W Welders	22	8	3	11	30	36	27
8	Coagh Utd.	22	6	6	10	32	41	24
9	Tobermore Utd.	22	5	5	12	39	54	20
10	Portstewart	22	6	2	14	29	44	20
11	Ballinamallard Utd.	22	4	3	15	14	42	15
12	Moyola Park	22	4	1	17	24	53	13

Leading scorer: 20 Paul McDowell (Bangor).

JJB SPORT IRISH CUP FINAL

Linfield 2 (Dickson, Ferguson), **Dungannon Swifts** 2 (Hamill, McAree), aet, **Linfield** won 3-2 on pens – Windsor Park, May 5, 2007.

Linfield: Mannus, Ervin, Murphy, Bailie, McShane, Dickson, Mulgrew, McAreavey (Gault), O'Kane (Stewart), Ferguson, Thompson.

Dungannon Swifts: Nelson, Wray, Gallagher, Montgomery, McMinn, McCluskey (McConkey), McCabe, McAree, Hamill, McAllister, Scullion (Everaldo).

Referee: M. Courtney (Cookstown).

CIS LEAGUE CUP FINAL

Glentoran 1 (Hamilton), **Cliftonville** 0 – Windsor Park, Belfast, December 2, 2006.

COUNTY ANTRIM SHIELD

Cliftonville 2 (Holland 2, 1 pen), **Lisburn Distillery** 1 (Muir) – The Oval, Belfast, January 23, 2007.

QUOTE-UNQUOTE

'I'm going to go home and freeze teletext' – **Steve Cotterill**, Burnley manager, after a 2-0 win over Q.P.R. on the opening day of the season puts his team top of the Championship.

'I'm looking to take the team in a different direction' – **Steve McClaren**, England's new coach, on his decision to drop David Beckham.

'What do you have to do to get a red card? Do you have to kill someone? Or maybe they just give them for pulling a shirt or kicking the ball away' – **Harry Redknapp**, Portsmouth manager, after Manchester City's Ben Thatcher escapes with a yellow card for a forearm smash which renders Pedro Mendes unconscious.

'The way Pedro Mendes has conducted himself is absolutely sensational. He could have hung Ben out to dry, but he hasn't. He deserves a lot of credit for that' – **Stuart Pearce**, Manchester City manager.

VASE HAT-TRICK FOR LEONARD

Manager Dave Leonard completed an F.A. Vase hat-trick when Truro City became the first Cornish side to win the trophy. Leonard, whose team beat AFC Totton 3-1 at Wembley, was a player with Tiverton Town when they were successful in 1998 and 1999.

UEFA CHAMPIONS LEAGUE 2006-07

FIRST QUALIFYING ROUND, FIRST LEG

Cork 1 (Woods 62), Apollon Limassol 0. **Linfield** 1 (Dickson 58 pen), Gorica 3 (Demirovic 14, 27, Sturm 66). MyPa 1 (Adriano 58), **TNS** 0.

FIRST QUALIFYING ROUND, SECOND LEG

Apollon Limassol 1 (Sosin 51), **Cork** 1 (Murray 75) – **Cork** won 2-1 on agg. Gorica 2 (Burgic 30, 83), **Linfield** 2 (Thompson 28, McAreavey 89) – Gorica won 5-3 on agg. **TNS** 0, MyPa 1 (Puhakainen 5) – MyPa won 2-0 on agg.

FIRST QUALIFYING ROUND, ON AGGREGATE

Ekranas 3, Elbasan 1; Hafnarfjordur 4, Tallinn 3; Metalurgs 2, Aktobe 1; Rabotnicki 1, Dudelange 0; Sheriff 2, Pyuniko 1; Sioni Bolnisi 2, Baku 1; Siroki Brijeg 2, Shakhtyor 0; Torshavn 5, Birkirkara 2.

SECOND QUALIFYING ROUND, FIRST LEG

Hearts 3 (Anic 53 og, Tall 79, Bednar 84), Siroki Brijeg 0. Att: 28,486 (at Murrayfield). **Cork** 0, Crvena Zvezda 1 (Behan 36 og). Att: 5,500.

SECOND QUALIFYING ROUND, SECOND LEG

Crvena Zvezda 3 (Milovanovic 2, Zigic 34, 59), **Cork** 0. Att: 30,000 (Red Star Belgrade won 4-0 on agg). Siroki Brijeg 0, **Hearts** 0. Att: 6,000 (**Hearts** won 3-0 on agg).

SECOND QUALIFYING ROUND, ON AGGREGATE

Copenhagen 4, MyPa 2; Dinamo Zagreb 9, Ekranas 3; Dynamo Kiev 8, Metalurgs 1; Fenerbahce 9, Torshavn 0; Legia Warsaw 3, Hafnarfjordur 0; Levski Sofia 4, Sioni Bolnisi 0. Mlada Boleslav 5, Valerenga 3; Rabotnicki 5, Debrecen 2; Ruzomberok 3, Djurgarden 2; Salzburg 3, Zurich 2; Spartak Moscow 1, Sheriff 1 (Spartak Moscow won on away goal); Steaua Bucharest 5, Gorica 0.

THIRD QUALIFYING ROUND, FIRST LEG

Dinamo Zagreb 0, **Arsenal** 3 (Fabregas 63, 79, Van Persie 64). Att: 28,500. **Hearts** 1 (Mikoliunas 62), AEK Athens 2 (Kapetanos 89, Berra 90 og). Att: 32,459 (at Murrayfield). **Liverpool** 2 (Bellamy 33, Gonzalez 88), Maccabi Haifa 1 (Boccoli 29). Att: 40,058.

THIRD QUALIFYING ROUND, SECOND LEG

AEK Athens 3 (Julio Cesar 79 pen, 86, Liberopoulos 82), **Hearts** 0. Att: 31,500 (AEK Athens won 5-1 on agg). **Arsenal** 2 (Ljungberg 77, Flamini 90), Dinamo Zagreb 1 (Eduardo 12). Att: 58,418 (**Arsenal** won 5-1 on agg). Maccabi Haifa 1 (Colautti 63), **Liverpool** 1 (Crouch 54). Att: 12,500 (**Liverpool** won 3-2 on agg).

THIRD QUALIFYING ROUND, ON AGGREGATE

AC Milan 3, Crvena Zvezda 1; Benfica 4, Austria Vienna 1; Copenhagen 3, Ajax 2; CSKA Moscow 5, Ruzomberok 0; Dynamo Kiev 5, Fenerbahce 3; Galatasaray 6, Mlada Boleslav 3; Hamburg 1, Osasuna 1 (Hamburg won on away goal); Levski Sofia 4, Chievo 2; Lille 4, Rabotnicki 0; Shakhtar Donetsk 4, Legia Warsaw 2; Spartak Moscow 2, Slovan Liberec 1; Steaua Bucharest 4, Standard Liege 3; Valencia 3, Salzburg 1.

GROUP STAGE

GROUP A

September 12, 2006
Barcelona 5 (Iniesta 7, Guily 39, Puyol 49, Eto'o 58, Ronaldinho 90), **Levski Sofia** 0. Att: 91,326.
Chelsea 2 (Essien 24, Ballack 68 pen), **Werder Bremen** 0. Att: 32,135.
Chelsea (4-1-3-2): Cech, Boulahrouz, Ricardo Carvalho, Terry, A. Cole, Makelele, Essien, Lampard, Ballack (Mikel 88), Drogba (Kalou 86), Shevchenko (J. Cole 78).

September 27, 2006
Levski Sofia 1 (Ognyanov 89), **Chelsea** 3 (Drogba 39, 52, 68). Att: 27,950.
Chelsea (4-1-3-2): Cech, Paulo Ferreira, Ricardo Carvalho, Terry, Bridge, Essien, Mikel (Kalou 63), Ballack, Lampard, Drogba (Robben 70), Shevchenko (Wright-Phillips 82).
Werder Bremen 1 (Puyol 56 og), **Barcelona** 1 (Messi 89). Att: 41,256.

October 18, 2006
Chelsea 1 (Drogba 46), **Barcelona** 0. Att: 40,599.
Chelsea (4-1-3-2): Hilario, Boulahrouz, Ricardo Carvalho, Terry, A. Cole, Makelele, Essien, Ballack, Lampard, Drogba (Kalou 90), Shevchenko (Robben 77).
Werder Bremen 2 (Naldo 45, Diego 74), **Levski Sofia** 0. Att: 41,000.

October 31, 2006
Barcelona 2 (Deco 3, Gudjohnsen 58), **Chelsea** 2 (Lampard 52, Drogba 90). Att: 98,000.
Chelsea (4-1-3-2): Hilario, Boulahrouz (J. Cole 74), Ricardo Carvalho, Terry, A. Cole, Makelele, Essien, Ballack (Paulo Ferreira 89), Lampard, Robben (Kalou 73), Drogba.
Levski Sofia 0, **Werder Bremen** 3 (Mihailov 34 og, Baumann 35, Frings 37).

November 22, 2006
Levski Sofia 0, **Barcelona** 2 (Giuly 5, Iniesta 65). Att: 38,000.
Werder Bremen 1 (Mertesacker 27), **Chelsea** 0. Att: 40,000.
Chelsea (4-1-4-1): Cudicini, Geremi, Boulahrouz, Terry, A. Cole, Makelele, Essien, Mikel (Robben 57), Ballack (Wright-Phillips 76), J. Cole, Drogba (Shevchenko 57).

December 5, 2006
Barcelona 2 (Ronaldinho 13, Gudjohnsen 19), **Werder Bremen** 0. Att: 95,500.
Chelsea 2 (Shevchenko 27, Wright-Phillips 83), **Levski Sofia** 0. Att: 33,358.
Chelsea (4-1-3-2): Hilario, Paulo Ferreira (Diarra 58), Boulahrouz, Ricardo Carvalho, Bridge, Essien, Ballack, Lampard, Robben (Wright-Phillips 69), Shevchenko (Kalou 69), Drogba.

FINAL TABLE

	P	*W*	*D*	*L*	*F*	*A*	*Pts*
CHELSEA	6	4	1	1	10	4	13
BARCELONA	6	3	2	1	12	4	11
Werder Bremen	6	3	1	2	7	5	10
Levski Sofia	6	0	0	6	1	17	0

GROUP B

September 12, 2006
Bayern Munich 4 (Pizarro 48, Santa Cruz 52, Schweinsteiger 71, Salihamidzic 85), **Spartak Moscow** 0. Att: 66,000.
Sporting Lisbon 1 (Caneira 64), **Inter Milan** 0. Att: 30,000.

September 27, 2006
Inter Milan 0, **Bayern Munich** 2 (Pizarro 81, Podolski 90). Att: 79,000.
Spartak Moscow 1 (Boyarintsev 4), **Sporting Lisbon** 1 (Nani 59). Att: 75,101.

October 18, 2006
Inter Milan 3 (Santa Cruz 2, 9, Stankovic 76), **Spartak Moscow** 1 (Pavluchenko 54). Att: 40,000.
Sporting Lisbon 0, **Bayern Munich** 1 (Schweinsteiger 19). Att: 48,000.

October 31, 2006
Bayern Munich 0, **Sporting Lisbon** 0. Att: 65,000.
Spartak Moscow 0, **Inter Milan** 1 (Cruz 1). Att: 60,000.

November 22, 2006
Inter Milan 1 (Crespo 36), **Sporting Lisbon** 0. Att: 69,000.
Spartak Moscow 2 (Kalinichenko 16, Kovac 73), **Bayern Munich** 2 (Pizarro 22, 39). Att: 38,000.

December 5, 2006
Bayern Munich 1(Makaay 62), **Inter Milan** 1 (Vieira 90). Att: 65,000.
Sporting Lisbon 1 (Bueno 31), **Spartak Moscow** 3 (Pavluchenko 8, Kalinichenko 16, Boyarintsev 89). Att: 40,000.

FINAL TABLE

	P	*W*	*D*	*L*	*F*	*A*	*Pts*
BAYERN MUNICH	6	3	3	0	10	3	12
INTER MILAN	6	3	1	2	5	5	10
Spartak Moscow	6	1	2	3	7	11	5
Sporting Lisbon	6	1	2	3	3	6	5

GROUP C

September 12, 2006
Galatasaray 0, **Bordeaux** 0. Att: 45,514.
PSV Eindhoven 0, **Liverpool** 0. Att: 35,000.
Liverpool (4-4-2): Reina, Finnan, Carragher, Agger, Warnock, Pennant, Sissoko (Xabi Alonso 62), Zenden, Aurelio (Gonzalez 81), Kuyt, Bellamy (Gerrard 71).

September 27, 2006
Bordeaux 0, **PSV Eindhoven** 1 (Vayrynen 65). Att: 26,000.
Liverpool 3 (Crouch 9, 52, Luis Garcia 14), **Galatasaray** 2 (Karan 59, 65). Att: 41,976.
Liverpool (4-4-2): Reina, Finnan, Carragher, Agger, Aurelio, Pennant (Sissoko 78), Gerrard, Xabi Alonso, Luis Garcia, Kuyt (Gonzalez 65), Crouch (Bellamy 90).

October 18, 2006
Bordeaux 0, **Liverpool** 1 (Crouch 58). Att: 33,000.
Liverpool (4-4-2): Reina, Finnan, Carragher, Hyypia, Riise, Luis Garcia, Xabi Alonso, Zenden, Gonzalez (Sissoko 68), Crouch (Kuyt 65), Bellamy.
Galatasaray 1 (Ilic 19), **PSV Eindhoven** 2 (Kromkamp 59, Kone 72). Att: 22,000.

October 31, 2006
Liverpool 3 (Luis Garcia 23, 76, Gerrard 71), **Bordeaux** 0. Att: 41,978.
Liverpool (4-4-2): Reina, Finnan, Carragher, Hyypia, Riise, Gerrard, Sissoko, Xabi Alonso (Zenden 57), Luis Garcia (Fowler 78), Kuyt, Crouch.
PSV Eindhoven 2 (Simons 59, Kone 84), **Galatasaray** 0. Att: 30,000.

November 22, 2006
Bordeaux 3 (Alonso 22, Laslandes 47, Faubert 50), **Galatasaray** 1 (Inamoto 72). Att: 30,000.
Liverpool 2 (Gerrard 65, Crouch 89), **PSV Eindhoven** 0. Att: 41,948.
Liverpool (4-4-2): Reina, Finnan, Carragher, Agger, Riise, Pennant (Bellamy 79), Gerrard, Xabi Alonso (Zenden 21), Gonzalez (Luis Garcia 36), Kuyt, Crouch.

December 5, 2006
Galatasaray 3 (Ates 24, Buruk 28, Ilic 79), **Liverpool** 2 (Fowler 22, 90). Att: 23,000.
Liverpool (4-4-2): Dudek, Peltier, Carragher, Agger, Riise, Pennant, Xabi Alonso (Roque 84), Paletta, Guthrie (Luis Garcia 66), Bellamy (Crouch 74), Fowler.
PSV Eindhoven 1 (Alex 87), **Bordeaux** 3 (Faubert 7, Dalmat 25, Darcheville 37). Att: 30,000.

FINAL TABLE

	P	*W*	*D*	*L*	*F*	*A*	*Pts*
LIVERPOOL	6	4	1	1	11	5	13
PSV EINDHOVEN	6	3	1	2	6	6	10
Bordeaux	6	2	1	3	6	7	7
Galatasaray	6	1	1	4	7	12	4

GROUP D

September 12, 2006
Olympiacos 2 (Konstantinou 28, Castillo 66), **Valencia** 4 (Morientes 34, 39, 90, Albiol 85). Att: 34,500.
Roma 4 (Taddei 67, Totti 76, De Rossi 79, Pizarro 89), **Shakhtar Donetsk** 0. Att: 75,000.

September 27, 2006
Shakhtar Donetsk 2 (Matuzalem 33, Marica 70), **Olympiacos** 2 (Konstantinou 74, Castillo 68). Att: 20,000.
Valencia 2 (Angulo 12, Villa 28), **Roma** 1 (Totti 19 pen). Att: 48,000.

October 18, 2006
Olympiacos 0, **Roma** 1 (Perrotta 76). Att: 30,000.
Valencia 2 (Villa 30, 45), **Shakhtar Donetsk** 0. Att: 45,000.

October 31, 2006
Roma 1 (Totti 66), **Olympiacos** 1 (Julio Cesar 19). Att: 20,000.
Shakhtar Donetsk 2 (Jadson 2, Fernandinho 28), **Valencia** 2 (Morientes 18, Ayala 68). Att: 21,000.

November 22, 2006
Shakhtar Donetsk 1 (Marica 61), **Roma** 0. Att: 18,673.
Valencia 2 (Angulo 45, Morientes 46), **Olympiacos** 0. Att: 38,000.

December 5, 2006
Olympiacos 1 (Castillo 54), **Shakhtar Donetsk** 1 (Matuzalem 27). Att: 27,500.
Roma 1 (Panucci 13), **Valencia** 0. Att: 45,000.

FINAL TABLE

	P	*W*	*D*	*L*	*F*	*A*	*Pts*
VALENCIA	6	4	1	1	12	6	13
ROMA	6	3	1	2	8	4	10
Shakhtar Donetsk	6	1	3	2	6	11	6
Olympiacos	6	0	3	3	6	11	3

GROUP E

September 13, 2006
Dynamo Kiev 1 (Rebrov 16), **Steaua Bucharest** 4 (Ghionea 3, Badea 24, Dica 43, 79). Att: 27,000.
Lyon 2 (Fred 11, Tiago 31), **Real Madrid** 0. Att: 35,814.

September 26, 2006
Real Madrid 5 (Van Nistelrooy 20, 70 pen, Raul 27, 61, Reyes 45), **Dynamo Kiev** 1 (Milevskiy 47). Att: 80,000.
Steaua Bucharest 0, **Lyon** 3 (Fred 44, Tiago 55, Malouda 90).

October 17, 2006
Dynamo Kiev 0, **Lyon** 3 (Juninho 31, Kallstrom 38, Malouda 51). Att: 24,000.
Steaua Bucharest 1 (Badea 64), **Real Madrid** 4 (Ramos 9, Raul 34, Robinho 56, Van Nistelrooy 76). Att: 20,000.

November 1, 2006
Lyon 1 (Benzema 14), **Dynamo Kiev** 0. Att: 41,000.
Real Madrid 1 (Nicolita 70 og), **Steaua Bucharest** 0. Att: 69,000.

November 21, 2006
Real Madrid 2 (Diarra 39, Van Nistelrooy 83), **Lyon** 2 (Carew 11, Malouda 32). Att: 78,677.
Steaua Bucharest 1 (Dica 69), **Dynamo Kiev** 1 (Cernat 29). Att: 20,000.

December 6, 2006
Dynamo Kiev 2 (Shatskikh 13, 27), **Real Madrid** 2 (Ronaldo 87, 88 pen). Att: 33,000.
Lyon 1 (Diarra 12), **Steaua Bucharest** 1 (Dica 3). Att: 40,000.

FINAL TABLE

FINAL TABLE

	P	*W*	*D*	*L*	*F*	*A*	*Pts*
LYON	6	4	2	0	12	3	14
REAL MADRID	6	3	2	1	14	8	11
Steaua Bucharest	6	1	2	3	7	11	5
Dynamo Kiev	6	0	2	4	5	16	2

GROUP F

September 13, 2006
Copenhagen 0, **Benfica** 0. Att: 40,000.
Manchester Utd. 3 (Saha 30 pen, 40, Solskjaer 47), **Celtic** 2 (Vennegoor of Hesselink 21, Nakamura 43).
Manchester Utd. (4-4-2): Van der Sar, Neville, Ferdinand, Brown, Silvestre, Fletcher, Carrick, Scholes (O'Shea 79), Giggs (Solskjaer 31), Rooney (Richardson 85), Saha.
Celtic (4-1-4-1): Boruc, Wilson (Telfer 50), Caldwell, McManus, Naylor, Lennon, Nakamura, Jarosik (Miller 55), Gravesen, McGeady (Maloney 68), Vennegoor of Hesselink.

September 26, 2006
Benfica 0, **Manchester Utd.** 1 (Saha 60). Att: 61,000.
Manchester Utd. (4-3-3): Van der Sar, Neville, Ferdinand, Vidic, Heinze, Carrick, O'Shea, Scholes, Ronaldo, Rooney (Fletcher 85), Saha (Smith 85).
Celtic 1 (Miller 36 pen), **Copenhagen** 0. Att: 57,598.
Celtic (4-4-2): Boruc, Telfer, Caldwell, McManus, Naylor; Nakamura, Gravesen, Lennon, McGeady (Pearson 87), Zurawski (Beattie 72), Miller (Maloney 81).

October 17, 2006
Celtic 3 (Miller 56, 66, Pearson 90), **Benfica** 0. Att: 58,313.
Celtic (4-4-2): Boruc, Telfer, Caldwell, McManus, Naylor, Maloney, Lennon, Sno (Pearson 86), Nakamura, Zurawski (Jarosik 83), Miller.
Manchester Utd. 3 (Scholes 39, O'Shea 46, Richardson 83), **Copenhagen** 0. Att: 72,020.
Manchester Utd. (4-4-2): Van der Sar, O'Shea, Brown, Vidic, Evra, Fletcher, Carrick (Smith 60), Scholes (Richardson 77), Ronaldo, Rooney, Saha (Solskjaer 60).

November 1, 2006
Benfica 3 (Caldwell 10 og, Nuno Gomes 22, Karyaka 76), **Celtic** 0. Att: 49,000.
Celtic (4-4-1-1): Boruc, Telfer, Caldwell, McManus, Naylor, Nakamura, Sno (Zurawski 71), Lennon, Pearson, Maloney (McGeady 64), Miller.
Copenhagen 1 (Allback 73), **Manchester Utd.** 0. Att: 40,000.
Manchester Utd. (4-4-1-1): Van der Sar, Brown, Vidic (Ferdinand 46), Silvestre, Heinze (Evra 80), Fletcher (Scholes 70), Carrick, O'Shea, Ronaldo, Rooney, Solskjaer.

November 21, 2006
Benfica 3 (Leo 14, Miccoli 16, 37), **Copenhagen** 1 (Allback 89). Att: 47,500.
Celtic 1 (Nakamura 81), **Manchester Utd.** 0. Att: 60,632.
Celtic (4-4-2): Boruc, Telfer, Balde, McManus, Naylor, Gravesen, Sno (Maloney 46), Lennon, Nakamura (Miller 84), Vennegoor of Hesselink, Zurawski (Jarosik 46).
Manchester Utd. (4-4-2): Van der Sar, Neville, Ferdinand, Vidic, Heinze (Evra 85), Ronaldo, Carrick (O'Shea 85), Scholes, Giggs, Rooney, Saha.

December 6, 2006
Copenhagen 3 (Hutchinson 2, Gronkjaer 27, Allback 57), **Celtic** 1 (Jarosik 75). Att: 41,500.
Celtic (4-4-2): Boruc, Wilson, Balde, McManus (O'Dea 73), Naylor, Gravesen (Nakamura 68), Lennon, Jarosik, McGeady (Pearson 68), Zurawski, Miller.
Manchester Utd. 3 (Vidic 45, Giggs 61, Saha 75), **Benfica** 1 (Nelson 27). Att: 74,955.
Manchester Utd. (4-4-2): Van der Sar, Neville, Ferdinand, Vidic, Evra (Heinze 67), Carrick, Scholes (Solskjaer 79), Giggs (Fletcher 74), Ronaldo, Rooney, Saha.

FINAL TABLE

	P	W	D	L	F	A	Pts
MANCHESTER UTD.	6	4	0	2	10	5	12
CELTIC	6	3	0	3	8	9	9
Benfica	6	2	1	3	7	8	7
Copenhagen	6	2	1	3	5	8	7

GROUP G

September 13, 2006
FC Porto 0, **CSKA Moscow** 0. Att: 28,500.
Hamburg 1 (Sanogo 90), **Arsenal** 2 (Gilberto Silva 12 pen, Rosicky 53).
Arsenal (4-4-2): Lehmann, Eboue, Toure (Hoyte 28), Djourou, Gallas, Hleb (Flamini 69), Fabregas, Gilberto Silva, Rosicky, Van Persie, Adebayor.

September 26, 2006
Arsenal 2 (Henry 38, Hleb 48), **FC Porto** 0. Att: 59,861.
Arsenal (4-4-2): Lehmann, Eboue, Toure, Gallas (Song 90), Hoyte, Hleb (Walcott 86), Fabregas, Gilberto Silva, Rosicky, Van Persie (Ljungberg 74), Henry.
CSKA Moscow 1 (Dudu 59), **Hamburg** 0. Att: 26,000.

October 17, 2006
CSKA Moscow 1 (Carvalho 24), **Arsenal** 0. Att: 36,500.
Arsenal (4-4-2): Lehmann, Hoyte, Toure, Djourou (Clichy 75), Gallas, Hleb, Fabregas, Gilberto, Silva, Rosicky (Walcott 80), Van Persie (Adebayor 80), Henry.
FC Porto 4 (Lopez 14, 81, Gonzalez 45 pen, Helder Postiga 69), **Hamburg** 1 (Trochowski 89). Att: 37,500.

November 1, 2006
Arsenal 0, **CSKA Moscow** 0. Att: 60,003.
Arsenal (4-4-2): Lehmann, Hoyte, Toure, Gallas, Clichy, Hleb (Walcott 70), Fabregas (Flamini 88), Gilberto Silva, Rosicky, Van Persie (Aliadiere 80), Henry.
Hamburg 1 (Van der Vaart 62), **FC Porto** 3 (Gonzalez 44, Lopez 61, Bruno Moraes 87). Att: 50,000.

November 21, 2006
Arsenal 3 (Van Persie 52, Eboue 83, Baptista 88), **Hamburg** 1 (Van der Vaart 4). Att: 59,962.
Arsenal (4-4-2): Lehmann, Eboue, Toure, Senderos, Clichy, Hleb, Fabregas, Flamini, Ljungberg, Van Persie (Adebayor 69), Henry.
CSKA Moscow 0, **FC Porto** 2 (Quaresma 2, Gonzalez 61). Att: 30,000.

December 6, 2006
FC Porto 0, **Arsenal** 0. Att: 41,500.
Arsenal (4-5-1): Lehmann, Eboue, Toure, Djourou, Clichy, Hleb, Fabregas, Gilberto Silva, Flamini, Ljungberg, Adebayor (Van Persie 79).
Hamburg 3 (Berisha 28, Van der Vaart 84, Sanogo 90), **CSKA Moscow** 2 (Olic 23 pen, Zhirkov 65). Att: 46,000.

FINAL TABLE

	P	W	D	L	F	A	Pts
ARSENAL	6	3	2	1	7	3	11
FC PORTO	6	3	2	1	9	4	11
CSKA Moscow	6	2	2	2	4	5	8
Hamburg	6	1	0	5	7	15	3

GROUP H

September 13, 2006
AC Milan 3 (Inzaghi 17, Gourcuff 41, Kaka 77 pen), **AEK Athens** 0. Att: 45,000.
Anderlecht 1 (Pareja 41), **Lille** 1 (Fauvergue 80). Att: 25,000.

September 26, 2006
AEK Athens 1 (Julio Cesar 28), **Anderlecht** 1 (Frutos 25). Att: 60,000
Lille 0, **AC Milan** 0. Att: 22,500.

October 17, 2006
Anderlecht 0, **AC Milan** 1 (Kaka 58). Att: 20,129.
Lille 3 (Robail 64, Gygax 82, Makoun 90), **AEK Athens** 1 (Ivic 68). Att: 15,000.

November 1, 2006
AC Milan 4 (Kaka 6 pen, 22, 56, Gilardino 88), **Anderlecht** 1 (Juhasz 61). Att: 42,300.
AEK Athens 1 (Liberopoulos 74), **Lille** 0. Att: 32,000.

November 22, 2006
AEK Athens 1 (Julio Cesar 32). **AC Milan** 0. Att: 70,000.
Lille 2 (Odemwingie 28, Fauvergue 47), **Anderlecht** 2 (Mpenza 38, 48). Att: 35,000.

December 6, 2006
AC Milan 0, **Lille** 2 (Odemwingie 8, Keita 67). Att: 40,000.
Anderlecht 2 (Van den Borre 38, Frutos 64), **AEK Athens** 2 (Lakis 76, Cirillo 81). Att: 18,000.

FINAL TABLE

	P	W	D	L	F	A	Pts
AC MILAN	6	3	1	2	8	4	10
LILLE	6	2	3	1	8	5	9
AEK Athens	6	2	2	2	6	9	8
Anderlecht	6	0	4	2	7	11	4

FIRST KNOCK-OUT ROUND, FIRST LEG

February 20, 2007
Celtic 0, **AC Milan** 0. Att: 58,785.
Celtic (4-4-2): Boruc, Wilson; McManus O'Dea, Naylor, Nakamura, Sno, Lennon, (Gravesen 81), McGeady, Vennegoor of Hesselink, Miller (Jarosik 63).
Lille 0, **Manchester Utd.** 1 (Giggs 83). Att: 41,000.
Manchester Utd. (4-4-2): Van der Sar, Neville, Ferdinand, Vidic, Evra, Ronaldo (Saha 67), Carrick, Scholes (O'Shea, 90), Giggs, Larsson, Rooney.
PSV Eindhoven 1 (Mendez 61), **Arsenal** 0. Att: 35,000.
Arsenal (4-4-2): Lehmann, Gallas, Toure, Senderos, Clichy, Hleb (Baptista 76), Fabregas, Gilberto Silva, Rosicky, Adebayor, Henry.
Real Madrid 3 (Raul 10, 28, Van Nistelrooy 34), **Bayern Munich** 2 (Lucio 23, Van Bommel 88). Att: 80,300.

February 21, 2007
Barcelona 1 (Deco 14), **Liverpool** 2 (Bellamy 43, Riise 74). Att: 88,000.
Liverpool (4-4-2): Reina, Finnan, Carragher, Agger, Arbeloa, Gerrard, Xabi Alonso, Sissoko (Zenden 84), Riise, Bellamy (Pennant 80), Kuyt (Crouch 90).
FC Porto 1 (Raul Meireles 12), **Chelsea** 1 (Shevchenko 16). Att: 49,000.
Chelsea (4-1-3-2): Cech, Diarra, Terry, Ricardo Carvalho (Robben 13, Mikel 46), Bridge, Makelele, Essien, Ballack, Lampard, Drogba, Shevchenko.
Inter Milan 2 (Cambiasso 29, Maicon 76), **Valencia** 2 (Villa 64, Silva 87). Att: 65,000.
Roma 0, **Lyon** 0. Att: 55,000.

FIRST KNOCK-OUT ROUND, SECOND LEG

March 6, 2007
Chelsea 2 (Robben 48, Ballack 79), **FC Porto** 1 (Quaresma 15). Att: 39,041 (**Chelsea** won 3-2 on agg).
Chelsea (4-1-3-2): Cech, Diarra (Paulo Ferreira 65), Ricardo Carvalho, Essien, A. Cole, Makelele (Mikel 46), Robben, Ballack, Lampard, Drogba, Shevchenko (Kalou 84).
Liverpool 0, **Barcelona** 1 (Gudjohnsen 75). Att: 45,000 (agg 2-2, **Liverpool** won on away goals).
Liverpool (4-4-2): Reina, Finnan, Carragher, Agger, Arbeloa, Gerrard, Sissoko, Xabi Alonso, Riise (Aurelio 76), Bellamy (Pennant 65), Kuyt (Crouch 89).
Lyon 0, **Roma** 2 (Totti 22, Mancini 44). Att: 41,000 (**Roma** won 2-0 on agg).
Valencia 0, **Inter Milan** 0. Att: 53,000 (agg 2-2, **Valencia** won on away goals).

March 7, 2007
AC Milan 1 (Kaka 93), **Celtic** 0. Att: 52,918 (aet, **AC Milan** won 1-0 on agg).
Celtic (4-4-1-1): Boruc, Telfer, McManus, O'Dea, Naylor, Nakamura, Lennon, Sno (Beattie 96), McGeady, Jarosik (Gravesen 52), Vennegoor of Hesselink.
Arsenal 1 (Alex 58 og), **PSV Eindhoven** 1 (Alex 83). Att: 60,073 (**PSV Eindhoven** won 2-1 on agg).
Arsenal (4-4-2): Lehmann, Toure, Gallas, Gilberto Silva, Clichy (Walcott 85), Hleb, Denilson, Fabregas, Ljungberg (Diaby 75), Baptista (Henry 66), Adebayor.
Bayern Munich 2 (Makaay 1, Lucio 66), **Real Madrid** 1 (Van Nistelrooy 83 pen). Att: 69,500 (Agg 4-4, Bayern Munich won on away goals).
Manchester Utd. 1 (Larsson 72), **Lille** 0. Att: 75,182 (**Manchester Utd.** won 2-0 on agg).
Manchester Utd. (4-4-2): Van der Sar, Neville, Ferdinand, Vidic, Silvestre, Ronaldo (Park 82), Carrick, Scholes, O'Shea, Larsson (Smith 73), Rooney (Richardson 82).

QUARTER-FINALS, FIRST LEG

April 3, 2007
AC Milan 2 (Pirlo 40, Kaka 84 pen), **Bayern Munich** 2 (Van Buyten 78, 90). Att: 77,700.
PSV Eindhoven 0, **Liverpool** 3 (Gerrard 27, Riise 49, Crouch 63). Att: 36,500.
Liverpool (4-4-2): Reina, Finnan, Carragher, Agger, Aurelio (Gonzalez 75), Gerrard, Mascherano, Xabi Alonso, Riise (Zenden 66), Crouch (Pennant 85), Kuyt.

April 4, 2007
Chelsea 1 (Drogba 53), **Valencia** 1 (Silva 30). Att: 38,065.
Chelsea (4-4-2): Cech, Diarra, Terry, Ricardo Carvalho, A. Cole, Kalou (Wright-Phillips 74), Ballack, Lampard, Mikel (J. Cole 74), Drogba, Shevchenko.
Roma 2 (Taddei 44, Vucinic 67), **Manchester Utd.** 1 (Rooney 60). Att: 77,000.
Manchester Utd. (4-4-1-1): Van der Sar, O'Shea, Ferdinand, Brown, Heinze, Ronaldo, Carrick, Scholes, Giggs (Saha 76), Rooney, Solskjaer (Fletcher 71).

QUARTER-FINALS, SECOND LEG

April 10, 2007
Manchester Utd. 7 (Carrick 11, 60, Smith 17, Rooney 19, Ronaldo 44, 49, Evra 81), **Roma** 1 (De Rossi 69). Att: 74,476 (**Manchester Utd.** won 8-3 on agg).
Manchester Utd. (4-4-2): Van der Sar, O'Shea (Evra 53), Ferdinand, Brown, Heinze, Ronaldo, Fletcher, Carrick (Richardson 72), Giggs (Solskjaer 60), Rooney, Smith.
Valencia 1 (Morientes 32), **Chelsea** 2 (Shevchenko 52, Essien 90). Att: 53,000 (**Chelsea** won 3-2 on agg).
Chelsea (4-1-3-2): Cech, Diarra (J. Cole 46), Ricardo Carvalho, Terry, A. Cole, Mikel, Essien, Lampard (Makelele 90), Ballack, Drogba, Shevchenko (Kalou 90).

April 11, 2007
Bayern Munich 0, **AC Milan** 2 (Seedorf 27, Inzaghi 31). Att: 65,000 (**AC Milan** won 4-2 on agg).
Liverpool 1 (Crouch 68), **PSV Eindhoven** 0. Att: 41,447 (**Liverpool** won 4-0 on agg).
Liverpool (4-4-2): Reina, Arbeloa, Hyypia, Agger (Paletta 78), Riise, Pennant, Sissoko, Xabi Alonso (Gonzalez 71), Zenden, Crouch, Bellamy (Fowler 16).

SEMI-FINALS, FIRST LEG

April 24, 2007
Manchester Utd. 3 (Ronaldo 6, Rooney 59, 90), **AC Milan** 2 (Kaka 22, 37). Att: 73,820.
Manchester Utd. (4-2-3-1): Van der Sar, O'Shea, Brown, Heinze, Evra, Fletcher, Carrick, Ronaldo, Scholes, Giggs, Rooney.

April 25, 2007
Chelsea 1 (J. Cole 29), **Liverpool** 0. Att: 39,483.
Chelsea (4-1-3-2): Cech, Paulo Ferreira, Ricarado Carvalho, Terry, A. Cole, Makelele, Mikel, Lampard, J. Cole (Wright-Phillips 84), Drogba, Shevchenko (Kalou 75).
Liverpool (4-4-2): Reina, Arbeloa, Carragher, Agger, Riise, Gerrard, Mascherano, Xabi Alonso (Pennant 83), Zenden, Kuyt, Bellamy (Crouch 52).

SEMI-FINALS, SECOND LEG

May 1, 2007
Liverpool 1 (Agger 22), **Chelsea** 0. Att: 42,554 (aet, agg 1-1, **Liverpool** won 4-1 on pens).
Liverpool (4-4-2): Reina, Finnan, Carragher, Agger, Riise, Pennant (Xabi Alonso 78), Gerrard, Mascherano (Fowler 118), Zenden, Kuyt, Crouch (Bellamy 105).
Chelsea (4-1-3-2): Cech, Paulo Ferreira, Essien, Terry, A. Cole, Makelele (Geremi 118), Mikel, Lampard, J. Cole (Robben 98), Drogba, Kalou (Wright-Phillips 107).

May 2, 2007
AC Milan 3 (Kaka 11, Seedorf 30, Gilardino 78), **Manchester Utd.** 0. Att: 78,500 (**AC Milan** won 5-3 on agg).
Manchester Utd. (4-2-3-1): Van der Sar, O'Shea (Saha 76), Brown, Vidic, Heinze, Fletcher, Carrick, Giggs, Scholes, Ronaldo, Rooney.

FINAL

AC MILAN 2, LIVERPOOL 1

Athens (67,000), Wedenesday, May 23, 2007

AC Milan (4-3-2-1): Dida, Oddo, Nesta, Maldini (capt), Jankulovski (Kaladze 79), Gattuso, Pirlo, Ambrosini, Seedorf (Favalli 90), Kaka, Inzaghi (Gilardino 88). **Subs not used:** Brocchi, Cafu, Serginho. **Scorer:** Inzaghi (45, 82). **Booked:** Gattuso, Jankulovski. **Coach:** Carlo Ancelotti.

Liverpool (4-4-1-1): Reina, Finnan (Arbeloa 88), Carragher, Agger, Riise, Pennant, Xabi Alonso, Mascherano (Crouch 78), Zenden (Kewell 57), Gerrard (capt), Kuyt. **Scorer:** Kuyt (89). **Booked:** Mascherano, Carragher. **Manager:** Rafael Benitez.

Referee: H. Fandel (Germany). **Half-time:** 1-0.

Same opponents, different result and plenty of soul-searching – that was the bottom line for Liverpool in a repeat of the 2005 Final. The drama of Istanbul was never likely to be recreated in Athens, but there was certainly plenty of controversy surrounding Milan's win and the organisation of the final itself.

For Filippo Inzaghi it provided the ultimate high, two years after he had suffered a massive low while sitting injured on the touchline as his team blew a three-goal lead, then lost in a penalty shoot-out. There was some luck involved, too, as the opening goal flew in off his arm after he inadvertently ran in front of an Andrea Pirlo free-kick just before half-time.

Until that point, Liverpool had enjoyed the majority of possession, but they failed to create any clear-cut chances or force goalkeeper Dida into making a decent save. After the heroics of 2005, a single-goal deficit seemed simple enough to overturn, but the Italians were in no mood to let another lead slip and, as Liverpool went for broke chasing the game, Inzaghi accepted an 82nd minute through ball from Kaka to apply a cool finish past Jose Reina.

Dirk Kuyt set up a tense finish by heading home in the 89th minute, but Liverpool could not fashion another sensational comeback, although Rafael Benitez was visibly fuming with the referee for failing to play the full amount of injury-time. As Paolo Maldini lifted the trophy, there were more dissenting voices questioning whether Milan – who after being caught up in the Italian match-fixing scandal had initially been banned from the Champions League – should have been allowed to compete in the tournament at all.

But the biggest row concerned UEFA's role in ugly scenes outside the ground before kick-off that saw hundreds of fans with tickets refused entry and, in some cases, attacked by police with tear gas. The governing body claimed the problem was largely caused by Liverpool fans with forged tickets, who had already filled the ground, but UEFA had reportedly been warned about that possibility weeks before and they were widely criticised for failing to provide adequate security at a stadium that some argued was ill-equipped to deal with a big European match.

There had already been plenty of complaints about the allocation of tickets for the big game, with both clubs being given only 17,000 each, despite the stadium holding 67,000 for the final. UEFA's 'Football Family' received the rest, much to the fury of fans on Merseyside.

FINAL FACTS AND FIGURES

* Milan's starting line-up was the oldest in the history of the European Cup/Champions League Final – an average age of 31 years, 34 days.

* Paolo Maldini was the oldest captain at 38 years, 331 days.

* Clarence Seedorf collected a fourth winners' medal, two with Milan, one with Ajax and another with Real Madrid.

* Carlo Ancelotti has also won the trophy four times – twice as Milan coach and twice as a player for the club.

* Italian clubs have now won the competition 11 times, equalling Spain's total and moving ahead of England's ten. Milan also moved to within two victories of Real Madrid's record of nine.

* Liverpool's five previous triumphs had come in red shirts against a team wearing white. This time the sequence was broken.

* They are now 2-2 in terms of finals against Italian opposition, having beaten Roma (1984) and Milan (2005) and lost to Juventus (1985).

* Only five players, Steve Finnan, Jamie Carragher, John Arne Riise, Xabi Alonso and Steven Gerrard, were in the Liverpool starting line-up for both the 2005 and 2007 finals.

* Dirk Kuyt became the first Dutch player to score in the final since Patrick Kluivert netted the only goal of the game for Ajax against AC Milan in 1995.

Leading scorers (from group stage): 10 Kaka (AC Milan), 6 Crouch (Liverpool), Drogba (Chelsea), Morientes (Valencia), Van Nistelrooy (Real Madrid); 5 Raul (Real Madrid); 4 Dica (Steaua Bucharest), Inzaghi (AC Milan), Pizarro (Bayern Munich), Rooney (Manchester Utd.), Saha (Manchester Utd.), Totti (Roma), Villa (Valencia).

EUROPEAN CUP FINALS

1956 Real Madrid 4, Reims 3 (Paris)
1957 Real Madrid 2, Fiorentina 0 (Madrid)
1958† Real Madrid 3, AC Milan 2 (Brussels)
1959 Real Madrid 2, Reims 0 (Stuttgart)
1960 Real Madrid 7, Eintracht Frankfurt 3 (Glasgow)
1961 Benfica 3, Barcelona 2 (Berne)
1962 Benfica 5, Real Madrid 3 (Amsterdam)
1963 AC Milan 2, Benfica 1 (Wembley)
1964 Inter Milan 3, Real Madrid 1 (Vienna)
1965 Inter Milan 1, Benfica 0 (Milan)
1966 Real Madrid 2, Partizan Belgrade 1 (Brussels)
1967 Celtic 2, Inter Milan 1 (Lisbon)
1968† Manchester Utd. 4, Benfica 1 (Wembley)
1969 AC Milan 4, Ajax 1 (Madrid)
1970† Feyenoord 2, Celtic 1 (Milan)
1971 Ajax 2, Panathinaikos 0 (Wembley)
1972 Ajax 2, Inter Milan 0 (Rotterdam)
1973 Ajax 1, Juventus 0 (Belgrade)
1974 Bayern Munich 4, Atletico Madrid 0 (replay Brussels, after a 1-1 draw, Brussels)
1975 Bayern Munich 2, Leeds Utd. 0 (Paris)
1976 Bayern Munich 1, St. Etienne 0 (Glasgow)
1977 Liverpool 3, Borussia Moenchengladbach 1 (Rome)
1978 Liverpool 1, Brugge 0 (Wembley)

1979 Nott'm. Forest 1, Malmo 0 (Munich)
1980 Nott'm. Forest 1, Hamburg 0 (Madrid)
1981 Liverpool 1, Real Madrid 0 (Paris)
1982 Aston Villa 1, Bayern Munich 0 (Rotterdam)
1983 SV Hamburg 1, Juventus 0 (Athens)
1984† Liverpool 1, AS Roma 1 (Liverpool won 4-2 on penalties) (Rome)
1985 Juventus 1, Liverpool 0 (Brussels)
1986† Steaua Bucharest 0, Barcelona 0 (Steaua won 2-0 on penalties) (Seville)
1987 Porto 2, Bayern Munich 1 (Vienna)
1988† PSV Eindhoven 0, Benfica 0 (PSV won 6-5 on penalties) (Stuttgart)
1989 AC Milan 4, Steaua Bucharest 0 (Barcelona)
1990 AC Milan 1, Benfica 0 (Vienna)
1991† Red Star Belgrade 0, Marseille 0 (Red Star won 5-3 on penalties) (Bari)
1992 Barcelona 1, Sampdoria 0 (Wembley)
1993 Marseille 1, AC Milan 0 (Munich)
1994 AC Milan 4, Barcelona 0 (Athens)
1995 Ajax 1, AC Milan 0 (Vienna)
1996† Juventus 1, Ajax 1 (Juventus won 4-2 on penalties) (Rome)
1997 Borussia Dortmund 3, Juventus 1 (Munich)
1998 Real Madrid 1, Juventus 0 (Amsterdam)
1999 Manchester Utd. 2, Bayern Munich 1 (Barcelona)
2000 Real Madrid 3, Valencia 0 (Paris)
2001 Bayern Munich 1, Valencia 1 (Bayern Munich won 5-4 on penalties) (Milan)
2002 Real Madrid 2, Bayer Leverkusen 1 (Glasgow)
2003† AC Milan 0, Juventus 0 (AC Milan won 3-2 on penalties) (Manchester)
2004 FC Porto 3, Monaco 0 (Gelsenkirchen)
2005† Liverpool 3, AC Milan 3 (Liverpool won 3-2 on penalties) (Istanbul)
2006 Barcelona 2, Arsenal 1 (Paris)
2007 AC Milan 2, Liverpool 1 (Athens)

(† After extra time)

GILBERTO'S RECORD GOES

Arsenal's Gilberto Silva lost his record as the Champions League's fastest scorer – 20 seconds against PSV Eindhoven in 2002 – when Roy Makaay netted for Bayern Munich in half that time last season against Real Madrid.

ALL FOREIGN FOR ARSENAL

Arsenal's multi-national team twice broke new ground in the Champions League last season. When London-born Justin Hoyte replaced Kolo Toure in a group victory in Hamburg, it was the first time a side had fielded 11 players of different nationalities. Their line-up after the substitution was: Lehmann (Germany), Eboue (Ivory Coast), Djourou (Switzerland), Hoyte (England), Gallas (France), Hleb (Belarus), Fabregas (Spain), Gilberto Silva (Brazil), Rosicky (Czech Republic), Van Persie (Holland), Adebayor (Togo). Later in the season, in a first knock-out round game, Arsenal and PSV Eindhoven had a record 21 foreign players in their starting line-ups. The exception was Eindhoven's Dutch midfielder Phillip Cocu.

UEFA CUP 2006-07

PRE-TOURNAMENT INTERTOTO CUP (SELECTED RESULTS)

FIRST ROUND

Keflavik 4, **Dungannon** 1 (4-1h, 0-0a); **Shelbourne** 5, Vetra 0 (4-0h, 1-0a); Tampere 8, **Carmarthen** 1 (5-0h, 3-1a).

SECOND ROUND

Hibernian 8, Dinaburg 0 (5-0h, 3-0a); Odense 3, **Shelbourne** 1 (3-0h, 0-1a).

THIRD ROUND

First leg: Newcastle Utd. 1 (Luque 50), Lillestrom 1 (Koren 24). Att: 31,059. Odense 1 (Sorensen 33 pen), **Hibernian** 0. Att: 2,341. **Second leg: Hibernian** 2 (Jones 51, Dalglish 79). Odense 1 (Grahn 50). Att: 10,640 (agg 2-2, Odense won on away goal). Lillestrom 0, **Newcastle Utd.** 3 (Ameobi 29, 36, Emre 90). Att: 8,742 (**Newcastle Utd.** won 4-1 on agg).

FIRST QUALIFYING ROUND, FIRST LEG

Gefle 1 (Viikmae 24), **Llanelli** 2 (Griffiths 82, Mingorance 87); **Glentoran** 0, Brann 1 (Memelli 69); Gothenburg 0, **Derry City** 1 (Hargan 80); HJK Helsinki 1 (Halsti 83), **Drogheda** 1 (Robinson 41); **Portadown** 1 (McCutcheon 65), Kaunas 3 (Manchkhava 2, Pehlic 9, Velicka 46); **Rhyl** 0, Suduva 0.

FIRST QUALIFYING ROUND, SECOND LEG

Brann 1 (Bjarnason 85 pen), **Glentoran** 0 (Brann won 2-0 on agg); **Derry** 1 (O'Flynn 32 pen), Gothenburg 0 (**Derry City** won 2-0 on agg); **Drogheda** 3 (Gartland 57, Lynch 96, 114), HJK Helsinki 1 (Ghazi 36) (aet, **Drogheda** won 4-2 on agg); Kaunas 1 (Ivaskevicius 43), **Portadown** 0 (Kaunas won 4-1 on agg); **Llanelli** 0, Gefle 0 (**Llanelli** won 2-1 on agg); Suduva 2 (Maciulevicius 18 pen, Mikuckis 25), **Rhyl** 1 (Grigas 80 og) (Suduva won 2-1 on agg).

FIRST QUALIFYING ROUND, ON AGGREGATE

Ameri Tbilisi 2, Banants Yerevan 2 (Ameri Tbilisi won on away goal); Apoel Nicosia 7, Murata 1; Artmedia Bratislava 3, Georgia Tbilisi 2; Atvidabergs 7, Etzella Ettelbruk 0; Basle 3, Tobol Kostanay 1; BATE 3, Nistru Otaci 0; Brondby 3, Valur Reykjavik 1; CSKA Sofia 5, Dinamo Tirana 1; Dinamo Bucharest 9, Hibernians 1; Dinamo Minsk 1, Zaglebie Lubin 1 (Dinamo Minski won on away goal); Domzale 7, Orasje 0; Fehervar 2, Kairat Almaty 2 (Feherva won on away goal; Flora Tallinn 1, Lyn Oslo 1 (Flora Tallinn won on away goal); IK Start 4, Skala 0; Karvan Evlakh 2, Spartak Trnava 0; Levadia Tallinn 2, Haka 1; Liteks Lovetch 6, Koper 0; Lokomotiv Sofia 3, Makedonija 1; Omonia Nicosia 4, Rijeka 3; Randers 2, Akranes 2 (Randers won on away goal); Rapid Bucharest 6, Sliema 0; Roeselare 7, Vardar 2; Sarajevo 5, Ranger's 0; Skonto Riga 5, Jeunesse Esch 0; SK Tirana 3, Varteks 1; Vaduz 4, Ujpest 1; Ventspils 4, Gota 1; Young Boys 4, Mika Ashtarak 1; Zimbru 3, Karabakh Azersun 2.

SECOND QUALIFYING ROUND, FIRST LEG

Gretna 1 (McGuffie 12), **Derry City** 5 (Kelly 22, Deery 54, 56, Martyn 63, 75). Att: 6,040. IK Start 1 (Stramstad 67), **Drogheda** 0. Att: 1,433. Odense 1 (Oliveira 30), **Llanelli** 0. Att: 2,000. Ventspils 0, **Newcastle Utd.** 1 (Bramble 70). Att: 6,000.

SECOND QUALIFYING ROUND, SECOND LEG

Derry 2 (Farren 37, Oman 69), **Gretna** 2 (Graham 17, Baldacchino 77). Att: 2,850 (**Derry** won 7-3 on agg). **Drogheda** 1 (Zayed 84), IK Start 0. Att: 4,154 (aet, agg 1-1, IK Start won 11-10 on pens). **Llanelli** 1 (Corbisiero 10), Odense 5 (Timm 15, Hansen 34, Christensen 59, Ophaug 65, Oliveira 90). Att: 2,759 (Odense won 6-1 on agg). **Newcastle Utd.** 0, Ventspils 0. Att: 30,498 (**Newcastle Utd.** won 1-0 on agg).

SECOND QUALIFYING ROUND, ON AGGREGATE

Artmedia Bratislava 5, Dinamo Minsk 3; Atvidabergs 4, Brann 4 (Atvidabergs won on away goals); Auxerre 5, OFK Belgrade 2; Basle 2, Vaduz 2 (Basle won on away goals); Brondby 4, Flora Tallinn 0; Club Bruges 7, Suduva 2; CSKA Sofia 1, Hajduk Kula 1 (CSKA Sofia won on away goal); Dinamo Bucharest 2, Beitar Jerusalem 1; Ethnikos Achnas 6, Roeselare 2; Grasshoppers 3, Videoton 1; Hapoel Tel-Aviv 4, Domzale 2; Hertha Berlin 3, Ameri Tbilisi 2; Kaunas 1, Randers 0; Kayserispor 5, Tirana 1; Levadia Tallinn 2, FC Twente 1; Liteks Lovetch 2, Omonia Nicosia 1; Lokomotiv Sofia 6, Bnei Yehuda 0; Marseille 3, Young Boys 3 (Marseille won on away goals); Metallurg 3, Zimbru 3 (metallurg won on away goals); Molde 2, Skonto Riga 1; Partizan Belgrade 3, Maribor 2; Rapid Bucharest 2, Sarajevo 1; Rubin Kazan 5, BATE 0; Slavia Prague 2, Karvan Evlakh 0; Sion 1, Ried 0; Trabzonspor 2, Apoel Nicosia 1; Wisla Krakow 2, Mattersburg 1; Chornomorets 1, Wisla Plock 1 (Chornomorets won on away goal).

FIRST ROUND, FIRST LEG

Derry City 0, Paris St-Germain 0. Att 3,000. **Hearts** 0, Sparta Prague 2 (Kolar 34, Matusovic 71. Att: 27,255 (at Murrayfield). Levadia Tallinn 0, **Newcastle Utd.** 1 (Sibierski 10). Att: 7,917. Molde 0, **Rangers** 0. Att: 6,569. Salzburg 2 (Zickler 30, Janko 90), **Blackburn Rov.** 2 (Savage 32, McCarthy 39). Att: 17,000. Slavia Prague 0, **Tottenham** 1 (Jenas 37). Att: 14,869. **West Ham Utd.** 0, Palermo 1 (Caracciolo 45). Att: 32,222.

FIRST ROUND, SECOND LEG

Blackburn Rov. 2 (McCarthy 32, Bentley 56), Salzburg 0. Att: 18,888 (**Blackburn Rov.** won 4-2 on agg). **Newcaste Utd.** 2 (Martins 47, 50), Levadia Tallinn 1 (Zelinski 65). Att: 27,012 (**Newcastle Utd.** won 3-1 on agg). Palermo 3 (Simplicio 35, 62, Di Michele 68), **West Ham Utd.** 0. Att: 19,284 (Palermo won 4-0 on agg). Paris St-Germain 2 (Cisse 6, Pauleta 41), **Derry City** 0. Att: 7,000 (Paris St-Germain won 2-0 on agg). **Rangers** 2 (Buffel 12, Ferguson 45), Molde 0. Att: 48,024 (**Rangers** won 2-0 on agg). Sparta Prague 0, **Hearts** 0. Att: 16,505 (Sparta Prague won 2-0 on agg). **Tottenham** 1 (Keane 80), Slavia Prague 0. Att: 35,191 (**Tottenham** won 2-0 on agg).

FIRST ROUND, ON AGGREGATE

Ajax 9, IK Start 2; Austria Magna 2, Legia Warsaw 1; Auxerre 5, Dinamo Zagreb 2; AZ Alkmaar 4, Kayserispor 3; Basle 7, Rabotnicki 2; Bayer Leverkusen 3, Sion 1; Besiktas 2, CSKA Sofia 2 (Besiktas won on away goal); Braga 3, Chievo 2; Celta Vigo 4, Standard Liege 0; Club Bruges 2, Ruzomberok 1; Dinamo Bucharest 8, Xanthi 4; Eintracht Frankfurt 6, Brondby 2; Espanyol 5, Artmedia Bratislava 3; Fenerbahce 5, Randers 1;

Feyenoord 2, Lokomotiv Sofia 2 (Feyenoord won on away goals); Grasshoppers 8, Atvidabergs 0; Hapoel Tel-Aviv 4, Chornomorets 1; Heerenveen 3, Vitoria Setubal 0; Lens 3, Ethnikos 1; Liberec 4, Crvena Zvezda 1; Livorno 3, Superfund 0; Maccabi Haifa 4, Liteks Lovetch 2; Mlada Boleslav 4, Marseille 3; Nancy 3, Schalke 2; Odense 3, Hertha Berlin 2; Osasuna 2, Trabzonspor 2 (Osasuna won on away goals); Panathinaikos 2, Metallurg 1; Parma 2, Rubin Kazan 0; Partizan Belgrade 4, Groningen 3; Rapid Bucharest 3, Nacional 1; Sevilla 6, Atromitos 1; Wisla Krakow 2, Iraklis 1; Zulte-Waregem 3, Lokomotiv Moscow 2.

GROUP STAGE

GROUP A

Match-day 1: Liverno 2 (Lucarelli 34 pen, 90), **Rangers** 3 (Adam 27, Boyd 30 pen, Novo 35). Att: 13,200. Maccabi Haifa 3 (Masudi 13, Boccoli 56, Colautti 58), Auxerre 1 (Niculae 29). Att: 13,500.

Match-day 2: Partizan Belgrade 1 (Mirosavljevic 70), Livorno 1 (Amelia 88). Att: 12,170. **Rangers** 2 (Novo 5, Adam 89 pen), Maccabi Haifa 0. Att: 43,062.

Match-day 3: Auxerre 2 (Jelen 31, Niculae 75), **Rangers** 2 (Novo 62, Boyd 84). Att: 8,305. Maccabi Haifa 1 (Anderson 21), Partizan Belgrade 0. Att: 13,500.

Match-day 4: Livorno 1 (Lucarelli 20), Maccabi Haifa 1 (Colautti 90). Att: 7,874. Partizan Belgrade 1 (Marinkovic 20), Auxerre 4 (Cheyrou 18, Niculae 24, Akale 36, Pieroni 82). Att: 7,000.

Match-day 5: Auxerre 0, Livorno 1 (Lucarelli 59). Att: 4,313. **Rangers** 1 (Hutton 55), Partizan Belgrade 0. Att: 45,129.

FINAL TABLE

	P	*W*	*D*	*L*	*F*	*A*	*Pts*
RANGERS	4	3	1	0	8	4	10
MACCABI HAIFA	4	2	1	1	5	4	7
LIVORNO	4	1	2	1	5	5	5
Auxerre	4	1	1	2	7	7	4
Partizan Belgrade	4	0	1	3	2	7	1

GROUP B

Match-day 1: Besiktas 0, **Tottenham** 2 (Ghaly 32, Berbatov 63). Att: 26,800. Club Bruges 1 (Clement 47), Bayer Leverkusen 1 (Schneider 35). Att: 17,789.

Match-day 2: Dinamo Bucharest 2 (Cristea 21, Niculescu 87 pen), Besiktas 1 (Bobo 58). Att: 12,000. **Tottenham** 3 (Berbatov 17, 73, Keane 63), Club Bruges 1 (Ibrahim 14). Att: 35,716.

Match-day 3: Bayer Leverkusen 0, **Tottenham** 1 (Berbatov 36). Att: 22,500. Club Bruges 1 (Vermant 62 pen), Dinamo Bucharest 1 (Niculescu 33). Att: 18,713.

Match-day 4: Besiktas 2 (Akin 32, Ricardinho 70 pen), Club Bruges 1 (Balaban 14 pen). Att: 19,668. Dinamo Bucharest 2 (Niculescu 37, 74), Bayer Leverkusen 1 (Barbarez 22). Att: 12,000.

Match-day 5: Bayer Leverkusen 2 (Schneider 78, Barbarez 87), Besiktas 1 (Ricardinho 90 pen). Att: 22,500. **Tottenham** 3 (Berbatov 16, Defoe 39, 50), Dinamo Bucharest 1 (Mendy 90). Att: 34,004.

FINAL TABLE

	P	W	D	L	F	A	Pts
TOTTENHAM	4	4	0	0	9	2	12
DIN. BUCHAREST	4	2	1	1	6	6	7
B. LEVERKUSEN	4	1	1	2	4	5	4
Besiktas	4	1	0	3	4	7	3
Club Bruges	4	0	2	2	4	7	2

GROUP C

Match-day 1: AZ Alkmaar 3 (Arveladze 37, Koevermans 75, Schaars 82), Braga 0. Att: 13,893. Liberec 0, Sevilla 0. Att: 7,023.

Match-day 2: Braga 4 (Ricardo Chaves 30, Marcel 33,Cesinha 54 pen, Bruno Gama 90), Liberec 0. Att: 15,000. Grasshoppers 2 (Biscotte 29, Eduardo 62), AZ Alkmaar 5 (Arveladze 48, De Zeeuw 56, Dembele 78, 90, Martens 90). Att: 5,500.

Match-day 3: Liberec 4 (Blazek 7, Zapotocny 21, Papousek 68, Frejlach 90), Grasshoppers 1 (Schwegler 9). Att: 6,670. Sevilla 2 (Luis Fabiano 40, Chevanton 76), Sporting Braga 0. Att: 37,000.

Match-day 4: AZ Alkmaar 2 (Steinsson 69, Jenner 89), Liberec 2 (Zapotocny 26, Papousek 85). Att: 16,000. Grasshoppers 0, Sevilla 4 (Daniel 12, 53, Chevanton 62, Kepa 84). Att: 7,300.

Match-day 5: Braga 2 (Joao Pinto 61, Castanheira 90), Grasshoppers 0. Att: 15,000. Sevilla 1 (Chevanton 52 pen), AZ Alkmaar 2 (Arveladze 62, 90). Att: 33,500.

FINAL TABLE

	P	W	D	L	F	A	Pts
AZ ALKMAAR	4	3	1	0	12	5	10
SEVILLA	4	2	1	1	7	2	7
BRAGA	4	2	0	2	6	5	6
Liberec	4	1	2	1	6	7	5
Grasshoppers	4	0	0	4	3	15	0

GROUP D

Match-day 1: Odense 1 (Hansen 7), Parma 2 (Dessena 41, Budan 51). Att: 12,559. Osasuna 0, Heerenveen 0. Att: 20,000.

Match-day 2: Heerenveen 0, Odense 2 (Lekic 45, 60). Att: 17,500. Lens 3 (Dindane 15, Cousin 74 pen, Boukari 88), Osasuna 1 (Valdo 80). Att: 33,833.

Match-day 3: Odense 1 (Grahn 58), Lens 1 (Jomaa 87). Att: 7,707. Parma 2 (Budan 24, 73), Heerenveen 1 (Pranjic 21). Att: 3,632.

Match-day 4: Lens 1 (Cousin 19), Parma 2 (Dedic 77, Paponi 90). Att: 32,341. Osasuna 3 (Punal 29, 67, Romeo 87), Odense 1 (Punal 75 og). Att: 13,000.

Match-day 5: Heerenveen 1 (Alves 90), Lens 0. Att: 23,000. Parma 0, Osasuna 3 (Lopez 33, 44, Juanfran 82). Att: 3,109.

FINAL TABLE

	P	W	D	L	F	A	Pts
PARMA	4	3	0	1	6	6	9
OSASUNA	4	2	1	1	7	4	7
LENS	4	1	1	2	5	5	4
Odense	4	1	1	2	5	6	4
Heerenveen	4	1	1	2	2	4	4

GROUP E

Match-day 1: Basle 1 (Eduardo 60), Feyenoord 1 (Huysegems 76). Att: 15,428. Wislaw Krakow 1 (Cantoro 28), **Blackburn Rov.** 2 (Savage 56, Bentley 90). Att: 14,000.

Match-day 2: Blackburn Rov. 3 (Tugay 75, Jeffers 89 pen, McCarthy 90), Basle 0. Att: 13,789. Nancy 2 (Berenguer 11, 58), Wisla Krakow 1 (Brozek 32). Att: 17,509.

Match-day 3: Basle 2 (Chipperfield 32, Sterjovski 56), Nancy 2 (Kim 31, Berenguer 34). Att: 14,497. Feyenoord 0, **Blackburn Rov.** 0. Att: 35,000.

Match-day 4: Nancy 3 (Puygrenier 22, Kim 42, Zerka 66 pen), Feyenoord 0. Att: 19,047. Wisla Krakow 3 (Brozek 11, 83, Paulista 71), Basle 1 (Petric 8). Att: 5,000.

Match-day 5: Blackburn Rov. 1 (Neill 90), Nancy 0. Att: 12,568. Feyenoord 3 (Hofs 16, De Guzman 41, Charisteas 67), Wisla Krakow 1 (Brozek 23). Att: 25,000.

FINAL TABLE

	P	*W*	*D*	*L*	*F*	*A*	*Pts*
BLACKBURN ROV.	4	3	1	0	6	1	10
NANCY	4	2	1	1	7	4	7
FEYENOORD	4	1	2	1	4	5	5
Wiska Krakow	4	1	0	3	6	8	3
Basle	4	0	2	2	4	9	2

GROUP F

Match-day 2: Austria Magna 1 (Lasnik 22), Zulte-Waregem 4 (Matthys 33, 56, 69, Van Den Driessche 90). Att: 11,100. Sparta Prague 0, Espanyol 2 (Luis Garcia 17 pen, Riera 85). Att: 11,020.

Match-day 2: Ajax 3 (Huntelaar 35, 68, Manucharyan 65), Austria Magner 0. Att: 32,285. Zulte-Waregem 3 (Roussel 4, Meert 17, Sergeant 63), Sparta Prague 1 (Lustinelli 85). Att: 6,000.

Match-day 3: Espanyol 6 (Coro 9, Pandiani 14, 83, Luis Garcia 19, 27 pen, 73), Zulte-Waregem 2 (Matthys 17, D'Haene 62). Sparta Prague 0, Ajax 0. Att: 12,000.

Match-day 4: Ajax 0, Espanyol 2 (Pandiani 36, Coro 78). Att: 41,248. Austria Magna 0, Sparta Prague 1 (Repka 11). Att: 8,600.

Match-day 5: Espanyol 1 (Pandiani 57), Austria Vienna 0. Att: 5,580. Zulte-Waregem 0, Ajax 3 (Huntelaar 4, 57, Heitinga 83). Att: 11,603.

FINAL TABLE

	P	*W*	*D*	*L*	*F*	*A*	*Pts*
ESPANYOL	4	4	0	0	11	2	12
AJAX	4	2	1	1	6	2	7
ZULTE-WAREGEM	4	2	0	2	9	11	6
Sparta Prague	4	1	1	2	2	5	4
Austria Vienna	4	0	0	4	1	9	0

GROUP G

Match-day 1: Panathinaikos 2 (Tel Chen 47 og, Romero 64), Hapoel Tel-Aviv 0. Att: 100. Rapid Bucharest 0, Paris St-Germain 0. Att: 15,000.

Match-day 2: Hapoel Tel-Aviv 2 (Ogbona 10, Badir 33), Rapid Bucharest 2 (Moldovan 14, Buga 53). Att: 12,000. Mlada Boleslav 0, Panathinaikos 1 (Salpigidis 64). Att: 4,280.

Match-day 3: Paris St-Germain 2 (Frau 14, Pauleta 25), Hapoel Tel-Aviv 4 (Toama 2, 6, Badir 44, Barda 57). Att: 35,000. Rapid Bucharest 1 (Constantin 52), Mlada Boleslav 1 (Rajnoch 42). Att: 6,600.

Match-day 4: Mlada Boleslav 0, Paris St-Germain 0. Att: 8,480. Panathinaikos 0, Rapid Bucharest 0. Att: 18,000.

Match-day 5: Hapoel Tel-Aviv 1 (Barda 27), Mlada Boleslav 1 (Kysela 39). Att: 8,000. Paris St-Germain 4 (Pauleta 29, 47, Kalou 52, 54), Panathinaikos 0. Att: 22,000.

FINAL TABLE

	P	*W*	*D*	*L*	*F*	*A*	*Pts*
PANATHINIAKOS	4	2	1	1	3	4	7
PARIS SG	4	1	2	1	6	4	5
HAPOEL TEL-AVIV	4	1	2	1	7	7	5
Rapid Bucharest	4	0	4	0	3	3	4
Mlada Boleslav	4	0	3	1	2	3	3

GROUP H

Match-day 1: Eintracht Frankfurt 1 (Streit 45), Palermo 2 (Brienza 50, Zaccardo 88). Att: 50,000. **Newcastle Utd.** 1 (Sibierski 79), Fenerbahce 0. Att: 30,035.

Match-day 2: Celta Vigo 1 (Jesue Perera 11), Eintracht Frankfurt 1 (Huber 17). Att: 10,000. Palermo 0, **Newcastle Utd.**1 (Luque 37). Att: 16,904.

Match-day 3: Fenerbahce 3 (Appiah 20, Lugano 62, Sanli 83), Palermo 0. Att: 39,071. **Newcastle Utd.** 2 (Sibierski 37, Taylor 86), Celta Vigo 1 (Canobbio 9). Att: 25,079.

Match-day 4: Celta Vigo 1 (Canobbio 77), Fenerbahce 0. Att: 12,000. Eintracht Frankfurt 0, **Newcastle Utd.** 0. Att: 47,000.

Match-day 5: Fenerbahce 2 (Sanli 64, Senturk 83), Eintracht Frankfurt 2 (Takara 7, 52). Att: 44,123. Palermo 1 (Tedesco 70), Celta Vigo 1 (Baiano 59). Att: 10,222.

FINAL TABLE

	P	*W*	*D*	*L*	*F*	*A*	*Pts*
NEWCASTLE UTD.	4	3	1	0	4	1	10
CELTA VIGO	4	1	2	1	4	4	5
FENERBAHCE	4	1	1	2	5	4	4
Palermo	4	1	1	2	3	6	4
Eintracht Frankfurt	4	0	3	1	4	5	3

ROUND OF 32

FIRST LEG

AEK Athens 0, Paris St-Germain 2 (Traore 45, Mendy 88). Att: 26,120. Bayer Leverkusen 3 (Callsen-Bracker 18, Ramelow 43, Schneider 56), **Blackburn Rov.** 2 (Bentley 39, Nonda 86). Att: 22,500. Benfica 1 (Miccoli 90), Dinamo Bucharest 0. 35,000. Bordeaux 0, Osasuna 0. Att: 16,029. Braga 1 (Ze Carlos 81), Parma 0. Att: 6,046. CSKA Moscow 0, Maccabi Haifa 0. Att: 18,102. Fenerbahce 3 (Metin 28, 75, Sanli 67), AZ Alkmaar 3 (De Zeeuw 15, Boukhari 62, Jenner 63). Att: 42,000. Hapoel Tel-Aviv 2 (Toama 43, Dago 76), **Rangers** 1 (Novo 53). Att: 13,000. Lens 3 (Jomaa 49, 70, Dindane 90 pen), Panathinaikos 1 (Salpigidis 65). Att: 29,449. Liverno 1 (Galante 82), Espanyol 2 (Pandiani 28 pen, Moha 59). Att: 15,000. Shakhtar Donetsk 1 (Srna 82), Nancy 1 (Fortune 81). Att: 45,000. Spartak Moscow 1 (Kalinichenko 64), Celta Vigo 1 (Nunez 41). Att: 30,000. Steaua Bucharest 0, Sevilla 2 (Poulsen 41, Kanoute 77 pen). Att: 30,000. Werder Bremen 3 (Mertesacker 48, Naldo 54, Frings 71), Ajax 0. Att: 37,500. Zulte-Waregem 1 (D'Haene 69), **Newcastle Utd.** 3 (Dindeleux 47 og, Martins 59 pen, Sibierski 76). Att: 8,015.

SECOND LEG

Ajax 3 (Leonardo 4, Huntelaar 60, Babel 74), Werder Bremen 1 (Hugo Almeida 14). Att: 30,000. (Werder Bremen won 4-3 on agg). AZ Alkmaar 2 (Martens 63, Opdam 86), Fenerbahce 2 (Metin 21, Alex 34). Att: 16,191 (Agg 5-5, AZ Alkmaar won on away goals). **Blackburn Rov.** 0, Bayer Leverkusen 0. Att: 25,124 (Bayer Leverkusen won 3-2 on agg). Celta Vigo 2 (Nene 19, Jonathan 78), Spartak Moscow 1 (Titov 88). Att: 8,000 (Celta Vigo won 3-2 on agg). Dinamo Bucharest 1 (Munteanu 23), Benfica 2 (Anderson 50, Katsouranis 64). Att: 15,300 (Benfica won 3-1 on agg). Espanyol 2 (Lacruz 16, Coro 49), Liverno 0. Att: 14,000 (Espanyol won 4-1 on agg). Nancy 0, Shakhtar Donetsk 1 (Fernandinho 70). Att: 17,000 (Shakhtar Donetsk won 2-1 on agg). Maccabi Haifa 1 (Colautti 14), CSKA Moscow 0. Att: 15,000 (Maccabi Haifa won 1-0 on agg). **Newcastle Utd.** 1 (Martins 68), Zulte-Waregem 0. Att: 30,083 (Newcastle Utd. won 4-1 on agg). Osasuna 1 (Nekounam 120), Bordeaux 0. Att: 17,000 (aet, Osasuna won 1-0 on agg). Paris St-Germain 2 (Frau 42, Mendy 90 pen), AEK Athens 0. Att: 30,000 (Paris St-Germain won 4-0 on agg). Panathinaikos 0, Lens 0. Att: 40,914 (Lens won 3-1 on agg). Parma 0, Braga 1 (Diego 89). Att: 3,861 (Braga won 2-0 on agg). **Rangers** 4 (Ferguson 24, 73, Boyd 35, Adam 90), Hapoel Tel-Aviv 0. Att: 46,213 (**Rangers** won 5-2 on agg). Sevilla 1 (Kerzhakov 45), Steaua Bucharest 0. Att: 20,000 (Sevilla won 3-0 on agg). * Bye: Tottenham (Feyenoord expelled for crowd trouble).

ROUND OF 16

FIRST LEG

Braga 2 (Paulo Jorge 76, Ze Carlos 81), **Tottenham** 3 (Keane 57, 90, Malbranque 72). Att: 15,000. Celta Vigo 0, Werder Bremen 1 (Almeida 84). Att: 9,236. Lens 2 (Monterrubio 17, Cousin 70 pen), Bayer Leverkusen 1 (Haggui 51). Att: 29,200. Maccabi Haifa 0, Espanyol 0. Att: 14,700. **Newcastle Utd.** 4 (Steinsson 8 og, Dyer 22, Martins 23, 37), AZ Alkmaar 2 (Arveladze 31, Koevermans 73). Att: 28,452. Paris St-Germain 2 (Pauleta 36, Frau 41), Benfica 1 (Simao 9). Att: 43,000. **Rangers** 1 (Hemdani 90), Osasuna 1 (Raul Garcia 17). Att: 50,290. Sevilla 2 (Marti 8 pen, Maresca 88 pen), Shakhtar Donetsk 2 (Hubschman 19, Matuzalem 60 pen). Att: 20,000.

SECOND LEG

AZ Alkmaar 2 (Arveladze 14, Koevermans 56), **Newcastle Utd.** 0. Att: 16,401 (agg 4-4, AZ Alkmaar won on away goals). Bayer Leverkusen 3 (Voronin 36, Barbarez 56, Juan 70), Lens 0. Att: 22,500 (Bayer Leverkusen won 4-2 on agg). Benfica 3 (Simao 12, 88 pen, Petit 27), Paris St-Germain 0. Att: 40,000 (Benfica won 4-3 on agg). Espanyol 4 (De la Pena 53, Tamudo 59, Luis Garcia 61, Pandiani 90), Maccabi Haifa 0. Att: 16,000 (Espanyol won 4-0 on agg). Osasuna 1 (Webo 71), **Rangers** 0. Att: 35,000 (Osasuna won 2-1 on agg). Shakhtar Donetsk 2 (Matuzalem 49, Elano 83), Sevilla 3 (Maresca 53, Palop 90, Chevanton 105). Att: 45,000 (aet, Sevilla won 5-4 on agg). **Tottenham** 3 (Berbatov 28, 42, Malbranque 76), Braga 2 (Huddlestone 24 og, Amaral 61). Att: 33,761 (**Tottenham** won 6-4 on agg). Werder Bremen 2 (Almeida 48, Fritz 61), Celta Vigo 0. Att: 35,278 (Werder Bremen won 3-0 on agg).

QUARTER-FINALS, FIRST LEG

AZ Alkmaar 0, Werder Bremen 0. Att: 16,401. Bayer Leverkusen 0, Osasuna 3 (Cuellar 1, Lopez 71,Webo 73). Att: 22,500. Espanyol 3 (Tamudo 15, Riera 33, Pandiani 59), Benfica 2 (Nuno Gomes 64, Simao 66). Att: 18,000. Sevilla 2 (Kanoute 19 pen, Kerzhakov 36), **Tottenham** 1 (Keane 2). Att: 32,000.

QUARTER-FINALS, SECOND LEG

Benfica 0, Espanyol 0. Att: 50,000 (Espanyol won 3-2 on agg). Osasuna 1 (Juanlu 62), Bayer Leverkusen 0. Att: 17,000 (Osasuna won 4-0 on agg). **Tottenham** 2 (Defoe 65, Lennon 67), Sevilla 2 (Malbranque 3 og, Kanoute 8). Att: 35,284 (Sevilla won 4-3 on agg). Werder Bremen 4 (Borowski 16, Klose 36, 61, Diego 80), AZ Alkmaar 1 (Dembele 32). Att: 35,000 (Werder Bremen won 4-1 on agg).

SEMI-FINALS, FIRST LEG

Espanyol 3 (Moises 21, Pandiani 50, Coro 88), Werder Bremen 0. Att: 40,000. Osasuna 1 (Soldado 55), Sevilla 0. Att: 19,800.

SEMI-FINALS, SECOND LEG

Sevilla 2 (Luis Fabiano 37, Renato 53), Osasuna 0. Att: 42,000 (Sevilla won 2-1 on agg). Werder Bremen 1 (Almeida 4), Espanyol 2 (Coro 50, Lacruz 61). Att: 36,000 (Espanyol won 5-1 on agg).

UEFA CUP FINAL

ESPANYOL 2, SEVILLA 2 (aet, Sevilla won 3-1 on pens)

Hampden Park (50,670), Wednesday, May 16, 2007

Espanyol (4-4-2): Iraizoz, Zabaleta, Jarque, Torrejon, D. Garcia, Rufete (Pandiani 56), Moises, De la Pena (Jonatas 86), Riera, L. Garcia, Tamudo (Lacruz 26). **Subs not used:** Kameni, Costa, Coro, Chica. **Scorers:** Riera (28), Jonatas (115). **Booked:** Moises. **Sent-off:** Moises. **Coach:** Ernesto Valverde.

Sevilla (4-1-3-2): Palop, Alves, Navarro, Puerta, Dragutinovic, Poulsen, Marti, Maresca (Jesus Navas 46), Adriano (Renato 75), Kanoute, Luis Fabiano (Kerzhakov 64). **Subs not used:** Cobeno, Castedo, Chevanton, Ocio. **Scorers:** Adriano (18), Kanoute (105). **Booked:** Luis Fabiano, Kanoute, Puerta. **Coach:** Juande Ramos.

Referee: M. Busacca (Switzerland). **Half-time:** 1-1.

UEFA CUP FINALS

1972 Tottenham beat Wolves 3-2 on agg. (2-1a, 1-1h)
1973 Liverpool beat Borussia Moenchengladbach 3-2 on agg. (3-0h, 0-2a)
1974 Feyenoord beat Tottenham 4-2 on agg. (2-2a, 2-0h)
1975 Borussia Moenchengladbach beat Twente Enschede 5-1 on agg. (0-0h, 5-1a)
1976 Liverpool beat Brugge 4-3 on agg. (3-2h, 1-1a)
1977 Juventus beat Atletico Bilbao on away goals after 2-2 agg. (1-0h, 1-2a)
1978 PSV Eindhoven beat Bastia 3-0 on agg. (0-0a, 3-0h)
1979 Borussia Moenchengladbach beat Red Star Belgrade 2-1 on agg. (1-1a, 1-0h)
1980 Eintracht Frankfurt beat Borussia Moenchengladbach on away goals after 3-3 agg. (2-3a, 1-0h)

1981 Ipswich Town beat AZ 67 Alkmaar 5-4 on agg. (3-0h, 2-4a)
1982 IFK Gothenburg beat SV Hamburg 4-0 on agg. (1-0h, 3-0a)
1983 Anderlecht beat Benfica 2-1 on agg. (1-0h, 1-1a)
1984 Tottenham beat Anderlecht 4-3 on penalties after 2-2 agg. (1-1a, 1-1h)
1985 Real Madrid beat Videoton 3-1 on agg. (3-0a, 0-1h)
1986 Real Madrid beat Cologne 5-3 on agg. (5-1h, 0-2a)
1987 IFK Gothenburg beat Dundee Utd. 2-1 on agg. (1-0h, 1-1a)
1988 Bayer Leverkusen beat Espanol 3-2 on penalties after 3-3 agg. (0-3a, 3-0h)
1989 Napoli beat VfB Stuttgart 5-4 on agg. (2-1h, 3-3a)
1990 Juventus beat Fiorentina 3-1 on agg. (3-1h, 0-0a)
1991 Inter Milan beat AS Roma 2-1 on agg. (2-0h, 0-1a)
1992 Ajax beat Torino on away goals after 2-2 agg. (2-2a, 0-0h)
1993 Juventus beat Borussia Dortmund 6-1 on agg. (3-1a, 3-0h)
1994 Inter Milan beat Salzburg 2-0 on agg. (1-0a, 1-0h)
1995 Parma beat Juventus 2-1 on agg. (1-0h, 1-1a)
1996 Bayern Munich beat Bordeaux 5-1 on agg. (2-0h, 3-1a)
1997 FC Schalke beat Inter Milan 4-1 on penalties after 1-1 agg. (1-0h, 0-1a)
1998 Inter Milan beat Lazio 3-0 (one match) – Paris
1999 Parma beat Marseille 3-0 (one match) – Moscow
2000 Galatasaray beat Arsenal 4-1 on penalties after 0-0 (one match) – Copenhagen
2001 Liverpool beat Alaves 5-4 on golden goal (one match) – Dortmund
2002 Feyenoord beat Borussia Dortmund 3-2 (one match) – Rotterdam
2003 FC Porto beat Celtic 3-2 on silver goal (one match) – Seville
2004 Valencia beat Marseille 2-0 (one match) – Gothenburg
2005 CSKA Moscow beat Sporting Lisbon 3-1 (one match) – Lisbon
2006 Sevilla beat Middlesbrough 4-0 (one match) – Eindhoven
2007 Sevilla beat Espanyol 3-1 on penalties after 2-2 (one match) – Hampden Park

FAIRS CUP FINALS

(As UEFA Cup previously known)

1958 Barcelona beat London 8-2 on agg. (2-2a, 6-0h)
1960 Barcelona beat Birmingham 4-1 on agg. (0-0a, 4-1h)
1961 AS Roma beat Birmingham City 4-2 on agg. (2-2a, 2-0h)
1962 Valencia beat Barcelona 7-3 on agg. (6-2h, 1-1a)
1963 Valencia beat Dynamo Zagreb 4-1 on agg. (2-1a, 2-0h)
1964 Real Zaragoza beat Valencia 2-1 (Barcelona)
1965 Ferencvaros beat Juventus 1-0 (Turin)
1966 Barcelona beat Real Zaragoza 4-3 on agg. (0-1h, 4-2a)
1967 Dynamo Zagreb beat Leeds Utd. 2-0 on agg. (2-0h, 0-0a)
1968 Leeds Utd. beat Ferencvaros 1-0 on agg. (1-0h, 0-0a)
1969 Newcastle Utd. beat Ujpest Dozsa 6-2 on agg. (3-0h, 3-2a)
1970 Arsenal beat Anderlecht 4-3 on agg. (1-3a, 3-0h)
1971 Leeds Utd. beat Juventus on away goals after 3-3 agg. (2-2a, 1-1h)

CUP-WINNERS' CUP FINALS

1961 Fiorentina beat Rangers 4-1 on agg. (2-0 Glasgow first leg, 2-1 Florence second leg)
1962 Atletico Madrid beat Fiorentina 3-0 (replay Stuttgart, after a 1-1 draw, Glasgow)
1963 Tottenham beat Atletico Madrid 5-1 (Rotterdam)
1964 Sporting Lisbon beat MTK Budapest 1-0 (replay Antwerp, after a 3-3 draw, Brussels)
1965 West Ham Utd. beat Munich 1860 2-0 (Wembley)
1966† Borussia Dortmund beat Liverpool 2-1 (Glasgow)
1967† Bayern Munich beat Rangers 1-0 (Nuremberg)
1968 AC Milan beat SV Hamburg 2-0 (Rotterdam)
1969 Slovan Bratislava beat Barcelona 3-2 (Basle)
1970 Manchester City beat Gornik Zabrze 2-1 (Vienna)
1971† Chelsea beat Real Madrid 2-1 (replay Athens, after a 1-1 draw, Athens)
1972 Rangers beat Moscow Dynamo 3-2 (Barcelona)
1973 AC Milan beat Leeds Utd. 1-0 (Salonika)
1974 Magdeburg beat AC Milan 2-0 (Rotterdam)
1975 Dynamo Kiev beat Ferencvaros 3-0 (Basle)
1976 Anderlecht beat West Ham Utd. 4-2 (Brussels)
1977 SV Hamburg beat Anderlecht 2-0 (Amsterdam)
1978 Anderlecht beat Austria WAC 4-0 (Paris)
1979† Barcelona beat Fortuna Dusseldorf 4-3 (Basle)
1980† Valencia beat Arsenal 5-4 on penalties after a 0-0 draw (Brussels)
1981 Dynamo Tbilisi beat Carl Zeiss Jena 2-1 (Dusseldorf)
1982 Barcelona beat Standard Liege 2-1 (Barcelona)
1983† Aberdeen beat Real Madrid 2-1 (Gothenburg)
1984 Juventus beat Porto 2-1 (Basle)
1985 Everton beat Rapid Vienna 3-1 (Rotterdam)
1986 Dynamo Kiev beat Atletico Madrid 3-0 (Lyon)
1987 Ajax beat Lokomotiv Leipzig 1-0 (Athens)
1988 Mechelen beat Ajax 1-0 (Strasbourg)
1989 Barcelona beat Sampdoria 2-0 (Berne)
1990 Sampdoria beat Anderlecht 2-0 (Gothenburg)
1991 Manchester Utd. beat Barcelona 2-1 (Rotterdam)
1992 Werder Bremen beat Monaco 2-0 (Lisbon)
1993 Parma beat Royal Antwerp 3-1 (Wembley)
1994 Arsenal beat Parma 1-0 (Copenhagen)
1995† Real Zaragoza beat Arsenal 2-1 (Paris)
1996 Paris St. Germain beat Rapid Vienna 1-0 (Brussels)
1997 Barcelona beat Paris St. Germain 1-0 (Rotterdam)
1998 Chelsea beat VfB Stuttgart 1-0 (Stockholm)
1999 Lazio beat Real Mallorca 2-1 (Villa Park, Birmingham)

(† After extra time)

INTER-CONTINENTAL CUP

Year	**Winners**	**Runners-up**	**Score**
1960	Real Madrid (Spa.)	Penarol (Uru.)	0-0 5-1
1961	Penarol (Uru.)	Benfica (Por.)	0-1 2-1 5-0
1962	Santos (Bra.)	Benfica (Por.)	3-2 5-2
1963	Santos (Bra.)	AC Milan (Ita.)	2-4 4-2 1-0

1964	Inter Milan (Ita.)	Independiente (Arg.)	0-1 2-0 1-0
1965	Inter Milan (Ita.)	Independiente (Arg.)	3-0 0-0
1966	Penarol (Uru.)	Real Madrid (Spa.)	2-0 2-0
1967	Racing (Arg.)	Celtic (Sco.)	0-1 2-1 1-0
1968	Estudiantes (Arg.)	Manchester Utd. (Eng.)	1-0 1-1
1969	AC Milan (Ita.)	Estudiantes (Arg.)	3-0 1-2
1970	Feyenoord (Hol.)	Estudiantes (Arg.)	2-2 1-0
1971	Nacional (Uru.)	Panathanaikos (Gre.)*	1-1 2-1
1972	Ajax (Hol.)	Independiente (Arg.)	1-1 3-0
1973	Independiente (Arg.)	Juventus (Ita.)*	1-0 #
1974	Atletico Madrid (Spa.)*	Independiente (Arg.)	0-1 2-0
1975	Not played		
1976	Bayern Munich (W.Ger.)	Cruzeiro (Bra.)	2-0 0-0
1977	Boca Juniors (Arg.)	Borussia Mönchengladbach (W.Ger.)*	2-2 3-0
1978	Not played		
1979	Olimpia Asuncion (Par.)	Malmö (Swe.)*	1-0 2-1
1980	Nacional (Arg.)	Nott'm. Forest (Eng.)	1-0
1981	Flamengo (Bra.)	Liverpool (Eng.)	3-0
1982	Penarol (Uru.)	Aston Villa (Eng.)	2-0
1983	Porto Alegre (Bra.)	SV Hamburg (W.Ger.)	2-1
1984	Independiente (Arg.)	Liverpool (Eng.)	1-0
1985	Juventus (Ita.)	Argentinos Juniors (Arg.)	2-2 (aet)
	(Juventus won 4-2 on penalties)		
1986	River Plate (Arg.)	Steaua Bucharest (Rum.)	1-0
1987	Porto (Por.)	Penarol (Uru.)	2-1 (aet)
1988	Nacional (Uru.)	PSV Eindhoven (Hol.)	1-1 (aet)
	(Nacional won 7-6 on penalties)		
1989	AC Milan (Ita.)	Nacional (Col.)	1-0 (aet)
1990	AC Milan (Ita.)	Olimpia Asuncion (Par.)	3-0
1991	Red Star (Yug.)	Colo Colo (Chi.)	3-0
1992	Sao Paulo (Bra.)	Barcelona (Spa.)	2-1
1993	Sao Paulo (Bra.)	AC Milan (Ita.)	3-2
1994	Velez Sarsfield (Arg.)	AC Milan (Ita.)	2-0
1995	Ajax (Hol.)	Gremio (Bra.)	0-0 (aet)
	(Ajax won 4-3 on penalties)		
1996	Juventus (Ita.)	River Plate (Arg.)	1-0
1997	Borussia Dortmund (Ger.)	Cruzeiro (Arg.)	2-0
1998	Real Madrid (Spa.)	Vasco da Gama (Bra.)	2-1
1999	Manchester Utd. (Eng.)	Palmeiras (Bra.)	1-0
2000	Boca Juniors (Arg.)	Real Madrid (Spa.)	2-1
2001	Bayern Munich (Ger.)	Boca Juniours (Arg.)	1-0

2002	Real Madrid (Spa.)	Olimpia Ascuncion (Par.)	2-0
2003	Boca Juniors (Arg.)	AC Milan (Ita.)	1-1
	(Boca Juniors won 3-1 on penalties)		
2004	FC Porto (Por.)	Caldas (Col.)	0-0
	(FC Porto won 8-7 on penalties)		

Played as a single match in Japan since 1980
* European Cup runners-up. # One match only.
Summary: 43 contests; South America 22 wins, Europe 23 wins.

WORLD CLUB CHAMPIONSHIP

2005	Sao Paulo beat Liverpool	1-0
2006	Internacional (Bra.) beat Barcelona	1-0

WORLD CLUB CHAMPIONSHIP FINAL

INTERNACIONAL 1, BARCELONA 0

Yokohama (67,128), Sunday, December 17, 2006

Internacional (4-3-3): Clemer, Ceara, Indio, Fabiano Eller, Rubens Cardoso, Wellington Monteiro, Alex (Vargas 46), Edinho, Fernandao (Adriano 76), Iarley, Pato (Luiz Adriano 61). **Scorer:** Adriano (82). **Booked:** Indio, Adriano, Iarley.

Barcelona (4-3-1-2): Valdes, Zambrotta (Belletti 46), Marquez, Puyol, Van Bronckhorst, Motta (Xavi 59), Deco, Iniesta, Ronaldinho, Gudjohnsen (Ezquerro 88), Giuly. **Booked:** Motta.

Referee: C. Batres (Guatemala). **Half-time:** 0-0.

EUROPEAN SUPERCUP

BARCELONA 0, SEVILLA 3

Monte Carlo (10,000), Friday, August 25, 2006

Barcelona (4-3-1-2): Valdes, Belletti, Marquez, Puyol, Sylvinho (Giuly 72), Motta (Gudjohnsen 57), Deco, Xavi (Iniesta 57), Ronaldinho, Eto'o, Messi. **Booked:** Sylvinho.

Sevilla (4-3-3): Palop, Alves, Navarro, Escude, Castedo, Jesus Navas (Maresca 75), Poulsen, Renato, Kanoute, Adriano (Puerta 81), Luis Fabiano (Marti 46). **Scorers:** Renato (7), Kanoute (45), Maresca (90 pen). **Booked:** Kanoute, Alves, Navarro, Palop, Escude, Maresca.

Referee: S. Farina (Italy). **Half-time:** 0-2.

EUROPEAN TABLES 2006-07

BELGIUM

		P	W	D	L	F	A	GD	Pts
1	Anderlecht	34	23	8	3	75	30	45	77
2	Genk	34	22	6	6	71	37	34	72
3	Standard Liège	34	19	7	8	62	38	24	64
4	Gent	34	18	6	10	56	40	16	60
5	Charleroi	34	17	9	8	51	40	11	60
6	Club Brugge	34	14	9	11	58	40	18	51
7	GBA	34	14	9	11	52	46	6	51
8	Westerlo	34	12	10	12	41	44	–3	46
9	Mons	34	12	8	14	41	41	0	44
10	Excelsior	34	10	12	12	51	55	–4	42
11	Roeselare	34	10	9	15	50	72	–22	39
12	Cercle Brugge	34	10	8	16	31	36	–5	38
13	Brussels	34	8	14	12	39	50	–11	38
14	Zulte Waregem	34	9	10	15	40	54	–14	37
15	Sint-Truiden	34	9	8	17	39	52	–13	35
16	Lokeren	34	5	15	14	32	48	–16	30
17	Lierse	34	6	8	20	33	66	–33	26
18	Beveren	34	5	10	19	31	64	–33	25

Leading scorers: 21 Sterchele (GBA); 20 Ogunsoto (Westerlo), Tchite (Anderlecht); 18 Custovic (Excelsior); 16 Balaban (Club Brugge); 15 Olufade (Gent); 14 Frutos (Anderlecht), Jovanovic (Standard Liege); 12 Hassan (Anderlecht).
Cup Final: Club Brugge 1, Standard Liege 0.

FRANCE

		P	W	D	L	F	A	GD	Pts
1	Lyon	38	24	9	5	64	27	37	81
2	Marseille	38	19	7	12	53	38	15	64
3	Toulouse	38	17	7	14	44	43	1	58
4	Rennes	38	14	15	9	38	30	8	57
5	Lens	38	15	12	11	47	41	6	57
6	Bordeaux	38	16	9	13	39	35	4	57
7	Sochaux	38	15	12	11	46	48	–2	57
8	Auxerre	38	13	15	10	41	41	0	54
9	Monaco	38	13	12	13	45	38	7	51
10	Lille	38	13	11	14	45	43	2	50
11	Saint-Etienne	38	14	7	17	52	50	2	49
12	Le Mans	38	11	16	11	45	46	–1	49
13	Nancy	38	13	10	15	37	44	–7	49
14	Lorient	38	12	13	13	33	40	–7	49
15	Paris SG	38	12	12	14	42	42	0	48
16	Nice	38	9	16	13	34	40	–6	43
17	Valenciennes	38	11	10	17	36	48	–12	43
18	Troyes	38	9	12	17	39	54	–15	39
19	Sedan	38	7	14	17	46	58	–12	35
20	Nantes	38	7	14	17	29	49	–20	35

Leading scorers: 15 Pauleta (Paris SG); 13 Savidan (Valenciennes); 12 Bangoura (Le Mans), Grafite (Le Mans), Niang (Marseille); 11 Dindane (Lens), Elmander (Toulouse), Fred (Lyon), Piquionne (St Etienne/Monaco), Utaka (Rennes).
Cup Final: Sochaux 2, Marseille 2 (aet, Sochaux won 5-4 on pens).

GERMANY

		P	W	D	L	F	A	GD	Pts
1	Stuttgart	34	21	7	6	61	37	24	70
2	Schalke	34	21	5	8	53	32	21	68
3	Werder Bremen	34	20	6	8	76	40	36	66
4	Bayern Munich	34	18	6	10	55	40	15	60
5	Bayer Leverkusen	34	15	6	13	54	49	5	51
6	Nuremberg	34	11	15	8	43	32	11	48
7	Hamburg	34	10	15	9	43	37	6	45
8	Bochum	34	13	6	15	49	50	–1	45
9	Borussia Dortmund	34	12	8	14	41	43	–2	44
10	Hertha	34	12	8	14	50	55	–5	44
11	Hannover	34	12	8	14	41	50	–9	44
12	Arminia Bielefeld	34	11	9	14	47	49	–2	42
13	Cottbus	34	11	8	15	38	49	–11	41
14	Eintracht Frankfurt	34	9	13	12	46	58	–12	40
15	Wolfsburg	34	8	13	13	37	45	–8	37
16	Mainz	34	8	10	16	34	57	–23	34
17	Alemannia Aachen	34	9	7	18	46	70	–24	34
18	Borussia Mönchengladbach	34	6	8	20	23	44	–21	26

Leading scorers: 20 Gekas (Bochum); 16 Frei (Borussia Dortmund), Makaay (Bayern Munich); 15 Kuranyi (Schalke); 14 Gomez (Stuttgart), Zidan (Werder Bremen/Mainz), Radu (Cottbus), Pantelic (Hertha); 13 Cacau (Stuttgart), Diego (Werder Bremen), Klose (Werder Bremen).
Cup Final: Nuremberg 3, Stuttgart 2 (aet).

HOLLAND

		P	W	D	L	F	A	GD	Pts
1	PSV Eindhoven	34	23	6	5	75	25	50	75
2	Ajax	34	23	6	5	84	35	49	75
3	AZ Alkmaar	34	21	9	4	83	31	52	72
4	FC Twente	34	19	9	6	67	37	30	66
5	Heerenveen	34	16	7	11	60	43	17	55
6	Roda	34	15	9	10	47	36	11	54
7	Feyenoord	34	15	8	11	56	66	–10	53
8	Groningen	34	15	6	13	54	54	0	51
9	Utrecht	34	13	9	12	41	44	–3	48
10	NEC	34	12	8	14	36	44	–8	44
11	Breda	34	12	7	15	43	54	–11	43
12	Vitesse	34	10	8	16	50	55	–5	38
13	Sparta Rotterdam	34	10	7	17	40	66	–26	37
14	Heracles	34	7	11	16	32	64	–32	32
15	Willem	34	8	7	19	31	64	–33	31
16	Excelsior	34	8	6	20	43	65	–22	30
17	Waalwijk	34	6	9	19	33	60	–27	27
18	Den Haag	34	3	8	23	40	72	–32	17

Leading scorers: 34 Alves (Heerenveen); 22 Koevermans (AZ Alkmaar), N'Kufo (FC Twente); 21 Farfan (PSV Eindhoven), Huntelaar (Ajax); 19 Lazovic (Arenhem); 18 Sneijder (Ajax); 15 Bakircioglu (FC Twente); 14 Arveladze (AZ Alkmaar); 13 Nevland (Groningen).
Cup Final: Ajax 1, AZ Alkmaar 1 (aet, Ajax won 8-7 on pens).

ITALY

		P	W	D	L	F	A	GD	Pts
1	Inter Milan	38	30	7	1	80	34	46	97
2	Roma	38	22	9	7	74	34	40	75
3	Lazio	38	18	11	9	59	33	26	62
4	AC Milan	38	19	12	7	57	36	21	61
5	Fiorentina	38	21	10	7	62	31	31	58
6	Palermo	38	16	10	12	58	51	7	58
7	Empoli	38	14	12	12	42	43	–1	54
8	Atalanta	38	12	14	12	56	54	2	50
9	Sampdoria	38	13	10	15	44	48	–4	49
10	Udinese	38	12	10	16	49	55	–6	46
11	Livorno	38	10	13	15	41	54	–13	43
12	Parma	38	10	12	16	41	56	–15	42
13	Catania	38	10	11	17	46	68	–22	41
14	Reggina	38	12	15	11	52	50	2	40
15	Siena	38	9	14	15	35	45	–10	40
16	Cagliari	38	9	13	16	35	46	–11	40
17	Torino	38	10	10	18	27	47	–20	40
18	Chievo	38	9	12	17	38	48	–10	39
19	Ascoli	38	5	12	21	36	67	–31	27
20	Messina	38	5	11	22	37	69	–32	26

Leading scorers: 26 Totti (Roma); 20 Lucarelli (Livorno); 19 Rigano (Messina); 18 Bianchi (Reggina); 17 Spinesi (Catania), Amoruso (Reggina); 16 Mutu (Fiorentina), Toni (Fiorentina), Rocchi (Lazio); 15 Ibrahimovic (Inter Milan).
Cup Final: Roma 7, Inter Milan 4 (on agg – 6-2h, 1-2a).

PORTUGAL

		P	W	D	L	F	A	GD	Pts
1	FC Porto	30	22	3	5	65	20	45	69
2	Sporting	30	20	8	2	54	15	39	68
3	Benfica	30	20	7	3	55	20	35	67
4	Sporting Braga	30	14	8	8	35	30	5	50
5	Belenenses	30	15	4	11	36	29	7	49
6	Paços de Ferreira	30	10	12	8	31	36	–5	42
7	Uniao Leiria	30	10	11	9	25	27	–2	41
8	Nacional	30	11	6	13	41	38	3	39
9	Boavista	30	8	11	11	32	34	–2	35
10	Estrêla Amadora	30	9	8	13	23	36	–13	35
11	Naval	30	7	11	12	28	37	–9	32
12	Marítimo	30	8	8	14	30	44	–14	32
13	Académica Coimbra	30	6	8	16	28	46	–18	26
14	Vitória Setúbal	30	5	9	16	21	45	–24	24
15	Beira-Mar	30	4	11	15	28	55	–27	23
16	Desportivo Aves	30	5	7	18	22	42	–20	22

Leading scorers: 15 Liedson (Sporting); 12 Dady (Belenenses); 11 Adriano (FC Porto), Simao (Benfica); 10 Helder Postiga (FC Porto), Linz (Boavista), Miccoli (Benfica), Nei (Naval); 9 Gonzalez (FC Porto).
Cup Final: Sporting 1, Belenenses 0.

SPAIN

		P	W	D	L	F	A	GD	Pts
1	Real Madrid	38	23	7	8	66	40	26	76
2	Barcelona	38	22	10	6	78	33	45	76
3	Sevilla	38	21	8	9	64	35	29	71
4	Valencia	38	20	6	12	57	42	15	66
5	Villarreal	38	18	8	12	48	44	4	62
6	Real Zaragoza	38	16	12	10	55	43	12	60
7	Atlético Madrid	38	17	9	12	46	39	7	60
8	Recreativo Huelva	38	15	9	14	54	52	2	54
9	Getafe	38	14	10	14	39	33	6	52
10	Racing Santander	38	12	14	12	42	48	–6	50
11	Espanyol	38	12	13	13	46	53	–7	49
12	Mallorca	38	14	7	17	41	47	–6	49
13	Deportivo La Coruña	38	12	11	15	32	45	–13	47
14	Osasuna	38	13	7	18	51	49	2	46
15	Levante	38	10	12	16	37	53	–16	42
16	Real Betis	38	8	16	14	36	49	–13	40
17	Athletic Bilbao	38	10	10	18	44	62	–18	40
18	Celta Vigo	38	10	9	19	40	59	–19	39
19	Real Sociedad	38	8	11	19	32	47	–15	35
20	Gimnàstic	38	7	7	24	34	69	–35	28

Leading scorers: 25 Van Nistelrooy (Real Madrid); 23 Milito (Real Zaragoza); 21 Kanoute (Sevilla), Ronaldinho (Barcelona); 19 Forlan (Villarreal); 15 Baiano (Celta Vigo), Tamudo (Espanyol), Villa (Valencia); 14 Messi (Barcelona), Torres (Atletico Madrid).
Cup Final: Sevilla 1, Getafe 0.

RECORD FOR VAN NISTELROOY

Ruud van Nistelrooy became the first player to finish leading marksman in three of Europe's top six leagues when netting 25 for Real Madrid last season. Van Nistelrooy had previously been top scorer with PSV Eindhoven (1999, 2000) and Manchester United (2003). He also joined four players in winning league titles in three of the top six – Claude Makelele (Nantes, Real Madrid, Chelsea), Clarence Seedorf (Ajax, Real Madrid, AC Milan), Jens Lehmann (AC Milan, Borussia Dortmund, Arsenal) and Michael Laudrup (Juventus, Barcelona/Real Madrid, Ajax).

NEW WEMBLEY HOLDS KEY TO ENGLAND'S CHANCES

England face a searching examination of their European Championship ambitions at the new Wembley in the months ahead. They will enjoy home advantage in four of the remaining five matches in Group E, but three of them are against teams still harbouring genuine hopes of reaching next summer's finals in Austria and Switzerland. Steve McClaren's side need quickly to turn the magnificent 90,000-capacity stadium into something of a fortress to see off the challenge presented by Israel, Russia and then the current group leaders Croatia in what could be a make-or-break match on November 21. England's one away fixture, against the Russians, also promises a stern test. Only the visit of Estonia looks to be relatively pressure-free thanks to the 3-0 victory in Tallinn, which took some of the heat off McClaren after less than convincing performances in previous matches.

The fortunes of Scotland and Northern Ireland are now in the hands of two former defensive stalwarts – and both Alex McLeish and Nigel Worthington have the opportunity to make an immediate name for themselves in international management. McLeish, who made 77 appearances for his country, must break the grip established by France and Italy at the top of Group B after taking over when Walter Smith decided to return to club football with Rangers. Scotland have a victory over France under their belt and may need a repeat of that display against Italy in their final fixture at Hampden Park on November 17.

Worthington, winner of 66 caps, will be looking to David Healy to maintain prolific scoring form for the Irish after replacing Lawrie Sanchez, who sacrificed his international ambitions for the chance to manage Fulham in the Premiership. UEFA's decision to hand Sweden a 3-0 victory over Denmark after referee Herbert Fandel was attacked by a fan in Copenhagen when the teams were set for a 3-3 draw in Group F was a blow. It put the Swedes top of the group, level on points with Spain. But if Healy can reproduce the sharpness which brought him hat-tricks against Spain and Liechtenstein last season – he now has 29 goals in 56 appearances – the Irish have a chance. The Republic of Ireland are disputing second place with the Czech Republic in Group D – the teams meet on September 12 – but Wales look to be playing for pride only after dropping five points at home against the Czechs and Slovakia.

The draw for the finals is in December. Joint hosts Switzerland kick off the tournament at Basle's St Jakob Park on June 7 next year. The final, on June 29, will be at the Ernst Happel Stadium in Vienna. Venues are: Austria – Vienna (50,000), Innsbruck (30,000), Klagenfurt (30,000), Salzburg (30,000). Switzerland – Basle (42,500), Berne (32,000), Geneva (30,000), Zurich (30,000).

MATCH SCHEDULE (UK TIMES)

GROUP STAGE

June 7: Switzerland v (Group) A2, Basle (5pm); A3 v A4, Geneva (7.45pm).
June 8: Austria v B2, Vienna (5pm); B3 v B4, Klagenfurt (7.45pm).
June 9: C3 v C4, Zurich (5pm); C1 v C2, Berne (7.45pm).
June 10: D3 v D4, Innsbruck (5pm); D1 v D2, Salzburg (7.45pm).
June 11: A2 v A3, Geneva (5pm); Switzerland v A4, Basle (7.45pm).
June 12: B2 v B3, Klagenfurt (5pm); Austria v B4, Vienna (7.45pm).
June 13: C2 v C3, Zurich (5pm); C1 v C4, Berne (7.45pm).
June 14: D2 v D3, Innsbruck (5pm); D1 v D4, Salzburg (7.45pm).
June 15: Switzerland v A3, Basle (7.45pm); A4 v A2, Geneva (7.45pm).
June 16: Austria v B3, Vienna (7.45pm); B4 v B2, Klagenfurt (7.45pm).
June 17: C1 v C3, Berne (7.45pm); C4 v C2, Zurich (7.45pm).
June 18: D1 v D3, Salzburg (7.45pm); D4 v D2, Innsbruck (7.45pm).

QUARTER-FINALS

June 19: Q-F 1, winner A v second B, Basle (7.45pm).
June 20: Q-F 2, winner B v second A, Vienna (7.45pm).
June 21: Q-F 3, winner C v second D, Basle (7.45pm).
June 22: Q-F 4, winner D v second C, Vienna (7.45pm).

REST DAYS

June 23-24

SEMI-FINALS

June 25: winner of 1 v winner of 2, Basle (7.45pm).
June 26: winner of 3 v winner of 4, Vienna (7.45pm).

REST DAYS

June 27-28

FINAL

June 29: Vienna (7.45pm).

QUALIFYING POSITIONS AFTER 2006-07 SEASON

GROUP A

	P	*W*	*D*	*L*	*F*	*A*	*Pts*
Poland	9	6	1	2	15	7	19
Serbia & Montenegro	7	4	2	1	10	4	14
Portugal	7	4	2	1	15	5	14
Finland	8	4	2	2	9	5	14
Belgium	8	2	1	5	5	10	7
Armenia	7	2	1	4	3	7	7
Kazakhstan	8	1	3	4	5	11	6
Azerbaijan	8	1	2	5	4	17	5

Results: Belgium 0, Kazakhstan 0; Serbia & Montenegro 1, Azerbaijan 0; Poland 1, Finland 3; Azerbaijan 1, Kazakhstan 1; Finland 1, Portugal 1; Poland 1, Serbia & Montenegro 1; Armenia 0, Belgium 1; Serbia & Montenegro 1, Belgium 0; Portugal 3, Azerbaijan 0; Armenia 0, Finland 0; Kazakhstan 0, Poland 1; Serbia & Montenegro 3, Armenia 0; Poland 2, Portugal 1; Belgium 3, Azerbaijan 0; Kazakhstan 0, Finland 2; Finland 1, Armenia 0; Belgium 0, Poland 1; Portugal 3, Kazakhstan 0; Poland 5, Azerbaijan 0; Kazakhstan 2, Serbia & Montenegro 1; Portugal 4, Belgium 0; Azerbaijan 1, Finland 0; Poland 1, Armenia 0; Serbia & Montenegro 1, Portugal 1; Finland 0, Serbia & Montenegro 2; Kazakhstan 1, Armenia 2; Azerbaijan 1, Poland 3; Belgium 1, Portugal 2; Armenia 1, Poland 0; Finland 2, Belgium 0; Kazakhstan 1, Azerbaijan 1.

To play: Aug. 22: Armenia v Portugal, Belgium v Serbia & Montenegro, Finland v Kazakhstan; Sept. 8: Azerbaijan v Armenia, Portugal v Poland, Serbia & Montenegro v Finland; Sept. 12: Armenia v Azerbaijan, Finland v Poland, Kazakhstan v Belgium, Portugal v Serbia & Montenegro; Oct. 13: Armenia v Serbia & Montenegro, Azerbaijan v Portugal, Belgium v Finland, Poland v Kazakhstan; Oct. 17: Azerbaijan v Serbia & Montenegro, Belgium v Armenia, Kazakhstan v Portugal; Nov. 17: Finland v

Azerbaijan, Poland v Belgium, Portugal v Armenia, Serbia & Montenegro v Kazakhstan; Nov. 21: Armenia v Kazakhstan, Azerbaijan v Belgium, Portugal v Finland, Serbia & Montenegro v Poland.

GROUP B

	P	*W*	*D*	*L*	*F*	*A*	*Pts*
France	7	6	0	1	15	2	18
Italy	7	5	1	1	13	6	16
Scotland	7	5	0	2	13	6	15
Ukraine	6	4	0	2	8	6	12
Lithuania	7	2	1	4	4	7	7
Georgia	8	2	0	6	13	14	6
Faroe Islands	8	0	0	8	2	27	0

Results: Faroe Islands 0, Georgia 6; **Scotland** 6, Faroe Islands 0; Georgia 0, France 3; Italy 1, Lithuania 1; Ukraine 3, Georgia 2; Lithuania 1, **Scotland** 2; France 3, Italy 1; Faroe Islands 0, Lithuania 1; **Scotland** 1, France 0; Italy 2, Ukraine 0; Ukraine 2, **Scotland** 0; France 5, Faroe Islands 0; Georgia 1, Italy 3; **Scotland** 2, Georgia 1; Faroe Islands 0, Ukraine 2; Lithuania 0, France 1; Ukraine 1, Lithuania 0; Georgia 3, Faroe Islands 1; Italy 2, **Scotland** 0; Faroe Islands 1, Italy 2; Lithuania 1, Georgia 0; France 2, Ukraine 0; Faroe Islands 0, **Scotland** 2; France 1, Georgia 0; Lithuania 0, Italy 2.

To play: Sept. 8: Georgia v Ukraine, Italy v France, **Scotland** v Lithuania; Sept. 12: France v **Scotland**, Lithuania v Faroe Islands, Ukraine v Italy; Oct. 13: Faroe Islands v France, Italy v Georgia, **Scotland** v Ukraine; Oct. 17: France v Lithuania, Georgia v **Scotland**, Ukraine v Faroe Islands; Nov. 17: **Scotland** v Italy, Lithuania v Ukraine. Nov. 21: Georgia v Lithuania, Italy v Faroe Islands, Ukraine v France.

GROUP C

	P	*W*	*D*	*L*	*F*	*A*	*Pts*
Greece	7	6	0	1	12	5	18
Bosnia-Herzegovina	7	4	1	2	14	14	13
Turkey	6	4	1	1	16	6	13
Norway	7	4	1	2	17	6	13
Hungary	7	2	0	5	7	14	6
Malta	7	1	1	5	5	15	4
Moldova	7	0	2	5	4	15	2

Results: Malta 2, Bosnia-Herzegovina 5; Hungary 1, Norway 4; Moldova 0, Greece 1; Norway 2, Moldova 0; Turkey 2, Malta 0; Bosnia-Herzegovina 1, Hungary 3; Moldova 2, Bosnia-Herzegovina 2; Hungary 0, Turkey 1; Greece 1, Norway 0; Malta 2, Hungary 1; Turkey 5, Moldova 0; Bosnia-Herzegovina 0, Greece 4; Moldova 1, Malta 1; Norway 1, Bosnia-Herzegovina 2; Greece 1, Turkey 4; Hungary 2, Moldova 0; Malta 0, Greece 1; Turkey 2, Norway 2; Norway 4, Malta 0; Bosnia-Herzegovina 3, Turkey 2; Greece 2, Hungary 0; Bosnia-Herzegovina 1, Malta 0; Greece 2, Moldova 1; Norway 4, Hungary 0.

To play: Sept. 8: Hungary v Bosnia-Herzegovina, Malta v Turkey, Moldova v Norway; Sept. 12: Bosnia-Herzegovina v Moldova, Norway v Greece, Turkey v Hungary; Oct. 13: Greece v Bosnia-Herzgovina, Hungary v Malta, Moldova v Turkey; Oct. 17: Bosnia-Herzegovina v Norway, Malta v Moldova, Turkey v Greece; Nov. 17: Greece v Malta, Moldova v Hungary, Norway v Turkey; Nov. 21: Hungary v Greece, Malta v Norway, Turkey v Bosnia-Herzegovina.

GROUP D

	P	W	D	L	F	A	Pts
Germany	7	6	1	0	29	4	19
Czech Republic	7	4	2	1	15	4	14
Republic of Ireland	7	4	1	2	12	8	13
Slovakia	7	3	0	4	16	13	9
Wales	6	2	1	3	8	9	7
Cyprus	6	1	1	4	9	16	4
San Marino	6	0	0	6	1	36	0

Results: Czech Republic 2, **Wales** 1; Slovakia 6, Cyprus 1; Germany 1, Republic of Ireland 0; Slovakia 0, Czech Republic 3; San Marino 0, Germany 13; **Wales** 1, Slovakia 5; Czech Republic 7, San Marino 0; Cyprus 5, **Republic of Ireland** 2; **Republic of Ireland** 1, Czech Republic 1; **Wales** 3, Cyprus 1; Slovakia 1, Germany 4; **Republic of Ireland** 5, San Marino 0; Cyprus 1, Germany 1; San Marino 1, **Republic of Ireland** 2; **Republic of Ireland** 1, **Wales** 0; Cyprus 1, Slovakia 3; Czech Republic 1, Germany 2; Czech Republic 1, Cyprus 0; **Republic of Ireland** 1, Slovakia 0; **Wales** 3, San Marino 0; Germany 6, San Marino 0; **Wales** 0, Czech Republic 0; Germany 2, Slovakia 1.

To play: Aug. 22: San Marino v Cyprus; Sept. 8: San Marino v Czech Republic, Slovakia v **Republic of Ireland**, **Wales** v Germany; Sept. 12: Cyprus v San Marino, Czech Republic v **Republic of Ireland**, Slovakia v **Wales**; Oct. 13: Cyprus v **Wales**, **Republic of Ireland** v Germany, Slovakia v San Marino; Oct. 17: Germany v Czech Republic, **Republic of Ireland** v Cyprus, San Marino v **Wales**; Nov. 17: Czech Republic v Slovakia, Germany v Cyprus, **Wales** v **Republic of Ireland**; Nov. 21: Cyprus v Czech Republic, Germany v **Wales**, San Marino v Slovakia.

GROUP E

	P	W	D	L	F	A	Pts
Croatia	7	5	2	0	16	4	17
Israel	8	5	2	1	17	7	17
Russia	7	4	3	0	11	1	15
England	7	4	2	1	12	2	14
Macedonia	7	2	1	4	6	7	7
Estonia	7	0	0	7	0	14	0
Andorra	7	0	0	7	1	28	0

Results: Estonia 0 Macedonia 1; **England** 5, Andorra 0; Estonia 0, Israel 1; Russia 0, Croatia 0; Israel 4, Andorra 1; Macedonia 0, **England** 1; **England** 0, Macedonia 0; Russia 1, Israel 1; Croatia 7, Andorra 0; Andorra 0, Macedonia 3; Croatia 2, **England** 0; Russia 2, Estonia 0; Macedonia 0, Russia 2; Israel 3, Croatia 4; Croatia 2, Macedonia 1; Israel 0, **England** 0; Estonia 0, Russia 2; Israel 4, Estonia 0; Andorra 0, **England** 3; Estonia 0, Croatia 1; Russia 4, Andorra 0; Macedonia 1, Israel 2; Andorra 0, Israel 2; Croatia 0, Russia 0; Estonia 0, **England** 3.

To play: Aug. 22: Estonia v Andorra; Sept. 8: Croatia v Estonia, **England** v Israel, Russia v Macedonia; Sept. 12: Andorra v Croatia, **England** v Russia, Macedonia v Estonia; Oct. 13: **England** v Estonia; Oct. 17: Croatia v Israel, Macedonia v Andorra, Russia v **England**; Nov. 17: Andorra v Estonia, Israel v Russia, Macedonia v Croatia; Nov. 21: Andorra v Russia, **England** v Croatia, Israel v Macedonia.

GROUP F

	P	W	D	L	F	A	Pts
Sweden	6	5	0	1	14	4	15
Spain	7	5	0	2	13	6	15
Northern Ireland	6	4	1	1	10	7	13
Denmark	5	3	1	1	9	2	10
Liechtenstein	7	1	1	5	4	18	4
Iceland	7	1	1	5	5	15	4
Latvia	6	1	0	5	4	7	3

Results: Northern Ireland 0, Iceland 3; Latvia 0, Sweden 1; Spain 4, Liechtenstein 0; Iceland 0, Denmark 2; Sweden 3, Liechtenstein 1; **Northern Ireland** 3, Spain 2; Sweden 2, Spain 0; Denmark 0, **Northern Ireland** 0; Latvia 4, Iceland 0; Iceland 1, Sweden 2; Liechtenstein 0, Denmark 4; **Northern Ireland** 1, Latvia 0; Liechtenstein 1, **Northern Ireland** 4; Spain 2, Denmark 1; Liechtenstein 1, Latvia 0; **Northern Ireland** 2, Sweden 1; Spain 1, Iceland 0; Latvia 0, Spain 2; Iceland 1, Liechtenstein 1; Denmark 3, Sweden 3*; Latvia 0, Denmark 2; Liechstenstein 0, Spain 2; Sweden 5, Iceland 0. *Sweden awarded match 3-0 after abandonment.

To play: Aug. 22: **Northern Ireland** v Liechtenstein; Sept. 8: Iceland v Spain, Latvia v **Northern Ireland**, Sweden v Denmark; Sept. 12: Denmark v Liechtenstein, Iceland v **Northern Ireland**, Spain v Latvia; Oct. 13: Denmark v Spain, Iceland v Latvia, Liechtenstein v Sweden; Oct. 17: Denmark v Latvia, Liechtenstein v Iceland, Sweden v **Northern Ireland**; Nov. 17: Latvia v Liechtenstein, **Northern Ireland** v Denmark, Spain v Sweden; Nov. 21: Denmark v Iceland, Spain v **Northern Ireland**, Sweden v Latvia.

GROUP G

	P	*W*	*D*	*L*	*F*	*A*	*Pts*
Romania	7	5	2	0	14	4	17
Bulgaria	7	4	3	0	11	4	15
Holland	6	4	2	0	8	2	14
Albania	7	2	3	2	8	6	9
Belarus	7	2	1	4	10	15	7
Slovenia	7	1	1	5	5	12	4
Luxembourg	7	0	0	7	1	14	0

Results: Belarus 2, Albania 2; Luxembourg 0, Holland 1; Romania 2, Bulgaria 2; Albania 0, Romania 2; Bulgaria 3, Slovenia 0; Holland 3, Belarus 0; Romania 3, Belarus 1; Slovenia 2, Luxembourg 0; Bulgaria 1, Holland 1; Belarus 4, Slovenia 2; Luxembourg 0, Bulgaria 1; Holland 2, Albania 1; Luxembourg 1, Belarus 2; Albania 0, Slovenia 0; Holland 0, Romania 0; Bulgaria 0, Albania 0; Romania 3, Luxembourg 0; Slovenia 0, Holland 1; Albania 2, Luxembourg 0; Belarus 0, Bulgaria 2; Slovenia 1, Romania 2; Bulgaria 2, Belarus 1; Luxembourg 0, Albania 3; Romania 2, Slovenia 0.

To play: Sept. 8: Belarus v Romania, Holland v Bulgaria, Luxembourg v Slovenia; Sept. 12: Albania v Holland, Bulgaria v Luxembourg, Slovenia v Belarus; Oct. 13: Belarus v Luxembourg, Romania v Holland, Slovenia v Albania; Oct. 17: Albania v Bulgaria, Holland v Slovenia, Luxembourg v Romania; Nov. 17: Albania v Belarus, Bulgaria v Romania, Holland v Luxembourg; Nov. 21: Belarus v Holland, Romania v Albania, Slovenia v Bulgaria.

PREVIOUS FINALS

1960	*USSR	2	Yugoslavia	1	(Paris)
1964	Spain	2	USSR	1	(Madrid)
1968	**Italy	2	Yugoslavia	0	(Rome)
1972	West Germany	3	USSR	0	(Brussels)
1976	***Czechoslovakia	2	West Germany	2	(Belgrade)
1980	West Germany	2	Belgium	1	(Rome)
1984	France	2	Spain	0	(Paris)
1988	Holland	2	USSR	0	(Munich)
1992	Denmark	2	Germany	0	(Gothenburg)
1996	+Germany	2	Czech Republic	1	(Wembley)
2000	+France	2	Italy	1	(Rotterdam)
2004	Greece	1	Portugal	0	(Lisbon)

* After extra-time. ** Replay after 1-1. *** Czechoslovakia won 5-3 on pens. + Golden goal winner.

Poland and the Ukraine will be joint hosts for the 2012 finals.

BRITISH AND IRISH INTERNATIONALS 2006-07

*(Denotes new cap)

EUROPEAN CHAMPIONSHIP 2008 – QUALIFYING

ENGLAND 5, ANDORRA 0

Group E, Old Trafford (56,290), Saturday, September 2, 2006

England (4-1-3-2): Robinson (Tottenham), Neville (Everton) (Lennon, Tottenham, 64), Brown (Manchester Utd.), Terry (Chelsea), A. Cole (Chelsea), Hargreaves (Bayern Munich), Gerrard (Liverpool), Lampard (Chelsea), Downing (Middlesbrough) (Richardson, Manchester Utd., 64), Crouch (Liverpool), Defoe (Tottenham) (Johnson, Everton, 71). **Scorers:** Crouch (5, 66), Gerrard (13), Defoe (38, 47). **Booked:** Brown

Andorra (4-5-1): Alvarez, Ayala, Lima Sola, Sonejee, J. Garcia, Javier Sanchez (Julio Sanchez 46), Ruiz, Vieira, Sivera (Genis Garcia 77), Pujol (Jimenez 48), Silva. **Booked:** Sivera, Jimenez, Lima Sola.

Referee: B. Brugger (Austria). **Half-time:** 3-0.

SCOTLAND 6, FAROE ISLANDS 0

Group B, Celtic Park (50,059), Saturday, September 2, 2006

Scotland (4-3-3): Gordon (Hearts), Dailly (West Ham Utd.), Pressley (Hearts), Weir (Everton), Naysmith (Everton), Fletcher (Manchester Utd.) (Teale, Wigan Athletic, 46), Hartley (Hearts), Quashie (W.B.A.) (Severin, Aberdeen, 84), Miller (Celtic) (O'Connor, Lokomotiv Moscow, 61), Boyd (Rangers), McFadden (Everton). **Scorers:** Fletcher (7), McFadden (10), Boyd (24 pen, 38), Miller (30 pen), O'Connor (85). **Booked:** Fletcher, Miller.

Faroe Islands (4-5-1): Mikkelsen, ABorg, Johannesen, Danielsen, Joensen, Hansen, Johnsson (Samuelsen 76), Benjaminsen, Frederiksberg (Thorleifsson 60), R. Jacobsen (Neilsen 84), C. Jacobsen. **Booked:** ABorg, Benjaminsen, Frederiksberg, Johannesen.

Referee: I. Egorov (Russia). **Half-time:** 5-0.

CZECH REPUBLIC 2, WALES 1

Group D, Teplice (16,204), Saturday, September 2, 2006

Czech Republic (4-4-2): Cech, Ujfalusi, Jiranez, Rozehnal, Jankulovski, Stajner (Sionko, 46), Rosicky, Galazek (Kovac, 88), Plasil, Koller, Kulic (Lafata, 75). **Scorer:** Lafata (76, 89).

Wales (3-5-2): Jones (Q.P.R.), Collins (West Ham Utd.), Gabbidon (West Ham Utd.), Nyatanga (Derby Co.), Delaney (Aston Villa) (Cotterill; Wigan Athletic, 79), Davies (Everton), Fletcher (Crystal Palace) (Ledley, Cardiff City, 46), Robinson (Norwich City), Ricketts (Hull City) (Earnshaw, Norwich City, 79), Bellamy (Liverpool), Giggs (Manchester Utd.). **Scorer:** Jiranek (85 og). **Booked:** Robinson.

Referee: J. Eriksson (Sweden). **Half-time:** 0-0.

NORTHERN IRELAND 0, ICELAND 3

Group F, Windsor Park (14,500), Saturday, September 2, 2006

Northern Ireland (4-4-2): Taylor (Birmingham City), Baird (Southampton), Hughes (Aston Villa), Craigan (Motherwell), Capaldi (Plymouth Argyle) (Duff, Burnley, 77), Gillespie (Sheffield Utd.), Clingan (Nott'm. Forest), Davis (Aston Villa), Elliott (Hull City) (Lafferty, Burnley, 64), Quinn (Northampton Town) (Feeney, Luton Town, 83), Healy (Leeds Utd.). **Booked:** Healy,

Iceland (4-4-1-1): Arason, Steinsson, Ingimarsson, Hreidarsson, I. Sigurdsson, Arnason (Danielsson 32), Gunnarsson (Gislason 75), Gudjonsson, H. Sigurdsson (Johnsson 64), Gudjohnsen, Thorvaldsson. **Scorers:** Thorvaldsson (13), Hreidarsson (20), Gudjohnsen (37). **Booked:** I. Sigurdsson.

Referee: T. Skjerven (Norway). **Half-time:** 0-3.

GERMANY 1, REPUBLIC OF IRELAND 0

Group D, Stuttgart (53,198), Saturday, September 2, 2006

Germany (4-4-2):Lehmann, Lahm, A. Friedrich, M. Friedrich, Jansen, Schneider (Borowski 83), Ballack, Frings, Schweinsteiger, Klose, Podolski (Neuville 76). **Scorer:** Podolski (57). **Booked:** Schweinsteiger, Klose, Schneider.

Republic of Ireland (4-4-1-1): Given (Newcastle Utd.), Carr (Newcastle Utd.), Dunne (Manchester City), Andy O'Brien (Portsmouth), Finnan (Liverpool), Reid (Blackburn Rov.), O'Shea (Manchester Utd.), Kilbane (Wigan Athletic) (Alan O'Brien, Newcastle Utd., 83), Duff (Newcastle Utd.) (McGeady, Celtic, 76), Keane (Tottenham), Doyle (Reading) (Elliott, Sunderland, 78). **Booked:** Given, Dunne, Reid.

Referee: L. Medina (Spain). **Half-time:** 0-0.

MACEDONIA 0, ENGLAND 1

Group E, Skopje (16,500), Wednesday, September 6, 2006

Macedonia (3-4-1-2): Nikolovski, Sedloski, Mitreski, Noveski, Lazarevski, Jancevski (Tasevski 51), Simulikoski, Petrov, Pandev, Naumoski, Maznov (Stojkov 56). **Booked:** Naumoski, Lazarevski, Pandev.

England (4-1-3-2): Robinson (Tottenham), Neville (Everton), Ferdinand (Manchester Utd.), Terry (Chelsea), A. Cole (Chelsea), Hargreaves (Bayern Munich), Gerrard (Liverpool), Lampard (Chelsea) (Carrick, Manchester Utd., 84), Downing (Middlesbrough), Crouch (Liverpool) (Johnson, Everton, 87), Defoe (Tottenham) (Lennon, Tottenham, 76). **Scorer:** Crouch (46). **Booked:** Crouch, Gerrard, A. Cole.

Referee: B. Layec (France). **Half-time:** 0-0.

LITHUANIA 1, SCOTLAND 2

Group B, Kaunas (6,500), Wednesday, September 6, 2006

Lithuania (4-4-2): Karcemarskas, Stankevicius, Skerla, Zvirgdauskas, Dziakjuaskas, Mikoliunas, Savenas (Tamosauskas, 55), Preiksaitis (Miceika 82), Kalonas, Poskus, Danilevicius. **Scorer:** Miceika (85). **Booked:** Zvirgdauskas, Preiksaitis, Poskus, Kalonas.

Scotland (4-1-4-1): Gordon (Hearts), Dailly (West Ham Utd.), Pressley (Hearts), Weir (Everton), Naysmith (Everton), Caldwell (Celtic), Fletcher (Manchester Utd.), Hartley (Hearts) (Severin, Aberdeen, 89), Quashie (W.B.A.) (Boyd, Rangers, 43), McFadden (Everton) (Alexander, Preston N.E., 22), Miller (Celtic). **Scorers:** Dailly (46), Miller (62). **Booked:** Miller, Dailly, Caldwell.

Referee: V. Hrinak (Slovakia). **Half-time:** 0-0.

NORTHERN IRELAND 3, SPAIN 2

Group F, Windsor Park (14,500), Wednesday, September 6, 2006

Northern Ireland (4-1-3-2) Carroll (West Ham Utd.) (Taylor, Birmingham City, 11), Duff (Burnley), Craigan (Motherwell), Hughes (Aston Villa), *Evans (Manchester Utd.), Baird (Southampton), Clingan (Nott'm Forest), Davis (Aston Villa), Gillespie (Sheffield Utd.), Healy (Leeds Utd.) (Feeney, Luton Town, 85), Lafferty (Burnley) (Quinn, Northampton Town, 81). **Scorer:** Healy (20, 64, 80). **Booked:** Duff, Feeney.

Spain (4-3-1-2): Casillas, Ramos (Salgado 46), Puyol, Pablo, Antonio Lopez, Xabi Alonso, Albelda (Fabregas 29), Xavi, Raul, Torres (Luis Garcia 63), Villa. **Scorers:** Xavi (14), Villa (52). **Booked:** Antonio Lopez, Puyol.

Referee: F. De Bleeckere (Belgium). **Half-time:** 1-1.

ENGLAND 0, MACEDONIA 0

Group E, Old Trafford (72,062), Saturday, October 7, 2006

England (4-4-2): Robinson (Tottenham), Neville (Manchester Utd.), Terry (Chelsea), King (Tottenham), A. Cole (Chelsea), Gerrard (Liverpool), Lampard (Chelsea), Carrick (Manchester Utd.), Downing (Middlesbrough) (Wright-Phillips, Chelsea, 69), Rooney (Manchester Utd.) (Defoe, Tottenham, 74), Crouch (Liverpool). **Booked:** Gerrard.

Macedonia (5-2-2-1): Nikolovski, Lazarevski, Sedloski, I. Mitreski, Noveski, Petrov, A. Mitrevski, Simulikovski, Maznov, Naumoski (Stojkov 46), Pandev (Tasevski 82). **Booked:** Petrov.

Referee: M. Merk (Germany). **Half-time:** 0-0.

SCOTLAND 1, FRANCE 0

Group B, Hampden Park (57,000), Saturday, October 7, 2006

Scotland (4-5-1): Gordon (Hearts), Dailly (West Ham Utd.), Pressley (Hearts), Caldwell (Celtic), Weir (Everton), Alexander (Preston N.E.), Hartley (Hearts), Fletcher (Manchester Utd.), Ferguson (Rangers), McCulloch (Wigan Athletic) (Teale, Wigan Athletic, 58), McFadden (Everton) (O'Connor, Lokomotiv Moscow, 72). **Scorer:** Caldwell (67). **Booked:** Dailly, McCulloch, McFadden.

France (4-4-2): Coupet, Sagnol, Thuram, Boumsong, Abidal, Ribery (Wiltord 73), Makelele, Vieira, Malouda, Trezeguet (Saha 62), Henry.

Referee: M. Busacca (Switzerland). **Half-time:** 0-0.

WALES 1, SLOVAKIA 5

Group D, Millennium Stadium (28,493), Saturday, October 7, 2006

Wales (5-3-2): Jones (Q.P.R.), Duffy (Portsmouth), Edwards (Wolves) (Ledley, Cardiff City, 58), Gabbidon (West Ham Utd.), Nyatanga (Derby Co.), Bale (Southampton), Davies (Everton) (Cotterill, Wigan Athletic, 88), Robinson (Norwich City), Koumas (W.B.A.), Earnshaw (Norwich City) (Parry, Cardiff City, 46), Bellamy (Liverpool). **Scorer:** Bale (37). **Booked:** Koumas, Davies.

Slovakia (4-3-2-1): Contofalsky, P. Petras, Kratochvil, Varga, Durica, Karhan (Krajik 67), M. Petras, Kozak, Mintal (Hodur 71), Svento, Vittek (Holosko 77). **Scorers:** Svento (14), Mintal (32, 38), Karhan (51), Vittek (59).

Referee: D. Van Egmond (Holland). **Half-time:** 1-3.

DENMARK 0, NORTHERN IRELAND 0

Group F, Copenhagen (41,482), Saturday, October 7, 2006

Denmark (4-3-3): Sorensen (Christiansen 68), Jacobsen, Agger, Gravgaard, N. Jensen (Bendtner 73), Poulsen, D. Jensen, Jorgensen, Kahlenberg, Tomasson, Lovenkrands (C. Jensen 56).

Northern Ireland (4-4-2): Taylor (Birmingham City), Duff (Burnley), Craigan (Motherwell), Hughes (Aston Villa), Evans (Manchester Utd.), Gillespie (Sheffield Utd.), Davis (Aston Villa), Clingan (Nott'm. Forest) (Johnson (Birmingham City, 56), Baird (Southampton), Healy (Leeds Utd.) (Feeney, Luton Town, 84), Lafferty (Burnley) (Jones, Burnley, 63). **Booked:** Taylor, Duff, Evans, Gillespie.

Referee: K. Plautz (Austria). **Half-time:** 0-0.

CYPRUS 5, REPUBLIC OF IRELAND 2

Group D, Nicosia (12,000), Saturday, October 7, 2006

Cyprus (4-1-4-1): Morphis, Theodotou, Louka, Lambrou, Garpozis (Charalambous 77), Satsias, Okkas (Yiasoumi 86), Makridis, Michail (Charalambidis 46), Aloneftis, Konstantinou. **Scorers:** Konstantinou (10, 50 pen), Garpozis (16), Charalambidis (60, 75). **Booked:** Morphis, Garpozis, Konstantinou, Stasias, Okkas, Aloneftis, Theodotou.

Republic of Ireland (4-4-2): Kenny (Sheffield Utd.), Finnan (Liverpool), Andy O'Brien (Portsmouth) (Lee, Ipswich Town, 72), Dunne (Manchester City), O'Shea (Manchester Utd.), McGeady (Celtic) (Alan O'Brien, Newcastle Utd., 81), Ireland (Manchester City) (Douglas, Leeds Utd., 83), Kilbane (Wigan Athletic), Duff (Newcastle Utd.), Morrison (Crystal Palace), Keane (Tottenham). **Scorers:** Ireland (8), Dunne (44). **Booked:** Dunne, O'Shea, Keane. **Sent-off:** Dunne.

Referee: L. Batista (Portugal). **Half-time:** 2-2.

CROATIA 2, ENGLAND 0

Group E, Zagreb (38,000), Wednesday, October 11, 2006

Croatia (4-1-3-2): Pletikosa, Corluka, R. Kovac, Simic, Simunic, N. Kovac, Rapaic (Olic 73), Modric, Kranjcar (Babic 89), Da Silva (Leko 82), Petric. **Scorers:** Da Silva (61), Neville (69 og). **Booked:** N. Kovac.

England (3-5-2): Robinson (Tottenham), Ferdinand (Manchester Utd.), Terry (Chelsea), Carragher (Liverpool) (Wright-Phillips, Chelsea, 72), Neville (Manchester Utd.), Carrick (Manchester Utd.), Parker (Newcastle Utd.) (Defoe, Tottenham, 72), Lampard (Chelsea), A. Cole (Chelsea), Rooney (Manchester Utd.), Crouch (Liverpool) (Richardson, Manchester Utd., 72). **Booked:** Ferdinand, A. Cole.

Referee: R. Rossetti (Italy). **Half-time:** 0-0.

UKRAINE 2, SCOTLAND 0

Group B, Kiev (40,000), Wednesday, October 11, 2006

Ukraine (4-4-2): Shovkovskiy, Sviderskiy, Kucher, Rusol, Nesmachniy, Gusev (Milevsky 62), Tymoschuk, Shelayev, Kalinichenko (Vorobey 76), Shevchenko, Voronin. **Scorers:** Kucher (60), Shevchenko (90 pen). **Booked:** Kucher.

Scotland (5-4-1): Gordon (Hearts), *Neilson (Hearts) (*McManus, Celtic, 89), Caldwell (Celtic), Pressley (Hearts), Weir (Everton), Alexander (Preston N.E.), Hartley (Hearts), Fletcher (Manchester Utd.), Ferguson (Rangers), McFadden (Everton) (Boyd, Rangers, 73), Miller (Celtic). **Booked:** McFadden, Fletcher, Neilson. **Sent-off:** Pressley.

Referee: M. Hansson (Sweden). **Half-time:** 0-0.

WALES 3, CYPRUS 1

Group D, Millennium Stadium (20,456), Wednesday, October 11, 2006

Wales (5-3-2): Price (Ipswich Town), Duffy (Portsmouth) (Edwards, Wolves, 79), *Morgan (MK Dons), Gabbidon (West Ham Utd.), Nyatanga (Derby Co.), Bale (Southampton), Davies (Everton), Robinson (Norwich City), Koumas (W.B.A.) (Ledley, Cardiff City, 76), Earnshaw (Norwich City), Bellamy (Liverpool) (Parry, Cardiff City, 90). **Scorers:** Koumas (33), Earnshaw (39), Bellamy (72). **Booked:** Koumas.

Cyprus (4-4-1-1): Morphis, Theodotou, Louka, Lambrou, Garpozis (Charalambidis 46), Michail (Charalambous 46), Satsias (Yiasoumi 84), Makridis, Aloneftis, Okkas, Konstantinou. **Scorer:** Okkas (83). **Booked:** Garpozis, Satsias.

Referee: J. Granat (Poland). **Half-time:** 2-0.

NORTHERN IRELAND 1, LATVIA 0

Group F, Windsor Park (14,500), Wednesday, October 11, 2006

Northern Ireland (4-4-2): Taylor (Birmingham City), Baird (Southampton), Craigan (Motherwell), Hughes (Aston Villa), Evans (Manchester Utd.), Gillespie (Sheffield Utd.), Johnson (Birmingham City), Davis (Aston Villa), Clingan (Nott'm. Forest), Healy (Leeds Utd.), (Feeney, Luton Town, 89), Lafferty (Burnley) (Quinn, Northampton Town, 88). **Scorer:** Healy (35). **Booked:** Lafferty.

Latvia (4-4-2): Kolinko, Smirnovs (Gorkss 46), Stepanovs, Kacanovs, Zimis, Pahars, Astafjevs, Laizans, Solonicins (Visnjakovs 86), Verpakovskis, Karlsons. **Booked:** Gorkss, Astafjevs.

Referee: H. Fleischer (Germany). **Half-time:** 1-0.

REPUBLIC OF IRELAND 1, CZECH REPUBLIC 1

Group D, Lansdowne Road (35,500), Wednesday, October 11, 2006

Republic of Ireland (4-5-1): Henderson (Brighton & H.A.), Finnan (Liverpool), *McShane (W.B.A.), O'Shea (Manchester Utd.), Kelly (Birmingham City), Duff (Newcastle Utd.), Douglas (Leeds Utd.), Reid (Charlton Athletic) (A. Quinn, Sheffield Utd., 71), Carsley (Everton), Kilbane (Wigan Athletic) (O'Brien, Newcastle Utd., 79), Keane (Tottenham). **Scorer:** Kilbane (62). **Booked:** Kilbane, Douglas, Carsley.

Czech Republic (4-3-3): Cech, Ujfalusi, Jiranek, Rozenhal, Jankulovski, Rosicky, Kovac, Polak, Plasil (Grygera 85), Koller, Baros (Jarolim 83). **Scorer:** Koller (64). **Booked:** Baros, Polak, Rozenhal, Kovac.

Referee: B. Layec (France). **Half-time:** 0-0.

REPUBLIC OF IRELAND 5, SAN MARINO 0

Group D, Lansdowne Road (34,018), Wednesday, November 15, 2006

Republic of Ireland (4-4-2): Given (Newcastle Utd.), O'Shea (Manchester Utd.), McShane (W.B.A.), Dunne (Manchester City), Finnan (Liverpool), Duff (Newcastle Utd.), Carsley (Everton) (Douglas, Leeds Utd., 50), Reid (Charlton Athletic), Kilbane (Wigan Athletic) (Lee, Ipswich Town, 79), Doyle (Reading) (McGeady, Celtic, 63), Keane (Tottenham). **Scorers:** Reid (7), Doyle (24), Keane (31, 58 pen, 85). **Booked:** McShane.

San Marino (5-4-1): F. Valentini, C. Valentini, Albani, Bacciocchi, D. Simoncini (Bonini 81), Vannucci (Crescentini 72), Andreini, Bugli, Manuel Marani, Mariotti (Michele Marani 59), Selva. **Booked:** Selva.

Referee: L. Isaksen (Faroe Islands). **Half-time:** 3-0.

SAN MARINO 1, REPUBLIC OF IRELAND 2

Group D, Rimini (3,294), Wednesday, February 7, 2007

San Marino (5-4-1): A. Simoncini, Valentini, D. Simoncini, Muccioli, Albani, Michele Marani, Bonini (Vannucci 76), Domeniconi (Bugli 86), Manuel Marani, Gasperoni (Andreini 66), Selva. **Scorer:** Manuel Marani (86). **Booked:** D. Simoncini, Selva.

Republic of Ireland (4-4-2): Henderson (Preston N.E.), Finnan (Liverpool), Dunne (Manchester City), O'Shea (Manchester Utd.) (McShane, W.B.A., 46), Harte (Levante) (*Hunt, Reading, 74), Duff (Newcastle Utd.), Ireland (Manchester City), Carsley (Everton), Kilbane (Wigan Athletic), *Long (Reading) (*Stokes, Sunderland, 81), Keane (Tottenham). **Scorers:** Kilbane (49), Ireland (90).

Referee: P. Rasmussen (Denmark). **Half-time:** 0-0.

ISRAEL 0, ENGLAND 0

Group E, Tel Aviv (35,000), Saturday, March 24, 2007

Israel (4-5-1): Aouate, Ben Haim, Gershon, Ziv, Benado, Shpungin, Badir, Benayoun, Ben Shushan (Alberman 87), Tamuz (Bardar 75), Balili (Sahar 69). **Booked:** Benado, Ben Haim.

England (4-1-3-2): Robinson (Tottenham), Neville (Everton) (Richards, Manchester City, 72), Ferdinand (Manchester Utd.), Terry (Chelsea), Carragher (Liverpool); Hargreaves (Bayern Munich), Gerrard (Liverpool), Lampard (Chelsea), Lennon (Tottenham) (Downing, Middlesbrough, 83) Rooney (Manchester Utd.), Johnson (Everton) (Defoe, Tottenham, 80). **Booked:** Carragher, Rooney.

Referee: T. Ovrebo (Norway). **Half-time:** 0-0.

SCOTLAND 2, GEORGIA 1

Group B, Hampden Park (50,850), Saturday, March 24, 2007

Scotland (4-4-2): Gordon (Hearts), Alexander (Preston N.E.), Weir (Rangers), McManus (Celtic), Naysmith (Everton), Teale (Derby Co.) (*Brown, Hibernian 60), Ferguson (Rangers), Hartley (Celtic), McCulloch (Wigan Athletic), Miller (Celtic) (Maloney, Aston Villa, 90), Boyd (Rangers) (Beattie, Celtic, 76). **Scorers:** Boyd (11), Beattie (89). **Booked:** Ferguson.

Georgia (4-4-2): Lomaia, Shashiashvili, Salukvadze, Khizanishvili, Eliava, Burduli (Siradze 57), Menteshasvili (Gogua 46), Tskitishvili (Mujiri 90), Kobiashvili, Demetradze, Arveladze. **Scorer:** Arveladze (41). **Booked:** Menteshashvili, Salukvadze, Demetradze.

Referee: N. Vollquartz (Denmark). **Half-time:** 1-1.

REPUBLIC OF IRELAND 1, WALES 0

Group D, Croke Park (72,539), Saturday, March 24, 2007

Republic of Ireland (4-4-2): Given (Newcastle Utd.), Finnan (Liverpool), McShane (W.B.A.), Dunne (Manchester City), O'Shea (Manchester Utd.), Douglas (Leeds Utd.) (Hunt, Reading, 80), Carsley (Everton), Ireland (Manchester City) (Doyle, Reading, 59), Kilbane (Wigan Athletic), Keane (Tottenham) (McGeady, Celtic, 89). Duff (Newcastle Utd.). **Scorer:** Ireland (39). **Booked:** Keane.

Wales (5-3-2): Coyne (Burnley), Ricketts (Hull City), J. Collins (West Ham Utd.), Evans (Wrexham), Nyatanga (Derby Co.), Bale (Southampton), (D. Collins, Sunderland, 74), Davies (Fulham), Robinson (Toronto) (Easter, Wycombe Wand., 90), Ledley (Cardiff City) (Fletcher, Crystal Palace, 46), Giggs (Manchester Utd.), Bellamy (Liverpool). **Booked:** Ricketts, Robinson.

Referee: T. Hauge (Norway). **Half-time:** 1-0.

LIECHTENSTEIN 1, NORTHERN IRELAND 4

Group F, Vaduz (4,340), Saturday, March 24, 2007

Liechtenstein (4-4-1-1): Jehle, Oehri (Tesler 67), Martin Stocklasa, Ritter, Michael Stocklasa, Rohrer (S. Buchel 87), R. Buchel (D. Frick 87), M. Buchel, Burgmeier, M. Frick, Beck. **Scorer:** Burgmeier (90). **Booked:** Burgmeier, M. Buchel.

Northern Ireland (4-4-2): Taylor (Birmingham City), Duff (Burnley), Hughes (Aston Villa), Craigan (Motherwell), Evans (Manchester Utd.), Gillespie (Sheffield Utd.), Johnson (Birmingham City), Davis (Aston Villa), Brunt (Sheffield Wed.) (McCann, Barnsley, 67), Healy (Leeds Utd.) (Jones, Burnley, 84), Lafferty (Burnley) (Feeney, Luton Town, 55). **Scorers:** Healy (52, 75, 83). McCann (90). **Booked:** Gillespie.

Referee: O. Oriekhov (Ukraine). **Half-time:** 0-0.

ANDORRA 0, ENGLAND 3

Group E, Barcelona (12,800), Wednesday, March 28, 2007

Andorra (4-5-1): Alvarez, Ayala, Sonejee, Lima Sola, Escura, Genis Garcia, Vieira, Justo (Fernandez 88), Pujol (Martinez 69), Bernaus, Toscano (Moreno 90). **Booked:** Lima Sola, Toscano, Sonejee, Genis Garcia.

England (4-4-2): Robinson (Tottenham), Richards (Manchester City) (Dyer, Newcastle Utd., 61), , Ferdinand (Manchester Utd.), Terry (Chelsea), A. Cole (Chelsea), Lennon (Tottenham), Gerrard (Liverpool), Hargreaves (Bayern Munich), Downing (Middlesbrough), Rooney (Manchester Utd.) (Defoe, Tottenham, 61), Johnson (Everton) (* Nugent, Preston N.E., 79). **Scorers:** Gerrard (54, 76), Nugent (90). **Booked:** Rooney, Hargreaves, A. Cole.

Referee: B. Duarte Paixao (Portugal). **Half-time:** 0-0.

ITALY 2, SCOTLAND 0

Group B, Bari (37,500), Wednesday, March 28, 2007

Italy (4-2-3-1): Buffon, Oddo, Cannavaro, Materazzi, Zambrotta, Gattuso, De Rossi, Camoranesi, Perrotta (Pirlo 77), Di Natale (Del Piero 66), Toni (Quagliarella 87). **Scorer:** Toni (12, 70).

Scotland (4-5-1): Gordon (Hearts), Alexander (Preston N.E.), Weir (Rangers), McManus (Celtic), Naysmith (Everton), Teale (Derby Co.) (Maloney, Aston Villa, 65), Brown (Hibernian) (Beattie, Celtic, 86), Hartley (Celtic), Ferguson (Rangers), McCulloch (Wigan Athletic) (Boyd, Rangers, 82), Miller (Celtic).

Referee: F. De Bleeckere (Belgium). **Half-time:** 1-0.

WALES 3, SAN MARINO 0

Group D, Millennium Stadium (18,752), Wednesday, March 28, 2007

Wales (4-4-2): Coyne (Burnley), Ricketts (Hull City), Evans (Wrexham) (Nyatanga, Derby Co., 62), Collins (West Ham Utd.), Bale (Southampton), Davies (Fulham), Fletcher (Crystal Palace), Koumas (W.B.A.), Giggs (Manchester Utd.) (Parry, Cardiff City, 73), Easter (Wycombe Wand.) (Cotterill, Wigan Athletic, 46), Bellamy (Liverpool). **Scorers:** Giggs (3), Bale (20), Koumas (63 pen). **Booked:** Koumas, Fletcher.

San Marino (5-4-1): Simoncini, Valentini (Toccaceli 85), Albani, Bacciocchi, Muccioli, Andreini, Negri (Nanni, 79), Domeniconi (Bugli 67), Marani, Gasperoni, Selva. **Booked:** Muccioli, Bacciocchi, Andreini

Referee: A. Tshagharyan (Armenia). **Half-time:** 2-0.

NORTHERN IRELAND 2, SWEDEN 1

Group F, Windsor Park (14,500), Wednesday, March 28, 2007

Northern Ireland (4-4-2): Taylor (Birmingham City), Duff (Burnley), Craigan (Motherwell), Hughes (Aston Villa), Evans (Manchester Utd.), Johnson (Birmingham City), McCann (Barnsley), Davis (Aston Villa), Brunt (Sheffield Wed.) (Sproule, Hibernian, 90), Healy (Leeds Utd.) (Webb, Ross Co., 89), Feeney (Luton Town) (Lafferty, Burnley, 71). **Scorer:** Healy (31, 58). **Booked:** Johnson

Sweden (4-1-3-2): Isaksson, Nilsson, Mellberg (Majstorovic 79), Hansson, Edman, Andersson, Alexandersson (Wilhelmsson 61), Svensson (Kallstrom 46). Ljungberg, Ibrahimovic, Elmander. **Scorer:** Elmander (26).

Referee: E. Braamhaar (Holland). **Half-time:** 1-1.

REPUBLIC OF IRELAND 1, SLOVAKIA 0

Group D, Croke Park (71,297), Wednesday, March 28, 2007

Republic of Ireland (4-4-1-1): Given (Newcastle Utd.), Finnan (Liverpool), McShane (W.B.A.), Dunne (Manchester City), O'Shea (Manchester Utd.), Carsley (Everton), Ireland (Manchester City) (Hunt, Reading, 70), McGeady (Celtic) (A. Quinn, Sheffield Utd., 86), Kilbane (Wigan Athletic), Duff (Newcastle Utd.), Doyle (Reading) (Long, Reading, 74). **Scorer:** Doyle (13).

Slovakia (4-1-4-1): Contofalsky, Singlar (Sestak 80), Skrtel, Klimpl, Gresko, Borbely, Zofcak, Sapara (Holosko 72), Vittek, Svento (Michalik 86), Jakubko. **Booked:** Klimpl.

Referee: Y. Baskakov (Russia). **Half-time:** 1-0.

WALES 0, CZECH REPUBLIC 0

Group D, Millennium Stadium (30,714), Saturday, June 2, 2007

Wales (3-5-1-1): Hennessey (Wolves), Collins (West Ham Utd.), Gabbidon (West Ham Utd.), Nyatanga (Derby Co.), Ricketts (Hull City), Davies (Fulham), Robinson (Toronto), Koumas (W.B.A.), Ledley (Cardiff City), Giggs (Manchester Utd.) (Earnshaw, Norwich City, 89), Bellamy (Liverpool).

Czech Republic (4-4-2): Cech, Ujfalusi, Kovac, Rozenhal, Jankulovski, Polak, Sivok (Matejovsky 83), Rosicky, Plasil, Baros (Kulic 46), Koller.

Referee: P. Allaerts (Belgium). **Half-time:** 0-0.

ESTONIA 0, ENGLAND 3

Group E, Tallinn (11,000), Wednesday, June 6, 2007

Estonia (4-2-3-1): Poom, Jaager, Stepanov, Klavan, Kruglov, Dmitrijev, Lindpere, Konsa (Neemolo 46), Vassiljev, Terehhov (Kink 64), Voskoboinikov.

England (4-4-2): Robinson (Tottenham), Brown (Manchester Utd.), King (Tottenham), Terry (Chelsea), Bridge (Chelsea), Beckham (Real Madrid) (Dyer, Newcastle Utd., 68), Gerrard (Liverpool), Lampard (Chelsea), J. Cole (Chelsea) (Downing, Middlesbrough, 76), Crouch (Liverpool), Owen (Newcastle Utd.) (Jenas, Tottenham, 88). **Scorers:** J. Cole (37), Crouch (54), Owen (62). **Booked:** Crouch.

Referee: G. Gilewski (Poland). **Half-time:** 0-1.

FAROE ISLANDS 0, SCOTLAND 2

Group B, Toftir (4,600), Wednesday, June 6, 2007

Faroe Islands (4-4-2): Mikkelsen, J. Jacobsen, Johanessen (Djurhuus 36) (Samuelsen 77), Benjaminsen, Danielsen, Aborg (Flotum 82), Olsen, Thomassen, C. Jacobsen, Holst, R. Jacobsen. **Booked:** Johanessen.

Scotland (4-4-2): Gordon (Hearts), Alexander (Preston N.E.), McManus (Celtic), Weir (Rangers), Naysmith (Everton), Fletcher (Manchester Utd.) (Teale, Derby Co., 68), Ferguson (Rangers), Hartley (Celtic), Maloney (Aston Villa) (Adam, Rangers, 77), Boyd (Rangers) (*Naismith, Kilmarnock, 83), O'Connor (Lokomotiv Moscow). **Scorers:** Maloney (31), O'Connor (35). **Booked:** Naysmith, O'Connor.

Referee: G. Kasnaferis (Greece). **Half-time:** 0-2.

FRIENDLY INTERNATIONALS

WALES 0, BULGARIA 0

Liberty Stadium, (8,200), Tuesday, August 15, 2006

Wales (4-4-2): Jones (Q.P.R.), Delaney (Aston Villa) (Duffy, Portsmouth, 61), Collins (West Ham Utd.), Gabbidon (West Ham Utd.) (Edwards, Wolves, 73), Ricketts (Hull City) (Vaughan, Crewe Alexandra, 69), Davies (Everton), Fletcher (Crystal Palace) (Ledley, Cardiff City, 52), Robinson (Norwich City), Giggs (Manchester Utd.) (Nyatanga, Derby Co., 52), Bellamy (Liverpool) (Parry, Cardiff City, 72), Earnshaw (Norwich City).

Bulgaria (4-2-3-1): Petkov (Ivankov 46), Angelov (Iliev 82), Kirilov, Tomasic, Vagner, S. Petrov, Kishishev (Y.Todorov 73), Peev (Georgiev 56), Iankovic (S. Todorov 64), M. Petrov (Lazarov 56), Berbatov. **Booked:** Tomasic.

Referee: J. Attard (Malta). **Half-time:** 0-0.

ENGLAND 4, GREECE 0

Old Trafford (45,864), Wednesday, August 16, 2006

England (4-1-3-2): Robinson (Tottenham) (Kirkland, Liverpool, 46), Neville (Manchester Utd.) (Carragher, Liverpool, 77), Ferdinand (Manchester Utd.), Terry (Chelsea), Cole (Arsenal) (Bridge, Chelsea, 80), Hargreaves (Bayern Munich), Gerrard (Liverpool) (D. Bent, Charlton Athletic, 77), Lampard (Chelsea), Downing (Middlesbrough) (Richardson, Manchester Utd., 68), Defoe (Tottenham) (Lennon, Tottenham, 68), Crouch (Liverpool). **Scorers:** Terry (14), Lampard (30), Crouch (35, 42).

Greece (5-4-1): Nikopolidis, Vyntra, Antzas (Kyrgiakos 46), Dellas (Anatolakis 63), Katsouranis, Fyssas (Lagos 28), Charisteas, Zagorakis (Basinas 46), Karagounis, Giannakopoulos (Salpigidis 46), Samaras (Amanatidis 46).

Referee: W. Stark (Germany). **Half-time:** 4-0 (Steve McClaren's first match as head coach),

FINLAND 1, NORTHERN IRELAND 2

Helsinki (12,500), Wednesday, August 16, 2006

Finland (4-4-2): Jaaskelainen, Pasanen, Tihinen, Hyypia (Pasoja 82), Kallio, Nurmela (Johansson 75), Riiihilahti (Wiss 46), Ilola (Vayrynen 46), Kolkka (Lagerblom 75), Eremenko, Forssell (Kuqi 58). **Scorer:** Vayrynen (74). **Booked:** Wiss.

Northern Ireland (4-4-2): Taylor (Birmingham City) (Carroll, West Ham Utd., 46) Baird (Southampton), Hughes (Aston Villa) (Duff, Burnley, 65), Craigan (Motherwell), Capaldi (Plymouth Argyle), Gillespie (Sheffield Utd.) (Jones, Burnley, 46), Clingan (Nott'm. Forest), McCann (Cheltenham Town), Elliott (Hull City) (Sproule, Hibernian, 65), Quinn (Northampton Town) (Lafferty, Burnley, 52), Healy (Leeds Utd.) (Feeney, Luton Town, 46). **Scorers:** Healy (34), Lafferty (64). **Booked:** Quinn, Carroll.

Referee: M. Svendsen (Denmark). **Half-time:** 0-1.

REPUBLIC OF IRELAND 0, HOLLAND 4

Lansdowne Road (42,400), Wednesday, August 16, 2006

Republic of Ireland (4-4-2): Kenny (Sheffield Utd.), Carr (Newcastle Utd.) (Doyle, Reading, 46), Andy O'Brien (Portsmouth), O'Shea (Manchester Utd.), Finnan (Liverpool) (Kelly, Birmingham City, 64), McGeady (Celtic), Reid (Blackburn Rov.) (Miller, Manchester Utd., 46), Kavanagh (Wigan Athletic) (*Alan O'Brien, Newcastle Utd., 46), Kilbane (Everton), Elliott (Sunderland), Morrison (Crystal Palace) (Douglas, Blackburn Rov., 46).

Holland (4-3-3): Van der Sar, Heitinga, Ooijer (Jaliens 77), Mathijsen, De Cler (Emanuelson 61), Landzaat (De Jong 61), Schaars (Janssen 83), Van der Vaart, Van Persie, Huntelaar, Robben (Kuyt 46). **Scorers:** Huntelaar (25, 53), Robben (41), Van Persie (70). **Booked:** Landzaat.

Referee: T. Overbo (Norway). **Half-time:** 0-2.

WALES 0, BRAZIL 2

White Hart Lane (22,008), Tuesday, September 5, 2006

Wales (3-5-2): Jones (Q.P.R.), Collins (West Ham Utd.), Gabbidon (West Ham Utd.), Nyatanga (Derby Co.), Duffy (Portsmouth) (Edwards, Wolves 63), Davies (Everton) (Vaughan, Crewe Alexandra, 67), Robinson (Norwich City) (Fletcher, Crystal Palace, 52), Giggs (Manchester Utd.) (Ricketts (Hull City, 46), Bale (Southampton) (Ledley, Cardiff City, 46), Bellamy (Liverpool), Earnshaw (Norwich City) (Cotterill, Wigan Athletic, 76).

Brazil (3-4-2-1): Gomes, Malcon (Cicinho 58), Luisao, Alex, Julio Baptista (Rafael Sobis 78), Edmilson (Gilberto Silva 46), Dudu Cearense, Marcelo (Gilberto 75), Kaka (Elano 71), Ronaldinho (Robinho 67), Vagner Love. **Scorers:** Marcelo (61), Vagner Love (74).

Referee: M. Riley (England). **Half-time:** 0-0.

WALES 4, LIECHTENSTEIN 0

Racecourse Ground (8,752), Tuesday, November 14, 2006

Wales (4-4-2): Brown (Blackburn Rov.), Duffy (Portsmouth) (Ledley, Cardiff City, 46), *Evans (Wrexham), Nyatanga (Derby Co.), Ricketts (Hull City), S. Davies (Everton) (*Jones, Wrexham, 70), Robinson (Norwich City) (Crofts, Gillingham, 81), Giggs (Manchester Utd.) (Fletcher, Crystal Palace, 46), Koumas (W.B.A.) (C. Davies, Wolves), Earnshaw (Norwich City) (Llewellyn, Wrexham, 59), Bellamy (Liverpool). **Scorers:** Koumas (9, 15), Bellamy (78), Llewellyn (90).

Leichtenstein (4-4-2): Jehle, Telser, Hasler, Ritter, Ritzberger (D. Frick 59), D'Elia (Rohrer 59), M. Buchel, Stocklasa, Burgmeier, Beck (Kieber 89), M. Frick (R. Buchel 82). **Booked:** Telser.

Referee: L. Wilmes (Luxembourg). **Half-time:** 2-0.

HOLLAND 1, ENGLAND 1

Amsterdam (44,000), Wednesday, November 15, 2006

Holland (4-3-3): Timmer (Stekelenburg 46), Boulahrouz,(Jaliens 61), Ooijer (Vennegoor of Hesselink 83), Mathijsen, Emanuelson, Landzaat, Schaars, Seedorf, Robben, Kuyt (Huntelaar 61), Van der Vaart. **Scorer:** Van der Vaart (86).

England (4-3-3): Robinson (Tottenham), *Richards (Manchester City), Ferdinand (Manchester Utd.), Terry (Chelsea), A. Cole (Chelsea), Gerrard (Liverpool), Carrick (Manchester Utd.), Lampard (Chelsea), Johnson (Everton) (Wright-Phillips, Chelsea, 73), Rooney (Manchester Utd.), J. Cole (Chelsea) (Richardson, Manchester Utd., 77). **Scorer:** Rooney (37). **Booked:** A. Cole.

Referee: L. Michel (Slovakia). **Half-time:** 0-1.

ENGLAND 0, SPAIN 1

Old Trafford (58,247), Wednesday, February 7, 2007

England (4-3-2-1): *Foster (Manchester Utd.), G.Neville (Manchester Utd.) (Richards, Manchester City, 65), Ferdinand (Manchester Utd.), Woodgate (Middlesbrough) (Carragher, Liverpool, 65), P. Neville (Everton) (Downing, Middlesbrough, 74), Gerrard (Liverpool) (Barry, Aston Villa, 46), Carrick (Manchester Utd.), Lampard (Chelsea) (*Barton, Manchester City, 79), Wright-Phillips (Chelsea) (Defoe, Tottenham, 70), Dyer (Newcastle Utd.), Crouch (Liverpool).

Spain (4-1-3-2): Casillas, Ramos (Navarro, 46), Puyol (Torres, 46), Ibanez, Capdevila, Albelda, Angulo (Iniesta 56), Xavi, Silva (Arizmendi 66), Morientes (Angel Lopez, 46), Villa (Fabregas 74). **Scorer:** Iniesta (63).

Referee: M. Weiner (Germany). **Half-time:** 0-0.

NORTHERN IRELAND 0, WALES 0

Windsor Park (10,000), Tuesday, February 7, 2007

Northern Ireland (4-4-2): Taylor (Birmingham City) (Ingham, Wrexham, 46), Duff (Burnley), Craigan (Motherwell) (Webb, Ross Co., 78), Hughes (Aston Villa), Capaldi (Plymouth Argyle), Gillespie (Sheffield Utd.), Davis (Aston Villa), Clingan (Nott'm. Forest) (McCann, Barnsley, 61), Brunt (Sheffield Wed.), Lafferty (Burnley) (Thompson, Linfield, 68), Sproule (Hibernian, 68) (Shiels, Hibernian, 67).

Wales (4-4-2): Coyne (Burnley), Duffy (Portsmouth) (Ricketts, Hull City, 46), Evans (Wrexham), Collins (Sunderland), Nyatanga (Derby Co.), Davies (Fulham), Koumas (W.B.A.), Robinson (Toronto), Vaughan (Crewe Alexandra) (Cotterill, Wigan Athletic, 46) (*Easter (Wycombe Wand., 69), Parry (Cardiff City) (Crofts, Gillingham, 81), Bellamy (Liverpool). **Booked:** Koumas.

Referee: C. Richmond (Scotland). **Half-time:** 0-0.

ECUADOR 1, REPUBLIC OF IRELAND 1

New York (20,823), Wednesday, May 23, 2007

Ecuador (4-4-2): Elizaga, Montano, Castr, Campos, Bagui, Quieroz (Salas 66), Caicedo, Umutia, Ayovi, Kaviedes (Palacios 77), Benitez. **Scorer:** Benitez (13). **Booked:** Castro. **Sent-off:** Castro

Republic of Ireland (4-4-2): *C. Doyle (Birmingham City), Kelly (Birmingham City), *Bruce (Ipswich Town), *Bennett (Reading), *O'Halloran (Aston Villa) (*O'Cearuill, Arsenal, 73), *Keogh (Wolves) (*Gamble, Cork City, 69), *Potter (Wolves), Kilbane (Wigan Athletic) (*Gleeson, Wolves, 79), Hunt (Reading) (Stokes, Sunderland, 69), K. Doyle (Reading) (Long, Reading, 60), *Murphy (Sunderland) (*Lapira, Notra Dame, 86). **Scorer:** Doyle (44).

Referee: J. Marrufo (United States). **Half-time:** 1-1.

WALES 2, NEW ZEALAND 2

Racecourse Ground (7,819), Saturday, May 26, 2007

Wales (4-4-2): Coyne (Burnley) (*Hennessey, Wolves, 46), *Gunter (Cardiff City) (Evans, Wrexham, 46), Collins (West Ham Utd.), Gabbidon (West Ham Utd.), Ricketts (Hull City), Davies (Fulham) (Crofts, Gillingham, 76), Fletcher (Crystal Palace) (Ledley, Cardiff City, 46), Robinson (Toronto), Giggs (Manchester Utd.) (Llewellyn, Wrexham, 76), Bellamy (Liverpool), Earnshaw (Norwich City) (*Nardiello, Barnsley, 64). **Scorer:** Bellamy (17, 37). **Booked:** Gunter.

New Zealand (4-4-2): Paston, Pritchett, Boyens, Fignund, Lochhead, Christie (Barron 58), Brown, Oughton, Bertos (Campbell 60), James, Smeltz. **Scorer:** Smeltz (2, 24). **Booked:** Boyens.

Referee: T. Fkjerven (Norway). **Half-time:** 2-2.

BOLIVIA 1, REPUBLIC OF IRELAND 1

Boston (10,000), Saturday, May 26, 2007

Bolivia (4-4-2): Suarez, Hoyos, Mendez, Pena, Alvarez, Garcia (Lima 61), Mojica, Reyes, Vaca (Galindo 74), Moreno (Cabrera 46), Arce (Pinedo 69). **Scorer:** Hoyos (14).

Republic of Ireland (4-4-2): Colgan (Barnsley) (Henderson, Preston N.E., 46), O'Cearuill (Arsenal), Bennett (Reading), *P. Murphy (Carlisle Utd.) (O'Halloran, Aston Villa, 46), Kelly (Birmingham City), Gamble (Cork City) (D. Murphy, Sunderland, 46), Kilbane (Wigan Athletic), (Hunt, Reading, 66), Potter (Wolves), O'Brien (Newcastle Utd.) (Gleeson, Wolves, 77), Long (Reading) (Doyle, Reading, 54), Stokes (Sunderland). **Scorer:** Long (12).

Referee: D. Murdoch (United States). **Half-time:** 1-1.

AUSTRIA 0, SCOTLAND 1

Vienna (13,200), Wednesday, May 30, 2007

Austria (4-4-2): Payer, Standfest, Hiden (Prodl 89), Patocka, Fuchs (Katzer 74), Ivanschitz, Aufhauser (Sariyar 74), Saumel, Leitgeb, Linz, Haas (Kulijic 60).

Scotland (4-4-2): *McGregor (Rangers) (Gordon, Hearts, 46), Alexander (Preston N.E.) (*Hutton, Rangers, 70), Weir (Rangers) (Dailly (West Ham Utd., 46), Caldwell (Celtic), Naysmith (Everton), Fletcher (Manchester Utd.), Maloney (Aston Villa) (*Adam, Rangers, 66), Ferguson (Rangers), McCulloch (Wigan Athletic) (Hartley, Celtic, 46), O'Connor (Lokomotiv Moscow) (McManus, Celtic, 86), Boyd (Rangers). **Scorer:** O'Connor (58).

Referee: Z. Szabo (Hungary). **Half-time:** 0-0.

ENGLAND 1, BRAZIL 1

Wembley (88,745), Friday, June 1, 2007

England (4-4-2): Robinson (Tottenham), Carragher (Liverpool), King (Tottenham), Terry (Chelsea) (Brown, Manchester Utd., 72), *Shorey (Reading), Beckham (Real Madrid) (Jenas, Tottenham, 77), Gerrard (Liverpool), Lampard (Chelsea) (Carrick, Manchester Utd., 88), J. Cole (Chelsea) (Downing, Middlesbrough, 62), Smith (Manchester Utd.) (Dyer, Newcastle Utd., 62), Owen (Newcastle Utd.) (Crouch, Liverpool, 83). **Scorer:** Terry (68).

Brazil (4-2-2-2): Helton, D. Alvez (Maicon 65), Naldo, Juan, Gilberto, Mineiro (Edmilson 62), Gilberto Silva, Kaka (A. Alves 71), Ronaldinho, Robinho (Diego 74), Vagner Love. **Scorer:** Diego (90).

Referee: M. Merk (Germany). **Half-time:** 0-0.

OTHER BRITISH & IRISH INTERNATIONAL RESULTS

ENGLAND

v. ALBANIA

		E	*A*
1989	Tirana (W.C.)	2	0
1989	Wembley (W.C.)	5	0
2001	Tirana (W.C.)	3	1
2001	Newcastle (W.C.)	2	0

v. ANDORRA

		E	*A*
2006	Old Trafford (E.C.)	5	0
2007	Barcelona (E.C.)	3	0

v. ARGENTINA

		E	*A*
1951	Wembley	2	1
1953*	Buenos Aires	0	0
1962	Rancagua (W.C.)	3	1
1964	Rio de Janeiro	0	1
1966	Wembley (W.C.)	1	0
1974	Wembley	2	2
1977	Buenos Aires	1	1
1980	Wembley	3	1
1986	Mexico City (W.C.)	1	2
1991	Wembley	2	2
1998†	St Etienne (W.C.)	2	2
2000	Wembley	0	0
2002	Sapporo (W.C.)	1	0
2005	Geneva	3	2

(* Abandoned after 21 mins. – rain)
(† England lost 3-4 on pens.)

v. AUSTRALIA

		E	*A*
1980	Sydney	2	1
1983	Sydney	0	0
1983	Brisbane	1	0
1983	Melbourne	1	1
1991	Sydney	1	0
2003	West Ham	1	3

v. AUSTRIA

		E	*A*
1908	Vienna	6	1
1908	Vienna	11	1
1909	Vienna	8	1
1930	Vienna	0	0
1932	Stamford Bridge	4	3
1936	Vienna	1	2
1951	Wembley	2	2
1952	Vienna	3	2
1958	Boras (W.C.)	2	2
1961	Vienna	1	3
1962	Wembley	3	1
1965	Wembley	2	3
1967	Vienna	1	0
1973	Wembley	7	0
1979	Vienna	3	4
2004	Vienna (W.C.)	2	2
2005	Old Trafford (W.C.)	1	0

v. AZERBAIJAN

		E	*A*
2004	Baku (W.C.)	1	0
2005	Newcastle (W.C.)	2	0

v. BELGIUM

		E	*B*
1921	Brussels	2	0
1923	Highbury	6	1
1923	Antwerp	2	2
1924	West Bromwich	4	0
1926	Antwerp	5	3
1927	Brussels	9	1
1928	Antwerp	3	1
1929	Brussels	5	1
1931	Brussels	4	1
1936	Brussels	2	3
1947	Brussels	5	2
1950	Brussels	4	1
1952	Wembley	5	0
1954	Basle (W.C.)	4	4
1964	Wembley	2	2
1970	Brussels	3	1
1980	Turin (E.C.)	1	1
1990	Bologna (W.C.)	1	0
1998*	Casablanca	0	0
1999	Sunderland	2	1

(* England lost 3-4 on pens.)

v. BOHEMIA

		E	*B*
1908	Prague	4	0

v. BRAZIL

		E	*B*
1956	Wembley	4	2
1958	Gothenburg (W.C.)	0	0
1959	Rio de Janeiro	0	2
1962	Vina del Mar (W.C.)	1	3
1963	Wembley	1	1
1964	Rio de Janeiro	1	5
1969	Rio de Janeiro	1	2
1970	Guadalajara (W.C.)	0	1
1976	Los Angeles	0	1
1977	Rio de Janeiro	0	0
1978	Wembley	1	1
1981	Wembley	0	1
1984	Rio de Janeiro	2	0
1987	Wembley	1	1
1990	Wembley	1	0
1992	Wembley	1	1
1993	Washington	1	1

		E	B
1995	Wembley	1	3
1997	Paris (T.F.)	0	1
2000	Wembley	1	1
2002	Shizuoka (W.C.)	1	2
2007	Wembley	1	1

v. BULGARIA

		E	B
1962	Rancagua (W.C.)	0	0
1968	Wembley	1	1
1974	Sofia	1	0
1979	Sofia (E.C.)	3	0
1979	Wembley (E.C.)	2	0
1996	Wembley	1	0
1998	Wembley (E.C.)	0	0
1999	Sofia (E.C.)	1	1

v. CAMEROON

		E	C
1990	Naples (W.C.)	3	2
1991	Wembley	2	0
1997	Wembley	2	0
2002	Kobe (Japan)	2	2

v. CANADA

		E	C
1986	Vancouver	1	0

v. CHILE

		E	C
1950	Rio de Janeiro (W.C.)	2	0
1953	Santiago	2	1
1984	Santiago	0	0
1989	Wembley	0	0
1998	Wembley	0	2

v. CHINA

		E	C
1996	Beijing	3	0

v. C.I.S.
(formerly Soviet Union)

		E	C
1992	Moscow	2	2

v. COLOMBIA

		E	C
1970	Bogota	4	0
1988	Wembley	1	1
1995	Wembley	0	0
1998	Lens (W.C.)	2	0
2005	New York	3	2

v. CROATIA

		E	C
1995	Wembley	0	0
2003	Ipswich	3	1
2004	Lisbon (E.C.)	4	2
2006	Zagreb (E.C.)	0	2

v. CYPRUS

		E	C
1975	Wembley (E.C.)	5	0
1975	Limassol (E.C.)	1	0

v. CZECH REPUBLIC

		E	C
1998	Wembley	2	0

v. CZECHOSLOVAKIA

		E	C
1934	Prague	1	2
1937	White Hart Lane	5	4
1963	Bratislava	4	2
1966	Wembley	0	0
1970	Guadalajara (W.C.)	1	0
1973	Prague	1	1
1974	Wembley (E.C.)	3	0
1975*	Bratislava (E.C.)	1	2
1978	Wembley (E.C.)	1	0
1982	Bilbao (W.C.)	2	0
1990	Wembley	4	2
1992	Prague	2	2

(* Aband. 0-0, 17 mins. prev. day – fog)

v. DENMARK

		E	D
1948	Copenhagen	0	0
1955	Copenhagen	5	1
1956	W'hampton (W.C.)	5	2
1957	Copenhagen (W.C.)	4	1
1966	Copenhagen	2	0
1978	Copenhagen (E.C.)	4	3
1979	Wembley (E.C.)	1	0
1982	Copenhagen (E.C.)	2	2
1983	Wembley (E.C.)	0	1
1988	Wembley	1	0
1989	Copenhagen	1	1
1990	Wembley	1	0
1992	Malmo (E.C.)	0	0
1994	Wembley	1	0
2002	Niigata (W.C.)	3	0
2003	Old Trafford	2	3
2005	Copenhagen	1	4

v. EAST GERMANY

		E	EG
1963	Leipzig	2	1
1970	Wembley	3	1
1974	Leipzig	1	1
1984	Wembley	1	0

v. ECUADOR

		E	Ec
1970	Quito	2	0
2006	Stuttgart (W.C.)	1	0

v. EGYPT

		E	Eg
1986	Cairo	4	0
1990	Cagliari (W.C.)	1	0

v. ESTONIA

		Eg	E
2007	Tallinn (E.C.)	3	0

v. F.I.F.A.

		E	F
1938	Highbury	3	0
1953	Wembley	4	4
1963	Wembley	2	1

v. FINLAND

		E	F
1937	Helsinki	8	0
1956	Helsinki	5	1
1966	Helsinki	3	0
1976	Helsinki (W.C.)	4	1
1976	Wembley (W.C.)	2	1
1982	Helsinki	4	1
1984	Wembley (W.C.)	5	0
1985	Helsinki (W.C.)	1	1
1992	Helsinki	2	1
2000	Helsinki (W.C.)	0	0
2001	Liverpool (W.C.)	2	1

v. FRANCE

		E	F
1923	Paris	4	1
1924	Paris	3	1
1925	Paris	3	2
1927	Paris	6	0
1928	Paris	5	1
1929	Paris	4	1
1931	Paris	2	5
1933	White Hart Lane	4	1
1938	Paris	4	2
1947	Highbury	3	0
1949	Paris	3	1
1951	Highbury	2	2
1955	Paris	0	1
1957	Wembley	4	0
1962	Hillsborough (E.C.)	1	1
1963	Paris (E.C.)	2	5
1966	Wembley (W.C.)	2	0
1969	Wembley	5	0
1982	Bilbao (W.C.)	3	1
1984	Paris	0	2
1992	Wembley	2	0
1992	Malmo (E.C.)	0	0
1997	Montpellier (T.F.)	1	0
1999	Wembley	0	2
2000	Paris	1	1
2004	Lisbon (E.C.)	1	2

v. GEORGIA

		E	G
1996	Tbilisi (W.C.)	2	0
1997	Wembley (W.C.)	2	0

v. GERMANY/WEST GERMANY

		E	G
1930	Berlin	3	3
1935	White Hart Lane	3	0
1938	Berlin	6	3
1954	Wembley	3	1
1956	Berlin	3	1
1965	Nuremberg	1	0
1966	Wembley	1	0
1966	Wembley (W.C.F.)	4	2
1968	Hanover	0	1
1970	Leon (W.C.)	2	3
1972	Wembley (E.C.)	1	3
1972	Berlin (E.C.)	0	0
1975	Wembley	2	0
1978	Munich	1	2
1982	Madrid (W.C.)	0	0
1982	Wembley	1	2
1985	Mexico City	3	0
1987	Dusseldorf	1	3
1990*	Turin (W.C.)	1	1
1991	Wembley	0	1
1993	Detroit	1	2
1996†	Wembley (E.C.)	1	1
2000	Charleroi (E.C.)	1	0
2000	Wembley (W.C.)	0	1
2001	Munich (W.C.)	5	1

(* England lost 3-4 on pens.)
(† England lost 5-6 on pens.)

v. GREECE

		E	G
1971	Wembley (E.C.)	3	0
1971	Athens (E.C.)	2	0
1982	Salonika (E.C.)	3	0
1983	Wembley (E.C.)	0	0
1989	Athens	2	1
1994	Wembley	5	0
2001	Athens (W.C.)	2	0
2001	Old Trafford (W.C.)	2	2
2006	Old Trafford	4	0

v. HOLLAND

		E	H
1935	Amsterdam	1	0
1946	Huddersfield	8	2
1964	Amsterdam	1	1
1969	Amsterdam	1	0
1970	Wembley	0	0
1977	Wembley	0	2
1982	Wembley	2	0
1988	Wembley	2	2
1988	Dusseldorf (E.C.)	1	3
1990	Cagliari (W.C.)	0	0
1993	Wembley (W.C.)	2	2
1993	Rotterdam (W.C.)	0	2
1996	Wembley (E.C.)	4	1
2001	White Hart Lane	0	2
2002	Amsterdam	1	1
2005	Villa Park	0	0
2006	Amsterdam	1	1

v. HUNGARY

		E	H
1908	Budapest	7	0
1909	Budapest	4	2
1909	Budapest	8	2
1934	Budapest	1	2
1936	Highbury	6	2
1953	Wembley	3	6
1954	Budapest	1	7
1960	Budapest	0	2
1962	Rancagua (W.C.)	1	2
1965	Wembley	1	0
1978	Wembley	4	1
1981	Budapest (W.C.)	3	1
1981	Wembley (W.C.)	1	0
1983	Wembley (E.C.)	2	0
1983	Budapest (E.C.)	3	0
1988	Budapest	0	0
1990	Wembley	1	0
1992	Budapest	1	0
1996	Wembley	3	0
1999	Budapest	1	1
2006	Old Trafford	3	1

v. ICELAND

		E	I
1982	Reykjavik	1	1
2004	City of Manchester	6	1

v. REPUBLIC OF IRELAND

		E	RI
1946	Dublin	1	0
1950	Goodison Park	0	2
1957	Wembley (W.C.)	5	1
1957	Dublin (W.C.)	1	1
1964	Dublin	3	1
1977	Wembley	1	1
1978	Dublin (E.C.)	1	1
1980	Wembley (E.C.)	2	0
1985	Wembley	2	1
1988	Stuttgart (E.C.)	0	1
1990	Cagliari (W.C.)	1	1
1990	Dublin (E.C.)	1	1
1991	Wembley (E.C.)	1	1
1995*	Dublin	0	1

(* Abandoned 27 mins. – crowd riot)

v. ISRAEL

		E	I
1986	Tel Aviv	2	1
1988	Tel Aviv	0	0
2006	Tel Aviv (E.C.)	0	0

v. ITALY

		E	I
1933	Rome	1	1
1934	Highbury	3	2
1939	Milan	2	2
1948	Turin	4	0
1949	White Hart Lane	2	0
1952	Florence	1	1
1959	Wembley	2	2
1961	Rome	3	2
1973	Turin	0	2
1973	Wembley	0	1
1976	New York	3	2
1976	Rome (W.C.)	0	2
1977	Wembley (W.C.)	2	0
1980	Turin (E.C.)	0	1
1985	Mexico City	1	2
1989	Wembley	0	0
1990	Bari (W.C.)	1	2
1996	Wembley (W.C.)	0	1
1997	Nantes (T.F.)	2	0
1997	Rome (W.C.)	0	0
2000	Turin	0	1
2002	Leeds	1	2

v. JAMAICA

		E	J
2006	Old Trafford	6	0

v. JAPAN

		E	J
1995	Wembley	2	1
2004	City of Manchester	1	1

v. KUWAIT

		E	K
1982	Bilbao (W.C.)	1	0

v. LIECHTENSTEIN

		E	L
2003	Vaduz (E.C.)	2	0
2003	Old Trafford (E.C.)	2	0

v. LUXEMBOURG

		E	L
1927	Luxembourg	5	2
1960	Luxembourg (W.C.)	9	0
1961	Highbury (W.C.)	4	1
1977	Wembley (W.C.)	5	0
1977	Luxembourg (W.C.)	2	0
1982	Wembley (E.C.)	9	0
1983	Luxembourg (E.C.)	4	0
1998	Luxembourg (E.C.)	3	0
1999	Wembley (E.C.)	6	0

v. MACEDONIA

		E	M
2002	Southampton (E.C.)	2	2
2003	Skopje (E.C.)	2	1
2006	Skopje (E.C.)	1	0
2006	Old Trafford (E.C.)	0	0

v. MALAYSIA

		E	M
1991	Kuala Lumpur	4	2

v. MALTA

		E	M
1971	Valletta (E.C.)	1	0

		E	M
1971	Wembley (E.C.)	5	0
2000	Valletta	2	1

v. MEXICO

		E	M
1959	Mexico City	1	2
1961	Wembley	8	0
1966	Wembley (W.C.)	2	0
1969	Mexico City	0	0
1985	Mexico City	0	1
1986	Los Angeles	3	0
1997	Wembley	2	0
2001	Derby	4	0

v. MOLDOVA

		E	M
1996	Kishinev	3	0
1997	Wembley (W.C.)	4	0

v. MOROCCO

		E	M
1986	Monterrey (W.C.)	0	0
1998	Casablanca	1	0

v. NEW ZEALAND

		E	NZ
1991	Auckland	1	0
1991	Wellington	2	0

v. NIGERIA

		E	N
1994	Wembley	1	0
2002	Osaka (W.C.)	0	0

v. NORWAY

		E	N
1937	Oslo	6	0
1938	Newcastle	4	0
1949	Oslo	4	1
1966	Oslo	6	1
1980	Wembley (W.C.)	4	0
1981	Oslo (W.C.)	1	2
1992	Wembley (W.C.)	1	1
1993	Oslo (W.C.)	0	2
1994	Wembley	0	0
1995	Oslo	0	0

v. PARAGUAY

		E	P
1986	Mexico City (W.C.)	3	0
2002	Anfield	4	0
2006	Frankfurt (W.C.)	1	0

v. PERU

		E	P
1959	Lima	1	4
1961	Lima	4	0

v. POLAND

		E	P
1966	Goodison Park	1	1
1966	Chorzow	1	0
1973	Chorzow (W.C.)	0	2
1973	Wembley (W.C.)	1	1
1986	Monterrey (W.C.)	3	0
1989	Wembley (W.C.)	3	0
1989	Katowice (W.C.)	0	0
1990	Wembley (E.C.)	2	0
1991	Poznan (E.C.)	1	1
1993	Chorzow (W.C.)	1	1
1993	Wembley (W.C.)	3	0
1996	Wembley (W.C.)	2	1
1997	Katowice (W.C.)	2	0
1999	Wembley (E.C.)	3	1
1999	Warsaw (E.C.)	0	0
2004	Katowice (W.C.)	2	1
2005	Old Trafford (W.C.)	2	1

v. PORTUGAL

		E	P
1947	Lisbon	10	0
1950	Lisbon	5	3
1951	Goodison Park	5	2
1955	Oporto	1	3
1958	Wembley	2	1
1961	Lisbon (W.C.)	1	1
1961	Wembley (W.C.)	2	0
1964	Lisbon	4	3
1964	Sao Paulo	1	1
1966	Wembley (W.C.)	2	1
1969	Wembley	1	0
1974	Lisbon	0	0
1974	Wembley (E.C.)	0	0
1975	Lisbon (E.C.)	1	1
1986	Monterrey (W.C.)	0	1
1995	Wembley	1	1
1998	Wembley	3	0
2000	Eindhoven (E.C.)	2	3
2002	Villa Park	1	1
2004	Faro	1	1
2004*	Lisbon (E.C.)	2	2
2006†	Gelsenkirchen (W.C.)	0	0

(† England lost 1–3 on pens)
(*England lost 5–6 on pens)

v. ROMANIA

		E	R
1939	Bucharest	2	0
1968	Bucharest	0	0
1969	Wembley	1	1
1970	Guadalajara (W.C.)	1	0
1980	Bucharest (W.C.)	1	2
1981	Wembley (W.C.)	0	0
1985	Bucharest (W.C.)	0	0
1985	Wembley (W.C.)	1	1
1994	Wembley	1	1
1998	Toulouse (W.C.)	1	2
2000	Charleroi (E.C.)	2	3

v. SAN MARINO

		E	SM
1992	Wembley (W.C.)	6	0
1993	Bologna (W.C.)	7	1

v. SAUDI ARABIA

		E	SA
1988	Riyadh	1	1
1998	Wembley	0	0

v. SERBIA-MONTENEGRO

		E	S-M
2003	Leicester	2	1

v. SLOVAKIA

		E	S
2002	Bratislava (E.C.)	2	1
2003	Middlesbrough (E.C.)	2	1

v. SOUTH AFRICA

		E	SA
1997	Old Trafford	2	1
2003	Durban	2	1

v. SOUTH KOREA

		E	SK
2002	Seoguipo	1	1

v. SOVIET UNION (see also C.I.S.)

		E	SU
1958	Moscow	1	1
1958	Gothenburg (W.C.)	2	2
1958	Gothenburg (W.C.)	0	1
1958	Wembley	5	0
1967	Wembley	2	2
1968	Rome (E.C.)	2	0
1973	Moscow	2	1
1984	Wembley	0	2
1986	Tbilisi	1	0
1988	Frankfurt (E.C.)	1	3
1991	Wembley	3	1

v. SPAIN

		E	S
1929	Madrid	3	4
1931	Highbury	7	1
1950	Rio de Janeiro (W.C.)	0	1
1955	Madrid	1	1
1955	Wembley	4	1
1960	Madrid	0	3
1960	Wembley	4	2
1965	Madrid	2	0
1967	Wembley	2	0
1968	Wembley (E.C.)	1	0
1968	Madrid (E.C.)	2	1
1980	Barcelona	2	0
1980	Naples (E.C.)	2	1
1981	Wembley	1	2
1982	Madrid (W.C.)	0	0
1987	Madrid	4	2
1992	Santander	0	1
1996*	Wembley (E.C.)	0	0
2001	Villa Park	3	0
2004	Madrid	0	1
2007	Old Trafford	0	1

(* England won 4-2 on pens.)

v. SWEDEN

		E	S
1923	Stockholm	4	2
1923	Stockholm	3	1
1937	Stockholm	4	0
1948	Highbury	4	2
1949	Stockholm	1	3
1956	Stockholm	0	0
1959	Wembley	2	3
1965	Gothenburg	2	1
1968	Wembley	3	1
1979	Stockholm	0	0
1986	Stockholm	0	1
1988	Wembley (W.C.)	0	0
1989	Stockholm (W.C.)	0	0
1992	Stockholm (E.C.)	1	2
1995	Leeds	3	3
1998	Stockholm (E.C.)	1	2
1999	Wembley (E.C.)	0	0
2001	Old Trafford	1	1
2002	Saitama (W.C.)	1	1
2004	Gothenburg	0	1
2006	Cologne (W.C.)	2	2

v. SWITZERLAND

		E	S
1933	Berne	4	0
1938	Zurich	1	2
1947	Zurich	0	1
1949	Highbury	6	0
1952	Zurich	3	0
1954	Berne (W.C.)	2	0
1962	Wembley	3	1
1963	Basle	8	1
1971	Basle (E.C.)	3	2
1971	Wembley (E.C.)	1	1
1975	Basle	2	1
1977	Wembley	0	0
1980	Wembley (W.C.)	2	1
1981	Basle (W.C.)	1	2
1988	Lausanne	1	0
1995	Wembley	3	1
1996	Wembley (E.C.)	1	1
1998	Berne	1	1
2004	Coimbra (E.C.)	3	0

v. TRINIDAD & TOBAGO

		E	T
2006	Nuremberg (W.C.)	2	0

v. TUNISIA

		E	T
1990	Tunis	1	1
1998	Marseille (W.C.)	2	0

v. TURKEY

		E	T
1984	Istanbul (W.C.)	8	0
1985	Wembley (W.C.)	5	0
1987	Izmir (E.C.)	0	0
1987	Wembley (E.C.)	8	0
1991	Izmir (E.C.)	1	0
1991	Wembley (E.C.)	1	0
1992	Wembley (W.C.)	4	0
1993	Izmir (W.C.)	2	0
2003	Sunderland (E.C.)	2	0
2003	Istanbul (E.C.)	0	0

v UKRAINE

		E	U
2000	Wembley	2	0
2004	Newcastle	3	0

v. URUGUAY

		E	U
1953	Montevideo	1	2
1954	Basle (W.C.)	2	4
1964	Wembley	2	1
1966	Wembley (W.C.)	0	0
1969	Montevideo	2	1
1977	Montevideo	0	0
1984	Montevideo	0	2
1990	Wembley	1	2
1995	Wembley	0	0
2006	Anfield	2	1

v. U.S.A.

		E	USA
1950	Belo Horizonte (W.C.)	0	1
1953	New York	6	3
1959	Los Angeles	8	1
1964	New York	10	0
1985	Los Angeles	5	0
1993	Boston	0	2
1994	Wembley	2	0
2005	Chicago	2	1

v. YUGOSLAVIA

		E	Y
1939	Belgrade	1	2
1950	Highbury	2	2
1954	Belgrade	0	1
1956	Wembley	3	0
1958	Belgrade	0	5
1960	Wembley	3	3
1965	Belgrade	1	1
1966	Wembley	2	0
1968	Florence (E.C.)	0	1
1972	Wembley	1	1
1974	Belgrade	2	2
1986	Wembley (E.C.)	2	0
1987	Belgrade (E.C.)	4	1
1989	Wembley	2	1

ENGLAND'S RECORD

England's first international was a 0-0 draw against Scotland in Glasgow, on the West of Scotland cricket ground, Partick, on November 30, 1872. Their complete record, at the start of 2007-08, is:

P	W	D	L	F	A
851	479	209	163	1893	863

ENGLAND "B" TEAM RESULTS

(England score shown first)

1949	Finland (A)	4	0
1949	Holland (A)	4	0
1950	Italy (A)	0	5
1950	Holland (H)	1	0
1950	Holland (A)	0	3
1950	Luxembourg (A)	2	1
1950	Switzerland (H)	5	0
1952	Holland (A)	1	0
1952	France (A)	1	7
1953	Scotland (A)	2	2
1954	Scotland (H)	1	1
1954	Germany (A)	4	0
1954	Yugoslavia (A)	1	2
1954	Switzerland (A)	0	2
1955	Germany (H)	1	1
1955	Yugoslavia (H)	5	1
1956	Switzerland (H)	4	1
1956	Scotland (A)	2	2
1957	Scotland (H)	4	1
1978	W. Germany (A)	2	1
1978	Czechoslovakia (A)	1	0
1978	Singapore (A)	8	0
1978	Malaysia (A)	1	1
1978	N. Zealand (A)	4	0
1978	N. Zealand (A)	3	1
1978	N. Zealand (A)	4	0
1979	Austria (A)	1	0
1979	N. Zealand (H)	4	1
1980	U.S.A. (H)	1	0
1980	Spain (H)	1	0

1980	Australia (H)	1	0
1981	Spain (A)	2	3
1984	N. Zealand (H)	2	0
1987	Malta (A)	2	0
1989	Switzerland (A)	2	0
1989	Iceland (A)	2	0
1989	Norway (A)	1	0
1989	Italy (H)	1	1
1989	Yugoslavia (H)	2	1
1990	Rep. of Ireland (A)	1	4
1990	Czechoslovakia (H)	2	0
1990	Algeria (A)	0	0
1991	Wales (A)	1	0
1991	Iceland (H)	1	0
1991	Switzerland (H)	2	1
1991	Spanish XI (A)	1	0
1992	France (H)	3	0
1992	Czechoslovakia (A)	1	0
1992	C.I.S. (A)	1	1
1994	N. Ireland (H)	4	2
1995	Rep. of Ireland (H)	2	0
1998	Chile (H)	1	2
1998	Russia (H)	4	1
2006	Belarus (H)	1	2
2007	Albania	3	1

GREAT BRITAIN V. REST OF EUROPE (F.I.F.A.)

		GB	*RofE*
1947	Glasgow	6	1
1955	Belfast	1	4

SCOTLAND

v. ARGENTINA

		S	*A*
1977	Buenos Aires	1	1
1979	Glasgow	1	3
1990	Glasgow	1	0

v. AUSTRALIA

		S	*A*
1985*	Glasgow (W.C.)	2	0
1985*	Melbourne (W.C.)	0	0
1996	Glasgow	1	0
2000	Glasgow	0	2

(* World Cup play-off)

v. AUSTRIA

		S	*A*
1931	Vienna	0	5
1933	Glasgow	2	2
1937	Vienna	1	1
1950	Glasgow	0	1
1951	Vienna	0	4
1954	Zurich (W.C.)	0	1
1955	Vienna	4	1
1956	Glasgow	1	1
1960	Vienna	1	4
1963*	Glasgow	4	1
1968	Glasgow (W.C.)	2	1
1969	Vienna (W.C.)	0	2
1978	Vienna (E.C.)	2	3
1979	Glasgow (E.C.)	1	1
1994	Vienna	2	1
1996	Vienna (W.C.)	0	0
1997	Glasgow (W.C.)	2	0

(* Abandoned after 79 minutes)

		S	*A*
2003	Glasgow	0	2
2005	Graz	2	2
2007	Vienna	1	0

v. BELARUS

		S	*B*
1997	Minsk (W.C.)	1	0
1997	Aberdeen (W.C.)	4	1
2005	Minsk (W.C.)	0	0
2005	Glasgow (W.C.)	0	1

v. BELGIUM

		S	*B*
1947	Brussels	1	2
1948	Glasgow	2	0
1951	Brussels	5	0
1971	Liege (E.C.)	0	3
1971	Aberdeen (E.C.)	1	0
1974	Brugge	1	2
1979	Brussels (E.C.)	0	2
1979	Glasgow (E.C.)	1	3
1982	Brussels (E.C.)	2	3
1983	Glasgow (E.C.)	1	1
1987	Brussels (E.C.)	1	4
1987	Glasgow (E.C.)	2	0
2001	Glasgow (W.C.)	2	2
2001	Brussels (W.C.)	0	2

v. BOSNIA

		S	*B*
1999	Sarajevo (E.C.)	2	1
1999	Glasgow (E.C.)	1	0

v. BRAZIL

		S	*B*
1966	Glasgow	1	1
1972	Rio de Janeiro	0	1
1973	Glasgow	0	1
1974	Frankfurt (W.C.)	0	0
1977	Rio de Janeiro	0	2
1982	Seville (W.C.)	1	4
1987	Glasgow	0	2

		S	B
1990	Turin (W.C.)	0	1
1998	St. Denis (W.C.)	1	2

v. BULGARIA

		S	B
1978	Glasgow	2	1
1986	Glasgow (E.C.)	0	0
1987	Sofia (E.C.)	1	0
1990	Sofia (E.C.)	1	1
1991	Glasgow (E.C.)	1	1
2006	Kobe	5	1

v. CANADA

		S	C
1983	Vancouver	2	0
1983	Edmonton	3	0
1983	Toronto	2	0
1992	Toronto	3	1
2002	Edinburgh	3	1

v. CHILE

		S	C
1977	Santiago	4	2
1989	Glasgow	2	0

v. C.I.S. (formerly Soviet Union)

		S	C
1992	Norrkoping (E.C.)	3	0

v. COLOMBIA

		S	C
1988	Glasgow	0	0
1996	Miami	0	1
1998	New York	2	2

v. COSTA RICA

		S	C
1990	Genoa (W.C.)	0	1

v. CROATIA

		S	C
2000	Zagreb (W.C.)	1	1
2001	Glasgow (W.C.)	0	0

v. CYPRUS

		S	C
1968	Nicosia (W.C.)	5	0
1969	Glasgow (W.C.)	8	0
1989	Limassol (W.C.)	3	2
1989	Glasgow (W.C.)	2	1

v. CZECH REPUBLIC

		S	C
1999	Glasgow (E.C.)	1	2
1999	Prague (E.C.)	2	3

v. CZECHOSLOVAKIA

		S	C
1937	Prague	3	1
1937	Glasgow	5	0
1961	Bratislava (W.C.)	0	4
1961	Glasgow (W.C.)	3	2
1961*	Brussels (W.C.)	2	4
1972	Porto Alegre	0	0
1973	Glasgow (W.C.)	2	1
1973	Bratislava (W.C.)	0	1
1976	Prague (W.C.)	0	2
1977	Glasgow (W.C.)	3	1

(* World Cup play-off)

v. DENMARK

		S	D
1951	Glasgow	3	1
1952	Copenhagen	2	1
1968	Copenhagen	1	0
1970	Glasgow (E.C.)	1	0
1971	Copenhagen (E.C.)	0	1
1972	Copenhagen (W.C.)	4	1
1972	Glasgow (W.C.)	2	0
1975	Copenhagen (E.C.)	1	0
1975	Glasgow (E.C.)	3	1
1986	Neza (W.C.)	0	1
1996	Copenhagen	0	2
1998	Glasgow	0	1
2002	Glasgow	0	1
2004	Copenhagen	0	1

v. EAST GERMANY

		S	EG
1974	Glasgow	3	0
1977	East Berlin	0	1
1982	Glasgow (E.C.)	2	0
1983	Halle (E.C.)	1	2
1986	Glasgow	0	0
1990	Glasgow	0	1

v. ECUADOR

		S	E
1995	Toyama, Japan	2	1

v. EGYPT

		S	E
1990	Aberdeen	1	3

v. ESTONIA

		S	E
1993	Tallinn (W.C.)	3	0
1993	Aberdeen	3	1
1996	Tallinn (W.C.)	* No result	
1997	Monaco (W.C.)	0	0
1997	Kilmarnock (W.C.)	2	0
1998	Edinburgh (E.C.)	3	2
1999	Tallinn (E.C.)	0	0
(* Estonia absent)			
2004	Tallinn	1	0

v. FAROE ISLANDS

		S	F
1994	Glasgow (E.C.)	5	1
1995	Toftir (E.C.)	2	0
1998	Aberdeen (E.C.)	2	1

		S	F
1999	Toftir (E.C.)	1	1
2002	Toftir (E.C.)	2	2
2003	Glasgow (E.C.)	3	1
2006	Glasgow (E.C.)	6	0
2007	Toftir (E.C.)	2	0

v. FINLAND

		S	F
1954	Helsinki	2	1
1964	Glasgow (W.C.)	3	1
1965	Helsinki (W.C.)	2	1
1976	Glasgow	6	0
1992	Glasgow	1	1
1994	Helsinki (E.C.)	2	0
1995	Glasgow (E.C.)	1	0
1998	Edinburgh	1	1

v. FRANCE

		S	F
1930	Paris	2	0
1932	Paris	3	1
1948	Paris	0	3
1949	Glasgow	2	0
1950	Paris	1	0
1951	Glasgow	1	0
1958	Orebro (W.C.)	1	2
1984	Marseilles	0	2
1989	Glasgow (W.C.)	2	0
1990	Paris (W.C.)	0	3
1997	St. Etienne	1	2
2000	Glasgow	0	2
2002	Paris	0	5
2006	Glasgow (E.C.)	1	0

v. GEORGIA

		S	G
2007	Glasgow (E.C.)	2	1

v. GERMANY/WEST GERMANY

		S	G
1929	Berlin	1	1
1936	Glasgow	2	0
1957	Stuttgart	3	1
1959	Glasgow	3	2
1964	Hanover	2	2
1969	Glasgow (W.C.)	1	1
1969	Hamburg (W.C.)	2	3
1973	Glasgow	1	1
1974	Frankfurt	1	2
1986	Queretaro (W.C.)	1	2
1992	Norrkoping (E.C.)	0	2
1993	Glasgow	0	1
1999	Bremen	1	0
2003	Glasgow (E.C.)	1	1
2003	Dortmund (E.C.)	1	2

v. GREECE

		S	G
1994	Athens (E.C.)	0	1
1995	Glasgow	1	0

v. HOLLAND

		S	H
1929	Amsterdam	2	0
1938	Amsterdam	3	1
1959	Amsterdam	2	1
1966	Glasgow	0	3
1968	Amsterdam	0	0
1971	Amsterdam	1	2
1978	Mendoza (W.C.)	3	2
1982	Glasgow	2	1
1986	Eindhoven	0	0
1992	Gothenburg (E.C.)	0	1
1994	Glasgow	0	1
1994	Utrecht	1	3
1996	Birmingham (E.C.)	0	0
2000	Arnhem	0	0
2003*	Glasgow (E.C.)	1	0
2003*	Amsterdam (E.C.)	0	6

(* Qual. Round play-off)

v. HUNGARY

		S	H
1938	Glasgow	3	1
1955	Glasgow	2	4
1955	Budapest	1	3
1958	Glasgow	1	1
1960	Budapest	3	3
1980	Budapest	1	3
1987	Glasgow	2	0
2004	Glasgow	0	3

v. ICELAND

		S	I
1984	Glasgow (W.C.)	3	0
1985	Reykjavik (W.C)	1	0
2002	Reykjavik (E.C)	2	0
2003	Glasgow (E.C)	2	1

v. IRAN

		S	I
1978	Cordoba (W.C.)	1	1

v. REPUBLIC OF IRELAND

		S	RI
1961	Glasgow (W.C.)	4	1
1961	Dublin (W.C.)	3	0
1963	Dublin	0	1
1969	Dublin	1	1
1986	Dublin (E.C.)	0	0
1987	Glasgow (E.C.)	0	1
2000	Dublin	2	1
2003	Glasgow (E.C.)	0	2

v. ISRAEL

		S	I
1981	Tel Aviv (W.C.)	1	0
1981	Glasgow (W.C.)	3	1
1986	Tel Aviv	1	0

v. ITALY

		S	I
1931	Rome	0	3
1965	Glasgow (W.C.)	1	0
1965	Naples (W.C.)	0	3
1988	Perugia	0	2
1992	Glasgow (W.C.)	0	0
1993	Rome (W.C.)	1	3
2005	Milan (W.C.)	0	2
2005	Glasgow (W.C.)	1	1
2007	Bari (E.C.)	0	2

v. JAPAN

		S	J
1995	Hiroshima	0	0
2006	Saitama	0	0

v. LATVIA

		S	L
1996	Riga (W.C.)	2	0
1997	Glasgow (W.C.)	2	0
2000	Riga (W.C.)	1	0
2001	Glasgow (W.C.)	2	1

v. LITHUANIA

		S	L
1998	Vilnius (E.C.)	0	0
1999	Glasgow (E.C.)	3	0
2003	Kaunus (E.C.)	0	1
2003	Glasgow (E.C.)	1	0
2006	Kaunas (E.C.)	2	1

v. LUXEMBOURG

		S	L
1947	Luxembourg	6	0
1986	Glasgow (E.C.)	3	0
1987	Esch (E.C.)	0	0

v. MALTA

		S	M
1988	Valletta	1	1
1990	Valletta	2	1
1993	Glasgow (W.C.)	3	0
1993	Valletta (W.C.)	2	0
1997	Valletta	3	2

v. MOLDOVA

		S	M
2004	Chisinau (W.C.)	1	1
2005	Glasgow (W.C.)	2	0

v. MOROCCO

		S	M
1998	St. Etienne (W.C.)	0	3

v. NEW ZEALAND

		S	NZ
1982	Malaga (W.C.)	5	2
2003	Edinburgh	1	1

v. NIGERIA

		S	N
2002	Aberdeen	1	2

v. NORWAY

		S	N
1929	Bergen	7	3
1954	Glasgow	1	0
1954	Oslo	1	1
1963	Bergen	3	4
1963	Glasgow	6	1
1974	Oslo	2	1
1978	Glasgow (E.C.)	3	2
1979	Oslo (E.C.)	4	0
1988	Oslo (W.C.)	2	1
1989	Glasgow (W.C.)	1	1
1992	Oslo	0	0
1998	Bordeaux (W.C.)	1	1
2003	Oslo	0	0
2004	Glasgow (W.C.)	0	1
2005	Oslo (W.C.)	2	1

v. PARAGUAY

		S	P
1958	Norrkoping (W.C.)	2	3

v. PERU

		S	P
1972	Glasgow	2	0
1978	Cordoba (W.C.)	1	3
1979	Glasgow	1	1

v. POLAND

		S	P
1958	Warsaw	2	1
1960	Glasgow	2	3
1965	Chorzow (W.C.)	1	1
1965	Glasgow (W.C.)	1	2
1980	Poznan	0	1
1990	Glasgow	1	1
2001	Bydgoszcz	1	1

v. PORTUGAL

		S	P
1950	Lisbon	2	2
1955	Glasgow	3	0
1959	Lisbon	0	1
1966	Glasgow	0	1
1971	Lisbon (E.C.)	0	2
1971	Glasgow (E.C.)	2	1
1975	Glasgow	1	0
1978	Lisbon (E.C.)	0	1
1980	Glasgow (E.C.)	4	1
1980	Glasgow (W.C.)	0	0
1981	Lisbon (W.C.)	1	2
1992	Glasgow (W.C.)	0	0
1993	Lisbon (W.C.)	0	5
2002	Braga	0	2

v. ROMANIA

		S	R
1975	Bucharest (E.C.)	1	1
1975	Glasgow (E.C.)	1	1
1986	Glasgow	3	0
1990	Glasgow (E.C.)	2	1

		S	R
1991	Bucharest (E.C.)	0	1
2004	Glasgow	1	2

v. RUSSIA

		S	R
1994	Glasgow (E.C.)	1	1
1995	Moscow (E.C.)	0	0

v. SAN MARINO

		S	SM
1991	Serravalle (E.C.)	2	0
1991	Glasgow (E.C.)	4	0
1995	Serravalle (E.C.)	2	0
1995	Glasgow (E.C.)	5	0
2000	Serravalle (W.C.)	2	0
2001	Glasgow (W.C.)	4	0

v. SAUDI ARABIA

		S	SA
1988	Riyadh	2	2

v. SLOVENIA

		S	SL
2004	Glasgow (W.C.)	0	0
2005	Celje (W.C.)	3	0

v. SOUTH AFRICA

		S	SA
2002	Hong Kong	0	2

v. SOUTH KOREA

		S	SK
2002	Busan	1	4

v. SOVIET UNION (see also C.I.S. and RUSSIA)

		S	SU
1967	Glasgow	0	2
1971	Moscow	0	1
1982	Malaga (W.C.)	2	2
1991	Glasgow	0	1

v. SPAIN

		S	Sp
1957	Glasgow (W.C.)	4	2
1957	Madrid (W.C.)	1	4
1963	Madrid	6	2
1965	Glasgow	0	0
1975	Glasgow (E.C.)	1	2
1975	Valencia (E.C.)	1	1
1982	Valencia	0	3
1985	Glasgow (W.C.)	3	1
1985	Seville (W.C.)	0	1
1988	Madrid	0	0
2004*	Valencia	1	1

(*Abandoned after 59 mins. – floodlight failure)

v. SWEDEN

		S	Swe
1952	Stockholm	1	3
1953	Glasgow	1	2
1975	Gothenburg	1	1
1977	Glasgow	3	1
1980	Stockholm (W.C.)	1	0
1981	Glasgow (W.C.)	2	0
1990	Genoa (W.C.)	2	1
1995	Solna	0	2
1996	Glasgow (W.C.)	1	0
1997	Gothenburg (W.C.)	1	2
2004	Edinburgh	1	4

v. SWITZERLAND

		S	Sw
1931	Geneva	3	2
1948	Berne	1	2
1950	Glasgow	3	1
1957	Basle (W.C.)	2	1
1957	Glasgow (W.C.)	3	2
1973	Berne	0	1
1976	Glasgow	1	0
1982	Berne (E.C.)	0	2
1983	Glasgow (E.C.)	2	2
1990	Glasgow (E.C.)	2	1
1991	Berne (E.C.)	2	2
1992	Berne (W.C.)	1	3
1993	Aberdeen (W.C.)	1	1
1996	Birmingham (E.C.)	1	0
2006	Glasgow	1	3

v. TRINIDAD + TOBAGO

		S	T
2004	Hibernian	4	1

v. TURKEY

		S	T
1960	Ankara	2	4

v. UKRAINE

		S	U
2006	Kiev (E.C.)	0	2

v. U.S.A.

		S	USA
1952	Glasgow	6	0
1992	Denver	1	0
1996	New Britain, Conn	1	2
1998	Washington	0	0
2005	Glasgow	1	1

v. URUGUAY

		S	U
1954	Basle (W.C.)	0	7
1962	Glasgow	2	3
1983	Glasgow	2	0
1986	Neza (W.C.)	0	0

v. YUGOSLAVIA

		S	Y
1955	Belgrade	2	2
1956	Glasgow	2	0

		S	Y
1958	Vaasteras (W.C.)	1	1
1972	Belo Horizonte	2	2
1974	Frankfurt (W.C.)	1	1
1984	Glasgow	6	1
1988	Glasgow (W.C.)	1	1
1989	Zagreb (W.C.)	1	3

v. ZAIRE

		S	Z
1974	Dortmund (W.C.)	2	0

WALES

v. ALBANIA

		W	A
1994	Cardiff (E.C.)	2	0
1995	Tirana (E.C.)	1	1

v. ARGENTINA

		W	A
1992	Gifu (Japan)	0	1
2002	Cardiff	1	1

v. ARMENIA

		W	A
2001	Yerevan (W.C.)	2	2
2001	Cardiff (W.C.)	0	0

v. AUSTRIA

		W	A
1954	Vienna	0	2
1955	Wrexham	1	2
1975	Vienna (E.C.)	1	2
1975	Wrexham (E.C.)	1	0
1992	Vienna	1	1
2005	Cardiff	0	2
2005	Vienna	0	1

v. AZERBAIJAN

		W	A
2002	Baku (E.C.)	2	0
2003	Cardiff (E.C.)	4	0
2004	Baku (W.C.)	1	1
2005	Cardiff (W.C.)	2	0

v. BELARUS

		W	B
1998	Cardiff (E.C.)	3	2
1999	Minsk (E.C.)	2	1
2000	Minsk (W.C.)	1	2
2001	Cardiff (W.C.)	1	0

v. BELGIUM

		W	B
1949	Liege	1	3
1949	Cardiff	5	1
1990	Cardiff (E.C.)	3	1
1991	Brussels (E.C.)	1	1
1992	Brussels (W.C.)	0	2
1993	Cardiff (W.C.)	2	0
1997	Cardiff (W.C.)	1	2
1997	Brussels (W.C.)	2	3

v. BOSNIA-HERZEGOVINA

		W	B-H
2003	Cardiff	2	2

v. BRAZIL

		W	B
1958	Gothenburg (W.C.)	0	1
1962	Rio de Janeiro	1	3
1962	Sao Paulo	1	3
1966	Rio de Janeiro	1	3
1966	Belo Horizonte	0	1
1983	Cardiff	1	1
1991	Cardiff	1	0
1997	Brasilia	0	3
2000	Cardiff	0	3
2006	White Hart Lane	0	2

v. BULGARIA

		W	B
1983	Wrexham (E.C.)	1	0
1983	Sofia (E.C.)	0	1
1994	Cardiff (E.C.)	0	3
1995	Sofia (E.C.)	1	3
2006	Swansea	0	0

v. CANADA

		W	C
1986	Toronto	0	2
1986	Vancouver	3	0
2004	Wrexham	1	0

v. CHILE

		W	C
1966	Santiago	0	2

v. COSTA RICA

		W	C
1990	Cardiff	1	0

v. CROATIA

		W	C
2002	Varazdin	1	1

v. CYPRUS

		W	C
1992	Limassol (W.C.)	1	0
1993	Cardiff (W.C.)	2	0
2005	Limassol	0	1
2006	Cardiff (E.C.)	3	1

v. CZECHOSLOVAKIA (see also R.C.S.)

		W	C
1957	Cardiff (W.C.)	1	0

		W	C
1957	Prague (W.C.)	0	2
1971	Swansea (E.C.)	1	3
1971	Prague (E.C.)	0	1
1977	Wrexham (W.C.)	3	0
1977	Prague (W.C.)	0	1
1980	Cardiff (W.C.)	1	0
1981	Prague (W.C.)	0	2
1987	Wrexham (E.C.)	1	1
1987	Prague (E.C.)	0	2

v. CZECH REPUBLIC

		W	CR
2002	Cardiff	0	0
2006	Teplice (E.C.)	1	2
2007	Cardiff (E.C.)	0	0

v. DENMARK

		W	D
1964	Copenhagen (W.C.)	0	1
1965	Wrexham (W.C.)	4	2
1987	Cardiff (E.C.)	1	0
1987	Copenhagen (E.C.)	0	1
1990	Copenhagen	0	1
1998	Copenhagen (E.C.)	2	1
1999	Anfield (E.C.)	0	2

v. EAST GERMANY

		W	EG
1957	Leipzig (W.C.)	1	2
1957	Cardiff (W.C.)	4	1
1969	Dresden (W.C.)	1	2
1969	Cardiff (W.C.)	1	3

v. ESTONIA

		W	E
1994	Tallinn	2	1

v. FAROE ISLANDS

		W	FI
1992	Cardiff (W.C.)	6	0
1993	Toftir (W.C.)	3	0

v. FINLAND

		W	F
1971	Helsinki (E.C.)	1	0
1971	Swansea (E.C.)	3	0
1986	Helsinki (E.C.)	1	1
1987	Wrexham (E.C.)	4	0
1988	Swansea (W.C.)	2	2
1989	Helsinki (W.C.)	0	1
2000	Cardiff	1	2
2002	Helsinki (E.C.)	2	0
2003	Cardiff (E.C.)	1	1

v. FRANCE

		W	F
1933	Paris	1	1
1939	Paris	1	2
1953	Paris	1	6
1982	Toulouse	1	0

v. GEORGIA

		W	G
1994	Tbilisi (E.C.)	0	5
1995	Cardiff (E.C.)	0	1

v. GERMANY/WEST GERMANY

		W	G
1968	Cardiff	1	1
1969	Frankfurt	1	1
1977	Cardiff	0	2
1977	Dortmund	1	1
1979	Wrexham (E.C.)	0	2
1979	Cologne (E.C.)	1	5
1989	Cardiff (W.C.)	0	0
1989	Cologne (W.C.)	1	2
1991	Cardiff (E.C.)	1	0
1991	Nuremberg (E.C.)	1	4
1995	Dusseldorf (E.C.)	1	1
1995	Cardiff (E.C.)	1	2
2002	Cardiff	1	0

v. GREECE

		W	G
1964	Athens (W.C.)	0	2
1965	Cardiff (W.C.)	4	1

v. HOLLAND

		W	H
1988	Amsterdam (W.C.)	0	1
1989	Wrexham (W.C.)	1	2
1992	Utrecht	0	4
1996	Cardiff (W.C.)	1	3
1996	Eindhoven (W.C.)	1	7

v. HUNGARY

		W	H
1958	Sanviken (W.C.)	1	1
1958	Stockholm (W.C.)	2	1
1961	Budapest	2	3
1963	Budapest (E.C.)	1	3
1963	Cardiff (E.C.)	1	1
1974	Cardiff (E.C.)	2	0
1975	Budapest (E.C.)	2	1
1986	Cardiff	0	3
2004	Budapest	2	1
2005	Cardiff	2	0

v. ICELAND

		W	I
1980	Reykjavik (W.C.)	4	0
1981	Swansea (W.C.)	2	2
1984	Reykjavik (W.C.)	0	1
1984	Cardiff (W.C.)	2	1
1991	Cardiff	1	0

v. IRAN

		W	I
1978	Tehran	1	0

v. REPUBLIC OF IRELAND

		W	RI
1960	Dublin	3	2

		W	RI
1979	Swansea	2	1
1981	Dublin	3	1
1986	Dublin	1	0
1990	Dublin	0	1
1991	Wrexham	0	3
1992	Dublin	1	0
1993	Dublin	1	2
1997	Cardiff	0	0
2007	Dublin (E.C.)	0	1

v. ISRAEL

		W	I
1958	Tel Aviv (W.C.)	2	0
1958	Cardiff (W.C.)	2	0
1984	Tel Aviv	0	0
1989	Tel Aviv	3	3

v. ITALY

		W	I
1965	Florence	1	4
1968	Cardiff (W.C.)	0	1
1969	Rome (W.C.)	1	4
1988	Brescia	1	0
1996	Terni	0	3
1998	Anfield (E.C.)	0	2
1999	Bologna (E.C.)	0	4
2002	Cardiff (E.C.)	2	1
2003	Milan (E.C.)	0	4

v. JAMAICA

		W	J
1998	Cardiff	0	0

v. JAPAN

		W	J
1992	Matsuyama	1	0

v. KUWAIT

		W	K
1977	Wrexham	0	0
1977	Kuwait City	0	0

v. LATVIA

		W	L
2004	Riga	2	0

v. LIECHTENSTEIN

		W	L
2006	Wrexham	4	0

v. LUXEMBOURG

		W	L
1974	Swansea (E.C.)	5	0
1975	Luxembourg (E.C.)	3	1
1990	Luxembourg (E.C.)	1	0
1991	Luxembourg (E.C.)	1	0

v. MALTA

		W	M
1978	Wrexham (E.C.)	7	0
1979	Valletta (E.C.)	2	0
1988	Valletta	3	2
1998	Valletta	3	0

v. MEXICO

		W	M
1958	Stockholm (W.C.)	1	1
1962	Mexico City	1	2

v. MOLDOVA

		W	M
1994	Kishinev (E.C.)	2	3
1995	Cardiff (E.C.)	1	0

v. NEW ZEALAND

		W	NZ
2007	Wrexham	2	2

v. NORWAY

		W	N
1982	Swansea (E.C.)	1	0
1983	Oslo (E.C.)	0	0
1984	Trondheim	0	1
1985	Wrexham	1	1
1985	Bergen	2	4
1994	Cardiff	1	3
2000	Cardiff (W.C.)	1	1
2001	Oslo (W.C.)	2	3
2004	Oslo	0	0

v. PARAGUAY

		W	P
2006	Cardiff	0	0

v. POLAND

		W	P
1973	Cardiff (W.C.)	2	0
1973	Katowice (W.C.)	0	3
1991	Radom	0	0
2000	Warsaw (W.C.)	0	0
2001	Cardiff (W.C.)	1	2
2004	Cardiff (W.C.)	2	3
2005	Warsaw (W.C.)	0	1

v. PORTUGAL

		W	P
1949	Lisbon	2	3
1951	Cardiff	2	1
2000	Chaves	0	3

v. QATAR

		W	Q
2000	Doha	1	0

v. R.C.S. (formerly Czechoslovakia)

		W	RCS
1993	Ostrava (W.C.)	1	1
1993	Cardiff (W.C.)	2	2

v. REST OF UNITED KINGDOM

		W	UK
1951	Cardiff	3	2
1969	Cardiff	0	1

v. ROMANIA

		W	R
1970	Cardiff (E.C.)	0	0
1971	Bucharest (E.C.)	0	2
1983	Wrexham	5	0
1992	Bucharest (W.C.)	1	5
1993	Cardiff (W.C.)	1	2

v. RUSSIA (See also Soviet Union)

		W	R
2003*	Moscow (E.C.)	0	0
2003*	Cardiff (E.C.)	0	1

(* Qual. Round play-offs)

v. SAN MARINO

		W	SM
1996	Serravalle (W.C.)	5	0
1996	Cardiff (W.C.)	6	0
2007	Cardiff (E.C.)	3	0

v. SAUDI ARABIA

		W	SA
1986	Dahran	2	1

v. SERBIA + MONTENEGRO

		W	S
2003	Belgrade (E.C.)	0	1
2003	Cardiff (E.C.)	2	3

v. SLOVAKIA

		W	S
2006	Cardiff (E.C.)	1	5

v. SLOVENIA

		W	S
2005	Swansea	0	0

v. SOVIET UNION (See also Russia)

		W	SU
1965	Moscow (W.C.)	1	2
1965	Cardiff (W.C.)	2	1
1981	Wrexham (W.C.)	0	0
1981	Tbilisi (W.C.)	0	3
1987	Swansea	0	0

v. SPAIN

		W	S
1961	Cardiff (W.C.)	1	2
1961	Madrid (W.C.)	1	1
1982	Valencia	1	1
1984	Seville (W.C.)	0	3
1985	Wrexham (W.C.)	3	0

v. SWEDEN

		W	S
1958	Stockholm (W.C.)	0	0
1988	Stockholm	1	4
1989	Wrexham	0	2
1990	Stockholm	2	4
1994	Wrexham	0	2

v. SWITZERLAND

		W	S
1949	Berne	0	4
1951	Wrexham	3	2
1996	Lugano	0	2
1999	Zurich (E.C.)	0	2
1999	Wrexham (E.C.)	0	2

v. TRINIDAD & TOBAGO

		W	T
2006	Graz	2	1

v. TUNISIA

		W	T
1998	Tunis	0	4

v. TURKEY

		W	T
1978	Wrexham (E.C.)	1	0
1979	Izmir (E.C.)	0	1
1980	Cardiff (W.C.)	4	0
1981	Ankara (W.C.)	1	0
1996	Cardiff (W.C.)	0	0
1997	Istanbul (W.C.)	4	6

v. UKRAINE

		W	U
2001	Cardiff (W.C.)	1	1
2001	Kiev (W.C.)	1	1

v. URUGUAY

		W	U
1986	Wrexham	0	0

v. U.S.A.

		W	USA
2003	San Jose	0	2

v. YUGOSLAVIA

		W	Y
1953	Belgrade	2	5
1954	Cardiff	1	3
1976	Zagreb (E.C.)	0	2
1976	Cardiff (E.C.)	1	1
1982	Titograd (E.C.)	4	4
1983	Cardiff (E.C.)	1	1
1988	Swansea	1	2

NORTHERN IRELAND

v. ALBANIA

		NI	A
1965	Belfast (W.C.)	4	1
1965	Tirana (W.C.)	1	1

		NI	A
1983	Tirana (E.C.)	0	0
1983	Belfast (E.C.)	1	0
1992	Belfast (W.C.)	3	0
1993	Tirana (W.C.)	2	1
1996	Belfast (W.C.)	2	0
1997	Zurich (W.C.)	0	1

v. ALGERIA

		NI	A
1986	Guadalajara (W.C.)	1	1

v. ARGENTINA

		NI	A
1958	Halmstad (W.C.)	1	3

v. ARMENIA

		NI	A
1996	Belfast (W.C.)	1	1
1997	Yerevan (W.C.)	0	0
2003	Yerevan (E.C.)	0	1
2003	Belfast (E.C.)	0	1

v. AUSTRALIA

		NI	A
1980	Sydney	2	1
1980	Melbourne	1	1
1980	Adelaide	2	1

v. AUSTRIA

		NI	A
1982	Madrid (W.C.)	2	2
1982	Vienna (E.C.)	0	2
1983	Belfast (E.C.)	3	1
1990	Vienna (E.C.)	0	0
1991	Belfast (E.C.)	2	1
1994	Vienna (E.C.)	2	1
1995	Belfast (E.C.)	5	3
2004	Belfast (W.C.)	3	3
2005	Vienna (W.C.)	0	2

v. AZERBAIJAN

		NI	A
2004	Baku (W.C.)	0	0
2005	Belfast (W.C.)	2	0

v. BARBADOS

		NI	B
2004	Bridgetown	1	1

v. BELGIUM

		NI	B
1976	Liege (W.C.)	0	2
1977	Belfast (W.C.)	3	0
1997	Belfast	3	0

v. BRAZIL

		NI	B
1986	Guadalajara (W.C.)	0	3

v. BULGARIA

		NI	B
1972	Sofia (W.C.)	0	3
1973	Sheffield (W.C.)	0	0
1978	Sofia (E.C.)	2	0
1979	Belfast (E.C.)	2	0
2001	Sofia (W.C.)	3	4
2001	Belfast (W.C.)	0	1

v. CANADA

		NI	C
1995	Edmonton	0	2
1999	Belfast	1	1
2005	Belfast	0	1

v. CHILE

		NI	C
1989	Belfast	0	1
1995	Edmonton, Canada	0	2

v. COLOMBIA

		NI	C
1994	Boston, USA	0	2

v. CYPRUS

		NI	C
1971	Nicosia (E.C.)	3	0
1971	Belfast (E.C.)	5	0
1973	Nicosia (W.C.)	0	1
1973	Fulham (W.C.)	3	0
2002	Belfast	0	0

v. CZECHOSLOVAKIA/CZECH REPUBLIC

		NI	C
1958	Halmstad (W.C.)	1	0
1958	Malmo (W.C.)	2	1
2001	Belfast (W.C.)	0	1
2001	Teplice (W.C.)	1	3

v. DENMARK

		NI	D
1978	Belfast (E.C.)	2	1
1979	Copenhagen (E.C.)	0	4
1986	Belfast	1	1
1990	Belfast (E.C.)	1	1
1991	Odense (E.C.)	1	2
1992	Belfast (W.C.)	0	1
1993	Copenhagen (W.C.)	0	1
2000	Belfast (W.C.)	1	1
2001	Copenhagen (W.C.)	1	1
2006	Copenhagen (E.C.)	0	0

v. ESTONIA

		NI	E
2004	Tallinn	1	0
2006	Belfast	1	0

v. FAROE ISLANDS

		NI	FI
1991	Belfast (E.C.)	1	1
1991	Landskrona, Sw. (E.C.)	5	0

v. FINLAND

		NI	F
1984	Pori (W.C.)	0	1
1984	Belfast (W.C.)	2	1
1998	Belfast (E.C.)	1	0
1999	Helsinki (E.C.)	1	4
2003	Belfast	0	1
2006	Helsinki	2	1

v. FRANCE

		NI	F
1951	Belfast	2	2
1952	Paris	1	3
1958	Norrkoping (W.C.)	0	4
1982	Paris	0	4
1982	Madrid (W.C.)	1	4
1986	Paris	0	0
1988	Belfast	0	0
1999	Belfast	0	1

v. GERMANY/WEST GERMANY

		NI	G
1958	Malmo (W.C.)	2	2
1960	Belfast (W.C.)	3	4
1961	Berlin (W.C.)	1	2
1966	Belfast	0	2
1977	Cologne	0	5
1982	Belfast (E.C.)	1	0
1983	Hamburg (E.C.)	1	0
1992	Bremen	1	1
1996	Belfast	1	1
1997	Nuremberg (W.C.)	1	1
1997	Belfast (W.C.)	1	3
1999	Belfast (E.C.)	0	3
1999	Dortmund (E.C.)	0	4
2005	Belfast	1	4

v. GREECE

		NI	G
1961	Athens (W.C.)	1	2
1961	Belfast (W.C.)	2	0
1988	Athens	2	3
2003	Belfast (E.C.)	0	2
2003	Athens (E.C.)	0	1

v. HOLLAND

		NI	H
1962	Rotterdam	0	4
1965	Belfast (W.C.)	2	1
1965	Rotterdam (W.C.)	0	0
1976	Rotterdam (W.C.)	2	2
1977	Belfast (W.C.)	0	1

v. HONDURAS

		NI	H
1982	Zaragoza (W.C.)	1	1

v. HUNGARY

		NI	H
1988	Budapest (W.C.)	0	1
1989	Belfast (W.C.)	1	2
2000	Belfast	0	1

v. ICELAND

		NI	I
1977	Reykjavik (W.C.)	0	1
1977	Belfast (W.C.)	2	0
2000	Reykjavik (W.C.)	0	1
2001	Belfast (W.C.)	3	0
2006	Belfast (E.C.)	0	3

v. REPUBLIC OF IRELAND

		NI	RI
1978	Dublin (E.C.)	0	0
1979	Belfast (E.C.)	1	0
1988	Belfast (W.C.)	0	0
1989	Dublin (W.C.)	0	3
1993	Dublin (W.C.)	0	3
1993	Belfast (W.C.)	1	1
1994	Belfast (E.C.)	0	4
1995	Dublin (E.C.)	1	1
1999	Dublin	1	0

v. ISRAEL

		NI	I
1968	Jaffa	3	2
1976	Tel Aviv	1	1
1980	Tel Aviv (W.C.)	0	0
1981	Belfast (W.C.)	1	0
1984	Belfast	3	0
1987	Tel Aviv	1	1

v. ITALY

		NI	I
1957	Rome (W.C.)	0	1
1957	Belfast	2	2
1958	Belfast (W.C.)	2	1
1961	Bologna	2	3
1997	Palermo	0	2
2003	Campobasso	0	2

v. LATVIA

		NI	L
1993	Riga (W.C.)	2	1
1993	Belfast (W.C.)	2	0
1995	Riga (E.C.)	1	0
1995	Belfast (E.C.)	1	2
2006	Belfast (E.C.)	1	0

v. LIECHTENSTEIN

		NI	L
1994	Belfast (E.C.)	4	1
1995	Eschen (E.C.)	4	0
2002	Vaduz	0	0
2007	Vaduz (E.C.)	4	1

v. LITHUANIA

		NI	L
1992	Belfast (W.C.)	2	2
1993	Vilnius (W.C.)	1	0

v. LUXEMBOURG

		NI	L
2000	Luxembourg	3	1

v. MALTA

		NI	M
1988	Belfast (W.C.)	3	0
1989	Valletta (W.C.)	2	0
2000	Ta'Qali	3	0
2000	Belfast (W.C.)	1	0
2001	Valletta (W.C.)	1	0
2005	Valletta	1	1

v. MEXICO

		NI	M
1966	Belfast	4	1
1994	Miami	0	3

v. MOLDOVA

		NI	M
1998	Belfast (E.C.)	2	2
1999	Kishinev (E.C.)	0	0

v. MOROCCO

		NI	M
1986	Belfast	2	1

v. NORWAY

		NI	N
1974	Oslo (E.C.)	1	2
1975	Belfast (E.C.)	3	0
1990	Belfast	2	3
1996	Belfast	0	2
2001	Belfast	0	4
2004	Belfast	1	4

v. POLAND

		NI	P
1962	Katowice (E.C.)	2	0
1962	Belfast (E.C.)	2	0
1988	Belfast	1	1
1991	Belfast	3	1
2002	Limassol (Cyprus)	1	4
2004	Belfast (W.C.)	0	3
2005	Warsaw (W.C.)	0	1

v. PORTUGAL

		NI	P
1957	Lisbon (W.C.)	1	1
1957	Belfast (W.C.)	3	0
1973	Coventry (W.C.)	1	1
1973	Lisbon (W.C.)	1	1
1980	Lisbon (W.C.)	0	1
1981	Belfast (W.C.)	1	0
1994	Belfast (E.C.)	1	2
1995	Oporto (E.C.)	1	1
1997	Belfast (W.C.)	0	0
1997	Lisbon (W.C.)	0	1
2005	Belfast	1	1

v. ROMANIA

		NI	R
1984	Belfast (W.C.)	3	2
1985	Bucharest (W.C.)	1	0
1994	Belfast	2	0
2006	Chicago	0	2

v. SERBIA + MONTENEGRO

		NI	S
2004	Belfast	1	1

v. SLOVAKIA

		NI	S
1998	Belfast	1	0

v. SOVIET UNION

		NI	SU
1969	Belfast (W.C.)	0	0
1969	Moscow (W.C.)	0	2
1971	Moscow (E.C.)	0	1
1971	Belfast (E.C.)	1	1

v. SPAIN

		NI	S
1958	Madrid	2	6
1963	Bilbao	1	1
1963	Belfast	0	1
1970	Seville (E.C.)	0	3
1972	Hull (E.C.)	1	1
1982	Valencia (W.C.)	1	0
1985	Palma, Majorca	0	0
1986	Guadalajara (W.C.)	1	2
1988	Seville (W.C.)	0	4
1989	Belfast (W.C.)	0	2
1992	Belfast (W.C.)	0	0
1993	Seville (W.C.)	1	3
1998	Santander	1	4
2002	Belfast	0	5
2002	Albacete (E.C.)	0	3
2003	Belfast (E.C.)	0	0
2006	Belfast (E.C.)	3	2

v. ST KITTS + NEVIS

		NI	SK
2004	Basseterre	2	0

v. SWEDEN

		NI	S
1974	Solna (E.C.)	2	0
1975	Belfast (E.C.)	1	2
1980	Belfast (W.C.)	3	0
1981	Stockholm (W.C.)	0	1
1996	Belfast	1	2
2007	Belfast (E.C.)	2	1

v. SWITZERLAND

		NI	S
1964	Belfast (W.C.)	1	0
1964	Lausanne (W.C.)	1	2
1998	Belfast	1	0
2004	Zurich	0	0

v. THAILAND

		NI	T
1997	Bangkok	0	0

v. TRINIDAD + TOBAGO

		NI	T
2004	Port of Spain	3	0

v. TURKEY

		NI	T
1968	Belfast (W.C.)	4	1
1968	Istanbul (W.C.)	3	0
1983	Belfast (E.C.)	2	1
1983	Ankara (E.C.)	0	1
1985	Belfast (W.C.)	2	0
1985	Izmir (W.C.)	0	0
1986	Izmir (E.C.)	0	0
1987	Belfast (E.C.)	1	0
1998	Istanbul (E.C.)	0	3
1999	Belfast (E.C.)	0	3

v. UKRAINE

		NI	U
1996	Belfast (W.C.)	0	1
1997	Kiev (W.C.)	1	2
2002	Belfast (E.C.)	0	0
2003	Donetsk (E.C.)	0	0

v. URUGUAY

		NI	U
1964	Belfast	3	0
1990	Belfast	1	0
2006	New Jersey	0	1

v.YUGOSLAVIA

		NI	Y
1975	Belfast (E.C.)	1	0
1975	Belgrade (E.C.)	0	1
1982	Zaragoza (W.C.)	0	0
1987	Belfast (E.C.)	1	2
1987	Sarajevo (E.C.)	0	3
1990	Belfast (E.C.)	0	2
1991	Belgrade (E.C.)	1	4
2000	Belfast	1	2

REPUBLIC OF IRELAND

v. ALBANIA

		RI	A
1992	Dublin (W.C.)	2	0
1993	Tirana (W.C.)	2	1
2003	Tirana (E.C.)	0	0
2003	Dublin (E.C.)	2	1

v. ALGERIA

		RI	A
1982	Algiers	0	2

v. ANDORRA

		RI	A
2001	Barcelona (W.C.)	3	0
2001	Dublin (W.C.)	3	1

v. ARGENTINA

		RI	A
1951	Dublin	0	1
1979*	Dublin	0	0
1980	Dublin	0	1
1998	Dublin	0	2

(* Not regarded as full Int.)

v. AUSTRALIA

		RI	A
2003	Dublin	2	1

v. AUSTRIA

		RI	A
1952	Vienna	0	6
1953	Dublin	4	0
1958	Vienna	1	3
1962	Dublin	2	3
1963	Vienna (E.C.)	0	0
1963	Dublin (E.C.)	3	2
1966	Vienna	0	1
1968	Dublin	2	2
1971	Dublin (E.C.)	1	4
1971	Linz (E.C.)	0	6
1995	Dublin (E.C.)	1	3
1995	Vienna (E.C.)	1	3

v. BELGIUM

		RI	B
1928	Liege	4	2
1929	Dublin	4	0
1930	Brussels	3	1
1934	Dublin (W.C.)	4	4
1949	Dublin	0	2
1950	Brussels	1	5
1965	Dublin	0	2
1966	Liege	3	2
1980	Dublin (W.C.)	1	1
1981	Brussels (W.C.)	0	1
1986	Brussels (E.C.)	2	2
1987	Dublin (E.C.)	0	0
1997*	Dublin (W.C.)	1	1
1997*	Brussels (W.C.)	1	2

(* World Cup play-off)

v. BOLIVIA

		RI	B
1994	Dublin	1	0
1996	East Rutherford, N.J.	3	0
2007	Boston	1	1

v. BRAZIL

		RI	B
1974	Rio de Janeiro	1	2
1982	Uberlandia	0	7

		RI	*B*
1987	Dublin	1	0
2004	Dublin	0	0

v. BULGARIA

		RI	*B*
1977	Sofia (W.C.)	1	2
1977	Dublin (W.C.)	0	0
1979	Sofia (E.C.)	0	1
1979	Dublin (E.C.)	3	0
1987	Sofia (E.C.)	1	2
1987	Dublin (E.C.)	2	0
2004	Dublin	1	1

v. CAMEROON

		RI	*C*
2002	Niigata (W.C.)	1	1

v. CANADA

		RI	*C*
2003	Dublin	3	0

v. CHILE

		RI	*C*
1960	Dublin	2	0
1972	Recife	1	2
1974	Santiago	2	1
1982	Santiago	0	1
1991	Dublin	1	1
2006	Dublin	0	1

v. CHINA

		RI	*C*
1984	Sapporo	1	0
2005	Dublin	1	0

v. CROATIA

		RI	*C*
1996	Dublin	2	2
1998	Dublin (E.C.)	2	0
1999	Zagreb (E.C.)	0	1
2001	Dublin	2	2
2004	Dublin	1	0

v. CYPRUS

		RI	*C*
1980	Nicosia (W.C.)	3	2
1980	Dublin (W.C.)	6	0
2001	Nicosia (W.C.)	4	0
2001	Dublin (W.C.)	4	0
2004	Dublin (W.C.)	3	0
2005	Nicosia (W.C.)	1	0
2006	Nicosia (E.C.)	2	5

v. CZECHOSLOVAKIA/CZECH REPUBLIC

		RI	*C*
1938	Prague	2	2
1959	Dublin (E.C.)	2	0
1959	Bratislava (E.C.)	0	4
1961	Dublin (W.C.)	1	3
1961	Prague (W.C.)	1	7
1967	Dublin (E.C.)	0	2
1967	Prague (E.C.)	2	1
1969	Dublin (W.C.)	1	2
1969	Prague (W.C.)	0	3
1979	Prague	1	4
1981	Dublin	3	1
1986	Reykjavik	1	0
1994	Dublin	1	3
1996	Prague	0	2
1998	Olomouc	1	2
2000	Dublin	3	2
2004	Dublin	2	1
2006	Dublin (E.C.)	1	1

v. DENMARK

		RI	*D*
1956	Dublin (W.C.)	2	1
1957	Copenhagen (W.C.)	2	0
1968*	Dublin (W.C.)	1	1
1969	Copenhagen (W.C.)	0	2
1969	Dublin (W.C.)	1	1
1978	Copenhagen (E.C.)	3	3
1979	Dublin (E.C.)	2	0
1984	Copenhagen (W.C.)	0	3
1985	Dublin (W.C.)	1	4
1992	Copenhagen (W.C.)	0	0
1993	Dublin (W.C.)	1	1
2002	Dublin	3	0

(* Abandoned after 51 mins. – fog)

v. ECUADOR

		RI	*E*
1972	Natal	3	2
2007	New York	1	1

v. EGYPT

		RI	*E*
1990	Palermo (W.C.)	0	0

v. ESTONIA

		RI	*E*
2000	Dublin (W.C.)	2	0
2001	Tallinn (W.C.)	2	0

v. FAROE ISLANDS

		RI	*F*
2004	Dublin (W.C.)	2	0
2005	Torshavn (W.C.)	2	0

v. FINLAND

		RI	*F*
1949	Dublin (W.C.)	3	0
1949	Helsinki (W.C.)	1	1
1990	Dublin	1	1
2000	Dublin	3	0
2002	Helsinki	3	0

v. FRANCE

		RI	*F*
1937	Paris	2	0

		RI	F
1952	Dublin	1	1
1953	Dublin (W.C.)	3	5
1953	Paris (W.C.)	0	1
1972	Dublin (W.C.)	2	1
1973	Paris (W.C.)	1	1
1976	Paris (W.C.)	0	2
1977	Dublin (W.C.)	1	0
1980	Paris (W.C.)	0	2
1981	Dublin (W.C.)	3	2
1989	Dublin	0	0
2004	Paris (W.C.)	0	0
2005	Dublin (W.C.)	0	1

v. GEORGIA

		RI	G
2002	Tbilisi (E.C.)	2	1
2003	Dublin (E.C.)	2	0

v. GERMANY/WEST GERMANY

		RI	G
1935	Dortmund	1	3
1936	Dublin	5	2
1939	Bremen	1	1
1951	Dublin	3	2
1952	Cologne	0	3
1955	Hamburg	1	2
1956	Dublin	3	0
1960	Dusseldorf	1	0
1966	Dublin	0	4
1970	Berlin	1	2
1979	Dublin	1	3
1981	Bremen	0	3
1989	Dublin	1	1
1994	Hanover	2	0
1995*	Dublin	1	0
2002	Ibaraki (W.C.)	1	1
2006	Stuttgart (E.C.)	0	1

(*v. W. Germany 'B')

v. GREECE

		RI	G
2000	Dublin	0	1
2002	Athens	0	0

v. HOLLAND

		RI	H
1932	Amsterdam	2	0
1934	Amsterdam	2	5
1935	Dublin	3	5
1955	Dublin	1	0
1956	Rotterdam	4	1
1980	Dublin (W.C.)	2	1
1981	Rotterdam (W.C.)	2	2
1982	Rotterdam (E.C.)	1	2
1983	Dublin (E.C.)	2	3
1988	Gelsenkirchen (E.C.)	0	1
1990	Palermo (W.C.)	1	1
1994	Tilburg	1	0
1994	Orlando (W.C.)	0	2
1995*	Liverpool (E.C.)	0	2
1996	Rotterdam	1	3

(* Qual. Round play-off)

		RI	H
2000	Amsterdam (W.C.)	2	2
2001	Dublin (W.C.)	1	0
2004	Amsterdam	1	0
2006	Dublin	0	4

v. HUNGARY

		RI	H
1934	Dublin	2	4
1936	Budapest	3	3
1936	Dublin	2	3
1939	Cork	2	2
1939	Budapest	2	2
1969	Dublin (W.C.)	1	2
1969	Budapest (W.C.)	0	4
1989	Budapest (W.C.)	0	0
1989	Dublin (W.C.)	2	0
1992	Gyor	2	1

v. ICELAND

		RI	I
1962	Dublin (E.C.)	4	2
1962	Reykjavik (E.C.)	1	1
1982	Dublin (E.C.)	2	0
1983	Reykjavik (E.C.)	3	0
1986	Reykjavik	2	1
1996	Dublin (W.C.)	0	0
1997	Reykjavik (W.C.)	4	2

v. IRAN

		RI	I
1972	Recife	2	1
2001*	Dublin (W.C.)	2	0
2001*	Tehran (W.C.)	0	1

(*Qual. Round play-off)

v. ISRAEL

		RI	I
1984	Tel Aviv	0	3
1985	Tel Aviv	0	0
1987	Dublin	5	0
2005	Tel Aviv (W.C.)	1	1
2005	Dublin (W.C.)	2	2

v. JAMAICA

		RI	J
2004	Charlton	1	0

v. ITALY

		RI	I
1926	Turin	0	3
1927	Dublin	1	2
1970	Florence (E.C.)	0	3
1971	Dublin (E.C.)	1	2
1985	Dublin	1	2
1990	Rome (W.C.)	0	1
1992	Boston, USA	0	2
1994	New York (W.C.)	1	0

		RI	I
2005	Dublin	1	2

v. LATVIA

		RI	L
1992	Dublin (W.C.)	4	0
1993	Riga (W.C.)	2	0
1994	Riga (E.C.)	3	0
1995	Dublin (E.C.)	2	1

v. LIECHTENSTEIN

		RI	L
1994	Dublin (E.C.)	4	0
1995	Eschen (E.C.)	0	0
1996	Eschen (W.C.)	5	0
1997	Dublin (W.C.)	5	0

v. LITHUANIA

		RI	L
1993	Vilnius (W.C.)	1	0
1993	Dublin (W.C.)	2	0
1997	Dublin (W.C.)	0	0
1997	Zalgiris (W.C.)	2	1

v. LUXEMBOURG

		RI	L
1936	Luxembourg	5	1
1953	Dublin (W.C.)	4	0
1954	Luxembourg (W.C.)	1	0
1987	Luxembourg (E.C.)	2	0
1987	Luxembourg (E.C.)	2	1

v. MACEDONIA

		RI	M
1996	Dublin (W.C.)	3	0
1997	Skopje (W.C.)	2	3
1999	Dublin (E.C.)	1	0
1999	Skopje (E.C.)	1	1

v. MALTA

		RI	M
1983	Valletta (E.C.)	1	0
1983	Dublin (E.C.)	8	0
1989	Dublin (W.C.)	2	0
1989	Valletta (W.C.)	2	0
1990	Valletta	3	0
1998	Dublin (E.C.)	1	0
1999	Valletta (E.C.)	3	2

v. MEXICO

		RI	M
1984	Dublin	0	0
1994	Orlando (W.C.)	1	2
1996	New Jersey	2	2
1998	Dublin	0	0
2000	Chicago	2	2

v. MOROCCO

		RI	M
1990	Dublin	1	0

v. NIGERIA

		RI	N
2002	Dublin	1	2
2004	Charlton	0	3

v. NORWAY

		RI	N
1937	Oslo (W.C.)	2	3
1937	Dublin (W.C.)	3	3
1950	Dublin	2	2
1951	Oslo	3	2
1954	Dublin	2	1
1955	Oslo	3	1
1960	Dublin	3	1
1964	Oslo	4	1
1973	Oslo	1	1
1976	Dublin	3	0
1978	Oslo	0	0
1984	Oslo (W.C.)	0	1
1985	Dublin (W.C.)	0	0
1988	Oslo	0	0
1994	New York (W.C.)	0	0
2003	Dublin	1	0

v. PARAGUAY

		RI	P
1999	Dublin	2	0

v. POLAND

		RI	P
1938	Warsaw	0	6
1938	Dublin	3	2
1958	Katowice	2	2
1958	Dublin	2	2
1964	Cracow	1	3
1964	Dublin	3	2
1968	Dublin	2	2
1968	Katowice	0	1
1970	Dublin	1	2
1970	Poznan	0	2
1973	Wroclaw	0	2
1973	Dublin	1	0
1976	Poznan	2	0
1977	Dublin	0	0
1978	Lodz	0	3
1981	Bydgoszcz	0	3
1984	Dublin	0	0
1986	Warsaw	0	1
1988	Dublin	3	1
1991	Dublin (E.C.)	0	0
1991	Poznan (E.C.)	3	3
2004	Bydgoszcz	0	0

v. PORTUGAL

		RI	P
1946	Lisbon	1	3
1947	Dublin	0	2
1948	Lisbon	0	2
1949	Dublin	1	0
1972	Recife	1	2
1992	Boston, USA	2	0

		RI	P
1995	Dublin (E.C.)	1	0
1995	Lisbon (E.C.)	0	3
1996	Dublin	0	1
2000	Lisbon (W.C.)	1	1
2001	Dublin (W.C.)	1	1
2005	Dublin	1	0

v. ROMANIA

		RI	R
1988	Dublin	2	0
1990*	Genoa	0	0
1997	Bucharest (W.C.)	0	1
1997	Dublin (W.C.)	1	1

(* Rep. won 5-4 on pens.)

v. RUSSIA (See also Soviet Union)

		RI	R
1994	Dublin	0	0
1996	Dublin	0	2
2002	Dublin	2	0
2002	Moscow (E.C.)	2	4
2003	Dublin (E.C.)	1	1

v. SAN MARINO

		RI	SM
2006	Dublin (E.C.)	5	0
2007	Rimini (E.C.)	2	1

v. SAUDI ARABIA

		RI	SA
2002	Yokohama (W.C.)	3	0

v. SLOVAKIA

		RI	S
2007	Dublin (E.C.)	1	0

v. SOUTH AFRICA

		RI	SA
2000	New Jersey	2	1

v. SOVIET UNION
(See also Russia)

		RI	SU
1972	Dublin (W.C.)	1	2
1973	Moscow (W.C.)	0	1
1974	Dublin (E.C.)	3	0
1975	Kiev (E.C.)	1	2
1984	Dublin (W.C.)	1	0
1985	Moscow (W.C.)	0	2
1988	Hanover (E.C.)	1	1
1990	Dublin	1	0

v. SPAIN

		RI	S
1931	Barcelona	1	1
1931	Dublin	0	5
1946	Madrid	1	0
1947	Dublin	3	2
1948	Barcelona	1	2
1949	Dublin	1	4
1952	Madrid	0	6
1955	Dublin	2	2
1964	Seville (E.C.)	1	5
1964	Dublin (E.C.)	0	2
1965	Dublin (W.C.)	1	0
1965	Seville (W.C.)	1	4
1965	Paris (W.C.)	0	1
1966	Dublin (E.C.)	0	0
1966	Valencia (E.C.)	0	2
1977	Dublin	0	1
1982	Dublin (E.C.)	3	3
1983	Zaragoza (E.C.)	0	2
1985	Cork	0	0
1988	Seville (W.C.)	0	2
1989	Dublin (W.C.)	1	0
1992	Seville (W.C.)	0	0
1993	Dublin (W.C.)	1	3
2002*	Suwon (W.C.)	1	1

(*Rep. lost 3-2 on pens.)

v. SWEDEN

		RI	S
1949	Stockholm (W.C.)	1	3
1949	Dublin (W.C.)	1	3
1959	Dublin	3	2
1960	Malmo	1	4
1970	Dublin (E.C.)	1	1
1970	Malmo (E.C.)	0	1
1999	Dublin	2	0
2006	Dublin	3	0

v. SWITZERLAND

		RI	S
1935	Basle	0	1
1936	Dublin	1	0
1937	Berne	1	0
1938	Dublin	4	0
1948	Dublin	0	1
1975	Dublin (E.C.)	2	1
1975	Berne (E.C.)	0	1
1980	Dublin	2	0
1985	Dublin (W.C.)	3	0
1985	Berne (W.C.)	0	0
1992	Dublin	2	1
2002	Dublin (E.C.)	1	2
2003	Basle (E.C.)	0	2
2004	Basle (W.C.)	1	1
2005	Dublin (W.C.)	0	0

v. TRINIDAD & TOBAGO

		RI	T&T
1982	Port of Spain	1	2

v. TUNISIA

		RI	T
1988	Dublin	4	0

v. TURKEY

		RI	T
1966	Dublin (E.C.)	2	1

		RI	T
1967	Ankara (E.C.)	1	2
1974	Izmir (E.C.)	1	1
1975	Dublin (E.C.)	4	0
1976	Ankara	3	3
1978	Dublin	4	2
1990	Izmir	0	0
1990	Dublin (E.C.)	5	0
1991	Istanbul (E.C.)	3	1
1999	Dublin (E.C.)	1	1
1999	Bursa (E.C.)	0	0
2003	Dublin	2	2

v. URUGUAY

		RI	U
1974	Montevideo	0	2
1986	Dublin	1	1

v. U.S.A.

		RI	USA
1979	Dublin	3	2
1991	Boston	1	1
1992	Dublin	4	1
1992	Washington	1	3
1996	Boston	1	2
2000	Foxboro	1	1
2002	Dublin	2	1

v. YUGOSLAVIA

		RI	Y
1955	Dublin	1	4
1988	Dublin	2	0
1998	Belgrade (E.C.)	0	1
1999	Dublin (E.C.)	2	1

BRITISH & IRISH INTERNATIONAL APPEARANCES SINCE THE WAR (1946-2007)

(As at start of season 2007-08. In year shown, 2007 = season 2006-07 etc. *Also a pre-war International player. Totals include appearances as substitute).

ENGLAND

A'Court, A. (Liverpool, 1958-9) 5
Adams, T. (Arsenal, 1987-2001) 66
Allen, A. (Stoke City, 1960) 3
Allen, C. (Q.P.R., Tottenham, 1984-8) 5
Allen, R. (W.B.A., 1952-5) 5
Anderson, S. (Sunderland, 1962) 2
Anderson, V. (Nott'm. Forest, Arsenal, Manchester Utd., 1979-88) 30
Anderton, D. (Tottenham, 1994-2002) 30
Angus, J. (Burnley, 1961) 1
Armfield, J. (Blackpool, 1959-66) 43
Armstrong, D. (Middlesbrough, Southampton, 1980-4) 3
Armstrong, K. (Chelsea, 1955) 1
Astall, G. (Birmingham City, 1956) 2
Astle, J. (W.B.A., 1969-70) 5
Aston, J. (Manchester Utd., 1949-51) 17
Atyeo, J. (Bristol City, 1956-7) 6

Bailey, G. (Manchester Utd., 1985) 2
Bailey, M. (Charlton Athletic, 1964-5) 2
Baily, E. (Tottenham, 1950-3) 9
Baker, J. (Hibernian, Arsenal, 1960-6) 8
Ball, A. (Blackpool, Everton, Arsenal, 1965-75) 72
Ball, M. (Everton, 2001) 1
Banks, G. (Leicester City, Stoke City, 1963-72) 73
Banks, T. (Bolton Wand., 1958-9) 6
Bardsley, D. (Q.P.R., 1993) 2
Barham, M. (Norwich City, 1983) 2
Barlow, R. (W.B.A., 1955) 1
Barmby, N. (Tottenham, Middlesbrough, Everton, Liverpool, 1995-2002) 23
Barnes, J. (Watford, Liverpool, 1983-96) 79
Barnes, P. (Manchester City, W.B.A., Leeds Utd., 1978-82) 22
Barrass, M. (Bolton Wand., 1952-3) ... 3
Barrett, E. (Oldham Athletic, Aston Villa, 1991-3) 3
Barry, G. (Aston Villa, 2000-7) 9
Barton, J. (Manchester City, 2007) 1
Barton, W. (Wimbledon, Newcastle Utd., 1995) 3
Batty, D. (Leeds Utd., Blackburn Rov., Newcastle Utd., Leeds Utd., 1991-2000) 42
Baynham, R. (Luton Town, 1956) 3
Beardsley, P. (Newcastle Utd., Liverpool, Newcastle Utd., 1986-96) 59
Beasant, D. (Chelsea, 1990) 2

Hodgkinson, A. (Sheffield Utd., 1957-61) 5
Holden, D. (Bolton Wand., 1959) 5
Holliday, E. (Middlesbrough, 1960) 3
Hollins, J. (Chelsea, 1967) 1
Hopkinson, E. (Bolton Wand., 1958-60) 14
Howe, D. (W.B.A., 1958-60) 23
Howe, J. (Derby Co., 1948-9) 3
Howey, S. (Newcastle Utd., 1995-6) .. 4
Hudson, A. (Stoke City, 1975) 2
Hughes, E. (Liverpool, Wolves, 1970-80) 62
Hughes, L. (Liverpool, 1950) 3
Hunt, R. (Liverpool, 1962-9) 34
Hunt, S. (W.B.A., 1984) 2
Hunter, N. (Leeds Utd., 1966-75) 28
Hurst, G. (West Ham Utd., 1966-72) 49

Ince, P. (Manchester Utd., Inter Milan, Liverpool, Middlesbrough, 1993-2000) 53

James, D. (Liverpool, Aston Villa, West Ham Utd., Manchester City, 1997-2006) 33
Jeffers, F. (Arsenal, 2003) 1
Jenas, J. (Newcastle Utd., Tottenham, 2003-7) 17
Jezzard, B. (Fulham, 1954-6) 2
Johnson, A. (Crystal Palace, Everton, 2005-7) 7
Johnson, D. (Ipswich Town, Liverpool, 1975-80) 8
Johnson, G (Chelsea, 2004-6) 5
Johnson, S. (Derby Co., 2001) 1
Johnston, H. (Blackpool, 1947-54) .. 10
Jones, M. (Leeds Utd., Sheffield Utd., 1965-70) 3
Jones, R. (Liverpool, 1992-5) 8
Jones, W.H. (Liverpool, 1950) 2

Kay, A. (Everton, 1963) 1
Keegan, K. (Liverpool, Hamburg, Southampton, 1973-82) 63
Kennedy, A. (Liverpool, 1984) 2
Kennedy, R. (Liverpool, 1976-80) 17
Keown, M. (Everton, Arsenal, 1992-2002) 43
Kevan, D. (W.B.A., 1957-61) 14
Kidd, B. (Manchester Utd., 1970) 2
King, L. (Tottenham, 2002-7) 19
Kirkland, C. (Liverpool, 2007) 1
Knight, Z. (Fulham, 2005) 2
Knowles, C. (Tottenham, 1968) 4
Konchesky, P. (Charlton Athletic, 2003–6) 2

Labone, B. (Everton, 1963-70) 26
Lampard, F., Snr. (West Ham Utd., 1973-80) 2
Lampard, F., Jnr. (West Ham Utd., Chelsea, 2000-7) 55
Langley, J. (Fulham, 1958) 3
Langton, R. (Blackburn Rov., Preston N.E., Bolton Wand., 1947-51) 11
Latchford, R. (Everton, 1978-9) 12
Lawler, C. (Liverpool, 1971-2) 4
*Lawton, T. (Chelsea, Notts Co., 1947-9) 15
Lee, F. (Manchester City, 1969-72) .. 27
Lee, J. (Derby Co., 1951) 1
Lee, R. (Newcastle Utd., 1995-9) 21
Lee, S. (Liverpool, 1983-4) 14
Lennon, A. (Tottenham, 2006-7) 9
Le Saux, G. (Blackburn Rov., Chelsea, 1994-2001) 36
Le Tissier, M. (Southampton, 1994-7) 8
Lindsay, A. (Liverpool, 1974) 4
Lineker, G. (Leicester City, Everton, Barcelona, Tottenham, 1985-92) .. 80
Little, B. (Aston Villa, 1975) 1
Lloyd, L. (Liverpool, Nott'm. Forest, 1971-80) 4
Lofthouse, N. (Bolton Wand., 1951-9) 33
Lowe, E. (Aston Villa, 1947) 3

Mabbutt, G. (Tottenham, 1983-92) .. 16
Macdonald, M. (Newcastle Utd., 1972-6) 14
Madeley, P. (Leeds Utd., 1971-7) 24
Mannion, W. (Middlesbrough, 1947-52) 26
Mariner, P. (Ipswich Town, Arsenal, 1977-85) 35
Marsh, R. (Q.P.R., Manchester City, 1972-3) 9
Martin, A. (West Ham Utd., 1981-7) 17
Martyn, N. (Crystal Palace, Leeds Utd., 1992-2002) 23
Marwood, B. (Arsenal, 1989) 1
Matthews, R. (Coventry City, 1956-7) . 5
*Matthews, S. (Stoke City, Blackpool, 1947-57) 37
McCann, G. (Sunderland, 2001) 1
McDermott, T. (Liverpool, 1978-82) . 25
McDonald, C. (Burnley, 1958-9) 8
McFarland, R. (Derby Co., 1971-7) .. 28
McGarry, W. (Huddersfield Town, 1954-6) 4
McGuinness, W. (Manchester Utd., 1959) 2
McMahon, S. (Liverpool, 1988-91) ... 17
McManaman, S. (Liverpool, Real Madrid, 1995-2002) 37
McNab, R. (Arsenal, 1969) 4
McNeil, M. (Middlesbrough, 1961-2) .. 9

Meadows, J. (Manchester City, 1955) . 1
Medley, L. (Tottenham, 1951-2) 6
Melia, J. (Liverpool, 1963) 2
Merrick, G. (Birmingham City, 1952-4) 23
Merson, P. (Arsenal, Middlesbrough, Aston Villa, 1992-9) 21
Metcalfe, V. (Huddersfield Town, 1951) 2
Milburn, J. (Newcastle Utd., 1949-56) 13
Miller, B. (Burnley, 1961) 1
Mills, D. (Leeds Utd., 2001-4) 19
Mills, M. (Ipswich Town, 1973-82) ... 42
Milne, G. (Liverpool, 1963-5) 14
Milton, A. (Arsenal, 1952) 1
Moore, R. (West Ham Utd., 1962-74) 108
Morley, A. (Aston Villa, 1982-3) 6
Morris, J. (Derby Co., 1949-50) 3
Mortensen, S. (Blackpool, 1947-54) . 25
Mozley, B. (Derby Co., 1950) 3
Mullen, J. (Wolves, 1947-54) 12
Mullery, A. (Tottenham, 1965-72) 35
Murphy, D. (Liverpool, 2002-4) 9

Neal, P. (Liverpool, 1976-84) 50
Neville, G. (Manchester Utd., 1995-2006) 81
Neville, P. (Manchester Utd., Everton, 1996-2007) 56
Newton, K. (Blackburn Rov., Everton, 1966-70) 27
Nicholls, J. (W.B.A., 1954) 2
Nicholson, W. (Tottenham, 1951) 1
Nish, D. (Derby Co., 1973-4) 5
Norman, M. (Tottenham, 1962-5) 23
Nugent, D. (Preston N.E., 2007) 1

O'Grady, M. (Huddersfield Town, Leeds Utd., 1963-9) 2
Osgood, P. (Chelsea, 1970-4) 4
Osman, R. (Ipswich Town, 1980-4) .. 11
Owen, M. (Liverpool, Real Madrid, Newcastle Utd., 1998-2007) 82
Owen, S. (Luton Town, 1954) 3

Paine, T. (Southampton, 1963-6) 19
Pallister, G. (Middlesbrough, Manchester Utd., 1988-97) 22
Palmer, C. (Sheffield Wed., 1992-4) . 18
Parker, P. (Q.P.R., Manchester Utd., 1989-94) 19
Parker, S (Charlton Athletic, Chelsea, Newcastle Utd., 2004-7) 3
Parkes, P. (Q.P.R., 1974) 1
Parlour, R. (Arsenal, 1999-2001) 10
Parry, R. (Bolton, 1960) 2
Peacock, A. (Middlesbrough, Leeds Utd., 1962-6) 6
Pearce, S. (Nott'm. Forest, West Ham Utd., 1987-2000) 78
Pearson, Stan (Manchester Utd., 1948-52) 8
Pearson, Stuart (Manchester Utd., 1976-8) 15
Pegg, D. (Manchester Utd., 1957) 1
Pejic, M. (Stoke City, 1974) 4
Perry, W. (Blackpool, 1956) 3
Perryman, S. (Tottenham, 1982) 1
Peters, M. (West Ham Utd., Tottenham, 1966-74) 67
Phelan, M. (Manchester Utd., 1990) .. 1
Phillips, K. (Sunderland, 1999-2002) 8
Phillips, L. (Portsmouth, 1952-5) 3
Pickering, F. (Everton, 1964-5) 3
Pickering, N. (Sunderland, 1983) 1
Pilkington, B. (Burnley, 1955) 1
Platt, D. (Aston Villa, Bari, Juventus, Sampdoria, Arsenal, 1990-6) 62
Pointer, R. (Burnley, 1962) 3
Powell, C. (Charlton Athletic, 2001-2) 5
Pye, J. (Wolves, 1950) 1

Quixall, A. (Sheffield Wed., 1954-5) ... 5

Radford, J. (Arsenal, 1969-72) 2
Ramsey, A. (Southampton, Tottenham, 1949-54) 32
Reaney, P. (Leeds Utd., 1969-71) 3
Redknapp, J. (Liverpool, 1996-2000) 17
Reeves, K. (Norwich City, Manchester City, 1980) 2
Regis, C. (W.B.A., Coventry City, 1982-8) 5
Reid, P. (Everton, 1985-8) 13
Revie, D. (Manchester City, 1955-7) ... 6
Richards, J. (Wolves, 1973) 1
Richards, M. (Manchester City, 2007) 4
Richardson, K. (Aston Villa, 1994) 1
Richardson, K. (Manchester Utd., 2005-7) 8
Rickaby, S. (W.B.A., 1954) 1
Ricketts, M. (Bolton Wand., 2002) 1
Rimmer, J. (Arsenal, 1976) 1
Ripley, S. (Blackburn Rov., 1994-7) ... 2
Rix, G. (Arsenal, 1981-4) 17
Robb, G. (Tottenham, 1954) 1
Roberts, G. (Tottenham, 1983-4) 6
Robinson, P. (Leeds Utd., Tottenham, 2003-7) 36
Robson, B. (W.B.A., Manchester Utd., 1980-92) 90
Robson, R. (W.B.A., 1958-62) 20
Rocastle, D. (Arsenal, 1989-92) 14
Rooney, W. (Everton, Manchester Utd., 2003-7) 38

Rowley, J. (Manchester Utd., 1949-52) 6
Royle, J. (Everton, Manchester City, 1971-7) 6
Ruddock, N. (Liverpool, 1995) 1

Sadler, D. (Manchester Utd., 1968-71) 4
Salako, J. (Crystal Palace, 1991-2) 5
Sansom, K. (Crystal Palace, Arsenal, 1979-88) 86
Scales, J. (Liverpool, 1995) 3
Scholes, P. (Manchester Utd., 1997-2004) 66
Scott, L. (Arsenal, 1947-9) 17
Seaman, D. (Q.P.R., Arsenal, 1989-2003) 75
Sewell, J. (Sheffield Wed., 1952-4) 6
Shackleton, L. (Sunderland, 1949-55) 5
Sharpe, L. (Manchester Utd., 1991-4) 8
Shaw, G. (Sheffield Utd., 1959-63) 5
Shearer, A. (Southampton, Blackburn Rov., Newcastle Utd., 1992-2000) 63
Shellito, K. (Chelsea, 1963) 1
Sheringham, E. (Tottenham, Manchester Utd., Tottenham, 1993-2002) 51
Sherwood, T. (Tottenham, 1999) 3
Shilton, P (Leicester City, Stoke City, Nott'm. Forest, Southampton, Derby Co., 1971-90) 125
Shimwell, E. (Blackpool, 1949) 1
Shorey, N. (Reading, 2007) 1
Sillett, P. (Chelsea, 1955) 3
Sinclair, T. (West Ham Utd., Manchester City, 2002-4) 12
Sinton, A. (Q.P.R., Sheffield Wed, 1992-4) 12
Slater, W. (Wolves, 1955-60) 12
Smith, A. (Arsenal, 1989-92) 13
Smith, A. (Leeds Utd., Manchester Utd., 2001-7) 17
Smith, L. (Arsenal, 1951-3) 6
Smith, R. (Tottenham, 1961-4) 15
Smith, T. (Birmingham City, 1960) 2
Smith, T. (Liverpool, 1971) 1
Southgate, G. (Aston Villa, Middlesbrough, 1996-2004) 57
Spink, N. (Aston Villa, 1983) 1
Springett, R. (Sheffield Wed., 1960-6) 33
Staniforth, R. (Huddersfield Town, 1954-5) 8
Statham, D. (W.B.A., 1983) 3
Stein, B. (Luton Town, 1984) 1
Stepney, A. (Manchester Utd., 1968) . 1
Sterland, M. (Sheffield Wed., 1989) ... 1
Steven, T. (Everton, Rangers, Marseille, 1985-92) 36
Stevens, G. (Everton, Rangers, 1985-92) 46
Stevens, G. (Tottenham, 1985-6) 7
Stewart, P. (Tottenham, 1992) 3
Stiles, N. (Manchester Utd., 1965-70) 28
Stone, S. (Nott'm. Forest, 1996) 9
Storey, P. (Arsenal, 1971-3) 19
Storey-Moore, I. (Nott'm. Forest, 1970) 1
Streten, B. (Luton Town, 1950) 1
Summerbee, M. (Manchester City, 1968-73) 8
Sunderland, A. (Arsenal, 1980) 1
Sutton, C. (Blackburn Rov., 1997) 1
Swan, P. (Sheffield Wed., 1960-2) ... 19
Swift, F. (Manchester City, 1947-9) .. 19

Talbot, B. (Ipswich Town, Arsenal, 1977-80) 6
Tambling, R. (Chelsea, 1963-6) 3
Taylor, E. (Blackpool, 1954) 1
Taylor, J. (Fulham, 1951) 2
Taylor, P. (Liverpool, 1948) 3
Taylor, P. (Crystal Palace, 1976) 4
Taylor, T. (Manchester Utd., 1953-8) 19
Temple, D. (Everton, 1965) 1
Terry, J. (Chelsea, 2003-7) 39
Thomas, D. (Coventry City, 1983) 2
Thomas, G. (Crystal Palace, 1991-2) .. 9
Thomas, D. (Q.P.R., 1975-6) 8
Thomas, M. (Arsenal, 1989-90) 2
Thompson, A. (Celtic, 2004) 1
Thompson, Peter (Liverpool, 1964-70) 16
Thompson, Phil (Liverpool, 1976-83) 42
Thompson, T. (Aston Villa, Preston N.E., 1952-7) 2
Thomson, R. (Wolves, 1964-5) 8
Todd, C. (Derby Co., 1972-7) 27
Towers, A. (Sunderland, 1978) 3
Tueart, D. (Manchester City, 1975-7) .. 6

Ufton, D. (Charlton Athletic, 1954) 1
Unsworth, D. (Everton, 1995) 1
Upson, M. (Birmingham City, 2003-5) 7

Vassell, D. (Aston Villa, 2002-4) 22
Venables, T. (Chelsea, 1965) 2
Venison, B. (Newcastle Utd., 1995) ... 2
Viljoen, C. (Ipswich Town, 1975) 2
Viollet, D. (Manchester Utd., 1960) 2

Waddle, C. (Newcastle Utd., Tottenham, Marseille, 1985-92) 62
Waiters, A. (Blackpool, 1964-5) 5
Walcott, T. (Arsenal, 2006) 1

Walker, D. (Nott'm. Forest, Sampdoria, Sheffield Wed., 1989-94) 59
Walker, I. (Tottenham, Leicester City, 1996-2004) 4
Wallace, D. (Southampton, 1986) 1
Walsh, P. (Luton Town, 1983-4) 5
Walters, M. (Rangers, 1991) 1
Ward, P. (Brighton & H.A., 1980) 1
Ward, T. (Derby Co., 1948) 2
Watson, D. (Sunderland, Manchester City, Werder Bremen, Southampton, Stoke City, 1974-82) 65
Watson, D. (Norwich City, Everton, 1984-8) 12
Watson, W. (Sunderland, 1950-1) 4
Webb, N. (Nott'm. Forest, Manchester Utd., 1988-92) 26
Weller, K. (Leicester City, 1974) 4
West, G. (Everton, 1969) 3
Wheeler, J. (Bolton Wand., 1955) 1
White, D. (Manchester City, 1993) 1
Whitworth, S. (Leicester City, 1975-6) 7
Whymark, T. (Ipswich Town, 1978) 1
Wignall, F. (Nott'm. Forest, 1965) 2
Wilcox, J. (Blackburn Rov., Leeds Utd., 1996-2000) 3
Wilkins, R. (Chelsea, Manchester Utd., AC Milan, 1976-87) 84
Williams, B. (Wolves, 1949-56) 24
Williams, S. (Southampton, 1983-5) .. 6
Willis, A. (Tottenham, 1952) 1
Wilshaw, D. (Wolves, 1954-7) 12
Wilson, R. (Huddersfield Town, Everton, 1960-8) 63
Winterburn, N. (Arsenal, 1990-3) 2
Wise, D. (Chelsea, 1991-2001) 21
Withe, P. (Aston Villa, 1981-5) 11
Wood, R. (Manchester Utd., 1955-6) .. 3
Woodcock, A. (Nott'm. Forest, Cologne, Arsenal, 1977-86) 42
Woodgate, J. (Leeds Utd., Newcastle Utd., Middlesbrough, 1999-2007) .. 6
Woods, C. (Norwich City, Rangers, Sheffield Wed., 1984-93) 43
Worthington, F. (Leicester City, 1974-5) 8
Wright, I. (Crystal Palace, Arsenal, West Ham Utd., 1991-9) 33
Wright, M. (Southampton, Derby Co., Liverpool, 1984-96) 45
Wright, R. (Ipswich Town, Arsenal, 2000-02) 2
Wright, T. (Everton, 1968-70) 11
Wright, W. (Wolves, 1947-59) 105
Wright-Phillips, S. (Manchester City, Chelsea, 2005-7) 12

Young, G. (Sheffield Wed., 1965) 1
Young, L. (Charlton Athletic, 2005) 7

NORTHERN IRELAND

Aherne, T. (Belfast Celtic, Luton Town, 1947-50) 4
Anderson, T. (Manchester Utd., Swindon Town, Peterborough Utd., 1973-9) 22
Armstrong, G. (Tottenham, Watford, Real Mallorca, W.B.A., 1977-86) 63

Baird, C. (Southampton, 2003-7) 25
Barr, H. (Linfield, Coventry City, 1962-3) 3
Best, G. (Manchester Utd., Fulham, 1964-77) 37
Bingham, W. (Sunderland, Luton Town, Everton, Port Vale, 1951-64) 56
Black, K. (Luton Town, Nott'm. Forest, 1988-94) 30
Blair, R. (Oldham Athletic, 1975-6) ... 5
Blanchflower, R.D. (Barnsley, Aston Villa, Tottenham, 1950-63) 56
Blanchflower, J. (Manchester Utd., 1954-8) 12
Blayney, A. (Doncaster Rov., 2006) 1
Bowler, G. (Hull City, 1950) 3
Braithwaite, R. (Linfield, Middlesbrough, 1962-5) 10
Brennan, R. (Luton Town, Birmingham City, Fulham, 1949-51) 5
Briggs, W. (Manchester Utd., Swansea City, 1962-5) 2
Brotherston, N. (Blackburn Rov., 1980-5) 27
Bruce, W. (Glentoran, 1961-7) 2
Brunt, C. (Sheffield Wed., 2005-7) .. 10

Campbell, D. (Nott'm. Forest, Charlton Athletic, 1987-8) 10
Campbell, J. (Fulham, 1951) 2
Campbell, R. (Crusaders, 1963-5) 2
Campbell, R. (Bradford City, 1982) 2
Campbell, W. (Dundee, 1968-70) 6
Capaldi, A. (Plymouth Argle, 2004-7) 21
Carey, J. (Manchester Utd., 1947-9) .. 7
Carroll, R. (Wigan Athletic, Manchester Utd., West Ham Utd., 1997-2007) 19
Casey, T. (Newcastle Utd., Portsmouth, 1955-9) 12
Caskey, W. (Derby Co., Tulsa Roughnecks, 1979-82) 7
Cassidy, T. (Newcastle Utd., Burnley, 1971-82) 24
Caughey, M. (Linfield, 1986) 2
Clarke, C. (Bournemouth, Southampton, Q.P.R., Portsmouth, 1986-93) 38

Cleary, J. (Glentoran, 1982-5) 5
Clements, D. (Coventry City, Sheffield Wed., Everton, New York City Cosmos, 1965-76) 48
Clingan, S. (Nott'm. Forest, 2006-7) .. 8
Clyde, M. (Wolves, 2005) 3
Cochrane, A. (Coleraine, Burnley, Middlesbrough, Gillingham, 1976-84) 26
Cochrane, D. (Leeds Utd., 1947-50) 10
Connell, T. (Coleraine, 1978) 1
Coote, A. (Norwich City, 1999-2000) . 6
Cowan, J. (Newcastle Utd., 1970) 1
Coyle, F. (Coleraine, Nott'm. Forest, 1956-8) 4
Coyle, L. (Derry C., 1989) 1
Coyle, R. (Sheffield Wed., 1973-4) 5
Craig, D. (Newcastle Utd., 1967-75) 25
Craigan, S. (Partick Thistle, Motherwell, 2003-7) 29
Crossan, E. (Blackburn Rov., 1950-5) . 3
Crossan, J. (Sparta Rotterdam, Sunderland, Manchester City, Middlesbrough, 1960-8) 24
Cunningham, W. (St Mirren, Leicester City, Dunfermline, 1951-62) 30
Cush, W. (Glenavon, Leeds Utd., Portadown, 1951-62) 26

D'Arcy, S. (Chelsea, Brentford, 1952-3) 5
Davis, S. (Aston Villa, 2005–7) 20
Davison, A. (Bolton Wand., Bradford City C., Grimsby Town, 1996-7) 3
Dennison, R. (Wolves, 1988-97) 18
Devine, J. (Glentoran, 1990) 1
Dickson, D. (Coleraine, 1970-3) 4
Dickson, T. (Linfield, 1957) 1
Dickson, W. (Chelsea, Arsenal, 1951-5) 12
Doherty, L. (Linfield, 1985-8) 2
*Doherty, P. (Derby Co., Huddersfield Town, Doncaster Rov., 1946-50) 6
Doherty, T. (Bristol City, 2003-5) 9
Donaghy, M. (Luton Town, Manchester Utd., Chelsea, 1980-94) 91
Dougan, D. (Portsmouth, Blackburn Rov., Aston Villa, Leicester City, Wolves, 1958-73) 43
Douglas, J. (Belfast Celtic, 1947) 1
Dowd, H. (Glenavon, 1974) 3
Dowie, I. (Luton Town, Southampton, Crystal Palace, West Ham Utd., Q.P.R., 1990-2000) 59
Duff, M. (Cheltenham Town, Burnley, 2002-7) 17
Dunlop, G. (Linfield, 1985-90) 4

Eglington, T. (Everton, 1947-9) 6
Elder, A. (Burnley, Stoke City, 1960-70) 40
Elliott, S. (Motherwell, Hull City, 2001-7) 36
Evans, J. (Manchester Utd., 2007) 5

Farrell, P. (Everton, 1947-9) 7
Feeney, J. (Linfield, Swansea City, 1947-50) 2
Feeney, W. (Glentoran, 1976) 1
Feeney, W. (Bournemouth, Luton Town, 2002-7) 18
Ferguson, G. (Linfield, 1999-2001) 5
Ferguson, W. (Linfield, 1966-7) 2
Ferris, R. (Birmingham City, 1950-2) . 3
Fettis, A. (Hull City, Nott'm. Forest, Blackburn Rov., 1992-9) 25
Finney, T. (Sunderland, Cambridge Utd., 1975-80) 14
Fleming, G. (Nott'm. Forest, Manchester City, Barnsley, 1987-95) 31
Forde, J. (Ards, 1959-61) 4

Gallogly, C. (Huddersfield Town, 1951) 2
Gaston, R. (Coleraine, 1969) 1
Gillespie, K. (Manchester Utd., Newcastle Utd., Blackburn Rov., Leicester City, Sheffield Utd., 1995-2007) 75
Gorman, W. (Brentford, 1947-8) 4
Graham, W. (Doncaster Rov., 1951-9) 14
Gray, P. (Luton Town, Sunderland, Nancy, Burnley, Oxford Utd., 1993-2001) 25
Gregg, H. (Doncaster Rov., Manchester Utd., 1954-64) 25
Griffin, D. (St Johnstone, Dundee Utd., Stockport Co., 1996-2004) 29

Hamill, R. (Glentoran, 1999) 1
Hamilton, B. (Linfield, Ipswich Town, Everton, Millwall, Swindon Town, 1969-80) 50
Hamilton, G. (Glentoran, Portadown, 2003-5) 4
Hamilton, W. (Q.P.R., Burnley, Oxford Utd., 1978-86) 41
Harkin, J. (Southport, Shrewsbury Town, 1968-70) 5
Harvey, M. (Sunderland, 1961-71) ... 34
Hatton, S. (Linfield, 1963) 2
Healy, D. (Manchester Utd., Preston N.E., Leeds Utd., 2000-7) 56
Healy, F. (Coleraine, Glentoran, 1982-3) 4
Hegan, D. (W.B.A., Wolves, 1970-3) ... 7
Hill, C. (Sheffield Utd., Leicester City, Trelleborg, Northampton Town, 1990-9) 27

Hill, J. (Norwich City, Everton, 1959-64) 7
Hinton, E. (Fulham, Millwall, 1947-51) 7
Holmes, S. (Wrexham, 2002) 1
Horlock, K. (Swindon Town, Manchester City, 1995-2003) 32
Hughes, A. (Newcastle Utd., Aston Villa, 1997-2007) 54
Hughes, J. (Lincoln City, 2006) 2
Hughes, M. (Oldham Athletic, 2006) .. 1
Hughes, M. (Manchester City, Strasbourg, West Ham Utd., Wimbledon, Crystal Palace, 1992-2005) 71
Hughes, P. (Bury, 1987) 3
Hughes, W. (Bolton Wand., 1951) 1
Humphries, W. (Ards, Coventry City, Swansea City, 1962-5) 14
Hunter, A. (Blackburn Rov., Ipswich Town, 1970-80) 53
Hunter, B. (Wrexham, Reading, 1995-2000) 15
Hunter, V. (Coleraine, 1962) 2

Ingham, M. (Sunderland, Wrexham, 2005–7) 3
Irvine, R. (Linfield, Stoke City, 1962-5) 8
Irvine, W. (Burnley, Preston N.E., Brighton & H.A., 1963-72) 23

Jackson, T. (Everton, Nott'm. Forest, Manchester Utd., 1969-77) 35
Jamison, J. (Glentoran, 1976) 1
Jenkins, I. (Chester City, Dundee Utd., 1997-2000) 6
Jennings, P. (Watford, Tottenham, Arsenal, Tottenham, 1964-86) 119
Johnson, D. (Blackburn Rov., Birmingham City, 1999-2007) 46
Johnston, W. (Glenavon, Oldham Athletic, 1962-6) 2
Jones, J. (Glenavon, 1956-7) 3
Jones, S. (Crewe Alexandra, Burnley, 2003-7) 27

Keane, T. (Swansea City, 1949) 1
Kee, P. (Oxford Utd., Ards, 1990-5) ... 9
Keith, R. (Newcastle Utd., 1958-62) 23
Kelly, H. (Fulham, Southampton, 1950-1) 4
Kelly, P. (Barnsley, 1950) 1
Kennedy, P. (Watford, Wigan Athletic, 1999-2004) 20
Kirk, A. (Hearts, Boston Utd., Northampton Town, 2000-05) 8

Lafferty, K. (Burnley, 2006-7) 10
Lawther, W. (Sunderland, Blackburn Rov., 1960-2) 4
Lennon, N. (Crewe Alexandra, Leicester City, Celtic, 1994-2002) 40
Lockhart, N. (Linfield, Coventry City, Aston Villa, 1947-56) 8
Lomas, S. (Manchester City, West Ham Utd., 1994-2003) 45
Lutton, B. (Wolves, West Ham Utd., 1970-4) 6

Magill, E. (Arsenal, Brighton & H.A., 1962-6) 26
Magilton, J. (Oxford Utd., Southampton, Sheffield Wed., Ipswich Town, 1991-2002) 52
Mannus, A. (Linfield, 2004) 1
Martin, C. (Glentoran, Leeds Utd., Aston Villa, 1947-50) 6
McAdams, W. (Manchester City, Bolton Wand., Leeds Utd., 1954-62) 15
*McAlinden, J. (Portsmouth, Southend Utd., 1947-9) 2
McAuley, G. (Lincoln City, 2005–6) 5
McBride, S. (Glenavon, 1991-2) 4
McCabe, J. (Leeds Utd., 1949-54) 6
McCann, G. (West Ham Utd., Cheltenham Town, Barnsley, 2002-7) 15
McCarthy, J. (Port Vale, Birmingham City, 1996-2001) 18
McCartney, G. (Sunderland, 2002-5) 20
McCavana, T. (Coleraine, 1954-5) 3
McCleary, J. (Cliftonville, 1955) 1
McClelland, J. (Arsenal, Fulham, 1961-7) 6
McClelland, J. (Mansfield Town, Rangers, Watford, Leeds Utd., 1980-90) 53
McCourt, F. (Manchester City, 1952-3) 6
McCourt, P. (Rochdale, 2002) 1
McCoy, R. (Coleraine, 1987) 1
McCreery, D. (Manchester Utd., Q.P.R., Tulsa Roughnecks, Newcastle Utd., 1976-90) 67
McCrory, S. (Southend Utd., 1958) 1
McCullough, W. (Arsenal, Millwall, 1961-7) 10
McCurdy, C. (Linfield, 1980) 1
McDonald, A. (Q.P.R., 1986-96) 52
McElhinney, G. (Bolton Wand., 1984-5) 6
McEvilly, L. (Rochdale, 2002) 1
McFaul, W. (Linfield, Newcastle Utd., 1967-74) 6
McGarry, J. (Cliftonville, 1951) 3
McGaughey, M. (Linfield, 1985) 1
McGibbon, P. (Manchester Utd., Wigan Athletic, 1995-2000) 7

Smith, A. (Glentoran, Preston N.E., 2003-5) 18
Smyth, S. (Wolves, Stoke City, 1948-52) 9
Smyth, W. (Distillery, 1949-54) 4
Sonner, D. (Ipswich Town, Sheffield Wed., Birmingham City, Nott'm. Forest, Peterborough Utd., 1997-2005) 13
Spence, D. (Bury, Blackpool, Southend Utd., 1975-82) 27
Sproule, I. (Hibernian, 2006-7) 8
*Stevenson, A. (Everton, 1947-8) 3
Stewart, A. (Glentoran, Derby Co., 1967-9) 7
Stewart, D. (Hull City, 1978) 1
Stewart, I. (Q.P.R., Newcastle Utd., 1982-7) 31
Stewart, T. (Linfield, 1961) 1

Taggart, G. (Barnsley, Bolton Wand., Leicester City, 1990-2003) 51
Taylor, M. (Fulham, Birmingham City, 1999-2007) 60
Thompson, P. (Linfield, 2006-7) 5
Todd, S. (Burnley, Sheffield Wed., 1966-71) 11
Toner, C. (Leyton Orient, 2003) 2
Trainor, D. (Crusaders, 1967) 1
Tully, C. (Glasgow Celtic, 1949-59) .. 10

Uprichard, W. (Swindon Town, Portsmouth, 1952-9) 18

Vernon, J. (Belfast Celtic, W.B.A., 1947-52) 17

Walker, J. (Doncaster Rov., 1955) 1
Walsh, D. (W.B.A., 1947-50) 9
Walsh, W. (Manchester City, 1948-9) .. 5
Watson, P. (Distillery, 1971) 1
Webb, S. (Ross Co., 2006-7) 4
Welsh, E. (Carlisle Utd., 1966-7) 4
Whiteside, N. (Manchester Utd., Everton, 1982-90) 38
Whitley, Jeff (Manchester City, Sunderland, Cardiff City, 1997-2006) 20
Whitley, Jim (Manchester City, 1998-2000) 3
Williams, M. (Chesterfield, Watford, Wimbledon, Stoke City, Wimbledon, MK Dons, 1999-2005) 36
Williams, P. (W.B.A., 1991) 1
Wilson, D. (Brighton & H.A., Luton Town, Sheffield Wed., 1987-92) ... 24
Wilson, K. (Ipswich Town, Chelsea, Notts Co., Walsall, 1987-95) 42
Wilson, S. (Glenavon, Falkirk, Dundee, 1962-8) 12
Wood, T. (Walsall, 1996) 1
Worthington, N. (Sheffield Wed., Leeds Utd., Stoke City, 1984-97) 66
Wright, T. (Newcastle Utd., Nott'm. Forest, Reading, Manchester City, 1989-2000) 31

SCOTLAND

Adam, C. (Rangers 2007) 2
Aird, J. (Burnley, 1954) 4
Aitken, G. (East Fife, 1949-54) 8
Aitken, R. (Celtic, Newcastle Utd., St Mirren, 1980-92) 57
Albiston, A. (Manchester Utd., 1982-6) 14
Alexander, G. (Preston N.E., 2002-7) 30
Alexander, N. (Cardiff City, 2006) 3
Allan, T. (Dundee, 1974) 2
Anderson, J. (Leicester City, 1954) 1
Anderson, R. (Aberdeen, 2003-6) 9
Archibald, S. (Aberdeen, Tottenham, Barcelona, 1980-6) 27
Auld, B. (Celtic, 1959-60) 3

Baird, H. (Airdrie, 1956) 1
Baird, S. (Rangers, 1957-8) 7
Bannon, E. (Dundee Utd., 1980-6) .. 11
Bauld, W. (Hearts, 1950) 3
Baxter, J. (Rangers, Sunderland, 1961-8) 34
Beattie, C. (Celtic, 2006-7) 4
Bell, W. (Leeds Utd., 1966) 2
Bernard, P. (Oldham Athletic, 1995) .. 2
Bett, J. (Rangers, Lokeren, Aberdeen, 1982-90) 26
Black, E. (Metz, 1988) 2
Black, I. (Southampton, 1948) 1
Blacklaw, A. (Burnley, 1963-6) 3
Blackley, J. (Hibernian, 1974-7) 7
Blair, J. (Blackpool, 1947) 1
Blyth, J. (Coventry City, 1978) 2
Bone, J. (Norwich City, 1972-3) 2
Booth, S. (Aberdeen, Borussia Dortmund, Twente Enschede, 1993-2002) 21
Bowman, D. (Dundee Utd., 1992-4) ... 6
Boyd, K. (Rangers, 2006-7) 9
Boyd, T. (Motherwell, Chelsea, Celtic, 1991-2002) 72
Brand, R. (Rangers, 1961-2) 8
Brazil, A. (Ipswich Town, Tottenham, 1980-3) 13
Bremner, D. (Hibernian, 1976) 1
Bremner, W. (Leeds Utd., 1965-76) . 54
Brennan, F. (Newcastle Utd., 1947-54) 7
Brogan, J. (Celtic, 1971) 4

Brown, A. (East Fife, Blackpool, 1950-4) 14
Brown, H. (Partick, 1947) 3
Brown, J. (Sheffield Utd., 1975) 1
Brown, R. (Rangers, 1947-52) 3
Brown, S. (Hibernian, 2007) 3
Brown, W. (Dundee, Tottenham, 1958-66) 28
Brownlie, J. (Hibernian, 1971-6) 7
Buchan, M. (Aberdeen, Manchester Utd., 1972-8) 34
Buckley, P. (Aberdeen, 1954-5) 3
Burchill, M. (Celtic, 2000) 6
Burke, C. (Rangers, 2006) 2
Burley, C. (Chelsea, Celtic, Derby Co., 1995-2003) 46
Burley, G. (Ipswich Town, 1979-82) . 11
Burns, F. (Manchester Utd.. 1970) 1
Burns, K. (Birmingham City, Nott'm. Forest, 1974-81) 20
Burns, T. (Celtic, 1981-8) 8

Calderwood, C. (Tottenham, Aston Villa, 1995-2000) 36
Caldow, E. (Rangers, 1957-63) 40
Caldwell, G. (Newcastle Utd., Hibernian, Celtic, 2002-7) 24
Caldwell, S. (Newcastle Utd., Sunderland, 2001-6) 9
Callaghan, T. (Dunfermline, 1970) 2
Cameron, C. (Hearts, Wolves, 1999-2005) 28
Campbell, R. (Falkirk, Chelsea, 1947-50) 5
Campbell, W. (Morton, 1947-8) 5
Canero, P. (Leicester City, 2004) 1
Carr, W. (Coventry City, 1970-3) 6
Chalmers, S. (Celtic, 1965-7) 5
Clark, J. (Celtic, 1966-7) 4
Clark, R. (Aberdeen, 1968-73) 17
Clarke, S. (Chelsea, 1988-94) 6
Collins, J. (Hibernian, Celtic, Monaco, Everton, 1988-2000) 58
Collins, R. (Celtic, Everton, Leeds Utd., 1951-65) 31
Colquhoun, E. (Sheffield Utd, 1972-3) 9
Colquhoun, J. (Hearts, 1988) 2
Combe, J. (Hibernian, 1948) 3
Conn, A. (Hearts, 1956) 1
Conn, A. (Tottenham, 1975) 2
Connachan, E. (Dunfermline, 1962) ... 2
Connelly, G. (Celtic, 1974) 2
Connolly, J. (Everton, 1973) 1
Connor, R. (Dundee, Aberdeen, 1986-91) 4
Cooke, C. (Dundee, Chelsea, 1966-75) 16
Cooper, D. (Rangers, Motherwell, 1980-90) 22
Cormack, P. (Hibernian, 1966-72) 9
Cowan, J. (Morton, 1948-52) 25
Cowie, D. (Dundee, 1953-8) 20
Cox, C. (Hearts, 1948) 1
Cox, S. (Rangers, 1948-54) 25
Craig, J.P. (Celtic, 1968) 1
Craig, J. (Celtic, 1977) 1
Craig, T. (Newcastle Utd., 1976) 1
Crainey, S. (Celtic, Southampton, 2002-4) 6
Crawford, S. (Raith, Dunfermline, Plymouth Argyle, 1995-2005) 25
Crerand, P. (Celtic, Manchester Utd., 1961-6) 16
Cropley, A. (Hibernian, 1972) 2
Cruickshank, J. (Hearts, 1964-76) 6
Cullen, M. (Luton Town, 1956) 1
Cumming, J. (Hearts, 1955-60) 9
Cummings, W. (Chelsea 2002) 1
Cunningham, W. (Preston N.E., 1954-5) 8
Curran, H. (Wolves, 1970-1) 5

Dailly, C. (Derby Co., Blackburn Rov., West Ham Utd., 1997-2007) 65
Dalglish, K. (Celtic, Liverpool, 1972-87) 102
Davidson, C. (Blackburn Rov., Leicester City, 1999-2003) 17
Davidson, J. (Partick, 1954-5) 8
Dawson, A. (Rangers, 1980-3) 5
Deans, J. (Celtic, 1975) 2
*Delaney, J. (Manchester Utd., 1947-8) 4
Devlin, P. (Birmingham, 2003-4) 10
Dick, J. (West Ham Utd., 1959) 1
Dickov, P. (Manchester City, Leicester City, Blackburn Rov. 2001-5) 10
Dickson, W. (Kilmarnock, 1970-1) 5
Dobie, S. (W.B.A., 2002-3) 6
Docherty, T. (Preston N.E., Arsenal, 1952-9) 25
Dodds, D. (Dundee Utd., 1984) 2
Dodds, W. (Aberdeen, Dundee Utd., Rangers, 1997-2002) 26
Donachie, W. (Manchester City, 1972-9) 35
Donnelly, S. (Celtic, 1997-9) 10
Dougall, C. (Birmingham City, 1947) .. 1
Dougan, R. (Hearts, 1950) 1
Douglas, R. (Celtic, Leicester City, 2002-6) 19
Doyle, J. (Ayr, 1976) 1
Duncan, A. (Hibernian, 1975-6) 6
Duncan, D. (East Fife, 1948) 3
Duncanson, J. (Rangers, 1947) 1
Durie, G. (Chelsea, Tottenham, Rangers, 1988-98) 43
Durrant, I. (Rangers, Kilmarnock, 1988-2000) 21

Elliott, M. (Leicester City, 1997-2002) 18
Evans, A. (Aston Villa, 1982) 4
Evans, R. (Celtic, Chelsea, 1949-60) 48
Ewing, T. (Partick, 1958) 2

Farm, G. (Blackpool, 1953-9) 10
Ferguson, B. (Rangers, Blackburn Rov., Rangers, 1999-2007) 39
Ferguson, D. (Dundee Utd., Everton, 1992-7) 7
Ferguson, D. (Rangers, 1988) 2
Ferguson, I. (Rangers, 1989-97) 9
Ferguson, R. (Kilmarnock, 1966-7) 7
Fernie, W. (Celtic, 1954-8) 12
Flavell, R. (Airdrie, 1947) 2
Fleck, R. (Norwich City, 1990-1) 4
Fleming, C. (East Fife, 1954) 1
Fletcher, D. (Manchester Utd., 2004-7) 29
Forbes, A. (Sheffield Utd., Arsenal, 1947-52) 14
Ford, D. (Hearts, 1974) 3
Forrest, J. (Motherwell, 1958) 1
Forrest, J. (Rangers, Aberdeen, 1966-71) 5
Forsyth, A. (Partick, Manchester Utd., 1972-6) 10
Forsyth, C. (Kilmarnock, 1964) 4
Forsyth, T. (Motherwell, Rangers, 1971-8) 22
Fraser, D. (W.B.A., 1968-9) 2
Fraser, W. (Sunderland, 1955) 2
Freedman, D. (Crystal Palace, 2002) .. 2

Gabriel, J. (Everton, 1961-4) 2
Gallacher, K. (Dundee Utd., Coventry City, Blackburn Rov., Newcastle Utd., 1988-2001) 53
Gallacher, P. (Dundee Utd., 2003-4) .. 8
Gallagher, P. (Blackburn Rov., 2004) .. 1
Galloway, M. (Celtic, 1992) 1
Gardiner, I. (Motherwell, 1958) 1
Gemmell, T. (St Mirren, 1955) 2
Gemmell, T. (Celtic, 1966-71) 18
Gemmill, A. (Derby Co., Nott'm. Forest, Birmingham City, 1971-81) 43
Gemmill, S. (Nott'm. Forest, Everton 1995-2003) 27
Gibson, D. (Leicester City, 1963-5) 7
Gillespie, G. (Liverpool, 1988-91) 13
Gilzean, A. (Dundee, Tottenham, 1964-71) 22
Glass, S. (Necastle Utd., 1999) 1
Glavin, R. (Celtic, 1977) 1
Glen, A. (Aberdeen, 1956) 2
Goram, A. (Oldham Athletic, Hibernian, Rangers, 1986-98) 43
Gordon, C. (Hearts, 2004-7) 23
Gough, R. (Dundee Utd., Tottenham, Rangers, 1983-93) 61
Gould, J. (Celtic, 2000-01) 2
Govan, J. (Hibernian, 1948-9) 6
Graham, A. (Leeds Utd., 1978-81) ... 10
Graham, G. (Arsenal, Manchester Utd., 1972-3) 12
Gray, A. (Aston Villa, Wolves, Everton, 1976-85) 20
Gray, A. (Bradford City, 2003) 2
Gray, E. (Leeds Utd., 1969-77) 12
Gray, F. (Leeds Utd., Nott'm. Forest, 1976-83) 32
Grant, J. (Hibernian, 1958) 2
Grant, P. (Celtic, 1989) 2
Green, A. (Blackpool, Newcastle Utd., 1971-2) 6
Greig, J. (Rangers, 1964-76) 44
Gunn, B. (Norwich City, 1990-4) 6

Haddock, H. (Clyde, 1955-8) 6
Haffey, F. (Celtic, 1960-1) 2
Hamilton, A. (Dundee, 1962-6) 24
Hamilton, G. (Aberdeen, 1947-54) 5
Hamilton, W. (Hibernian, 1965) 1
Hammell, S. (Motherwell, 2005) 1
Hansen, A. (Liverpool, 1979-87) 26
Hansen, J. (Partick, 1972) 2
Harper, J. (Aberdeen, Hibernian, 1973-8) 4
Hartford, A. (W.B.A., Manchester City, Everton, 1972-82) 50
Hartley, P. (Hearts, Celtic, 2005-7) .. 15
Harvey, D. (Leeds Utd., 1973-7) 16
Haughney, M. (Celtic, 1954) 1
Hay, D. (Celtic, 1970-4) 27
Hegarty, P. (Dundee Utd., 1979-83) ... 8
Henderson, J. (Portsmouth, Arsenal, 1953-9) 7
Henderson, W. (Rangers, 1963-71) .. 29
Hendry, C. (Blackburn Rov., Rangers, Coventry City, Bolton Wand., 1994-2001) 51
Herd, D. (Arsenal, 1959-61) 5
Herd, G. (Clyde, 1958-61) 5
Herriot, J. (Birmingham City, 1969-70) 8
Hewie, J. (Charlton Athletic, 1956-60) 19
Holt, D. (Hearts, 1963-4) 5
Holt, G. (Kilmarnock, Norwich City, 2001-5) 10
Holton, J. (Manchester Utd., 1973-5) 15
Hope, R. (W.B.A., 1968-9) 2
Hopkin, D. (Crystal Palace, Leeds Utd., 1997-2000) 7
Houliston, W. (Queen of the South, 1949) 3
Houston, S. (Manchester Utd., 1976) . 1
Howie, H. (Hibernian, 1949) 1

Hughes, J. (Celtic, 1965-70) 8
Hughes, R. (Portsmouth, 2004-6) 5
Hughes, W. (Sunderland, 1975) 1
Humphries, W. (Motherwell, 1952) 1
Hunter, A. (Kilmarnock, Celtic, 1972-4) 4
Hunter, W. (Motherwell, 1960-1) 3
Husband, J. (Partick, 1947) 1
Hutchison, D. (Everton, Sunderland, West Ham Utd., 1999-2004) 26
Hutchison, T. (Coventry City, 1974-6) 17
Hutton, A. (Rangers, 2007) 1

Imlach, S. (Nott'm. Forest, 1958) 4
Irvine, B. (Aberdeen, 1991-4) 9

Jackson, C. (Rangers, 1975-7) 21
Jackson, D. (Hibernian, Celtic, 1995-9) 29
Jardine, A. (Rangers, 1971-80) 38
Jarvie, A. (Airdrie, 1971) 3
Jess, E. (Aberdeen, Coventry City, Aberdeen, 1993-9) 17
Johnston, A. (Sunderland, Rangers, Middlesbrough, 1999-2003) 18
Johnston, M. (Watford, Celtic, Nantes, Rangers, 1984-92) 38
Johnston, W. (Rangers, WBA, 1966-78) 22
Johnstone, D. (Rangers, 1973-80) 14
Johnstone, J. (Celtic, 1965-75) 23
Johnstone, L. (Clyde, 1948) 2
Johnstone, R. (Hibernian, Manchester City, 1951-6) 17
Jordan, J. (Leeds Utd., Manchester Utd., AC Milan, 1973-82) 52

Kelly, H. (Blackpool, 1952) 1
Kelly, J. (Barnsley, 1949) 2
Kennedy, J. (Celtic, 1964-5) 6
Kennedy, J. (Celtic, 2004) 1
Kennedy, S. (Rangers, 1975) 5
Kennedy, S. (Aberdeen, 1978-82) 8
Kerr, A. (Partick, 1955) 2
Kerr, B. (Newcastle Utd, 2003-4) 3
Kyle, K. (Sunderland, 2002-4) 9

Lambert P. (Motherwell, Borussia Dortmund, Celtic, 1995-2003) 40
Law, D. (Huddersfield Town, Manchester City, Torino, Manchester Utd., 1959-74) 55
Lawrence T. (Liverpool, 1963-9) 3
Leggat, G. (Aberdeen, Fulham, 1956-60) 18
Leighton, J. (Aberdeen, Manchester Utd., Hibernian, Aberdeen, 1983-99) 91
Lennox, R. (Celtic, 1967-70) 10
Leslie, L. (Airdrie, 1961) 5
Levein, C. (Hearts, 1990-5) 16
Liddell, W. (Liverpool, 1947-55) 28
Linwood, A. (Clyde, 1950) 1
Little, R. (Rangers, 1953) 1
Logie, J. (Arsenal, 1953) 1
Long, H. (Clyde, 1947) 1
Lorimer, P. (Leeds Utd., 1970-6) 21

Macari, L. (Celtic, Manchester Utd., 1972-8) 24
Macaulay, A. (Brentford, Arsenal, 1947-8) 7
MacDonald, A. (Rangers, 1976) 1
MacDougall, E. (Norwich City, 1975-6) 7
Mackay, D. (Hearts, Tottenham, 1957-66) 22
Mackay, G. (Hearts, 1988) 4
Mackay, M. (Norwich City, 2004-5) 5
MacLeod, J. (Hibernian, 1961) 4
MacLeod, M. (Celtic, Borussia Dort., Hibernian, 1985-91) 20
Maloney, S. (Celtic, Aston Villa, 2006-7) 6
Malpas, M. (Dundee Utd., 1984-93) 55
Marshall, D. (Celtic, 2005) 2
Marshall, G. (Celtic, 1992) 1
Martin, B. (Motherwell, 1995) 2
Martin, F. (Aberdeen, 1954-5) 6
Martin, N. (Hibernian, Sunderland, 1965-6) 3
Martis, J. (Motherwell, 1961) 1
Mason, J. (Third Lanark, 1949-51) 7
Masson, D. (Q.P.R., Derby Co., 1976-8) 17
Mathers, D. (Partick, 1954) 1
Matteo, D. (Leeds Utd., 2001-2) 6
McAllister, B. (Wimbledon, 1997) 3
McAllister, G. (Leicester City, Leeds Utd., Coventry City, 1990-9) 57
McAllister, J. (Livingston, 2004) 1
McAvennie, F. (West Ham Utd., Celtic, 1986-8) 5
McBride, J. (Celtic, 1967) 2
McCall, S. (Everton, Rangers, 1990-8) 40
McCalliog, J. (Sheffield Wed., Wolves, 1967-71) 5
McCann, N. (Hearts, Rangers, Southampton, 1999-2006) 26
McCann, R. (Motherwell, 1959-61) 5
McClair, B. (Celtic, Manchester Utd., 1987-93) 30
McCloy, P. (Rangers, 1973) 4
McCoist, A. (Rangers, Kilmarnock, 1986-99) 61
McColl, I. (Rangers, 1950-8) 14
McCreadie, E. (Chelsea, 1965-9) 23
McCulloch, L. (Wigan Athletic, 2005–7) 11

McDonald, J. (Sunderland, 1956) 2
McFadden, J. (Motherwell, Everton 2002-7) 31
McFarlane, W. (Hearts, 1947) 1
McGarr, E. (Aberdeen, 1970) 2
McGarvey, F. (Liverpool, Celtic, 1979-84) 7
McGhee, M. (Aberdeen, 1983-4) 4
McGinlay, J. (Bolton Wand., 1995-7) 14
McGrain, D. (Celtic, 1973-82) 62
McGregor, A. (Rangers, 2007) 1
McGrory, J. (Kilmarnock, 1965-6) 3
McInally, A. (Aston Villa, Bayern Munich, 1989-90) 8
McInally, J. (Dundee Utd., 1987-93) 10
McInnes, D. (W.B.A., 2003) 2
McKay, D. (Celtic, 1959-62) 14
McKean, R. (Rangers, 1976) 1
McKenzie, J. (Partick, 1954-6) 9
McKimmie, S. (Aberdeen, 1989-96) . 40
McKinlay, T. (Celtic, 1996-8) 22
McKinlay, W. (Dundee Utd., Blackburn Rov., 1994-9) 29
McKinnon, R. (Rangers, 1966-71) ... 28
McKinnon, R. (Motherwell, 1994-5) ... 3
McLaren, A. (Preston N.E., 1947-8) ... 4
McLaren, A. (Hearts, Rangers, 1992-6) 24
McLaren, A. (Kilmarnock, 2001) 1
McLean, G. (Dundee, 1968) 1
McLean, T. (Kilmarnock, Rangers, 1969-71) 6
McLeish, A. (Aberdeen, 1980-93) 77
McLintock, F. (Leicester City, Arsenal, 1963-71) 9
McManus, S. (Celtic, 2007) 5
McMillan, I. (Airdrie, 1952-61) 6
McNamara, J. (Celtic, Wolves, 1997-2006) 33
McNamee, D. (Livingston, 2004–6) 4
McNaught, W. (Raith, 1951-5) 5
McNaughton, K. (Aberdeen, 2002-5) .. 3
McNeill, W. (Celtic, 1961-72) 29
McPhail, J. (Celtic, 1950-4) 5
McPherson, D. (Hearts, Rangers, 1989-93) 27
McQueen, G. (Leeds Utd., Manchester Utd., 1974-81) 30
McStay, P. (Celtic, 1984-97) 76
McSwegan, G. (Hearts, 2000) 2
Millar, J. (Rangers, 1963) 2
Miller, C. (Dundee Utd., 2001) 1
Miller, K. (Rangers, Wolves, Celtic 2001-7) 31
Miller, L. (Dundee Utd., 2006) 1
Miller, W. (Celtic, 1946-7) 6
Miller, W. (Aberdeen, 1975-90) 65
Mitchell, R. (Newcastle Utd., 1951) ... 2
Mochan, N. (Celtic, 1954) 3
Moir, W. (Bolton Wand., 1950) 1
Moncur, R. (Newcastle Utd., 1968-72) 16
Morgan, W. (Burnley, Manchester Utd., 1968-74) 21
Morris, H. (East Fife, 1950) 1
Mudie, J. (Blackpool, 1957-8) 17
Mulhall, G. (Aberdeen, Sunderland, 1960-4) 3
Munro, F. (Wolves, 1971-5) 9
Munro, I. (St Mirren, 1979-80) 7
Murdoch, R. (Celtic, 1966-70) 12
Murray, I. (Hibernian, Rangers, 2003-6) 6
Murray, J. (Hearts, 1958) 5
Murray, S. (Aberdeen, 1972) 1
Murty, G. (Reading, 2004–6) 3

Naismith, S. (Kilmarnock, 2007) 1
Narey, D. (Dundee Utd., 1977-89) ... 35
Naysmith, G. (Hearts, Everton, 2000-7) 36
Neilson, R. (Hearts, 2007) 1
Nevin, P. (Chelsea, Everton, Tranmere Rov., 1987-96) 26
Nicholas, C. (Celtic, Arsenal, Aberdeen, 1983-9) 20
Nicholson, B. (Dunfermline, 2001-5) .. 3
Nicol, S. (Liverpool, 1985-92) 27

O'Connor, G. (Hibernian, Lokomotiv Moscow, 2002-7) 11
O'Donnell, P. (Motherwell, 1994) 1
O'Hare, J. (Derby Co., 1970-2) 13
O'Neil, B. (Celtic, VfL Wolfsburg, Derby Co., Preston N.E., 1996-2006) 7
O'Neil, J. (Hibernian, 2001) 1
Ormond, W. (Hibernian, 1954-9) 6
Orr, T. (Morton, 1952) 2

Parker, A. (Falkirk, Everton, 1955-6) 15
Parlane, D. (Rangers, 1973-7) 12
Paton, A. (Motherwell, 1952) 2
Pearson, S. (Motherwell, Celtic, 2004-5) 6
Pearson, T. (Newcastle Utd., 1947) 2
Penman, A. (Dundee, 1966) 1
Pettigrew, W. (Motherwell, 1976-7) 5
Plenderleith, J. (Manchester City, 1961) 1
Pressley, S. (Hearts, 2000-7) 32
Provan, D. (Rangers, 1964-6) 5
Provan, D. (Celtic, 1980-2) 10

Quashie, N. (Portsmouth, Southampton, W.B.A., 2004-7) 14
Quinn, P. (Motherwell, 1961-2) 9

Rae, G. (Dundee, Rangers 2001-6) .. 11

Redpath, W. (Motherwell, 1949-52) ... 9
Reilly, L. (Hibernian, 1949-57) 38
Ring, T. (Clyde, 1953-8) 12
Rioch, B. (Derby Co., Everton, 1975-8) 24
Riordan, D. (Hibernian, 2006) 1
Ritchie, P. (Hearts, Bolton Wand., 1999-2000) 6
Ritchie, W. (Rangers, 1962) 1
Robb, D. (Aberdeen, 1971) 5
Robertson, A. (Clyde, 1955) 5
Robertson, D. (Rangers, 1992-4) 3
Robertson, H. (Dundee, 1962) 1
Robertson, J. (Tottenham, 1964) 1
Robertson, J. (Nott'm. Forest, Derby Co., 1978-84) 28
Robertson, J. (Hearts, 1991-6) 14
Robinson, R. (Dundee, 1974-5) 4
Ross, M. (Rangers, 2002-4) 12
Rough, A. (Partick, Hibernian, 1976-86) 53
Rougvie, D. (Aberdeen, 1984) 1
Rutherford, E. (Rangers, 1948) 1

Schaedler, E. (Hibernian, 1974) 1
Scott, A. (Rangers, Everton, 1957-66) 16
Scott, J. (Hibernian, 1966) 1
Scott, J. (Dundee, 1971) 2
Scoular, J. (Portsmouth, 1951-3) 9
Severin, S. (Hearts, Aberdeen, 2002-7) 15
Sharp, G. (Everton, 1985-8) 12
Shaw, D. (Hibernian, 1947-9) 8
Shaw, J. (Rangers, 1947) 4
Shearer, D. (Aberdeen, 1994-6) 7
Shearer, R. (Rangers, 1961) 4
Simpson, N. (Aberdeen, 1983-8) 4
Simpson, R. (Celtic, 1967-9) 5
Sinclair, J. (Leicester City, 1966) 1
Smith, D. (Aberdeen, Rangers, 1966-8) 2
Smith, G. (Hibernian, 1947-57) 18
Smith, H. (Hearts, 1988-92) 3
Smith, J.E. (Celtic, 1959) 2
Smith, J. (Aberdeen, Newcastle Utd., 1968-74) 4
Smith, J. (Celtic, 2003) 2
Souness, G. (Middlesbrough, Liverpool, Sampdoria, Rangers, 1975-86) 54
Speedie, D. (Chelsea, Coventry City, 1985-9) 10
Spencer, J. (Chelsea, Q.P.R., 1995-7) 14
Stanton, P. (Hibernian, 1966-74) 16
Steel, W. (Morton, Derby Co., Dundee, 1947-53) 30
Stein, C. (Rangers, Coventry City, 1969-73) 21
Stephen, J. (Bradford City, 1947-8) ... 2
Stewart, D. (Leeds Utd., 1978) 1
Stewart, J. (Kilmarnock, Middlesbrough, 1977-9) 2
Stewart, M. (Manchester Utd., 2002) . 3
Stewart, R. (West Ham Utd., 1981-7) 10
St John, I. (Motherwell, Liverpool, 1959-65) 21
Stockdale, R. (Middlesbrough, 2002-3) 5
Strachan, G. (Aberdeen, Manchester Utd., Leeds Utd., 1980-92) 50
Sturrock, P. (Dundee Utd., 1981-7) .. 20
Sullivan, N. (Wimbledon, Tottenham, 1997-2003) 28

Teale, G. (Wigan Athletic, Derby Co., 2006-7) 8
Telfer, P. (Coventry City, 2000) 1
Telfer, W. (St Mirren, 1954) 1
Thompson, S. (Dundee Utd., Rangers, 2002-5) 16
Thomson, W. (St Mirren, 1980-4) 7
Thornton, W. (Rangers, 1947-52) 7
Toner, W. (Kilmarnock, 1959) 2
Turnbull, E. (Hibernian, 1948-58) 8

Ure, I. (Dundee, Arsenal, 1962-8) 11

Waddell, W. (Rangers, 1947-55) 17
Walker, A. (Celtic, 1988-95) 3
Walker, N. (Hearts, 1993-6) 2
Wallace, I. (Coventry City, 1978-9) 3
Wallace, W. (Hearts, Celtic, 1965-9) .. 7
Wardhaugh, J. (Hearts, 1955-7) 2
Wark, J. (Ipswich Town, Liverpool, 1979-85) 29
Watson, J. (Motherwell, Huddersfield Town, 1948-54) 2
Watson, R. (Motherwell, 1971) 1
Webster, A. (Hearts, 2003-6) 22
Weir, A. (Motherwell, 1959-60) 6
Weir, D. (Hearts, Everton, Rangers, 1997-2007) 56
Weir, P. (St Mirren, Aberdeen, 1980-4) 6
White, J. (Falkirk, Tottenham, 1959-64) 22
Whyte, D. (Celtic, Middlesbrough, Aberdeen, 1988-99) 12
Wilkie, L. (Dundee, 2002-3) 11
Williams, G. (Nott'm. Forest, 2002-3) 5
Wilson, A. (Portsmouth, 1954) 1
Wilson, D. (Rangers, 1961-5) 22
Wilson, I. (Leicester City, Everton, 1987-8) 5
Wilson, P. (Celtic, 1975) 1
Wilson, R. (Arsenal, 1972) 2
Wood, G. (Everton, Arsenal, 1978-82) 4
Woodburn, W. (Rangers, 1947-52) ... 24

Wright, K. (Hibernian, 1992) 1
Wright, S. (Aberdeen, 1993) 2
Wright, T. (Sunderland, 1953) 3

Yeats, R. (Liverpool, 1965-6) 2

Yorston, H. (Aberdeen, 1955) 1
Young, A. (Hearts, Everton, 1960-6) ... 8
Young, G. (Rangers, 1947-57) 53
Younger, T. (Hibernian, Liverpool, 1955-8) 24

WALES

Aizlewood, M. (Charlton Athletic, Leeds Utd., Bradford City, Bristol C., Cardiff City, 1986-95) 39
Allchurch, I. (Swansea City, Newcastle Utd., Cardiff City, 1951-66) 68
Allchurch, L. (Swansea City, Sheffield Utd., 1955-64) 11
Allen, B. (Coventry City, 1951) 2
Allen, M. (Watford, Norwich City, Millwall, Newcastle Utd., 1986-94) 14

Baker, C. (Cardiff City, 1958-62) 7
Baker, W. (Cardiff City, 1948) 1
Bale, G. (Southampton, 2006-7) 6
Barnard, D. (Barnsley, Bradford City, Barnsley, Grimsby Town, 1998-2004) 22
Barnes, W. (Arsenal, 1948-55) 22
Bellamy, C. (Norwich City, Coventry City, Newcastle Utd., Blackburn Rov., Liverpool, 1998-2007) 46
Berry, G. (Wolves, Stoke City, 1979-83) 5
Blackmore, C. (Manchester Utd., Middlesbrough, 1985-97) 39
Blake, N. (Sheffield Utd., Bolton Wand., Blackburn Rov., Wolves, 1994-2004) 29
Bodin, P. (Swindon Town, Crystal Palace, Swindon Town, 1990-5) 23
Bowen, D. (Arsenal, 1955-9) 19
Bowen, J. (Swansea City, Birmingham City, 1994-7) 2
Bowen, M. (Tottenham, Norwich City, West Ham Utd., 1986-97) 41
Boyle, T. (Crystal Palace, 1981) 2
Brown, J. (Gillingham, Blackburn Rov., 2006-7) 2
Browning, M. (Bristol R., Huddersfield Town, 1996-7) 5
Burgess, R. (Tottenham, 1947-54) ... 32
Burton, A. (Norwich City, Newcastle Utd., 1963-72) 9

Cartwright, L. (Coventry City, Wrexham, 1974-9) 7
Charles, Jeremy (Swansea City, Q.P.R., Oxford Utd., 1981-7) 19
Charles, John (Leeds Utd., Juventus, Cardiff City, 1950-65) 38
Charles, M. (Swansea City, Arsenal, Cardiff City, 1955-63) 31
Clarke, R. (Manchester City, 1949-56) 22
Coleman, C. (Crystal Palace, Blackburn Rov., Fulham, 1992-2002) 32
Collins, D. (Sunderland, 2005–7) 16
Collins, J. (Cardiff City, West Ham Utd., 2004-7) 19
Cornforth, J. (Swansea City, 1995) 2
Cotterill, D. (Bristol City, Wigan Athletic, 2006-7) 8
Coyne, D. (Tranmere Rov., Grimsby Town, Leicester City, Burnley, 1996-2007) 15
Crofts, A. (Gillingham, 2006-7) 6
Crossley, M. (Nott'm. Forest, Middlesbrough, Fulham, 1997-2005) 8
Crowe, V. (Aston Villa, 1959-63) 16
Curtis, A. (Swansea City, Leeds Utd., Southampton, Cardiff City, 1976-87) 35

Daniel, R. (Arsenal, Sunderland, 1951-7) 21
Davies, A. (Manchester Utd., Newcastle Utd., Swansea City, Bradford City, 1983-90) 13
Davies, A. (Yeovil Town, 2006) 1
Davies, C. (Charlton Athletic, 1972) ... 1
Davies, C. (Oxford Utd., Verona, Wolves, 2006-7) 4
Davies, D. (Everton, Wrexham, Swansea City, 1975-83) 52
Davies, E.R. (Newcastle Utd., 1953-8) 6
Davies, G. (Fulham, Chelsea, Manchester City, 1980-6) 16
Davies, R.T. (Norwich City, Southampton, Portsmouth, 1964-74) 29
Davies, R.W. (Bolton Wand., Newcastle Utd., Manchester Utd., Manchester City, Blackpool, 1964-74) 34
Davies, S. (Manchester Utd., 1996) ... 1
Davies, S. (Tottenham, Everton, Fulham, 2001-7) 41
Davis, G. (Wrexham, 1978) 3
Deacy, N. (PSV Eindhoven, Beringen, 1977-9) 12
Delaney, M. (Aston Villa, 2000-7) 36
Derrett, S. (Cardiff City, 1969-71) 4
Dibble, A. (Luton Town, Manchester City, 1986-9) 3

Duffy, R. (Portsmouth, 2006-7) 12
Durban, A. (Derby Co., 1966-72) 27
Dwyer, P. (Cardiff City, 1978-80) 10

Earnshaw, R. (Cardiff City, W.B.A., Norwich City, 2002-7) 34
Easter, J. (Wycombe Wand., 2007) 3
Edwards, C. (Swansea City, 1996) 1
Edwards, G. (Birmingham City, Cardiff City, 1947-50) 12
Edwards, I. (Chester City, Wrexham, 1978-80) 4
Edwards, L. (Charlton Athletic, 1957) 2
Edwards, R. (Bristol City, 1997-8) 4
Edwards, R. (Aston Villa, Wolves, 2003-7) 15
Emmanuel, W. (Bristol City, 1973) 2
England, M. (Blackburn Rov., Tottenham, 1962-75) 44
Evans, B. (Swansea City, Hereford, 1972-4) 7
Evans, I. (Crystal Palace, 1976-8) 13
Evans, P. (Brentford, Bradford City, 2002-3) 2
Evans, R. (Swansea City, 1964) 1
Evans, S. (Wrexham, 2007) 5

Felgate, D. (Lincoln City, 1984) 1
Fletcher, C. (Bournemouth, West Ham Utd., Crystal Palace, 2004-7) 22
Flynn, B. (Burnley, Leeds Utd., 1975-84) 66
Ford, T. (Swansea City, Sunderland, Aston Villa, Cardiff City, 1947-57) 38
Foulkes, W. (Newcastle Utd., 1952-4) 11
Freestone, R. (Swansea City, 2000-03) 1

Gabbidon, D. (Cardiff City, West Ham Utd., 2002-7) 33
Garner, G. (Leyton Orient, 2006) 1
Giggs, R. (Manchester Utd., 1992-2007) 64
Giles, D. (Swansea City, Crystal Palace, 1980-3) 12
Godfrey, B. (Preston N.E., 1964-5) 3
Goss, J. (Norwich City, 1991-6) 9
Green, C. (Birmingham City, 1965-9) 15
Green, R. (Wolves, 1998) 2
Griffiths, A. (Wrexham, 1971-7) 17
Griffiths, H. (Swansea City, 1953) 1
Griffiths, M. (Leicester City, 1947-54) 11
Gunter, C. (Cardiff City, 2007) 1

Hall, G. (Chelsea, 1988-92) 9
Harrington, A. (Cardiff City, 1956-62) 11
Harris, C. (Leeds Utd., 1976-82) 23
Harris, W. (Middlesbrough, 1954-8) ... 6
Hartson, J. (Arsenal, West Ham Utd., Wimbledon, Coventry City, Celtic, 1995-2006) 51
Haworth, S. (Cardiff City, Coventry City, 1997-8) 5
Hennessey, T. (Birmingham City, Nott'm Forest, Derby Co., 1962-73) 39
Hennessey, W. (Wolves, 2007) 2
Hewitt, R. (Cardiff City, 1958) 5
Hill, M. (Ipswich Town, 1972) 2
Hockey, T. (Sheffield Utd., Norwich City, Aston Villa, 1972-4) 9
Hodges, G. (Wimbledon, Newcastle Utd., Watford, Sheffield Utd., 1984-96) 18
Holden, A. (Chester City, 1984) 1
Hole, B. (Cardiff City, Blackburn Rov., Aston Villa, Swansea City, 1963-71) 30
Hollins, D. (Newcastle Utd., 1962-6) 11
Hopkins, J. (Fulham, Crystal Palace, 1983-90) 16
Hopkins, M. (Tottenham, 1956-63) .. 34
Horne, B. (Portsmouth, Southampton, Everton, Birmingham City, 1988-97) 59
Howells, R. (Cardiff City, 1954) 2
Hughes, C. (Luton Town, Wimbledon, 1992-7) 8
Hughes, I. (Luton Town, 1951) 4
Hughes, M. (Manchester Utd., Barcelona, Bayern Munich, Manchester Utd., Chelsea, Southampton, 1984-99) 72
*Hughes, W. (Birmingham City, 1947) 3
Hughes, W.A. (Blackburn Rov., 1949) . 5
Humphreys, J. (Everton, 1947) 1

Jackett, K. (Watford, 1983-8) 31
James, E.G. (Blackpool, 1966-71) 9
James, L. (Burnley, Derby Co., Q.P.R., Swansea City, Sunderland, 1972-83) 54
James, R. (Swansea City, Stoke City, Q.P.R., Leicester City, Swansea City, 1979-88) 47
Jarvis, A. (Hull City, 1967) 3
Jenkins, S. (Swansea City, Huddersfield Town, 1996-2002) 16
Johnson, A. (Nott'm. Forest, W.B.A., 1999-2005) 15
Johnson, M. (Swansea City, 1964) 1
Jones, A. (Port Vale, Charlton Athletic, 1987-90) 6

Jones, Barrie (Swansea City, Plymouth Argyle, Cardiff City, 1963-9) 15
*Jones, Bryn (Arsenal, 1947-9) 4
Jones, C. (Swansea City, Tottenham, Fulham, 1954-69) 59
Jones, D. (Norwich City, 1976-80) 8
Jones, E. (Swansea City, Tottenham, 1947-9) 4
Jones, J. (Liverpool, Wrexham, Chelsea, Huddersfield Town, 1976-86) 72
Jones, K. (Aston Villa, 1950) 1
Jones, L. (Liverpool, Tranmere Rov., 1997) 2
Jones, M. (Leeds Utd., Leicester City, 2000-03) 13
Jones, M. (Wrexham, 2007) 1
Jones, P. (Stockport Co., Southampton, Wolves, Millwall, Q.P.R., 1997-2007) 50
Jones, R. (Sheffield Wed., 1994) 1
*Jones, T.G. (Everton, 1946-9) 13
Jones, V. (Wimbledon, 1995-7) 9
Jones, W. (Bristol Rov., 1971) 1

Kelsey, J. (Arsenal, 1954-62) 41
King, J. (Swansea City, 1955) 1
Kinsey, N. (Norwich City, Birmingham City, 1951-6) 7
Knill, A. (Swansea City, 1989) 1
Koumas, J. (Tranmere Rov., W.B.A., 2001-7) 23
Krzywicki, R. (W.B.A., Huddersfield Town, 1970-2) 8

Lambert, R. (Liverpool, 1947-9) 5
Law, B. (Q.P.R., 1990) 1
Ledley, J. (Cardiff City, 2006-7) 12
Lee, C. (Ipswich Town, 1965) 2
Leek, K. (Leicester City, Newcastle Utd., Birmingham City, Northampton Town, 1961-5) 13
Legg, A. (Birmingham City, Cardiff City, 1996-2001) 6
Lever, A. (Leicester City, 1953) 1
Lewis, D. (Swansea City, 1983) 1
Llewellyn, C. (Norwich City, Wrexham, 1998-2007) 6
Lloyd, B. (Wrexham, 1976) 3
Lovell, S. (Crystal Palace, Millwall, 1982-6) 6
Lowndes, S. (Newport, Millwall, Brighton & H.A., Barnsley, 1983-8) 10
Lowrie, G. (Coventry City, Newcastle Utd., 1948-9) 4
Lucas, M. (Leyton Orient, 1962-3) 4
Lucas, W. (Swansea City, 1949-51) 7

Maguire, G. (Portsmouth, 1990-2) 7
Mahoney, J. (Stoke City, Middlesbrough, Swansea City, 1968-83) 50
Mardon, P. (W.B.A., 1996) 1
Margetson, M. (Cardiff City, 2004) 1
Marriott, A. (Wrexham, 1996-8) 5
Marustik, C. (Swansea City, 1982-3) .. 6
Medwin, T. (Swansea City, Tottenham, 1953-63) 29
Melville, A. (Swansea City, Oxford Utd., Sunderland, Fulham, West Ham Utd., 1990-2005) 65
Mielczarek, R. (Rotherham Utd., 1971) 1
Millington, A. (W.B.A., Peterborough Utd., Swansea City, 1963-72) 21
Moore, G. (Cardiff City, Chelsea, Manchester Utd., Northampton Town, Charlton Athletic, 1960-71) 21
Morgan, C. (MK Dons, 2007) 1
Morris, W. (Burnley, 1947-52) 5

Nardiello, D. (Coventry City, 1978) 2
Nardiello, D. (Barnsley, 2007) 1
Neilson, A. (Newcastle Utd., Southampton, 1992-7) 5
Nicholas, P. (Crystal Palace, Arsenal, Crystal Palace, Luton Town, Aberdeen, Chelsea, Watford, 1979-92) 73
Niedzwiecki, E. (Chelsea, 1985-8) 2
Nogan, L. (Watford, Reading, 1991-6) 2
Norman, T. (Hull City, 1986-8) 5
Nurse, M. (Swansea City, Middlesbrough, 1960-3) 12
Nyatanga, L. (Derby Co., 2006-7) 12

O'Sullivan, P. (Brighton & H.A., 1973-8) 3
Oster, J. (Everton, Sunderland, 1997-2005) 13

Page, M. (Birmingham City, 1971-9) 28
Page, R. (Watford, Sheffield Utd., Cardiff City, Coventry City, 1997-2006) 41
Palmer, D. (Swansea City, 1957) 3
Parry, J. (Swansea City, 1951) 1
Parry, P, (Cardiff City, 2004-7) 11
Partridge, D. (Motherwell, Bristol City, 2005–6) 7
Pascoe, C. (Swansea City, Sunderland, 1984-92) 10
Paul, R. (Swansea City, Manchester City, 1949-56) 33
Pembridge, M. (Luton Town, Derby Co., Sheffield Wed., Benfica, Everton, Fulham, 1992-2005) 54
Perry, J. (Cardiff City, 1994) 1
Phillips, D. (Plymouth Argyle, Manchester City, Coventry City, Norwich City, Nott'm. Forest, 1984-96) 62
Phillips, J. (Chelsea, 1973-8) 4

Phillips, L. (Cardiff City, Aston Villa, Swansea City, Charlton Athletic, 1971-82) 58
Pipe, D. (Coventry City, 2003) 1
Pontin, K. (Cardiff City, 1980) 2
Powell, A. (Leeds Utd., Everton, Birmingham City, 1947-51) 8
Powell, D. (Wrexham, Sheffield Utd. 1968-71) 11
Powell, I. (Q.P.R., Aston Villa, 1947-51) 8
Price, L. (Ipswich Town, 2006-7) 3
Price, P. (Luton Town, Tottenham, 1980-4) 25
Pring, K. (Rotherham Utd., 1966-7) ... 3
Pritchard, H. (Bristol City, 1985) 1

Rankmore, F. (Peterborough Utd., 1966) 1
Ratcliffe, K. (Everton, Cardiff City, 1981-93) 59
Ready, K. (Q.P.R., 1997-8) 5
Reece, G. (Sheffield Utd., Cardiff City, 1966-75) 29
Reed, W. (Ipswich Town, 1955) 2
Rees, A. (Birmingham City, 1984) 1
Rees, J. (Luton Town, 1992) 1
Rees, R. (Coventry City, W.B.A., Nott'm. Forest, 1965-72) 39
Rees, W. (Cardiff City, Tottenham, 1949-50) 4
Richards, S. (Cardiff City, 1947) 1
Ricketts, S. (Swansea City, Hull City, 2005–7) 19
Roberts, A. (Q.P.R., 1993) 1
Roberts, D. (Oxford Utd., Hull City, 1973-8) 17
Roberts, G. (Tranmere Rov., 2000-6) .. 8
Roberts, I. (Watford, Huddersfield Town, Leicester City, Norwich City, 1990-2002) 15
Roberts, J. (Arsenal, Birmingham City, 1971-6) 21
Roberts, J. (Bolton Wand., 1949) 1
Roberts, M. (Q.P.R., 1997) 1
Roberts, N. (Wrexham, Wigan Athletic, 2000-4) 4
Roberts, P. (Portsmouth, 1974) 4
Roberts, S. (Wrexham, 2005) 1
Robinson, C. (Wolves, Portsmouth, Sunderland, Norwich City, Toronto, 2000-7) 39
Robinson, J. (Charlton Athletic, 1996-2002) 30
Rodrigues, P. (Cardiff City, Leicester City, Sheffield Wed. 1965-74) 40
Rouse, V. (Crystal Palace, 1959) 1
Rowley, T. (Tranmere Rov., 1959) 1
Rush, I. (Liverpool, Juventus, Liverpool, 1980-96) 73

Saunders, D. (Brighton & H.A., Oxford Utd., Derby Co., Liverpool, Aston Villa, Galatasaray, Nott'm. Forest, Sheffield Utd., Benfica, Bradford City, 1986-2001) 75
Savage, R. (Crewe Alexandra, Leicester City, Birmingham City, 1996-2005) 39
Sayer, P. (Cardiff City, 1977-8) 7
Scrine, F. (Swansea City, 1950) 2
Sear, C. (Manchester City, 1963) 1
Sherwood, A. (Cardiff City, Newport, 1947-57) 41
Shortt, W. (Plymouth Argyle, 1947-53) 12
Showers, D. (Cardiff City, 1975) 2
Sidlow, C. (Liverpool, 1947-50) 7
Slatter, N. (Bristol Rov., Oxford Utd., 1983-9) 22
Smallman, D. (Wrexham, Everton, 1974-6) 7
Southall, N. (Everton, 1982-97) 92
Speed, G. (Leeds Utd., Everton, Newcastle Utd., 1990-2004) 85
Sprake, G. (Leeds Utd., Birmingham City, 1964-75) 37
Stansfield, F. (Cardiff City, 1949) 1
Stevenson, B. (Leeds Utd., Birmingham City, 1978-82) 15
Stevenson, N. (Swansea City, 1982-3) 4
Stitfall, R. (Cardiff City, 1953-7) 2
Sullivan, D. (Cardiff City, 1953-60) .. 17
Symons, K. (Portsmouth, Manchester City, Fulham, Crystal Palace, 1992-2004) 37

Tapscott, D. (Arsenal, Cardiff City, 1954-9) 14
Taylor, G. (Crystal Palace, Sheffield Utd., Burnley, Nott'm. Forest, 1996-2005) 15
Thatcher, B (Leicester City, Manchester City, 2004-5) 7
Thomas, D. (Swansea City, 1957-8) ... 2
Thomas, M. (Wrexham, Manchester Utd., Everton, Brighton & H.A., Stoke City, Chelsea, W.B.A., 1977-86) ... 51
Thomas, M. (Newcastle Utd., 1987) ... 1
Thomas, R. (Swindon Town, Derby Co., Cardiff City, 1967-78) 50
Thomas, S. (Fulham, 1948-9) 4
Toshack, J. (Cardiff City, Liverpool, Swansea City, 1969-80) 40
Trollope, P. (Derby Co., Fulham, Northampton Town, 1997-2003) 9

Van den Hauwe, P. (Everton, 1985-9) 13
Vaughan, D. (Crewe Alexandra, 2003-7) 10

Vaughan, N. (Newport, Cardiff City, 1983-5) 10
Vearncombe, G. (Cardiff City, 1958-61) 2
Vernon, R. (Blackburn Rov., Everton, Stoke City, 1957-68) 32
Villars, A. (Cardiff City, 1974) 3

Walley, T. (Watford, 1971) 1
Walsh, I. (Crystal Palace, 1980-2) 18
Ward, D. (Bristol Rov., Cardiff City, 1959-62) 2
Ward, D. (Notts Co., Nott'm. Forest, 2000-4) 5
Webster, C. (Manchester Utd., 1957-8) 4
Weston, R. (Arsenal, Cardiff City, 2000-5) 7
Williams, A. (Reading, Wolves, Reading, 1994-2003) 13
Williams, A. (Southampton, 1997-8) .. 2
Williams, D. (Norwich City, 1986-7) ... 5
Williams, G. (Cardiff City, 1951) 1
Williams, G. (Derby Co., Ipswich Town, 1988-96) 13
Williams, G. (West Ham Utd., 2006) .. 2
Williams, G.E. (W.B.A., 1960-9) 26
Williams, G.G. (Swansea City, 1961-2) 5
Williams, H.J. (Swansea City, 1965-72) 3
Williams, H.T. (Newport, Leeds Utd., 1949-50) 4
Williams, S. (W.B.A., Southampton, 1954-66) 43
Witcomb, D. (W.B.A., Sheffield Wed., 1947) 3
Woosnam, P. (Leyton Orient, West Ham Utd., Aston Villa, 1959-63) 17

Yorath, T. (Leeds Utd., Coventry City, Tottenham, Vancouver Whitecaps, 1970-81) 59
Young, E. (Wimbledon, Crystal Palace, Wolves, 1990-6) 21

REPUBLIC OF IRELAND

Aherne, T. (Belfast Celtic, Luton Town, 1946-54) 16
Aldridge, J. (Oxford Utd., Liverpool, Real Sociedad, Tranmere Rov., 1986-97) 69
Ambrose, P. (Shamrock R., 1955-64) . 5
Anderson, J. (Preston N.E., Newcastle Utd., 1980-9) 16

Babb, P. (Coventry City, Liverpool, Sunderland, 1994-2003) 35
Bailham, E. (Shamrock R., 1964) 1
Barber, E. (Bohemians, Birmingham City, 1966) 2
Barrett, G. (Arsenal, Coventry City, 2003-5) 6
Beglin, J. (Liverpool, 1984-7) 15
Bennett, A. (Reading, 2007) 2
Braddish, S. (Dundalk, 1978) 2
Branagan, K. (Bolton Wand., 1997) 1
Bonner, P. (Celtic, 1981-96) 80
Brady, L. (Arsenal, Juventus, Sampdoria, Inter-Milan, Ascoli, West Ham Utd., 1975-90) 72
Brady, R. (Q.P.R., 1964) 6
Breen, G. (Birmingham City, Coventry City, West Ham Utd., Sunderland 1996-2006) 63
*Breen, T. (Shamrock R., 1947) 3
Brennan, F. (Drumcondra, 1965) 1
Brennan, S. (Manchester Utd., Waterford, 1965-71) 19
Browne, W. (Bohemians, 1964) 3
Bruce, A. (Ipswich Town, 2007) 1
Buckley, L. (Shamrock R., Waregem, 1984-5) 2
Burke, F. (Cork Ath., 1952) 1
Butler, P. (Sunderland, 2000) 1
Butler, T. (Sunderland, 2003) 2
Byrne, A. (Southampton, 1970-4) 14
Byrne, J. (Shelbourne, 2004–6) 2
Byrne, J. (Q.P.R., Le Havre, Brighton & H.A., Sunderland, Millwall, 1985-93) 23
Byrne, P. (Shamrock R., 1984-6) 8

Campbell, A. (Santander, 1985) 3
Campbell, N. (St Patrick's Ath., Fortuna Cologne, 1971-7) 11
Cantwell, N. (West Ham Utd., Manchester Utd., 1954-67) 36
Carey, B. (Manchester Utd., Leicester City, 1992-4) 3
*Carey, J. (Manchester Utd., 1946-53) 21
Carolan, J. (Manchester Utd., 1960) .. 2
Carr, S. (Tottenham, Newcastle Utd., 1999-2007) 43
Carroll, B. (Shelbourne, 1949-50) 2
Carroll, T. (Ipswich Town, 1968-73) . 17
Carsley, L. (Derby Co., Blackburn Rov., Coventry City, Everton, 1997-2007) 34
Cascarino, A. (Gillingham, Millwall, Aston Villa, Chelsea, Marseille, Nancy, 1986-2000) 88
Chandler, J. (Leeds Utd., 1980) 2
Clarke, C. (Stoke City, 2004) 2
Clarke, J. (Drogheda, 1978) 1
Clarke, K. (Drumcondra, 1948) 2
Clarke, M. (Shamrock R., 1950) 1
Clinton, T. (Everton, 1951-4) 3

Coad, P. (Shamrock R., 1947-52) 11
Coffey, T. (Drumcondra, 1950) 1
Colfer, M. (Shelbourne, 1950-1) 2
Colgan, N. (Hibernian, 2002-4) 8
Conmy, O. (Peterborough Utd., 1965-70) 5
Connolly, D. (Watford, Feyenoord, Excelsior, Feyenoord, Wimbledon, West Ham Utd., Wigan Athletic, 1996-2006) 41
Conroy, G. (Stoke City, 1970-7) 27
Conway, J. (Fulham, Manchester City, 1967-77) 20
Corr, P. (Everton, 1949-50) 4
Courtney, E. (Cork Utd., 1946) 1
Coyle, O. (Bolton Wand., 1994) 1
Coyne, T. (Celtic, Tranmere Rov., Motherwell, 1992-8) 22
Crowe, G. (Bohemians, 2003) 2
Cummins, G. (Luton Town, 1954-61) 19
Cuneen, T. (Limerick, 1951) 1
Cunningham, K. (Wimbledon, Birmingham City, 1996-2006) 72
Curtis, D. (Shelbourne, Bristol City, Ipswich Town, Exeter City) 17
Cusack, S. (Limerick, 1953) 1

Daish, L. (Cambridge Utd., Coventry City, 1992-6) 5
Daly, G. (Manchester Utd., Derby Co., Coventry City, Birmingham City, Shrewsbury Town, 1973-87) 48
Daly, M. (Wolves, 1978) 2
Daly, P. (Shamrock R., 1950) 1
Deacy, E. (Aston Villa, 1982) 4
Delap, R. (Derby Co., Southampton, 1998-2004) 11
De Mange, K. (Liverpool, Hull City, 1987-9) 2
Dempsey, J. (Fulham, Chelsea, 1967-72) 19
Dennehy, J. (Cork Hibs., Nott'm Forest, Walsall, 1972-7) 11
Desmond, P. (Middlesbrough, 1950) ... 4
Devine, J. (Arsenal, 1980-5) 13
Doherty, G. (Tottenham, Norwich City, 2000-6) 33
Donovan, D. (Everton, 1955-7) 5
Donovan, T. (Aston Villa, 1980) 2
Douglas, J. (Blackburn Rov., Leeds Utd., 2004-7) 7
Doyle, C. (Shelbourne, 1959) 1
Doyle, C. (Birmingham City, 2007) 1
Doyle, K. (Reading, 2006-7) 9
Doyle, M. (Coventry City, 2004) 1
Duff, D. (Blackburn Rov., Chelsea, Newcastle Utd., 1998-2007) 66
Duffy, B. (Shamrock R., 1950) 1
Dunne, A. (Manchester Utd., Bolton Wand., 1962-76) 33
Dunne, J. (Fulham, 1971) 1
Dunne, P. (Manchester Utd., 1965-7) . 5
Dunne, R. (Everton, Manchester City, 2000-7) 35
Dunne, S. (Luton Town, 1953-60) 15
Dunne, T. (Bolton Wand., 1975) 1
Dunning, P. (Shelbourne, 1971) 2
Dunphy, E. (York City, Millwall, 1966-71) 23
Dwyer, N. (West Ham Utd., Swansea City, 1960-5) 14

Eccles, P. (Shamrock R., 1986) 1
Eglington, T. (Shamrock R., Everton, 1946-56) 24
Elliott, S. (Sunderland, 2005–7) 9
Evans, M. (Southampton, 1997) 1

Fagan, E. (Shamrock R., 1973) 1
Fagan, F. (Manchester City, Derby Co., 1955-61) 8
Fairclough, M. (Dundalk, 1982) 2
Fallon, S. (Celtic, 1951-5) 8
Farrell, P. (Shamrock R., Everton, 1946-57) 28
Farrelly, G. (Aston Villa, Everton, Bolton Wand., 1996-2000) 6
Finnan, S. (Fulham, Liverpool, 2000-7) 46
Finucane, A. (Limerick, 1967-72) 11
Fitzgerald, F. (Waterford, 1955-6) 2
Fitzgerald, P. (Leeds Utd., 1961-2) 5
Fitzpatrick, K. (Limerick, 1970) 1
Fitzsimons, A. (Middlesbrough, Lincoln City, 1950-9) 26
Fleming, C. (Middlesbrough, 1996-8) 10
Fogarty, A. (Sunderland, Hartlepool Utd., 1960-4) 11
Foley, D. (Watford, 2000-01) 6
Foley, T. (Northampton Town, 1964-7) 9
Fullam, J. (Preston N.E., Shamrock R., 1961-70) 11

Gallagher, C. (Celtic, 1967) 2
Gallagher, M. (Hibernian, 1954) 1
Galvin, A. (Tottenham, Sheffield Wed., Swindon Town, 1983-90) 29
Gamble, J. (Cork City, 2007) 2
Gannon, E. (Notts. Co., Sheffield Wed., Shelbourne, 1949-55) 14
Gannon, M. (Shelbourne, 1972) 1
Gavin, J. (Norwich City, Tottenham, Norwich City, 1950-7) 7
Gibbons, A. (St Patrick's Ath., 1952-6) 4
Gilbert, R. (Shamrock R., 1966) 1
Giles, C. (Doncaster Rov., 1951) 1
Giles, J. (Manchester Utd., Leeds Utd., W.B.A., Shamrock R., 1960-79) ... 59

Given, S. (Blackburn Rov., Newcastle Utd., 1996-2007) 80
Givens, D. (Manchester Utd., Luton Town, Q.P.R., Birmingham City, Neuchatel, Switz., 1969-82) 56
Gleeson, S. (Wolves, 2007) 2
Glynn, D. (Drumcondra, 1952-5) 2
Godwin, T. (Shamrock R., Leicester City, Bournemouth, 1949-58) 13
Goodman, J. (Wimbledon, 1997) 4
Goodwin, J. (Stockport Co., 2003) 1
*Gorman, W. (Brentford, 1947) 2
Grealish, A. (Orient, Luton Town, Brighton & H.A., W.B.A., 1976-86) 45
Gregg, E. (Bohemians, 1978-80) 8
Grimes, A. (Manchester Utd., Coventry City, Luton Town, 1978-88) 18

Hale, A. (Aston Villa, Doncaster Rov., Waterford, 1962-72) 13
Hamilton, T. (Shamrock R., 1959) 2
Hand, E. (Portsmouth, 1969-76) 20
Harte, I. (Leeds Utd., Levante, 1996-2007) 64
Hartnett, J. (Middlesbrough, 1949-54) 2
Haverty, J. (Arsenal, Blackburn Rov., Millwall, Celtic, Bristol R., Shelbourne, 1956-67) 32
Hayes, A. (Southampton, 1979) 1
*Hayes, W. (Huddersfield Town, 1947) 2
Hayes, W. (Limerick, 1949) 1
Healey, R. (Cardiff City, 1977-80) 2
Healy, C. (Celtic, Sunderland, 2002-4) 13
Heighway, S. (Liverpool, Minnesota, 1971-82) 34
Henderson, B. (Drumcondra, 1948) 2
Henderson, W. (Brighton & H.A., Preston N.E., 2006-7) 5
Hennessy, J. (Shelbourne, St Patrick's Ath., 1956-69) 5
Herrick, J. (Cork Hibs., Shamrock R., 1972-3) 3
Higgins, J. (Birmingham City, 1951) ... 1
Holland, M. (Ipswich Town, Charlton Athletic, 2000-6) 49
Holmes, J. (Coventry City, Tottenham, Vancouver W'caps, 1971-81) 30
Houghton, R. (Oxford Utd., Liverpool, Aston Villa, Crystal Palace, Reading, 1986-97) 73
Howlett, G. (Brighton & H.A., 1984) .. 1
Hughton, C. (Tottenham, West Ham Utd., 1980-92) 53
Hunt, S. (Reading, 2007) 5
Hurley, C. (Millwall, Sunderland, Bolton Wand., 1957-69) 40

Ireland, S. (Manchester City, 2006-7) . 5
Irwin, D. (Manchester Utd., 1991-2000) 56

Kavanagh, G. (Stoke City, Cardiff City, Wigan Athletic, 1998-2007) 16
Keane, Robbie (Wolves, Coventry City, Inter Milan, Leeds Utd., Tottenham, 1998-2007) 72
Keane, Roy (Nott'm. Forest, Manchester Utd., 1991-2006) 67
Keane, T. (Swansea City, 1949) 4
Kearin, M. (Shamrock R., 1972) 1
Kearns, F. (West Ham Utd., 1954) 1
Kearns, M. (Oxford Utd., Walsall, Wolves, 1970-80) 18
Kelly, A. (Sheffield Utd., Blackburn Rov., 1993-2002) 34
Kelly, D. (Walsall, West Ham Utd., Leicester City, Newcastle Utd., Wolves, Sunderland, Tranmere Rov., 1988-98) 26
Kelly, G. (Leeds Utd., 1994-2003) ... 52
Kelly, J.A. (Drumcondra, Preston N.E., 1957-73) 47
Kelly, J. (Wolves, 1961-2) 5
Kelly, M. (Portsmouth, 1988-91) 4
Kelly, N. (Nott'm. Forest, 1954) 1
Kelly, S. (Tottenham, Birmingham City, 2006-7) 5
Kenna, J. (Blackburn Rov., 1995-2000) 27
Kennedy, M. (Portsmouth, 1986) 2
Kennedy, M. (Liverpool, Wimbledon, Manchester City, Wolves, 1996-2004) 34
Kenny, P. (Sheffield Utd., 2004-7) 7
Keogh, A. (Wolves, 2007) 1
Keogh, J. (Shamrock R., 1966) 1
Keogh, S. (Shamrock R., 1959) 1
Kernaghan, A. (Middlesbrough, Man. C., 1993-6) 22
Kiely, D. (Charlton Athletic, 2000-03) 8
Kiernan, F. (Shamrock R., Southampton, 1951-2) 5
Kilbane, K. (W.B.A., Sunderland, Everton, Wigan Athletic, 1997-2007) 80
Kinnear, J. (Tottenham, Brighton & H.A., 1967-76) 26
Kinsella, M. (Charlton Athletic, Aston Villa, W.B.A., 1998-2004) 48

Langan, D. (Derby Co., Birmingham City, Oxford Utd., 1978-88) 26
Lapira, J. (Notre Dame, 2007) 1
Lawler, R. (Fulham, 1953-6) 8
Lawlor, J. (Drumcondra, Doncaster Rov., 1949-51) 3
Lawlor, M. (Shamrock R., 1971-3) 5

Lawrenson, M. (Preston N.E., Brighton & H.A., Liverpool, 1977-88) 39
Lee, A. (Rotherham Utd., Cardiff City, Ipswich Town, 2003-7) 10
Leech, M. (Shamrock R., 1969-73) 8
Long, S. (Reading, 2007) 4
Lowry, D. (St Patrick's Ath., 1962) 1

McAlinden, J. (Portsmouth, 1946) 2
McAteer, J. (Bolton Wand., Liverpool, Blackburn Rov., Sunderland, 1994-2004) 52
McCann, J. (Shamrock R., 1957) 1
McCarthy, M. (Manchester City, Celtic, Lyon, Millwall, 1984-92) 57
McConville, T. (Dundalk, Waterford, 1972-3) 6
McDonagh, J. (Everton, Bolton Wand., Sunderland, Notts. Co., 1981-6) ... 25
McDonagh, J. (Shamrock R., 1984-5) 3
McEvoy, A. (Blackburn Rov., 1961-7) 17
McGeady, A. (Celtic, 2004-7) 10
McGee, P. (Q.P.R., Preston N.E., 1978-81) 15
McGoldrick, E. (Crystal Palace, Arsenal, 1992-5) 15
McGowan, D. (West Ham Utd., 1949) 3
McGowan, J. (Cork Utd., 1947) 1
McGrath, M. (Blackburn Rov., Bradford City, 1958-66) 22
McGrath, P. (Manchester Utd., Aston Villa, Derby Co., 1985-97) 83
Macken, J. (Manchester City, 2005) ... 1
Mackey, G. (Shamrock R., 1957) 3
McLoughlin, A. (Swindon Town, Southampton, Portsmouth, 1990-2000) 42
McMillan, W. (Belfast Celtic, 1946) 2
McNally, B. (Luton Town, 1959-63) ... 3
McPhail, S. (Leeds Utd., 2000-4) 10
McShane, P. (W.B.A., 2007) 5
Macken, A. (Derby Co., 1977) 1
Mahon, A. (Tranmere Rov., 2000) 3
Malone, G. (Shelbourne, 1949) 1
Mancini, T. (Q.P.R., Arsenal, 1974-5) . 5
Martin, C. (Glentoran, Leeds Utd., Aston Villa, 1946-56) 30
Martin, M. (Bohemians, Manchester Utd., 1972-83) 52
Maybury, A. (Leeds Utd., Hearts, Leicester City, 1998-2005) 10
Meagan, M. (Everton, Huddersfield Town, Drogheda, 1961-70) 17
Miller, L. (Celtic, Manchester Utd., 2004-7) 13
Milligan, M. (Oldham Athletic, 1992) . 1
Mooney, J. (Shamrock R., 1965) 2
Moore, A. (Middlesbrough, 1996-7) 8
Moran, K. (Manchester Utd., Sporting Gijon, Blackburn Rov., 1980-94) .. 71
Moroney, T. (West Ham Utd., 1948-54) 12
Morris, C. (Celtic, Middlesbrough, 1988-93) 35
Morrison, C. (Crystal Palace, Birmingham City, Crystal Palace, 2002-7) 36
Moulson, G. (Lincoln City, 1948-9) 3
Mucklan, C. (Drogheda, 1978) 1
Mulligan, P. (Shamrock R., Chelsea, Crystal Palace, W.B.A., Shamrock R., 1969-80) 50
Munroe, L. (Shamrock R., 1954) 1
Murphy, A. (Clyde, 1956) 1
Murphy, B. (Bohemians, 1986) 1
Murphy, D. (Sunderland, 2007) 2
Murphy, J. (Crystal Palace, 1980) 3
Murphy, J. (W.B.A., 2004) 1
Murphy, P. (Carlisle Utd., 2007) 1
Murray, T. (Dundalk, 1950) 1

Newman, W. (Shelbourne, 1969) 1
Nolan, R. (Shamrock R., 1957-63) .. 10

O'Brien, Alan (Newcastle Utd., 2007) 4
O'Brien, Andy (Newcastle Utd., Portsmouth, 2001-7) 26
O'Brien, F. (Philadelphia Forest, 1980) 3
O'Brien, J. (Bolton Wand., 2006) 1
O'Brien, L. (Shamrock R., Manchester Utd., Newcastle Utd., Tranmere Rov., 1986-97) 16
O'Brien, R. (Notts Co., 1976-7) 5
O'Byrne, L. (Shamrock R., 1949) 1
O'Callaghan, B. (Stoke City, 1979-82) 6
O'Callaghan, K. (Ipswich Town, Portsmouth, 1981-7) 21
O'Cearuill, J. (Arsenal, 2007) 2
O'Connell, A. (Dundalk, Bohemians, 1967-71) 2
O'Connor, T. (Shamrock R., 1950) 4
O'Connor, T. (Fulham, Dundalk, Bohemians, 1968-73) 7
O'Driscoll, J. (Swansea City, 1949) 3
O'Driscoll, S. (Fulham, 1982) 3
O'Farrell, F. (West Ham Utd., Preston N.E., 1952-9) 9
*O'Flanagan, Dr. K. (Arsenal, 1947) ... 3
O'Flanagan, M. (Bohemians, 1947) 1
O'Halloran, S. (Aston Villa, 2007) 2
O'Hanlon, K (Rotherham Utd., 1988) . 1
O'Keefe, E. (Everton, Port Vale, 1981-5) 5
O'Leary, D. (Arsenal, 1977-93) 68
O'Leary, P. (Shamrock R., 1980-1) 7
O'Neill, F. (Shamrock R., 1962-72) .. 20

O'Neill, J. (Everton, 1952-9) 17
O'Neill, J. (Preston N.E., 1961) 1
O'Neill, K. (Norwich City, Middlesbrough, 1996-2000) 13
O'Regan, K. (Brighton & H.A., 1984-5) 4
O'Reilly, J. (Cork Utd., 1946) 3
O'Shea, J. (Manchester Utd., 2002-7) 38

Peyton, G. (Fulham, Bournemouth, Everton, 1977-92) 33
Peyton, N. (Shamrock R., Leeds Utd., 1957-61) 6
Phelan, T. (Wimbledon, Manchester City, Chelsea, Everton, Fulham, 1992-2000) 42
Potter, D. (Wolves, 2007) 2

Quinn, A. (Sheffield Wed., Sheffield Utd., 2003-7) 8
Quinn, B. (Coventry City, 2000) 4
Quinn, N. (Arsenal, Manchester City, Sunderland, 1986-2002) 91

Reid, A. (Nott'm. Forest, Tottenham, 2004-7) 24
Reid, S. (Millwall, Blackburn Rov., 2002-7) 18
Richardson, D. (Shamrock R., Gillingham, 1972-80) 3
Ringstead, A. (Sheffield Utd., 1951-9) 20
Robinson, M. (Brighton & H.A., Liverpool, Q.P.R., 1981-6) 24
Roche, P. (Shelbourne, Manchester Utd., 1972-6) 8
Rogers, E. (Blackburn Rov., Charlton Athletic, 1968-73) 19
Rowlands, M. (Q.P.R, 2004) 3
Ryan, G. (Derby Co., Brighton & H.A., 1978-85) 18
Ryan, R. (W.B.A., Derby Co., 1950-56) 16

Sadlier, R. (Millwall, 2002) 1
Savage, D. (Millwall, 1996) 5
Saward, P. (Millwall, Aston Villa, Huddersfield Town, 1954-63) 18
Scannell, T. (Southend Utd., 1954) 1
Scully, P. (Arsenal, 1989) 1
Sheedy, K. (Everton, Newcastle Utd., 1984-93) 46
Sheridan, J. (Leeds Utd., Sheffield Wed., 1988-96) 34
Slaven, B. (Middlesbrough, 1990-3) ... 7
Sloan, P. (Arsenal, 1946) 2
Smyth, M. (Shamrock R., 1969) 1
Stapleton, F. (Arsenal, Manchester Utd., Ajax, Derby Co., Le Havre, Blackburn Rov., 1977-90) 71
Staunton, S. (Liverpool, Aston Villa, Liverpool, Crystal Palace, Aston Villa, 1989-2002) 102
*Stevenson, A. (Everton, 1947-9) 6
Stokes, A. (Sunderland, 2007) 3
Strahan, F. (Shelbourne, 1964-5) 5
Swan, M. (Drumcondra, 1960) 1
Synnott, N. (Shamrock R., 1978-9) 3

Thomas, P. (Waterford, 1974) 2
Thompson, J. (Nott'm. Forest, 2004) .. 1
Townsend, A. (Norwich City, Chelsea, Aston Villa, Middlesbrough, 1989-97) 70
Traynor, T. (Southampton, 1954-64) ... 8
Treacy, R. (W.B.A., Charlton Athletic, Swindon Town, Preston N.E., Shamrock R., 1966-80) 42
Tuohy, L. (Shamrock R., Newcastle Utd., Shamrock R., 1956-65) 8
Turner, A. (Celtic, 1963) 2

Vernon, J. (Belfast Celtic, 1946) 2

Waddock, G. (Q.P.R., Millwall, 1980-90) 21
Walsh, D. (W.B.A., Aston Villa, 1946-54) 20
Walsh, J. (Limerick, 1982) 1
Walsh, M. (Blackpool, Everton, Q.P.R., Porto, 1976-85) 21
Walsh, M. (Everton, Norwich City, 1982-3) 4
Walsh, W. (Manchester City, 1947-50) 9
Waters, J. (Grimsby Town, 1977-80) ... 2
Whelan, R. (St Patrick's Ath., 1964) .. 2
Whelan, R. (Liverpool, Southend Utd., 1981-95) 53
Whelan, L. (Manchester Utd., 1956-7) 4
Whittaker, R. (Chelsea, 1959) 1

INTERNATIONAL GOALSCORERS 1946-2007

(As at start of season 2007-08)

ENGLAND

Charlton, R 49
Lineker 48
Greaves 44
Owen 37
Finney 30
Lofthouse 30
Shearer 30
Platt 27
Robson, B 26
Hurst 24
Mortensen 23

Name	Goals
Channon	21
Keegan	21
Peters	20
Haynes	18
Hunt, R	18
Beckham	17
Lawton	16
Taylor, T	16
Woodcock	16
Scholes	14
Chivers	13
Mariner	13
Smith, R	13
Crouch	12
Francis, T	12
Gerrard	12
Lampard, Frank Jnr.	12
Rooney	12
Barnes, J	11
Douglas	11
Mannion	11
Sheringham	11
Clarke, A	10
Flowers, R	10
Gascoigne	10
Lee, F	10
Milburn	10
Wilshaw	10
Beardsley	9
Bell	9
Bentley	9
Hateley	9
Wright, I	9
Ball	8
Broadis	8
Byrne, J	8
Hoddle	8
Kevan	8
Anderton	7
Cole, J	7
Connelly	7
Coppell	7
Fowler	7
Paine	7
Charlton, J	6
Johnson	6
Macdonald	6
Mullen	6
Rowley	6
Vassell	6
Waddle	6
Adams	5
Atyeo	5
Baily	5
Brooking	5
Carter	5
Edwards	5
Ferdinand, L	5
Heskey	5
Hitchens	5
Latchford	5
Neal	5
Pearce	5
Pearson, Stan	5
Pearson, Stuart	5
Pickering, F	5
Barmby	4
Barnes, P	4
Bull	4
Dixon, K	4
Hassall	4
Revie	4
Robson, R	4
Steven	4
Watson, Dave (Sunderland)	4
Webb	4
Baker	3
Blissett	3
Butcher	3
Currie	3
Defoe	3
Elliott	3
Francis, G	3
Grainger	3
Kennedy, R	3
McDermott	3
McManaman	3
Matthews, S	3
Merson	3
Morris	3
O'Grady	3
Peacock	3
Ramsey	3
Sewell	3
Terry	3
Wilkins	3
Wright, W	3
Allen, R	2
Anderson	2
Bradley	2
Broadbent	2
Brooks	2
Cowans	2
Eastham	2
Froggatt, J	2
Froggatt, R	2
Haines	2
Hancocks	2
Hunter	2
Ince	2
Keown	2
Lee, R	2
Lee, S	2
Moore	2
Perry	2
Pointer	2
Richardson	2
Royle	2
Southgate	2
Stone	2
Taylor, P	2
Tueart	2
Wignall	2
Worthington	2
A'Court	1
Astall	1
Beattie, K	1
Bowles	1
Bradford	1
Bridge	1
Bridges	1
Campbell	1
Chamberlain	1
Cole, Andy	1
Crawford	1
Dixon, L	1
Ehiogu	1
Ferdinand, R	1
Goddard	1
Hirst	1
Hughes, E	1
Jeffers	1
Kay	1
Kidd	1
King	1
Langton	1
Lawler	1
Lee, J	1
Le Saux	1
Mabbutt	1
Marsh	1
Medley	1
Melia	1
Mullery	1
Murphy	1
Nicholls	1
Nicholson	1
Nugent	1
Palmer	1
Parry	1
Redknapp	1
Sansom	1
Shackleton	1
Smith, A (1989-92)	1
Smith, A (2001-5)	1
Stiles	1
Summerbee	1
Tambling	1
Thompson, Phil	1
Viollet	1
Wallace	1
Walsh	1
Weller	1
Wise	1
Withe	1
Wright, M	1

Wright-Phillips, S 1

N. IRELAND

Healy 29
Clarke 13
Armstrong 12
Quinn, J.M. 12
Dowie 11
Bingham 10
Crossan, J 10
McIlroy, J 10
McParland 10
Best 9
Whiteside 9
Dougan 8
Irvine, W 8
O'Neill, M (1972-85) .. 8
McAdams 7
Taggart, G 7
Wilson, S 7
Gray 6
McLaughlin 6
Nicholson, J 6
Wilson, K 6
Cush 5
Hamilton, W 5
Hughes, M 5
Magilton 5
McIlroy, S 5
Simpson 5
Smyth, S 5
Walsh, D 5
Anderson, T 4
Elliott 4
Hamilton, B 4
McGrath 4
McMorran 4
O'Neill, M. (1989-96) . 4
Quinn, S.J. 4
Brotherston 3
Harvey, M 3
Lockhart 3
Lomas 3
McDonald 3
McMordie 3
Morgan, S 3
Mulryne 3
Nicholl, C 3
Spence, D 3
Tully 3
Blanchflower, D 2
Casey 2
Clements 2
Doherty, P 2
Feeney (2002–6) 2
Finney 2
Gillespie 2
Harkin 2
Lennon 2
McMahon 2
Neill, W 2
O'Neill, J 2
Peacock 2
Penney 2
Stewart, I 2
Whitley 2
Barr 1
Black 1
Blanchflower, J 1
Brennan 1
Campbell, W 1
Caskey 1
Cassidy 1
Cochrane, T 1
Crossan, E 1
D'Arcy 1
Davis 1
Doherty, L 1
Elder 1
Ferguson 1
Ferris 1
Griffin 1
Hill, C 1
Humphries 1
Hunter, A 1
Hunter, B 1
Johnston 1
Jones, J 1
Jones,S 1
Lafferty 1
McCann 1
McCartney 1
McClelland (1961) 1
McCrory 1
McCurdy 1
McGarry 1
McVeigh 1
Moreland 1
Morrow 1
Murdock 1
Nelson 1
Nicholl, J 1
O'Boyle 1
O'Kane 1
Patterson, D 1
Rowland 1
Sproule 1
Stevenson 1
Walker 1
Welsh 1
Williams 1
Wilson, D 1

SCOTLAND

Dalglish 30
Law 30
Reilly 22
McCoist 19
Johnston, M 14
Collins, J 12
Gilzean 12
Steel 12
Jordan 11
Collins, R 10
Johnstone, R 10
McFadden 10
Stein 10
Gallacher 9
McStay 9
Miller, K 9
Mudie 9
St John 9
Brand 8
Gemmill, A 8
Leggat 8
Robertson, J (1978-84) . 8
Wilson, D 8
Dodds 7
Durie 7
Gray, A 7
Wark 7
Booth 6
Brown, A 6
Cooper 6
Dailly 6
Gough 6
Liddell 6
Murdoch 6
Rioch 6
Waddell 6
Boyd, K 5
Henderson, W 5
Hutchison 5
Macari 5
Masson 5
McAllister G. 5
McQueen 5
Nevin 5
Nicholas 5
O'Hare 5
Scott, A 5
Strachan 5
Young, A 5
Archibald 4
Caldow 4
Crawford 4
Fletcher 4
Hamilton 4
Hartford 4
Herd, D. 4
Jackson, D 4
Johnstone, J 4
Lorimer 4
Mackay, D 4
Mason 4

McGinlay 4
McKinlay, W. 4
McLaren 4
O'Connor 4
Smith, G 4
Souness 4
Baxter 3
Bremner, W 3
Burley, C 3
Chalmers 3
Gibson 3
Graham, G 3
Gray, E 3
Greig 3
Hendry 3
Lennox 3
MacDougall 3
McCann 3
McInally, A 3
McNeill 3
McPhail 3
Morris 3
Robertson, J (1991-5) .. 3
Sturrock 3
Thompson, ... 3
White 3
Baird, S 2
Bauld 2
Burke 2
Caldwell, G 2
Cameron 2
Ferguson, B 2
Flavell 2
Fleming 2
Graham, A 2
Harper 2
Hewie 2
Holton 2
Hopkin 2
Houliston 2
Jess 2
Johnstone, A 2
Johnstone, D 2
McClair 2
McGhee 2
McMillan 2
Pettigrew 2
Ring 2
Robertson, A 2
Shearer, D 2
Aitken, R 1
Bannon 1
Beattie 1
Bett 1
Bone 1
Boyd 1
Brazil 1
Buckley 1
Burns 1
Calderwood 1
Campbell, R 1
Combe 1
Conn 1
Craig 1
Curran 1
Davidson 1
Dickov 1
Dobie 1
Docherty 1
Duncan, M 1
Elliott 1
Fernie 1
Freedman 1
Gray, F 1
Gemmell, T 1
Hartley 1
Henderson, J 1
Holt 1
Howie 1
Hughes, J 1
Hunter, W 1
Hutchison, T 1
Jackson, C 1
Jardine 1
Johnstone, L 1
Kyle 1
Lambert 1
Linwood 1
Mackay, G 1
MacLeod 1
Maloney 1
McAvennie 1
McCall 1
McCalliog 1
McKenzie 1
McKimmie 1
McKinnon 1
McLean 1
McLintock 1
McSwegan 1
Miller, W 1
Mitchell 1
Morgan 1
Mulhall 1
Murray, J 1
Narey 1
Naysmith 1
Ormond 1
Orr 1
Parlane 1
Provan, D 1
Quashie 1
Quinn 1
Ritchie, P 1
Sharp 1
Stewart, R 1
Thornton 1
Wallace, I 1
Webster 1
Weir, A 1
Weir, D 1
Wilkie 1

WALES

Rush 28
Allchurch, I 23
Ford 23
Saunders 22
Hughes, M 16
Charles, John 15
Jones, C 15
Hartson 14
Bellamy 13
Toshack 13
Earnshaw 12
Giggs 12
James, L 10
Davies, R.T 8
James, R 8
Vernon 8
Davies, R.W 7
Flynn 7
Speed 7
Walsh, I 7
Charles, M 6
Curtis, A 6
Griffiths, A 6
Medwin 6
Pembridge 6
Clarke, R 5
Davies, S 5
Koumas 5
Leek 5
Blake 4
Coleman 4
Deacy 4
Edwards, I 4
Tapscott 4
Thomas, M 4
Woosnam 4
Allen, M 3
Bodin 3
Bowen, M 3
England 3
Melville 3
Palmer, D 3
Rees, R 3
Robinson, J 3
Bale 2
Davies, G 2
Durban, A 2
Dwyer 2
Edwards, G 2
Giles, D 2
Godfrey 2
Griffiths, M 2

Hodges 2
Horne 2
Jones, Barrie 2
Jones, Bryn 2
Lowrie 2
Nicholas 2
Phillips, D 2
Reece, G 2
Savage 2
Slatter 2
Symons 2
Yorath 2
Barnes 1
Blackmore 1
Bowen, D 1
Boyle, T 1
Burgess, R 1
Charles, Jeremy 1
Evans, I 1
Foulkes 1
Harris, C 1
Hewitt, R 1
Hockey 1
Jones, A 1
Jones, D 1
Jones, J 1
Krzywicki 1
Llewellyn 1
Lovell 1
Mahoney 1
Moore, G. 1
O'Sullivan 1
Parry 1
Paul 1
Powell, A 1
Powell, D 1
Price, P 1
Roberts, P 1
Robinson, C 1
Smallman 1
Taylor 1
Williams, A 1
Williams, G.E 1
Williams, G.G 1
Young 1

REP. OF IRELAND

Keane, Robbie 29
Quinn, N 21
Stapleton 20
Aldridge 19
Cascarino 19
Givens 19
Cantwell 14
Daly 13
Harte 11
Brady 9
Connolly 9
Keane, Roy 9
Kelly, D 9
Morrison 9
Sheedy 9
Curtis 8
Grealish 8
McGrath, P 8
Staunton 8
Duff 7
Fitzsimons 7
Kilbane 7
Ringstead 7
Townsend 7
Breen G 6
Coyne 6
Houghton 6
McEvoy 6
Martin, C 6
Moran 6
Cummins 5
Dunne, R 5
Fagan, F 5
Giles 5
Holland 5
Lawrenson 5
Rogers 5
Sheridan 5
Treacy 5
Walsh, D 5
Byrne, J 4
Doherty 4
Irwin 4
McGee 4
Martin, M 4
O'Neill, K 4
Reid, A 4
Robinson 4
Tuohy 4
Carey, J 3
Coad 3
Conway 3
Doyle 3
Farrell 3
Fogarty 3
Haverty 3
Ireland 3
Kennedy, Mark 3
Kinsella 3
McAteer 3
Ryan, R 3
Waddock 3
Walsh, M 3
Whelan 3
Barrett 2
Conroy 2
Dennehy 2
Eglington 2
Fallon 2
Fitzgerald, P 2
Foley 2
Gavin 2
Hale 2
Hand 2
Hurley 2
Kelly, G 2
Leech 2
McCarthy 2
McLoughlin 2
O'Connor 2
O'Farrell 2
O'Reilly, J 2
Reid, S 2
Ambrose 1
Anderson 1
Carroll 1
Dempsey 1
Duffy 1
Elliott 1
Finnan 1
Fitzgerald, J 1
Fullam, J 1
Galvin 1
Glynn 1
Grimes 1
Healy 1
Holmes 1
Hughton 1
Kavanagh 1
Kernaghan 1
Long 1
Mancini 1
McCann 1
McPhail 1
Miller 1
Mooney 1
Moroney 1
Mulligan 1
O'Brien 1
O'Callaghan, K 1
O'Keefe 1
O'Leary 1
O'Neill, F 1
O' Shea 1
Ryan, G 1
Slaven 1
Sloan 1
Strahan 1
Waters 1

HOME INTERNATIONAL RESULTS

Note: In the results that follow, W.C. = World Cup, E.C. = European Championship. TF = Tournoi de France. For Northern Ireland read Ireland before 1921.

ENGLAND V. SCOTLAND

Played 110; England 45; Scotland 41; drawn 24. Goals: England 192, Scotland 169.

		E	S			E	S
1872	Glasgow	0	0	1932	Wembley	3	0
1873	The Oval	4	2	1933	Glasgow	1	2
1874	Glasgow	1	2	1934	Wembley	3	0
1875	The Oval	2	2	1935	Glasgow	0	2
1876	Glasgow	0	3	1936	Wembley	1	1
1877	The Oval	1	3	1937	Glasgow	1	3
1878	Glasgow	2	7	1938	Wembley	0	1
1879	The Oval	5	4	1939	Glasgow	2	1
1880	Glasgow	4	5	1947	Wembley	1	1
1881	The Oval	1	6	1948	Glasgow	2	0
1882	Glasgow	1	5	1949	Wembley	1	3
1883	Sheffield	2	3	1950	Glasgow (W.C.)	1	0
1884	Glasgow	0	1	1951	Wembley	2	3
1885	The Oval	1	1	1952	Glasgow	2	1
1886	Glasgow	1	1	1953	Wembley	2	2
1887	Blackburn	2	3	1954	Glasgow (W.C.)	4	2
1888	Glasgow	5	0	1955	Wembley	7	2
1889	The Oval	2	3	1956	Glasgow	1	1
1890	Glasgow	1	1	1957	Wembley	2	1
1891	Blackburn	2	1	1958	Glasgow	4	0
1892	Glasgow	4	1	1959	Wembley	1	0
1893	Richmond	5	2	1960	Glasgow	1	1
1894	Glasgow	2	2	1961	Wembley	9	3
1895	Goodison Park	3	0	1962	Glasgow	0	2
1896	Glasgow	1	2	1963	Wembley	1	2
1897	Crystal Palace	1	2	1964	Glasgow	0	1
1898	Glasgow	3	1	1965	Wembley	2	2
1899	Birmingham	2	1	1966	Glasgow	4	3
1900	Glasgow	1	4	1967	Wembley (E.C.)	2	3
1901	Crystal Palace	2	2	1968	Glasgow (E.C.)	1	1
1902	Birmingham	2	2	1969	Wembley	4	1
1903	Sheffield	1	2	1970	Glasgow	0	0
1904	Glasgow	1	0	1971	Wembley	3	1
1905	Crystal Palace	1	0	1972	Glasgow	1	0
1906	Glasgow	1	2	1973	Glasgow	5	0
1907	Newcastle	1	1	1973	Wembley	1	0
1908	Glasgow	1	1	1974	Glasgow	0	2
1909	Crystal Palace	2	0	1975	Wembley	5	1
1910	Glasgow	0	2	1976	Glasgow	1	2
1911	Goodison Park	1	1	1977	Wembley	1	2
1912	Glasgow	1	1	1978	Glasgow	1	0
1913	Stamford Bridge	1	0	1979	Wembley	3	1
1914	Glasgow	1	3	1980	Glasgow	2	0
1920	Sheffield	5	4	1981	Wembley	0	1
1921	Glasgow	0	3	1982	Glasgow	1	0
1922	Birmingham	0	1	1983	Wembley	2	0
1923	Glasgow	2	2	1984	Glasgow	1	1
1924	Wembley	1	1	1985	Glasgow	0	1
1925	Glasgow	0	2	1986	Wembley	2	1
1926	Manchester	0	1	1987	Glasgow	0	0
1927	Glasgow	2	1	1988	Wembley	1	0
1928	Wembley	1	5	1989	Glasgow	2	0
1929	Glasgow	0	1	1996	Wembley (E.C.)	2	0
1930	Wembley	5	2	1999	Glasgow (E.C.)	2	0
1931	Glasgow	0	2	1999	Wembley (E.C.)	0	1

ENGLAND V. WALES

Played 99; England won 64; Wales 14; drawn 21. Goals: England 242, Wales 90.

		E	W
1879	The Oval	2	1
1880	Wrexham	3	2
1881	Blackburn	0	1
1882	Wrexham	3	5
1883	The Oval	5	0
1884	Wrexham	4	0
1885	Blackburn	1	1
1886	Wrexham	3	1
1887	The Oval	4	0
1888	Crewe	5	1
1889	Stoke	4	1
1890	Wrexham	3	1
1891	Sunderland	4	1
1892	Wrexham	2	0
1893	Stoke	6	0
1894	Wrexham	5	1
1895	Queens Club, London	1	1
1896	Cardiff	9	1
1897	Bramall Lane	4	0
1898	Wrexham	3	0
1899	Bristol	4	0
1900	Cardiff	1	1
1901	Newcastle	6	0
1902	Wrexham	0	0
1903	Portsmouth	2	1
1904	Wrexham	2	2
1905	Anfield	3	1
1906	Cardiff	1	0
1907	Fulham	1	1
1908	Wrexham	7	1
1909	Nottingham	2	0
1910	Cardiff	1	0
1911	Millwall	3	0
1912	Wrexham	2	0
1913	Bristol	4	3
1914	Cardiff	2	0
1920	Highbury	1	2
1921	Cardiff	0	0
1922	Anfield	1	0
1923	Cardiff	2	2
1924	Blackburn	1	2
1925	Swansea	2	1
1926	Selhurst Park	1	3
1927	Wrexham	3	3
1927	Burnley	1	2
1928	Swansea	3	2
1929	Stamford Bridge	6	0
1930	Wrexham	4	0
1931	Anfield	3	1
1932	Wrexham	0	0

		E	W
1933	Newcastle	1	2
1934	Cardiff	4	0
1935	Wolverhampton	1	2
1936	Cardiff	1	2
1937	Middlesbrough	2	1
1938	Cardiff	2	4
1946	Maine Road	3	0
1947	Cardiff	3	0
1948	Villa Park	1	0
1949	Cardiff (W.C.)	4	1
1950	Sunderland	4	2
1951	Cardiff	1	1
1952	Wembley	5	2
1953	Cardiff (W.C.)	4	1
1954	Wembley	3	2
1955	Cardiff	1	2
1956	Wembley	3	1
1957	Cardiff	4	0
1958	Villa Park	2	2
1959	Cardiff	1	1
1960	Wembley	5	1
1961	Cardiff	1	1
1962	Wembley	4	0
1963	Cardiff	4	0
1964	Wembley	2	1
1965	Cardiff	0	0
1966	Wembley (E.C.)	5	1
1967	Cardiff (E.C.)	3	0
1969	Wembley	2	1
1970	Cardiff	1	1
1971	Wembley	0	0
1972	Cardiff	3	0
1972	Cardiff (W.C.)	1	0
1973	Wembley (W.C.)	1	1
1973	Wembley	3	0
1974	Cardiff	2	0
1975	Wembley	2	2
1976	Wrexham	2	1
1976	Cardiff	1	0
1977	Wembley	0	1
1978	Cardiff	3	1
1979	Wembley	0	0
1980	Wrexham	1	4
1981	Wembley	0	0
1982	Cardiff	1	0
1983	Wembley	2	1
1984	Wrexham	0	1
2004	Old Trafford (W.C.)	2	0
2005	Cardiff (W.C.)	1	0

ENGLAND V. N. IRELAND

Played 98; England won 75; Ireland 7; drawn 16. Goals: England 323, Ireland 81.

		E	I
1882	Belfast	13	0
1883	Aigburth, Liverpool	7	0
1884	Belfast	8	1
1885	Whelley Range, Manchester	4	0
1886	Belfast	6	1
1887	Bramall Lane	7	0
1888	Belfast	5	1
1889	Goodison Park	6	1
1890	Belfast	9	1
1891	Wolverhampton	6	1
1892	Belfast	2	0
1893	Perry Barr, Birmingham	6	1
1894	Belfast	2	2
1895	Derby	9	0
1896	Belfast	2	0
1897	Nottingham	6	0
1898	Belfast	3	2
1899	Sunderland	13	2
1900	Dublin	2	0
1901	Southampton	3	0
1902	Belfast	1	0
1903	Wolverhampton	4	0
1904	Belfast	3	1
1905	Middlesbrough	1	1
1906	Belfast	5	0
1907	Goodison Park	1	0
1908	Belfast	3	1
1909	Bradford P.A.	4	0
1910	Belfast	1	1
1911	Derby	2	1
1912	Dublin	6	1
1913	Belfast	1	2
1914	Middlesbrough	0	3
1919	Belfast	1	1
1920	Sunderland	2	0
1921	Belfast	1	1
1922	West Bromwich	2	0
1923	Belfast	1	2
1924	Goodison Park	3	1
1925	Belfast	0	0
1926	Anfield	3	3
1927	Belfast	0	2
1928	Goodison Park	2	1
1929	Belfast	3	0
1930	Bramall Lane	5	1
1931	Belfast	6	2
1932	Blackpool	1	0
1933	Belfast	3	0
1935	Goodison Park	2	1
1935	Belfast	3	1
1936	Stoke	3	1
1937	Belfast	5	1
1938	Old Trafford	7	0
1946	Belfast	7	2
1947	Goodison Park	2	2
1948	Belfast	6	2
1949	Maine Road (W.C.)	9	2
1950	Belfast	4	1
1951	Villa Park	2	0
1952	Belfast	2	2
1953	Goodison Park (W.C.)	3	1
1954	Belfast	2	0
1955	Wembley	3	0
1956	Belfast	1	1
1957	Wembley	2	3
1958	Belfast	3	3
1959	Wembley	2	1
1960	Belfast	5	2
1961	Wembley	1	1
1962	Belfast	3	1
1963	Wembley	8	3
1964	Belfast	4	3
1965	Wembley	2	1
1966	Belfast (E.C.)	2	0
1967	Wembley (E.C.)	2	0
1969	Belfast	3	1
1970	Wembley	3	1
1971	Belfast	1	0
1972	Wembley	0	1
1973	*Goodison Park	2	1
1974	Wembley	1	0
1975	Belfast	0	0
1976	Wembley	4	0
1977	Belfast	2	1
1978	Wembley	1	0
1979	Wembley (E.C.)	4	0
1979	Belfast	2	0
1979	Belfast (E.C.)	5	1
1980	Wembley	1	1
1982	Wembley	4	0
1983	Belfast	0	0
1984	Wembley	1	0
1985	Belfast (W.C.)	1	0
1985	Wembley (W.C.)	0	0
1986	Wembley (E.C.)	3	0
1987	Belfast (E.C.)	2	0
2005	Old Trafford (W.C.)	4	0
2005	Belfast (W.C.)	0	1

(* Switched from Belfast because of political situation in N. Ireland)

SCOTLAND V. WALES

Played 103; Scotland won 60; Wales 20; drawn 23. Goals: Scotland 237, Wales 116.

		S	W
1876	Glasgow	4	0
1877	Wrexham	2	0
1878	Glasgow	9	0
1879	Wrexham	3	0
1880	Glasgow	5	1
1881	Wrexham	5	1
1882	Glasgow	5	0
1883	Wrexham	3	0
1884	Glasgow	4	1
1885	Wrexham	8	1
1886	Glasgow	4	1
1887	Wrexham	2	0
1888	Edinburgh	5	1
1889	Wrexham	0	0
1890	Paisley	5	0
1891	Wrexham	4	3
1892	Edinburgh	6	1
1893	Wrexham	8	0
1894	Kilmarnock	5	2
1895	Wrexham	2	2
1896	Dundee	4	0
1897	Wrexham	2	2
1898	Motherwell	5	2
1899	Wrexham	6	0
1900	Aberdeen	5	2
1901	Wrexham	1	1
1902	Greenock	5	1
1903	Cardiff	1	0
1904	Dundee	1	1
1905	Wrexham	1	3
1906	Edinburgh	0	2
1907	Wrexham	0	1
1908	Dundee	2	1
1909	Wrexham	2	3
1910	Kilmarnock	1	0
1911	Cardiff	2	2
1912	Tynecastle	1	0
1913	Wrexham	0	0
1914	Glasgow	0	0
1920	Cardiff	1	1
1921	Aberdeen	2	1
1922	Wrexham	1	2
1923	Paisley	2	0
1924	Cardiff	0	2
1925	Tynecastle	3	1
1926	Cardiff	3	0
1927	Glasgow	3	0
1928	Wrexham	2	2
1929	Glasgow	4	2
1930	Cardiff	4	2
1931	Glasgow	1	1
1932	Wrexham	3	2
1933	Edinburgh	2	5
1934	Cardiff	2	3
1935	Aberdeen	3	2
1936	Cardiff	1	1
1937	Dundee	1	2
1938	Cardiff	1	2
1939	Edinburgh	3	2
1946	Wrexham	1	3
1947	Glasgow	1	2
1948	Cardiff (W.C.)	3	1
1949	Glasgow	2	0
1950	Cardiff	3	1
1951	Glasgow	0	1
1952	Cardiff (W.C.)	2	1
1953	Glasgow	3	3
1954	Cardiff	1	0
1955	Glasgow	2	0
1956	Cardiff	2	2
1957	Glasgow	1	1
1958	Cardiff	3	0
1959	Glasgow	1	1
1960	Cardiff	0	2
1961	Glasgow	2	0
1962	Cardiff	3	2
1963	Glasgow	2	1
1964	Cardiff	2	3
1965	Glasgow (E.C.)	4	1
1966	Cardiff (E.C.)	1	1
1967	Glasgow	3	2
1969	Wrexham	5	3
1970	Glasgow	0	0
1971	Cardiff	0	0
1972	Glasgow	1	0
1973	Wrexham	2	0
1974	Glasgow	2	0
1975	Cardiff	2	2
1976	Glasgow	3	1
1977	Glasgow (W.C.)	1	0
1977	Wrexham	0	0
1977	Anfield (W.C.)	2	0
1978	Glasgow	1	1
1979	Cardiff	0	3
1980	Glasgow	1	0
1981	Swansea	0	2
1982	Glasgow	1	0
1983	Cardiff	2	0
1984	Glasgow	2	1
1985	Glasgow (W.C.)	0	1
1985	Cardiff (W.C.)	1	1
1997	Kilmarnock	0	1
2004	Cardiff	0	4

SCOTLAND V. N. IRELAND

Played 93; Scotland won 62; Ireland 15; drawn 16. Goals: Scotland 257, Ireland 81.

		S	I			S	I
1884	Belfast	5	0	1934	Glasgow	1	2
1885	Glasgow	8	2	1935	Belfast	1	2
1886	Belfast	7	2	1936	Edinburgh	2	1
1887	Belfast	4	1	1937	Belfast	3	1
1888	Belfast	10	2	1938	Aberdeen	1	1
1889	Glasgow	7	0	1939	Belfast	2	0
1890	Belfast	4	1	1946	Glasgow	0	0
1891	Glasgow	2	1	1947	Belfast	0	2
1892	Belfast	3	2	1948	Glasgow	3	2
1893	Glasgow	6	1	1949	Belfast	8	2
1894	Belfast	2	1	1950	Glasgow	6	1
1895	Glasgow	3	1	1951	Belfast	3	0
1896	Belfast	3	3	1952	Glasgow	1	1
1897	Glasgow	5	1	1953	Belfast	3	1
1898	Belfast	3	0	1954	Glasgow	2	2
1899	Glasgow	9	1	1955	Belfast	1	2
1900	Belfast	3	0	1956	Glasgow	1	0
1901	Glasgow	11	0	1957	Belfast	1	1
1902	Belfast	5	1	1958	Glasgow	2	2
1902	Belfast	3	0	1959	Belfast	4	0
1903	Glasgow	0	2	1960	Glasgow	5	1
1904	Dublin	1	1	1961	Belfast	6	1
1905	Glasgow	4	0	1962	Glasgow	5	1
1906	Dublin	1	0	1963	Belfast	1	2
1907	Glasgow	3	0	1964	Glasgow	3	2
1908	Dublin	5	0	1965	Belfast	2	3
1909	Glasgow	5	0	1966	Glasgow	2	1
1910	Belfast	0	1	1967	Belfast	0	1
1911	Glasgow	2	0	1969	Glasgow	1	1
1912	Belfast	4	1	1970	Belfast	1	0
1913	Dublin	2	1	1971	Glasgow	0	1
1914	Belfast	1	1	1972	Glasgow	2	0
1920	Glasgow	3	0	1973	Glasgow	1	2
1921	Belfast	2	0	1974	Glasgow	0	1
1922	Glasgow	2	1	1975	Glasgow	3	0
1923	Belfast	1	0	1976	Glasgow	3	0
1924	Glasgow	2	0	1977	Glasgow	3	0
1925	Belfast	3	0	1978	Glasgow	1	1
1926	Glasgow	4	0	1979	Glasgow	1	0
1927	Belfast	2	0	1980	Belfast	0	1
1928	Glasgow	0	1	1981	Glasgow (W.C.)	1	1
1929	Belfast	7	3	1981	Glasgow	2	0
1930	Glasgow	3	1	1981	Belfast (W.C.)	0	0
1931	Belfast	0	0	1982	Belfast	1	1
1932	Glasgow	3	1	1983	Glasgow	0	0
1933	Belfast	4	0	1984	Belfast	0	2
				1992	Glasgow	1	0

WALES V. N. IRELAND

Played 93; Wales won 43; Ireland 27; drawn 23. Goals: Wales 187, Ireland 131.

		W	I
1882	Wrexham	7	1
1883	Belfast	1	1
1884	Wrexham	6	0
1885	Belfast	8	2
1886	Wrexham	5	0
1887	Belfast	1	4
1888	Wrexham	11	0
1889	Belfast	3	1
1890	Shrewsbury	5	2
1891	Belfast	2	7
1892	Bangor	1	1
1893	Belfast	3	4
1894	Swansea	4	1
1895	Belfast	2	2
1896	Wrexham	6	1
1897	Belfast	3	4
1898	Llandudno	0	1
1899	Belfast	0	1
1900	Llandudno	2	0
1901	Belfast	1	0
1902	Cardiff	0	3
1903	Belfast	0	2
1904	Bangor	0	1
1905	Belfast	2	2
1906	Wrexham	4	4
1907	Belfast	3	2
1908	Aberdare	0	1
1909	Belfast	3	2
1910	Wrexham	4	1
1911	Belfast	2	1
1912	Cardiff	2	3
1913	Belfast	1	0
1914	Wrexham	1	2
1920	Belfast	2	2
1921	Swansea	2	1
1922	Belfast	1	1
1923	Wrexham	0	3
1924	Belfast	1	0
1925	Wrexham	0	0
1926	Belfast	0	3
1927	Cardiff	2	2
1928	Belfast	2	1
1929	Wrexham	2	2
1930	Belfast	0	7
1931	Wrexham	3	2
1932	Belfast	0	4

		W	I
1933	Wrexham	4	1
1934	Belfast	1	1
1935	Wrexham	3	1
1936	Belfast	2	3
1937	Wrexham	4	1
1938	Belfast	0	1
1939	Wrexham	3	1
1947	Belfast	1	2
1948	Wrexham	2	0
1949	Belfast	2	0
1950	Wrexham (W.C.)	0	0
1951	Belfast	2	1
1952	Swansea	3	0
1953	Belfast	3	2
1954	Wrexham (W.C.)	1	2
1955	Belfast	3	2
1956	Cardiff	1	1
1957	Belfast	0	0
1958	Cardiff	1	1
1959	Belfast	1	4
1960	Wrexham	3	2
1961	Belfast	5	1
1962	Cardiff	4	0
1963	Belfast	4	1
1964	Swansea	2	3
1965	Belfast	5	0
1966	Cardiff	1	4
1967	Belfast (E.C.)	0	0
1968	Wrexham (E.C.)	2	0
1969	Belfast	0	0
1970	Swansea	1	0
1971	Belfast	0	1
1972	Wrexham	0	0
1973	*Goodison Park	0	1
1974	Wrexham	1	0
1975	Belfast	0	1
1976	Swansea	1	0
1977	Belfast	1	1
1978	Wrexham	1	0
1979	Belfast	1	1
1980	Cardiff	0	1
1982	Wrexham	3	0
1983	Belfast	1	0
1984	Swansea	1	1
2004	Cardiff (W.C.)	2	2
2005	Belfast (W.C.)	3	2
2007	Belfast	0	0

(* Switched from Belfast because of political situation in N. Ireland)

BRITISH AND IRISH UNDER-21 INTERNATIONALS 2006-07

EUROPEAN UNDER-21 CHAMPIONSHIP QUALIFYING

ENGLAND 2, MOLDOVA 2

Group 8, Portman Road (13,556), Tuesday, August 15, 2006

England: Carson (Liverpool), Richards (Manchester City), Taylor (Newcastle Utd.), Ferdinand (West Ham Utd.), Baines (Wigan Athletic), Routledge (Tottenham), Reo-Coker (West Ham Utd.), Huddlestone (Tottenham), Bentley (Blackburn Rov.) (Ambrose, Charlton Athletic, 78), Walcott (Arsenal) (Jerome, Birmingham City, 67), Nugent (Preston N.E.).

Scorers – England: Walcott (3), Nugent (76). **Moldova:** Alexeev (75), Zislis (86). **Half-time:** 1-0.

SLOVENIA 1, SCOTLAND 0

Group 14, Murska Sobota (2,250), Wednesday, August 16, 2006

Scotland: Marshall (Celtic),Whittaker (Hibernian), Diamond (Aberdeen), Broadfoot (St Mirren), Wilson (Celtic), Brown (Hibernian), Adam (Rangers) (Beattie, Celtic, 66),Thomson (Hibernian), Wallace (Celtic) (Quinn, Celtic, 66), Naismith (Kilmarnock), Elliott (Hearts) (Foster, Aberdeen, 75).

Scorer – Slovenia: Burgic (57). **Half-time:** 0.0

ISRAEL 3, WALES 2

Group 13, Waalwijk, Hol (100), Wednesday, August 16, 2006

Wales: Price (Ipswich Town), Eardley (Oldham Athletic), Jacobson (Cardiff City), Critchell (Southampton) (Marc Williams, Wrexham, 52), Morgan (MK Dons) (James, Southampton, 86), Mike Williams (Wrexham), Blake (Cardiff City) (Gunter, Cardiff City, 49), Crofts (Gillingham), C. Davies (Verona), Edwards (Shrewsbury Town), A. Davies (Yeovil Town). **Sent-off:** Marc Williams, C. Davies.

Scorers – Israel: Tamuz (26), Srur (64), Rafaelov (78 pen). **Wales:** Marc Williams (60, 66). **Half-time:** 1-0.

ROMANIA 3, NORTHERN IRELAND 0

Group 10, Urzoceni (1,000), Wednesday, August 16, 2006

Northern Ireland: McGovern (Celtic), Ward (Glentoran), Hughes (Lincoln City), McArdle (Sheffield Wed.), McChrystal (Derry City), Evans (Manchester Utd.), Gilfillan (Gretna) (Clarke, Newry, 65), Brunt (Sheffield Wed.), Thompson (Linfield) (Stewart, unatt, 82), Shiels (Hibernian), Scullion (Dungannon) (Turner, Sligo Rov., 76).

Scorers – Romania: Pulhac (33), Keseru (41), Florescu (84). **Half-time:** 2-0.

GREECE 0, REPUBLIC OF IRELAND 2

Group 4, Athens (3,000), Wednesday, August 16, 2006

Republic of Ireland: Doyle (Birmingham City), Foley (Luton Town), Painter (Birmingham City), Bruce (Ipswich Town), McShane (W.B.A.), Keegan (Drogheda Utd.), Flood (Cardiff City), Whelan (Sheffield Wed.), Timlin (Fulham), Deery (Derry City), Ward (Bohemians) (Keogh, Scunthorpe Utd., 80).

Scorers – Republic of Ireland: McShane (10), Whelan (52). **Half-time:** 0-1.

SCOTLAND 1, FRANCE 3

Group 14, Pittodrie (11,950), Friday, September 1, 2006

Scotland: Marshall (Celtic), Wilson (Celtic), Smith (Rangers), Thomson (Hibernian) (Wallace, Sunderland, 46), Diamond (Aberdeen) (Hutton, Rangers, 46), Broadfoot (St Mirren), Whittaker (Hibernian), Brown (Hibernian), Beattie (Celtic) (Fletcher, Hibernian, 64).Adam (Rangers), Naismith (Kilmarnock).

Scorers – Scotland: Adam (86 pen). **France:** Briand (3), Sinama Pongolle (16), Gourcuff (83). **Half-time:** 0-2.

NORTHERN IRELAND 2, GERMANY 3

Group 10, Lurgan (1,500), Friday, September 1, 2006

Northern Ireland: McGovern (Celtic), Ward (Glentoran) (Stewart, unatt, 75), Hughes (Lincoln City), Evans (Manchester Utd.), McArdle (Sheffield Wed.), Smylie (Livingston) (Turner, Sligo Rov., 57), Gilfillan (Gretna), Clarke (Newry), Thompson (Linfield), Shiels (Hibernian), Scullion (Dungannon) (Buchanan, Bury, 59).

Scorers – Northern Ireland: Shiels (69 pen), Stewart (81). **Germany:** Hilbert (13), Helmes (36), Trochowski 66). **Half-time:** 0-2.

REPUBLIC OF IRELAND 0, BELGIUM 1

Group 4, Galway (1,500), Friday, September 1, 2006

Republic of Ireland: Doyle (Birmingham City), Foley (Luton Town), Painter (Birmingham City), Bruce (Ipswich Town), McShane (W.B.A.), Keegan (Drogheda Utd.), Deery (Derry City) (O'Donovan, Cork City, 78), Whelan (Sheffield Wed.), Flood (Cardiff City), Ward (Bohemians) (Dixon, Tottenham, 88), Timlin (Fulham) (Keogh, Scunthorpe Utd., 68).

Scorer – Belgium: Martens (58). **Half-time:** 0-0.

WALES 0, TURKEY 0

Group 13, Ninian Park (731), Saturday, September 2, 2006

Wales: (Price, Ipswich Town), Eardley (Oldham Athletic), Bale (Southampton), James (Southampton), Morgan (MK Dons), Mike Williams (Wrexham), Macdonald (Swansea City), Edwards (Shrewsbury Town), Fleetwood (Cardiff City) (Haldane, Bristol Rov., 73), Davies (Yeovil Town), Jacobson (Cardiff City).

SWITZERLAND 2, ENGLAND 3

Group 8, Lucerne (8,500), Wednesday, September 6, 2006

England: Carson (Liverpool), Hoyte (Arsenal), Ferdinand (West Ham Utd.), Taylor (Newcastle Utd.), Baines (Wigan Athletic), Huddlestone (Tottenham). Reo-Coker (West Ham Utd.), Bentley (Blackburn Rov.) (Milner, Newcastle Utd., 46), Walcott (Arsenal), Nugent (Preston N.E.) (Jerome, Birmingham City, 68), Routledge (Tottenham) (Young, Watford, 78).

Scorers – Switzerland: Vonlanthen (28), Barnetta (70). **England:** Walcott (13), Nugent (18), Milner (88). **Half-time:** 1-2.

ENGLAND 1, GERMANY 0

Play-off, first leg, Ricoh Arena (30,919), Friday, October 6, 2006

England: Carson (Liverpool), Richards (Manchester City), Taylor (Newcastle Utd.), Ferdinand (West Ham Utd.), Baines (Wigan Athletic), Huddlestone (Tottenham), Reo-Coker (West Ham Utd.), Milner (Newcastle Utd.), Walcott (Arsenal) (Young, Watford, 65), Nugent (Preston N.E.) (Watson, Crystal Palace, 80), Routledge (Tottenham) (Agbonlahor, Aston Villa, 70).

Scorer – England: Baines (77). **Half-time:** 0-0.

GERMANY 0, ENGLAND 2

Play-off, second leg, Leverkusen (20,800), Tuesday, October 10, 2006

England: Carson (Liverpool), Richards (Manchester City), Taylor (Newcastle Utd.), Ferdinand (West Ham Utd.), Baines (Wigan Athletic), Agbonlahor (Aston Villa) (Walcott, Arsenal, 77), Reo-Coker (West Ham Utd.), Huddlestone (Tottenham), Milner (Newcastle Utd.), Young (Watford) (Jerome, Birmingham City, 90), Nugent (Preston N.E.) (Hoyte, Arsenal, 67). **Sent-off:** Taylor.

Scorer – England: Walcott (84, 90). **Half-time:** 0-0.

QUALIFYING TABLES

GROUP 1

	P	W	D	L	F	A	Pts
Bosnia-Hertz.	2	1	1	0	4	3	4
Armenia	2	1	0	1	3	3	3
Norway	2	0	1	1	1	2	1

GROUP 2

	P	W	D	L	F	A	Pts
Spain	2	2	0	0	7	2	6
Slovakia	2	0	1	1	2	4	1
Albania	2	0	1	1	0	3	1

GROUP 3

	P	W	D	L	F	A	Pts
Serbia & Mont.	2	2	0	0	5	1	6
Lithuania	2	1	0	1	1	2	3
Georgia	2	0	0	2	1	4	0

GROUP 4

	P	W	L	D	F	A	Pts
Belgium	2	2	0	0	3	1	6
Republic of Ireland	2	1	0	1	2	1	3
Greece	2	0	0	2	1	4	0

GROUP 5

	P	W	D	L	F	A	Pts
Italy	2	2	0	0	2	0	6
Austria	2	0	1	1	0	1	1
Iceland	2	0	1	1	0	1	1

GROUP 6

	P	W	D	L	F	A	Pts
Russia	2	2	0	0	8	2	6
Hungary	2	1	0	1	6	3	3
Finland	2	0	0	2	1	10	0

GROUP 7

	P	W	D	L	F	A	Pts
Portugal	2	2	0	0	4	0	6
Poland	2	1	0	1	3	3	3
Latvia	2	0	0	2	1	5	0

GROUP 8

	P	W	D	L	F	A	Pts
England	2	1	1	0	5	4	4
Switzerland	2	1	0	1	5	4	3
Moldova	2	0	1	1	3	5	1

GROUP 9

	P	W	D	L	F	A	Pts
Czech Republic	2	2	0	0	4	1	6
Belarus	2	1	0	1	2	2	3
Cyprus	2	0	0	2	0	3	0

GROUP 10

	P	W	D	L	F	A	Pts
Germany	2	2	0	0	8	3	6
Romania	2	1	0	1	4	5	3
Northern Ireland	2	0	0	2	2	6	0

GROUP 11

	P	W	D	L	F	A	Pts
Sweden	2	2	0	0	5	1	6
Denmark	2	1	0	1	3	2	3
Macedonia	2	0	0	2	1	6	0

GROUP 12

	P	W	D	L	F	A	Pts
Bulgaria	2	2	0	0	5	1	6
Ukraine	2	1	0	1	2	4	3
Croatia	2	0	0	2	2	4	0

GROUP 13

	P	W	D	L	F	A	Pts
Israel	2	1	1	0	3	2	4
Turkey	2	0	2	0	0	0	2
Wales	2	0	1	1	2	3	1

GROUP 14

	P	W	D	L	F	A	Pts
France	2	2	0	0	5	1	6
Slovenia	2	1	0	1	1	2	3
Scotland	2	0	0	2	1	4	0

Play-offs to decide Championship finalists (on agg): Belgium 5, Bulgaria 2; Czech Republic 3, Bosnia-Herzegovina 2; **England** 3, Germany 0; Israel 2, France 1; Italy 2, Spain 1; Portugal 4, Russia 4 (Portugal through on away goal); Serbia & Montenegro 5, Sweden 3.

FINALS – HOLLAND

GROUP A

Holland 1 (Maduro 10), Israel 0 – Heerenveen. Att: 23,000. Portugal 0, Belgium 0 – Groningen. Att:12,000. Holland 2 (Babel 33 pen, Rigters 75), Portugal 1 (Veloso 77) – Heerenveen. Att: 19,498. Israel 0, Belgium 1 (Mirallas 82) – Groningen. Att: 5,239. Belgium 2 (Mirallas 9, Pocognoli 70), Holland 2 (Rigters 13, Drenthe 37) – Heerenveen. Att: 24,799. Israel 0, Portugal 4 (Fernandes 37, Vaz Te 45, Veloso 49, Nani 52) – Groningen. Att: 10,883.

GROUP TABLE

	P	W	D	L	F	A	Pts
HOLLAND	3	2	1	0	5	3	7
BELGIUM	3	1	2	0	3	2	5
Portugal	3	1	1	1	5	2	4
Israel	3	0	0	3	0	6	0

GROUP B

ENGLAND 0, CZECH REPUBLIC 0

Arnhem (9,382), Monday, June 11, 2007

England (4-1-4-1): Carson (Liverpool), Hoyte (Arsenal), Onuoha (Manchester City), Cahill (Aston Villa), Baines (Wigan Athletic), Huddlestone (Tottenham) (Noble, West Ham Utd., 82), Milner (Newcastle Utd.) (Lita, Reading, 63), Reo-Coker (West Ham Utd.), Richardson (Manchester Utd.) (Routledge, Tottenham, 56), Young (Aston Villa), Nugent (Preston N.E.).

ENGLAND 2, ITALY 2

Arnhem (21,000), Thursday, June 14, 2007

England (4-4-2): Carson (Liverpool), Hoyte (Arsenal). Taylor (Newcastle Utd.), Onuoha (Manchester City), Baines (Wigan Athletic), Milner (Newcastle Utd.), Reo-Coker (West Ham Utd.) (Richardson, Manchester Utd., 89), Noble (West Ham Utd.), Young (Aston Villa), Nugent (Preston N.E.) (Whittingham, Cardiff City, 68), Lita (Reading) (Vaughan, Everton, 83).

Scorers – England: Nugent (24), Lita (26); **Italy:** Chiellini (36), Aquilani (69). **Half-time:** 2-1.

ENGLAND 2, SERBIA & MONTENEGRO 0

Nijmegen (9,133), Sunday, June 17, 2007

England (4-4-2): Carson (Liverpool), Hoyte (Arsenal), Taylor (Newcastle Utd.), Onuoha (Manchester City), Baines (Wigan Athletic), Richardson (Manchester Utd.), Reo-Coker (West Ham Utd.) (Huddlestone, Tottenham, 88), Noble (West Ham Utd.), Milner (Newcastle Utd.), Lita (Reading) (Derbyshire, Blackburn Rov., 70), Nugent (Preston N.E.). **Sent-off:** Huddlestone.

Scorers – England: Lita (5), Derbyshire (76). **Half-time:** 1-0.

Other Group B results: Serbia & Montenegro 1 (Milovanovic 63), Italy 0 – Nijmegen. Att: 6,000; Czech Republic 0, Serbia & Montenegro 1 (Jankovic 90) – Nijmegen. Att: 6,103. Italy 3 (Aquilani 3, Chiellini 29, Rossi 45), Czech Republic 1 Papadopulos 14) – Arnhem. Att: 7,167.

GROUP TABLE

	P	W	D	L	F	A	Pts
SERBIA & MONT.	3	2	0	1	2	2	6
ENGLAND	3	1	2	0	4	2	5
Italy	3	1	1	1	5	4	4
Czech Republic	3	0	1	2	1	4	1

SEMI-FINALS

ENGLAND 1, HOLLAND 1 (aet, Holland won 13-12 on pens)

Heerenveen (23,467), Wednesday, June 20, 2007

England (4-4-2): Carson (Liverpool), Hoyte (Arsenal), Taylor (Newcastle Utd.), Onuoha (Manchester City), Baines (Wigan Athletic) (Rosenior, Fulham, 46), Milner (Newcastle Utd.), Reo-Coker (West Ham Utd.), Noble (West Ham Utd.), Young (Aston Villa), Lita (Reading) (Ferdinand, West Ham Utd., 86), Nugent (Preston N.E.) (Derbyshire, Blackburn Rov., 77).

Scorers – England: Lita (39). Holland – Rigters (89). **Half-time:** 1-0.

Other Semi-final: Serbia & Montenegro 2 (Kolarov 4, Mrdja 87), Belgium 0 –Arnhem. Att: 17,438.

FINAL

Holland 4 (Bakkal 16, Babel 60, Rigters 67, Bruins 87), **Serbia & Montenegro** 1 (Mrdja 79) – Groningen (19,800), Saturday, June 23, 2007

Stuart Pearce experienced penalty shoot-out heartbreak as a player in the semi-finals of Italia 90 and Euro 96. Now Pearce has tasted disappointment as a manager in charge of England Under-21s for the European Championship in Holland. This time, his injury-hit side lost a marathon series of 32 spot-kicks 13-12 to the host nation, who went on to beat Serbia and Montenegro 4-1 in the final. It was a traumatic end to the season for Pearce, who a month earlier had been sacked by Manchester City after a poor Premiership campaign. But he was full of praise for his young team, who lost a first-half lead established by Leroy Lita to a Dutch equaliser in the 89th minute, were down to ten men in extra-time with the loss of Nedum Onuoha and had Steven Taylor a virtual passenger after another injury.

England's preparations for the tournament had also been disrupted when two potentially key players, Blackburn's David Bentley and Aston Villa's Gabriel Agbonlahor, declined places in the squad. They opened their group series with a goalless draw against the Czech Republic, Lita missing a penalty which could have put them in control. The Reading striker then gave his team a 2-0 lead against Italy two minutes after David Nugent had opened the scoring, but they eventually had to be satisfied with a 2-2 scoreline. Lita was again on the mark against the Serbs and a second goal by Matt Derbyshire ensured England would go through. This victory, however, was soured by racial abuse from Serb supporters and the dismissal of Tom Huddlestone for offensive language two minutes after he came off the bench.

FRIENDLY INTERNATIONALS

LUXEMBOURG 0, REPUBLIC OF IRELAND 2

Mamer (500), Wednesday, October 18, 2006

Republic of Ireland: Quigley (UCD) (Randolph, Charlton Athletic, 46), Kane (Blackburn Rov.), O'Cearuill (Arsenal), R. Keogh (Bristol City) (O'Halloran, Aston Villa, 56), Stapleton (unatt) (Powell, Bohemians, 46), Cregg (Falkirk), Morris (Scunthorpe Utd.) (Hand, Huddersfield Town, 46), Dicker (UCD) (Wilson, Portsmouth, 46), Kelly (Bohemians), A. Keogh (Scunthorpe Utd.), Stokes (Arsenal).

Scorers – Republic of Ireland: Stokes (47), A. Keogh (67). **Half-time:** 0-0.

HOLLAND 0, ENGLAND 1

Alkmaar (15,000), Tuesday, November 14, 2006

England: Carson (Liverpool), Hoyte (Arsenal), Davies (W.B.A.), Kilgallon (Leeds Utd.), Baines (Wigan Athletic) (Rosenior, Fulham, 46), Routledge (Tottenham) (Welsh, Hull City, 78), Milner (Newcastle Utd.) (Whittingham, Aston Villa, 64), Huddlestone (Tottenham), Young (Watford), Nugent (Preston N.E.) (Onuoha, Manchester City, 85), Walcott (Arsenal) (Jerome, Birmingham City, 82).

Scorer – England: Hoyte (10). **Half-time:** 0-1.

ENGLAND 2, SPAIN 2

Pride Park (28,295), Tuesday, February 6, 2007

England: Carson (Liverpool) (Hart, Manchester City, 81), Hoyte (Arsenal), S. Taylor (Newcastle Utd.), Davies (W.B.A.), A. Taylor (Middlesbrough) (Rosenior, Fulham, 62), Milner (Newcastle Utd.) (Lita, Reading, 60), Huddlestone (Tottenham) (Richardson, Manchester Utd., 51), Reo-Coker (West Ham Utd.), Bentley (Blackburn Rov.), Nugent (Preston N.E.), Young (Aston Villa) (Walcott, Arsenal, 46).

Scorers – England: Nugent (50), Lita (79). **Spain:** Soldado (34), Jurado (45). **Half-time:** 0-2.

SCOTLAND 0, GERMANY 2

Broadwood Stadium (2,326), Tuesday, February 6, 2007

Scotland: McNeil (Hibernian) (McDonald, Hearts, 46), Ross (Dunfermline Athletic), Wallace (Hearts), Fitzpatrick (Motherwell) (Considine, Aberdeen, 85), Cuthbert (Celtic), Reynolds (Motherwell), McGlinchey (Celtic) (Smith, Motherwell, 46), Robertson (Dundee Utd.) (Dorrans, Livingston, 46), Naismith (Kilmarnock), Quinn (Celtic) (Adams, Kilmarnock), Conroy (Celtic).

Scorers – Germany: Hunt (22), Flessers (74). **Half-time:** 0-1.

NORTHERN IRELAND 0, WALES 4

Oval (1,200), Tuesday, February 6, 2007

Northern Ireland: Tuffey (Partick Thistle) (Carson, Sunderland, 63), Casement (Ipswich Town), McCaffrey (Queen of South) (Armstrong, Hearts, 46), Cathcart (Manchester Utd.), McArdle (Rochdale) (Taylor, Hearts, 46), Howland (Birmingham City) (Callaghan, Ballymena, 46), Mulgrew (Linfield) (Ward, Torquay Utd., 46), McKenna (Tottenham), Stewart (Linfield), Fordyce (Portsmouth) (Paterson, Grimsby Town, 46), Hazley (Stoke City) (Buchanan, Bury, 55).

Wales: Hennessey (Wolves) (fon Williams, Crewe Alexandra, 57), Gunter (Cardiff City) (Bradley, Walsall, 46), Jacobson (Cardiff City), Edwards (Shrewsbury Town) (Flynn, Crewe Alexandra, 57), R. Williams (Middlesbrough), Mike Williams (Wrexham), Grubb (Bristol City) (C. Jones, Swansea City, 46), Collins (Fulham) (Davies, W.B.A., 46), Vokes (Bournemouth) (Blake, Cardiff City, 66), Evans (Manchester City), Warlow (Lincoln City) (James, Southampton, 71).

Scorers – Northern Ireland: Vokes (1), Jacobson (11), Evans 31, 46). **Half-time:** 0-3.

REPUBLIC OF IRELAND 1, SLOVAKIA 0

Madeira Tournament (1,000), Tuesday, February 27, 2007

Republic of Ireland: Russell (Chelsea), Kane (Blackburn Rov.), Powell (Bohemians), O'Cearuill (Arsenal) (Murphy, MK Dons, 46), O'Halloran (Aston Villa), Kelly (Bohemians) (Simmonds, Chelsea 75), Chambers (Shelbourne) (Curran, Sligo Rov., 56), Morris (Scunthorpe Utd.), O'Brien (Celtic), Bracken (Glenavon) (Hayes, Reading, 45), Clarke (Ipswich Town) (Dennehy, Sunderland, 89).

Scorer – Republic of Ireland: Murphy (61). **Half-time:** 0-0.

MADEIRA 2, REPUBLIC OF IRELAND 2

Madeira Tournament (2,000), Wednesday, February 28, 2007

Republic of Ireland: Gilmartin (Walsall), Kane (Blackburn Rov.) (Synnott, Ipswich Town, 67), Powell (Bohemians) (Finn, UCD, 46), Murphy (MK Dons), O'Halloran (Aston Villa), Kelly (Bohemians), Simmonds (Chelsea), Morris (Scunthorpe Utd.), O'Brien (Celtic) (Chambers, Shelbourne 46), Gaynor (Millwall), Hayes (Reading) (Dennehy, Sunderland, 52).

Scorers – Madeira: Costa (15), Sousa (44). **Republic of Ireland:** Gaynor (19, 75). **Half-time:** 2-1.

PORTUGAL 1, REPUBLIC OF IRELAND 0

Madeira Tournament (2,000), Friday, March 2, 2007

Republic of Ireland: Russell (Chelsea), O'Cearuill (Arsenal) (Curran, Sligo Rov., 70), Powell (Bohemians), Murphy (MK Dons), O'Halloran (Aston Villa), Simmonds (Chelsea), Chambers (Shelbourne), Kelly (Bohemians) (Hayes, Reading, 54), Morris (Scunthorpe Utd.), O'Brien (Celtic), Gaynor (Millwall) (Bracken, Glenavon 80).

Scorer – Portugal: Celestino (30). **Half-time:** 1-0.

ENGLAND 3, ITALY 3

Wembley (55,700), Saturday, March 24, 2007

England: Camp (Q.P.R.), Rosenior (Fulham) (Hoyte, Arsenal, 57), Ferdinand (West Ham Utd.), Cahill (Aston Villa), Baines (Wigan Athletic), Bentley (Blackburn Rov.) (Young, Aston Villa, 88), Reo-Coker (West Ham Utd.), Richardson (Manchester Utd.) (Huddlestone, Tottenham, 80), Routledge (Tottenham) (Milner, Newcastle Utd., 57), Agbonlahor (Aston Villa) (Derbyshire, Blackburn Rov., 46), Lita (Reading).

Scorers – England: Bentley (31), Routledge (52), Derbyshire (58). **Italy:** Pazzini (1, 53, 68). **Half-time:** 1-1.

HOLLAND 1, REPUBLIC OF IRELAND 0

Venlo (3,000), Tuesday, March 27, 2007

Republic of Ireland: Quigley (UCD) (Randolph, Charlton Athletic, 46), Kane (Blackburn Rov.), O'Halloran (Aston Villa), O'Cearuill (Arsenal) (Keogh, Bristol City, 81), O'Dea (Celtic), Gibson (Manchester Utd.), Keegan (Drogheda Utd.), Quinn (Sheffield Utd.), O'Brien (Celtic) (Powell, Bohemians, 83), Ward (Wolves) (Rooney, Stoke City, 72), Clarke (Ipswich Town).

Scorer – Holland: Drenthe (72). **Half-time:** 0-0.

ROMANIA 2, NORTHERN IRELAND 0

Pitesti (1,500), Saturday, March 24, 2007

Northern Ireland: Tuffey (Partick Thistle) (Carson, Sunderland), Callaghan, (Ballymena) (Paterson, Grimsby Town), Taylor (Hearts) (Cathcart, Manchester Utd.), Casement (Ipswich Town) (Meenan, Monaghan Utd.), McArdle (Rochdale), Garrett (Stoke City), Turner (Sligo Rov.), McKenna (Tottenham) (Howland, Birmingham City), Stewart (Linfield), Fordyce (Portsmouth), Buchanan (Bury) (Mulgrew, Linfield).

Scorers – Romania: McArdle (30 og), Tincu (85). **Half-time:** 1-0.

WORLD CUP SUMMARIES 1930-2006

1930 IN URUGUAY

WINNERS: Uruguay. RUNNERS-UP: Argentina. THIRD: U.S.A. FOURTH: Yugoslavia.
Other countries taking part: Belgium, Bolivia, Brazil, Chile, France, Mexico, Paraguay, Peru, Rumania, Yugoslavia. **Total entries**: 13.
Venue: All matches played in Montevideo.
Top scorer: Stabile (Argentina) 8 goals.
Final (30.7.30): **Uruguay 4** (Dorado 12, Cea 55, Iriarte 64, Castro 89), **Argentina 2** (Peucelle 29, Stabile 35). **Att**: 90,000.
Uruguay: Ballesteros; Nasazzi (Capt.), Mascheroni, Andrade, Fernandez, Gestido, Dorado, Scarone, Castro, Cea, Iriarte.
Argentina: Botasso; Della Torre, Paternoster, Evaristo (J.), Monti, Suarez, Peucelle, Varallo, Stabile, Ferreira (Capt.), Evaristo (M.).
Referee: Langenus (Belgium). **Half-time**: 1-2.

1934 IN ITALY

WINNERS: Italy. RUNNERS-UP: Czechoslovakia. THIRD: Germany. FOURTH: Austria.
Other countries in finals: Argentina, Austria, Belgium, Brazil, Egypt, France, Holland, Hungary, Romania, Spain, Sweden, Switzerland, U.S.A. **Total entries**: 29 (16 qualifiers).
Venues: Bologna, Florence, Genoa, Milan, Naples, Rome, Trieste, Turin.
Top scorers: Conen (Germany), Nejedly (Czechoslovakia), Schiavio (Italy), each 4 goals.
Final (Rome, 10.6.34): **Italy 2** (Orsi 82, Schiavio 97), **Czechoslovakia 1** (Puc 70), **after extra-time. Att**: 50,000.
Italy: Combi (Capt.); Monzeglio, Allemandi, Ferraris, Monti, Bertolini, Guaita, Meazza, Schiavio, Ferrari, Orsi.
Czechoslovakia: Planicka (Capt.); Zenisek, Ctyroky, Kostalek, Cambal, Krcil, Junek, Svoboda, Sobotka, Nejedly, Puc.
Referee: Eklind (Sweden). **Half-time**: 0-0. **90 mins**: 1-1.

1938 IN FRANCE

WINNERS: Italy. RUNNERS-UP: Hungary. THIRD: Brazil. FOURTH: Sweden.
Other countries in finals: Belgium, Cuba, Czechoslovakia, Dutch East Indies, France, Germany, Holland, Norway, Poland, Rumania, Sweden, Switzerland. **Total entries**: 25 (15 qualifiers).
Venues: Antibes, Bordeaux, Le Havre, Lille, Marseilles, Paris, Reims, Strasbourg, Toulouse.
Top scorer: Leonidas (Brazil) 8 goals.
Final (Paris, 19.6.38): **Italy 4** (Colaussi 6, 36, Piola 15, 81), **Hungary 2** (Titkos 7, Sarosi 65). **Att**: 45,000.
Italy: Olivieri; Foni, Rava, Serantoni, Andreolo, Locatelli, Biavati, Meazza (Capt.), Piola, Ferrari, Colaussi.
Hungary: Szabo; Polgar, Biro, Szalay, Szucs, Lazar, Sas, Vincze, Sarosi (Capt.), Szengeller, Titkos.
Referee: Capdeville (France). **Half-time**: 3-1.

1950 IN BRAZIL

WINNERS: Uruguay. RUNNERS-UP: Brazil. THIRD: Sweden. FOURTH: Spain.
Other countries in finals: Bolivia, Chile, England, Italy, Mexico, Paraguay, Spain, Switzerland, U.S.A., Yugoslavia. **Total entries**: 29 (13 qualifiers).
Venues: Belo Horizonte, Curitiba, Porto Alegre, Recife, Rio de Janeiro, Sao Paulo.
Top scorer: Ademir (Brazil) 9 goals.
Deciding Match (Rio de Janeiro, 16.7.50): **Uruguay 2** (Schiaffino 64, Ghiggia 79), **Brazil 1** (Friaca 47). **Att**: 199,850.
(For the only time, the World Cup was decided on a final pool system, in which the winners of the four qualifying groups met in a six-match series. So, unlike previous and subsequent tournaments, there was no official Final as such, but Uruguay v Brazil was the deciding final match in the final pool).
Uruguay: Maspoli; Gonzales, Tejera, Gambetta, Varela (Capt.), Andrade, Ghiggia, Perez, Miguez, Schiaffino, Moran.
Brazil: Barbosa; Augusto (Capt.), Juvenal, Bauer, Danilo, Bigode, Friaca, Zizinho, Ademir, Jair, Chico.
Referee: Reader (England). **Half-time**: 0-0.

1954 IN SWITZERLAND

WINNERS: West Germany. RUNNERS-UP: Hungary. THIRD: Austria. FOURTH: Uruguay.
Other countries in finals: Belgium, Brazil, Czechoslovakia, England, France, Italy, Korea, Mexico, Scotland, Switzerland, Turkey, Uruguay, Yugoslavia. **Total entries**: 35 (16 qualifiers).
Venues: Basle, Berne, Geneva, Lausanne, Lugano, Zurich.
Top scorer: Kocsis (Hungary) 11 goals.
Final (Berne, 4.7.54): **West Germany 3** (Morlock 12, Rahn 17, 84), **Hungary 2** (Puskas 4, Czibor 9). **Att**: 60,000.
West Germany: Turek; Posipal, Kohlmeyer, Eckel, Liebrich, Mai, Rahn, Morlock, Walter (O.), Walter (F.) (Capt.), Schaefer.
Hungary: Grosics; Buzansky, Lantos, Bozsik, Lorant, Zakarias, Czibor, Kocsis, Hidegkuti, Puskas (Capt.), Toth (J.).
Referee: Ling (England). **Half-time**: 2-2.

1958 IN SWEDEN

WINNERS: Brazil. RUNNERS-UP: Sweden. THIRD: France. FOURTH: West Germany.
Other countries in finals: Argentina, Austria, Czechoslovakia, England, Hungary, Mexico, Northern Ireland, Paraguay, Scotland, Soviet Union, Wales, West Germany, Yugoslavia. **Total entries**: 47 (16 qualifiers).
Venues: Boras, Eskilstuna, Gothenburg, Halmstad, Helsingborg, Malmo, Norrkoping, Orebro, Sandviken, Stockholm, Vasteras.
Top scorer: Fontaine (France) 13 goals.
Final (Stockholm, 29.6.58): **Brazil 5** (Vava 10, 32, Pele 55, 88, Zagalo 76), **Sweden 2** (Liedholm 4, Simonsson 83). **Att**: 49,737.
Brazil: Gilmar; Santos (D.), Santos (N.), Zito, Bellini (Capt.), Orlando, Garrincha, Didi, Vava, Pele, Zagalo.
Sweden: Svensson; Bergmark, Axbom, Boerjesson, Gustavsson, Parling, Hamrin, Gren, Simonsson, Liedholm (Capt.), Skoglund.
Referee: Guigue (France). **Half-time**: 2-1.

1962 IN CHILE

WINNERS: Brazil. RUNNERS-UP: Czechoslovakia. THIRD: Chile. FOURTH: Yugoslavia.
Other countries in finals: Argentina, Bulgaria, Colombia, England, Hungary, Italy, Mexico, Soviet Union, Spain, Switzerland, Uruguay, West Germany, Yugoslavia. **Total entries**: 53 (16 qualifiers).
Venues: Arica, Rancagua, Santiago, Vina del Mar.
Top scorer: Jerkovic (Yugoslavia), 5 goals.
Final (Santiago, 17.6.62): **Brazil 3** (Amarildo 17, Zito 69, Vava 77), **Czechoslovakia 1** (Masopust 16). **Att**: 68,679.
Brazil: Gilmar; Santos (D.), Mauro (Capt.), Zozimo, Santos (N.), Zito, Didi, Garrincha, Vava, Amarildo, Zagalo.
Czechoslovakia: Schroiff; Tichy, Novak, Pluskal, Popluhar, Masopust (Capt.), Pospichal, Scherer, Kvasnak, Kadraba, Jelinek.
Referee: Latychev (Soviet Union). **Half-time**: 1-1.

1966 IN ENGLAND

WINNERS: England. RUNNERS-UP: West Germany. THIRD: Portugal. FOURTH: USSR.
Other countries in finals: Argentina, Brazil, Bulgaria, Chile, France, Hungary, Italy, Mexico, North Korea, Soviet Union, Spain, Switzerland, Uruguay. **Total entries**: 53 (16 qualifiers).
Venues: Birmingham (Villa Park), Liverpool (Goodison Park), London (Wembley and White City), Manchester (Old Trafford), Middlesbrough, Sheffield (Hillsborough), Sunderland.
Top scorer: Eusebio (Portugal) 9 goals.
Final (Wembley, 30.7.66): **England 4** (Hurst 19, 100, 120, Peters 78), **West Germany 2** (Haller 13, Weber 89), **after extra-time. Att**: 93,802.
England: Banks; Cohen, Wilson, Stiles, Charlton (J.), Moore (Capt.), Ball, Hurst, Hunt, Charlton (R.), Peters.
West Germany: Tilkowski; Hottges, Schnellinger, Beckenbauer, Schulz, Weber, Haller, Held, Seeler (Capt.), Overath, Emmerich.
Referee: Dienst (Switzerland). **Half-time**: 1-1. **90 mins**: 2-2.

1970 IN MEXICO

WINNERS: Brazil. RUNNERS-UP: Italy. THIRD: West Germany. FOURTH: Uruguay.
Other countries in finals: Belgium, Bulgaria, Czechoslovakia, El Salvador, England, Israel, Mexico, Morocco, Peru, Romania, Soviet Union, Sweden, Uruguay. **Total entries**: 68 (16 qualifiers).
Venues: Guadalajara, Leon, Mexico City, Puebla, Toluca.
Top scorer: Muller (West Germany) 10 goals.
Final (Mexico City, 21.6.70): **Brazil 4** (Pele 18, Gerson 66, Jairzinho 71, Carlos Alberto 87), **Italy 1** (Boninsegna 38). **Att**: 107,412.
Brazil: Felix; Carlos Alberto (Capt.), Brito, Piazza, Everaldo, Clodoaldo, Gerson, Jairzinho, Tostao, Pele, Rivelino.
Italy: Albertosi; Burgnich, Facchetti (Capt.), Cera, Rosato, Bertini (Juliano 72), Domenghini, De Sisti, Mazzola, Boninsegna (Rivera 84), Riva.
Referee: Glockner (East Germany). **Half-time**: 1-1.

1974 IN WEST GERMANY

WINNERS: West Germany. RUNNERS-UP: Holland. THIRD: Poland. FOURTH: Brazil.
Other countries in finals: Argentina, Australia, Brazil, Bulgaria, Chile, East Germany, Haiti, Italy, Scotland, Sweden, Uruguay, Yugoslavia, Zaire. **Total entries**: 98 (16 qualifiers).
Venues: Berlin, Dortmund, Dusseldorf, Frankfurt, Gelsenkirchen, Hamburg, Hanover, Munich, Stuttgart.
Top scorer: Lato (Poland) 7 goals
Final (Munich, 7.7.74): **West Germany 2** (Breitner 25 pen., Muller 43), **Holland 1** (Neeskens 2 pen.). **Att**: 77,833.
West Germany: Maier; Vogts, Schwarzenbeck, Beckenbauer (Capt.), Breitner, Bonhof, Hoeness, Overath, Grabowski, Muller, Holzenbein.
Holland: Jongbloed; Suurbier, Rijsbergen (De Jong 69), Haan, Krol, Jansen, Van Hanegem, Neeskens, Rep, Cruyff (Capt.), Rensenbrink (Van der Kerkhof (R.) 46).
Referee: Taylor (England). **Half-time**: 2-1.

1978 IN ARGENTINA

WINNERS: Argentina. RUNNERS-UP: Holland. THIRD: Brazil. FOURTH: Italy.
Other countries in finals: Austria, France, Hungary, Iran, Italy, Mexico, Peru, Poland, Scotland, Spain, Sweden, Tunisia, West Germany. **Total entries**: 102 (16 qualifiers).
Venues: Buenos Aires, Cordoba, Mar del Plata, Mendoza, Rosario.
Top scorer: Kempes (Argentina) 6 goals.
Final (Buenos Aires, 25.6.78): **Argentina 3** (Kempes 38, 104, Bertoni 115), **Holland 1** (Nanninga 82), **after extra-time. Att**: 77,000.
Argentina: Fillol; Passarella (Capt.), Olguin, Galvan, Tarantini, Ardiles (Larrosa 66), Gallego, Ortiz (Houseman 74), Bertoni, Luque, Kempes.
Holland: Jongbloed; Krol (Capt.), Poortvliet, Brandts, Jansen (Suurbier 73), Haan, Neeskens, Van der Kerkhof (W.), Rep (Nanninga 58), Van der Kerkhof (R.), Rensenbrink.
Referee: Gonella (Italy). **Half-time**: 1-0. **90 mins**: 1-1.

1982 IN SPAIN

WINNERS: Italy. RUNNERS-UP: West Germany. THIRD: Poland. FOURTH: France.
Other countries in finals: Algeria, Argentina, Austria, Belgium, Brazil, Cameroon, Chile, Czechoslovakia, El Salvador, England, France, Honduras, Hungary, Kuwait, New Zealand, Northern Ireland, Peru, Scotland, Soviet Union, Spain, Yugoslavia. **Total entries**: 109 (24 qualifiers).
Venues: Alicante, Barcelona, Bilbao, Coruna, Elche, Gijon, Madrid, Malaga, Oviedo, Seville, Valencia, Valladolid, Vigo, Zaragoza.
Top scorer: Rossi (Italy) 6 goals.
Final (Madrid, 11.7.82): **Italy 3** (Rossi 57, Tardelli 69, Altobelli 81), **West Germany 1** (Breitner 84). **Att**: 90,089.
Italy: Zoff (Capt.); Bergomi, Scirea, Collovati, Cabrini, Oriali, Gentile, Tardelli, Conti, Rossi, Graziani (Altobelli 18 – Causio 88).
West Germany: Schumacher; Kaltz, Stielike, Forster (K-H.), Forster (B.), Dremmler (Hrubesch 63), Breitner, Briegel, Rummenigge (Capt.) (Muller 70), Fischer, Littbarski.
Referee: Coelho (Brazil). **Half-time**: 0-0.

1986 IN MEXICO

WINNERS: Argentina. RUNNERS-UP: West Germany. THIRD: France. FOURTH: Belgium.
Other countries in finals: Algeria, Belgium, Brazil, Bulgaria, Canada, Denmark, England, Hungary, Iraq, Italy, Mexico, Morocco, Northern Ireland, Paraguay, Poland, Portugal, Scotland, South Korea, Soviet Union, Spain, Uruguay. **Total entries**: 118 (24 qualifiers).
Venues: Guadalajara, Irapuato, Leon, Mexico City, Monterrey, Nezahualcoyotl, Puebla, Queretaro, Toluca.
Top scorer: Lineker (England) 6 goals.
Final (Mexico City, 29.6.86): **Argentina 3** (Brown 23, Valdano 56, Burruchaga 85), **West Germany 2** (Rummenigge 74, Voller 82). **Att**: 115,026.
Argentina: Pumpido; Cuciuffo, Brown, Ruggeri, Olarticoechea, Batista, Giusti, Maradona (Capt.), Burruchaga (Trobbiani 89), Enrique, Valdano.
West Germany: Schumacher; Berthold, K-H.Forster, Jakobs, Brehme, Briegel, Eder, Matthaus, Magath (Hoeness 62), Allofs (Voller 45), Rummenigge (Capt.).
Referee: Filho (Brazil). **Half-time**: 1-0.

1990 IN ITALY

WINNERS: West Germany. RUNNERS-UP: Argentina. THIRD: Italy. FOURTH: England.
Other countries in finals: Austria, Belgium, Brazil, Cameroon, Colombia, Costa Rica, Czechoslovakia, Egypt, England, Holland, Rep. of Ireland, Romania, Scotland, Spain, South Korea, Soviet Union, Sweden, United Arab Emirates, U.S.A., Uruguay, Yugoslavia. **Total entries**: 103 (24 qualifiers).
Venues: Bari, Bologna, Cagliari, Florence, Genoa, Milan, Naples, Palermo, Rome, Turin, Udine, Verona.
Top scorer: Schillaci (Italy) 6 goals.
Final (Rome, 8.7.90): **Argentina 0, West Germany 1** (Brehme 85 pen.). **Att**: 73,603.
Argentina: Goycochea; Ruggeri (Monzon 45), Simon, Serrizuela, Lorenzo, Basualdo, Troglio, Burruchaga (Calderon 53), Sensini, Maradona (Capt.), Dezotti. **Sent-off**: Monzon (65), Dezotti (86) – first players ever to be sent off in World Cup Final.
West Germany: Illgner; Berthold (Reuter 75), Buchwald, Augenthaler, Kohler, Brehme, Matthaus (Capt.), Littbarski, Hassler, Klinsmann, Voller.
Referee: Codesal (Mexico). **Half-time**: 0-0.

1994 IN U.S.A.

WINNERS: Brazil. RUNNERS-UP: Italy. THIRD: Sweden. FOURTH: Bulgaria.
Other countries in finals: Argentina, Belgium, Bolivia, Bulgaria, Cameroon, Colombia, Germany, Greece, Holland, Mexico, Morocco, Nigeria, Norway, Rep. of Ireland, Romania, Russia, Saudi Arabia, South Korea, Spain, Switzerland, U.S.A. **Total entries**: 144 (24 qualifiers).
Venues: Boston, Chicago, Dallas, Detroit, Los Angeles, New York City, Orlando, San Francisco, Washington.
Top scorers: Salenko (Russia), Stoichkov (Bulgaria), each 6 goals.
Final (Los Angeles, 17.7.94): **Brazil 0, Italy 0, after extra-time; Brazil** won 3-2 on pens. **Att**: 94,194.
Brazil: Taffarel; Jorginho (Cafu 21), Aldair, Marcio Santos, Branco, Mazinho, Mauro Silva, Dunga (Capt.), Zinho (Viola 105), Romario, Bebeto.
Italy: Pagliuca; Mussi (Apolloni 35), Baresi (Capt.), Maldini, Benarrivo, Berti, Albertini, D. Baggio (Evani 95), Donadoni, R. Baggio, Massaro.
Referee: Puhl (Hungary).
Shoot-out: Baresi missed, Marco Santos saved, Albertini 1-0, Romario 1-1, Evani 2-1, Branco 2-2, Massaro saved, Dunga 2-3, R Baggio over.

1998 IN FRANCE

WINNERS: France. RUNNERS-UP: Brazil. THIRD: Croatia. FOURTH: Holland.
Other countries in finals: Argentina, Austria, Belgium, Bulgaria, Cameroon, Chile, Colombia, Denmark, England, Germany, Holland, Iran, Italy, Jamaica, Japan, Mexico, Morocco, Nigeria, Norway, Paraguay, Romania, Saudi Arabia, Scotland, South Africa, South Korea, Spain, Tunisia, U.S.A., Yugoslavia. **Total entries**: 172 (32 qualifiers).
Venues: Bordeaux, Lens, Lyon, Marseille, Montpellier, Nantes, Paris (St Denis, Parc des Princes), Saint-Etienne, Toulouse.
Top scorer: Davor Suker (Croatia) 6 goals.
Final (Paris St Denis, 12.7.98): **Brazil 0, France 3** (Zidane 27, 45, Petit 90). **Att**: 75,000.
Brazil: Traffarel; Cafu, Junior Baiano, Aldair, Roberto Carlos; Dunga (Capt.), Leonardo (Denilson 46), Cesar Sampaio (Edmundo 74), Rivaldo; Bebeto, Ronaldo.
France: Barthez; Thuram, Leboeuf, Desailly, Lizarazu; Karembeu (Boghossian 56), Deschamps (Capt.), Petit, Zidane, Djorkaeff (Viera 75); Guivarc'h (Dugarry 66). **Sent-off**: Desailly (68).
Referee: Belqola (Morocco). **Half-time**: 0-2.

2002 IN JAPAN/SOUTH KOREA

WINNERS: Brazil. RUNNERS-UP: Germany. THIRD: Turkey. FOURTH: South Korea.
Other countries in finals: Argentina, Belgium, Cameroon, China, Costa Rica, Croatia, Denmark, Ecuador, England, France, Italy, Japan, Mexico, Nigeria, Paraguay, Poland, Portugal, Republic of Ireland, Russia, Saudi Arabia, Senegal, Slovenia, South Africa, Spain, Sweden, Tunisia, United States, Uruguay. **Total entries**: 195 (32 qualifiers).
Venues: Japan – Ibaraki, Kobe, Miyagi, Niigata, Oita, Osaka, Saitama, Sapporo, Shizuoka, Yokohama. **South Korea** – Daegu, Daejeon, Gwangju, Incheon, Jeonju, Busan, Seogwipo, Seoul, Suwon. Ulsan.
Top scorer: Ronaldo (Brazil) 8 goals.
Final (Yokohama, 30.6.02): **Germany** 0, **Brazil** 2 (Ronaldo 67, 79). **Att:** 69,029.
Germany: Kahn (Capt.), Linke, Ramelow, Metzelder, Frings, Jeremies (Asamoah 77), Hamann, Schneider, Bode (Zeige 84), Klose (Bierhoff 74), Neuville.
Brazil: Marcos, Lucio, Edmilson, Roque Junior, Cafu (Capt.) Kleberson, Gilberto Silva, Roberto Carlos, Ronaldinho (Juninho 85), Rivaldo, Ronaldo (Denilson 90).
Referee: Collina (Italy). **Half-time:** 0-0.

2006 IN GERMANY

WINNERS: Italy. RUNNERS-UP: France THIRD: Germany. FOURTH: Portugal.
Other countries in finals: Angola, Argentina, Australia, Brazil, Costa Rica, Croatia, Czech Republic, Ecuador, England, Ghana, Holland, Iran, Ivory Coast, Japan, Mexico, Paraguay, Poland, Saudi Arabia, Serbia & Montenegro, South Korea, Spain, Sweden, Switzerland, Trinidad & Tobago, Togo, Tunisia, Ukraine, United States. **Total entres:**198 (32 qualifiers).
Venues: Berlin, Cologne, Dortmund, Frankfurt, Gelsenkirchen, Hamburg, Hanover, Kaiserslautern, Leipzig, Munich, Nuremberg, Stuttgart.
Top scorer: Klose (Germany) 5 goals.
Final (Berlin, 9.7.06): **Italy** 1 (Materazzi 19), **France** 1 (Zidane 7 pen), **after extra-time; Italy** won 5-3 on pens. **Att:** 69,000.
Italy: Buffon; Zambrotta, Cannavaro (Capt.), Materazzi, Grosso, Perrotta (De Rossi 61), Pirlo, Gattuso, Camoranesi (Del Piero 86), Totti (Iaquinta 61), Toni.
France: Barthez; Sagnol, Thuram, Gallas, Abidal, Makelele, Vieira (Diarra 56), Ribery (Trezeguet 100), Malouda, Zidane (Capt.), Henry (Wiltord 107). **Sent-off:** Zidane (110).
Referee: Elizondo (Argentina). **Half-time:** 1-1. **90 mins:** 1-1.
Shoot-out: Pirlo 1-0, Wiltord 1-1, Materazzi 2-1, Trezeguet missed, De Rossi 3-1, Abidal 3-2, Del Piero 4-2, Sagnol 4-3, Grosso 5-3.

TRANSFER TRAIL

★ = British record fee
A = Record all-British deal
B = British record for goalkeeper
C = Record deal between English and Scottish clubs
D = Record fee paid by Scottish club
E = Record fee to Scottish club
F = Record for teenager
G = Most expensive foreign import
(• Re dates, 1/00 = Jan 2000 etc)

	Player	From	To	Date	£
★G	Andriy Shevchenko	AC Milan	Chelsea	5/06	30,800,000
★A	Rio Ferdinand	Leeds Utd.	Manchester Utd.	7/02	29,100,000
	Juan Sebastian Veron	Lazio	Manchester Utd.	7/01	28,100,000
F	Wayne Rooney	Everton	Manchester Utd.	8/04	27,000,000
	Marc Overmars	Arsenal	Barcelona	7/00	25,000,000
	Michael Essien	Lyon	Chelsea	8/05	24,400,000
	David Beckham	Manchester Utd.	Real Madrid	7/03	23,300,000
	Didier Drogba	Marseille	Chelsea	7/04	23,200,000
	Nicolas Anelka	Arsenal	Real Madrid	8/99	22,500,000
	Fernando Torres	Atletico Madrid	Liverpool		22,000,000
	Shaun Wright-Phillips	Manchester City	Chelsea	7/05	21,000,000
	Ruud van Nistelrooy	PSV Eindhoven	Manchester Utd.	4/01	19,000,000
	Michael Carrick	Tottenham	Manchester Utd.	8/06	18,600,000
	Rio Ferdinand	West Ham Utd.	Leeds Utd.	11/00	18,000,000
	Anderson	FC Porto	Manchester Utd.	7/07	18,000,000
	Jose Reyes	Sevilla	Arsenal	1/04	17,400,000
	Damien Duff	Blackburn Rov.	Chelsea	7/03	17,000,000
	Owen Hargreaves	Bayern Munich	Manchester Utd.	6/07	17,000,000
	Hernan Crespo	Inter Milan	Chelsea	8/03	16,800,000
	Claude Makelele	Real Madrid	Chelsea	9/03	16,600,000
	Ricardo Carvalho	FC Porto	Chelsea	7/04	16,500,000
	Darren Bent	Charlton Athletic	Tottenham	6/07	16,500,000
	Michael Owen	Real Madrid	Newcastle Utd.	8/05	16,000,000
	Thierry Henry	Arsenal	Barcelona	6/07	16,000,000
	Adrian Mutu	Parma	Chelsea	8/03	15,800,000
	Alan Shearer	Blackburn Rov.	Newcastle Utd.	7/96	15,000,000
	Jimmy F. Hasselbaink	Atl. Madrid	Chelsea	6/00	15,000,000
	Juan Sebastian Veron	Manchester Utd.	Chelsea	8/03	15,000,000
	Djibril Cisse	Auxerre	Liverpool	7/04	14,000,000
	Patrick Vieira	Arsenal	Juventus	7/05	13,700,000
	Paulo Ferreira	Porto	Chelsea	7/04	13,500,000
	Florent Malouda	Lyon	Chelsea	7/07	13,500,000
	Jonathan Woodgate	Newcastle Utd.	Real Madrid	8/04	13,400,000
	Jaap Stam	Manchester Utd.	Lazio	8/01	13,300,000
	Robbie Keane	Coventry City	Inter Milan	7/00	13,000,000
	Sylvain Wiltord	Bordeaux	Arsenal	8/00	13,000,000
	Nicolas Anelka	Paris St. Germain	Manchester City	5/02	13,000,000
	Louis Saha	Fulham	Manchester Utd.	1/04	12,825,000
	Dwight Yorke	Aston Villa	Manchester Utd.	8/98	12,600,000
	Cristiano Ronaldo	Sporting Lisbon	Manchester Utd.	8/03	12,240,000
	Juninho	Middlesbrough	Atl. Madrid	7/97	12,000,000
	Jimmy F. Hasselbaink	Leeds Utd.	Atl. Madrid	8/99	12,000,000
CD	Tore Andre Flo	Chelsea	Rangers	11/00	12,000,000
	Robbie Keane	Inter Milan	Leeds Utd.	12/00	12,000,000
	Arjen Robben	PSV Eindhoven	Chelsea	4/04	12,000,000
	Theo Walcott	Southampton	Arsenal	1/06	12,000,000

	Nani	Sporting Lisbon	Manchester Utd.	7/07	12,000,000
	Steve Marlet	Lyon	Fulham	8/01	11,500,000
	Sergei Rebrov	Dynamo Kiev	Tottenham	5/00	11,000,000
	Frank Lampard	West Ham Utd.	Chelsea	6/01	11,000,000
	Robbie Fowler	Liverpool	Leeds Utd.	11/01	11,000,000
	Dimitar Berbatov Bayer	Leverkusen	Tottenham	5/06	10,900,000
	Jaap Stam	PSV Eindhoven	Manchester Utd.	5/98	10,750,000
	Xabi Alonso	Real Sociedad	Liverpool	8/04	10,700,000
	Thierry Henry	Juventus	Arsenal	8/99	10,500,000
	Laurent Robert	Paris St. Germain	Newcastle Utd.	8/01	10,500,000
	Ruud van Niestelrooy	Manchester Utd.	Real Madrid	7/06	10,200,000
	Dirk Kuyt	Feyenoord	Liverpool	8/06	10,200,000
	Chris Sutton	Blackburn Rov.	Chelsea	7/99	10,000,000
	Emile Heskey	Leicester City	Liverpool	2/00	10,000,000
	El Hadji Diouf	Lens	Liverpool	6/02	10,000,000
	Scott Parker	Charlton Athletic	Chelsea	1/04	10,000,000
	Alexander Hleb	Stuttgart	Arsenal	6/05	10,000,000
	Obafemi Martins	Inter Milan	Newcastle Utd.	8/06	10,000,000
	Juan Pablo Angel	River Plate (Arg.)	Aston Villa	1/01	9,500,000
	Albert Luque	Dep. La Coruna	Newcastle Utd.	8/05	9,500,000
	Jonathan Woodgate	Leeds Utd.	Newcastle Utd.	1/03	9,000,000
	Andy Johnson	Crystal Palace	Everton	5/06	8,600,000
E	Giovanni van Bronckhorst	Rangers	Arsenal	6/01	8,500,000
	Stan Collymore	Nott'm Forest	Liverpool	6/95	8,500,000
	Hugo Viana	Sporting Lisbon	Newcastle Utd.	6/02	8,500,000
	Nigel Reo-Coker	West Ham Utd.	Aston Villa	7/07	8,500,000
	Dean Richards	Southampton	Tottenham	9/01	8,100,000
	Massimo Maccarone	Empoli	Middlesbrough	7/02	8,100,000
	Andrei Kanchelskis	Everton	Fiorentina	1/97	8,000,000
	Dietmar Hamann	Newcastle Utd.	Liverpool	7/99	8,000,000
	Ugo Ehiogu	Aston Villa	Middlesbrough	10/00	8,000,000
	Francis Jeffers	Everton	Arsenal	6/01	8,000,000
	Andy Cole	Manchester Utd.	Blackburn Rov.	12/01	8,000,000
	Tiago	Benfica	Chelsea	7/04	8,000,000
	Michael Owen	Liverpool	Real Madrid	8/04	8,000,000
	Jean-Alain Boumsong	Rangers	Newcastle Utd.	1/05	8,000,000
	Asier del Horno	Athletic Bilbao	Chelsea	6/05	8,000,000
	Eidur Gudjohnsen	Chelsea	Barcelona	6/06	8,000,000
	Nicolas Anelka	Fenerbahce	Bolton Wand.	8/06	8,000,000
	Eduardo da Silva	Dinamo Zagreb	Arsenal	7/07	8,000,000
B	Fabien Barthez	Monaco	Manchester Utd.	5/00	7,800,000
	Jesper Gronkjaer	Ajax Amsterdam	Chelsea	10/00	7,800,000
	Dennis Bergkamp	Inter Milan	Arsenal	6/95	7,500,000
	Kevin Davies	Southampton	Blackburn Rov.	6/98	7,500,000
	John Hartson	West Ham Utd.	Wimbledon	1/99	7,500,000
	Emmanuel Petit	Barcelona	Chelsea	6/01	7,500,000
	Diego Forlan	Independiente (Arg.)	Manchester Utd.	1/02	7,500,000
	Barry Ferguson	Rangers	Blackburn Rov.	8/03	7,500,000
	Aiyegbeni Yakubu	Porstmouth	Middlesbrough	6/05	7,500,000
	Matthew Upson	Birmingham City	West Ham Utd.	1/07	7,500,000
	Craig Bellamy	Liverpool	West Ham Utd.	7/07	7,500,000
	Dean Ashton	Norwich City	West Ham Utd.	1/06	7,250,000
	Olivier Dacourt	Lens	Leeds Utd.	5/00	7,200,000
	Andy Cole	Newcastle Utd.	Manchester Utd.	1/95	7,000,000

Fabrizio Ravanelli	Juventus	Middlesbrough	7/96	7,000,000
Stan Collymore	Liverpool	Aston Villa	5/97	7,000,000
Marc Overmars	Ajax Amsterdam	Arsenal	6/97	7,000,000
Duncan Ferguson	Everton	Newcastle Utd.	11/98	7,000,000
Lauren	Real Mallorca	Arsenal	5/00	7,000,000
Carl Cort	Wimbledon	Newcastle Utd.	7/00	7,000,000
Edwin Van der Sar	Juventus	Fulham	8/01	7,000,000
Boudewijn Zenden	Barcelona	Chelsea	8/01	7,000,000
Seth Johnson	Derby Co.	Leeds Utd.	10/01	7,000,000
Robbie Keane	Leeds Utd.	Tottenham	8/02	7,000,000
Wayne Bridge	Southampton	Chelsea	7/03	7,000,000
Jermain Defoe	West Ham Utd.	Tottenham	2/04	7,000,000
Alan Smith	Leeds Utd.	Manchester Utd.	5/04	7,000,000
Jermaine Jenas	Newcastle Utd.	Tottenham	8/05	7,000,000
Nemanja Vidic	Spartak Moscow	Manchester Utd.	1/06	7,000,000
Jonathan Woodgate	Real Madrid	Middlesbrough	4/07	7,000,000
Sulley Muntari	Udinese	Portsmouth	5/07	7,000,000
Geremi	Real Madrid	Chelsea	7/03	6,900,000
Petr Cech	Rennes	Chelsea	7/04	6,900,000
Gabriel Heinze	Paris St. Germain	Manchester Utd.	6/04	6,900,000
Tomas Rosicky	Borussia Dortmund	Arsenal	5/06	6,800,000
Paul Merson	Middlesbrough	Aston Villa	8/98	6,750,000
Corrado Grabbi	Ternana (It.)	Blackburn Rov.	6/01	6,750,000
Tore Andre Flo	Rangers	Sunderland	8/02	6,750,000
Faustino Asprilla	Parma	Newcastle Utd.	2/96	6,700,000
Jermaine Pennant	Birmingham City	Liverpool	7/06	6,700,000
David Platt	Bari	Juventus	6/92	6,500,000
Olivier Dacourt	Everton	Lens	6/99	6,500,000
Kieron Dyer	Ipswich Town	Newcastle Utd.	7/99	6,500,000
Craig Bellamy	Coventry City	Newcastle Utd.	6/01	6,500,000
Gareth Southgate	Aston Villa	Middlesbrough	7/01	6,500,000
Michael Ball	Everton	Rangers	8/01	6,500,000
John Hartson	Coventry City	Celtic	8/01	6,500,000
Fernando Morientes	Real Madrid	Liverpool	1/05	6,500,000
Scott Parker	Chelsea	Newcastle Utd.	6/05	6,500,000
Milan Baros	Liverpool	Aston Villa	8/05	6,500,000
Tiago	Chelsea	Lyon	8/05	6,500,000

BRITISH RECORD TRANSFERS FROM FIRST £1,000 DEAL

Player	From	To	Date	£
Alf Common	Sunderland	Middlesbrough	2/1905	1,000
Syd Puddefoot	West Ham Utd.	Falkirk	2/22	5,000
Warney Cresswell	S. Shields	Sunderland	3/22	5,500
Bob Kelly	Burnley	Sunderland	12/25	6,500
David Jack	Bolton Wand.	Arsenal	10/28	10,890
Bryn Jones	Wolves	Arsenal	8/38	14,500
Billy Steel	Morton	Derby Co.	9/47	15,000
Tommy Lawton	Chelsea	Notts Co.	11/47	20,000
Len Shackleton	Newcastle Utd.	Sunderland	2/48	20,500
Johnny Morris	Manchester Utd.	Derby Co.	2/49	24,000
Eddie Quigley	Sheffield Wed.	Preston N.E.	12/49	26,500

Trevor Ford	Aston Villa	Sunderland	10/50	30,000
Jackie Sewell	Notts Co.	Sheffield Wed.	3/51	34,500
Eddie Firmani	Charlton Athletic	Sampdoria	7/55	35,000
John Charles	Leeds Utd.	Juventus	4/57	65,000
Denis Law	Manchester City	Torino	6/61	100,000
Denis Law	Torino	Manchester Utd.	7/62	115,000
Allan Clarke	Fulham	Leicester City	6/68	150,000
Allan Clarke	Leicester City	Leeds Utd.	6/69	165,000
Martin Peters	West Ham Utd.	Tottenham	3/70	200,000
Alan Ball	Everton	Arsenal	12/71	220,000
David Nish	Leicester City	Derby Co.	8/72	250,000
Bob Latchford	Birmingham City	Everton	2/74	350,000
Graeme Souness	Middlesbrough	Liverpool	1/78	352,000
Kevin Keegan	Liverpool	Hamburg	6/77	500,000
David Mills	Middlesbrough	W.B.A.	1/79	516,000
Trevor Francis	Birmingham City	Nott'm. Forest	2/79	1,180,000
Steve Daley	Wolves	Manchester City	9/79	1,450,000
Andy Gray	Aston Villa	Wolves	9/79	1,469,000
Bryan Robson	W.B.A.	Manchester Utd.	10/81	1,500,000
Ray Wilkins	Manchester Utd.	AC Milan	5/84	1,500,000
Mark Hughes	Manchester Utd.	Barcelona	5/86	2,300,000
Ian Rush	Liverpool	Juventus	6/87	3,200,000
Chris Waddle	Tottenham	Marseille	7/89	4,250,000
David Platt	Aston Villa	Bari	7/91	5,500,000
Paul Gascoigne	Tottenham	Lazio	6/92	5,500,000
Andy Cole	Newcastle Utd.	Manchester Utd.	1/95	7,000,000
Dennis Bergkamp	Inter Milan	Arsenal	6/95	7,500,000
Stan Collymore	Nott'm. Forest	Liverpool	6/95	8,500,000
Alan Shearer	Blackburn Rov.	Newcastle Utd.	7/96	15,000,000
Nicolas Anelka	Arsenal	Real Madrid	8/99	22,500,000
Juan Sebastian Veron	Lazio	Manchester Utd.	7/01	28,100,000
Rio Ferdinand	Leeds Utd.	Manchester Utd.	7/02	29,100,000
Andriy Shevchenko	AC Milan	Chelsea	5/06	30,800,000

• **World's first £1m. transfer:** Guiseppe Savoldi, Bologna to Napoli, July 1975.

TOP FOREIGN SIGNINGS

Player	From	To	Date	£
Zinedine Zidane	Juventus	Real Madrid	7/01	47,200,000
Luis Figo	Barcelona	Real Madrid	7/00	37,200,000
Hernan Crespo	Parma	Lazio	7/00	35,000,000
Ronaldo	Inter Milan	Real Madrid	8/02	33,000,000
Gianluigi Buffon	Parma	Juventus	7/01	32,600,000
Christian Vieri	Lazio	Inter Milan	6/99	31,000,000
Alessandro Nesta	Lazio	AC Milan	8/02	30,200,000
Hernan Crespo	Lazio	Inter Milan	8/02	29,000,000
Gaizka Mendieta	Valencia	Lazio	7/01	28,500,000
Pavel Nedved	Lazio	Juventus	7/01	25,000,000
Rui Costa	Fiorentina	AC Milan	7/01	24,500,000
Gabriel Batistuta	Fiorentina	Roma	5/00	22,000,000

Lilian Thuram	Parma	Juventus	6/01	22,000,000
Nicolas Anelka	Real Madrid	Paris St. Germain	7/00	21,700,000
Filippo Inzaghi	Juventus	AC Milan	7/01	21,700,000
Denilson	Sao Paulo	Real Betis	7/97	21,400,000
Claudio Lopez	Valencia	Lazio	7/00	21,200,000
Marcio Amoroso	Udinese	Parma	6/99	21,000,000
Ronaldinho	Paris St Germain	Barcelona	7/03	21,000,000
Antonio Cassano	Bari	Roma	3/01	20,000,000
Javier Saviola	River Plate	Barcelona	7/01	20,000,000
Juan Sebastian Veron	Parma	Lazio	6/99	19,800,000
Mohamadou Diarra	Lyon	Real Madrid	8/06	19,300,000
Hidetoshi Nakata	Roma	Parma	7/01	19,100,000
Marcelo Salas	River Plate	Lazio	8/98	19,000,000
Emerson	Roma	Juventus	7/04	18,600,000
Alberto Gilardino	Parma	AC Milan	7/05	18,600,000
Marcio Do Amoroso	Udinese	Parma	6/99	18,100,000
Marcio Jardel	FC Porto	Galatasaray	6/00	18,100,000
Juan Veron	Parma	Lazio	6/99	18,100,000
Ronaldo	Barcelona	Inter Milan	6/97	18,000,000
Francesco Toldo	Fiorentina	Inter Milan	7/01	18,000,000

WORLD RECORD FEE FOR TEENAGER

£27m. for **Wayne Rooney**, aged 18, Everton to Manchester Utd., Aug. 2004.

WORLD RECORD FOR 16-YEAR-OLD

£12m. for **Theo Walcott**, Southampton to Arsenal, Jan. 2006.

RECORD FEE BETWEEN SCOTTISH CLUBS

£4.4m. for **Scott Brown**, Hibernian to Celtic, May 2007.

RECORD CONFERENCE FEE

£260,000: **George Boyd**, Stevenage to Peterborough Utd., Jan. 2007.

RECORD FEE BETWEEN NON-LEAGUE CLUBS

£180,000 for **Justin Jackson**, Morecambe to Rushden & Diamonds (Conference), June 2000.

MILESTONES OF SOCCER

1848 First code of rules compiled at Cambridge University.

1857 Sheffield F.C., world's oldest football club, formed.

1862 Notts Co. (oldest League club) formed.

1863 Football Association founded – their first rules of game agreed.

1871 F.A. Cup introduced.

1872 First official International: Scotland 0, England 0. Corner-kick introduced.

1873 Scottish F.A. formed; Scottish Cup introduced.

1874 Shinguards introduced.

1875 Crossbar introduced (replacing tape).

1876 F.A. of Wales formed.

1877 Welsh Cup introduced.

1878 Referee's whistle first used.

1880 Irish F.A. founded; Irish Cup introduced.

1883 Two-handed throw-in introduced.

1885 Record first-class score (Arbroath 36, Bon Accord 0 – Scottish Cup). Professionalism legalised.

1886 International Board formed.

1887 Record F.A. Cup score (Preston N.E. 26, Hyde 0).

1888 Football League founded by Wm. McGregor. First matches on Sept. 8.

1889 Preston N.E. win Cup and League (first club to complete Double).

1890 Scottish League and Irish League formed.

1891 Goal-nets introduced. Penalty-kick introduced.

1892 Inter-League games began. Football League Second Division formed.

1893 F.A. Amateur Cup launched.

1894 Southern League formed.

1895 F.A. Cup stolen from Birmingham shop window – never recovered.

1897 First Players' Union formed. Aston Villa win Cup and League.

1898 Promotion and relegation introduced.

1901 Maximum wage rule in force (£4 a week). Tottenham first professional club to take F.A. Cup South. First six-figure attendance (110,802) at F.A. Cup Final.

1902 Ibrox Park disaster (25 killed). Welsh League formed.

1904 F.I.F.A. founded (7 member countries).

1905 First £1,000 transfer (Alf Common, Sunderland to Middlesbrough).

1907 Players' Union revived.

1908 Transfer fee limit (£350) fixed in January and withdrawn in April.

1911 New F.A. Cup trophy – in use to 1991. Transfer deadline introduced.

1914 King George V first reigning monarch to attend F.A. Cup Final.

1916 Entertainment Tax introduced.

1919 League extended to 44 clubs.

1920 Third Division (South) formed.

1921 Third Division (North) formed.

1922 Scottish League (Div. II) introduced.

1923 Beginning of football pools. First Wembley Cup Final.

1924 First International at Wembley (England 1, Scotland 1). Rule change allows goals to be scored direct from corner-kicks.

1925 New offside law.

1926 Huddersfield Town complete first League Championship hat-trick.

1927 First League match broadcast (radio): Arsenal v Sheff. Utd. First radio broadcast of Cup Final (winners Cardiff City). Charles Clegg, president of F.A., becomes first knight of football.

1928 First £10,000 transfer – David Jack (Bolton Wand. to Arsenal). W.R. ('Dixie') Dean (Everton) creates League record – 60 goals in season. Britain withdraws from F.I.F.A.

1930 Uruguay first winners of World Cup.

1931 W.B.A. win Cup and promotion.

1933 Players numbered for first time in Cup Final (1-22).

1934 Sir Frederick Wall retires as F.A. secretary; successor Stanley Rous. Death of Herbert Chapman (Arsenal manager).

1935 Arsenal equal Huddersfield Town's Championship hat-trick record. Official two-referee trials.

1936 Joe Payne's 10-goal League record (Luton Town 12, Bristol Rov. 0).

1937 British record attendance: 149,547 at Scotland v England match.

1938 First live TV transmission of F.A. Cup Final. Football League 50th Jubilee. New pitch marking – arc on edge of penalty-area. Laws of Game re-drafted by Stanley Rous. Arsenal pay record £14,500 fee for Bryn Jones (Wolves).

1939 Compulsory numbering of players in Football League. First six-figure attendance for League match (Rangers v Celtic, 118,567). All normal competitions suspended for duration of Second World War.

1945 Scottish League Cup introduced.

1946 British associations rejoin F.I.F.A. Bolton Wand. disaster (33 killed) during F.A. Cup tie with Stoke City. Walter Winterbottom appointed England's first director of coaching.

1947 Great Britain beat Rest of Europe 6-1 at Hampden Park, Glasgow. First £20,000 transfer – Tommy Lawton, Chelsea to Notts Co.

1949 Stanley Rous, secretary F.A., knighted. England's first home defeat outside British Champ. (0-2 v Eire).

1950 Football League extended from 88 to 92 clubs. World record crowd (203,500) at World Cup Final, Brazil v Uruguay, in Rio. Scotland's first home defeat by foreign team (0-1 v Austria).

1951 White ball comes into official use.

1952 Newcastle Utd. first club to win F.A. Cup at Wembley in successive seasons.

1953 England's first Wembley defeat by foreign opponents (3-6 v Hungary).

1954 Hungary beat England 7-1 in Budapest.

1955 First F.A. Cup match under floodlights (prelim. round replay): Kidderminster Harriers v Brierley Hill Alliance.

1956 First F.A. Cup ties under floodlights in competition proper. First League match by floodlight (Portsmouth v Newcastle Utd.). Real Madrid win the first European Cup.

1957 Last full Football League programme on Christmas Day. Entertainment Tax withdrawn.

1958 Manchester Utd. air crash at Munich. League re-structured into four divisions.

1960 Record transfer fee: £55,000 for Denis Law (Huddersfield Town to Manchester City). Wolves win Cup, miss Double and Championship hat-trick by one goal. For fifth time in ten years F.A. Cup Final team reduced to ten men by injury. F.A. recognise Sunday football. Football League Cup launched.

1961 Tottenham complete the first Championship-F.A. Cup double this century. Maximum wage (£20 a week) abolished in High Court challenge by George Eastham. First British £100-a-week wage paid (by Fulham to Johnny Haynes). First £100,000 British transfer – Denis Law, Manchester City to Torino. Sir Stanley Rous elected president of F.I.F.A.

1962 Manchester Utd. raise record British transfer fee to £115,000 for Denis Law.

1963 F.A. Centenary. Season extended to end of May due to severe winter. First pools panel. English "retain and transfer" system ruled illegal in High Court test case.

1964 Rangers' second great hat-trick – Scottish Cup, League Cup and League. Football League and Scottish League guaranteed £500,000 a year in new fixtures copyright agreement with Pools. First televised 'Match of the Day' (BBC2): Liverpool 3, Arsenal 2.

1965 Bribes scandal – ten players jailed (and banned for life by F.A.) for match-fixing 1960-3. Stanley Matthews knighted in farewell season. Arthur Rowley (Shrewsbury Town) retires with record of 434 League goals. Substitutes allowed for injured players in Football League matches (one per team).

1966 England win World Cup (Wembley).

1967 Alf Ramsey, England manager, knighted; O.B.E. for captain Bobby Moore. Celtic become first British team to win European Cup. First substitutes allowed in F.A. Cup Final (Tottenham v Chelsea) but not used. Football League permit loan transfers (two per club).

1968 First F.A. Cup Final televised live in colour (BBC2 – W.B.A. v Everton). Manchester Utd. first English club to win European Cup.

1970 F.I.F.A/U.E.F.A approve penalty shoot-out in deadlocked ties.

1971 Arsenal win League Championship and F.A. Cup.

1973 Football League introduce 3-up, 3-down promotion/relegation between Divisions 1, 2 and 3 and 4-up, 4-down between Divisions 3 and 4.

1974 First F.A. Cup ties played on Sunday. League football played on Sunday for first time. Last F.A. Amateur Cup Final. Joao Havelange (Brazil) succeeds Sir Stanley Rous as F.I.F.A. president.

1975 Scottish Premier Division introduced.

1976 Football League introduce goal difference (replacing goal average) and red/yellow cards.

1977 Liverpool achieve the double of League Championship and European Cup. Don Revie defects to United Arab Emirates when England manager – successor Ron Greenwood.

1978 Freedom of contract for players accepted by Football League. P.F.A. lifts ban on foreign players in English football. Football League introduce Transfer Tribunal. Viv Anderson (Nott'm. Forest) first black player to win a full England cap. Willie Johnston (Scotland) sent home from World Cup Finals in Argentina after failing dope test.

1979 First all-British £500,000 transfer – David Mills, M'bro' to W.B.A. First British million pound transfer (Trevor Francis – B'ham to Nott'm. Forest). Andy Gray moves from Aston Villa to Wolves for a record £1,469,000 fee.

1981 Tottenham win 100th F.A. Cup Final. Liverpool first British side to win European Cup three times. Three points for a win introduced by Football League. Q.P.R. install Football League's first artificial pitch. Death of Bill Shankly, manager-legend of Liverpool 1959-74. Record British transfer – Bryan Robson (W.B.A. to Manchester Utd.), £1,500,000.

1982 Aston Villa become sixth consecutive English winners of European Cup. Tottenham retain F.A. Cup – first club to do so since Tottenham 1961 and 1962. Football League Cup becomes the (sponsored) Milk Cup.

1983 Liverpool complete League Championship-Milk Cup double for second year running. Manager Bob Paisley retires. Aberdeen first club to do Cup-Winners' Cup and domestic Cup double. Football League clubs vote to keep own match receipts. Football League sponsored by Canon, Japanese camera and business equipment manufacturers – 3-year agreement starting 1983-4. Football League agree 2-year contract for live TV coverage of ten matches per season (5 Friday night, BBC, 5 Sunday afternoon, ITV).

1984 One F.A. Cup tie in rounds 3, 4, 5 and 6 shown live on TV (Friday or Sunday). Aberdeen take Scottish Cup for third successive season, win Scottish Championship, too. Tottenham win UEFA Cup on penalty shoot-out. Liverpool win European Cup on penalty shoot-out to complete unique treble with Milk Cup and League title (as well as Championship hat-trick). N. Ireland win the final British Championship. France win European Championship – their first honour. F.A. National Soccer School opens at Lilleshall. Britain's biggest score this century: Stirling Alb. 20, Selkirk 0 (Scottish Cup).

1985 Bradford City fire disaster – 56 killed. First £1m. receipts from match in Britain (F.A. Cup Final). Kevin Moran (Manchester Utd.) first player to be sent off in F.A. Cup Final. Celtic win 100th Scottish F.A. Cup Final. European Cup Final horror (Liverpool v Juventus, riot in Brussels) 39 die. UEFA ban all English clubs indefinitely from European competitions. No TV coverage at start of League season – first time since 1963 (resumption delayed until January 1986). Sept: first ground-sharing in League history – Charlton Athletic move from The Valley to Selhurst Park (Crystal Palace).

1986 Liverpool complete League and Cup double in player-manager Kenny Dalglish's first season in charge. Swindon Town (4th Div. Champions) set League points record (102). League approve reduction of First Division to 20 clubs by 1988. Everton chairman Philip Carter elected president of Football League. Death of Sir Stanley Rous (91). 100th edition of *News of the World* Football Annual. League Cup sponsored for next three years by Littlewoods (£2m.). Football League voting majority (for rule changes) reduced from ¾ to ⅔. Wales move HQ from Wrexham to Cardiff City after 110 years. Two substitutes in F.A. Cup and League (Littlewoods) Cup. Two-season League/TV deal (£6.2m.):- BBC and ITV each show seven live League matches per season, League Cup semi-finals and Final. Football League sponsored by *Today* newspaper. Luton Town first club to ban all visiting supporters; as sequel are themselves banned from League Cup. Oldham Athletic and Preston N.E. install artificial pitches, making four in F. League (following Q.P.R. and Luton Town).

1987 League introduce play-off matches to decide final promotion/relegation places in all divisions. Re-election abolished – bottom club in Div. 4 replaced by winners of GM Vauxhall Conference. Two substitutes approved for Football League 1987-8. Red and yellow disciplinary cards (scrapped 1981) re-introduced by League and F.A. Football League sponsored by Barclays. First Div. reduced to 21 clubs.

1988 Football League Centenary. First Division reduced to 20 clubs.

1989 Soccer gets £74m. TV deal: £44m. over 4 years, ITV; £30m. over 5 years, BBC/BSB. But it costs Philip Carter the League Presidency. Ted Croker retires as F.A. chief executive; successor Graham Kelly, from Football League. Hillsborough disaster: 95 die at F.A. Cup semi-final (Liverpool v Nott'm. Forest). Arsenal win closest-ever Championship with last kick. Peter Shilton sets England record with 109 caps.

1990 Nott'm. Forest win last Littlewoods Cup Final. Both F.A. Cup semi-finals played on Sunday and televised live. Play-off finals move to Wembley; Swindon Town win place in Div. 1, then relegated back to Div. 2 (breach of financial regulations) – Sunderland promoted instead. England reach World Cup semi-final in Italy and win F.I.F.A. Fair Play Award. Peter Shilton retires as England goalkeeper with 125 caps (world record). Graham Taylor (Aston Villa) succeeds Bobby Robson as England manager. Int. Board amend offside law (player 'level' no longer offside). F.I.F.A. make "pro foul" a sending-off offence. English clubs back in Europe (Manchester Utd. and Aston Villa) after 5-year exile.

1991 First F.A. Cup semi-final at Wembley (Tottenham 3, Arsenal 1). Bert Millichip (F.A. chairman) and Philip Carter (Everton chairman) knighted. End of artificial pitches in

Div. 1 (Luton Town, Oldham Athletic). Scottish League reverts to 12-12-14 format (as in 1987-8). Penalty shoot-out introduced to decide F.A. Cup ties level after one replay.

1992 Introduction of fourth F.A. Cup (previous trophy withdrawn). F.A. launch Premier League (22 clubs). Football League reduced to three divisions (71 clubs). Record TV-sport deal: BSkyB/BBC to pay £304m. for 5-year coverage of Premier League. ITV do £40m., 4-year deal with F. League. Channel 4 show Italian football live (Sundays). F.I.F.A. approve new back-pass rule (goalkeeper must not handle ball kicked to him by team-mate). New League of Wales formed. Record all-British transfer, £3.3m.: Alan Shearer (Southampton to Blackburn Rov.). Charlton Athletic return to The Valley after 7-year absence.

1993 Barclays end 6-year sponsorship of F. League. For first time both F.A. Cup semi-finals at Wembley (Sat., Sun.). Arsenal first club to complete League Cup/F.A. Cup double. Rangers pull off Scotland's domestic treble for fifth time. F.A. in record British sports sponsorship deal (£12m. over 4 years) with brewers Bass for F.A. Carling Premiership, from Aug. Brian Clough retires after 18 years as Nott'm. Forest manager; as does Jim McLean (21 years manager of Dundee Utd.). Football League agree 3-year, £3m. sponsorship with Endsleigh Insurance. Premier League introduce squad numbers with players' names on shirts. Record British transfer: Duncan Ferguson, Dundee Utd. to Rangers (£4m.). Record English-club signing: Roy Keane, Nott'm. Forest to Manchester Utd. (£3.75m.). Graham Taylor resigns as England manager after World Cup exit (Nov.). Death in Feb. of Bobby Moore (51), England World-Cup winning captain 1966.

1994 Death of Sir Matt Busby. Terry Venables appointed England coach. Manchester Utd. complete the Double. Last artificial pitch in English football goes – Preston N.E. revert to grass, summer 1994. Bobby Charlton knighted. Scottish League format changes to four divisions of ten clubs. Record British transfer: Chris Sutton, Norwich City to Blackburn Rov. (£5m.). Sept: F.A. announce first sponsorship of F.A. Cup – Littlewoods Pools (4-year, £14m. deal, plus £6m. for Charity Shield). Death of Billy Wright.

1995 New record British transfer: Andy Cole, Newcastle Utd. to Manchester Utd. (£7m.). First England match abandoned through crowd trouble (v Rep. of Ireland, Dublin). Blackburn Rov. Champions for first time since 1914. Premiership reduced to 20 clubs. British transfer record broken again: Stan Collymore, Nott'm. Forest to Liverpool (£8½m.). Starting season 1995-6, teams allowed to use 3 substitutes per match, not necessarily including a goalkeeper. European Court of Justice upholds Bosman ruling, barring transfer fees for players out of contract and removing limit on number of foreign players clubs can field.

1996 Death of Bob Paisley (77), ex-Liverpool, most successful manager in English Football. F.A. appoint Chelsea manager Glenn Hoddle to succeed Terry Venables as England coach after Euro 96. Manchester Utd. first English club to achieve Double twice (and in 3 seasons). Football League completes £125m., 5-year TV deal with BSkyB starting 1996-7. England stage European Championship, reach semi-finals, lose on pens to tournament winners Germany. Keith Wiseman succeeds Sir Bert Millichip as F.A. Chairman. Linesmen become known as "referees' assistants". Coca-Cola Cup experiment with own disciplinary system (red, yellow cards). Alan Shearer football's first £15m. player (Blackburn Rov. to Newcastle Utd.). Nigeria first African country to win Olympic soccer. Nationwide Building Society sponsor Football League in initial 3-year deal worth £5.25m. Peter Shilton first player to make 1000 League apps.

1997 Howard Wilkinson appointed English football's first technical director. England's first home defeat in World Cup (0-1 v Italy). Ruud Gullit (Chelsea) first foreign coach to win F.A. Cup. Rangers equal Celtic's record of 9 successive League titles. Manchester Utd. win Premier League for fourth time in 5 seasons. New record World Cup score: Iran 17, Maldives 0 (qual. round). Season 1997-8 starts Premiership's record £36m., 4-year sponsorship extension with brewers Bass (Carling).

1998 In French manager Arsene Wenger's second season at Highbury, Arsenal become second English club to complete the Double twice. Chelsea also win two trophies under new player-manager Gianluca Vialli (Coca-Cola Cup, Cup Winners' Cup). France win 16th World Cup competition. In breakaway from Scottish League, top ten clubs form new Premiership under SFA, starting season 1998-9. Football League celebrates its 100th season, 1998-9. New F.A. Cup sponsors – French insurance giants AXA (25m., 4-year deal). League Cup becomes Worthington Cup in £23m., 5-year contract with brewers Bass. Nationwide Building Society's sponsorship of Football League extended to season 2000-1.

1999 F.A. buy Wembley Stadium (£103m.) for £320m., plan rebuilding (Aug. 2000-March 2003) as new national stadium (Lottery Sports fund contributes £110m.) Scotland's new Premier League takes 3-week mid-season break in January. Sky screen Oxford Utd. v Sunderland (Div. 1) as first pay-per-view match on TV. F.A. sack England coach Glenn Hoddle; Fulham's Kevin Keegan replaces him at £1m. a year until 2003. Sir Alf Ramsey, England's World Cup-winning manager, dies aged 79. With effect 1999, F.A. Cup Final to be decided on day (via penalties, if necessary). Hampden Park re-opens for Scottish Cup Final after £63m. refit. Alex Ferguson knighted after Manchester Utd. complete Premiership, F.A. Cup, European Cup treble. Starting season 1999-2000, UEFA increase Champions League from 24 to 32 clubs. End of Cup-Winners' Cup (merged into 121-club UEFA Cup). F.A. allow holders Manchester Utd. to withdraw from F.A. Cup to participate in FIFA's inaugural World Club Championship in Brazil in January. Chelsea first British club to field an all-foreign line-up at Southampton (Prem). F.A. vote in favour of streamlined 14-man board of directors to replace its 92-member council.

2000 Scot Adam Crozier takes over as F.A. chief executive. Wales move to Cardiff's £125m. Millennium Stadium (v Finland). Brent Council approve plans for new £475m. Wembley Stadium (completion target spring 2003); demolition of old stadium to begin after England v Germany (World Cup qual.). Fulham Ladies become Britain's first female professional team. F.A. Premiership and Nationwide League to introduce (season 2000-01) rule whereby referees advance free-kick by 10 yards and caution player who shows dissent, delays kick or fails to retreat 10 yards. Scottish football increased to 42 League clubs in 2000-01 (12 in Premier League and 3 divisions of ten; Peterhead and Elgin City elected from Highland League). France win European Championship – first time a major Int. tournament has been jointly hosted (Holland/Belgium). England's £10m. bid to stage 2006 World Cup fails; vote goes to Germany. England manager Kevin Keegan resigns after 1-0 World Cup defeat by Germany in Wembley's last International. Lazio's Swedish coach Sven-Goran Eriksson agrees to become England head coach.

2001 Scottish Premier League experiment with split into two 5-game mini leagues (6 clubs in each) after 33 matches completed. New transfer system agreed by FIFA/UEFA is ratified. Barclaycard begin £48m., 3-year sponsorship of the Premiership, and Nationwide's contract with the Football League is extended by a further 3 years (£12m.). ITV, after winning auction against BBC's Match of the Day, begin £183m., 3-season contract for highlights of Premiership matches; BSkyB's live coverage (66 matches per season) for next 3 years will cost £1.1bn. BBC and BSkyB pay £400m. (3-year contract) for live coverage of F.A. Cup and England home matches. ITV and Ondigital pay £315m. to screen Nationwide League and Worthington Cup matches. In new charter for referees, top men can earn up to £60,000 a season in Premiership. Real Madrid break world transfer record, buying Zinedine Zidane from Juventus for £47.2m. F.A. introduce prize money, round by round, in F.A. Cup.

2002 Scotland appoint their first foreign manager, Germany's former national coach Bertie Vogts replacing Craig Brown. Collapse of ITV Digital deal, with Football League owed £178m., threatens lower-division clubs. Arsenal complete Premiership/F.A. Cup Double for second time in 5 seasons, third time in all. Newcastle Utd. manager Bobby Robson knighted in Queen's Jubilee Honours. Brazil win World Cup for fifth time. New record British transfer and world record for defender, £28.25m. Rio

Ferdinand (Leeds Utd. to Manchester Utd.). Transfer window introduced to British football. F.A. Charity Shield renamed F.A. Community Shield. After 2-year delay, demolition of Wembley Stadium begins. October: Adam Crozier, F.A. chief executive, resigns.

2003 F.A. Cup draw (from 4th. Round) reverts to Monday lunchtime. Scottish Premier League decide to end mid-winter shut-down. Mark Palios appointed F.A. chief executive. For first time, two Football League clubs demoted (replaced by two from Conference). Ban lifted on loan transfers between Premiership clubs. July: David Beckham becomes record British export (Man. Utd. to Real Madrid, £23.3m.). Biggest takeover in British football history – Russian oil magnate Roman Abramovich buys control of Chelsea for £150m. Wimbledon leave rented home at Selhurst Park, become England's first franchised club in 68-mile move to Milton Keynes.

2004 Arsenal first club to win Premiership with unbeaten record and only the third in English football history to stay undefeated through League season. Trevor Brooking knighted in Queen's Birthday Honours. Wimbledon change name to Milton Keynes Dons. Greece beat hosts Portugal to win European Championship as biggest outsiders (80-1 at start) ever to succeed in major Int. tournament. New contracts – Premiership in £57m. deal with Barclays, seasons 2004-07. Coca-Cola replace Nationwide as Football League sponsors (£15m. over 3 years), rebranding Div. 1 as Football League Championship, with 2nd. and 3rd. Divs, becoming Leagues 1 and 2. After 3 years, BBC Match of the Day wins back Premiership highlights from ITV with 3-year, £105m. contract (2004-07). All-time League record of 49 unbeaten Premiership matches set by Arsenal. Under new League rule, Wrexham forfeit 10 points for going into administration.

2005 Brian Barwick, controller of ITV Sport, becomes F.A. chief executive. Foreign managers take all major trophies for English clubs: Chelsea, in Centenary year, win Premiership (record 95 points) and League Cup in Jose Mourinho's first season; Arsene Wenger's Arsenal win F.A. Cup in Final's first penalty shoot-out; under new manager Rafael Benitez, Liverpool lift European Cup on penalties after trailing 0-3 in Champions League Final. Wigan Athletic, a League club only since 1978, promoted to Premiership. In new record British-club take-over, American tycoon Malcolm Glazer buys Manchester Utd. for £790m. Bury become the first club to score 1,000 goals in each of the four divisions. Tributes are paid world-wide to George Best, who dies aged 59.

2006 Steve Staunton succeeds Brian Kerr as Republic of Ireland manager. Chelsea post record losses of £140m. Sven-Goran Eriksson agrees a settlement to step down as England coach. Steve McClaren replaces him. The Premier League announce a new 3-year TV deal worth £1.7 billion under which Sky lose their monopoly of coverage. Chelsea smash the British transfer record, paying £30.8m. for Andriy Shevchenko. Italy win the World Cup on penalties. Aston Villa are taken over by American billionaire Randy Lerner. Clydesdale Bank replace Bank of Scotland as sponsor of the SPL. An Icelandic consortium buy West Ham.

2007 Michel Platini becomes the new president of UEFA. Walter Smith resigns as Scotland manager to return to Rangers and is replaced by Alex McLeish. American tycoons George Gillett and Tom Hicks finalise a £450m. takeover of Liverpool. The new £800m. Wembley Stadium is finally completed. The BBC and Sky lose TV rights for England's home matches and F.A. Cup ties to ITV and Setanta. World Cup-winner Alan Ball dies aged 61. Lawrie Sanchez resigns as Northern Ireland manager to take over at Fulham. Nigel Worthington succeeds him. Lord Stevens names five clubs in his final report into alleged transfer irregularities. Former Thai Prime Minister Thaksin Shinawatra becomes Manchester City's new owner.

FINAL WHISTLE – OBITUARIES 2006-07

JULY 2006

JIMMY LEADBETTER, 78, developed from a journeyman left-winger into an inspirational League Championship winner, who made a major contribution to England's World Cup triumph of 1966 – after he retired. The Scot had largely undistinguished spells with Chelsea and Brighton before joining Ipswich where, under manager Alf Ramsey, he collected Division Three South, Two and One title medals in the space of five years. Leadbetter, who made 344 league appearances for the club and scored 41 goals, was used by Ramsey in a deep-lying role, forgoing runs along the touchline to concentrate on collecting the ball out of defence and spraying passes to his forwards. When Ramsey left to become England manager in 1963, he took with him the idea of playing without orthodox wingers. And during that golden summer three years later, he successfully used Alan Ball and Martin Peters as wide players in what was effectively a 4-3-3 system.

ROGER GRIFFITHS, 61, played right-back in the Hereford team that scored one of the greatest of all F.A. Cup giant-killing victories. It came in 1972 when the Southern League side held Newcastle 2-2 at St James' Park and won the replay 2-1 in extra-time. Griffiths, who was born in Hereford and supported the club as a boy, played in both matches. Remarkably, after sustaining a fractured leg in a collision with his own goalkeeper Fred Potter six minutes into the replay, he carried on for nearly 80 minutes.

TERRY SPRINGTHORPE, 82, was a member of the Wolves team that beat Leicester 3-1 in the 1949 F.A. Cup Final. The full-back came to Molineux ten years earlier, shortly before the outbreak of the Second World War, during which he 'guested' for Leicester and Wrexham. He signed a full professional contract with Wolves in 1947 and later had a short spell with Coventry. Then he played in South Africa and the United States.

JOE KIERNAN, 63, made 308 league appearances for Northampton after beginning his career as an apprentice with Sunderland. The wing-half with a sweet left foot was a key figure in the club's promotion to the old First Division in 1965 and the only player who figured in all 42 matches during their one season in the top flight. He was also tipped for Scotland honours, but his chance disappeared as Northampton tumbled back down the divisions. Later, he captained Kettering under Ron Atkinson, served as Northampton's youth team coach and was No 2 when Theo Foley became manager.

EDDIE KILSHAW, 86, was a right-winger who joined Bury in 1937 from Prescot Cables. His career at the club was interrupted by the Second World War, but he returned in 1946 and made a total of 147 league appearances before moving to Sheffield Wednesday in 1948.

JOHN LAKIN, 59, was a defender who made more than 500 appearances for Boston between 1964 and 1975. He won five championship medals as the club made their way up the non-league ladder.

AUGUST 2006

HERMAN VAN DEN BERG, 88, played 22 league matches at outside-left for Liverpool in three seasons prior to the Second World War. He also played some war-time football for the club while working as a carpenter on the docks refitting ships, before returning to his native Cape Town.

SEPTEMBER 2006

GEORGE HESLOP, 66, missed only one game during Manchester City's League Championship-winning season of 1967-68 when they finished two points ahead of Manchester United. When the teams met at Old Trafford in March that season, he scored with a header in a 3-1 victory. The centre-half played in the Cup-Winners' Cup Final in 1970 when City beat Gornik Zabrze 2-1 and also collected League Cup, Division Two and Charity Shield winners' medals. He made 203 appearances for the club after spells with Newcastle and Everton. Heslop had one season on loan in South Africa before leaving Maine Road permanently for a spell with Bury.

GIACINTO FACCHETTI, 64, was one of finest defenders Italy has produced, a strong, speedy left-back who made 94 international appearances, 70 of them as captain. He was taken from his local club, Treviglio, by the fabled Inter Milan coach Helenio Herrera and schooled in the man-for-man defensive system called the 'catenaccio,' which brought major success for club and country. Facchetti played in three World Cups, including the 1970 tournament when Italy lost 4-1 to Brazil in a classic final. He was a European Championship winner in 1968, when Italy beat Yugoslavia 2-0, lifted the European Cup twice and accumulated four Italian title medals. He became Inter president in 2004.

CHARLIE WILLIAMS, 77, made 157 league appearances for Doncaster after being spotted playing for a colliery team. The centre-half made his debut in 1950 and was at Belle Vue until the 1958-59 season. He then went into showbusiness and was a regular on the popular TV programme, *The Comedians*.

LIONEL PICKERING, 74, bought Derby for £13m. in 1991, invested about £10m. in the team over the next two years and supervised the club's move from the Baseball Ground to Pride Park in 1997. Derby were relegated from the Premiership in 2002 with huge debts and Pickering, a pioneer of free newspapers, stepped down the following year.

PETER FOAKES, 60, trained as a referee as part of his job as a PE teacher. He rose through the ranks to take charge of Premiership and Football League matches and ended his career with two finals at Wembley in 1995 – the First Division play-off between Bolton and Reading and the Auto Windscreens Shield game between Birmingham and Carlisle. Foakes, from Essex, later coached referees and the day before he died had taken part in a seminar for league officials.

MATT GADSBY, 27, collapsed after 20 minutes of Hinckley's Conference North match at Harrogate and died soon after. The game was abandoned. The defender started his career as a trainee with Walsall and had also played for Mansfield and Kidderminster.

NOVEMBER 2006

FERENC PUSKAS, 79, was short and stocky, barrel-chested and overweight. But he was also one of football's all-time greats, a player whose appearance disguised a magical left foot, wonderful skills on the ball and a ruthless touch in front of goal. The 6-3 win at Wembley in 1953 by his Hungary side not only destroyed England's air of invincibility in their own stadium but sent shock waves around the world. For good measure, the 'Magical Magyars,' as that team became known, thrashed England 7-1 in Budapest the following year. 'I came away wondering to myself what we had been doing all these years,' said Tom Finney, later knighted for his services to the English game. When Puskas returned in 1960, this time to Hampden Park, the effect was no less dazzling as he scored four times and Alfredo Di Stefano three for Real Madrid, who beat Eintracht

Frankfurt 7-3 in the European Cup Final watched by a crowd of 135,000. By the time a glittering career ended in 1967, Puskas could look back on 83 goals in 84 internationals for Hungary, 357 in 354 matches for the army club Honved and 512 in 528 games for Real Madrid. That record was accompanied by ten domestic titles and three European Cup successes, along with a hat-trick in a fourth final, which Real lost 5-3 to Benfica. He had also opened the scoring for Hungary in the 1954 World Cup Final, although his side were beaten 3-2 by West Germany. In later years, Puskas was briefly in charge of his national team, led Panathinaikos to a European Cup Final (0-2 v Ajax) and coached clubs in several other parts of the world.

BOBBY SHEARER, 74, made 407 appearances for Rangers between 1955-65 and was known as 'Captain Cutlass' for his combative style. The tough-tackling full-back won five league titles, the Scottish Cup three times and the League Cup on four occasions. He skippered the side that won the Treble in 1964, a clean sweep completed in the Scottish Cup Final when two goals in the last two minutes delivered a 3-1 win over Dundee.

ERNIE TAGG, 89, served Crewe as ball-boy, player, trainer, manager, secretary and groundsman. 'I think I filled almost every position except chairman,' he once said. He was manager between 1964-71 and served a second spell in 1975. He also played for Bournemouth and Carlisle.

PIETRO RAVA, 90, was the last surviving member of Italy's 1938 World Cup triumph, a defender in the team that beat Hungary 4-2 in the final. He also won a gold medal at the 1936 Olympics and the Italian title with Juventus in 1950 before coaching Sampdoria and Palermo.

DECEMBER 2006

HARRY LEYLAND, 76, was Blackburn's goalkeeper in the 1960 F.A. Cup Final which they lost 3-0 to Wolves. He helped them to promotion from the old Second Division two years earlier after moving from Everton, where the presence of Ted Sagar and Jimmy O'Neill meant his first team chances were restricted. Leyland also played for Tranmere before becoming player-manager of Wigan.

DEREK HUNT, 69, played left-back in the Barnet side of the late 1950s. He also managed Kingsbury Town.

JANUARY 2007

JOHNNY SPUHLER, 89, was the oldest surviving Middlesbrough player, a centre-forward or winger who made 241 appearances and scored 81 goals in the late 1940s and early 1950s. Only Wilf Mannion accumulated more post-war goals in the top flight for the club than Spuhler's total of 69. He later moved to Darlington, was player-manager of Spennymoor and had a short spell as Shrewsbury manager in 1958.

BOBBY DALE, 75, joined Bury from Altrincham in 1951 and moved to Colchester two years later. He was an inside forward whose career was ended by illness in 1958.

DEREK WALLIS, 79, was a leading football reporter with the *Daily Mirror*, where he spent more than three decades and became northern chief sports writer. He began his career with the *Slough Observer* and *Portsmouth Evening News* and in 1986 contributed to the launch of *The Independent*.

FEBRUARY 2007

HAROLD ROBERTS, 87, joined Chesterfield in 1939 shortly before the outbreak of war, but had to wait until it ended before making his debut seven years later. The left-winger joined Birmingham for a then club-record fee of £10,600 and also played for Shrewsbury and Scunthorpe before returning to Saltergate in the late 1960s as youth coach.

BOBBY BELL, 72, was a right-back who joined Watford in 1957 from home-town club Ayr and over the next seven years made nearly 300 appearances. His career at Vicarage Road came to an end when Ken Furphy took over as manager, but he continued to live in the area, playing for and coaching local clubs.

DANNY WHITE, 17, was a first-year Walsall apprentice, who died of cancer. The popular striker progressed through the club's Centre of Excellence after being released by Birmingham and was tipped for a bright future in the game. A minute's silence was observed before Walsall's home game against Barnet and flags around the Stadium flew at half-mast.

JOHN RITCHIE, 65, scored 176 goals in 343 games for Stoke and remains the club's leading marksman. He was signed by manager Tony Waddington, on a scout's recommendation, in 1962, joined Sheffield Wednesday for £70,000 in 1966 and returned to the Victoria Ground for £45,000 three years later. During that second spell, Stoke won the League Cup, beating Chelsea 2-1 in 1972, and twice reached F.A. Cup semi-finals. His career was ended in 1975 by a double leg fracture. After that he concentrated on his pottery business in Stoke.

TOM GARNEYS, 83, was a free-scoring centre-forward who netted 143 goals in 274 matches for Ipswich in the 1950s. He was the team's leading marksman for four successive seasons and twice won Division Three South Championship medals – in 1954 and 1957. Garneys, previously with Brentford and Notts County, once scored four times in a 5-1 victory over Doncaster.

STAN JACKSON, 77, was president of Wigan, a lifelong fan and the man who played a major role in transforming the club's fortunes in the mid-90s. He was involved in approaches to Dave Whelan, which led to the local businessman taking control and delivering Premiership football to the club.

EPHRAIM DODDS, 91, was a powerfully-built centre-forward who played for Sheffield United and Blackpool pre-war and for Everton and Lincoln City afterwards. Known as Jock, he won war-time honours with Scotland, scoring a hat-trick in a 5-4 win over England at Hampden Park in 1942.

APRIL 2007

ALAN BALL, 61, was the youngest member of England's World Cup-winning team of 1966 and rated by many, including hat-trick hero Geoff Hurst, as the outstanding player of the 4-2 win over West Germany in the final at Wembley. Ball, socks round his ankles, ran ceaselessly along the right flank, his energy into extra-time proving a crucial factor. It was his cross that Hurst drove against the crossbar and, according to the linesman, over the line for 3-2. And it was Ball who kept pace with Hurst on the breakaway for the fourth goal seconds from the end. He made his international debut against Yugoslavia a year before the tournament and the last of his 72 appearances in a 5-1 win over Scotland at Wembley in 1975. The low point came two years earlier when, in a World

Cup qualifier in Poland, he became only the second England player to be sent off. Ball was twice involved in British transfer record moves – £110,000 from Blackpool to Everton and £220,000 from Everton to Arsenal. He won the League Championship with Everton in 1970 and also played for Southampton and Bristol Rovers, as well as in Philadelphia, Vancouver and Hong Kong. Ball's career spanned 975 games. His managerial appointments included Manchester City, Portsmouth, Southampton and Stoke. But it was not until 2000 that he was rewarded for his services to the game, with an MBE. In 2005, he auctioned his World Cup medal for £140,000 to provide for his family's future.

BRIAN MILLER, 70, was one of Burnley's finest servants, a one-club man who spent four decades at Turf Moor in various capacities. The wing-half was an ever-present in the side that won the League Championship by a point from Wolves in 1959-60, played in the F.A. Cup Final two years later when Burnley lost 2-1 to Tottenham and won one England cap, against Austria in 1961. Miller was twice manager, from 1979-83 and 1986-89. During his second spell in charge, Burnley preserved their league status with victory over Orient. He also had spells as coach and chief scout.

ARTHUR MILTON, 79, was the last man to play football and cricket for England, a fleet-footed winger and stylish batsman who became a hugely popular figure in Bristol sporting circles. He scored 21 goals in 84 appearances for Arsenal and was part of their Championship-winning side in the 1952-53 season. Later, he helped Bristol City finish top of the Third Division South. Milton's one England cap came in a 2-2 draw with Austria in 1951 at Wembley. He made six Test appearances between 1958-59 in a cricketing career which produced more than 32,000 first-class runs before retirement at 46 after 26 years with Gloucestershire.

BILL AXBEY, 102, was one of football's longest-serving supporters, following Brentford from the age of three. He became an honorary vice-president of the club and at the age of 95 was mascot for a match at Griffin Park.

MAY 2007

BOBBY CRAM, 68, captained Colchester to one of the F.A. Cup's most famous giant-killing feats – the 3-2 victory over Don Revie's Leeds in a fifth round tie at Layer Road in 1971. The defender, uncle of former athletics star Steve Cram, joined the club after eight years with West Bromwich Albion.

BRIAN WOODALL, 58, was a right winger who started his career with Sheffield Wednesday and had spells with Oldham, his home-town club Chester and Crewe. One of his best performance was for Wednesday in an F.A. Cup third round replay against Leeds when he scored twice in a 3-1 win at Elland Road in 1969.

KAI JOHANSEN, 67, was a Denmark international full-back who played 238 matches for Rangers after a £20,000 move from Morton in 1965. He scored the only goal in a Scottish Cup Final replay against Celtic in 1966 and helped the Ibrox club reach the European Cup-Winners' Cup Final the following year when they lost 1-0 to Bayern Munich after extra-time. Johansen made 20 appearances for his country.

JUNE 2007

DEREK DOUGAN, 69, was a much-travelled centre-forward whose strength in the air, sureness of touch and outspoken opinions made him of the game's great characters in the 1960s and 1970s. Nicknamed The Doog, he started with the Irish League club Distillery before embarking on a career in England which took in Portsmouth, Blackburn, Aston Villa, Peterborough, Leicester and finally Wolves, where he made the biggest impression. Dougan scored 123 goals in 323 appearances for the Molineux club, forming a flourishing attacking partnership with John Richards. He helped them regain their top-flight status in 1967 and was a League Cup winner in 1974. But a second spell at the club, fronting a takeover consortium, proved unsuccessful, with Wolves falling from Division One to Division Four in successive seasons. He played 43 times for Northern Ireland, many of them alongside George Best, and was one of the pall bearers at Best's funeral in November 2005. 'He carried us for years, so it was an honour to carry him,' said Dougan afterwards. His playing days ended in the United States and there was a spell as manager of Kettering. As chairman of the Professional Footballers' Association, Dougan fought hard for players' rights and conditions. He was involved in charity work and politics, appearing on BBC's Question Time in 2006 for the fringe party UKIP.

FRANK GRIFFIN, 79, scored the winning goal for West Bromwich Albion against Preston in the 1954 F.A. Cup Final three minutes from the end of a game deadlocked at 2-2. Right-winger Griffin outshone his opposite number, the great Tom Finney, who along with Stanley Matthews denied him the England recognition many felt he deserved. It was the most important of 52 goals in 275 games for the club. He joined them from Shrewsbury and later played for Northampton after sustaining a broken leg that cost him the burst of acceleration for which he was renowned.

BILLY HOGAN, 83, was a club-record buy by Carlisle in 1949 when manager Bill Shankly paid £4,000 for his services. The former Manchester City right-winger made 202 appearances and scored 27 goals in a career which would have prospered even more but for a serious knee injury which forced his retirement in 1956

WARREN BRADLEY, 75, was one of the great names in Amateur football's golden period. A teacher by profession, he left Bishop Auckland to play on the right wing for Manchester United, making 63 league appearances and scoring 20 goals between 1958-61. Bradley graduated from England Amateurs to win three caps as a full International. He also had a spell with Bury.

JULY 2007

DAVE SIMMONS, 58, scored Colchester's third goal in their shock 3-2 F.A. Cup fifth round win over Leeds in 1971, giving them a 3-0 lead before Don Revie's side made a game of it. The centre-forward began his career as an apprentice with Arsenal and went on to play for Bournemouth, Aston Villa and Walsall. After leaving Colchester, he had two spells with Cambridge and two years at Brentford, where he enjoyed his most prolific time, scoring 17 league goals in 52 appearances for the London club.

WEMBLEY LEADS THE WAY AFTER YEARS OF DELAYS

A new era for English football began in March 2007 with the completion of the new Wembley Stadium. The 90,000-seater arena is being hailed as one of the finest in the world – but has come at a price. Costs spiralled, completion was years behind schedule and disputes involving the F.A., builders Multiplex and the Government were rife. Here is the timetable of events spanning the last nine years.

March 1998: The old stadium, opened in 1923 and costing £750,000, is sold to a consortium of the F.A. and English Sports Council for £103m.

September 2000: Australian construction company Multiplex sign an agreement to build the new venue for a maximum price of £326m. But plans to stage the 2003 F.A. Cup Final there are scrapped.

October 2000: In the old Wembley's last international, England are beaten by Dietmar Hamann's goal for Germany in a World Cup qualifier, prompting coach Kevin Keegan to resign.

February 2001: Former chairman Ken Bates resigns from the board of Wembley National Stadium Limited, claiming he has been undermined by Government and F.A. figures.

May 2001: Amid growing financial worries, F.A. chief executive Adam Crozier warns that the project faces collapse unless the Government bail it out.

June 2001: Ministers refuse assistance and the project is put on hold while a review is carried out by Lord Patrick Carter.

May 2002: The F.A. sign an agreement with German bank WestLB for a loan of £426m. and set a starting date for three months' time.

September 2002: Work finally gets under way on the massive project, which includes demolishing the famous twin towers.

February 2004: An influential group of MPs comes out with strong criticism of the F.A.'s handling of the project.

May 2004: Wembley's new landmark, a 440ft high steel arch weighing 2,000 tons, is raised into position.

September 2004: Prime Minister Tony Blair and the England captain David Beckham attend a 'topping out' ceremony on site.

August 2005: More delays and cost overruns raise fears about the planned completion date. The F.A. book Cardiff's Millennium Stadium as back up for the following year's F.A. Cup Final.

February 2006: The governing body reveal that the new stadium will not be ready for May's showpiece match. The new deadline for completion is September.

June 2006: The first strips of turf, grown at a secret location, are laid as construction moves into the final stage.

August 2006: The F.A. express confidence that everything will be ready for the 2007 F.A. Cup Final.

October 2006: The F.A. resolve a long-running dispute with Multiplex, agreeing an extra payment of £36m. to the builders.

March 2007: The keys to the stadium are finally handed over, with costs having soared to around £800m.

March 2007: The doors are opened to thousands of local residents – and former Crystal Palace and Sheffield Wednesday striker Mark Bright scores the first goal in a charity match.

March 2007: A crowd of 55,700 at the first international see Giampaolo Pazzini score a hat-trick for Italy in a 3-3 draw with England in an Under-21 friendly.

May 2007: In the first final of the new era, Stevenage Borough beat Conference rivals Kidderminster Harriers 3-2 to win the F.A. Trophy.

May 2007: The F.A. Cup Final returns to its spiritual home, with Chelsea beating Manchester United 1-0 in extra-time, watched by a crowd of 89,826.

June 2007: Brazil provide the opposition for the England senior team's first match, a 1-1 draw in front of 88,745 spectators.

RECORDS SECTION

INDEX

GOALSCORING

(† Football League pre 1992-3. * Home team)

Highest: *Arbroath 36, Bon Accord (Aberdeen) 0, in **Scottish Cup** 1st Round, Sept. 12, 1885. On same day, also in Scottish Cup 1st Round, Dundee Harp beat Aberdeen Rov. 35-0.

Internationals: England 15, *France 0, in Paris, 1906 (Amateur); England 13 *Ireland 0, in Belfast, Feb. 18, 1882 (record in U.K.); *England 9, Scotland 3, at Wembley, Apr. 15, 1961; Biggest England win at Wembley: 9-0 v Luxembourg (E.Champ), Dec. 15, 1982.

Other record wins: Scotland: 11-0 v Ireland (Glasgow, Feb. 23, 1901); **Northern Ireland:** 7-0 v Wales (Belfast, Feb. 1, 1930); **Wales:** 11-0 v Ireland (Wrexham, Mar. 3, 1888); **Rep. of Ireland:** 8-0 v Malta (E. Champ., Dublin, Nov. 16, 1983).

Record International defeats: England: 1-7 v Hungary (Budapest, May 23, 1954); **Scotland:** 3-9 v England (Wembley, Apr. 15, 1961); **Ireland:** 0-13 v England (Belfast, Feb. 18, 1882); **Wales:** 0-9 v Scotland (Glasgow, Mar. 23, 1878); **Rep. of Ireland:** 0-7 v Brazil (Uberlandia, May 27, 1982).

World Cup: Qualifying round – Australia 31, American Samoa 0, world record Int. score (Apr. 11, 2001); Australia 22, Tonga 0 (Apr. 9, 2001); Iran 19, Guam 0 (Nov. 25, 2000); Maldives 0, Iran 17 (Jun. 2, 1997). **Finals – highest scores:** Hungary 10, El Salvador 1 (Spain, Jun. 15, 1982); Hungary 9, S. Korea 0 (Switzerland, Jun. 17, 1954); Yugoslavia 9, Zaire 0 (W. Germany, Jun. 18, 1974).

European Championship: Qualifying round – highest scorers: San Marino 0, Germany 13 (Serravalle, Sept. 6, 2006). **Finals – highest score:** Holland 6, Yugoslavia 1 (Quarter-final, Rotterdam, Jun. 25, 2000).

F.A. Cup: *Preston N.E. 26, Hyde 0, 1st Round, Oct. 15, 1887.

League Cup: *West Ham Utd. 10, Bury 0 (2nd Round, 2nd Leg, Oct 25, 1983); *Liverpool 10, Fulham 0 (2nd Round, 1st Leg, Sept. 23, 1986). **Record Aggregates:** Liverpool 13, Fulham 2 (10-0h, 3-2a), Sept. 23-Oct. 7, 1986; West Ham Utd. 12, Bury 1 (2-1a, 10-0h), Oct. 4-25, 1983; Liverpool 11, Exeter City 0 (5-0h, 6-0a), Oct. 7-28, 1981.

F.A. Premier League (beginning 1992-3): *Manchester Utd. 9, Ipswich Town 0, Mar. 4, 1995. **Record away win:** Manchester Utd. 8, *Nott'm. Forest 1, Feb. 6, 1999.

Highest aggregate scores in Premier League – 9: Manchester Utd. 9, Ipswich Town 0, Mar. 4, 1995; Nott'm. Forest 1, Manchester Utd. 8, Feb. 6, 1999; Blackburn Rov. 7, Sheffield Wed. 2, Aug. 25, 1997; Southampton 6, Manchester Utd. 3, Oct. 26, 1996; Tottenham 7, Southampton 2, Mar. 11, 2000; Tottenham 4, Arsenal 5, Nov. 13, 2004.

†Football League (First Division): *Aston Villa 12, Accrington 2, Mar. 12, 1892; *Tottenham 10, Everton 4, Oct. 11, 1958 (highest 1st. Div. aggregate that century); *W.B.A. 12, Darwen 0, Apr. 4, 1892; *Nott'm. Forest 12, Leicester Fosse 0, Apr. 21, 1909. **Record away win:** Sunderland 9, *Newcastle Utd. 1, Dec. 5, 1908; Wolves 9, *Cardiff City 1, Sept. 3, 1955; W.B.A 8, *Wolves 0, Dec. 27, 1893.

New First Division (beginning 1992-3): *Bolton Wand. 7, Swindon Town 0, Mar. 8, 1997; Sunderland 7, Oxford Utd. 0, Sept. 19, 1998. **Record away win:** Birmingham City 7, *Stoke City 0, Jan. 10, 1998; Birmingham City 7, *Oxford Utd. 0, Dec. 12, 1998.

Record aggregates (11 goals): *Grimsby Town 6, Burnley 5, Oct. 29, 2002; *Burnley 4, Watford 7, Apr. 5, 2003.

†**Second Division:** *Manchester City 11, Lincoln City 3, Mar. 23, 1895; *Newcastle Utd. 13, Newport County 0, Oct. 5, 1946; *Small Heath 12, Walsall Town Swifts 0, Dec. 17, 1892; *Darwen 12, Walsall 0, Dec. 26, 1896; *Small Heath 12, Doncaster Rov. 0, Apr. 11, 1903. **Record away win:** Sheffield Utd. 10, *Burslem Port Vale 0, Dec. 10, 1892.

New Second Division (beginning 1992-3): *Hartlepool Utd. 1, Plymouth Argyle 8, May 7, 1994; *Hartlepool Utd. 8, Grimsby Town 1, Sept. 12, 2003.

†**Third Division:** *Gillingham 10, Chesterfield 0, Sept. 5, 1987; *Tranmere Rov. 9, Accrington Stanley 0, Apr. 18, 1959; *Brighton & H.A. 9, Southend Utd. 1, Nov. 22, 1965; *Brentford 9, Wrexham 0, Oct. 15, 1963. **Record away win:** Fulham 8, *Halifax Town 0, Sept. 16, 1969.

New Third Division (beginning 1992-3): *Barnet 1, Peterborough Utd. 9, Sept. 5, 1998.

†**Third Division (North):** *Stockport Co. 13, Halifax Town 0 (still joint biggest win in F. League – see Div. 2) Jan. 6, 1934; *Tranmere Rov. 13, Oldham Athletic 4, Dec. 26, 1935. *(17 is highest Football League aggregate score).* **Record away win:** Barnsley 9, *Accrington Stanley 0, Feb. 3, 1934.

†**Third Division (South):** *Luton Town 12, Bristol Rov. 0, Apr. 13, 1936; *Bristol City 9, Gillingham 4, Jan. 15, 1927; *Gillingham 9, Exeter City 4, Jan. 7, 1951. **Record away win:** Walsall 8, *Northampton Town 0, Apr. 8, 1947.

†**Fourth Division:** *Oldham Athletic 11, Southport 0, Dec. 26, 1962; *Hartlepool Utd. 10, Barrow 1, Apr. 4, 1959; *Wrexham 10, Hartlepool Utd. 1, Mar. 3, 1962. **Record away win:** Rotherham Utd. 8, *Crewe Alexandra 1, Sept. 8, 1973.

Scottish Premier Division – Highest aggregate: 11 goals – Celtic 8, Hamilton 3, Jan. 3, 1987; Motherwell 5, Aberdeen 6, Oct. 20, 1999. **Other highest team scores:** Aberdeen 8, Motherwell 0 (Mar. 26, 1979); Hamilton 0, Celtic 8 (Nov. 5, 1988).

Scottish League Div. 1: *Celtic 11, Dundee 0, Oct. 26, 1895. **Record away win:** Hibs 11, *Airdrie 1, Oct. 24, 1959.

Scottish League Div. 2: *Airdrieonians 15, Dundee Wanderers 1, Dec. 1, 1894. (biggest win in history of League football in Britain).

Record modern Scottish League aggregate (12 goals): Brechin City 5, Cowdenbeath 7, Div. 2, Jan. 18, 2003.

Record British score since 1900: Stirling Albion 20, Selkirk 0 (Scottish Cup 1st. Round, Dec. 8, 1984). Winger Davie Thompson (7 goals) was one of 9 Stirling players to score.

LEAGUE GOALS – BEST IN SEASON (Before restructure in 1992)

Div.		*Goals*	*Games*
1	W.R. (Dixie) Dean, Everton, 1927-8	60	39
2	George Camsell, Middlesbrough, 1926-7	59	37
3(S)	Joe Payne, Luton Town, 1936-7	55	39
3(N)	Ted Harston, Mansfield Town, 1936-7	55	41
3	Derek Reeves, Southampton, 1959-60	39	46
4	Terry Bly, Peterborough Utd., 1960-1	52	46

(Since restructure in 1992)

Div.		*Goals*	*Games*
1	Guy Whittingham, Portsmouth, 1992-3	42	46
2	Jimmy Quinn, Reading, 1993-4	35	46
3	Andy Morrell, Wrexham, 2002-03	34	45

F.A. PREMIER LEAGUE – BEST IN SEASON

Andy Cole **34 goals** (Newcastle Utd. – 40 games, 1993-4); Alan Shearer **34 goals** (Blackburn Rov. – 42 games, 1994-5).

FOOTBALL LEAGUE – BEST MATCH HAULS
(Before restructure in 1992)

Div.		*Goals*
1	Ted Drake (Arsenal), away to Aston Villa, Dec. 14, 1935	7
	James Ross (Preston N.E.) v Stoke City, Oct 6, 1888	7
2	*Neville (Tim) Coleman (Stoke City) v Lincoln City, Feb. 23, 1957	7
	Tommy Briggs (Blackburn Rov.) v Bristol Rov., Feb. 5, 1955	7
3(S)	Joe Payne (Luton Town) v Bristol Rov., Apr. 13, 1936	10
3(N)	Robert ('Bunny') Bell (Tranmere Rov.) v Oldham Athletic, Dec. 26, 1935 – he also missed a penalty	9
3	Barrie Thomas (Scunthorpe Utd.) v Luton Town, Apr. 24, 1965	5
	Keith East (Swindon Town) v Mansfield Town, Nov. 20, 1965	5
	Steve Earle (Fulham) v Halifax Town, Sept. 16, 1969	5
	Alf Wood (Shrewsbury Town) v Blackburn Rov., Oct. 2, 1971	5
	Tony Caldwell (Bolton Wand.) v Walsall, Sept. 10, 1983	5
	Andy Jones (Port Vale) v Newport Co., May 4, 1987	5
4	Bert Lister (Oldham Athletic) v Southport, Dec. 26, 1962	6

* Scored from the wing

(SINCE RESTRUCTURE IN 1992)

Div.	*Goals*
1	**4** in match – John Durnin (Oxford Utd. v Luton Town, 1992-3); Guy Whittingham (Portsmouth v Bristol Rov. 1992-3); Craig Russell (Sunderland v Millwall, 1995-6); David Connolly (Wolves at Bristol City 1998-9); Darren Byfield (Rotherham Utd. at Millwall, 2002–03); David Connolly (Wimbledon at Bradford City, 2002–03); Marlon Harewood (Nott'm. F. v Stoke City, 2002–03); Michael Chopra (Watford at Burnley, 2002–03); Robert Earnshaw (Cardiff City v Gillingham, 2003–04).
2	**5** in match – Paul Barnes (Burnley v Stockport Co., 1996-7); Robert Taylor (all 5, Gillingham at Burnley, 1998-9); Lee Jones (all 5, Wrexham v Cambridge Utd., 2001-02).
3	**5** in match – Tony Naylor (Crewe Alexandra v Colchester Utd., 1992-3); Steve Butler (Cambridge Utd. v Exeter City, 1993-4); Guiliano Grazioli (Peterborough Utd. at Barnet, 1998-9).
Lge. 1	**5** in match – Juan Ugarte (Wrexham at Hartlepool Utd., 2004-05).

F.A. PREMIER LEAGUE – BEST MATCH HAUL

5 goals in match: Andy Cole (Manchester Utd. v Ipswich Town, Mar. 4, 1995); Alan Shearer (Newcastle Utd. v Sheffield Wed., Sept. 19, 1999).

SCOTTISH LEAGUE

Div.		*Goals*
	Kris Boyd (Kilmarnock) v Dundee Utd., Sept. 25, 2004	5
Prem.	Kenny Miller (Rangers) v St. Mirren, Nov. 4, 2000	5
	Marco Negri (Rangers) v Dundee Utd., Aug. 23, 1997	5
	Paul Sturrock (Dundee Utd.) v Morton, Nov. 17, 1984	5
1	Jimmy McGrory (Celtic) v Dunfermline Athletic, Jan. 14, 1928	8
1	Owen McNally (Arthurlie) v Armadale, Oct. 1, 1927	8
2	Jim Dyet (King's Park) v Forfar Athletic, Jan. 2, 1930, on his debut for the club	8
2	John Calder (Morton) v Raith Rov., Apr. 18, 1936	8
2	Norman Haywood (Raith Rov.) v Brechin, Aug. 20, 1937	8

SCOTTISH LEAGUE – BEST IN SEASON

Prem.	Brian McClair (Celtic, 1986-7)	**35**
	Henrik Larsson (Celtic, 2000-01)	**35**
1	William McFadyen (Motherwell, 1931-2)	**53**
2	*Jimmy Smith (Ayr, 1927-8 – 38 appearances)	**66**

(*British record)

CUP FOOTBALL

Scottish Cup: John Petrie (Arbroath) v Bon Accord, at Arbroath, 1st Round, Sept. 12, 1885 .... **13**

F.A. Cup: Ted MacDougall (Bournemouth) v Margate, 1st Round, Nov. 20, 1971 .... **9**

F.A. Cup Final: Billy Townley (Blackburn Rov.) v Sheffield Wed., at Kennington Oval, 1890; Jimmy Logan (Notts Co.) v Bolton Wand., at Everton, 1894; Stan Mortensen (Blackpool) v Bolton Wand., at Wembley, 1953 .... **3**

League Cup: Frank Bunn (Oldham Athletic) v Scarborough (3rd Round), Oct. 25, 1989 .... **6**

Scottish League Cup: Jim Fraser (Ayr) v Dumbarton, Aug. 13, 1952; Jim Forrest (Rangers) v Stirling Albion, Aug. 17, 1966 .... **5**

Scottish Cup: Most goals in match since war: **10** by **Gerry Baker** (St. Mirren) in 15-0 win (1st. Round) v Glasgow Univ., Jan. 30, 1960; **9** by his brother **Joe Baker** (Hibernian) in 15-1 win (2nd. Round) v Peebles Rov., Feb. 11, 1961.

AGGREGATE LEAGUE SCORING RECORDS

	Goals
* Arthur Rowley (1947-65, WBA, Fulham, Leicester City, Shrewsbury Town)	**434**
† Jimmy McGrory (1922-38, Celtic, Clydebank)	**410**
Hughie Gallacher (1921-39, Airdrieonians, Newcastle Utd., Chelsea, Derby Co., Notts Co., Grimsby Town, Gateshead)	**387**
William ('Dixie') Dean (1923-37, Tranmere Rov., Everton, Notts County)	**379**
Hugh Ferguson (1916-30, Motherwell, Cardiff City, Dundee)	**362**
▪ Jimmy Greaves (1957-71, Chelsea, Tottenham, West Ham Utd.)	**357**
Steve Bloomer (1892-1914, Derby Co., Middlesbrough, Derby Co.)	**352**
George Camsell (1923-39, Durham City, Middlesbrough)	**348**
Dave Halliday (1920-35, St. Mirren, Dundee, Sunderland, Arsenal, Manchester City, Clapton Orient)	**338**
John Aldridge (1979-98, Newport, Oxford Utd., Liverpool, Tranmere Rov.)	**329**
John Atyeo (1951-66, Bristol City)	**315**
Joe Smith (1908-29, Bolton Wand., Stockport Co.)	**315**
Victor Watson (1920-36, West Ham Utd., Southampton)	**312**
Harry Johnson (1919-36, Sheffield Utd., Mansfield Town)	**309**
Bob McPhail (1923–1939, Airdrie, Rangers)	**306**

(* **Rowley** scored 4 for WBA, 27 for Fulham, 251 for Leicester City, 152 for Shrewsbury Town. ▪ **Greaves's** 357 is record top-division total (he also scored 9 League goals for AC Milan). **Aldridge** also scored 33 League goals for Real Sociedad. † **McGrory** scored 397 for Celtic, 13 for Clydebank.)

Most League goals for one club: 349 – Dixie Dean (Everton 1925-37); **326 – George Camsell** (Middlesbrough 1925-39); **315 – John Atyeo** (Bristol City 1951-66); **306 – Vic Watson** (West Ham Utd. 1920-35); **291 – Steve Bloomer** (Derby Co. 1892-1906, 1910-14); **259 – Arthur Chandler** (Leicester City 1923-35); **255 – Nat Lofthouse** (Bolton Wand. 1946-61); **251 – Arthur Rowley** (Leicester City 1950-58).

Over 500 Goals: Jimmy McGrory (Celtic, Clydebank and Scotland) scored a total of 550 goals in his first-class career (1922-38).

Over 1,000 goals: Brazil's **Pele** is reputedly the game's all-time highest scorer with 1,282 goals in 1,365 matches (1956-77), but many of them were scored in friendlies for his club, Santos. He scored his 1,000th goal, a penalty, against Vasco da Gama in the Maracana Stadium, Rio, on Nov. 19, 1969. Pele (born Oct. 23, 1940) played regularly for Santos from the age of 16. During his career, he was sent off only once. He played 95 'A' Internationals for Brazil and in their World Cup-winning teams in 1958 and 1970. • Pele (Edson Arantes do Nascimento) was subsequently Brazil's Minister for Sport. He never played at Wembley, apart from being filmed there scoring a goal for a commercial. Aged 57, Pele received an 'honorary knighthood' (Knight Commander of the British Empire) from the Queen at Buckingham Palace on Dec. 3, 1997.

MOST LEAGUE GOALS IN SEASON: DEAN'S 60

W.R. ('Dixie') Dean, Everton centre-forward, created a League scoring record in 1927-8 with an aggregate of 60 in 39 First Division matches. He also scored three goals in F.A. Cup-ties, and 19 in representative games (total for the season 82).

George Camsell, of Middlesbrough, previously held the record with 59 goals in 37 Second Division matches in 1926-7, his total for the season being 75.

SHEARER'S RECORD 'FIRST'

Alan Shearer (Blackburn Rov.) is the only player to score more than 30 top-division goals in 3 successive seasons since the war: 31 in 1993-4, 34 in 1994-5, 31 in 1995-6. **Thierry Henry** (Arsenal) is the first player to score more than 20 Premiership goals in five consecutive seasons (2002–6). **David Halliday** (Sunderland) topped 30 First Div. goals in 4 consecutive seasons with totals of 38, 36, 36 and 49 from 1925-26 to 1928-29.

MOST GOALS IN A MATCH

September 12, 1885: John Petrie set the all-time British individual record for a first-class match when, in Arbroath's 36-0 win against Bon Accord (Scottish Cup first round), he scored **13**

April 13, 1936: Joe Payne set the still-existing individual record on his debut as a centre-forward, for Luton Town v Bristol Rov. (Div. III South). In a 12-0 win he scored **10**

ROWLEY'S ALL-TIME RECORD

Arthur Rowley is English football's **top club scorer** with a total of 464 goals for W.B.A., Fulham, Leicester City and Shrewsbury Town (1947-65). They comprised 434 in the League, 26 F.A. Cup, 4 League Cup.

Jimmy Greaves is second with a total of 420 goals for Chelsea, AC Milan, Tottenham and West Ham Utd., made up of 366 League, 35 F.A. Cup, 10 League Cup and 9 in Europe. He also scored nine goals for AC Milan.

John Aldridge retired as a player at the end of the season 1997-98 with a career total of 329 Football League goals for Newport, Oxford Utd., Liverpool and Tranmere Rov. (1979-98). In all competitions for those clubs he scored 410 goals in 737 apps. He also scored 45 goals in 63 games for Real Sociedad.

MOST GOALS IN INTERNATIONAL MATCHES

THIRTEEN BY

Archie Thompson for Australia v American Samoa in World Cup (Oceania Group qualifier) at Coff's Harbour, New South Wales, Apr. 11, 2001. Result: 31-0.

SEVEN BY

Stanley Harris for England v France in Amateur International in Paris, Nov. 1, 1906. Result: 15-0.

SIX BY

Nat Lofthouse for Football League v Irish League, at Wolves, Sept. 24, 1952. Result: 7-1.

Joe Bambrick for Ireland against Wales, in Belfast, Feb. 1, 1930. Result: 7-0.
W.C. Jordan in Amateur International for England v France, at Park Royal, Mar. 23, 1908. Result: 12-0.
Vivian Woodward for England v Holland in Amateur International, at Chelsea, Dec. 11, 1909. Result: 9-1.

FIVE BY

Howard Vaughton for England v Ireland (Belfast) Feb. 18, 1882. Result: 13-0.
Steve Bloomer for England v Wales (Cardiff City) Mar. 16, 1896. Result: 9-1.
Hughie Gallacher for Scotland against Ireland (Belfast), Feb. 23, 1929. Result: 7-3.
Willie Hall for England v Northern Ireland, at Old Trafford, Nov. 16, 1938. Five in succession (first three in 3½ mins. – fastest International hat-trick). Result: 7-0.
Malcolm Macdonald for England v Cyprus (Wembley) Apr. 16, 1975. Result: 5-0.
Hughie Gallacher for Scottish League against Irish League (Belfast) Nov. 11, 1925. Result: 7-3.
Barney Battles for Scottish League against Irish League (Firhill Park, Glasgow) Oct. 31, 1928. Result: 8-2.
Bobby Flavell for Scottish League against Irish League (Belfast) Apr. 30, 1947. Result: 7-4.
Joe Bradford for Football League v Irish League (Everton) Sept. 25, 1929. Result: 7-2.
Albert Stubbins for Football League v Irish League (Blackpool) Oct. 18, 1950. Result: 6-3.
Brian Clough for Football League v Irish League (Belfast) Sept. 23, 1959. Result: 5-0.

LAST ENGLAND PLAYER TO SCORE . . .

3 goals: Peter Crouch v Jamaica (6–0), friendly, Old Trafford, Jun. 3, 2006.
4 goals: Ian Wright v San Marino (7-1), World Cup qual., Bologna, Nov. 17, 1993.
5 goals: Malcolm Macdonald v Cyprus (5-0), Eur. Champ. qual., Wembley, Apr. 16, 1975.

INTERNATIONAL TOP SHOTS

		Goals	*Games*
England	– Bobby Charlton (1958-70)	49	106
N. Ireland	– David Healy (2000-7)	29	56
Scotland	– Denis Law (1958-74)	30	55
	– Kenny Dalglish (1971-86)	30	102
Wales	– Ian Rush (1980-96)	28	73
Rep. of I.	– Robbie Keane (1998-2007)	29	72

ENGLAND'S TOP MARKSMEN

(As at start of season 2007-08)

	Goals	*Games*
Bobby Charlton (1958-70)	49	106
Gary Lineker (1984-92)	48	80
Jimmy Greaves (1959-67)	44	57
Michael Owen (1998-2007)	37	82
Tom Finney (1946-58)	30	76
Nat Lofthouse (1950-58)	30	33
Alan Shearer (1992-2000)	30	63
Vivian Woodward (1903-11)	29	23
Steve Bloomer (1895-1907)	28	23
David Platt (1989-96)	27	62
Bryan Robson (1979-91)	26	90
Geoff Hurst (1966-72)	24	49
Stan Mortensen (1947-53)	23	25
Tommy Lawton (1938-48)	22	23
Mike Channon (1972-77)	21	46
Kevin Keegan (1972-82)	21	63

CONSECUTIVE GOALS FOR ENGLAND

Steve Bloomer scored in **TEN** consecutive appearances (19 goals) for **England** between March 1895 and March 1899.

Jimmy Greaves scored 11 goals in five consecutive England matches from the start of season 1960–61.

Paul Mariner scored in five consecutive **England** appearances (7 goals) between November 1981 and June 1982.

ENGLAND'S TOP FINAL SERIES MARKSMAN

Gary Lineker with 6 goals at 1986 World Cup in Mexico.

ENGLAND TOP SCORERS IN COMPETITIVE INTERNATIONALS

Gary Lineker 22 goals in 39 matches; **Michael Owen** 23 in 49; **Alan Shearer** 20 in 31.

MOST ENGLAND HAT-TRICKS

Jimmy Greaves 6; **Gary Lineker** 5.

MOST GOALS FOR ENGLAND U-21S

13 – Alan Shearer (11 apps.) Francis Jeffers (13 apps.)

'GOLDEN GOAL' DECIDERS

The Football League, in an experiment to avoid penalty shoot-outs, introduced a new 'golden goal' system in the 1994-95 **Auto Windscreens Shield** to decide matches in the knock-out stages of the competition in which scores were level after 90 minutes. The first goal scored in overtime ended play.

Iain Dunn (Huddersfield Town) became the first player in British football to settle a match by this sudden-death method. His 107th-minute goal beat Lincoln City 3-2 on Nov. 30, 1994, and to mark his 'moment in history' he was presented with a golden football trophy.

The AWS Final of 1995 was decided when **Paul Tait** headed the only goal for Birmingham City against Carlisle Utd. 13 minutes into overtime – the first time a match at Wembley had been decided by the 'golden goal' formula.

First major International tournament match to be decided by sudden death was the Final of the **1996 European Championship** at Wembley in which Germany beat Czech Rep. 2-1 by **Oliver Bierhoff's** goal in the 95th minute.

In the **1998 World Cup Finals** (2nd Round), host country France beat Paraguay 1-0 on **Laurent Blanc's** Golden Goal (114 mins.).

France won the **2000 European Championship** with Golden Goals in the semi-final, 2-1 v Portugal (Zinedine Zidane pen, 117 mins), and in the Final, 2-1 v Italy (David Trezeguet, 103 mins).

Galatasaray (Turkey) won the **European Super Cup** 2-1 against Real Madrid (Monaco, August 25, 2000) with a 103rd min Golden Goal, a penalty.

Liverpool won the **UEFA Cup** 5-4 against Alaves with a 117th min Golden Goal, an own goal, in the Final in Dortmund (May 19, 2001).

In the **2002 World Cup Finals,** 3 matches were decided by Golden Goals: in the 2nd Round Senegal beat Sweden 2-1 (Henri Camara, 104 mins) and South Korea beat Italy 2-1 (Ahn Jung – hwan, 117 mins); in the Quarter-final, Turkey beat Senegal 1-0 (Ilhan Mansiz, 94 mins).

France won the 2003 FIFA Confederations Cup Final against Cameroon (Paris, June 29) with a 97th-minute Golden Goal by Thierry Henry.

Doncaster Rov. won promotion to Football League with a 110th-minute Golden Goal winner (3–2) in the Conference Play-off Final against Dagenham & Redbridge at Stoke (May 10, 2003).

Germany won the **Women's World Cup Final** 2-1 v Sweden (Los Angeles, October 12, 2003) with a 98th-minute Golden Goal.

GOLD TURNS TO SILVER

Starting with the 2003 Finals of the UEFA Cup and Champions' League/European Cup, UEFA introduced a new rule by which a Silver Goal could decide the winners if the scores were 'level' after 90 minutes.

Team leading after 15 minutes' extra time win match. If sides level, a second period of 15 minutes to be played. If still no winner, result to be decided by penalty shoot-out.

UEFA said the change was made because the Golden Goal put too much pressure on referees and prompted teams to play negative football.

Although both 2003 Euro Finals went to extra time, neither was decided by a Silver Goal. The new rule applied in the 2004 European Championship Finals, and Greece won their Semi-final against the Czech Republic with a 105th-minute Silver Goal.

The **International Board** decided (Feb. 28 2004) that the Golden/Silver Goal rule was 'unfair' and that from July 1 competitive International matches level after extra time would, when necessary, be settled on penalties.

PREMIERSHIP TOP SHOTS (1992-2007)

Alan Shearer	260
Andy Cole	188
Thierry Henry	174
Robbie Fowler	163
Les Ferdinand	150
Teddy Sheringham	147
Jimmy Floyd Hasselbaink	127
Michael Owen	125
Dwight Yorke	122
Ian Wright	113
Dion Dublin	111
Matthew Le Tissier	101

(As at start of season 2007-08)

LEAGUE GOAL RECORDS

The highest goal-scoring aggregates in the Football League, Premier and Scottish League are as follows:

FOR

	Goals	*Games*	*Club*	*Season*
Prem.	97	38	Manchester Utd.	1999-2000
Div. 1	128	42	Aston Villa	1930-1
New Div. 1	108	46	Manchester City	2001-02
New Champ.	99	46	Reading	2005-06
Div. 2	122	42	Middlesbrough	1926-7
New Div. 2	89	46	Millwall	2000-01
New Lge. 1	87	46	Luton Town	2004-05
Div. 3(S)	127	42	Millwall	1927-8
Div. 3(N)	128	42	Bradford City	1928-9
Div. 3	111	46	Q.P.R.	1961-2
New Div. 3	96	46	Luton Town	2001-02
New Lge. 2	90	46	Yeovil Town	2004-05
Div. 4	134	46	Peterborough Utd.	1960-1
Scot. Prem.	105	38	Celtic	2003-04
Scot. L. 1	132	34	Hearts	1957-8
Scot. L. 2	142	34	Raith Rov.	1937-8
Scot. L. 3 (Modern)	130	36	Gretna	2004-05

AGAINST

	Goals	*Games*	*Club*	*Season*
Prem.	100	42	Swindon Town	1993-4
Div. 1	125	42	Blackpool	1930-1
New Div. 1	102	46	Stockport Co.	2001-02

New Champ.	86	46	Crewe Alexandra	2004-05
Div. 2	141	34	Darwen	1898-9
New Div. 2	102	46	Chester City	1992-3
New Lge. 1	98	46	Stockport Co.	2004-05
Div. 3(S)	135	42	Merthyr T.	1929-30
Div. 3(N)	136	42	Nelson	1927-8
Div. 3	123	46	Accrington S.	1959-60
New Div. 3	113	46	Doncaster Rov.	1997-8
New Lge. 2	85	46	Kidderminster Harriers	2004-05
Div. 4	109	46	Hartlepool Utd.	1959-60
Scot. Prem.	100	36	Morton	1984-5
Scot. Prem.	100	44	Morton	1987-8
Scot. L. 1	137	38	Leith A.	1931-2
Scot. L. 2	146	38	Edinburgh City	1931-2
Scot. L. 3 (Modern)	118	36	East Stirling	2003-04

BEST DEFENSIVE RECORDS – *Denotes under old offside law

Div.	*Goals Agst.*	*Games*	*Club*	*Season*
Prem.	15	38	Chelsea	2004-05
1	16	42	Liverpool	1978-9
1	*15	22	Preston N.E.	1888-9
New Div. 1	28	46	Sunderland	1998-9
New Champ.	30	46	Preston N.E.	2005-06
2	18	28	Liverpool	1893-4
2	*22	34	Sheffield Wed.	1899-1900
2	24	42	Birmingham City	1947-8
2	24	42	Crystal Palace	1978-9
New Div. 2	25	46	Wigan Athletic	2002-03
New Lge. 1	35	46	Scunthorpe Utd.	2006-07
3(S)	*21	42	Southampton	1921-2
3(S)	30	42	Cardiff City	1946-7
3(N)	*21	38	Stockport Co.	1921-2
3(N)	21	46	Port Vale	1953-4
3	30	46	Middlesbrough	1986-7
New Div. 3	20	46	Gillingham	1995-6
New Lge. 2	34	46	Walsall	2006-07
4	25	46	Lincoln City	1980-1

SCOTTISH LEAGUE

Div.	*Goals Agst.*	*Games*	*Club*	*Season*
Prem.	18	38	Celtic	2001-02
1	*12	22	Dundee	1902-3
1	*14	38	Celtic	1913-14
2	20	38	Morton	1966-7
2	*29	38	Clydebank	1922-3
2	29	36	East Fife	1995-6
New Div. 3	21	36	Brechin	1995-6

TOP SCORERS (LEAGUE ONLY)

		Goals	*Div.*
2006–07	Billy Sharp (Scunthorpe Utd.)	30	Lge. 1
2005–06	Thierry Henry (Arsenal)	27	Prem.

2004-05	Stuart Elliott (Hull City)	27	Lge. 1
	Phil Jevons (Yeovil Town)	27	Lge. 2
	Dean Windass (Bradford City)	27	Lge. 1
2003-04	Thierry Henry (Arsenal)	30	Prem.
2002-03	Andy Morrell (Wrexham)	34	3
2001-02	Shaun Goater (Manchester City)	28	1
	Bobby Zamora (Brighton & H.A.)	28	2
2000-01	Bobby Zamora (Brighton & H.A.)	28	3
1999-00	Kevin Phillips (Sunderland)	30	Prem.
1998-9	Lee Hughes (W.B.A.)	31	1
1997-8	Pierre van Hooijdonk (Nott'm Forest)	29	1
	Kevin Phillips (Sunderland)	29	1
1996-7	Graeme Jones (Wigan Athletic)	31	3
1995-6	Alan Shearer (Blackburn Rov.)	31	Prem.
1994-5	Alan Shearer (Blackburn Rov.)	34	Prem.
1993-4	Jimmy Quinn (Reading)	35	2
1992-3	Guy Whittingham (Portsmouth)	42	1
1991-2	Ian Wright (Crystal Palace 5, Arsenal 24)	29	1
1990-1	Teddy Sheringham (Millwall)	33	2
1989-90	Mick Quinn (Newcastle Utd.)	32	2
1988-9	Steve Bull (Wolves)	37	3
1987-8	Steve Bull (Wolves)	34	4
1986-7	Clive Allen (Tottenham)	33	1
1985-6	Gary Lineker (Everton)	30	1
1984-5	Tommy Tynan (Plymouth Argyle)	31	3
	John Clayton (Tranmere Rov.)	31	4
1983-4	Trevor Senior (Reading)	36	4
1982-3	Luther Blissett (Watford)	27	1
1981-2	Keith Edwards (Hull City 1, Sheffield Utd. 35)	36	4
1980-1	Tony Kellow (Exeter City)	25	3
1979-80	Clive Allen (Queens Park Rangers)	28	2
1978-9	Ross Jenkins (Watford)	29	3
1977-8	Steve Phillips (Brentford)	32	4
	Alan Curtis (Swansea City)	32	4
1976-7	Peter Ward (Brighton & H.A.)	32	3
1975-6	Dixie McNeil (Hereford)	35	3
1974-5	Dixie McNeil (Hereford)	31	3
1973-4	Brian Yeo (Gillingham)	31	4
1972-3	Bryan (Pop) Robson (West Ham Utd.)	28	1
1971-2	Ted MacDougall (Bournemouth)	35	3
1970-1	Ted MacDougall (Bournemouth)	42	4
1969-70	Albert Kinsey (Wrexham)	27	4
1968-9	Jimmy Greaves (Tottenham)	27	1
1967-8	George Best (Manchester Utd.)	28	1
	Ron Davies (Southampton)	28	1
1966-7	Ron Davies (Southampton)	37	1
1965-6	Kevin Hector (Bradford P.A.)	44	4
1964-5	Alick Jeffrey (Doncaster Rov.)	36	4
1963-4	Hugh McIlmoyle (Carlisle Utd.)	39	4
1962-3	Jimmy Greaves (Tottenham)	37	1
1961-2	Roger Hunt (Liverpool)	41	2
1960-1	Terry Bly (Peterborough Utd.)	52	4

100 LEAGUE GOALS IN SEASON

Manchester City, First Div. Champions in 2001-02, scored 108 goals.

Bolton Wand., First Div. Champions in 1996-7, reached 100 goals, the first side to complete a century in League football since 103 by Northampton Town (Div. 4 Champions) in 1986-7.

Last League Champions to reach **100** League goals: **Tottenham** (115 in 1960-1). Last century of goals in the top division: **111** by runners-up **Tottenham** in 1962-3.

Wolves topped 100 goals in four successive First Division seasons (1957-8, 1958-9, 1959-60, 1960-1).

In **1930-1**, the Championship top three all scored a century of League goals: 1 Arsenal (127), 2 Aston Villa (128), 3 Sheffield Wed. (102).

100 GOALS AGAINST

Swindon Town, relegated with 100 goals against in 1993-4, were the first top-division club to concede a century of League goals since **Ipswich Town** (121) went down in 1964. Most goals conceded in the top division: 125 by **Blackpool** in 1930-31, but they avoided relegation.

MOST LEAGUE GOALS ON ONE DAY

A record of 209 goals in the four divisions of the Football League (43 matches) was set on **Jan. 2, 1932**: 56 in Div. 1, 53 in Div. 2, 57 in Div. 3 South and 43 in Div. 3 North. There were two 10-goal aggregates: Bradford City 9, Barnsley 1 in Div. 2 and Coventry City 5, Fulham 5 in Div. 3 South.

That total of 209 League goals on one day was equalled on **Feb. 1, 1936** (44 matches): 46 in Div. 1, 46 in Div. 2, 49 in Div. 3 South and 69 in Div. 3 North. Two matches in the Northern Section produced 23 of the goals: Chester 12, York City 0 and Crewe Alexandra 5, Chesterfield 6.

MOST GOALS IN TOP DIV. ON ONE DAY

This record has stood since Dec. 26, 1963, when **66 goals** were scored in the ten First Division matches played.

MOST F.A. PREMIER LEAGUE GOALS ON ONE DAY

47, in nine matches on May 8, 1993 (last day of season).

FEWEST PREMIERSHIP GOALS IN ONE WEEK-END

10, in 10 matches on Nov. 24/25, 2001

FEWEST FIRST DIV. GOALS ON ONE DAY

For full/near full programme: **Ten goals,** all by home clubs, in ten matches on April 28, 1923 (day of Wembley's first F.A. Cup Final).

SCORERS IN CONSECUTIVE TOP-DIVISION MATCHES

Stan Mortensen scored in 11 consecutive Division One games for Blackpool in season 1950–51. **Ruud van Nistelrooy** (Manchester Utd.) scored 13 goals in last 8 games of season 2002-03 and in first 2 of 2003-04. Since the last war, 3 other players scored in 10 successive matches in the old First Division: **Billy McAdams** (Man. City, 1957-58), **Ron Davies** (Southampton, 1966-67) and **John Aldridge** (Liverpool, May-Oct. 1987).

SCORERS FOR 6 PREMIERSHIP CLUBS

Les Ferdinand (Q.P.R., Newcastle Utd., Tottenham, West Ham Utd., Leicester City, Bolton Wand.); **Andy Cole** (Newcastle Utd., Manchester Utd., Blackburn Rov., Fulham, Manchester City, Portsmouth).

SCORERS FOR 5 PREMIERSHIP CLUBS

Stan Collymore (Nott'm. Forest, Liverpool, Aston Villa, Leicester City, Bradford City); **Mark Hughes** (Manchester Utd., Chelsea, Southampton, Everton, Blackburn Rov.); **Nick Barmby** (Tottenham, Middlesbrough, Everton, Liverpool, Leeds Utd.); **Benito Carbone** (Sheff. Wed., Aston Villa, Bradford City, Derby Co., Middlesbrough); **Ashley Ward** (Norwich City, Derby Co., Barnsley, Blackburn Rov. Bradford City); **Teddy Sheringham**

(Nottm. Forest, Tottenham, Manchester Utd., Portsmouth, West Ham Utd.); **Marcus Bent** (Crystal Palace, Ipswich Town, Leicester City, Everton, Charlton Althetic); **Chris Sutton** (Norwich City, Blackburn Rov., Chelsea, Birmingham City, Aston Villa).

SCORERS IN MOST CONSECUTIVE LEAGUE MATCHES

Arsenal broke the record by scoring in 55 successive Premiership fixtures: the last match in season 2000-01, then all 38 games in winning the Championship in 2001–02, and the first 16 in season 2002–03. The sequence ended with a 2–0 defeat away to Manchester Utd. on December 7, 2002.

Chesterfield previously held the record, having scored in 46 consecutive matches in Div. 3 (North), starting on Christmas Day 1929 and ending on December 27, 1930.

SIX-OUT-OF-SIX HEADERS

When **Oxford Utd.** beat Shrewsbury Town 6-0 (Div. 2) on Apr. 23, 1996, all six goals were headers.

FIVE IN A MATCH

Latest players to score 5 goals in a top-division match: **Tony Woodcock** (for Arsenal in 6-2 win away to Aston Villa) and **Ian Rush** (Liverpool 6, Luton Town 0), both on October 29, 1983; **Andy Cole** (Manchester Utd. 9, Ipswich Town 0) on Mar. 4, 1995; **Alan Shearer** (Newcastle Utd. 8, Sheffield Wed. 0) on Sept. 19, 1999.

ALL–ROUND MARKSMAN

Alan Cork scored in four divisions of the Football League and in the F.A. Premier League in his 18-season career with Wimbledon, Sheffield Utd. and Fulham (1977-95).

MOST CUP GOALS

F.A. Cup – most goals in one season: 20 by Jimmy Ross (Preston N.E., runners-up 1887-8); 15 by Alex (Sandy) Brown (Tottenham, winners 1900-1).

Most F.A. Cup goals in individual careers: 49 by Harry Cursham (Notts Co. 1877-89); this century: 44 by Ian Rush (39 for Liverpool, 4 for Chester City, 1 for Newcastle Utd. 1979-98). Denis Law was the previous highest F.A. Cup scorer in the 20th century with 41 goals for Huddersfield Town, Manchester City and Manchester Utd. (1957-74).

Most F.A. Cup Final goals by individual: 5 by Ian Rush for Liverpool (2 in 1986, 2 in 1989, 1 in 1992).

HOTTEST CUP HOT-SHOT

Geoff Hurst scored 21 cup goals in season 1965-66: 11 League Cup, 4 F.A. Cup and 2 Cup-Winners' Cup for West Ham Utd., and 4 in the World Cup for England.

SCORERS IN EVERY ROUND

Twelve players have scored in **every round** of the F.A. Cup in one season, from opening to Final inclusive: **Archie Hunter** (Aston Villa, winners 1887); **Sandy Brown** (Tottenham, winners 1901); **Harry Hampton** (Aston Villa, winners 1905); **Harold Blackmore** (Bolton Wand., winners 1929); **Ellis Rimmer** (Sheffield Wed., winners 1935); **Frank O'Donnell** (Preston N.E., beaten 1937); **Stan Mortensen** (Blackpool, beaten 1948); **Jackie Milburn** (Newcastle Utd., winners 1951); **Nat Lofthouse** (Bolton Wand., beaten 1953); **Charlie Wayman** (Preston N.E., beaten 1954); **Jeff Astle** (W.B.A., winners 1968); **Peter Osgood** (Chelsea, winners 1970).

Blackmore and the next seven completed their 'set' in the Final at Wembley; Osgood did so in the Final replay at Old Trafford.

Only player to score in every **Football League Cup** round possible in one season: **Tony Brown** for W.B.A., winners 1965-6, with 9 goals in 10 games (after bye in Round 1).

TEN IN A ROW

Dixie McNeill scored for Wrexham in **ten successive** F.A. Cup rounds (18 goals): 11 in Rounds 1-6, 1977-8; 3 in Rounds 3-4, 1978-9; 4 in Rounds 3-4, 1979-80.

Stan Mortensen (Blackpool) scored 25 goals in 16 F.A. Cup rounds out of 17 (1946-51).

TOP MATCH HAULS IN F.A. CUP

Ted MacDougall scored nine goals, a record for the competition proper, in the F.A. Cup first round on Nov. 20, 1971, when Bournemouth beat Margate 11-0. On Nov. 23, 1970 he had scored six in an 8-1 first round replay against Oxford City.

Other six-goal F.A. Cup scorers include **George Hilsdon** (Chelsea v Worksop, 9-1, 1907-8), **Ronnie Rooke** (Fulham v Bury, 6-0, 1938-9), **Harold Atkinson** (Tranmere Rov. v Ashington, 8-1, 1952-3), **George Best** (Manchester Utd. v Northampton Town 1969-70, 8-2 away), and **Duane Darby** (Hull City v Whitby, 8-4, 1996-7).

Denis Law scored all **six** for Manchester City at Luton Town (6-2) in an F.A. Cup 4th Round tie on Jan. 28, 1961, but none of them counted – the match was abandoned (69 mins.) because of a waterlogged pitch. He also scored City's goal when the match was played again, but they lost 3-1.

Tony Philliskirk scored **five** when Peterborough Utd. beat Kingstonian 9-1 in an F.A. Cup 1st Round replay on November 25, 1992, but had them wiped from the records. With the score at 3-0, the Kingstonian goalkeeper was concussed by a coin thrown from the crowd and unable to play on. The F.A. ordered the match to be replayed at Peterborough behind closed doors, and Kingstonian lost 1-0.

• Two players have scored **ten goals** in F.A. Cup preliminary round matches: **Chris Marron** for South Shields against Radcliffe in September 1947; **Paul Jackson** when Sheffield-based club Stocksbridge Park Steels beat Oldham Town 17–1 on August 31, 2002. He scored 5 in each half and all ten with his feet – goal times 6, 10, 22, 30, 34, 68, 73, 75, 79, 84 mins.

QUICKEST GOALS AND RAPID SCORING

A goal in **4 seconds** was claimed by **Jim Fryatt,** for Bradford P.A. v Tranmere Rov. (Div. 4, April 25, 1965), and by **Gerry Allen** for Whitstable Town v Danson (Kent League, March 3,1989). **Damian Mori** scored in 4 seconds for Adelaide City v Sydney Utd. (Australian National League, December 6, 1995).

Goals after 6 seconds – **Albert Mundy** for Aldershot v Hartlepool Utd., October 25, 1958; **Barrie Jones** for Notts County v Torquay Utd., March 31, 1962; **Keith Smith** for Crystal Palace v Derby Co., December 12, 1964.

9.6 seconds by **John Hewitt** for Aberdeen at Motherwell, 3rd Round, January 23, 1982 (fastest goal in Scottish Cup history).

Colin Cowperthwaite reputedly scored in **3½ seconds** for Barrow v Kettering (Alliance Premier League) on December 8, 1979, but the timing was unofficial.

Phil Starbuck scored for Huddersfield Town only **3 seconds** after entering the field as 54th min. substitute at home to Wigan Athletic (Div. 2) on Easter Monday, April 12, 1993. A corner-kick was delayed, awaiting his arrival, and he scored with a header.

Malcolm Macdonald scored after **5 seconds** (officially timed) in Newcastle Utd.'s 7-3 win in a pre-season friendly at St. Johnstone on July 29, 1972.

Scored first kick: Billy Foulkes (Newcastle Utd.) for Wales v England at Cardiff, October 20, 1951, in his first International match.

Six goals in seven minutes in Preston N.E.'s record 26-0 F.A. Cup 1st Round win v Hyde, October 15, 1887.

Five in 20 minutes: Frank Keetley in Lincoln City's 9-1 win over Halifax Town in Div. 3 (North), January 16, 1932; **Brian Dear** for West Ham Utd. v W.B.A. (6-1, Div.1) April 16, 1965. **Kevin Hector** for Bradford P.A. v Barnsley (7–2, Div. 4) November 20, 1965.

Four in five minutes: by **John McIntyre** for Blackburn Rov. v Everton (Div. 1), September 16, 1922; **W.G. (Billy) Richardson** for W.B.A. v West Ham Utd. (Div. 1), November 7, 1931.

Three in three minutes: Billy Lane for Watford v Clapton Orient (Div.3S), December 20, 1933; **Johnny Hartburn** for Leyton Orient v Shrewsbury Town (Div. 3S), January 22, 1955;

Gary Roberts for Brentford v Newport, (Freight Rover Trophy, South Final), May 17, 1985; **Gary Shaw** for Shrewsbury Town v Bradford City (Div. 3), December 22, 1990.

Fastest hat-trick in League History: 2 mins. 20 secs. by Bournemouth's 84th-minute substitute **James Hayter** in 6-0 home win v Wrexham (Div. 2) on February 24, 2004 (goal times 86, 87, 88 mins.).

Three in 2½ minutes: Jimmy Scarth for Gillingham v Leyton Orient (Div. 3S), November 1, 1952.

Two in nine seconds: Jamie Bates with last kick of first half, **Jermaine McSporran** 9 seconds into second half when Wycombe Wand. beat Peterborough Utd. 2-0 at home (Div. 2) on September 23, 2000.

Arsenal scored six goals in 18 minutes (71-89 mins.) in 7-1 home win (Div. 1) v Sheffield Wed., February 15, 1992.

Plymouth Argyle scored five goals in first 18 minutes in 7-0 home win v Chesterfield (Div. 2), January 3, 2004.

Sunderland scored eight goals in 28 minutes at Newcastle Utd. (9-1 Div 1), December 5, 1908. Newcastle went on to win the Championship.

Southend Utd. scored all seven goals in 29 minutes in 7-0 win at home to Torquay Utd. (Leyland Daf Cup, Southern quarter-final), February 26, 1991. Score was 0-0 until 55th. minute.

Six goals in first 19 minutes by Tranmere Rov. when they beat Oldham Athletic 13-4 (Div. 3 North) on December 26, 1935.

Notts Co. scored six second-half goals in 12 minutes (Tommy Lawton 3, Jackie Sewell 3) when they beat Exeter City 9-0 (Div. 3 South) at Meadow Lane on October 16, 1948.

World's fastest goal: 2.8 seconds, direct from kick-off, by Argentinian **Ricardo Olivera** for Rio Negro v Soriano (Uruguayan League), December 26, 1998.

Fastest International goal: 8.3 secs. by **Davide Gualtieri** for San Marino v England (World Cup qual., Bologna, November 17, 1993).

Fastest International hat-trick: 3 minutes 15 seconds by **Masashi Nakayami** for Japan in 9-0 win v Brunei in Macao (Asian Cup), February 16, 2000.

Fastest International hat-trick in British matches: 3½ minutes by **Willie Hall** for England v N. Ireland at Old Trafford, Manchester, November 16, 1938. (Hall scored 5 in 7-0 win); 4½ minutes by **Arif Erdem** for Turkey v N. Ireland, European Championship, at Windsor Park, Belfast, on September 4, 1999.

Fastest International goal by substitute: 5 seconds by **John Jensen** for Denmark v Belgium (Eur. Champ.), October 12, 1994.

Fastest England goals: 17 seconds by **Tommy Lawton** v Portugal in Lisbon, May 25, 1947. 27 seconds by **Bryan Robson** v. France in World Cup at Bilbao, Spain on June 16, 1982; 37 seconds by **Gareth Southgate** v South Africa in Durban, May 22, 2003; 30 seconds by **Jack Cock** v Ireland, Belfast, October 25, 1919; 30 seconds by **Bill Nicholson** v Portugal at Goodison Park, May 19, 1951. 38 seconds by **Bryan Robson** v Yugoslavia at Wembley, December 13, 1989; 42 seconds by **Gary Lineker** v Malaysia in Kuala Lumpur, June 12, 1991.

Fastest goal by England substitute: 10 seconds by **Teddy Sheringham** v Greece (World Cup qualifying match) at Old Trafford, October 6, 2001.

Fastest F.A. Cup Final goals: 30 seconds by **John Devey**, for Aston Villa v W.B.A., 1895; at Wembley: 42 seconds by **Roberto di Matteo**, for Chelsea v Middlesbrough, 1997.

Fastest goal by substitute in F.A. Cup Final: 96 seconds by **Teddy Sheringham** for Manchester Utd. v Newcastle Utd. at Wembley, May 22, 1999.

Fastest League Cup Final goal: 45 seconds by **John Arne Riise** for Liverpool v Chelsea, 2005.

Fastest goal on full League debut: 7.7 seconds by **Freddy Eastwood** for Southend Utd. v Swansea City (Lge. 2), October 16, 2004. He went on to score hat-trick in 4-2 win.

Fastest goal in cup final: 4.07 seconds by 14-year-old **Owen Price** for Ernest Bevin College, Tooting, beaten 3-1 by Barking Abbey in Heinz Ketchup Cup Final at Arsenal Stadium on May 18, 2000. Owen, on Tottenham's books, scored from inside his own half when the ball was played back to him from kick-off.

Fastest F.A. Cup hat-tricks: In 3 minutes by **Billy Best** for Southend Utd. v Brentford (2nd. Round, December 7, 1968); 2 minutes 20 seconds by **Andy Locke** for Nantwich v Droylesden (1st. Qual. Round, September 9, 1995).

F.A. Premier League – fastest scoring: Four goals in 4 minutes, 44 seconds by Tottenham at home to Southampton on Sunday, February 7, 1993.

Premiership – fast scoring away: When Aston Villa won 5-0 at Leicester (January 31, 2004), all the goals were scored in 18 second-half minutes (50-68).

Fastest First Division hat-tricks since war: Graham Leggat, 3 goals in 3 minutes (first half) when Fulham beat Ipswich Town 10-1 on Boxing Day, 1963; **Nigel Clough,** 3 goals in 4 minutes (81, 82, 85 pen) when Nott'm. Forest beat Q.P.R. 4-0 on December 13, 1987.

Fastest goal in Champions League: 10 seconds by **Roy Makaay** for Bayern Munich v Real Madrid (1st. ko rd.), March 7, 2007.

F.A. Premier League – fastest hat-trick: 4½ minutes (26, 29, 31) by **Robbie Fowler** in Liverpool 3, Arsenal 0 on Sunday, August 28, 1994.

Fastest hat-trick of headers: Dixie Dean's 5 goals in Everton's 7–2 win at home to Chelsea (Div. 1) on November 14, 1931 included 3 headers between 5th and 15th-minutes.

Fastest Premier League goals: 10 seconds by **Ledley King** for Tottenham away to Bradford City, December 9, 2000; 10.4 seconds by **Alan Shearer** for Newcastle Utd. v Manchester City, January 18, 2003: 11 seconds by **Mark Viduka** for Leeds Utd. v Charlton Athletic, March 17, 2001; 12.5 seconds by **James Beattie** for Southampton at Chelsea, August 28, 2004; 13 seconds by **Chris Sutton** for Blackburn Rov. at Everton, April 1, 1995; 13 seconds by **Dwight Yorke** for Aston Villa at Coventry City, September 30, 1995.

Fastest top-division goal: 7 seconds by **Bobby Langton** for Preston N.E. v Manchester City (Div. 1), August 25, 1948.

Fastest Premier League goal by substitute: 9 seconds by **Shaun Goater**, Manchester City's equaliser away to Manchester Utd. (1–1), Feb. 9, 2003.

Four in 13 minutes by Premier League substitute: Ole Gunnar Solskjaer for Manchester Utd. away to Nott'm. Forest, Feb. 6, 1999.

Fastest Scottish hat-trick: 2½ mins. by **Ian St. John** for Motherwell away to Hibernian (Scottish League Cup), August 15, 1959.

Fastest all-time hat-trick: Reported at 1 min. 50 secs. by **Eduardo Maglioni** for Independiente against Gimnasia de la Plata in Argentina First Division, March 18, 1973.

Fastest goal in Women's Football: 7 seconds by **Angie Harriott** for Launton Ladies v Thame Utd. (Southern League, Prem. Div.), season 1998-9.

FASTEST GOALS IN WORLD CUP FINAL SERIES

10.8 secs. by **Hakan Sukur** for Turkey against South Korea in 3rd/4th-place match at Taegu, June 29, 2002.

15 secs. by **Vaclav Masek** for Czechoslovakia v Mexico (in Vina, Chile, 1962).

27 secs. by **Bryan Robson** for England v France (in Bilbao, Spain, 1982).

TOP MATCH SCORES SINCE WAR

By English clubs: **13-0** by Newcastle Utd. v Newport (Div. 2, Oct. 1946); **13-2** by Tottenham v Crewe Alexandra (F.A. Cup 4th. Rd. replay, Feb. 1960); **13-0** by Chelsea v Jeunesse Hautcharage, Lux. (Cup-Winners' Cup 1st. Rd., 2nd. Leg, Sept. 1971).

By Scottish club: **20-0** by Stirling Albion v Selkirk (E. of Scotland League) in Scottish Cup 1st. Rd. (Dec. 1984). That is the highest score in British first-class football since Preston N.E. beat Hyde 26-0 in F.A. Cup, Oct. 1887.

GOALS BY WINGERS

	Season	*Matches*	*Goals*
Cliff Bastin (Arsenal)	(Div. I) 1932-3	42	33
Bob Ferrier (Motherwell)	(Div. I) 1929-30	27	32
Ken Dawson (Falkirk)	(Div. II) 1935-6	34	39

GOALS BY GOALKEEPERS

Goalkeepers who have scored with long clearances include:

Pat Jennings for Tottenham away to Manchester Utd. (goalkeeper Alex Stepney) on August 12, 1967 (F.A. Charity Shield).

Peter Shilton for Leicester City at Southampton (goalkeeper Campbell Forsyth) on October 14, 1967 (Div. 1).

Ray Cashley for Bristol City at home to Hull City (goalkeeper Jeff Wealands) on September 18, 1973 (Div. 2).

Steve Sherwood for Watford away to Coventry City (goalkeeper Raddy Avramovic) on January 14, 1984 (Div. 1).

Steve Ogrizovic for Coventry City away to Sheffield Wed. (goalkeeper Martin Hodge) on October 25, 1986 (Div. 1).

Andy Goram for Hibernian at home to Morton (goalkeeper David Wylie) on May 7, 1988 (Scottish Premier Div.).

Andy McLean, on Irish League debut, for Cliftonville v Linfield (goalkeeper George Dunlop) on August 20, 1988.

Alan Paterson for Glentoran against Linfield (goalkeeper George Dunlop) on November 30, 1988 (Irish League Cup Final at The Oval, Belfast). His long punt (87 mins) gave Glentoran a 2-1 victory – the only instance of a goalkeeper scoring the winning goal in a senior cup final in the UK.

Ray Charles for East Fife at Stranraer (goalkeeper Bernard Duffy) on February 28, 1990 (Scottish Div. 2).

Iain Hesford scored Maidstone's winner (3-2 v Hereford, Div. 4, November 2, 1991) with long kick-out that went first bounce past Tony Elliott in opposite goal.

Chris Mackenzie for Hereford at home to Barnet (goalkeeper Mark Taylor) in Div. 3, August 12, 1995.

Mark Bosnich (Aston Villa) scored the last goal (a penalty) when Australia beat Solomon Islands 13-0 in World Cup Oceania Zone qualifier in Sydney on June 11, 1997.

Steve Mildenhall (Notts Co.) scored with a free-kick from his own half past Mansfield Town's Kevin Pilkington for the winning goal (4-3, away) in the Worthington Cup 1st Round on August 21, 2001.

Mart Poom headed Sunderland's last-seconds equaliser (1-1) away to his former club Derby Co. (goalkeeper Andy Oakes), Div. 1, September 20, 2003.

Brad Friedel (Blackburn Rov.) shot late equaliser against Charlton Athletic 'keeper Dean Kiely at The Valley (Premiership, February 21, 2004) but finished on losing side, 2-3.

Paul Robinson (Leeds Utd.) headed last-minute equaliser (2-2) at home to Swindon Town (Carling Cup, 2nd Round, September 24, 2003). Leeds won 4-3 on penalties. Robinson scored again with a 90-yard free-kick in Tottenham's 3-1 Premiership win over Watford on March 17 2007. The ball bounced over his England rival Ben Foster, who was ten yards off his line.

Andy Lonergan (Preston) scored equaliser (1-1) at Leicester, in Coca-Cola Championship on October 2, 2004 with 95-yard punt past 'keeper Kevin Pressman, who slipped on wet turf.

Gavin Ward (Tranmere Rov.) scored first goal in 3-0 win over Leyton Orient (lge. 1) on September 2, 2006 with 80-yard indirect free-kick which Glenn Morris parried into own net.

Mark Crossley (Sheffield Wed.) headed injury-time equalist from corner past Southampton's Kelvin Davis (Champ. 3-3) on December 23, 2006.

Most goals by a goalkeeper in a League season: 5 (all penalties) by **Arthur Birch** for Chesterfield (Div. 3 North), 1923-4.

Arthur Wilkie, Reading's goalkeeper at home to Halifax Town (Div. 3) on August 31, 1962, injured a hand, then played as a forward and scored twice in a 4-2 win.

Alex Stepney was Manchester Utd.'s joint top scorer for two months in season 1973-4 with two penalties.

Alan Fettis, N. Ireland goalkeeper, scored twice for Hull City in Div. 2 in season 1994-5: as a substitute in 3-1 home win v Oxford Utd. (Dec. 17) and, when selected outfield, with last-minute winner (2-1) at Blackpool on May 6.

Peter Schmeichel, Manchester Utd.'s goalkeeper, headed an 89th minute equaliser (2-2) from Ryan Giggs' corner in the UEFA Cup 1st. Round, 2nd leg against Rotor Volgograd (Russia) on September 26, 1995, but United lost the tie on away goals.

On October 20, 2001, **Schmeichel** became the first goalkeeper to score in the Premiership when, following a corner, he volleyed Aston Villa's second goal in their 3-2 defeat at Everton.

In League matches for Swansea City, **Roger Freestone** scored with a penalty at Oxford Utd. (Div. 2, April 30, 1995) and, in 1995-6 (Div. 2) with penalties at home to Shrewsbury Town (August 12) and Chesterfield (August 26).

Jimmy Glass, on loan from Swindon Town, scored the winner that kept Carlisle Utd. in the Football League on May 8, 1999. With only ten seconds of injury time left, he went upfield for a corner and shot the goal that beat Plymouth Argyle 2-1 at Brunton Park. It preserved Carlisle's League existence since 1928 and sent Scarborough down to the Conference.

Tony Roberts (Dagenham & Redbridge), only known goalkeeper to score from open play in the F.A. Cup, away to Basingstoke in 4th Qual. Round on October 27, 2001. His last-minute equaliser (2-2) forced a replay, which Dagenham won 3-0 and went on to the 3rd Round proper.

Jose Luis Chilavert, Paraguay's Int. goalkeeper, scored a hat-trick of penalties when his club Velez Sarsfield beat Ferro Carril Oeste 6-1 in the Argentine League on November 28, 1999. In all, he scored 8 goals in his 72 Internationals.

OWN GOALS

Most by player in one season: 5 by **Robert Stuart** (Middlesbrough) in 1934-35.

Three in match by one team: Sheffield Wed.'s Vince Kenny, Norman Curtis and Eddie Gannon in 5–4 defeat at home to W.B.A. (Div. 1) on December 26, 1952; **Rochdale's** George Underwood, Kenny Boyle and Danny Murphy in 7–2 defeat at Carlisle (Div. 3 North), December 25, 1954; **Sunderland's** Stephen Wright and Michael Proctor (2) in 24, 29, 32 minutes at home to Charlton Athletic (1–3, Premiership), February 1, 2003.

Two in match by one player: Chris Nicholl (Aston Villa) scored all 4 goals in 2-2 draw away to Leicester City (Div. 1), March 20, 1976; **Jamie Carragher** (Liverpool) in first half at home to Manchester Utd. (2-3) in Premiership, September 11, 1999; **Jim Goodwin** (Stockport Co.) in 1–4 defeat away to Plymouth Argyle (Div. 2), September 23, 2002; **Michael Proctor** (Sunderland) in 1–3 defeat at home to Charlton Athletic Ath. (Premiership), February 1, 2003.

Fastest own goals: 8 seconds by **Pat Kruse** of Torquay Utd., for Cambridge Utd. (Div. 4), January 3, 1977; in **First Division**, 16 seconds by **Steve Bould** (Arsenal) away to Sheffield Wed., February 17, 1990.

Late own-goal man: Frank Sinclair (Leicester City) put through his own goal in the 90th minute of Premiership matches away to Arsenal (L1-2) and at home to Chelsea (D2-2) in August 1999.

Half an own goal each: Chelsea's second goal in a 3-1 home win against Leicester City on December 18, 1954 was uniquely recorded as 'shared own goal'. Leicester City defenders **Stan Milburn** and **Jack Froggatt**, both lunging at the ball in an attempt to clear, connected simultaneously and sent it rocketing into the net.

Match of 149 own goals: When Adama, Champions of Malagasy (formerly Madagascar) won a League match 149-0 on October 31, 2002, all 149 were **own goals** scored by opponents Stade Olympique De L'Emryne. They repeatedly put the ball in their own net in protest at a refereeing decision.

MOST SCORERS IN MATCH

Liverpool set a Football League record with **EIGHT** scorers when they beat Crystal Palace 9-0 (Div.1) on September 12, 1989. Their marksmen were: Steve Nicol (7 and 88 mins), Steve McMahon (16), Ian Rush (45), Gary Gillespie (56), Peter Beardsley (61), John Aldridge pen. (67), John Barnes (79) and Glenn Hysen (82).

Fifteen years earlier, **Liverpool** had gone one better with **NINE** different scorers when they achieved their record win, 11-0 at home to Stromsgodset (Norway) in the Cup-Winners' Cup 1st. round, 1st leg on September 17, 1974.

Eight players scored for **Swansea City** when they beat Sliema, Malta, 12-0 in the Cup-Winners' Cup 1st round, 1st leg on September 15, 1982.

Nine **Stirling Albion** players scored in the 20-0 win against Selkirk in the Scottish Cup 1st. Round on December 8, 1984.

LONG SCORING RUNS

Tom Phillipson scored in 13 consecutive matches for Wolves (Div. 2) in season 1926-27, which is still an English League record. **Bill Prendergast** scored in 13 successive League and Cup appearances for Chester City (Div. 3 North) in season 1938-39.

Dixie Dean scored in 12 consecutive games (23 goals) for Everton in Div. 2 in 1930-1.

Danish striker **Finn Dossing** scored in 15 consecutive matches (Scottish record) for Dundee Utd. (Div. 1) in 1964-5.

Marco Negri (Rangers) scored in all the first 10 Premier games of 1997-8, a total of 12 goals.

Jermain Defoe, 18, on loan from West Ham Utd., equalled a single-season post-war record by scoring for Bournemouth in 10 consecutive matches (Div. 2), October-January 2000-01. **Billy McAdams** did likewise for Manchester City (1957-8), as did **Ron Davies** for Southampton (1966-7).

John Aldridge (Liverpool) scored in 10 successive First Division matches – the last game of season 1986-7 and the first nine in 1987-8.

Kevin Russell (Wrexham) scored in nine consecutive matches in Div. 4, March-May, 1988.

Ruud van Nistelrooy (Manchester Utd.) holds the record for scoring in most consecutive Premiership matches in one season – 8 (11 goals) in December-January, 2001-02. He repeated the feat in the last 8 Premiership games (13 goals, including 5 penalties and 2 hat-tricks) of season 2002–03.

Ian Wright scored on 12 successive first-team appearances, including 7 Premiership, for Arsenal (Sept. 15-Nov. 23, 1994).

50-GOAL PLAYERS

With **52** goals for **Wolves** in 1987-8 (34 League, 12 Sherpa Van Trophy, 3 Littlewoods Cup, 3 F.A. Cup), **Steve Bull** became the first player to score 50 in a season for a League club since **Terry Bly** for 4th Division newcomers Peterborough Utd. in 1960-1. Bly's 54 comprised 52 League goals and 2 in the F.A. Cup, and included 7 hat-tricks, still a post-war League record.

Bull was again the country's top scorer with 50 goals in season 1988-9: 37 League, 2 Littlewoods Cup and 11 Sherpa Van Trophy.

Between Bly and Bull, the highest individual scoring total for a season was 49 by two players: Ted MacDougall (Bournemouth 1970-1, 42 League, 7 F.A. Cup) and Clive Allen (Tottenham 1986-7, 33 League, 12 Littlewoods Cup, 4 F.A. Cup).

HOT SHOTS

Jimmy Greaves was First Division top scorer (League goals) six times in 11 seasons: 32 for Chelsea (1958-9), 41 for Chelsea (1960-1) and, for Tottenham, 37 in 1962-3, 35 in 1963-4, 29 in 1964-5 (joint top) and 27 in 1968-9.

Brian Clough (Middlesbrough) was the Second Division's leading scorer in three successive seasons: 40 goals in 1957-8, 42 in 1958-9 and 39 in 1959-60.

John Hickton (Middlesbrough) was top Div. 2 scorer three times in four seasons: 24 goals in 1967-8, 24 in 1969-70 and 25 in 1970-1.

MOST HAT-TRICKS

Nine by **George Camsell** (Middlesbrough) in Div. 2, 1926-7, is the record for one season. Most League hat-tricks in career: 37 by **Dixie Dean** for Tranmere Rov. and Everton (1924-38).

Most **top division** hat-tricks in a season since last war: six by **Jimmy Greaves** for Chelsea (1960-1). **Alan Shearer** scored five hat-tricks for Blackburn Rov. in the Premier League, season 1995-96.

Frank Osborne (Tottenham) scored three consecutive hat-tricks in Div. 1 in October-November 1925, against Liverpool, Leicester City (away) and West Ham Utd.

Tom Jennings (Leeds Utd.) scored hat-tricks in three successive First Div. matches (Sept-Oct, 1926): 3 goals v Arsenal, 4 at Liverpool, 4 v Blackburn Rov. Leeds Utd. were relegated at the end of the season.

Jack Balmer (Liverpool) scored only three hat-tricks in a 17-year career - in successive First Div. matches (Nov. 1946): 3 v Portsmouth, 4 at Derby Co., 3 v Arsenal. No other Liverpool player scored during that 10-goal sequence by Balmer.

Gilbert Alsop scored hat-tricks in three successive matches for Walsall in Div. 3 South in April 1939: 3 at Swindon Town, 3 v Bristol City and 4 v Swindon Town.

Alf Lythgoe scored hat-tricks in three successive games for Stockport Co. (Div. 3 North) in March 1934: 3 v Darlington, 3 at Southport and 4 v Wrexham.

TRIPLE HAT-TRICKS

There have been at least three instances of **3 hat-tricks being scored** for **one team** in a Football League match:-

April 21, 1909: Enoch West, Billy Hooper and Alfred Spouncer scored 3 apiece for Nott'm. Forest (12-0 v Leicester Fosse, Div. 1).

March 3, 1962: Ron Barnes, Wyn Davies and Roy Ambler registered hat-tricks in Wrexham's 10-1 win against Hartlepool Utd. (Div. 4).

November 7, 1987: Tony Adcock, Paul Stewart and David White each scored 3 goals for Manchester City in 10-1 win at home to Huddersfield Town (Div. 2).

For the first time in the Premiership, **three hat-tricks** were completed **on one day** (September 23, 1995): Tony Yeboah for Leeds Utd. at Wimbledon; Alan Shearer for Blackburn Rov. v Coventry City; and Robbie Fowler with 4 goals for Liverpool v Bolton Wand.

In the F.A. Cup, **Jack Carr**, **George Elliott** and **Walter Tinsley** each scored 3 in Middlesbrough's 9-3 first round win against Goole in Jan. 1915. **Les Allen** scored 5, **Bobby Smith** 4 and **Cliff Jones** 3 when Tottenham beat Crewe Alexandra 13-2 in a fourth-round replay in February 1960.

HAT-TRICKS v THREE 'KEEPERS

When West Ham Utd. beat Newcastle Utd. 8-1 (Div.1) at home on April 21, 1986 **Alvin Martin** scored 3 goals against different 'keepers: Martin Thomas injured a shoulder and was replaced, in turn, by outfield players Chris Hedworth and Peter Beardsley.

Jock Dodds of Lincoln City had done the same **against** West Ham Utd. on December 18, 1948, scoring past **Ernie Gregory**, **Tommy Moroney** and **George Dick**. The Hammers lost 3-4.

David Herd (Manchester Utd.) scored against three Sunderland goalkeepers (Jim Montgomery, Charlie Hurley and Johnny Parke) in 5-0 First Division home win on Nov. 26, 1966.

Brian Clark, of Bournemouth, scored against three Rotherham Utd. goalkeepers (Jim McDonagh,, Conal Gilbert and Michael Leng twice) in 7-2 win at Rotherham Utd. (Div. 3) on Oct. 10, 1972.

On Oct. 16, 1993 (Div.3) **Chris Pike** (Hereford) scored a hat-trick against different goalkeepers. Opponents Colchester Utd., beaten 5-0, became the first team in League history to have two 'keepers sent off in the same game.

On Dec. 18, 2004 (League 1), in 6-1 defeat at Hull, Tranmere Rov. used three goalkeepers: **John Achterberg** and **Russell Howarth** both retired injured, and defender **Theo Whitmore** kept goal for the second half.

EIGHT-DAY HAT-TRICK TREBLE

Joe Bradford of Birmingham City scored three hat-tricks in eight days in September 1929-30 v Newcastle Utd. (won 5-1) on the 21st, 5 for the Football League v Irish League (7-2) on the 25th, and 3 in his club's 5-7 defeat away to Blackburn Rov. on the 28th.

PREMIERSHIP DOUBLE HAT-TRICK

Robert Pires and **Jermaine Pennant** each scored 3 goals in Arsenal's 6–1 win at home to Southampton (May 7, 2003).

TON UP – BOTH ENDS

Manchester City are the only club to **score and concede** a century of League goals in the same season. When fifth in the 1957-8 Championship, they scored 104 goals and gave away 100.

TOURNAMENT TOP SHOTS

Most individual goals in a World Cup Final series: 13 by **Just Fontaine** for France, in Sweden 1958. Most in European Championship Finals: 9 by **Michel Platini** for France, in France 1984.

MOST GOALS ON CLUB DEBUT

Jim Dyet scored **eight** in King's Park's 12-2 win against Forfar Athletic (Scottish Div. 2, Jan. 2, 1930).

Len Shackleton scored **six** times in Newcastle Utd.'s 13-0 win v Newport County (Div. 2, Oct. 5, 1946) in the week he joined them from Bradford Park Avenue.

MOST GOALS ON LEAGUE DEBUT

Five by **George Hilsdon**, for Chelsea (9-2) v Glossop, Div. 2 Sept. 1, 1906. **Alan Shearer**, with three goals for Southampton (4-2) v Arsenal, April 9, 1988, became, at 17, the youngest player to score a First Division hat-trick on his full debut.

CLEAN-SHEET RECORDS

On the way to promotion from Div. 3 in season 1995-6, **Gillingham's** ever-present goalkeeper **Jim Stannard** set a clean-sheet record. In 46 matches, he achieved 29 shut-outs (17 at home, 12 away), beating the 28 by Ray Clemence for Liverpool (42 matches in Div. 1, 1978-9) and the previous best in a 46-match programme of 28 by Port Vale (Div. 3 North, 1953-4). In conceding only 20 League goals in 1995-6, Gillingham created a defensive record for the lower divisions.

Chris Woods, Rangers' England goalkeeper, set a British record in season 1986-7 by going 1,196 minutes without conceding a goal. The sequence began in the UEFA Cup match against Borussia Moenchengladbach on Nov. 26, 1986 and ended when Rangers were sensationally beaten 1-0 at home by Hamilton in the Scottish Cup 3rd. Round on Jan. 31, 1987 with a 70th.-minute goal by Adrian Sprott.

The previous British record of 1,156 minutes without a goal conceded was held by Aberdeen goalkeeper **Bobby Clark** (season 1970-1).

Chelsea goalkeeper **Petr Cech** set a Premiership clean-sheet record of 1,024 consecutive minutes (including 10 complete matches) in season 2004-05.

Most clean sheets in season in top English division: 28 by **Liverpool** (42 matches) in 1978-79; 25 by Chelsea (38 matches) in 2004-05.

There have been three instances of clubs keeping 11 consecutive clean sheets in the Football League: Millwall (Div. 3 South, 1925-6), York City (Div. 3, 1973-4) and Reading (Div. 4, 1978-9). In his sequence, Reading goalkeeper **Steve Death** set the existing League shut-out record of 1,103 minutes.

Mark Leonard (Chesterfield) kept a clean sheet in 8 consecutive Div.3 away games (Jan-April 1994).

Sasa Ilic remained unbeaten for over 14 hours with 9 successive shut-outs (7 in FL Div. 1, 2 in play-offs) to equal a Charlton Athletic club record in Apr./May 1998. He had 12 clean sheets in 17 first team games after winning promotion from the reserves with 6 successive clean sheets.

Sebastiano Rossi kept a clean sheet in 8 successive away matches for AC Milan (Nov. 1993-Apr. 1994).

A world record of 1,275 minutes without conceding a goal was set in 1990-1 by **Abel Resino**, the Atletico Madrid goalkeeper. He was finally beaten by Sporting Gijon's Enrique in Atletico's 3-1 win on March 19, 1991.

In International football, the record is held by **Dino Zoff** with a shut-out for Italy (Sept. 1972 to June 1974) lasting 1,142 minutes.

LOW SCORING

Fewest goals by any club in season in Football League: **24** by **Stoke City** (Div. 1, 42 matches, 1984-5); **24** by **Watford** (Div. 2, 42 matches, 1971-2). In 46-match programme, **27** by **Stockport Co.** (Div. 3, 1969-70).

Arsenal were the lowest Premier League scorers in its opening season (1992-3) with 40 goals in 42 matches, but won both domestic cup competitions. In subsequent seasons the lowest Premier League scorers were **Ipswich Town** (35) in 1993-4, **Crystal Palace** (34) in 1994-5, **Manchester City** (33) in 1995-6 and **Leeds Utd.** (28) in 1996–7 until **Sunderland** set the Premiership's new fewest-goals record with only 21 in 2002–03.

LONG TIME NO SCORE

The world International non-scoring record was set by **Northern Ireland** when they played 13 matches and 1,298 minutes without a goal. The sequence began against Poland on Feb. 13, 2002 and ended 2 years and 5 days later when David Healy scored against Norway (1-4) in Belfast on Feb. 18, 2004.

Longest non-scoring sequences in Football League: 11 matches by **Coventry City** in 1919-20 (Div. 2); 11 matches by **Hartlepool Utd.** in 1992-3 (Div. 2). After beating Crystal Palace 1-0 in the F.A. Cup 3rd round on Jan. 2, they went 13 games and 2 months without scoring (11 League, 1 F.A. Cup, 1 Autoglass Trophy). The sequence ended after 1,227 blank minutes with a 1-1 draw at Blackpool (League) on March 6.

In the **Premier League** (Oct.-Jan. season 1994-5) Crystal Palace failed to score in nine consecutive matches.

The British non-scoring club record is held by **Stirling Albion**: 14 consecutive matches (13 League, 1 Scottish Cup) and 1,292 minutes play, from Jan. 31, 1981 until Aug. 8, 1981 (when they lost 4-1 to Falkirk in the League Cup).

In season 1971-2, **Mansfield Town** did not score in any of their first nine home games in Div. 3. They were relegated on goal difference of minus two.

F.A. CUP CLEAN SHEETS

Most consecutive F.A. Cup matches without conceding a goal: 11 by **Bradford City**. The sequence spanned 8 rounds, from 3rd. in 1910-11 to 4th. Round replay in 1911-12, and included winning the Cup in 1911.

GOALS THAT WERE WRONGLY GIVEN

Tottenham's last-minute winner at home to Huddersfield (Div. 1) on April 2, 1952: Eddie Baily's corner-kick struck referee W.R. Barnes in the back, and the ball rebounded to Baily, who centred for Len Duquemin to head into the net. Baily had infringed the Laws by playing the ball twice, but the result (1-0) stood. Those two points helped Spurs to finish Championship runners-up; Huddersfield were relegated.

The second goal (66 mins) in **Chelsea's** 2-1 home win v Ipswich Town (Div. 1) on Sept. 26, 1970: Alan Hudson's low shot from just beyond the penalty-area hit the stanchion on the outside of goal and the ball rebounded on to the pitch. But instead of the goal-kick, referee Roy Capey gave a goal, on a linesman's confirmation. TV pictures proved otherwise. But the Football League quoted from the Laws of the Game: 'The referee's decision on all matters is final.' And though it was wrong, the goal stood and sent Chelsea on the way to victory.

• The most notorious goal in World Cup history was fisted in by Diego Maradona in Argentina's 2-1 quarter-final win over England in Mexico City on June 22, 1986.

ATTENDANCES

GREATEST WORLD CROWDS

World Cup, Maracana Stadium, Rio de Janeiro, July 16, 1950. Final match (Brazil v Uruguay) attendance 199,850; receipts £125,000.

Total attendance in three matches (including play-off) between Santos (Brazil) and AC Milan for the Inter-Continental Cup (World Club Championship) 1963, exceeded 375,000.

BRITISH RECORD CROWDS

Most to pay: 149,547, Scotland v England, at Hampden Park, Glasgow, April 17, 1937. This was the first all-ticket match in Scotland (receipts £24,000).

At Scottish F.A. Cup Final: 146,433, Celtic v Aberdeen, at Hampden Park, April 24, 1937. Estimated another 20,000 shut out.

For British club match (apart from a Cup Final): 143,470, Rangers v Hibernian, at Hampden Park, March 27, 1948 (Scottish Cup semi-final).

F.A. Cup Final: 126,047, Bolton Wand. v West Ham Utd., April 28, 1923. Estimated 150,000 in ground at opening of Wembley Stadium.

New Wembly: 89,826, F.A. Cup Final, Chelsea v Manchester Utd., May 19, 2007.

World Cup Qualifying Ties: 120,000, Cameroon v Morocco, Yaounde, November 29, 1981; 107,580, Scotland v Poland, Hampden Park, October 13, 1965.

European Cup: 135,826, Celtic v Leeds Utd. (semi-final, 2nd. leg) at Hampden Park, Glasgow, April 15, 1970.

European Cup Final: 127,621, Real Madrid v Eintracht Frankfurt, at Hampden Park, Glasgow, May 18, 1960.

European Cup-Winners' Cup Final: 100,000, West Ham Utd. v TSV Munich, at Wembley, May 19, 1965.

Scottish League: 118,567, Rangers v Celtic, January 2, 1939.

Scottish League Cup Final: 107,609, Celtic v Rangers, at Hampden Park, October 23, 1965.

Football League old format: First Div.: 83,260, Manchester Utd. v Arsenal, January 17, 1948 (at Maine Road); **Second Div.:** 70,302 Tottenham v Southampton, February 25, 1950; **Third Div. South:** 51,621, Cardiff City v Bristol City, April 7, 1947; **Third Div. North:** 49,655, Hull City v Rotherham Utd., December 25, 1948; **Third Div.:** 49,309, Sheffield Wed. v Sheffield Utd., December 26, 1979; **Fourth Div.:** 37,774, Crystal Palace v Millwall, March 31, 1961.

Premier League: 76,098, Manchester Utd. v Blackburn Rov., March 31, 2007.

Football League – New Div. 1: 41,214, Sunderland v Stoke City, April 25, 1998; **New Div. 2:** 32,471, Manchester City v York City, May 8, 1999; **New Div. 3:** 22,319 Hull City v Hartlepool Utd., December 26, 2002. **New Champs:** 47,350 Sunderland v Stoke City, May 8, 2005; **New Lge. 1** 28,798 Sheffield Wed. v Bristol City, May 7, 2005; **New Lge. 2:** 13,467 Carlisle Utd. v Torquay Utd., April 29, 2006.

In English Provinces: 84,569, Manchester City v Stoke City (F.A. Cup 6th Round), March 3, 1934.

Record for Under-21 International: 55,700, England v Italy, first match at New Wembley, March 24, 2007.

Record for friendly match: 104,679, Rangers v Eintracht Frankfurt, at Hampden Park, Glasgow, October 17, 1961.

F.A. Youth Cup: 38,187, Arsenal v Manchester Utd., at Emirates Stadium, March 14, 2007.

Record Football League aggregate (season): 41,271,414 (1948-9) – 88 clubs.

Record Football League aggregate (single day): 1,269,934, December 27, 1949, previous day, 1,226,098.

Record average home League attendance for season: 68,764 by Manchester Utd. in 2005–06.

Long-ago League attendance aggregates: 10,929,000 in 1906-07 (40 clubs); 28,132,933 in 1937-8 (88 clubs).

Last 1m. crowd aggregate, League (single day): 1,007,200, December 27, 1971.

Record Amateur match attendance: 100,000 for F.A. Amateur Cup Final, Pegasus v Harwich & Parkeston at Wembley, April 11, 1953.

Record Cup-tie aggregate: 265,199, at two matches between Rangers and Morton, in the Scottish Cup Final, 1947-8.

Abandoned match attendance records: In **England** – 63,480 at Newcastle Utd. v Swansea City F.A. Cup 3rd round, Jan. 10, 1953, abandoned 8 mins (0-0), fog.

In Scotland: 94,596 at Scotland v Austria (4-1), Hampden Park, May 8, 1963. Referee Jim Finney ended play (79 minutes) after Austria had two players sent off and one carried off.

Colchester Utd.'s record crowd (19,072) was for the F.A. Cup 1st round tie v Reading on Nov. 27, 1948, abandoned 35 minutes (0-0), fog.

SMALLEST CROWDS

Smallest League attendances: 13, Stockport Co. v Leicester City (Div. 2, May 7, 1921; played at Old Trafford – Stockport ground closed); 469, Thames v Luton Town (Div. 3 South, December 6, 1930).

Lowest post-war League attendance: 450 Rochdale v Cambridge Utd. (Div. 3, February 5, 1974).

Lowest Premier League crowd: 3,039 for Wimbledon v Everton, Jan. 26, 1993 (smallest top-division attendance since war).

Lowest Saturday post-war top-division crowd: 3,231 for Wimbledon v Luton Town, Sept. 7, 1991 (Div. 1).

Lowest Football League crowds, new format – Div. 1: 849 for Wimbledon v Rotherham Utd., (Div. 1) October 29, 2002 (smallest att. in top two divisions since war); 1,054 Wimbledon v Wigan Athletic (Div. 1), Sept. 13, 2003 in club's last home match when sharing Selhurst Park; **Div. 2:** 1,077, Hartlepool Utd. v Cardiff City, March 22, 1994; **Div. 3:** 739, Doncaster Rov. v Barnet, March 3, 1998.

Lowest top-division crowd at a major ground since the war: 4,554 for Arsenal v Leeds Utd. (May 5, 1966) – fixture clashed with live TV coverage of Cup-Winners' Cup Final (Liverpool v Borussia Dortmund).

Smallest League Cup attendances: 612, Halifax Town v Tranmere Rov. (1st Round, 2nd Leg) September 6, 2000; 664, Wimbledon v Rotherham Utd. (3rd Round), November 5, 2002.

Smallest League Cup attendance at top-division ground: 1,987 for Wimbledon v Bolton Wand. (2nd Round, 2nd Leg) Oct. 6, 1992.

Smallest Wembley crowds for England matches: 15,628 v Chile (Rous Cup, May 23, 1989 – affected by Tube strike); 20,038 v Colombia (Friendly, Sept. 6, 1995); 21,432 v Czech. (Friendly, Apr. 25, 1990); 21,142 v Japan (Umbro Cup, June 3, 1995); 23,600 v Wales (British Championship, Feb. 23, 1983); 23,659 v Greece (Friendly, May 17, 1994); 23,951 v East Germany (Friendly, Sept. 12, 1984); 24,000 v N. Ireland (British Championship, Apr. 4, 1984); 25,756 v Colombia (Rous Cup, May 24, 1988); 25,837 v Denmark (Friendly, Sept. 14, 1988).

Smallest Int. modern crowd: 221 for Poland v N. Ireland (4-1, friendly) at Limassol, Cyprus, on February 13, 2002. Played at neutral venue at Poland's World Cup training base.

Smallest Int. modern crowds at home: N.Ireland: 2,500 v Chile (Belfast, May 26, 1989 – clashed with ITV live screening of Liverpool v Arsenal Championship decider); **Scotland:** 7,843 v N.Ireland (Hampden Park, May 6, 1969); **Wales:** 2,315 v N.Ireland (Wrexham, May 27, 1982).

Smallest attendance for post-war England match: 2,378 v San Marino (World Cup) at Bologna (Nov. 17, 1993). Tie clashed with Italy v Portugal (World Cup) shown live on Italian TV.

Smallest paid attendance for British first-class match: 29 for Clydebank v East Stirling, CIS Scottish League Cup 1st Round, July 31, 1999. Played at Morton's Cappielow Park ground, shared by Clydebank, the match clashed with the Tall Ships Race which attracted 200,000 to the area.

F.A. CUP CROWD RECORD (OUTSIDE FINAL)

The first F.A. Cup-tie shown on closed-circuit TV (5th. Round, Saturday, March 11, 1967, kick-off 7pm) drew a total of 105,000 spectators to Goodison Park and Anfield. This is the biggest attendance for a single F.A. Cup match other than the Final. At Goodison, 64,851 watched the match 'for real', while 40,149 saw the TV version on eight giant screens at Anfield. Everton beat Liverpool 1-0.

LOWEST SEMI-FINAL CROWD

The smallest F.A. Cup semi-final attendance since the war was 17,987 for Manchester Utd. v Crystal Palace replay, at Villa Park on April 12, 1995. Crystal Palace supporters largely boycotted tie after a fan died in car-park clash outside pub in Walsall before first match. Previous lowest: 25,963 for Wimbledon v Luton Town, at Tottenham on April 9, 1988.

Lowest quarter-final crowd since the war: 8,735 for Chesterfield v Wrexham on March 9, 1997.

Smallest F.A. Cup 3rd. Round attendances for matches between League clubs: 1,833 for Chester City v Bournemouth (at Macclesfield Town) Jan. 5, 1991; 1,966 for Aldershot v Oxford Utd., Jan. 10, 1987.

PRE-WEMBLEY CUP FINAL CROWDS

AT CRYSTAL PALACE

1895	42,560	1902	48,036	1908	74,967
1896	48,036	Replay	33,050	1909	67,651
1897	65,891	1903	64,000	1910	76,980
1898	62,017	1904	61,734	1911	69,098
1899	73,833	1905	101,117	1912	54,434
1900	68,945	1906	75,609	1913	120,028
1901	110,802	1907	84,584	1914	72,778

AT OLD TRAFFORD

1915 50,000

AT STAMFORD BRIDGE

1920	50,018	1921	72,805	1922	53,000

RECEIPTS RECORDS

Wembley Stadium underwent its first considerable alteration during 1962-3 in preparation for the World Cup in 1966. Higher admission fees at the 1963 F.A. Cup Final resulted in 100,000 spectators paying a record £89,000.

This is how Wembley's receipts records subsequently rose:

1968	F.A. Cup Final (Everton v W.B.A.)	£110,000
1968	European Cup Final (Manchester Utd. v Benfica)	£120,000
1976	F.A. Cup Final (Southampton v Manchester Utd.)	£420,000
1978	F.A. Cup Final (Ipswich Town v Arsenal)	£500,000
1981	England v Hungary (World Cup)	£671,000
1982	F.A. Cup Final (Tottenham v Q.P.R.) (plus £605,000 for replay)	£886,000
1984	F.A. Cup Final (Everton v Watford)	£919,000
*1985	F.A. Cup Final (Manchester Utd. v Everton)	£1,100,000
1986	F.A. Cup Final (Liverpool v Everton)	£1,100,000
†1987	League Cup Final (Arsenal v Liverpool)	£1,000,000
1987	F.A. Cup Final (Coventry City v Tottenham)	£1,286,737
1988	F.A. Cup Final (Wimbledon v Liverpool)	£1,422,814
1989	F.A. Cup Final (Liverpool v Everton)	£1,600,000
1990	League Cup Final (Nott'm Forest v Oldham Athletic)	£1,650,000
1990	F.A. Cup Final (Manchester Utd. v Crystal Palace – first match)	£2,000,000
1991	League Cup Final (Manchester Utd. v Sheffield Wed.)	£2,000,000
1991	F.A. Cup Final (Nott'm F. v Tottenham)	£2,016,000
1992	F.A. Cup Final (Liverpool v Sunderland)	£2,548,174
1993	F.A. Cup Final (Arsenal v Sheffield W. – first match) (Replay took receipts for both matches to £4,695,200)	£2,818,000
1994	F.A. Cup Final record (Manchester Utd. v Chelsea)	£2,962,167

1997 League Cup Final record (Leicester City v Middlesbrough) £2,750,000
1998 League Cup Final record (Chelsea v Middlesbrough) £2,983,000
•2000 F.A. Cup Final record (Chelsea v Aston Villa) £3,100,000

EARLY CUP FINAL RECEIPTS

1885 Blackburn Rov. v Queens Park £442
1913 Aston Villa v Sunderland £9,406
1923 Bolton Wand. v West Ham Utd., first Wembley Final £27,776
1939 Portsmouth v Wolves £29,000
1946 Derby Co. v Charlton Athletic £45,000

INTERNATIONAL RECORDS

MOST APPEARANCES

Peter Shilton, England goalkeeper, then aged 40, retired from International football after the 1990 World Cup Finals with the European record number of caps – 125. Previous record (119) was set by **Pat Jennings**, Northern Ireland's goalkeeper from 1964-86, who retired on his 41st birthday during the 1986 World Cup in Mexico. Shilton's England career spanned 20 seasons from his debut against East Germany at Wembley on Nov. 25, 1970.

Four players have completed a century of appearances in full International matches for England. **Billy Wright** of Wolves, was the first, retiring in 1959 with a total of 105 caps.

Bobby Charlton, of Manchester Utd., beat Wright's record in the World Cup match against West Germany in Leon, Mexico, in June 1970 and **Bobby Moore,** of West Ham Utd., overtook Charlton's 106 caps against Italy in Turin, in June 1973. Moore played 108 times for England, a record that stood until **Shilton** reached 109 against Denmark in Copenhagen (June 7, 1989).

Kenny Dalglish became Scotland's first 100-cap International v Romania (Hampden Park, March 26, 1986).

World's most-capped player: Mohamed Al-Deayea (Saudi Arabia goalkeeper) 173 caps (1990–2004).

Most-capped European player: Lothar Matthaus 150 Internationals for Germany (1980-2000).

Most-capped European goalkeeper: Thomas Ravelli, 143 Internationals for Sweden (1981-97).

Gillian Coultard, (Doncaster Belles), England Women's captain, received a special presentation from Geoff Hurst to mark 100 caps when England beat Holland 1-0 at Upton Park on October 30, 1997. She made her Int. debut at 18 in May 1981, and retired at the end of season 1999-2000 with a record 119 caps (30 goals).

BRITAIN'S MOST-CAPPED PLAYERS

(As at start of season 2007-08)

England

Peter Shilton 125
Bobby Moore 108
Bobby Charlton 106
Billy Wright 105
David Beckham 96

Scotland

Kenny Dalglish 102
Jim Leighton 91
Alex McLeish 77
Paul McStay 76
Tommy Boyd 72

Wales

Neville Southall	92
Gary Speed	85
Dean Saunders	75
Peter Nicholas	73
Ian Rush	73

Northern Ireland

Pat Jennings	119
Mal Donaghy	91
Sammy McIlroy	88
Keith Gillespie	75
Jimmy Nicholl	73

Republic of Ireland

Steve Staunton	102
Niall Quinn	91
Tony Cascarino	88
Paul McGrath	83
Pat Bonner	80
Shay Given	80
Kevin Kilbane	80

MOST ENGLAND CAPS IN ROW

Most consecutive International appearances: 70 by **Billy Wright**, for England from October 1951 to May 1959. He played 105 of England's first 108 post-war matches.

England captains most times: Billy Wright and **Bobby Moore**, 90 each.

England captains – 4 in match (v Serbia & Montenegro at Leicester June 3, 2003): **Michael Owen** was captain for the first half and after the interval the armband passed to **Emile Heskey** (for 15 minutes), **Philip Neville** (26 minutes) and substitute **Jamie Carragher** (9 minutes, including time added).

ENGLAND'S TALLEST

At 6ft. 7in., Southampton striker **Peter Crouch** became England's tallest-ever International when he made his debut against Colombia in New Jersey, USA on May 31, 2005.

MOST PLAYERS FROM ONE CLUB IN ENGLAND SIDES

Arsenal supplied seven men (a record) to the England team v Italy at Highbury on November 14, 1934. They were: Frank Moss, George Male, Eddie Hapgood, Wilf Copping, Ray Bowden, Ted Drake and Cliff Bastin. In addition, Arsenal's Tom Whittaker was England's trainer.

Since then until 2001, the most players from one club in an England team was six from **Liverpool** against Switzerland at Wembley in September 1977. The side also included a Liverpool old boy, Kevin Keegan (Hamburg).

Seven **Arsenal** men took part in the England – France (0-2) match at Wembley on February 10, 1999. Goalkeeper David Seaman and defenders Lee Dixon, Tony Adams and Martin Keown lined up for England. Nicolas Anelka (2 goals) and Emmanuel Petit started the match for France and Patrick Vieira replaced Anelka.

Manchester Utd. equalled Arsenal's 1934 record by providing England with seven players in the World Cup qualifier away to Albania on March 28, 2001. Five started the match – David Beckham (captain), Gary Neville, Paul Scholes, Nicky Butt and Andy Cole – and two went on as substitutes: Wes Brown and Teddy Sheringham.

INTERNATIONAL SUBS RECORDS

Malta substituted all 11 players in their 1-2 home defeat against England on June 3, 2000. Six substitutes by England took the total replacements in the match to 17, then an International record.

Most substitutions in match by **England**: 11 in second half by Sven-Goran Eriksson against Holland at Tottenham on August 15, 2001; 11 against Italy at Leeds on March 27, 2002; Italy sent on 8 players from the bench – the total of 19 substitutions was then a record for an England match; 11 against Australia at Upton Park on February 12, 2003 (entire England team changed at half-time); 11 against Iceland at City of Manchester Stadium on June 5, 2004.

Forty-three players, a record for an England match, were used in the International against Serbia & Montenegro at Leicester on June 3, 2003. England sent on 10 substitutes in the second half and their opponents changed all 11 players.

The **Republic of Ireland** sent on 12 second-half substitutes, using 23 players in all, when they beat Russia 2-0 in a friendly International in Dublin on February 13, 2002.

First England substitute: Wolves winger **Jimmy Mullen** replaced injured Jackie Milburn (15 mins.) away to Belgium on May 18, 1950. He scored in a 4-1 win.

ENGLAND'S WORLD CUP-WINNERS

At Wembley, July 30, 1966, 4-2 v West Germany (2-2 after 90 mins), scorers Hurst 3, Peters. Team: Banks; Cohen, Wilson, Stiles, Charlton (J.), Moore (Captain), Ball, Hurst, Charlton (R.), Hunt, Peters. Manager **Alf Ramsey** fielded that same eleven in six successive matches (an England record): the World Cup quarter-final, semi-final and Final, and the first three games of the following season. England wore red shirts in the Final and Her Majesty the Queen presented the Cup to Bobby Moore. The players each received a £1,000 bonus, plus £60 World Cup Final appearance money, all less tax, and Ramsey a £6,000 bonus from the F.A. The match was shown live on TV (in black and white).

BRAZIL'S RECORD RUN

Brazil hold the record for the longest unbeaten sequence in International football: 45 matches from 1993-7. The previous record of 31 matches undefeated was held by Hungary between June 1950 and July 1954.

ENGLAND MATCHES ABANDONED

May 17, 1953 v **Argentina** (Friendly, Buenos Aires) after 23 mins. (0–0) – rain.

Oct. 29, 1975 v **Czechoslovakia** (Eur. Champ. Qual., Bratislava) after 17 mins. (0–0) – fog. Played next day.

Feb. 15, 1995 v **Rep. of Ireland** (Friendly, Dublin) after 27 mins. (1–0) – crowd disturbance.

ENGLAND POSTPONEMENT

Nov 21, 1979 v **Bulgaria** (Eur. Champ. qual., Wembley postponed for 24 hours – fog.

ENGLAND UNDER COVER

England played indoors for the first time when they beat Argentina 1-0 in the World Cup at the Sapporo Dome, Japan, on June 7, 2002.

ALL-SEATED INTERNATIONALS

The first **all-seated crowd** (30,000) for a full International in Britain saw **Wales** and **West Germany** draw 0-0 at Cardiff City Arms Park on May 31, 1989. The terraces were closed.

England's first all-seated International at Wembley was against Yugoslavia (2-1) on December 13, 1989 (attendance 34,796). The terracing behind the goals was closed for conversion to seating.

The first **full-house all-seated** International at Wembley was for England v Brazil (1-0) on March 28, 1990, when a capacity 80,000 crowd paid record British receipts of £1,200,000.

ENGLAND 'ON THE ROAD'

Since Wembley Stadium closed in October 2000, England have played home fixtures at 14 club grounds (to end of season 2004-05): Manchester Utd. (10), Aston Villa (3), Liverpool (3), Newcastle (3), Manchester City (2), Derby, Tottenham, Leeds, Southampton, West Ham, Sunderland, Leicester, Middlesbrough and Ipswich.

FIRST BLACK CAPS

First black player for **England** in a senior International was Nott'm. Forest full-back **Viv Anderson** against Czechoslovakia at Wembley on November 29, 1978.

Aston Villa's **Ugo Ehiogu** was **England's** first black captain (U-21 v Holland at Portsmouth, April 27, 1993).

Paul Ince (Manchester Utd.) became the first black player to captain **England** in a **full International** (v U.S.A., Boston, June 9, 1993).

First black British International was **Eddie Parris** (Bradford Park Avenue) for Wales against N. Ireland in Belfast on December 5, 1931.

MOST NEW CAPS IN ENGLAND TEAM

6, by Sir Alf Ramsey (v Portugal, April 3, 1974) and **by Sven-Goran Eriksson** (v Australia, February 12, 2003; 5 at half-time when 11 changes made).

PLAYED FOR MORE THAN ONE COUNTRY

Multi-nationals in senior International football include: **Johnny Carey** (1938-53) – caps Rep. of Ireland 29, N. Ireland 7; **Ferenc Puskas** (1945-62) – caps Hungary 84, Spain 4; **Alfredo di Stefano** (1950-6) – caps Argentina 7, Spain 31; **Ladislav Kubala** (1948-58) – caps, Hungary 3, Czechoslovakia 11, Spain 19, only player to win full Int. honours with 3 countries. Kubala also played in a fourth Int. team, scoring twice for FIFA v England at Wembley in 1953.

Eleven players, including Carey, appeared for both N. Ireland and the Republic of Ireland in seasons directly after the last war.

Cecil Moore, capped by N. Ireland in 1949 when with Glentoran, played for USA v England in 1953.

Hawley Edwards played for England v Scotland in 1874 and for Wales v Scotland in 1876.

Jack Reynolds (Distillery and W.B.A.) played for both Ireland (5 times) and England (8) in the 1890s.

Bobby Evans (Sheffield Utd.) had played 10 times for Wales when capped for England, in 1910-11. He was born in Chester of Welsh parents.

In recent years several players have represented USSR and one or other of the breakaway republics. The same applies to Yugoslavia and its component states. **Josip Weber** played for Croatia in 1992 and made a 5-goal debut for Belgium in 1994.

3-GENERATION INTERNATIONAL FAMILY

When Bournemouth striker **Warren Feeney** was capped away to Liechtenstein on March 27, 2002, he became the third generation of his family to play for Northern Ireland. He followed in the footsteps of his grandfather James (capped twice in 1950) and father Warren Snr. (1 in 1976).

FATHERS & SONS CAPPED BY ENGLAND

George Eastham senior (pre-war) and **George Eastham junior**; **Brian Clough** and **Nigel Clough**; **Frank Lampard** senior and **Frank Lampard** junior.

FATHER & SON SAME-DAY CAPS

Iceland made father-and-son Int. history when they beat Estonia 3-0 in Tallin on April 24, 1996. Arnor Gudjohnsen (35) started the match and was replaced (62 mins.) by his 17-year-old son Eidur.

LONGEST UNBEATEN START TO ENGLAND CAREER

Steven Gerrard, 21 matches (W16, D5) 2000–03.

SUCCESSIVE ENGLAND HAT-TRICKS

The last player to score a hat-trick in consecutive England matches was **Dixie Dean** on the summer tour in May 1927, against Belgium (9-1) and Luxembourg (5-2).

POST-WAR HAT-TRICKS v ENGLAND

November 25, 1953, scorer **Nandor Hidegkuti** (England 3, Hungary 6, Wembley); May 11, 1958, scorer **Aleksandar Petakovic** (Yugoslavia 5, England 0, Belgrade); May 17, 1959, scorer **Juan Seminario** (Peru 4, England 1, Lima); June 15, 1988, scorer **Marco Van Basten** (Holland 3, England 1, European Championship, Dusseldorf).

NO-SAVE GOALKEEPERS

Chris Woods did not have one save to make when England beat San Marino 6-0 (World Cup) at Wembley on February 17, 1993. He touched the ball only six times throughout the match.

Gordon Banks had a similar no-save experience when England beat Malta 5-0 (European Championship) at Wembley on May 12, 1971. Malta did not force a goal-kick or corner, and the four times Banks touched the ball were all from back passes.

FOOTBALL'S GOVERNING BODIES

By June 2005, a total of 205 National Associations were members of the Federation Internationale de Football Association (**F.I.F.A.**, founded May, 1904), and the Union of European Football Associations (**U.E.F.A.**, founded June, 1954) embraced 52 countries.

The seven original members of the F.I.F.A. were Belgium, Denmark, France, Holland, Spain, Sweden and Switzerland.

FIFA WORLD YOUTH CHAMPIONSHIP (UNDER-20)

Finals: 1977 (Tunis) Soviet Union 2, Mexico 2 (Soviet won 9-8 on pens.); **1979** (Tokyo) Argentina 3, Soviet Union 1; **1981** (Sydney) W. Germany 4, Qatar 0; **1983** (Mexico City) Brazil 1, Argentina 0; **1985** (Moscow) Brazil 1, Spain 0; **1987** (Santiago) Yugoslavia 1, W. Germany 1 (Yugoslavia won 5-4 on pens.); **1989** (Riyadh) Portugal 2, Nigeria 0; **1991** (Lisbon) Portugal 0, Brazil 0 (Portugal won 4-2 on pens.); **1993** (Sydney) Brazil 2, Ghana 1; **1995** (Qatar) Argentina 2, Brazil 0; **1997** (Kuala Lumpur) Argentina 2, Uruguay 1; **1999** (Lagos) Spain 4, Japan 0; **2001** (Buenos Aires) Argentina 3, Ghana 0; **2003** (Dubai) Brazil 1, Spain 0; **2005** (Utrecht) Argentina 2, Nigeria 1.

FAMOUS CLUB FEATS

Chelsea were Premiership winners in 2004-05, their centenary season with the highest points total (95) ever recorded by England Champions. They set these other records: Most Premiership wins in season (29); most clean sheets (25) and fewest goals conceded (15) in top-division history. They also won the League Cup in 2005.

Arsenal created an all-time English League record sequence of 49 unbeaten Premiership matches (W36, D13), spanning 3 seasons, from May 7, 2003 until losing 2-0 away to Manchester United on October 24, 2004. It included all 38 games in season 2003-04.

The Double: There have been ten instances of a club winning the Football League/ Premiership title and the F.A. Cup in the same season. **Manchester Utd.** and **Arsenal** have each done so three times:-

Preston N.E. 1888-89; **Aston Villa** 1896-97; **Tottenham** 1960-61; **Arsenal** 1970-71, 1997-98, 2001-02; **Liverpool** 1985-86; **Manchester Utd.** 1993-94, 1995-96, 1998-99.

The Treble: Liverpool were the first English club to win three major competitions in one season when in 1983-84, Joe Fagan's first season as manager, they were League Champions, League Cup winners and European Cup winners.

Sir Alex Ferguson's **Manchester Utd.** achieved an even more prestigious treble in 1998-99, completing the domestic double of Premiership and F.A. Cup and then winning the European Cup.

Liverpool completed a unique treble by an English club with three cup successes under Gerard Houllier in season 2000-01: the League Cup, F.A. Cup and UEFA Cup.

Liverpool the first English club to win five major trophies in one calendar year (February-August 2001): League Cup, F.A. Cup, UEFA Cup, Charity Shield, UEFA Super Cup.

As Champions in season 2001-02, **Arsenal** set a Premiership record by winning the last 13 matches. They were the first top-division club since Preston N.E. in the League's inaugural season (1888-9) to maintain an unbeaten away record.

(See Scottish section for treble feats by Rangers and Celtic.)

Home Runs: Sunderland lost only one home Div. 1 game out of 73 in five seasons, 1891 to 1896. **Brentford** won all 21 home games in 1929-30 in the Third Division (South). Others have won all home games in a smaller programme.

Record Home Run: Liverpool went 85 competitive first-team games unbeaten at home between losing 2-3 to Birmingham City on January 21, 1978 and 1-2 to Leicester City on January 31, 1981. They comprised 63 in the League, 9 League Cup, 7 in European competition and 6 F.A. Cup. Leicester were relegated that season. **Chelsea** equalled Liverpool's record sequence of 63 unbeaten home League matches, from 2004 to end of season 2006-07.

Millwall were unbeaten at home in the League for 59 consecutive matches from 1964-67.

Third to First: Charlton Athletic, in 1936, became the first club to advance from the Third to First Division in successive seasons. **Queens Park Rangers** were the second club to achieve the feat in 1968, and **Oxford Utd.** did it in 1984 and 1985 as Champions of each division. Subsequently, **Derby Co.** (1987), **Middlesbrough** (1988), **Sheffield Utd.** (1990) and **Notts Co.** (1991) climbed from Third Division to First in consecutive seasons.

Watford won successive promotions from the modern Second Division to the Premier League in 1997-8, 1998-9. **Manchester City** equalled the feat in 1998-9, 1999-2000.

Fourth to First: Northampton Town, in 1965 became the first club to rise from the Fourth to the First Division. **Swansea City** climbed from the Fourth Division to the First (three promotions in four seasons), 1977-8 to 1980-1. **Wimbledon** repeated the feat, 1982-3 to 1985-6 **Watford** did it in five seasons, 1977-8 to 1981-2. **Carlisle Utd.** climbed from Fourth Division to First, 1964-74.

Non-League to First: When **Wimbledon** finished third in the Second Division in 1986, they completed the phenomenal rise from non-League football (Southern League) to the First Division in nine years. Two years later they won the F.A. Cup.

Tottenham, in 1960-1, not only carried off the First Division Championship and the F.A. Cup for the first time that century but set up other records by opening with 11 successive wins, registering most First Division wins (31), most away wins in the League's history (16), and equalling Arsenal's First Division records of 66 points and 33 away points. They already held the Second Division record of 70 points (1919-20).

Arsenal, in 1993, became the first club to win both English domestic cup competitions (F.A. Cup and League Cup) in the same season. **Liverpool** repeated the feat in 2000-01.

Preston N.E., in season 1888-9, won the first League Championship without losing a match and the F.A. Cup without having a goal scored against them. Only other English clubs to remain unbeaten through a League season were **Liverpool** (Div. 2 Champions in 1893-4) and **Arsenal** (Premiership Champions 2003-04).

Bury, in 1903, also won the F.A. Cup without conceding a goal.

Everton won Div. 2, Div. 1 and the F.A. Cup in successive seasons, 1930-1, 1931-2, 1932-3.

Liverpool won the League Championship in 1964, the F.A. Cup in 1965 and the Championship again in 1966. In 1978 they became the first British club to win the European Cup in successive seasons. **Nott'm. Forest** repeated the feat in 1979 and 1980.

Liverpool won the League Championship six times in eight seasons (1976-83) under **Bob Paisley's** management.

Sir Alex Ferguson's **Manchester Utd.** have won the F.A. Premier League in nine of its 15 seasons (1993-2007). They were runners-up twice and third three times.

Most Premiership wins in season: 29 by Chelsea in 2004-05, 2005–06.

Biggest points-winning margin by League Champions: 18 by Manchester Utd. (1999-2000).

COVENTRY UNIQUE

Coventry City are the only club to have played in the Premier League, all four previous divisions of the Football League, in both sections (North and South) of the old Third Division and in the Coca-Cola Championship.

FAMOUS UPS & DOWNS

Sunderland: Relegated in 1958 after maintaining First Division status since their election to the Football League in 1890. They dropped into Division 3 for the first time in 1987.

Aston Villa: Relegated with **Preston N.E.** to the Third Division in 1970.

Arsenal up: When the League was extended in 1919, Woolwich Arsenal (sixth in Division Two in 1914-15, last season before the war) were elected to Division One. Arsenal have been in the top division ever since.

Tottenham down: At that same meeting in 1919 Chelsea (due for relegation) retained their place in Division One but the bottom club (Tottenham) had to go down to Division Two.

Preston N.E. and Burnley down: Preston N.E., the first League Champions in season 1888-9, dropped into the Fourth Division in 1985. So did Burnley, also among the League's original members in 1888. In 1986, Preston N.E. had to apply for re-election.

Wolves' fall: Wolves, another of the Football League's original members, completed the fall from First Division to Fourth in successive seasons (1984-5-6).

Lincoln City out: Lincoln City became the first club to suffer automatic demotion from the Football League when they finished bottom of Div. 4, on goal difference, in season 1986-7. They were replaced by Scarborough, champions of the GM Vauxhall Conference. Lincoln City regained their place a year later.

Swindon Town up and down: In the 1990 play-offs, Swindon Town won promotion to the First Division for the first time, but remained in the Second Division because of financial irregularities.

MOST CHAMPIONSHIP WINS

Liverpool, by winning the First Division in 1976-7, established a record of 10 Championship victories. They later increased the total to 18. **Manchester Utd.** are second with 16 League titles (7 Football League, 9 Premier League) and **Arsenal** third with 13 (10 Football League, 3 Premier League).

LONGEST CURRENT MEMBERS OF TOP DIVISION

Arsenal (since 1919), **Everton** (1954), **Liverpool** (1962), **Manchester Utd.** (1975).

CHAMPIONS: FEWEST PLAYERS

Liverpool used only 14 players (five ever-present) when they won the League Championship in season 1965-6. **Aston Villa** also called on no more than 14 players to win the title in 1980-81, with seven ever-present.

UNBEATEN CHAMPIONS

Only two clubs have become Champions of England with an unbeaten record: **Preston N.E.** as the Football League's first winners in 1888-9 (22 matches) and **Arsenal**, Premiership winners in 2003-04 (38 matches).

LEAGUE HAT-TRICKS

Huddersfield Town created a record in 1924-5-6 by winning the League Championship three years in succession.

Arsenal equalled this League hat-trick in 1933-4-5, **Liverpool** in 1982-3-4 and **Manchester United** in 1999-2000-01.

'SUPER DOUBLE' WINNERS

Since the war, there have been three instances of players appearing in and then managing F.A. Cup and Championship-winning teams:

Joe Mercer: Player in Arsenal Championship teams 1948, 1953 and in their 1950 F.A. Cup side; manager of Manchester City when they won Championship 1968, F.A. Cup 1969.

Kenny Dalglish: Player in Liverpool Championship-winning teams 1979, 1980, 1982, 1983, 1984, player-manager 1986, 1988, 1990: player-manager when Liverpool won F.A. Cup (to complete Double) 1986; manager of Blackburn Rov., Champions 1995.

George Graham: Played in Arsenal's Double-winning team in 1971, and as manager took them to Championship success in 1989 and 1991 and the F.A. Cup – League Cup double in 1993.

ORIGINAL TWELVE

The original 12 members of the Football League (formed in 1888) were: **Accrington, Aston Villa, Blackburn Rov., Bolton Wand., Burnley, Derby Co., Everton, Notts Co., Preston N.E., Stoke City, W.B.A.** and **Wolves.**

Results on the opening day (September 8, 1888): Bolton Wand. 3, Derby Co. 6; Everton 2, Accrington 1; Preston N.E. 5, Burnley 2; Stoke City 0, W.B.A. 2; Wolves 1, Aston Villa 1. Preston N.E. had the biggest first-day crowd: 6,000. Blackburn Rov. and Notts Co. did not play that day. They kicked off a week later (September 15) – Blackburn Rov. 5, Accrington 5; Everton 2, Notts Co. 1.

FASTEST CLIMBS

Three promotions in four seasons by two clubs – **Swansea City:** 1978 third in Div.4; 1979 third in Div.3; 1981 third in Div.2; **Wimbledon:** 1983 Champions of Div.4; 1984 second in Div.3; 1986 third in Div.2.

MERSEYSIDE RECORD

Liverpool is the only city to have staged top-division football – through Everton and/or Liverpool – in **every season** since League football began in 1888.

EARLIST PROMOTIONS TO TOP DIVISION POST-WAR

March 23, 1974, Middlesbrough; March 25, 2006, Reading.

EARLIEST RELEGATIONS POST-WAR

From top division: **Q.P.R.** went down from the old First Division on March 29, 1969. From modern First Division: **Stockport Co.** on March 16, 2002, with 7 matches still to play; **Wimbledon** on April 6, 2004, with 7 matches to play.

LEAGUE RECORDS

DOUBLE CHAMPIONS

Nine men have played in and managed League Championship-winning teams:

Ted Drake Player – Arsenal 1934, 1935, 1938. Manager – Chelsea 1955.
Bill Nicholson Player – Tottenham 1951. Manager – Tottenham 1961.
Alf Ramsey Player – Tottenham 1951. Manager – Ipswich Town 1962.

Joe Mercer Player – Everton 1939, Arsenal 1948, 1953. Manager – Manchester City 1968.
Dave Mackay Player – Tottenham 1961. Manager – Derby Co. 1975.
Bob Paisley Player – Liverpool 1947. Manager – Liverpool 1976, 1977, 1979, 1980, 1982, 1983.
Howard Kendall Player – Everton 1970. Manager – Everton 1985, 1987.
Kenny Dalglish Player – Liverpool 1979, 1980, 1982, 1983, 1984. Player-manager – Liverpool 1986, 1988, 1990. Manager – Blackburn Rov. 1995.
George Graham Player – Arsenal 1971. Manager – Arsenal 1989, 1991.

MOST LEAGUE CHAMPIONSHIP MEDALS

Kenny Dalglish: 9 – 8 for Liverpool (5 as player, 1979-80-82-83-84; 3 as player-manager, 1986-88-90); 1 for Blackburn Rov. (as manager, 1995). As a player he also won 4 Scottish Championship medals with Celtic (1972-73-74-77). **Phil Neal**: 8 for Liverpool (1976-77-79-80-82-83-84-86); **Alan Hansen**: 8 for Liverpool (1979-80-82-83-84-86-88-90); **Ryan Giggs**: 9 for Manchester Utd. (1993–94–96–97–99–2000–01–03–07); **Sir Alex Ferguson:** 9 as Manchester Utd. manager (1993–94–96–97–99–2000–01–03–07).

CANTONA'S FOUR-TIMER

Eric Cantona played in four successive Championship-winning teams: Marseille 1990-1, Leeds Utd. 1991-2, Manchester Utd. 1992-3 and 1993-4.

ARRIVALS AND DEPARTURES

The following are the Football League arrivals and departures since 1923:

Year	*In*	*Out*
1923	Doncaster Rov.	Stalybridge Celtic
	New Brighton	
1927	Torquay Athletic	Aberdare Athletic
1928	Carlisle Utd.	Durham City
1929	York City	Ashington
1930	Thames	Merthyr Tydfil
1931	Mansfield Town	Newport County
	Chester City	Nelson
1932	Aldershot	Thames
	Newport County	Wigan Borough
1938	Ipswich Town	Gillingham
1950	Colchester Utd.	
	Gillingham	
	Scunthorpe Utd.	
	Shrewsbury Town	
1951	Workington	New Brighton
1960	Peterborough Utd.	Gateshead
1962	Oxford Utd.	Accrington Stanley (resigned)
1970	Cambridge Utd.	Bradford P.A.
1972	Hereford Utd.	Barrow
1977	Wimbledon	Workington
1978	Wigan Athletic	Southport
1987	Scarborough	Lincoln City
1988	Lincoln City	Newport County
1989	Maidstone Utd.	Darlington
1990	Darlington	Colchester Utd.
1991	Barnet	
1992	Colchester Utd.	Aldershot, Maidstone (resigned)
1993	Wycombe Wand.	Halifax Town
1997	Macclesfield Town	Hereford Utd.
1998	Halifax Town	Doncaster Rov.
1999	Cheltenham Town	Scarborough
2000	Kidderminster Harriers	Chester City
2001	Rushden & Diamonds	Barnet

2002	Boston Utd.	Halifax Town
2003	Yeovil Town, Doncaster Rov.	Exeter City, Shrewsbury Town
2004	Chester City, Shrewsbury Town	Carlisle Utd., York City
2005	Barnet, Carlisle Utd.	Kidderminster, Cambridge Utd.
2006	Accrington Stanley, Hereford Utd.	Oxford Utd., Rushden & Diamonds
2007	Dag. and Redbridge, Morecambe	Torquay Utd., Boston Utd.

Leeds City were expelled from Div. 2 in October, 1919; Port Vale took over their fixtures.

EXTENSIONS TO FOOTBALL LEAGUE

Clubs	*Season*	*Clubs*	*Season*
12 to 14	1891-2	44 to 66+	1920-1
14 to 28*	1892-3	66 to 86†	1921-2
28 to 31	1893-4	86 to 88	1923-4
31 to 32	1894-5	88 to 92	1950-1
32 to 36	1898-9	92 to 93	1991-2
36 to 40	1905-6	(Reverted to 92 when Aldershot closed,	
40 to 44	1919-20	March 1992)	

* Second Division formed. + Third Division (South) formed from Southern League clubs.
† Third Division (North) formed.
Football League reduced to 70 clubs and three divisions on the formation of the F.A. Premier League in 1992; increased to 72 season 1994-5, when Premier League reduced to 20 clubs.

RECORD RUNS

Arsenal hold the record unbeaten sequence in the English League – 49 Premiership matches (36 wins, 13 draws) from May 7, 2003 until October 24, 2004 when beaten 2-0 away to Manchester United.

The record previously belonged to **Nott'm. Forest** – 42 First Division matches (21 wins, 21 draws) from November 19, 1977 until beaten 2-0 at Liverpool on December 9, 1978.

Best debuts: Ipswich Town won the First Division at their first attempt in 1961-2. **Peterborough Utd.** in their first season in the Football League (1960-1) not only won the Fourth Division but set the all-time scoring record for the League of 134 goals. **Hereford Utd.** were promoted from the Fourth Division in their first League season, 1972-3. **Wycombe Wand.** were promoted from the Third Division (via the play-offs) in their first League season, 1993-4.

Record winning sequence in a season: 14 consecutive League victories (all in Second Division): **Manchester Utd.** 1904-5, **Bristol City** 1905-6 and **Preston N.E.** 1950-1.

Best winning start to League season: 13 successive victories in Div. 3 by **Reading**, season 1985-6.

Best starts in 'old' First Division: 11 consecutive victories by **Tottenham** in 1960-1; 10 by **Manchester Utd.** in 1985-6. **Newcastle Utd.** won their first 11 matches in the **'new' First Division** in 1992-3.

Longest unbeaten sequence (all competitions): 40 by **Nott'm. Forest**, March-December 1978. It comprised 21 wins, 19 draws (in 29 League matches, 6 League Cup, 4 European Cup, 1 Charity Shield).

Longest unbeaten starts to League season: 38 matches (26 wins, 12 draws) in **Arsenal's** undefeated Premiership season, 2003-4; 29 matches – **Leeds Utd.,** Div. 1 1973-4 (19 wins, 10 draws); **Liverpool,** Div. 1 1987-8 (22 wins, 7 draws).

Most consecutive League matches unbeaten in a season: 38 **Arsenal** Premiership season 2003-4 (see above); 33 **Reading** (25 wins, 8 draws) 2005–6.

Longest winning sequence in Div. 1: 13 matches by **Tottenham** – last two of season 1959-60, first 11 of 1960-1.

Longest winning one-season sequences in Championship: 13 matches by **Preston N.E.** in 1891-2; 13 by **Sunderland**, also in 1891-2.

Longest unbeaten home League sequence in top division: 63 matches (49 wins, 14 draws) by **Liverpool** (February 1978–December 1980). **Chelsea** 63 matches (48 wins, 15 draws) Mar. 2004–May 2007.

League's longest winning sequence with clean sheets: 9 matches by Stockport Co. (Lge. 2, 2006-7 season).

Premier League – best starts to season: (before **Arsenal** unbeaten through season 2003-4): 12 games unbeaten – **Nott'm. Forest** in 1995-6, **Arsenal** in 1997-8, **Aston Villa** in 1998-9, **Liverpool** 2002-3.

Best winning start to Premiership season: 9 consecutive victories by Chelsea in 2005-06.

Premier League – most consecutive wins (two seasons): 14 by **Arsenal,** February-August, 2002.

Premier League's record unbeaten run: 40 matches (W28, D12) by **Arsenal** (May 7, 2003–May 15, 2004). **In one season**, all 38 matches by Arsenal (W26, D12) in 2003-4.

Premier League – longest unbeaten away run: 23 matches (W16, D7) by **Arsenal** (Aug. 18, 2001–Sept. 28, 2002); and by **Arsenal** again (W13, D10), April 5 2003–May 15, 2004.

Record home-win sequences: Bradford Park Avenue won 25 successive home games in Div. 3 North – the last 18 in 1926-7 and the first 7 the following season. Longest run of home wins in the top division is 21 by **Liverpool** – the last 9 of 1971-2 and the first 12 of 1972-3.

British record for successive League wins: 25 by **Celtic** (Scottish Premier League), 2003-4.

WORST SEQUENCES

Cambridge Utd. experienced the longest run without a win in Football League history in season 1983-4: 31 matches (21 lost, 10 drawn). They finished bottom of the Second Division.

Worst losing start to a League season: 12 consecutive defeats by **Manchester Utd.** (Div. 1), 1930-1.

Worst Premier League start: **Swindon Town** 15 matches without win (6 draws, 9 defeats), 1993-4.

Worst Premier League sequence: Sunderland 26 matches without win (3 draws, 23 defeats), December 2002 – September 2005.

Premier League – most consecutive defeats: 20 **Sunderland** last 15 matches, 2002-3, first five matches 2005-06.

Longest non-winning start to League season: 25 matches (4 draws, 21 defeats) by **Newport County**, Div. 4. Worst no-win League starts since then: 16 matches by **Burnley** (9 draws, 7 defeats in Div. 2, 1979-80); 16 by **Hull City** (10 draws, 6 defeats in Div. 2, 1989-90); 16 by **Sheffield Utd.** (4 draws, 12 defeats in Div. 1, 1990-91).

Most League defeats in season: 34 by **Doncaster Rov.** (Div. 3) 1997-8; 33 by **Wimbledon** (Div. 1) 2003-4.

Fewest League wins in season: 1 by **Loughborough Town** (Div. 2, season 1899-1900). They lost 27, drew 6, goals 18-100 and dropped out of the League. (See also Scottish section).

Fewest home League wins in season: 1 by **Loughborough Town** (Div. 2, 1899-1900), **Notts Co.** (Div. 1, 1904-5), **Woolwich Arsenal** (Div. 1, 1912-13), **Blackpool** (Div. 1, 1966-7), **Rochdale** (Div. 3, 1973-4), **Sunderland** (Premiership; 2005-06).

Most home League defeats in season: 18 by **Cambridge Utd.** (Div. 3, 1984-5).

Away League defeats record: 24 in row by **Nelson** (Div. 3 North) – 3 in April 1930 followed by all 21 in season 1930-31. They then dropped out of the League.

Biggest defeat in Champions' season: During **Newcastle Utd.'s** Championship-winning season in 1908-9, they were beaten 9-1 at home by Sunderland on December 5.

WORST START BY EVENTUAL CHAMPIONS

Sunderland took only 2 points from their first 7 matches in season 1912-13 (2 draws, 5 defeats). They won 25 of the remaining 31 games to clinch their fifth League title.

SUNDERLAND'S WOE

Sunderland were relegated in season 2002–03 as the worst-ever team in the Premiership: fewest wins (4), fewest points (19), fewest goals (21) and with the longest run of consecutive defeats (15). They were relegated again in 2005-06 with three wins and 15 points.

UNBEATEN LEAGUE SEASON

Only three clubs have completed an English League season unbeaten: **Preston N.E.** (22 matches in 1888-9, the League's first season), **Liverpool** (28 matches in Div. 2, 1893-4) and **Arsenal** (38 matches in Premiership, 2003-4).

100 PER CENT HOME RECORDS

Five clubs have won every home League match in a season, four of them in the old Second Division: **Liverpool** (14) in 1893-4, **Bury** (15) in 1894-5, **Sheffield Wed.** (17) in 1899-1900 and **Small Heath**, subsequently Birmingham (17) in 1902-3. The last club to do it, **Brentford**, won all 21 home games in Div. 3 South in 1929-30.

Rotherham Utd. just failed to equal that record in 1946-7. They won their first 20 home matches in Div. 3 North, then drew the last 3-3 v Rochdale.

BEST HOME LEAGUE RECORDS IN TOP FLIGHT

Newcastle Utd., 1906-07 (P19, W18, D1); **Chelsea** 2005-6 (P19, W18, D1).

MOST CONSECUTIVE CLEAN SHEETS

Football League – **11**: **Millwall** (Div. 3 South 1925-26); **York City** (Div. 3 1973-74); **Reading** (Div. 4, 1978-79). **Premiership** – **10**: **Chelsea** (2004-05).

WORST HOME RUNS

Most consecutive home League defeats: 8 by **Rochdale,** who took only 11 points in Div. 3 North in season 1931-2; 8 by **Stockport Co.** (Div.1) in season 2001-02; 8 by **Sunderland** (Premiership), season 2002–03.

Between November 1958 and October 1959 **Portsmouth** drew 2 and lost 14 out of 16 consecutive home games.

West Ham Utd. did not win in the Premiership at Upton Park in season 2002–03 until the 13th. home match on January 29.

MOST AWAY WINS IN SEASON

Doncaster Rovers won 18 of their 21 away League fixtures when winning Div. 3 North in 1946-7.

AWAY WINS RECORD

Most **consecutive away League wins**: **10 by Tottenham** (Div. 1) – 8 at start of 1960-1, after ending previous season with 2 away victories.

100 PER CENT HOME WINS ON ONE DAY

Div. 1 – All 11 home teams won on Feb. 13, 1926 and on Dec. 10, 1955. **Div. 2** – All 12 home teams won on Nov. 26, 1988. **Div. 3**, all 12 home teams won in the week-end programme of Oct. 18-19, 1968.

NO HOME WINS IN DIV. ON ONE DAY

Div. 1 – 8 away wins, 3 draws in 11 matches on Sept. 6, 1986. **Div. 2** – 7 away wins, 4 draws in 11 matches on Dec. 26, 1987. **Premier League** – 6 away wins, 5 draws in 11 matches on Dec. 26, 1994.

The week-end **Premiership** programme on Dec. 7-8-9, 1996 produced no home win in the ten games (4 aways, 6 draws). There was again no home victory (3 away wins, 7 draws) in the week-end **Premiership** fixtures on September 23-24, 2000.

MOST DRAWS IN A SEASON (FOOTBALL LEAGUE)

23 by **Norwich City** (Div. 1, 1978-9), **Exeter City** (Div. 4, 1986-7). **Cardiff City** and **Hartlepool Utd.** (both Div. 3, 1997-8). Norwich City played 42 matches, the others 46.

MOST DRAWS IN ONE DIV. ON ONE DAY

On September 18, 1948 **nine** out of 11 First Division matches were drawn.

MOST DRAWS IN PREMIER DIV. PROGRAMME

Over the week-ends of December 2-3-4, 1995, and September 23-24, 2000, seven out of the ten matches finished level.

FEWEST DRAWS IN SEASON (46 MATCHES)

3 by **Reading** (Div. 3 South, 1951–2); **Bradford City Park Avenue** (Div. 3 North, 1956–7); **Tranmere Rov.** (Div. 4, 1984–5); **Southend Utd.** (Div. 3, 2002–3).

HIGHEST-SCORING DRAWS IN LEAGUE

Leicester City 6, Arsenal 6 (Div. 1 April 21, 1930) and **Charlton Athletic 6, Middlesbrough 6** (Div 2. October 22, 1960)

Latest 6-6 draw in first-class football was between Tranmere Rov. and Newcastle Utd. in the Zenith Data Systems Cup 1st. Round on October 1, 1991. The score went from 3-3 at 90 minutes to 6-6 after extra time, and Tranmere Rov. won 3-2 on penalties. In Scotland: Queen of the South 6, Falkirk 6 (Div. 1, September 20, 1947).'

Most recent 5-5 draws in top division: Southampton v Coventry City (Div. 1, May 4, 1982); Q.P.R. v Newcastle Utd. (Div. 1, Sept. 22, 1984).

DRAWS RECORDS

Most consecutive drawn matches in Football League: 8 by **Torquay Utd.** (Div. 3), Oct. 25 – Dec. 13, 1969; Chesterfield (Lge. 1), Nov. 26 – Jan. 2 (2005-6).

Longest sequence of draws by the same score: six 1-1 results by **Q.P.R.** in season 1957-8.

Tranmere Rov. became the first club to play **five consecutive 0-0 League draws**, in season 1997-8.

IDENTICAL RECORDS

There is only **one instance** of two clubs in one division finishing a season with identical records. In 1907-8, **Blackburn Rov.** and **Woolwich Arsenal** were bracketed equal 14th. in the First Division with these figures: P38, W12, D12, L14, Goals 51-63, Pts. 36.

The total of **1195 goals** scored in the Premier League in season 1993-4 was **repeated** in 1994-5.

DEAD LEVEL

Millwall's record in Division Two in season 1973-74 was P42, W14, D14, L14, F51, A51, Pts 42.

CHAMPIONS OF ALL DIVISIONS

Wolves and **Burnley** are the only clubs to have won the Championships of the old **Divisions 1, 2, 3 and 4**. Wolves were also **Champions** of the **Third Division North**.

POINTS DEDUCTIONS

Season 2000–1: Chesterfield (Div. 3) had 9 points deducted (plus £20,000 fine) for breach of transfer regulations and falsifying gate receipts. They finished in third (promotion) place.

Season 2002–3: Boston Utd. entered the Football League under a double penalty. On charges of contractual irregularities, they were fined £100,000 by the F.A. and deducted 4 points.

Season 2004-5: Wrexham were deducted 10 points in December 2004 after going into administration. The penalty resulted in their being relegated from League One. **Cambridge United** were deducted 10 points for going into administration in April 2005 after finishing bottom of League Two.

Season 2005-6: Rotherham Utd. were deducted 10 points from the start of following season for going into administration.

Season 2006-7: Leeds Utd. and **Boston Utd.** were both deducted 10 points for going into administration.

Bury were deducted 1 point from 2005-6 season for fielding an unregistered player.

Among previous points penalties imposed:

Nov. 1990: **Arsenal** deducted 2 points and **Man. United** 1 point following mass player brawl at Old Trafford.

Dec. 1996: **Brighton** docked 2 points for two pitch invasions by fans.

Jan. 1997: **Middlesbrough** deducted 3 points for refusing to play Premiership match at Blackburn because of injuries and illness.

• June 1994: **Tottenham** deducted 12 points (reduced to 6) and banned from next season's F.A. Cup for making illegal payments to players. On appeal, points deduction annulled and Spurs re-instated in Cup.

NIGHTMARE STARTS

Most goals conceded by a goalkeeper on League debut: 13 by **Steve Milton** when Halifax Town lost 13-0 at Stockport Co. (Div. 3 North) on January 6, 1934.

Post-war: 11 by Crewe Alexandra's new goalkeeper **Dennis Murray** (Div. 3 North) on September 29, 1951, when Lincoln City won 11-1.

RELEGATION ODD SPOTS

None of the Barclays Premiership relegation places in season 2004-5 were decided until the last day (Sunday, May 15). **WBA** (botton at kick-off) survived with a 2-0 home win against Portsmouth, and the three relegated clubs were Southampton (1-2 v Man. United), Norwich City (0-6 at Fulham) and Crystal Palace (2-2 at Charlton).

In season 1937-8, **Manchester City** were the highest-scoring team in the First Division with 80 goals (3 more than Champions Arsenal), but they finished in 21st place and were relegated – a year after winning the Championship. They scored more goals than they conceded (77).

That season produced the **closest relegation battle** in top-division history, with only 4 points spanning the bottom 11 clubs in Div. 1. WBA went down with Manchester City.

Twelve years earlier, in 1925-6, City went down to Division 2 despite totalling 89 goals – still the most scored in any division by a relegated team. Manchester City also scored 31 F.A. Cup goals that season, but lost the Final 1-0 to Bolton Wanderers.

Cardiff City were relegated from Div. 1 in season 1928-9, despite conceding fewest goals in the division (59). They also scored fewest (43).

On their way to relegation from the First Division in season 1984–85, **Stoke City** twice lost ten matches in a row.

RELEGATION TREBLES

Two Football League clubs have been relegated three seasons in succession. **Bristol City** fell from First Division to Fourth in 1980-1-2, and **Wolves** did the same in 1984-5-6.

END OF CHRISTMAS 'CERTAINTY'

In season 2004-5, **W.B.A.** became the first Premiership club to avoid relegation after being bottom of the table at Christmas.

OLDEST CLUBS

Oldest Association Football Club is **Sheffield F.C.** (formed in 1857). The oldest Football League clubs are **Notts Co.**, 1862; **Nott'm. Forest**, 1865; and **Sheffield Wed.**, 1866.

FOUR DIVISIONS

In **May, 1957**, the Football League decided to re-group the two sections of the Third Division into Third and Fourth Divisions in **season 1958-9**.

The Football League was reduced to three divisions on the formation of the F.A. Premier League in **1992**.

In season 2004-5, under new sponsors Coca-Cola, the titles of First, Second and Third Divisions were changed to League Championship, League One and League Two.

THREE UP – THREE DOWN

The Football League Annual General Meeting of June 1973 agreed to adopt the promotion and relegation system of three up and three down.

The **new system** came into effect in **season 1973-4** and applied only to the first three divisions; four clubs were still relegated from the Third and four promoted from the Fourth.

It was the first change in the promotion and relegation system for the top two divisions in 81 years.

PLAY-OFF FINALS
HIGHEST SCORES

Div. 1	1993	(Wembley)	Swindon Town 4, Leicester City 3
	1995	(Wembley)	Bolton Wand. 4, Reading 3
	1998	(Wembley)	Charlton Athletic 4, Sunderland 4 (Charlton Athletic won 7–6 on pens.)
Div. 2	1993	(Wembley)	W.B.A. 3, Port Vale 0
	2000	(Wembley)	Gillingham 3, Wigan Athletic 2
	2001	(Cardiff)	Walsall 3, Reading 2
Div. 3	2003	(Cardiff)	Bournemouth 5, Lincoln City 2

BIGGEST ATTENDANCES

Div. 1	1998	(Wembley)	Charlton Athletic v Sunderland	77,739
Div. 2	1999	(Wembley)	Manchester City v Gillingham	76,935
Div. 3	2007	(Wembley)	Bristol Rov. v Shrewsbury Town	61,589

MOST LEAGUE APPEARANCES

Players with more than 700 English League apps. (as at end of season 2005-06).

1005 **Peter Shilton** 1966-97 (286 Leicester City, 110 Stoke City, 202 Nott'm. Forest, 188 Southampton, 175 Derby Co., 34 Plymouth Argyle, 1 Bolton Wand., 9 Leyton Orient).

931 **Tony Ford** 1975-2002 (423 Grimsby Town, 9 Sunderland, 112 Stoke City, 114 W.B.A., 5 Bradford City, 76 Scunthorpe Utd., 103 Mansfield Town, 89 Rochdale).

824 **Terry Paine** 1956-77 (713 Southampton, 111 Hereford).

795 **Tommy Hutchison** 1968-91 (165 Blackpool, 314 Coventry City, 46 Manchester City, 92 Burnley, 178 Swansea City). In addition, 68 Scottish League apps. for Alloa 1965-68, giving career League app. total of 863.

790 **Neil Redfearn** 1982-2004 (35 Bolton Wand., 100 Lincoln City, 46 Doncaster Rov., 57 Crystal Palace, 24 Watford, 62 Oldham Athletic, 292 Brnsley, 30 Charlton Athletic, 17 Bradford City, 22 Wigan Athletic, 42 Halifax Town, 54 Boston Utd., 9 Rochdale).

782 **Robbie James** 1973-94 (484 Swansea City, 48 Stoke City, 87 Q.P.R., 23 Leicester City, 89 Bradford City, 51 Cardiff City).

777 **Alan Oakes** 1959-84 (565 Manchester City, 211 Chester City, 1 Port Vale).

773 **Dave Beasant** 1980-2003 (340 Wimbledon, 20 Newcastle Utd., 6 Grimsby Town, 4 Wolves, 133 Chelsea, 88 Southampton, 139 Nott'm. F., 27 Portsmouth, 16 Brighton).

770 **John Trollope** 1960-80 (all for Swindon Town, record total for one club).

764 **Jimmy Dickinson** 1946-65 (all for Portsmouth).

761 **Roy Sproson** 1950-72 (all for Port Vale).

760 **Mick Tait** 1974-97 (64 Oxford Utd., 106 Carlisle Utd., 33 Hull City, 240 Portsmouth, 99 Reading, 79 Darlington, 139 Hartlepool Utd.).

758 **Billy Bonds** 1964-88 (95 Charlton Athletic, 663 West Ham Utd.).

758 **Ray Clemence** 1966-88 (48 Scunthorpe Utd., 470 Liverpool, 240 Tottenham).

757 **Pat Jennings** 1963-86 (48 Watford, 472 Tottenham, 237 Arsenal).

757 **Frank Worthington** 1966-88 (171 Huddersfield Town, 210 Leicester City, 84 Bolton Wand., 75 Birmingham City, 32 Leeds Utd., 19 Sunderland, 34 Southampton, 31 Brighton & H.A., 59 Tranmere Rov., 23 Preston N.E., 19 Stockport Co.).

749 **Ernie Moss** 1968-88 (469 Chesterfield, 35 Peterborough Utd., 57 Mansfield Town, 74 Port Vale, 11 Lincoln City, 44 Doncaster Rov., 26 Stockport Co., 23 Scarborough, 10 Rochdale).

746 **Les Chapman** 1966-88 (263 Oldham Athletic, 133 Huddersfield Town, 70 Stockport Co., 139 Bradford City, 88 Rochdale, 53 Preston N.E.).

744 **Asa Hartford** 1967-90 (214 W.B.A., 260 Manchester City, 3 Nott'm. F., 81 Everton, 28 Norwich City, 81 Bolton Wand., 45 Stockport Co., 7 Oldham Athletic, 25 Shrewsbury Town).

743 **Alan Ball** 1963-84 (146 Blackpool, 208 Everton, 177 Arsenal, 195 Southampton, 17 Bristol Rov.).

743 **John Hollins** 1963-84 (465 Chelsea, 151 Q.P.R., 127 Arsenal).

743 **Phil Parkes** 1968-91 (52 Walsall, 344 Q.P.R., 344 West Ham Utd., 3 Ipswich Town).

737 **Steve Bruce** 1979-99 (205 Gillingham, 141 Norwich City, 309 Manchester Utd. 72 Birmingham City, 10 Sheffield Utd.).

732 **Mick Mills** 1966-88 (591 Ipswich Town, 103 Southampton, 38 Stoke City).

731 **Ian Callaghan** 1959-81 (640 Liverpool, 76 Swansea City, 15 Crewe Alexandra).

731 **David Seaman** 1982-2003 (91 Peterborough Utd, 75 Birmingham City, 141 Q.P.R., 405 Arsenal, 19 Manchester City).

725 **Steve Perryman** 1969-90 (655 Tottenham, 17 Oxford Utd., 53 Brentford).

722 **Martin Peters** 1961-81 (302 West Ham Utd., 189 Tottenham, 207 Norwich City, 24 Sheffield Utd.).

718 **Mike Channon** 1966-86 (511 Southampton, 72 Manchester City, 4 Newcastle Utd., 9 Bristol Rov., 88 Norwich City, 34 Portsmouth).

716 **Ron Harris** 1961-83 (655 Chelsea, 61 Brentford).

716 **Mike Summerbee** 1959-79 (218 Swindon Town, 357 Manchester City, 51 Burnley, 3 Blackpool, 87 Stockport Co.).

715 **Teddy Sheringham** 1983-2007 (220 Millwall, 5 Aldershot, 42 Nott'm. Forest, 104 Manchester Utd., 236 Tottenham, 32 Portsmouth, 76 West Ham Utd.).

714 **Glenn Cockerill** 1976-98 (186 Lincoln City, 26 Swindon Town, 62 Sheffield Utd., 387 Southampton, 90 Leyton Orient, 40 Fulham, 23 Brentford).

705 **Keith Curle** 1981-2003 (32 Bristol Rov., 16 Torquay Utd., 121 Bristol City, 40 Reading, 93 Wimbledon, 171 Manchester City, 150 Wolves, 57 Sheffield Utd., 11 Barnsley, 14 Mansfield Town.

705 **Phil Neal** 1968-89 (186 Northampton Town, 455 Liverpool, 64 Bolton Wand.).

705 **John Wile** 1968-86 (205 Peterborough Utd., 500 W.B.A.).

701 **Neville Southall** 1980-2000 (39 Bury, 578 Everton, 9 Port Vale, 9 Southend, 12 Stoke, 53 Torquay, 1 Bradford City).

• **Stanley Matthews** made 701 League apps. 1932-65 (322 Stoke City, 379 Blackpool), incl. 3 for Stoke City at start of 1939-40 before season abandoned (war).

• Goalkeeper **John Burridge** made a total of 771 League appearances in a 28-season career in English and Scottish football (1968-96). He played 691 games for 15 English clubs (Workington, Blackpool, Aston Villa, Southend Utd., Crystal Palace, Q.P.R., Wolves, Derby Co., Sheffield Utd., Southampton, Newcastle Utd., Scarborough, Lincoln City, Manchester City and Darlington) and 80 for 5 Scottish clubs (Hibernian, Aberdeen, Dumbarton, Falkirk and Queen of the South).

LONGEST LEAGUE APPEARANCE SEQUENCE

Harold Bell, centre-half of Tranmere Rov., was ever-present for the first nine post-war seasons (1946-55), achieving a League record of 401 consecutive matches. Counting F.A. Cup and other games, his run of successive appearances totalled 459.

The longest League sequence since Bell's was 394 appearances by goalkeeper **Dave Beasant** for Wimbledon, Newcastle Utd. and Chelsea. His nine-year run began on August 29, 1981 and was ended by a broken finger sustained in Chelsea's League Cup-tie against Portsmouth on October 31, 1990. Beasant's 394 consecutive League games comprised 304 for Wimbledon (1981-8), 20 for Newcastle Utd. (1988-9) and 70 for Chelsea (1989-90).

Phil Neal made 366 consecutive First Division appearances for Liverpool between December 1974 and September 1983, a remarkable sequence for an outfield player in top-division football.

MOST CONSECUTIVE PREMIERSHIP APPEARANCES

164 by **Frank Lampard** (Chelsea) October 2001 – December 2005.

EVER-PRESENT DEFENCE

The **entire defence** of Huddersfield Town played in all 42 Second Division matches in season 1952-3, namely, Bill Wheeler (goal), Ron Staniforth and Laurie Kelly (full-backs), Bill McGarry, Don McEvoy and Len Quested (half-backs). In addition, Vic Metcalfe played in all 42 League matches at outside-left.

FIRST SUBSTITUTE USED IN LEAGUE

Keith Peacock (Charlton Athletic), away to Bolton Wand. (Div. 2) on August 21, 1965.

FROM PROMOTION TO CHAMPIONS

Clubs who have become Champions of England a year after winning promotion: **Liverpool** 1905, 1906; **Everton** 1931, 1932; **Tottenham** 1950, 1951; **Ipswich Town** 1961, 1962; **Nott'm. Forest** 1977, 1978. The first four were placed top in both seasons: Forest finished third and first.

PREMIERSHIP'S FIRST MULTI-NATIONAL LINE-UP

Chelsea made history on December 26, 1999 when starting their Premiership match at Southampton without a single British player in the side.

Fulham's Unique XI: In the Worthington Cup 3rd. Round at home to Bury on November 6, 2002, **Fulham** fielded 11 players of 11 different nationalities. Ten were full Internationals, with Lee Clark an England U–21 cap.

On February 14, 2005 **Arsenal** became the first English club to select an all-foreign match squad when Arsene Wenger named 16 non-British players at home to Crystal Palace (Premiership).

THREE-NATION CHAMPION

Trevor Steven earned eight Championship medals, in three countries: two with Everton (1985, 1987); five with Rangers (1990, 1991, 1993, 1994, 1995) and one with Marseille in 1992.

LEEDS NO-WAY AWAY

Leeds Utd., in 1992-3, provided the first instance of a club failing to win an away League match as reigning Champions.

PIONEERS IN 1888 AND 1992

Three clubs among the twelve who formed the Football League in 1888 were also founder members of the F.A. Premier League: **Aston Villa**, **Blackburn Rov.** and **Everton**.

CHAMPIONS (MODERN) WITH TWO CLUBS – PLAYERS

Francis Lee (Manchester City 1968, Derby Co. 1975); **Ray Kennedy** (Arsenal 1971, Liverpool 1979, 1980, 1982); **Archie Gemmill** (Derby Co. 1972, 1975, Nott'm. F. 1978); **John McGovern** (Derby Co. 1972, Nott'm. F. 1978) **Larry Lloyd** (Liverpool 1973, Nott'm. F. 1978); **Peter Withe** (Nott'm. F. 1978, Aston Villa 1981); **John Lukic** (Arsenal 1989, Leeds Utd. 1992); **Kevin Richardson** (Everton 1985, Arsenal 1989); **Eric Cantona** (Leeds Utd. 1992, Manchester Utd. 1993, 1994, 1996, 1997); **David Batty** (Leeds Utd. 1992, Blackburn Rov. 1995), **Bobby Mimms** (Everton 1987, Blackburn Rov. 1995), **Henning Berg** (Blackburn Rov. 1995, Manchester United 1999, 2001).

TITLE TURNABOUTS

In January 1996, **Newcastle Utd.** led the Premier League by 13 points. They finished runners-up to Manchester Utd.

At Christmas 1997, **Arsenal** were 13 points behind leaders Manchester Utd. and still 11 points behind at the beginning of March 1998. But a run of 10 wins took the title to Highbury.

On March 2, 2003, **Arsenal**, with 9 games left, went 8 points clear of Manchester Utd., who had a match in hand. United won the Championship by 5 points.

• In March 2002, **Wolves** were in second (automatic promotion) place in Nationwide Div. 1, 11 points ahead of W.B.A., who had 2 games in hand. They were overtaken by Albion on the run-in, finished third, then failed in the play-offs. A year later they won promotion to the Premiership via the play-offs.

CLUB CLOSURES

Four clubs have left the Football League in mid-season: **Leeds City** (expelled Oct. 1919); **Wigan Borough** (Oct. 1931, debts of £20,000); **Accrington Stanley** (March 1962, debts £62,000); **Aldershot** (March 1992, debts £1.2m.). **Maidstone Utd.**, with debts of £650,000, closed August 1992, on the eve of the season.

FOUR-DIVISION MEN

In season 1986-7, goalkeeper **Eric Nixon,** became the first player to appear in **all four divisions** of the Football League **in one season**. He served two clubs in Div. 1: Manchester City (5 League games) and Southampton (4); in Div. 2 Bradford City (3); in Div. 3 Carlisle Utd. (16); and in Div. 4 Wolves (16). Total appearances: 44.

Harvey McCreadie, a teenage forward, played in four divisions over two seasons inside a calendar year – from Accrington (Div. 3) to Luton Town (Div. 1) in January 1960, to Div. 2 with Luton Town later that season and to Wrexham (Div. 4) in November.

Tony Cottee played in all four divisions in season 2000-01, for Leicester City (Premiership), Norwich City (Div. 1), Barnet (Div. 3, player-manager) and Millwall (Div. 2).

FATHERS & SONS

When player-manager **Ian Bowyer** (39) and **Gary Bowyer** (18) appeared together in the **Hereford Utd.** side at Scunthorpe Utd. (Div.4, April 21, 1990), they provided the first instance of father and son playing in the same team in a Football League match for 39 years. Ian Bowyer played as substitute, and Gary scored Hereford's injury-time equaliser in a 3-3 draw.

Alec (39) and **David** (17) **Herd** were the previous father-and-son duo in League football – for **Stockport Co.**, 2-0 winners at Hartlepool Utd. (Div.3 North) on May 5, 1951.

When **Preston N.E.** won 2-1 at Bury in Div. 3 on January 13, 1990, the opposing goalkeepers were brothers: **Alan Kelly** (21) for Preston N.E. and **Gary** (23) for Bury. Their father, **Alan Kelly Senior** (who kept goal for Preston N.E. in the 1964 F.A. Cup Final and won 47 Rep. of Ireland caps) flew from America to watch the sons he taught to keep goal line up on opposite sides.

George Eastham Snr. (manager) and son **George Eastham Jnr.** were inside-forward partners for Ards in the Irish League in season 1954-5.

FATHER & SON BOTH CHAMPIONS

John Aston Snr. won a Championship medal with Manchester Utd. in 1952 and **John Aston Jnr.** did so with the club in 1967.

FATHER & SON RIVAL MANAGERS

When **Bill Dodgin senior** took Bristol Rov. to Fulham for an F.A. Cup 1st Round tie in Nov. 1970, the opposing manager was his son, **Bill junior**.

FATHER & SON ON OPPOSITE SIDES

It happened for the first time in F.A. Cup history (1st. Qual. Round on Sept. 14, 1996) when 21-year-old **Nick Scaife** (Bishop Auckland) faced his father **Bobby** (41), who played for Pickering. Both were in midfield. Home side Bishops won 3-1.

THREE BROTHERS IN SAME SIDE

Southampton provided the first instance for 65 years of three brothers appearing together in a First Division side when **Danny Wallace** (24) and his 19-year-old twin brothers **Rodney** and **Ray** played against Sheffield Wed.on October 22, 1988. In all, they made 25 appearances together for Southampton until September 1989.

A previous instance in Div. 1 was provided by the Middlesbrough trio, **William**, **John** and **George Carr** with 24 League appearances together from January 1920 to October 1923.

The **Tonner** brothers, **Sam, James** and **Jack**, played together in 13 Second Division matches for Clapton Orient in season 1919-20.

Brothers **David**, **Donald** and **Robert Jack** played together in Plymouth Argyle's League side in 1920.

TWIN TEAM-MATES (see also **Wallace twins** above)

Twin brothers **David** and **Peter Jackson** played together for three League clubs (Wrexham, Bradford City and Tranmere Rov.) from 1954-62.

The **Morgan** twins, **Ian** and **Roger**, played regularly in the Q.P.R. forward line from 1964-68.

W.B.A's **Adam** and **James Chambers**, 18, were the first twins to represent England (v Cameroon in World Youth Championship, April 1999). They first played together in Albion's senior team, aged 19, in the League Cup 2nd. Round against Derby Co. in September 2000.

SIR TOM DOES THE HONOURS

Sir Tom Finney, England and Preston N.E. legend, opened the Football League's new headquarters on their return to Preston on Feb. 23, 1999. Preston had been the League's original base for 70 years before the move to Lytham St. Annes in 1959.

SHORTENED MATCHES

The 0-0 score in the **Bradford City v Lincoln City Third Division fixture** on May 11, 1985, abandoned through fire after 40 minutes, was subsequently confirmed as a result. It is the shortest officially completed League match on record, and was the fourth of only five instances in Football League history of the score of an unfinished match being allowed to stand.

The other occasions: **Middlesbrough 4, Oldham Athletic 1** (Div. 1, April 3, 1915), abandoned after 55 minutes when Oldham Athletic defender Billy Cook refused to leave the field after being sent off; **Barrow 7, Gillingham 0** (Div. 4, Oct. 9, 1961), abandoned after 75 minutes because of bad light, the match having started late because of Gillingham's delayed arrival.

A crucial **Manchester derby** (Div.1) was abandoned after 85 minutes, and the result stood, on April 27, 1974, when a pitch invasion at Old Trafford followed the only goal, scored for City by Denis Law, which relegated Manchester Utd., Law's former club.

The only instance of a first-class match in England being abandoned **'through shortage of players'** occurred in the First Division at Bramall Lane on March 16, 2002. Referee Eddie Wolstenholme halted play after 82 minutes because **Sheffield Utd.** were reduced to 6 players against **W.B.A.** They had had 3 men sent off (goalkeeper and 2 substitutes), and with all 3 substitutes used and 2 players injured, were left with fewer than the required minimum of 7 on the field. Promotion contenders W.B.A. were leading 3-0, and the League ordered the result to stand.

The last 60 seconds of **Birmingham City v Stoke City** (Div. 3, 1-1, on Feb. 29, 1992) were played behind locked doors. The ground had been cleared after a pitch invasion.

A First Division fixture, **Sheffield Wed. v Aston Villa** (Nov. 26, 1898), was abandoned through bad light after 79½ mins. with Wed. leading 3-1. The Football League ruled that the match should be completed, and the remaining 10½ minutes were played **four months later** (Mar. 13, 1899), when Wed. added another goal to make the result 4-1.

F.A. CUP RECORDS

(See also Goalscoring section)

CHIEF WINNERS

Eleven Times: Manchester Utd.
Ten Times: Arsenal.
Eight Times: Tottenham.
Seven Times: Aston Villa, Liverpool.
Three Times in Succession: The Wanderers (1876-7-8) and Blackburn Rov. (1884-5-6).
Trophy Handed Back: The F.A. Cup became the Wanderers' absolute property in 1878, but they handed it back to the Association on condition that it was not to be won outright by any club.
In Successive Years by Professional Clubs: Blackburn Rov. (in 1890 and 1891); Newcastle Utd. (in 1951 and 1952); Tottenham (in 1961 and 1962); Tottenham again (in 1981 and 1982) and Arsenal (in 2002 and 2003).
Record Final-tie score: Bury 6, Derby Co. 0 (1903).
Most F.A. Cup wins at Wembley: Manchester Utd. 9, Arsenal 7, Tottenham 6, Newcastle Utd. 5, Liverpool 5.

SECOND DIVISION WINNERS

Notts Co. (1894), Wolves (1908), Barnsley (1912), West Bromwich Albion (1931), Sunderland (1973), Southampton (1976), West Ham Utd. (1980). When Tottenham won the Cup in 1901 they were a Southern League club.

'OUTSIDE' SEMI-FINALISTS

Wycombe Wand., in 2001, became the eighth team from outside the top two divisions to reach the semi-finals, following Millwall (1937), Port Vale (1954), York City (1955), Norwich City (1959), Crystal Palace (1976), Plymouth Argyle (1984) and Chesterfield (1997). None reached the Final.

FOURTH DIVISION QUARTER-FINALISTS

Oxford Utd. (1964), Colchester Utd. (1971), Bradford City (1976), Cambridge Utd. (1990).

FOUR TROPHIES

The latest F.A. Cup, first presented at Wembley in 1992, is a replica of the one it replaced, which had been in existence since 1911. 'It was falling apart and was not going to last much longer,' said the FA.

The new trophy is the fourth F.A. Cup. These were its predecessors:

1895 First stolen from shop in Birmingham while held by Aston Villa. Never seen again.
1910 Second presented to Lord Kinnaird on completing 21 years as F.A. president. This trophy was bought by Birmingham City chairman David Gold at Christie's (London) for £420,000 in May 2005 and presented to the National Football Museum at Preston.
1992 Third 'gracefully retired' after 80 years' service (1911-91).

There are three F.A. Cups currently in existence. The retired model is still used for promotional work. The present trophy stays with the winners until the following March. A third, identical Cup is secreted in the F.A. vaults as cover against loss of the existing trophy.

FINALISTS RELEGATED

Four clubs have reached the F.A. Cup Final in a season of relegation, and all lost at Wembley: Manchester City 1926, Leicester City 1969, Brighton & H.A. 1983, Middlesbrough 1997.

GIANT-KILLING

(* Home team; R = Replay; Season 2007 = 2006-07)

Season	Team	Score	Team	Score
2007	*Chesterfield	0	Basingstoke	1
2007	*Rushden & D	3	Yeovil	1
2006	*Bournemouth	1	Tamworth	2
2006	*Burscough	3	Gillingham	2
2006	*Burton	1	Peterborough	0R
2006	*Hartlepool Utd.	1	Tamworth	2
2006	*Fulham	1	Leyton Orient	2
2006	*Colchester Utd.	3	Derby Co.	1
2005	*Hinckley	2	Torquay Utd.	0
2005	*Histon	2	Shrewsbury T.	0
2005	*Slough	2	Walsall	1
2005	*Exeter City	1	Grimsby Town	0
2005	*Carlisle Utd.	1	Bristol Rov.	0R
2005	*Exeter City	2	Doncaster Rov.	1
2005	*Oldham Ath.	1	Manchester City	0
2005	*Rotherham Utd.	0	Yeovil	3
2004	*Hornchurch	2	Darlington	0
2004	*Scarborough	1	Doncaster Rov.	0
2004	*Port Vale	0	Scarborough	1
2004	*Scarborough	1	Southend Utd.	0R
2004	*Accrington	1	Huddersfield T.	0
2004	*Accrington	0	Bournemouth	0R
	(Accrington won on pens).			
2004	*Stevenage	2	Stockport Co.	1
2004	*Torquay Utd.	1	Burton Alb.	2
2004	*Telford	3	Brentford	0
2004	*Crewe Alex.	0	Telford	1
2004	*Colchester Utd.	3	Coventry City	1R
2004	*Bolton Wand.	1	Tranmere Rov.	2R
2004	*Gillingham	3	Charlton Ath.	2
2003	*Chesterfield	1	Morecambe	2
2003	*Colchester Utd.	0	Chester City	1
2003	*Southport	4	Notts Co.	2
2003	Margate	1	Leyton Orient	0R
	(at Dover)			
2003	*Q.P.R.	1	Vauxhall Mot	1 R
	(Vauxhall won on pens.)			
2003	*Shrewsbury T.	2	Everton	1
2003	*Dagenham & R.	2	Plymouth	0 R
2003	*Darlington	2	Farnborough	3
2003	*Rochdale	2	Coventry City	0
2003	*Liverpool	0	Crystal Palace	2
2003	*Sunderland	0	Watford	1
2002	*Wigan Athletic	0	Canvey Island	1
2002	*Canvey Island	1	Northampton T.	0
2002	*Dagenham & R	3	Exeter City	0R
2002	*Cardiff City	2	Leeds Utd.	1
2002	*Derby Co.	1	Bristol Rov.	3
2001	*Wycombe Wand.	2	Wolves	1
2001	*Wimbledon	2	Wycombe Wand.	2R
	(Wycombe Wand. won on pens).			
2001	*Leicester City	1	Wycombe Wand.	2
2001	*Brentford	1	Kingstonian	3
2001	*Yeovil	5	Colchester Utd.	1
2001	*Southend Utd.	0	Kingstonian	1
2001	*Nuneaton	1	Stoke City	0R
2001	*Hull City	0	Kettering	1R
2001	*Northwich Vic.	1	Bury	0R
2001	*Port Vale	1	Canvey Island	2R
2001	*Lincoln City	0	Dagenham & R.	1

2001 *Morecambe .... 2 Cambridge Utd. ... 1
2001 *Blackpool .... 0 Yeovil 1
2001 *Everton .... 0 Tranmere Rov. 3
2001 *Tranmere Rov. .... 4 Southampton 3R
2000 *Rushden & D ..... 2 Scunthorpe Utd. .. 0
2000 *Chesterfield .... 1 Enfield 2
2000 *Hereford .... 1 York City 0
2000 *Ilkeston Town .... 2 Carlisle Utd. 1
2000 *Hereford .... 1 Hartlepool Utd. ... 0
1999 *Bedlington T ...... 4 Colchester Utd. ... 1
1999 *Hednesford .... 3 Barnet 1
1999 *Mansfield Town .. 1 Southport 2
1999 *Rushden & D ..... 1 Shrewsbury Town . 0
1999 *Southend Utd. ... 0 Doncaster Rov. 1
1999 *Yeovil Town .... 2 Northampton T 0
1999 *Aston Villa .... 0 Fulham 2
1998 *Hull City .... 0 Hednesford 2
1998 Lincoln City .... 3 Emley 3R
(at Huddersfield; Emley won on pens).
1998 *Leyton O .... 0 Hendon 1R
1998 *Swindon Town ... 1 Stevenage 2
1998 *Stevenage .... 2 Cambridge Utd. ... 1
1997 *Millwall .... 0 Woking 1R
1997 *Brighton & H.A. . 1 Sudbury Town ... 1R
(Sudbury won on pens).
1997 *Blackpool .... 0 Hednesford 1
1997 *Cambridge Utd. . 0 Woking 2
1997 *Leyton O. .... 1 Stevenage 2
1997 *Hednesford .... 1 York City 0
1997 *Chesterfield ...... 1 Nott'm. Forest 0
1996 *Hitchin .... 2 Bristol Rov. 1
1996 *Woking .... 2 Barnet 1R
1996 *Bury .... 0 Blyth Spartans 2
1996 *Gravesend .... 2 Colchester Utd. ... 0
1995 *Kingstonian .... 2 Brighton & H.A. ... 1
1995 *Enfield .... 1 Cardiff City 0
1995 *Marlow .... 2 Oxford Utd. 0
1995 *Woking .... 1 Barnet 0R
1995 *Hitchin .... 4 Hereford 2R
1995 *Torquay Utd. ...... 0 Enfield 1R
1995 *Altrincham .... 1 Wigan Athletic 0
1995 *Wrexham .... 2 Ipswich Town 1
1995 *Scarborough ...... 1 Port Vale 0
1994 *Colchester Utd. .. 3 Sutton 4
1994 *Yeovil .... 1 Fulham 0
1994 *Torquay Utd. ...... 0 Sutton 1
1994 *Halifax Town ...... 2 W.B.A. 1
1994 *Birmingham C. .. 1 Kidderminster 2
1994 *Stockport Co. ..... 2 Q.P.R. 1
1994 *Liverpool .... 0 Bristol City 1R
1994 *Arsenal .... 1 Bolton Wand. 3R
1994 *Leeds Utd. .... 2 Oxford Utd. 3R
1994 *Luton Town .... 2 Newcastle Utd. . 0R
1994 *Kidderminster .... 1 Preston N.E. 0
1994 *Cardiff City .... 1 Manchester City .. 0
1993 *Hereford .... 1 Yeovil 2R
1993 *Torquay Utd. ...... 2 Yeovil 5
1993 *Altrincham .... 2 Chester City 0R
1993 *Cardiff City .... 2 Bath 3
1993 *Chesterfield .... 2 Macclesfield 2R
(Macclesfield Town won on pens).
1993 *Marine .... 4 Halifax Town 1
1993 *Stafford .... 2 Lincoln City 1R
1993 *Hartlepool Utd. .. 1 Crystal Palace 0
1993 *Liverpool .... 0 Bolton Wand. 2R
1992 *Fulham .... 0 Hayes 2
1992 *Crawley .... 4 Northampton 2
1992 *Telford .... 2 Stoke City 1R
1992 *Aldershot .... 0 Enfield 1
1992 *Halifax Town ...... 1 Witton A. 2R
1992 *Maidstone .... 1 Kettering 2
1992 *Walsall .... 0 Yeovil 1R
1992 *Farnborough ...... 4 Torquay Utd. 3
1992 *Wrexham .... 2 Arsenal 1
1991 *Scarborough ...... 0 Leek 2
1991 *Northampton ..... 0 Barnet 1R
1991 *Hayes .... 1 Cardiff City 0R
1991 *Chorley .... 2 Bury 1
1991 *Shrewsbury T ..... 1 Wimbledon 0
1991 *W.B.A. .... 2 Woking 4
1990 *Aylesbury .... 1 Southend Utd. 0
1990 *Scarborough ...... 0 Whitley Bay 1
1990 *Welling .... 1 Gillingham 0R
1990 *Whitley Bay .... 2 Preston N.E. 0
1990 *Northampton ..... 1 Coventry City 0
1990 *Cambridge Utd. . 1 Millwall 0R
1989 *Sutton .... 2 Coventry City 1
1989 *Halifax Town ...... 2 Kettering 3R
1989 *Kettering .... 2 Bristol Rov. 1
1989 *Bognor .... 2 Exeter City 1
1989 *Leyton Orient ..... 0 Enfield 1R
1989 *Altrincham .... 3 Lincoln City 2
1989 *Wrexham .... 2 Runcorn 3R
1988 *Sutton .... 3 Aldershot 0
1988 *Peterborough ..... 1 Sutton 3
1988 *Carlisle Utd. ...... 2 Maccesfield 4
1988 *Macclesfield ...... 4 Rotherham Utd. ... 0
1988 *Chester City .... 0 Runcorn 1
1988 *Cambridge Utd. . 0 Yeovil 1
1987 *Caernarfon .... 1 Stockport Co. 0
1987 Chorley .... 3 Wolves 0R
(at Bolton)
1987 *Telford .... 3 Burnley 0
1987 *York City .... 1 Caernarfon 2R
1987 *Aldershot .... 3 Oxford Utd. 0
1987 *Wigan Athletic ... 1 Norwich City 0
1987 *Charlton Ath. ..... 1 Walsall 2
1986 *Stockport Co. ..... 0 Telford 1
1986 *Wycombe W. ...... 2 Colchester Utd. ... 0
1986 *Dagenham .... 2 Cambridge Utd. 1
1986 *Blackpool .... 1 Altrincham 2
1986 *Birmingham C. .. 1 Altrincham 2
1986 *Peterborough ..... 1 Leeds Utd. 0
1985 *Telford .... 2 Lincoln City 1
1985 *Preston N.E. ...... 1 Telford 4
1985 *Telford .... 2 Bradford City 1
1985 *Telford .... 3 Darlington 0R
1985 *Blackpool .... 0 Altrincham 1

1985	*Wimbledon	1	Nott'm. Forest	0R	
1985	*Orient	2	W.B.A.	1	
1985	*Dagenham	1	Peterborough	0	
1985	*Swindon Town	1	Dagenham	2R	
1985	*York City	1	Arsenal	0	
1984	*Halifax Town	2	Whitby	3	
1984	*Bournemouth	2	Manchester Utd.	0	
1984	*Telford	3	Stockport Co.	0	
1984	*Telford	3	Northampton	2R	
1984	Telford	4	*Rochdale	1	
1983	*Cardiff City	2	Weymouth	3	
1981	*Exeter City	3	Leicester City	1R	
1981	*Exeter City	4	Newcastle Utd.	0R	
1980	*Halifax Town	1	Manchester City	0	
1980	*Harlow	1	Leicester City	0R	
1980	*Chelsea	0	Wigan Athletic	1	
1979	*Newport	2	West Ham Utd.	1	
1978	*Wrexham	4	Newcastle	1R	
1978	*Stoke City	2	Blyth Spartans	3	
1976	*Leeds Utd.	0	Crystal Palace	1	
1975	*Brighton & H.A.	0	Leatherhead	1	
1975	*Burnley	0	Wimbledon	1	
1972	*Hereford	2	Newcastle	1R	
1971	*Colchester Utd.	3	Leeds Utd.	2	
1969	*Mansfield Town	3	West Ham Utd.	0	
1967	*Swindon Town	3	West Ham Utd.	0R	
1967	*Manchester U.	1	Norwich City	2	
1966	*Ipswich Town	2	Southport	3R	
1965	*Peterborough	2	Arsenal	1	
1964	*Newcastle Utd.	1	Bedford Town	2	
1964	*Aldershot	2	Aston Villa	1R	
1961	*Coventry City	1	Kings Lynn	2	
1961	*Chelsea	1	Crewe Alex.	2	
1960	*Manchester City	1	South'ton	5	
1959	*Norwich City	3	Manchester U	0	
1959	*Worcester	2	Liverpool	1	
1959	*Tooting	3	Bournemouth	1	
1959	*Tooting	2	Northampton	1	
1958	*Newcastle Utd.	1	Scunthorpe Utd.	3	
1957	*Wolves	0	Bournemouth	1	
1957	*Bournemouth	3	Tottenham	1	
1957	*Derby Co.	1	New Brighton	3	
1956	*Derby Co.	1	Boston United	6	
1955	*York City	2	Tottenham	1	
1955	*Blackpool	0	York City	2	
1954	*Arsenal	1	Norwich City	2	
1954	*Port Vale	2	Blackpool	0	
1952	*Everton	1	Leyton Orient	3	
1949	*Yeovil Town	2	Sunderland	1	
1948	*Colchester Utd.	1	Huddersfield	0	
1948	*Arsenal	0	Bradford P.A.	1	
1938	*Chelmsford	4	Southampton	1	
1933	*Walsall	2	Arsenal	0	
1922	*Everton	0	Crystal Palace	6	

YEOVIL TOP GIANT-KILLERS

Yeovil's victories over Colchester Utd. and Blackpool in season 2000-01 gave them a total of 20 F.A. Cup wins against League opponents. They set another non-League record by reaching the third round 13 times.

This was Yeovil's triumphant (non-League) Cup record against League clubs: 1924-5 Bournemouth 3-2; 1934-5 Crystal Palace 3-0, Exeter City 4-1; 1938-9 Brighton & H.A. 2-1; 1948-9 Bury 3-1, Sunderland 2-1; 1958-9 Southend Utd. 1-0; 1960-1 Walsall 1-0; 1963-4 Southend Utd. 1-0, Crystal Palace 3-1; 1970-1 Bournemouth 1-0; 1972-3 Brentford 2-1; 1987-8 Cambridge Utd. 1-0; 1991-2 Walsall 1-0; 1992-3 Torquay Utd. 5-2, Hereford 2-1; 1993-4 Fulham 1-0; 1998-9 Northampton 2-0; 2000-01 Colchester Utd. 5-1, Blackpool 1-0.

NON-LEAGUE BEST

Since League football began in 1888, three non-League clubs have reached the F.A. Cup Final. **Sheffield Wed.** (Football Alliance) were runners-up in 1890, as were **Southampton** (Southern League) in 1900 and 1902. **Tottenham** won the Cup as a Southern League team in 1901.

Otherwise, the **furthest progress** by non-League clubs has been to the **5th. Round** on 5 occasions: Colchester Utd. 1948, Yeovil 1949, Blyth Spartans 1978, Telford 1985 and Kidderminster 1994.

Greatest number of non-League sides to reach the **3rd. Round** is 6 in 1978: Blyth, Enfield, Scarborough, Tilbury, Wealdstone and Wigan Athletic. Since then, 5 in 1988: Bath City, Macclesfield Town, Maidstone, Sutton and Yeovil.

Most to reach **Round 4**: 3 in 1957 (Rhyl, New Brighton, Peterborough Utd.) and 1975 (Leatherhead, Stafford and Wimbledon).

Five non-League clubs reaching **Round 3** in 2001 was a Conference record. They were Chester City, Yeovil, Dagenham & Redbridge, Morecambe and Kingstonian.

In season 2002–3, **Team Bath** became the first University-based side to reach the F.A. Cup 1st. Round since Oxford University (Finalists in 1880).

NON-LEAGUE 'LAST TIMES'

Last time no non-League club reached Round 3: 1951. Last time only one did so: 1969 (Kettering Town).

TOP-DIVISION SCALPS

Victories in F.A. Cup by non-League clubs over top-division teams since 1900 include:- 1900-1 (Final, replay); **Tottenham** 3, Sheffield Utd. 1 (Tottenham then in Southern League); 1919-20 **Cardiff City** 2, Oldham Athletic 0, and Sheffield Wed. 0, **Darlington** 2; 1923-4 **Corinthians** 1, Blackburn Rov. 0; 1947-8 **Colchester Utd.** 1, Huddersfield Town 0; 1948-9 **Yeovil Town** 2, Sunderland 1; 1971-2 **Hereford Utd.** 2, Newcastle Utd. 1; 1974-5 Burnley 0, **Wimbledon** 1; 1985-6 Birmingham City 1, **Altrincham** 2; 1988-9 **Sutton Utd.** 2, Coventry City 1.

FIVE WINNING MEDALS

The Hon. Arthur Kinnaird (The Wanderers and Old Etonians), **Charles Wollaston** (The Wanderers) and **Jimmy Forrest** (Blackburn Rov.) each earned five F.A. Cup winners' medals. Kinnaird, later president of the F.A., played in nine of the first 12 F.A. Cup Finals, and was on the winning side three times for The Wanderers, in 1873 (captain), 1877, 1878 (captain), and twice as captain of Old Etonians (1879, 1882).

MOST WINNERS' MEDALS AT WEMBLEY

4 – **Mark Hughes** (3 for Manchester Utd., 1 for Chelsea).

3 – **Dick Pym** (3 clean sheets in Finals), **Bob Haworth**, **Jimmy Seddon**, **Harry Nuttall**, **Billy Butler** (all Bolton Wand.); **David Jack** (2 Bolton Wand., 1 Arsenal); **Bob Cowell**, **Jack Milburn**, **Bobby Mitchell** (all Newcastle Utd.); **Dave Mackay** (Tottenham); **Frank Stapleton** (1 Arsenal, 2 Manchester Utd.); **Bryan Robson** (3 times winning captain), **Arthur Albiston**, **Gary Pallister** (all Manchester Utd.); **Bruce Grobbelaar**, **Steve Nicol**, **Ian Rush** (all Liverpool); **Roy Keane**, **Peter Schmeichel**; **Ryan Giggs** (all Manchester Utd.); **Dennis Wise** (1 Wimbledon, 2 Chelsea).

- Arsenal's **David Seaman** and **Ray Parlour** have each earned 4 winners' medals (2 at Wembley, 2 at Cardiff) as have Manchester Utd's **Roy Keane** and **Ryan Giggs** (3 at Wembley, 1 at Cardiff).

MOST WEMBLEY FINALS

Nine players appeared in five F.A. Cup Finals at Wembley, replays excluded:-

- Joe Hulme (Arsenal: 1927, lost; 1930 won; 1932 lost; 1936 won; Huddersfield Town: 1938 lost).
- Johnny Giles (Manchester Utd.: 1963 won; Leeds Utd.: 1965 lost; 1970 drew at Wembley, lost replay at Old Trafford; 1972 won; 1973 lost).
- Pat Rice (all for Arsenal: 1971 won; 1972 lost; 1978 lost; 1979 won; 1980 lost).
- Frank Stapleton (Arsenal: 1978 lost; 1979 won; 1980 lost; Manchester Utd.; 1983 won; 1985 won).
- Ray Clemence (Liverpool: 1971 lost; 1974 won; 1977 lost; Tottenham: 1982 won; 1987 lost).
- Mark Hughes (Manchester Utd.: 1985 won; 1990 won; 1994 won; 1995 lost; Chelsea: 1997 won).
- John Barnes (Watford: 1984 lost; Liverpool: 1988 lost; 1989 won; 1996 lost; Newcastle Utd.: 1998, sub, lost): he was the first player to lose Wembley F.A. Cup Finals with three different clubs.
- Roy Keane (Nott'm Forest: 1991 lost; Manchester Utd.: 1994 won; 1995 lost; 1996 won; 1999 won).
- Ryan Giggs (Manchester Utd: 1994 won; 1995 lost; 1996 won; 1999 won; 2007 lost).

Stapleton, Clemence and Hughes also played in a replay, making six actual F.A. Cup Final appearances for each of them.

Glenn Hoddle also made six F.A. Cup Final appearances at Wembley: 5 for Tottenham (incl. 2 replays), in 1981, 1982 and 1987, and 1 for Chelsea as sub in 1994.
▲Paul Bracewell played in four F.A. Cup Finals without being on the winning side – for Everton 1985, 1986, 1989, Sunderland 1992.

MOST WEMBLEY/CARDIFF FINAL APPEARANCES

7 by **Roy Keane** (Nott'm F: 1991 lost; Manchester Utd.: 1994 won; 1995 lost; 1996 won; 1999 won; 2004 won; 2005 lost).

7 by **Ryan Giggs** (Manchester Utd.): 1994 won; 1995 lost; 1996 won; 1999 won; 2004 won; 2005 lost; 2007 lost.

5 by **David Seaman** and **Ray Parlour** (Arsenal): 1993 won; 1998 won; 2001 lost; 2002 won; 2003 won; **Dennis Wise** (Wimbledon 1988 won; Chelsea 1994 lost; 1997 won; 2000 won; Millwall 2004 lost).

WINNING GOALKEEPER-CAPTAINS

1988 **Dave Beasant** (Wimbledon); 2003 **David Seaman** (Arsenal).

MOST-WINNING MANAGER

Sir Alex Ferguson (Man. Utd.) 5 times (1990, 1994, 1996, 1999, 2004).

PLAYER-MANAGERS IN FINAL

Kenny Dalglish (Liverpool, 1986); **Glenn Hoddle** (Chelsea, 1994); **Dennis Wise** (Millwall, 2004).

DEBUTS IN FINAL

Alan Davies (Manchester Utd. v Brighton & H.A., 1983); **Chris Baird** (Southampton v Arsenal, 2003); **Curtis Weston** (Millwall substitute v Manchester Utd., 2004).

SEMI-FINALS AT WEMBLEY

1991 Tottenham 3, Arsenal 1; **1993** Sheffield Wed. 2, Sheffield Utd. 1; Arsenal 1, Tottenham 0; **1994** Chelsea 2, Luton 0; Manchester Utd. 1, Oldham 1; **2000** Aston Villa beat Bolton 4-1 on pens. (after 0-0); Chelsea 2, Newcastle Utd 1.

FIRST ENTRANTS (1871-2)

Barnes, Civil Service, Crystal Palace, Clapham Rov., Donnington School (Spalding), Hampstead Heathens, Harrow Chequers, Hitchin, Maidenhead, Marlow, Queen's Park (Glasgow), Reigate Priory, Royal Engineers, Upton Park and Wanderers. Total 15. Three scratched. 2006-7 entry: 687.

F.A. CUP FIRSTS

Out of country: Cardiff City, by defeating Arsenal 1-0 in the 1927 Final at Wembley, became the first and only club to take the F.A. Cup out of England.

All-English Winning XI: First club to win the F.A. Cup with all-English XI: Blackburn Olympic in 1883. Others since: W.B.A. in 1888 and 1931, Bolton Wand. (1958), Manchester City (1969), West Ham Utd. (1964 and 1975).

Non-English Winning XI: Liverpool in 1986 (Mark Lawrenson, born Preston, was a Rep. of Ireland player).

Won both Cups: Old Carthusians won the F.A. Cup in 1881 and the F.A. Amateur Cup in 1894 and 1897. **Wimbledon** won Amateur Cup in 1963, F.A. Cup in 1988.

MOST GAMES NEEDED TO WIN

Barnsley played a record 12 matches (20 hours' football) to win the F.A. Cup in season 1911-12. All six replays (one in Rd. 1, three in Rd. 4 and one in each of semi-final and Final) were brought about by goalless draws.

Arsenal played 11 F.A. Cup games when winning the trophy in 1979. Five of them were in the 3rd. Rd. against Sheffield Wed..

LONGEST TIES

6 matches (11 hours): **Alvechurch v Oxford City** (4th. qual. round, 1971-2). Alvechurch won 1-0.

5 matches (9 hours, 22 mins – record for competition proper): **Stoke City v Bury** (3rd. round, 1954-5). Stoke City won 3-2.

5 matches: Chelsea v Burnley (4th. round, 1955-6). Chelsea won 2-0.

5 matches: Hull City v Darlington (2nd. round, 1960-1). Hull City won 3-0.

5 matches: Arsenal v Sheffield Wed. (3rd. round, 1978-9). Arsenal won 2-0.

Other marathons (qualifying comp., all 5 matches, 9 hours): **Barrow v Gillingham** (last qual. round, 1924-5) – winners Barrow; **Leyton v Ilford** (3rd. qual. round, 1924-5) – winners Leyton; **Falmouth Town v Bideford** (3rd. qual. round, 1973-4) – winners Bideford.

End of Cup Final replays: The F.A. decided that, with effect from 1999, there would be no Cup Final replays. In the event of a draw after extra-time, the match would be decided on penalties. This happened for the first time in 2005, when **Arsenal** beat **Manchester United** 5-4 on penalties after a 0-0 draw. A year later, Liverpool beat West Ham United 3-1 on penalties after a 3-3 draw.

F.A. Cup marathons ended in season 1991-2, when the penalty shoot-out was introduced to decide ties still level after one replay and extra-time.

- In 1932-3 **Brighton & H.A.** (Div. 3 South) played 11 F.A. Cup games, including replays, and scored 43 goals, without getting past Rd 5. They forgot to claim exemption and had to play from 1st Qual. Round.

LONGEST ROUND

The longest round in F.A. Cup history was the **third round** in **season 1962-3**. It took 66 days to complete, lasting from January 5 to March 11, and included 261 postponements because of bad weather.

LONGEST UNBEATEN RUN

23 matches by **Blackburn Rov.** In winning the Cup in three consecutive years (1884-5-6), they won 21 ties (one in a replay), and their first Cup defeat in four seasons was in a first round replay of the next competition.

RE-STAGED TIES

Sixth round, March 9, 1974: Newcastle Utd. 4, Nott'm. Forest 3. Match declared void by F.A. and ordered to be replayed following a pitch invasion after Newcastle had a player sent off. Forest claimed the hold-up caused the game to change its pattern. The tie went to two further matches at Goodison Park (0-0, then 1-0 to Newcastle).

Third round, January 5, 1985: Burton Albion 1, Leicester City 6 (at Derby Co.). Burton goalkeeper Paul Evans was hit on the head by a missile thrown from the crowd, and continued in a daze. The F.A. ordered the tie to be played again, behind closed doors at Coventry City (Leicester won 1- 0).

First round replay, November 25, 1992: Peterborough Utd. 9 (Tony Philliskirk 5), Kingstonian 1. Match expunged from records because, at 3-0 after 57 mins, Kingstonian were reduced to ten men when goalkeeper Adrian Blake was concussed by a 50 pence coin thrown from the crowd. The tie was re-staged on the same ground behind closed doors (Peterborough won 1-0).

Fifth round: Within an hour of holders Arsenal beating Sheffield Utd. 2-1 at Highbury on February 13, 1999, the Football Association took the unprecedented step of declaring the match void because an unwritten rule of sportsmanship had been broken. With United's Lee Morris lying injured, their goalkeeper Alan Kelly kicked the ball into touch. Play resumed with Arsenal's Ray Parlour throwing it in the direction of Kelly, but Nwankwo Kanu took possession and centred for Marc Overmars to score the 'winning' goal. After four minutes of protests by manager Steve Bruce and his players, referee

Peter Jones confirmed the goal. Both managers absolved Kanu of cheating but Arsenal's Arsene Wenger offered to replay the match. With the F.A. immediately approving, it was re-staged at Highbury ten days later (ticket prices halved) and Arsenal again won 2-1.

PRIZE FUND

The makeover of the F.A. Cup competition took off in 2001-02 with the introduction of round-by-round prize-money.

F.A. CUP FOLLIES 1999-2000

The F.A. broke with tradition by deciding the 3rd. Round be moved from its regular January date and staged before Christmas. Criticism was strong, gates poor and the 3rd. Round in 2000-01 reverted to the New Year.

By allowing the holders Manchester Utd. to withdraw from the 1999-2000 Cup competition in order to play in FIFA's inaugural World Club Championship in Brazil in January, the F.A. were left with an odd number of clubs in the 3rd. Round. Their solution was a **'lucky losers'** draw among clubs knocked out in Round 2. Darlington, beaten at Gillingham, won it to re-enter the competition, then lost 2-1 away to Aston Villa.

HAT-TRICKS IN FINAL

There have been three in the history of the competition: **Billy Townley** (Blackburn Rov., 1890), **Jimmy Logan** (Notts Co., 1894) and **Stan Mortensen** (Blackpool, 1953).

MOST APPEARANCES

88 by **Ian Callaghan** (79 for Liverpool, 7 for Swansea City, 2 for Crewe Alexandra); 87 by **John Barnes** (31 for Watford, 51 for Liverpool, 5 for Newcastle Utd.); 86 by **Stanley Matthews** (37 for Stoke City, 49 for Blackpool); 84 by **Bobby Charlton** (80 for Manchester Utd., 4 for Preston N.E.); 84 by **Pat Jennings** (3 for Watford, 43 for Tottenham, 38 for Arsenal); 84 by **Peter Shilton** for seven clubs (30 for Leicester City, 7 for Stoke City, 18 for Nottm. Forest, 17 for Southampton, 10 for Derby Co., 1 for Plymouth Argyle, 1 for Leyton Orient); 82 by **David Seaman** (5 for Peterborough Utd., 5 for Birmingham City, 17 for Q.P.R., 54 for Arsenal, 1 for Manchester City.

THREE-CLUB FINALISTS

Four players have appeared in the F.A. Final for three clubs: **Harold Halse** for Manchester Utd. (1909), Aston Villa (1913) and Chelsea (1915); **Ernie Taylor** for Newcastle Utd. (1951), Blackpool (1953) and Manchester Utd. (1958); **John Barnes** for Watford (1984), Liverpool (1988, 1989, 1996) and Newcastle Utd. (1998); **Dennis Wise** for Wimbledon (1988), Chelsea (1994, 1997, 2000), Millwall (2004)..

CUP MAN WITH TWO CLUBS IN SAME SEASON

Stan Crowther, who played for Aston Villa against Manchester Utd. in the 1957 F.A. Cup Final, appeared for both Villa and United in the 1957-8 competition. United signed him directly after the Munich air crash and, in the circumstances, he was given special dispensation to play for them in the Cup, including the Final.

CAPTAIN'S CUP DOUBLE

Martin Buchan is the only player to have captained Scottish and English F.A. Cup-winning teams – Aberdeen in 1970 and Manchester Utd. in 1977.

MEDALS BEFORE AND AFTER

Two players appeared in F.A. Cup Final teams before and after the war: **Raich Carter** was twice a winner (Sunderland 1937, Derby Co. 1946) and **Willie Fagan** twice on the losing side (Preston N.E. 1937, Liverpool 1950).

DELANEY'S COLLECTION

Scotland winger **Jimmy Delaney** uniquely earned Scottish, English, Northern Ireland and Republic of Ireland cup medals. He was a winner with Celtic (1937), Manchester Utd. (1948) and Derry City (1954) and a runner-up with Cork City (1956).

STARS WHO MISSED OUT

Internationals who never won an F.A. Cup winner's medal include: **Tommy Lawton, Tom Finney, Johnny Haynes, Gordon Banks, George Best, Terry Butcher, Peter Shilton, Martin Peters, Nobby Stiles, Alan Ball, Malcolm Macdonald, Alan Shearer.**

CUP WINNERS AT NO COST

Not one member of **Bolton's** 1958 F.A. Cup-winning team cost the club a transfer fee. Each joined the club for a £10 signing-on fee.

ALL-INTERNATIONAL CUP WINNERS

In **Manchester Utd.'s** 1985 Cup-winning team v Everton, all 11 players were full Internationals, as was the substitute who played. So were ten of Everton's team.

Arsenal's Cup-winning line-ups in the 2002 and 2003 Finals were all full Internationals, as were all 14 players who appeared for **Manchester Utd.** in the 2004 final.

NO-CAP CUP WINNERS

Sunderland, in 1973, were the last F.A. Cup-winning team not to include an International player, although some were capped later.

11-NATIONS LINE-UP

Liverpool fielded a team of 11 different nationalities in the F.A. Cup 3rd Round at Yeovil on Jan. 4, 2004.

HIGH-SCORING SEMI-FINALS

The **record team score** in F.A. Cup semi-finals is 6: 1891-2 WBA 6, Nott'm. Forest 2; 1907-8 Newcastle Utd. 6, Fulham 0; 1933-4 Manchester City 6, Aston Villa 1.

Most goals in semi-finals (aggregate): 17 in 1892 (4 matches) and 1899 (5 matches). In modern times: 15 in 1958 (3 matches, including Manchester Utd. 5, Fulham 3 – highest-scoring semi-final since last war); 16 in 1989-90 (Crystal Palace 4, Liverpool 3; Manchester Utd. v Oldham Athletic 3-3, 2-1. **All 16 goals** in those three matches were scored by **different players**.

Last hat-trick in an F.A. Cup semi-final was scored by **Alex Dawson** for Manchester Utd. in 5-3 replay win against Fulham at Highbury in 1958.

SEMI-FINAL VENUES

Villa Park has staged more such matches (55 including replays) than any other ground. Next is Hillsborough (33).

FOUR SPECIAL AWAYS

For the only time in F.A. Cup history, **all four quarter-finals** in season 1986-7 were won by the away team.

DRAWS RECORD

In season 1985-6, **seven** of the eight F.A. Cup 5th. Round ties went to replays – a record for that stage of the competition.

LUCK OF THE DRAW

In the F.A. Cup on Jan. 11, 1947, eight of **London**'s ten Football League clubs involved in the 3rd. Round were drawn at home (including Chelsea v Arsenal). Only Crystal Palace played outside the capital (at Newcastle Utd.).

Contrast: In the 3rd. Round in Jan. 1992, Charlton Athletic were the only London club drawn at home (against Barnet), but the venue of the Farnborough v West Ham Utd. tie was reversed on police instruction. So Upton Park staged Cup-ties on successive days, with West Ham Utd. at home on the Saturday and Charlton Athletic (who shared the ground) on Sunday.

Arsenal were drawn away in every round on the way to reaching the F.A. Cup Finals of 1971 and 1972. **Manchester Utd.** won the Cup in 1990 without playing once at home.

The 1999 F.A. Cup finalists **Manchester Utd.** and **Newcastle Utd.** were both drawn at home every time in Rounds 3-6.

On their way to the semi-finals of both domestic Cup competitions in season 2002–03, **Sheffield Utd.** were drawn at home ten times out of ten and won all ten matches – six in the League's Worthington Cup and four in the F.A. Cup.

ALL TOP-DIVISION VICTIMS

The only instance of an F.A. Cup-winning club meeting top-division opponents in every round was provided by Manchester Utd. in 1947-8. They beat Aston Villa, Liverpool, Charlton Athletic, Preston N.E., then Derby Co. in the semi-final and Blackpool in the Final.

In **contrast**, these clubs have reached the Final without playing top-division opponents on the way: West Ham Utd. (1923), Bolton Wand. (1926), Blackpool (1948), Bolton Wand. (1953), Millwall (2004).

WON CUP WITHOUT CONCEDING GOAL

1873 **The Wanderers** (1 match; as holders, exempt until Final); 1889 **Preston N.E.** (5 matches); 1903 **Bury** (5 matches). In 1966 **Everton** reached Final without conceding a goal (7 matches), then beat Sheffield Wed. 3-2 at Wembley.

HOME ADVANTAGE

For the first time in F.A. Cup history, all eight ties in the 1992-3 5th. Round were won (no replays) by the **clubs drawn at home**. Only other instance of eight home wins at the 'last 16' stage of the F.A. Cup was in 1889-90, in what was then the 2nd. Round.

FEWEST TOP-DIVISION CLUBS IN LAST 16 (5TH. ROUND)

5 in 1958; **6** in 1927, 1970, 1982; **7** in 1994, 2003; **8** in 2002, 2004.

SIXTH-ROUND ELITE

For the first time in F.A. Cup 6th. Round history, dating from 1926, when the format of the competition changed, **all eight quarter-finalists** in 1995-6 were from the top division.

SEMI-FINAL – DOUBLE DERBIES

There have been only two instances of both F.A. Cup semi-finals in the same year being local derbies: **1950** Liverpool beat Everton 2-0 (Maine Road), Arsenal beat Chelsea 1-0 after 2-2 draw (both at Tottenham); **1993** Arsenal beat Tottenham 1-0 (Wembley), Sheffield Wed. beat Sheffield Utd. 2-1 (Wembley).

TOP CLUB DISTINCTION

Since the Football League began in 1888, there has never been an F.A. Cup Final in which **neither club** represented the top division.

SPURS OUT – AND IN

Tottenham were banned, pre-season, from the 1994-5 F.A. Cup competition because of financial irregularities, but were readmitted on appeal and reached the semi-finals.

BROTHERS IN F.A. CUP FINAL TEAMS (Modern Times)

1950 Denis and Leslie Compton (Arsenal); **1952** George and Ted Robledo (Newcastle Utd.); **1967** Ron and Allan Harris (Chelsea); **1977** Jimmy and Brian Greenhoff (Manchester Utd.); **1996** and **1999** Gary and Phil Neville (Manchester Utd.)

FIRST SPONSORS

Littlewoods Pools became the first sponsors of the F.A. Cup in season 1994-5 in a £14m., 4-year deal. French insurance giants **AXA** took over (season 1998-9) in a sponsorship worth £25m. over 4 years. German energy company **E.ON** agreed a 4-year sponsorship (worth £32m.) from season 2006-07.

FIRST GOALKEEPER-SUBSTITUTE IN FINAL

Paul Jones (Southampton), who replaced injured Antti Niemi against Arsenal in 2003.

LEAGUE CUP RECORDS

(See also Goalscoring section)

Highest scores: West Ham Utd. 10-0 v Bury (2nd. Rd., 2nd. Leg 1983-4; agg. 12-1); Liverpool 10-0 v Fulham (2nd. Rd., 1st. Leg 1986-7; agg. 13-2).
Most League Cup goals (career): 49 Geoff Hurst (43 West Ham Utd., 6 Stoke City, 1960-75); 49 Ian Rush (48 Liverpool, 1 Newcastle Utd., 1981-98).
Highest scorer (season): 12 Clive Allen (Tottenham 1986-7 in 9 apps).
Most goals in match: 6 Frank Bunn (Oldham Athletic v Scarborough, 3rd. Rd., 1989-90).
Fewest goals conceded by winners: 3 by Leeds Utd. (1967-8), Tottenham (1970-1), Aston Villa (1995-6).
Most winner's medals: 5 Ian Rush (Liverpool).
Most appearances in Final: 6 Kenny Dalglish (Liverpool 1978-87), Ian Rush (Liverpool 1981-95).
League Cup sponsors: Milk Cup 1981-6, Littlewoods Cup 1987-90, Rumbelows Cup 1991-2, Coca-Cola Cup 1993-8. Worthington Cup 1999-2003, Carling Cup from season 2003-4.
Norwich City unique: In 1985, Norwich City became (and they remain) the only club to win a major domestic cup and be relegated in the same season. They won the League's Milk Cup and went down from the old First Division.
Liverpool's League Cup records: Winners a record 7 times. **Ian Rush** only player to win 5 times. Rush also first to play in 8 winning teams in Cup Finals **at Wembley**, all with Liverpool (F.A. Cup 1986-89-92; League Cup 1981-82-83-84-95).
Britain's first under-cover Cup Final: Worthington Cup Final between Blackburn Rov. and Tottenham at Cardiff's Millennium Stadium on Sunday, February 24, 2002. With rain forecast, the retractable roof was closed on the morning of the match.

DISCIPLINE

SENDINGS-OFF

Season 2003-4 set an **all-time record** of 504 players sent off in English domestic football competitions. There were 58 in the Premiership, 390 Nationwide League, 28 F.A. Cup (excluding non-League dismissals), 22 League Cup, 2 in Nationwide play-offs, 4 in LDV Vans Trophy.

The 58 Premiership red cards was 13 fewer than the record English **top-division** total of 71 in 2002-03. **Bolton Wand.** were the only club in the English divisions without a player sent off in any first-team competition that season.

Worst day for dismissals in English football history was December 13, 2003 with 19 red cards (2 Premiership and the 17 in the Nationwide League setting a **Football League record** for one day).

Previous worst overall total was 18 on November 16, 2002 (1 Premier League, 5 Nationwide League, 12 in F.A. Cup 1st. Round – 7 of those non-League). That equalled the **F.A. Cup's worst disciplinary day** (12 dismissals in 1st. Round on November 20, 1982).

Most players ordered off in **Anglo-Scottish football on one day**: 25, all League, on Oct. 16, 1999 (14 in England, 11 in Scotland).

• In the entire first season of post-war League football (1946-7) only 12 players were sent off, followed by 14 in 1949-50, and the total League dismissals for the first nine seasons after the war was 104.

The worst pre-war total was 28 in each of seasons 1921-2 and 1922-3.

ENGLAND SENDINGS-OFF

Wayne Rooney's red card aginst Portugal in the World Cup quarter-final was England's 11th sending off in their international history. In the qualifying match against Austria, David Beckham became the first England captain to be dismissed and the first England player to be sent off twice.

June 5, 1968 **Alan Mullery**	v Yugoslavia (Florence, Eur. Champ.)
June 6, 1973 **Alan Ball**	v Poland (Chorzow, World Cup qual.)
June 15, 1977 **Trevor Cherry**	v Argentina (Buenos Aires, friendly)
June 6, 1986 **Ray Wilkins**	v Morocco (Monterrey, World Cup Finals)
June 30, 1998 **David Beckham**	v Argentina (St. Etienne, World Cup Finals)
Sept. 5, 1998 **Paul Ince**	v Sweden (Stockholm, Eur. Champ. qual.)
June 5, 1999 **Paul Scholes**	v Sweden (Wembley, Eur. Champ. qual.)
Sept. 8, 1999 **David Batty**	v Poland (Warsaw, Eur. Champ. qual.)
Oct. 16, 2002 **Alan Smith**	v Macedonia (Southampton, Eur. Champ. qual.)
Oct. 8, 2005 **David Beckham**	v Austria (Old Trafford, World Cup qual.)
July 1, 2006 **Wayne Rooney**	v Portugal (Gelsenkirchen, World Cup Finals)

Other countries: Most recent sendings-off of players representing other Home Countries: **N. Ireland – James Quinn** (friendly v Romania, Chicago, May 2006); **Scotland – Steven Pressley** (European Champ. qual. v Ukraine, Oct. 11, 2006); **Wales – Robbie Savage** (World Cup qual. v N. Ireland, Cardiff, Sept. 8, 2004); **Rep. of Ireland – Richard Dunne** (European Champ. qual. v Cyprus, Nicosia, Oct. 7, 2006).

England dismissals at other levels:-

U-23: Stan Anderson (v Bulgaria, Sofia, May 19, 1957); **Alan Ball** (v Austria, Vienna, June 2, 1965); **Kevin Keegan** (v E. Germany, Magdeburg, June 1, 1972); **Steve Perryman** (v Portugal, Lisbon, Nov. 19, 1974).

U-21: Sammy Lee (v Hungary, Keszthely, June 5, 1981); **Mark Hateley** (v Scotland, Hampden Park, April 19, 1982); **Paul Elliott** (v Denmark, Maine Road, Manchester, Mar. 26, 1986); **Tony Cottee** (v W. Germany, Ludenscheid, Sept. 8, 1987); **Julian Dicks** (v Mexico, Toulon, France, Jun. 12, 1988); **Jason Dodd** (v Mexico, Toulon, May 29, 1991; 3 Mexico players also sent off in that match); **Matthew Jackson** (v France, Toulon, May 28, 1992); **Robbie Fowler** (v Austria, Kafkenberg, Oct. 11, 1994); **Alan Thompson** (v Portugal, Oporto, Sept. 2, 1995); **Terry Cooke** (v Portugal, Toulon, May 30, 1996); **Ben Thatcher** (v Italy, Rieti, Oct. 10, 1997); **John Curtis** (v Greece, Heraklion, Nov. 13, 1997); **Jody Morris** (v Luxembourg, Grevenmacher, Oct. 13, 1998); **Stephen Wright** (v Germany, Derby, Oct. 6, 2000); **Alan Smith** (v Finland, Valkeakoski, Oct. 10, 2000); **Luke Young** and **John Terry** (v Greece, Athens, Jun. 5, 2001); **Shola Ameobi** (v Portugal, Rio Maior, Mar. 28, 2003); **Jermaine Pennant** (v Croatia, Upton Park, Aug. 19, 2003); **Glen Johnson** (v Turkey, Istanbul, Oct. 10, 2003); **Nigel Reo-Coker** (v Azerbaijan, Baku, Oct. 12, 2004); **Glen Johnson** (v Spain, Henares, Nov. 16, 2004); **Steven Taylor** (v Germany, Leverkusen, Oct. 10, 2006); **Tom Huddlestone** (v Serbia & Montenegro, Nijmegen, Jun. 17, 2007).

England 'B' (1): **Neil Webb** (v Algeria, Algiers, December 11, 1990).

MOST DISMISSALS IN INTERNATIONAL MATCHES

19 (10 Chile, 9 Uruguay), June 25, 1975; **6** (2 Mexico, 4 Argentina), 1956; **6** (5 Ecuador, 1 Uruguay), Jan. 4, 1977 (4 Ecuadorians sent off in 78th min., match abandoned, 1-1); **5** (Holland 3, Brazil 2), June 6, 1999 in Goianio, Brazil.

INTERNATIONAL STOPPED THROUGH DEPLETED SIDE

Portugal v Angola (5-1), friendly International in Lisbon on November 14, 2001, abandoned (68 mins) because Angola were down to 6 players (4 sent off, 1 carried off, no substitutes left).

MOST 'CARDS' IN WORLD CUP FINALS MATCH

20 in Portugal v Holland quarter-final, Nuremberg, June 25, 2006 (9 yellow, 2 red, Portugal; 7 yellow, 2 red, Holland).

FIVE OFF IN ONE MATCH

For the first time since League football began in 1888, **five** players were sent off in one match (two Chesterfield, three Plymouth Argyle) in Div. 2 at Saltergate on **Feb. 22, 1997**. Four were dismissed (two from each side) in a goalmouth brawl in the last minute.

Second instance of **five** sent off in a League match was on **Dec. 2, 1997**: 4 Bristol Rov. players, 1 Wigan Athletic in Div. 2 match at Wigan. Four of those dismissals came in the 45th minute.

Third instance occurred on **Nov. 23, 2002**: Exeter City 3, Cambridge Utd. 2 (Div. 3) – all in the last minute.

Matches with **four** Football League club players being sent off in one match:

Jan. 8, 1955 Crewe Alexandra v Bradford City (Div. 3 North), two players from each side.

Dec. 13, 1986 Sheffield Utd. (1 player) v Portsmouth (3) in Div. 2.

Aug. 18, 1987 Port Vale v Northampton Town (Littlewoods Cup 1st. Round, 1st. Leg), two players from each side.

Dec. 12, 1987 Brentford v Mansfield Town (Div. 3), two players from each side.

Sept. 6, 1992 First instance in British first-class football of **four players from one side** being sent off in one match. Hereford Utd.'s seven survivors, away to Northampton Town (Div. 3), held out for a 1-1 draw.

Mar. 1, 1977 Norwich City v Huddersfield Town (Div. 1), two from each side.

Oct. 4, 1977 Shrewsbury Town (1 player), Rotherham Utd. (3) in Div. 3.

Aug. 22, 1998 Gillingham v Bristol Rov. (Div. 2), two from each side, all after injury-time brawl.

Mar. 16, 2001 Bristol City v Millwall (Div. 2), two from each side.

Aug. 17, 2002 Lincoln City (1 player), Carlisle Utd. (3) in Div. 3.

Aug. 26, 2002 (Wycombe Wand. v Q.P.R. (Div. 2), two from each side.

Nov. 1, 2005 Burnley (1 player) v Millwall (3) in Championship.

Four Stranraer players were sent off away to Airdrie (Scottish Div. 1) on Dec. 3, 1994, and that Scottish record was equalled when **four Hearts men** were ordered off away to Rangers (Prem. Div.) on **Sept. 14, 1996**. **Albion Rov.** had **four players** sent off (3 in last 8 mins) away to Queen's Park (Scottish Div. 3) on **August 23, 1997**.

In the **Island Games** in Guernsey (July 2003), five players (all from Rhodes) were sent off against Guernsey for violent conduct and the match was abandoned by referee Wendy Toms.

Most dismissals one team, one match: Five players of America Tres Rios in first ten minutes after disputed goal by opponents Itaperuna in Brazilian cup match in Rio de Janeiro on Nov. 23, 1991. Tie then abandoned and awarded to Itaperuna.

Eight dismissals in one match: Four on each side in S. American Super Cup quarter-final (Gremio, Brazil v Penarol, Uruguay) in Oct. 1993.

Five dismissals in one season – **Dave Caldwell** (2 with Chesterfield, 3 with Torquay Utd.) in 1987-88.

First instance of **four dismissals in Scottish match**: three **Rangers** players (all English – Terry Hurlock, Mark Walters, Mark Hateley) and **Celtic's** Peter Grant in Scottish Cup quarter-final at Parkhead on Mar. 17, 1991 (Celtic won 2-0).

Four players (3 Hamilton, 1 Airdrie) were sent off in Scottish Div. 1 match on Oct. 30, 1993.

Four players (3 Ayr, 1 Stranraer) were sent off in Scottish Div. 1 match on Aug. 27, 1994.

In Scottish Cup first round replays on Dec. 16, 1996, there were two instances of **three players of one side sent off**: Albion Rov. (away to Forfar) and Huntly (away to Clyde).

FASTEST SENDINGS-OFF

World record – 10 secs: Giuseppe Lorenzo (Bologna) for striking opponent in Italian League match v Parma, December 9, 1990.

Domestic – 13 secs: Kevin Pressman (Sheffield Wed. goalkeeper at Wolves, Div. 1, Sunday, Aug. 14, 2000); **15 secs: Simon Rea** (Peterborough Utd. at Cardiff, Div. 2, Nov. 2, 2002). **19 secs: Mark Smith** (Crewe Alexandra goalkeeper at Darlington, Div. 3, Mar. 12, 1994). **Premier League – 72 secs: Tim Flowers** (Blackburn Rov. goalkeeper v Leeds Utd., Feb. 1, 1995).

In World Cup – 55 secs: Jose Batista (Uruguay v Scotland at Neza, Mexico, June 13, 1986).

In European competition – 90 secs: Sergei Dirkach (Dynamo Moscow v Ghent UEFA Cup 3rd round, 2nd leg, December 11, 1991).

Fastest F.A. Cup dismissal – 52 secs: Ian Culverhouse (Swindon Town defender, deliberate hand-ball on goal-line, away to Everton, 3rd. Round, Sunday Jan. 5, 1997).

Fastest League Cup dismissal – 33 secs: Jason Crowe (Arsenal substitute v Birmingham City, 3rd Round, Oct. 14, 1997).

Fastest Sending-off on debut: See **Jason Crowe** (above).

Fastest Sending-off of substitute – 0 secs: Walter Boyd (Swansea City) for striking opponent before ball in play after he went on (83 mins) at home to Darlington, Div. 3, Nov. 23, 1999. **15 secs: Keith Gillespie** (Sheffield Utd.) for striking an opponent at Reading (Premiership), Jan. 20, 2007. **90 secs: Andreas Johansson** (Wigan Athletic), without kicking a ball, for shirt-pulling (penalty) away to Arsenal (Premiership), May 7, 2006.

MOST SENDINGS-OFF IN CAREER

21 – Willie Johnston (Rangers 7, WBA 6, Vancouver Whitecaps 4, Hearts 3, Scotland 1)
21 – Roy McDonough (13 in Football League – Birmingham City, Walsall, Chelsea, Colchester Utd., Southend Utd., Exeter City, Cambridge Utd. + 8 non-league).
13 – Steve Walsh (Wigan Athletic, Leicester City, Norwich City, Coventry City).
13 – Martin Keown (Arsenal, Aston Villa, Everton).
12 – Dennis Wise (Wimbledon, Chelsea, Leicester City, Millwall).
12 – Vinnie Jones (Wimbledon, Leeds Utd., Sheffield Utd., Chelsea, Q.P.R.).
12 – Mark Dennis (Birmingham City, Southampton, Q.P.R.).
12 – Roy Keane (Manchester Utd., Rep. of Ireland).
12 – Alan Smith (Leeds Utd., Manchester Utd., England U–21, England).
10 – Patrick Vieira (Arsenal).

Most Premiership Sendings-off: Patrick Vieira 9, Duncan Ferguson 8, Vinnie Jones 7, Roy Keane 7.

- **Carlton Palmer** holds the unique record of having been sent off with each of his five Premiership clubs: Sheffield Wed., Leeds Utd., Southampton, Nott'm. Forest and Coventry City.

F.A. CUP FINAL SENDINGS-OFF

Kevin Moran (Man. United) v Everton, Wembley, 1985; **Jose Antonio Reyes** (Arsenal) v Man. United, Cardiff, 2005.

WEMBLEY SENDINGS-OFF

Manchester Utd.'s **Kevin Moran**, first player to be sent off in the F.A. Cup Final (v Everton, 1985), was one of 22 dismissals in major matches at Wembley:

Aug. 1948 **Branko Stankovic** (Yugoslavia) v Sweden, Olympic Games.

July 1966 **Antonio Rattin** (Argentina captain) v England, World cup q-final.
Aug. 1974 **Billy Bremner** (Leeds Utd.) and **Kevin Keegan** (Liverpool), Charity Shield.
Mar. 1977 **Gilbert Dresch** (Luxembourg) v England, World Cup.
May 1985 **Kevin Moran** (Manchester Utd.) v Everton, F.A. Cup Final.
Apr. 1993 **Lee Dixon** (Arsenal) v Tottenham, F.A. Cup semi-final.
May 1993 **Peter Swan** (Port Vale) v W.B.A., Div. 2 Play-off Final.
Mar. 1994 **Andrei Kanchelskis** (Manchester Utd.) v Aston Villa, League Cup Final.
May 1994 **Mike Wallace, Chris Beaumont** (Stockport) v Burnley, Div. 2 Play-off Final.
June 1995 **Tetsuji Hashiratani** (Japan) v England, Umbro Cup.
May 1997 **Brian Statham** (Brentford) v Crewe Alexandra, Div. 2 Play-off Final.
Apr. 1998 **Capucho** (Portugal) v England, friendly.
Nov. 1998 **Ray Parlour** (Arsenal) and Tony Vareilles (Lens), Champions League.
Mar. 1999 **Justin Edinburgh** (Tottenham) v Leicester City, League Cup Final.
June 1999 **Paul Scholes** (England) v Sweden, European Championship qual.
Feb. 2000 **Clint Hill** (Tranmere) v Leicester City, League Cup Final.
Apr. 2000 **Mark Delaney** (Aston Villa) v Bolton Wand., F.A. Cup semi-final.
May 2000 **Kevin Sharp** (Wigan Athletic) v Gillingham, Div. 2 Play-off Final.
Aug. 2000 **Roy Keane** (Manchester Utd. captain) v Chelsea, Charity Shield.
May 2007 **Marc Tierney** (Shrewsbury Town) v Bristol Rov., Lge. 2 Play-off Final.
May 2007 **Malt Gill** (Exeter City) v Morecambe, Conf. Play-off Final.

WEMBLEY'S SUSPENDED CAPTAINS

Suspension prevented four **club captains** playing at Wembley in modern finals, in successive years.

Three were in F.A. Cup Finals – **Glenn Roeder** (Q.P.R., 1982), **Steve Foster** (Brighton & H.A., 1983) and **Wilf Rostron** (Watford, 1984) – and Sunderland's **Shaun Elliott** was barred from the 1985 Milk Cup Final.

Roeder was banned from Q.P.R.'s 1982 Cup Final replay against Tottenham, and Foster was ruled out of the first match in Brighton & H.A.'s 1983 Final against Manchester Utd.

BOOKINGS RECORDS

Most players of one Football League club booked in one match is **TEN** – members of the Mansfield Town team away to Crystal Palace in F.A. Cup third round, January 1963.

Fastest bookings – 3 seconds after kick-off, **Vinnie Jones** (Chelsea, home to Sheffield Utd., F.A. Cup fifth round, February 15, 1992); 5 seconds after kick-off: **Vinnie Jones** (Sheffield Utd., away to Manchester City, Div. 1, January 19, 1991). He was sent-off (54 mins) for second bookable offence.

FIGHTING TEAM-MATES

Charlton Athletic's **Mike Flanagan** and **Derek Hales** were sent off for fighting each other five minutes from end of F.A. Cup 3rd Round tie at home to Southern League Maidstone on Jan. 9, 1979.

Bradford City's **Andy Myers** and **Stuart McCall** had a fight during the 1-6 Premiership defeat at Leeds on Sunday, May 13, 2001.

On Sept. 28, 1994 the Scottish F.A. suspended Hearts players **Graeme Hogg** and **Craig Levein** for ten matches for fighting each other in a pre-season 'friendly' v Raith.

Blackburn Rovers' England Internationals **Graeme Le Saux** and **David Batty** clashed away to Spartak Moscow (Champions League) on Nov. 22, 1995. Neither was sent off.

Newcastle United's England Internationals **Lee Bowyer** and **Kieron Dyer** were sent off for fighting each other at home to Aston Villa (Premiership on Apr. 2, 2005).

FOOTBALL'S FIRST BETTING SCANDAL

A Football League investigation into the First Division match which ended Manchester Utd 2, Liverpool 0 at Old Trafford on Good Friday, April 2, 1915 proved that the result had been 'squared' by certain players betting on the outcome. Four members of each team were suspended for life, but some of the bans were lifted when League football resumed in 1919 in recognition of the players' war service.

PLAYERS JAILED

Ten professional footballers found guilty of conspiracy to fraud by 'fixing' matches for betting purposes were given prison sentences at Nottingham Assizes on Jan. 26, 1965.

Jimmy Gauld (Mansfield Town), described as the central figure, was given four years. Among the others sentenced, Tony Kay (Sheffield Wed., Everton & England), Peter Swan (Sheffield Wed. & England) and David 'Bronco' Layne (Sheffield Wed.) were suspended from football for life by the F.A.

DRUGS BAN

Abel Xavier (Middlesbrough) was the first Premiership player found to have taken a performancing-enchancing drug. He was banned by UEFA for 18 months in November 2005 after testing positive for an anabolic steroid. The ban was reduced to a year in July 2006 by the Court of Arbitration for Sport.

LONG SUSPENSIONS

The longest suspension (8 months) in modern times for a player in British football has been imposed on two Manchester Utd. footballers. First, French international captain **Eric Cantona**, following his attack on a spectator as he left the pitch after being sent off at Crystal Palace (Prem. League) on Jan. 25, 1995.

The club immediately suspended him to the end of the season and fined him 2 weeks' wages (est. £20,000). Then, on a disrepute charge, the F.A. fined him £10,000 (February 1995) and extended the ban to September 30 (which FIFA confirmed as world wide).

A subsequent 2-weeks' jail sentence on Cantona for assault was altered, on appeal, to 120 hours' community service, which took the form of coaching schoolboys in the Manchester area.

On December 19, 2003 an F.A. commission, held at Bolton F.C., suspended **Rio Ferdinand** (Manchester Utd. & England) from football for 8 months (plus £50,000 fine) for failing to take a random drug test at the club's training ground on September 23. The ban operated from January 12, 2004.

October 1998: Paolo Di Canio (Sheff. Wed.) banned for 11 matches and fined £10,000 for pushing referee Paul Alcock after being sent off at home to Arsenal (Prem.), Sept. 26.

March 2005: David Prutton (Southampton) banned for 10 matches (plus 1 for red card) and fined £6,000 by F.A. for shoving referee Alan Wiley when sent off at home to Arsenal (Prem.), Feb. 26.

Seven-month ban: Frank Barson, 37-year-old Watford centre-half, sent off at home to Fulham (Div. 3 South) on September 29, 1928, was suspended by the F.A. for the remainder of the season.

Twelve-month ban: Oldham Athletic full-back **Billy Cook** was given a 12-month suspension for refusing to leave the field when sent off at Middlesbrough (Div. 1), on April 3, 1915. The referee abandoned the match with 35 minutes still to play, and the score (4-1 to Middlesbrough) was ordered to stand.

Long Scottish bans: September 1954: Willie Woodburn, Rangers and Scotland centre-half, suspended for rest of career after fifth sending-off in 6 years.

Billy McLafferty, Stenhousemuir striker, was banned (April 14) for 8½ months, to Jan. 1, 1993, and fined £250 for failing to appear at a disciplinary hearing after being sent off against Arbroath on Feb. 1.

Twelve-match ban: On May 12, 1994 Scottish F.A. suspended Rangers forward **Duncan Ferguson** for 12 matches for violent conduct v Raith on Apr. 16. On Oct. 11, 1995, Ferguson (then with Everton) sent to jail for 3 months for the assault (served 44 days); Feb. 1, 1996 Scottish judge quashed 7 matches that remained of SFA ban on Ferguson.

On September 29, 2001 the SFA imposed a **17-match suspension** on Forfar Athletic's former Scottish International **Dave Bowman** for persistent foul and abusive language when sent off against Stranraer on September 22. As his misconduct continued, he was shown **5 red cards** by the referee.

TOP FINES

Clubs: £1,500,000 (increased from original £600,000) Tottenham: Dec. 1994, financial irregularities.; **£300,000** (reduced to £75,000 on appeal) Chelsea: June 2005, illegal approach to Arsenal's Ashley Cole.; **£175,000** Arsenal: Oct. 2003, players' brawl v Manchester Utd.; **£150,000** Leeds Utd.: Mar. 2000, players' brawl v Tottenham; **£150,000** Tottenham: Mar. 2000, players brawl v Leeds Utd.; **£105,000** Chelsea: Jan 1991, irregular payments.; **£100,000** Boston Utd.: July 2002, contract irregularities.; **£100,000** Arsenal and Chelsea: Mar. 2007 for mass brawl after Carling Cup Final. **£62,000** Macclesfield Town: Dec. 2005, funding of a stand at club's ground.

Players: £150,000 Roy Keane (Manchester Utd.): Oct. 2002, disrepute offence over autobiography.; **£100,000** (reduced to £75,000 on appeal) Ashley Cole (Arsenal): June 2005, illegal approach by Chelsea.; **£45,000** Patrick Vieira (Arsenal): Oct. 1999, tunnel incidents v West Ham Utd.; **£40,000** Lauren (Arsenal): Oct. 2003, players' fracas v Manchester Utd.; **£32,000** Robbie Fowler (Liverpool): Apr. 1999, simulating drug-taking and incident with Graeme Le Saux v Chelsea.; **£30,000** Lee Bowyer (Newcastle Utd.): Apr. 2005, fighting with team-mate Kieron Dyer v Aston Villa.

* In eight seasons with Arsenal (1996-2004) Patrick Vieira was fined a toal of £122,000 by the F.A. for disciplinary offences.

Managers: £200,000 (reduced to £75,000 on appeal) Jose Mourinho (Chelsea): June 2005, illegal approach to Arsenal's Ashley Cole.; **£20,000** Graeme Souness (Newcastle Utd.): June 2005, criticising referee v Everton.; **£15,000** Graeme Souness (Blackburn Rov.): Oct. 2002, sent off v Liverpool.; **£15,000** Arsene Wenger (Arsenal): Dec 2004, comments about Manchester Utd.'s Ruud van Nistelrooy.; **£10,000** Arsene Wenger (Arsenal): Feb. 2001, incident with fourth official v Sunderland.; **£10,000** Graeme Souness (Blackburn Rov.): Apr. 2002, verbal abusing referee v Middlesbrough.; **£10,000** Sir Alex Ferguson (Manchester Utd.): Oct. 2003, verbally abusing match officials v Newcastle Utd.; **£10,000** Graeme Souness (Blackburn Rov.): May 2004, verbally abusing referee v Tottenham.; **£10,000** Graeme Souness (Newcastle Utd.): Dec. 2004, altercation with referee v Fulham; **£10,000** Arsene Wenger (Arsenal): Dec. 2006, for altercation with West Ham Utd. manager Alan Pardew.

• Johnathan Barnett, Ashley Cole's agent was fined **£100,000** in September 2006 for his role in the 'tapping up' affair involving the player and Chelsea.

*£68,000 F.A: May 2003, pitch invasions and racist chanting by fans during England v Turkey, Stadium of Light.

MANAGERS

INTERNATIONAL RECORDS

(As at start of season 2007-08)

	P	*W*	*D*	*L*	*F*	*A*
Nigel Worthington (Northern Ireland – appointed May 2007)	–	–	–	–	–	–
Alex McLeish (Scotland – appointed Jan. 2007)	4	3	0	1	5	3
John Toshack (Wales – appointed Nov. 2004)	22	7	6	9	23	22
Steve Staunton (Rep. of Ireland-appointed Jan. 2006)	12	5	3	4	17	15
Final records						
Lawrie Sanchez (Northern Ireland, Jan. 2004 – May 2007)	32	11	10	11	35	42
Walter Smith (Scotland, Dec. 2004 – Jan. 2007)	16	7	5	4	26	15

ENGLAND'S MANAGERS

		P	W	D	L
1946-62	**Walter Winterbottom**	139	78	33	28
1963-74	**Sir Alf Ramsey**	113	69	27	17
1974	**Joe Mercer**, caretaker	7	3	3	1
1974-77	**Don Revie**	29	14	8	7
1977-82	**Ron Greenwood**	55	33	12	10
1982-90	**Bobby Robson**	95	47	30	18
1990-93	**Graham Taylor**	38	18	13	7
1994-96	**Terry Venables**, coach	23	11	11	1
1996-99	**Glenn Hoddle**, coach	28	17	6	5
1999	**Howard Wilkinson**, caretaker	1	0	0	1
1999-2000	**Kevin Keegan**, coach	18	7	7	4
2000	**Howard Wilkinson**, caretaker	1	0	1	0
2000	**Peter Taylor**, caretaker	1	0	0	1
2001-2006	**Sven-Goran Eriksson**, coach	67	40	17	10
2006	**Steve McClaren**, coach	11	5	4	2

INTERNATIONAL MANAGER CHANGES

England: Walter Winterbottom 1946-62 (initially coach); **Alf Ramsey** (Feb. 1963-May 1974); **Joe Mercer** (caretaker May 1974); **Don Revie** (July 1974-July 1977); **Ron Greenwood** (Aug. 1977-July 1982); **Bobby Robson** (July 1982-July 1990); **Graham Taylor** (July 1990-Nov. 1993); **Terry Venables**, coach (Jan. 1994-June 1996); **Glenn Hoddle**, coach (June 1996-Feb. 1999); **Howard Wilkinson** (caretaker Feb. 1999); **Kevin Keegan** coach (Feb. 1999-Oct. 2000); **Howard Wilkinson** (caretaker Oct. 2000); **Peter Taylor** (caretaker Nov. 2000); **Sven-Goran Eriksson** (Jan. 2001 – Aug. 2006); **Steve McClaren** (since Aug. 2006).

N. Ireland (modern): **Peter Doherty** (1951-62); **Bertie Peacock** (1962-67); **Billy Bingham** (1967-Aug. 1971); **Terry Neill** (Aug. 1971-Mar. 1975); **Dave Clements** (player-manager Mar. 1975-1976); **Danny Blanchflower** (June 1976-Nov. 1979); **Billy Bingham** (Feb. 1980-Nov. 1993); **Bryan Hamilton** Feb. 1994-Feb. 1998); **Lawrie McMenemy** (Feb. 1998-Nov. 1999); **Sammy McIlroy** (Jan. 2000-Oct. 2003); **Lawrie Sanchez** (Jan. 2004-May 2007); **Nigel Worthington** (since May 2007).

Scotland (modern): **Bobby Brown** (Feb. 1967-July 1971); **Tommy Docherty** (Sept. 1971- Dec. 1972); **Willie Ormond** (Jan. 1973-May 1977); **Ally MacLeod** (May 1977-Sept.1978); **Jock Stein** (Oct. 1978-Sept. 1985); **Alex Ferguson** (caretaker Oct. 1985-June 1986); **Andy Roxburgh**, coach (July 1986-Sept. 1993); **Craig Brown** (Sept. 1993-Oct. 2001); **Berti Vogts** (Feb. 2002 – Oct. 2004); **Walter Smith** (Dec. 2004-Jan. 2007); **Alex McLeish** (since Jan. 2007).

Wales (modern): **Mike Smith** (July 1974-Dec. 1979); **Mike England** (Mar. 1980-Feb. 1988); **David Williams** (caretaker Mar. 1988); **Terry Yorath** (Apr. 1988-Nov. 1993); **John Toshack** (Mar. 1994, one match); **Mike Smith** (Mar. 1994-June 1995); **Bobby Gould** (Aug. 1995-June 1999); **Mark Hughes** (Aug. 1999 – Oct. 2004); **John Toshack** (since Nov. 2004).

Rep. of Ireland (modern): **Liam Tuohy** (Sept. 1971-Nov. 1972); **Johnny Giles** (Oct. 1973-Apr. 1980, initially player-manager); **Eoin Hand** (June 1980-Nov. 1985); **Jack Charlton** (Feb. 1986-Dec. 1995); **Mick McCarthy** (Feb. 1996-Oct. 2002); **Brian Kerr** (Jan. 2003 – Oct. 2005); **Steve Staunton** (since Jan. 2006).

FIRST BLACK ENGLAND MANAGER

Chris Ramsey, 36, in charge of England's U-20 squad for the World Youth Championship in Nigeria, April 1999. He was Brighton & H.A.'s right-back in the 1983 F.A. Cup Final v Manchester Utd.

YOUNGEST LEAGUE MANAGERS

Ivor Broadis, 23, appointed player-manager of Carlisle Utd., August 1946; **Chris Brass**, 27, appointed player-manager of York City, June 2003; **Terry Neill**, 28, appointed player manager of Hull City, June 1970;

Graham Taylor, 28, appointed manager of Lincoln City, December 1972.

LONGEST-SERVING LEAGUE MANAGERS – ONE CLUB

Fred Everiss, secretary-manager of W.B.A. for 46 years (1902-48); **George Ramsay**, secretary-manager of Aston Villa for 42 years (1884-1926); **John Addenbrooke**, Wolves, for 37 years (1885-1922). Since last war, **Sir Matt Busby**, in charge of Manchester Utd. for 25 seasons (1945-69, 1970-71; **Dario Gradi** at Crewe Alexandra for 24 years (1983–2007); **Jimmy Seed** at Charlton Athletic for 23 years (1933-56).

LAST ENGLISH MANAGER TO WIN CHAMPIONSHIP

Howard Wilkinson (Leeds Utd.), season 1991–92.

1,000-TIME MANAGERS

Only five have managed in more than 1,000 English League games: **Alec Stock**, **Brian Clough**, **Jim Smith**, **Graham Taylor** and **Dario Gradi**.

Sir Matt Busby, **Dave Bassett**, **Lennie Lawrence**, **Alan Buckley**, **Denis Smith**, **Joe Royle**, **Sir Alex Ferguson**, **Brian Horton**, **Neil Warnock** and **Harry Redknapp** have each managed more than 1,000 matches in all first class competitions.

SHORT-TERM MANAGERS

		Departed
3 Days	Bill Lambton (Scunthorpe Utd.)	April 1959
7 Days	Tim Ward (Exeter City)	March 1953
7 Days	Kevin Cullis (Swansea City)	February 1996
10 Days	Dave Cowling (Doncaster Rov.)	October 1997
10 Days	Peter Cormack (Cowdenbeath)	December 2000
13 Days	Johnny Cochrane (Reading)	April 1939
13 Days	Micky Adams (Swansea City)	October 1997
16 Days	Jimmy McIlroy (Bolton Wand.)	November 1970
20 Days	Paul Went (Leyton Orient)	October 1981
27 Days	Malcolm Crosby (Oxford Utd.)	January 1998
28 Days	Tommy Docherty (Q.P.R.)	December 1968
32 Days	Steve Coppell (Manchester City)	November 1996
34 Days	Niall Quinn (Sunderland)	August 2006
36 Days	Steve Claridge (Millwall)	July 2005
39 Days	Paul Gascoigne (Kettering)	December 2005
41 Days	Steve Wicks (Lincoln City)	October 1995
41 Days	Les Reed (Charlton Athletic)	December 2006
44 Days	Brian Clough (Leeds Utd.)	September 1974
44 Days	Jock Stein (Leeds Utd.)	October 1978
48 Days	John Toshack (Wales)	March 1994
48 Days	David Platt (Sampdoria coach)	February 1999
49 Days	Brian Little (Wolves)	October 1986
49 Days	Terry Fenwick (Northampton Town)	February 2003
61 Days	Bill McGarry (Wolves)	November 1985

• In May 1984, Crystal Palace named **Dave Bassett** as manager, but he changed his mind four days later, without signing the contract, and returned to Wimbledon.

• In May 2007, **Leroy Rosenior** was reportedly appointed manager of Torquay Utd. after relegation and sacked ten minutes later when the club came under new ownership.

• **Brian Laws** lost his job at Scunthorpe Utd. on March 25, 2004 and was re-instated three weeks later.

• In an angry outburst after a play-off defeat in May 1992, Barnet chairman Stan Flashman sacked manager **Barry Fry** and re-instated him a day later.

EARLY-SEASON MANAGER SACKINGS

2004 Paul Sturrock (Southampton) 9 days; **2004** Sir Bobby Robson (Newcastle Utd.) 16 days; **2003** Glenn Roeder (West Ham) 15 days; **2000** Alan Buckley (Grimsby Town) 10 days; **1997** Kerry Dixon (Doncaster Rov.) 12 days; **1996** Sammy Chung (Doncaster Rov.)

on morning of season's opening League match; **1996** Alan Ball (Manchester City) 12 days; **1994** Kenny Hibbitt (Walsall) and Kenny Swain (Wigan Athletic) 20 days; **1993** Peter Reid (Manchester City) 12 days; **1991** Don Mackay (Blackburn Rov.) 14 days; **1989** Mick Jones (Peterborough Utd.) 12 days; **1980** Bill McGarry (Newcastle Utd.) 13 days; **1979** Dennis Butler (Port Vale) 12 days; **1977** George Petchey (Leyton O.) 13 days; **1977** Willie Bell (Birmingham City) 16 days; **1971** Len Richley (Darlington) 12 days.

FEWEST MANAGERS

West Ham Utd. have had only 11 managers in their 106-year history: Syd King, Charlie Paynter, Ted Fenton, Ron Greenwood, John Lyall, Lou Macari, Billy Bonds, Harry Redknapp, Glenn Roeder, Alan Pardew and Alan Curbishley.

RECORD START FOR MANAGER

Arsenal were unbeaten in 17 League matches from the start of season 1947-8 under new manager Tom Whittaker.

MANAGER CHOSEN BY POLL

A month after being sacked by Third Division promotion winners Hartlepool Utd., **Mike Newell** became manager of Luton Town in June 2003. He was appointed via a telephone poll which the club, under a new board, conducted among fans, players, shareholders and season-ticket holders.

MANAGER DOUBLES

Four managers have won the League Championship with different clubs: **Tom Watson**, secy-manager with Sunderland (1892-3-5) and Liverpool (1901); **Herbert Chapman** with Huddersfield Town (1923-4, 1924-5) and Arsenal (1930-1, 1932-3); **Brian Clough** with Derby Co. (1971-2) and Nott'm. Forest (1977-8); **Kenny Dalglish** with Liverpool (1985-6, 1987-8, 1989-90) and Blackburn Rov. (1994-5).

Managers to win the F.A. Cup with different clubs: **Billy Walker** (Sheffield Wed. 1935, Nott'm. Forest 1959); **Herbert Chapman** (Huddersfield Town 1922, Arsenal 1930).

Kenny Dalglish (Liverpool) and **George Graham** (Arsenal) completed the Championship/F.A. Cup double as both player and manager with a single club. **Joe Mercer** won the Championship as a player with Everton, the Championship twice and F.A. Cup as a player with Arsenal and both competitions as manager of Manchester City.

CHAIRMAN-MANAGER

On December 20, 1988, after two years on the board, Dundee Utd. manager **Jim McLean** was elected chairman, too. McLean, Scotland's longest-serving manager (appointed on November 24, 1971), resigned at end of season 1992-3 (remained chairman).

Ron Noades was chairman-manager of Brentford from July 1998 – March 2001. **Niall Quinn** did both jobs for five weeks in 2006 before appointing Roy Keane as manager of Sunderland.

TOP DIVISION PLAYER–MANAGERS

Les Allen (Q.P.R. 1968-9); **Johnny Giles** (W.B.A. 1976-7); **Howard Kendall** (Everton 1981-2); **Kenny Dalglish** (Liverpool, 1985-90); **Trevor Francis** (Q.P.R., 1988-9); **Terry Butcher** (Coventry City, 1990-1), **Peter Reid** (Manchester City, 1990-93), **Trevor Francis** (Sheffield Wed., 1991-4), **Glenn Hoddle**, (Chelsea, 1993-5), **Bryan Robson** (Middlesbrough, 1994-7), **Ray Wilkins** (Q.P.R., 1994-6), **Ruud Gullit** (Chelsea, 1996-8), **Gianluca Vialli** (Chelsea, 1998-2000).

FIRST FOREIGN MANAGER IN ENGLISH LEAGUE

Uruguayan **Danny Bergara** (Rochdale 1988-9).

FOREIGN TRIUMPH

Former Dutch star **Ruud Gullit** became the first foreign manager to win a major English competition when Chelsea took the F.A. Cup in 1997.

Arsene Wenger and **Gerard Houllier** became the first foreign managers to receive recognition when they were awarded honorary OBEs in the Queen's Birthday Honours in June 2003 'for their contribution to English football and Franco–British relations.'

MANAGERS OF POST-WAR CHAMPIONS (*Double Winners)

1947 George Kay (Liverpool); **1948** Tom Whittaker (Arsenal); **1949** Bob Jackson (Portsmouth); **1950** Bob Jackson (Portsmouth); **1951** Arthur Rowe (Tottenham); **1952** Matt Busby (Manchester Utd.); **1953** Tom Whittaker (Arsenal).

1954 Stan Cullis (Wolves); **1955** Ted Drake (Chelsea); **1956** Matt Busby (Manchester Utd.); **1957** Matt Busby (Manchester Utd.); **1958** Stan Cullis (Wolves); **1959** Stan Cullis (Wolves); **1960** Harry Potts (Burnley).

1961 *Bill Nicholson (Tottenham); **1962** Alf Ramsey (Ipswich Town); **1963** Harry Catterick (Everton); **1964** Bill Shankly (Liverpool); **1965** Matt Busby (Manchester Utd.); **1966** Bill Shankly (Liverpool); **1967** Matt Busby (Manchester Utd.).

1968 Joe Mercer (Manchester City); **1969** Don Revie (Leeds Utd.); **1970** Harry Catterick (Everton); **1971** *Bertie Mee (Arsenal); **1972** Brian Clough (Derby Co.); **1973** Bill Shankly (Liverpool); **1974** Don Revie (Leeds Utd.).

1975 Dave Mackay (Derby Co.); **1976** Bob Paisley (Liverpool); **1977** Bob Paisley (Liverpool); **1978** Brian Clough (Nott'm. Forest); **1979** Bob Paisley (Liverpool); **1980** Bob Paisley (Liverpool); **1981** Ron Saunders (Aston Villa).

1982 Bob Paisley (Liverpool); **1983** Bob Paisley (Liverpool); **1984** Joe Fagan (Liverpool); **1985** Howard Kendall (Everton); **1986** *Kenny Dalglish (Liverpool – player/manager); **1987** Howard Kendall (Everton).

1988 Kenny Dalglish (Liverpool – player/manager); **1989** George Graham (Arsenal); **1990** Kenny Dalglish (Liverpool); **1991** George Graham (Arsenal); **1992** Howard Wilkinson (Leeds Utd.); **1993** Alex Ferguson (Manchester Utd.).

1994 *Alex Ferguson (Manchester Utd.); **1995** Kenny Dalglish (Blackburn Rov.); **1996** *Alex Ferguson (Manchester Utd.); **1997** Alex Ferguson (Manchester Utd.); **1998** *Arsene Wenger (Arsenal); **1999** *Alex Ferguson (Manchester Utd.); **2000** Sir Alex Ferguson (Manchester Utd.); **2001** Sir Alex Ferguson (Manchester Utd.); **2002** *Arsene Wenger (Arsenal); **2003** Sir Alex Ferguson (Manchester Utd.); **2004** Arsene Wenger (Arsenal); **2005** Jose Mourinho (Chelsea); **2006** Jose Mourinho (Chelsea); **2007** Sir Alex Ferguson (Manchester Utd.).

SIR ALEX IS TOPS

With 28 major prizes **Sir Alex Ferguson** has the most successful managerial record with Scottish and English clubs combined. At **Aberdeen** (1978-86) he won ten top prizes: 3 Scottish Championships, 4 Scottish Cups, 1 Scottish League Cup, 1 Cup-Winners' Cup, 1 European Super Cup.

Manchester Utd. winning the Premiership in 2001 made Sir Alex the outright most successful manager in English football, the first to win seven League titles, and the first to win three in a row. He achieved a ninth Premiership success in 2007.

His title success in 2007 was United's 18th major trophy in 17 seasons: 1990 F.A. Cup; 1991 Cup-Winners' Cup; 1992 League Cup; 1993 Championship; 1994 Championship and F.A. Cup; 1996 Championship and F.A. Cup; 1997 Championship; 1999 Championship, F.A. Cup and European Cup; 2000 Championship; 2001 Championship; 2003 Championship; 2004 F.A. Cup; 2006 Carling Cup; 2007 Championship.

BOB PAISLEY'S HONOURS

Bob Paisley won 13 major competitions for Liverpool (1974-83): 6 League Championships, 3 European Cups, 3 League Cups, 1 UEFA Cup.

FOUR FOR MOURINHO

Jose Mourinho has led four consecutive title-winning teams – FC Porto (2002-3, 2003-4) and Chelsea (2004-5, 2005-6). He also won the League Cup with Chelsea in 2005 and 2007 and the F.A. Cup in 2007.

MANAGERS WITH MOST F.A. CUP SUCCESSES

5 Sir Alex Ferguson (Manchester Utd.); **4** Arsene Wenger (Arsenal); **3** Charles Foweraker (Bolton Wand.), John Nicholson (Sheffield Utd.), Bill Nicholson (Tottenham).

HOLE-IN-ONE MANAGER

Three days after appointing **Bobby Williamson** manager, from Hibernian, **Plymouth Argyle** clinched promotion and the Second Division Championship by beating Q.P.R. 2-1 on April 24, 2004.

RELEGATION 'DOUBLES'

Managers associated with two clubs relegated in same season: **John Bond** in 1985-6 (Swansea City and Birmingham City); **Ron Saunders** in 1985-6 (W.B.A. – and their reserve team – and Birmingham City); **Bob Stokoe** in 1986-7 (Carlisle Utd. and Sunderland); **Billy McNeill** in 1986-7 (Manchester City and Aston Villa); **Dave Bassett** in 1987-8 (Watford and Sheffield Utd.); **Mick Mills** in 1989-90 (Stoke City and Colchester Utd.).

WEMBLEY STADIUM

(For New Wembley see page 325)

INVASION DAY

Memorable scenes were witnessed at the **first F.A. Cup Final at Wembley, April 28, 1923**, between **Bolton** and **West Ham**. An accurate return of the attendance could not be made owing to thousands breaking in, but there were probably more than 200,000 spectators present. The match was delayed for 40 minutes by the crowd invading the pitch. Official attendance was 126,047.

Gate receipts totalled £27,776. The two clubs and the Football Association each received £6,365 and the F.A. refunded £2,797 to ticket-holders who were unable to get to their seats. Cup Final admission has since been by ticket only.

REDUCED CAPACITY

Capacity of the all-seated **Wembley Stadium** was 78,000. The last 100,000 attendance was for the 1985 F.A. Cup Final between Manchester Utd. and Everton.

WEMBLEY'S FIRST UNDER LIGHTS

November 30, 1955 (England 4, Spain 1), when the floodlights were switched on after 73 minutes (afternoon match played in damp, foggy conditions).

First Wembley International played throughout under lights: England 8, N. Ireland 3 on evening of November 20, 1963 (att: 55,000).

MOST WEMBLEY APPEARANCES BY PLAYER

59 by Tony Adams (24 Arsenal, 35 England).

WEMBLEY HAT-TRICKS

Three players have scored hat-tricks in major cup finals at Wembley: **Stan Mortensen** for Blackpool v Bolton Wand. (F.A. Cup Final, 1953), **Geoff Hurst** for England v West Germany (World Cup Final, 1966) and **David Speedie** for Chelsea v Manchester City (Full Members Cup, 1985).

ENGLAND'S WEMBLEY DEFEATS

England have lost 18 matches to foreign opponents at Wembley:

Nov.	1953	3-6 v Hungary	Sept.	1983	0-1 v Denmark
Oct.	1959	2-3 v Sweden	June	1984	0-2 v Russia
Oct.	1965	2-3 v Austria	May	1990	1-2 v Uruguay
Apr.	1972	1-3 v W. Germany	Sept.	1991	0-1 v Germany
Nov.	1973	0-1 v Italy	June	1995	1-3 v Brazil
Feb.	1977	0-2 v Holland	Feb.	1997	0-1 v Italy
Mar.	1981	1-2 v Spain	Feb.	1998	0-2 v Chile
May	1981	0-1 v Brazil	Feb.	1999	0-2 v France
Oct.	1982	1-2 v W. Germany	Oct.	2000	0-1 v Germany

A further defeat came in **Euro 96**. After drawing the semi-final with Germany 1-1, England went out 6-5 on penalties.

FASTEST GOALS AT WEMBLEY

In first-class matches: **38 seconds** by **Bryan Robson** in England's 2-1 win against Yugoslavia on December 13, 1989; **44 seconds** by **Bryan Robson** for England in 4-0 win v N. Ireland on February 23, 1982; **42 seconds** by **Roberto di Matteo** for Chelsea in the 1997 F.A. Cup Final v Middlesbrough.

Fastest goal in **any** match at Wembley: **20 seconds** by **Maurice Cox** for Cambridge University against Oxford on December 5, 1979.

FOUR WEMBLEY HEADERS

When **Wimbledon** beat Sutton Utd. 4-2 in the F.A. Amateur Cup Final at Wembley on May 4, 1963, Irish centre-forward **Eddie Reynolds** headed all four goals.

WEMBLEY ONE-SEASON DOUBLES

In 1989, **Nott'm. Forest** became the first club to win two Wembley Finals in the same season (Littlewoods Cup and Simod Cup).

In 1993, **Arsenal** made history there as the first club to win the League (Coca-Cola) Cup and the F.A. Cup in the same season. They beat Sheffield Wed. 2-1 in both finals.

SUDDEN-DEATH DECIDERS

First Wembley Final decided on sudden death (first goal scored in overtime): April 23, 1995 – **Birmingham City** beat Carlisle Utd. (1-0, Paul Tait 103 mins.) to win Auto Windscreens Shield.

First instance of a 'golden goal' deciding a major International tournament was at Wembley on June 30, 1996, when **Germany** beat the Czech Republic 2-1 in the European Championship Final with Oliver Bierhoff's goal in the 95th. minute.

SHADOWS OVER SOCCER

DAYS OF TRAGEDY – CLUBS

Season 1988-9 brought the worst disaster in the history of British sport, with the death of 96 Liverpool supporters (200 injured) at the **F.A. Cup semi-final** against Nott'm. Forest at **Hillsborough, Sheffield**, on Saturday, April 15. The tragedy built up in the minutes preceding kick-off, when thousands surged into the ground at the Leppings Lane end. Many were crushed in the tunnel between entrance and terracing, but most of the victims were trapped inside the perimeter fencing behind the goal. The match was abandoned without score after six minutes' play. The dead included seven women and girls, two teenage sisters and two teenage brothers. The youngest victim was a boy of ten, the oldest 67-year-old Gerard Baron, whose brother Kevin played for Liverpool in the 1950 Cup Final. (*Total became 96 in March 1993, when Tony Bland died after being in a coma for nearly four years.)

The two worst disasters in one season in British soccer history occurred at the end of 1984-5. On May 11, the last Saturday of the League season, 56 people (two of them visiting supporters) were burned to death – and more than 200 taken to hospital – when fire destroyed the main stand at the **Bradford City-Lincoln City** match at Valley Parade.

The wooden, 77-year-old stand was full for City's last fixture before which, amid scenes of celebration, the club had been presented with the Third Division Championship trophy. The fire broke out just before half-time and, within five minutes, the entire stand was engulfed.

Eighteen days later, on May 29, at the European Cup Final between **Liverpool** and **Juventus** at the Heysel Stadium, Brussels, 39 spectators (31 of them Italian) were crushed or trampled to death and 437 injured. The disaster occurred an hour before the scheduled kick-off when Liverpool supporters charged a Juventus section of the crowd at one end of the stadium, and a retaining wall collapsed.

The sequel was a 5-year ban by UEFA on English clubs generally in European competition, with a 6-year ban on Liverpool.

On May 26, 1985 ten people were trampled to death and 29 seriously injured in a crowd panic on the way into the **Olympic Stadium, Mexico City** for the Mexican Cup Final between local clubs National University and America.

More than 100 people died and 300 were injured in a football disaster at **Nepal's national stadium** in Katmandu in March 1988. There was a stampede when a violent hailstorm broke over the capital. Spectators rushed for cover, but the stadium exits were locked, and hundreds were trampled in the crush.

In South Africa, on January 13, 1991 40 black fans were trampled to death (50 injured) as they tried to escape from fighting that broke out at a match in the gold-mining town of Orkney, 80 miles from Johannesburg. The friendly, between top teams **Kaiser Chiefs** and **Orlando Pirates**, attracted a packed crowd of 20,000. Violence erupted after the referee allowed Kaiser Chiefs a disputed second-half goal to lead 1-0.

Disaster struck at the French Cup semi-final (May 5, 1992), with the death of 15 spectators and 1,300 injured when a temporary metal stand collapsed in the Corsican town of Bastia. The tie between Second Division **Bastia** and French Champions **Marseille** was cancelled. **Monaco**, who won the other semi-final, were allowed to compete in the next season's Cup-Winners' Cup.

A total of 318 died and 500 were seriously injured when the crowd rioted over a disallowed goal at the National Stadium in Lima, Peru, on May 24, 1964. **Peru** and **Argentina** were competing to play in the Olympic Games in Tokyo.

That remained sport's heaviest death toll until October 20, 1982, when (it was revealed only in July 1989) 340 Soviet fans were killed in Moscow's Lenin Stadium at the UEFA Cup second round first leg match between **Moscow Spartak** and **Haarlem (Holland)**. They were crushed on an open stairway when a last-minute Spartak goal sent departing spectators surging back into the ground.

Among other crowd disasters abroad: **June 1968** – 74 died in **Argentina**. Panic broke out at the end of a goalless match between River Plate and Boca Juniors at Nunez, Buenos Aires, when Boca supporters threw lighted newspaper torches on to fans in the tiers below.

February 1974 – 49 killed in **Egypt** in crush of fans clamouring to see Zamalek play Dukla Prague.

September 1971 – 44 died in **Turkey**, when fighting among spectators over a disallowed goal (Kayseri v Siwas) led to a platform collapsing.

The then worst disaster in the history of British football, in terms of loss of life, occurred at Glasgow Rangers' ground at **Ibrox Park**, January 2, 1971.

Sixty-six people were trampled to death (100 injured) as they tumbled down Stairway 13 just before the end of the **Rangers v Celtic** New Year's match. That disaster led to the 1975 Safety of Sports Grounds legislation.

The Ibrox tragedy eclipsed even the Bolton disaster in which 33 were killed and about 500 injured when a wall and crowd barriers collapsed near a corner-flag at the **Bolton Wand. v Stoke City** F.A. Cup sixth round tie on March 9, 1946. The match was completed after half an hour's stoppage.

In a previous crowd disaster at **Ibrox** on April 5, 1902, part of the terracing collapsed during the Scotland v England International and 25 people were killed. The match, held up for 20 minutes, ended 1-1, but was never counted as an official International.

Eight leading players and three officials of **Manchester Utd.** and eight newspaper representatives were among the 23 who perished in the air crash at Munich on February 6, 1958, during take-off following a European Cup-tie in Belgrade. The players were Roger Byrne, Geoffrey Bent, Eddie Colman, Duncan Edwards, Mark Jones, David Pegg, Tommy Taylor and Liam Whelan, and the officials were Walter Crickmer (secretary), Tom Curry (trainer) and Herbert Whalley (coach). The newspaper representatives were Alf Clarke, Don Davies, George Follows, Tom Jackson, Archie Ledbrooke, Henry Rose, Eric Thompson and Frank Swift (former England goalkeeper of Manchester City).

On May 14, 1949, the entire team of Italian Champions **Torino,** 8 of them Internationals, were killed when the aircraft taking them home from a match against Benfica in Lisbon crashed at Superga, near Turin. The total death toll of 28 included all the club's reserve players, the manager, trainer and coach.

On February 8, 1981, 24 spectators died and more than 100 were injured at a match **in Greece**. They were trampled as thousands of the 40,000 crowd tried to rush out of the stadium at Piraeus after Olympiakos beat AEK Athens 6-0.

On November 17, 1982, 24 people (12 of them children) were killed and 250 injured when fans stampeded at the end of a match at the Pascual Guerrero stadium in **Cali, Colombia**. Drunken spectators hurled fire crackers and broken bottles from the higher stands on to people below and started a rush to the exits.

On December 9, 1987, the 18-strong team squad of **Alianza Lima,** one of Peru's top clubs, were wiped out, together with 8 officials and several youth players, when a military aircraft taking them home from Puccalpa crashed into the sea off Ventillana, ten miles from Lima. The only survivor among 43 on board was a member of the crew.

On April 28, 1993, 18 members of **Zambia's International** squad and 5 ZFA officials died when the aircraft carrying them to a World Cup qualifying tie against Senegal crashed into the Atlantic soon after take-off from Libreville, Gabon.

On October 16, 1996, 81 fans were crushed to death and 147 seriously injured in the 'Guatemala Disaster' at the World Cup qualifier against Costa Rica in Mateo Flores stadium. The tragedy happened an hour before kick-off, allegedly caused by ticket forgery and overcrowding – 60,000 were reported in the 45,000-capacity ground – and safety problems related to perimeter fencing.

On July 9, 1996, 8 people died, 39 injured in riot after derby match between **Libya's two top clubs** in Tripoli. Al-Ahli had beaten Al-Ittihad 1-0 by a controversial goal.

On April 6, 1997, 5 spectators were crushed to death at **Nigeria's national stadium** in Lagos after the 2-1 World Cup qualifying victory over Guinea. Only two of five gates were reported open as the 40,000 crowd tried to leave the ground.

It was reported from the **Congo** (October 29, 1998) that a bolt of lightning struck a village match, killing all 11 members of the home team Benatshadi, but leaving the opposing players from Basangana unscathed. It was believed the surviving team wore better-insulated boots.

On January 10, 1999 eight fans died and 13 were injured in a stampede at **Egypt's Alexandria Stadium**. Some 25,000 spectators had pushed into the ground. Despite the tragedy, the cup-tie between Al-Ittihad and Al-Koroum was completed.

Three people suffocated and several were seriously injured when thousands of fans forced their way into **Liberia's national stadium** in Monrovia at a goalless World Cup qualifying match against Chad on April 23, 2000. The stadium (capacity 33,000) was reported 'heavily overcrowded'.

On Sunday, July 9, 2000 12 spectators died from crush injuries when police fired tear gas into the 50,000 crowd after South Africa scored their second goal in a World Cup group qualifier against Zimbabwe in **Harare**. A stampede broke out as fans scrambled to leave the national stadium. Players of both teams lay face down on the pitch as fumes swept over them. FIFA launched an investigation and decided that the result would stand, with South Africa leading 2-0 at the time of the 84th-minute abandonment.

On April 11, 2001, at one of the biggest matches of the South African season, 43 died and 155 were injured in a crush at **Ellis Park, Johannesburg**. After tearing down a fence, thousands of fans surged into a stadium already packed to its 60,000 capacity for the Premiership derby between top Soweto teams Kaizer Chiefs and Orlando Pirates.

The match was abandoned at 1-1 after 33 minutes. In January 1991, 40 died in a crowd crush at a friendly between the same clubs at Orkney, 80 miles from Johannesburg.

On April 29, 2001, seven people were trampled to death and 51 injured when a riot broke out at a match between two of Congo's biggest clubs, Lupopo and Mazembe at **Lubumbashi**, southern Congo.

On May 6, 2001, two spectators were killed in Iran and hundreds were injured when a glass fibre roof collapsed at the over-crowded Mottaqi Stadium at **Sari** for the match between Pirouzi and Shemshak Noshahr.

On May 9, 2001, in Africa's worst football disaster, 123 died and 93 were injured in a stampede at the national stadium in **Accra, Ghana**. Home team Hearts of Oak were leading 2-1 against Asante Kotoko five minutes from time, when Asanti fans started hurling bottles on to the pitch. Police fired tear gas into the stands, and the crowd panicked in a rush for the exits, which were locked. It took the death toll at three big matches in Africa in April/May to 173.

On August 12, 2001, two players were killed by lightning and ten severely burned at a **Guatemala** Third Division match between Deportivo Culquimulilla and Pueblo Nuevo Vinas.

On November 1, 2002, two players died from injuries after lightning struck Deportivo Cali's training ground in **Colombia**.

On March 12, 2004, five people were killed and more than 100 injured when spectators stampeded shortly before the Syrian Championship fixture between Al-Jihad and Al-Fatwa in **Qameshli**, Northern Syria. The match was cancelled.

On October 10, 2004, three spectators died in a crush at the African Zone World Cup qualifier between **Guinea** and **Morocco** (1-1) at Conakry, Guinea.

On March 25, 2005, five were killed as 100,000 left the Azadi Stadium, **Tehran**, after Iran's World Cup qualifying win (2-1) against Japan.

On June 2, 2007 12 spectators were killed and 46 injured in a crush at the Chillabombwe Stadium, **Zambia**, after an African Nations Cup qualifier against Congo.

DAYS OF TRAGEDY – PERSONAL

Sam Wynne, Bury right-back, collapsed five minutes before half-time in the First Division match away to Sheffield Utd. on April 30, 1927, and died in the dressing-room.

John Thomson, Celtic and Scotland goalkeeper, sustained a fractured skull when diving at an opponent's feet in the Rangers v Celtic League match on September 5, 1931, and died the same evening.

Sim Raleigh (Gillingham), injured in a clash of heads at home to Brighton & H.A. (Div. 3 South) on December 1, 1934, continued to play but collapsed in second half and died in hospital the same night.

James Thorpe, Sunderland goalkeeper, was injured during the First Division match at home to Chelsea on February 1, 1936 and died in a diabetic coma three days later.

Derek Dooley, Sheffield Wed. centre-forward and top scorer in 1951-52 in the Football League with 46 goals in 30 matches, broke a leg in the League match at Preston N.E. on February 14, 1953, and, after complications set in, had to lose the limb by amputation.

John White Tottenham's Scottish International forward, was killed by lightning on a golf course at Enfield, North London in July, 1964.

Tommy Allden Highgate Utd. centre-half was struck by lightning during an Amateur Cup quarter-final with Enfield Town on February 25, 1967. He died the following day. Four other players were also struck but recovered.

Roy Harper died while refereeing the York City–Halifax Town (Div. 4) match on May 5, 1969.

Jim Finn collapsed and died from a heart attack while refereeing Exeter City v Stockport Co. (Div. 4) on September 16, 1972.

Scotland manager **Jock Stein**, 62, collapsed and died at the end of the Wales-Scotland World Cup qualifying match (1-1) at Ninian Park, Cardiff on September 10, 1985.

David Longhurst, York City forward, died after being carried off two minutes before half-time in the Fourth Division fixture at home to Lincoln City on September 8, 1990. The match was abandoned (0-0). The inquest revealed that Longhurst suffered from a rare heart condition.

Mike North collapsed while refereeing Southend Utd. v Mansfield Town (Div. 3) on April 16, 2001 and died shortly afterwards. The match was abandoned and re-staged on May 8, with the receipts donated to his family.

Marc-Vivien Foe, on his 63rd appearance in Cameroon's midfield, collapsed unchallenged in the centre circle after 72 minutes of the FIFA Confederations Cup semi-final against Colombia in Lyon, France, on June 26, 2003, and despite the efforts of the stadium medical staff he could not be revived. He had been on loan to Manchester City from Olympique Lyonnais in season 2002–03, and poignantly scored the club's last goal at Maine Road.

Paul Sykes, Folkestone Invicta (Ryman league) striker, died on the pitch during the Kent Senior Cup semi-final against Margate on April 12, 2005. He collapsed after an innocuous off-the-ball incident.

Craig Gowans, Falkirk apprentice, was killed at the club's training ground on July 8, 2005 when he came into contact with power lines.

Peter Wilson, Mansfield Town goalkeeping coach, died of a heart attack after collapsing during the warm-up of the League Two game away to Shrewsbury on November 19, 2005.

Matt Gadsby, Hinckley defender, collapsed and died while playing in a Conference North match at Harrogate on September 9, 2006.

GREAT SERVICE

'For services to Association Football', **Stanley Matthews** (Stoke City, Blackpool and England), already a C.B.E., became the first professional footballer to receive a knighthood. This was bestowed in 1965, his last season.

Before he retired and five days after his 50th birthday, he played for Stoke City to set a record as the oldest First Division footballer (v. Fulham, February 6, 1965).

Over a brilliant span of 33 years, he played in 886 first-class matches, including 54 full Internationals (plus 31 in war time), 701 League games (including 3 at start of season 1939-40, which was abandoned on the outbreak of war) and 86 F.A. Cup-ties, and scored 95 goals. He was never booked in his career.

Sir Stanley died on February 23 2000, three weeks after his 85th birthday. His ashes were buried under the centre circle of Stoke's Britannia Stadium. After spending a number of years in Toronto, he made his home back in the Potteries in 1989, having previously returned to his home town, Hanley, Stoke-on-Trent in October, 1987 to unveil a life-size bronze statue of himself.

The inscription reads: 'Sir Stanley Matthews, CBE. Born Hanley, 1 February 1915. His name is symbolic of the beauty of the game, his fame timeless and international, his sportsmanship and modesty universally acclaimed. A magical player, of the people, for the people.'

On his home-coming in 1989, Sir Stanley was made President of Stoke City, the club he joined as a boy of 15 and served as a player for 20 years between 1931 and 1965, on either side of his spell with Blackpool.

In July 1992 FIFA honoured him with their 'Gold merit award' for outstanding services to the game.

Former England goalkeeper **Peter Shilton** has made more first-class appearances (1,387) than any other footballer in British history. He played his 1,000th. League game in Leyton Orient's 2-0 home win against Brighton & H.A. on Dec. 22, 1996 and in all played 9 times for Orient in his final season. He retired from International football after the 1990 World Cup in Italy with 125 caps, then a world record.

Shilton's career spanned 32 seasons, 20 of them on the International stage. He made his League debut for Leicester City in May 1966, two months before England won the World Cup.

His 1,387 first-class appearances comprise a record 1,005 in the Football League, 125 Internationals, 102 League Cup, 86 F.A. Cup, 13 for England U-23s, 4 for the Football League and 52 other matches (European Cup, UEFA Cup, World Club Championship, Charity Shield, European Super Cup, Full Members' Cup, Play-offs, Screen Sports Super Cup, Anglo-Italian Cup, Texaco Cup, Simod Cup, Zenith Data Systems Cup and Autoglass Trophy).

Shilton appeared more times at Wembley (57) than any other player: 52 for England, 2 League Cup Finals, 1 F.A. Cup Final, 1 Charity Shield match, and 1 for the Football League. He passed a century of League appearances with each of his first five clubs: Leicester City (286), Stoke City (110), Nott'm. Forest (202), Southampton (188) and Derby Co. (175) and subsequently played for Plymouth Argyle, Bolton Wand. and Leyton Orient.

His club honours, all gained with Nott'm. Forest: League Championship 1978, League Cup 1979, European Cup 1979 and 1980, PFA Player of Year 1978.

Five other British footballers have made more than 1,000 first-class appearances:

Ray Clemence, formerly with Tottenham, Liverpool and England, retired through injury in season 1987-8 after a goalkeeping career of 1,119 matches starting in 1965-6. Clemence played 50 times for his first club, Scunthorpe Utd.; 665 for Liverpool; 337 for Tottenham; his 67 representative games included 61 England caps.

A third great British goalkeeper, **Pat Jennings**, ended his career (1963-86) with a total of 1,098 first-class matches for Watford, Tottenham, Arsenal and N. Ireland. They were made up of 757 in the Football League, 119 full Internationals, 84 F.A. Cup appearances, 72 League/Milk Cup, 55 European club matches, 2 Charity Shield, 3 Other Internationals, 1 Under-23 cap, 2 Texaco Cup, 2 Anglo-Italian Cup and 1 Super Cup. Jennings played his 119th. and final International on his 41st birthday, June 12, 1986, against Brazil in Guadalajara in the Mexico World Cup.

Yet another outstanding 'keeper, **David Seaman**, passed the 1,000 appearances milestone for clubs and country in season 2002–03, reaching 1,004 when aged 39, he captained Arsenal to F.A. Cup triumph against Southampton.

With Arsenal, Seaman won 3 Championship medals, the F.A. Cup 4 times, the Double twice, the League Cup and Cup-Winners' Cup once each. After 13 seasons at Highbury, he joined Manchester City (June 2003) on a free transfer. He played 26 matches for City before a shoulder injury forced his retirement in January 2004, aged 40.

Seaman's 22-season career composed 1,046 first-class matches: 955 club apps. (Peterborough Utd. 106, Birmingham City 84, Q.P.R. 175, Arsenal 564, Manchester City 26); 75 senior caps for England, 6 'B' caps and 10 at U-21 level.

Defender **Graeme Armstrong**, 42-year-old commercial manager for an Edinburgh whisky company and part-time assistant-manager and captain of Scottish Third Division club Stenhousemuir, made the 1000th first team appearance of his career in the Scottish Cup 3rd Round against Rangers at Ibrox on January 23, 1999. He was presented with the Man of the Match award before kick-off.

Against East Stirling on Boxing Day, he had played his 864th League game, breaking the British record for an outfield player set by another Scot, Tommy Hutchison, with Alloa, Blackpool, Coventry City, Manchester City, Burnley and Swansea City.

Armstrong's 24-year career, spent in the lower divisions of the Scottish League, began as a 1-match trialist with Meadowbank Thistle in 1975 and continued via Stirling Albion, Berwick Rangers, Meadowbank and, from 1992, Stenhousemuir.

Tony Ford became the first English outfield player to reach 1000 senior appearances in Rochdale's 1-0 win at Carlisle (Auto Windscreens Shield) on March 7, 2000. Grimsby-born, he began his 26-season midfield career with Grimsby Town and played for 7 other League clubs: Sunderland (loan), Stoke City, W.B.A., Bradford City (loan), Scunthorpe Utd., Mansfield Town and Rochdale. He retired, aged 42, in 2001 with a career record of 1072 appearances (121 goals) and his total of 931 League games is exceeded only by Peter Shilton's 1005.

TEN KNIGHTS OF SOCCER

Dave Richards, chairman of the Premier League and of the Football Foundation, became the tenth senior football figure to receive a knighthood when he was honoured in the Queen's Birthday Honours in June, 2006 for services to sport.

The elite list reads: **Stanley Matthews** (1965), **Alf Ramsey** (1967), **Matt Busby** (1968), **Bobby Charlton** (1994), **Tom Finney** (1998), **Geoff Hurst** (1998), **Alex Ferguson** (1999), **Bobby Robson** (2002), **Trevor Brooking** (2004), **Dave Richards** (2006).

PENALTIES

The **penalty-kick** was introduced to the game, following a proposal to the Irish F.A. in 1890 by William McCrum, son of the High Sheriff for Co. Omagh, and approved by the International Football Board on June 2, 1891.

First penalty scored in a first-class match in England was by John Heath, for Wolves v Accrington Stanley (5-0 in Div. 1, September 14, 1891).

The greatest influence of the penalty has come since the 1970s, with the introduction of the shoot-out to settle deadlocked ties in various competitions.

Manchester Utd. were the first club to win a competitive match in British football via a shoot-out (4-3 away to Hull City, Watney Cup semi-final, August 5, 1970); in that penalty contest, George Best was the first player to score, Denis Law the first to miss.

The shoot-out was adopted by FIFA and UEFA the same year (1970).

In season 1991-2, penalty shoot-outs were introduced to decide **F.A. Cup ties** still level after one replay and extra time.

Wembley saw its first penalty contest in the 1974 Charity Shield. Since then many major matches across the world have been settled in this way, including:

1974 **F.A. Charity Shield** (Wembley): Liverpool beat Leeds Utd. 6-5 (after 1-1).
1976 **Eur. Champ. Final** (Belgrade): Czech. beat W. Germany 5-3 (after 2-2).
1980 **Cup-Winners' Cup Final** (Brussels): Valencia beat Arsenal 5-4 (0-0).
1980 **Eur. Champ. 3rd/4th place play-off** (Naples): Czechoslovakia beat Italy 9-8 (after 1-1).
1982 **World Cup s-final** (Seville): West Germany beat France 5-4 (after 3-3).
1984 **European Cup Final** (Rome): Liverpool beat AS Roma 4-2 (after 1-1).
1984 **UEFA Cup Final**: Tottenham (home) beat Anderlecht 4-3 (2-2 agg.).
1984 **Eur. Champ. s-final** (Lyon): Spain beat Denmark 5-4 (after 1-1).
1986 **European Cup Final** (Seville): Steaua Bucharest beat Barcelona 2-0 (0-0). Barcelona's four penalties were all saved.
1987 **Freight Rover Trophy Final** (Wembley): Mansfield Town beat Bristol City 5-4 (after 1-1).
1987 **Scottish League (Skol) Cup Final** (Hampden Park): Rangers beat Aberdeen 5-3 (after 3-3).
1988 **European Cup Final** (Stuttgart): PSV Eindhoven beat Benfica 6-5 (after 0-0).
1988 **UEFA Cup Final**: Bayer Leverkusen (home) beat Espanyol 3-2 after 3-3 (0-3a, 3-0h).
1990 **Scottish F.A. Cup Final** (Hampden Park): Aberdeen beat Celtic 9-8 (0-0).
1990 **World Cup** (in Italy): 2nd. Round: Rep. of Ireland beat Romania 5-4 (after 0-0); q-final: Argentina beat Yugoslavia 3-2 (after 0-0); s-finals: Argentina beat Italy 4-3 (after 1-1); West Germany beat England 4-3 (1-1).
1991 **European Cup Final** (Bari): Red Star Belgrade beat Marseille 5-3 (after 0-0).
1991 **Barclays League Play-off** (4th. Div. Final – Wembley): Torquay Utd. beat Blackpool 5-4 (after 2-2).
1992 **F.A. Cup s-final** replay (Villa Park): Liverpool beat Portsmouth 3-1 (after 0-0).
1992 **Barclays League Play-off** (4th. Div. Final – Wembley): Blackpool beat Scunthorpe Utd. 4-3 (after 1-1).
1992 **Eur. Champ. s-final** (Gothenburg): Denmark beat Holland 5-4 (after 2-2).
1993 **Barclays League Play-off**: (3rd Div. Final – Wembley): York City beat Crewe Alexandra 5-3 (after 1-1).
1993 **F.A. Charity Shield** (Wembley): Manchester Utd. beat Arsenal 5-4 (after 1-1).
1994 **League (Coca-Cola) Cup s-final**: Aston Villa beat Tranmere Rov. 5-4 (after 4-4, 1-3a, 3-1h).
1994 **Autoglass Trophy Final** (Wembley): Swansea City beat Huddersfield Town 3-1 (after 1-1).
1994 **World Cup** (Los Angeles): **Final**: Brazil beat Italy 3-2 (after 0-0).
1994 **Scottish League (Coca-Cola) Cup Final** (Ibrox Park): Raith beat Celtic 6-5 (after 2-2).
1995 **Cup-Winners' Cup s-final**: Arsenal beat Sampdoria away 3-2 (5-5 agg.)

1995 **Copa America Final** (Montevideo): Uruguay beat Brazil 5-3 (after 1-1).
1996 **European Cup Final** (Rome): Juventus beat Ajax 4-2 (after 1-1).
1996 **European U-21 Champ. Final** (Barcelona): Italy beat Spain 4-2 (after 1-1).
1996 **Eur. Champ. q-finals**: England beat Spain (Wembley) 4-2 after 0-0; **s-finals**: Germany beat England (Wembley) 6-5 after 1-1; Czech Republic beat France (Old Trafford) 6-5 after 0-0.
1997 **Auto Windscreens Shield Final** (Wembley): Carlisle Utd. beat Colchester Utd. 4-3 (after 0-0)
1997 **UEFA Cup Final**: FC Schalke beat Inter Milan 4-1 (after 1-1 agg.).
1998 **Nationwide League play-off** (1st Div. Final Wembley): Charlton Athletic beat Sunderland 7-6 (after 4-4).
1998 **World Cup Finals**: (St Etienne): Argentina beat England (2nd Round) 4-3 (after 2-2).
1999 **Nationwide League play-offs Div. 1 s-final**: Watford beat Birmingham City 7-6 away (after 1-1); **Div. 2 Final (Wembley)**: Manchester City beat Gillingham 3-1 (after 2-2).
1999 **Women's World Cup Final** (Pasedena): U.S.A. beat China 5-4 (after 0-0).
2000 **African Nations Cup Final** (Lagos): Cameroon beat Nigeria 4-3 (after 0-0).
2000 **F.A. Cup s-final** (Wembley): Aston Villa beat Bolton Wand. 4-1 (after 0-0).
2000 **UEFA Cup Final** (Copenhagen): Galatasaray beat Arsenal 4-1 (after 0-0).
2000 **Eur. Champ. s-final** (Amsterdam): Italy beat Holland 3-1 (after 0-0). Holland missed 5 penalties in match – 2 in normal play, 3 in shoot-out. Italy survived with ten men after 33rd minute sending-off.
2000 **Olympic Final** (Sydney): Cameroon beat Spain 5-3 (after 2-2). Spain led 2-0, then had 2 men sent off.
2001 **League (Worthington) Cup Final** (Millennium Stadium, Cardiff): Liverpool beat Birmingham City 5-4 (after 1-1).
2001 **Champions League Final** (Milan): Bayern Munich beat Valencia 5-4 (after 1-1).
2002 **Eur. U-21 Champ. Final** (Basle): Czech Republic beat France 3-1 (after 0-0).
2002 **Nationwide League** play-off (1st Div. Final, Millennium Stadium, Cardiff): Birmingham City beat Norwich City 4-2 (after 1-1).
2002 **World Cup Finals**: (Suwon): Spain beat Rep. of Ireland (2nd Round) 3-2 (after 1-1).
2003 **Champions League Final** (Old Trafford): AC Milan beat Juventus 3–2 (after 0–0).
2003 **F.A. Community Shield** (Millennium Stadium): Manchester Utd. beat Arsenal 4-3 (after 1-1).
2004 **Nationwide League play-off Div. 3 Final** (Millennium Stadium): Huddersfield Town beat Mansfield Town 4-1 (after 0-0).
2004 **Eur. Champ. q-finals**: Portugal beat England (Lisbon) 6-5 after 2-2.
2004 **Copa America Final** (Lima): Brazil beat Argentina 4-2 (after 2-2).
2005 **Coca-Cola League 1 play-off s-final**: Hartlepool Utd. beat Tranmere Rov. 6-5 away (after 2-2 agg.)
2005 **F.A. Cup Final** (Cardiff): Arsenal beat Manchester Utd. 5-4 (after 0-0).
2005 **Champions League Final** (Istanbul): Liverpool beat AC Milan 3-2 (after 3-3).
2005 **World Cup qual.** (Sydney): Australia beat Uruguay 4-2 (after 1-1).
2006 **African Cup of Nations Final** (Cairo): Egypt beat Ivory Coast 4-2 (after 0-0).
2006 **F.A. Cup Final** (Millennium Stadium): Liverpool beat West Ham Utd. 3-1 (after 3-3).
2006 **Scottish Cup Final** (Hampden Park): Hearts beat Gretna 4-2 (after 1-1).
2006 **Coca-Cola League 1 play-off Final** (Millennium Stadium): Barnsley beat Swansea City 4-3 (after 2-2).
2006 **World Cup Finals** (Germany): Ukraine beat Switzerland 3-0 (after 0-0, 2nd rd.); Germany beat Argentina 4-2 (after 1-1, q. final); Portugal beat England 3-1 (after 0-0, q. final); Italy beat France 5-3 (after 1-1, final).
2007 **UEFA Cup Final** (Hampden Park): Sevilla beat Espanyol 3-1 (after 2-2).

Footnote: Highest-recorded score in a penalty shoot-out between Football League clubs was **Aldershot's 11-10** victory at home to **Fulham** after their 1-1 draw in the Freight Rover

Trophy Southern quarter-final on February 10, 1987. Seven spot-kicks were missed or saved in a record 28-penalty shoot-out at senior level.

In South America in 1992, in a 26-shot competition, **Newell's Old Boys** beat America 11-10 in the Copa Libertadores.

Longest-recorded penalty contest in first-class matches was in Argentina in 1988 – from 44 shots, **Argentinos Juniors** beat **Racing Club 20-19**. **Genclerbirligi** beat **Galatasaray** 17-16 in a Turkish Cup-tie in 1996. Only one penalty was missed.

Highest-scoring shoot-outs in **Int. football**: North Korea beat Hong Kong 11-10 (after 3-3 draw) in an Asian Cup match in 1975; and Ivory Coast beat Ghana 11-10 (after 0-0 draw) in African Nations Cup Final, 1992.

Most penalties needed to settle an adult game in Britain: 44 in Norfolk Primary Cup 4th Round replay, December 2000. Aston Village side **Freethorpe** beat Foulsham 20-19 (5 kicks missed). All 22 players took 2 penalties each, watched by a crowd of 20. The sides had drawn 2-2, 4-4 in a tie of 51 goals.

Penalty that took 24 days: That is how long elapsed between the award and the taking of a penalty in an Argentine Second Division match between **Atalanta** and **Defensores** in 2003. A riot ended the original match with 5 minutes left, and the game was resumed on 30 April behind closed doors with the penalty that caused the abandonment. Lucas Ferreiro scored it to give Atalanta a 1–0 win.

INTERNATIONAL PENALTIES, MISSED

Four penalties out of five were missed when **Colombia** beat **Argentina** 3-0 in a Copa America group tie in Paraguay in July 1999. Martin Palmeiro missed three for Argentina and Colombia's Hamilton Ricard had one spot-kick saved.

In the European Championship semi-final against Italy in Amsterdam on June 29, 2000, **Holland** missed five penalties – two in normal time, three in the penalty contest which Italy won 3-1 (after 0-0). Dutch captain Frank de Boer missed twice from the spot.

ENGLAND'S SHOOT-OUT RECORD

England have been beaten in six out of seven penalty shoot-outs in major tournaments:

1990 (World Cup semi-final, Turin) 3-4 v West Germany after 1-1.
1996 (Euro Champ. quarter-final, Wembley) 4-2 v Spain after 0-0.
1996 (Euro Champ. semi-final, Wembley) 5-6 v Germany after 1-1.
1998 (World Cup 2nd rd., St Etienne) 3-4 v Argentina after 2-2.
2004 (Euro Champ. quarter-final, Lisbon) 5-6 v Portugal after 2-2.
2006 (World Cup quarter-final, Gelsenkirchen) 1-3 v Portugal after 0-0.
2007 (Euro U-21 Champ. semi-final, Heerenveen) 12-13 v Holland after 1-1.

F.A. CUP SHOOT-OUTS

The **first** penalty contest in the F.A. Cup took place in **1972**. In the days of the play-off for third place, the match was delayed until the eve of the following season when losing semi-finalists Birmingham City and Stoke City met at St Andrews on Aug. 5. The score was 0-0 and Birmingham City won 4-3 on penalties.

Record Shoot-out: 40 kicks, Tunbridge Wells beating Littlehampton 16-15 (9 missed) in prelim. round replay (2-2 aet) on August 30, 2005. In competition proper Macclesfield Town beat Forest Green Rov. (away) 11-10 in 1st Round replay (1-1 aet) on November 28, 2001 which stretched to 24 kicks.

Shoot-out abandoned: The F.A. Cup 1st Round replay between Oxford City and Wycombe Wand. at Wycombe on November 9, 1999 was abandoned (1-1) after extra time because, as the penalty shoot-out was about to begin, a fire broke out under a stand. Wycombe won the second replay 1-0 at Oxford Utd.'s ground.

First F.A. Cup Final to be decided by shoot-out was in 2005 (May 21), when Arsenal beat Manchester Utd. 5-4 on penalties at Cardiff's Millennium Stadium (0-0 after extra time). A year later (May 13) Liverpool beat West Ham Utd. 3-1 (3-3 after extra-time).

MISSED CUP FINAL PENALTIES

John Aldridge (Liverpool) became the first player to miss a penalty in the F.A. Cup Final at Wembley – and the second in the competition's history (previously Charlie Wallace, of

Aston Villa, in the 1913 Final against Sunderland at Crystal Palace) – when Wimbledon's Dave Beasant saved his shot in May 1988. Seven previous penalties had been scored in this Final at Wembley.

Another crucial penalty miss at Wembley was by Arsenal's **Nigel Winterburn,** Luton Town's Andy Dibble saving his spot-kick in the 1988 Littlewoods Cup Final, when a goal would have put Arsenal 3-1 ahead. Instead, they lost 3-2.

Winterburn was the third player to fail with a League Cup Final penalty at Wembley, following **Ray Graydon** (Aston Villa) against Norwich City in 1975 and **Clive Walker** (Sunderland), who shot wide in the 1985 Milk Cup Final, also against Norwich City (won 1-0). Graydon had his penalty saved by Kevin Keelan, but scored from the rebound and won the cup for Aston Villa (1-0).

Tottenham's **Gary Lineker** saw his penalty saved by Nott'm. Forest goalkeeper Mark Crossley in the 1991 F.A. Cup Final.

Derby Co.'s Martin Taylor saved a penalty from **Eligio Nicolini** in the Anglo-Italian Cup Final at Wembley on March 27, 1993, but Cremonese won 3-1.

LEAGUE PENALTIES RECORD

Most penalties in Football League match: Five – 4 to Crystal Palace (3 missed), 1 to Brighton & H.A. (scored) in Div. 2 match at Selhurst Park on March 27 (Easter Monday), 1989. Crystal Palace won 2-1. Three of the penalties were awarded in a 5-minute spell. The match also produced 5 bookings and a sending-off.

Other teams missing 3 penalties in a match: **Burnley** v Grimsby Town (Div. 2), February 13, 1909; **Manchester City** v Newcastle Utd. (Div. 1), January 17, 1912.

HOTTEST MODERN SPOT-SHOT

Matthew Le Tissier ended his career in season 2001-02 with the distinction of having netted 48 out of 49 first-team penalties for Southampton. He scored the last 27 after his only miss when Nott'm. Forest keeper Mark Crossley saved in a Premier League match at The Dell on March 24, 1993.

SPOT-KICK HAT-TRICKS

Right-back **Joe Willetts** scored three penalties when Hartlepool Utd. beat neighbours Darlington 6–1 (Div. 3N) on Good Friday 1951.

Danish International **Jan Molby**'s only hat-trick in English football, for Liverpool in a 3-1 win at home to Coventry City (Littlewoods Cup, 4th round replay, Nov. 26, 1986) comprised three goals from the penalty spot.

It was the first such hat-trick in a major match for two years – since **Andy Blair** scored three penalties for Sheffield Wed. against Luton Town (Milk Cup 4th. round, Nov. 20 1984).

Portsmouth's **Kevin Dillon** scored a penalty hat-trick in the Full Members Cup (2nd rd.) at home to Millwall (3-2) on Nov. 4, 1986.

Alan Slough scored a hat-trick of penalties in an away game and was on the losing side, when Peterborough Utd. were beaten 4-3 at Chester City (Div. 3, Apr. 29, 1978).

Penalty hat-tricks in **International football**: **Dimitris Saravakos** (in 9 mins.) for Greece v Egypt in 1990. He scored 5 goals in match. **Henrik Larsson**, among his 4 goals in Sweden's 6-0 home win v Moldova in World Cup qualifying match, June 6, 2001.

MOST PENALTY GOALS (LEAGUE) IN SEASON

Thirteen out of 13 by **Francis Lee** for Manchester City (Div. 1) in 1971-2. His goal total for the season was 33. In season 1988-9, **Graham Roberts** scored 12 League penalties for Second Division Champions Chelsea. In season 2004-5, **Andrew Johnson** scored 11 Premiership penalties for Crystal Palace, who were relegated.

PENALTY-SAVE SEQUENCES

Ipswich Town goalkeeper **Paul Cooper** saved eight of the ten penalties he faced in 1979-80. **Roy Brown** (Notts Co.) saved six in a row in season 1972-3.

Andy Lomas, goalkeeper for Chesham Utd. (Diadora League) claimed a record eight **consecutive** penalty saves – three at the end of season 1991-2 and five in 1992-3.

Mark Bosnich (Aston Villa) saved five in two consecutive matches in 1993-4: three in Coca-Cola Cup semi-final penalty shoot-out v Tranmere Rov. (Feb. 26), then two in Premiership at Tottenham (Mar. 2).

MISSED PENALTIES SEQUENCE

Against Wolves in Div. 2 on Sept. 28, 1991, **Southend Utd.** missed their seventh successive penalty (five of them the previous season).

SCOTTISH RECORDS

(See also under 'Goals' & 'Discipline')

RANGERS' MANY RECORDS

Rangers' record-breaking feats include:-

League Champions: 51 times (once joint holders) – world record.

Winning every match in Scottish League (18 games, 1898-9 season).

Major hat-tricks: Rangers have completed the domestic treble (League Championship, League Cup and Scottish F.A. Cup) a record seven times (1948-9, 1963-4, 1975-6, 1977-8, 1992-3, 1998-9, 2002-3).

League & Cup double: 16 times.

Nine successive Championships (1989-97). Four men played in all nine sides: Richard Gough, Ally McCoist, Ian Ferguson and Ian Durrant.

107 major trophies: Championships 51, Scottish Cup 31, League Cup 24, Cup-Winners' Cup 1.

CELTIC'S GRAND SLAM

Celtic's record in 1966-7 was the most successful by a British club in one season. They won the **Scottish League**, the **Scottish Cup**, the **Scottish League Cup** and became the first British club to win the **European Cup**. They also won the **Glasgow Cup**.

Celtic have 3 times achieved the Scottish treble (League Championship, League Cup and F.A. Cup), in 1966-7, 1968-9 and 2000-01 (in Martin O'Neill's first season as their manager). They became Scottish Champions for 2000-01 with a 1-0 home win against St. Mirren on April 7 – the earliest the title had been clinched for 26 years, since Rangers' triumph on March 29, 1975.

They have won the Scottish Cup 34 times, and have completed the League and Cup double 14 times.

Celtic won nine consecutive Scottish League titles (1966-74) under Jock Stein.

They set a **British record** of 25 consecutive League wins in season 2003-04 (Aug. 15 to Mar. 14). They were unbeaten for 77 matches (all competitions) at Celtic Park from August 22, 2001, to April 21, 2004.

UNBEATEN SCOTTISH CHAMPIONS

Celtic and **Rangers** have each won the Scottish Championship with an unbeaten record: Celtic in 1897-98 (P18, W15, D3), Rangers in 1898-99 (P18, W18).

LARSSON SUPREME

After missing most of the previous campaign with a broken leg, Swedish International **Henrik Larsson**, with 53 goals in season 2000-01, set a post-war record for Celtic and equalled the Scottish Premier League record of 35 by Brian McClair (Celtic) in 1986-7. Larsson's 35 earned him Europe's Golden Shoe award.

His 7 seasons as a Celtic player ended, when his contract expired in May 2004, with a personal total of 242 goals in 315 apps. (third-highest scorer in the club's history). He helped Celtic win 4 League titles, and at 32 he moved to Barcelona (free) on a 2-year contract.

SCOTTISH CUP HAT-TRICKS

Aberdeen's feat of winning the Scottish F.A. Cup in 1982-3-4 made them only the third club to achieve that particular hat-trick.

Queen's Park did it twice (1874-5-6 and 1880-1-2), and **Rangers** have won the Scottish Cup three years in succession on three occasions: 1934-5-6, 1948-9-50 and 1962-3-4.

SCOTTISH CUP FINAL DISMISSALS

Four players have been sent off in the Scottish F.A. Cup Final: **Jock Buchanan** (Rangers v. Kilmarnock, 1929), **Roy Aitken** (Celtic v Aberdeen, 1984), **Walter Kidd** (Hearts captain v Aberdeen, 1986), **Paul Hartley** (Hearts v Gretna, 2006).

RECORD SEQUENCES

Celtic hold Britain's League record of 62 matches undefeated, from November 13, 1915 to April 21, 1917, when Kilmarnock won 2-0 at Parkhead. They won 49, drew 13 (111 points) and scored 126 goals to 26.

Greenock Morton in 1963-4 accumulated 67 points out of 72 and scored 135 goals.

Queens Park did not have a goal scored against them during the first seven seasons of their existence (1867-74, before the Scottish League was formed).

EARLIEST PROMOTIONS IN SCOTLAND

Dundee promoted from Div. 2, February 1, 1947; **Greenock Morton** promoted from Div. 2, March 2, 1964; **Gretna** promoted from Div. 3, March 5, 2005.

WORST HOME SEQUENCE

After gaining promotion to Div. 1 in 1992, **Cowdenbeath** went a record 38 consecutive home League matches without a win. They ended the sequence (drew 8, lost 30) when beating Arbroath 1-0 on April 2, 1994, watched by a crowd of 225.

ALLY'S RECORDS

Ally McCoist became the first player to complete 200 goals in the Premier Division when he scored Rangers' winner (2-1) at Falkirk on December 12, 1992. His first was against Celtic in September 1983, and he reached 100 against Dundee on Boxing Day 1987.

When McCoist scored twice at home to Hibernian (4-3) on December 7, 1996, he became Scotland's record post-war League marksman, beating Gordon Wallace's 264.

Originally with St. Johnstone (1978-81), he spent two seasons with Sunderland (1981-3), then joined Rangers for £200,000 in June 1983.

In 15 seasons at Ibrox, he scored 355 goals for Rangers (250 League), and helped them win 10 Championships (9 in succession), 3 Scottish Cups and earned a record 9 League Cup winner's medals. He won the European Golden Boot in consecutive seasons (1991-2, 1992-3).

His 9 Premier League goals in three seasons for Kilmarnock gave him a career total of 281 Scottish League goals when he retired at the end of 2000-01.

FIVE IN A MATCH

Paul Sturrock set an individual scoring record for the Scottish Premier Division with 5 goals in Dundee Utd.'s 7-0 win at home to Morton on November 17, 1984. **Marco Negri** equalled the feat with all 5 when Rangers beat Dundee Utd. 5-1 at Ibrox (Premier Division) on August 23, 1997, and **Kenny Miller** scored 5 in Rangers' 7-1 win at home to St. Mirren on November 4, 2000. **Kris Boyd** scored all Kilmarnock's goals in a 5-2 SPL win at home to Dundee Utd. on September 25, 2004.

NEGRI'S TEN-TIMER

Marco Negri scored in Rangers' first ten League matches (23 goals) in season 1997-8 – a Premier Division record. The previous best sequence was 8 by Ally MacLeod for Hibernian in 1978.

DOUBLE SCOTTISH FINAL

Rangers v Celtic drew **129,643** and **120,073** people to the Scottish Cup Final and replay at Hampden Park, Glasgow, in 1963. Receipts for the two matches totalled £50,500.

MOST SCOTTISH CHAMPIONSHIP MEDALS

13 by **Sandy Archibald** (Rangers, 1918-34). Post-war record: **10** by **Bobby Lennox** (Celtic, 1966-79).

Alan Morton won **nine** Scottish Championship medals with Rangers in 1921-23-24-25-27-28-29-30-31. **Ally McCoist** played in the Rangers side that won nine successive League titles (1989-97).

Between 1927 and 1939 **Bob McPhail** helped Rangers win nine Championships, finish second twice and third once. He scored 236 League goals but was never top scorer in a single season.

TOP SCOTTISH LEAGUE SCORERS IN SEASON

Raith Rovers (Div. 2) 142 goals in 1937-38; **Morton** (Div. 2) 135 goals in 1963-64; **Hearts** (Div. 1) 132 goals in 1957-58; **Falkirk** (Div. 2) 132 goals in 1935-36; **Gretna** (Div. 3) 130 goals in 2004-05.

SCOTTISH CUP – NO DECISION

The **Scottish F.A.** withheld their Cup and medals in 1908-9 after Rangers and Celtic played two drawn games in the Final. Spectators rioted.

FEWEST LEAGUE WINS IN SEASON

Clydebank won only one of 36 matches in Div. 1, season 1999-2000. It came on March 7 (2-1 at home to Raith).

HAMPDEN'S £63M. REDEVELOPMENT

On completion of redevelopment costing £63m. **Hampden Park**, home of Scottish football and the oldest first-class stadium in the world, was re-opened full scale for the Rangers-Celtic Cup Final on May 29, 1999.

Work on the 'new Hampden' (capacity 52,000) began in 1992. The North and East stands were restructured (£12m.); a new South stand and improved West stand cost £51m. The Millennium Commission contributed £23m. and the Lottery Sports Fund provided a grant of £3.75m.

GRETNA'S RISE

Gretna, who joined the Scottish League in 2002, won the Bell's Third, Second and First Division titles in successive seasons (2005-6-7). They also become the first team from the third tier to reach the Scottish Cup Final, taking Hearts to penalties (2006).

DEMISE OF AIRDRIE AND CLYDEBANK

In May 2002, First Division **Airdrieonians**, formed in 1878, went out of business. They had debts of £3m. Their place in the Scottish League was taken by **Gretna**, from the English Unibond League, who were voted into Div. 3. Second Division **Clydebank** folded in July 2002 and were taken over by the new **Airdrie United** club.

GREAT SCOTS

In February 1988, the Scottish F.A. launched a national **Hall of Fame**, initially comprising the first 11 Scots to make 50 International appearances, to be joined by all future players to reach that number of caps. Each member receives a gold medal, invitation for life at all Scotland's home matches, and has his portrait hung at Scottish F.A. headquarters in Glasgow.

MORE CLUBS IN 2000

The **Scottish Premier League** increased from 10 to 12 clubs in season 2000-1.

The **Scottish Football League** admitted two new clubs – Peterhead and Elgin City from the Highland League – to provide three divisions of 10 in 2000-1.

NOTABLE SCOTTISH 'FIRSTS'

- The father of League football was a Scot, **William McGregor**, a draper in Birmingham. The 12-club Football League kicked off in September 1888, and McGregor was its first president.
- **Hibernian** were the first British club to play in the European Cup, by invitation. They reached the semi-final when it began in 1955-6.
- **Celtic** were Britain's first winners of the European Cup, in 1967.
- Scotland's First Division became the **Premier Division** in season 1975-6.
- Football's **first International** was staged at the West of Scotland cricket ground, Partick, on November 30, 1872: Scotland 0, England 0.
- Scotland introduced its **League Cup** in 1945-6, the first season after the war. It was another 15 years before the Football League Cup was launched.
- The Scottish F.A. Cup has been **sponsored** by Tennents for the last 16 seasons.
- Scotland pioneered the use in British football of **two substitutes** per team in League and Cup matches.
- The world's **record football score** belongs to Scotland: Arbroath 36, Bon Accord 0 (Scottish Cup first round) on September 12, 1885.
- The Scottish F.A. introduced the **penalty shoot-out** to their Cup Final in 1990.
- On Jan. 22, 1994 all six matches in the **Scottish Premier Division** ended as draws.
- Scotland's new Premier League introduced a **3-week shut-down** in January 1999 – first instance of British football adopting the winter break system that operates in a number of European countries. The SPL ended its New Year closure after 2003.
- **Rangers** made history at home to St. Johnstone (Premier League, 0-0, March 4, 2000) when fielding a team entirely without Scottish players.

SCOTTISH CUP SHOCK RESULTS

1885-86 (1) Arbroath 36, Bon Accord 0
1921-22 (F) Morton 1, Rangers 0
1937-38 (F) East Fife 4, Kilmarnock 2 (replay, after 1-1)
1960-61 (F) Dunfermline 2, Celtic 0 (replay, after 0-0)
1966-67 (1) Berwick Rangers 1, Rangers 0
1979-80 (3) Hamilton 2, Keith 3
1984-85 (1) Stirling Albion 20, Selkirk 0
1984-85 (3) Inverness Thistle 3, Kilmarnock 0
1986-87 (3) Rangers 0, Hamilton 1
1994-95 (4) Stenhousemuir 2, Aberdeen 0
1998-99 (3) Aberdeen 0, Livingston 1
1999-2000 (3) Celtic 1, Inverness Caledonian Thistle 3
2002-03 (5) Inverness Caledonian Thistle 1, Celtic 0
2005-06 (3) Clyde 2, Celtic 1

Scottish League (Coca-Cola) Cup Final shock
1994-95 Raith 2, Celtic 2 (Raith won 6-5 on pens.)

SCOTTISH DISCIPLINE (MODERN) – MAJOR PUNISHMENTS

1989 (June) fine **Hearts** £93,000, following TV infringement at UEFA Cup q-final.
1994 (August) Scottish League fine **Celtic** record £100,000 for poaching manager Tommy Burns from Kilmarnock.
1996 (November) UEFA fine **Celtic** £42,000 and **Alan Stubbs** £28,000 for using unlicensed agents in summer transfer from Bolton Wanderers.
1999 (August) Scottish Premier League fine **Celtic** £45,000 for their part in disturbances at home match with Rangers, May 2.

2000 (April) Scottish League deduct a record 15 points from **Hamilton Academical**, following their players (in protest over unpaid wages) refusing to turn up for Div. 2 fixture at Stenhousemuir on April 1. As a result, Hamilton relegated at end of season.

MISCELLANEOUS

NATIONAL ASSOCIATIONS FORMED

F.A. **1863**
F.A. of Wales **1876**
Scottish F.A. **1873**
Irish F.A. **1904**
Federation of International Football Associations (FIFA) **1904**

NATIONAL & INTERNATIONAL COMPETITIONS LAUNCHED

F.A. Cup **1871**
Welsh Cup **1877**
Scottish Cup **1873**
Irish Cup **1880**
Football League **1888**
F.A. Premier League **1992**
Scottish League **1890**
Scottish Premier League **1998**
Scottish League Cup **1945**
Football League Cup **1960**
Home International Championship **1883-4**
World Cup **1930**
European Championship **1958**
European Cup **1955**
Fairs/UEFA Cup **1955**
Cup-Winners' Cup **1960**
European Champions League **1992**
Olympic Games Tournament, at Shepherd's Bush **1908**

INNOVATIONS

Size of Ball: Fixed in **1872.**
Shinguards: Introduced and registered by Sam Weller Widdowson (Nott'm. Forest & England) in **1874.**
Referee's Whistle: First used on Nott'm. Forest's ground in **1878.**
Professionalism: Legalised in England in the summer of **1885** as a result of agitation by Lancashire clubs.
Goal-nets: Invented and patented in **1890** by Mr. J. A. Brodie of Liverpool. They were first used in the North v South match in January, **1891.**
Referees and Linesmen: Replaced umpires and referees in January, **1891.**
Penalty-kick: Introduced at Irish F.A.'s request in the season **1891-2.** The penalty law ordering the goalkeeper to remain on the goal-line came into force in September, **1905,** and the order to stand on his goal-line until the ball is kicked arrived in **1929-30.**
White ball: First came into official use in **1951.**
Floodlighting: First F.A. Cup-tie (replay), Kidderminster Harriers v Brierley Hill Alliance, **1955**. First Football League match: Portsmouth v Newcastle Utd. (Div. 1), 1956.
Heated pitch to beat frost tried by Everton at Goodison Park in **1958.**
First Soccer Closed-circuit TV: At Coventry City ground in October **1965** (10,000 fans saw their team win at Cardiff City, 120 miles away).

Substitutes (one per team) were first allowed in Football League matches at the start of season **1965-6**. Three substitutes (one a goalkeeper) allowed, two of which could be used, in Premier League matches, **1992-93**. The Football League introduced three substitutes for **1993-94**.

Three points for a win: This was introduced by the Football League in **1981-2,** by FIFA in World Cup games in 1994, and by the Scottish League in the same year.

Offside law amended, player 'level' no longer offside, and 'professional foul' made sending-off offence, **1990**.

Penalty shoot-outs introduced to decide F.A. Cup ties level after one replay and extra time, **1991-2**.

New back-pass rule – goalkeeper must not handle ball kicked to him by team-mate, **1992**.

Linesmen became 'referees' assistants', **1998**.

Goalkeepers not to hold ball longer than 6 seconds, **2000**.

Free-kicks advanced by ten yards against opponents failing to retreat, **2000**.

DERBY DAYS: COMPLETE LEAGUE RESULTS

Arsenal v Tottenham: Played 140 (all top div.); Arsenal 57 wins, Tottenham 45, Drawn 38.

Aston Villa v Birmingham City: Played 104; Aston Villa 41, Birmingham City 36, Drawn 27.

Everton v Liverpool: Played 176 (all top div.); Liverpool 65, Everton 56, Drawn 55.

Ipswich Town v Norwich City: Played 76; Ipswich Town 36, Norwich City 27, Drawn 13.

Manchester City v Manchester Utd.: Played 136; United 53, City 35, Drawn 48.

Middlesbrough v Newcastle Utd.: Played 108; Newcastle Utd. 43, Middlesbrough 34, Drawn 31.

Newcastle Utd. v Sunderland: Played 128; Newcastle Utd. 48, Sunderland 41, Drawn 39 (incl. 1990 play-offs – Sunderland win and draw).

Middlesbrough v Sunderland: Played 124; Sunderland 54, Middlesbrough 39, Drawn 31.

Nott'm. Forest v Notts Co.: Played 86; Forest 35, County 28, Drawn 23.

Sheffield Utd. v Sheffield Wed.: Played 106; United 41, Wednesday 32, Drawn 33.

Portsmouth v Southampton: Played 30; Southampton 14, Portsmouth 8, Drawn 8.

Port Vale v Stoke City: Played 44; Stoke City 16, Port Vale 14, Drawn 14.

Bristol City v Bristol Rovers: Played 86; City 33, Rovers 25, Drawn 28.

Celtic v Rangers: Played 283; Rangers 109, Celtic 92, Drawn 82.

Dundee v Dundee Utd.: Played 123; United 58, Dundee 38, Drawn 27.

Hearts v Hibernian: Played 242; Hearts 99, Hibernian 71, Drawn 72.

YOUNGEST AND OLDEST

Youngest Caps	*Age*
Gareth Bale (Wales v Trinidad & Tobago, May 27, 2006)	**16** years **315** days
Norman Whiteside (N. Ireland v Yugoslavia, June 17, 1982)	**17** years **41** days
Theo Walcott (England v Hungary, May 30, 2006)	**17** years **75** days
Johnny Lambie (Scotland v Ireland, March 20, 1886)	**17** years **92** days
Jimmy Holmes (Rep. of Ireland v Austria, May 30, 1971)	**17** years **200** days

Youngest England scorer: Wayne Rooney (17 years, 317 days) v Macedonia, Skopje, September 6, 2003.

Youngest England captains: Bobby Moore (v Czech., Bratislava, May 29, 1963), 22 years, 47 days; Michael Owen (v Paraguay, Anfield, April 17, 2002), 22 years, 117 days.

Youngest England players to reach 50 caps: Michael Owen (23 years, 6 months) v Slovakia at Middlesbrough, June 11, 2003; Bobby Moore (25 years, 7 months) v Wales at Wembley, November 16, 1966.

Youngest player in World Cup Final: Pele (Brazil) aged 17 years, 237 days v Sweden in Stockholm, June 12, 1958.

Youngest player to appear in World Cup Finals: Norman Whiteside (N. Ireland v Yugoslavia in Spain – June 17, 1982, age 17 years and 42 days.

Youngest First Division player: Derek Forster (Sunderland goalkeeper v Leicester City, August 22, 1964) aged 15 years, 185 days.

Youngest First Division scorer: At 16 years and 57 days, schoolboy Jason Dozzell (substitute after 30 minutes for Ipswich Town at home to Coventry City on February 4, 1984). Ipswich Town won 3-1 and Dozzell scored their third goal.
Youngest F.A. Premier League player: Matthew Briggs (Fulham sub. at Middlesbrough, May 13, 2007) aged 16 years and 65 days.
Youngest F.A. Premier League scorer: James Vaughan (Everton, home to Crystal Palace, April 10, 2005), 16 years, 271 days.
Youngest F.A. Premier League captain: Lee Cattermole (Middlesbrough away to Fulham, May 7, 2006) aged 18 years, 47 days.
Youngest player sent off in Premier League: Wayne Rooney (Everton, away to Birmingham City, December 26, 2002) aged 17 years, 59 days.
Youngest First Division hat-trick scorer: Alan Shearer, aged 17 years, 240 days, in Southampton's 4-2 home win v Arsenal (April 9, 1988) on his full debut. Previously, Jimmy Greaves (17 years, 309 days) with 4 goals for Chelsea at home to Portsmouth (7-4), Christmas Day, 1957.
Youngest to complete 100 Football League goals: Jimmy Greaves (20 years, 261 days) when he did so for Chelsea v Manchester City, November 19, 1960.
Youngest players in Football League: Albert Geldard (Bradford Park Avenue v Millwall, Div. 2, September 16, 1929) aged 15 years, 158 days; Ken Roberts (Wrexham v Bradford Park Avenue, Div. 3 North, September 1, 1951) also 15 years, 158 days.
Youngest Football League scorer: Ronnie Dix (for Bristol Rov. v Norwich City, Div. 3 South, March 3, 1928) aged 15 years, 180 days.
Youngest player in Scottish League: Goalkeeper Ronnie Simpson (Queens Park) aged 15 in 1946.
Youngest player in F.A. Cup: Andy Awford, Worcester City's England Schoolboy defender, aged 15 years, 88 days when he substituted in second half away to Boreham Wood (3rd. qual. round) on October 10, 1987.
Youngest player in F.A. Cup proper: Schoolboy Lee Holmes (15 years, 277 days) for Derby Co. away to Brentford in 3rd. Round on January 4, 2003.
Youngest Wembley Cup Final captain: Barry Venison (Sunderland v Norwich City, Milk Cup Final, March 24, 1985 – replacing suspended captain Shaun Elliott) – aged 20 years, 220 days.
Youngest F.A. Cup-winning captain: Bobby Moore (West Ham Utd., 1964, v Preston N.E.), aged 23 years, 20 days.
Youngest F.A. Cup Final captain: David Nish aged 21 years and 212 days old when he captained Leicester City against Manchester City at Wembley on April 26, 1969.
Youngest F.A. Cup Final player: Curtis Weston (Millwall sub. last 3 mins v Manchester Utd., 2004) aged 17 years, 119 days.
Youngest F.A. Cup Final scorer: Norman Whiteside (Manchester Utd. v Brighton & H.A. in 1983 replay at Wembley), aged 18 years, 19 days.
Youngest F.A. Cup Final managers: Stan Cullis, Wolves (33) v Leicester City, 1949; Steve Coppell, Crystal Palace (34) v Manchester Utd., 1990; Ruud Gullit, Chelsea (34) v Mid'bro', 1997.
Youngest player in Football League Cup: Kevin Davies (Chesterfield sub at West Ham Utd., 2nd Round, 2nd Leg on September 22, 1993) aged 16 years, 180 days.
Youngest Wembley scorer: Norman Whiteside (Manchester Utd. v Liverpool, Milk Cup Final, March 26, 1983) aged 17 years, 324 days.
Youngest Wembley Cup Final goalkeeper: Chris Woods (18 years, 125 days) for Nott'm Forest v Liverpool, League Cup Final on March 18, 1978.
Youngest Wembley F.A. Cup Final goalkeeper: Peter Shilton (19 years, 219 days) for Leicester City v Manchester City, April 26, 1969.
Youngest senior International at Wembley: Salomon Olembe (sub for Cameroon v England, November 15, 1997), aged 16 years, 342 days.
Youngest winning manager at Wembley: Roy McDonough, aged 33 years. 6 months, 24 days as player-manager of Colchester Utd., F.A. Trophy winners on May 10, 1992.
Youngest scorer in full International: Mohamed Kallon (Sierra Leone v Congo, African Nations Cup, April 22, 1995), reported as aged 15 years, 192 days.
Youngest player sent off in World Cup Final series: Rigobert Song (Cameroon v Brazil, in USA, June 1994) aged 17 years, 358 days.
Youngest F.A. Cup Final referee: Kevin Howley, of Middlesbrough, aged 35 when in charge of Wolves v Blackburn Rov., 1960.

Youngest player in England U-23 team: Duncan Edwards (v. Italy, Bologna, January 20, 1954), aged 17 years, 112 days.
Youngest player in England U-21 team: Theo Walcott (v Moldova, Ipswich, August 15, 2006), aged 17 years, 152 days.
Youngest player in Scotland U-21 team: Christian Dailly (v Romania, Hampden Park, Sept. 11, 1990), aged 16 years, 330 days.
Youngest player in senior football: Cameron Campbell Buchanan, Scottish-born outside right, aged 14 years, 57 days when he played for Wolves v W.B.A. in War-time League match, September 26, 1942.
Youngest player in peace-time senior match: Eamon Collins (Blackpool v Kilmarnock, Anglo-Scottish Cup quarter-final 1st. leg, September 9, 1980) aged 14 years, 323 days.
World's youngest player in top-division match: Centre-forward Fernando Rafael Garcia, aged 13, played for 23 minutes for Peruvian club Juan Aurich in 3-1 win against Estudiantes on May 19, 2001.
Oldest player to appear in Football League: New Brighton manager Neil McBain (51 years, 120 days) as emergency goalkeeper away to Hartlepool Utd. (Div. 3 North, March 15, 1947).
Other oldest post-war League players: Sir Stanley Matthews (Stoke City, 1965, 50 years, 5 days); Peter Shilton (Leyton Orient 1997, 47 years, 126 days); Dave Beasant (Brighton & H.A. 2003, 44 years, 46 days); Alf Wood (Coventry City, 1958, 43 years, 199 days); Tommy Hutchison (Swansea City, 1991, 43 years, 172 days).
Oldest Football League debutant: Andy Cunningham, for Newcastle Utd. at Leicester City (Div. 1) on February 2, 1929, aged 38 years, 2 days.
Oldest post-war debut in English League: Defender David Donaldson (35 years, 7 months, 23 days) for Wimbledon on entry to Football League (Div. 4) away to Halifax Town, August 20, 1977.
Oldest player to appear in First Division: Sir Stanley Matthews (Stoke City v Fulham, February 6, 1965), aged 50 years, 5 days – on that his last League appearance, the only 50-year-old ever to play in the top division.
Oldest players in Premier League: Goalkeepers John Burridge (Manchester City v Q.P.R., May 14, 1995), aged 43 years, 5 months, 11 days; Alec Chamberlain (Watford v Newcastle Utd., May 13, 2007) aged 42 years, 11 months, 23 days; Steve Ogrizovic (Coventry City v Sheffield Wed., May 6, 2000), aged 42 years, 7 months, 24 days; Neville Southall (Bradford City v Leeds Utd., March 12, 2000), aged 41 years, 5 months, 26 days. Outfield: Teddy Sheringham (West Ham Utd. v Manchester City, December 30, 2006), aged 40 years, 8 months, 28 days. Gordon Strachan (Coventry City v Derby Co., May 3, 1997), aged 40 years, 2 months, 24 days.
Oldest player for British professional club: John Ryan (owner-chairman of Conference club Doncaster Rov., played as substitute for last minute in 4–2 win at Hereford on April 26, 2003), aged 52 years, 11 months, 3 weeks.
Oldest F.A. Cup Final player: Walter (Billy) Hampson (Newcastle Utd. v Aston Villa on April 26, 1924), aged 41 years, 257 days.
Oldest F.A. Cup Final scorers: Bert Turner (Charlton Athletic v Derby Co., April 27, 1946) aged 36 years, 312 days. Scored for both sides. Teddy Sherringham (West Ham Utd. v Liverpool, May 13, 2006) aged 40 years, 41 days. Scored in penalty shoot-out.
Oldest F.A. Cup-winning team: Arsenal 1950 (average age 31 years, 2 months). Eight of the players were over 30, with the three oldest centre-half Leslie Compton 37, and skipper Joe Mercer and goalkeeper George Swindin, both 35.
Oldest World Cup-winning captain: Dino Zoff, Italy's goalkeeper v W. Germany in 1982 Final, aged 40 years, 92 days.
Oldest player capped by England: Stanley Matthews (v. Denmark, Copenhagen, May 15, 1957), aged 42 years, 103 days.
Oldest England scorer: Stanley Matthews (v N. Ireland, Belfast, October 6, 1956), aged 41 years, 248 days.
Oldest British International player: Billy Meredith (Wales v England at Highbury, March 15, 1920), aged 45 years, 229 days.
Oldest 'new caps': Goalkeeper Alexander Morten, aged 41 years, 113 days when earning his only England Cap against Scotland on March 8, 1873; Arsenal centre-half Leslie Compton, at 38 years, 64 days when he made his England debut in 4-2 win against

Wales at Sunderland on November 15, 1950. **For Scotland:** Goalkeeper Ronnie Simpson (Celtic) at 36 years, 186 days v England at Wembley, April 15, 1967.
Longest Football League career: This spanned 32 years and 10 months, by Stanley Matthews (Stoke City, Blackpool, Stoke City) from March 19, 1932 until February 6, 1965.
Smallest F.A. Cup-winning captain: 5ft. 4in. – Bobby Kerr (Sunderland v Leeds Utd., 1973).

SHIRT NUMBERING

Numbering players in Football League matches was made compulsory in 1939. Players wore numbered shirts (1-22) in the F.A. Cup Final as an experiment in 1933 (Everton 1-11 v Manchester City 12-22).

Squad numbers for players were introduced by the F.A. Premier League at the start of season 1993-4. They were optional in the Football League until made compulsory in 1999-2000.

Names on shirts: For first time, players wore names as well as numbers on shirts in League Cup and F.A. Cup Finals, 1993.

SUBSTITUTES

In **1965**, the Football League, by 39 votes to 10, agreed that **one substitute** be allowed for an injured player at any time during a League match. First substitute used in Football League: Keith Peacock (Charlton Athletic), away to Bolton Wand. in Div. 2, August 21, 1965.

Two substitutes per team were approved for the League (Littlewoods) Cup and F.A. Cup in season 1986-7 and two were permitted in the Football League for the first time in 1987-8.

Three substitutes (one a goalkeeper), two of which could be used, introduced by the Premier League for 1992-3. The Football League followed suit for 1993-4.

Three substitutes (one a goalkeeper) were allowed at the World Cup Finals for the first time at US '94.

Three substitutes (any position) introduced by Premier League and Football League in 1995-6.

First substitute to score in F.A. Cup Final: Eddie Kelly (Arsenal v Liverpool, 1971).

The **first recorded use of a substitute was in 1889** (Wales v Scotland at Wrexham on April 15) when Sam Gillam arrived late – although he was a Wrexham player – and Allen Pugh (Rhostellyn) was allowed to keep goal until he turned up. The match ended 0-0.

When Dickie Roose, the Welsh goalkeeper, was injured against England at Wrexham, March 16, 1908, Dai Davies (Bolton Wand.) was allowed to take his place as substitute. Thus Wales used 12 players. England won 7-1.

END OF WAGE LIMIT

Freedom from the maximum wage system – in force since the formation of the Football League in 1888 – was secured by the Professional Footballers' Association in 1961. About this time Italian clubs renewed overtures for the transfer of British stars and Fulham's **Johnny Haynes** became the first British player to earn £100 a week.

THE BOSMAN RULING

On December 15, 1995 the **European Court of Justice** ruled that clubs had no right to transfer fees for out-of-contract players, and the outcome of the 'Bosman case' irrevocably changed football's player-club relationship. It began in 1990, when the contract of 26-year-old **Jean-Marc Bosman**, a midfield player with FC Liege, Belgium, expired. French club Dunkirk wanted him but were unwilling to pay the £500,000 transfer fee, so Bosman was compelled to remain with Liege. He responded with a lawsuit against his club and UEFA on the grounds of 'restriction of trade', and after five years at various court levels the European Court of Justice ruled not only in favour of Bosman but of all professional footballers.

The end of restrictive labour practices revolutionised the system. It led to a proliferation of transfers, rocketed the salaries of elite players who, backed by an increasing army of agents, found themselves in a vastly improved bargaining position as they moved from team to team, league to league, nation to nation. Removing the limit on the number of foreigners clubs could field brought an increasing ratio of such signings, not least in England and Scotland.

Bosman's one-man stand opened the way for footballers to become millionaires, but ended his own career. All he received for his legal conflict was 16 million Belgian francs (£312,000) in compensation, a testimonial of poor reward and martyrdom as the man who did most to change the face of football.

INTERNATIONAL SHOCK RESULTS

1950 U.S.A. 1, England 0 (World Cup Finals).
1953 England 3, Hungary 6 (International friendly).
1954 Hungary 7, England 1 (International friendly)
1966 North Korea 1, Italy 0 (World Cup Finals).
1982 Spain 0, Northern Ireland 1; Algeria 2, West Germany 1 (World Cup Finals).
1990 Cameroon 1, Argentina 0; Scotland 0, Costa Rica 1; Sweden 1 Costa Rica 2 (World Cup Finals).
1990 Faroe Islands 1, Austria 0 (European Championship qualifying).
1992 Denmark 2, Germany 0 (European Championship Final).
1993 U.S.A. 2, England 0 (U.S. Cup tournament).
1993 Argentina 0, Colombia 5 (World Cup qualifying).
1993 France 2, Israel 3 (World Cup qualifying).
1994 Bulgaria 2, Germany 1 (World Cup Finals).
1994 Moldova 3, Wales 2; Georgia 5 Wales 0 (European Championship qualifying).
1995 Belarus 1, Holland 0 (European Championship qualifying).
1996 Nigeria 4, Brazil 3 (Olympic Games).
1998 U.S.A. 1, Brazil 0 (Concacaf Gold Cup).
1998 Croatia 3, Germany 0 (World Cup Finals).
2000 Scotland 0, Australia 2 (International friendly).
2001 Australia 1, France 0; Australia 1, Brazil 0 (Confederations Cup).
2001 Honduras 2, Brazil 0 (Copa America).
2001 Germany 1 England 5 (World Cup qualifying).
2002 France 0 Senegal 1; South Korea 2,Italy 1 (World Cup Finals).
2003: England 1, Australia 3 (Friendly international).
2004: Portugal 0, Greece 1 (European Championship Final).
2005: Northern Ireland 1, England 0 (World Cup qualifying).

GREAT RECOVERIES

On December 21, 1957, Charlton Athletic were losing 5-1 against Huddersfield Town (Div. 2) at The Valley with only 28 minutes left, and from the 15th minute, had been reduced to ten men by injury, but they won 7-6, with left-winger Johnny Summers scoring five goals. Huddersfield Town (managed by Bill Shankly) remain the only team to score six times in a League match and lose.

Among other notable comebacks: on November 12, 1904 (Div. 1), Sheffield Wed. were losing 0-5 at home to Everton, but drew 5-5. At Anfield on December 4, 1909 (Div.1), Liverpool trailed 2-5 to Newcastle Utd. at half-time, then won 6-5. On Boxing Day, 1927, in Div. 3 South, Northampton Town won 6-5 at home to Luton Town after being 1-5 down at half-time. On September 22, 1984 (Div. 1), Q.P.R. drew 5-5 at home to Newcastle Utd. after trailing 0-4 at half-time. On April 12, 1993 (Div. 1) Swindon Town were 1-4 down at Birmingham City with 30 minutes left, but won 6-4.

Other astonishing turnabouts in Div.1 include: Grimsby Town (3-5 down) won 6-5 at W.B.A. on Apr. 30, 1932; and Derby Co. beat Manchester Utd. 5-4 (from 1-4) on Sept. 5, 1936.

With 5 minutes to play, Ipswich Town were losing 3-0 at Barnsley (Div. 1, March 9, 1996), but drew 3-3.

On Sunday, Jan. 19, 1997 (Div. 1), Q.P.R. were 0-4 down away to Port Vale at half-time and still trailing 1-4 with 5 minutes left. They drew 4-4.

Tranmere Rov. retrieved a 3-0 half-time deficit to beat Southampton 4-3 in an F.A. Cup fifth round replay at home on Feb. 20, 2001.

Premier League comebacks: Jan. 4, 1994 – Liverpool were 3 down after 24 mins. at home to Manchester Utd., drew 3-3; Nov. 8, 1997 – Derby Co. led 3-0 after 33 mins. at Elland Road, but Leeds Utd. won 4-3 with last-minute goal; Sept. 29, 2001 – Manchester Utd. won 5-3 at Tottenham after trailing 3-0 at half-time.

Season 2003-04 produced some astonishing turn-rounds. **Premiership** (Oct. 25): In bottom-two clash at Molineux, Wolves were 3 down at half-time v Leicester City, but won 4-3. Feb. 22: Leicester City, down to 10 men, rallied from 3-1 down at Tottenham to lead 4-3. Result 4-4.

First Division (Nov. 8): West Ham Utd. led 3-0 after 18 mins at home to WBA, but lost 4-3.

F.A. Cup 4th **Round replay** (Feb. 4): At half-time, Tottenham led 3-0 at home to Manchester City, but City, reduced to 10 men, won 4-3.

In the 1966 World Cup quarter-final (July 23) at Goodison Park, North Korea led Portugal 3-0, but Eusebio scored 4 times to give Portugal a 5-3 win.

Liverpool produced the most extraordinary recovery in the 50-year history of **European Cup Finals**. In the **Champions League Final** against AC Milan in Istanbul on May 25, 2005, they were 0-3 down at half-time, drew 3-3 after extra time and then won the trophy for the fifth time, 3-2 on penalties.

On November 19, 2005 **Leeds Utd.** retrieved a 3-0 deficit against Southampton in the final 20 minutes to win their **Championship** game 4-3.

MATCHES OFF

Worst day for postponements: Feb. 9, 1963, when 57 League fixtures in England and Scotland were frozen off. Only 7 Football League matches took place, and the entire Scottish programme was wiped out

Worst other weather-hit days:

Jan. 12, 1963 and Feb. 2, 1963 – on both those Saturdays, only 4 out of 44 Football League matches were played.

Jan. 1, 1979 – 43 out of 46 Football League fixtures postponed.

Jan. 17, 1987 – 37 of 45 scheduled Football League fixtures postponed; only 2 Scottish matches survived.

Feb. 8-9, 1991 – only 4 of the week-end's 44 Barclays League matches survived the freeze-up (4 of the postponements were on Friday night). In addition, 11 Scottish League matches were off.

Jan. 27, 1996 – 44 Cup and League matches in England and Scotland were frozen off. The ten fixtures played comprised 3 F.A. Cup (4th. Round), 1 in Div. 1, 5 in Scottish Cup (3rd. Round), 1 in Scottish Div. 2.

Fewest matches left on one day by postponements was during the Second World War – Feb. 3, 1940 when, because of snow, ice and fog only one out of 56 regional league fixtures took place. It resulted Plymouth Argyle 10, Bristol City 3.

The Scottish Cup second round tie between Inverness Thistle and Falkirk in season 1978-9 was **postponed 29 times** because of snow and ice. First put off on Jan. 6, it was eventually played on Feb. 22. Falkirk won 4-0.

Pools Panel's busiest days: Jan. 17, 1987 and Feb. 9, 1991 – on both dates they gave their verdict on 48 postponed coupon matches.

FEWEST 'GAMES OFF'

Season 1947-8 was the best since the war for English League fixtures being played to schedule. Only **six** were postponed.

LONGEST SEASON

The latest that League football has been played in a season was **June 7, 1947** (six weeks after the F.A. Cup Final). The season was extended because of mass postponements caused by bad weather in mid-winter.

The latest the F.A. Cup competition has ever been completed was in season 1981-2, when Tottenham beat Q.P.R. 1-0 in a Final replay at Wembley on May 27.

Worst winter hold-up was in season 1962-3. The Big Freeze began on Boxing Day and lasted until March, with nearly 500 first-class matches postponed. The F.A. Cup 3rd. Round was the longest on record – it began with only three out of 32 ties playable on January 5 and ended 66 days and 261 postponements later on March 11. The Lincoln City-Coventry City tie was put off 15 times. The Pools Panel was launched that winter, on January 26, 1963.

HOTTEST DAYS

The Nationwide League kicked off season 2003-04 on August 9 with pitch temperatures of 102 degrees recorded at Luton Town v Rushden & Diamonds and Bradford City v Norwich City.

On the following day, there was a pitch temperature of 100 degrees for the Community Shield match between Manchester Utd. and Arsenal at Cardiff's Millennium Stadium.

FOOTBALL ASSOCIATION SECRETARIES/ CHIEF EXECUTIVES

Ebenezer Morley (1863-66), **Robert Willis** (1866-68), **R.G. Graham** (1868-70), **Charles Alcock** (1870-95, paid from 1887), 1895-1934 **Sir Frederick Wall**, 1934-62 **Sir Stanley Rous**, 1962-73 **Denis Follows**, 1973-89 **Ted Croker** (latterly chief executive), 1989-99 **Graham Kelly** (chief executive), 2000-02 **Adam Crozier** (chief executive), 2003-04 **Mark Palios** (chief executive). Since January 2005 **Brian Barwick** (chief executive).

FOOTBALL'S SPONSORS

Football League: Canon 1983-6; Today Newspaper 1986-7; Barclays 1987-93; Endsleigh Insurance 1993-6; Nationwide Building Society 1996-2004; Coca-Cola from 2004.

League Cup: Milk Cup 1982-6; Littlewoods 1987-90; Rumbelows 1991-2; Coca-Cola 1993-8; Worthington 1998-2003; Carling from 2003.

Premier League: Carling 1993-2001; Barclaycard 2001-04; Barclays from 2004.

F.A. Cup: Littlewoods 1994-8; AXA 1998-2002; E.ON from 2006.

SOCCER HEADQUARTERS

Football Association: 25 Soho Square, London W1D 4FA (moved from Lancaster Gate, London W2, September 2000).

F.A. Premier League: 11 Connaught Place, London W1 2ET.

Football League: Edward VII Quay, Navigation Way, Preston PR2 2YF. **London Office:** 11 Connaught Place, London W2 2ET.

Professional Footballers' Association: 2 Oxford Court, Bishopsgate, Manchester M2 3WQ.

Scottish Football Association: Hampden Park, Glasgow G42 9AY.

Scottish Premier League: National Stadium, Hampden Park, Glasgow G42 9EB.

Scottish Football League: Hampden Park, Glasgow G42 9EB.

Irish Football Association: 20 Windsor Avenue, Belfast BT9 6EG.

Irish Football League: 96 University Street, Belfast BT7 1HE.

League of Ireland: 80 Merrion Square, Dublin 2.

Football Association of Ireland: 80 Merrion Square, Dublin 2.

Welsh Football Association: 3 Westgate Street, Cardiff CF1 1DD.

Football Conference: Collingwood House, Schooner Court, Crossways, Dartford, Kent DAZ 6QQ.

FIFA: P.O. Box 85, 8030 Zurich, Switzerland.

UEFA: Route de Geneve, CH-1260, Nyon, Geneva, Switzerland.

NEW HOMES OF SOCCER

Newly-constructed League grounds in England since the war: 1946 Hull City (Boothferry Park); 1950 Port Vale (Vale Park); 1955 Southend Utd. (Roots Hall); 1988 Scunthorpe Utd. (Glanford Park); 1990 Walsall (Bescot Stadium); 1990 Wycombe Wand. (Adams Park); 1992 Chester City (Deva Stadium, Bumpers Lane); 1993 Millwall (New Den); 1994 Huddersfield Town (Alfred McAlpine Stadium, Kirklees); 1994 Northampton Town (Sixfields Stadium); 1995 Middlesbrough (Riverside Stadium); 1997 Bolton Wand. (Reebok Stadium); 1997 Derby Co. (Pride Park); 1997 Stoke City (Britannia Stadium); 1997 Sunderland (Stadium of Light); 1998 Reading (Madejski Stadium); 1999 Wigan Athletic (JJB Stadium); 2001 Southampton (St. Mary's Stadium); 2001 Oxford Utd. (Kassam Stadium); 2002 Leicester City (Walkers Stadium); 2002 Hull City (Kingston Communications Stadium); 2003 Manchester City (City of Manchester Stadium); 2003 Darlington (New Stadium); 2005 Coventry City (Ricoh Arena); Swansea City (Stadium of Swansea, Morfa); 2006 Arsenal (Emirates Stadium); 2007 Milton Keynes Dons (Stadium: MK); Shrewsbury Town (New Meadow).

• Wycombe Wand. now Causeway Stadium; Chester City now Saunders Honda Stadium; Huddersfield Town now Galpharm Stadium; Swansea City now Liberty Stadium; Walsall now Banks's Stadium.

GROUND-SHARING

Crystal Palace and **Charlton Athletic** (Selhurst Park, 1985-91); **Bristol Rov.** and **Bath City** (Twerton Park, Bath, 1986-96); **Partick Thistle** and **Clyde** (Firhill Park, Glasgow, 1986-91; in seasons 1990-1, 1991-2 **Chester City** shared **Macclesfield Town's** ground (Moss Rose). **Crystal Palace** and **Wimbledon** shared Selhurst Park, from season 1991-2, when **Charlton Athletic** (tenants) moved to rent Upton Park from **West Ham Utd. Clyde** moved to Douglas Park, **Hamilton Academicals'** home, in 1991-2. **Stirling Albion** shared **Stenhousemuir's** ground, Ochilview Park, in 1992-3. In 1993-4, **Clyde** shared **Partick's** home until moving to Cumbernauld. In 1994-5, **Celtic** shared Hampden Park with **Queen's Park** (while Celtic Park was redeveloped); **Hamilton** shared **Partick's** ground. **Airdrie** shared **Clyde's** Broadwood Stadium. **Bristol Rov.** left Bath City's ground at the start of season 1996-7, sharing Bristol Rugby Club's Memorial Ground. **Clydebank** shared **Dumbarton's** Boghead Park from 1996-7 until renting **Greenock Morton's** Cappielow Park in season 1999-2000. **Brighton** shared **Gillingham's** ground in seasons 1997-8, 1998-9. **Fulham** shared Q.P.R.'s home at Loftus Road in seasons 2002–3, 2003–4, returning to Craven Cottage in August 2004.

Inverness Caledonian Thistle moved to share Aberdeen's Pittodrie Stadium in 2004-5 after being promoted to the SPL.

ARTIFICIAL TURF

Q.P.R. were the first British club to install an artificial pitch, in 1981. They were followed by **Luton Town** in 1985, and **Oldham Athletic** and **Preston N.E. in 1986**. Q.P.R. reverted to grass in 1988, as did Luton Town and promoted Oldham Athletic in season 1991-2 (when artificial pitches were banned in Div. 1). **Preston N.E.** were the last Football League club playing 'on plastic' in 1993-4, and their Deepdale ground was restored to grass for the start of 1994-5.

Stirling Albion were the **first Scottish club** to play on plastic, in season 1987-8.

DOUBLE RUNNERS-UP

There have been nine instances of clubs finishing **runner-up in both the League Championship and F.A. Cup in the same season**: 1928 Huddersfield Town; 1932 Arsenal; 1939 Wolves; 1962 Burnley; 1965 and 1970 Leeds Utd.; 1986 Everton; 1995 Manchester Utd; 2001 Arsenal.

CORNER-KICK RECORDS

Not a single corner-kick was recorded when **Newcastle Utd.** drew 0-0 at home to **Portsmouth** (Div.1) on December 5, 1931.

The record for **most corners** in a match for one side is believed to be **Sheffield Utd.'s 28** to West Ham Utd.'s 1 in Div.2 at Bramall Lane on October 14, 1989. For all their pressure, Sheffield Utd. lost 2-0.

Nott'm. Forest led Southampton 22-2 on corners (Premier League, Nov. 28, 1992) but lost the match 1-2.

Tommy Higginson (Brentford, 1960s) once passed back to his own goalkeeper from a corner kick.

When **Wigan Athletic** won 4–0 at home to Cardiff City (Div. 2) on February 16, 2002, all four goals were headed in from corners taken by N. Ireland International **Peter Kennedy**.

Steve Staunton (Rep. of Ireland) is believed to be the only player to score direct from a corner in **two** Internationals.

NO OFFSIDE

Not one offside decision was given in the **Brazil-Turkey** World Cup semi-final at Saitama, Japan, on June 26, 2002.

SACKED AT HALF-TIME

Leyton Orient sacked **Terry Howard** on his 397th. appearance for the club – at half-time in a Second Division home defeat against Blackpool (Feb. 7, 1995) for 'an unacceptable performance'. He was fined two weeks' wages, given a free transfer and moved to Wycombe Wanderers.

Bobby Gould resigned as **Peterborough United's** head coach at half-time in their 1-0 defeat in the LDV Vans Trophy 1st Round at Bristol City on Sept. 29, 2004.

Harald Schumacher, former Germany goalkeeper, was sacked as Fortuna Koln coach when they were two down at half-time against Waldhof Mannheim (Dec. 15, 1999). They lost 5-1.

MOST GAMES BY 'KEEPER FOR ONE CLUB

Alan Knight made 683 League appearances for Portsmouth, over 23 seasons (1978-2000), a record for a goalkeeper at one club. The previous holder was Peter Bonetti with 600 League games for Chelsea (20 seasons, 1960-79).

PLAYED TWO GAMES ON SAME DAY

Jack Kelsey played full-length matches for both club and country on Wed., November 26, 1958. In the afternoon he kept goal for Wales in a 2-2 draw against England at Villa Park, and he then drove to Highbury to help Arsenal win 3-1 in a prestigious floodlit friendly against Juventus.

On the same day, winger **Danny Clapton** played for England (against Wales and Kelsey) and then in part of Arsenal's match against Juventus.

On November 11, 1987, **Mark Hughes** played for Wales against Czechoslovakia (European Championship) in Prague, then flew to Munich and went on as substitute that night in a winning Bayern Munich team, to whom he was on loan from Barcelona.

On February 16, 1993 goalkeeper **Scott Howie** played in Scotland's 3-0 U-21 win v Malta at Tannadice Park, Dundee (k.o. 1.30pm) and the same evening played in Clyde's 2-1 home win v Queen of South (Div. 2).

Ryman League **Hornchurch**, faced by end-of-season fixture congestion, played **two matches on the same night** (May 1, 2001). They lost 2-1 at home to Ware and drew 2-2 at Clapton.

RECORD CLUB LOSSES

Fulham, brokered by Harrods owner Mohamed Al Fayed, made British football's then record loss of £23.3m. in the year to June 30, 2001 (in which they won promotion to the Premiership as Div. 1 Champions). The club's debts rose to £61.7m. Previous highest loss was £18.7m. by **Newcastle Utd.** in 2000. In September 2002, **Leeds Utd.**

reported a loss of £33.9m. for the year ending June 30. It took their debts to £77m. A year later, in October 2003, **Leeds** declared a loss of £49.5m. (debts £78m). **Chelsea** made losses of £87.8m. in seasons 2003-4 (their first under the ownership of Roman Abramovich) and £140m. in 2004-5.

FIRST 'MATCH OF THE DAY'

BBC TV (recorded highlights): Liverpool 3, Arsenal 2 on August 22, 1964. **First complete match to be televised:** Arsenal 3, Everton 2 on August 29, 1936. **First League match televised in colour:** Liverpool 2, West Ham Utd. 0 on November 15, 1969.

'MATCH OF THE DAY' – BIGGEST SCORES

Football League: Tottenham 9, Bristol Rov. 0 (Div. 2, 1977-8). **Premier League:** Nott'm Forest 1, Manchester Utd. 8 (1998-9).

FIRST COMMENTARY ON RADIO

Arsenal 1, **Sheffield Utd.** 1 (Div. 1) broadcast on BBC, January 22, 1927.

OLYMPIC SOCCER WINNERS

1908 Great Britain (in London); **1912** Great Britain (Stockholm); **1920** Belgium (Antwerp); **1924** Uruguay (Paris); **1928** Uruguay (Amsterdam); **1932** No soccer in Los Angeles Olympics.

1936 Italy (Berlin); **1948** Sweden (London); **1952** Hungary (Helsinki); **1956** USSR (Melbourne); **1960** Yugoslavia (Rome); **1964** Hungary (Tokyo); **1968** Hungary (Mexico); **1972** Poland (Munich); **1976** E. Germany (Montreal); **1980** Czechoslovakia (Moscow); **1984** France (Los Angeles); **1988** USSR (Seoul); **1992** Spain (Barcelona); **1996** Nigeria (Atlanta); **2000** Cameroon (Sydney); **2004** Argentina (Athens).

Highest scorer in Final tournament: Ferenc Bene (Hungary) 12 goals, 1964.

Record crowd for Olympic Soccer Final: 108,800 (France v Brazil, Los Angeles 1984).

MOST AMATEUR CUP WINS

Bishop Auckland set the F.A. Amateur Cup record with 10 wins, and in 1957 became the only club to carry off the trophy in three successive seasons. The competition was discontinued after the Final on April 20, 1974. (Bishop's Stortford 4, Ilford 1, at Wembley).

FOOTBALL FOUNDATION

This was formed (May 2000) to replace the **Football Trust**, which had been in existence since 1975 as an initiative of the Pools companies to provide financial support at all levels, from schools football to safety and ground improvement work throughout the game.

SEVEN-FIGURE TESTIMONIALS

The first was **Sir Alex Ferguson's** at Old Trafford on October 11, 1999, when a full-house of 54,842 saw a Rest of the World team beat Manchester Utd. 4-2. United's manager pledged that a large percentage of the estimated £1m. receipts would go to charity.

Estimated receipts of £1m. and over came from testimonials for **Denis Irwin** (Manchester Utd.) against Manchester City at Old Trafford on August 16, 2000 (45,158); **Tom Boyd** (Celtic) against Manchester Utd. at Celtic Park on May 15, 2001 (57,000) and **Ryan Giggs** (Manchester Utd.) against Celtic on August 1, 2001 (66,967).

Tony Adams' second testimonial (1-1 v Celtic on May 13, 2002) two nights after Arsenal completed the Double, was watched by 38,021 spectators at Highbury. Of £1m. receipts, he donated £500,000 to Sporting Chance, the charity that helps sportsmen/women with drink, drug, gambling problems.

Sunderland and a Republic of Ireland XI drew 0-0 in front of 35,702 at the Stadium of Light on May 14, 2002. The beneficiary, **Niall Quinn**, donated his testimonial proceeds, estimated at £1m., to children's hospitals in Sunderland and Dublin, and to homeless children in Africa and Asia.

A record testimonial crowd of 69,591 for **Roy Keane** at Old Trafford on May 9, 2006 netted more than £2m. for charities in Dublin, Cork and Manchester. Manchester United beat Celtic 1-0, with Keane playing for both teams.

Alan Shearer's testimonial on May 11, 2006, watched by a crowd of 52,275 at St James' Park, raised more than £1m. The club's record scorer, in his farewell match, came off the bench in stoppage time to score the penalty that gave Newcastle a 3-2 win over Celtic. Total proceeds from his testimonial events, £1.64m., were donated to 14 charities in the north-east.

WHAT IT USED TO COST

Minimum admission to League football was one shilling in 1939. After the war, it was increased to 1s. 3d. in 1946; 1s. 6d. in 1951; 1s. 9d. in 1952; 2s. in 1955; 2s. 6d. in 1960; 4s. in 1965; 5s. in 1968; 6s. in 1970; and 8s. (40p) in 1972. After that, the fixed minimum charge was dropped.

Wembley's first Cup Final programme in 1923 cost three pence (1¼p in today's money). The programme for the 'farewell' F.A. Cup Final in May, 2000 was priced £10.

WHAT THEY USED TO EARN

In the 1930s, First Division players were on £8 a week (£6 in close season) plus bonuses of £2 win, £1 draw. The maximum wage went up to £12 when football resumed post-war in 1946 and had reached £20 by the time the limit was abolished in 1961.

EUROPEAN TROPHY WINNERS

European Cup: 9 Real Madrid; **7** AC Milan; **5** Liverpool; **4** Ajax; Bayern Munich; **2** Benfica, Inter Milan, Juventus, Manchester Utd., Nott'm. Forest, FC Porto; **1** Aston Villa, Borussia Dortmund, Celtic, Feyenoord, Hamburg, Marseille, PSV Eindhoven, Red Star Belgrade, Steaua Bucharest.

Cup-Winners' Cup: 4 Barcelona; **2** Anderlecht, Chelsea, Dynamo Kiev, AC Milan; **1** Aberdeen, Ajax Amsterdam, Arsenal, Atletico Madrid, Bayern Munich, Borussia Dortmund, Dynamo Tbilisi, Everton, Fiorentina, Hamburg SV, Juventus, Lazio, Magdeburg, Manchester City, Manchester Utd., Mechelen, Paris St. Germain, Parma, Rangers, Real Zaragoza, Sampdoria, Slovan Bratislava, Sporting Lisbon, Tottenham, Valencia, Werder Bremen, West Ham Utd.

UEFA Cup: 3 Barcelona, Inter Milan, Juventus, Liverpool, Valencia; **2** Borussia Moenchengladbach, Feyenoord, Gothenburg, Leeds Utd., Parma, Real Madrid, Sevilla, Tottenham; **1** Ajax, Anderlecht, Arsenal, Bayer Leverkusen, Bayern Munich, Dynamo Zagreb, Eintracht Frankfurt, PSV Eindhoven, Ferencvaros, Ipswich Town, Napoli, Newcastle Utd., Real Zaragoza, Roma, Schalke, Galatasaray, FC Porto, CSKA Moscow.

- The Champions League was introduced into the European Cup in 1992-3 to counter the threat of a European Super League.

BRITAIN'S 31 TROPHIES IN EUROPE

Liverpool's success in the 2004-05 Champions League/European Cup took the number of **British** club triumphs in European Football to 31:

European Cup (11)
1967 Celtic
1968 Manchester Utd.
1977 Liverpool
1978 Liverpool
1979 Nott'm. Forest
1980 Nott'm. Forest
1981 Liverpool

Cup-Winners' Cup (10)
1963 Tottenham
1965 West Ham Utd.
1970 Manchester City
1971 Chelsea
1972 Rangers
1983 Aberdeen
1985 Everton

Fairs/UEFA Cup (10)
1968 Leeds Utd.
1969 Newcastle Utd.
1970 Arsenal
1971 Leeds Utd.
1972 Tottenham
1973 Liverpool
1976 Liverpool

1982 Aston Villa
1984 Liverpool
1999 Manchester Utd.
2005 Liverpool

1991 Manchester Utd.
1994 Arsenal
1998 Chelsea

1981 Ipswich Town
1984 Tottenham
2001 Liverpool

END OF CUP-WINNERS' CUP

The **European Cup-Winners' Cup**, inaugurated in 1960-61, terminated with the 1999 final. The competition merged into a revamped, 121-club **UEFA Cup**.

From its inception in 1955, the **European Cup** comprised only championship-winning clubs until 1998-9, when selected runners-up were introduced. Further expansion came in 1999-2000 with the inclusion of clubs finishing third in certain leagues and fourth in 2002.

EUROPEAN CLUB COMPETITIONS – SCORING RECORDS

European Cup – Record aggregate: 18-0 by Benfica v Dudelange (Lux) (8-0a, 10-0h), prelim. round, 1965-6.

Record single-match score: 12-0 by Feyenoord v KR Reykjavik (Ice), 1st. round, 1st. leg, 1969-70 (aggregate was 16-0).

Champions League – highest match aggregates: 11 goals – Monaco 8, Deportivo La Coruna 3 (Nov. 5, 2003); 9 goals – Paris St. Germain 7, Rosenborg 2 (Oct. 24. 2000).

Cup-Winners' Cup – *Record aggregate: 21-0 by Chelsea v Jeunesse Hautcharage (Lux) (8-0a, 13-0h), 1st. round, 1971-2.

Record single-match score: 16-1 by Sporting Lisbon v Apoel Nicosia, 2nd. round, 1st. leg, 1963-4 (aggregate was 18-1).

UEFA Cup (prev. Fairs Cup) – *Record aggregate: 21-0 by Feyenoord v US Rumelange (Lux) (9-0h, 12-0a), 1st. round, 1972-3.

Record single-match score: 14-0 by Ajax Amsterdam v Red Boys (Lux) 1st. round, 2nd leg, 1984-5 (aggregate also 14-0).

Record British score in Europe: 13-0 by **Chelsea** at home to Jeunesse Hautcharage (Lux) in Cup-Winners' Cup 1st. round, 2nd. leg, 1971-2. Chelsea's overall 21-0 win in that tie is highest aggregate by British club in Europe.

Individual scoring record for European tie (over two legs): **10 goals** (6 home, 4 away) by **Kiril Milanov** for Levski Spartak in 19-3 agg. win CWC 1st round v Lahden Reipas, 1976-7. Next highest: **8 goals** by **Jose Altafini** for AC Milan v US Luxembourg (European Cup, prelim. round, 1962-3, agg. 14-0) and by **Peter Osgood** for Chelsea v Jeunesse Hautcharage (Cup-Winners' Cup, 1st. round 1971-2, agg. 21-0). Altafini and Osgood each scored 5 goals at home, 3 away.

Individual single-match scoring record in European competition: **6** goals by **Mascarenhas** for Sporting Lisbon in 16-1 Cup-Winner's Cup 2nd. round, 1st. leg win v Apoel, 1963-4; **6** by **Lothar Emmerich** for Borussia Dortmund in 8-0 CWC 1st. round, 2nd. leg win v Floriana 1965-6; **6** by **Kiril Milanov** for Levski Spartak in 12-2 CWC 1st. round, 1st. leg win v Lahden Reipas, 1976-7.

Most goals in single European campaign: **15** by **Jurgen Klinsmann** for Bayern Munich (UEFA Cup 1995-6).

Most goals by British player in European competition: **30** by **Peter Lorimer** (Leeds Utd., in 9 campaigns).

Most European Cup goals by individual player: **49** by **Alfredo di Stefano** in 58 apps. for Real Madrid (1955-64).

(*Joint record European aggregate)

First European 'Treble': Clarence Seedorf became the first player to win the European Cup with three clubs: Ajax in 1995, Real Madrid in 1998 and AC Milan in 2003.

EUROPEAN FOOTBALL – BIG RECOVERIES

In the most astonishing Final in the 51-year history of the **European Cup, Liverpool** became the first club to win it from a 3-0 deficit when they beat AC Milan 3-2 on penalties after a 3-3 draw in Istanbul on May 25, 2005. Liverpool's fifth triumph in the competition meant that they would keep the trophy.

The following season, **Middlesbrough** twice recovered from three-goal aggregate deficits in the **UEFA Cup**, beating Basle 4-3 in the quarter finals and Steaua Bucharest by the same scoreline in the semi-finals.

Only four clubs have survived a **4-goal** deficit in any of the European club competitions after the first leg had been completed:

1961-2 (Cup-Winners' Cup 1st. Rd.): Leixoes (Portugal) beat Chaux de Fonds (Luxembourg) 7-6 on agg. (lost 2-6a, won 5-0h).

1962-3 (Fairs Cup 2nd. Rd.): Valencia (Spain) beat **Dunfermline** 1-0 in play-off in Lisbon after 6-6 agg. (Valencia won 4-0h, lost 2-6a).

1984-5 (UEFA Cup 2nd. Rd.): Partizan Belgrade beat **Q.P.R.** on away goals (lost 2-6 away, at Highbury, won 4-0 home).

1985-6 (UEFA Cup 3rd. Rd.): Real Madrid beat Borussia Moenchengladbach on away goals (lost 1-5a, won 4-0h) and went on to win competition.

In the **Champions League** quarter-final, 2003-04, Deportivo La Coruna lost the first leg 4-1 away to Inter Milan, then won the return match 4-0 to go through 5-4 on agg. This was the first instance in the Champions League of a team over-turning a 3-goal deficit.

In the **European Cup**, there are eight instances of clubs reaching the next round after **arrears of three goals** in the first leg:

1958-9 (Prel. Rd.) Schalke beat KB Copenhagen (0-3, 5-2, 3-1).
1965-6 (Q-final) Partizan Belgrade beat Sparta Prague (1-4, 5-0).
1970-1 (S-final) Panathinaikos beat Red Star Belgrade on away goal (1-4, 3-0).
1975-6 (2nd. Rd.) Real Madrid beat **Derby Co.** (1-4, 5-1).
1985-6 (S-final) Barcelona beat IFK Gothenburg on pens. (0-3, 3-0).
1988-9 (1st. Rd.) Werder Bremen beat Dynamo Berlin (0-3, 5-0).
1988-9 (2nd. Rd.) Galatasaray (Turkey) beat Neuchatel Xamax (Switz.) (0-3, 5-0).
1992-3 (1st. Rd.) **Leeds Utd.** beat VfB Stuttgart 2-1 in play-off in Barcelona. Over two legs, VfB won on away goal (3-0h, 1-4 away) but a third match was ordered because they broke 'foreigners' rule in team selection.

In the **Cup-Winners' Cup**, six clubs survived a **3-goal** deficit:

1963-4 (Q-final) Sporting Lisbon beat **Manchester Utd.** (1-4, 5-0).
1963-4 (S-final) MTK Budapest beat **Celtic** (0-3, 4-0).
1978-9 (2nd. Rd.) Barcelona beat Anderlecht on pens. (0-3, 3-0).
1980-1 (1st. Rd.) Carl Zeiss Jena beat AS Roma (0-3, 4-0).
1984-5 (Q-final) Rapid Vienna beat Dynamo Dresden (0-3, 5-0).
1989-90 (1st. Rd.) Grasshoppers (Switz.) beat Slovan Bratislava (0-3, 4-0).

In the **Fairs Cup/UEFA Cup**, there have been more than 20 occasions when clubs have survived a deficit of **3 goals**, the most notable example being the 1988 UEFA Cup Final, which Bayer Leverkusen won 3-2 on pens., having lost the first leg 0-3 away to Espanol and won the return 3-0 to level the aggregate.

Two Scottish clubs have won a European tie from a 3-goal, first leg deficit: **Kilmarnock** 0-3, 5-1 v Eintracht Frankfurt (Fairs Cup 1st. Round, 1964-5); **Hibernian** 1-4, 5-0 v Napoli (Fairs Cup 2nd. Round, 1967-8).

English clubs have three times gone out of the **UEFA Cup** after leading 3-0 from the first leg: 1975-6 (2nd. Rd.) **Ipswich Town** lost 3-4 on agg. to Bruges; 1976-7 (Q-final) **Q.P.R.** lost on pens. to AEK Athens after 3-3 agg; 1977-8 (3rd. Rd.) **Ipswich Town** lost on pens. to Barcelona after 3-3 agg.

HEAVIEST ENGLISH-CLUB DEFEATS IN EUROPE

(Single-leg scores)

European Cup: Artmedia Bratislava 5, Celtic 0 (2nd. Q. Rd.), July 2005 (agg. 5-4); Ajax 5, Liverpool 1 (2nd. Rd.), Dec. 1966 (agg. 7-3); Real Madrid 5, Derby Co. 1 (2nd. Rd.), Nov. 1975 (agg. 6-5).

Cup-Winners' Cup: Sporting Lisbon 5, Manchester Utd. 0 (Q-final), Mar. 1964 (agg. 6-4).

Fairs/UEFA Cup: Bayern Munich 6, Coventry City 1 (2nd. Rd.), Oct. 1970 (agg. 7-3). Combined London team lost 6-0 (agg. 8-2) in first Fairs Cup Final in 1958. Barcelona 5, Chelsea 0 in Fairs Cup Semi-final play-off, 1966, in Barcelona (after 2-2 agg.).

SHOCK ENGLISH-CLUB DEFEATS

1968-69 (E. Cup, 1st. Rd.): Manchester City beaten by Fenerbahce, 1-2 agg.
1971-72 (CWC, 2nd. Rd.): Chelsea beaten by Atvidaberg on away goals.
1993-94 (E. Cup, 2nd. Rd.): Manchester Utd. beaten by Galatasaray on away goals.
1994-95 (UEFA Cup, 1st. Rd.): Blackburn Rov. beaten by Trelleborgs, 2-3 agg.
2000-01 (UEFA Cup, 1st Rd.): Chelsea beaten by St. Gallen, Swit. 1-2 agg.

P.F.A. FAIR PLAY AWARD (Bobby Moore Trophy from 1993)

1988	Liverpool	1998	Cambridge Utd.
1989	Liverpool	1999	Grimsby Town
1990	Liverpool	2000	Crewe Alexandra
1991	Nott'm. Forest	2001	Crewe Alexandra
1992	Portsmouth	2002	Crewe Alexandra
1993	Norwich City	2003	Crewe Alexandra
1994	Crewe Alexandra	2004	Crewe Alexandra
1995	Crewe Alexandra	2005	Crewe Alexandra
1996	Crewe Alexandra	2006	Crewe Alexandra
1997	Crewe Alexandra	2007	Crewe Alexandra

RECORD MEDAL SALES

West Ham Utd. bought (June 2000) the late **Bobby Moore's** collection of medals and trophies for £1.8m. at Christie's auction in London. It was put up for sale by his first wife Tina and included his World Cup winner's medal.

A No. 6 duplicate red shirt made for England captain **Bobby Moore** for the 1966 World Cup Final fetched £44,000 at an auction at Wolves' ground in Sept. 1999. Moore kept the shirt he wore in that Final and gave the replica to England physio Harold Shepherdson.

Sir Geoff Hurst's 1966 World Cup-winning shirt fetched a record £91,750 at Christie's on September 28, 2000. His World Cup Final cap fetched £37,600 and his Man of the Match trophy £18,800. Proceeds totalling £274,410 from the 129 lots went to Hurst's three daughters and charities of his choice, including the Bobby Moore Imperial Cancer Research Fund.

In August 2001, Sir Geoff sold his World Cup-winner's medal to his former club West Ham Utd. (for their museum) at a reported £150,000.

'The **Billy Wright Collection**' – caps, medals and other memorabilia from his illustrious career – fetched over £100,000 at Christie's in Glasgow on Nov. 21, 1996.

At the sale in Oct. 1993, trophies, caps and medals earned by **Ray Kennedy**, former England, Arsenal and Liverpool player, fetched a then record total of £88,407. Kennedy, suffering from Parkinson's Disease, received £73,000 after commission.

The P.F.A. paid £31,080 for a total of 60 lots – including a record £16,000 for his 1977 European Cup winner's medal – to be exhibited at their Manchester museum. An anonymous English collector paid £17,000 for the medal and plaque commemorating Kennedy's part in the Arsenal Double in 1971.

Previous record for one player's medals, shirts etc. collection: £30,000 (**Bill Foulkes**, Manchester Utd. in 1992). The sale of **Dixie Dean**'s medals etc. in 1991 realised £28,000.

In March 2001, **Gordon Banks**' 1966 World Cup-winner's medal fetched a new record £124,750, and at auctions in season 2001-02: In London on Sept. 21, TV's Nick Hancock, a Stoke City fan, paid £23,500 for **Sir Stanley Matthews**' 1953 F.A. Cup-winner's medal. He also bought one of Matthews' England caps for £3,525 and paid £2,350 for a Stoke Div. 2 Championship medal (1963).

Dave Mackay's 1961 League Championship and F.A. Cup winner's medals sold for £18,000 at Sotherby's. Tottenham bought them for their museum.

A selection of England World Cup-winning manager **Sir Alf Ramsey**'s memorabilia – England caps, championship medals with Ipswich Town etc. – fetched more than £80,000 at Christie's. They were offered for sale by his family, and his former clubs Tottenham and Ipswich Town were among the buyers.

Ray Wilson's 1966 England World Cup-winning shirt fetched £80,750. Also in March 2002, the No. 10 shirt worn by **Pele** in Brazil's World Cup triumph in 1970 was sold for a record £157,750 at Christies. It went to an anonymous telephone bidder.

In October 2003, **George Best's** European Footballer of the Year (1968) trophy was sold to an anonymous British bidder for £167,250 at Bonham's, Chester. It was the then most expensive item of sporting memorabilia ever auctioned in Britain.

England captain **Bobby Moore's** 1970 World Cup shirt, which he swapped with Pele after Brazil's 1-0 win in Mexico, was sold for £60,000 at Christie's in London in March 2004.

September 2004: England shirt worn by tearful **Paul Gascoigne** in 1990 World Cup semi-final v Germany sold at Christie's for £28,680. At same auction, shirt worn by Brazil's **Pele** in 1958 World Cup Final in Sweden sold for £70,505.

May 2005: The **second F.A. Cup** (which was presented to winning teams from 1896 to 1909) was bought for £420,000 at Christie's by Birmingham City chairman David Gold, a world record for an item of football memorabilia. It was presented to the National Football Museum, Preston. At the same aution, the World Cup-winner's medal earned by England's **Alan Ball** in 1966 was sold for £140,000.

October 2005: At auction at Bonham's (London) the medals and other memorabilia of Hungary and Real Madrid legend Ferenc Puskas were sold for £85,000 to help pay for hospital treatment.

November 2006: A ball used in the 2006 World Cup Final and signed by the winning Italy team was sold for £1.2m. (a world record for football memorabilia) at a charity auction in Qatar. It was bought by the Qatar Sports Academy.

LONGEST UNBEATEN CUP RUN

Liverpool established the longest unbeaten Cup sequence by a Football League club: 25 successive rounds in the League/Milk Cup between semi-final defeat by Nott'm. Forest (1-2 agg.) in 1980 and defeat at Tottenham (0-1) in the third round on October 31, 1984. During this period Liverpool won the tournament in four successive seasons, a feat no other Football League club has achieved in any competition.

NEAR £1M. RECORD DAMAGES

A High Court judge in Newcastle (May 7, 1999) awarded Bradford City's 28-year-old striker **Gordon Watson** record damages for a football injury: £909,143. He had had his right leg fractured in two places by Huddersfield Town's Kevin Gray on Feb. 1, 1997.

Huddersfield Town were 'proven negligent for allowing their player to make a rushed tackle'. The award was calculated at £202,643 for loss of earnings, £730,500 for 'potential career earnings' if he had joined a Premiership club, plus £26,000 to cover medical treatment and care.

Watson, awarded £50,000 in an earlier legal action, had a 6-inch plate inserted in the leg. He resumed playing for City in season 1998-9.

BIG HALF-TIME SCORES

Tottenham 10, Crewe Alexandra 1 (F.A. Cup 4th. Rd. replay, Feb. 3, 1960; result 13-2); Tranmere Rov. 8, Oldham Athletic 1 (Div. 3N., Dec. 26, 1935; result 13-4); Chester City 8, York City 0 (Div. 3N., Feb. 1, 1936; result 12-0; believed to be record half-time scores in League football).

Nine goals were scored in the first half – Burnley 4, Watford 5 in Div. 1 on April 5, 2003. Result: 4–7.

Stirling Albion led Selkirk 15-0 at half-time (result 20-0) in the Scottish Cup 1st. Rd., Dec. 8, 1984.

World record half-time score: 16-0 when Australia beat American Samoa 31-0 (another world record) in the World Cup Oceania qualifying group at Coff's Harbour, New South Wales, on April 11, 2001.

• On March 4, 1933 Coventry City beat Q.P.R. (Div. 3 South) 7-0, having led by that score at half-time. This repeated the half-time situation in Bristol City's 7-0 win over Grimsby Town on Dec. 26, 1914.

TOP SECOND-HALF TEAM

Most goals scored by a team in one half of a League match is eleven. Stockport Co. led Halifax Town 2-0 at half-time in Div. 3 North on Jan. 6, 1934 and won 13-0.

FIVE NOT ENOUGH

Last team to score 5 in League match and lose: Reading, beaten 7-5 at Doncaster Rov. (Div. 3, Sept. 25, 1982).

LONG SERVICE WITH ONE CLUB

Bill Nicholson, OBE, was associated with Tottenham for 67 years – as a wing-half (1938-55), then the club's most successful manager (1958-74) with 8 major prizes, subsequently chief advisor and scout. He became club president, and an honorary freeman of the borough, had an executive suite named after him at the club, and the stretch of roadway from Tottenham High Road to the main gates has the nameplate Bill Nicholson Way. He died, aged 85, in October 2004.

Ted Bates, the Grand Old Man of Southampton with 66 years of unbroken service to the club, was awarded the Freedom of the City in April, 2001. He joined Saints as an inside-forward from Norwich City in 1937, made 260 peace-time appearances for the club, became reserve-team trainer in 1953 and manager at The Dell for 18 years (1955-73), taking Southampton into the top division in 1966. He was subsequently chief executive, director and club president. He died in October 2003, aged 85.

Dario Gradi, MBE, stepped down after completing 24 seasons and more than 1,000 matches as manager of Crewe Alexandra (appointed June 1983). Never a League player, he previously managed Wimbledon and Crystal Palace. At Crewe, his policy of finding and grooming young talent has earned the club more than £20m. in transfer fees. His new position is technical director.

Bob Paisley was associated with Liverpool for 57 years from 1939, when he joined them from Bishop Auckland, until he died in February 1996. He served them as player, trainer, coach, assistant-manager, manager, director and vice-president. He was Liverpool's most successful manager, winning 13 major trophies for the club (1974-83).

Ronnie Moran, who joined Liverpool in as a player 1952, retired from the Anfield coaching staff in season 1998-9.

Ernie Gregory served West Ham Utd. for 52 years as goalkeeper and coach. He joined them as boy of 14 from school in 1935, retired in May 1987.

Ted Sagar, Everton goalkeeper, 23 years at Goodison Park (1929-52, but only 16 League seasons because of War).

Alan Knight, goalkeeper, played 23 seasons (1977-2000) for his only club, Portsmouth.

Roy Sproson, defender, played 21 League seasons for his only club, Port Vale (1950-71).

Allan Ball, goalkeeper, 20 seasons with Queen of the South (1963-83).

Pat Bonner, goalkeeper, 19 seasons with Celtic (1978-97).

Danny McGrain, defender, 17 years with Celtic (1970-87).

TIGHT AT HOME

Fewest home goals conceded in League season (modern times): 4 by **Liverpool** (Div. 1, 1978-9); 4 by **Manchester Utd.** (Premier League, 1994-5) – both in 21 matches.

FOOTBALL POOLS

Littlewoods launched them in 1923 with a capital of £100. Coupons were first issued (4,000 of them) outside Manchester Utd.'s ground, the original 35 investors staking a total of £4-7s.-6d (pay-out £2-12s).

Vernons joined Littlewoods as the leading promoters. The Treble Chance, leading to bonanza dividends, was introduced in 1946 and the Pools Panel began in January 1963, to counter mass fixture postponements caused by the Big Freeze winter.

But business was hard hit by the launch of the National Lottery in 1994. Dividends slumped, the work-force was drastically cut and in June 2000 the Liverpool-based Moores family sold Littlewoods Pools in a £161m. deal.

The record prize remains the £2,924,622 paid to a Worsley, Manchester, syndicate in November 1994.

Fixed odds football – record pay-out: £654,375 by Ladbrokes (May 1993) to Jim Wright, of Teignmouth, Devon. He placed a £1,000 each-way pre-season bet on the champions of the three Football League divisions – Newcastle Utd. (8–1), Stoke City (6–1) and Cardiff City (9–1).

Record for match accumulator: **£164,776** to £4 stake on 18 correct results, October 5, 6, 7, 2002. The bet, with Ladbrokes in Colchester, was made by Army chef Mark Simmons.

TRANSFER WINDOW

This was introduced to Britain in September 2002 via FIFA regulations to bring uniformity across Europe (the rule previously applied in a number of other countries). The transfer of contracted players is restricted to two periods: June 1–August 31 and January 1–31).

On appeal, Football League clubs continued to sign/sell players through seasons 2002–03, 2003-04, 2004-05, 2005-06 (excluding deals with Premiership clubs).

PROGRAMME PIONEERS

Chelsea pioneered football's magazine-style programme when they introduced a 16-page issue for their First Division match against Portsmouth on Christmas Day 1948. It cost sixpence (2½p).

TRIBUNAL-FEE RECORDS

Top tribunal fee: £2.5m for **Chris Bart-Williams** (Sheffield Wed. to Nott'm. Forest, June 1995).

Biggest discrepancy: **Andy Walker**, striker, Bolton Wand. to Celtic, June 1994: Bolton Wand. asked £2.2m, Celtic offered £250,000. Tribunal decided £550,000.

LONGEST THROW-IN?

That by Notts Co.'s **Andy Legg** was measured (season 1994-5) at 41 metres (45 yards) and claimed as the longest throw by any footballer in the world, until 1997-8, when **Dave Challinor** (Tranmere Rov.) reached 46.3 metres (50½ yards).

BALL JUGGLING: WORLD RECORD CLAIMS

Sam Ik (South Korea) juggled a ball non-stop for 18 hours, 11 minutes, 4 seconds in March 1995. Thai footballer **Sam-Ang Sowanski** juggled a ball for 15 hours without letting it touch the ground in Bangkok in April 2000.

Milene Domingues, wife of Brazilian star Ronaldo and a player for Italian women's team Fiammamonza, Milan, became the 'Queen of Keepy Uppy' when for 9 hours, 6 minutes she juggled a ball 55,187 times.

SUBS' SCORING RECORD

Barnet's 5-4 home win v Torquay Utd. (Div. 3, Dec. 28, 1993) provided the first instance of **all four substitutes** scoring in a major League match in England.

FOOTBALL'S OLDEST ANNUAL

Now in its 121st edition, this publication began as the 16-page ***Athletic News Football Supplement & Club Directory*** in 1887. From the long-established ***Athletic News***, it became the ***Sunday Chronicle Annual*** in 1946, the ***Empire News*** in 1956, the ***News of the World & Empire News*** in 1961 and, since 1965, the ***News of the World Annual***.

BARCLAYS PREMIERSHIP CLUB DETAILS AND SQUADS 2007-08

(At time of going to press)

ARSENAL

Ground: Emirates Stadium, Highbury, London, N5 1BU.
Telephone: 0207 704 4000. **Club nickname:** Gunners.
First-choice colours: Red and white shirts; white shorts; white socks.
Record transfer fee: £17,400,000 to Seville for Jose Antonio Reyes, January 2004.
Record fee received: £25,000,000 from Barcelona for Marc Overmars, July 2000.
Record attendance: At Highbury: 73,295 v Sunderland (Div.1) 9 March, 1935. At Wembley: 73,707 v Lens (Champions League) November 1998. At Emirates Stadium: 60,132 v Reading (Premier League) 3 March, 2007.
Capacity for 2007-08: 60,432. **Sponsors:** Emirates.
League Championship: Winners 1930-31, 1932-33, 1933-34, 1934-35, 1937-38, 1947-48, 1952-53, 1970-71, 1988-89, 1990-91, 1997-98, 2001-02, 2003-04.
F.A. Cup: Winners 1930, 1936, 1950, 1971, 1979, 1993, 1998, 2002, 2003, 2005.
League Cup: Winners 1987, 1993.
European Competitions: Winners Fairs Cup 1969-70, Cup-Winners' Cup 1993-94.
Finishing positions in Premiership: 1992-93 10th, 1993-94 4th, 1994-95 12th, 1995-96 5th, 1996-97 3rd, 1997-98 1st, 1998-99 2nd, 1999-2000 2nd, 2000-01 2nd, 2001-02 1st, 2002-03 2nd, 2003-04 1st, 2004-05 2nd, 2005-06 4th, 2006-07 4th.
Biggest win: 12-0 v Loughborough Town, Div. 2, 12.3.1900.
Biggest defeat: 0-8 v Loughborough Town, Div. 2, 12.12.1896.
Highest League scorer in a season: Ted Drake, 42, 1934-35.
Most League goals in aggregate: Thierry Henry, 174, 1999-2007.
Most capped player: Patrick Vieira (France) 79.
Longest unbeaten League sequence: 49 matches (October 2004).
Longest sequence without a League win: 23 matches (March 1913).

Name	Height ft. in.	Previous club	Birthplace	Birthdate
Goalkeepers				
Almunia, Manuel	6. 3	Celta Vigo	Pamplona	19.05.77
Fabianski, Lukasz	6. 3	Legia Warsaw	Kostrzyn, Pol.	18.04.85
Lehmann, Jens	6. 3	Borussia Dortmund	Essen	11.10.69
Defenders				
Clichy, Gael	5.11	Cannes	Paris	26.07.85
Connolly, Matthew	6. 1	–	Barnet	24.09.87
Djourou, Johan	6. 3	Etoile Carouge	Ivory Coast	18.01.87
Eboue, Emmanuel	5.10	Beveren	Abidjan, Iv.	4.06.83
Gallas, William	6. 1	Chelsea	Asnieres, Fra.	17.08.77
Gilbert, Kerrea	5. 6	–	Hammersmith	28.02.87
Hoyte, Justin	5.11	–	Waltham Forest	20.11.84
Senderos, Philippe	6. 3	Servette	Geneva	14.02.85
Toure, Kolo	5.11	Mimosa	Abidjan, Iv.	19.03.81
Traore, Armand	6. 1	Monaco	Paris	8.10.89
Midfielders				
Denilson	5.10	Sao Paulo	Brazil	16.02.88
Diaby, Abou	6. 2	Auxerre	Paris	11.05.86
Fabregas, Francesc	5.10	Barcelona	Vilessoc, Sp.	4.05.87
Flamini, Mathieu	5.10	Marseille	Marseilles	7.03.84
Gilberto Silva	6. 3	Atletico Mineiro	Lagoa Prata, Bra.	7.10.76
Hleb, Alexandr	5.10	Stuttgart	Minsk	1.05.81
Ljungberg, Freddie	5.11	Halmstad	Halmstad	16.04.77

Rosicky, Tomas	5.10	Borussia Dortmund	Prague	4.10.80
Randall, Mark	6. 0	–	Milton Keynes	28.09.89
Song, Alexandre	6. 1	Bastia	Douala, Cam.	9.09.87
Walcott, Theo	5. 8	Southampton	Newbury	16.03.89
Forwards				
Adebayor, Emmanuel	6. 3	Monaco	Lome, Togo	26.02.85
Bendtner, Nicklas	6. 3	–	Copenhagen	16.01.88
Da Silva, Eduardo	5.10	Dinamo Zagreb	Rio de Janeiro	25.02.83
Van Persie, Robin	6. 0	Feyenoord	Rotterdam	6.08.83

ASTON VILLA

Ground: Villa Park, Trinity Road, Birmingham, B6 6HE.
Telephone: 0121 327 2299. **Club nickname:** Villans.
First-choice colours: Claret and blue shirts; white shorts; blue socks.
Record transfer fee: £9,600,000 to Watford for Ashley Young, January 2007.
Record fee received: £12,600,000 for Dwight Yorke from Manchester Utd., August 1998.
Record attendance: 76,588 v Derby Co. (F.A. Cup 6) 2 March, 1946.
Capacity for 2007-08: 42,614. **Sponsors:** 32 Red.com.
League Championship: Winners 1893-94, 1895-96, 1896-97, 1898-99, 1899-1900, 1909-10, 1980-81.
F.A. Cup: Winners 1887, 1895, 1897, 1905, 1913, 1920, 1957.
League Cup: Winners 1961, 1975, 1977, 1994, 1996.
European Competitions: Winners European Cup 1981-82, European Super Cup 1982-83.
Finishing positions in Premiership: 1992-93 2nd, 1993-94 10th, 1994-95 18th, 1995-96 4th, 1996-97 5th, 1997-98 7th, 1998-99 6th, 1999-2000 6th, 2000-01 8th, 2001-02 8th, 2002-03 16th, 2003-04 6th, 2004-05 10th, 2005-06 16th, 2006-07 11th.
Biggest win: 12-2 v Accrington, Div. 1, 12.3.1892; 11-1 v Charlton Athletic, Div. 2, 24.11.1959; 10-0 v Sheffield Wed., Div. 1, 5.10.1912, v Burnley, Div. 1, 29.8.1925.
Biggest defeat: 0-7 in five League matches from Blackburn Rov., Div. 1, 19.10.1889 to Manchester Utd., Div. 1, 24.10.1964.
Highest League scorer in a season: 'Pongo' Waring, 49, 1930-31.
Most League goals in aggregate: Harry Hampton, 215, 1904-1915.
Most capped player: Steve Staunton (Rep. of Ireland) 64.
Longest unbeaten League sequence: 15 matches (January 1897, December 1909 and March 1949).
Longest sequence without a League win: 12 matches (November 1973 and December 1986).

Name	Height ft. in.	Previous club	Birthplace	Birthdate
Goalkeepers				
Sorensen, Thomas	6. 4	Sunderland	Odense	12.06.76
Taylor, Stuart	6. 4	Aston Villa	Romford	28.11.81
Defenders				
Bouma, Wilfred	6. 0	PSV Eindhoven	Helmond, Hol.	15.06.78
Cahill, Gary	6. 2	–	Dronfield	19.12.85
Delaney, Mark	6. 1	Cardiff City	Haverfordwest	13.05.76
Laursen, Martin	6. 2	AC Milan	Farvoug, Den.	26.07.77
Mellberg, Olof	6. 1	Racing Santander	Stockholm	9.03.77
O'Halloran, Stephen	6. 0	–	Cork	29.11.87
Ridgewell, Liam	5.10	–	Bexley	21.07.84
Midfielders				
Barry, Gareth	6. 0	–	Hastings	23.02.81
Berger, Patrik	6. 1	Portsmouth	Prague	10.11.73
Djemba-Djemba, Eric	5. 9	Manchester Utd.	Douala	4.05.81
Gardner, Craig	5.10	–	Solihull	25.11.86
Osbourne, Isaiah	6. 2	–	Birmingham	15.11.87

Petrov, Stililyan	5.10	Celtic	Bulgaria	5.07.79
Reo-Coker, Nigel	5. 8	West Ham Utd.	Thornton Heath	14.05.84
Young, Ashley	5.10	Watford	Stevenage	9.07.85
Forwards				
Agbonlahor, Gabriel	5.11	–	Birmingham	13.10.86
Carew, John	6. 4	Lyon	Lorenskog, Nor.	5.09.79
Maloney, Shaun	5. 7	Celtic	Mirri, Mal.	24.01.83
Moore, Luke	5.10	–	Birmingham	13.02.86
Williams, Sam	5.11	–	London	9.06.87

BIRMINGHAM CITY

Ground: St Andrews, Birmingham B9 4NH.
Telephone: 0844 557 1875.
First-choice colours: Blue and white shirts; blue shorts; blue socks.
Record transfer fee: £6,250,000 to Liverpool for Emile Heskey, May 2004.
Record fee received: £6,700,000 from Liverpool for Jermaine Pennant, July 2006.
Record attendance: 66,844 v Everton (F.A. Cup 5), 11 February, 1939.
Capacity for 2007-08: 30,009. **Sponsors:** F&C Investments.
League Championship: 6th 1955-56.
F.A. Cup: Runners-up 1931, 1956.
League Cup: Winners 1963.
European Competitions: Runners-up Fairs Cup, 1958-60, 1960-61.
Finishing positions in Premiership: 2002-03 13th, 2003-04 10th, 2004-05 12th, 2005-06 18th.
Biggest win: 12-0 v Walsall, Div. 2, 17.12.1892. 12-0 v Doncaster Rov., Div. 2, 11.4.1903.
Biggest defeat: 1-9 v Sheffield Wed., Div. 1, 13.12.30. 1-9 v Blackburn Rov., Div. 1, 5.1.1895.
Highest League scorer in a season: Joe Bradford City, 29, 1927-28.
Most League goals in aggregate: Joe Bradford City, 249, 1920-35.
Most capped player: Kenny Cunningham (Republic. of Ireland) 32.
Longest unbeaten League sequence: 20 matches (January 1995).
Longest sequence without a League win: 17 matches (January 1986).

Name	Height ft. in.	Previous club	Birthplace	Birthdate
Goalkeepers				
Doyle, Colin	6. 5	–	Cork	12.08.85
Taylor, Maik	6. 4	Fulham	Hildeshein, Ger.	4.09.71
Defenders				
Jaidi, Radhi	6. 4	Bolton Wand.	Tunis	30.05.75
Kelly, Stephen	5.11	Tottenham	Dublin	6.09.83
Oji, Samuel	6. 0	Arsenal	Westminster	9.10.85
Parnaby, Stuart	5.11	Middlesbrough	Durham	19.07.82
Sadler, Matthew	5.11	–	Solihull	26.02.85
Taylor, Martin	6. 4	Blackburn Rov.	Ashington	9.11.79
Tebily, Olivier	6. 0	Celtic	Abidjan, Iv.	19.12.75
Midfielders				
Birley, Matthew	5.10	–	Birmingham	26.07.86
Clemence, Stephen	5.11	Tottenham	Liverpool	31.03.78
Danns, Neil	5. 9	Colchester Utd.	Liverpool	23.11.82
Johnson, Damien	5.10	Blackburn Rov.	Lisburn	18.11.78
Kapo, Olivier	6. 2	Juventus	Abidjan, Iv.	27.09.80
Kilkenny, Neil	5. 8	–	Enfield	19.12.85
Larsson, Sebastian	5.10	Arsenal	Eskiltuna, Swe.	6.06.85
Muamba, Fabrice	5.11	Arsenal	Congo	6.04.88
Nafti, Medhi	5. 9	Racing Santander	Toulouse	28.11.78
Forwards				
Aluko, Sone	5. 8	–	Birmingham	19.02.89
Campbell, Dudley	5.11	Brentford	London	12.11.81

Forssell, Mikael	6. 0	Chelsea	Steinfurt, Ger.	15.03.81
Jerome, Cameron	6. 1	Cardiff City	Huddersfield	14.08.86
McSheffrey, Gary	5. 8	Coventry City	Coventry	13.08.72
O'Connor, Garry	6. 1	Lokomotiv Moscow	Edinburgh	7.05.83
Vine, Rowan	6. 1	Luton Town	Basingstoke	21.09.82

BLACKBURN ROVERS

Ground: Ewood Park, Blackburn BB2 4JF.
Telephone: 08701 113232. **Club nickname:** Rovers.
First-choice colours: Blue and white shirts; white shorts; white socks.
Record transfer fee: £8,000,000 to Manchester Utd. for Andy Cole, December 2001.
Record fee received: £17,000,000 from Chelsea for Damien Duff, July 2003.
Record attendance: 62,522 v Bolton Wand., (F.A. Cup 6) 2 March, 1929.
Capacity for 2007-08: 31,367. **Sponsors:** Bet24.
League Championship: Winners 1911-12, 1913-14, 1994-95.
F.A. Cup: Winners 1884, 1885, 1886, 1890, 1891, 1928.
League Cup: Winners 2002.
European Competitions: Champions League 1st group stage 1995-96.
Finishing positions in Premiership: 1992-93 4th, 1993-94 2nd, 1994-95 1st, 1995-96 7th, 1996-97 13th, 1997-98 6th, 1998-99 19th, 2001-02 10th, 2002-03 6th, 2003-04 15th, 2004-05 15th, 2005-06 6th, 2006-07 10th.
Biggest win: 9-0 v Middlesbrough, Div. 2, 6.11.1954. Also 11-0 v Rossendale, F.A. Cup 1st Rd, 13.10.1884.
Biggest defeat: 0-8 v Arsenal, Div. 1, 25.2.1933.
Highest League scorer in a season: Ted Harper, 43, 1925-26.
Most League goals in aggregate: Simon Garner, 168, 1978-92.
Most capped player: Henning Berg (Norway) 58.
Longest unbeaten League sequence: 23 matches (September 1987).
Longest sequence without a League win: 16 matches (November 1978).

Goalkeepers	**Height ft. in.**	**Previous club**	**Birthplace**	**Birthdate**
Brown, Jason	6. 0	Gillingham	Bermondsey	18.05.82
Enckelman, Peter	6. 2	Aston Villa	Turku, Fin.	10.03.77
Fielding, Frank	5.11	–	Blackburn	4.04.88
Friedel, Brad	6. 3	Liverpool	Lakewood, USA	18.05.71
Nielsen, Gunnar	6. 5	BK Copenhagen	Faroe Is.	7.10.86
Defenders				
Berner, Bruno	6. 1	Basle	Zurich	21.11.77
Gray, Michael	5. 7	Sunderland	Sunderland	3.08.74
Henchoz, Stephane	6. 1	Wigan Athletic	Billens, Switz.	7.09.74
Khishanishvili, Zurab	6. 1	Rangers	Tblisi	6.10.81
Kane, Tony	5. 8	–	Belfast	29.08.87
Mokoena, Aaron	6. 1	Genk	Johannesburg	25.11.80
Nelsen, Ryan	6. 0	DC Utd.	Christchurch, NZ	18.10.77
Nolan, Eddie	6. 0	–	Waterford	5.08.88
Ooijer, Andre	6. 1	PSV Eindhoven	Amsterdam	11.07.74
Samba, Chris	6. 5	Hertha Berlin	Creteil, Fr.	28.03.84
Taylor, Andy	5.11	–	Blackburn	14.03.86
Warnock, Stephen	5.10	Liverpool	Ormskirk	12.12.81
Midfielders				
Bentley, David	5.10	Arsenal	Peterborough	27.08.84
Dunn, David	5.10	Birmingham City	Blackburn	27.12.79
Emerton, Brett	6. 1	Feyenoord	Bankstown, Aus.	22.02.79
Pedersen, Morten Gamst	5.11	Tromso	Vadso, Nor.	8.09.81
Peter, Sergio	5. 8	–	Ludwigshafen, Ger.	12.10.86
Reid, Steven	6. 1	Millwall	Kingston	10.03.81
Savage, Robbie	5.11	Birmingham City	Wrexham	18.10.74
Treacy, Keith	6. 0	–	Dublin	13.09.88

Tugay, Kerimoglu	5. 9	Rangers	Istanbul	24.08.70
Forwards				
Derbyshire, Matt	5.10	Great Harwood	Blackburn	14.04.86
Gallagher, Paul	6. 0	–	Blackburn	9.08.84
Jeffers, Francis	5. 9	Charlton Athletic	Liverpool	25.01.81
McCarthy, Benni	6. 0	Porto	Cape Town	12.11.77
Rigters, Maceo	5.10	Breda	Amsterdam	22.01.84
Roberts, Jason	5.11	Wigan Athletic	Park Royal	25.01.78

BOLTON WANDERERS

Ground: Reebok Stadium, Burnden Way, Lostock, Bolton BL6 6JW.
Telephone: 01204 673673. **Club nickname:** Trotters.
First-choice colours: White shirts; white shorts; white socks.
Record transfer fee: £8,000,000 to Fenerbahce for Nicolas Anelka, August 2006.
Record fee received: £4,500,000 from Liverpool for Jason McAteer, September 1995.
Record attendance: At Reebok Stadium: 28,353 v Leicester City (Premier League) 28 December, 2003. At Burnden Park: 69,912 v Manchester City, (F.A. Cup 5) 18 February, 1933.
Capacity for 2007-08: 28,500. **Sponsors:** Reebok.
League Championship: 3rd 1891-92, 1920-21, 1924-25.
F.A. Cup: Winners 1923, 1926, 1929, 1958.
League Cup: Runners-up 1995, 2004.
European Competitions: UEFA Cup rd. of 32 2005-06.
Finishing positions in Premiership: 1995-96 20th, 1997-98 18th, 2001-02 16th, 2002-03 17th, 2003-04 8th, 2004-05 6th, 2005-06 8th, 2006-07 7th.
Biggest win: 8-0 v Barnsley, Div. 2, 6.10.1934. Also 13-0 v Sheffield Utd., F.A. Cup 2nd Rd, 1.1.1890.
Biggest defeat: 1-9 v Preston N.E., F.A. Cup 2nd Rd, 10.12.1887.
Highest League scorer in a season: Joe Smith, 38, 1920-21.
Most League goals in aggregate: Nat Lofthouse, 255, 1946-61.
Most capped player: Mark Fish (South Africa) 34.
Longest unbeaten League sequence: 23 matches (October 1990).
Longest sequence without a League win: 26 matches (April 1902).

Name	Height ft. in.	Previous club	Birthplace	Birthdate
Goalkeepers				
Al Habsi, Ali	6. 5	Lyn Oslo	Oman	30.12.81
Jaaskelainen, Jussi	6. 4	VPS	Vaasa, Fin.	17.04.75
Walker, Iain	6. 2	Leicester City	Watford	31.10.71
Defenders				
Cid, Gerald	6. 2	Bordeaux	Talence, Fr.	17.02.83
Gardner, Ricardo	5. 9	Harbour View	St Andrews, Jam.	25.09.78
Hunt, Nicky	6. 1	–	Bolton	3.09.83
Meite, Abdoulaye	6. 1	Marseille	Paris	6.10.80
Samuel, Jlloyd	5.11	Aston Villa	Trinidad	29.03.81
Midfielders				
Campo, Ivan	6. 1	Real Madrid	San Sebastian	21.02.74
Dzemaili, Blerim	5.11	Zurich	Switzerland	12.04.86
Faye, Abdoulaye	6. 3	Lens	Dakar	26.02.78
Giannakopoulos, Stelios	5.10	Olympiakos	Athens	12.07.74
McCann, Gavin	5.11	Aston Villa	Blackpool	10.01.78
Michalik, Lubomir	6. 6	Senec	Slovakia	13.08.83
Nolan, Kevin	6. 1	–	Liverpool	24.06.82
O'Brien Joey	6. 2	–	Dublin	17.02.86
Speed, Gary	5.10	Newcastle Utd.	Deeside	8.09.69
Tal, Idan	5.11	Rayo Vallecano	Petah Tikva, Isr.	12.12.75
Teymourian, Andranik	5.11	Abu Moslem	Tehran	6.03.83
Forwards				
Anelka, Nicolas	6. 1	Fenerbahce	Versailles	14.03.79

Davies, Kevin	6. 0	Southampton	Sheffield	26.03.77
Diouf, El-Hadji	5.11	Liverpool	Dakar	15.01.81
Harsanyi, Zoltan	6. 1	Senec	Slovakia	1.06.87
Sinclair, James	5. 6	–	Newcastle	22.10.87
Smith, Johann	5.11	–	Harford, USA	25.04.87
Vaz Te, Ricardo	6. 2	Farense	Lisbon	1.10.86

CHELSEA

Ground: Stamford Bridge Stadium, London SW6 1HS.
Telephone: 0870 300 1212. **Club nickname:** Blues.
First-choice colours: Blue shirts; blue shorts; white socks.
Record transfer fee: £30,800,000 to AC Milan for Andriy Shevchenko, May 2006.
Record fee received: £12,000,000 from Rangers for Tore Andre Flo, November 2000.
Record attendance: 82,905 v Arsenal (Div. 1) 12 October, 1935.
Capacity for 2007-08: 42,449. **Sponsors:** Samsung.
League Championship: Winners 1954-55, 2004-05, 2005-06.
F.A. Cup: Winners 1970, 1997, 2000, 2007.
League Cup: Winners 1965, 1998, 2005, 2007.
European Competitions: Winners Cup-Winners' Cup 1970-71, 1997-98.
Finishing positions in Premiership: 1992-93 11th, 1993-94 14th, 1994-95 11th, 1995-96 11th, 1996-97 6th, 1997-98 4th, 1998-99 3rd, 1999-2000 5th, 2000-01 6th, 2001-02 6th, 2002-03 4th, 2003-04 2nd, 2004-05 1st, 2005-06 1st, 2006-07 2nd.
Biggest win: 7-0 in four League matches from Lincoln City, Div. 2, 29.10.1910 to Walsall, Div. 2, 4.2.1989. Also 9-2 v Glossop N.E. Div. 2, 1.9.1906. Europe: 13-0 v Jeunesse Hautcharage, Cup-Winners' Cup 1st rd, 29.9.1971.
Biggest defeat: 1-8 v Wolves, Div. 1, 26.9.1923. Also 0-7 v Leeds Utd., Div. 1, 7.10.1967 and v Nott'm. Forest Div. 1, 20.4.1991.
Highest League scorer in a season: Jimmy Greaves, 41, 1960-61.
Most League goals in aggregate: Bobby Tambling, 164, 1958-70.
Most capped player: Marcel Desailly (France) 67.
Longest unbeaten League sequence: 27 matches (October 1988).
Longest sequence without a League win: 21 matches (November 1987).

Name	Height ft. in.	Previous club	Birthplace	Birthdate
Goalkeepers				
Cech, Petr	6. 5	Rennes	Plzen, Cz.	20.05.82
Cudicini, Carlo	6. 1	Castel di Sangro	Milan	6.09.73
Hilario, Henrique	6. 3	–	Sao Pedro, Por.	21.10.75
Defenders				
Ben Haim, Tal	5.11	Bolton Wand.	Rishon le Zion, Isr.	31.03.82
Boulahrouz, Khalid	5. 9	Hamburg	Maassluis, Hol.	28.12.81
Bridge, Wayne	5.10	Southampton	Southampton	5.08.80
Carvalho, Ricardo	6. 0	Porto	Amarante, Por.	18.05.78
Cole, Ashley	5. 8	Chelsea	Stepney	20.12.80
Ferreira, Paulo	6. 0	Porto	Lisbon	18.01.79
Johnson, Glen	6. 0	West Ham Utd.	Greenwich	23.08.84
Terry, John	6. 1	–	Barking	7.12.80
Midfielders				
Ballack, Michael	6. 2	Bayern Munich	Gorlitz, Ger.	26.09.76
Cole, Joe	5. 9	West Ham Utd.	Islington	8.11.81
Diarra, Lassana	5. 8	Le Havre	Paris	10.03.85
Essien, Michael	6. 0	Lyon	Accra	3.12.82
Lampard, Frank	6. 0	West Ham Utd.	Romford	20.06.78
Makelele, Claude	5. 7	Real Madrid	Kinshasa	18.02.73
Malouda, Florent	5.11	Lyon	Cayenne, Guiana	13.06.80
Mikel, John Obi	6. 2	Lyn Oslo	Plato State, Nig.	22.04.87
Robben, Arjen	5.11	PSV Eindhoven	Bedum, Hol.	23.01.84
Sidwell, Steve	5.10	Reading	Wandsworth	14.12.82

Wright-Phillips, Shaun	5. 6	Manchester City	Greenwich	25.10.81
Forwards				
Drogba, Didier	6. 2	Marseille	Abidjan, Iv.	11.03.78
Kalou, Salomon	5.10	Feyenoord	Oume, Iv.	5.08.85
Pizarro, Claudio	6. 0	Bayern Munich	Lima	3.20.78
Shevchenko, Andriy	6. 0	AC Milan	Dvirkivshchyna, Ukr.	29.09.76

DERBY COUNTY

Ground: Pride Park Stadium, Pride Park, Derby DE24 8XL.
Telephone: 0870 444 1884.
First-choice colours: White and black shirts; black shorts; black and white socks.
Record transfer fee: £3,500,000 to Norwich City for Robert Earnshaw, June 2007.
Record fee received: £7,000,000 from Leeds Utd. for Seth Johnson, October 2001.
Record attendance: At Pride Park: 33,475 v Rangers (Ted McMinn testimonial) 1 May, 2006. At Baseball Ground: 41,826 v Tottenham (Division 1) 20 September 1969.
Capacity for 2007-08: 33,597. **Sponsors:** Derbyshire Building Society.
League Championship: 1971-72, 1974-75.
F.A. Cup: Winners 1946.
League Cup: Semi-finals 1968.
European Competitions: European Cup semi-finals 1972-73.
Finishing positions in Premiership: 1996-97 12th, 1997-98 9th, 1998-99 8th, 1999-2000 16th, 2000-01 17th, 2001-02 19th.
Biggest win: 9-0 v Wolves, Div. 1, 10.1.1891. 9-0 v Sheffield Wed., Div. 1, 21.1.1899. Also 12-0 v Finn Harps, UEFA Cup 1st rd. 1st leg, 15.9.76.
Biggest defeat: 0-8 v Blackburn Rov., Div. 1, 3.1.1891. 0-8 v Sunderland, Div. 1, 1.9.1894. Also 2-11 v Everton, F.A. Cup 1st rd., 1889-90.
Highest League scorer in a season: Jack Bowers, 37, 1930-31 and Ray Straw, 37, 1956-57.
Most League goals in aggregate: Steve Bloomer, 292, 1892-1906 and 1910-14.
Most capped player:.Deon Burton (Jamaica) and Mart Poom (Estonia).
Longest unbeaten League sequence: 22 matches (September 1969).
Longest sequence without a League win: 20 matches (April 1991).

Name	Height ft. in.	Previous club	Birthplace	Birthdate
Goalkeepers				
Bywater, Stephen	6. 2	West Ham Utd.	Manchester	7.06.81
Camp, Lee	5.11	–	Derby	22.08.84
Defenders				
Camara, Mo	5.11	Celtic	Conakry, Guin.	25.06.75
Edworthy, Marc	5. 9	Norwich City	Barnstaple	24.12.72
Jackson, Richard	5. 7	Scarborough	Whitby	18.04.80
Johnson, Michael	5.11	Birmingham City	Nottingham	4.07.73
Leacock, Dean	6. 2	Fulham	Croydon	10.06.84
Malcolm, Robert	5.11	Rangers	Glasgow	12.11.80
McEveley, Jay	6. 1	Blackburn Rov.	Liverpool	11.02.85
Meredith, James	6. 1	–	Albury	4.04.88
Moore, Darren	6. 2	W.B.A.	Birmingham	22.04.74
Nyatanga, Lewin	6. 2	–	Burton	18.08.88
Todd, Andy	5.10	Blackburn Rov.	Derby	21.09.74
Midfielders				
Barnes, Giles	6. 0	–	Barking	5.08.88
Holmes, Lee	5. 8	–	Mansfield	2.04.87
Jones, David	5.10	Manchester Utd.	Southport	4.11.84
Mears, Tyrone	5.11	West Ham Utd.	Stockport	18.02.83
Oakley, Matt	5.10	Southampton	Peterborough	17.08.77
Pearson, Stephen	6. 0	Celtic	Lanark	2.10.82
Teale, Gary	5.11	Wigan Athletic	Glasgow	21.07.78
Forwards				
Earnshaw, Robert	5. 8	Norwich City	Zambia	6.04.81

Fagan, Craig	5.11	Hull City	Birmingham	11.12.82
Howard, Steve	6. 2	Luton Town	Durham	10.05.76
Macken, Jon	6. 2	Crystal Palace	Manchester	9.07.77

EVERTON

Ground: Goodison Park, Liverpool L4 4EL.
Telephone: 0870 442 1878. **Club nickname:** Toffees.
First-choice colours: Royal blue shirts; white shorts; white socks.
Record transfer fee: £8,500,000 to Crystal Palace for Andy Johnson, June 2006.
Record fee received: £27,000,000 from Manchester Utd. for Wayne Rooney, August 2004.
Record attendance: 78,299 v Liverpool (Div. 1) 18 September, 1948.
Capacity for 2007-08: 40,565. **Sponsors:** Chang.
League Championship: Winners 1890-91, 1914-15, 1927-28, 1931-31, 1938-39, 1962-63, 1969-70, 1984-85, 1986-87.
F.A. Cup: Winners 1906, 1933, 1966, 1984, 1995.
League Cup: Runners up 1977, 1984.
European Competitions: Winners Cup-Winners' Cup 1984-85.
Finishing positions in Premiership: 1992-93 13th, 1993-94 17th, 1994-95 15th 1995-96 6th 1996-97 15th 1997-98 17th 1998-99 14th, 1999-2000 13th, 2000-01 16th, 2001-02 15th, 2002-03 7th, 2003-04 17th, 2004-05 4th, 2005-06 11th, 2006-07 6th.
Biggest win: 9-1 v Manchester City, Div. 1, 3.9.1906, v Plymouth Argyle, Div. 2, 27.12.1930. Also 11-2 v Derby Co., F.A. Cup 1st rd, 18.1.1890.
Biggest defeat: 0-7 v Portsmouth, Div. 1, 10.9.1949 and v Arsenal, Prem., 11.5.2005.
Highest League scorer in a season: Ralph 'Dixie' Dean, 60, 1927-28.
Most League goals in aggregate: Ralph 'Dixie' Dean, 349, 1925-37.
Most capped player: Neville Southall (Wales) 92.
Longest unbeaten League sequence: 20 matches (April 1978).
Longest sequence without a League win: 14 matches (March 1937).

Name	Height ft. in.	Previous club	Birthplace	Birthdate
Goalkeepers				
Howard, Tim	6. 3	Manchester Utd.	New Jersey	03.06.79
Ruddy, John	6. 4	Cambridge Utd.	St Ives, Cambs.	24.10.86
Turner, Iain	6. 4	Stirling Alb.	Stirling	26.01.84
Defenders				
Boyle, Patrick	5.10	–	Glasgow	20.03.87
Hibbert, Tony	5.10	–	Liverpool	20.02.81
Jagielka, Phil	5.11	Sheffield Utd.	Manchester	17.08.82
Lescott, Joleon	6. 2	Wolves	Birmingham	16.08.82
Stubbs, Alan	6. 2	Sunderland	Liverpool	6.10.71
Valente, Nuno	6. 0	Porto	Lisbon	12.09.74
Yobo, Joseph	6. 2	Marseille	Kano, Nig.	6.09.80
Midfielders				
Arteta, Mikel	5. 9	Real Sociedad	San Sebastian	28.03.82
Cahill, Tim	5.10	Millwall	Sydney	6.12.79
Carsley, Lee	5. 9	Coventry City	Birmingham	28.02.74
Neville, Phil	5.11	Manchester Utd.	Bury	21.01.77
Osman, Leon	5. 8	–	Billinge	17.05.81
Van der Meyde, Andy	5.10	Inter Milan	Arnhem	30.09.79
Vidarsson, Bjarni	6. 1	–	Iceland	5.03.88
Forwards				
Anderson Silva	6. 2	Racing Santander	Sao Paulo	29.08.82
Anichebe, Victor	6. 1	–	Lagos	23.04.88
Beattie, James	6. 1	Southampton	Lancaster	27.02.78
Johnson, Andy	5. 9	Crystal Palace	Bedford	10.02.81
Jutkiewicz, Lukas	6. 1	Swindon Town	Southampton	20.03.89

McFadden, James	5.10	Motherwell	Glasgow	14.04.83
Vaughan, James	5.11	–	Birmingham	14.07.88

FULHAM

Ground: Craven Cottage, Stevenage Road, London SW6 6HH.
Telephone: 0870 442 1222. **Club nickname:** Cottagers.
First-choice colours: White shirts; black shorts; white socks.
Record transfer fee: £11,500,000 to Lyon for Steve Marlet, August 2001.
Record fee received: £12,825,000 from Manchester Utd. for Louis Saha, January 2004.
Record attendance: 49,335 v Millwall (Div. 2) 8 October, 1938.
Capacity for 2007-08: 24,600. **Sponsors:** LG.
League Championship: 9th 2003-04.
F.A. Cup: Runners-up 1975.
League Cup: 5th rd. 1968, 1971, 2000.
Finishing positions in Premiership: 2001-02 13th, 2002-03 14th, 2003-04 9th, 2004-05 13th, 2005-06 12th, 2006-07 16th.
Biggest win: 10-1 v Ipswich Town, Div. 1, 26.12.1963.
Biggest defeat: 0-10 v Liverpool, League Cup 2nd Rd 1st leg, 23.9.1986.
Highest League scorer in a season: Frank Newton, 43, 1931-32.
Most League goals in aggregate: Gordon Davies, 159, 1978-84 and 1986-91.
Most capped player: Johnny Haynes (England) 56.
Longest unbeaten League sequence: 15 matches (January 1999).
Longest sequence without a League win: 15 matches (February 1950).

Name	Height ft. in.	Previous club	Birthplace	Birthdate
Goalkeepers				
Batista, Ricardo	6. 1	Vitoria Setubal	Setubal, Por.	18.11.86
Niemi, Antti	6. 1	Southampton	Oulu, Fin.	31.05.72
Warner, Tony	6. 4	Millwall	Liverpool	11.05.74
Defenders				
Bocanegra, Carlos	6. 0	Chicago Fire	Alta Loma, USA	25.05.79
Christanval, Philippe	6. 1	Marseille	Paris	31.08.78
Hughes, Aaron	6. 1	Aston Villa	Cookstown	8.11.79
Knight, Zat	6. 6	–	Solihull	2.05.80
Pearce, Ian	6. 3	West Ham Utd.	Bury St Edmunds	7.05.74
Queudrue, Franck	5.10	Middlesbrough	Paris	27.08.78
Rosenior, Liam	5. 9	Bristol City	Wandsworth	9.07.84
Volz, Moritz	5.11	Arsenal	Siegen, Ger.	21.01.83
Zakuani, Gabriel	6. 0	Leyton Orient	Congo	31.05.86
Midfielders				
Bullard, Jimmy	5.10	Wigan Athletic	Newham	23.10.78
Brown, Michael	5. 9	Tottenham	Hartlepool	25.01.77
Davis, Steven	5. 7	Aston Villa	Ballymena	1.01.85
Davies, Simon	5.11	Everton	Haverfordwest	23.10.79
Diop, Papa Bouba	6. 4	Lens	Dakar	28.01.78
Elrich, Ahmad	5.11	Buscan Icons	Sydney	30.05.81
Elliott, Simon	6. 0	Columbus Crew	Wellington, NZ	10.06.74
Forwards				
Dempsey, Clint	6. 1	New England	Nacogdoches, USA	9.03.83
Helguson, Heidar	6. 0	Watford	Akureyri, Ice.	22.08.77
John, Collins	6. 0	FC Twente	Zwandru, Lib.	7.10.85
Kamara, Diomansy	5.11	W.B.A.	Paris	8.11.80
McBride, Brian	6. 1	Columbus	Arlington Hgts, USA	19.06.72
Runstrom, Bjorn	6. 1	Hammarby	Stockholm	1.03.84

LIVERPOOL

Ground: Anfield, Liverpool L4 0TH.
Telephone: 0151 263 2361. **Club nickname:** Reds or Pool.
First-choice colours: Red shirts; red shorts; red socks.
Record transfer fee: £14,000,000 to Auxerre for Djibril Cisse, July 2004.
Record fee received: £11,000,000 from Leeds Utd. for Robbie Fowler, November 2001.
Record attendance: 61,905 v Wolves, (F.A. Cup 4), 2 February, 1952.
Capacity for 2007-08: 45,362. **Sponsors:** Carlsberg.
League Championship: Winners 1900-01, 1905-06, 1921-22, 1922-23, 1946-47, 1963-64, 1965-66, 1972-73, 1975-76, 1976-77, 1978-79, 1979-80, 1981-82, 1982-83, 1983-84, 1985-86, 1987-88, 1989-90.
F.A. Cup: Winners 1965, 1974, 1986, 1989, 1992, 2001, 2006.
League Cup: Winners 1981, 1982, 1983, 1984, 1995, 2001, 2003.
European Competitions: Winners European Cup 1976-77, 1977-78, 1980-81, 1983-84, 2004-05; UEFA Cup 1972-73, 1975-76, 2000-01; European Super Cup 1977, 2005.
Finishing positions in Premiership:1992-93 6th, 1993-94 8th, 1994-95 4th, 1995-96 3rd, 1996-97 4th, 1997-98 3rd, 1998-99 7th, 1999-2000 4th, 2000-01 3rd, 2001-02 2nd, 2002-03 5th, 2003-04 4th, 2004-05 5th, 2005-06 3rd, 2006-07 3rd.
Biggest win: 10-1 v Rotherham Utd., Div. 2, 18.2.1896. Europe: 11-0 v Stromsgodset, CWC, 17.9.1974.
Biggest defeat: 1-9 v Birmingham City, Div. 2, 11.12.1954.
Highest League scorer in a season: Roger Hunt, 41, 1961-62.
Most League goals in aggregate: Roger Hunt, 245, 1959-69.
Most capped player: Ian Rush (Wales) 67.
Longest unbeaten League sequence: 31 matches (May 1987).
Longest sequence without a League win: 14 (December 1953).

Name	Height ft. in.	Previous club	Birthplace	Birthdate
Goalkeepers				
Carson, Scott	6. 3	Leeds Utd.	Whitehaven	3.09.85
Mihaylov, Nikolay	6. 4	Levski Sofia	Sofia	28.06.88
Martin, David	6. 1	MK Dons	Romford	22.01.86
Reina, Jose	6. 2	Aston Villarreal	Madrid	31.08.82
Defenders				
Agger, Daniel	6. 3	Brondby	Hvidovre, Den.	12.12.84
Arbeloa, Alvaro	6. 1	Deportivo La Coruna	Salamanca, Sp.	17.01.83
Aurelio, Fabio	5.10	Valencia	Sao Carlos, Br.	24.09.79
Finnan, Steve	5.10	Fulham	Limerick	20.04.76
Carragher, Jamie	6. 1	–	Liverpool	28.01.78
Darby, Stephen	5.11	–	Liverpool	6.10.88
Hyypia, Sami	6. 4	Willem II	Porvoo, Fin.	7.10.73
Hobbs, Jack	5.11	Lincoln City	Portsmouth	18.08.88
Insua, Emiliano	5.10	Boca Juniors	Buenos Aires	7.01.89
Paletta, Gabriel	6. 1	Banfield	Longchamps, Arg.	15.02.86
Roque, Miki	6. 2	Lleida	Tremp, Sp.	8.07.88
Midfielders				
Anderson, Paul	5. 9	Hull City	Leicester	23.07.88
El Zhar, Nabil	5. 7	St Etienne	Ales, Fr.	27.08.86
Gerrard, Steven	6. 1	–	Whiston	30.05.80
Gonzalez, Mark	5. 9	Albacete	Durban	10.07.84
Guthrie, Danny	5. 9	–	Shrewsbury	18.04.87
Kewell, Harry	6. 0	Leeds Utd.	Sydney	22.09.78
Mascherano, Javier	5. 7	West Ham Utd.	Rosario, Arg.	8.06.84
Peltier, Lee	5.10	–	Liverpool	11.12.86
Pennant, Jermaine	5. 6	Birmingham City	Nottingham	15.01.83
Riise, John Arne	6. 1	Monaco	Molde, Nor.	24.09.80
Sissoko, Mohamed	6. 2	Valencia	Mont St Agnain, Fr.	22.01.85

Xabi Alonso	6. 0	Real Sociedad	Tolosa, Sp.	25.11.81
Forwards				
Crouch, Peter	6. 7	Southampton	Macclesfield	30.01.81
Kuyt, Dirk	6. 0	Feyenoord	Katwijk, Hol.	22.07.80
Lindfield, Craig	5.11	–	Liverpool	7.09.88
Torres, Fernando	6. 1	Atletico Madrid	Madrid	20.03.84
Voronin, Andrey	5.10	Bayer Leverkusen	Odessa	21.07.79

MANCHESTER CITY

Ground: City of Manchester Stadium, Sportcity, Manchester M11 3FF.
Telephone: 0870 062 1894. **Club nickname:** City.
First-choice-colours: Sky blue shirts; white shorts; sky blue socks.
Record transfer fee: £10,000,000 to Paris St Germain for Nicolas Anelka, June 2002.
Record fee received: £21,000,000 from Chelsea for Shaun Wright-Phillips, July 2005.
Record attendance: At City of Manchester Stadium: 47,304 v Chelsea (Premier League) 28 February, 2004. At Maine Road: 84,569 v Stoke City (F.A. Cup 6) 3 March, 1934 (British record for any game outside London or Glasgow).
Capacity for 2007-08: 47,715. **Sponsors:** Thomas Cook.
League Championship: Winners 1936-37, 1967-68.
F.A. Cup: Winners 1904, 1934, 1956, 1969.
League Cup: Winners 1970, 1976.
European Competitions: Winners Cup-Winners' Cup 1969-70.
Finishing positions in Premiership: 1992-93 9th, 1993-94 16th, 1994-95 17th, 1995-96 18th, 2000-01: 18th, 2002-03 9th, 2003-04 16th, 2004-05 8th, 2005-06 15th, 2006-07 14th.
Biggest win: 10-1 Huddersfield Town, Div. 2, 7.11.1987. Also 10-1 v Swindon Town, F.A. Cup 4th rd. 29.1.1930.
Biggest defeat: 1-9 v Everton, Div. 1, 3.9,1906.
Highest League scorer in a season: Tommy Johnson, 38, 1928-29.
Most League goals in aggregate: Tommy Johnson, 158, 1919-30.
Most capped player: Colin Bell (England) 48.
Longest unbeaten League sequence: 22 matches (April 1947).
Longest sequence without a League win: 17 matches (April 1980).

Name	Height ft. in.	Previous club	Birthplace	Birthdate
Goalkeepers				
Hart, Joe	6. 3	Shrewsbury Town	Shrewsbury	19.04.87
Isaksson, Andreas	6. 6	Rennes	Trelleborg, Swe.	3.10.81
Schmeichel, Kasper	6. 0	–	Copenhagen	5.11.86
Defenders				
Ball, Michael	5.10	PSV Eindhoven	Liverpool	2.10.79
Dunne, Richard	6. 2	Everton	Dublin	21.09.79
Mills, Danny	6. 0	Leeds Utd.	Norwich	18.05.77
Mills, Matthew	6. 3	Southampton	Swindon	14.07.86
Onuoha, Nedum	6. 2	–	Nigeria	12.11.86
Richards, Micah	5.11	–	Birmingham	24.06.88
Sun Jihai	5.10	Dalian Wanda	Dalian, Chi.	30.09.77
Midfielders				
Dabo, Ousmane	6. 1	Lazio	France	8.02.77
Hamann, Dietmar	6. 2	Liverpool	Waldasson, Ger.	27.08.73
Ireland, Stephen	5. 8	–	Cork	22.08.86
Johnson, Michael	6. 0	–	Urmston	3.03.88
Miller, Ishmael	6. 3	–	Manchester	5.03.87
Forwards				
Corradi, Bernado	6. 2	Valencia	Siena	30.03.76
Dickov, Paul	5. 6	Blackburn Rov.	Livingston	1.11.72
Mpenza, Emile	5.10	Al Rayyan	Brussels	4.07.78
Samaras, Georgios	6. 4	Heerenveen	Heraklion, Gre.	21.02.85
Vassell, Darius	5. 7	Aston Villa	Birmingham	13.06.80

MANCHESTER UNITED

Ground: Old Trafford Stadium, Sir Matt Busby Way, Manchester, M16 ORA.
Telephone: 0161 868 8000. **Club nickname:** Red Devils.
First-choice colours: Red shirts; white shorts; black socks.
Record transfer fee: £28,250,000 to Leeds Utd. for Rio Ferdinand, July 2002.
Record fee received: £25,000,000 from Real Madrid for David Beckham, July 2003.
Record attendance: Club: 76,098 v Blackburn Rov. (Premier League), 31 March 2007. F.A. Cup (semi-final): 76,962, Wolves v Grimsby Town, 25 March, 1939. Note: 83,260 saw Manchester Utd. v Arsenal, Div. 1, 17 January, 1948 at Maine Road. Old Trafford was out of action through bomb damage.
Capacity for 2007-08: 76,212. **Sponsors:** AIG.
League Championship: Winners 1907-08, 1910-11, 1951-52, 1955-56, 1956-7, 1964-65, 1966-67, 1992-93, 1993-94, 1995-96, 1996-97, 1998-99, 1999-2000, 2000-01, 2002-03, 2006-07.
F.A. Cup: Winners 1909, 1948, 1963, 1977, 1983, 1985, 1990, 1994, 1996, 1999, 2004.
League Cup: Winners 1992, 2006.
European Competitions: Winners European Cup 1967-68, 1998-99; Cup-Winners' Cup 1990-91; European Super Cup 1991.
Finishing positions in Premiership: 1992-93 1st, 1993-94 1st, 1994-95 2nd, 1995-96 1st, 1996-97 1st, 1997-98 2nd, 1998-99 1st, 1999-2000 1st, 2000-01 1st, 2001-02 3rd, 2002-03 1st, 2003-04 3rd, 2004-05 3rd, 2005-06 2nd, 2006-07 1st.
Biggest win: (while Newton Heath) 10-1 v Wolves, Div.1, 15.10.1892, (as Manchester Utd.) 9-0 v Ipswich Town, Premier League, 4.3.1995. Europe: 10-0 v Anderlecht, European Cup prelim. round, 26.9.1956.
Biggest defeat: 0-7 v Wolves Div 2, 26.12.1931, v Aston Villa, Div. 1, 27.12.1930 and v Blackburn Rov. Div. 1, 10.4.1926.
Highest League scorer in a season: Dennis Viollet, 32, 1959-60.
Most League goals in aggregate: Bobby Charlton, 199, 1956-73.
Most capped player: Bobby Charlton (England) 106.
Longest unbeaten League sequence: 26 matches (February 1956).
Longest sequence without a League win: 16 matches (November 1928 and April 1930).

Name	Height ft. in.	Previous club	Birthplace	Birthdate
Goalkeepers				
Foster, Ben	6. 2	Stoke City	Leamington Spa	3.04.83
Heaton, Tom	6. 1	–	Chester	15.04.86
Kuszczak, Tomasz	6. 3	W.B.A.	Krosno, Pol.	20.03.82
Van der Sar, Edwin	6. 6	Fulham	Voorhout, Hol.	29.10.70
Defenders				
Bardsley, Phillip	5.10	–	Manchester	28.06.85
Brown, Wes	6. 1	–	Manchester	13.10.79
Cathcart, Craig	6. 2	–	Belfast	6.02.89
Evra, Patrice	5. 8	Monaco	Dakar	15.05.81
Ferdinand, Rio	6. 2	Leeds Utd.	Peckham	8.11.78
Heinze, Gabriel	5.11	Paris SG	Crespo, Arg.	19.04.78
Neville, Gary	5.11	–	Bury	18.02.75
O'Shea, John	6. 3	Waterford	Waterford	30.04.81
Pique, Gerard	6. 2	Barcelona	Barcelona	02.02.87
Silvestre, Mikael	6. 0	Inter Milan	Chambray, Fr.	9.08.77
Vidic, Nemanja	6. 3	Spartak Moscow	Uzice, Serbia	21.10.81
Midfielders				
Anderson	5.10	Porto	Alegre, Br.	13.04.88
Carrick, Michael	6. 0	Tottenham	Wallsend	28.07.81
Eagles, Chris	5.11	–	Hemel Hempstead	19.11.85
Fletcher, Darren	6. 0	–	Edinburgh	1.02.84
Giggs, Ryan	5.11	–	Cardiff	29.11.73
Hargreaves, Owen	5. 9	Bayern Munich	Calgary	20.01.81

Ji-Sung Park	5. 9	PSV Eindhoven	Seoul	25.02.81
Nani	5.10	Sporting Lisbon	Amadora, Por.	17.11.86
Richardson, Kieran	5.10	–	Greenwich	21.10.84
Ronaldo, Cristiano	6. 1	Sporting Lisbon	Madeira	5.02.85
Rossi, Giuseppe	5. 9	Parma	New Jersey	1.02.87
Scholes, Paul	5. 7	–	Salford	16.11.74
Forwards				
Fangzhuo Dong	6. 2	–	Dalian, Chi.	23.01.85
Rooney, Wayne	5.10	Everton	Liverpool	24.10.85
Rossi, Giuseppe	5. 8	Parma	Teaneck, USA	1.02.87
Saha, Louis	5.11	Fulham	Paris	8.08.78
Smith, Alan	5. 9	Leeds Utd.	Leeds	28.10.80
Solskjaer, Ole Gunnar	5.10	Molde	Kristiansund, Nor.	26.02.73

MIDDLESBROUGH

Ground: Cellnet Riverside Stadium, Middlesbrough, TS3 6RS.
Telephone: 0844 499 6789. **Club nickname:** Boro.
First-choice colours: Red and white shirts; red shorts; red socks.
Record transfer fee: £8,150,000 to Empoli for Massimo Maccarone, July 2002.
Record fee received: £12,000,000 from Atletico Madrid for Juninho, July 1997.
Record attendance: At Riverside Stadium: 34,836 v Norwich City (Premier League) 28 December, 2004. 35,000 England v Slovakia 11 June, 2003. At Ayresome Park: 53,596 v Newcastle Utd. (Div.1) 27 December, 1949.
Capacity for 2007-08: 35,041. **Sponsors:** 888.com.
League Championship: 3rd 1913-14.
F.A. Cup: Runners-up 1997.
League Cup: Winners 2004.
European Competitions: UEFA Cup Final 2005-06.
Finishing positions in Premiership: 1992-93 21st, 1995-96 12th, 1996-97 19th, 1998-99 9th, 1999-2000 12th, 2000-01 14th, 2001-02 12th, 2002-03 11th, 2003-04 11th, 2004-05 7th, 2005-06 14th, 2006-07 12th.
Biggest win: 9-0 v Brighton & H.A., Div 2, 23.8.1958.
Biggest defeat: 0-9 v Blackburn Rov., Div 2, 6.11.1954.
Highest League scorer in a season: George Camsell, 59, 1926-27.
Most League goals in aggregate: George Camsell, 326, 1925-39.
Most capped player: Wilf Mannion (England) 26.
Longest unbeaten League sequence: 24 matches (September 1973).
Longest sequence without a League win: 19 matches (October 1981).

Name	Height ft. in.	Previous club	Birthplace	Birthdate
Goalkeepers				
Jones, Bradley	6. 3	–	Armadale, Aus.	19.03.82
Knight, David	6. 0	–	Houghton	15.01.87
Schwarzer, Mark	6. 4	Bradford City	Sydney	6.10.72
Turnbull, Ross	6. 1	–	Bishop Auckland	4.01.85
Defenders				
Arca, Julio	5.10	Sunderland	Quilmes Bernal, Arg.	31.01.81
Bates, Matthew	5.10	–	Stockton	10.12.86
Davies, Andrew	5.11	–	Stockton	17.12.84
Huth, Robert	6. 2	Chelsea	Berlin	18.08.84
McMahon, Tony	5.10	–	Bishop Auckland	24.03.86
Pogatetz, Emanuel	6. 4	Bayer Leverkusen	Steinbock, Aut.	16.01.83
Riggott, Chris	6. 2	Derby Co.	Derby	1.09.80
Taylor, Andrew	5.10	–	Hartlepool	01.08.86
Wheater, David	6. 4	–	Redcar	14.02.87
Woodgate, Jonathan	6. 2	Real Madrid	Middlesbrough	22.01.80
Midfielders				
Boateng, George	5. 9	Aston Villa	Nkawka, Gh.	5.09.75
Cattermole, Lee	5.10	–	Stockton	21.03.88

Downing, Stewart	6. 0	–	Middlesbrough	22.07.84
Hines, Sebastian	6. 2	–	Wetherby	29.05.88
Johnson, Adam	5. 9	–	Sunderland	14.07.87
Kennedy, Jason	6. 1	–	Stockton	11.09.86
Mendieta, Gaizka	5. 8	Lazio	Bilbao	27.03.74
Morrison, James	5.10	–	Darlington	25.05.86
Owens, Graeme	5.10	–	Cramlington	1.06.88
Rochemback, Fabio	6. 1	Barcelona	Soledade, Br.	10.12.81
Forwards				
Aliadiere, Jeremie	6. 0	Arsenal	Rambouillet, Fr.	30.03.83
Craddock, Tom	5.11	–	Durham	14.10.86
Dong Gook Lee	6. 1	Pohang	Pohang	29.04.79
Euell, Jason	5.11	Charlton Athletic	Lambeth	6.02.77
Sanli, Tuncay	6. 0	Fenerbahce	Sakarya, Tur.	16.01.82
Yakubu, Aiyegbeni	6. 0	Portsmouth	Benin, Nig.	22.11.82

NEWCASTLE UNITED

Ground: St James' Park, Newcastle-upon-Tyne, NE1 4ST.
Telephone: 0191 201 8400. **Club nickname:** Magpies.
First-choice colours: Black and white shirts; black shorts; black socks.
Record transfer fee: £16,500,000 to Real Madrid for Michael Owen, August 2005.
Record fee received: £13,400,000 from Real Madrid for Jonathan Woodgate, August 2004.
Record attendance: 68,386 v Chelsea (Div. 1) 3 September, 1930.
Capacity for 2007-08: 52,387. **Sponsors:** Northern Rock.
League Championship: Winners 1904-05, 1906-07, 1908-09, 1926-27.
F.A. Cup: Winners 1910, 1924, 1932, 1951, 1952, 1955.
League Cup: Runners-up 1976.
European Competitions: Winners Fairs Cup 1968-69, Anglo-Italian Cup 1972-73.
Finishing positions in Premiership: 1993-94 3rd 1994-95 6th 1995-96 2nd 1996-97 2nd 1997-98 13th 1998-99 13th, 1999-2000 11th, 2000-01 11th, 2001-02 4th, 2002-03 3rd, 2003-04 5th, 2004-05 14th, 2005-06 7th, 2006-07 13th.
Biggest win: 13-0 v Newport County, Div. 2, 5.10.1946.
Biggest defeat: 0-9 v Burton Wanderers, Div. 2, 15.4.1895.
Highest League scorer in a season: Hughie Gallacher, 36, 1926-27.
Most League goals in aggregate: Jackie Milburn, 177, 1946-57.
Most capped player: Shay Given (Rep. of Ireland) 71.
Longest unbeaten League sequence: 14 matches (April 1950).
Longest sequence without a League win: 21 matches (January 1978).

Name	Height ft. in.	Previous club	Birthplace	Birthdate
Goalkeepers				
Forster, Fraser	6. 0	–	Hexham	17.03.88
Given, Shay	6. 1	Blackburn Rov.	Lifford	20.04.76
Harper, Steve	6. 2	–	Easington	14.03.75
Krul, Tim	6. 3	Den Haag	Den Haag	3.04.88
Defenders				
Babayaro, Celestine	5. 9	Newcastle Utd.	Kaduna, Nig.	29.08.78
Carr, Stephen	5. 8	Tottenham	Dublin	29.08.76
Edgar, David	6. 2	–	Kitchener, Can.	19.05.87
Geremi	5.11	Chelsea	Batousam, Cam.	20.12.78
Huntington, Paul	6. 3	–	Carlisle	17.09.87
Gate, Kris	5. 7	–	Newcastle	1.01.85
Ramage, Peter	6. 1	–	Newcastle	22.11.83
Rozehnal, David	6. 3	Paris SG	Sternberk, Cz.	5.07.80
Taylor, Steven	6. 2	–	Greenwich	23.01.86
Midfielders				
Barton, Joey	5. 9	Manchester City	Huyton	2.09.82
Butt, Nicky	5.10	Manchester Utd.	Manchester	21.01.75

Duff, Damien	5.10	Chelsea	Dublin	2.03.79
Dyer, Kieron	5. 7	Ipswich Town	Ipswich	29.12.78
Emre	5.10	Inter Milan	Istanbul	7.09.80
Milner, James	5.11	Leeds Utd.	Leeds	4.01.86
N'Zogbia, Charles	5. 7	–	Harfleur, Fr.	28.05.86
Pattison, Matthew	5. 8	–	Johannesburg	27.10.86
Solano, Nolberto	5. 8	Aston Villa	Lima	12.12.74
Troisi, James	5.11	–	Adelaide, Aus.	3.07.88
Forwards				
Ameobi, Shola	6. 3	–	Zaria, Nig.	12.10.81
Carroll, Andrew	6. 3	–	Gateshead	6.01.89
LuaLua, Kazenga	5.11	–	Kinshasa	10.12.90
Luque, Albert	6. 0	Dep. La Coruna	Barcelona	11.03.78
Martins, Obafemi	5. 8	Inter Milan	Lagos	28.10.84
Owen, Michael	5. 8	Real Madrid	Chester	14.12.79
Viduka, Mark	6. 2	Middlesbrough	Melbourne	9.10.75

PORTSMOUTH

Ground: Fratton Park, Frogmore Road, Portsmouth, PO4 8RA.
Telephone: 0239 273 1204. **Club nickname:** Pompey.
First choice colours: Royal blue shirts; white shorts; red socks.
Record transfer fee: £7,000,000 to Udinese for Sulley Muntari, May 2007.
Record fee received: £7,500,000 from Middlesbrough for Aiyegbeni Yakubu, June 2005.
Record attendance: 51,385 v Derby Co. (F.A. Cup 6) 26 February, 1949.
Capacity for 2007-08: 20,388. **Sponsors:** OKI.
League Championships: winners 1948-49, 1949-50.
F.A. Cup: Winners 1939.
League Cup: 5th rd. 1961, 1986.
Finishing positions in Premiership: 2003-04 13th, 2004-05 16th, 2005-06 17th, 2006-07 9th.
Biggest win: 9-1 v Notts Co., Div. 1, 09.04.1927.
Biggest defeat: 0-10 v Leicester City, Div. 1, 20.10.1928.
Highest League scorer in a season: Guy Whittingham, 42, Div. 1, 1992-93.
Most League goals in aggregate: Peter Harris, 194, 1946-60.
Most capped player: Jimmy Dickinson (England) 48.
Longest unbeaten League sequence: 15 matches (October 1924).
Longest sequence without a League win: 25 matches (August 1959).

Name	Height ft. in.	Previous club	Birthplace	Birthdate
Goalkeepers				
Ashdown, Jamie	6. 3	Reading	Reading	30.11.80
Begovic, Asmir	6. 5	–	Trebinje, Bosnia	20.06.87
James, David	6. 5	Manchester City	Welwyn Garden City	1.08.70
Jordan, Nicholas	5.11	–	Aldershot	13.11.89
Defenders				
Campbell, Sol	6. 2	Arsenal	Newham	18.09.74
Distin, Sylvain	6. 4	Manchester City	Paris	16.12.77
Duffy, Richard	5.10	Swansea City	Swansea	30.08.85
Griffin, Andy	5. 9	Newcastle Utd.	Billinge	7.03.79
Hreidarsson, Hermann	6. 1	Charlton Athletic	Iceland	11.07.74
Koroman, Ognjen	5.10	Terek Grozny	Sarajevo	19.09.78
Lauren	5.11	Arsenal	Londi Kribi, Cam.	19.01.77
O'Brien, Andy	5.10	Newcastle Utd.	Harrogate	29.06.79
Pamarot, Noe	6. 2	Tottenham	Paris	14.04.79
Primus, Linvoy	5.11	Reading	Forest Gate	14.07.73
Stefanovic, Dejan	5.11	Vitesse Arnhem	Belgrade	28.10.74
Traore, Djimi	6. 1	Charlton Athletic	Saint-Ouen, Fr.	1.03.80

Midfielders

Davis, Sean	5.11	Tottenham	Clapham	20.09.79
Douala, Roudolphe	5.10	Sporting Lisbon	Cam.	25.09.78
Hughes, Richard	5. 9	Bournemouth	Glasgow	25.06.79
Kranjcar, Niko	6. 1	Hajduk Split	Zagreb	13.08.84
Mendes, Pedro	5.10	Tottenham	Guimaraes, Por.	26.02.79
Muntari, Sulley	5.11	Udinese	Konongo, Gh.	27.08.84
Mvuemba, Arnold	5. 7	Rennes	Alencon, Fr.	28.01.85
O'Neil, Gary	5. 9	–	Beckenham	18.05.83
Taylor, Matthew	5.11	Luton Town	Oxford	27.11.81
Forwards				
Cole, Andrew	5.11	Manchester City	Nottingham	15.10.71
Kanu, Nwankwo	6. 4	W.B.A.	Owerri, Nig.	1.08.76
LuaLua, Lomana	5. 8	Newcastle Utd.	Kinshasa	28.12.80
Mwaruwari, Benjani	6. 2	Auxerre	Bulawayo	13.08.78

READING

Ground: Madejski Stadium, Junction 11 M4, Reading RG2 OFL.
Telephone: 0118 968 1100. **Club nickname:** Royals.
First-choice colours: Blue and white shirts; blue and white shorts; blue socks.
Record transfer fee: £1,000,000 to Bristol City for Leroy Lita, July 2005.
Record fee received: £1,750,000 from Newcastle Utd. for Shaka Hislop, August 1995.
Record attendance: At Elm Park: 33,042 v Brentford (F.A. Cup 5) 19 February, 1927. At Madejski Stadium: 24,122 v Aston Villa (Premier League) 10 February, 2007.
Capacity for 2007-08: 24,200. **Sponsors:** Kyocera.
F.A. Cup: Semi-finals 1927.
League Cup: 5th rd. 1996.
Finishing position in Premiership: 2006-07 8th.
Biggest win: 10-2 v Crystal Palace, Div. 3 (South), 04.09.1946.
Biggest defeat: 0-18 v Preston N.E., F.A. Cup 1st rd., 1893-94.
Highest League scorer in a season: Ronnie Blackman, 39, 1951-52.
Most League goals in aggregate: Ronnie Blackman, 158, 1947-54.
Most capped player: Jimmy Quinn (Northern Ireland) 17.
Longest unbeaten League sequence: 19 matches (October 1973).
Longest sequence without a League win: 14 matches (October 1927).

Name	Height ft. in.	Previous club	Birthplace	Birthdate
Goalkeepers				
Andersen, Mikkel	6. 5	AB Copenhagen	Herlev, Den.	17.12.88
Federici, Adam	6. 2	Sardenga	Nowra, Aus.	31.01.85
Hahnemann, Marcus	6. 3	Fulham	Seattle	15.06.72
Stack, Graham	6. 2	Arsenal	Hampstead	26.09.81
Defenders				
Bennett, Alan	6. 2	Cork City	Cork	4.10.81
Bikey, Andre	6. 0	–	Douala, Cam.	8.01.85
De la Cruz, Ulises	5.11	Aston Villa	Piqulucho, Ec.	08.02.74
Duberry, Michael	6. 1	Stoke City	Enfield	14.10.75
Golbourne, Scott	5. 8	Bristol City	Bristol	29.02.88
Halls, John	6. 0	Stoke City	Islington	14.02.82
Ingimarsson, Ivar	6. 0	Wolves	Iceland	20.08.77
Murty, Graeme	5.10	York City	Saltburn	13.11.74
Pearce, Alex	6. 0	–	Oxford	9.11.88
Shorey, Nicky	5. 9	Leyton Orient	Romford	19.02.81
Sodje, Sam	6. 1	Brentford	Greenwich	29.05.79
Sonko, Ibrahima	5.10	Brentford	Bignaolo, Sen.	22.01.81
Midfielders				
Bozanic, Oliver	6. 0	Central Coast	Sydney	8.01.89
Brown, Aaron	6. 4	Tamworth	Birmingham	23.06.83

Cisse, Kalifa	6. 1	Boavista	Dreux, Fr.	9.01.84
Convey, Bobby	5. 8	DC Utd.	Philadelphia	27.05.83
Cox, Simon	5.10	–	Reading	28.04.87
Davies, Scott	5.11	Wycombe Wand.		10.03.88
Gunnarsson, Brynjar	6. 1	Watford	Reykjavik	16.10.75
Harper, James	5.11	Arsenal	Chelmsford	9.11.80
Henry, James	6. 1	–	Reading	10.06.89
Hunt, Stephen	5. 8	Brentford	Port Laoise	1.08.80
Little, Glen	6. 3	Burnley	Wimbledon	15.10.75
Oster, John	5. 9	Burnley	Boston	8.12.78
Seol Ki-Hyeon	6. 0	Wolves	South Korea	8.01.79
Forwards				
Doyle, Kevin	5.11	Cork City	Ireland	18.09.83
Kitson, Dave	6. 3	Cambridge Utd.	Hitchin	21.01.80
Lita, Leroy	5. 9	Bristol City	Congo	28.12.84
Long, Shane	5.10	Cork City	Gortnahoe, Ire.	22.01.87

SUNDERLAND

Ground: Stadium of Light, Sunderland SR5 1SU.
Telephone: 0191 551 5000.
First-choice colours: Red and white shirts; black shorts; black socks.
Record transfer fee: £8,000,000 to Rangers for Tore Andre Flo, August 2002.
Record fee received: £5,000,000 from Leeds Utd. for Michael Bridges, July 1999.
Record attendance: At Stadium of Light: 48,353 v Liverpool (Premier League) 13 April 2002. At Roker Park: 75,118 v Derby Co. (F.A. Cup 6 replay) 8 March 1933.
Capacity for 2007-08: 49,000. **Sponsors:** Boylesports.
League Championship: Winners 1891-92, 1892-93, 1894-95, 1901-02, 1912-13, 1935-36.
F.A. Cup: Winners 1937, 1973.
League Cup: Runners-up 1985.
European Competitions: Cup-Winners' Cup rd. 2, 1973-74.
Finishing positions in Premiership: 1996-97 18th, 1999-2000 7th, 2000-01 7th, 2001-02 17th, 2002-03 20th, 2005-06 20th.
Biggest win: 9-1 v Newcastle Utd., Div. 1, 5.12, 1908. Also 11-1 v Fairfield, F.A. Cup, 1st rd., 2.2.1895.
Biggest defeat: 0-8 v Sheffield Wed., Div.1, 26.12.1911. 0-8 v West Ham Utd., Div. 1, 19.10.68. 0-8 v Watford, Div. 1, 25.9.82.
Highest League scorer in a season: Dave Halliday, 43, 1928-29.
Most League goals in aggregate: Charlie Buchan, 209, 1911-25.
Most capped player:.Charlie Hurley (Republic of Ireland) 38.
Longest unbeaten League sequence: 19 matches (November 1998).
Longest sequence without a League win: 22 matches (August 2003).

Name	**Height ft. in.**	**Previous club**	**Birthplace**	**Birthdate**
Goalkeepers				
Carson, Trevor	6. 0	–	Downpatrick	5.03.88
Fulop, Marton	6. 6	Tottenham	Budapest	3.05.83
Ward, Darren	5.11	Norwich City	Worksop	11.05.74
Defenders				
Anderson, Russell	6. 1	Aberdeen	Aberdeen	25.10.78
Clarke, Clive	6. 1	West Ham Utd.	Dublin	14.01.80
Collins, Danny	5.11	Chester City	Chester	6.08.80
Halford, Greg	6. 4	Reading	Chelmsford	8.12.84
Hartley, Peter	6. 0	–	Hartlepool	3.04.88
Nosworthy, Nyron	6. 0	Gillingham	Brixton	11.10.80
Varga, Stanislav	6. 4	Celtic	Lipany	8.10.72
Wright, Stephen	6. 0	Liverpool	Liverpool	8.02.80
Midfielders				
Dennehy, Billy	5.10	Shelbourne	Tralee	17.02.87

Edwards, Carlos	5.11	Luton Town	Port of Spain, Trin.	24.10.78
Hysen, Tobias	5.10	Djurgarden	Gothenburg	9.03.82
Kavanagh, Graham	5.10	Wigan Athletic	Dublin	2.12.73
Leadbitter, Grant	5. 9	–	Sunderland	7.01.86
Miller, Liam	5. 8	Manchester Utd.	Cork	13.02.81
Richardson, Jake	5. 8	Sutton Coldfield	Watford	22.10.88
Riera, Arnau	5. 9	Barcelona	Mallorca	1.10.81
Wallace, Ross	5. 6	Celtic	Dundee	23.05.85
Welsh, Andrew	5.10	Stockport Co.	Manchester	24.01.83
Whitehead, Dean	5.11	Oxford Utd.	Abingdon	12.01.82
Forwards				
Connolly, David	5. 8	Wigan Athletic Athetic	Willesden	6.06.77
Elliott, Stephen	5.11	Manchester City	Dublin	6.01.84
John, Stern	6. 1	Coventry City	Tunapuna, Trin.	30.10.76
Murphy, Daryl	6. 2	Waterford	Waterford	15.03.83
Stokes, Anthony	5.11	Arsenal	Dublin	25.07.88
Yorke, Dwight	5.10	Sydney	Canaan, Tob.	3.11.71

TOTTENHAM HOTSPUR

Ground: White Hart Lane, Tottenham, London N17 OAP.
Telephone: 0208 365 5000. **Club nickname:** Spurs.
First-choice colours: White shirts; navy shorts; white socks.
Record transfer fee: £16,500,000 to Charlton Athletic for Darren Bent, June 2007.
Record fee received: £18,600,000 from Manchester Utd. for Michael Carrick, August 2006.
Record attendance: 75,038 v Sunderland (F.A. Cup 6) 5 March 1938.
Capacity for 2007-08: 36,252. **Sponsors:** Mansion.
League Championship: Winners 1950-51, 1960-61.
F.A. Cup: Winners 1901, 1921, 1961, 1962, 1967, 1981, 1982, 1991.
League Cup: Winners 1971, 1973, 1999.
European Competitions: Winners Cup-Winners' Cup 1962-63, UEFA Cup 1971-72, 1983-84.
Finishing positions in Premiership: 1992-93 8th, 1993-94 15th, 1994-95 7th, 1995-96 8th, 1996-97 10th, 1997-98 14th, 1998-99 11th, 1999-2000 10th, 2000-01 12th, 2001-02 9th, 2002-03 10th, 2003-04 14th, 2004-05 9th, 2005-06 5th, 2006-07 5th.
Biggest win: 9-0 v Bristol Rov., Div.2, 22.10.1977, F.A. Cup 13-2 v Crewe Alexandra, round four replay, 3.2.1960, Europe 9-0 v Keflavik, UEFA Cup, round one, 28.9.1971.
Biggest defeat: 0-7 v Liverpool, Div.1, 2.9.1979.
Highest League scorer in a season: Jimmy Greaves, 37, 1962-63.
Most League goals in aggregate: Jimmy Greaves, 220, 1961-70.
Most capped player: Pat Jennings (Northern Ireland) 74.
Longest unbeaten League sequence: 22 matches (August 1949).
Longest sequence without a League win: 16 matches (December 1934).

Name	Height ft. in.	Previous club	Birthplace	Birthdate
Goalkeepers				
Alnwick, Ben	6. 0	Sunderland	Gateshead	1.01.87
Cerny, Radek	6. 4	Slavia Prague	Czech Rep.	18.02.74
Robinson, Paul	6. 2	Leeds Utd.	Beverley	15.10.79
Defenders				
Assou-Ekotto, Benoit	5.10	Lens	Arras, Fr.	24.03.84
Bale, Gareth	6. 0	Southampton	Cardiff	16.07.89
Berchiche, Yuri	5.11	Athletic Bilbao	Zarautz, Sp.	10.02.90
Chimbonda, Pascal	5.11	Wigan Athletic	Les Abymes, Fr.	21.02.79
Dawson, Michael	6. 2	Nott'm. Forest	Northallerton	18.11.83
Dervite, Dorian	6. 3	Lille	Lille	25.07.88
Gardner, Anthony	6. 5	Port Vale	Stafford	19.09.80

Ifil, Phil	5. 9	–	Brent	18.11.86
Kaboul, Younes	6. 3	Auxerre	Saint Julien, Fr.	4.01.86
King, Ledley	6. 2	–	Bow	12.10.80
Rocha, Ricardo	6. 0	Benfica	Braga, Por.	3.10.78
Stalteri, Paul	5.11	Werder Bremen	Etobicoke, Can.	18.10.77
Young-Pyo Lee	5. 9	PSV Eindhoven	Hong Chung, S. Kor.	23.04.77
Midfielders				
Ghaly, Hossam	6. 0	Feyenoord	Kafr El-Sheikh, Egy.	15.12.81
Jenas, Jermaine	6. 0	Newcastle Utd.	Nottingham	18.02.83
Lennon, Aaron	5. 5	Leeds Utd.	Leeds	16.04.87
Malbranque, Steed	5. 8	Fulham	Mouscron, Bel.	6.01.80
Murphy, Danny	5.10	Charlton Athletic	Chester	18.03.77
O'Hara, Jamie	5.11	–	London	25.09.86
Routledge, Wayne	5. 6	Crystal Palace	Sidcup	7.01.85
Tainio, Teemu	5. 8	Auxerre	Tornio, Fin.	27.11.79
Taarabt, Adel	5.11	Lens	Berre-l'Etang, Fr.	24.05.89
Zokora, Didier	5.11	St Etienne	Abidjan, Iv.	14.12.80
Forwards				
Barcham, Andy	5. 9	–	Basildon	16.12.86
Barnard, Lee	5.10	–	Romford	18.07.84
Bent, Darren	5.11	Charlton Athletic	Wandsworth	6.02.84
Berbatov, Dimitar	6. 2	Bayer Leverkusen	Bulgaria	30.01.81
Defoe, Jermain	5. 7	West Ham Utd.	Beckton	7.10.82
Keane, Robbie	5. 9	Leeds Utd.	Dublin	8.07.80
Mido, Ahmed	6. 2	Roma	Cairo	23.2.83

WEST HAM UNITED

Ground: Boleyn Ground, Green Street, Upton Park, London E13 9AZ.
Telephone: 0208 548 2748. **Club nickname:** Hammers.
First-choice colours: Claret and blue shirts; white shorts; white socks.
Record transfer fee: £7,250,000 to Norwich City for Dean Ashton, January 2006.
Record fee received: £18,000,000 from Leeds Utd. for Rio Ferdinand, November 2000.
Record attendance: 43,322 v Tottenham (Div. 1) 17 October, 1970.
Capacity for 2007-08: 35,056. **Sponsors:** XL Airways.
League Championship: 3rd 1985-86.
F.A. Cup: Winners 1964, 1975, 1980.
League Cup: Runners-up 1966, 1981.
European Competitions: Winners Cup-Winners' Cup 1964-65.
Finishing positions in Premiership: 1993-94 13th, 1994-95 14th, 1995-96 10th, 1996-97 14th, 1997-98 8th, 1998-99 5th, 1999-2000 9th, 2000-01 15th, 2001-02 7th, 2002-03 18th, 2005-06 9th, 2006-07 15th.
Biggest win: 8-0 v Rothham Utd., Div. 2, 8.3.1958 and v Sunderland, Div. 1, 19.10.1968. League Cup 10-0 v Bury, round 2, 25.10.83.
Biggest defeat: 0-7 v Sheffield Wed., Div. 1, 28.11.1959, v Everton, Div. 1, 22.10.1927, v Barnsley, Div. 2, 1.9.1919.
Highest League scorer in a season: Vic Watson, 42, 1929-30.
Most League goals in aggregate: Vic Watson, 298, 1920-35.
Most capped player: Bobby Moore (England) 108.
Longest unbeaten League sequence: 27 matches (October 1981).
Longest sequence without a League win: 17 matches (August 1976).

Name	Height ft. in.	Previous club	Birthplace	Birthdate
Goalkeepers				
Green, Robert	6. 2	Norwich City	Chertsey	18.01.80
Walker, James	5.11	Walsall	Sutton-in-Ashfield	9.07.73
Wright, Richard	6. 2	Everton	Ipswich	5.11.77
Defenders				
Collins, James	6. 2	Cardiff City	Newport	23.08.83
Dailly, Christian	6. 0	Blackburn Rov.	Dundee	23.10.73

Davenport, Calum	6. 4	Tottenham	Bedford	1.01.83
Ferdinand, Anton	6. 0	–	Peckham	18.02.85
Gabbidon, Danny	6. 1	Cardiff City	Cwmbran	8.08.79
Konchesky, Paul	5.10	Charlton Athletic	Barking	15.05.81
McCartney, George	6. 0	Sunderland	Belfast	29.04.81
Neill, Lucas	6. 1	Blackburn Rov.	Sydney	9.03.78
Pantsil, John	5.10	Hapoel Tel Aviv	Ghana	15.06.81
Spector, Jonathan	6. 1	Manchester Utd.	Arlington Hts., USA	3.01.86
Upson, Matthew	6. 1	Birmingham City	Eye	18.04.79
Midfielders				
Benayoun, Yossi	5.10	Racing Santander	Dimona, Isr.	5.05.80
Boa Morte, Luis	5. 9	Fulham	Lisbon	4.08.77
Bowyer, Lee	5. 9	Newcastle Utd.	Canning Town	3.01.77
Etherington, Matthew	5.10	Tottenham	Truro	14.08.81
Faubert, Julien	5.11	Bordeaux	Le Havre	1.08.83
Mullins, Hayden	6. 0	Crystal Palace	Reading	27.03.79
Noble, Mark	5.11	–	West Ham	8.05.87
Parker, Scott	5. 7	Newcastle Utd.	Lambeth	13.10.80
Quashie, Nigel	6. 0	W.B.A.	Peckham	20.07.78
Reid, Kyel	5. 8	–	London	26.11.87
Forwards				
Ashton, Dean	6. 1	Norwich City	Crewe	24.11.83
Bellamy, Craig	5. 9	Liverpool	Cardiff	13.07.79
Cole, Carlton	6. 3	Chelsea	Croydon	12.10.83
Ephraim, Hogan	5. 9	–	Islington	31.03.88
Harewood, Marlon	6. 1	Nott'm. Forest	Hampstead	25.08.79
Tevez, Carlos	5. 6	Corinthians	Buenos Aires	5.02.84
Zamora, Bobby	6. 0	Tottenham	Barking	16.01.81

WIGAN ATHLETIC

Ground: JJB Stadium, Robin Park, Wigan WN5 0UZ.
Telephone: 01942 774000. Club nickname: Latics.
First-choice colours: Blue and white shirts; blue shorts; white socks.
Record transfer fee: £5,500,000 to Birmingham City for Emile Heskey July 2006.
Record fee received: £4,500,000 from Tottenham for Pascal Chimbonda, August 2006.
Record attendance: At Springfield Park: 27,526 v Hereford Utd. (F.A. Cup 2) 12 December, 1953. At JJB Stadium: 25,023 v Liverpool (Premier League) 11 February, 2006.
Capacity for 2007-08: 25,000. **Sponsors:** JJB Sports.
F.A. Cup: 6th Rd. 1987.
League Cup: Final, 2006.
Finishing positions in Premiership: 2005-06 10th, 2006-07 17th.
Biggest win: 7-1 v Scarborough, Div. 3, 11.3.1997, 6-0 v Carlisle Utd., F.A. Cup2 nd Rd., 24.11.1934.
Biggest defeat: 1-6 v Bristol Rov., Div. 3, 3.3.1990.
Highest League scorer in a season: Graeme Jones, 31, 1996-97.
Most League goals in aggregate: Andy Liddell, 70, 1998-2004.
Most capped player: Roy Carroll (Northern Ireland) 9.
Longest unbeaten League sequence: 25 matches (January 2000).
Longest sequence without a League win: 14 (October 1989).

Name	Height ft. in.	Previous club	Birthplace	Birthdate
Goalkeepers				
Kirkland, Chris	6. 3	Liverpool	Leicester	2.05.81
Nash, Carlo	6. 5	Preston N.E.	Bolton	13.09.73
Pollitt, Mike	6. 4	Rotherham Utd.	Farnworth	29.02.72
Defenders				
Baines, Leighton	5. 7	–	Liverpool	11.12.84
Boyce, Emmerson	5.11	Crystal Palace	Aylesbury	24.09.79

Bramble, Titus	6. 1	Newcastle Utd.	Ipswich	21.07.81
Granqvist, Andreas	6. 4	Helsingborgs	Helsingborg, Swe.	16.04.85
Hall, Fitz	6. 1	Crystal Palace	Leytonstone	20.12.80
Melchiot, Mario	6. 2	Rennes	Amsterdam	4.11.76
Scharner, Paul	6. 3	SK Brann	Scheibbs, Aut.	11.03.80
Taylor, Ryan	5. 8	Tranmere Rov.	Liverpool	19.08.84
Midfielders				
Cotterill, David	5.10	Bristol City	Cardiff	4.12.87
Johansson, Andreas	5.10	Djurgardens	Vanersborg, Swe.	5.07.78
Koumas, Jason	5.10	W.B.A.	Wrexham	25.09.79
Kilbane, Kevin	6. 0	Everton	Preston	1.02.77
Landzaat, Denny	5.10	AZ Alkmaar	Amsterdam	28.12.81
Montrose, Lewis	6. 0	–	Manchester	17.11.88
Skoko, Josip	5.10	Genclerbirligi	Mt. Gambier, Aus.	10.12.75
Valencia, Antonio	5.10	Villarreal	Lago Agrio, Sp.	4.08.85
Forwards				
Aghahowa, Julius	6. 0	Shakhtar Donetsk	Benin, Nig.	12.02.82
Camara, Henri	5.10	Wolves	Dakar	10.05.77
Folan, Caleb	6. 1	Chesterfield	Leeds	26.10.82
Heskey, Emile	6. 2	Birmingham City	Leicester	11.01.78
McCulloch, Lee	6. 1	Motherwell	Bellshill	14.05.78
Sibierski, Antoine	6. 2	Newcastle Utd.	Lille	5.08.74

COCA-COLA LEAGUE CLUB DETAILS AND SQUADS 2007-08 – CHAMPIONSHIP

BARNSLEY

Ground: Oakwell Stadium, Barnsley S71 1ET.
Telephone: 01226 211211. **Club nickname:** Tykes.
First-choice colours: Red shirts; white shorts; red socks.
Main Sponsor: Barnsley Building Society. **Capacity for 2007-08:** 23,186.
Record attendance: 40,255 v Stoke City (F.A. Cup 5) 15 February, 1936.

Name	Height ft. in.	Previous club	Birthplace	Birthdate
Goalkeepers				
Colgan, Nick	6. 1	Hibernian	Drogheda	19.09.73
Letheren, Kyel	6. 2	Swansea City	Barnsley	26.12.87
Lucas, David	6. 0	Sheffield Wed.	Preston	23.11.77
Defenders				
Atkinson, Robert	6. 1	–	Beverley	29.04.87
Bruma, Marciano	5.11	Sparta Rotterdam	Rotterdam	7.03.84
Harban, Thomas	6. 0	–	Barnsley	12.11.85
Hassell, Bobby	5. 9	Mansfield Town	Derby	4.06.80
Heckingbottom, Paul	6. 0	Sheffield Wed.	Barnsley	17.07.77
Kozluk, Robert	5. 8	Sheffield Utd.	Sutton-in-Ashfield	5.08.77
Reid, Paul	6. 2	Northampton Town	Carlisle	18.02.82
Togwell, Sam	5.11	Crystal Palace	Beaconsfield	14.10.84
Werling, Dominik	5. 9	Sakaryaspor	Ludwigshafen, Ger.	13.12.82
Midfielders				
Devaney, Martin	5.10	Cheltenham Town	Cheltenham	1.06.80
Heslop, Simon	5.11	–	York	1.05.87
Howard, Brian	5. 8	Swindon Town	Winchester	23.01.83
Johnson, Andy	6. 1	Leicester City	Bristol	2.05.74
Mattis, Dwayne	6. 1	Bury	Huddersfield	31.07.81
McCann, Grant	5.10	Cheltenham Town	Belfast	14.04.80

Name	Height ft. in.	Previous club	Birthplace	Birthdate
Forwards				
Coulson, Michael	5.10	Scarborough	Scarborough	4.04.88
Ferenczi, Istvan	6. 3	Zalaegerszeg	Hungary	14.09.77
Joynes, Nathan	6. 1	–	Barnsley	7.08.85
McGrory, Scott	5.11	–	Aberdeen	5.04.87
Mostto, Miguel	5.10	Cienciano	Ica, Per.	11.11.79
Odejayi, Kayode	6. 2	Cheltenham Town	Ibadon, Nig.	21.02.82

BLACKPOOL

Ground: Bloomfield Road, Blackpool FY1 6JJ.
Telephone: 0870 443 1953. **Club nickname:** Seasiders.
First-choice colours: Tangerine shirts; white shorts; tangerine socks.
Main sponsor: Floors 260. **Capacity for 2007-08:** 9,469.
Record attendance: 38,098 v Wolves (Div. 1) 17 September, 1955

Name	Height ft. in.	Previous club	Birthplace	Birthdate
Goalkeepers				
Clancy, Kyle	6. 0	–	Barking	16.11.89
Edge, Lewis	6. 1	–	Lancaster	12.01.87
Evans, Rhys	6. 1	Swindon Town	Swindon	27.01.82
Gorkss, Kaspars	6. 3	Ventspils	Riga	6.11.81
Rachubka, Paul	6. 1	Huddersfield Town	San Luis, USA,	21.05.81
Defenders				
Barker, Shaun	6. 2	Rotherham Utd.	Nottingham	19.09.82
Crainey, Stephen	5. 9	Leeds Utd.	Glasgow	22.06.81
Evatt, Ian	6. 3	Q.P.R.	Coventry	19.11.81
Hills, John	5. 9	Sheffield Wed.	Blackpool	21.04.78
Jackson, Michael	5.11	Tranmere Rov.	Chester	4.12.73
Williams, Robbie	5.10	Barnsley	Pontefract	2.10.84
Midfielders				
Bean, Marcus	5.11	Q.P.R.	Hammersmith	2.11.84
Coid, Danny	5.11	–	Liverpool	3.10.81
Flynn, Michael	5.10	Gillingham	Newport	17.10.80
Fox, David	5. 9	Manchester Utd.	Leek	13.12.83
Hoolahan, Wesley	5. 6	Livingston	Dublin	10.08.83
Kay, Matthew	6. 0	–	Blackpool	12.10.89
Jorgensen, Claus	5.11	Bournemouth	Holstebro	27.04.79
Southern, Keith	5.10	Everton	Gateshead	21.04.84
Tierney, Paul	5.10	Livingston	Salford	15.09.82
Wiles, Simon	5.11	–	Preston	22.04.85
Forwards				
Burgess, Ben	6. 3	Hull City	Buxton	9.11.81
Forbes, Adrian	5. 8	Swansea City	Ealing	23.01.79
Morrell, Andy	5.11	Coventry City	Doncaster	28.09.74
Parker, Keigan	5. 7	St Johnstone	Livingston	8.06.82
Taylor-Fletcher, Gary	6. 0	Huddersfield Town	Liverpool	4.06.81
Vernon, Scott	6. 1	Oldham Athletic	Manchester	13.12.83

BRISTOL CITY

Ground: Ashton Gate, Bristol BS3 2EJ.
Telephone: 0117 963 0630. **Club nickname:** Robins.
First-choice colours: Red shirts; white shorts; red and white socks.
Main sponsor: Bristol Trade Centre. **Capacity for 2007-08:** 21,698.
Record attendance: 43,335 v Preston N.E. (F.A. Cup 5) 16 February 1935.

Name	Height ft. in.	Previous club	Birthplace	Birthdate
Goalkeepers				
Basso, Adriano	6. 1	Woking	Brazil	18.04.75
Henderson, Stephen	6. 3	Aston Villa	Dublin	2.05.88
Weale, Chris	6. 2	Yeovil Town	Chard	9.02.82
Defenders				
Carey, Louis	5.10	Coventry City	Bristol	22.01.77
Fontaine, Liam	6. 3	Fulham	Beckenham	7.01.83
Keogh, Richard	6. 2	Stoke City	Harlow	11.08.86
McAllister, Jamie	5.11	Hearts	Glasgow	26.04.78
McCombe, Jamie	6. 5	Lincoln City	Pontefract	1.01.83
Partridge, David	6. 1	Motherwell	Westminster	26.11.78
Wilson, James		–	Chepstow	26.02.89
Midfielders				
Artus, Frankie		–	Bristol	27.09.88
Betsy, Kevin	6. 1	Wycombe Wand.	Seychelles	20.03.78
Johnson, Lee	5. 6	Yeovil Town	Newmarket	7.06.81
Murray, Scott	5. 8	Reading	Aberdeen	26.05.74
Noble, David	6. 0	Boston Utd.	Hitchin	2.02.82
Orr, Bradley	6. 0	Newcastle Utd.	Liverpool	1.11.82
Russell, Alex	5.10	Torquay Utd.	Crosby	17.03.73
Skuse, Cole	5. 9	–	Bristol	29.03.86
Wilson, Brian	5.10	Cheltenham Town	Manchester	9.05.83
Forwards				
Brooker, Stephen	5.10	Port Vale	Newport Pagnell	21.05.81
Jevons, Phil	5.11	Yeovil Town	Liverpool	1.08.79
Myrie-Williams, Jennison	5.11	–	Bristol	17.05.88
Showunmi, Enoch	6. 4	Luton Town	Kilburn	21.04.82
Sproule, Ivan	5. 9	Hibernian	Castlederg, NI	18.02.81

BURNLEY

Ground: Turf Moor, Harry Potts Way, Burnley BB10 4BX.
Telephone: 0870 443 1882. **Club nickname:** Clarets.
First-choice colours: Claret shirts; white shorts; white socks.
Main sponsor: Holland. **Capacity for 2007-08:** 22,619.
Record attendance: 54,775 v Huddersfield Town (F.A. Cup 4) 23 February, 1924.

Name	Height ft. in.	Previous club	Birthplace	Birthdate
Goalkeepers				
Jensen, Brian	6. 1	W.B.A.	Copenhagen	8.06.75
Kiralry, Gabor	6. 4	Crystal Palace	Szombathely, Hun.	1.04.76
Defenders				
Caldwell, Steve	6. 0	Sunderland	Stirling	12.09.80
Duff, Mike	6. 1	Cheltenham Town	Belfast	11.01.78
Foster, Steve	6. 0	Crewe Alexandra	Warrington	10.09.80
Gudjonsson, Joey	5. 8	AZ Alkmaar	Akranes, Ice.	25.05.80
Harley, Jon	5. 8	Sheffield Utd.	Maidstone	26.09.79
Thomas, Wayne	6. 2	Stoke City	Gloucester	17.05.79
Midfielders				
Elliott, Wade	5.10	Bournemouth	Eastleigh	14.12.78
Mahon, Alan	5.10	Wigan Athletic	Dublin	4.04.78
McCann, Chris	6. 1	–	Dublin	21.07.87
O'Connor, Garreth	5. 7	Bournemouth	Dublin	10.11.78
O'Connor, James	5. 8	W.B.A.	Dublin	1.09.79
Spicer, John	5.11	Bournemouth	Romford	13.09.83
Forwards				
Akinbiyi, Ade	6. 1	Sheffield Utd.	Hackney	10.10.74
Berisha, Besart	6. 0	SV Hamburg	Pristina, Yug.	29.07.85

Gray, Andy	6. 1	Sunderland	Harrogate	15.11.77
Jones, Steve	5. 4	Crewe Alexandra	Londonderry	25.10.76
Lafferty, Kyle	6. 4	–	Enniskillen	16.09.87

CARDIFF CITY

Ground: Ninian Park, Sloper Road, Cardiff CF11 8SX.
Telephone: 02920 221001. **Club nickname:** Bluebirds.
First-choice colours: Blue shirts; white shorts; blue socks.
Main sponsor: Communications Direct. **Capacity for 2007-08:** 20,324.
Record attendance: 61,566 Wales v England, 14 October, 1961. Club: 57,800 v Arsenal (Div. 1) 22 April, 1953.

Name	Height ft. in.	Previous club	Birthplace	Birthdate
Goalkeepers				
Forde, David	6. 2	Derry City	Galway	20.12.79
Oakes, Michael	6. 2	Wolves	Northwich	30.10.73
Defenders				
Capaldi, Tony	6. 0	Plymouth Argyle	Porsgrunn, Nor.	12.08.81
Johnson, Roger	6. 3	Wycombe Wand.	Ashford	28.04.83
Loovens, Glenn	6. 1	Feyenoord	Doetinchem, Hol.	22.09.83.
McNaughton, Kevin	5.10	Aberdeen	Dundee	28.08.82
Purse, Darren	6. 2	W.B.A.	Stepney	14.02.77
Scimeca, Riccardo	6. 1	W.B.A.	Leamington Spa	13.06.75
Midfielders				
Cooper, Kevin	5. 8	Wolves	Derby	23.02.78
Flood, Willo	5. 6	Manchester City	Dublin	10.04.85
Ledley, Joe	6. 0	–	Cardiff	23.01.87
McPhail, Stephen	5.10	Barnsley	Westminster	9.12.79
Parry, Paul	5.10	Hereford Utd.	Chepstow	19.08.80
Rae, Gavin	5.11	Rangers	Aberdeen	28.11.77
Ramsey, Aaron	5.11	–	Caerphilly	26.12.90
Whittingham, Peter	5.10	Aston Villa	Nuneaton	8.09.84
Forwards				
Bryne, Jason	5.11	Shelbourne	Tallaght, Ire.	23.02.78
Chopra, Michael	5.10	Newcastle Utd.	Newcastle	23.12.83
Feeney, Warren	5.10	Luton Town	Belfast	17.01.81
Green, Matt	5. 8	Newport Co.	Bath	2.01.87
MacLean, Steven	6. 0	Sheffield Wed.	Edinburgh	23.08.82
Thompson, Steven	6. 2	Rangers	Paisley	14.10.78

CHARLTON ATHLETIC

Ground: The Valley, Floyd Road, London SE7 8BL.
Telephone: 0208 333 4000. **Club nickname:** Addicks.
First-choice colours: Red shirts; white shorts; red socks.
Main sponsor: Llanera. **Capacity for 2007-08:** 27,111.
Record attendance: 75,031 v Aston Villa (F.A. Cup 5) 12 February, 1938

Name	Height ft. in.	Previous club	Birthplace	Birthdate
Goalkeepers				
Elliot, Robert	6. 2	–	Chatham	30.04.86
Randolph, Darren	6. 1	–	Dublin	12.05.87
Weaver, Nicky	6. 3	Manchester City	Sheffield	2.03.79
Defenders				
Bougherra, Madjid	6. 2	Sheffield Wed.	Longvic, Fr.	7.10.82
Diawara, Souleymane	6. 1	Sochaux	Gabou, Sen.	24.12.78
Faye, Amdy	6. 0	Newcastle Utd.	Dakar	12.03.77
Fortune, Jonathan	6. 2	–	Islington	28.08.80
McCarthy, Patrick	6. 1	Leicester City	Dublin	31.05.83

Moutaouakil, Yassin	5.11	Chateauroux	Nice	18.07.86
Powell, Chris	5.10	Watford	Lambeth	8.09.69
Semedo, Jose		Sporting Lisbon	Setubal, Por.	11.01.85
Sankofa, Osei	6. 0	–	Streatham	19.03.85
Thatcher, Ben	5.10	Manchester City	Swindon	30.11.75
Youga, Kelly	6. 1	Lyon	Bangui, CAF Rep.	22.09.85
Young, Luke	6. 0	Tottenham	Harlow	19.07.79
Midfielders				
Ambrose, Darren	5.11	Newcastle Utd.	Harlow	29.02.84
Christensen, Martin	5.11	Herfolge	Denmark	23.12.87
Holland, Matt	5. 9	Ipswich Town	Bury	11.04.74
Reid, Andy	5. 7	Tottenham	Dublin	29.07.82
Sam, Lloyd	5. 8	–	Leeds	27.09.84
Thomas, Jerome	6. 1	Arsenal	Brent	23.03.83
Walton, Simon	6. 1	Leeds Utd.	Sherburn	13.09.87
Forwards				
Bent, Marcus	6. 2	Everton	Hammersmith	19.05.78
Iwelumo, Chris	6. 3	Colchester Utd.	Coatbridge	1.08.78
Rommedahl, Dennis	5.10	PSV Eindhoven	Copenhagen	22.07.79
Todorov, Svetoslav	6. 0	Portsmouth	Dobrich, Bul.	30.08.78
Varney, Luke	5.11	Crewe Alexandra	Leicester	27.12.84

COLCHESTER UNITED

Ground: Layer Road, Colchester CO2 7JJ.
Telephone: 0871 226 2161. **Club nickname:** U's.
First-choice-colours: Blue and white shirts; blue shorts; white socks.
Main sponsor: haart. **Capacity for 2007-08:** 6,300.
Record attendance: 19,072 v Reading (F.A. Cup 1) 27 November, 1948.

Name	Height ft. in.	Previous club	Birthplace	Birthdate
Goalkeepers				
Davison, Aidan	6. 1	Grimsby Town	Sedgefield	11.05.68
Gerken, Dean	6. 2	–	Southend	4.08.85
Defenders				
Baldwin, Pat	6. 0	Chelsea	London	12.11.82
Brown, Wayne	6. 0	Watford	Banbury	20.08.77
Elokobi, George	6. 1	Dulwich Hamlet	Cameroon	31.01.86
Granville, Danny	5.11	Crystal Palace	Islington	19.01.75
Richards, Garry	5.11	–	Romford	11.05.86
White, John	6. 0	–	Colchester	25.07.86
Midfielders				
Duguid, Karl	5.11	–	Hitchin	21.03.78
Izzet, Kemal	5. 8	Charlton Athetic	Whitechapel	29.09.80
Jackson, Johnnie	6. 1	Tottenham	Camden	15.08.82
Guttridge, Luke	5. 5	Leyton Orient	Barnstaple	27.03.82
McLeod, Kevin	5.11	Swansea City	Liverpool	12.09.80
Watson, Kevin	6. 0	Reading	Hackney	3.01.74
Forwards				
Guy, Jamie	6. 1	–	Barking	1.08.87
Platt, Clive	6. 4	MK Dons	Wolverhampton	27.10.77
Sheringham, Teddy	5.11	West Ham Utd.	Highams Park	2.04.66
Yeates, Mark	5. 9	Tottenham	Dublin	11.01.85

COVENTRY CITY

Ground: Ricoh Arena, Foleshill, Coventry CV6 6GE.
Telephone: 0870 421 1987. **Club nickname:** Sky Blues.
First-choice colours: Sky blue shirts; sky blue shorts; sky blue socks.
Main sponsor: Cassidy Group. **Capacity for 2007-08:** 32,500.

Record attendance: (Highfield Road) 51,455 v Wolves (Div. 2) 29 April, 1967. (Ricoh Arena) 26,851 v Wolves (Championship) 2 January, 2006.

Name	Height ft. in.	Previous club	Birthplace	Birthdate
Goalkeepers				
Konstantopoulos, Dimi	6. 4	Hartlepool Utd.	Kalamata, Gre.	29.11.78
Marshall, Andy	6. 2	Millwall	Bury St Edmunds	14.04.75
Defenders				
Borrowdale, Gary	6. 0	Crystal Palace	Sutton	16.07.85
De Zeeuw, Arjan	6. 1	Wigan Athletic	Castricum, Hol.	16.04.70
Giddings, Stuart	6. 0	–	Coventry	27.03.86
Hall, Marcus	6. 1	Stoke City	Coventry	24.03.76
Hawkins, Colin	6. 1	Shelbourne	Galway	17.08.77
McNamee, David	5.11	Livingston	Glasgow	10.10.80
Page, Robert	6. 0	Cardiff City	Llwynpia	3.09.74
Ward, Elliott	6. 1	West Ham Utd.	Harrow	19.01.85
Midfielders				
Birchall, Chris	5. 9	Port Vale	Stafford	5.05.84
Cairo, Ellery	5.10	Hertha Berlin	Rotterdam	3.08.78
Davis, Liam	5. 8	–	Wandsworth	23.11.86
Doyle, Michael	5.10	Celtic	Dublin	8.07.81
Hughes, Michael	5. 7	Crystal Palace	Larne	2.08.71
Hughes, Stephen	6. 0	Charlton Athletic	Wokingham	18.09.76
Mifsud, Michael	5. 6	Lillestrom	Pieta, Malt.	17.04.81
Osbourne, Isaac	5.10	–	Birmingham	22.06.86
Tabb, Jay	5. 6	Brentford	Tooting	21.02.84
Thornton, Kevin	5. 7	–	Drogheda	9.07.86
Forwards				
Adebola, Dele	6. 3	Crystal Palace	Lagos	23.06.75
Andrews, Wayne	5.10	Crystal Palace	Paddington	25.11.77
Best, Leon	6. 1	Southampton	Nottingham	19.09.86
Kyle, Kevin	6. 3	Sunderland	Stranraer	7.06.81
McKenzie, Leon	5.11	Norwich City	Croydon	17.05.78
Simpson, Robbie	5.11	Cambridge Utd.		15.03.85

CRYSTAL PALACE

Ground: Selhurst Park, London SE25, 6PU.
Telephone: 0208 768 6000. **Club nickname:** Eagles.
First-choice colours: Red and blue shirts; red shorts; red socks.
Main sponsor: GAC Logistics. **Capacity for 2007-08:** 26,309.
Record attendance: 51,482 v Burnley (Div. 2), 11 May, 1979.

Name	Height ft. in.	Previous club	Birthplace	Birthdate
Goalkeepers				
Flinders, Scott	6. 4	Barnsley	Rotherham	12.06.86
Speroni, Julian	6. 1	Dundee	Federal, Arg.	18.05.79
Wilkinson, David	6. 0	–	Croydon	19.04.88
Defenders				
Butterfield, Danny	5.10	Grimsby Town	Boston	21.11.79
Cort, Leon	6. 3	Hull City	Bermondsey	11.07.79
Craig, Tony	6. 0	Millwall	Greenwich	20.04.85
Fray, Arron	5.11	–	Bromley	1.05.87
Hudson, Mark	6. 3	Fulham	Guildford	30.03.82
Hughes, Jeff	6. 1	Lincoln City	Larne	29.05.85
Lawrence, Matt	6. 1	Millwall	Northampton	19.06.74
Midfielders				
Fletcher, Carl	5.10	West Ham Utd.	Camberley	7.04.80
Green, Stuart	5.10	Hull City	Whitehaven	15.06.81
Hall, Ryan	5.10	–	Dulwich	4.01.88

Ifill, Paul	6. 0	Sheffield Utd.	Brighton	20.10.79
Kennedy, Mark	5.11	Wolves	Dublin	15.05.76
Soares, Tom	6. 0	–	Reading	10.07.86
Starkey, Phil	6. 0	–	Dartford	10.09.87
Watson, Ben	5.10	–	Camberwell	9.07.85
Forwards				
Freedman, Dougie	5. 9	Nott'm. Forest	Glasgow	21.01.74
Grabban, Lewis	6. 0	–	Croydon	12.01.88
Kuqi, Shefki	6. 2	Blackburn Rov.	Albania	10.11.76
Martin, David	5. 9	Dartford		3.06.85
Morrison, Clinton	6. 1	Birmingham City	Wandsworth	14.05.79
Scowcroft, James	6. 1	Leicester City	Bury St Edmunds	15.11.75
Sheringham, Charlie	6. 0	Ipswich Town	Chingford	17.04.88

HULL CITY

Ground: Kingston Communications Stadium, The Circle, Walton Street, Anlaby Road, Hull, HU3 6HU.
Telephone: 0870 837 0003. **Club nickname:** Tigers.
First-choice colours: Amber shirts; black shorts; black socks.
Main sponsor: Kingston Communications. **Capacity for 2007-08:** 25,417.
Record attendance: (Boothferry Park) 55,019 v Manchester Utd. (F.A. Cup 6) 28 February, 1949. (Kingston Communications Stadium) 24,277 v Sheffield Wed. (League 1) 30 April, 2005. 25,280 England U-21 v Holland, 17 February, 2004.

Name	Height ft. in.	Previous club	Birthplace	Birthdate
Goalkeepers				
Aspden, Curtis	6. 0	–	Blackburn	16.11.87
Duke, Matt	6. 5	Burton Albion	Sheffield	16.07.77
Myhill, Boaz	6. 3	Aston Villa	Modesto, USA	9.11.82
Defenders				
Coles, Danny	6. 1	Bristol City	Bristol	31.10.81
Collins, Sam	6. 2	–	Pontefract	5.06.77
Dawson, Andy	5. 9	Scunthorpe Utd.	Northallerton	20.10.78
Delaney, Damien	6. 3	Leicester City	Cork	20.07.81
Doyle, Nathan	5.11	Derby Co.	Derby	12.01.87
Plummer, Matt	6. 1	–	Hull	18.01.89
Ricketts, Sam	6. 0	Swansea City	Aylesbury	11.10.81
Turner, Michael	6. 4	Brentford	Lewisham	9.11.83
Midfielders				
Ashbee, Ian	6. 1	Cambridge Utd.	Birmingham	6.09.76
Barmby, Nick	5. 7	Leeds Utd.	Hull	11.02.74
Elliott, Stuart	5.10	Motherwell	Belfast	23.07.78
France, Ryan	5.11	Alfreton Town	Sheffield	13.12.80
Hughes, Bryan	5. 9	Charlton Athletic	Liverpool	19.06.76
Livermore, David	6. 0	Leeds Utd.	Edmonton	20.05.80
Marney, Dean	5.11	Tottenham	Barking	31.01.84
Welsh, John	6. 0	Liverpool	Liverpool	10.01.84
Wilkinson, Ben		–	Sheffield	25.04.87
Forwards				
Bridges, Michael	6. 1	Carlisle Utd.	North Shields	5.08.78
Featherstone, Nicky	5. 9	–	Goole	18.01.89
Garcia, Richard	5.11	Colchester Utd.	Perth, Aus.	9.04.81
McPhee, Stephen	5. 7	Port Vale	Glasgow	5.06.81
Windass, Dean	5.10	Bradford City	Hull	1.04.69

IPSWICH TOWN

Ground: Portman Road, Ipswich IP1 2DA.
Telephone: 01473 400500. **Club nickname:** Blues/Town.
First-choice colours: Blue shirts; white shorts; blue socks.

Main sponsor: E.ON. **Capacity for 2007-08:** 30,300.
Record attendance: 38,010 v Leeds Utd. (F.A. Cup 6) 8 March, 1975.

Name	Height ft. in.	Previous club	Birthplace	Birthdate
Goalkeepers				
Plummer, Andrew	6. 0	–	Ipswich	3.10.89
Price, Lewis	6. 3	Southampton	Bournemouth	19.07.84
Supple, Shane	6. 0	–	Dublin	4.05.87
Defenders				
Bruce, Alex	5.11	Birmingham City	Norwich	28.09.84
Casement, Chris	6. 0	–	Northern Ireland	12.01.88
De Vos, Jason	6. 4	Wigan Athletic	Ontario	2.01.74
Harding, Dan	6. 0	Leeds Utd.	Gloucester	23.12.83
Miller, Ian	6. 2	Bury Town	Colchester	23.11.83
Naylor, Richard	6. 1	–	Leeds	28.02.77
Richards, Matt	5. 8	–	Harlow	26.12.84
Sito, Luis Castro	5. 9	Racing Ferrol	La Coruna	21.05.80
Synnott, Michael	5. 7	Home Farm	Dublin	20.01.87
Wilnis, Fabian	5.10	De Graafschap	Surinam	23.08.70
Wright, David	5.11	Wigan Athletic	Warrington	1.05.80
Midfielders				
Bowditch, Dean	5.11	–	Bishop's Stortford	15.06.86
Garvan, Owen	6. 0	–	Dublin	29.01.88
Haynes, Danny	5.11	–	Peckham	19.01.88
Legwinski, Sylvain	6. 3	Fulham	Clermond-Ferrand	6.10.73
Moore, Sammy	5. 8	Chelsea	Dover	7.09.87
O'Callaghan, George	6. 1	Cork City	Whitechurch	5.09.79
Peters, Jaime	5. 7	–	Ontario	4.05.87
Roberts, Gary	5.10	Accrington Stanley	Chester	18.03.84
Trotter, Liam	6. 2	–	Ipswich	24.08.88
Williams, Gavin	5.10	West Ham Utd.	Pontypridd	20.07.80
Forwards				
Clarke, Billy	5. 7	–	Cork	13.12.87
Lee, Alan	6. 2	Cardiff City	Galway	21.08.78
Rhodes, Jordan	6. 1	Barnsley	Oldham	5.02.90
Walters, Jonathan	6. 0	Chester City	Birkenhead	20.09.83

LEICESTER CITY

Ground: Walkers Stadium, Filbert Way, Leicester, LE2 7FL.
Telephone: 0870 040 6000. **Club nickname:** Foxes.
First choice colours: Blue shirts; blue shorts; blue socks.
Main sponsor: Topps Tiles. **Capacity for 2007-08**: 32,500.
Record attendance: (Filbert Street) 47,298 v. Tottenham (F.A. Cup 5) 18 February 1928. (Walkers Stadium) 32,148 v Newcastle Utd. (Premier League) 26 December, 2003.

Name	Height ft. in.	Previous club	Birthplace	Birthdate
Goalkeepers				
Douglas, Rob	6. 3	Celtic	Lanark	24.04.72
Henderson, Paul	6. 1	Bradford City	Sydney	22.04.76
Logan, Conrad	6. 2	–	Letterkenny	18.04.86
Nielsen, Jimmy	6. 3	Aalborg	Aalborg	6.08.77
Defenders				
Chambers, James	5.10	Watford	West Bromwich	20.11.80
Gerrbrand, Patrick	6. 2	Hammarby	Sweden	27.04.81
Kenton, Darren	5.10	Southampton	Wandsworth	13.09.78
Kishishev, Radostin	5.11	Charlton Athletic	Burgas, Bul.	30.07.74
Kisnorbo, Patrick	6. 2	Hearts	Australia	24.03.81
Maltock, Joe	5.11	–	Leicester	15.05.90
Maybury, Alan	5.11	Hearts	Dublin	8.08.78

McAuley, Gareth	6. 3	Lincoln City	Larne	5.12.79
N'Gotty, Bruno	6. 1	Birmingham City	Lyon	10.06.71
Sheehan, Alan	5.11	–	Athlone	14.09.86
Stearman, Richard	6. 2	–	Wolverhampton	19.08.87
Midfielders				
Hellings, Sergio	6. 0	Anderlecht	Amsterdam	11.10.84
Hughes, Stephen	5.11	Rangers	Motherwell	14.11.82
Kaebi, Hoessein	5. 6	Persepolis	Ahvez, Iran	23.09.85
Newton, Shaun	5. 8	West Ham Utd.	Camberwell	20.08.75
Porter, Levi	5. 3	–	Leicester	6.04.87
Wesolowski, James	5.10	Northern Spirit	Sydney	25.08.87
Forwards				
Cort, Carl	6. 4	Wolves	Southwark	1.11.77
De Vries, Mark	6. 3	Hearts	Surinam	24.08.75
Dodds, Louis	5.11	–	Sheffield	8.10.86
Fryatt, Matty	5.10	Walsall	Nuneaton	5.03.86
Hammond, Elvis	5.10	Fulham	Accra	6.10.80
Hayes, Jonathan	5. 9	Reading	Balleyfermot, Ire.	9.07.87
Hume, Iain	5. 7	Tranmere Rov.	Brampton, Can.	31.10.83

NORWICH CITY

Ground: Carrow Road, Norwich NR1 1JE.
Telephone: 01603 760760. **Club nickname:** Canaries.
First-choice colours: Yellow shirts; green and yellow shorts; yellow socks.
Main sponsor: Flybe.com. **Capacity for 2007-08:** 26,034.
Record attendance: 43,984 v Leicester City (F.A. Cup 6), 30 March, 1963.

Name	Height ft. in.	Previous club	Birthplace	Birthdate
Goalkeepers				
Gallacher, Paul	6. 0	Dundee Utd.	Glasgow	16.08.79
Gilks, Matthew	6. 1	Rochdale	Rochdale	4.06.82
Lewis, Joe	6. 5	–	Bury St Edmunds	7.07.85
Marshall, David	6. 3	Celtic	Glasgow	5.03.85
Defenders				
Colin, Jurgen	5.10	PSV Eindhoven	Holland	20.01.81
Doherty, Gary	6. 1	Tottenham	Carndonagh	31.01.80
Drury, Adam	5.10	Peterborough Utd.	Cambridge	29.08.78
Dublin, Dion	6. 2	Leicester City	Leicester	22.04.69
Etuhu, Dickson	6. 2	Preston N.E.	Kano, Nig.	8.06.82
Halliday, Matthew	5.11	–	Norwich	23.01.87
Jarvis, Rossi	5.11	–	Fakenham	11.03.88
Otsemobor, Jon	5.10	Crewe Alexandra	Liverpool	23.03.83
Shackell, Jason	5.11	–	Stevenage	27.09.83
Midfielders				
Brellier, Julien	6. 0	Hearts	Echirolles, Fr.	10.01.82
Cave-Brown, Andrew	5.10	–	Gravesend	5.08.88
Chadwick, Luke	5.11	Stoke City	Cambridge	18.11.80
Croft, Lee	5. 9	Manchester City	Wigan	21.06.85
Eagle, Robert	5. 9	Ipswich Town	Leiston	23.02.87
Fotheringham, Mark	5. 7	Aarau	Dundee	22.10.83
Hughes, Andy	5.11	Reading	Manchester	2.01.78
Lappin, Simon	5.11	St Mirren	Glasgow	25.01.83
Safri, Youssef	6. 2	Coventry City	Casablanca	1.03.77
Smart, Bally	5.10	–	Polokwane	27.04.89
Spillane, Michael	5. 9	–	Cambridge	23.03.89
Forwards				
Brown, Chris	6. 1	Sunderland	Doncaster	11.12.84
Cureton, Jamie	5. 8	Colchester Utd.	Bristol	28.08.75
Huckerby, Darren	5.10	Manchester City	Nottingham	23.04.76
Martin, Chris	5.10	–	Beccles	4.11.88

Jarvis, Ryan	5.11	–	Fakenham	11.07.86
Renton, Kris	6. 2	–	Musselburgh	12.07.90

PLYMOUTH ARGYLE

Ground: Home Park, Plymouth PL2 3DQ.
Telephone: 01752 562561. **Club nickname:** Pilgrims.
First-choice colours: Green shirts; white shorts; green socks.
Main sponsor: Ginsters. **Capacity for 2007-08:** 20,000.
Record attendance: 42,684 v Aston Villa (Div. 2) 10 October, 1936.

Name	Height ft. in.	Previous club	Birthplace	Birthdate
Goalkeepers				
Larrieu, Romain	6. 2	Valence	Mont de Marsan, Fr.	31.08.76
McCormick, Luke	6. 0	–	Coventry	15.08.83
Defenders				
Connolly, Paul	6. 0	–	Liverpool	29.09.83
Doumbe, Mathias	6. 0	Hibernian	Drancy, Fr.	28.20.79
Laird, Scott		–	Taunton	15.05.88
Sawyer, Gary	5.10	Exeter City	Bideford	5.07.85
Seip, Marcel	6. 0	Heerenveen	Winschoten, Hol.	5.04.82
Timar, Krisztian	6. 3	Ferencvaros	Hungary	4.10.79
Wotton, Paul	5.11	–	Plymouth	17.08.77
Midfielders				
Buzsaky, Akos	5.11	Porto	Hungary	7.05.82
Djordjic, Bojan	5.10	Manchester Utd.	Belgrade	6.02.82
Dickson, Ryan	5.10	–	Saltash	14.12.86
Gosling, Dan	5.10	–	Brixham	2.02.90
Halmosi, Peter	5.10	Debreceni	Szombathely, Hun.	25.09.79
Hodges, Lee	6. 0	Reading	Epping	4.09.73
Nalis, Lilian	6. 1	Leicester City	Paris	29.09.71
Norris, David	5. 7	Bolton Wand.	Stamford	22.02.81
Summerfield, Luke	6. 0	–	Ivybridge	6.12.87
Forwards				
Chadwick, Nick	5.11	Everton	Market Drayton	26.10.82
Ebanks-Blake, Sylvain	5.10	Manchester Utd.	Cambridge	29.03.86
Fallon, Rory	6. 2	Swansea City	Gisborne, NZ	20.03.82
Hayles, Barry	5. 9	Millwall	Lambeth	17.05.72
Reid, Reuben	6. 0	–	Bristol	26.07.88
Samba, Cherno	5.10	Cadiz	Banjul, Gam.	10.01.85

PRESTON NORTH END

Ground: Deepdale, Sir Tom Finney Way, Preston PR1 6RU.
Telephone: 0870 442 1964. **Club nickname:** Lilywhites.
First-choice colours: White shirts; navy blue shorts; white socks.
Main sponsor: Enterprise. **Capacity for 2007-08:** 19,525.
Record attendance: 42,684 v Arsenal (Div. 1) 23 April, 1938.

Name	Height ft. in.	Previous club	Birthplace	Birthdate
Goalkeepers				
Henderson, Wayne	5.11	Brighton & H.A.	Dublin	16.09.83
Lonergan, Andy	6. 4	–	Preston	19.10.83
Neal, Chris	6. 2	–	St Albans	23.10.85
Defenders				
Alexander, Graham	5.11	Luton Town	Coventry	10.10.71
Chilvers, Liam	6. 2	Colchester Utd.	Chelmsford	6.11.81
Davidson, Callum	5.10	Leicester City	Stirling	25.06.76
Hill, Matt	5. 8	Bristol City	Bristol	26.03.81

Jarrett, Jason	6. 0	Norwich City	Bury	14.09.79
Mawene, Youl	6. 1	Derby Co.	Caen	16.07.79
St Ledger, Sean	6. 0	Peterborough Utd.	Birmingham	28.12.84
Wilson, Kelvin	6. 2	Notts Co.	Nottingham	3.09.85
Midfielders				
Anyinsah, Joe	5. 8	Bristol City	Bristol	8.10.84
Jones, Billy	5.11	Crewe Alexandra	Shrewsbury	24.03.87
McKenna, Paul	5. 8	–	Chorley	20.10.77
Neal, Lewis	6. 0	Stoke City	Leicester	14.07.81
Nicholls, Kevin	6. 0	Leeds Utd.	Newham	2.01.79
Pugh, Danny	6. 0	Leeds Utd.	Manchester	19.10.82
Sedgwick, Chris	5.11	Rotherham Utd.	Sheffield	28.04.80
Whaley, Simon	5.11	Bury	Bolton	7.06.85
Forwards				
Agyemang, Patrick	6. 1	Gillingham	Walthamstow	29.09.80
Hawley, Karl	5. 7	Carlisle Utd.	Walsall	6.12.81
McGrail, Chris	5.10	–	Preston	
Mellor, Neil	6. 0	Liverpool	Sheffield	4.11.82
Nowland, Adam	5.11	Nott'm. Forest	Preston	6.07.81
Nugent, David	5.11	Bury	Liverpool	2.05.85
Ormerod, Brett	5.11	Southampton	Blackburn	18.10.76

QUEENS PARK RANGERS

Ground: Loftus Road Stadium, South Africa Road, London W12 7PA.
Telephone: 0208 743 0262. **Club nickname:** Hoops.
First-choice colours: Blue and white shirts; white shorts; white socks.
Main sponsor: Car Giant. **Capacity for 2007-08:** 18,420.
Record attendance: 35,353 v Leeds Utd. (Div. 1) 27 April, 1974.

Name	**Height ft. in.**	**Previous club**	**Birthplace**	**Birthdate**
Goalkeepers				
Cole, Jake	6. 2	–	Hammersmith	11.09.85
Thomas, Sean	6. 1	–	Edgware	5.09.86
Defenders				
Barker, Chris	6. 0	Cardiff City	Sheffield	02.03.80
Bignot, Marcus	5.10	Rushden & Diamonds	Birmingham	22.08.74
Cullip, Danny	6. 1	Nott'm. Forest	Bracknell	17.09.76
Curtis, John	5.10	Nott'm. Forest	Nuneaton	3.09.78
Kanyuka, Patrick	6. 0	–	Kinshasa	19.07.87
Rehman, Zesh	6. 2	Fulham	Birmingham	14.10.83
Shimmin, Dominic	6. 0	–	Bermondsey	13.10.87
Timoska, Sampsa	6. 0	MyPa	Kokemaki, Fin.	12.12.79
Midfielders				
Ainsworth, Gareth	5. 9	Cardiff City	Blackburn	10.05.73
Baidoo, Shabazz	5. 8	–	Hackney	13.04.88
Bailey, Stefan	5.11	–	Brent	10.11.87
Bolder, Adam	5. 8	Derby Co.	Hull	25.10.80
Cook, Lee	5. 9	Watford	Hammersmith	3.08.82
Doherty, Tommy	5. 8	Bristol City	Bristol	17.03.79
Rowlands, Martin	5. 9	Brentford	Hammersmith	8.02.79
St Aimie, Kieron	5.10	–	Brent	4.05.89
Stewart, Damion	6. 3	Bradford City	Jamaica	8.08.80
Ward, Nick	6. 0	Perth Glory	Perth, Aus.	24.03.85
Forwards				
Blackstock, Dexter	6. 2	Southampton	Oxford	20.05.86
Jones, Ray	6. 4	–	East Ham	28.08.88
Moore, Stefan	5.10	Aston Villa	Birmingham	28.09.83
Nardiello, Danny	5.11	Barnsley	Coventry	22.10.82
Nygaard, Marc	6. 5	Brescia	Copenhagen	9.01.76

SCUNTHORPE UNITED

Ground: Glanford Park, Doncaster Road, Scunthorpe DN15 8TD.
Telephone: 0871 221.1899 **Club nickname:** Iron.
First-choice colours: Claret and blue shirts, shorts and socks.
Main sponsor: Rainham Steel. **Capacity for 2007-08:** 9,194.
Record attendance: (Old Show Ground) 23,935 v Portsmouth (F.A. Cup 4) 30 January, 1954. (Glanford Park) 8,906 v Nott'm Forest (Lge. 1) 10, March 2007.

Name	Height ft. in.	Previous club	Birthplace	Birthdate
Goalkeepers				
Lillis, Josh	6. 0	–	Derby	24.06.87
Murphy, Joe	6. 2	Sunderland	Dublin	21.08.81
Defenders				
Butler, Andy	6. 0	–	Doncaster	4.11.83
Byrne, Cliff	6. 0	Sunderland	Dublin	26.04.82
Crosby, Andy	6. 2	Oxford Utd.	Rotherham	3.03.73
Iriekpen, Izzy	6. 1	Swansea City	London	14.05.82
Mulligan, Dave	5. 8	Doncaster Rov.	Bootle	24.03.82
Wilcox, Joe	6. 1	–		18.04.89
Williams, Marcus	5. 8	–	Doncaster	8.04.86
Midfielders				
Baraclough, Ian	6. 1	Notts Co.	Leicester	4.12.70
Goodwin, Jim	5. 9	Stockport Co.	Waterford	20.11.81
Hurst, Kevan	6. 0	Sheffield Utd.	Chesterfield	27.08.85
Morris, Ian	6. 0	Leeds Utd.	Dublin	27.02.87
Sparrow, Matt	5.10	–	Wembley	3.10.81
Taylor, Cleveland	5. 8	Bolton Wand.	Leicester	9.09.83
Forwards				
Forte, Jonathan	6. 0	Sheffield Utd.	Sheffield	25.07.86
Hayes, Paul	6. 0	Barnsley	Dagenham	20.09.83
McBreen, Daniel	6. 1	Falkirk	Burnley	23.03.77
Paterson, Martin	5.10	Stoke City	Tunstall	13.05.87
Winn, Peter	6. 0	–	Grimsby	19.12.88

SHEFFIELD UNITED

Ground: Bramall Lane, Sheffield S2 4SU.
Telephone: 0870 787 1960. **Club nickname:** Blades.
First-choice colours: Red and white shirts; black and red shorts; black and red socks.
Main sponsor: Capital One. **Capacity for 2007-08:** 32,609.
Record attendance: 68,287 v Leeds Utd. (F.A. Cup 5) 15 February, 1936.

Name	Height ft. in.	Previous club	Birthplace	Birthdate
Goalkeepers				
Annerson, Jamie	6. 2	–	Sheffield	21.06.88
Bennett, Ian	6. 0	Leeds Utd.	Worksop	10.10.71
Kenny, Paddy	6. 1	Sheffield Utd.	Halifax	17.05.78
Defenders				
Armstrong, Chris	5. 9	Oldham Athletic	Newcastle	5.08.82
Bromby, Leigh	6. 0	Sheffield Wed.	Dewsbury	2.06.80
Davis, Claude	6. 3	Preston N.E.	Jamaica	6.03.79
Geary, Derek	5. 6	Stockport Co.	Dublin	19.06.80
Kilgallon, Matthew	6. 1	Leeds Utd.	York	8.01.84
Law, Nicky	5.11	–	Nottingham	29.03.88
Lucketti, Chris	6. 0	Preston N.E.	Rochdale	28.09.71
Morgan, Chris	6. 1	Barnsley	Barnsley	9.11.77
Naysmith, Gary	5.11	Everton	Edinburgh	16.11.78
Seck, Mamadou	6. 3	Le Havre	Rufisque	26.08.79
Sommeil, David	5.11	Manchester City	Point-a-Pitre, Guad.	10.08.74

Midfielders				
Fathi, Ahmed	5. 9	Ismailly	Egypt	10.11.84
Gillespie, Keith	5.10	Leicester City	Bangor, N.I.	18.02.75
Leigertwood, Mikele	6. 1	Crystal Palace	Enfield	12.11.82
Li Tie	6. 0	Everton	Liaoning, Chi.	18.09.77
Montgomery, Nick	5. 9	–	Leeds	28.10.81
Quinn, Alan	5. 9	Sheffield Wed.	Dublin	13.06.79
Quinn, Stephen	5. 6	–	Dublin	4.04.86
Ross, Ian	5.11	–	Sheffield	13.01.86
Tonge, Michael	5.11	–	Manchester	7.04.83
Forwards				
Hulse, Rob	6. 1	Leeds Utd.	Crewe	25.10.79
Sharp, Billy	5. 8	Scunthorpe Utd.	Sheffield	5.02.86
Shelton, Luton	5.11	Helsingborg	Jamaica	11.11.85
Stead, Jon	6. 3	Sunderland	Huddersfield	7.04.83
Webber, Danny	5. 9	Watford	Manchester	28.12.81

SHEFFIELD WEDNESDAY

Ground: Hillsborough, Sheffield, S6 1SW.
Telephone: 0870 999 1867. **Club nickname:** Owls.
First-choice colours: Blue and white shirts; black shorts; black socks.
Main Sponsor: Plusnet. **Capacity for 2007-08:** 39,814.
Record attendance: 72,841 v Manchester City (F.A. Cup 5) 17 February, 1934.

Name	Height ft. in.	Previous club	Birthplace	Birthdate
Goalkeepers				
Burch, Rob	6. 0	Tottenham	Yeovil	8.02.84
Grant, Lee	6. 2	Derby Co.	Hemel Hempstead	27.01.83
Defenders				
Beevers, Mark	6. 4	–	Barnsley	21.11.89
Bullen, Lee	6. 1	Dumfermline Ath.	Edinburgh	29.03.71
Gilbert, Peter	5. 9	Plymouth Argyle	Newcastle	31.07.83
Hinds, Richard	6. 2	Scunthorpe Utd.	Sheffield	22.08.80
Simek, Frankie	6. 0	Arsenal	St Louis	13.10.84
Spurr, Tommy	6. 1	–	Leeds	13.09.87
Wood, Richard	6. 3	–	Wakefield	5.07.85
Midfielders				
Boden, Luke	6. 1	–	Sheffield	26.11.88
Brunt, Chris	6. 1	Middlesbrough	Belfast	14.12.84
Folly, Yoann	5.11	Southampton	Togo	6.06.85
Johnson, Jermaine	5. 9	Bradford City	Kingston	25.06.80
Lunt, Kenny	5.10	Crewe Alexandra	Runcorn	20.11.79
McAllister, Sean	5. 8	Bolton Wand.	Bolton	15.08.87
O'Brien, Burton	5.11	Livingston	Johannesburg	10.06.81
Small, Wade	5.10	MK Dons	Croydon	23.02.84
Whelan, Glenn	5.11	Manchester City	Dublin	13.01.84
Forwards				
Burton, Deon	5. 9	Rotherham Utd.	Ashford	25.10.76
Clarke, Leon	6. 2	Wolves	Birmingham	10.02.85
Graham, David	5.10	Wigan Athletic	Edinburgh	6.10.78
Tudgay, Marcus	5.10	Derby Co.	Worthing	3.02.83

SOUTHAMPTON

Ground: The Friends Provident St Mary's Stadium, Britannia Road, Southampton, SO14 5FP.
Telephone: 0845 688 9448. **Club nickname:** Saints.
First-choice colours: Red and white shirts; black shorts; white socks.
Main sponsor: Flybe. **Capacity for 2007-08:** 32,689.

Record attendance: At St Mary's: 32,151 v Arsenal (Premier League) 29 December, 2003. At The Dell: 31,044 v Manchester Utd. (Div. 1) 8 October 1969.

Name	Height ft. in.	Previous club	Birthplace	Birthdate
Goalkeepers				
Bialkowski, Bartosz	6. 0	Gornik Zabrze	Poland	6.07.87
Davis, Kelvin	6. 1	Sunderland	Bedford	29.09.76
Poke, Michael	6. 1	–	Spelthorne	21.11.85
Defenders				
Baird, Chris	5.10	–	Ballymoney	25.02.82
Lundekvam, Claus	6. 4	Brann	Austevoll, Nor.	22.02.73
Makin, Chris	5.10	Reading	Manchester	8.05.73
Ostlund, Alexandre	6. 0	Feyenoord	Sweden	2.11.78
Pele	5.11	Belenenses	Albufeira	2.05.78
Powell, Darren	6. 3	Crystal Palace	Hammersmith	10.03.76
Midfielders				
Dyer, Nathan	5.10	–	Trowbridge	29.11.87
Idiakez, Inigo	6. 0	Derby Co.	Spain	8.11.73
Licka, Mario	5.11	Slovacko	Ostrava	30.04.82
Gillett, Simon	5. 6	–	Oxford	6.11.85
Skacel, Rudi	5.10	Hearts	Trutnov, Cz.	17.07.79
Surman, Andrew	5.11	–	Johannsburg	20.08.86
Viafara, John	6. 1	Caldas	Robles, Col.	27.10.78
Wright, Jermaine	5. 9	Leeds Utd.	Greenwich	21.10.75
Forwards				
Jones, Kenwyne	6. 2	W-Connection	Trinidad	5.10.84
Lallana, Adam		–	Bournemouth	10.05.88
McGoldrick, David	6. 1	Notts Co.	Nottingham	29.11.87
Rasiak, Grzegorz	6. 3	Derby Co.	Szczecin, Pol.	12.01.79
Saganowski, Marek	5.10	Troyes	Lodz, Pol.	31.10.78
Wright-Phillips, Bradley	5. 8	Manchester City	Lewisham	12.03.85

STOKE CITY

Ground: Britannia Stadium, Stanley Matthews Way, Stoke-on-Trent ST4 7EG.
Telephone: 0871 663 2008. **Club nickname:** Potters.
First-choice colours: Red and white shirts; white shorts; white socks.
Main sponsor: Britannia. **Capacity for 2007-08:** 28,000.
Record attendance: (Victoria Ground) 51,380 v Arsenal (Div. 1) 29 March, 1937. (Britannia Stadium) 27,109 v Liverpool (League Cup 4) 29 November, 2000.

Name	Height ft. in.	Previous club	Birthplace	Birthdate
Goalkeepers				
Hoult, Russell	6. 3	W.B.A.	Ashby-de-la-Zouch	22.11.72
Simonsen, Steve	6. 3	Everton	South Shields	3.04.79
Defenders				
Broomes, Marlon	6. 0	Preston N.E.	Birmingham	28.11.77
Buxton, Lewis	6. 1	Portsmouth	Newport, IOW	10.12.83
Delap, Rory	6. 0	Sunderland	Sutton Coldfield	6.07.76
Dickinson, Carl	6. 0	–	Swadlincote	31.03.87
Higginbotham, Danny	6. 1	Southampton	Manchester	29.12.78
Hill, Clint	6. 0	Oldham Athletic	Liverpool	19.10.78
Hoefkens, Carl	6. 1	Germinal	Belgium	6.10.78
Matteo, Dominic	6. 1	Blackburn Rov.	Dumfries	24.04.74
Wilkinson, Andy	5.11	–	Stone	6.08.84
Midfielders				
Diao, Salif	6. 0	Liverpool	Kedougou, Sen.	10.02.77
Eustace, John	5.11	Coventry City	Solihull	3.11.79
Hazley, Matthew	6. 1	–	Banbridge	30.12.87
Lawrence, Liam	5. 9	Sunderland	Retford	14.12.81

Russell, Darel	6. 0	Norwich City	Stepney	22.10.80
Sweeney, Peter	6. 0	Millwall	Glasgow	25.09.84
Forwards				
Bangoura, Sambegou	6. 1	Standard Liege	Guinea	3.04.82
Fuller, Ricardo	6. 3	Southampton	Kingston, Jam.	31.10.79
Parkin, Jon	6. 4	Hull City	Barnsley	30.12.81
Pericard, Vincent	6. 1	Portsmouth	Efok, Cam.	3.10.82
Pulis, Anthony	5.10	Portsmouth	Bristol	21.07.84
Rooney, Adam	5.10	–	Dublin	21.04.87
Sidibe, Mamady	6. 4	Gillingham	Mali	18.12.79

WATFORD

Ground: Vicarage Road Stadium, Vicarage Road, Watford WD18 OER.
Telephone: 0870 111 1881. **Club nickname:** Hornets.
First-choice colours: Yellow shirts, black shorts, yellow socks.
Main sponsor: Beko. **Capacity for 2007-08:** 19,920.
Record attendance: 34,099 v Manchester Utd. (F.A. Cup 4 replay) 3 February 1969.

Name	Height ft. in.	Previous club	Birthplace	Birthdate
Goalkeepers				
Lee, Richard	5.11	–	Oxford	5.10.82
Loach, Scott	6. 2	Lincoln City	Nottingham	14.10.79
Poom, Mart	6. 4	Arsenal	Tallinn	3.02.72
Defenders				
Carlisle, Clarke	6. 2	Leeds Utd.	Preston	14.10.79
DeMerit, Jay	5.11	Chicago Fire	Green Bay, USA	4.12.79
Doyley, Lloyd	5.10	–	Whitechapel	1.12.82
Jackson, Matt	6. 1	Wigan Athletic	Leeds	19.10.71
Mackay, Malky	6. 1	West Ham Utd.	Bellshill	19.02.72
Mariappa, Adrian	5.11	–	Harrow	3.10.86
Osborne, Junior	5.10	–	Watford	12.02.88
Parkes, Jordan	6. 0	–	Watford	26.07.89
Shittu, Danny	6. 3	Q.P.R.	Lagos	2.09.80
Stewart, Jordan	5.11	Leicester City	Birmingham	3.03.82
Midfielders				
Avinel, Cedric	6. 2	Creteil	Paris	11.09.86
Bangura, Alhassan	6. 2	–	Freestown, SL	24.01.88
Campana, Alexa	5.11	–	Harrow	11.10.88
Cavalli, Johan	5. 7	Istres	Ajaccio	12.09.81
Diagouraga, Toumani	5.11	–	Paris	9.06.87
Francis, Damien	6. 1	Wigan Athletic	Wandsworth	27.02.79
Mahon, Gavin	6. 0	Brentford	Birmingham	2.01.77
McAnuff, Jobi	5.11	Crystal Palace	Edmonton	9.11.81
McNamee, Anthony	5. 6	–	Kensington	13.07.84
Rinaldi, Douglas	6. 0	Veranopolis	Erval Seco, Br.	10.02.84
Williams, Gareth	5.11	Leicester City	Glasgow	16.12.81
Williamson, Lee	5.10	Rotherham Utd.	Derby	7.06.82
Forwards				
Ashikodi, Moses	5.10	Rangers	Lagos	27.06.87
Bouazza, Hameur	5.11	–	Evry, Fr.	22.02.85
Henderson, Darius	6. 0	Gillingham	Sutton	7.09.81
Hoskins, Will	5.10	Rotherham Utd.	Nottingham	6.05.86
Kabba, Steve	5. 8	Sheffield Utd.	Lambeth	7.03.81
King, Marlon	6. 1	Nott'm. Forest	Dulwich	26.04.80
Priskin, Tamas	6. 2	Guyon	Komarno, Slovak.	27.09.87
Robinson, Theo	5. 9	–	Birmingham	22.01.89
Smith, Tommy	5.10	Derby Co.	Hemel Hempstead	22.05.80

WEST BROMWICH ALBION

Ground: The Hawthorns, Halford Lane, West Bromwich B71 4LF.
Telephone: 0871 271 1100. **Club nickname:** Baggies.
First-choice colours: Navy and white shirts; white shorts; navy socks.
Main sponsor: T-Mobile. **Capacity for 2007-08:** 27,500.
Record attendance: 64,815 v Arsenal (F.A. Cup 6) 6 March, 1937.

Name	Height ft. in.	Previous club	Birthplace	Birthdate
Goalkeepers				
Kiely, Dean	6. 0	Portsmouth	Salford	10.10.70
Steele, Luke	6. 2	Manchester Utd.	Peterborough	24.09.84
Defenders				
Albrechtsen, Martin	6. 2	FC Copenhagen	Denmark	31.03.80
Clement, Neil	6. 0	Chelsea	Reading	3.10.78
Davies, Curtis	6. 1	Luton Town	Waltham Forest	15.03.85
Gaardsoe, Thomas	6. 2	Ipswich Town	Randers, Den.	23.11.79
Hodgkiss, Jared	5. 8	–	Stafford	15.11.86
Martis, Shelton	6. 2	Hibernian	Willemstad, Cur.	29.11.82
McShane, Paul	5.11	Manchester Utd.	Wicklow	6.01.86
Robinson, Paul	5. 9	Watford	Watford	14.12.78
Watson, Steve	6. 0	Everton	North Shields	1.04.74
Midfielders				
Carter, Darren	6. 2	Birmingham City	Solihull	18.12.83
Chaplow, Richard	5. 9	Burnley	Accrington	2.02.85
Davies, Rob	5. 9	Wrexham	Tywyn	24.03.87
Gera, Zoltan	6. 0	Ferencvaros	Pecs, Hun.	22.04.79
Greening, Jonathan	6. 0	Middlesbrough	Scarborough	2.01.79
Koren, Robert	5.10	Lillestrom	Slovenia	20.09.80
Wallwork, Ronnie	5.10	Manchester Utd.	Manchester	10.09.77
Forwards				
Beattie, Craig	6. 0	Celtic	Glasgow	16.01.84
Ellington, Nathan	5.10	Wigan Athletic	Bradford	2.07.81
Hartson, John	6. 1	Celtic	Swansea	5.04.75
Nicholson, Stuart	5.10	–	Newcastle	3.02.87
Nardiello, Michael	6. 0	Liverpool	Torquay	9.05.89
Phillips, Kevin	5. 7	Aston Villa	Hitchin	25.07.73

WOLVERHAMPTON WANDERERS

Ground: Molineux Stadium, Wolverhampton, WV1 4QR.
Telephone: 0871 880 8442. **Club nickname:** Wolves.
First choice colours: Gold and black shirts; black shorts; black socks.
Main sponsor: Chaucer. **Capacity for 2007-08:** 28,565.
Record attendance: 61,315 v Liverpool (F.A. Cup 5) 11 February 1939.

Name	Height ft. in.	Previous club	Birthplace	Birthdate
Goalkeepers				
Hennessey, Wayne	6. 0	–	Anglesey	24.01.87
Ikeme, Carl	6. 2	–	Sutton Coldfield	8.06.86
Murray, Matt	6. 4	–	Solihull	2.05.81
Defenders				
Breen, Gary	6. 1	Sunderland	Hendon	12.12.73
Clapham, Jamie	5. 9	Birmingham City	Lincoln	7.12.75
Collins, Lee		–	Telford	28.09.88
Collins, Neil	5.11	Sunderland	Troon	2.09.83
Craddock, Jody	6. 2	Sunderland	Redditch	25.07.75
Edwards, Rob	6. 1	Aston Villa	Telford	25.12.82
Henry, Karl	6. 1	Stoke City	Wolverhampton	26.11.82
Little, Mark	6. 1	–	Worcester	20.08.88

Mulgrew, Charlie	6. 3	Celtic	Glasgow	6.03.86
O'Connor, Kevin	5.11	–	Dublin	19.10.85
Riley, Martin	6. 0	–	Wolverhampton	5.12.86
Ward, Darren	6. 0	Crystal Palace	Harrow	13.09.78
Midfielders				
Davies, Mark	5.11	–	Wolverhampton	18.12.88
Gobern, Lewis	5.10	–	Birmingham	28.01.85
Jarvis, Matthew	5. 8	Gillingham	Middlesbrough	22.05.86
Jones, Daniel	6. 2	–	Wordsley	14.07.86
McIndoe, Michael	5. 8	Barnsley	Edinburgh	2.12.79
Olofinjana, Seyi	6. 4	Brann Bergen	Lagos	30.06.80
Potter, Darren	5.10	Liverpool	Liverpool	21.12.84
Rosa, Denes	5. 9	Ferencvaros	Hungary	7.04.77
Forwards				
Bothroyd, Jay	6. 3	Charlton Athletic	Islington	7.05.82
Eastwood, Freddy	5.11	Southend Utd.	Epsom	29.10.83
Frankowski, Tomasz	5. 9	Elche	Poland	16.08.74
Gleeson, Stephen	6. 2	Cherry Orchard	Dublin	3.08.88
Johnson, Jemal	5. 9	Blackburn Rov.	New Jersey	3.05.84
Keogh, Andrew	6. 0	Scunthorpe Utd.	Dublin	16.05.86
Kightly, Michael	5.11	Grays	Basildon	24.01.86
Ward, Stephen	5.11	Bohemians	Dublin	20.08.85

LEAGUE ONE

AFC BOURNEMOUTH

Ground: Fitness First Stadium, Dean Court, Bournemouth BH7 7AF.
Telephone: 01202 726300. **Club nickname:** Cherries.
First-choice colours: Red and black shirts; black shorts; black socks.
Main sponsor: Focal Point. **Capacity for 2007-08:** 10,375.
Record attendance: 28,799 v Manchester Utd. (F.A. Cup 6) 2 March, 1957.

Name	**Height ft. in.**	**Previous club**	**Birthplace**	**Birthdate**
Goalkeepers				
Moss, Neil	6. 3	Southampton	New Milton	10.05.75
Pryce, Ryan	6. 0	–		20.09.86
Stewart, Gareth	6. 0	Blackburn Rov.	Preston	3.02.80
Defenders				
Cummings, Warren	5. 9	Chelsea	Aberdeen	15.10.80
Gowling, Joshua	6. 3	Herfolge	Coventry	29.11.83
Perrett, Russell	6. 3	Luton Town	Barton-on-Sea	18.06.73
Young, Neil	5. 9	Tottenham	Harlow	31.08.73
Midfielders				
Anderton, Darren	6. 1	Wolves	Southampton	3.3.72
Cooper, Shaun	5.10	Portsmouth	Isle of Wight	5.10.83
Foley, Steve	5. 4	Aston Villa	Dublin	10.02.86
Hollands, Danny	5.11	Chelsea	Ashford	6.11.85
McQuoid, Josh	5.11	–		15.12.89
Forwards				
Kuffour, Jo	5. 7	Brentford	Edmonton	17.11.81
Pitman, Brett	6. 0	–	Jersey	31.01.88
Vokes, Sam	5.11	–	Lymington	21.10.89

BRIGHTON AND HOVE ALBION

Ground: Withdean Stadium, Tongdean Lane, Brighton BN1 5JD.
Telephone: 01273 695400. **Club nickname:** Seagulls.
First-choice colours: Blue and white shirts; white shorts; white socks.
Main sponsor: Skint. **Capacity for 2007-08:** 8,850.
Record attendance: (Goldstone Ground) 36,747 v Fulham (Div. 2) 27 December, 1958; (Withdean Stadium) 7,999 v Southampton (Championship) 8 April, 2006.

Name	Height ft. in.	Previous club	Birthplace	Birthdate
Goalkeepers				
Kuipers, Michel	6. 2	Bristol Rov.	Amsterdam	26.06.74
Martin, Richard	6. 2	–	Brighton	1.09.87
Sullivan, John	5.10	–	Brighton	8.03.88
Defenders				
Butters, Guy	6. 3	Gillingham	Hillingdon	30.10.69
El-Abd, Adam	6. 0	–	Brighton	11.09.84
Elphick, Tommy	5.11	–	Brighton	7.09.87
Hinshelwood, Adam	5.10	–	Oxford	8.01.84
Hinshelwood, Paul	6. 2	–	Chatham	11.10.87
Lynch, Joel	6. 1	–	Eastbourne	3.10.87
Mayo, Kerry	5. 9	–	Cuckfield	21.09.77
Reid, Paul	5.10	Bradford City	Sydney	6.07.79
Rents, Sam	5.11	–	Brighton	22.06.87
Midfielders				
Bertin, Alexis	5. 8	Le Havre	Le Havre	13.05.80
Chamberlain, Scott	5.11	–	Brighton	15.01.88
Cox, Dean	5. 5	–	Cookfield	12.08.87
Fogden, Wes	5. 9	–	Brighton	12.04.88
Fraser, Tommy	5.11	–	Brighton	5.12.87
Frutos, Alexandre	5. 9	Metz	France	23.04.82
Gatting, Joe	5.11	–	Brighton	25.11.87
Hammond, Dean	5.11	–	Hastings	7.03.83
Hart, Gary	5. 9	Stansted	Harlow	21.09.76
Loft, Doug	6. 0	Hastings	Maidstone	25.12.86
Oatway, Charlie	5. 7	Brentford	Hammersmith	28.11.73
Whing, Andy	6. 0	Coventry City	Birmingham	20.09.84
Forwards				
Elder, Nathan	5. 9	Billericay	Hornchurch	1.08.87
Forster, Nicky	5. 9	Hull City	Caterham	8.09.73
Revell, Alex	6. 3	Braintree	Cambridge	7.07.83
Robinson, Jake	5. 7	–	Brighton	23.10.86
Savage, Bas	6. 1	Bristol City	Wandsworth	7.01.82

BRISTOL ROVERS

Ground: Memorial Ground, Filton Avenue, Horfield, Bristol BS7 0BF (sharing Cheltenham Town's ground from Jan. 2008).
Telephone: 0117 909 6648. **Club nickname:** Pirates.
First-choice colours: Blue and white shirts; white shorts; blue socks.
Main sponsor: Cowlin Construction. **Capacity for 2007-08:** 11,717.
Record attendance: (Eastville) 38,472 v Preston N.E. (F.A. Cup 4) 30 January, 1960. (Memorial Ground) 11,530 v Bristol City (Johnstone's Paint Trophy, Southern Final, 2nd. Leg) 27 February, 2007.

Name	Height ft. in.	Previous club	Birthplace	Birthdate
Goalkeepers				
Green, Mike	6. 0	–		23.07.89
Phillips, Steve	6. 1	Bristol City	Bath	6.05.78

Defenders				
Byron, Anthony	6. 1	Cardiff City	Newport	20.09.84
Carruthers, Chris	6. 1	Northampton Town	Kettering	19.08.83
Elliott, Steve	6. 1	Blackpool	Derby	29.10.78
Green, Ryan	5. 8	Hereford Utd.	Cardiff	20.10.80
Hinton, Craig	5.11	Kidderminster Harr.	Wolverhampton	26.11.77
Jacobson, Joe	5.11	Cardiff City	Cardiff	17.11.86
Parrinello, Tom	5. 6	–		11.11.89
Ryan, Robbie	5.10	Millwall	Dublin	16.05.77
Midfielders				
Campbell, Stuart	5.10	Grimsby Town	Corby	9.12.77
Disley, Craig	5. 1	Mansfield Town	Worksop	24.08.81
Igoe, Sammy	5. 6	Millwall	Staines	30.09.75
Lescott, Aaron	5. 8	Stockport Co.	Birmingham	2.12.77
Lines, Chris	6. 2	–	Bristol	30.11.85
Sandell, Andy	5.10	Bath City	Swindon	8.09.83
Trollope, Paul	6. 0	Northampton Town	Swindon	3.06.72
Willshire, Ben		–		5.10.86
Forwards				
Haldane, Lewis	6. 0	–	Trowbridge	13.03.85
Lambert, Rickie	5.10	Rochdale	Liverpool	16.02.82
Powell, Lewis	5.10	Swansea City	Caerphilly	14.01.88
Rigg, Sean	5.11	Forest Green		1.10.88
Walker, Richard	6. 0	Oxford Utd.	Birmingham	8.11.77
Williams, Andy	5.11	Hereford Utd.	Hereford	14.08.86

CARLISLE UNITED

Ground: Brunton Park, Warwick Road, Carlisle Utd. CA1 1LL.
Telephone: 01228 526237. **Club nickname**: Cumbrians.
First-choice colours: Blue and white shirts; blue and white shorts; blue socks.
Main sponsor: Stobart Ltd. **Capacity for 2007-08:** 16,982.
Record attendance: 27,500 v Birmingham City (F.A. Cup 3) 5 January, 1957, and v Middlesbrough (F.A. Cup 5) 7 January, 1970.

Name	Height ft. in.	Previous club	Birthplace	Birthdate
Goalkeepers				
Howarth, Chris	6. 0	Bolton Wand.	Bolton	23.05.86
Westwood, Kieren	6. 1	Manchester City	Manchester	23.10.84
Defenders				
Aranalde, Zigor	6. 1	Walsall	Guipuzcoa, Sp.	28.02.73
Arnison, Paul	5.10	Hartlepool Utd.	Hartlepool	18.09.77
Kirkup, Dan	6. 3	–	Hexham	19.05.88
Livesey, Danny	6. 3	Bolton Wand.	Salford	31.12.84
Raven, David	6. 0	Liverpool	Birkenhead	10.03.85
Midfielders				
Bridge-Wilkinson, Marc	5. 6	Bradford City	Nuneaton	16.03.79
Hackney, Simon	5. 8	Woodley Sports	Manchester	5.02.84
Joyce, Luke		Wigan Athletic		9.07.87
Lumsdon, Chris	5.11	Barnsley	Newcastle	15.12.79
Thirlwell, Paul	5.11	Derby Co.	Springwell	13.02.79
Forwards				
Carlton, Danny	6. 0	Morecambe	Leeds	22.12.83
Gall, Kevin	5. 9	Yeovil Town	Merthyr Tydfil	4.02.82
Graham, Danny	5.11	Middlesbrough	Gateshead	12.08.85

CHELTENHAM TOWN

Ground: Whaddon Road, Cheltenham GL52 5NA.
Telephone: 01242 573558. **Club nickname:** Town.
First-choice colours: Red and white shirts; white shorts; red socks.

Main Sponsor: George Bence. **Capacity for 2007-08:** 7,136.
Record attendance: 8,326 v Reading (F.A. Cup 1) 17 November, 1956.

Name	Height ft. in.	Previous club	Birthplace	Birthdate
Goalkeepers				
Brown, Scott	6. 0	Bristol City	Wolves	26.04.85
Higgs, Shane	6. 2	Worcester City	Oxford	13.05.77
Puddy, Will	5.11	Bristol City	Salisbury	4.10.87
Defenders				
Caines, Gavin	6. 1	Walsall	Birmingham	20.09.83
Duff, Shane	6. 1	–	Wroughton	2.04.82
Gallinagh, Andy	5.10	–	Sutton Coldfield	16.03.85
Gill, Jerry	5. 7	Northampton Town	Clevedon	8.09.70
Ridley, Lee	5. 9	Scunthorpe Utd.	Scunthorpe	5.12.81
Townsend, Michael	6. 2	Wolves	Walsall	17.05.86
Wylde, Michael	6. 2	–	Birmingham	6.01.87
Midfielders				
Bird, David	5. 8	Cinderford Town	Gloucester	26.12.84
Connolly, Adam	5. 9	–	Manchester	10.04.86
Finnigan, John	5. 8	Lincoln City	Wakefield	20.03.76
Foley, Sam	6. 0	–	Upton	17.10.86
Gill, Ben	5. 9	Watford	Harrow	4.10.87
Yao, Sosthene	5. 4	West Ham Utd.	Iv.	7.08.87
Forwards				
Connor, Paul	6. 2	Leyton Orient	Bishop Auckland	12.01.79
Gillespie, Steven	5. 9	Bristol City	Liverpool	4.06.85
Reid, Craig	5.10	Coventry City	Coventry	17.12.88
Spencer, Damian	6. 1	Bristol City	Ascot	19.09.81
Vincent, Ashley	6. 0	Wolves	Birmingham	26.05.85

CREWE ALEXANDRA

Ground: Alexandra Stadium, Gresty Road, Crewe CW2 6EB.
Telephone: 01270 213014. **Club nickname:** Railwaymen.
First-choice colours: Red shirts; white shorts; red socks.
Main sponsor: Mornflake Oats. **Capacity for 20067-08:** 10,107.
Record attendance: 20,000 v Tottenham (F.A. Cup 4) 30 January,1960.

Name	Height ft. in.	Previous club	Birthplace	Birthdate
Goalkeepers				
Tomlinson, Stuart	6. 0	–	Chester	10.05.85
Williams, Ben	6. 0	Manchester Utd.	Manchester	27.08.82
Williams, Owain fon	6. 4	–	Gwynedd	17.03.87
Defenders				
Baudet, Julien	6. 3	Notts Co.	Grenoble	13.01.79
Cox, Neil	6. 0	Cardiff City	Scunthorpe	8.10.71
Dugdale, Adam	6. 3	–	Liverpool	12.09.87
Jones, Billy	5.11	–	Shrewsbury	24.03.87
McCready, Chris	6. 0	Tranmere Rov.	Chester	5.07.81
O'Donnell, Daniel	6. 1	Liverpool	Liverpool	10.03.86
Sutton, Ritchie	6. 0	–	Stoke	29.04.86
Woodards, Danny	5.11	Exeter City	Forest Gate	7.10.83
Midfielders				
Bopp, Eugene	5.10	Rotherham Utd.	Kiev	5.09.83
Carrington, Mark	6. 0	–	Warrington	4.05.87
Lowe, Ryan	5.11	Chester City	Liverpool	18.09.78
O'Connor, Michael	6. 1	–	Belfast	6.10.87
Rix, Ben	5.10	–	Wolves	11.12.83
Roberts, Gary	5. 9	–	Chester	4.02.87
Schumacher, Steven	6. 0	Bradford City	Liverpool	30.04.84

Vaughan, David	5. 6	–	St Asaph	18.02.83
Forwards				
Bailey, Matthew	6. 4	Northwich Victoria	Crewe	12.03.86
Maynard, Nicky	5.11	–	Winsford	11.12.86
Miller, Shaun	5.10	–	Alsager	25.09.87
Pope, Tom	6. 3	Biddulph	Stoke	27.08.85

DONCASTER ROVERS

Ground: Keepmoat Stadium, Stadium Way, Doncaster DN4 5JW.
Telephone: 01302 764664. **Club nickname:** Rovers.
First-choice colours: Red and white shirts; black shorts; black socks.
Main sponsor: Wright Investments. **Capacity for 2007-08:** 15,269.
Record attendance: (Belle Vue): 37,149 v Hull City (Div.3N) 2 October, 1948. (Keepmoat Stadium): 14,470 v Huddersfield Town (Lge. 1) 1 January, 2007.

Name	Height ft. in.	Previous club	Birthplace	Birthdate
Goalkeepers				
Smith, Ben	6. 0	Stockport Co.	Newcastle	5.09.86
Sullivan, Neil	6. 0	Leeds Utd.	Sutton	24.02.70
Defenders				
Griffith, Anthony	6. 0	–	Huddersfield	28.10.86
Lee, Graeme	6. 2	Sheffield Wed.	Middlesbrough	31.05.78
Lockwood, Adam	6. 0	Yeovil Town	Wakefield	26.10.81
McDaid, Sean	5. 6	Leeds Utd.	Harrogate	6.03.86
Noble, Matt		–		23.11.88
O'Connor, James	5.10	Bournemouth	Birmingham	20.11.84
Roberts, Gareth	5. 8	Tranmere Rov.	Wrexham	6.02.78
Midfielders				
Green, Paul	5.10	Sheffield Wed.	Sheffield	10.04.83
Horlock, Kevin	6. 0	Ipswich Town	Erith	1.11.72
Nelthorpe, Craig	5.10	–	Doncaster	10.06.87
Price, Jason	6. 2	Hull City	Pontypridd	12.04.77
Roberts, Stephen	6. 2	Wrexham	Wrexham	24.02.80
Stock, Brian	5.10	Preston N.E.	Winchester	24.12.81
Wellens, Ritchie	5. 9	Oldham Athletic	Manchester	26.03.80
Wilson, Mark	6. 0	Dallas	Scunthorpe	9.02.79
Woods, Martin	5.11	Rotherham Utd.	Airdrie	1.01.86
Forwards				
Coppinger, James	5. 7	Exeter City	Middlesbrough	10.01.81
Dyer, Bruce	6. 0	Sheffield Utd.	Ilford	13.04.75
Guy, Lewis	5.10	Newcastle Utd.	Penrith	27.08.85
Hayter, James	5. 9	Bournemouth	Newport, IOW	9.04.79
Heffernan, Paul	5.10	Notts Co.	Dublin	29.12.81
McCammon, Mark	6. 2	Brighton & H.A.	Barnet	7.08.78

GILLINGHAM

Ground: Priestfield Stadium, Redfern Avenue, Gillingham ME7 4DD.
Telephone: 01634 300000. **Club nickname:** Gills.
First-choice colours: Blue shirts; blue shorts; blue socks.
Main sponsor: krbs.com. **Capacity for 2007-08:** 11,440.
Record attendance: 23,002 v Q.P.R. (F.A. Cup 3) 10 January, 1948.

Name	Height ft. in.	Previous club	Birthplace	Birthdate
Goalkeepers				
Jack, Kelvin	6. 3	Dundee	Trincity	29.04.76
Defenders				
Clohessy, Sean	5.11	Arsenal	Croydon	12.12.86

Cox, Ian	6. 0	Burnley	Croydon	25.03.71
Easton, Clint	5.11	Wycombe Wand.	Barking	1.10.77
Jupp, Duncan	6. 0	Southend Utd.	Guildford	25.01.75
King, Simon	5.11	Barnet	Oxford	11.04.83
Sancho, Brent	6. 1	Dundee	Trinidad & Tobago	13.03.77
Sodje, Efe	6. 1	Southend Utd.	Greenwich	5.10.72
Midfielders				
Armstrong, Craig	5.11	Cheltenham Town	South Shields	23.05.75
Bentley, Mark	6. 2	Southend Utd.	Hertford	7.01.78
Brown, Aaron	5.10	Swindon Town	Bristol	14.03.80
Cogan, Barry	5. 9	Barnet	Sligo	4.11.84
Crofts, Andrew	5.11	–	Chatham	29.05.84
Pouton, Alan	6. 0	Grimsby Town	Newcastle	1.02.77
Southall, Nicky	5.10	Nott'm. Forest	Middlesbrough	28.01.72
Stone, Craig	6. 0	–	Gravesend	29.12.88
Forwards				
Collin, Frannie	5.11	–	Chatham	20.04.87
Cumbers, Luis	6. 0	–	Chelmsford	6.09.88
Facey, Delroy	5.11	Rotherham Utd.	Huddersfield	22.04.80
Mulligan, Gary	6. 1	Sheffield Utd.	Dublin	23.04.85
N'Dumbu-Nsungu, Guylain	6. 1	Cardiff City	Kinshasa	26.12.82
Pugh, Andy	5. 9	–	Gravesend	28.01.89

HARTLEPOOL UNITED

Ground: Victoria Park, Clarence Road, Hartlepool TS24 8BZ.
Telephone: 01429 272584. **Club nickname:** Pool.
First-choice colours: Blue and white shirts; blue shorts; white socks.
Main Sponsor: Dove Energy. **Capacity for 2007-08:** 7,629.
Record attendance: 17,426 v Manchester Utd. (F.A. Cup 3) 5 January, 1957.

Name	Height ft. in.	Previous club	Birthplace	Birthdate
Goalkeepers				
Budtz, Jan	6. 5	Doncaster Rov.	Denmark	20.04.79
Lee-Barrett, Arran	6. 2	Coventry City	Chertsey	28.02.84
Provett, Jim	5.11	–	Trimdon	22.12.82
Defenders				
Barron, Michael	5.11	Middlesbrough	Lumley	22.12.74
Clark, Ben	6. 2	Sunderland	Shotley Bridge	24.01.83
Nelson, Michael	5. 9	Bury	Gateshead	15.03.82
Midfielders				
Boland, Willie	5. 9	Cardiff City	Ennis	6.08.75
Bullock, Lee	6. 1	Cardiff City	Stockton	22.05.81
Liddle, Gary	6. 1	Middlesbrough	Middlesbrough	15.06.86
McCunnie, Jamie	5.10	Dunfermline	Glasgow	15.04.83
Monkhouse, Andy	6. 1	Swindon Town	Leeds	23.10.80
Robson, Matty	5.10	–	Durham	23.01.85
Sweeney, Anthony	6. 0	–	Stockton	5.09.83
Turnbull, Stephen	5.10	–	South Shields	7.01.87
Forwards				
Barker, Richie	6. 0	Mansfield Town	Sheffield	30.05.75
Brown, James	5.11	–	Cramlington	3.01.87
Foley, David	5. 6	–	South Shields	12.07.87
Humphreys, Richie	5.11	Cambridge Utd.	Sheffield	30.11.77
Porter, Joel	5. 9	West Adelaide	Sydney	25.12.78

HUDDERSFIELD TOWN

Ground: Galpharm Stadium, Huddersfield HD1 6PX.
Telephone: 0970 444 4677. **Club nickname:** Terriers.
First-choice colours: Blue and white shirts; white and blue shorts; white and blue socks.

Main Sponsor: Yorkshire Building Society. **Capacity for 2007-08:** 24,554.
Record attendance: (Leeds Road) 67,037 v Arsenal (F.A. Cup 6) 27 February, 1932; (Galpharm Stadium) 23,678 v Liverpool (F.A. Cup 3) 12 December, 1999.

Name	Height ft. in.	Previous club	Birthplace	Birthdate
Goalkeepers				
Eastwood, Simon	6. 2	–	Luton	26.06.89
Glennon, Matt	6. 2	St Johnstone	Stockport	8.10.78
Defenders				
Clarke, Nathan	6. 2	–	Halifax	30.11.83
Clarke, Tom	5.11	–	Halifax	21.12.87
Mirfin, David	6. 2	–	Sheffield	18.04.85
Sinclair, Frank	5. 9	Burnley	Lambeth	3.12.71
Skarz, Joe	5.10	–	Huddersfield	13.07.89
Midfielders				
Collins, Michael	6. 0	–	Halifax	30.04.86
Hand, James	5. 9	–	Ireland	22.10.86
Hardy, Aaron	5. 8	–	South Elmsall	26.05.86
Holdsworth, Andy	5. 9	–	Pontefract	29.01.84
Kamara, Malvin	5.11	Port Vale	Southwark	17.11.83
Worthington, Jon	5. 9	–	Dewsbury	16.04.83
Young, Matthew	5. 9	–	Leeds	25.10.85
Forwards				
Beckett, Luke	5.11	Sheffield Utd.	Sheffield	25.11.76
Booth, Andy	6. 1	Sheffield Wed.	Huddersfield	6.12.73
Cadamarteri, Danny	5. 7	Leicester City	Cleckheaton	12.10.79
Schofield, Danny	5.10	Brodsworth	Doncaster	10.04.80

LEEDS UNITED

Ground: Elland Road, Leeds LS11 OES.
Telephone: 0113 367 6000. **Club nickname:** Whites.
First-choice colours: White shirts; white shorts; white socks.
Main sponsor: Bet24. **Capacity for 2007-08:** 39,457.
Record attendance: 57,892 v Sunderland, 15 March, 1967.

Name	Height ft. in.	Previous club	Birthplace	Birthdate
Goalkeepers				
Lund, Jonathan		–	Leeds	1.11.88
Defenders				
Delph, Fabian	5.10	–		5.05.91
Heath, Matt	6. 4	Coventry City	Leicester	1.11.81
Richardson, Frazer	5.10	–	Rotherham	29.10.82
Rui Marques, Manuel	5.11	Maritimo	Luanda, Ang.	3.09.77
Midfielders				
Carole, Sebastien	5. 7	Brighton & H.A.	France	8.09.82
Derry, Shaun	5.10	Crystal Palace	Nottingham	6.12.77
Douglas, Jonathan	5.10	Blackburn Rov.	Monaghan	22.11.81
Einarsson, Gylfi	6. 1	Lillestrom	Iceland	27.10.78
Lewis, Eddie	5. 9	Preston N.E.	Cerritos, US	17.05.74
Rose, Danny	5.11	–	Doncaster	2.07.90
Westlake, Ian	5.10	Ipswich Town	Clacton	10.07.83
Forwards				
Beckford, Jermaine	6. 2	Wealdstone		9.12.83
Blake, Robbie	5. 9	Birmingham City	Middlesbrough	4.03.76
Cresswell, Richard	6. 0	Preston N.E.	Bridlington	20.09.77
Flo, Tore Andre	6. 4	Valerenga	Stryn, Nor.	15.06.73
Healy, David	5. 8	Preston N.E.	Downpatrick	5.08.79
Kandol, Tresor	6. 1	Barnet	Banga, Con.	30.08.81

LEYTON ORIENT

Ground: Matchroom Stadium, Brisbane Road, London E10 5NE.
Telephone: 0871 310 1881. **Club nickname:** O's.
First-choice colours: Red and white shirts; red shorts; red socks.
Main Sponsor: Party Poker.com. **Capacity for 2007-08:** 9,271.
Record attendance: 34,345 v West Ham Utd. (F.A. Cup 4) 25 January 1964.

Name	Height ft. in.	Previous club	Birthplace	Birthdate
Goalkeepers				
Morris, Glenn	6. 0	–	Woolwich	20.12.83
Nelson, Stuart	6. 1	Brentford	Stroud	17.09.81
Defenders				
Chambers, Adam	5.10	Kidderminster	Sandwell	20.11.80
Demetriou, Jason	5.11	–		18.11.87
Fortune, Clayton	6. 3	Bristol City	Forest Gate	10.11.82
Mkandawire, Tamika	5.11	Hereford Utd.	Malawi	28.05.83
Palmer, Aiden	5. 8	–	Enfield	2.01.87
Purches, Stephen	5.11	Bournemouth	Ilford	14.01.80
Thelwell, Alton	6. 0	Hull City	Islington	5.09.80
Midfielders				
Corden, Wayne	5. 9	Scunthorpe Utd.	Leek	1.11.75
Melligan, John	5. 9	Cheltenham Town	Dublin	11.02.82
Saah, Brian	6. 1	–	Rush Green	16.12.86
Simpson, Michael	5. 8	Wycombe Wand.	Nottingham	28.02.74
Terry, Paul	5.10	Yeovil Town	Dagenham	3.04.79
Thornton, Sean	5.10	Doncaster Rov.	Drogheda	18.05.83
Forwards				
Echanomi, Efe	6. 1	–	Nigeria	27.09.86
Ibehre, Jabo	6. 2	–	Islington	28.01.83

LUTON TOWN

Ground: Kenilworth Stadium, Maple Road, Luton LU4 8AW.
Telephone: 01582 411622. **Club nickname:** Hatters.
First-choice colours: White shirts; black shorts; white socks.
Main sponsor: Electrolux. **Capacity for 2007-08:** 10,226.
Record attendance: 30,069 v Blackpool (F.A. Cup 6) 4 March, 1959.

Name	Height ft. in.	Previous club	Birthplace	Birthdate
Goalkeepers				
Beresford, Marlon	6. 1	Barnsley	Lincoln	2.09.69
Brill, Dean	6. 2	–	Luton	10.02.85
Defenders				
Barnett, Leon	6. 1	–	Stevenage	30.11.85
Coyne, Chris	6. 3	Dundee	Brisbane	28.12.78
Davis, Sol	5. 8	Swindon Town	Cheltenham	4.09.79
Foley, Kevin	5. 9	–	Luton	1.11.84
Goodall, Alan	6. 0	Rochdale	Liverpool	2.12.81
Heikkinen, Markus	6. 1	Aberdeen	Sweden	13.10.78
Perry, Chris	5. 9	W.B.A.	Carshalton	26.04.73
Underwood, Paul	5.11	Rushden & Diamonds	Wimbledon	16.08.73
Midfielders				
Bell, David	5.10	Rushden & Diamonds		21.01.84
Brkovic, Ahmet	5. 7	Leyton Orient	Dubrovnic	23.09.74
Currie, Darren	5.11	Ipswich Town	Hampstead	29.11.74
Edwards, David	5.11	Shrewsbury Town	Pontesbury	3.02.86
Keane, Keith	5. 9	–	Luton	20.11.86
Morgan, Dean	6. 0	Reading	Enfield	3.10.83
O'Leary, Stephen	5.10	–	London	12.02.85

Robinson, Steve	5. 9	Preston N.E.	Lisburn	10.12.74
Spring, Matthew	5.11	Watford	Harlow	17.11.79
Forwards				
Andrew, Calvin	6. 0	–	Luton	19.12.86
Boyd, Adam	5. 9	Hartlepool Utd.	Hartlepool	25.05.82
Parkin, Sam	6. 2	Ipswich Town	Roehampton	14.03.81
Talbot, Drew	5.10	Sheffield Wed.	Barnsley	19.07.86

MILLWALL

Ground: The New Den, Zampa Road, London SE16 3LN.
Telephone: 0207 232 1222. **Club nickname:** Lions.
First-choice colours: Blue and white shirts; white and blue shorts; blue socks.
Main sponsor: Oppida. **Capacity for 2007-08:** 19,734.
Record attendance: (The Den) 48,672 v Derby Co. (F.A. Cup 5) 20 February, 1937. (New Den) 20,093 v Arsenal (F.A. Cup 3) 10 January, 1994.

Name	Height ft. in.	Previous club	Birthplace	Birthdate
Goalkeepers				
Day, Chris	6. 3	Oldham Athletic	Walthamstow	28.07.75
Pidgeley, Lenny	6. 4	Chelsea	Twickenham	7.02.84
Defenders				
Barron, Scott	5.10	Ipswich Town	Preston	2.09.85
Dunne, Alan	5.10	–	Dublin	23.08.82
Frampton, Andy	5.11	Brentford	Wimbledon	3.09.79
Robinson, Paul	6. 1	–	Barnet	7.01.82
Phillips, Mark	6. 2	–	Lambeth	27.01.82
Whitbread, Zak	6. 2	Liverpool	Houston	4.03.84
Midfielders				
Elliott, Marvin	6. 0	–	Wandsworth	15.09.84
Hackett, Chris	6. 0	Hearts	Oxford	1.03.83
Morais, Filipe	5. 9	Chelsea	Lisbon	21.11.85
Smith, Ryan	5.10	Derby Co.	Islington	10.11.86
Spiller, Danny	5. 9	Gillingham	Maidstone	10.10.81
Williams, Marvin	5.11	–	Hammersmith	12.08.87
Forwards				
Alexander, Gary	5.11	Leyton Orient	Lambeth	15.08.79
Byfield, Darren	5.11	Gillingham	Sutton Coldfield	29.09.76
Harris, Neil	5.11	Nott'm. Forest	Orsett	12.07.77
May, Ben	6. 1	–	Gravesend	10.03.84

NORTHAMPTON TOWN

Ground: Sixfields Stadium, Upton Way, Northampton NN5 5QA.
Telephone: 0870 822 1997. **Club nickname:** Cobblers.
First-choice colours: Claret shirts; white shorts; claret socks.
Main sponsor: Jackson Grundy. **Capacity for 2007-08:** 7,653.
Record attendance: (County Ground) 24,523 v Fulham (Div. 1) 23 April, 1966. (Sixfields Stadium) 7,557 v Manchester City (Div. 2) 26 September, 1998.

Name	Height ft. in.	Previous club	Birthplace	Birthdate
Goalkeepers				
Bunn, Mark	6. 0	–	Camden	16.11.84
Dunn, Chris	6. 4	–		23.10.87
Defenders				
Crowe, Jason	5. 9	Grimsby Town	Sidcup	30.09.78
Doig, Chris	6. 2	Nott'm. Forest	Dumfries	13.02.81
Holt, Andrew	6. 1	Wrexham	Manchester	21.05.78
Hughes, Mark	6. 2	Everton	Liverpool	9.12.86
Jackman, Danny	5. 5	Gillingham	Worcester	3.01.83

Johnson, Brett	6. 1	Aldershot	Hammersmith	15.08.85
May, Danny		–		19.11.88
Midfielders				
Aiston, Sam	6. 2	Tranmere Rov.	Newcastle	21.11.76
Burnell, Joe	5. 9	Wycombe Wand.	Bristol	10.10.80
Coke, Giles	5.11	Mansfield Town	Westminster	3.06.86
Gilligan, Ryan	5.10	Watford	Swindon	18.01.87
Johnson, Bradley	5.10	Cambridge Utd.	Hackney	28.04.87
Forwards				
Henderson, Ian	5. 8	Norwich City	Bury St Edmunds	24.01.85
Kirk, Andy	5.10	Boston Utd.	Belfast	29.05.79
Larkin, Colin	5. 9	Chesterfield	Dundalk	27.04.82
Quinn, James	6. 1	Peterborough	Coventry	15.12.74

NOTTINGHAM FOREST

Ground: City Ground, Pavilion Road, Nottingham NG2 5FJ.
Telephone: 0115 982 4444. **Club nickname:** Forest.
First-choice colours: Red shirts; white shorts; red socks.
Main sponsor: Capital One. **Capacity for 2007-08:** 30,576.
Record attendance: 49,945 v Manchester Utd. (Div. 1) 28 October, 1967.

Name	Height ft. in.	Previous club	Birthplace	Birthdate
Goalkeepers				
Redmond, Shane		Cherry Orchard	Rathcoole, Ire.	23.03.89
Roberts, Dale	6. 3	Middlesbrough	Horden	22.10.86
Smith, Paul	6. 3	Southampton	Epsom	17.12.79
Defenders				
Bennett, Julian	6. 1	Walsall	Nottingham	17.12.84
Breckin, Ian	5.11	Wigan Athletic	Rotherham	24.02.75
Chambers, Luke	5.11	Northampton Town	Kettering	29.08.85
Lockwood, Matt	5. 9	Leyton Orient	Southend	17.10.76
Morgan, Wes	5.11	–	Nottingham	21.01.84
Perch, James	6. 0	–	Mansfield	28.09.85
Midfielders				
Bastians, Felix	6. 2	Borussia Dortmund	Bochum	9.05.88
Clingan, Sammy	5.11	Wolves	Belfast	13.01.84
Cohen, Chris	5.11	Yeovil	Norwich	5.03.87
Commons, Kris	5. 6	Stoke City	Mansfield	30.08.83
Davies, Arron	5. 9	Yeovil	Cardiff	22.06.84
Lennon, Neil	5. 9	Celtic	Lurgan	25.06.71
Forwards				
Agogo, Junior	5.10	Bristol Rov.	Accra, Gh.	1.08.79
Dobie, Scott	6. 1	Millwall	Workington	10.10.78
Holt, Grant	6. 0	Rochdale	Carlisle	12.04.81
Tyson, Nathan	6. 0	Wycombe Wand.	Reading	4.05.82

OLDHAM ATHLETIC

Ground: Boundary Park, Oldham OL1 2PA.
Telephone: 0871 226 2235. **Club nickname:** Latics.
First-choice colours: Blue shirts; blue shorts; white socks.
Main sponsor: Hillstone Development. **Capacity for 2007-08:** 13,500.
Record attendance: 47,761 v Sheffield Wed. (F.A. Cup 4) 25 January, 1930.

Name	Height ft. in.	Previous club	Birthplace	Birthdate
Goalkeepers				
Crossley, Mark	6. 0	Fulham	Barnsley	16.06.69
Pogliacomi, Leslie	6. 5	Parramatta	Perth, Aus.	3.05.76

Defenders				
Gregan, Sean	6. 2	Leeds Utd.	Stockton	29.03.74
Stam, Stefan	6. 2	Huizen	Amersfoot, Hol.	14.09.79
Thompson, John	6. 1	Nott'm. Forest	Dublin	12.10.81
Midfielders				
Allott, Mark	5.11	Chesterfield	Manchester	3.10.77
Kalala, Jean-Paul	5.10	Yeovil Town	Lubumbashi, Con.	16.02.82
Lomax, Kelvin	5.11	–	Bury	12.11.86
McDonald, Gary	6. 1	Kilmarnock	Irvine	10.04.82
Taylor, Chris	5.11	–	Oldham	20.12.86
Forwards				
Davies, Craig	6. 2	Verona	Burton	9.01.86
Liddell, Andy	5. 8	Sheffield Utd.	Leeds	28.06.73
Ricketts, Michael	6. 2	Preston N.E.	Birmingham	4.12.78
Wolfenden, Matthew	5. 9	–	Oldham	23.07.87

PORT VALE

Ground: Vale Park, Hamil Road, Burslem, Stoke-on-Trent ST6 1AW.
Telephone: 01782 655800. **Club nickname:** Valiants.
First-choice colours: White, black and gold shirts, shorts and socks.
Main sponsor: Sennheiser. **Capacity for 2007-08:** 18,947.
Record attendance: 50,000 v Aston Villa (F.A. Cup 5) 20 February, 1960.

Name	Height ft. in.	Previous club	Birthplace	Birthdate
Goalkeepers				
Goodlad, Mark	6. 0	Nott'm Forest	Barnsley	9.09.80
Defenders				
Edwards, Paul	5.11	Oldham Athletic	Manchester	1.1.80
Lowe, Keith	6. 2	Wolves	Wolves	13.09.85
McGregor, Mark	5.11	Blackpool	Chester	16.02.77
Miller, Justin	6. 0	Leyton Orient	Johannesburg	16.12.80
Pilkington, George	6. 0	Everton	Rugeley	1.11.81
Talbot, Jason	5. 8	Mansfield Town	Irlam	30.09.75
Midfielders				
Harsley, Paul	5. 8	Macclesfield Town	Scunthorpe	29.05.78
Hulbert, Robin	5. 9	Telford Utd.	Plymouth	14.03.80
Rocastle, Craig	6. 1	Oldham Athletic	Lewisham	17.08.81
Tudor, Shane	5. 8	Leyton Orient	Wolves	10.02.82
Forwards				
Richards, Marc	5.11	Barnsley	Wolverhampton	8.07.82
Rodgers, Luke	5. 8	Crewe Alexandra	Birmingham	1.01.82
Sodje, Akpo	6. 2	Darlington	Greenwich	31.01.81

SOUTHEND UNITED

Ground: Roots Hall, Victoria Avenue, Southend SS2 6NQ.
Telephone: 01702 304050. **Club nickname:** Shrimpers.
First-choice colours: Navy shirts; navy shorts; navy socks.
Main sponsor: Insure and Go. **Capacity for 2007-08:** 12,392.
Record attendance: 31,033 v Liverpool (F.A. Cup 3) 10 January, 1979.

Name	Height ft. in.	Previous club	Birthplace	Birthdate
Goalkeepers				
Collis, Steve	6. 2	Yeovil Town	Harrow	18.03.81
Flahavan, Darryl	5.10	Southampton	Southampton	28.11.78
Welch, Joe	6. 3	–	Welwyn Garden City	29.11.88
Defenders				
Barrett, Adam	5.10	Bristol Rov.	Dagenham	29.11.79
Clarke, Peter	6. 0	Blackpool	Southport	3.01.82

Francis, Simon	6. 0	Sheffield Utd.	Nottingham	16.02.85
Hammell, Steven	5.10	St Mirren	Rutherglen	18.02.82
Hunt, Lewis	5.11	Derby Co.	Birmingham	25.08.82
Prior, Spencer	6. 3	Cardiff City	Southend	22.04.71
Midfielders				
Bailey, Nicky	5.10	Barnet	Putney	10.06.84
Black, Tommy	5. 7	Crystal Palace	Chigwell	26.11.79
Campbell-Ryce, Jamal	5. 7	Rotherham Utd.	Lambeth	6.04.83
Gower, Mark	5.11	Barnet	Edmonton	5.10.78
Maher, Kevin	5.11	Tottenham	Ilford	17.10.76
Forwards				
Bradbury, Lee	6. 2	Oxford Utd.	Isle of Wight	3.07.75
Foran, Richie	6. 0	Motherwell	Dublin	16.06.80
Harrold, Matt	6. 1	Yeovil Town	Leyton	25.07.84
Hooper, Gary	5. 9	Grays	Loughton	26.01.88
Lawson, James	5.10	–	Basildon	21.01.87
MacDonald, Charlie	5.10	Ebbsfleet	Southwark	13.02.81
McCormack, Alan	5. 8	Preston N.E.	Dublin	10.01.84
Paynter, Billy	6. 0	Hull City	Liverpool	13.07.84

SWANSEA CITY

Ground: Liberty Stadium, Morfa, Swansea SA1 2FA.
Telephone: 01792 616600. **Club nickname:** Swans.
First-choice colours: White shirts; white shorts; white and black socks.
Main sponsor: Swansea.com. **Capacity for 2007-08:** 20,520.
Record attendance: (Vetch Field) 32,786 v Arsenal (F.A. Cup 4) 17 February, 1968. (Liberty Stadium) 19,288 v Yeovil Town (Lg.1) 18 November, 2005.

Name	Height ft. in.	Previous club	Birthplace	Birthdate
Goalkeepers				
Devries, Dorus	5.11	Dunfermline	Beverwijk, Hol.	29.12.80
Gueret, Willy	6. 1	Millwall	Guadaloupe	3.08.73
Defenders				
Austin, Kevin	6. 0	Bristol Rov.	Hackney	12.02.73
Collins, Matty	5. 9	Fulham	Merthyr	31.03.86
Monk, Garry	6. 0	Barnsley	Bedford	6.03.79
Tate, Alan	6. 1	Manchester Utd.	Easington	2.09.82
Watt, Steven	6. 2	Chelsea	Aberdeen	1.05.85
Williams, Tom	6. 0	Barnsley	Carshalton	8.07.80
Midfielders				
Britton, Leon	5. 5	West Ham Utd.	London	16.09.82
Tudur-Jones, Owain	6. 2	–	Bangor	15.10.84
Way, Darren	5. 7	Yeovil Town	Plymouth	21.11.79
Forwards				
Bauza, Guillem	5.11	Espanyol	Palma	25.10.84
Duffy, Daryl	5.11	Hull City	Glasgow	16.04.84
MacDonald, Shaun	6. 1	–	Swansea	17.06.88
Pratley, Darren	6. 0	Fulham	Barking	22.04.85
Robinson, Andy	5. 8	Cammell Laird	Birkenhead	3.11.79
Scotland, Jason	5. 8	St Johnstone	Morvant, Trin.	18.02.79
Trundle, Lee	5.11	Wrexham	Liverpool	10.10.76

SWINDON TOWN

Ground: County Ground, County Road, Swindon SN1 2ED.
Telephone: 0870 443 1969. **Club nickname:** Robins.
First-choice colours: Red shirts; white shorts; red socks.
Main sponsor: Nationwide. **Capacity for 2007-08:** 14,225.
Record attendance: 32,000 v Arsenal (F.A. Cup 3) 15 January, 1972.

Name	Height ft. in.	Previous club	Birthplace	Birthdate
Goalkeepers				
Smith, Phil	6. 1	Crawley	Harrow	14.12.79
Defenders				
Aljofree, Hasney	6. 0	Plymouth Argyle	Manchester	11.07.78
Ifil, Jerel	6. 1	Watford	London	27.06.82
Nicholas, Andrew	6. 2	Liverpool	Liverpool	10.10.83
Smith, Jack	5.11	Watford	Hemel Hempstead	14.10.83
Williams, Adrian	6. 2	Coventry City	Reading	16.08.71
Midfielders				
Easton, Craig	5.10	Leyton Orient	Bellshill	26.02.79
Pook, Michael	5.11	–	Swindon	24.06.86
Forwards				
Corr, Barry	6. 4	Sheffield Wed.	Wicklow	2.04.85
Peacock, Lee	6. 0	Sheffield Wed.	Paisley	9.10.76
Roberts, Christian	5.11	Bristol City	Cardiff	22.10.79
Shakes, Ricky	5.10	Bolton Wand.	Brixton	26.01.85

TRANMERE ROVERS

Ground: Prenton Park, Prenton Road West, Birkenhead CH42 9PY.
Telephone: 0870 460 3333. **Club nickname:** Rovers.
First-choice colours: White shirts; white shorts; white socks.
Mian Sponsor: Wirral Borough Council. **Capacity for 2007-08:** 16,567.
Record attendance: 24,424 v Stoke City (F.A. Cup 4) 5 February, 1972.

Name	Height ft. in.	Previous club	Birthplace	Birthdate
Goalkeepers				
Achterberg, John	6. 1	Eindhoven	Liverpool	8.07.71
Coyne, Danny	5. 11	Burnley	Prestatyn	27.08.73
Defenders				
Cansdell-Sherriff, Shane	6. 0	Aarhus	Sydney	10.11.82
Chorley, Ben	6. 3	MK Dons	Sidcup	30.09.82
Goodison, Ian	6. 3	Hull City	Kingston, Jam.	21.11.72
Johnston, Michael	5. 10	–	Liverpool	16.12.87
Stockdale, Robbie	6. 0	Hull City	Redcar	30.11.79
Tremarco, Carl	5. 11	–	Liverpool	11.10.85
Midfielders				
Ahmed, Adnan	5. 10	Huddersfield Town	Burnley	7.06.84
Henry, Paul	5. 8	–	Liverpool	28.01.88
Jennings, Steven	5. 7	–	Liverpool	28.10.84
Jones, Mike	6. 0	–	Birkenhead	15.08.87
Kay, Anthony	5. 11	Barnsley	Barnsley	21.10.82
McLaren, Paul	6. 1	Rotherham	High Wycombe	17.11.76
Mullin, John	6. 0	Rotherham Utd.	Bury	11.08.75
Forwards				
Curran, Craig	5. 9	–	Liverpool	23.08.89
Davies, Steve	6. 1	–	Liverpool	29.12.87
Greenacre, Chris	5. 11	Stoke City	Halifax	23.12.77
Shuker, Chris	5. 5	Barnsley	Liverpool	9.05.82
Taylor, Gareth	6. 1	Nott'm. Forest	Weston-Super-Mare	25.02.73
Zola, Calvin	6. 2	Newcastle Utd.	Kinshasa	31.12.84

WALSALL

Ground: Banks's Stadium, Bescot Crescent, Walsall WS1 4SA.
Telephone: 0871 221 0442. **Club nickname:** Saddlers.
First-choice colours: White shirts; red shorts; red socks.

Main Sponsor: Easy Fit Conservatories. **Capacity for 2007-08:** 11,300.
Record attendance: (Fellows Park) 25,433 v Newcastle Utd. (Div. 2) 29 August, 1961. (Bescot Stadium) 11,307 v Wolves (Div. 1) 11 January, 2003.

Name	Height ft. in.	Previous club	Birthplace	Birthdate
Goalkeepers				
Gilmartin, Rene	6. 5	–	Ireland	31.05.87
Ince, Clayton	6. 3	Coventry City	Trinidad	13.07.72
Mckeown, James	6. 1	–	Birmingham	24.07.89
Defenders				
Bradley, Mark	6. 0	–	Wordsley	14.01.88
Dann, Scott	6. 2	–	Liverpool	14.02.87
Dobson, Michael	5.11	Brentford	Isleworth	9.04.81
Fox, Daniel	6. 0	Everton		29.05.86
Gerrard, Anthony	6. 2	Everton	Liverpool	6.02.86
Roper, Ian	6. 3	–	Nuneaton	20.06.77
Sonner, Danny	5.11	Port Vale	Wigan	9.01.72
Midfielders				
Demontagnac, Ishmel	5.10	Charlton Athletic	London	15.06.88
Wrack, Darren	5. 9	Grimsby Town	Cleethorpes	5.05.76
Forwards				
Hall, Paul	5. 9	Chesterfield	Manchester	3.07.72

YEOVIL TOWN

Ground: Huish Park, Lufton Way, Yeovil BA22 8YF.
Telephone: 01935 423662. **Club nickname:** Glovers.
First-choice colours: Green and white shirts; green shorts; white socks.
Main sponsor: Bradfords Building Supplies. **Capacity for 2007-08:** 9,665.
Record attendance: 9,348 v Liverpool (F.A. Cup 3) 4 January, 2004.

Name	Height ft. in.	Previous club	Birthplace	Birthdate
Goalkeepers				
Behcet, Darren	6. 0	West Ham Utd.		8.10.86
Mildenhall, Steve	6. 4	Grimsby Town	Swindon	13.05.78
Defenders				
Guyett, Scott	6. 2	Chester City	Ascot	20.01.76
Forbes, Terrell	6. 0	Oldham Athletic	Southwark	17.08.81
Lynch, Mark	5.11	Hull City	Manchester	2.09.81
Rose, Matthew	5.11	Q.P.R.	Dartford	24.09.75
Skiverton, Terry	6. 1	Welling	Mile End	20.06.75
Midfielders				
Jones, Nathan	5. 7	Brighton & H.A.	Rhondda	28.05.73
Morris, Lee	5.10	Leicester City	Driffield	30.04.80
Forwards				
Gray, Wayne	5.10	Southend Utd.	Dulwich	7.11.80
Knights, Darryl	5. 7	Ipswich Town	Ipswich	1.05.88
Owusu, Lloyd	6. 1	Brentford	Slough	12.12.76
Stewart, Marcus	5.10	Bristol City	Bristol	7.11.72

LEAGUE TWO

ACCRINGTON STANLEY

Ground: Fraser Eagle Stadium, Livingstone Road, Accrington BB5 5BX.
Telephone: 01254 356950. **Club nickname:** Stanley.

First-choice colours: Red shirts; white shorts; red socks.
Main sponsor: Fraser Eagle. **Capacity for 2007-08:** 5,057.
Record attendance: 4,368 v Colchester Utd. (F.A. Cup 3) 3 January, 2003.

Name	Height ft. in.	Previous club	Birthplace	Birthdate
Goalkeepers				
Arthur, Kenny	6. 3	Partick Thistle	Bellshill	7.12.78
Dunbavin, Ian	6. 1	Halifax Town	Knowsley	27.05.80
Fearon, Martin	5.11	–	Blackburn	30.10.88
Defenders				
Cavanagh, Peter	5.10	Liverpool	Liverpool	14.10.81
Edwards, Phil	5. 8	Wigan Athletic	Kirkby	8.11.85
Richardson, Leam	5. 7	Blackpool	Leeds	19.11.79
Williams, Robbie	5.10	St Dominics	Liverpool	12.04.79
Midfielders				
Boco, Romuald	5.10	Niort	France	8.07.85
Branch, Graham	6. 2	Burnley	Liverpool	12.02.72
Carden, Paul	5. 8	Burton	Liverpool	29.03.79
Harris, Jay	5. 7	Everton	Liverpool	15.04.07
Procter, Andrew	5.11	Great Harwood	Lancashire	13.03.83
Whalley, Shaun	5. 9	Witton	Whiston	7.08.87
Forwards				
Brown, David	5.10	Hereford Utd.	Bolton	2.10.78
Dsane, Roscoe	5. 5	AFC Wimbledon	Epsom	16.10.80
McGivern, Leighton	5. 8	Vauxhall Motors	Liverpool	2.06.84
Miles, John	5.10	Macclesfield Town	Fazackerley	28.09.81
Mullin, Paul	6. 0	Radcliffe	Bury	16.03.74

BARNET

Ground: Underhill Stadium, Barnet EN5 2DN.
Telephone: 0208 441 6932. **Club nickname:** Bees.
First-choice colours: Black and gold shirts; black shorts; black socks.
Main sponsor: Mortgage Express. **Capacity for 2007-08:** 5,300.
Record attendance: 11,026 v Wycombe Wand. (F.A. Amateur Cup 4), January 1954.

Name	Height ft. in.	Previous club	Birthplace	Birthdate
Goalkeepers				
Harrison, Lee	6. 2	Peterborough Utd.	Billericay	12.09.71
Defenders				
Devera, Joe	6. 2	–	Southgate	6.02.87
Hendon, Ian	6. 0	Peterborough Utd.	Ilford	5.12.71
Ioannou, Nicky	5.11	Rushden & Diamonds	Camden	3.07.87
Nicolau, Nicky	5. 8	Swindon Town	St Pancras	12.10.83
Yakubu, Ismail	5.11	–	London	8.04.85
Midfielders				
Bishop, Neil	6. 1	York City	Stockton	7.08.81
Leary, Michael	5.11	Luton Town	Ealing	17.04.83
Porter, Max	5.10	Bishop's Stortford		29.06.87
Puncheon, Jason	5.11	MK Dons	Croydon	26.06.86
Sinclair, Dean	5. 9	Norwich City	Luton	17.12.84
Forwards				
Birchall, Adam	5. 7	Mansfield Town	Maidstone	2.12.84
Grazioli, Giuliano	5.11	Bristol Rov.	Marylebone	23.03.75
Hatch, Liam	6. 3	Gravesend	Kent	3.04.84

BRADFORD CITY

Ground: Intersonic Stadium, Valley Parade, Bradford BD8 7DY.
Telephone: 0870 822 0000. **Club nickname:** Bantams.
First-choice colours: Claret and amber shirts; black and claret shorts; claret and amber socks.
Main Sponsor: Bradford and Bingley. **Capacity for 2007-08:** 25,132.
Record attendance: 39,146 v Burnley (F.A. Cup 4) 11 March, 1911.

Name	Height ft. in.	Previous club	Birthplace	Birthdate
Goalkeepers				
Ricketts, Donovan	6. 3	Bolton Wand.	Kingston, Jam.	7.06.77
Saynor, Ben	6. 3	–		6.03.89
Defenders				
Ainge, Simon	6. 1	–		18.02.88
Bentham, Craig	5. 9	–	Bradford	7.03.85
Bower, Mark	5.10	–	Bradford	23.01.80
Clarke, Matt	6. 3	Darlington	Leeds	18.12.80
Wetherall, David	6. 3	Leeds Utd.	Sheffield	14.03.71
Midfielders				
Colbeck, Joe	5.11	–	Bradford	29.11.86
Daley, Omar	5. 9	Charleston	Kingston	25.04.81
Penford, Tom	5.10	–	Leeds	5.01.85
Forwards				
Conlon, Barry	6. 3	Mansfield Town	Drogheda	1.10.78
Johnson, Eddie	5.10	Manchester Utd.	Chester	20.09.84
Thorne, Peter	6. 0	Norwich City	Manchester	21.06.73

BRENTFORD

Ground: Griffin Park, Braemar Road, Brentford TW8 0NT.
Telephone: 0845 345 6442. **Club nickname:** Bees.
First-choice colours: Red and white shirts; black shorts; red stockings.
Main sponsor: Samvo. **Capacity for 2007-08:** 12,400.
Record attendance: 39,626 v Preston N.E. (F.A. Cup 6) 5 March, 1938.

Name	Height ft. in.	Previous club	Birthplace	Birthdate
Goalkeepers				
Brown, Sebastian	6. 0	–		24.11.89
Masters, Clark	6. 3	–	Hastings	31.05.87
Defenders				
Charles, Darius	5.11	–	Ealing	10.12.87
Falco, Bradley	5.10	–		18.09.89
Heywood, Matt	6. 2	Bristol City	Chatham	26.08.79
Mackie, John	6. 0	Leyton Orient	Whitechapel	5.07.76
Pead, Craig	5. 9	Walsall	Bromsgrove	15.09.81
Osborne, Karleigh	6. 2	–	Southall	19.03.88
Tillen, Sam	5.10	Chelsea	Reading	16.04.85
Midfielders				
Brooker, Paul	5. 8	Reading	Hammersmith	25.11.76
Keith, Joe	5. 8	Leyton Orient	Plaistow	1.10.78
Mousinho, John	6. 1	Notre Dame	Isleworth	30.04.86
O'Connor, Kevin	5.11	–	Blackburn	24.02.82
Poole, Glenn	5. 8	Grays	London	3.02.81
Forwards				
Connell, Alan	5.11	Hereford Utd.	Enfield	15.02.83
Ide, Charlie	5. 8	–	Sunbury	10.05.88
Montague, Ross	6.00	–		1.11.88
Peters, Ryan	5.11	–	Wandsworth	21.08.87

BURY

Ground: Gigg Lane, Bury BL9 9HR.
Telephone: 0161 764 4881. **Club nickname:** Shakers.
First-choice colours: White shirts; blue shorts; blue socks.
Main Sponsor: Bury Metro. **Capacity for 2007-08:** 11,669.
Record attendance: 35,000 v Bolton Wand. (F.A. Cup 3) 9 January, 1960.

Name	Height ft. in.	Previous club	Birthplace	Birthdate
Goalkeepers				
Grundy, Aaron	6. 1	–	Bolton	21.01.88
Defenders				
Challinor, Dave	6. 1	Stockport Co.	Chester	2.10.75
Futcher, Ben	6. 4	Peterborough Utd.	Manchester	20.02.81
Morgan, Paul	5.11	Lincoln City	Belfast	23.10.78
Parrish, Andy	6. 0	–	Bolton	22.06.88
Scott, Paul	5.11	Huddersfield Town	Wakefield	5.11.79
Woodthorpe, Colin	6. 1	Stockport Co.	Ellesmere Port	13.01.69
Midfielders				
Adams, Nicky	5.10	–	Bolton	16.10.86
Barry-Murphy, Brian	6. 0	Sheffield Wed.	Cork	27.07.78
Buchanan, David	5. 8	–	Rochdale	6.05.86
Forwards				
Bishop, Andy	6. 0	York City	Stone	19.10.82
Hurst, Glynn	5.10	Shrewsbury Town	Barnsley	17.01.76

CHESTER CITY

Ground: Saunders Honda Stadium, Bumpers Lane, Chester CH1 4LT.
Telephone: 01244 371376. **Club nickname:** Blues.
First-choice colours: Blue and white shirts; blue shorts; blue socks.
Main sponsor: UK Sameday. **Capacity for 2007-08:** 6,012.
Record attendance: (Sealand Road): 20,500 v Chelsea (F.A. Cup 3) 16 January, 1952. (Deva Stadium): 5,987 v Scarborough (Conference) 17 April, 2004.

Name	Height ft. in.	Previous club	Birthplace	Birthdate
Goalkeepers				
Danby, John	6. 2	Kidderminster Harr.	Stoke	20.09.81
Palethorpe, Phillip	6. 2	Tranmere Rov.	Liverpool	17.09.86
Ward, Gavin	6. 3	Tranmere Rov.	Sutton Coldfield	30.06.70
Defenders				
Bolland, Phil	6. 2	Peterborough Utd.	Liverpool	26.08.76
Hessey, Sean	5.10	Blackpool	Whiston	19.09.78
Linwood, Paul	6. 2	Tranmere Rov.	Birkenhead	24.10.83
Marples, Simon	5.10	Doncaster Rov.	Sheffield	30.07.75
Sandwith, Kevin	5.11	Macclesfield Town	Workington	30.04.78
Vaughan, James	5. 8	Tranmere Rov.	Liverpool	6.12.86
Westwood, Ashley	5.11	Northampton Town	Bridgnorth	31.08.76
Midfielders				
Bennett, Dean	5.10	Wrexham	Wolverhampton	13.12.77
Cronin, Glenn	5. 9	Exeter City	Dublin	14.09.81
Hand, Jamie	5.11	Watford	Uxbridge	7.02.84
Partridge, Richie	5. 8	Rotherham Utd.	Dublin	12.09.80
Wilson, Laurence	5.10	Everton	Liverpool	10.10.86
Forwards				
Brownlie, Royce	6. 0	Swindon Town	Coffs Harbour, Aus.	28.01.80
Ellison, Kevin	6. 1	Tranmere Rov.	Liverpool	23.02.79
Holroyd, Chris	5.11	–	Nantwich	24.10.86
Lowndes, Nathan	5.11	Port Vale	Salford	2.06.77
Murphy, John	6. 2	Macclesfield Town	Whiston	18.10.76

Rutherford, Paul	5. 9	–	Moreton	10.07.87
Steele, Lee	5. 9	Leyton Orient	Liverpool	8.12.73
Yeo, Simon	5.10	Peterborough Utd.	Stockport	20.10.73

CHESTERFIELD

Ground: Recreation Ground, Chesterfield S40 4SX.
Telephone: 01246 209765. **Club nickname:** Spireites.
First-choice colours: Blue shirts; white shorts; blue socks.
Main Sponsor: Autoworld. **Capacity for 2007-08:** 8,502.
Record attendance: 30,698 v Newcastle Utd. (Div. 2) 7 April, 1939.

Name	Height ft. in.	Previous club	Birthplace	Birthdate
Goalkeepers				
Jordan, Michael	6. 2	Arsenal	Enfield	7.04.86
Roche, Barry	6. 4	Nott'm. Forest	Dublin	6.04.82
Defenders				
Downes, Aaron	6. 1	Frickley	Mudgee, Aus.	15.05.85
Gray, Kevin	6. 0	Carlisle Utd.	Sheffield	7.01.72
Kovacs, Janos	6. 4	MTK Hungaria	Budapest, Hung.	11.09.85
Lowry, Jamie	6. 0	–	Newquay	18.03.87
O'Hare, Alan	6. 2	Bolton Wand.	Drogheda	31.07.82
Picken, Phil	5. 9	Manchester Utd.	Manchester	12.11.85
Robertson, Gregor	6. 0	Rotherham Utd.	Edinburgh	19.01.84
Midfielders				
Davies, Gareth	6. 1	–	Chesterfield	4.02.83
Niven, Derek	5.10	Raith Rov.	Falkirk	12.12.83
Forwards				
Allison, Wayne	6. 1	Sheffield Utd.	Huddersfield	16.10.68
Fletcher, Steve	6. 2	Bournemouth	Hartlepool	26.06.72
Jackson, Jamie	6. 0	–	Sheffield	1.11.86
Lester, Jack	5.10	Nott'm. Forest	Sheffield	8.10.75
Shaw, Paul	5.11	Sheffield Utd.	Burnham	4.09.73
Smith, Adam	5.10	–	Huddersfield	20.02.85
Ward, Jamie	5. 5	Torquay Utd.	Birmingham	12.05.86

DAGENHAM AND REDBRIDGE

Ground: Glyn Hopkin Stadium, Victoria Road, Da genham RM10 7XL.
Telephone: 0208 592 1549. **Club nickname:** Daggers.
First-choice colours: Red and white shirts, red shorts, red socks.
Main sponsor: West & Coe. **Capacity 2007-08:** 6,000.
Record attendance: 5,949 v Ipswich Town (F.A. Cup 3), 5 January, 2002.

Name	Height ft. in.	Previous club	Birthplace	Birthdate
Goalkeepers				
Eyre, Nicky	5.10	Rushden & Dmnds.	Braintree	7.09.85
Roberts, Tony	6. 0	St Albans	Bangor	4.08.69
Defenders				
Boardman, Jon	6. 2	Rochdale	Reading	27.01.81
Foster, Danny	6. 0	Tottenham	Enfield	23.09.84
Goodwin, Lee	6. 0	West Ham Utd.	Stepney	5.09.78
Griffiths, Scott	5.11	Aveley	Essex	10.02.86
Uddin, Anwar	5.11	Bristol Rov.	Whitechapel	1.11.81
Midfielders				
Bruce, Paul	5.10	Q.P.R.	London	18.02.78
Graham, Richard	5. 8	Barnet	Newry	5.8.79
Huke, Shane	5.10	Peterborough Utd.	Hammersmith	2.11.76
Leberl, Jake		Margate	Morden	2.04.77

Rainford, Dave	6. 0	Bishop's Stortford	Stepney	21.04.79
Saunders, Sam	5.11	Carshalton		29.08.83
Sloma, Sam		Thurrock	London	29.10.82
Southam, Glen	6. 0	Bishop's Stortford	London	10.06.80
Forwards				
Akurang, Cliff	6. 0	Heybridge	Ghana	27.02.81
Batt, Shaun		Stevenage	Luton	22.02.87
Benson, Paul	6. 2	White Ensign		23.06.80
Lawson, James	6. 0	Southend Utd.	Basildon	21.01.87
Lettejallow, Bai Mas	5. 9	Harlow	London	16.04.84
Moore, Chris	6. 0	Brentford	London	13.01.80
Strevens, Ben	6. 1	Crawley	Edgeware	24.05.80
Taylor, Jamie		Woking	Crawley	16.12.82

DARLINGTON

Ground: The Arena, Hurworth Moor, Neasham Road, Darlington, DL2 1GR.
Telephone: 01325 387000. **Club nickname:** Quakers.
First-choice colours: Black and white shirts; black shorts; black and white socks.
Main sponsor: Darlington Building Society. **Capacity for 2007-08:** 25,000.
Record attendance: (Feethams) 21,023 v Bolton Wand. (League Cup 3) 14 November, 1960. (The Arena), 11,600 v Kidderminstre Harr. (Div. 3) 16 August, 2003.

Name	Height ft. in.	Previous club	Birthplace	Birthdate
Goalkeepers				
Oakes, Andy	6. 4	Swansea City	Northwich	11.01.77
Stockdale, David	6. 3	York City	Leeds	28.09.85
Defenders				
Austin, Neil	5.10	Barnsley	Barnsley	26.04.83
Brackstone, John	5.11	Hartlepool Utd.	Hartlepool	9.02.85
Burgess, Kevin		Middlesbrough	Eston	8.01.88
Collins, Patrick	6. 2	Sheffield Wed.	Oman	4.02.85
Foster, Steve	6. 1	Scunthorpe Utd.	Mansfield	3.12.74
Ryan, Tim	5.10	Boston Utd.	Stockport	10.12.74
White, Alan	6. 0	Notts Co.	Darlington	22.03.76
Midfielders				
Cummins, Michael	6. 0	Port Vale	Dublin	1.06.78
Keltie, Clark	6. 1	–	Newcastle	31.08.83
McBride, Kevin	5.11	Motherwell	Bellshill	14.06.81
Purdie, Rob	5. 9	Hereford Utd.	Leicester	28.09.82
Ravenhill, Ricky	5.10	Grimsby Town	Doncaster	16.01.81
Wainwright, Neil	6. 0	Sunderland	Warrington	4.11.77
Wiseman, Scott	6. 0	Hull City	Hull	9.10.85
Forwards				
Blundell, Gregg	5.10	Chester City	Liverpool	3.10.77
Joachim, Julian	5. 6	Boston Utd.	Boston	20.09.74
Smith, Martin	5.11	Northampton Town	Sunderland	13.11.74
Wright, Tommy	6. 0	Barnsley	Kirby Muxloe	28.09.84

GRIMSBY TOWN

Ground: Blundell Park, Cleethorpes, DN35 7PY.
Telephone: 01472 605050. **Club nickname:** Mariners.
First-choice colours: Black and white shirts; black shorts; white and black socks.
Main sponsor: Young's. **Capacity for 2007-08:** 9,106.
Record attendance: 31,651 v Wolves (F.A. Cup 5) 20 February, 1937.

Name	Height ft. in.	Previous club	Birthplace	Birthdate
Goalkeepers				
Barnes, Phil	6. 1	Sheffield Utd.	Sheffield	2.03.79

Defenders				
Bennett, Ryan		Ipswich Town	Orsett	6.03.90
Clarke, Jamie	6. 2	Boston Utd.	Sunderland	18.09.82
Fenton, Nick	6. 1	Doncaster Rov.	Preston	23.11.79
Hunt, James	5. 8	Bristol Rov.	Derby	17.12.76
Newey, Tom	5.10	Leyton Orient	Huddersfield	31.10.82
Whittle, Justin	6. 1	Hull City	Derby	18.03.71
Midfielders				
Bolland, Paul	5.11	Notts Co.	Bradford	23.12.79
Bore, Peter	6. 0	–	Grimsby	4.11.87
Boshell, Danny	5.11	Stockport Co.	Bradford	30.05.81
Harkins, Gary	6. 2	Blackburn Rov.	Greenock	2.01.85
Hegarty, Nick	5.10	Sheffield Wed.	Hemsworth	25.06.86
Till, Peter	5.11	Birmingham City	Walsall	7.09.85
Toner, Ciaran	6. 1	Lincoln City	Craigavon	30.06.81
Forwards				
Jones, Gary	6. 3	Tranmere Rov.	Chester	10.05.75
North, Danny	5.11	–	Grimsby	7.09.87
Taylor, Andy	6. 2	–	Grimsby	30.10.88

HEREFORD UNITED

Ground: Edgar Street Ground, Edgar Street, Hereford HR4 9JU.
Telephone: 01432 276666. **Club nickname:** Bulls.
First-choice colours: White and black shirts, black shorts, white socks.
Main sponsor: Sun Valley. **Capacity for 2007-08:** 7,873.
Record attendance: 18,114 v Sheffield Wed. (F.A. Cup 3) 4 January, 1958.

Name	Height ft. in.	Previous club	Birthplace	Birthdate
Goalkeepers				
Brown, Wayne	6. 1	Chester City	Southampton	14.01.77
Defenders				
Broadhurst, Karl	6. 1	Bournemouth	Portsmouth	18.03.80
Beckwith, Dean	6. 3	Gillingham	Southwark	19.09.83
McClenahan, Trent	5. 9	West Ham Utd.	Australia	4.02.85
McCombe, John	6. 2	Huddersfield Town	Pontefract	7.05.85
Midfielders				
Fitzpatrick, Jordan	6. 0	Wolves	Stourbridge	15.06.88
Gwynne, Sam	5. 9	–	Hereford	17.12.87
Rose, Richard	6. 0	Gillingham	Pembury	8.09.82
Smith, Ben	5. 9	Weymouth	Chelmsford	23.11.78
Taylor, Kris	5. 9	Walsall	Stafford	12.01.84
Webb, Luke	6. 0	Coventry City	Nottingham	12.09.86
Forwards				
Guinan, Steve	6. 1	Cheltenham Town	Birmingham	24.12.75
Palmer, Marcus	6. 0	Cheltenham Town	Gloucester	6.01.88

LINCOLN CITY

Ground: Sincil Bank, Lincoln LN5 8LD.
Telephone: 0870 899 2005. **Club nickname:** Imps.
First-choice colours: Red and white shirts; black shorts; red socks.
Main sponsor: Starglaze Windows. **Capacity for 2007-08:** 10,120.
Record attendance: 23,196 v Derby Co. (League Cup 4) 15 November, 1967.

Name	Height ft. in.	Previous club	Birthplace	Birthdate
Goalkeepers				
Marriott, Alan	6. 0	Tottenham	Bedford	3.09.78

Defenders				
Amoo, Ryan	5.10	Northampton Town	Leicester	11.10.83
Beevers, Lee	6. 3	Boston Utd.	Doncaster	4.12.83
Green, Paul	5.11	Doncaster Rov.	Sheffield	10.04.83
Moses, Adie	6. 1	Crewe Alexandra	Doncaster	4.05.75
Watt, Phil	6. 1	Rotherham Utd.	Rotherham	10.01.88
Midfielders				
Frecklington, Lee	5. 8	–	Lincoln	8.09.85
Kerr, Scott	5. 9	Scarborough	Leeds	11.12.81
King, Gary		–	Grimsby	27.01.90
N'Guessan, Dany	6. 1	Rangers	Ivry-sur-Seine, Fr.	11.08.87
Semple, Ryan	5.11	Peterborough Utd.	Belfast	14.07.85
Sherlock, Jamie	6. 1	Gainsborough	Hull	25.04.83
Toyne, Andy	6. 1	–	Lincoln	15.07.88
Forwards				
Bacon, Danny	5.10	Mansfield Town	Mansfield	20.09.80
Brown, Nat	6. 2	Huddersfield Town	Sheffield	15.06.81
Forrester, Jamie	5. 6	Bristol Rov.	Bradford	1.11.74
Lenell, John-Lewis		–	London	17.05.89
Ryan, Oliver	5.11	–	Boston	26.09.85
Stallard, Mark	6. 0	Shrewsbury Town	Derby	24.10.74

MACCLESFIELD TOWN

Ground: Moss Rose, London Road, Macclesfield SK11 7SP.
Telephone: 01625 264686. **Club nickname:** Silkmen.
First-choice colours: Blue shirts; white shorts; blue socks.
Main sponsor: Cheshire Building Society. **Capacity for 2007-08:** 6,141.
Record attendance: 9,003 v Winsford Town (Cheshire Senior Cup 2) 14 February, 1948.

Name	**Height ft. in.**	**Previous club**	**Birthplace**	**Birthdate**
Goalkeepers				
Brain, Jonny	6. 4	Port Vale	Carlisle	11.02.83
Lee, Tommy	6. 2	Manchester Utd.		3.01.86
Defenders				
McNulty, James	6. 1	Caernarfon	Liverpool	13.02.85
Morley, David	6. 1	Doncaster Rov.	St Helens	25.09.77
Regan, Carl	6. 0	Chester City	Liverpool	14.01.80
Scott, Rob	6. 1	Oldham Athletic	Epsom	15.08.73
Swailes, Danny	6. 3	Bury	Bolton	1.04.79
Teague, Andrew	6. 2	–	Preston	5.02.86
Midfielders				
Hadfield, Jordan	5. 9	Stockport Co.	Swinton	1.08.87
Jennings, James	5.10	Manchester City		2.09.87
McIntyre, Kevin	6. 0	Chester City	Liverpool	23.12.77
Murray, Adam	5. 8	Torquay Utd.	Birmingham	30.09.81
Navarro, Alan	5.11	Tranmere Rov.	Liverpool	31.05.81
Thomas, Danny	5. 7	Hereford Utd.	Leamington Spa	1.05.81
Tolley, Jamie	6. 1	Shrewsbury Town	Shrewsbury	12.05.83
Forwards				
Green, Francis	5. 9	Boston Utd.	Nottingham	25.04.80
Gritton, Martin	6. 1	Lincoln City	Glasgow	1.06.78
Murphy, John	6. 1	Blackpool	Whiston	18.10.76

MANSFIELD TOWN

Ground: Field Mill, Quarry Lane, Mansfield NG18 5DA.
Telephone: 0870 756 3160 **Club nickname:** Stags.

First-choice colours: Amber, white and blue shirts; blue shorts; yellow socks.
Main sponsor: Perry Electrical. **Capacity for 2007-08:** 9,954.
Record attendance: 24,467 v Nott'm. Forest (F.A. Cup 3) 10 January, 1953.

Name	Height ft. in.	Previous club	Birthplace	Birthdate
Goalkeepers				
Muggleton, Carl	6. 2	Chesterfield	Leicester	13.09.68
White, Jason	6. 2	–	Mansfield	28.01.86
Defenders				
Baptise, Alex	5.11	–	Sutton-in-Ashfield	31.01.86
Buxton, Jake	6. 0	–	Sutton-in-Ashfield	4.03.85
Hjelde, Jon Olav	6. 1	Nott'm. Forest	Levanger, Nor.	30.07.72
Jelleyman, Gareth	5.10	Peterborough Utd.	Holywell	14.11.80
Kitchen, Ashley	5.11	–	Mansfield	10.10.88
McIntosh, Martin	6. 2	Huddersfield Town	East Kilbride	19.03.71
Mullins, John	5.11	Reading	Hampstead	6.11.85
Midfielders				
Arnold, Nathan	5. 8	–	Mansfield	26.07.87
Brown, Simon	5. 7	Kidderminster Harr.	West Bromwich	18.09.83
D'Laryea, Jonathan	5.10	Manchester City	Manchester	3.09.85
Dawson, Stephen	5. 6	–	Ireland	4.12.85
Hamshaw, Matt	5. 9	Stockport Co.	Rotherham	1.01.82
Hodge, Bryan		Blackburn Rov.	Hamilton	23.09.87
Sleath, Danny	5. 8	–	Derby	14.12.86
Trimmer, Lewis	5. 7	–	Norwich	30.10.89
Forwards				
Boulding, Rory	5.10	–	Sheffield	4.03.87
McAliskey, John	6. 5	Huddersfield Town	Huddersfield	2.09.84
Reet, Danny	6. 1	Sheffield Wed.	Sheffield	31.01.87
Wood, Chris	5.11	–	Worksop	24.01.87

MILTON KEYNES DONS

Ground: National Hockey Stadium, Silbury Boulevard, Milton Keynes MK9 1FA.
Telephone: 01908 607090. **Club nickname:** Dons.
First-choice colours: White shirts; white shorts; white socks.
Main sponsor: Marshalls Amplification. **Capacity for 2007-08:** 8,786.
Record attendance: (Milton Keynes): 7,620 v Luton Town (League 1) 20 November, 2004. (Wimbledon): 8,118 v West Ham Utd. (Div. 1), 25 November, 2003.

Name	Height ft. in.	Previous club	Birthplace	Birthdate
Goalkeepers				
Bankole, Ademole	6. 3	Brentford	Lagos	9.09.69
Defenders				
Diallo, Drissa	6. 1	Sheffield Wed.	Nouadhibou, Maur.	4.01.73
Edds, Gareth	5. 11	Bradford City	Sydney	3.02.81
Lewington, Dean	5. 11	–	London	18.05.84
Murphy, Kieron	5. 11	–		31.12.87
O'Hanlon, Sean	6. 1	Swindon Town	Liverpool	2.01.83
Page, Sam	5. 7	–	Buckingham	15.03.89
Stirling, Jude	6. 2	Peterborough Utd.	Highgate	29.06.82
Midfielders				
Andrews, Keith	5. 11	Hull City	Dublin	13.09.80
Blizzard, Dominic	6. 2	Watford	High Wycombe	2.09.83
Dyer, Lloyd	5. 10	Millwall	Birmingham	13.09.82
Lewis, Junior	6. 3	Brentford	Wembley	9.10.73
McGovern, Jon-Paul	5. 7	Sheffield Wed.	Glasgow	3.10.80
Mitchell, Paul	5. 9	Wigan Athletic	Manchester	26.08.81

Forwards				
Baldock, Sam	5. 7	–	Bedford	15.03.89
Gallen, Kevin	5.11	Q.P.R.	Chiswick	21.09.75
Knight, Leon	5. 4	Swansea City	Hackney	16.09.82
McLeod, Izale	6. 1	Derby Co.	Birmingham	15.10.84
Taylor, Scott	5.10	Plymouth Argyle	Chertsey	5.05.76
Wilbraham, Aaron	6. 3	Hull City	Knutsford	21.10.79

MORECAMBE

Ground: Christie Park, Lancaster Road, Morecambe LA4 5TJ.
Telephone: 01524 411797. **Club nickname:** Shrimps.
First-choice colours: Red shirts, white shorts, red socks.
Main sponsor: Umbro. **Capacity for 2007-08:** 6,000.
Record attendance: 9,383 v Weymouth (F.A. Cup 3) 6 January 1962.

Name	Height ft. in.	Previous club	Birthplace	Birthdate
Goalkeepers				
Davies, Scott	6. 0	–	Blackpool	27.02.87
Drench, Steven	5.11	Blackburn Rov.	Manchester	11.09.85
Defenders				
Adams, Danny	5. 8	Huddersfield Town	Altrincham	3.01.76
Bentley, Jim	6. 1	Telford	Liverpool	11.06.76
Blackburn Chris	5. 7	Northwich	Chester	2.08.82
Brannan, Ged	6. 0	Radcliffe	Prescot	15.01.72
Davies, Jamie	6. 0	–	Preston	11.08.87
Howard, Michael	5. 6	Swansea City	Birkenhead	2.12.78
Langford, Andy		–	Manchester	3.07.88
Walmsley, Keiran	5.11	–	Preston	11.12.83
Yates, Adam	5.10	Leek	Stoke	28.05.83
Midfielders				
Burns, Jamie	5. 9	Blackpool	Blackpool	6.03.84
Hunter, Garry	5.10	–	Morecambe	1.01.85
Lloyd, Paul	5.11	–	Preston	26.03.87
McLachlan, Fraser	5.11	Mansfield Town	Manchester	9.11.82
Sorvel, Neil	6. 0	Shrewsbury Town	Whiston	2.03.73
Stanley, Craig	5. 8	Hereford Utd.	Bedworth	3.03.83
Thompson, Garry	6. 0	–	Kendal	24.11.80
West, Michael		–	Burnley	1.02.88
Forwards				
Blinkhorn, Matthew	5.11	Blackpool	Blackpool	2.03.85
Curtis, Wayne	6. 0	–	Barrow	6.03.80
McNiven, David	5.10	Scarborough	Leeds	27.05.78
Twiss, Michael	5.11	Chester City	Manchester	26.10.77

NOTTS COUNTY

Ground: Meadow Lane, Nottingham NG2 3HJ.
Telephone: 0115 952 9000. **Club nickname:** Magpies.
First-choice colours: Black and white shirts; black shorts; black socks.
Main sponsor: Medoc. **Capacity for 2007-08:** 20,300.
Record attendance: 47,310 v York City (F.A. Cup 6) 12 March, 1955.

Name	Height ft. in.	Previous club	Birthplace	Birthdate
Goalkeepers				
Pilkington, Kevin	6. 2	Mansfield Town	Hitchin	8.03.74
Sandercombe, Tim	6. 4	Plymouth Argyle		15.06.89
Defenders				
Edwards, Mike	6. 1	Grimsby Town	Hessle	25.04.80

Hunt, Stephen	6. 1	Colchester Utd.	Southampton	11.11.84
Mayo, Paul	5.11	Lincoln City	Lincoln	13.10.81
McCann, Austin	5. 9	Boston Utd.	Alexandria	21.01.80
Silk, Gary	5.10	Portsmouth	Newport, IOW	13.07.84
Tann, Adam	6. 0	Leyton Orient	Fakenham	12.05.82
Midfielders				
Frost, Stef	6. 2	–	Nottingham	3.07.89
MacKenzie, Neil	6. 1	Scunthorpe Utd.	Birmingham	15.04.76
Parkinson, Andy	5. 8	Grimsby Town	Liverpool	27.05.79
Pipe, David	5. 9	Coventry City	Caerphilly	5.11.83
Smith, Jay	5. 7	Southend Utd.	Lambeth	24.09.81
Somner, Matt	6. 0	Aldershot	Isleworth	8.12.82
Weston, Myles	5.10	Charlton Athletic	Lewisham	12.03.88
Forwards				
Dudfield, Lawrie	6. 1	Boston Utd.	Southwark	7.05.80
Lee, Jason,	6. 3	Northampton Town	Forest Gate	9.05.71
Mendes, Junior	5.10	Huddersfield Town	London	15.09.76
Sam, Hector,	5. 9	Walsall	Mount Hope, Trin.	25.02.78
Weir-Daley, Spencer	5. 9	Nott'm. Forest	Leicester	5.09.85

PETERBOROUGH UNITED

Ground: London Road Stadium, Peterborough PE2 8AL.
Telephone: 01733 563947. **Club nickname:** Posh.
First-choice colours: Blue shirts; blue shorts; blue socks.
Main sponsor: MRI Overseas Property. **Capacity for 2007-08:** 15,460.
Record attendance: 30,096 v Swansea City (F.A. Cup 5) 20 February, 1965.

Name	Height ft. in.	Previous club	Birthplace	Birthdate
Goalkeepers				
Jalal, Shwan	6. 2	Woking	Baghdad	14.08.83
McShane, Luke	6. 1	–	Peterborough	6.11.85
Tyler, Mark	5.11	–	Norwich	2.04.77
Defenders				
Arber, Mark	6. 1	Oldham Athletic	Johannesburg	9.10.77
Blackett, Shane	5.11	Dag. & Red.	Luton	3.10.82
Branston, Guy	6. 0	Oldham Athletic	Leicester	9.01.79
Morgan, Craig	6. 0	MK Dons	St Asaph	18.06.85
Smith, Adam	5.11	King's Lynn	Lingwood	11.09.85
Westwood, Chris	6. 0	Walsall	Dudley	13.02.77
Midfielders				
Butcher, Richard	6. 0	Oldham Athletic	Peterborough	22.01.81
Day, Jamie	5. 9	–	High Wycombe	7.05.86
Gain, Peter	6. 1	Lincoln City	Hammersmith	2.11.76
Hyde, Micah	5.11	Burnley	Newham	10.11.74
Keates, Dean	5. 6	Walsall	Walsall	30.06.78
Lee, Charlie	5.11	Tottenham	Whitechapel	5.01.87
Low, Josh	6. 1	Leicester City	Bristol	15.02.79
Newton, Adam	5.10	West Ham Utd.	Ascot	4.12.80
Strachan, Gavin	5.11	Hartlepool Utd.	Aberdeen	23.12.78
Forwards				
Boyd, George	5.11	Stevenage	Medway	2.10.85
Crow, Danny	5.10	Norwich City	Great Yamouth	26.01.86
Howe, Rene	6. 0	Kettering	Bedford	22.10.86
Mackail-Smith, Craig	5.11	Dag. & Red.	Herts	25.02.84
McLean, Aaron	5. 6	Grays	Hammersmith	25.05.83

ROCHDALE

Ground: Spotland, Wilbutts Lane, Rochdale OL11 5DS.
Telephone: 0870 822 1969. **Club nickname:** Dale.

First-choice colours: Black and white shirts; white shorts; black socks.
Main Sponsor: MMC Estates. **Capacity for 2007-08:** 10,249.
Record attendance: 24,231 v Notts Co. (F.A. Cup 2) 10 December, 1949.

Name	Height ft. in.	Previous club	Birthplace	Birthdate
Goalkeepers				
Rigby, Lloyd	6. 2	–		12.03.87
Spencer, James	6. 5	Stockport Co.	Stockport	11.04.85
Defenders				
Brown, Gary	5. 6	–	Darwen	29.10.85
Goodall, Alan	5. 9	Bangor	Birkenhead	2.12.81
Kennedy, Thomas	5.11	Bury	Bury	24.06.85
McArdle, Rory	6. 1	Sheffield Wed.	Sheffield	1.05.87
Ramsden, Simon	6. 0	Grimsby Town	Bishop Auckland	17.12.81
Stanton, Nathan	5. 9	Scunthorpe Utd.	Nottingham	6.05.81
Midfielders				
Bates, Tom	5.10	Leamington	Coventry	31.08.85
Crooks, Lee	6. 0	Bradford City	Wakefield	14.01.78
Doolan, John	6. 1	Doncaster Rov.	Liverpool	7.05.74
Flitcroft, David	5.11	Bury	Bolton	14.01.74
Jones, Gary	5.10	Barnsley	Birkenhead	3.06.77
Rundle, Adam	5.10	Mansfield Town	Durham	8.07.84
Perkins, David	6. 2	Morecambe	Heysham	21.06.82
Prendergast, Rory	5. 9	Blackpool	Pontefract	6.04.78
Thompson, Joe	6. 0	–	Rochdale	5.03.89
Forwards				
Dagnall, Chris	5. 8	Tranmere Rov.	Liverpool	15.04.86
Muirhead, Ben	5. 9	Bradford City	Doncaster	5.01.83
Murray, Glenn	6. 0	Carlisle Utd.	Workington	25.09.83

ROTHERHAM UNITED

Ground: Millmoor, Rotherham S60 1HR.
Telephone: 01709 512434. **Club nickname:** Millers.
First-choice colours: Red and white shirts; white shorts; red socks.
Main sponsor: Parkgate Shopping. **Capacity for 2007-08:** 7,902.
Record attendance: 25,000 v Sheffield Wed. (Div. 2) 26 January, 1952 and v Sheffield Wed. (Div. 2) 13 December, 1952.

Name	Height ft. in.	Previous club	Birthplace	Birthdate
Goalkeepers				
Liversidge, Andy	6. 0	–	Wakefield	11.11.89
Warrington, Andy	6. 3	Bury	Sheffield	10.06.76
Defenders				
Joseph, Marc	6. 0	Blackpool	Leicester	10.11.76
Brogan, Stephen	5. 7	–	Rotherham	12.04.88
Fleming, Craig	6. 0	Norwich City	Halifax	6.10.71
Hurst, Paul	5. 4	–	Sheffield	25.09.74
Kerr, Nat	6. 0	Crewe Alexandra	Manchester	31.10.87
King, Liam	5. 9	–	Rotherham	31.12.87
Mills, Pablo	6. 0	Derby Co.	Birmingham	27.05.84
Sharps, Ian	6. 4	Tranmere Rov.	Warrington	23.10.80
Midfielders				
Duncum, Sam	5. 9	–	Sheffield	18.02.87
Harrison, Danny	5.11	Tranmere Rov.	Liverpool	4.11.82
Harrison, Simon	5. 9	–	Nether Edge	14.06.89
Holmes, Peter	5.10	Luton Town	Bishop Auckland	18.11.80
Hudson, Mark	5.10	Huddersfield Town	Bishop Auckland	24.10.80
Newsham, Marc	5.10	–	Hatfield, Yorks.	24.03.87
Tonge, Dale	5.10	Barnsley	Doncaster	7.05.85

Forwards				
Green, Jamie	5. 7	–		18.08.89
O'Grady, Chris	6. 1	Leicester City	Nottingham	25.01.86
Taylor, Ryan	6. 2	–	Rotherham	4.05.88
Todd, Andy	6. 0	Accrington Stanley	Nottingham	22.02.79
Yates, Jamie	5. 8	–	Sheffield	24.12.88

SHREWSBURY TOWN

Ground: Gay Meadow, Shrewsbury SY2 6AB.
Telephone: 01743 360111. **Club nickname:** Shrews.
First-choice colours: Blue and amber shirts, shorts and socks.
Main sponsor: Morris Lubricants. **Capacity for 2007-08:** 8,000.
Record attendance: 18,917 v Walsall (Div. 3) 26 April, 1961.

Name	**Height ft. in.**	**Previous club**	**Birthplace**	**Birthdate**
Esson, Ryan	6. 2	Aberdeen	Aberdeen	19.03.80
Garner, Glyn	6. 2	Leyton Orient	Pontypool	9.12.76
MacKenzie, Chris	6. 0	Chester City	Birmingham	14.05.72
Defenders				
Ashton, Neil	5.10	Tranmere Rov.	Liverpool	15.01.85
Canoville, Lee	6. 1	Boston Utd.	Ealing	14.03.81
Hall, Danny	6. 2	Oldham Athletic	Ashton-under-Lyne	14.11.83
Herd, Ben	5. 9	Watford	Welwyn	21.06.85
Kempson, Darren	6. 2	Crewe Alexandra	Blackpool	6.12.84
Jones, Luke	5. 9	Blackburn Rov.	Blackburn	10.04.87
Moss, Darren	5.10	Crewe Alexandra	Wrexham	24.05.81
Tierney, Marc	6. 0	Oldham Athletic	Prestwich	23.08.85
Midfielders				
Davies, Ben	5. 6	Chester City	Birmingham	27.05.81
Drummond, Stewart	6. 2	Chester City	Preston	11.12.75
Hunt, David	5.11	Northampton Town	Dulwich	10.09.82
Leslie, Steven	5.10	–	Shrewsbury	5.11.87
Pugh, Marc	5.11	Bury	Bacup	2.04.87
Williams, Dale	6. 1	Yeovil Town	Swindon	25.02.87
Forwards				
Asamoah, Derek	5. 6	Lincoln City	Ghana	1.05.81
Cooke, Andy	6. 0	Bradford City	Shrewsbury	20.01.74
Langmead, Kelvin	6. 1	–	Coventry	23.03.85
Symes, Michael	6. 3	Everton	Great Yarmouth	31.10.83

STOCKPORT COUNTY

Ground: Edgeley Park, Hardcastle Road, Edgeley, Stockport SK3 9DD.
Telephone: 0161 286 8888. **Club nickname:** County.
First-choice colours: Blue and white shirts; blue shorts; white socks.
Main Sponsor: Scandia. **Capacity for 2007-08:** 10,641.
Record attendance: 27,833 v Liverpool (F.A. Cup 5) 11 February, 1950.

Name	**Height ft. in.**	**Previous club**	**Birthplace**	**Birthdate**
Goalkeepers				
Adamson, Chris	6. 1	Sheffield Wed.	Ashington	4.11.78
Defenders				
Briggs, Keith	5.10	Norwich City	Glossop	11.12.81
Clare, Rob	6. 2	–	Belper	28.02.83
Dinning, Tony	6. 0	Port Vale	Wallsend	12.04.75
Owen, Gareth	6. 1	Oldham Athletic	Pontypridd	21.09.82
Raynes, Michael	6. 2	–	Wythenshawe	15.10.87

Rose, Michael	5.10	Yeovil Town	Salford	28.07.82
Tunnicliffe, James	6. 4	–	Denton	17.1.89
Williams, Ashley	6. 0	Hednesford Town	Wolves	23.08.84
Midfielders				
Allen, Damien	5.10	–	Cheadle	1.08.86
Crowther, Ryan	5.11	–	Stockport	17.09.88
Ellis, Danny	5.10	–	Stockport	18.11.88
Griffin, Adam	5. 7	Oldham Athletic	Salford	26.08.84
Taylor, Jason	6. 1	Oldham Athletic	Ashton-under-Lyme	28.01.87
Forwards				
Bramble, Tes	6. 2	Southend Utd.	Ipswich	20.07.80
Dickinson, Liam	6. 4	–	Salford	4.10.85
Elding, Anthony	6. 2	Boston Utd.	Boston	16.04.82
Le Fondre, Adam	5.11	–	Stockport	2.12.86
Malcolm, Michael	5.10	Tottenham	Harrow	13.10.85
Poole, David	5. 8	Yeovil Town	Manchester	12.11.84
Proudlock, Adam	6. 0	Ipswich Town	Telford	9.05.81

WREXHAM

Ground: Racecourse Ground, Mold Road, Wrexham LL11 2AH.
Telephone: 01978 262129. **Club nickname:** Robins.
First-choice-colours: Red shirts; white shorts; red socks.
Main sponsor: Lease Direct Finance. **Capacity for 2007-08:** 10,500.
Record attendance: 34,445 v Manchester Utd. (F.A. Cup 4) 26 January, 1957.

Name	Height ft. in.	Previous club	Birthplace	Birthdate
Goalkeepers				
Ingham, Michael	6. 4	Sunderland	Belfast	9.07.80
Jones, Michael	6. 3	–	Liverpool	3.12.87
Williams, Anthony	6. 1	Carlisle Utd.	Maesteg	20.09.77
Defenders				
Evans, Gareth	6. 1	–	Wrexham	10.01.87
Evans, Steve	6. 0	TNS	Wrexham	26.02.79
Hope, Richard	6. 2	Shrewsbury Town	Stockton	22.06.78
Pejic, Shaun	6. 1	–	Hereford	16.11.82
Roche, Lee	5.10	Burnley	Bolton	28.10.80
Spender, Simon	5.11	–	Mold	15.11.85
Valentine, Ryan	5.10	Darlington	Wrexham	19.08.82
Walker, Richard	6. 2	Port Vale	Stafford	17.09.80
Williams, Mike	5.11	–	Colwyn Bay	27.10.86
Midfielders				
Crowell, Matt	5. 9	Southampton	Bridgend	3.07.84
Done, Matt	5.10	–	Oswestry	22.07.88
Jones, Mark	5.11	–	Wrexham	15.08.83
Mackin, Levi	6. 0	–	Chester	4.04.86
Murtagh, Conall	6. 0	Southport	Belfast	29.06.85
Williams, Danny	6. 1	Bristol Rov.	Wrexham	12.07.79
Forwards				
Johnson, Josh	5. 5	San Juan	Carenage, St Vinc.	16.04.81
Llewellyn, Chris	5.11	Hartlepool Utd.	Swansea	29.08.79
McEvilly, Lee	6. 0	Accrington	Liverpool	15.04.82
Proctor, Michael	5.11	Hartlepool Utd.	Sunderland	3.10.80
Reed, Jamie	5.11	–	Chester	13.08.87
Roberts, Neil	5.10	Doncaster Rov.	Wrexham	7.04.78
Ugarte, Juan	5.10	Crewe Alexandra	San Sebastian	7.11.80
Williams, Eifion	5.11	Hartlepool Utd.	Anglesey	15.11.75
Williams, Marc	5.10	–	Colwyn Bay	27.07.88

WYCOMBE WANDERERS

Ground: Causeway Stadium, Hillbottom Road, High Wycombe HP12 4HJ.
Telephone: 01494 472100. **Club nickname:** Chairboys.
First-choice colours: Light and dark blue shirts; light blue shorts; light and dark blue socks.
Main sponsor: Dreams. **Capacity for 2007-08:** 10,000.
Record attendance: 9,921 v Fulham (F.A. Cup 3) 8 January, 2002.

Name	Height ft. in.	Previous club	Birthplace	Birthdate
Goalkeepers				
Shearer, Scott	6. 3	Bristol Rov.	Glasgow	15.02.81
Young, Jamie	5.11	Reading	Brisbane	25.08.85
Defenders				
Antwi, Will	6. 3	Aldershot	Ashford	19.10.82
Christon, Lewis	5.11	–	Milton Keynes	21.01.89
Crooks, Leon	5.11	MK Dons	–	21.11.85
McCracken, David	6. 2	Dundee Utd.	Glasgow	16.10.81
Stockley, Sam	6. 0	Colchester Utd.	Tiverton	5.09.77
Williamson, Mike	6. 3	Southampton	Stoke	8.11.83
Woodman, Craig	5. 9	Bristol City	Tiverton	22.12.82
Midfielders				
Bloomfield, Matt	5. 8	Ipswich Town	Felixstowe	8.02.84
Duncan, Derek	5. 9	Leyton Orient	Newham	23.04.87
Johnson, Leon	6. 0	Gillingham	Shoreditch	10.05.81
Martin, Russell	6. 0	Lewes	Brighton	4.01.86
Oakes, Stefan	5.11	Notts Co.	Leicester	6.09.78
Palmer, Chris	5. 7	Notts Co.	Derby	16.10.83
Torres, Sergio	6. 2	Basingstoke	Mar Del Plata, Arg.	11.07.81
Forwards				
Easter, Jermaine	5. 8	Boston Utd.	Cardiff	15.01.82
McGleish, Scott	5. 9	Northampton Town	Barnet	10.02.74
Mooney, Tommy	5.11	Oxford Utd.	Billingham	11.08.71
Onibuje, Fola	6. 7	Swindon Town	Lagos	25.09.84
Sutton, John	6. 0	St Mirren	Norwich	26.12.83

CLYDESDALE SCOTTISH PREMIER LEAGUE SQUADS 2007-08

(at time of going to press)

ABERDEEN

Goalkeepers: Jamie Langfield, Greg Kelly, Derek Soutar.
Defenders: Richie Byrne, Andrew Considine, Alexander Diamond, David Donald, Richard Foster, Michael Hart, Johnathan Kurrant, Lee Mair, Jackie McNamara, Neil McVitie, Daniel Smith.
Midfielders: Chris Clark, Jeffrey De Visscher, Barry Nicholson, Scott Severin, Jamie Smith, Stuart Smith, Karim Touzani.
Forwards: Craig Brewster, Steve Lovell, Darren Mackie, Chris Maguire, Lee Miller, Michael Paton.

CELTIC

Goalkeepers: Artur Boruc, Mark Brown, Michael McGovern.
Defenders: Bobo Balde, Gary Caldwell, Scott Cuthbert, John Kennedy, Stephen McManus, Lee Naylor, Darren O'Dea, Steven Pressley, Mark Wilson.
Midfielders: Scott Brown, Simon Ferry, Thomas Gravesen, Paul Hartley, Jiri Jarosik, Paul Lawson, Shunsuke Nakamura, Evander Sno.
Forwards: Chris Killen, Scott McDonald, Aiden McGeady, Michael McGlinchey, Kenny Miller, Rocco Quinn, Nicholas Riley, Derek Riordan, Cillian Sheridan, Jan Vennegoor of Hesselink, Maciej Zurawski.

DUNDEE UNITED

Goalkeepers: Euan McLean, Lukasz Zaluska.
Defenders: Sean Dillon, Darren Dods, Christian Kalvenes, Gary Kenneth, Lee Wilkie.
Midfielders: Greg Cameron, Craig Conway, Stuart Duff, Morgaro Gomis, William Easton, Mark Kerr, David Proctor, Steven Robb, David Robertson, Barry Robson.
Forwards: Jon Daly, Noel Hunt, David Goodwillie.

FALKIRK

Goalkeepers: Robert Olejnik.
Defenders: Darren Barr, Dean Holden, Kenny Milne, Jack Ross, Thomas Scobbie, Cedric Uras.
Midfielders: Patrick Cregg, Liam Craig, Russell Latapy, Steven Thomson.
Forwards: Graham Barratt, Graeme Churchill, Carl Finnigan, Michael Higdon, Pedro Moutinho, John Stewart.

GRETNA

Goalkeepers: Greg Fleming, Alan Main, David Mathieson.
Defenders: Craig Barr, Mark Birch, Martin Canning, Danny Grainger, Chris Innes.
Midfielders: Ryan Baldacchino, Allan Jenkins, Niall Henderson, Steven Hogg, Brendan McGill, Ryan McGuffie, Paul Murray, Abdul Osman, Erik Paartalu, Gavin Skelton.
Forwards: David Bingham, Kenny Deuchar, David Graham, James Grady, Colin McMenamin.

HEARTS

Goalkeepers: Steve Banks, Craig Gordon, Mark Ridgers.
Defenders: John Armstrong, Nerijus Barasa, Christophe Berra, Mirsad Beslija, Jose Goncalves, Christos Karipidis, Alan Lithgow, Sean Mackle, Ibrahim Tall, Lee Wallace, Marius Zaliukas.
Midfielders: Bruno Aguiar, Matthew Doherty, Andrew Driver, Gary Glen, Kestutis Ivaskevicius, Eggert Jonsson, Tomas Kancelsku, Shaun Kelly, Laryea Kingston, Neil McCann, Denis McLaughlin, Michael Stewart.
Forwards: John Armstrong, Roman Bednar, Calum Elliot, Saulius Mikoliunas, Jamie Mole, Robbie Neilson, Michal Pospisil, Andrius Velicka.

HIBERNIAN

Goalkeepers: Alastair Brown, David Grof, Yves Makaba-Makalamby, Zbigniew Malkowski, Andrew McNeil.
Defenders: Chris Hogg, Rob Jones, Dermot McCaffrey, Kevin McCann, David Murphy, Lewis Stevenson, Steven Whittaker.

Midfielders: Keegan Ayre, Guillaume Beuzelin, Ross Chisholm, Stephen Glass, Brian Kerr, Sean Lynch, Alan O'Brien, Merouane Zemmama.
Forwards: Abdessalam Benjelloun, Ross Campbell, Clayton Donaldson, Steven Fletcher, Damon Gray, Darren McCormack, Dean Shiels.

INVERNESS CALEDONIAN THISTLE

Goalkeepers: Michael Fraser, Ally Ridgers.
Defenders: Jamie Duff, Stuart McCaffrey, Grant Munro, Ross Tokely.
Midfielders: Ian Black, Russell Duncan, Richard Hart, Roy McBain, Alan Morgan, Markus Paatelainen, John Rankin, Barry Wilson, Garry Wood.
Forwards: Graham Bayne, Rory McAllister, Zander Sutherland, Dennis Wyness.

KILMARNOCK

Goalkeepers: Cameron Bell, Alan Combe, Jamie Donnelly, Chad Harpur.
Defenders: Scott Anson, Iain Campbell, Simon Ford, James Fowler, Garry Hay, Jamie Hamill, David Lilley, Sean McGhee, Grant Murray, Thomas Nolan, Ryan O'Leary, Gary Wild, Frazer Wright, Kyle Wright.
Midfielders: Niall Blair, Rhian Dodds, Iain Flannigan, Georgios Fotakis, William Gibson, Danny Invincibile, Allan Johnston, Gary Locke, Paul McInnes, Colin Nish, Eric Skora, Momo Sylla.
Forwards: Andrew Barrowman, David Cox, Robert Campbell, Paul Di Giacomo, David Fernandez, Aime Koudou. Steven Naismith, Gary Wales.

MOTHERWELL

Goalkeepers: Colin Meldrum, Graeme Smith.
Defenders: Martyn Corrigan, Stephen Craigan, Bobby Donnelly, Marc Fitzpatrick, William Kinniburgh, Brian McLean, Danny Murphy, Paul Quinn, Mark Reynolds.
Midfielders: Kenny Connolly, Keith Lasley, Simon Mensing, Phil O'Donnell, Jim Paterson.
Forwards: David Clarkson, Paul Keegan, Ross McCormack, Steven McGarry, Trevor Molloy, Chris Porter, Darren Smith.

RANGERS

Goalkeepers: Roy Carroll, Scott Gallacher, Allan McGregor, Lee Robinson, Graeme Smith.
Defenders: Kirk Broadfoot, Steven Campbell, Ugo Ehiogu, Brahim Hemdani, Alan Hutton, Alan Lowing, Jordan McMillan, Sasa Papac, Ross Perry, Antoine Ponroy, Steven Smith, David Weir.
Midfielders: Charlie Adam, DaMarcus Beasley, Thomas Buffel, Chris Burke, Georgios Efrem, Paul Emslie, Barry Ferguson, Dean Furman, Brian Gilmour, Steven Lennon, Ian Murray, Andrew Shinnie, Libor Sionko, Kevin Thomson.
Forwards: Kris Boyd, Jean Claude Darcheville, Alan Gow, Nacho Novo, Filip Sebo.

ST MIRREN

Goalkeepers: Mark Howard, Danny McColgan, Chris Smith.
Defenders: Stuart Balmer, Will Haining, Eddie Malone, Ian Maxwell, Andy Millen, John-Paul Potter, David Van Zanten.
Midfielders: Iain Anderson, David Barron, Garry Brady, Richard Brittain, Gary Mason, Stephen McGinn, Craig Molloy, Hugh Murray, Stephen O'Donnell, Alan Reid.
Forwards: Alex Burke, Marc Corcoran, Craig Dargo, Stewart Kean, Billy Mehmet.

LEAGUE FIXTURES 2007-08

Saturday, 11 August
Barclays Premiership
Arsenal v Fulham
Aston Villa v Liverpool
Bolton Wand. v Newcastle Utd.
Derby Co. v Portsmouth
Everton v Wigan Athletic
Middlesbrough v Blackburn Rov.
Sunderland v Tottenham
West Ham Utd. v Manchester City

Coca-Cola League Championship
Barnsley v Coventry City
Bristol City v Q.P.R.
Burnley v W.B.A.
Cardiff City v Stoke City
Charlton Athletic v Scunthorpe Utd.
Hull City v Plymouth Argyle
Ipswich Town v Sheffield Wed.
Leicester City v Blackpool
Preston N.E. v Norwich City
Sheffield Utd. v Colchester Utd.
Southampton v Crystal Palace
Wolves v Watford

Coca-Cola League One
Cheltenham Town v Gillingham
Crewe Alexandra v Brighton & H.A.
Doncaster Rov. v Millwall
Huddersfield Town v Yeovil
Luton Town v Hartlepool Utd.
Northampton Town v Swindon Town
Nott'm. Forest v Bournemouth
Oldham Athletic v Swansea City
Port Vale v Bristol Rov.
Southend Utd. v Leyton Orient
Tranmere Rov. v Leeds Utd.
Walsall v Carlisle Utd.

Coca-Cola League Two
Bradford City v Macclesfield Town
Brentford v Mansfield Town
Chester City v Chesterfield
Darlington v Wrexham
Grimsby Town v Notts Co.
Hereford v Rotherham Utd.
Lincoln City v Shrewsbury Town
Milton Keynes Dons v Bury
Morecambe v Barnet
Peterborough Utd. v Rochdale
Stockport Co. v Dag & Red
Wycombe Wand. v Accrington Stanley

Sunday, 12 August
Barclays Premiership
Chelsea v Birmingham City
Manchester Utd. v Reading

Tuesday, 14 August
Barclays Premiership
Birmingham City v Sunderland
Portsmouth v Manchester Utd.
Reading v Chelsea
Tottenham v Everton

Wednesday, 15 August
Barclays Premiership
Blackburn Rov. v Aston Villa
Fulham v Bolton Wand.
Liverpool v West Ham Utd.
Manchester City v Derby Co.
Newcastle Utd. v Arsenal
Wigan Athletic v Middlesbrough

Saturday, 18 August
Barclays Premiership
Birmingham City v West Ham Utd.
Blackburn Rov. v Arsenal
Fulham v Middlesbrough
Newcastle Utd. v Aston Villa
Portsmouth v Bolton Wand.
Reading v Everton
Tottenham v Derby Co.
Wigan Athletic v Sunderland

Coca-Cola League Championship
Blackpool v Bristol City
Colchester Utd. v Barnsley
Coventry City v Hull City
Crystal Palace v Leicester City
Norwich City v Southampton
Plymouth Argyle v Ipswich Town
Q.P.R. v Cardiff City
Scunthorpe Utd. v Burnley
Sheffield Wed. v Wolves
Stoke City v Charlton Athletic
Watford v Sheffield Utd.
W.B.A. v Preston N.E.

Coca-Cola League One
Bournemouth v Huddersfield Town
Brighton & H.A. v Northampton Town
Bristol Rov. v Crewe Alexandra
Carlisle Utd. v Oldham Athletic
Gillingham v Tranmere Rov.
Hartlepool Utd. v Doncaster Rov.
Leeds Utd. v Southend Utd.
Leyton Orient v Walsall
Millwall v Cheltenham Town
Swansea City v Nott'm. Forest
Swindon Town v Luton Town
Yeovil v Port Vale

Coca-Cola League Two
Accrington Stanley v Darlington
Barnet v Hereford
Bury v Grimsby Town
Chesterfield v Stockport Co.
Dag & Red v Wycombe Wand.
Macclesfield Town v Milton Keynes Dons
Mansfield Town v Lincoln City
Notts Co. v Brentford
Rochdale v Chester City
Shrewsbury Town v Bradford City
Wrexham v Morecambe

Sunday, 19 August
Barclays Premiership
Liverpool v Chelsea
Manchester City v Manchester Utd.

Coca-Cola League Two
Rotherham Utd. v Peterborough Utd.

Saturday, 25 August
Barclays Premiership
Arsenal v Manchester City
Aston Villa v Fulham
Bolton Wand. v Reading
Chelsea v Portsmouth
Derby Co. v Birmingham City
Everton v Blackburn Rov.
Sunderland v Liverpool
West Ham Utd. v Wigan Athletic

Coca-Cola League Championship
Barnsley v Plymouth Argyle
Bristol City v Scunthorpe Utd.
Burnley v Q.P.R.
Cardiff City v Coventry City
Charlton Athletic v Sheffield Wed.
Hull City v Norwich City
Leicester City v Watford
Preston N.E. v Colchester Utd.
Sheffield Utd. v W.B.A.
Southampton v Stoke City
Wolves v Blackpool

Coca-Cola League One
Cheltenham Town v Swindon Town
Crewe Alexandra v Leyton Orient
Doncaster Rov. v Bournemouth
Huddersfield Town v Carlisle Utd.
Luton Town v Gillingham
Northampton Town v Yeovil
Nott'm. Forest v Leeds Utd.
Oldham Athletic v Bristol Rov.
Port Vale v Hartlepool Utd.
Southend Utd. v Millwall
Tranmere Rov. v Brighton & H.A.
Walsall v Swansea City

Coca-Cola League Two
Bradford City v Wrexham
Brentford v Barnet
Chester City v Dag & Red
Darlington v Notts Co.
Grimsby Town v Macclesfield Town
Hereford v Rochdale
Lincoln City v Accrington Stanley
Milton Keynes Dons v Shrewsbury Town
Morecambe v Mansfield Town
Peterborough Utd. v Chesterfield
Stockport Co. v Rotherham Utd.
Wycombe Wand. v Bury

Sunday, 26 August
Barclays Premiership
Manchester Utd. v Tottenham
Middlesbrough v Newcastle Utd.

Coca-Cola League Championship
Ipswich Town v Crystal Palace

Saturday, 1 September
Barclays Premiership
Blackburn Rov. v Manchester City
Bolton Wand. v Everton
Fulham v Tottenham
Liverpool v Derby Co.
Manchester Utd. v Sunderland
Middlesbrough v Birmingham City
Newcastle Utd. v Wigan Athletic
Reading v West Ham Utd.

Coca-Cola League Championship
Colchester Utd. v Burnley
Coventry City v Preston N.E.
Crystal Palace v Charlton Athletic
Norwich City v Cardiff City
Plymouth Argyle v Leicester City

Q.P.R. v Southampton
Scunthorpe Utd. v Sheffield Utd.
Sheffield Wed. v Bristol City
Stoke City v Wolves
Watford v Ipswich Town
W.B.A. v Barnsley

Coca-Cola League One
Bournemouth v Port Vale
Brighton & H.A. v Southend Utd.
Bristol Rov. v Nott'm. Forest
Carlisle Utd. v Cheltenham Town
Gillingham v Walsall
Hartlepool Utd. v Oldham Athletic
Leeds Utd. v Luton Town
Leyton Orient v Northampton Town
Millwall v Huddersfield Town
Swansea City v Doncaster Rov.
Swindon Town v Crewe Alexandra
Yeovil v Tranmere Rov.

Coca-Cola League Two
Accrington Stanley v Peterborough Utd.
Barnet v Bradford City
Bury v Brentford
Chesterfield v Wycombe Wand.
Dag & Red v Lincoln City
Macclesfield Town v Darlington
Mansfield Town v Stockport Co.
Notts Co. v Morecambe
Rochdale v Milton Keynes Dons
Rotherham Utd. v Chester City
Shrewsbury Town v Grimsby Town
Wrexham v Hereford

Sunday, 2 September
Barclays Premiership
Arsenal v Portsmouth
Aston Villa v Chelsea

Monday, 3 September
Coca-Cola League Championship
Blackpool v Hull City

Friday, 7 September
Coca-Cola League One
Brighton & H.A. v Millwall
Cheltenham Town v Swansea City
Northampton Town v Doncaster Rov.

Coca-Cola League Two
Chester City v Morecambe
Chesterfield v Bury
Lincoln City v Bradford City
Milton Keynes Dons v Notts Co.

Saturday, 8 September
Coca-Cola League One
Carlisle Utd. v Tranmere Rov.
Crewe Alexandra v Huddersfield Town
Leeds Utd. v Hartlepool Utd.
Leyton Orient v Bournemouth
Luton Town v Bristol Rov.
Nott'm. Forest v Oldham Athletic
Southend Utd. v Gillingham
Walsall v Port Vale

Coca-Cola League Two
Accrington Stanley v Grimsby Town
Dag & Red v Barnet
Hereford v Macclesfield Town
Peterborough Utd. v Mansfield Town
Rochdale v Wrexham
Rotherham Utd. v Darlington
Stockport Co. v Shrewsbury Town

Sunday, 9 September
Coca-Cola League One
Swindon Town v Yeovil

Coca-Cola League Two
Wycombe Wand. v Brentford

Friday, 14 September
Coca-Cola League One
Bristol Rov. v Leeds utd.
Swansea City v Carlisle Utd.
Tranmere Rov. v Luton Town

Saturday, 15 September
Barclays Premiership
Birmingham City v Bolton Wand.
Chelsea v Blackburn Rov.
Everton v Manchester Utd.
Portsmouth v Liverpool
Sunderland v Reading
Tottenham v Arsenal
West Ham Utd. v Middlesbrough
Wigan Athletic v Fulham

Coca-Cola League Championship
Barnsley v Scunthorpe Utd.
Burnley v Blackpool
Colchester Utd. v Charlton Athletic
Coventry City v Bristol City
Hull City v Stoke City
Leicester City v Q.P.R.
Norwich City v Crystal Palace
Plymouth Argyle v Cardiff City
Preston N.E. v Sheffield Wed.
Sheffield Utd. v Wolves

Watford v Southampton
W.B.A. v Ipswich Town

Coca-Cola League One
Bournemouth v Northampton Town
Gillingham v Brighton & H.A.
Hartlepool Utd. v Swindon Town
Huddersfield Town v Cheltenham Town
Millwall v Walsall
Oldham Athletic v Southend Utd.
Port Vale v Nott'm. Forest
Yeovil v Leyton Orient

Coca-Cola League Two
Barnet v Rochdale
Bradford City v Peterborough Utd.
Brentford v Milton Keynes Dons
Bury v Chester City
Darlington v Lincoln City
Grimsby Town v Stockport Co.
Macclesfield Town v Wycombe Wand.
Mansfield Town v Chesterfield
Morecambe v Hereford
Notts Co. v Dag & Red
Shrewsbury Town v Accrington Stanley
Wrexham v Rotherham Utd.

Sunday, 16 September
Barclays Premiership
Manchester City v Aston Villa

Coca-Cola League One
Doncaster Rov. v Crewe Alexandra

Monday, 17 September
Barclays Premiership
Derby Co. v Newcastle Utd.

Tuesday, 18 September
Coca-Cola League Championship
Blackpool v Sheffield Utd.
Bristol City v W.B.A.
Cardiff City v Watford
Charlton Athletic v Norwich City
Crystal Palace v Coventry City
Ipswich Town v Leicester City
Q.P.R. v Plymouth Argyle
Scunthorpe Utd. v Preston N.E.
Sheffield Wed. v Burnley
Southampton v Colchester Utd.
Stoke City v Barnsley
Wolves v Hull City

Saturday, 22 September
Barclays Premiership
Arsenal v Derby Co.
Aston Villa v Everton
Blackburn Rov. v Portsmouth
Bolton Wand. v Tottenham
Fulham v Manchester City
Liverpool v Birmingham City
Middlesbrough v Sunderland
Reading v Wigan Athletic

Coca-Cola League Championship
Blackpool v Colchester Utd.
Bristol City v Burnley
Cardiff City v Preston N.E.
Charlton Athletic v Leicester City
Crystal Palace v Sheffield Utd.
Ipswich Town v Coventry City
Q.P.R. v Watford
Scunthorpe Utd. v W.B.A.
Sheffield Wed. v Hull City
Southampton v Barnsley
Stoke City v Plymouth Argyle
Wolves v Norwich City

Coca-Cola League One
Brighton & H.A. v Yeovil
Carlisle Utd. v Bristol Rov.
Cheltenham Town v Tranmere Rov.
Crewe Alexandra v Millwall
Leeds Utd. v Swansea City
Leyton Orient v Hartlepool Utd.
Luton Town v Port Vale
Northampton Town v Huddersfield Town
Nott'm. Forest v Gillingham
Southend Utd. v Doncaster Rov.
Swindon Town v Bournemouth
Walsall v Oldham Athletic

Coca-Cola League Two
Accrington Stanley v Mansfield Town
Chester City v Brentford
Chesterfield v Barnet
Dag & Red v Bury
Hereford v Bradford City
Lincoln City v Grimsby Town
Milton Keynes Dons v Darlington
Peterborough Utd. v Morecambe
Rochdale v Macclesfield Town
Rotherham Utd. v Notts Co.
Stockport Co. v Wrexham
Wycombe Wand. v Shrewsbury Town

Sunday, 23 September
Barclays Premiership
Manchester Utd. v Chelsea
Newcastle Utd. v West Ham Utd.

Saturday, 29 September
Barclays Premiership
Birmingham City v Manchester Utd.
Chelsea v Fulham
Derby Co. v Bolton Wand.
Manchester City v Middlesbrough
Portsmouth v Reading
Sunderland v Blackburn Rov.
West Ham Utd. v Arsenal
Wigan Athletic v Liverpool

Coca-Cola League Championship
Barnsley v Cardiff City
Burnley v Crystal Palace
Colchester Utd. v Scunthorpe Utd.
Coventry City v Charlton Athletic
Hull City v Ipswich Town
Leicester City v Stoke City
Norwich City v Sheffield Wed.
Plymouth Argyle v Wolves
Preston N.E. v Bristol City
Sheffield Utd. v Southampton
Watford v Blackpool
W.B.A. v Q.P.R.

Coca-Cola League One
Bournemouth v Carlisle Utd.
Bristol Rov. v Leyton Orient
Doncaster Rov. v Cheltenham Town
Gillingham v Leeds Utd.
Hartlepool Utd. v Walsall
Huddersfield Town v Luton Town
Millwall v Swindon Town
Oldham Athletic v Crewe Alexandra
Port Vale v Southend Utd.
Swansea City v Brighton & H.A.
Tranmere Rov. v Northampton Town
Yeovil v Nott'm. Forest

Coca-Cola League Two
Barnet v Rotherham Utd.
Bradford City v Wycombe Wand.
Brentford v Stockport Co.
Bury v Accrington Stanley
Darlington v Peterborough Utd.
Grimsby Town v Hereford
Macclesfield Town v Chester City
Mansfield Town v Dag & Red
Morecambe v Milton Keynes Dons
Notts Co. v Chesterfield
Shrewsbury Town v Rochdale
Wrexham v Lincoln City

Sunday, 30 September
Barclays Premiership
Everton v Newcastle Utd.

Monday, 1 October
Barclays Premiership
Tottenham v Aston Villa

Tuesday, 2 October
Coca-Cola League Championship
Barnsley v Bristol City
Burnley v Ipswich Town
Colchester Utd. v Q.P.R.
Coventry City v Blackpool
Hull City v Charlton Athletic
Leicester City v Wolves
Norwich City v Scunthorpe Utd.
Plymouth Argyle v Crystal Palace
Preston N.E. v Southampton
Sheffield Utd. v Cardiff City
Watford v Sheffield Wed.
W.B.A. v Stoke City

Coca-Cola League One
Bournemouth v Brighton & H.A.
Bristol Rov. v Southend Utd.
Doncaster Rov. v Walsall
Gillingham v Leyton Orient
Hartlepool Utd. v Carlisle Utd.
Huddersfield Town v Nott'm. Forest
Millwall v Northampton Town
Oldham Athletic v Leeds Utd.
Port Vale v Cheltenham Town
Swansea City v Swindon Town
Tranmere Rov. v Crewe Alexandra
Yeovil v Luton Town

Coca-Cola League Two
Barnet v Wycombe Wand.
Bradford City v Accrington Stanley
Brentford v Dag & Red
Bury v Lincoln City
Darlington v Rochdale
Grimsby Town v Chester City
Macclesfield Town v Rotherham Utd.
Mansfield Town v Milton Keynes Dons
Morecambe v Stockport Co.
Notts Co. v Hereford
Shrewsbury Town v Peterborough Utd.
Wrexham v Chesterfield

Saturday, 6 October
Barclays Premiership
Aston Villa v West Ham Utd.
Blackburn Rov. v Birmingham City
Bolton Wand. v Chelsea
Liverpool v Tottenham
Manchester Utd. v Wigan Athletic
Middlesbrough v Everton
Newcastle Utd. v Manchester City

Coca-Cola League Championship
Blackpool v Plymouth Argyle
Bristol City v Sheffield Utd.
Cardiff City v Burnley
Charlton Athletic v Barnsley
Crystal Palace v Hull City
Ipswich Town v Preston N.E.
Scunthorpe Utd. v Watford
Sheffield Wed. v Leicester City
Southampton v W.B.A.
Stoke City v Colchester Utd.
Wolves v Coventry City

Coca-Cola League One
Brighton & H.A. v Bristol Rov.
Carlisle Utd. v Millwall
Cheltenham Town v Oldham Athletic
Crewe Alexandra v Bournemouth
Leeds Utd. v Yeovil
Leyton Orient v Swansea City
Luton Town v Doncaster Rov.
Northampton Town v Port Vale
Nott'm. Forest v Hartlepool Utd.
Southend Utd. v Tranmere Rov.
Swindon Town v Gillingham
Walsall v Huddersfield Town

Coca-Cola League Two
Accrington Stanley v Wrexham
Chesterfield v Macclesfield Town
Dag & Red v Darlington
Hereford v Brentford
Lincoln City v Morecambe
Milton Keynes Dons v Bradford City
Peterborough Utd. v Grimsby Town
Rochdale v Bury
Rotherham Utd. v Mansfield Town
Stockport Co. v Barnet
Wycombe Wand. v Notts Co.

Sunday, 7 October
Barclays Premiership
Arsenal v Sunderland
Fulham v Portsmouth
Reading v Derby Co.

Coca-Cola League Two
Chester City v Shrewsbury Town

Monday, 8 October
Coca-Cola League Championship
Q.P.R. v Norwich City

Friday, 12 October
Coca-Cola League One
Hartlepool Utd. v Bristol Rov.

Coca-Cola League Two
Brentford v Rotherham Utd.
Chester City v Hereford
Grimsby Town v Rochdale
Morecambe v Bradford City

Saturday, 13 October
Coca-Cola League One
Bournemouth v Swansea City
Cheltenham Town v Nott'm. Forest
Gillingham v Millwall
Leeds Utd. v Leyton Orient
Port Vale v Brighton & H.A.
Southend Utd. v Crewe Alexandra
Tranmere Rov. v Walsall
Yeovil v Carlisle Utd.

Coca-Cola League Two
Barnet v Mansfield Town
Dag & Red v Accrington Stanley
Darlington v Stockport Co.
Macclesfield Town v Wrexham
Notts Co. v Bury
Peterborough Utd. v Wycombe Wand.
Shrewsbury Town v Chesterfield

Sunday, 14 October
Coca-Cola League One
Doncaster Rov. v Huddersfield Town
Oldham Athletic v Swindon Town

Coca-Cola League Two
Milton Keynes Dons v Lincoln City

Monday, 15 October
Coca-Cola League One
Luton Town v Northampton Town

Saturday, 20 October
Barclays Premiership
Arsenal v Bolton Wand.
Aston Villa v Manchester Utd.
Blackburn Rov. v Reading
Everton v Liverpool
Fulham v Derby Co.
Manchester City v Birmingham City
Middlesbrough v Chelsea
Wigan Athletic v Portsmouth

Coca-Cola League Championship
Barnsley v Burnley
Blackpool v Crystal Palace
Colchester Utd. v W.B.A.
Norwich City v Bristol City
Plymouth Argyle v Coventry City

Q.P.R. v Ipswich Town
Scunthorpe Utd. v Leicester City
Sheffield Utd. v Preston N.E.
Southampton v Cardiff City
Stoke City v Sheffield Wed.
Watford v Hull City
Wolves v Charlton Athletic

Coca-Cola League One
Brighton & H.A. v Leeds Utd.
Bristol Rov. v Yeovil
Carlisle Utd. v Gillingham
Crewe Alexandra v Luton Town
Huddersfield Town v Oldham Athletic
Leyton Orient v Port Vale
Millwall v Bournemouth
Northampton Town v Cheltenham Town
Nott'm. Forest v Doncaster Rov.
Swansea City v Hartlepool Utd.
Swindon Town v Tranmere Rov.
Walsall v Southend Utd.

Coca-Cola League Two
Accrington Stanley v Macclesfield Town
Bradford City v Darlington
Bury v Shrewsbury Town
Chesterfield v Dag & Red
Hereford v Milton Keynes Dons
Lincoln City v Peterborough Utd.
Mansfield Town v Notts Co.
Rochdale v Brentford
Rotherham Utd. v Morecambe
Stockport Co. v Chester City
Wrexham v Barnet
Wycombe Wand. v Grimsby Town

Sunday, 21 October
Barclays Premiership
West Ham Utd. v Sunderland

Monday, 22 October
Barclays Premiership
Newcastle Utd. v Tottenham

Coca-Cola League Championship
Hull City v Barnsley

Tuesday, 23 October
Coca-Cola League Championship
Bristol City v Southampton
Burnley v Norwich City
Cardiff City v Wolves
Charlton Athletic v Plymouth Argyle
Coventry City v Watford
Crystal Palace v Stoke City
Ipswich Town v Colchester Utd.
Leicester City v Sheffield Utd.
Preston N.E. v Q.P.R.
Sheffield Wed. v Scunthorpe Utd.
W.B.A. v Blackpool

Friday, 26 October
Coca-Cola League One
Tranmere Rov. Huddersfield Town

Saturday, 27 October
Barclays Premiership
Birmingham City v Wigan Athletic
Chelsea v Manchester City
Derby Co. v Everton
Manchester Utd. v Middlesbrough
Portsmouth v West Ham Utd.
Reading v Newcastle Utd.
Sunderland v Fulham
Tottenham v Blackburn Rov.

Coca-Cola League Championship
Bristol City v Stoke City
Burnley v Southampton
Cardiff City v Scunthorpe Utd.
Charlton Athletic v Q.P.R.
Coventry City v Colchester Utd.
Crystal Palace v Watford
Hull City v Sheffield Utd.
Ipswich Town v Wolves
Leicester City v Barnsley
Preston N.E. v Plymouth Argyle
Sheffield Wed. v Blackpool
W.B.A. v Norwich City

Coca-Cola League One
Bournemouth v Walsall
Cheltenham Town v Crewe Alexandra
Gillingham v Bristol Rov.
Hartlepool Utd. v Brighton & H.A.
Leeds Utd. v Millwall
Luton Town v Nott'm. Forest
Oldham Athletic v Northampton Town
Port Vale v Swindon Town
Southend Utd. v Carlisle Utd.
Yeovil v Swansea City

Coca-Cola League Two
Barnet v Accrington Stanley
Brentford v Lincoln City
Chester City v Wycombe Wand.
Dag & Red v Rotherham Utd.
Darlington v Chesterfield
Grimsby Town v Bradford City
Macclesfield Town v Bury
Milton Keynes Dons v Stockport Co.
Morecambe v Rochdale

Notts Co. v Wrexham
Peterborough Utd. v Hereford
Shrewsbury Town v Mansfield Town

Sunday, 28 October
Barclays Premiership
Bolton Wand. v Aston Villa
Liverpool v Arsenal

Coca-Cola League One
Doncaster Rov. Leyton Orient

Friday, 2 November
Coca-Cola League Two
Lincoln City v Chester City

Saturday, 3 November
Barclays Premiership
Arsenal v Manchester Utd.
Aston Villa v Derby Co.
Blackburn Rov. v Liverpool
Everton v Birmingham City
Fulham v Reading
Middlesbrough v Tottenham
Newcastle Utd. v Portsmouth
Wigan Athletic v Chelsea

Coca-Cola League Championship
Barnsley v Preston N.E.
Blackpool v Cardiff City
Colchester Utd. v Leicester City
Norwich City v Ipswich Town
Plymouth Argyle v Sheffield Wed.
Q.P.R. v Hull City
Scunthorpe Utd. v Crystal Palace
Sheffield Utd. v Burnley
Southampton v Charlton Athletic
Stoke City v Coventry City
Watford v W.B.A.
Wolves v Bristol City

Coca-Cola League One
Brighton & H.A. v Luton Town
Bristol Rov. v Bournemouth
Carlisle Utd. v Leeds Utd.
Crewe Alexandra v Yeovil
Huddersfield Town v Port Vale
Leyton Orient v Oldham Athletic
Millwall v Hartlepool Utd.
Northampton Town v Southend Utd.
Nott'm. Forest v Tranmere Rov.
Swansea City v Gillingham
Swindon Town v Doncaster Rov.
Walsall v Cheltenham Town

Coca-Cola League Two
Accrington Stanley v Notts Co.
Bradford City v Brentford
Bury v Barnet
Chesterfield v Morecambe
Hereford v Darlington
Mansfield Town v Macclesfield Town
Rochdale v Dag & Red
Rotherham Utd. v Grimsby Town
Stockport Co. v Peterborough Utd.
Wycombe Wand. v Milton Keynes Dons

Sunday, 4 November
Barclays Premiership
West Ham Utd. v Bolton Wand.

Coca-Cola League Two
Wrexham v Shrewsbury Town

Monday, 5 November
Barclays Premiership
Manchester City v Sunderland

Tuesday, 6 November
Coca-Cola League Championship
Barnsley v Blackpool
Bristol City v Charlton Athletic
Burnley v Hull City
Cardiff City v Crystal Palace
Colchester Utd. v Plymouth Argyle
Norwich City v Watford
Preston N.E. v Leicester City
Q.P.R. v Coventry City
Scunthorpe Utd. v Stoke City
Sheffield Utd. v Ipswich Town
Southampton v Wolves
W.B.A. v Sheffield Wed.

Coca-Cola League One
Bournemouth v Leeds Utd.
Brighton & H.A. v Walsall
Cheltenham Town v Yeovil
Gillingham v Doncaster Rov.
Huddersfield Town v Hartlepool Utd.
Luton Town v Carlisle Utd.
Millwall v Swansea City
Northampton Town v Bristol Rov.
Nott'm. Forest v Southend Utd.
Port Vale v Crewe Alexandra
Swindon Town v Leyton Orient
Tranmere Rov. v Oldham Athletic

Coca-Cola LeagueTwo
Barnet v Notts Co.
Bradford City v Chester City
Darlington v Shrewsbury Town

Hereford v Mansfield Town
Lincoln City v Chesterfield
Macclesfield Town v Brentford
Milton Keynes Dons v Grimsby Town
Morecambe v Accrington Stanley
Peterborough Utd. v Dag & Red
Rochdale v Stockport Co.
Rotherham Utd. v Bury

Wednesday, 7 November
Coca-Cola League Two
Wrexham v Wycombe Wand.

Saturday, 10 November
Barclays Premiership
Bolton Wand. v Middlesbrough
Chelsea v Everton
Derby Co. v West Ham Utd.
Liverpool v Fulham
Manchester Utd. v Blackburn Rov.
Sunderland v Newcastle Utd.
Tottenham v Wigan Athletic

Coca-Cola League Championship
Blackpool v Scunthorpe Utd.
Charlton Athletic v Cardiff City
Crystal Palace v Q.P.R.
Hull City v Preston N.E.
Ipswich Town v Bristol City
Leicester City v Burnley
Plymouth Argyle v Norwich City
Sheffield Wed. v Southampton
Stoke City v Sheffield Utd.
Watford v Colchester Utd.
Wolves v Barnsley

Sunday, 11 November
Barclays Premiership
Birmingham City v Aston Villa
Portsmouth v Manchester City

Monday, 12 November
Barclays Premiership
Reading v Arsenal

Coca-Cola League Championship
Coventry City v W.B.A.

Friday, 16 November
Coca-Cola League One
Swansea City v Huddersfield Town

Saturday, 17 November
Coca-Cola League One
Bristol Rov. v Millwall
Crewe Alexandra v Northampton Town
Doncaster Rov. v Tranmere Rov.
Hartlepool Utd. v Bournemouth
Leeds Utd. v Swindon Town
Leyton Orient v Brighton & H.A.
Oldham Athletic v Port Vale
Southend Utd. v Cheltenham Town
Walsall v Luton Town

Coca-Cola League Two
Accrington Stanley v Rotherham Utd.
Brentford v Darlington
Bury v Peterborough Utd.
Chester City v Milton Keynes Dons
Chesterfield v Rochdale
Dag & Red v Bradford City
Grimsby Town v Morecambe
Mansfield Town v Wrexham
Notts Co. v Macclesfield Town
Shrewsbury Town v Barnet
Stockport Co. v Hereford
Wycombe Wand. v Lincoln City

Sunday, 18 November
Coca-Cola League One
Carlisle Utd. v Nott'm. Forest
Yeovil v Gillingham

Saturday, 24 November
Barclays Premiership
Arsenal v Wigan Athletic
Birmingham City v Portsmouth
Bolton Wand. v Manchester Utd.
Derby Co. v Chelsea
Everton v Sunderland
Manchester City v Reading
Middlesbrough v Aston Villa
Newcastle Utd. v Liverpool

Coca-Cola League Championship
Barnsley v Watford
Bristol City v Leicester City
Burnley v Stoke City
Cardiff City v Ipswich Town
Colchester Utd. v Crystal Palace
Norwich City v Coventry City
Preston N.E. v Charlton Athletic
Q.P.R. v Sheffield Wed.
Scunthorpe Utd. v Hull City
Sheffield Utd. v Plymouth Argyle
Southampton v Blackpool
W.B.A. v Wolves

Coca-Cola League One
Bournemouth v Oldham Athletic
Brighton & H.A. v Carlisle Utd.
Cheltenham Town v Leeds Utd.

Gillingham v Hartlepool Utd.
Huddersfield Town v Leyton Orient
Luton Town v Southend Utd.
Millwall v Yeovil
Northampton Town v Walsall
Nott'm. Forest v Crewe Alexandra
Port Vale v Doncaster Rov.
Swindon Town v Bristol Rov.
Tranmere Rov. v Swansea City

Coca-Cola League Two
Barnet v Grimsby Town
Bradford City v Stockport Co.
Darlington v Wycombe Wand.
Hereford v Accrington Stanley
Lincoln City v Notts Co.
Macclesfield Town v Dag & Red
Milton Keynes Dons v Chesterfield
Morecambe v Bury
Peterborough Utd. v Brentford
Rochdale v Mansfield Town
Rotherham Utd. v Shrewsbury Town

Sunday, 25 November
Barclays Premiership
Fulham v Blackburn Rov.
West Ham Utd. v Tottenham

Coca-Cola League Two
Wrexham v Chester City

Tuesday, 27 November
Coca-Cola League Championship
Blackpool v Norwich City
Charlton Athletic v Sheffield Utd.
Coventry City v Scunthorpe Utd.
Crystal Palace v Preston N.E.
Hull City v Bristol City
Ipswich Town v Southampton
Leicester City v Cardiff City
Plymouth Argyle v W.B.A.
Sheffield Wed. v Barnsley
Stoke City v Q.P.R.
Watford v Burnley
Wolves v Colchester Utd.

Saturday, 1 December
Barclays Premiership
Aston Villa v Arsenal
Blackburn Rov. v Newcastle Utd.
Chelsea v West Ham Utd.
Liverpool v Bolton Wand.
Manchester Utd. v Fulham
Portsmouth v Everton
Reading v Middlesbrough
Sunderland v Derby Co.
Tottenham v Birmingham City
Wigan Athletic v Manchester City

Coca-Cola League Championship
Blackpool v Q.P.R.
Charlton Athletic v Burnley
Coventry City v Sheffield Utd.
Crystal Palace v W.B.A.
Hull City v Cardiff City
Ipswich Town v Barnsley
Leicester City v Southampton
Plymouth Argyle v Scunthorpe Utd.
Sheffield Wed. v Colchester Utd.
Stoke City v Norwich City
Watford v Bristol City
Wolves v Preston N.E.

Tuesday, 4 December
Coca-Cola League Championship
Barnsley v Wolves
Bristol City v Ipswich Town
Burnley v Leicester City
Cardiff City v Charlton Athletic
Colchester Utd. v Watford
Norwich City v Plymouth Argyle
Preston N.E. v Hull City
Q.P.R. v Crystal Palace
Scunthorpe Utd. v Blackpool
Sheffield Utd. v Stoke City
Southampton v Sheffield Wed.
W.B.A. v Coventry City

Coca-Cola League One
Carlisle Utd. v Swindon Town
Crewe Alexandra v Gillingham
Doncaster Rov. v Brighton & H.A.
Hartlepool Utd. v Tranmere Rov.
Leeds Utd. v Port Vale
Leyton Orient v Millwall
Oldham Athletic v Luton Town
Swansea City v Northampton Town
Walsall v Nott'm. Forest
Yeovil v Bournemouth

Coca-Cola League Two
Brentford v Morecambe
Bury v Wrexham
Chester City v Barnet
Dag & Red v Milton Keynes Dons
Grimsby Town v Darlington
Mansfield Town v Bradford City
Notts Co. v Peterborough Utd.
Shrewsbury Town v Macclesfield Town
Stockport Co. v Lincoln City
Wycombe Wand. v Hereford

Wednesday, 5 December
Coca-Cola League One
Bristol Rov. v Cheltenham Town
Southend Utd. v Huddersfield Town

Coca-Cola League Two
Accrington Stanley v Rochdale
Chesterfield v Rotherham Utd.

Friday, 7 December
Coca-Cola League One
Brighton & H.A. v Nott'm. Forest

Saturday, 8 December
Barclays Premiership
Aston Villa v Portsmouth
Blackburn Rov. v West Ham Utd.
Bolton Wand. v Wigan Athletic
Chelsea v Sunderland
Everton v Fulham
Manchester Utd. v Derby Co.
Middlesbrough v Arsenal
Newcastle Utd. v Birmingham City
Reading v Liverpool
Tottenham v Manchester City

Coca-Cola League Championship
Barnsley v Crystal Palace
Cardiff City v Colchester Utd.
Charlton Athletic v Ipswich Town
Leicester City v W.B.A.
Norwich City v Sheffield Utd.
Plymouth Argyle v Bristol City
Preston N.E. v Blackpool
Scunthorpe Utd. v Q.P.R.
Sheffield Wed. v Coventry City
Southampton v Hull City
Stoke City v Watford
Wolves v Burnley

Coca-Cola League One
Bristol Rov. v Swansea City
Crewe Alexandra v Walsall
Gillingham v Port Vale
Leeds Utd. v Huddersfield Town
Leyton Orient v Cheltenham Town
Luton Town v Millwall
Northampton Town v Carlisle Utd.
Oldham Athletic v Doncaster Rov.
Southend Utd. v Swindon Town
Tranmere Rov. v Bournemouth
Yeovil v Hartlepool Utd.

Coca-Cola League Two
Barnet v Macclesfield Town
Brentford v Grimsby Town
Chester City v Peterborough Utd.
Chesterfield v Bradford City
Dag & Red v Wrexham
Hereford v Lincoln City
Mansfield Town v Bury
Milton Keynes Dons v Accrington Stanley
Morecambe v Darlington
Notts Co. v Shrewsbury Town
Rotherham Utd. v Rochdale
Stockport Co. v Wycombe Wand.

Friday, 14 December
Coca-Cola League One
Cheltenham Town v Luton Town

Saturday, 15 December
Barclays Premiership
Arsenal v Chelsea
Birmingham City v Reading
Derby Co. v Middlesbrough
Fulham v Newcastle Utd.
Liverpool v Manchester Utd.
Manchester City v Bolton Wand.
Portsmouth v Tottenham
Sunderland v Aston Villa
West Ham Utd. v Everton
Wigan Athletic v Blackburn Rov.

Coca-Cola League Championship
Blackpool v Stoke City
Bristol City v Cardiff City
Burnley v Preston N.E.
Colchester Utd. v Norwich City
Coventry City v Southampton
Crystal Palace v Sheffield Wed.
Hull City v Leicester City
Ipswich Town v Scunthorpe Utd.
Q.P.R. v Wolves
Sheffield Utd. v Barnsley
Watford v Plymouth Argyle
W.B.A. v Charlton Athletic

Coca-Cola League One
Bournemouth v Gillingham
Carlisle Utd. v Leyton Orient
Hartlepool Utd. v Crewe Alexandra
Huddersfield Town v Bristol Rov.
Millwall v Oldham Athletic
Nott'm. Forest v Northampton Town
Port Vale v Tranmere Rov.
Swansea City v Southend Utd.
Swindon Town v Brighton & H.A.
Walsall v Leeds Utd.

Coca-Cola League Two
Accrington Stanley v Chesterfield
Bradford City v Rotherham Utd.
Bury v Hereford
Darlington v Chester City
Grimsby Town v Mansfield Town
Lincoln City v Barnet
Macclesfield Town v Stockport Co.
Peterborough Utd. v Milton Keynes Dons
Rochdale v Notts Co.
Shrewsbury Town v Dag & Red
Wrexham v Brentford
Wycombe Wand. v Morecambe

Sunday, 16 December
Coca-Cola League One
Doncaster Rov. v Yeovil

Friday, 21 December
Coca-Cola League One
Brighton & H.A. v Gillingham
Northampton Town v Bournemouth

Coca-Cola League Two
Chesterfield v Mansfield Town
Milton Keynes Dons v Brentford

Saturday, 22 December
Barclays Premiership
Arsenal v Tottenham
Aston Villa v Manchester City
Blackburn Rov. v Chelsea
Bolton Wand. v Birmingham City
Fulham v Wigan Athletic
Liverpool v Portsmouth
Manchester Utd. v Everton
Middlesbrough v West Ham Utd.
Newcastle Utd. v Derby Co.
Reading v Sunderland

Coca-Cola League Championship
Blackpool v Coventry City
Bristol City v Barnsley
Cardiff City v Sheffield Utd.
Charlton Athletic v Hull City
Crystal Palace v Plymouth Argyle
Ipswich Town v Burnley
Q.P.R. v Colchester Utd.
Scunthorpe Utd. v Norwich City
Sheffield Wed. v Watford
Southampton v Preston N.E.
Stoke City v W.B.A.
Wolves v Leicester City

Coca-Cola League One
Carlisle Utd. v Swansea City
Cheltenham Town v Huddersfield Town
Crewe Alexandra v Doncaster Rov.
Leeds Utd. v Bristol Rov.
Leyton Orient v Yeovil
Luton Town v Tranmere Rov.
Nott'm. Forest v Port Vale
Southend Utd. v Oldham Athletic
Swindon Town v Hartlepool Utd.
Walsall v Millwall

Coca-Cola League Two
Accrington Stanley v Shrewsbury Town
Chester City v Bury
Dag & Red v Notts Co.
Hereford v Morecambe
Lincoln City v Darlington
Peterborough Utd. v Bradford City
Rochdale v Barnet
Rotherham Utd. v Wrexham
Stockport Co. v Grimsby Town
Wycombe Wand. v Macclesfield Town

Wednesday, 26 December
Barclays Premiership
Birmingham City v Middlesbrough
Chelsea v Aston Villa
Derby Co. v Liverpool
Everton v Bolton Wand.
Manchester City v Blackburn Rov.
Portsmouth v Arsenal
Sunderland v Manchester Utd.
Tottenham v Fulham
West Ham Utd. v Reading
Wigan Athletic v Newcastle Utd.

Coca-Cola League Championship
Barnsley v Stoke City
Burnley v Sheffield Wed.
Colchester Utd. v Southampton
Coventry City v Crystal Palace
Hull City v Wolves
Leicester City v Ipswich Town
Norwich City v Charlton Athletic
Plymouth Argyle v Q.P.R.
Preston N.E. v Scunthorpe Utd.
Sheffield Utd. v Blackpool
Watford v Cardiff City
W.B.A. v Bristol City

Coca-Cola League One
Bournemouth v Leyton Orient
Bristol Rov. v Luton Town
Doncaster Rov. v Northampton Town
Gillingham v Southend Utd.
Hartlepool Utd. v Leeds Utd.

Huddersfield Town v Crewe Alexandra
Millwall v Brighton & H.A.
Oldham Athletic v Nott'm. Forest
Port Vale v Walsall
Swansea City v Cheltenham Town
Tranmere Rov. v Carlisle Utd.
Yeovil v Swindon Town

Coca-Cola League Two
Barnet v Dag & Red
Bradford City v Lincoln City
Brentford v Wycombe Wand.
Bury v Chesterfield
Darlington v Rotherham Utd.
Grimsby Town v Accrington Stanley
Macclesfield Town v Hereford
Mansfield Town v Peterborough Utd.
Morecambe v Chester City
Notts Co. v Milton Keynes Dons
Shrewsbury Town v Stockport Co.
Wrexham v Rochdale

Saturday, 29 December
Barclays Premiership
Birmingham City v Fulham
Chelsea v Newcastle Utd.
Derby Co. v Blackburn Rov.
Everton v Arsenal
Manchester City v Liverpool
Portsmouth v Middlesbrough
Sunderland v Bolton Wand.
Tottenham v Reading
West Ham Utd. v Manchester Utd.
Wigan Athletic v Aston Villa

Coca-Cola League Championship
Barnsley v Southampton
Burnley v Bristol City
Colchester Utd. v Blackpool
Coventry City v Ipswich Town
Hull City v Sheffield Wed.
Leicester City v Charlton Athletic
Norwich City v Wolves
Plymouth Argyle v Stoke City
Preston N.E. v Cardiff City
Sheffield Utd. v Crystal Palace
Watford v Q.P.R.
W.B.A. v Scunthorpe Utd.

Coca-Cola League One
Bournemouth v Swindon Town
Bristol Rov. v Carlisle Utd.
Doncaster Rov. v Southend Utd.
Gillingham v Nott'm. Forest
Hartlepool Utd. v Leyton Orient
Huddersfield Town v Northampton Town
Millwall v Crewe Alexandra
Oldham Athletic v Walsall
Port Vale v Luton Town
Swansea City v Leeds Utd.
Tranmere Rov. v Cheltenham Town
Yeovil v Brighton & H.A.

Coca-Cola League Two
Barnet v Chesterfield
Bradford City v Hereford
Brentford v Chester City
Bury v Dag & Red
Darlington v Milton Keynes Dons
Grimsby Town v Lincoln City
Macclesfield Town v Rochdale
Mansfield Town v Accrington Stanley
Morecambe v Peterborough Utd.
Notts Co. v Rotherham Utd.
Shrewsbury Town v Wycombe Wand.
Wrexham v Stockport Co.

Tuesday, 1 January
Barclays Premiership
Arsenal v West Ham Utd.
Aston Villa v Tottenham
Blackburn Rov. v Sunderland
Bolton Wand. v Derby Co.
Fulham v Chelsea
Liverpool v Wigan Athletic
Manchester Utd. v Birmingham City
Middlesbrough v Manchester City
Newcastle Utd. v Everton
Reading v Portsmouth

Coca-Cola League Championship
Blackpool v Burnley
Bristol City v Coventry City
Cardiff City v Plymouth Argyle
Charlton Athletic v Colchester Utd.
Crystal Palace v Norwich City
Ipswich Town v W.B.A.
Q.P.R. v Leicester City
Scunthorpe Utd. v Barnsley
Sheffield Wed. v Preston N.E.
Southampton v Watford
Stoke City v Hull City
Wolves v Sheffield Utd.

Coca-Cola League One
Brighton & H.A. v Bournemouth
Carlisle Utd. v Hartlepool Utd.
Crewe Alexandra v Tranmere Rov.
Leeds Utd. v Oldham Athletic
Leyton Orient v Gillingham
Luton Town v Yeovil
Northampton Town v Millwall
Nott'm. Forest v Huddersfield Town
Southend Utd. v Bristol Rov.

Swindon Town v Swansea City
Walsall v Doncaster Rov.

Coca-Cola League Two
Accrington Stanley v Bradford City
Chester City v Grimsby Town
Chesterfield v Wrexham
Dag & Red v Brentford
Hereford v Notts Co.
Lincoln City v Bury
Milton Keynes Dons v Mansfield Town
Peterborough Utd. v Shrewsbury Town
Rochdale v Darlington
Rotherham Utd. v Macclesfield Town
Stockport Co. v Morecambe
Wycombe Wand. v Barnet

Wednesday, 2 January
Coca-Cola League One
Cheltenham Town v Port Vale

Saturday, 5 January
Coca-Cola League One
Bournemouth v Luton Town
Brighton & H.A. v Cheltenham Town
Bristol Rov. v Doncaster Rov.
Carlisle Utd. v Port Vale
Gillingham v Oldham Athletic
Hartlepool Utd. v Southend Utd.
Leeds Utd. v Northampton Town
Leyton Orient v Tranmere Rov.
Millwall v Nott'm. Forest
Swansea City v Crewe Alexandra
Swindon Town v Huddersfield Town
Yeovil v Walsall

Coca-Cola League Two
Accrington Stanley v Chester City
Barnet v Darlington
Bury v Bradford City
Chesterfield v Grimsby Town
Dag & Red v Hereford
Macclesfield Town v Morecambe
Mansfield Town v Wycombe Wand.
Notts Co. v Stockport Co.
Rochdale v Lincoln City
Rotherham Utd. v Milton Keynes Dons
Shrewsbury Town v Brentford
Wrexham v Peterborough Utd.

Friday, 11 January
Coca-Cola League One
Tranmere Rov. Bristol Rov.

Saturday, 12 January
Barclays Premiership
Arsenal v Birmingham City
Aston Villa v Reading
Bolton Wand. v Blackburn Rov.
Chelsea v Tottenham
Derby Co. v Wigan Athletic
Everton v Manchester City
Manchester Utd. v Newcastle Utd.
Middlesbrough v Liverpool
Sunderland v Portsmouth
West Ham Utd. v Fulham

Coca-Cola League Championship
Barnsley v Norwich City
Bristol City v Colchester Utd.
Burnley v Plymouth Argyle
Cardiff City v Sheffield Wed.
Charlton Athletic v Blackpool
Hull City v W.B.A.
Ipswich Town v Stoke City
Leicester City v Coventry City
Preston N.E. v Watford
Sheffield Utd. v Q.P.R.
Southampton v Scunthorpe Utd.
Wolves v Crystal Palace

Coca-Cola League One
Cheltenham Town v Bournemouth
Crewe Alexandra v Leeds Utd.
Doncaster Rov. v Carlisle Utd.
Huddersfield Town v Gillingham
Luton Town v Swansea City
Northampton Town v Hartlepool Utd.
Nott'm. Forest v Leyton Orient
Oldham Athletic v Brighton & H.A.
Port Vale v Millwall
Southend Utd. v Yeovil
Walsall v Swindon Town

Coca-Cola League Two
Bradford City v Notts Co.
Brentford v Chesterfield
Chester City v Mansfield Town
Darlington v Bury
Grimsby Town v Wrexham
Lincoln City v Rotherham Utd.
Milton Keynes Dons v Barnet
Morecambe v Dag & Red
Peterborough Utd. v Macclesfield Town
Stockport Co. v Accrington Stanley
Wycombe Wand. v Rochdale

Sunday, 13 January
Coca-Cola League Two
Hereford Utd. v Shrewsbury Town

Friday, 18 January
Coca-Cola League One
Hartlepool Utd. v Cheltenham Town

Saturday, 19 January
Barclays Premiership
Birmingham City v Chelsea
Blackburn Rov. v Middlesbrough
Fulham v Arsenal
Liverpool v Aston Villa
Manchester City v West Ham Utd.
Newcastle Utd. v Bolton Wand.
Portsmouth v Derby Co.
Reading v Manchester Utd.
Tottenham v Sunderland
Wigan Athletic v Everton

Coca-Cola League Championship
Blackpool v Ipswich Town
Colchester Utd. v Hull City
Coventry City v Burnley
Crystal Palace v Bristol City
Norwich City v Leicester City
Plymouth Argyle v Southampton
Q.P.R. v Barnsley
Scunthorpe Utd. v Wolves
Sheffield Wed. v Sheffield Utd.
Stoke City v Preston N.E.
Watford v Charlton Athletic
W.B.A. v Cardiff City

Coca-Cola League One
Bournemouth v Southend Utd.
Brighton & H.A. v Huddersfield Town
Bristol Rov. v Walsall
Carlisle Utd. v Crewe Alexandra
Gillingham v Northampton Town
Leeds Utd. v Doncaster Rov.
Leyton Orient v Luton Town
Millwall v Tranmere Rov.
Swansea City v Port Vale
Swindon Town v Nott'm. Forest
Yeovil v Oldham Athletic

Coca-Cola League Two
Accrington Stanley v Brentford
Barnet v Peterborough Utd.
Bury v Stockport Co.
Chesterfield v Hereford
Dag & Red v Grimsby Town
Macclesfield Town v Lincoln City
Mansfield Town v Darlington
Notts Co. v Chester City
Rochdale v Bradford City
Rotherham Utd. v Wycombe Wand.
Shrewsbury Town v Morecambe
Wrexham v Milton Keynes Dons

Friday, 25 January
Coca-Cola League One
Cheltenham Town v Carlisle Utd.
Northampton Town v Leyton Orient

Saturday, 26 January
Coca-Cola League One
Crewe Alexandra v Swindon Town
Doncaster Rov. v Swansea City
Huddersfield Town v Millwall
Luton Town v Leeds Utd.
Nott'm. Forest v Bristol Rov.
Oldham Athletic v Hartlepool Utd.
Port Vale v Bournemouth
Southend Utd. v Brighton & H.A.
Tranmere Rov. v Yeovil
Walsall v Gillingham

Coca-Cola League Two
Bradford City v Barnet
Brentford v Bury
Chester City v Rotherham Utd.
Darlington v Macclesfield Town
Grimsby Town v Shrewsbury Town
Hereford v Wrexham
Lincoln City v Dag & Red
Milton Keynes Dons v Rochdale
Morecambe v Notts Co.
Peterborough Utd. v Accrington Stanley
Stockport Co. v Mansfield Town
Wycombe Wand. v Chesterfield

Tuesday, 29 January
Barclays Premiership
Arsenal v Newcastle Utd.
Bolton Wand. v Fulham
Derby Co. v Manchester City
Middlesbrough v Wigan Athletic
Sunderland v Birmingham City
West Ham Utd. v Liverpool
Wednesday, 30 January 2008
Barclays Premiership
Aston Villa v Blackburn Rov.
Chelsea v Reading
Everton v Tottenham
Manchester Utd. v Portsmouth

Coca-Cola League Championship
Barnsley v Colchester Utd.
Bristol City v Blackpool
Burnley v Scunthorpe Utd.
Cardiff City v Q.P.R.
Charlton Athletic v Stoke City
Hull City v Coventry City
Ipswich Town v Plymouth Argyle
Leicester City v Crystal Palace
Preston N.E. v W.B.A.

Sheffield Utd. v Watford
Southampton v Norwich City
Wolves v Sheffield Wed.

Coca-Cola League One
Cheltenham Town v Millwall
Crewe Alexandra v Bristol Rov.
Doncaster Rov. v Hartlepool Utd.
Huddersfield Town v Bournemouth
Luton Town v Swindon Town
Northampton Town v Brighton & H.A.
Nott'm. Forest v Swansea City
Oldham Athletic v Carlisle Utd.
Port Vale v Yeovil
Southend Utd. v Leeds Utd.
Tranmere Rov. v Gillingham
Walsall v Leyton Orient

Coca-Cola League Two
Bradford City v Shrewsbury Town
Brentford v Notts Co.
Chester City v Rochdale
Darlington v Accrington Stanley
Grimsby Town v Bury
Hereford v Barnet
Lincoln City v Mansfield Town
Milton Keynes Dons v Macclesfield Town
Morecambe v Wrexham
Peterborough Utd. v Rotherham Utd.
Stockport Co. v Chesterfield
Wycombe Wand. v Dag & Red

Saturday, 2 February
Barclays Premiership
Birmingham City v Derby Co.
Blackburn Rov. v Everton
Fulham v Aston Villa
Liverpool v Sunderland
Manchester City v Arsenal
Newcastle Utd. v Middlesbrough
Portsmouth v Chelsea
Reading v Bolton Wand.
Tottenham v Manchester Utd.
Wigan Athletic v West Ham Utd.

Coca-Cola League Championship
Blackpool v Leicester City
Colchester Utd. v Sheffield Utd.
Coventry City v Barnsley
Crystal Palace v Southampton
Norwich City v Preston N.E.
Plymouth Argyle v Hull City
Q.P.R. v Bristol City
Scunthorpe Utd. v Charlton Athletic
Sheffield Wed. v Ipswich Town
Stoke City v Cardiff City

Watford v Wolves
W.B.A. v Burnley

Coca-Cola League One
Bournemouth v Nott'm. Forest
Brighton & H.A. v Crewe Alexandra
Bristol Rov. v Port Vale
Carlisle Utd. v Walsall
Gillingham v Cheltenham Town
Hartlepool Utd. v Luton Town
Leeds Utd. v Tranmere Rov.
Leyton Orient v Southend Utd.
Millwall v Doncaster Rov.
Swansea City v Oldham Athletic
Swindon Town v Northampton Town
Yeovil v Huddersfield Town

Coca-Cola League Two
Accrington Stanley v Wycombe Wand.
Barnet v Morecambe
Bury v Milton Keynes Dons
Chesterfield v Chester City
Dag & Red v Stockport Co.
Macclesfield Town v Bradford City
Mansfield Town v Brentford
Notts Co. v Grimsby Town
Rochdale v Peterborough Utd.
Rotherham Utd. v Hereford
Shrewsbury Town v Lincoln City
Wrexham v Darlington

Saturday, 9 February
Barclays Premiership
Arsenal v Blackburn Rov.
Aston Villa v Newcastle Utd.
Bolton Wand. v Portsmouth
Chelsea v Liverpool
Derby Co. v Tottenham
Everton v Reading
Manchester Utd. v Manchester City
Middlesbrough v Fulham
Sunderland v Wigan Athletic
West Ham Utd. v Birmingham City

Coca-Cola League Championship
Barnsley v W.B.A.
Bristol City v Sheffield Wed.
Burnley v Colchester Utd.
Cardiff City v Norwich City
Charlton Athletic v Crystal Palace
Hull City v Blackpool
Ipswich Town v Watford
Leicester City v Plymouth Argyle
Preston N.E. v Coventry City
Sheffield Utd. v Scunthorpe Utd.
Southampton v Q.P.R.
Wolves v Stoke City

Coca-Cola League One
Cheltenham Town v Brighton & H.A.
Crewe Alexandra v Swansea City
Doncaster Rov. v Bristol Rov.
Huddersfield Town v Swindon Town
Luton Town v Bournemouth
Northampton Town v Leeds Utd.
Nott'm. Forest v Millwall
Oldham Athletic v Gillingham
Port Vale v Carlisle Utd.
Southend Utd. v Hartlepool Utd.
Tranmere Rov. v Leyton Orient
Walsall v Yeovil

Coca-Cola League Two
Bradford City v Bury
Brentford v Shrewsbury Town
Chester City v Accrington Stanley
Darlington v Barnet
Grimsby Town v Chesterfield
Hereford v Dag & Red
Lincoln City v Rochdale
Milton Keynes Dons v Rotherham Utd.
Morecambe v Macclesfield Town
Peterborough Utd. v Wrexham
Stockport Co. v Notts Co.
Wycombe Wand. v Mansfield Town

Tuesday, 12 February
Coca-Cola League Championship
Blackpool v Wolves
Colchester Utd. v Preston N.E.
Coventry City v Cardiff City
Crystal Palace v Ipswich Town
Norwich City v Hull City
Plymouth Argyle v Barnsley
Q.P.R. v Burnley
Scunthorpe Utd. v Bristol City
Sheffield Wed. v Charlton Athletic
Stoke City v Southampton
Watford v Leicester City
W.B.A. v Sheffield Utd.

Coca-Cola League One
Bournemouth v Doncaster Rov.
Brighton & H.A. v Tranmere Rov.
Bristol Rov. v Oldham Athletic
Carlisle Utd. v Huddersfield Town
Gillingham v Luton Town
Hartlepool Utd. v Port Vale
Leeds Utd. v Nott'm. Forest
Leyton Orient v Crewe Alexandra
Millwall v Southend Utd.
Swansea City v Walsall
Swindon Town v Cheltenham Town
Yeovil v Northampton Town

Coca-Cola League Two
Accrington Stanley v Lincoln City
Barnet v Brentford
Bury v Wycombe Wand.
Dag & Red v Chester City
Macclesfield Town v Grimsby Town
Mansfield Town v Morecambe
Notts Co. v Darlington
Rochdale v Hereford
Rotherham Utd. v Stockport Co.
Shrewsbury Town v Milton Keynes Dons
Wrexham v Bradford City

Wednesday, 13 February
Coca-Cola League Two
Chesterfield v Peterborough Utd.

Saturday, 16 February
Coca-Cola League Championship
Barnsley v Q.P.R.
Bristol City v Crystal Palace
Burnley v Coventry City
Cardiff City v W.B.A.
Charlton Athletic v Watford
Hull City v Colchester Utd.
Ipswich Town v Blackpool
Leicester City v Norwich City
Preston N.E. v Stoke City
Sheffield Utd. v Sheffield Wed.
Southampton v Plymouth Argyle
Wolves v Scunthorpe Utd.

Coca-Cola League One
Cheltenham Town v Hartlepool Utd.
Crewe Alexandra v Carlisle Utd.
Doncaster Rov. v Leeds Utd.
Huddersfield Town v Brighton & H.A.
Luton Town v Leyton Orient
Northampton Town v Gillingham
Nott'm. Forest v Swindon Town
Oldham Athletic v Yeovil
Port Vale v Swansea City
Southend Utd. v Bournemouth
Tranmere Rov. v Millwall
Walsall v Bristol Rov.

Coca-Cola League Two
Bradford City v Rochdale
Brentford v Accrington Stanley
Chester City v Notts Co.
Darlington v Mansfield Town
Grimsby Town v Dag & Red
Hereford v Chesterfield
Lincoln City v Macclesfield Town
Milton Keynes Dons v Wrexham
Morecambe v Shrewsbury Town
Peterborough Utd. v Barnet

Stockport Co. v Bury
Wycombe Wand. v Rotherham Utd.

Friday, 22 February
Coca-Cola League One
Hartlepool Utd. v Northampton Town
Swansea City v Luton Town

Coca-Cola League Two
Wrexham v Grimsby Town

Saturday, 23 February
Barclays Premiership
Birmingham City v Arsenal
Blackburn Rov. v Bolton Wand.
Fulham v West Ham Utd.
Liverpool v Middlesbrough
Manchester City v Everton
Newcastle Utd. v Manchester Utd.
Portsmouth v Sunderland
Reading v Aston Villa
Tottenham v Chelsea
Wigan Athletic v Derby Co.

Coca-Cola League Championship
Blackpool v Charlton Athletic
Colchester Utd. v Bristol City
Coventry City v Leicester City
Crystal Palace v Wolves
Norwich City v Barnsley
Plymouth Argyle v Burnley
Q.P.R. v Sheffield Utd.
Scunthorpe Utd. v Southampton
Sheffield Wed. v Cardiff City
Stoke City v Ipswich Town
Watford v Preston N.E.
W.B.A. v Hull City

Coca-Cola League One
Bournemouth v Cheltenham Town
Brighton & H.A. v Oldham Athletic
Bristol Rov. v Tranmere Rov.
Carlisle Utd. v Doncaster Rov.
Gillingham v Huddersfield Town
Leeds Utd. v Crewe Alexandra
Leyton Orient v Nott'm. Forest
Millwall v Port Vale
Swindon Town v Walsall
Yeovil v Southend Utd.

Coca-Cola League Two
Accrington Stanley v Stockport Co.
Barnet v Milton Keynes Dons
Bury v Darlington
Chesterfield v Brentford
Dag & Red v Morecambe
Macclesfield Town v Peterborough Utd.
Mansfield Town v Chester City
Notts Co. v Bradford City
Rochdale v Wycombe Wand.
Rotherham Utd. v Lincoln City
Shrewsbury Town v Hereford

Friday, 29 February
Coca-Cola League One
Cheltenham Town v Southend Utd.

Saturday, 1 March
Barclays Premiership
Arsenal v Aston Villa
Birmingham City v Tottenham
Bolton Wand. v Liverpool
Derby Co. v Sunderland
Everton v Portsmouth
Fulham v Manchester Utd.
Manchester City v Wigan Athletic
Middlesbrough v Reading
Newcastle Utd. v Blackburn Rov.
West Ham Utd. v Chelsea

Coca-Cola League Championship
Barnsley v Sheffield Wed.
Bristol City v Hull City
Burnley v Watford
Cardiff City v Leicester City
Colchester Utd. v Wolves
Norwich City v Blackpool
Preston N.E. v Crystal Palace
Q.P.R. v Stoke City
Scunthorpe Utd. v Coventry City
Sheffield Utd. v Charlton Athletic
Southampton v Ipswich Town
W.B.A. v Plymouth Argyle

Coca-Cola League One
Bournemouth v Hartlepool Utd.
Brighton & H.A. v Leyton Orient
Gillingham v Yeovil
Huddersfield Town v Swansea City
Luton Town v Walsall
Millwall v Bristol Rov.
Northampton Town v Crewe Alexandra
Nott'm. Forest v Carlisle Utd.
Port Vale v Oldham Athletic
Swindon Town v Leeds Utd.
Tranmere Rov. v Doncaster Rov.

Coca-Cola League Two
Barnet v Shrewsbury Town
Bradford City v Dag & Red
Darlington v Brentford
Hereford v Stockport Co.

Lincoln City v Wycombe Wand.
Macclesfield Town v Notts Co.
Milton Keynes Dons v Chester City
Morecambe v Grimsby Town
Peterborough Utd. v Bury
Rochdale v Chesterfield
Rotherham Utd. v Accrington Stanley
Wrexham v Mansfield Town

Tuesday, 4 March
Coca-Cola League Championship
Blackpool v Barnsley
Charlton Athletic v Bristol City
Coventry City v Q.P.R.
Crystal Palace v Cardiff City
Hull City v Burnley
Ipswich Town v Sheffield Utd.
Leicester City v Preston N.E.
Plymouth Argyle v Colchester Utd.
Sheffield Wed. v W.B.A.
Stoke City v Scunthorpe Utd.
Watford v Norwich City
Wolves v Southampton

Coca-Cola League One
Bristol Rov. v Northampton Town

Saturday, 8 March
Barclays Premiership
Aston Villa v Middlesbrough
Blackburn Rov. v Fulham
Chelsea v Derby Co.
Liverpool v Newcastle Utd.
Manchester Utd. v Bolton Wand.
Portsmouth v Birmingham City
Reading v Manchester City
Sunderland v Everton
Tottenham v West Ham Utd.
Wigan Athletic v Arsenal

Coca-Cola League Championship
Blackpool v Southampton
Charlton Athletic v Preston N.E.
Coventry City v Norwich City
Crystal Palace v Colchester Utd.
Hull City v Scunthorpe Utd.
Ipswich Town v Cardiff City
Leicester City v Bristol City
Plymouth Argyle v Sheffield Utd.
Sheffield Wed. v Q.P.R.
Stoke City v Burnley
Watford v Barnsley
Wolves v W.B.A.

Coca-Cola League One
Bristol Rov. v Swindon Town
Carlisle Utd. v Brighton & H.A.
Crewe Alexandra v Nott'm. Forest
Doncaster Rov. v Port Vale
Hartlepool Utd. v Gillingham
Leeds Utd. v Bournemouth
Leyton Orient v Huddersfield Town
Oldham Athletic v Tranmere Rov.
Southend Utd. v Luton Town
Swansea City v Millwall
Walsall v Northampton Town
Yeovil v Cheltenham Town

Coca-Cola League Two
Accrington Stanley v Hereford
Brentford v Macclesfield Town
Bury v Morecambe
Chesterfield v Lincoln City
Dag & Red v Peterborough Utd.
Grimsby Town v Milton Keynes Dons
Mansfield Town v Rochdale
Notts Co. v Barnet
Shrewsbury Town v Rotherham Utd.
Stockport Co. v Bradford City
Wycombe Wand. v Darlington

Sunday, 9 March
Coca-Cola League Two
Chester City v Wrexham

Tuesday, 11 March
Coca-Cola League Championship
Barnsley v Ipswich Town
Bristol City v Watford
Burnley v Charlton Athletic
Cardiff City v Hull City
Colchester Utd. v Sheffield Wed.
Norwich City v Stoke City
Preston N.E. v Wolves
Q.P.R. v Blackpool
Scunthorpe Utd. v Plymouth Argyle
Sheffield Utd. v Coventry City
Southampton v Leicester City
W.B.A. v Crystal Palace

Coca-Cola League One
Carlisle Utd. v Luton Town
Crewe Alexandra v Port Vale
Doncaster Rov. v Gillingham
Hartlepool Utd. v Huddersfield Town
Leeds Utd. v Cheltenham Town
Leyton Orient v Swindon Town
Oldham Athletic v Bournemouth
Southend Utd. v Nott'm. Forest
Swansea City v Tranmere Rov.
Walsall v Brighton & H.A.
Yeovil v Millwall

Coca-Cola League Two
Brentford v Peterborough Utd.
Bury v Rotherham Utd.
Dag & Red v Macclesfield Town
Grimsby Town v Barnet
Mansfield Town v Hereford
Notts Co. v Lincoln City
Shrewsbury Town v Darlington
Stockport Co. v Rochdale
Wycombe Wand. v Wrexham

Wednesday, 12 March
Coca-Cola League Two
Accrington Stanley v Morecambe
Chester City v Bradford City
Chesterfield v Milton Keynes Dons

Saturday, 15 March
Barclays Premiership
Arsenal v Middlesbrough
Birmingham City v Newcastle Utd.
Derby Co. v Manchester Utd.
Fulham v Everton
Liverpool v Reading
Manchester City v Tottenham
Portsmouth v Aston Villa
Sunderland v Chelsea
West Ham Utd. v Blackburn Rov.
Wigan Athletic v Bolton Wand.

Coca-Cola League Championship
Blackpool v Preston N.E.
Bristol City v Plymouth Argyle
Burnley v Wolves
Colchester Utd. v Cardiff City
Coventry City v Sheffield Wed.
Crystal Palace v Barnsley
Hull City v Southampton
Ipswich Town v Charlton Athletic
Q.P.R. v Scunthorpe Utd.
Sheffield Utd. v Norwich City
Watford v Stoke City
W.B.A. v Leicester City

Coca-Cola League One
Bournemouth v Yeovil
Brighton & H.A. v Doncaster Rov.
Cheltenham Town v Bristol Rov.
Gillingham v Crewe Alexandra
Huddersfield Town v Southend Utd.
Luton Town v Oldham Athletic
Millwall v Leyton Orient
Northampton Town v Swansea City
Nott'm. Forest v Walsall
Port Vale v Leeds Utd.
Swindon Town v Carlisle Utd.
Tranmere Rov. v Hartlepool Utd.

Coca-Cola League Two
Barnet v Chester City
Bradford City v Mansfield Town
Darlington v Grimsby Town
Hereford v Wycombe Wand.
Lincoln City v Stockport Co.
Macclesfield Town v Shrewsbury Town
Milton Keynes Dons v Dag & Red
Morecambe v Brentford
Peterborough Utd. v Notts Co.
Rochdale v Accrington Stanley
Rotherham Utd. v Chesterfield
Wrexham v Bury

Friday, 21 March
Coca-Cola League One
Northampton Town v Nott'm. Forest
Yeovil v Doncaster Rov.

Saturday, 22 March
Barclays Premiership
Aston Villa v Sunderland
Blackburn Rov. v Wigan Athletic
Bolton Wand. v Manchester City
Chelsea v Arsenal
Everton v West Ham Utd.
Manchester Utd. v Liverpool
Middlesbrough v Derby Co.
Newcastle Utd. v Fulham
Reading v Birmingham City
Tottenham v Portsmouth

Coca-Cola League Championship
Barnsley v Sheffield Utd.
Cardiff City v Bristol City
Charlton Athletic v W.B.A.
Leicester City v Hull City
Norwich City v Colchester Utd.
Plymouth Argyle v Watford
Preston N.E. v Burnley
Scunthorpe Utd. v Ipswich Town
Sheffield Wed. v Crystal Palace
Southampton v Coventry City
Stoke City v Blackpool
Wolves v Q.P.R.

Coca-Cola League One
Brighton & H.A. v Swindon Town
Bristol Rov. v Huddersfield Town
Crewe Alexandra v Hartlepool Utd.
Gillingham v Bournemouth
Leeds Utd. v Walsall
Leyton Orient v Carlisle Utd.
Luton Town v Cheltenham Town
Oldham Athletic v Millwall
Southend Utd. v Swansea City
Tranmere Rov. v Port Vale

Coca-Cola League Two
Barnet v Lincoln City
Brentford v Wrexham
Chester City v Darlington
Chesterfield v Accrington Stanley
Dag & Red v Shrewsbury Town
Hereford v Bury
Mansfield Town v Grimsby Town
Milton Keynes Dons v Peterborough Utd.
Morecambe v Wycombe Wand.
Notts Co. v Rochdale
Rotherham Utd. v Bradford City
Stockport Co. v Macclesfield Town

Monday, 24 March
Coca-Cola League One
Bournemouth v Tranmere Rov.
Carlisle Utd. v Northampton Town
Cheltenham Town v Leyton Orient
Doncaster Rov. v Oldham Athletic
Hartlepool Utd. v Yeovil
Millwall v Luton Town
Nott'm. Forest v Brighton & H.A.
Port Vale v Gillingham
Swansea City v Bristol Rov.
Swindon Town v Southend Utd.
Walsall v Crewe Alexandra

Coca-Cola League Two
Accrington Stanley v Milton Keynes Dons
Bradford City v Chesterfield
Bury v Mansfield Town
Darlington v Morecambe
Grimsby Town v Brentford
Lincoln City v Hereford
Macclesfield Town v Barnet
Peterborough Utd. v Chester City
Rochdale v Rotherham Utd.
Shrewsbury Town v Notts Co.
Wrexham v Dag & Red
Wycombe Wand. v Stockport Co.

Tuesday, 25 March
Coca-Cola League One
Huddersfield Town v Leeds Utd.

Friday, 28 March
Coca-Cola League One
Doncaster Rov. v Nott'm. Forest
Tranmere Rov. v Swindon Town

Saturday, 29 March
Barclays Premiership
Birmingham City v Manchester City
Bolton Wand. v Arsenal
Chelsea v Middlesbrough
Derby Co. v Fulham
Liverpool v Everton
Manchester Utd. v Aston Villa
Portsmouth v Wigan Athletic
Reading v Blackburn Rov.
Sunderland v West Ham Utd.
Tottenham v Newcastle Utd.

Coca-Cola League Championship
Bristol City v Norwich City
Burnley v Barnsley
Cardiff City v Southampton
Charlton Athletic v Wolves
Coventry City v Plymouth Argyle
Crystal Palace v Blackpool
Hull City v Watford
Ipswich Town v Q.P.R.
Leicester City v Scunthorpe Utd.
Preston N.E. v Sheffield Utd.
Sheffield Wed. v Stoke City
W.B.A. v Colchester Utd.

Coca-Cola League One
Bournemouth v Millwall
Cheltenham Town v Northampton Town
Gillingham v Carlisle Utd.
Hartlepool Utd. v Swansea City
Leeds Utd. v Brighton & H.A.
Luton Town v Crewe Alexandra
Oldham Athletic v Huddersfield Town
Port Vale v Leyton Orient
Southend Utd. v Walsall
Yeovil v Bristol Rov.

Coca-Cola League Two
Barnet v Wrexham
Brentford v Rochdale
Chester City v Stockport Co.
Dag & Red v Chesterfield
Darlington v Bradford City
Grimsby Town v Wycombe Wand.
Macclesfield Town v Accrington Stanley
Milton Keynes Dons v Hereford
Morecambe v Rotherham Utd.
Notts Co. v Mansfield Town
Peterborough Utd. v Lincoln City
Shrewsbury Town v Bury

Friday, 4 April
Coca-Cola League Two
Lincoln City v Milton Keynes Dons

Saturday, 5 April
Barclays Premiership
Arsenal v Liverpool
Aston Villa v Bolton Wand.

Blackburn Rov. v Tottenham
Everton v Derby Co.
Fulham v Sunderland
Manchester City v Chelsea
Middlesbrough v Manchester Utd.
Newcastle Utd. v Reading
West Ham Utd. v Portsmouth
Wigan Athletic v Birmingham City

Coca-Cola League Championship
Barnsley v Hull City
Blackpool v W.B.A.
Colchester Utd. v Ipswich Town
Norwich City v Burnley
Plymouth Argyle v Charlton Athletic
Q.P.R. v Preston N.E.
Scunthorpe Utd. v Sheffield Wed.
Sheffield Utd. v Leicester City
Southampton v Bristol City
Stoke City v Crystal Palace
Watford v Coventry City
Wolves v Cardiff City

Coca-Cola League One
Brighton & H.A. v Port Vale
Bristol Rov. v Hartlepool Utd.
Carlisle Utd. v Yeovil
Crewe Alexandra v Southend Utd.
Huddersfield Town v Doncaster Rov.
Leyton Orient v Leeds Utd.
Millwall v Gillingham
Northampton Town v Luton Town
Nott'm. Forest v Cheltenham Town
Swansea City v Bournemouth
Swindon Town v Oldham Athletic
Walsall v Tranmere Rov.

Coca-Cola League Two
Accrington Stanley v Dag & Red
Bradford City v Morecambe
Bury v Notts Co.
Chesterfield v Shrewsbury Town
Hereford v Chester City
Mansfield Town v Barnet
Rochdale v Grimsby Town
Rotherham Utd. v Brentford
Stockport Co. v Darlington
Wrexham v Macclesfield Town
Wycombe Wand. v Peterborough Utd.

Saturday, 12 April
Barclays Premiership
Birmingham City v Everton
Bolton Wand. v West Ham Utd.
Chelsea v Wigan Athletic
Derby Co. v Aston Villa
Liverpool v Blackburn Rov.
Manchester Utd. v Arsenal
Portsmouth v Newcastle Utd.
Reading v Fulham
Sunderland v Manchester City
Tottenham v Middlesbrough

Coca-Cola League Championship
Bristol City v Wolves
Burnley v Sheffield Utd.
Cardiff City v Blackpool
Charlton Athletic v Southampton
Coventry City v Stoke City
Crystal Palace v Scunthorpe Utd.
Hull City v Q.P.R.
Ipswich Town v Norwich City
Leicester City v Colchester Utd.
Preston N.E. v Barnsley
Sheffield Wed. v Plymouth Argyle
W.B.A. v Watford

Coca-Cola League One
Bournemouth v Bristol Rov.
Cheltenham Town v Walsall
Doncaster Rov. v Swindon Town
Gillingham v Swansea City
Hartlepool Utd. v Millwall
Leeds Utd. v Carlisle Utd.
Luton Town v Brighton & H.A.
Oldham Athletic v Leyton Orient
Port Vale v Huddersfield Town
Southend Utd. v Northampton Town
Tranmere Rov. v Nott'm. Forest
Yeovil v Crewe Alexandra

Coca-Cola League Two
Barnet v Bury
Brentford v Bradford City
Chester City v Lincoln City
Dag & Red v Rochdale
Darlington v Hereford
Grimsby Town v Rotherham Utd.
Macclesfield Town v Mansfield Town
Milton Keynes Dons v Wycombe Wand.
Morecambe v Chesterfield
Notts Co. v Accrington Stanley
Peterborough Utd. v Stockport Co.

Sunday, 13 April
Coca-Cola League Two
Shrewsbury Town v Wrexham

Saturday, 19 April
Barclays Premiership
Arsenal v Reading
Aston Villa v Birmingham City
Blackburn Rov. v Manchester Utd.

Everton v Chelsea
Fulham v Liverpool
Manchester City v Portsmouth
Middlesbrough v Bolton Wand.
Newcastle Utd. v Sunderland
West Ham Utd. v Derby Co.
Wigan Athletic v Tottenham

Coca-Cola League Championship
Barnsley v Leicester City
Blackpool v Sheffield Wed.
Colchester Utd. v Coventry City
Norwich City v W.B.A.
Plymouth Argyle v Preston N.E.
Q.P.R. v Charlton Athletic
Scunthorpe Utd. v Cardiff City
Sheffield Utd. v Hull City
Southampton v Burnley
Stoke City v Bristol City
Watford v Crystal Palace
Wolves v Ipswich Town

Coca-Cola League One
Brighton & H.A. v Hartlepool Utd.
Bristol Rov. v Gillingham
Carlisle Utd. v Southend Utd.
Crewe Alexandra v Cheltenham Town
Huddersfield Town v Tranmere Rov.
Leyton Orient v Doncaster Rov.
Millwall v Leeds Utd.
Northampton Town v Oldham Athletic
Nott'm. Forest v Luton Town
Swansea City v Yeovil
Swindon Town v Port Vale
Walsall v Bournemouth

Coca-Cola League Two
Accrington Stanley v Barnet
Bradford City v Grimsby Town
Bury v Macclesfield Town
Chesterfield v Darlington
Hereford v Peterborough Utd.
Lincoln City v Brentford
Mansfield Town v Shrewsbury Town
Rochdale v Morecambe
Rotherham Utd. v Dag & Red
Stockport Co. v Milton Keynes Dons
Wrexham v Notts Co.
Wycombe Wand. v Chester City

Saturday, 26 April
Barclays Premiership
Birmingham City v Liverpool
Chelsea v Manchester Utd.
Derby Co. v Arsenal
Everton v Aston Villa
Manchester City v Fulham
Portsmouth v Blackburn Rov.
Sunderland v Middlesbrough
Tottenham v Bolton Wand.
West Ham Utd. v Newcastle Utd.
Wigan Athletic v Reading

Coca-Cola League Championship
Barnsley v Charlton Athletic
Burnley v Cardiff City
Colchester Utd. v Stoke City
Coventry City v Wolves
Hull City v Crystal Palace
Leicester City v Sheffield Wed.
Norwich City v Q.P.R.
Plymouth Argyle v Blackpool
Preston N.E. v Ipswich Town
Sheffield Utd. v Bristol City
Watford v Scunthorpe Utd.
W.B.A. v Southampton

Coca-Cola League One
Bournemouth v Crewe Alexandra
Bristol Rov. v Brighton & H.A.
Doncaster Rov. v Luton Town
Gillingham v Swindon Town
Hartlepool Utd. v Nott'm. Forest
Huddersfield Town v Walsall
Millwall v Carlisle Utd.
Oldham Athletic v Cheltenham Town
Port Vale v Northampton Town
Swansea City v Leyton Orient
Tranmere Rov. v Southend Utd.
Yeovil v Leeds Utd.

Coca-Cola League Two
Barnet v Stockport Co.
Bradford City v Milton Keynes Dons
Brentford v Hereford
Bury v Rochdale
Darlington v Dag & Red
Grimsby Town v Peterborough Utd.
Macclesfield Town v Chesterfield
Mansfield Town v Rotherham Utd.
Morecambe v Lincoln City
Notts Co. v Wycombe Wand.
Shrewsbury Town v Chester City
Wrexham v Accrington Stanley

Saturday, 3 May
Barclays Premiership
Arsenal v Everton
Aston Villa v Wigan Athletic
Blackburn Rov. v Derby Co.
Bolton Wand. v Sunderland
Fulham v Birmingham City
Liverpool v Manchester City
Manchester Utd. v West Ham Utd.

Middlesbrough v Portsmouth
Newcastle Utd. v Chelsea
Reading v Tottenham

Coca-Cola League One
Brighton & H.A. v Swansea City
Carlisle Utd. v Bournemouth
Cheltenham Town v Doncaster Rov.
Crewe Alexandra v Oldham Athletic
Leeds Utd. v Gillingham
Leyton Orient v Bristol Rov.
Luton Town v Huddersfield Town
Northampton Town v Tranmere Rov.
Nott'm. Forest v Yeovil
Southend Utd. v Port Vale
Swindon Town v Millwall
Walsall v Hartlepool Utd.

Coca-Cola League Two
Accrington Stanley v Bury
Chester City v Macclesfield Town
Chesterfield v Notts Co.
Dag & Red v Mansfield Town
Hereford v Grimsby Town
Lincoln City v Wrexham
Milton Keynes Dons v Morecambe
Peterborough Utd. v Darlington
Rochdale v Shrewsbury Town
Rotherham Utd. v Barnet

Stockport Co. v Brentford
Wycombe Wand. v Bradford City

Sunday, 4 May
Coca-Cola League Championship
Blackpool v Watford
Bristol City v Preston N.E.
Cardiff City v Barnsley
Charlton Athletic v Coventry City
Crystal Palace v Burnley
Ipswich Town v Hull City
Q.P.R. v W.B.A.
Scunthorpe Utd. v Colchester Utd.
Sheffield Wed. v Norwich City
Southampton v Sheffield Utd.
Stoke City v Leicester City
Wolves v Plymouth Argyle

Sunday, 11 May
Barclays Premiership
Birmingham City v Blackburn Rov.
Chelsea v Bolton Wand.
Derby Co. v Reading
Everton v Middlesbrough
Manchester City v Newcastle Utd.
Portsmouth v Fulham
Sunderland v Arsenal
Tottenham v Liverpool
West Ham Utd. v Aston Villa
Wigan Athletic v Manchester Utd.

SCOTTISH LEAGUE FIXTURES 2007-08

Saturday, 4 August
Clydesdale Bank Premier League
Dundee Utd v Aberdeen
Gretna v Falkirk
Inverness CT v Rangers
St Mirren v Motherwell

First Division
Hamilton v Dunfermline
Livingston v Dundee
Morton v Clyde
Queen of South v St Johnstone
Stirling v Partick

Second Division
Airdrie Utd v Raith
Berwick v Cowdenbeath
Peterhead v Alloa
Queens Park v Brechin
Ross County v Ayr

Third Division
Dumbarton v Elgin
East Fife v East Stirling
Montrose v Albion
Stenhousemuir v Arbroath
Stranraer v Forfar

Sunday, 5 August
Clydesdale Bank Premier League
Celtic v Kilmarnock

Monday, 6 August
Clydesdale Bank Premier League
Hearts v Hibernian

Saturday, 11 August
Clydesdale Bank Premier League
Falkirk v Celtic
Hibernian v Gretna
Motherwell v Inverness CT
Rangers v St Mirren

First Division
Clyde v Hamilton
Dundee v Queen of South
Dunfermline v Morton
Partick v Livingston
St Johnstone v Stirling

Second Division
Alloa v Airdrie Utd
Ayr v Queens Park
Brechin v Peterhead
Cowdenbeath v Ross County
Raith v Berwick

Third Division
Albion v Stranraer
Arbroath v East Fife
East Stirling v Dumbarton
Elgin v Montrose
Forfar v Stenhousemuir

Sunday 12 August
Clydesdale Bank Premier League
Aberdeen v Hearts

Monday, 13 August
Clydesdale Bank Premier League
Kilmarnock v Dundee Utd.

Saturday, 18 August
Clydesdale Bank Premier League
Dundee Utd v Hibernian
Hearts v Gretna
Motherwell v Kilmarnock
Rangers v Falkirk
St Mirren v Inverness CT

First Division
Hamilton v Queen of South
Livingston v Dunfermline
Partick v Clyde
St Johnstone v Dundee
Stirling v Morton

Second Division
Berwick v Airdrie Utd
Brechin v Ayr
Peterhead v Cowdenbeath
Queens Park v Ross County
Raith v Alloa

Third Division
Albion v Stenhousemuir
Arbroath v Dumbarton
East Stirling v Forfar
Elgin v East Fife
Stranraer v Montrose

Sunday, 19 August
Clydesdale Bank Premier League
Aberdeen v Celtic

Saturday, 25 August
Clydesdale Bank Premier League
Celtic v Hearts
Falkirk v St Mirren
Gretna v Motherwell
Hibernian v Aberdeen
Inverness CT v Dundee Utd
Kilmarnock v Rangers

First Division
Clyde v St Johnstone
Dundee v Partick
Dunfermline v Stirling
Morton v Hamilton
Queen of South v Livingston

Second Division
Airdrie Utd v Queens Park
Alloa v Brechin
Ayr v Berwick
Cowdenbeath v Raith
Ross County v Peterhead

Third Division
Dumbarton v Albion
East Fife v Stranraer
Forfar v Elgin
Montrose v Arbroath
Stenhousemuir v East Stirling

Saturday, 1 September
Clydesdale Bank Premier League
Dundee Utd v Falkirk
Hibernian v Inverness CT
Kilmarnock v Aberdeen
Rangers v Gretna

First Division
Clyde v Dundee
Dunfermline v St Johnstone
Morton v Queen of South

Partick v Hamilton
Stirling v Livingston

Second Division
Ayr v Alloa
Brechin v Cowdenbeath
Peterhead v Berwick
Queens Park v Raith
Ross County v Airdrie Utd

Third Division
Albion v East Stirling
Arbroath v Elgin
East Fife v Forfar
Stenhousemuir v Montrose
Stranraer v Dumbarton

Sunday, 2 September
Clydesdale Bank Premier League
St Mirren v Celtic

Monday, 3 September
Clydesdale Bank Premier League
Motherwell v Hearts

Saturday, 15 September
Clydesdale Bank Premier League
Aberdeen v Motherwell
Celtic v Inverness CT
Falkirk v Hibernian
Gretna v Kilmarnock
Hearts v Rangers

First Division
Dundee v Dunfermline
Hamilton v Stirling
Livingston v Morton
Queen of South v Clyde
St Johnstone v Partick

Second Division
Airdrie Utd v Peterhead
Alloa v Queens Park
Berwick v Brechin
Cowdenbeath v Ayr
Raith v Ross County

Third Division
Dumbarton v Stenhousemuir
East Stirling v Stranraer
Elgin v Albion
Forfar v Arbroath
Montrose v East Fife

Sunday, 16 September
Clydesdale Bank Premier League
Dundee Utd. v St Mirren

Saturday, 22 September
Clydesdale Bank Premier League
Falkirk v Motherwell
Gretna v Dundee Utd
Inverness CT v Hearts
Kilmarnock v St Mirren

First Division
Clyde v Dunfermline
Hamilton v Livingston
Morton v St Johnstone
Partick v Queen of South
Stirling v Dundee

Second Division
Airdrie Utd v Brechin
Alloa v Cowdenbeath
Berwick v Ross County
Peterhead v Queens Park
Raith v Ayr

Third Division
Arbroath v Albion
Dumbarton v East Fife
Elgin v East Stirling
Forfar v Montrose
Stenhousemuir v Stranraer

Sunday, 23 September
Clydesdale Bank Premier League
Hibernian v Celtic
Rangers v Aberdeen

Saturday, 29 September
Clydesdale Bank Premier League
Aberdeen v Gretna
Celtic v Dundee Utd
Hibernian v Kilmarnock
Inverness CT v Falkirk
Motherwell v Rangers
St Mirren v Hearts

First Division
Dundee v Morton
Dunfermline v Partick
Livingston v Clyde
Queen of South v Stirling
St Johnstone v Hamilton

Second Division
Ayr v Peterhead
Brechin v Raith

Cowdenbeath v Airdrie Utd
Queens Park v Berwick
Ross County v Alloa

Third Division
Albion v Forfar
East Fife v Stenhousemuir
East Stirling v Arbroath
Montrose v Dumbarton
Stranraer v Elgin

Saturday, 6 October
Clydesdale Bank Premier League
Dundee Utd v Motherwell
Hearts v Falkirk
Kilmarnock v Inverness CT
Rangers v Hibernian

First Division
Hamilton v Dundee
Livingston v St Johnstone
Morton v Partick
Queen of South v Dunfermline
Stirling v Clyde

Second Division
Airdrie Utd v Ayr
Berwick v Alloa
Peterhead v Raith
Queens Park v Cowdenbeath
Ross County v Brechin

Third Division
Dumbarton v Forfar
East Fife v Albion
Montrose v East Stirling
Stenhousemuir v Elgin
Stranraer v Arbroath

Sunday, 7 October
Clydesdale Bank Premier League
Aberdeen v St Mirren
Gretna v Celtic

Saturday, 20 October
Clydesdale Bank Premier League
Falkirk v Kilmarnock
Hearts v Dundee Utd
Inverness CT v Aberdeen
Motherwell v Hibernian
Rangers v Celtic
St Mirren v Gretna

First Division
Clyde v Morton
Dundee v Livingston
Dunfermline v Hamilton
Partick v Stirling
St Johnstone v Queen of South

Second Division
Alloa v Peterhead
Ayr v Ross County
Brechin v Queens Park
Cowdenbeath v Berwick
Raith v Airdrie Utd

Third Division
Albion v Montrose
Arbroath v Stenhousemuir
East Stirling v East Fife
Elgin v Dumbarton
Forfar v Stranraer

Saturday, 27 October
Clydesdale Bank Premier League
Aberdeen v Falkirk
Celtic v Motherwell
Gretna v Inverness CT
Hibernian v St Mirren
Kilmarnock v Hearts

First Division
Hamilton v Morton
Livingston v Queen of South
Partick v Dundee
St Johnstone v Clyde
Stirling v Dunfermline

Second Division
Airdrie Utd v Berwick
Alloa v Raith
Ayr v Brechin
Cowdenbeath v Peterhead
Ross County v Queens Park

Sunday, 28 October
Clydesdale Bank Premier League
Dundee Utd. v Rangers

Saturday, 3 November
Clydesdale Bank Premier League
Aberdeen v Dundee Utd
Falkirk v Gretna
Kilmarnock v Celtic
Motherwell v St Mirren
Rangers v Inverness CT

First Division
Clyde v Partick
Dundee v St Johnstone

Dunfermline v Livingston
Morton v Stirling
Queen of South v Hamilton

Second Division
Berwick v Ayr
Brechin v Alloa
Peterhead v Ross County
Queens Park v Airdrie Utd
Raith v Cowdenbeath

Third Division
Dumbarton v Arbroath
East Fife v Elgin
Forfar v East Stirling
Montrose v Stranraer
Stenhousemuir v Albion

Sunday, 4 November
Clydesdale Bank Premier League
Hibernian v Hearts

Saturday, 10 November
Clydesdale Bank Premier League
Celtic v Falkirk
Dundee Utd v Kilmarnock
Gretna v Hibernian
Hearts v Aberdeen
Inverness CT v Motherwell

First Division
Dundee v Clyde
Hamilton v Partick
Livingston v Stirling
Queen of South v Morton
St Johnstone v Dunfermline

Second Division
Airdrie Utd v Ross County
Alloa v Ayr
Berwick v Peterhead
Cowdenbeath v Brechin
Raith v Queens Park

Third Division
Albion v Dumbarton
Arbroath v Montrose
East Stirling v Stenhousemuir
Elgin v Forfar
Stranraer v East Fife

Sunday, 11 November
Clydesdale Bank Premier League
St Mirren v Rangers

Saturday, 24 November
Clydesdale Bank Premier League
Celtic v Aberdeen
Falkirk v Rangers
Gretna v Hearts
Hibernian v Dundee Utd
Inverness CT v St Mirren
Kilmarnock v Motherwell

Saturday, 1 December
Clydesdale Bank Premier League
Aberdeen v Hibernian
Dundee Utd v Inverness CT
Hearts v Celtic
Motherwell v Gretna
Rangers v Kilmarnock
St Mirren v Falkirk

First Division
Clyde v Queen of South
Dunfermline v Dundee
Morton v Livingston
Partick v St Johnstone
Stirling v Hamilton

Second Division
Ayr v Cowdenbeath
Brechin v Berwick
Peterhead v Airdrie Utd
Queens Park v Alloa
Ross County v Raith

Third Division
Albion v Elgin
Arbroath v Forfar
East Fife v Montrose
Stenhousemuir v Dumbarton
Stranraer v East Stirling

Saturday, 8 December
Clydesdale Bank Premier League
Aberdeen v Kilmarnock
Celtic v St Mirren
Falkirk v Dundee Utd
Gretna v Rangers
Hearts v Motherwell
Inverness CT v Hibernian

First Division
Dundee v Stirling
Dunfermline v Clyde
Livingston v Hamilton
Queen of South v Partick
St Johnstone v Morton

Second Division
Airdrie Utd v Cowdenbeath
Alloa v Ross County
Berwick v Queens Park
Peterhead v Ayr
Raith v Brechin

Third Division
Dumbarton v Stranraer
East Stirling v Albion
Elgin v Arbroath
Forfar v East Fife
Montrose v Stenhousemuir

Saturday, 15 December
Clydesdale Bank Premier League
Hibernian v Falkirk
Inverness CT v Celtic
Kilmarnock v Gretna
Motherwell v Aberdeen
Rangers v Hearts
St Mirren v Dundee Utd

First Division
Clyde v Livingston
Hamilton v St Johnstone
Morton v Dundee
Partick v Dunfermline
Stirling v Queen of South

Second Division
Ayr v Raith
Brechin v Airdrie Utd
Cowdenbeath v Alloa
Queens Park v Peterhead
Ross County v Berwick

Third Division
Albion v Arbroath
East Fife v Dumbarton
East Stirling v Elgin
Montrose v Forfar
Stranraer v Stenhousemuir

•

Saturday, 22 December
Clydesdale Bank Premier League
Aberdeen v Rangers
Celtic v Hibernian
Dundee Utd v Gretna
Hearts v Inverness CT
Motherwell v Falkirk
St Mirren v Kilmarnock

First Division
Clyde v Stirling
Dundee v Hamilton
Dunfermline v Queen of South
Partick v Morton
St Johnstone v Livingston

Second Division
Alloa v Berwick
Ayr v Airdrie Utd
Brechin v Ross County
Cowdenbeath v Queens Park
Raith v Peterhead

Third Division
Arbroath v East Stirling
Dumbarton v Montrose
Elgin v Stranraer
Forfar v Albion
Stenhousemuir v East Fife

Wednesday, 26 December
Clydesdale Bank Premier League
Dundee Utd v Celtic
Falkirk v Inverness CT
Gretna v Aberdeen
Hearts v St Mirren
Kilmarnock v Hibernian
Rangers v Motherwell

First Division
Hamilton v Clyde
Livingston v Partick
Morton v Dunfermline
Queen of South v Dundee
Stirling v St Johnstone

Second Division
Airdrie Utd v Alloa
Berwick v Raith
Peterhead v Brechin
Queens Park v Ayr
Ross County v Cowdenbeath

Third Division
Dumbarton v East Stirling
East Fife v Arbroath
Montrose v Elgin
Stenhousemuir v Forfar
Stranraer v Albion

Saturday, 29 December
Clydesdale Bank Premier League
Celtic v Gretna
Falkirk v Hearts
Hibernian v Rangers
Inverness CT v Kilmarnock

Motherwell v Dundee Utd
St Mirren v Aberdeen

First Division
Clyde v St Johnstone
Dundee v Partick
Dunfermline v Stirling
Morton v Hamilton
Queen of South v Livingston

Second Division
Berwick v Airdrie Utd
Brechin v Ayr
Peterhead v Cowdenbeath
Queens Park v Ross County
Raith v Alloa

Third Division
Albion v East Fife
Arbroath v Stranraer
East Stirling v Montrose
Elgin v Stenhousemuir
Forfar v Dumbarton

Wednesday, 2 January
Clydesdale Bank Premier League
Aberdeen v Inverness CT
Celtic v Rangers
Dundee Utd v Hearts
Gretna v St Mirren
Hibernian v Motherwell
Kilmarnock v Falkirk

First Division
Hamilton v Queen of South
Livingston v Dunfermline
Partick v Clyde
St Johnstone v Dundee
Stirling v Morton

Second Division
Airdrie Utd v Queens Park
Alloa v Brechin
Ayr v Berwick
Cowdenbeath v Raith
Ross County v Peterhead

Third Division
Dumbarton v Albion
East Fife v Stranraer
Forfar v Elgin
Montrose v Arbroath
Stenhousemuir v East Stirling

Saturday, 5 January
Clydesdale Bank Premier League
Falkirk v Aberdeen
Hearts v Kilmarnock
Inverness CT v Gretna
Motherwell v Celtic
Rangers v Dundee Utd
St Mirren v Hibernian

First Division
Dundee v Dunfermline
Hamilton v Stirling
Livingston v Morton
Queen of South v Clyde
St Johnstone v Partick

Second Division
Airdrie Utd v Peterhead
Alloa v Queens Park
Berwick v Brechin
Cowdenbeath v Ayr
Raith v Ross County

Third Division
Albion v Stenhousemuir
Arbroath v Dumbarton
East Stirling v Forfar
Elgin v East Fife
Stranraer v Montrose

Saturday, 12 January
Third Division
Dumbarton v Stenhousemuir
East Stirling v Stranraer
Elgin v Albion
Forfar v Arbroath
Montrose v East Fife

Saturday, 19 January
Clydesdale Bank Premier League
Celtic v Kilmarnock
Dundee Utd v Aberdeen
Gretna v Falkirk
Hearts v Hibernian
Inverness CT v Rangers
St Mirren v Motherwell

First Division
Clyde v Dundee
Dunfermline v St Johnstone
Morton v Queen of South
Partick v Hamilton
Stirling v Livingston

Second Division
Ayr v Alloa
Brechin v Cowdenbeath
Peterhead v Berwick
Queens Park v Raith
Ross County v Airdrie Utd

Third Division
Albion v East Stirling
Arbroath v Elgin
East Fife v Forfar
Stenhousemuir v Montrose
Stranraer v Dumbarton

Saturday, 26 January
Clydesdale Bank Premier League
Aberdeen v Hearts
Falkirk v Celtic
Hibernian v Gretna
Kilmarnock v Dundee Utd
Motherwell v Inverness CT
Rangers v St Mirren

First Division
Clyde v Hamilton
Dundee v Queen of South
Dunfermline v Morton
Partick v Livingston
St Johnstone v Stirling

Second Division
Alloa v Airdrie Utd
Ayr v Queens Park
Brechin v Peterhead
Cowdenbeath v Ross County
Raith v Berwick

Third Division
Albion v Stranraer
Arbroath v East Fife
East Stirling v Dumbarton
Elgin v Montrose
Forfar v Stenhousemuir

Saturday, 2 February
Second Division
Airdrie Utd v Raith
Berwick v Cowdenbeath
Peterhead v Alloa
Queens Park v Brechin
Ross County v Ayr

Third Division
Dumbarton v Elgin
East Fife v East Stirling
Montrose v Albion
Stenhousemuir v Arbroath
Stranraer v Forfar

Saturday, 9 February
Clydesdale Bank Premier League
Aberdeen v Celtic
Dundee Utd v Hibernian
Hearts v Gretna
Motherwell v Kilmarnock
Rangers v Falkirk
St Mirren v Inverness CT

First Division
Hamilton v Dunfermline
Livingston v Dundee
Morton v Clyde
Queen of South v St Johnstone
Stirling v Partick

Second Division
Ayr v Peterhead
Brechin v Raith
Cowdenbeath v Airdrie Utd
Queens Park v Berwick
Ross County v Alloa

Third Division
Albion v Forfar
East Fife v Stenhousemuir
East Stirling v Arbroath
Montrose v Dumbarton
Stranraer v Elgin

Saturday, 16 February
Clydesdale Bank Premier League
Celtic v Hearts
Falkirk v St Mirren
Gretna v Motherwell
Hibernian v Aberdeen
Inverness CT v Dundee Utd
Kilmarnock v Rangers

First Division
Dundee v Morton
Dunfermline v Partick
Livingston v Clyde
Queen of South v Stirling
St Johnstone v Hamilton

Second Division
Airdrie Utd v Brechin
Alloa v Cowdenbeath
Berwick v Ross County

Peterhead v Queens Park
Raith v Ayr

Third Division
Arbroath v Albion
Dumbarton v East Fife
Elgin v East Stirling
Forfar v Montrose
Stenhousemuir v Stranraer

Saturday, 23 February
Clydesdale Bank Premier League
Dundee Utd v Falkirk
Hibernian v Inverness CT
Kilmarnock v Aberdeen
Motherwell v Hearts
Rangers v Gretna
St Mirren v Celtic

First Division
Clyde v Dunfermline
Hamilton v Livingston
Morton v St Johnstone
Partick v Queen of South
Stirling v Dundee

Second Division
Airdrie Utd v Berwick
Alloa v Raith
Ayr v Brechin
Cowdenbeath v Peterhead
Ross County v Queens Park

Third Division
Dumbarton v Arbroath
East Fife v Elgin
Forfar v East Stirling
Montrose v Stranraer
Stenhousemuir v Albion

Wednesday, 27 February
Clydesdale Bank Premier League
Aberdeen v Motherwell
Celtic v Inverness CT
Dundee Utd v St Mirren
Falkirk v Hibernian
Gretna v Kilmarnock
Hearts v Rangers

Saturday, 1 March
Clydesdale Bank Premier League
Falkirk v Motherwell
Gretna v Dundee Utd
Hibernian v Celtic
Inverness CT v Hearts
Kilmarnock v St Mirren
Rangers v Aberdeen

First Division
Clyde v Partick
Dundee v St Johnstone
Dunfermline v Livingston
Morton v Stirling
Queen of South v Hamilton

Second Division
Berwick v Ayr
Brechin v Alloa
Peterhead v Ross County
Queens Park v Airdrie Utd
Raith v Cowdenbeath

Third Division
Albion v Dumbarton
Arbroath v Montrose
East Stirling v Stenhousemuir
Elgin v Forfar
Stranraer v East Fife

Saturday, 8 March
First Division
Hamilton v Morton
Livingston v Queen of South
Partick v Dundee
St Johnstone v Clyde
Stirling v Dunfermline

Second Division
Airdrie Utd v Ayr
Berwick v Alloa
Peterhead v Raith
Queens Park v Cowdenbeath
Ross County v Brechin

Third Division
Dumbarton v Forfar
East Fife v Albion
Montrose v East Stirling
Stenhousemuir v Elgin
Stranraer v Arbroath

Tuesday, 11 March
First Division
Clyde v Morton
Dundee v Livingston
Partick v Stirling
St Johnstone v Queen of South

Wednesday, 12 March
First Division
Dunfermline v Hamilton

Saturday, 15 March
Clydesdale Bank Premier League
Aberdeen v Gretna
Celtic v Dundee Utd
Hibernian v Kilmarnock
Inverness CT v Falkirk
Motherwell v Rangers
St Mirren v Hearts

First Division
Hamilton v Dundee
Livingston v St Johnstone
Morton v Partick
Queen of South v Dunfermline
Stirling v Clyde

Second Division
Alloa v Peterhead
Ayr v Ross County
Brechin v Queens Park
Cowdenbeath v Berwick
Raith v Airdrie Utd

Third Division
Albion v Montrose
Arbroath v Stenhousemuir
East Stirling v East Fife
Elgin v Dumbarton
Forfar v Stranraer

Saturday, 22 March
Clydesdale Bank Premier League
Aberdeen v St Mirren
Dundee Utd v Motherwell
Gretna v Celtic
Hearts v Falkirk
Kilmarnock v Inverness CT
Rangers v Hibernian

First Division
Clyde v Queen of South
Dunfermline v Dundee
Morton v Livingston
Partick v St Johnstone
Stirling v Hamilton

Second Division
Ayr v Cowdenbeath
Brechin v Berwick
Peterhead v Airdrie Utd
Queens Park v Alloa
Ross County v Raith

Third Division
Albion v Elgin
Arbroath v Forfar
East Fife v Montrose
Stenhousemuir v Dumbarton
Stranraer v East Stirling

Saturday, 29 March
Clydesdale Bank Premier League
Falkirk v Kilmarnock
Hearts v Dundee Utd
Inverness CT v Aberdeen
Motherwell v Hibernian
Rangers v Celtic
St Mirren v Gretna

First Division
Dundee v Clyde
Hamilton v Partick
Livingston v Stirling
Queen of South v Morton
St Johnstone v Dunfermline

Second Division
Airdrie Utd v Ross County
Alloa v Ayr
Berwick v Peterhead
Cowdenbeath v Brechin
Raith v Queens Park

Third Division
Dumbarton v Stranraer
East Stirling v Albion
Elgin v Arbroath
Forfar v East Fife
Montrose v Stenhousemuir

Saturday, 5 April
Clydesdale Bank Premier League
Aberdeen v Falkirk
Celtic v Motherwell
Dundee Utd v Rangers
Gretna v Inverness CT
Hibernian v St Mirren
Kilmarnock v Hearts

First Division
Clyde v Livingston
Hamilton v St Johnstone
Morton v Dundee
Partick v Dunfermline
Stirling v Queen of South

Second Division
Ayr v Raith
Brechin v Airdrie Utd
Cowdenbeath v Alloa

Queens Park v Peterhead
Ross County v Berwick

Third Division
Albion v Arbroath
East Fife v Dumbarton
East Stirling v Elgin
Montrose v Forfar
Stranraer v Stenhousemuir

Saturday, 12 April
First Division
Dundee v Stirling
Dunfermline v Clyde
Livingston v Hamilton
Queen of South v Partick
St Johnstone v Morton

Second Division
Airdrie Utd v Cowdenbeath
Alloa v Ross County
Berwick v Queens Park
Peterhead v Ayr
Raith v Brechin

Third Division
Arbroath v East Stirling
Dumbarton v Montrose
Elgin v Stranraer
Forfar v Albion
Stenhousemuir v East Fife

Saturday, 19 April
First Division
Hamilton v Clyde
Livingston v Partick
Morton v Dunfermline
Queen of South v Dundee
Stirling v St Johnstone

Second Division
Airdrie Utd v Alloa
Berwick v Raith
Peterhead v Brechin
Queens Park v Ayr
Ross County v Cowdenbeath

Third Division
Dumbarton v East Stirling
East Fife v Arbroath
Montrose v Elgin
Stenhousemuir v Forfar
Stranraer v Albion

Saturday, 26 April
First Division
Clyde v Stirling
Dundee v Hamilton
Dunfermline v Queen of South
Partick v Morton
St Johnstone v Livingston

Second Division
Alloa v Berwick
Ayr v Airdrie Utd
Brechin v Ross County
Cowdenbeath v Queens Park
Raith v Peterhead

Third Division
Albion v East Fife
Arbroath v Stranraer
East Stirling v Montrose
Elgin v Stenhousemuir
Forfar v Dumbarton

BLUE SQUARE PREMIER LEAGUE FIXTURES 2007-08

Saturday, 11 August
Altrincham v Exeter City
Crawley v Stevenage
Droylsden v Salisbury
Ebbsfleet v Northwich
Farsley v Stafford
Histon v Burton
Kidderminster Harr. v Aldershot
Oxford Utd. v Forest Green
Torquay Utd. v Grays
Weymouth v Halifax Town
Woking v Rushden
York City v Cambridge Utd.

Tuesday, 14 August
Aldershot v Torquay Utd.
Burton v York City
Cambridge Utd. v Oxford Utd.
Exeter City v Crawley
Forest Green v Weymouth
Grays v Woking
Halifax Town v Altrincham
Northwich v Droylsden
Rushden v Farsley
Salisbury v Ebbsfleet
Stafford v Kidderminster Harr.
Stevenage v Histon

Saturday, 18 August
Aldershot v Droylsden
Burton v Oxford Utd.
Cambridge Utd. v Farsley
Exeter City v York City
Forest Green v Altrincham
Grays v Kidderminster Harr.
Halifax Town v Histon
Northwich v Torquay Utd.
Rushden v Ebbsfleet
Salisbury v Crawley
Stafford v Woking
Stevenage v Weymouth

Friday, 24 August
Histon v Aldershot

Saturday, 25 August
Altrincham v Grays
Crawley v Northwich
Droylsden v Exeter City
Ebbsfleet v Halifax Town
Farsley v Salisbury
Kidderminster Harr. v Stevenage
Oxford Utd. v Stafford
Torquay Utd. v Rushden
Weymouth v Burton
Woking v Cambridge Utd.
York City v Forest Green

Monday, 27 August
Aldershot v Crawley
Burton v Farsley
Cambridge Utd. v Ebbsfleet
Exeter City v Weymouth
Forest Green v Torquay Utd.
Grays v Histon
Halifax Town v Droylsden
Northwich v York City
Rushden v Kidderminster Harr.
Salisbury City v. Woking
Stafford v Altrincham
Stevenage v Oxford Utd.

Friday, 31 August
Weymouth v Cambridge Utd.

Saturday, 1 September
Altrincham v Aldershot
Crawley v Burton
Droylsden v Grays
Ebbsfleet v Stevenage
Farsley v Northwich
Histon v Salisbury
Kidderminster Harr. v Exeter City
Oxford Utd. v Halifax Town
Torquay Utd. v Stafford
Woking v Forest Green
York City v Rushden

Tuesday, 4 September
Cambridge Utd. v Grays
Droylsden v Stevenage
Ebbsfleet v Histon
Farsley v Kidderminster Harr.
Forest Green v Aldershot
Northwich v Burton
Oxford Utd. v Exeter City
Rushden v Crawley
Stafford v Halifax Town
Torquay Utd. v Salisbury
Woking v Weymouth
York City v Altrincham

Saturday, 8 September
Aldershot v Northwich Victoria
Altrincham v Oxford Utd.
Burton v Torquay Utd.
Crawley v Droylsden
Exeter City v Cambridge Utd.
Grays v Forest Green
Halifax Town v Woking
Histon v Farsley
Kidderminster Harr. v York City
Salisbury v Rushden
Stevenage v Stafford
Weymouth v Ebbsfleet

Saturday, 15 September
Cambridge Utd. v Crawley
Droylsden v Weymouth
Ebbsfleet v Kidderminster Harr.
Farsley v Exeter City
Forest Green v Salisbury
Northwich v Histon
Oxford Utd. v Aldershot
Rushden v Burton
Stafford v Grays
Torquay Utd. v Halifax Town
Woking v Altrincham
York City v Stevenage

Tuesday, 18 September
Aldershot v York City
Altrincham v Cambridge Utd.
Burton v Ebbsfleet
Crawley v Woking
Exeter City v Forest Green
Grays v Oxford Utd.
Halifax Town v Northwich
Histon v Torquay Utd.
Kidderminster Harr. v Droylsden
Salisbury v Stafford
Stevenage v Farsley
Weymouth v Rushden

Friday, 21 September
Histon v Oxford Utd.

Saturday, 22 September
Aldershot v Farsley
Altrincham v Droylsden
Burton v Woking
Crawley v Forest Green
Exeter City v Ebbsfleet
Grays v York City
Halifax Town v Rushden
Kidderminster Harr. v Torquay Utd.
Salisbury v Northwich
Stevenage v Cambridge Utd.
Weymouth v Stafford

Tuesday, 25 September
Cambridge Utd. v Aldershot
Droylsden v Burton
Ebbsfleet v Crawley
Farsley v Altrincham
Forest Green v Stevenage
Northwich v Kidderminster Harr.
Oxford Utd. v Salisbury
Rushden v Grays
Stafford v Histon
Torquay Utd. v Weymouth
Woking v Exeter City
York City v Halifax Town

Saturday, 29 September
Aldershot v Exeter City
Crawley v Altrincham
Farsley v Ebbsfleet
Forest Green v Cambridge Utd.
Grays v Stevenage
Halifax Town v Burton
Histon v Weymouth
Northwich v Woking
Oxford Utd. v York City
Rushden v Stafford
Salisbury v Kidderminster Harr.
Torquay Utd. v Droylsden

Saturday, 6 October
Altrincham v Rushden
Burton v Salisbury
Cambridge Utd. v Halifax Town
Droylsden v Oxford Utd.
Ebbsfleet v Torquay Utd.
Exeter City v Grays
Kidderminster Harr. v Crawley
Stafford v Forest Green
Stevenage v Aldershot
Weymouth v Northwich
Woking v Farsley
York City v Histon

Tuesday, 9 October
Aldershot v Ebbsfleet
Altrincham v Burton
Cambridge Utd. v Rushden
Crawley v Histon
Droylsden v Farsley
Exeter City v Salisbury
Forest Green v Northwich
Grays v Weymouth
Kidderminster Harr. v Halifax Town
Oxford Utd. v Torquay Utd.
Stevenage v Woking
York City v Stafford

Friday, 12 October
Weymouth v Crawley

Saturday, 13 October
Burton v Aldershot
Ebbsfleet v Droylsden
Farsley v Oxford Utd.
Halifax Town v Grays
Histon v Kidderminster Harr.
Northwich v Exeter City
Rushden v Forest Green
Salisbury v Altrincham
Stafford v Cambridge Utd.
Torquay Utd. v Stevenage
Woking v York City

Saturday, 20 October
Aldershot v Halifax Town
Altrincham v Ebbsfleet
Cambridge Utd. v Salisbury
Crawley v Stafford
Droylsden v Histon
Exeter City v Rushden
Forest Green v Farsley
Grays v Northwich
Kidderminster Harr. v Weymouth
Oxford Utd. v Woking
Stevenage v Burton
York City v Torquay Utd.

Saturday, 3 November
Burton v Kidderminster Harr.
Ebbsfleet v Forest
Farsley v York City
Halifax Town v Crawley
Histon v Altrincham
Northwich v Stevenage
Rushden v Oxford Utd.
Salisbury v Grays
Stafford v Exeter City
Torquay Utd. v Cambridge Utd.
Weymouth v Aldershot
Woking v Droylsden

Saturday, 17 November
Aldershot v Rushden
Altrincham v Weymouth
Cambridge Utd. v Northwich
Crawley v Torquay Utd.
Droylsden v Stafford
Exeter City v Burton
Forest Green v Histon
Grays v Farsley
Kidderminster Harr. v Woking
Oxford Utd. v Ebbsfleet
Stevenage v Halifax Town
York City v Salisbury

Saturday, 24 November
Aldershot v Grays
Burton v Cambridge Utd.
Crawley v Farsley
Droylsden v Forest Green
Ebbsfleet v Stafford
Halifax Town v Salisbury
Histon v Exeter City
Kidderminster Harr. v Oxford Utd.
Northwich v Rushden
Stevenage v Altrincham
Torquay Utd. v Woking
Weymouth v York City

Saturday, 1 December
Altrincham v Kidderminster Harr.
Cambridge Utd. v Droylsden
Exeter City v Stevenage
Farsley v Torquay Utd.
Forest Green v Halifax Town
Grays v Burton
Oxford Utd. v Weymouth
Rushden v Histon
Salisbury v Aldershot
Stafford v Northwich
Woking v Ebbsfleet
York City v Crawley

Saturday, 8 December
Aldershot v Stafford
Burton v Forest Green
Crawley v Grays
Droylsden v Rushden
Ebbsfleet v York City
Halifax Town v Exeter City
Histon v Woking
Kidderminster Harr. v Cambridge Utd.
Northwich v Oxford Utd.
Stevenage v Salisbury
Torquay Utd. v Altrincham
Weymouth v Farsley

Wednesday, 26 December
Altrincham v Northwich
Cambridge Utd. v Histon
Exeter City v Torquay Utd.
Farsley v Halifax Town
Forest Green v Kidderminster Harr.
Grays v Ebbsfleet
Oxford Utd. v Crawley
Rushden v Stevenage
Salisbury v Weymouth
Stafford v Burton
Woking v Aldershot
York City v Droylsden

Saturday, 29 December
Altrincham v Stevenage
Cambridge Utd. v Burton
Exeter City v Histon
Farsley v Crawley
Forest Green v Droylsden
Grays v Aldershot
Oxford Utd. v Kidderminster Harr.
Rushden v Northwich
Salisbury v Halifax Town
Stafford v Ebbsfleet
Woking v Torquay Utd.
York City v Weymouth

Tuesday, 1 January
Aldershot v Woking
Burton v Stafford
Crawley v Oxford Utd.
Droylsden v York City
Ebbsfleet v Grays
Halifax Town v Farsley
Histon v Cambridge Utd.
Kidderminster Harr. v Forest Green
Northwich v Altrincham
Stevenage v Rushden
Torquay Utd. v Exeter City
Weymouth v Salisbury

Saturday, 5 January
Cambridge Utd. v Exeter City
Droylsden v Crawley
Ebbsfleet v Weymouth
Farsley v Histon
Forest Green v Grays
Northwich v Aldershot
Oxford Utd. v Altrincham
Rushden v Salisbury
Stafford v Stevenage
Torquay Utd. v Burton
Woking v Halifax Town
York City v Kidderminster Harr.

Saturday, 19 January
Aldershot v Forest Green
Altrincham v York City
Burton v Northwich
Crawley v Rushden
Exeter City v Oxford Utd.
Grays v Cambridge Utd.
Halifax Town v Stafford
Histon v Ebbsfleet
Kidderminster Harr. v Farsley
Salisbury v Torquay Utd.
Stevenage v Droylsden
Weymouth v Woking

Saturday, 26 January
Cambridge Utd. v Altrincham
Droylsden v Kidderminster Harr.
Ebbsfleet v Burton
Farsley v Stevenage
Forest Green v Exeter City
Northwich v Halifax Town
Oxford Utd. v Grays
Rushden v Weymouth
Stafford v Salisbury
Torquay Utd. v Histon
Woking v Crawley
York City v Aldershot

Saturday, 2 February
Aldershot v Oxford Utd.
Altrincham v Woking
Burton v Rushden
Crawley v Cambridge Utd.
Exeter City v Farsley
Grays v Stafford
Halifax Town v Torquay Utd.
Histon v Northwich
Kidderminster Harr. v Ebbsfleet
Salisbury v Forest Green
Stevenage v York City
Weymouth v Droylsden

Saturday, 9 February
Cambridge Utd. v Stevenage
Droylsden v Altrincham
Ebbsfleet v Exeter City
Farsley v Aldershot
Forest Green v Crawley
Northwich v Salisbury
Oxford Utd. v Histon
Rushden v Halifax Town
Stafford v Weymouth
Torquay Utd. v Kidderminster Harr.
Woking v Burton
York City v Grays

Tuesday, 12 February
Aldershot v Cambridge Utd.
Altrincham v Farsley
Burton Albion v Droylsden
Crawley v Ebbsfleet
Exeter City v Woking
Grays v Rushden
Halifax Town v York City
Histon v Stafford
Kidderminster Harr. v Northwich
Salisbury v Oxford Utd.
Stevenage v Forest Green
Weymouth v Torquay Utd.

Saturday, 16 February
Aldershot v Stevenage
Crawley v Kidderminster Harr.
Farsley v Woking
Forest Green v Stafford
Grays v Exeter City
Halifax Town v Cambridge Utd.
Histon v York City
Northwich v Weymouth
Oxford Utd. v Droylsden
Rushden v Altrincham
Salisbury v Burton
Torquay Utd. v Ebbsfleet

Saturday, 23 February
Altrincham v Crawley
Burton v Halifax Town
Cambridge Utd. v Forest Green
Droylsden v Torquay Utd.
Ebbsfleet v Farsley
Exeter City v Aldershot
Kidderminster Harr. v Salisbury
Stafford v Rushden
Stevenage v Grays
Weymouth v Histon
Woking v Northwich
York City v Oxford Utd.

Saturday, 1 March
Aldershot v Kidderminster Harr.
Burton v Histon
Cambridge Utd. v York City
Exeter City v Altrincham
Forest Green v Oxford Utd.
Grays v Torquay Utd.
Halifax Town v Weymouth
Northwich v Ebbsfleet
Rushden v Woking
Salisbury v Droylsden
Stafford v Farsley
Stevenage v Crawley

Tuesday, 4 March
Altrincham v Halifax Town
Crawley v Exeter City
Droylsden v Northwich
Ebbsfleet v Salisbury
Farsley v Rushden
Histon v Stevenage
Kidderminster Harr. v Stafford
Oxford Utd. v Cambridge Utd.
Torquay Utd. v Aldershot
Weymouth v Forest Green
Woking v Grays
York City v Burton

Saturday, 8 March
Altrincham v Forest Green
Crawley v Salisbury
Droylsden v Aldershot
Ebbsfleet v Rushden
Farsley v Cambridge Utd.
Histon v Halifax Town
Kidderminster Harr. v Grays
Oxford Utd. v Burton
Torquay Utd. v Northwich
Weymouth v Stevenage
Woking v Stafford
York City v Exeter City

Saturday, 15 March
Aldershot v Histon
Burton v Weymouth
Cambridge Utd. v Woking
Exeter City v Droylsden
Forest Green v York City
Grays v Altrincham
Halifax Town v Ebbsfleet
Northwich v Crawley
Rushden v Torquay Utd.
Salisbury v Farsley
Stafford v Oxford Utd.
Stevenage v Kidderminster Harr.

Saturday, 22 March
Aldershot v Altrincham
Burton v Crawley
Cambridge Utd. v Weymouth
Exeter City v Kidderminster Harr.
Forest Green v Woking
Grays v Droylsden
Halifax Town v Oxford Utd.
Northwich v Farsley
Rushden v York City
Salisbury v Histon
Stafford v Torquay Utd.
Stevenage v Ebbsfleet

Monday, 24 March
Altrincham v Stafford
Crawley v Aldershot
Droylsden v Halifax Town
Ebbsfleet v Cambridge Utd.
Farsley v Burton
Histon v Grays
Kidderminster Harr. v Rushden
Oxford Utd. v Stevenage
Torquay Utd. v Forest
Weymouth v Exeter City
Woking v Salisbury
York City v Northwich

Saturday, 29 March
Altrincham v Torquay Utd.
Cambridge Utd. v Kidderminster Harr.
Exeter City v Halifax Town
Farsley v Weymouth
Forest Green v Burton
Grays v. Crawley
Oxford Utd. v Northwich
Rushden v Droylsden
Salisbury v Stevenage
Stafford v. Aldershot
Woking v Histon
York City v Ebbsfleet

Saturday, 5 April
Aldershot v Salisbury
Burton v Grays
Crawley v York City
Droylsden v Cambridge Utd.
Ebbsfleet v Woking
Halifax Town v Forest Green
Histon v Rushden
Kidderminster Harr. v Altrincham
Northwich v Stafford
Stevenage v Exeter City
Torquay Utd. v Farsley
Weymouth v Oxford Utd.

Tuesday, 8 April
Burton v Altrincham
Ebbsfleet v Aldershot
Farsley v Droylsden
Halifax Town v Kidderminster Harr.
Histon v Crawley
Northwich v Forest Green
Rushden v Cambridge Utd.
Salisbury v Exeter City
Stafford v York City
Torquay Utd. v Oxford Utd.
Weymouth v Grays
Woking v Stevenage

Saturday, 12 April
Aldershot v Burton
Altrincham v Salisbury
Cambridge Utd. v Stafford
Crawley v Weymouth
Droylsden v Ebbsfleet
Exeter City v Northwich
Forest Green v Rushden
Grays v Halifax Town
Kidderminster Harr. v Histon
Oxford Utd. v Farsley
Stevenage Borough v Torquay Utd.
York City v Woking

Saturday, 19 April
Burton v Stevenage
Ebbsfleet v. Altrincham
Farsley v Forest Green
Halifax Town v Aldershot
Histon v Droylsden
Northwich v Grays
Rushden v Exeter City
Salisbury v Cambridge Utd.
Stafford v Crawley
Torquay Utd. v York City
Weymouth v Kidderminster Harr.
Woking v Oxford Utd.

Saturday, 26 April
Aldershot v Weymouth
Altrincham v Histon
Cambridge Utd. v Torquay Utd.
Crawley v Halifax Town
Droylsden v Woking
Exeter City v Stafford
Forest Green v Ebbsfleet
Grays v Salisbury
Kidderminster Harr. v Burton
Oxford Utd. v Rushden
Stevenage v Northwich
York City v Farsley

Saturday, 3 May
Burton v Exeter City
Ebbsfleet v Oxford Utd.
Farsley v Grays
Halifax Town v Stevenage
Histon v Forest Green
Northwich v Cambridge Utd.
Rushden v Aldershot
Salisbury v York City
Stafford v Droylsden
Torquay Utd. v Crawley
Weymouth v Altrincham
Woking v Kidderminster Harr.